OSW

OFFICIAL SCRABBLE® WORDS

D1189186

OSW

OFFICIAL SCRABBLE® WORDS

Chambers

Scrabble® is a registered trade mark owned in the USA and Canada by Selchow & Righter Company, New York, in Australia by Murfett Regency Pty Ltd, Victoria, and elsewhere by J W Spear & Sons PLC, Enfield, EN3 7TB, England.

First published 1988 by W & R Chambers Ltd Edinburgh

This paperback edition published 1989 by W & R Chambers Ltd, 43-45 Annandale Street, Edinburgh EH7 4AZ

British Library Cataloguing in Publication Data

OSW : Official Scrabble words.
  1. Scrabble – Manuals
  793.73

ISBN 0-550-19021-X

Cover design by John Marshall

Typeset by Waddie & Co. Ltd., Edinburgh.
Printed in Great Britain by
Richard Clay Ltd, Bungay, Suffolk

Preface

At last we have the book which Scrabble® players have been wanting for many years. *Official Scrabble® Words (OSW)* is the definitive work which will save family arguments in social games and enable challenges to be dealt with quickly and efficiently in Scrabble Clubs and tournaments.

J W Spear & Sons and Chambers have had a close relationship going back to when the UK Scrabble Club movement adopted *Chambers 20th Century Dictionary* as its reference work. *Chambers* (now published as *Chambers English Dictionary*) is loved by Scrabble players throughout most of the English-speaking world because of the rich fund of useful Scrabble words it contains.

Official Scrabble Words uses this source so it almost certainly contains your pet Scrabble words and thousands of others. *OSW* is complementary to *Chambers English Dictionary* which remains the reference work when you want to check a definition.

The task of adjudicating on well over 150,000 words was a mammoth one. I would like to thank the main adjudicating committee, the groups of volunteer Scrabble players who acted as the initial adjudicators (all named on p. vi) and, of course, Catherine Schwarz and her colleagues at Chambers for the dedicated way they handled the many problems. I also thank the members of the Australian Scrabble Players' Association who have made their contribution in helping Chambers' editorial team.

I am sure that the work they all have done will add to the enjoyment and satisfaction that you obtain from playing Scrabble.

Francis A Spear
Chairman and Chief Executive
J W Spear & Sons PLC

Main Committee:

Darryl Francis, *London Scrabble League*
Leonard Hodge, *Scrabble Club Co-ordinator and Chairman*
Angus Macdonald, *Mapperley Scrabble Club*
Philip Nelkon, *London Scrabble League*
Allan Simmons, *Postal Scrabble Club*

Initial Adjudicating Committee:

Steve Ablitt-Jones *Croydon SC*
Olive Behan *Glenthorn SC*
Jackie Fallows *Isle of Wight SC*
Raye Green *Leicester SC*
Mary Grylls *Grantham SC*
Ian Gucklhorn *London Scrabble League*
Dorothy Harrison *Plymouth SC*
Josef Kollar *Hythe SC*
Kevin Morris *Bristol SC*
Jane McLeman *Frodsham SC*
Norman Smith *Edinburgh SC*
Roy Upton *Derby SC*
Mike Willis *Milton Keynes SC*

The publishers wish to acknowledge the computing help of Peter Schwarz in the compilation of *Official Scrabble® Words*.

The book was prepared on a Sirius microcomputer using programs run under the UCSD-p system and the large-file editor ASE. The final text was sorted on the Edinburgh University Multi-Access System (EMAS).

Introduction

Official Scrabble® Words is the final authority on allowed Scrabble® words. It is based on the 1988 edition of *Chambers English Dictionary*. All words listed in that dictionary are permitted in Scrabble except:

> those only spelt with an initial capital letter;
> abbreviations;
> prefixes and suffixes;
> those requiring apostrophes and hyphens.

Official Scrabble Words fully takes account of the 1988 revision of the rules used for the National Scrabble Championship and other official Scrabble events. The differences between the new, revised rules and the earlier rules can be summarised here:

> foreign words are now allowed;
> names of letters and letter sounds are now allowed;
> obsolete words and words from the works of Shakespeare, Spenser and Milton are now allowed;
> adverbs are only allowed if in *Chambers*.

Let us look at these differences in slightly more detail, as well as at the approaches that have been taken towards certain groups of words.

Foreign words

Foreign words appearing in *Chambers English Dictionary* have been included in *Official Scrabble Words*. Where a specific plural form appears in *Chambers*, we have included only that form, but where no plural is shown in the dictionary, we have used our judgment, and the appropriate plural form has been included. In some instances, this will be a foreign plural; in others, it will be an English plural (usually the addition of an -S); occasionally both types of plural will be included. Do be aware that not all plural forms in *OSW* are explicitly shown in *Chambers*.

Letters and letter sounds

Names of letters and letter sounds appearing in *Chambers English Dictionary* are included in *Official Scrabble Words*. The reasons for barring these from the National Scrabble Championship and other official events were never clear, and these words are now welcomed back into the realm of valid Scrabble words. This allows the inclusion here of a flurry of words such as MU, NU and XI, as well as AITCH, VAU and YPSILON. Their plural forms are also included.

Obsolete words

Obsolete words are included in *Official Scrabble Words*, along with many of their relevant inflected forms (such as plurals and verb inflections). We have included plurals of most obsolete nouns. We have included verb inflections of many, but certainly not all, obsolete verbs. We have not included comparative and superlative forms of obsolete adjectives. We have not included derivatives of obsolete words, unless explicitly shown in *Chambers*. (For example, BROACH and BROACHER are both allowable words, and BROCH is in the dictionary as an obsolete spelling of BROACH – so BROACH, BROACHER and BROCH are all allowable, but we have not included the assumed BROCHER.)

Words marked in *Chambers* as being from the works of Shakespeare, Spenser and Milton have been treated in the same way as obsolete words.

Adverbs

Adverbs have only been included in *Official Scrabble Words* if they are included in *Chambers*. No attempt has been made to include adverbial forms which are not explicitly shown in the dictionary.

Users of *OSW* may find it helpful if we outline our thinking on certain other groups of words, as well as on the word lengths included in the book.

Plurals

With very few exceptions, we have included in *Official Scrabble Words* the plurals of all nouns. Plural forms have been shown for all nouns ending in -ISM, -ITY and -NESS. While these plurals may be little used in regular English, all are available for use if needed in the English language. We have also included the plural forms of chemicals, chemical elements, minerals, man-made materials, natural materials, fibres, drugs, gases, rocks, oils, vitamins, enzymes, diseases, illnesses, and the like.

Comparatives and superlatives

We have included a wide range of comparatives and super-latives in *Official Scrabble Words*. We have considered the possible comparative and superlative forms of all adjectives in *OSW,* and we have based our final selection on a range of criteria. These have included commonness or familiarity of the adjective, number of syllables, meaning, and whether the adjective is dialect, obsolete or foreign. We also took into account the euphony of the -ER and -EST forms, current usage, and listings in other dictionaries. We cannot say that we have applied a mechanical formula in deciding which comparatives and superlatives to include. We have allowed the -IER and -IEST forms of many adjectives ending in -Y, but by no means all. We have not excluded the comparatives and superlatives of all adjectives of three syllables or more – some have been included. We have not excluded the comparatives and super-latives of all adjectives ending with certain specific groups of letters, such as -ATE, -ENT, -ETE and -ID. We have certainly included some of these comparatives and superlatives. Overall we think you will find our selection of comparatives and super-latives more than adequate for Scrabble games, whether played at a cosy social level or a cut-throat championship level.

Interjections

Interjections are treated not as nouns, but as parts of speech which do not permit plurals. In *Official Scrabble Words*, an inter-jection has no inflected forms, unless explicitly indicated in *Chambers*. A plural is only allowed if an interjection is also shown to be a noun; and verb forms are only allowed if an interjection is shown to be a verb. Some examples:

> AH, QUOTHA and UM are interjections only,
> so no inflected forms are allowed;

EH is an interjection and a verb, so the
inflected verb forms **EHS, EHED** and **EHING**
are allowed;

OOH is an interjection, verb and noun, so the
verb forms **OOHS, OOHED** and **OOHING** are
allowed; **OOHS** is also the plural form of the
noun.

If *Chambers* quite clearly lists a plural form of an interjection
(for example, as at LO), then that is allowable.

Accents

Accented letters have been retained in *Official Scrabble Words*,
even though there are no accents in English-language Scrabble
sets. Accents are to be ignored. Occasionally, two forms of an
allowable Scrabble word are given in *OSW*, one accented, one
not. An example is PATE and PÂTÉ. Retention of accents has
been considered desirable because we have anticipated that
OSW may well be used as the authority for other word-games
which do *not* allow accented words. Inclusion of the accents will
enable the players of those other games to discard accented
words if they wish to.

Word lengths

Official Scrabble Words users may well want to understand what
criteria have been employed in considering word lengths. In
compiling *OSW* we began by listing all the valid but uninflected
words of length up to (and including) 9 letters. We then
allowed the relevant inflections of these (namely plurals, verb
forms, and comparatives and superlatives), resulting in words
up to 13 letters long. (It is possible for a 9-letter verb to double a
final consonant before adding -ING, giving 13 letters in all!)
Here are some examples:

the 9-letter noun CACODEMON gives rise to
the 10-letter plural CACODEMONS;

the 9-letter noun CACOPHONY gives rise to
the 11-letter plural CACOPHONIES;

the 9-letter noun CANTHARIS gives rise to
the 11-letter plural CANTHARIDES;

the 9-letter verb CALCULATE gives rise to
these verb inflections: CALCULATED,
CALCULATES and CALCULATING, having
10 or 11 letters;

the 8-letter verb CARBURET gives rise to
these verb inflections: CARBURETS,
CARBURETTED and CARBURETTING, having
9, 11 or 12 letters.

If any inflected form of 9 letters is also a singular noun in its
own right, then a plural form of that noun is also included. For
example:

the 9-letter verb CATERWAUL gives rise to
these verb inflections: CATERWAULS,
CATERWAULED and CATERWAULING; but
since CATERWAULING is also shown in
Chambers as a noun, the plural form
CATERWAULINGS has been included here;

the 8-letter verb CROSSCUT gives rise to
these verb inflections: CROSSCUTS and
CROSSCUTTING; but since CROSSCUTTING is
also shown in *Chambers* as a noun, the plural
form CROSSCUTTINGS has been included
here.

There are a few instances of 9-letter adjectives which add an -S
to become 10-letter nouns. For example, CANONICAL is an
adjective only, yet CANONICALS is a noun. In such cases, we
have included the -S form. After all, if CANONICAL was a noun
rather than an adjective, we would have included its plural
form CANONICALS. There are instances of singular nouns
having more than 9 letters, but with plurals of 9 letters or less.
The singulars have not been included here, but the plurals
have. For example, the singular CYNOMOLGUS has 10 letters,
so hasn't been included, but its plural CYNOMOLGI has 9 letters,
so is included.

Order of words

All the words in *Official Scrabble Words* are listed in strict
alphabetical sequence regardless of length. It is important to

bear this in mind, particularly when checking the validity of plurals. For example:

> the plural of FAD is not listed immediately after FAD but is shown at its correct alphabetical place between FADQS and FADY;

> to determine whether FAB has a plural or not, it is necessary to check between the entries FABRICS and FABULAR. It is not listed there, so FABS is not allowed.

Official Scrabble Words does not list the definitions of any words. If you wish to discover the meaning of a word included, then it is necessary to consult *Chambers English Dictionary*.

Apparent misspellings

There are some instances where it may appear that a word has been misspelt. This can occur when the normal spelling is greater than 9 letters and therefore excluded, but an older or obsolete spelling of the same word qualifies for inclusion. For example:

> SENSUALTY and its plural form SENSUALTIES both appear in *Official Scrabble Words* because SENSUALTY is a 9-letter noun. The regular spelling SENSUALITY and its plural form SENSUALITIES are not listed because SENSUALITY is longer than 9 letters.

Official Scrabble Words will not answer every possible enquiry regarding the validity of words. For uninflected words longer than 9 letters, you will have to turn to *Chambers* itself. For example, CYNOMOLGUS, mentioned above, is perfectly valid for use in Scrabble; it's just that it isn't included here. There are plenty of other 10-15 letter words which could be played on a Scrabble board and are in *Chambers*. However, we felt that such words fell outside the scope of *OSW*.

If after considering the guidelines here you believe you have found an error, either of inclusion or omission, then please write to Catherine Schwarz at W and R Chambers, Edinburgh.

Darryl Francis, Leonard Hodge,
Angus Macdonald, Philip Nelkon,
Allan Simmons
UK *Official Scrabble® Words Committee*

A

AA
AARDVARK
AARDVARKS
AARDWOLF
AARDWOLVES
AAS
AASVOGEL
AASVOGELS
ABA
ABAC
ABACA
ABACAS
ABACI
ABACK
ABACS
ABACTINAL
ABACTOR
ABACTORS
ABACUS
ABACUSES
ABAFT
ABALONE
ABALONES
ABAMPERE
ABAMPERES
ABAND
ABANDED
ABANDING
ABANDON
ABANDONED
ABANDONEE
ABANDONEES
ABANDONING
ABANDONS
ABANDO
ABAC
ABASE
ABASED
ABASEMENT
ABASEMENTS
ABASES
ABASH
ABASHED
ABASHES
ABASHING
ABASHLESS
ABASHMENT
ABASHMENTS
ABASING
ABASK
ABATABLE
ABATE
ABATED
ABATEMENT
ABATEMENTS
ABATES
ABATING
ABATIS
ABATOR
ABATORS
ABATTIS
ABATTOIR
ABATTOIRS
ABATTU

ABATURE
ABATURES
ABAXIAL
ABAYA
ABAYAS
ABB
ABBA
ABBACIES
ABBACY
ABBAS
ABBATIAL
ABBÉ
ABBÉS
ABBESS
ABBESSES
ABBEY
ABBEYS
ABBOT
ABBOTS
ABBOTSHIP
ABBOTSHIPS
ABBS
ABCEE
ABCEES
ABDABS
ABDICABLE
ABDICANT
ABDICATE
ABDICATED
ABDICATES
ABDICATING
ABDOMEN
ABDOMENS
ABDOMINAL
ABDUCE
ABDUCED
ABDUCENT
ABDUCES
ABDUCING
ABDUCT
ABDUCTED
ABDUCTEE
ABDUCTEES
ABDUCTING
ABDUCTION
ABDUCTIONS
ABDUCTOR
ABDUCTORS
ABDUCTS
ABEAM
ABEAR
ABEARING
ABEARS
ABED
ABEIGH
ABELE
ABELES
ABELIA
ABELIAS
ABERRANCE
ABERRANCES
ABERRANCIES
ABERRANCY
ABERRANT

ABERRATE
ABERRATED
ABERRATES
ABERRATING
ABESSIVE
ABESSIVES
ABET
ABETMENT
ABETMENTS
ABETS
ABETTED
ABETTER
ABETTERS
ABETTING
ABETTOR
ABETTORS
ABEYANCE
ABEYANCES
ABEYANCIES
ABEYANCY
ABEYANT
ABHOR
ABHORRED
ABHORRENT
ABHORRER
ABHORRERS
ABHORRING
ABHORRINGS
ABHORS
ABID
ABIDANCE
ABIDANCES
ABIDDEN
ABIDE
ABIDED
ABIDER
ABIDING
ABIDINGLY
ABIDINGS
ABIES
ABIGAIL
ABIGAILS
ABILITIES
ABILITY
ABIOSES
ABIOSIS
ABIOTIC
ABJECT
ABJECTED
ABJECTING
ABJECTION
ABJECTIONS
ABJECTLY
ABJECTS
ABJOINT
ABJOINTED
ABJOINTING
ABJOINTS
ABJURE
ABJURED
ABJURER
ABJURERS
ABJURES
ABJURING

ABLATE
ABLATED
ABLATES
ABLATING
ABLATION
ABLATIONS
ABLATIVAL
ABLATIVE
ABLATIVES
ABLATOR
ABLATORS
ABLAUT
ABLAUTS
ABLAZE
ABLE
ABLED
ABLER
ABLES
ABLEST
ABLET
ABLETS
ABLING
ABLINS
ABLOOM
ABLOW
ABLUSH
ABLUTION
ABLUTIONS
ABLY
ABNEGATE
ABNEGATED
ABNEGATES
ABNEGATING
ABNEGATOR
ABNEGATORS
ABNORMAL
ABNORMITIES
ABNORMITY
ABNORMOUS
ABOARD
ABODE
ABODED
ABODEMENT
ABODEMENTS
ABODES
ABODING
ABOIDEAU
ABOIDEAUS
ABOIL
ABOITEAU
ABOITEAUS
ABOLISH
ABOLISHED
ABOLISHES
ABOLISHING
ABOLITION
ABOLITIONS
ABOLLA
ABOLLAE
ABOLLAS
ABOMASA
ABOMASUM
ABOMASUS
ABOMASUSES

ABOMINATE
ABOMINATED
ABOMINATES
ABOMINATING
ABONDANCE
ABONDANCES
ABORAL
ABORD
ABORDED
ABORDING
ABORDS
ABORE
ABORIGEN
ABORIGENS
ABORIGIN
ABORIGINE
ABORIGINES
ABORIGINS
ABORNE
ABORT
ABORTED
ABORTING
ABORTION
ABORTIONS
ABORTIVE
ABORTS
ABOUGHT
ABOULIA
ABOULIAS
ABOUND
ABOUNDED
ABOUNDING
ABOUNDS
ABOUT
ABOUTS
ABOVE
ABRADANT
ABRADANTS
ABRADE
ABRADED
ABRADES
ABRADING
ABRAID
ABRAIDED
ABRAIDING
ABRAIDS
ABRAM
ABRASION
ABRASIONS
ABRASIVE
ABRASIVES
ABRAXAS
ABRAXASES
ABRAY
ABRAYED
ABRAYING
ABRAYS
ABRAZO
ABRAZOS
ABREACT
ABREACTED
ABREACTING
ABREACTS
ABREAST

ABRÉGÉ
ABRÉGÉS
ABRICOCK
ABRICOCKS
ABRIDGE
ABRIDGED
ABRIDGER
ABRIDGERS
ABRIDGES
ABRIDGING
ABRIM
ABRIN
ABRINS
ABROACH
ABROAD
ABROGATE
ABROGATED
ABROGATES
ABROGATING
ABROGATOR
ABROGATORS
ABROOKE
ABROOKED
ABROOKES
ABROOKING
ABRUPT
ABRUPTER
ABRUPTEST
ABRUPTION
ABRUPTIONS
ABRUPTLY
ABRUPTS
ABSCESS
ABSCESSES
ABSCIND
ABSCINDED
ABSCINDING
ABSCINDS
ABSCISE
ABSCISED
ABSCISES
ABSCISIN
ABSCISING
ABSCISINS
ABSCISS
ABSCISSA
ABSCISSAE
ABSCISSAS
ABSCISSE
ABSCISSES
ABSCISSIN
ABSCISSINS
ABSCOND
ABSCONDED
ABSCONDER
ABSCONDERS
ABSCONDING
ABSCONDS
ABSEIL
ABSEILED
ABSEILING
ABSEILINGS
ABSEILS
ABSENCE
ABSENCES
ABSENT
ABSENTED
ABSENTEE
ABSENTEES
ABSENTING

ABSENTLY
ABSENTS
ABSEY
ABSEYS
ABSINTH
ABSINTHE
ABSINTHES
ABSINTHS
ABSIT
ABSITS
ABSOLUTE
ABSOLUTES
ABSOLVE
ABSOLVED
ABSOLVER
ABSOLVERS
ABSOLVES
ABSOLVING
ABSONANT
ABSORB
ABSORBATE
ABSORBATES
ABSORBED
ABSORBENT
ABSORBENTS
ABSORBER
ABSORBERS
ABSORBING
ABSORBS
ABSTAIN
ABSTAINED
ABSTAINER
ABSTAINERS
ABSTAINING
ABSTAINS
ABSTERGE
ABSTERGED
ABSTERGES
ABSTERGING
ABSTINENT
ABSTRACT
ABSTRACTED
ABSTRACTER
ABSTRACTEST
ABSTRACTING
ABSTRACTS
ABSTRICT
ABSTRICTED
ABSTRICTING
ABSTRICTS
ABSTRUSE
ABSTRUSER
ABSTRUSEST
ABSURD
ABSURDER
ABSURDEST
ABSURDITIES
ABSURDITY
ABSURDLY
ABTHANE
ABTHANES
ABULIA
ABULIAS
ABUNA
ABUNAS
ABUNDANCE
ABUNDANCES
ABUNDANCIES
ABUNDANCY
ABUNDANT

ABUNE
ABURST
ABUSAGE
ABUSAGES
ABUSE
ABUSED
ABUSER
ABUSERS
ABUSES
ABUSING
ABUSION
ABUSIONS
ABUSIVE
ABUSIVELY
ABUT
ABUTILON
ABUTILONS
ABUTMENT
ABUTMENTS
ABUTS
ABUTTAL
ABUTTALS
ABUTTED
ABUTTER
ABUTTERS
ABUTTING
ABUZZ
ABVOLT
ABVOLTS
ABY
ABYE
ABYEING
ABYES
ABYING
ABYSM
ABYSMAL
ABYSMALLY
ABYSMS
ABYSS
ABYSSAL
ABYSSES
ACACIA
ACACIAS
ACADEME
ACADEMES
ACADEMIA
ACADEMIAS
ACADEMIC
ACADEMICS
ACADEMIES
ACADEMIST
ACADEMISTS
ACADEMY
ACAJOU
ACAJOUS
ACALEPH
ACALEPHA
ACALEPHAN
ACALEPHANS
ACALEPHAS
ACALEPHE
ACALEPHES
ACALEPHS
ACANTH
ACANTHA
ACANTHAS
ACANTHIN
ACANTHINE
ACANTHINS
ACANTHOID

ACANTHOUS
ACANTHS
ACANTHUS
ACANTHUSES
ACAPNIA
ACAPNIAS
ACARI
ACARIAN
ACARIASES
ACARIASIS
ACARICIDE
ACARICIDES
ACARID
ACARIDAN
ACARIDANS
ACARIDEAN
ACARIDEANS
ACARIDIAN
ACARIDIANS
ACARIDS
ACARINE
ACAROID
ACAROLOGIES
ACAROLOGY
ACARPOUS
ACARUS
ACATER
ACATERS
ACATES
ACATOUR
ACATOURS
ACAUDAL
ACAUDATE
ACAULINE
ACAULOSE
ACCABLÉ
ACCEDE
ACCEDED
ACCEDENCE
ACCEDENCES
ACCEDER
ACCEDERS
ACCEDES
ACCEDING
ACCEND
ACCENDED
ACCENDING
ACCENDS
ACCENSION
ACCENSIONS
ACCENT
ACCENTED
ACCENTING
ACCENTOR
ACCENTORS
ACCENTS
ACCENTUAL
ACCEPT
ACCEPTANT
ACCEPTANTS
ACCEPTED
ACCEPTER
ACCEPTERS
ACCEPTING
ACCEPTIVE
ACCEPTOR
ACCEPTORS
ACCEPTS
ACCESS
ACCESSARIES

ACCESSARY
ACCESSED
ACCESSES
ACCESSING
ACCESSION
ACCESSIONS
ACCESSORIES
ACCESSORY
ACCIDENCE
ACCIDENCES
ACCIDENT
ACCIDENTS
ACCIDIE
ACCIDIES
ACCINGE
ACCINGED
ACCINGES
ACCINGING
ACCITE
ACCITED
ACCITES
ACCITING
ACCLAIM
ACCLAIMED
ACCLAIMING
ACCLAIMS
ACCLIMATE
ACCLIMATED
ACCLIMATES
ACCLIMATING
ACCLIVITIES
ACCLIVITY
ACCLIVOUS
ACCLOY
ACCLOYED
ACCLOYING
ACCLOYS
ACCOAST
ACCOASTED
ACCOASTING
ACCOASTS
ACCOIED
ACCOIL
ACCOILS
ACCOLADE
ACCOLADES
ACCOMPANIED
ACCOMPANIES
ACCOMPANY
ACCOMPANYING
ACCOMPT
ACCOMPTED
ACCOMPTING
ACCOMPTS
ACCORAGE
ACCORAGED
ACCORAGES
ACCORAGING
ACCORD
ACCORDANT
ACCORDED
ACCORDER
ACCORDERS
ACCORDING
ACCORDION
ACCORDIONS
ACCORDS
ACCOST
ACCOSTED
ACCOSTING

ACCOSTS
ACCOUNT
ACCOUNTED
ACCOUNTING
ACCOUNTINGS
ACCOUNTS
ACCOURAGE
ACCOURAGED
ACCOURAGES
ACCOURAGING
ACCOURT
ACCOURTED
ACCOURTING
ACCOURTS
ACCOUTRE
ACCOUTRED
ACCOUTRES
ACCOUTRING
ACCOY
ACCOYED
ACCOYING
ACCOYLD
ACCOYS
ACCREDIT
ACCREDITED
ACCREDITING
ACCREDITS
ACCRETE
ACCRETED
ACCRETES
ACCRETING
ACCRETION
ACCRETIONS
ACCRETIVE
ACCREW
ACCREWED
ACCREWING
ACCREWS
ACCRUAL
ACCRUALS
ACCRUE
ACCRUED
ACCRUES
ACCRUING
ACCUMBENT
ACCURACIES
ACCURACY
ACCURATE
ACCURSE
ACCURSED
ACCURSES
ACCURSING
ACCURST
ACCUSABLE
ACCUSAL
ACCUSALS
ACCUSE
ACCUSED
ACCUSER
ACCUSERS
ACCUSES
ACCUSING
ACCUSTOM
ACCUSTOMED
ACCUSTOMING
ACCUSTOMS
ACE
ACED
ACEDIA
ACEDIAS

ACELLULAR
ACERB
ACERBATE
ACERBATED
ACERBATES
ACERBATING
ACERBER
ACERBEST
ACERBIC
ACERBITIES
ACERBITY
ACEROSE
ACEROUS
ACERVATE
ACES
ACESCENCE
ACESCENCES
ACESCENCIES
ACESCENCY
ACESCENT
ACETABULA
ACETAL
ACETALS
ACETAMIDE
ACETAMIDES
ACETATE
ACETATES
ACETIC
ACETIFIED
ACETIFIES
ACETIFY
ACETIFYING
ACETONE
ACETONES
ACETOSE
ACETOUS
ACETYL
ACETYLENE
ACETYLENES
ACETYLS
ACHAENIUM
ACHAENIUMS
ACHAGE
ACHAGES
ACHARNÉ
ACHARYA
ACHARYAS
ACHATES
ACHE
ACHED
ACHENE
ACHENES
ACHENIAL
ACHENIUM
ACHENIUMS
ACHES
ACHIER
ACHIEST
ACHIEVE
ACHIEVED
ACHIEVER
ACHIEVERS
ACHIEVES
ACHIEVING
ACHIMENES
ACHING
ACHINGS
ACHKAN
ACHKANS
ACHROMAT

ACHROMATS
ACHY
ACICULAR
ACICULATE
ACID
ACIDER
ACIDEST
ACIDFREAK
ACIDFREAKS
ACIDIC
ACIDIFIED
ACIDIFIES
ACIDIFY
ACIDIFYING
ACIDITIES
ACIDITY
ACIDOSES
ACIDOSIS
ACIDS
ACIDULATE
ACIDULATED
ACIDULATES
ACIDULATING
ACIDULOUS
ACIERAGE
ACIERAGES
ACIERATE
ACIERATED
ACIERATES
ACIERATING
ACIFORM
ACING
ACINI
ACINIFORM
ACINOSE
ACINOUS
ACINUS
ACKEE
ACKEES
ACKERS
ACKNEW
ACKNOW
ACKNOWING
ACKNOWN
ACKNOWNE
ACKNOWS
ACLINIC
ACME
ACMES
ACMITE
ACMITES
ACNE
ACNES
ACOCK
ACOEMETI
ACOLD
ACOLUTHIC
ACOLYTE
ACOLYTES
ACOLYTH
ACOLYTHS
ACONITE
ACONITES
ACONITIC
ACONITINE
ACONITINES
ACONITUM
ACONITUMS
ACORN
ACORNED

ACORNS
ACOSMISM
ACOSMISMS
ACOSMIST
ACOSMISTS
ACOUCHIES
ACOUCHY
ACOUSTIC
ACOUSTICS
ACQUAINT
ACQUAINTED
ACQUAINTING
ACQUAINTS
ACQUEST
ACQUESTS
ACQUIESCE
ACQUIESCED
ACQUIESCES
ACQUIESCING
ACQUIGHT
ACQUIGHTED
ACQUIGHTING
ACQUIGHTS
ACQUIRAL
ACQUIRALS
ACQUIRE
ACQUIRED
ACQUIRES
ACQUIRING
ACQUIST
ACQUISTS
ACQUIT
ACQUITE
ACQUITED
ACQUITES
ACQUITING
ACQUITS
ACQUITTAL
ACQUITTALS
ACQUITTED
ACQUITTING
ACRAWL
ACRE
ACREAGE
ACREAGES
ACRED
ACRES
ACRID
ACRIDER
ACRIDEST
ACRIDIN
ACRIDINE
ACRIDINES
ACRIDINS
ACRIDITIES
ACRIDITY
ACRIMONIES
ACRIMONY
ACROBAT
ACROBATIC
ACROBATICS
ACROBATS
ACROGEN
ACROGENS
ACROLEIN
ACROLEINS
ACROLITH
ACROLITHS
ACROMIAL
ACROMION

ACROMIONS
ACRONYM
ACRONYMIC
ACRONYMS
ACROPETAL
ACROPHONIES
ACROPHONY
ACROPOLIS
ACROPOLISES
ACROSPIRE
ACROSPIRES
ACROSS
ACROSTIC
ACROSTICS
ACROTER
ACROTERIA
ACROTERS
ACROTISM
ACROTISMS
ACRYLIC
ACRYLICS
ACT
ACTA
ACTED
ACTIN
ACTINAL
ACTING
ACTINGS
ACTINIA
ACTINIAE
ACTINIAN
ACTINIANS
ACTINIAS
ACTINIC
ACTINIDE
ACTINIDES
ACTINISM
ACTINISMS
ACTINIUM
ACTINIUMS
ACTINOID
ACTINOIDS
ACTINON
ACTINONS
ACTINS
ACTION
ACTIONIST
ACTIONISTS
ACTIONS
ACTIVATE
ACTIVATED
ACTIVATES
ACTIVATING
ACTIVATOR
ACTIVATORS
ACTIVE
ACTIVELY
ACTIVISM
ACTIVISMS
ACTIVIST
ACTIVISTS
ACTIVITIES
ACTIVITY
ACTON
ACTONS
ACTOR
ACTORS
ACTRESS
ACTRESSES
ACTS

ACTUAL
ACTUALISE
ACTUALISED
ACTUALISES
ACTUALISING
ACTUALIST
ACTUALISTS
ACTUALITIES
ACTUALITY
ACTUALIZE
ACTUALIZED
ACTUALIZES
ACTUALIZING
ACTUALLY
ACTUARIAL
ACTUARIES
ACTUARY
ACTUATE
ACTUATED
ACTUATES
ACTUATING
ACTUATION
ACTUATIONS
ACTUATOR
ACTUATORS
ACTURE
ACTURES
ACUITIES
ACUITY
ACULEATE
ACULEATED
ACUMEN
ACUMENS
ACUMINATE
ACUMINATED
ACUMINATES
ACUMINATING
ACUPOINT
ACUPOINTS
ACUSHLA
ACUSHLAS
ACUTE
ACUTELY
ACUTENESS
ACUTENESSES
ACUTER
ACUTES
ACUTEST
ACYCLIC
ACYCLOVIR
ACYCLOVIRS
ACYL
ACYLS
AD
ADAGE
ADAGES
ADAGIO
ADAGIOS
ADAMANT
ADAMANTS
ADAPT
ADAPTABLE
ADAPTED
ADAPTER
ADAPTERS
ADAPTING
ADAPTION
ADAPTIONS
ADAPTIVE
ADAPTOR

ADAPTORS
ADAPTS
ADAW
ADAWED
ADAWING
ADAWS
ADAXIAL
ADAYS
ADD
ADDAX
ADDAXES
ADDED
ADDEEM
ADDEEMED
ADDEEMING
ADDEEMS
ADDEND
ADDENDA
ADDENDS
ADDENDUM
ADDER
ADDERS
ADDERWORT
ADDERWORTS
ADDICT
ADDICTED
ADDICTING
ADDICTION
ADDICTIONS
ADDICTIVE
ADDICTS
ADDING
ADDIO
ADDIOS
ADDITION
ADDITIONS
ADDITIVE
ADDITIVES
ADDLE
ADDLED
ADDLEMENT
ADDLEMENTS
ADDLES
ADDLING
ADDOOM
ADDOOMED
ADDOOMING
ADDOOMS
ADDORSED
ADDRESS
ADDRESSED
ADDRESSEE
ADDRESSEES
ADDRESSER
ADDRESSERS
ADDRESSES
ADDRESSING
ADDRESSOR
ADDRESSORS
ADDREST
ADDS
ADDUCE
ADDUCED
ADDUCENT
ADDUCER
ADDUCERS
ADDUCES
ADDUCIBLE
ADDUCING
ADDUCT

ADDUCTED
ADDUCTING
ADDUCTION
ADDUCTIONS
ADDUCTIVE
ADDUCTOR
ADDUCTORS
ADDUCTS
ADEEM
ADEEMED
ADEEMING
ADEEMS
ADEMPTION
ADEMPTIONS
ADENINE
ADENINES
ADENITIS
ADENITISES
ADENOID
ADENOIDAL
ADENOIDS
ADENOMA
ADENOMAS
ADENOMATA
ADENOSINE
ADENOSINES
ADEPT
ADEPTER
ADEPTEST
ADEPTS
ADEQUACIES
ADEQUACY
ADEQUATE
ADERMIN
ADERMINS
ADESPOTA
ADESSIVE
ADESSIVES
ADHARMA
ADHARMAS
ADHERE
ADHERED
ADHERENCE
ADHERENCES
ADHERENT
ADHERENTS
ADHERER
ADHERERS
ADHERES
ADHERING
ADHESION
ADHESIONS
ADHESIVE
ADHESIVES
ADHIBIT
ADHIBITED
ADHIBITING
ADHIBITS
ADIABATIC
ADIAPHORA
ADIEU
ADIEUS
ADIEUX
ADIOS
ADIPIC
ADIPOCERE
ADIPOCERES
ADIPOSE
ADIPOSITIES
ADIPOSITY

ADIT
ADITS
ADJACENCIES
ADJACENCY
ADJACENT
ADJECTIVE
ADJECTIVES
ADJOIN
ADJOINED
ADJOINING
ADJOINS
ADJOINT
ADJOINTS
ADJOURN
ADJOURNED
ADJOURNING
ADJOURNS
ADJUDGE
ADJUDGED
ADJUDGES
ADJUDGING
ADJUNCT
ADJUNCTLY
ADJUNCTS
ADJURE
ADJURED
ADJURES
ADJURING
ADJUST
ADJUSTED
ADJUSTER
ADJUSTERS
ADJUSTING
ADJUSTOR
ADJUSTORS
ADJUSTS
ADJUTAGE
ADJUTAGES
ADJUTANCIES
ADJUTANCY
ADJUTANT
ADJUTANTS
ADJUVANCIES
ADJUVANCY
ADJUVANT
ADJUVANTS
ADMASS
ADMASSES
ADMEASURE
ADMEASURED
ADMEASURES
ADMEASURING
ADMIN
ADMINICLE
ADMINICLES
ADMINS
ADMIRABLE
ADMIRABLY
ADMIRAL
ADMIRALS
ADMIRANCE
ADMIRANCES
ADMIRE
ADMIRED
ADMIRER
ADMIRERS
ADMIRES
ADMIRING
ADMISSION
ADMISSIONS

ADMISSIVE
ADMIT
ADMITS
ADMITTED
ADMITTING
ADMIX
ADMIXED
ADMIXES
ADMIXING
ADMIXTURE
ADMIXTURES
ADMONISH
ADMONISHED
ADMONISHES
ADMONISHING
ADMONITOR
ADMONITORS
ADNASCENT
ADNATE
ADNATION
ADNATIONS
ADO
ADOBE
ADOBES
ADONISE
ADONISED
ADONISES
ADONISING
ADONIZE
ADONIZED
ADONIZES
ADONIZING
ADOORS
ADOPT
ADOPTED
ADOPTER
ADOPTERS
ADOPTING
ADOPTION
ADOPTIONS
ADOPTIOUS
ADOPTIVE
ADOPTS
ADORABLE
ADORABLY
ADORATION
ADORATIONS
ADORE
ADORED
ADORER
ADORERS
ADORES
ADORING
ADORINGLY
ADORN
ADORNED
ADORNING
ADORNMENT
ADORNMENTS
ADORNS
ADOS
ADOWN
ADPRESS
ADPRESSED
ADPRESSES
ADPRESSING
ADRAD
ADREAD
ADREADED
ADREADING

ADREADS
ADRED
ADRENAL
ADRENALS
ADRIFT
ADROIT
ADROITER
ADROITEST
ADROITLY
ADRY
ADS
ADSCRIPT
ADSCRIPTS
ADSORB
ADSORBATE
ADSORBATES
ADSORBED
ADSORBENT
ADSORBENTS
ADSORBING
ADSORBS
ADSUM
ADULARIA
ADULARIAS
ADULATE
ADULATED
ADULATES
ADULATING
ADULATION
ADULATIONS
ADULATOR
ADULATORS
ADULATORY
ADULT
ADULTERER
ADULTERERS
ADULTERIES
ADULTERY
ADULTHOOD
ADULTHOODS
ADULTS
ADUMBRATE
ADUMBRATED
ADUMBRATES
ADUMBRATING
ADUNC
ADUNCATE
ADUNCATED
ADUNCITIES
ADUNCITY
ADUNCOUS
ADUST
ADUSTED
ADUSTING
ADUSTS
ADVANCE
ADVANCED
ADVANCES
ADVANCING
ADVANTAGE
ADVANTAGED
ADVANTAGES
ADVANTAGING
ADVECTION
ADVECTIONS
ADVENE
ADVENED
ADVENES
ADVENING
ADVENT

ADVENTIVE
ADVENTIVES
ADVENTS
ADVENTURE
ADVENTURED
ADVENTURES
ADVENTURING
ADVERB
ADVERBIAL
ADVERBS
ADVERSARIES
ADVERSARY
ADVERSE
ADVERSELY
ADVERSER
ADVERSEST
ADVERSITIES
ADVERSITY
ADVERT
ADVERTED
ADVERTENT
ADVERTING
ADVERTISE
ADVERTISED
ADVERTISES
ADVERTISING
ADVERTISINGS
ADVERTS
ADVEW
ADVEWED
ADVEWING
ADVEWS
ADVICE
ADVICEFUL
ADVICES
ADVISABLE
ADVISABLY
ADVISE
ADVISED
ADVISEDLY
ADVISER
ADVISERS
ADVISES
ADVISING
ADVISINGS
ADVISOR
ADVISORS
ADVISORY
ADVOCAAT
ADVOCAATS
ADVOCACIES
ADVOCACY
ADVOCATE
ADVOCATED
ADVOCATES
ADVOCATING
ADVOCATOR
ADVOCATORS
ADVOUTRER
ADVOUTRERS
ADVOUTRIES
ADVOUTRY
ADVOWSON
ADVOWSONS
ADWARD
ADWARDED
ADWARDING
ADWARDS
ADYNAMIA
ADYNAMIAS

ADYNAMIC
ADYTA
ADYTUM
ADZE
ADZES
AE
AECIA
AECIDIA
AECIDIUM
AECIUM
AEDILE
AEDILES
AEFALD
AEFAULD
AEFAWLD
AEGIRINE
AEGIRINES
AEGIRITE
AEGIRITES
AEGIS
AEGISES
AEGLOGUE
AEGLOGUES
AEGROTAT
AEGROTATS
AEMULE
AEMULED
AEMULES
AEMULING
AEOLIAN
AEOLIPILE
AEOLIPILES
AEOLIPYLE
AEOLIPYLES
AEON
AEONIAN
AEONS
AERATE
AERATED
AERATES
AERATING
AERATION
AERATIONS
AERATOR
AERATORS
AERIAL
AERIALIST
AERIALISTS
AERIALITIES
AERIALITY
AERIALLY
AERIALS
AERIE
AERIER
AERIES
AERIEST
AERIFORM
AEROBE
AEROBES
AEROBIC
AEROBICS
AEROBIONT
AEROBIONTS
AEROBOMB
AEROBOMBS
AEROBUS
AEROBUSES
AERODART
AERODARTS
AERODROME

AERODROMES
AERODYNE
AERODYNES
AEROFOIL
AEROFOILS
AEROGRAM
AEROGRAMS
AEROGRAPH
AEROGRAPHS
AEROLITE
AEROLITES
AEROLITH
AEROLITHS
AEROLITIC
AEROLOGIES
AEROLOGY
AEROMANCIES
AEROMANCY
AEROMETER
AEROMETERS
AEROMETRIES
AEROMETRY
AEROMOTOR
AEROMOTORS
AERONAUT
AERONAUTS
AERONOMIES
AERONOMY
AEROPHONE
AEROPHONES
AEROPHYTE
AEROPHYTES
AEROPLANE
AEROPLANES
AEROSHELL
AEROSHELLS
AEROSOL
AEROSOLS
AEROSPACE
AEROSPACES
AEROSTAT
AEROSTATS
AEROTAXES
AEROTAXIS
AEROTRAIN
AEROTRAINS
AERY
AESC
AESCES
AESCULIN
AESCULINS
AESIR
AESTHESES
AESTHESIA
AESTHESIAS
AESTHESIS
AESTHETE
AESTHETES
AESTHETIC
AESTHETICS
AESTIVAL
AESTIVATE
AESTIVATED
AESTIVATES
AESTIVATING
AETHER
AETHERS
AETIOLOGIES
AETIOLOGY
AFALD

AFAR
AFARA
AFARAS
AFAWLD
AFEAR
AFEARD
AFEARED
AFEARING
AFEARS
AFFABLE
AFFABLY
AFFAIR
AFFAIRE
AFFAIRES
AFFAIRS
AFFEAR
AFFEARD
AFFEARE
AFFEARED
AFFEARES
AFFEARING
AFFEARS
AFFECT
AFFECTED
AFFECTER
AFFECTERS
AFFECTING
AFFECTION
AFFECTIONED
AFFECTIONING
AFFECTIONS
AFFECTIVE
AFFECTS
AFFEER
AFFEERED
AFFEERING
AFFEERS
AFFERENT
AFFIANCE
AFFIANCED
AFFIANCES
AFFIANCING
AFFICHE
AFFICHES
AFFIDAVIT
AFFIDAVITS
AFFIED
AFFIES
AFFILIATE
AFFILIATED
AFFILIATES
AFFILIATING
AFFINE
AFFINED
AFFINES
AFFINITIES
AFFINITY
AFFIRM
AFFIRMANT
AFFIRMANTS
AFFIRMED
AFFIRMER
AFFIRMERS
AFFIRMING
AFFIRMS
AFFIX
AFFIXED
AFFIXES
AFFIXING
AFFLATED

AFFLATION	AFLATOXINS	AGATE	AGGRY	AGNISING
AFFLATIONS	AFLOAT	AGATES	AGHA	AGNIZE
AFFLATUS	AFOOT	AGAVE	AGHAS	AGNIZED
AFFLATUSES	AFORE	AGAVES	AGHAST	AGNIZES
AFFLICT	AFOREHAND	AGAZE	AGILA	AGNIZING
AFFLICTED	AFORESAID	AGAZED	AGILAS	AGNOMEN
AFFLICTING	AFORETIME	AGE	AGILE	AGNOMENS
AFFLICTS	AFOUL	AGED	AGILELY	AGNOMINA
AFFLUENCE	AFRAID	AGEDNESS	AGILER	AGNOSTIC
AFFLUENCES	AFREET	AGEDNESSES	AGILEST	AGNOSTICS
AFFLUENT	AFREETS	AGEE	AGILITIES	AGO
AFFLUENTS	AFRESH	AGEING	AGILITY	AGOG
AFFLUX	AFRIT	AGEINGS	AGIN	AGOGE
AFFLUXES	AFRITS	AGEISM	AGING	AGOGES
AFFLUXION	AFRO	AGEISMS	AGINGS	AGOGIC
AFFLUXIONS	AFRONT	AGEIST	AGINIZE	AGOGICS
AFFOORD	AFROS	AGEISTS	AGINIZED	AGOING
AFFOORDED	AFT	AGELAST	AGINIZES	AGON
AFFOORDING	AFTER	AGELASTIC	AGINIZING	AGONE
AFFOORDS	AFTERCARE	AGELASTS	AGINNER	AGONIC
AFFORCE	AFTERCARES	AGELESS	AGINNERS	AGONIES
AFFORCED	AFTEREYE	AGELONG	AGIO	AGONISE
AFFORCES	AFTEREYED	AGEN	AGIOS	AGONISED
AFFORCING	AFTEREYES	AGENCIES	AGIOTAGE	AGONISES
AFFORD	AFTEREYING	AGENCY	AGIOTAGES	AGONISING
AFFORDED	AFTERGAME	AGENDA	AGIST	AGONIST
AFFORDING	AFTERGAMES	AGENDAS	AGISTED	AGONISTES
AFFORDS	AFTERGLOW	AGENE	AGISTER	AGONISTIC
AFFOREST	AFTERGLOWS	AGENES	AGISTERS	AGONISTICS
AFFORESTED	AFTERINGS	AGENT	AGISTING	AGONISTS
AFFORESTING	AFTERMATH	AGENTED	AGISTMENT	AGONIZE
AFFORESTS	AFTERMATHS	AGENTIAL	AGISTMENTS	AGONIZED
AFFRAP	AFTERMOST	AGENTING	AGISTOR	AGONIZES
AFFRAPPED	AFTERNOON	AGENTS	AGISTORS	AGONIZING
AFFRAPPING	AFTERNOONS	AGES	AGISTS	AGONS
AFFRAPS	AFTERS	AGGER	AGITATE	AGONY
AFFRAY	AFTERTIME	AGGERS	AGITATED	AGOOD
AFFRAYED	AFTERTIMES	AGGRACE	AGITATES	AGORA
AFFRAYING	AFTERWARD	AGGRACED	AGITATING	AGORAS
AFFRAYS	AFTERWARDS	AGGRACES	AGITATION	AGOROT
AFFRENDED	AFTERWORD	AGGRACING	AGITATIONS	AGOUTA
AFFRET	AFTERWORDS	AGGRADE	AGITATIVE	AGOUTAS
AFFRETS	AFTMOST	AGGRADED	AGITATO	AGOUTI
AFFRICATE	AGA	AGGRADES	AGITATOR	AGOUTIES
AFFRICATED	AGAÇANT	AGGRADING	AGITATORS	AGOUTIS
AFFRICATES	AGAÇANTE	AGGRATE	AGITPROP	AGOUTY
AFFRIGHT	AGACERIE	AGGRATED	AGITPROPS	AGRAFFE
AFFRIGHTED	AGACERIES	AGGRATES	AGLEE	AGRAFFES
AFFRIGHTING	AGAIN	AGGRATING	AGLET	AGRAPHA
AFFRIGHTS	AGAINST	AGGRAVATE	AGLETS	AGRAPHIA
AFFRONT	AGALACTIA	AGGRAVATED	AGLEY	AGRAPHIAS
AFFRONTÉ	AGALACTIAS	AGGRAVATES	AGLIMMER	AGRAPHIC
AFFRONTED	AGALLOCH	AGGRAVATING	AGLITTER	AGRAPHON
AFFRONTÉE	AGALLOCHS	AGGREGATE	AGLOW	AGRARIAN
AFFRONTEE	AGAMI	AGGREGATED	AGMA	AGRASTE
AFFRONTING	AGAMIC	AGGREGATES	AGMAS	AGRAVIC
AFFRONTINGS	AGAMID	AGGREGATING	AGNAIL	AGREE
AFFRONTS	AGAMIDS	AGGRESS	AGNAILS	AGREEABLE
AFFUSION	AGAMIS	AGGRESSED	AGNAME	AGREEABLY
AFFUSIONS	AGAMOID	AGGRESSES	AGNAMED	AGREED
AFFY	AGAMOIDS	AGGRESSING	AGNAMES	AGREEING
AFFYDE	AGAMOUS	AGGRESSOR	AGNATE	AGREEMENT
AFFYING	AGAPAE	AGGRESSORS	AGNATES	AGREEMENTS
AFGHAN	AGAPE	AGGRI	AGNATIC	AGREES
AFGHANS	AGAR	AGGRIEVE	AGNATICAL	AGRÉGÉ
AFIELD	AGARIC	AGGRIEVED	AGNATION	AGRÉGÉS
AFIRE	AGARICS	AGGRIEVES	AGNATIONS	AGRÉMENS
AFLAJ	AGARS	AGGRIEVING	AGNISE	AGRÉMENT
AFLAME	AGAS	AGGRO	AGNISED	AGRÉMENTS
AFLATOXIN	AGAST	AGGROS	AGNISES	AGRESTAL

AGRESTIAL
AGRESTIC
AGRIMONIES
AGRIMONY
AGRIN
AGRIOLOGIES
AGRIOLOGY
AGRISE
AGRISED
AGRISES
AGRISING
AGRIZE
AGRIZED
AGRIZES
AGRIZING
AGROLOGIES
AGROLOGY
AGRONOMIC
AGRONOMICS
AGRONOMIES
AGRONOMY
AGROUND
AGRYZE
AGRYZED
AGRYZES
AGRYZING
AGUACATE
AGUACATES
AGUE
AGUED
AGUES
AGUISE
AGUISED
AGUISES
AGUISH
AGUISHLY
AGUISING
AGUIZE
AGUIZED
AGUIZES
AGUIZING
AGUTI
AGUTIO
AH
AHA
AHEAD
AHEAP
AHEIGHT
AHEM
AHIGH
AHIMSA
AHIMSAS
AHIND
AHINT
AHOLD
AHORSE
AHOY
AHULL
AHUNGERED
AHUNGRY
AI
AIA
AIAS
AIBLINS
AID
AIDANCE
AIDANCES
AIDANT
AIDE
AIDED

AIDER
AIDERS
AIDES
AIDFUL
AIDING
AIDLESS
AIDOI
AIDOS
AIDS
AIERIES
AIERY
AIGLET
AIGLETS
AIGRETTE
AIGRETTES
AIGUILLE
AIGUILLES
AIKIDO
AIKIDOS
AIKONA
AIL
AILANTHUS
AILANTHUSES
AILANTO
AILANTOS
AILED
AILERON
AILERONS
AILETTE
AILETTES
AILING
AILMENT
AILMENTS
AILS
AIM
AIMED
AIMING
AIMLESS
AIMLESSLY
AIMS
AIN
AINE
AINEE
AIOLI
AIOLIS
AIR
AIRBORNE
AIRBURST
AIRBURSTS
AIRCRAFT
AIRDRAWN
AIRDROME
AIRDROMES
AIRED
AIRER
AIRERS
AIRFIELD
AIRFIELDS
AIRFRAME
AIRFRAMES
AIRGAP
AIRGAPS
AIRGRAPH
AIRGRAPHS
AIRHOLE
AIRHOLES
AIRIER
AIRIEST
AIRILY
AIRINESS

AIRINESSES
AIRING
AIRINGS
AIRLESS
AIRLIFT
AIRLIFTED
AIRLIFTING
AIRLIFTS
AIRLINE
AIRLINER
AIRLINERS
AIRLINES
AIRMAIL
AIRMAILED
AIRMAILING
AIRMAILS
AIRMAN
AIRMEN
AIRN
AIRNED
AIRNING
AIRNS
AIRPLANE
AIRPLANES
AIRPORT
AIRPORTS
AIRS
AIRSCREW
AIRSCREWS
AIRSHAFT
AIRSHAFTS
AIRSHIP
AIRSHIPS
AIRSICK
AIRSPACE
AIRSPACES
AIRSTOP
AIRSTOPS
AIRSTREAM
AIRSTREAMS
AIRSTRIP
AIRSTRIPS
AIRT
AIRTED
AIRTIGHT
AIRTIME
AIRTIMES
AIRTING
AIRTS
AIRWARD
AIRWARDS
AIRWAVE
AIRWAVES
AIRWAY
AIRWAYS
AIRWOMAN
AIRWOMEN
AIRWORTHY
AIRY
AIS
AISLE
AISLED
AISLES
AISLING
AISLINGS
AIT
AITCH
AITCHBONE
AITCHBONES
AITCHES

AITS
AITU
AITUS
AIZLE
AIZLES
AJAR
AJEE
AJOWAN
AJOWANS
AJUTAGE
AJUTAGES
AJWAN
AJWANS
AKE
AKED
AKEE
AKEES
AKENE
AKENES
AKES
AKIMBO
AKIN
AKINESES
AKINESIA
AKINESIAS
AKINESIS
AKING
AKKAS
AKOLUTHOS
AKOLUTHOSES
AKVAVIT
AKVAVITS
ALA
ALAAP
ALAAPS
ALABAMINE
ALABAMINES
ALABASTER
ALABASTERS
ALACK
ALACRITIES
ALACRITY
ALAE
ALAIMENT
ALAIMENTS
ALALAGMOI
ALALAGMOS
ALALIA
ALALIAS
ALAMEDA
ALAMEDAS
ALAMODE
ALAMODES
ALAMORT
ALAND
ALANG
ALANGS
ALANNAH
ALANNAHS
ALAP
ALAPA
ALAPAS
ALAPS
ALAR
ALARM
ALARMED
ALARMEDLY
ALARMING
ALARMISM
ALARMISMS

ALARMIST
ALARMISTS
ALARMS
ALARUM
ALARUMED
ALARUMING
ALARUMS
ALARY
ALAS
ALASTRIM
ALASTRIMS
ALATE
ALATED
ALAY
ALAYED
ALAYING
ALAYS
ALB
ALBACORE
ALBACORES
ALBARELLI
ALBARELLO
ALBARELLOS
ALBATA
ALBATAS
ALBATROSS
ALBATROSSES
ALBE
ALBEDO
ALBEDOS
ALBEE
ALBEIT
ALBERGI
ALBERGO
ALBERT
ALBERTITE
ALBERTITES
ALBERTS
ALBESCENT
ALBESPINE
ALBESPINES
ALBESPYNE
ALBESPYNES
ALBICORE
ALBICORES
ALBINESS
ALBINESSES
ALBINISM
ALBINISMS
ALBINO
ALBINOISM
ALBINOISMS
ALBINOS
ALBINOTIC
ALBITE
ALBITES
ALBITISE
ALBITISED
ALBITISES
ALBITISING
ALBITIZE
ALBITIZED
ALBITIZES
ALBITIZING
ALBRICIAS
ALBS
ALBUGO
ALBUGOS
ALBUM
ALBUMEN

ALBUMENS
ALBUMIN
ALBUMINS
ALBUMS
ALBURNOUS
ALBURNUM
ALBURNUMS
ALCAHEST
ALCAHESTS
ALCAIDE
ALCAIDES
ALCALDE
ALCALDES
ALCARRAZA
ALCARRAZAS
ALCATRAS
ALCATRASES
ALCAYDE
ALCAYDES
ALCÁZAR
ALCÁZARS
ALCHEMIC
ALCHEMIES
ALCHEMIST
ALCHEMISTS
ALCHEMY
ALCHERA
ALCHERAS
ALCHYMIES
ALCHYMY
ALCOHOL
ALCOHOLIC
ALCOHOLICS
ALCOHOLS
ALCORZA
ALCORZAS
ALCOVE
ALCOVES
ALDEA
ALDEAS
ALDEHYDE
ALDEHYDES
ALDER
ALDERMAN
ALDERMEN
ALDERN
ALDERS
ALDOSE
ALDOSES
ALDRIN
ALDRINS
ALE
ALEATORIC
ALEATORIES
ALEATORY
ALEBENCH
ALEBENCHES
ALECOST
ALECOSTS
ALECTRYON
ALECTRYONS
ALEE
ALEFT
ALEGAR
ALEGARS
ALEGGE
ALEGGED
ALEGGES
ALEGGING
ALEMBIC

ALEMBICS
ALEMBROTH
ALEMBROTHS
ALENGTH
ALEPH
ALEPHS
ALEPINE
ALEPINES
ALERCE
ALERCES
ALERION
ALERIONS
ALERT
ALERTED
ALERTER
ALERTEST
ALERTING
ALERTLY
ALERTNESS
ALERTNESSES
ALERTS
ALES
ALEURON
ALEURONE
ALEURONES
ALEURONS
ALEVIN
ALEVINS
ALEW
ALEWASHED
ALEWIFE
ALEWIVES
ALEWS
ALEXIA
ALEXIAS
ALEXIC
ALEXIN
ALEXINS
ALEYE
ALEYED
ALEYES
ALEYING
ALFA
ALFALFA
ALFALFAS
ALFAQUÍ
ALFAQUÍS
ALFAS
ALFÉRECES
ALFÉREZ
ALFORJA
ALFORJAS
ALFRESCO
ALGA
ALGAE
ALGAL
ALGAROBA
ALGAROBAS
ALGARROBA
ALGARROBAS
ALGARROBO
ALGARROBOS
ALGATE
ALGATES
ALGEBRA
ALGEBRAIC
ALGEBRAS
ALGERINE
ALGERINES
ALGESES

ALGESIA
ALGESIAS
ALGESIS
ALGICIDE
ALGICIDES
ALGID
ALGIDITIES
ALGIDITY
ALGIN
ALGINATE
ALGINATES
ALGINIC
ALGINS
ALGOID
ALGOLOGIES
ALGOLOGY
ALGORISM
ALGORISMS
ALGORITHM
ALGORITHMS
ALGUACIL
ALGUACILS
ALGUAZIL
ALGUAZILS
ALGUM
ALGUMS
ALIAS
ALIASES
ALIBI
ALIBIS
ALICANT
ALICANTS
ALICYCLIC
ALIDAD
ALIDADE
ALIDADES
ALIDADS
ALIEN
ALIENABLE
ALIENAGE
ALIENAGES
ALIENATE
ALIENATED
ALIENATES
ALIENATING
ALIENATOR
ALIENATORS
ALIENED
ALIENEE
ALIENEES
ALIENING
ALIENISM
ALIENISMS
ALIENIST
ALIENISTS
ALIENOR
ALIENORS
ALIENS
ALIFORM
ALIGARTA
ALIGARTAS
ALIGHT
ALIGHTED
ALIGHTING
ALIGHTS
ALIGN
ALIGNED
ALIGNING
ALIGNMENT
ALIGNMENTS

ALIGNS
ALIKE
ALIMENT
ALIMENTAL
ALIMENTED
ALIMENTING
ALIMENTS
ALIMONIES
ALIMONY
ALINE
ALINED
ALINEMENT
ALINEMENTS
ALINES
ALINING
ALIPED
ALIPEDS
ALIPHATIC
ALIQUANT
ALIQUOT
ALISMA
ALISMAS
ALIT
ALIUNDE
ALIVE
ALIZARE
ALIZARES
ALIZARIN
ALIZARINE
ALIZARINES
ALIZARINS
ALKAHEST
ALKAHESTS
ALKALI
ALKALIES
ALKALIFIED
ALKALIFIES
ALKALIFY
ALKALIFYING
ALKALINE
ALKALIS
ALKALISE
ALKALISED
ALKALISES
ALKALISING
ALKALIZE
ALKALIZED
ALKALIZES
ALKALIZING
ALKALOID
ALKALOIDS
ALKALOSES
ALKALOSIS
ALKANE
ALKANES
ALKANET
ALKANETS
ALKENE
ALKENES
ALKYD
ALKYDS
ALKYL
ALKYLS
ALKYNE
ALKYNES
ALL
ALLANTOIC
ALLANTOID
ALLANTOIDS
ALLANTOIS

ALLANTOISES
ALLATIVE
ALLATIVES
ALLAY
ALLAYED
ALLAYER
ALLAYERS
ALLAYING
ALLAYINGS
ALLAYMENT
ALLAYMENTS
ALLAYS
ALLEDGE
ALLEDGED
ALLEDGES
ALLEDGING
ALLÉE
ALLÉES
ALLEGE
ALLEGED
ALLEGEDLY
ALLEGER
ALLEGERS
ALLEGES
ALLEGGE
ALLEGGED
ALLEGGES
ALLEGGING
ALLEGIANT
ALLEGING
ALLEGORIC
ALLEGORIES
ALLEGORY
ALLEGRO
ALLEGROS
ALLEL
ALLELE
ALLELES
ALLELS
ALLELUIA
ALLELUIAH
ALLELUIAHS
ALLELUIAS
ALLEMANDE
ALLEMANDES
ALLENARLY
ALLERGEN
ALLERGENS
ALLERGIC
ALLERGIES
ALLERGY
ALLERION
ALLERIONS
ALLEVIATE
ALLEVIATED
ALLEVIATES
ALLEVIATING
ALLEY
ALLEYED
ALLEYS
ALLEYWAY
ALLEYWAYS
ALLHEAL
ALLHEALS
ALLIANCE
ALLIANCES
ALLICE
ALLICES
ALLICHOLIES
ALLICHOLY

ALLIED
ALLIES
ALLIGARTA
ALLIGARTAS
ALLIGATE
ALLIGATED
ALLIGATES
ALLIGATING
ALLIGATOR
ALLIGATORS
ALLIS
ALLISES
ALLNESS
ALLNESSES
ALLNIGHT
ALLOCABLE
ALLOCARPIES
ALLOCARPY
ALLOCATE
ALLOCATED
ALLOCATES
ALLOCATING
ALLOD
ALLODIAL
ALLODIUM
ALLODIUMS
ALLODS
ALLOGAMIES
ALLOGAMY
ALLOGRAPH
ALLOGRAPHS
ALLOMETRIES
ALLOMETRY
ALLOMORPH
ALLOMORPHS
ALLONGE
ALLONGES
ALLONS
ALLONYM
ALLONYMS
ALLOPATH
ALLOPATHIES
ALLOPATHS
ALLOPATHY
ALLOPHONE
ALLOPHONES
ALLOPLASM
ALLOPLASMS
ALLOSAUR
ALLOSAURS
ALLOSTERIES
ALLOSTERY
ALLOT
ALLOTMENT
ALLOTMENTS
ALLOTROPE
ALLOTROPES
ALLOTROPIES
ALLOTROPY
ALLOTS
ALLOTTED
ALLOTTEE
ALLOTTEES
ALLOTTERIES
ALLOTTERY
ALLOTTING
ALLOW
ALLOWABLE
ALLOWABLY
ALLOWANCE

ALLOWANCES
ALLOWED
ALLOWEDLY
ALLOWING
ALLOWS
ALLOY
ALLOYED
ALLOYING
ALLOYS
ALLS
ALLSEED
ALLSEEDS
ALLSPICE
ALLSPICES
ALLUDE
ALLUDED
ALLUDES
ALLUDING
ALLURE
ALLURED
ALLURER
ALLURERS
ALLURES
ALLURING
ALLUSION
ALLUSIONS
ALLUSIVE
ALLUVIA
ALLUVIAL
ALLUVION
ALLUVIONS
ALLUVIUM
ALLY
ALLYCHOLIES
ALLYCHOLY
ALLYING
ALLYL
ALLYLS
ALMA
ALMAH
ALMAHS
ALMAIN
ALMAINS
ALMANAC
ALMANACS
ALMANDINE
ALMANDINES
ALMAS
ALME
ALMEH
ALMEHS
ALMERIES
ALMERY
ALMES
ALMIGHTY
ALMIRAH
ALMIRAHS
ALMOND
ALMONDS
ALMONER
ALMONERS
ALMONRIES
ALMONRY
ALMOST
ALMOUS
ALMS
ALMUG
ALMUGS
ALNAGE
ALNAGER

ALNAGERS
ALNAGES
ALOD
ALODIAL
ALODIUM
ALODIUMS
ALODS
ALOE
ALOED
ALOES
ALOETIC
ALOETICS
ALOFT
ALOGIA
ALOGIAS
ALOGICAL
ALOHA
ALOHAS
ALONE
ALONELY
ALONENESS
ALONENESSES
ALONG
ALONGSIDE
ALONGST
ALOOF
ALOOFLY
ALOOFNESS
ALOOFNESSES
ALOPECIA
ALOPECIAS
ALOPECOID
ALOUD
ALOW
ALOWE
ALP
ALPACA
ALPACAS
ALPARGATA
ALPARGATAS
ALPEEN
ALPEENS
ALPENHORN
ALPENHORNS
ALPHA
ALPHABET
ALPHABETS
ALPHAS
ALPHASORT
ALPHASORTED
ALPHASORTING
ALPHASORTS
ALPHORN
ALPHORNS
ALPINE
ALPINES
ALPINISM
ALPINISMS
ALPINIST
ALPINISTS
ALPS
ALREADY
ALRIGHT
ALS
ALSIKE
ALSIKES
ALSO
ALSOON
ALSOONE
ALT

ALTAR
ALTARAGE
ALTARAGES
ALTARS
ALTARWISE
ALTER
ALTERABLE
ALTERANT
ALTERANTS
ALTERCATE
ALTERCATED
ALTERCATES
ALTERCATING
ALTERED
ALTERING
ALTERITIES
ALTERITY
ALTERN
ALTERNANT
ALTERNANTS
ALTERNAT
ALTERNATE
ALTERNATED
ALTERNATES
ALTERNATING
ALTERNATS
ALTERNE
ALTERNES
ALTERS
ALTESSE
ALTESSES
ALTEZA
ALTEZAS
ALTEZZA
ALTEZZAS
ALTHAEA
ALTHAEAS
ALTHORN
ALTHORNS
ALTHOUGH
ALTIMETER
ALTIMETERS
ALTISSIMO
ALTITUDE
ALTITUDES
ALTO
ALTOS
ALTRICES
ALTRICIAL
ALTRUISM
ALTRUISMS
ALTRUIST
ALTRUISTS
ALTS
ALUDEL
ALUDELS
ALULA
ALULAS
ALUM
ALUMINA
ALUMINAS
ALUMINATE
ALUMINATES
ALUMINISE
ALUMINISED
ALUMINISES
ALUMINISING
ALUMINIUM
ALUMINIUMS
ALUMINIZE

ALUMINIZED
ALUMINIZES
ALUMINIZING
ALUMINOUS
ALUMINUM
ALUMINUMS
ALUMISH
ALUMIUM
ALUMIUMS
ALUMNA
ALUMNAE
ALUMNI
ALUMNUS
ALUMS
ALUNITE
ALUNITES
ALURE
ALURES
ALVEARIES
ALVEARY
ALVEATED
ALVEOLAR
ALVEOLATE
ALVEOLE
ALVEOLES
ALVEOLI
ALVEOLUS
ALVINE
ALWAY
ALWAYS
ALYSSUM
ALYSSUMS
AM
AMABILE
AMADAVAT
AMADAVATS
AMADOU
AMADOUS
AMAH
AMAHS
AMAIN
AMALGAM
AMALGAMS
AMANDINE
AMANDINES
AMANITA
AMANITAS
AMARACUS
AMARACUSES
AMARANT
AMARANTH
AMARANTHS
AMARANTIN
AMARANTS
AMARYLLID
AMARYLLIDS
AMARYLLIS
AMARYLLISES
AMASS
AMASSABLE
AMASSED
AMASSES
AMASSING
AMASSMENT
AMASSMENTS
AMATE
AMATED
AMATES
AMATEUR
AMATEURS

AMATING	AMBLES	AMENE *	AMMONALS	AMORTISED
AMATION	AMBLING	AMENED	AMMONIA	AMORTISES
AMATIONS	AMBLINGS	AMENING	AMMONIAC	AMORTISING
AMATIVE	AMBLYOPIA	AMENITIES	AMMONIAS	AMORTIZE
AMATOL	AMBLYOPIAS	AMENITY	AMMONITE	AMORTIZED
AMATOLS	AMBO	AMENS	AMMONITES	AMORTIZES
AMATORIAL	AMBONES	AMENT	AMMONIUM	AMORTIZING
AMATORIAN	AMBOS	AMENTA	AMMONIUMS	AMOSITE
AMATORY	AMBRIES	AMENTAL	AMMONOID	AMOSITES
AMAUROSES	AMBROID	AMENTIA	AMMONOIDS	AMOUNT
AMAUROSIS	AMBROIDS	AMENTIAS	AMMONS	AMOUNTED
AMAUROTIC	AMBROSIA	AMENTS	AMMOS	AMOUNTING
AMAZE	AMBROSIAL	AMENTUM	AMNESIA	AMOUNTS
AMAZED	AMBROSIAN	AMERCE	AMNESIAC	AMOUR
AMAZEDLY	AMBROSIAS	AMERCED	AMNESIACS	AMOURETTE
AMAZEMENT	AMBROTYPE	AMERCES	AMNESIAS	AMOURETTES
AMAZEMENTS	AMBROTYPES	AMERCING	AMNESIC	AMOURS
AMAZES	AMBRY	AMERICIUM	AMNESICS	AMOVE
AMAZING	AMBULACRA	AMERICIUMS	AMNESTIED	AMOVED
AMAZINGLY	AMBULANCE	AMETHYST	AMNESTIES	AMOVES
AMAZON	AMBULANCES	AMETHYSTS	AMNESTY	AMOVING
AMAZONIAN	AMBULANT	AMI	AMNESTYING	AMP
AMAZONITE	AMBULANTS	AMIABLE	AMNIA	AMPASSIES
AMAZONITES	AMBULATE	AMIABLY	AMNION	AMPASSY
AMAZONS	AMBULATED	AMIANTHUS	AMNIOTIC	AMPERAGE
AMBAGE	AMBULATES	AMIANTHUSES	AMOEBA	AMPERAGES
AMBAGES	AMBULATING	AMIANTUS	AMOEBAE	AMPERE
AMBAGIOUS	AMBULATOR	AMIANTUSES	AMOEBAEAN	AMPERES
AMBAN	AMBULATORS	AMICABLE	AMOEBIC	AMPERSAND
AMBANS	AMBUSCADE	AMICABLY	AMOEBOID	AMPERSANDS
AMBASSAGE	AMBUSCADED	AMICE	AMOK	AMPERZAND
AMBASSAGES	AMBUSCADES	AMICES	AMOMUM	AMPERZANDS
AMBASSIES	AMBUSCADING	AMID	AMOMUMS	AMPHIBIAN
AMBASSY	AMBUSCADO	AMIDE	AMONG	AMPHIBIANS
AMBATCH	AMBUSCADOES	AMIDES	AMONGST	AMPHIBOLE
AMBATCHES	AMBUSCADOS	AMIDMOST	AMOOVE	AMPHIBOLES
AMBER	AMBUSH	AMIDSHIPS	AMOOVED	AMPHIBOLIES
AMBERED	AMBUSHED	AMIDST	AMOOVES	AMPHIBOLY
AMBERGRIS	AMBUSHES	AMIE .	AMOOVING	AMPHIGORIES
AMBERGRISES	AMBUSHING	AMIES	AMORAL	AMPHIGORY
AMBERITE	AMEARST	AMIGO	AMORALISM	AMPHIOXUS
AMBERITES	AMEBA	AMIGOS	AMORALISMS	AMPHIOXUSES
AMBERJACK	AMEBAS	AMILDAR	AMORALIST	AMPHIPOD
AMBERJACKS	AMEBIC	AMILDARS	AMORALISTS	AMPHIPODS
AMBEROID	AMEER	AMINE	AMORCE	AMPHOLYTE
AMBEROIDS	AMEERS	AMINES	AMORCES	AMPHOLYTES
AMBEROUS	AMELCORN	AMIR	AMORET	AMPHORA
AMBERS	AMELCORNS	AMIRS	AMORETS	AMPHORAE
AMBERY	AMELIA	AMIS	AMORETTI	AMPHORIC
AMBIANCE	AMELIAS	AMISES	AMORETTO	AMPLE
AMBIANCES	AMEN	AMISS	AMORINI	AMPLENESS
AMBIENCE	AMENABLE	AMISSES	AMORINO	AMPLENESSES
AMBIENCES	AMENABLY	AMISSIBLE	AMORISM	AMPLER
AMBIENT	AMENAGE	AMISSING	AMORISMS	AMPLEST
AMBIENTS	AMENAGED	AMITIES	AMORIST	AMPLIFIED
AMBIGUITIES	AMENAGES	AMITOSES	AMORISTS	AMPLIFIER
AMBIGUITY	AMENAGING	AMITOSIS	AMORNINGS	AMPLIFIERS
AMBIGUOUS	AMENAUNCE	AMITOTIC	AMOROSA	AMPLIFIES
AMBIT	AMENAUNCES	AMITY	AMOROSAS	AMPLIFY
AMBITION	AMEND	AMLA	AMOROSITIES	AMPLIFYING
AMBITIONS	AMENDABLE	AMLAS	AMOROSITY	AMPLITUDE
AMBITIOUS	AMENDE	AMMAN	AMOROSO	AMPLITUDES
AMBITS	AMENDED	AMMANS	AMOROSOS	AMPLOSOME
AMBITTY	AMENDER	AMMETER	AMOROUS	AMPLOSOMES
AMBIVERT	AMENDERS	AMMETERS	AMOROUSLY	AMPLY
AMBIVERTS	AMENDES	AMMIRAL	AMORPHISM	AMPOULE
AMBLE	AMENDING	AMMIRALS	AMORPHISMS	AMPOULES
AMBLED	AMENDMENT	AMMO	AMORPHOUS	AMPS
AMBLER	AMENDMENTS	AMMON	AMORT	AMPUL
AMBLERS	AMENDS	AMMONAL	AMORTISE	AMPULE

AMPULES
AMPULLA
AMPULLAE
AMPULS
AMPUTATE
AMPUTATED
AMPUTATES
AMPUTATING
AMPUTATOR
AMPUTATORS
AMPUTEE
AMPUTEES
AMRIT
AMRITA
AMRITAS
AMRITS
AMTMAN
AMTMANS
AMTRACK
AMTRACKS
AMUCK
AMULET
AMULETIC
AMULETS
AMUSABLE
AMUSE
AMUSED
AMUSEDLY
AMUSEMENT
AMUSEMENTS
AMUSER
AMUSERS
AMUSES
AMUSETTE
AMUSETTES
AMUSING
AMUSINGLY
AMUSIVE
AMYGDAL
AMYGDALA
AMYGDALAS
AMYGDALE
AMYGDALES
AMYGDALIN
AMYGDALINS
AMYGDALS
AMYGDULE
AMYGDULES
AMYL
AMYLASE
AMYLASES
AMYLENE
AMYLENES
AMYLOID
AMYLOIDAL
AMYLOPSIN
AMYLOPSINS
AMYLS
AMYLUM
AMYLUMS
AN
ANA
ANABAS
ANABASES
ANABASIS
ANABATIC
ANABIOSES
ANABIOSIS
ANABIOTIC
ANABLEPS

ANABLEPSES
ANABOLIC
ANABOLISM
ANABOLISMS
ANABRANCH
ANABRANCHES
ANACHARIS
ANACHARISES
ANACONDA
ANACONDAS
ANACRUSES
ANACRUSIS
ANADEM
ANADEMS
ANAEMIA
ANAEMIAS
ANAEMIC
ANAEROBE
ANAEROBES
ANAEROBIC
ANAGLYPH
ANAGLYPHS
ANAGLYPTA
ANAGLYPTAS
ANAGOGE
ANAGOGES
ANAGOGIC
ANAGOGIES
ANAGOGY
ANAGRAM
ANAGRAMMED
ANAGRAMMING
ANAGRAMS
ANAI
ANALCIME
ANALCIMES
ANALCITE
ANALCITES
ANALECTA
ANALECTIC
ANALECTS
ANALEPTIC
ANALOGGIA
ANALGESIAS
ANALGESIC
ANALGESICS
ANALLY
ANALOG
ANALOGIC
ANALOGIES
ANALOGISE
ANALOGISED
ANALOGISES
ANALOGISING
ANALOGIST
ANALOGISTS
ANALOGIZE
ANALOGIZED
ANALOGIZES
ANALOGIZING
ANALOGON
ANALOGONS
ANALOGOUS
ANALOGS
ANALOGUE
ANALOGUES
ANALOGY
ANALYSAND
ANALYSANDS
ANALYSE

ANALYSED
ANALYSER
ANALYSERS
ANALYSES
ANALYSING
ANALYSIS
ANALYST
ANALYSTS
ANALYTIC
ANALYTICS
ANALYZE
ANALYZED
ANALYZER
ANALYZERS
ANALYZES
ANALYZING
ANAMNESES
ANAMNESIS
ANAN
ANANA
ANANAS
ANANASES
ANANDROUS
ANANKE
ANANKES
ANANTHOUS
ANAPAEST
ANAPAESTS
ANAPEST
ANAPESTS
ANAPHASE
ANAPHASES
ANAPHORA
ANAPHORAS
ANAPHORIC
ANAPLASTIES
ANAPLASTY
ANAPTYXES
ANAPTYXIS
ANARAK
ANARAKS
ANARCH
ANARCHAL
ANARCHIAL
ANARCHIC
ANARCHIES
ANARCHISE
ANARCHISED
ANARCHISES
ANARCHISING
ANARCHISM
ANARCHISMS
ANARCHIST
ANARCHISTS
ANARCHIZE
ANARCHIZED
ANARCHIZES
ANARCHIZING
ANARCHS
ANARCHY
ANAS
ANASARCA
ANASARCAS
ANASTASES
ANASTASIS
ANASTATIC
ANATASE
ANATASES
ANATHEMA
ANATHEMAS

ANATOMIC
ANATOMIES
ANATOMISE
ANATOMISED
ANATOMISES
ANATOMISING
ANATOMIST
ANATOMISTS
ANATOMIZE
ANATOMIZED
ANATOMIZES
ANATOMIZING
ANATOMY
ANATROPIES
ANATROPY
ANATTA
ANATTAS
ANATTO
ANATTOS
ANBURIES
ANBURY
ANCE
ANCESTOR
ANCESTORS
ANCESTRAL
ANCESTRIES
ANCESTRY
ANCHOR
ANCHORAGE
ANCHORAGES
ANCHORED
ANCHORESS
ANCHORESSES
ANCHORET
ANCHORETS
ANCHORING
ANCHORITE
ANCHORITES
ANCHORS
ANCHOVETA
ANCHOVETAS
ANCHOVIES
ANCHOVY
ANCHYLOSE
ANCHYLOSED
ANCHYLOSES
ANCHYLOSING
ANCHYLOSIS
ANCIENT
ANCIENTLY
ANCIENTRIES
ANCIENTRY
ANCIENTS
ANCILE
ANCILES
ANCILLARIES
ANCILLARY
ANCIPITAL
ANCLE
ANCLES
ANCOME
ANCOMES
ANCON
ANCONES
ANCORA
ANCRESS
ANCRESSES
AND
ANDANTE
ANDANTES

ANDANTINO
ANDANTINOS
ANDESINE
ANDESINES
ANDESITE
ANDESITES
ANDESITIC
ANDIRON
ANDIRONS
ANDROGEN
ANDROGENS
ANDROGYNE
ANDROGYNES
ANDROGYNIES
ANDROGYNY
ANDROID
ANDROIDS
ANDROLOGIES
ANDROLOGY
ANDROMEDA
ANDROMEDAS
ANDS
ANDVILE
ANDVILES
ANE
ANEAR
ANEARED
ANEARING
ANEARS
ANEATH
ANECDOTAL
ANECDOTE
ANECDOTES
ANECHOIC
ANELACE
ANELACES
ANELE
ANELED
ANELES
ANELING
ANEMIA
ANEMIAS
ANEMIC
ANEMOGRAM
ANEMOGRAMS
ANEMOLOGIES
ANEMOLOGY
ANEMONE
ANEMONES
ANENT
ANERLY
ANEROID
ANEROIDS
ANES
ANESTRA
ANESTRI
ANESTROUS
ANESTRUM
ANESTRUS
ANETIC
ANEURIN
ANEURINS
ANEURISM
ANEURISMS
ANEURYSM
ANEURYSMS
ANEW
ANGARIES
ANGARY
ANGEKKOK

ANGEKKOKS
ANGEKOK
ANGEKOKS
ANGEL
ANGELHOOD
ANGELHOODS
ANGELIC
ANGELICA
ANGELICAL
ANGELICAS
ANGELS
ANGELUS
ANGELUSES
ANGER
ANGERED
ANGERING
ANGERLESS
ANGERLY
ANGERS
ANGICO
ANGICOS
ANGINA
ANGINAL
ANGINAS
ANGIOGRAM
ANGIOGRAMS
ANGIOMA
ANGIOMAS
ANGIOMATA
ANGLE
ANGLED
ANGLER
ANGLERS
ANGLES
ANGLESITE
ANGLESITES
ANGLEWISE
ANGLICE
ANGLICISE
ANGLICISED
ANGLICISES
ANGLICISING
ANGLICISM
ANGLICISMS
ANGLICIST
ANGLICISTS
ANGLICIZE
ANGLICIZED
ANGLICIZES
ANGLICIZING
ANGLIFIED
ANGLIFIES
ANGLIFY
ANGLIFYING
ANGLING
ANGLINGS
ANGLIST
ANGLISTS
ANGLOPHIL
ANGLOPHILS
ANGORA
ANGORAS
ANGRIER
ANGRIES
ANGRIEST
ANGRILY
ANGRINESS
ANGRINESSES
ANGRY
ANGST

ANGSTROM
ANGSTROMS
ANGSTS
ANGUIFORM
ANGUINE
ANGUIPED
ANGUIPEDE
ANGUISH
ANGUISHED
ANGUISHES
ANGUISHING
ANGULAR
ANGULATED
ANHEDONIA
ANHEDONIAS
ANHEDRAL
ANHUNGRED
ANHYDRIDE
ANHYDRIDES
ANHYDRITE
ANHYDRITES
ANHYDROUS
ANICONIC
ANICONISM
ANICONISMS
ANICONIST
ANICONISTS
ANICUT
ANICUTS
ANIGH
ANIGHT
ANIL
ANILE
ANILINE
ANILINES
ANILITIES
ANILITY
ANILS
ANIMA
ANIMAL
ANIMALIC
ANIMALISE
ANIMALISED
ANIMALISES
ANIMALISING
ANIMALISM
ANIMALISMS
ANIMALIST
ANIMALISTS
ANIMALITIES
ANIMALITY
ANIMALIZE
ANIMALIZED
ANIMALIZES
ANIMALIZING
ANIMALLY
ANIMALS
ANIMAS
ANIMATE
ANIMATED
ANIMATES
ANIMATING
ANIMATION
ANIMATIONS
ANIMATISM
ANIMATISMS
ANIMATOR
ANIMATORS
ANIMÉ
ANIME

ANIMÉS
ANIMES
ANIMISM
ANIMISMS
ANIMIST
ANIMISTIC
ANIMISTS
ANIMOSITIES
ANIMOSITY
ANIMUS
ANIMUSES
ANION
ANIONIC
ANIONS
ANISE
ANISEED
ANISEEDS
ANISES
ANISETTE
ANISETTES
ANKER
ANKERITE
ANKERITES
ANKERS
ANKH
ANKHS
ANKLE
ANKLED
ANKLES
ANKLET
ANKLETS
ANKUS
ANKUSES
ANKYLOSE
ANKYLOSED
ANKYLOSES
ANKYLOSING
ANKYLOSIS
ANLACE
ANLACES
ANLAGE
ANLAGES
ANN
ANNA
ANNAL
ANNALISE
ANNALISED
ANNALISES
ANNALISING
ANNALIST
ANNALISTS
ANNALIZE
ANNALIZED
ANNALIZES
ANNALIZING
ANNALS
ANNAS
ANNAT
ANNATES
ANNATS
ANNATTA
ANNATTAS
ANNATTO
ANNATTOS
ANNEAL
ANNEALED
ANNEALER
ANNEALERS
ANNEALING
ANNEALINGS

ANNEALS
ANNECTENT
ANNELID
ANNELIDS
ANNEX
ANNEXE
ANNEXED
ANNEXES
ANNEXING
ANNEXION
ANNEXIONS
ANNEXMENT
ANNEXMENTS
ANNEXURE
ANNEXURES
ANNICUT
ANNICUTS
ANNO
ANNOTATE
ANNOTATED
ANNOTATES
ANNOTATING
ANNOTATOR
ANNOTATORS
ANNOUNCE
ANNOUNCED
ANNOUNCER
ANNOUNCERS
ANNOUNCES
ANNOUNCING
ANNOY
ANNOYANCE
ANNOYANCES
ANNOYED
ANNOYING
ANNOYS
ANNS
ANNUAL
ANNUALISE
ANNUALISED
ANNUALISES
ANNUALISING
ANNUALIZE
ANNUALIZED
ANNUALIZES
ANNUALIZING
ANNUALLY
ANNUALS
ANNUITANT
ANNUITANTS
ANNUITIES
ANNUITY
ANNUL
ANNULAR
ANNULARS
ANNULATE
ANNULATED
ANNULATES
ANNULET
ANNULETS
ANNULI
ANNULLED
ANNULLING
ANNULMENT
ANNULMENTS
ANNULOSE
ANNULS
ANNULUS
ANOA
ANOAS

ANODAL
ANODE
ANODES
ANODIC
ANODISE
ANODISED
ANODISES
ANODISING
ANODIZE
ANODIZED
ANODIZES
ANODIZING
ANODYNE
ANODYNES
ANOESES
ANOESIS
ANOESTRA
ANOESTRI
ANOESTRUM
ANOESTRUS
ANOETIC
ANOINT
ANOINTED
ANOINTING
ANOINTS
ANOMALIES
ANOMALOUS
ANOMALY
ANOMIC
ANOMIE
ANOMIES
ANOMY
ANON
ANONYM
ANONYMA
ANONYMAS
ANONYMITIES
ANONYMITY
ANONYMOUS
ANONYMS
ANOPHELES
ANORAK
ANORAKS
ANORECTIC
ANORECTICS
ANORETIC
ANORETICS
ANOREXIA
ANOREXIAS
ANOREXIC
ANOREXICS
ANOREXIES
ANOREXY
ANORTHIC
ANORTHITE
ANORTHITES
ANOSMIA
ANOSMIAS
ANOTHER
ANOUGH
ANOUROUS
ANOW
ANOXIA
ANOXIAS
ANOXIC
ANSATE
ANSATED
ANSERINE
ANSWER
ANSWERED

ANSWERER	ANTHOID	ANTIPODAL	ANXIETIES	APEMEN
ANSWERERS	ANTHOLOGIES	ANTIPODE	ANXIETY	APEPSIA
ANSWERING	ANTHOLOGY	ANTIPODES	ANXIOUS	APEPSIAS
ANSWERS	ANTHRACIC	ANTIPOLE	ANXIOUSLY	APEPSIES
ANT	ANTHRAX	ANTIPOLES	ANY	APEPSY
ANTA	ANTHRAXES	ANTIPOPE	ANYBODIES	APERÇU
ANTACID	ANTHROPIC	ANTIPOPES	ANYBODY	APERÇUS
ANTACIDS	ANTHURIUM	ANTIQUARIES	ANYHOW	APERIENT
ANTAE	ANTHURIUMS	ANTIQUARK	ANYONE	APERIENTS
ANTAR	ANTI	ANTIQUARKS	ANYONES	APERIES
ANTARS	ANTIAR	ANTIQUARY	ANYROAD	APERIODIC
ANTBEAR	ANTIARS	ANTIQUATE	ANYTHING	APÉRITIF
ANTBEARS	ANTIBODIES	ANTIQUATED	ANYTHINGS	APÉRITIFS
ANTE	ANTIBODY	ANTIQUATES	ANYTIME	APERITIVE
ANTECEDE	ANTIC	ANTIQUATING	ANYWAY	APERITIVES
ANTECEDED	ANTICHLOR	ANTIQUE	ANYWAYS	APERT
ANTECEDES	ANTICHLORS	ANTIQUED	ANYWHEN	APERTNESS
ANTECEDING	ANTICIVIC	ANTIQUELY	ANYWHERE	APERTNESSES
ANTECHOIR	ANTICIZE	ANTIQUES	ANYWISE	APERTURE
ANTECHOIRS	ANTICIZED	ANTIQUING	ANZIANI	APERTURES
ANTED	ANTICIZES	ANTIQUITIES	AORIST	APERY
ANTEDATE	ANTICIZING	ANTIQUITY	AORISTIC	APES
ANTEDATED	ANTICK	ANTIS	AORISTS	APETALIES
ANTEDATES	ANTICKE	ANTISCIAN	AORTA	APETALOUS
ANTEDATING	ANTICKED	ANTISCIANS	AORTAL	APETALY
ANTEFIX	ANTICKES	ANTISERA	AORTAS	APEX
ANTEFIXA	ANTICKING	ANTISERUM	AORTIC	APEXES
ANTEFIXAL	ANTICKS	ANTISERUMS	AORTITIS	APHAGIA
ANTEFIXES	ANTICLINE	ANTISHIP	AORTITISES	APHAGIAS
ANTEING	ANTICLINES	ANTISPAST	AOUDAD	APHANITE
ANTELOPE	ANTICOUS	ANTISPASTS	AOUDADS	APHANITES
ANTELOPES	ANTICS	ANTISTAT	APACE	APHASIA
ANTELUCAN	ANTIDOTAL	ANTISTATS	APACHE	APHASIAC
ANTENATAL	ANTIDOTE	ANTITHET	APACHES	APHASIACS
ANTENATI	ANTIDOTES	ANTITHETS	APAGE	APHASIAS
ANTENNA	ANTIENT	ANTITOXIC	APAGOGE	APHASIC
ANTENNAE	ANTIENTS	ANTITOXIN	APAGOGES	APHELIA
ANTENNAL	ANTIGEN	ANTITOXINS	APAGOGIC	APHELIAN
ANTENNARY	ANTIGENIC	ANTITRADE	APAID	APHELIC
ANTENNAS	ANTIGENS	ANTITRADES	APANAGE	APHELION
ANTENNULE	ANTIHELICES	ANTITYPAL	APANAGED	APHERESES
ANTENNULES	ANTIHELIX	ANTITYPE	APANAGES	APHERESIS
ANTEPAST	ANTIKNOCK	ANTITYPES	APART	APHESES
ANTEPASTS	ANTIKNOCKS	ANTITYPIC	APARTHEID	APHESIS
ANTERIOR	ANTILOG	ANTIVENIN	APARTHEIDS	APHETIC
ANTEROOM	ANTILOGIES	ANTIVENINS	APARTMENT	APHETISE
ANTEROOMS	ANTILOGS	ANTIVIRAL	APARTMENTS	APHETISED
ANTES	ANTILOGY	ANTLER	APARTNESS	APHETISES
ANTEVERT	ANTIMASK	ANTLERED	APARTNESSES	APHETISING
ANTEVERTED	ANTIMASKS	ANTLERS	APATETIC	APHETIZE
ANTEVERTING	ANTIMONIC	ANTLIA	APATHATON	APHETIZED
ANTEVERTS	ANTIMONIES	ANTLIAE	APATHATONS	APHETIZES
ANTHELIA	ANTIMONY	ANTLIATE	APATHETIC	APHETIZING
ANTHELICES	ANTING	ANTONYM	APATHIES	APHICIDE
ANTHELION	ANTINGS	ANTONYMS	APATHY	APHICIDES
ANTHELIX	ANTINODAL	ANTRE	APATITE	APHID
ANTHEM	ANTINODE	ANTRES	APATITES	APHIDES
ANTHEMED	ANTINODES	ANTRORSE	APAY	APHIDIAN
ANTHEMIA	ANTINOMIC	ANTRUM	APAYD	APHIDIANS
ANTHEMING	ANTINOMIES	ANTRUMS	APAYING	APHIDICAL
ANTHEMION	ANTINOMY	ANTS	APAYS	APHIDS
ANTHEMS	ANTIPAPAL	ANUCLEATE	APE	APHIS
ANTHER	ANTIPASTO	ANUCLEATED	APEAK	APHONIA
ANTHERS	ANTIPASTOS	ANURIA	APED	APHONIAS
ANTHESES	ANTIPATHIES	ANURIAS	APEDOM	APHONIC
ANTHESIS	ANTIPATHY	ANUROUS	APEDOMS	APHONIES
ANTHOCARP	ANTIPHON	ANUS	APEEK	APHONOUS
ANTHOCARPS	ANTIPHONIES	ANUSES	APEHOOD	APHONY
ANTHOCYAN	ANTIPHONS	ANVIL	APEHOODS	APHORISE
ANTHOCYANS	ANTIPHONY	ANVILS	APEMAN	APHORISED

APHORISER	APODES	APOTHEGM	APPERIL	APPOSES
APHORISERS	APODICTIC	APOTHEGMS	APPERILL	APPOSING
APHORISES	APODOSES	APOTHEM	APPERILLS	APPOSITE
APHORISING	APODOSIS	APOTHEMS	APPERILS	APPRAISAL
APHORISM	APODOUS	APOZEM	APPERTAIN	APPRAISALS
APHORISMS	APODS	APOZEMS	APPERTAINED	APPRAISE
APHORIST	APOENZYME	APPAID	APPERTAINING	APPRAISED
APHORISTS	APOENZYMES	APPAIR	APPERTAINS	APPRAISER
APHORIZE	APOGAEIC	APPAIRED	APPESTAT	APPRAISERS
APHORIZED	APOGAMIES	APPAIRING	APPESTATS	APPRAISES
APHORIZER	APOGAMOUS	APPAIRS	APPETENCE	APPRAISING
APHORIZERS	APOGAMY	APPAL	APPETENCES	APPREHEND
APHORIZES	APOGEAL	APPALLED	APPETENCIES	APPREHENDED
APHORIZING	APOGEAN	APPALLING	APPETENCY	APPREHENDING
APHOTIC	APOGEE	APPALS	APPETENT	APPREHENDS
APHTHA	APOGEES	APPALTI	APPETIBLE	APPRESS
APHTHAE	APOGRAPH	APPALTO	APPETISE	APPRESSED
APHTHOUS	APOGRAPHS	APPANAGE	APPETISED	APPRESSES
APHYLLIES	APOLLINE	APPANAGED	APPETISER	APPRESSING
APHYLLOUS	APOLLO	APPANAGES	APPETISERS	APPRISE
APHYLLY	APOLLOS	APPARAT	APPETISES	APPRISED
APIAN	APOLOGIA	APPARATS	APPETISING	APPRISES
APIARIAN	APOLOGIAS	APPARATUS	APPETITE	APPRISING
APIARIES	APOLOGIES	APPARATUSES	APPETITES	APPRIZE
APIARIST	APOLOGISE	APPAREL	APPETIZE	APPRIZED
APIARISTS	APOLOGISED	APPARELLED	APPETIZED	APPRIZER
APIARY	APOLOGISES	APPARELLING	APPETIZER	APPRIZERS
APICAL	APOLOGISING	APPARELS	APPETIZERS	APPRIZES
APICALLY	APOLOGIST	APPARENCIES	APPETIZES	APPRIZING
APICES	APOLOGISTS	APPARENCY	APPETIZING	APPRIZINGS
APICULATE	APOLOGIZE	APPARENT	APPLAUD	APPRO
APIECE	APOLOGIZED	APPARENTS	APPLAUDED	APPROACH
APING	APOLOGIZES	APPARITOR	APPLAUDER	APPROACHED
APIOL	APOLOGIZING	APPARITORS	APPLAUDERS	APPROACHES
APIOLS	APOLOGUE	APPAY	APPLAUDING	APPROACHING
APISH	APOLOGUES	APPAYD	APPLAUDS	APPROBATE
APISHLY	APOLOGY	APPAYING	APPLAUSE	APPROBATED
APISHNESS	APOMICTIC	APPAYS	APPLAUSES	APPROBATES
APISHNESSES	APOMIXES	APPEACH	APPLE	APPROBATING
APISM	APOMIXIS	APPEACHED	APPLES	APPROOF
APISMS	APOOP	APPEACHES	APPLIABLE	APPROOFS
APIVOROUS	APOPHATIC	APPEACHING	APPLIANCE	APPROS
APLANAT	APOPHYGE	APPEAL	APPLIANCES	APPROVAL
APLANATIC	APOPHYGES	APPEALED	APPLICANT	APPROVALS
APLANATS	APOPHYSES	APPEALING	APPLICANTS	APPROVE
APLASIA	APOPHYSIS	APPEALS	APPLICATE	APPROVED
APLASIAS	APOPLEX	APPEAR	APPLIED	APPROVER
APLASTIC	APOPLEXES	APPEARED	APPLIES	APPROVERS
APLENTY	APOPLEXIES	APPEARER	APPLIQUÉ	APPROVES
APLITE	APOPLEXY	APPEARERS	APPLIQUÉS	APPROVING
APLITES	APORIA	APPEARING	APPLY	APPUI
APLOMB	APORIAS	APPEARS	APPLYING	APPUIED
APLOMBS	APORT	APPEASE	APPOINT	APPUIS
APLUSTRE	APOSITIA	APPEASED	APPOINTED	APPULSE
APLUSTRES	APOSITIAS	APPEASES	APPOINTEE	APPULSES
APNEA	APOSPORIES	APPEASING	APPOINTEES	APPUY
APNEAS	APOSPORY	APPELLANT	APPOINTING	APPUYED
APNOEA	APOSTASIES	APPELLANTS	APPOINTOR	APPUYING
APNOEAS	APOSTASY	APPELLATE	APPOINTORS	APPUYS
APOCOPATE	APOSTATE	APPEND	APPOINTS	APRAXIA
APOCOPATED	APOSTATES	APPENDAGE	APPORT	APRAXIAS
APOCOPATES	APOSTATIC	APPENDAGES	APPORTION	APRÈS
APOCOPATING	APOSTIL	APPENDANT	APPORTIONED	APRICATE
APOCOPE	APOSTILLE	APPENDANTS	APPORTIONING	APRICATED
APOCOPES	APOSTILLES	APPENDED	APPORTIONS	APRICATES
APOCRINE	APOSTILS	APPENDICES	APPORTS	APRICATING
APOCRYPHA	APOSTLE	APPENDING	APPOSE	APRICOCK
APOD	APOSTLES	APPENDIX	APPOSED	APRICOCKS
APODAL	APOSTOLIC	APPENDIXES	APPOSER	APRICOT
APODE	APOTHECIA	APPENDS	APPOSERS	APRICOTS

APRIORISM
APRIORISMS
APRIORIST
APRIORISTS
APRIORITIES
APRIORITY
APRON
APRONED
APRONFUL
APRONFULS
APRONING
APRONS
APROPOS
APSE
APSES
APSIDAL
APSIDES
APSIDIOLE
APSIDIOLES
APSIS
APT
APTED
APTER
APTERAL
APTERIA
APTERIUM
APTEROUS
APTERYX
APTERYXES
APTEST
APTING
APTITUDE
APTITUDES
APTLY
APTNESS
APTNESSES
APTOTE
APTOTES
APTOTIC
APTS
APYRETIC
APYREXIA
APYREXIAS
AQUA
AQUABATIC
AQUABATICS
AQUABOARD
AQUABOARDS
AQUACADE
AQUACADES
AQUADROME
AQUADROMES
AQUAE
AQUAFER
AQUAFERS
AQUALUNG
AQUALUNGS
AQUANAUT
AQUANAUTS
AQUAPLANE
AQUAPLANES
AQUARELLE
AQUARELLES
AQUARIA
AQUARIAN
AQUARIANS
AQUARIIST
AQUARIISTS
AQUARIST
AQUARISTS

AQUARIUM
AQUARIUMS
AQUAS
AQUATIC
AQUATICS
AQUATINT
AQUATINTA
AQUATINTAS
AQUATINTED
AQUATINTING
AQUATINTS
AQUAVIT
AQUAVITS
AQUEDUCT
AQUEDUCTS
AQUEOUS
AQUIFER
AQUIFERS
AQUILEGIA
AQUILEGIAS
AQUILINE
AQUIVER
AR
ARABA
ARABAS
ARABESQUE
ARABESQUED
ARABESQUES
ARABICA
ARABICAS
ARABIN
ARABINOSE
ARABINOSES
ARABINS
ARABISE
ARABISED
ARABISES
ARABISING
ARABIZE
ARABIZED
ARABIZES
ARABIZING
ARABLE
ARACEAE
ARACEOUS
ARACHIS
ARACHISES
ARACHNID
ARACHNIDS
ARACHNOID
ARACHNOIDS
ARAGONITE
ARAGONITES
ARAISE
ARAISED
ARAISES
ARAISING
ARAK
ARAKS
ARALIA
ARALIAS
ARAME
ARAMES
ARANEID
ARANEIDS
ARANEOUS
ARAPAIMA
ARAPAIMAS
ARAPONGA
ARAPONGAS

ARAPUNGA
ARAPUNGAS
ARAR
ARAROBA
ARAROBAS
ARARS
ARAUCARIA
ARAUCARIAS
ARAYSE
ARAYSED
ARAYSES
ARAYSING
ARBA
ARBALEST
ARBALESTS
ARBALIST
ARBALISTS
ARBAS
ARBITER
ARBITERS
ARBITRAGE
ARBITRAGED
ARBITRAGES
ARBITRAGING
ARBITRAL
ARBITRARY
ARBITRATE
ARBITRATED
ARBITRATES
ARBITRATING
ARBITRESS
ARBITRESSES
ARBITRIUM
ARBITRIUMS
ARBLAST
ARBLASTER
ARBLASTERS
ARBLASTS
ARBOR
ARBOREAL
ARBOREOUS
ARBORET
ARBORETA
ARBORETS
ARBORETUM
ARBORIST
ARBORISTS
ARBOROUS
ARBORS
ARBOUR
ARBOURED
ARBOURS
ARBUTE
ARBUTES
ARBUTUS
ARBUTUSES
ARC
ARCADE
ARCADED
ARCADES
ARCADING
ARCADINGS
ARCANA
ARCANE
ARCANELY
ARCANER
ARCANEST
ARCANIST
ARCANISTS
ARCANUM

ARCCOS
ARCCOSES
ARCED
ARCH
ARCHAEI
ARCHAEUS
ARCHAIC
ARCHAISE
ARCHAISED
ARCHAISER
ARCHAISERS
ARCHAISES
ARCHAISING
ARCHAISM
ARCHAISMS
ARCHAIST
ARCHAISTS
ARCHAIZE
ARCHAIZED
ARCHAIZER
ARCHAIZERS
ARCHAIZES
ARCHAIZING
ARCHANGEL
ARCHANGELS
ARCHDUCAL
ARCHDUCHIES
ARCHDUCHY
ARCHDUKE
ARCHDUKES
ARCHED
ARCHEI
ARCHER
ARCHERESS
ARCHERESSES
ARCHERIES
ARCHERS
ARCHERY
ARCHES
ARCHEST
ARCHETYPE
ARCHETYPES
ARCHEUS
ARCHIL
ARCHILOWE
ARCHILOWES
ARCHILS
ARCHIMAGE
ARCHIMAGES
ARCHING
ARCHITECT
ARCHITECTED
ARCHITECTING
ARCHITECTS
ARCHIVAL
ARCHIVE
ARCHIVES
ARCHIVIST
ARCHIVISTS
ARCHIVOLT
ARCHIVOLTS
ARCHLET
ARCHLETS
ARCHLUTE
ARCHLUTES
ARCHLY
ARCHNESS
ARCHNESSES
ARCHOLOGIES
ARCHOLOGY

ARCHON
ARCHONS
ARCHONTIC
ARCHWAY
ARCHWAYS
ARCHWISE
ARCING
ARCINGS
ARCKED
ARCKING
ARCKINGS
ARCO
ARCS
ARCSECOND
ARCSECONDS
ARCSIN
ARCSINS
ARCTAN
ARCTANS
ARCTIC
ARCTICS
ARCTOID
ARCTOPHIL
ARCTOPHILS
ARCUATE
ARCUATED
ARCUATION
ARCUATIONS
ARCUS
ARCUSES
ARDEB
ARDEBS
ARDENCIES
ARDENCY
ARDENT
ARDENTLY
ARDOUR
ARDOURS
ARDRI
ARDRIGH
ARDRIGHS
ARDRIS
ARDUOUS
ARDUOUSLY
ARE
AREA
AREACH
AREACHED
AREACHES
AREACHING
AREAD
AREADING
AREADS
AREAL
AREAR
AREAS
ARECA
ARECAS
ARED
AREDD
AREDE
AREDES
AREDING
AREFIED
AREFIES
AREFY
AREFYING
ARENA
ARENAS
ARENATION

ARENATIONS
AREOLA
AREOLAE
AREOLAR
AREOLATE
AREOLATED
AREOLE
AREOLES
AREOMETER
AREOMETERS
AREOSTYLE
AREOSTYLES
ARERE
ARES
ARET
ARÊTE
ARÊTES
ARETS
ARETT
ARETTED
ARETTING
ARETTS
AREW
ARGAL
ARGALA
ARGALAS
ARGALI
ARGALIS
ARGAN
ARGAND
ARGANDS
ARGANS
ARGEMONE
ARGEMONES
ARGENT
ARGENTINE
ARGENTINES
ARGENTITE
ARGENTITES
ARGENTS
ARGHAN
ARGHANS
ARGIL
ARGILLITE
ARGILLITES
ARGILS
ARGININE
ARGININES
ARGOL
ARGOLS
ARGON
ARGONAUT
ARGONAUTS
ARGONS
ARGOSIES
ARGOSY
ARGOT
ARGOTS
ARGUABLE
ARGUABLY
ARGUE
ARGUED
ARGUER
ARGUERS
ARGUES
ARGUFIED
ARGUFIES
ARGUFY
ARGUFYING
ARGUING

ARGULI
ARGULUS
ARGUMENT
ARGUMENTS
ARGUS
ARGUSES
ARGUTE
ARGUTELY
ARGYLE
ARGYLES
ARGYRIA
ARGYRIAS
ARGYRITE
ARGYRITES
ARHYTHMIA
ARHYTHMIAS
ARHYTHMIC
ARIA
ARIAS
ARID
ARIDER
ARIDEST
ARIDITIES
ARIDITY
ARIDLY
ARIDNESS
ARIDNESSES
ARIEL
ARIELS
ARIETTA
ARIETTAS
ARIETTE
ARIETTES
ARIGHT
ARIL
ARILLARY
ARILLATE
ARILLATED
ARILLI
ARILLODE
ARILLODES
ARILLUS
ARILS
ARIOSI
ARIOSO
ARIOSOS
ARIOT
ARIPPLE
ARIS
ARISE
ARISEN
ARISES
ARISH
ARISHES
ARISING
ARISTA
ARISTAE
ARISTAS
ARISTATE
ARISTO
ARISTOS
ARK
ARKED
ARKING
ARKITE
ARKITES
ARKOSE
ARKOSES
ARKS
ARLES

ARLESED
ARLESES
ARLESING
ARM
ARMADA
ARMADAS
ARMADILLO
ARMADILLOS
ARMAMENT
ARMAMENTS
ARMATURE
ARMATURES
ARMBAND
ARMBANDS
ARMCHAIR
ARMCHAIRS
ARMED
ARMET
ARMETS
ARMFUL
ARMFULS
ARMGAUNT
ARMHOLE
ARMHOLES
ARMIES
ARMIGER
ARMIGERAL
ARMIGERO
ARMIGEROS
ARMIGERS
ARMIL
ARMILLA
ARMILLAE
ARMILLARY
ARMILLAS
ARMILS
ARMING
ARMISTICE
ARMISTICES
ARMLESS
ARMLET
ARMLETS
ARMLOCK
ARMLOCKS
ARMOIRE
ARMOIRES
ARMOR
ARMORIAL
ARMORIES
ARMORIST
ARMORISTS
ARMORS
ARMORY
ARMOUR
ARMOURED
ARMOURER
ARMOURERS
ARMOURIES
ARMOURS
ARMOURY
ARMOZEEN
ARMOZEENS
ARMOZINE
ARMOZINES
ARMPIT
ARMPITS
ARMS
ARMURE
ARMURES
ARMY

ARNA
ARNAS
ARNICA
ARNICAS
ARNOTTO
ARNOTTOS
ARNUT
ARNUTS
AROBA
AROBAS
AROID
AROIDS
AROINT
AROINTED
AROINTING
AROINTS
AROLLA
AROLLAS
AROMA
AROMAS
AROMATIC
AROMATICS
AROMATISE
AROMATISED
AROMATISES
AROMATISING
AROMATIZE
AROMATIZED
AROMATIZES
AROMATIZING
AROSE
AROUND
AROUSAL
AROUSALS
AROUSE
AROUSED
AROUSER
AROUSERS
AROUSES
AROUSING
AROW
AROYNT
AROYNTED
AROYNTING
AROYNTS
ARPEGGIO
ARPEGGIOS
ARPENT
ARPENTS
ARQUEBUS
ARQUEBUSE
ARQUEBUSES
ARRACACHA
ARRACACHAS
ARRACK
ARRACKS
ARRAH
ARRAIGN
ARRAIGNED
ARRAIGNER
ARRAIGNERS
ARRAIGNING
ARRAIGNINGS
ARRAIGNS
ARRANGE
ARRANGED
ARRANGER
ARRANGERS
ARRANGES
ARRANGING

ARRANT
ARRANTLY
ARRAS
ARRASED
ARRASENE
ARRASENES
ARRASES
ARRAUGHT
ARRAY
ARRAYED
ARRAYING
ARRAYMENT
ARRAYMENTS
ARRAYS
ARREAR
ARREARAGE
ARREARAGES
ARREARS
ARRECT
ARREDD
ARREEDE
ARREEDES
ARREEDING
ARREST
ARRESTED
ARRESTEE
ARRESTEES
ARRESTER
ARRESTERS
ARRESTING
ARRESTIVE
ARRESTOR
ARRESTORS
ARRESTS
ARRÊT
ARRÊTS
ARRIAGE
ARRIAGES
ARRIDE
ARRIDED
ARRIDES
ARRIDING
ARRIÉRÉ
ARRIERO
ARRIEROS
ARRIS
ARRISES
ARRISH
ARRISHES
ARRIVAL
ARRIVALS
ARRIVANCE
ARRIVANCES
ARRIVANCIES
ARRIVANCY
ARRIVE
ARRIVED
ARRIVES
ARRIVING
ARRIVISME
ARRIVISMES
ARRIVISTE
ARRIVISTES
ARROBA
ARROBAS
ARROGANCE
ARROGANCES
ARROGANCIES
ARROGANCY
ARROGANT

ARROGATE
ARROGATED
ARROGATES
ARROGATING
ARROW
ARROWED
ARROWING
ARROWROOT
ARROWROOTS
ARROWS
ARROWWOOD
ARROWWOODS
ARROWY
ARROYO
ARROYOS
ARS
ARSE
ARSEHOLE
ARSEHOLES
ARSENAL
ARSENALS
ARSENATE
ARSENATES
ARSENIATE
ARSENIATES
ARSENIC
ARSENICAL
ARSENICS
ARSENIDE
ARSENIDES
ARSENIOUS
ARSENITE
ARSENITES
ARSES
ARSHEEN
ARSHEENS
ARSHIN
ARSHINE
ARSHINES
ARSHINS
ARSINE
ARSINES
ARSIS
ARSON
ARSONIST
ARSONISTS
ARSONITE
ARSONITES
ARSONS
ART
ARTAL
ARTEFACT
ARTEFACTS
ARTEL
ARTELS
ARTEMISIA
ARTEMISIAS
ARTERIAL
ARTERIES
ARTERIOLE
ARTERIOLES
ARTERITIS
ARTERITISES
ARTERY
ARTESIAN
ARTFUL
ARTFULLY
ARTHRITIC
ARTHRITICS
ARTHRITIS

ARTHROPOD
ARTHROPODS
ARTHROSES
ARTHROSIS
ARTIC
ARTICHOKE
ARTICHOKES
ARTICLE
ARTICLED
ARTICLES
ARTICLING
ARTICS
ARTICULAR
ARTIER
ARTIEST
ARTIFACT
ARTIFACTS
ARTIFICE
ARTIFICER
ARTIFICERS
ARTIFICES
ARTILLERIES
ARTILLERY
ARTISAN
ARTISANAL
ARTISANS
ARTIST
ARTISTE
ARTISTES
ARTISTIC
ARTISTRIES
ARTISTRY
ARTISTS
ARTLESS
ARTLESSLY
ARTS
ARTSIER
ARTSIEST
ARTSMAN
ARTSMEN
ARTSY
ARTWORK
ARTWORKS
ARTY
ARUM
ARUMS
ARVAL
ARVO
ARVOS
ARY
ARYBALLOS
ARYBALLOSES
ARYL
ARYLS
ARYTENOID
ARYTENOIDS
AS
ASAFETIDA
ASAFETIDAS
ASANA
ASANAS
ASAR
ASARUM
ASARUMS
ASBESTIC
ASBESTINE
ASBESTOS
ASBESTOSES
ASBESTOUS
ASCARID

ASCARIDES
ASCARIDS
ASCARIS
ASCAUNT
ASCEND
ASCENDANT
ASCENDANTS
ASCENDED
ASCENDENT
ASCENDENTS
ASCENDER
ASCENDERS
ASCENDING
ASCENDS
ASCENSION
ASCENSIONS
ASCENSIVE
ASCENT
ASCENTS
ASCERTAIN
ASCERTAINED
ASCERTAINING
ASCERTAINS
ASCESES
ASCESIS
ASCETIC
ASCETICAL
ASCETICS
ASCI
ASCIAN
ASCIANS
ASCIDIA
ASCIDIAN
ASCIDIANS
ASCIDIUM
ASCITES
ASCITIC
ASCITICAL
ASCLEPIAD
ASCLEPIADS
ASCLEPIAS
ASCLEPIASES
ASCONCE
ASCORBATE
ASCORBATES
ASCORBIC
ASCOSPORE
ASCOSPORES
ASCOT
ASCOTS
ASCRIBE
ASCRIBED
ASCRIBES
ASCRIBING
ASCUS
ASEISMIC
ASEITIES
ASEITY
ASEPALOUS
ASEPSES
ASEPSIS
ASEPTATE
ASEPTIC
ASEPTICS
ASEXUAL
ASEXUALLY
ASH
ASHAKE
ASHAME
ASHAMED

ASHAMEDLY
ASHAMES
ASHAMING
ASHEN
ASHERIES
ASHERY
ASHES
ASHET
ASHETS
ASHIER
ASHIEST
ASHINE
ASHIVER
ASHLAR
ASHLARED
ASHLARING
ASHLARINGS
ASHLARS
ASHLER
ASHLERED
ASHLERING
ASHLERINGS
ASHLERS
ASHORE
ASHRAM
ASHRAMA
ASHRAMAS
ASHRAMS
ASHY
ASIDE
ASIDES
ASINICO
ASINICOS
ASININE
ASININITIES
ASININITY
ASK
ASKANCE
ASKANCED
ASKANCES
ASKANCING
ASKANT
ASKANTED
ASKANTS
ASKARI
ASKARIS
ASKED
ASKER
ASKERS
ASKESES
ASKESIS
ASKEW
ASKING
ASKLENT
ASKS
ASLAKE
ASLAKED
ASLAKES
ASLAKING
ASLANT
ASLEEP
ASLOPE
ASMEAR
ASMOULDER
ASOCIAL
ASP
ASPARAGUS
ASPARAGUSES
ASPARTAME

ASPARTAMES
ASPECT
ASPECTED
ASPECTING
ASPECTS
ASPECTUAL
ASPEN
ASPENS
ASPER
ASPERATE
ASPERATED
ASPERATES
ASPERATING
ASPERGE
ASPERGED
ASPERGER
ASPERGERS
ASPERGES
ASPERGILL
ASPERGILLS
ASPERGING
ASPERITIES
ASPERITY
ASPEROUS
ASPERS
ASPERSE
ASPERSED
ASPERSES
ASPERSING
ASPERSION
ASPERSIONS
ASPERSIVE
ASPERSOIR
ASPERSORY
ASPHALT
ASPHALTED
ASPHALTIC
ASPHALTING
ASPHALTS
ASPHALTUM
ASPHALTUMS
ASPHODEL
ASPHODELS
ASPHYXIA
ASPHYXIAS
ASPHYXIES
ASPHYXY
ASPIC
ASPICK
ASPICKS
ASPICS
ASPIDIA
ASPIDIOID
ASPIDIUM
ASPINE
ASPINES
ASPIRANT
ASPIRANTS
ASPIRATE
ASPIRATED
ASPIRATES
ASPIRATING
ASPIRATOR
ASPIRATORS
ASPIRE
ASPIRED
ASPIRES
ASPIRIN
ASPIRING

ASPIRINS
ASPORT
ASPORTED
ASPORTING
ASPORTS
ASPOUT
ASPRAWL
ASPREAD
ASPROUT
ASPS
ASQUAT
ASQUINT
ASS
ASSAGAI
ASSAGAIED
ASSAGAIING
ASSAGAIS
ASSAI
ASSAIL
ASSAILANT
ASSAILANTS
ASSAILED
ASSAILING
ASSAILS
ASSAIS
ASSART
ASSARTED
ASSARTING
ASSARTS
ASSASSIN
ASSASSINS
ASSAULT
ASSAULTED
ASSAULTER
ASSAULTERS
ASSAULTING
ASSAULTS
ASSAY
ASSAYABLE
ASSAYED
ASSAYER
ASSAYERS
ASSAYING
ASSAYINGS
ASSAYS
ASSEGAAI
ASSEGAAIED
ASSEGAAIING
ASSEGAAIS
ASSEGAI
ASSEGAIED
ASSEGAIING
ASSEGAIS
ASSEMBLE
ASSEMBLÉ
ASSEMBLED
ASSEMBLER
ASSEMBLERS
ASSEMBLES
ASSEMBLÉS
ASSEMBLIES
ASSEMBLING
ASSEMBLY
ASSENT
ASSENTED
ASSENTER
ASSENTERS
ASSENTING
ASSENTIVE
ASSENTOR
ASSENTORS

ASSENTS
ASSERT
ASSERTED
ASSERTER
ASSERTERS
ASSERTING
ASSERTION
ASSERTIONS
ASSERTIVE
ASSERTOR
ASSERTORS
ASSERTORY
ASSERTS
ASSES
ASSESS
ASSESSED
ASSESSES
ASSESSING
ASSESSOR
ASSESSORS
ASSET
ASSETS
ASSEVER
ASSEVERED
ASSEVERING
ASSEVERS
ASSHOLE
ASSHOLES
ASSIDUITIES
ASSIDUITY
ASSIDUOUS
ASSIEGE
ASSIEGED
ASSIEGES
ASSIEGING
ASSIENTO
ASSIENTOS
ASSIGN
ASSIGNAT
ASSIGNATS
ASSIGNED
ASSIGNEE
ASSIGNEES
ASSIGNING
ASSIGNOR
ASSIGNORS
ASSIGNS
ASSIST
ASSISTANT
ASSISTANTS
ASSISTED
ASSISTING
ASSISTS
ASSIZE
ASSIZED
ASSIZER
ASSIZERS
ASSIZES
ASSIZING
ASSOCIATE
ASSOCIATED
ASSOCIATES
ASSOCIATING
ASSOIL
ASSOILED
ASSOILING
ASSOILS
ASSOILZIE
ASSOILZIED
ASSOILZIEING
ASSOILZIES

ASSONANCE
ASSONANCES
ASSONANT
ASSONATE
ASSONATED
ASSONATES
ASSONATING
ASSORT
ASSORTED
ASSORTER
ASSORTERS
ASSORTING
ASSORTS
ASSOT
ASSOTS
ASSOTT
ASSOTTED
ASSOTTING
ASSUAGE
ASSUAGED
ASSUAGES
ASSUAGING
ASSUAGINGS
ASSUASIVE
ASSUETUDE
ASSUETUDES
ASSUMABLE
ASSUMABLY
ASSUME
ASSUMED
ASSUMEDLY
ASSUMES
ASSUMING
ASSUMINGS
ASSUMPSIT
ASSUMPSITS
ASSURABLE
ASSURANCE
ASSURANCES
ASSURE
ASSURED
ASSUREDLY
ASSUREDS
ASSURER
ASSURERS
ASSURES
ASSURGENT
ASSURING
ASSWAGE
ASSWAGED
ASSWAGES
ASSWAGING
ASTABLE
ASTARE
ASTART
ASTARTED
ASTARTING
ASTARTS
ASTATIC
ASTATINE
ASTATINES
ASTATKI
ASTATKIS
ASTEISM
ASTEISMS
ASTELIC
ASTELIES
ASTELY
ASTER
ASTERIA
ASTERIAS

ASTERID
ASTERIDS
ASTERISK
ASTERISKED
ASTERISKING
ASTERISKS
ASTERISM
ASTERISMS
ASTERN
ASTEROID
ASTEROIDS
ASTERS
ASTERT
ASTERTED
ASTERTING
ASTERTS
ASTHENIA
ASTHENIAS
ASTHENIC
ASTHENICS
ASTHMA
ASTHMAS
ASTHMATIC
ASTHORE
ASTHORES
ASTICHOUS
ASTIGMIA
ASTIGMIAS
ASTILBE
ASTILBES
ASTIR
ASTOMOUS
ASTONE
ASTONED
ASTONES
ASTONIED
ASTONIES
ASTONING
ASTONISH
ASTONISHED
ASTONISHES
ASTONISHING
ASTONY
ASTONYING
ASTOOP
ASTOUND
ASTOUNDED
ASTOUNDING
ASTOUNDS
ASTRADDLE
ASTRAGAL
ASTRAGALS
ASTRAKHAN
ASTRAKHANS
ASTRAL
ASTRAND
ASTRAY
ASTREX
ASTREXES
ASTRICT
ASTRICTED
ASTRICTING
ASTRICTS
ASTRIDE
ASTRINGE
ASTRINGED
ASTRINGER
ASTRINGERS
ASTRINGES
ASTRINGING
ASTRODOME

ASTRODOMES
ASTROFELL
ASTROFELLS
ASTROID
ASTROIDS
ASTROLABE
ASTROLABES
ASTROLOGIES
ASTROLOGY
ASTRONAUT
ASTRONAUTS
ASTRONOMIES
ASTRONOMY
ASTROPHEL
ASTROPHELS
ASTRUT
ASTUCIOUS
ASTUCITIES
ASTUCITY
ASTUN
ASTUNNED
ASTUNNING
ASTUNS
ASTUTE
ASTUTELY
ASTUTER
ASTUTEST
ASTYLAR
ASUDDEN
ASUNDER
ASWARM
ASWAY
ASWIM
ASWING
ASWIRL
ASWOON
ASYLUM
ASYLUMS
ASYMMETRIES
ASYMMETRY
ASYMPTOTE
ASYMPTOTES
ASYNDETIC
ASYNDETON
ASYNDETONS
ASYNERGIA
ASYNERGIAS
ASYSTOLE
ASYSTOLES
AT
ATABAL
ATABALS
ATABEG
ATABEGS
ATABEK
ATABEKS
ATABRIN
ATABRINS
ATACAMITE
ATACAMITES
ATACTIC
ATAGHAN
ATAGHANS
ATALAYA
ATALAYAS
ATAMAN
ATAMANS
ATAP
ATAPS
ATARACTIC
ATARACTICS

ATARAXIA	ATHRILL	ATONEMENTS	ATTEMPERING	ATTRAP
ATARAXIAS	ATHROB	ATONER	ATTEMPERS	ATTRAPPED
ATARAXIC	ATHROCYTE	ATONERS	ATTEMPT	ATTRAPPING
ATARAXICS	ATHROCYTES	ATONES	ATTEMPTED	ATTRAPS
ATARAXIES	ATHWART	ATONIC	ATTEMPTER	ATTRIBUTE
ATARAXY	ATILT	ATONICITIES	ATTEMPTERS	ATTRIBUTED
ATAVISM	ATIMIES	ATONICITY	ATTEMPTING	ATTRIBUTES
ATAVISMS	ATIMY	ATONIES	ATTEMPTS	ATTRIBUTING
ATAVISTIC	ATINGLE	ATONING	ATTEND	ATTRIST
ATAXIA	ATLAS	ATONINGLY	ATTENDANT	ATTRISTED
ATAXIAS	ATLASES	ATONY	ATTENDANTS	ATTRISTING
ATAXIC	ATMAN	ATOP	ATTENDED	ATTRISTS
ATAXIES	ATMANS	ATOPIC	ATTENDEE	ATTRITE
ATAXY	ATMOLOGIES	ATOPIES	ATTENDEES	ATTRITION
ATCHIEVE	ATMOLOGY	ATOPY	ATTENDER	ATTRITIONS
ATCHIEVED	ATMOLYSE	ATRAMENT	ATTENDERS	ATTUENT
ATCHIEVES	ATMOLYSED	ATRAMENTS	ATTENDING	ATTUITE
ATCHIEVING	ATMOLYSES	ATREMBLE	ATTENDS	ATTUITED
ATE	ATMOLYSING	ATRESIA	ATTENT	ATTUITES
ATEBRIN	ATMOLYSIS	ATRESIAS	ATTENTAT	ATTUITING
ATEBRINS	ATMOLYZE	ATRIA	ATTENTATS	ATTUITION
ATELIER	ATMOLYZED	ATRIAL	ATTENTION	ATTUITIONS
ATELIERS	ATMOLYZES	ATRIP	ATTENTIONS	ATTUITIVE
ATHANASIES	ATMOLYZING	ATRIUM	ATTENTIVE	ATTUNE
ATHANASY	ATMOMETER	ATROCIOUS	ATTENTS	ATTUNED
ATHANOR	ATMOMETERS	ATROCITIES	ATTENUANT	ATTUNES
ATHANORS	ATOC	ATROCITY	ATTENUANTS	ATTUNING
ATHEISE	ATOCIA	ATROPHIED	ATTENUATE	ATWAIN
ATHEISED	ATOCIAS	ATROPHIES	ATTENUATED	ATWEEL
ATHEISES	ATOCS	ATROPHY	ATTENUATES	ATWEEN
ATHEISING	ATOK	ATROPHYING	ATTENUATING	ATWIXT
ATHEISM	ATOKAL	ATROPIA	ATTERCOP	ATYPICAL
ATHEISMS	ATOKE	ATROPIAS	ATTERCOPS	AUBADE
ATHEIST	ATOKES	ATROPIN	ATTEST	AUBADES
ATHEISTIC	ATOKOUS	ATROPINE	ATTESTED	AUBERGE
ATHEISTS	ATOKS	ATROPINES	ATTESTER	AUBERGES
ATHEIZE	ATOLL	ATROPINS	ATTESTERS	AUBERGINE
ATHEIZED	ATOLLS	ATROPISM	ATTESTING	AUBERGINES
ATHEIZES	ATOM	ATROPISMS	ATTESTOR	AUBRIETIA
ATHEIZING	ATOMIC	ATROPOUS	ATTESTORS	AUBRIETIAS
ATHELING	ATOMICAL	ATTABOY	ATTESTS	AUBURN
ATHELINGS	ATOMICITIES	ATTACH	ATTIC	AUCEPS
ATHEMATIC	ATOMICITY	ATTACHÉ	ATTICS	AUCEPSES
ATHEOLOGIES	ATOMIES	ATTACHED	ATTIRE	AUCTION
ATHEOLOGY	ATOMISE	ATTACHES	ATTIRED	AUCTIONED
ATHEOUS	ATOMISED	ATTACHÉS	ATTIRES	AUCTIONING
ATHERINE	ATOMISER	ATTACHING	ATTIRING	AUCTIONS
ATHERINES	ATOMISERS	ATTACK	ATTIRINGS	AUCTORIAL
ATHEROMA	ATOMISES	ATTACKED	ATTITUDE	AUCUBA
ATHEROMAS	ATOMISING	ATTACKER	ATTITUDES	AUCUBAS
ATHETESES	ATOMISM	ATTACKERS	ATTOLLENT	AUDACIOUS
ATHETESIS	ATOMISMS	ATTACKING	ATTOLLENTS	AUDACITIES
ATHETISE	ATOMIST	ATTACKS	ATTONCE	AUDACITY
ATHETISED	ATOMISTIC	ATTAIN	ATTONE	AUDIBLE
ATHETISES	ATOMISTS	ATTAINDER	ATTONED	AUDIBLY
ATHETISING	ATOMIZE	ATTAINDERS	ATTONES	AUDIENCE
ATHETIZE	ATOMIZED	ATTAINED	ATTONING	AUDIENCES
ATHETIZED	ATOMIZER	ATTAINING	ATTORN	AUDIENT
ATHETIZES	ATOMIZERS	ATTAINS	ATTORNED	AUDIENTS
ATHETIZING	ATOMIZES	ATTAINT	ATTORNEY	AUDILE
ATHETOID	ATOMIZING	ATTAINTED	ATTORNEYS	AUDILES
ATHETOIDS	ATOMS	ATTAINTING	ATTORNING	AUDIO
ATHETOSES	ATOMY	ATTAINTS	ATTORNS	AUDIOGRAM
ATHETOSIS	ATONAL	ATTAP	ATTRACT	AUDIOGRAMS
ATHIRST	ATONALISM	ATTAPS	ATTRACTED	AUDIOLOGIES
ATHLETA	ATONALISMS	ATTAR	ATTRACTING	AUDIOLOGY
ATHLETAS	ATONALITIES	ATTARS	ATTRACTOR	AUDIOPHIL
ATHLETE	ATONALITY	ATTASK	ATTRACTORS	AUDIOPHILS
ATHLETES	ATONE	ATTASKT	ATTRACTS	AUDIOS
ATHLETIC	ATONED	ATTEMPER	ATTRAHENT	AUDIPHONE
ATHLETICS	ATONEMENT	ATTEMPERED	ATTRAHENTS	AUDIPHONES

AUDIT
AUDITED
AUDITING
AUDITION
AUDITIONED
AUDITIONING
AUDITIONS
AUDITIVE
AUDITOR
AUDITORIA
AUDITORIES
AUDITORS
AUDITORY
AUDITRESS
AUDITRESSES
AUDITS
AUF
AUFGABE
AUFGABES
AUFS
AUGER
AUGERS
AUGHT
AUGHTS
AUGITE
AUGITES
AUGITIC
AUGMENT
AUGMENTED
AUGMENTER
AUGMENTERS
AUGMENTING
AUGMENTOR
AUGMENTORS
AUGMENTS
AUGUR
AUGURAL
AUGURED
AUGURER
AUGURERS
AUGURIES
AUGURING
AUGURS
AUGURSHIP
AUGURSHIPS
AUGURY
AUGUST
AUGUSTE
AUGUSTER
AUGUSTES
AUGUSTEST
AUGUSTLY
AUGUSTS
AUK
AUKLET
AUKLETS
AUKS
AULA
AULARIAN
AULARIANS
AULAS
AULD
AULDER
AULDEST
AULIC
AULOI
AULOS
AUMAIL
AUMAILED
AUMAILING
AUMAILS

AUMBRIES
AUMBRY
AUMIL
AUMILS
AUNT
AUNTER
AUNTERS
AUNTIE
AUNTIES
AUNTS
AUNTY
AURA
AURAE
AURAL
AURALLY
AURAS
AURATE
AURATED
AURATES
AUREATE
AUREI
AUREITIES
AUREITY
AURELIA
AURELIAN
AURELIANS
AURELIAS
AUREOLA
AUREOLAS
AUREOLE
AUREOLED
AUREOLES
AUREUS
AURIC
AURICLE
AURICLED
AURICLES
AURICULA
AURICULAR
AURICULAS
AURIFIED
AURIFIES
AURIFORM
AURIFY
AURIFYING
AURISCOPE
AURISCOPES
AURIST
AURISTS
AUROCHS
AUROCHSES
AURORA
AURORAE
AURORAL
AURORALLY
AURORAS
AUROREAN
AUROUS
AUSPICATE
AUSPICATED
AUSPICATES
AUSPICATING
AUSPICE
AUSPICES
AUSTENITE
AUSTENITES
AUSTERE
AUSTERELY
AUSTERER
AUSTEREST
AUSTERITIES

AUSTERITY
AUTACOID
AUTACOIDS
AUTARCHIC
AUTARCHIES
AUTARCHY
AUTARKIC
AUTARKIES
AUTARKIST
AUTARKISTS
AUTARKY
AUTEUR
AUTEURS
AUTHENTIC
AUTHOR
AUTHORED
AUTHORESS
AUTHORESSES
AUTHORIAL
AUTHORING
AUTHORINGS
AUTHORISE
AUTHORISED
AUTHORISES
AUTHORISH
AUTHORISING
AUTHORISM
AUTHORISMS
AUTHORITIES
AUTHORITY
AUTHORIZE
AUTHORIZED
AUTHORIZES
AUTHORIZING
AUTHORS
AUTISM
AUTISMS
AUTISTIC
AUTO
AUTOBUS
AUTOBUSES
AUTOCADE
AUTOCADES
AUTOCAR
AUTOCARP
AUTOCARPS
AUTOCARS
AUTOCLAVE
AUTOCLAVES
AUTOCRACIES
AUTOCRACY
AUTOCRAT
AUTOCRATS
AUTOCROSS
AUTOCROSSES
AUTOCUE
AUTOCUES
AUTOCYCLE
AUTOCYCLES
AUTODYNE
AUTOFLARE
AUTOFLARES
AUTOGAMIC
AUTOGAMIES
AUTOGAMY
AUTOGENIC
AUTOGENIES
AUTOGENY
AUTOGIRO
AUTOGIROS
AUTOGRAFT

AUTOGRAFTED
AUTOGRAFTING
AUTOGRAFTS
AUTOGRAPH
AUTOGRAPHED
AUTOGRAPHING
AUTOGRAPHS
AUTOGYRO
AUTOGYROS
AUTOHARP
AUTOHARPS
AUTOLATRIES
AUTOLATRY
AUTOLOGIES
AUTOLOGY
AUTOLYSE
AUTOLYSED
AUTOLYSES
AUTOLYSING
AUTOLYSIS
AUTOLYTIC
AUTOLYZE
AUTOLYZED
AUTOLYZES
AUTOLYZING
AUTOMAT
AUTOMATA
AUTOMATE
AUTOMATED
AUTOMATES
AUTOMATIC
AUTOMATICS
AUTOMATING
AUTOMATON
AUTOMATONS
AUTOMATS
AUTONOMIC
AUTONOMICS
AUTONOMIES
AUTONOMY
AUTONYM
AUTONYMS
AUTOPHAGIES
AUTOPHAGY
AUTOPHOBIES
AUTOPHOBY
AUTOPHONIES
AUTOPHONY
AUTOPILOT
AUTOPILOTS
AUTOPISTA
AUTOPISTAS
AUTOPOINT
AUTOPOINTS
AUTOPSIA
AUTOPSIAS
AUTOPSIED
AUTOPSIES
AUTOPSY
AUTOPSYING
AUTOPTIC
AUTOROUTE
AUTOROUTES
AUTOS
AUTOSCOPIES
AUTOSCOPY
AUTOSOMAL
AUTOSOME
AUTOSOMES
AUTOTELIC
AUTOTIMER

AUTOTIMERS
AUTOTOMIES
AUTOTOMY
AUTOTOXIN
AUTOTOXINS
AUTOTROPH
AUTOTROPHS
AUTOTYPE
AUTOTYPED
AUTOTYPES
AUTOTYPING
AUTOVAC
AUTOVACS
AUTUMN
AUTUMNAL
AUTUMNS
AUTUMNY
AUTUNITE
AUTUNITES
AUXESES
AUXESIS
AUXETIC
AUXETICS
AUXILIAR
AUXILIARIES
AUXILIARS
AUXILIARY
AUXIN
AUXINS
AUXOMETER
AUXOMETERS
AVA
AVADAVAT
AVADAVATS
AVAIL
AVAILABLE
AVAILABLY
AVAILE
AVAILED
AVAILES
AVAILFUL
AVAILING
AVAILS
AVAL
AVALANCHE
AVALANCHED
AVALANCHES
AVALANCHING
AVALE
AVALED
AVALES
AVALING
AVANT
AVANTI
AVARICE
AVARICES
AVAS
AVAST
AVATAR
AVATARS
AVAUNT
AVAUNTED
AVAUNTING
AVAUNTS
AVE
AVENGE
AVENGED
AVENGEFUL
AVENGEING
AVENGER
AVENGERS

AVENGES
AVENGING
AVENIR
AVENIRS
AVENS
AVENSES
AVENTAIL
AVENTAILE
AVENTAILES
AVENTAILS
AVENTRE
AVENTRED
AVENTRES
AVENTRING
AVENTURE
AVENTURES
AVENUE
AVENUES
AVER
AVERAGE
AVERAGED
AVERAGES
AVERAGING
AVERMENT
AVERMENTS
AVERRED
AVERRING
AVERS
AVERSE
AVERSELY
AVERSION
AVERSIONS
AVERSIVE
AVERT
AVERTABLE
AVERTED
AVERTEDLY
AVERTIBLE
AVERTING
AVERTS
AVES
AVGAS
AVGASES
AVIAN
AVIARIES
AVIARIST
AVIARISTS
AVIARY
AVIATE
AVIATED
AVIATES
AVIATING
AVIATION
AVIATIONS
AVIATOR
AVIATORS
AVIATRIX
AVIATRIXES
AVID
AVIDER
AVIDEST
AVIDITIES
AVIDITY
AVIDLY
AVIETTE
AVIETTES
AVIFAUNA
AVIFAUNAS
AVIFORM
AVINE
AVION

AVIONIC
AVIONICS
AVIONS
AVISANDUM
AVISANDUMS
AVISE
AVISED
AVISEMENT
AVISEMENTS
AVISES
AVISING
AVISO
AVISOS
AVITAL
AVIZANDUM
AVIZANDUMS
AVIZE
AVIZED
AVIZEFULL
AVIZES
AVIZING
AVOCADO
AVOCADOS
AVOCATION
AVOCATIONS
AVOCET
AVOCETS
AVOID
AVOIDABLE
AVOIDANCE
AVOIDANCES
AVOIDED
AVOIDING
AVOIDS
AVOISION
AVOISIONS
AVOSET
AVOSETS
AVOUCH
AVOUCHED
AVOUCHES
AVOUCHING
AVOUE
AVOUCO
AVOURE
AVOURES
AVOUTERER
AVOUTERERS
AVOUTRER
AVOUTRERS
AVOUTRIES
AVOUTRY
AVOW
AVOWABLE
AVOWAL
AVOWALS
AVOWED
AVOWEDLY
AVOWING
AVOWRIES
AVOWRY
AVOWS
AVOYER
AVOYERS
AVULSE
AVULSED
AVULSES
AVULSING
AVULSION
AVULSIONS
AVUNCULAR

AVYZE
AVYZED
AVYZES
AVYZING
AW
AWA
AWAIT
AWAITED
AWAITING
AWAITS
AWAKE
AWAKED
AWAKEN
AWAKENED
AWAKENING
AWAKENINGS
AWAKENS
AWAKES
AWAKING
AWAKINGS
AWANTING
AWARD
AWARDED
AWARDING
AWARDS
AWARE
AWARENESS
AWARENESSES
AWARER
AWAREST
AWARN
AWARNED
AWARNING
AWARNS
AWASH
AWATCH
AWAVE
AWAY
AWAYES
AWAYS
AWDL
AWDLS
AWE
AWEARIED
AWEARY
AWED
AWEEL
AWELESS
AWES
AWESOME
AWESOMELY
AWESTRIKE
AWESTRIKES
AWESTRIKING
AWESTRUCK
AWETO
AWETOS
AWFUL
AWFULLY
AWFULNESS
AWFULNESSES
AWHAPE
AWHAPED
AWHAPES
AWHAPING
AWHEEL
AWHEELS
AWHILE
AWING
AWKWARD
AWKWARDER

AWKWARDEST
AWKWARDLY
AWL
AWLBIRD
AWLBIRDS
AWLS
AWMOUS
AWMRIE
AWMRIES
AWMRY
AWN
AWNED
AWNER
AWNERS
AWNIER
AWNIEST
AWNING
AWNINGS
AWNLESS
AWNS
AWNY
AWOKE
AWOKEN
AWORK
AWRACK
AWRONG
AWRY
AWSOME
AX
AXE
AXED
AXEL
AXELS
AXES
AXIAL
AXIALLY
AXIL
AXILE
AXILLA
AXILLAE
AXILLAR
AXILLARY
AXILS
AXING
AXINITE
AXINITES
AXIOLOGIES
AXIOLOGY
AXIOM
AXIOMATIC
AXIOMATICS
AXIOMS
AXIS
AXISES
AXLE
AXLES
AXOID
AXOIDS
AXOLOTL
AXOLOTLS
AXON
AXONS
AXOPLASM
AXOPLASMS
AY
AYAH
AYAHS
AYAHUASCO
AYAHUASCOS
AYATOLLAH
AYATOLLAHS

AYE
AYELP
AYENBITE
AYENBITES
AYES
AYGRE
AYONT
AYRE
AYRES
AYRIE
AYRIES
AYU
AYURVEDIC
AYUS
AYWORD
AYWORDS
AZALEA
AZALEAS
AZAN
AZANS
AZEOTROPE
AZEOTROPES
AZIDE
AZIDES
AZIMUTH
AZIMUTHAL
AZIMUTHS
AZIONE
AZIONES
AZOIC
AZOLLA
AZOLLAS
AZONAL
AZONIC
AZOTE
AZOTES
AZOTH
AZOTHS
AZOTIC
AZOTISE
AZOTISED
AZOTISES
AZOTISING
AZOTIZE
AZOTIZED
AZOTIZES
AZOTIZING
AZOTOUS
AZULEJO
AZULEJOS
AZURE
AZUREAN
AZURES
AZURINE
AZURINES
AZURITE
AZURITES
AZURN
AZURY
AZYGIES
AZYGOUS
AZYGY
AZYM
AZYME
AZYMES
AZYMITE
AZYMITES
AZYMOUS
AZYMS

B

BA
BAA
BAAED
BAAING
BAAINGS
BAAS
BAASES
BAASSKAP
BAASSKAPS
BABA
BABACOOTE
BABACOOTES
BABAS
BABASSU
BABASSUS
BABBIT
BABBITS
BABBITTED
BABBITTING
BABBLE
BABBLED
BABBLER
BABBLERS
BABBLES
BABBLIER
BABBLIEST
BABBLING
BABBLINGS
BABBLY
BABE
BABELDOM
BABELDOMS
BABELISH
BABELISM
BABELISMS
BABES
BABICHE
BABICHES
BABIED
BABIER
BABIES
BABIEST
BABIRUSSA
BABIRUSSAS
BABLAH
BABLAHS
BABOO
BABOON
BABOONERIES
BABOONERY
BABOONISH
BABOONS
BABOOS
BABOOSH
BABOOSHES
BABOUCHE
BABOUCHES
BABU
BABUCHE
BABUCHES
BABUDOM
BABUDOMS
BABUISM
BABUISMS

BABUL
BABULS
BABUS
BABUSHKA
BABUSHKAS
BABY
BABYFOOD
BABYFOODS
BABYHOOD
BABYHOODS
BABYING
BABYISH
BACCA
BACCAE
BACCARA
BACCARAS
BACCARAT
BACCARATS
BACCARE
BACCAS
BACCATE
BACCHANAL
BACCHANALS
BACCHANT
BACCHANTE
BACCHANTES
BACCHANTS
BACCHIAC
BACCHII
BACCHIUS
BACCIES
BACCIFORM
BACCO
BACCOES
BACCOS
BACCY
BACH
BACHARACH
BACHARACHS
BACHED
BACHELOR
BACHELORS
BACHES
BACHING
BACHS
BACILLAR
BACILLARY
BACILLI
BACILLUS
BACK
BACKACHE
BACKACHES
BACKARE
BACKBAND
BACKBANDS
BACKBIT
BACKBITE
BACKBITER
BACKBITERS
BACKBITES
BACKBITING
BACKBITTEN
BACKBOND
BACKBONDS

BACKBONE
BACKBONED
BACKBONES
BACKCHAT
BACKCHATS
BACKCHATTED
BACKCHATTING
BACKCOURT
BACKCOURTS
BACKDOWN
BACKDOWNS
BACKDROP
BACKDROPS
BACKED
BACKER
BACKERS
BACKET
BACKETS
BACKFALL
BACKFALLS
BACKFILL
BACKFILLED
BACKFILLING
BACKFILLS
BACKFIRE
BACKFIRED
BACKFIRES
BACKFIRING
BACKFISCH
BACKFISCHES
BACKHAND
BACKHANDS
BACKHOE
BACKHOES
BACKING
BACKINGS
BACKLASH
BACKLASHES
BACKLIST
BACKLISTS
BACKLOG
BACKLOGS
BACKMOST
BACKPACK
BACKPACKED
BACKPACKING
BACKPACKINGS
BACKPACKS
BACKPAY
BACKPAYS
BACKPIECE
BACKPIECES
BACKROOM
BACKS
BACKSAW
BACKSAWS
BACKSET
BACKSETS
BACKSEY
BACKSEYS
BACKSHISH
BACKSHISHES
BACKSIDE
BACKSIDES

BACKSIGHT
BACKSIGHTS
BACKSLID
BACKSLIDE
BACKSLIDES
BACKSLIDING
BACKSPACE
BACKSPACED
BACKSPACES
BACKSPACING
BACKSPEER
BACKSPEERED
BACKSPEERING
BACKSPEERS
BACKSPEIR
BACKSPEIRED
BACKSPEIRING
BACKSPEIRS
BACKSPIN
BACKSPINS
BACKSTAGE
BACKSTALL
BACKSTALLS
BACKSTAYS
BACKSTOP
BACKSTOPS
BACKSWORD
BACKSWORDS
BACKTRACK
BACKTRACKED
BACKTRACKING
BACKTRACKS
BACKVELD
BACKVELDS
BACKWARD
BACKWARDS
BACKWASH
BACKWASHED
BACKWASHES
BACKWASHING
BACKWATER
BACKWATERS
BACKWOODS
BACKWORD
BACKWORDS
BACKWORK
BACKWORKS
BACKYARD
BACKYARDS
BACLAVA
BACLAVAS
BACON
BACONS
BACTERIA
BACTERIAL
BACTERIAN
BACTERIC
BACTERISE
BACTERISED
BACTERISES
BACTERISING
BACTERIUM
BACTERIZE
BACTERIZED

BACTERIZES
BACTERIZING
BACTEROID
BACTEROIDS
BACULINE
BACULITE
BACULITES
BAD
BADDIE
BADDIES
BADDISH
BADDY
BADE
BADGE
BADGER
BADGERED
BADGERING
BADGERLY
BADGERS
BADGES
BADINAGE
BADINAGES
BADIOUS
BADLANDS
BADLY
BADMAN
BADMASH
BADMASHES
BADMEN
BADMINTON
BADMINTONS
BADMOUTH
BADMOUTHED
BADMOUTHING
BADMOUTHS
BADNESS
BADNESSES
BAEL
BAELS
BAETYL
BAETYLS
BAFF
BAFFED
BAFFIES
BAFFING
BAFFLE
BAFFLED
BAFFLEGAB
BAFFLEGABS
BAFFLER
BAFFLERS
BAFFLES
BAFFLING
BAFFS
BAFFY
BAFT
BAFTS
BAG
BAGARRE
BAGARRES
BAGASSE
BAGASSES
BAGATELLE
BAGATELLES

BAGEL	BAILORS	BALANCED	BALKING	BALLOTING
BAGELS	BAILS	BALANCER	BALKINGLY	BALLOTS
BAGFUL	BAILSMAN	BALANCERS	BALKINGS	BALLOW
BAGFULS	BAILSMEN	BALANCES	BALKLINE	BALLOWS
BAGGAGE	BAININ	BALANCING	BALKLINES	BALLPARK
BAGGAGES	BAININS	BALANITIS	BALKS	BALLS
BAGGED	BAIRN	BALANITISES	BALKY	BALLY
BAGGIER	BAIRNLIKE	BALAS	BALL	BALLYHOO
BAGGIEST	BAIRNLY	BALASES	BALLABILE	BALLYHOOS
BAGGILY	BAIRNS	BALATA	BALLABILES	BALLYRAG
BAGGING	BAISEMAIN	BALATAS	BALLABILI	BALLYRAGGED
BAGGINGS	BAISEMAINS	BALBOA	BALLAD	BALLYRAGGING
BAGGIT	BAIT	BALBOAS	BALLADE	BALLYRAGS
BAGGITS	BAITED	BALCONET	BALLADED	BALM
BAGGY	BAITER	BALCONETS	BALLADEER	BALMED
BAGMAN	BAITERS	BALCONIED	BALLADEERED	BALMIER
BAGMEN	BAITFISH	BALCONIES	BALLADEERING	BALMIEST
BAGNIO	BAITFISHES	BALCONY	BALLADEERS	BALMILY
BAGNIOS	BAITING	BALD	BALLADES	BALMINESS
BAGPIPE	BAITINGS	BALDACHIN	BALLADING	BALMINESSES
BAGPIPER	BAITS	BALDACHINS	BALLADIST	BALMING
BAGPIPERS	BAIZE	BALDAQUIN	BALLADISTS	BALMORAL
BAGPIPES	BAIZED	BALDAQUINS	BALLADRIES	BALMORALS
BAGPIPING	BAIZES	BALDER	BALLADRY	BALMS
BAGPIPINGS	BAIZING	BALDEST	BALLADS	BALMY
BAGS	BAJADA	BALDING	BALLAN	BALNEAL
BAGUETTE	BAJADAS	BALDISH	BALLANS	BALNEARIES
BAGUETTES	BAJAN	BALDLY	BALLANT	BALNEARY
BAGUIO	BAJANS	BALDMONEY	BALLANTS	BALONEY
BAGUIOS	BAJRA	BALDMONEYS	BALLAST	BALONEYS
BAGWASH	BAJRAS	BALDNESS	BALLASTED	BALOO
BAGWASHES	BAJREE	BALDNESSES	BALLASTING	BALOOS
BAGWIG	BAJREES	BALDPATE	BALLASTS	BALSA
BAGWIGS	BAJRI	BALDPATED	BALLAT	BALSAM
BAH	BAJRIS	BALDPATES	BALLATS	BALSAMED
BAHADA	BAKE	BALDRIC	BALLCOCK	BALSAMIC
BAHADAS	BAKEAPPLE	BALDRICK	BALLCOCKS	BALSAMING
BAHT	BAKEAPPLES	BALDRICKS	BALLED	BALSAMS
BAHTS	BAKEBOARD	BALDRICS	BALLERINA	BALSAMY
BAHUVRIHI	BAKEBOARDS	BALE	BALLERINAS	BALSAS
BAHUVRIHIS	BAKED	BALECTION	BALLERINE	BALTHASAR
BAIGNOIRE	BAKEHOUSE	BALECTIONS	BALLET	BALTHASARS
BAIGNOIRES	BAKEHOUSES	BALED	BALLETIC	BALTHAZAR
BAIL	BAKEMEAT	BALEEN	BALLETS	BALTHAZARS
BAILABLE	BAKEMEATS	BALEENS	BALLING	BALU
BAILBOND	BAKEN	BALEFUL	BALLINGS	BALUS
BAILBONDS	BAKER	BALEFULLY	BALLISTA	BALUSTER
BAILED	BAKERIES	BALER	BALLISTAE	BALUSTERS
BAILEE	BAKERS	BALERS	BALLISTAS	BALZARINE
BAILER	BAKERY	BALES	BALLISTIC	BALZARINES
BAILERS	BAKES	BALING	BALLISTICS	BAM
BAILEY	BAKESTONE	BALISTA	BALLIUM	BAMBINI
BAILEYS	BAKESTONES	BALISTAE	BALLIUMS	BAMBINO
BAILIE	BAKEWARE	BALISTAS	BALLOCKS	BAMBINOS
BAILIES	BAKEWARES	BALK	BALLOCKSED	BAMBOO
BAILIFF	BAKHSHISH	BALKANISE	BALLOCKSES	BAMBOOS
BAILIFFS	BAKHSHISHES	BALKANISED	BALLOCKSING	BAMBOOZLE
BAILING	BAKING	BALKANISES	BALLON	BAMBOOZLED
BAILIWICK	BAKINGS	BALKANISING	BALLONET	BAMBOOZLES
BAILIWICKS	BAKLAVA	BALKANIZE	BALLONETS	BAMBOOZLING
BAILLI	BAKLAVAS	BALKANIZED	BALLONS	BAMMED
BAILLIAGE	BAKSHEESH	BALKANIZES	BALLOON	BAMMER
BAILLIAGES	BAKSHEESHES	BALKANIZING	BALLOONED	BAMMERS
BAILLIE	BALADIN	BALKED	BALLOONING	BAMMING
BAILLIES	BALADINE	BALKER	BALLOONINGS	BAMPOT
BAILLIS	BALADINES	BALKERS	BALLOONS	BAMPOTS
BAILMENT	BALADINS	BALKIER	BALLOT	BAMS
BAILMENTS	BALALAIKA	BALKIEST	BALLOTED	BAN
BAILOR	BALALAIKAS	BALKINESS	BALLOTEE	BANAL
	BALANCE	BALKINESSES	BALLOTEES	BANALER

BANALEST
BANALITIES
BANALITY
BANALLY
BANANA
BANANAS
BANAUSIAN
BANAUSIC
BANC
BANCO
BANCOS
BANCS
BAND
BANDAGE
BANDAGED
BANDAGES
BANDAGING
BANDALORE
BANDALORES
BANDANA
BANDANAS
BANDANNA
BANDANNAS
BANDAR
BANDARS
BANDBRAKE
BANDBRAKES
BANDEAU
BANDEAUX
BANDED
BANDELET
BANDELETS
BANDELIER
BANDELIERS
BANDEROL
BANDEROLE
BANDEROLES
BANDEROLS
BANDH
BANDHED
BANDHING
BANDHS
BANDICOOT
BANDICOOTED
BANDICOOTING
BANDICOOTS
BANDIED
BANDIER
BANDIES
BANDIEST
BANDING
BANDINGS
BANDIT
BANDITRIES
BANDITRY
BANDITS
BANDITTI
BANDITTIS
BANDOBAST
BANDOBASTS
BANDOG
BANDOGS
BANDOLEER
BANDOLEERS
BANDOLERO
BANDOLEROS
BANDOLIER
BANDOLIERS
BANDOLINE
BANDOLINES

BANDOOK
BANDOOKS
BANDORA
BANDORAS
BANDORE
BANDORES
BANDROL
BANDROLS
BANDS
BANDSMAN
BANDSMEN
BANDSTAND
BANDSTANDS
BANDSTER
BANDSTERS
BANDURA
BANDURAS
BANDWAGON
BANDWAGONS
BANDWIDTH
BANDWIDTHS
BANDY
BANDYING
BANDYINGS
BANDYMAN
BANDYMEN
BANE
BANEBERRIES
BANEBERRY
BANED
BANEFUL
BANEFULLY
BANES
BANG
BANGED
BANGER
BANGERS
BANGING
BANGLE
BANGLED
BANGLES
BANGS
BANGSRING
BANGSRINGS
BANGSTER
BANGSTERS
BANI
BANIA
BANIAN
BANIANS
BANIAS
BANING
BANISH
BANISHED
BANISHES
BANISHING
BANISTER
BANISTERS
BANJAX
BANJAXED
BANJAXES
BANJAXING
BANJO
BANJOES
BANJOIST
BANJOISTS
BANJOS
BANJULELE
BANJULELES
BANK

BANKABLE
BANKED
BANKER
BANKERS
BANKET
BANKETS
BANKING
BANKINGS
BANKROLL
BANKROLLS
BANKRUPT
BANKRUPTED
BANKRUPTING
BANKRUPTS
BANKS
BANKSIA
BANKSIAS
BANKSMAN
BANKSMEN
BANLIEUE
BANLIEUES
BANNED
BANNER
BANNERALL
BANNERALLS
BANNERED
BANNERET
BANNERETS
BANNEROL
BANNEROLS
BANNERS
BANNING
BANNOCK
BANNOCKS
BANNS
BANQUET
BANQUETED
BANQUETER
BANQUETERS
BANQUETING
BANQUETINGS
BANQUETS
BANQUETTE
BANQUETTES
BANS
BANSHEE
BANSHEES
BANT
BANTAM
BANTAMS
BANTED
BANTENG
BANTENGS
BANTER
BANTERED
BANTERER
BANTERERS
BANTERING
BANTERINGS
BANTERS
BANTING
BANTINGS
BANTLING
BANTLINGS
BANTS
BANXRING
BANXRINGS
BANYAN
BANYANS
BANZAI

BAOBAB
BAOBABS
BAP
BAPS
BAPTISE
BAPTISED
BAPTISES
BAPTISING
BAPTISM
BAPTISMAL
BAPTISMS
BAPTIST
BAPTISTRIES
BAPTISTRY
BAPTISTS
BAPTIZE
BAPTIZED
BAPTIZES
BAPTIZING
BAPU
BAPUS
BAR
BARACAN
BARACANS
BARAGOUIN
BARAGOUINS
BARATHEA
BARATHEAS
BARATHRUM
BARATHRUMS
BARB
BARBARIAN
BARBARIANS
BARBARIC
BARBARISE
BARBARISED
BARBARISES
BARBARISING
BARBARISM
BARBARISMS
BARBARITIES
BARBARITY
BARBARIZE
BARBARIZED
BARBARIZES
BARBARIZING
BARBAROUS
BARBASCO
BARBASCOS
BARBASTEL
BARBASTELS
BARBATE
BARBATED
BARBE
BARBECUE
BARBECUED
BARBECUES
BARBECUING
BARBED
BARBEL
BARBELS
BARBER
BARBERED
BARBERING
BARBERRIES
BARBERRY
BARBERS
BARBES
BARBET
BARBETS

BARBETTE
BARBETTES
BARBICAN
BARBICANS
BARBICEL
BARBICELS
BARBING
BARBITAL
BARBITALS
BARBITONE
BARBITONES
BARBOLA
BARBOLAS
BARBOTINE
BARBOTINES
BARBS
BARBULE
BARBULES
BARCA
BARCAROLE
BARCAROLES
BARCAS
BARCHAN
BARCHANE
BARCHANES
BARCHANS
BARD
BARDED
BARDIC
BARDING
BARDLING
BARDLINGS
BARDS
BARDSHIP
BARDSHIPS
BARDY
BARE
BAREBACK
BAREBOAT
BAREBONE
BAREBONES
BARED
BAREFACED
BAREFOOT
BAREGE
BAREGES
BAREGINE
BAREGINES
BARELY
BARENESS
BARENESSES
BARER
BARES
BARESARK
BARESARKS
BAREST
BARF
BARFED
BARFING
BARFLIES
BARFLY
BARFS
BARFUL
BARGAIN
BARGAINED
BARGAINER
BARGAINERS
BARGAINING
BARGAINS
BARGAIST

BARGAISTS
BARGANDER
BARGANDERS
BARGE
BARGED
BARGEE
BARGEES
BARGEESE
BARGELLO
BARGELLOS
BARGEMAN
BARGEMEN
BARGEPOLE
BARGEPOLES
BARGES
BARGEST
BARGESTS
BARGHEST
BARGHESTS
BARGING
BARGOOSE
BARIC
BARILLA
BARILLAS
BARING
BARISH
BARITE
BARITES
BARITONE
BARITONES
BARIUM
BARIUMS
BARK
BARKAN
BARKANS
BARKED
BARKEEPER
BARKEEPERS
BARKEN
BARKENED
BARKENING
BARKENS
BARKER
BARKERS
BARKHAN
BARKHANS
BARKIER
BARKIEST
BARKING
BARKLESS
BARKS
BARKY
BARLEY
BARLEYS
BARM
BARMAID
BARMAIDS
BARMAN
BARMBRACK
BARMBRACKS
BARMEN
BARMIER
BARMIEST
BARMINESS
BARMINESSES
BARMIZVAH
BARMIZVAHS
BARMKIN
BARMKINS
BARMS

BARMY
BARN
BARNACLE
BARNACLED
BARNACLES
BARNED
BARNEY
BARNEYS
BARNING
BARNS
BARNSTORM
BARNSTORMED
BARNSTORMING
BARNSTORMS
BARNYARD
BARNYARDS
BAROCCO
BAROCCOS
BAROCK
BAROCKS
BAROGRAM
BAROGRAMS
BAROGRAPH
BAROGRAPHS
BAROMETER
BAROMETERS
BAROMETRIES
BAROMETRY
BAROMETZ
BAROMETZES
BARON
BARONAGE
BARONAGES
BARONESS
BARONESSES
BARONET
BARONETCIES
BARONETCY
BARONETS
BARONIAL
BARONIES
BARONNE
BARONNES
BARONS
BARONY
BAROQUE
BAROQUES
BAROSCOPE
BAROSCOPES
BAROSTAT
BAROSTATS
BAROUCHE
BAROUCHES
BARP
BARPERSON
BARPERSONS
BARPS
BARQUE
BARQUES
BARRACAN
BARRACANS
BARRACE
BARRACES
BARRACK
BARRACKED
BARRACKER
BARRACKERS
BARRACKING
BARRACKINGS
BARRACKS

BARRACOON
BARRACOONS
BARRACUDA
BARRACUDAS
BARRAGE
BARRAGES
BARRANCA
BARRANCAS
BARRANCO
BARRANCOS
BARRAT
BARRATOR
BARRATORS
BARRATRIES
BARRATRY
BARRATS
BARRÉ
BARRE
BARRED
BARREFULL
BARREL
BARRELAGE
BARRELAGES
BARRELFUL
BARRELFULS
BARRELLED
BARRELLING
BARRELS
BARREN
BARRENER
BARRENEST
BARRES
BARRET
BARRETS
BARRETTE
BARRETTES
BARRICADE
BARRICADED
BARRICADES
BARRICADING
BARRICADO
BARRICADOED
BARRICADOES
BARRICADOING
BARRICADOS
BARRICO
BARRICOES
BARRICOS
BARRIER
BARRIERED
BARRIERING
BARRIERS
BARRING
BARRINGS
BARRIO
BARRIOS
BARRISTER
BARRISTERS
BARROW
BARROWS
BARRULET
BARRULETS
BARS
BARTENDER
BARTENDERS
BARTER
BARTERED
BARTERER
BARTERERS
BARTERING

BARTERS
BARTISAN
BARTISANED
BARTISANS
BARTIZAN
BARTIZANS
BARTON
BARTONS
BARWOOD
BARWOODS
BARYE
BARYES
BARYON
BARYONS
BARYTA
BARYTAS
BARYTES
BARYTIC
BARYTON
BARYTONE
BARYTONES
BARYTONS
BAS
BASAL
BASALT
BASALTIC
BASALTS
BASAN
BASANITE
BASANITES
BASANS
BASBLEU
BASBLEUS
BASCULE
BASCULES
BASE
BASEBALL
BASEBALLS
BASEBOARD
BASEBOARDS
BASECOURT
BASECOURTS
BASED
BASELARD
BASELARDS
BASELESS
BASELY
BASEMAN
BASEMEN
BASEMENT
BASEMENTS
BASENESS
BASENESSES
BASENJI
BASENJIS
BASEPLATE
BASEPLATES
BASER
BASES
BASEST
BASH
BASHAW
BASHAWISM
BASHAWISMS
BASHAWS
BASHED
BASHER
BASHERS
BASHES
BASHFUL

BASHFULLY
BASHING
BASHINGS
BASHLESS
BASHLYK
BASHLYKS
BASIC
BASICALLY
BASICITIES
BASICITY
BASICS
BASIDIA
BASIDIAL
BASIDIUM
BASIFIXED
BASIFUGAL
BASIL
BASILAR
BASILICA
BASILICAL
BASILICAN
BASILICAS
BASILICON
BASILICONS
BASILISK
BASILISKS
BASILS
BASIN
BASINET
BASINETS
BASINFUL
BASINFULS
BASING
BASINS
BASIPETAL
BASIS
BASK
BASKED
BASKET
BASKETFUL
BASKETFULS
BASKETRIES
BASKETRY
BASKING
BASKS
BASMIZVAH
BASMIZVAHS
BASNET
BASNETS
BASOCHE
BASOCHES
BASON
BASONS
BASQUE
BASQUED
BASQUES
BASQUINE
BASQUINES
BASS
BASSE
BASSED
BASSER
BASSES
BASSEST
BASSET
BASSETED
BASSETING
BASSETS
BASSI

BASSIER	BATHE	BATTED	BAUKING	BAYT
BASSIEST	BATHED	BATTEL	BAUKS	BAYTED
BASSINET	BATHER	BATTELED	BAULK	BAYTING
BASSINETS	BATHERS	BATTELER	BAULKED	BAYTS
BASSING	BATHES	BATTELERS	BAULKING	BAZAAR
BASSIST	BATHETIC	BATTELING	BAULKS	BAZAARS
BASSISTS	BATHHOUSE	BATTELS	BAUR	BAZAR
BASSO	BATHHOUSES	BATTEMENT	BAURS	BAZARS
BASSOON	BATHING	BATTEMENTS	BAUSOND	BAZAZZ
BASSOONS	BATHMIC	BATTEN	BAUXITE	BAZAZZES
BASSOS	BATHMISM	BATTENED	BAUXITES	BAZOOKA
BASSWOOD	BATHMISMS	BATTENING	BAUXITIC	BAZOOKAS
BASSWOODS	BATHOLITE	BATTENINGS	BAVARDAGE	BDELLIUM
BASSY	BATHOLITES	BATTENS	BAVARDAGES	BDELLIUMS
BAST	BATHOLITH	BATTER	BAVIN	BE
BASTA	BATHOLITHS	BATTERED	BAVINS	BEACH
BASTARD	BATHORSE	BATTERIE	BAWBEE	BEACHED
BASTARDIES	BATHORSES	BATTERIES	BAWBEES	BEACHES
BASTARDLY	BATHOS	BATTERING	BAWBLE	BEACHHEAD
BASTARDS	BATHOSES	BATTERO	BAWBLES	BEACHHEADS
BASTARDY	BATHROBE	BATTEROS	BAWCOCK	BEACHIER
BASTE	BATHROBES	BATTERS	BAWCOCKS	BEACHIEST
BASTED	BATHROOM	BATTERY	BAWD	BEACHING
BASTER	BATHROOMS	BATTIER	BAWDIER	BEACHY
BASTERS	BATHS	BATTIEST	BAWDIES	BEACON
BASTES	BATHTUB	BATTILL	BAWDIEST	BEACONED
BASTIDE	BATHTUBS	BATTILLED	BAWDILY	BEACONING
BASTIDES	BATHYAL	BATTILLING	BAWDINESS	BEACONS
BASTILLE	BATHYBIUS	BATTILLS	BAWDINESSES	BEAD
BASTILLES	BATHYBIUSES	BATTING	BAWDKIN	BEADED
BASTINADE	BATHYLITE	BATTINGS	BAWDKINS	BEADIER
BASTINADED	BATHYLITES	BATTLE	BAWDRIES	BEADIEST
BASTINADES	BATHYLITH	BATTLED	BAWDRY	BEADING
BASTINADING	BATHYLITHS	BATTLER	BAWDS	BEADINGS
BASTINADO	BATIK	BATTLERS	BAWDY	BEADLE
BASTINADOED	BATIKS	BATTLES	BAWL	BEADLEDOM
BASTINADOES	BATING	BATTLING	BAWLED	BEADLEDOMS
BASTINADOING	BATISTE	BATTOLOGIES	BAWLER	BEADLES
BASTINADOS	BATISTES	BATTOLOGY	BAWLERS	BEADMAN
BASTING	BATLER	BATTS	BAWLEY	BEADMEN
BASTINGS	BATLERS	BATTUE	BAWLEYS	BEADS
BASTION	BATLET	BATTUES	BAWLING	BEADSMAN
BASTIONED	BATLETS	BATTUTA	BAWLINGS	BEADSMEN
BASTIONS	BATMAN	BATTUTAS	BAWLS	BEADY
BASTLE	BATMEN	BATTY	BAWN	BEAGLE
BASTLES	BATMIZVAH	BATWOMAN	BAWNS	BEAGLED
BASTO	BATMIZVAHS	BATWOMEN	BAWR	BEAGLER
BASTOS	BATOLOGIES	BAUBLE	BAWRS	BEAGLERS
BASTS	BATOLOGY	BAUBLES	BAXTER	BEAGLES
BAT	BATON	BAUBLING	BAXTERS	BEAGLING
BATABLE	BATONED	BAUCHLE	BAY	BEAGLINGS
BATATA	BATONING	BAUCHLED	BAYADÈRE	BEAK
BATATAS	BATONS	BAUCHLES	BAYADÈRES	BEAKED
BATCH	BATOON	BAUCHLING	BAYARD	BEAKER
BATCHED	BATOONED	BAUD	BAYARDS	BEAKERS
BATCHES	BATOONING	BAUDEKIN	BAYBERRIES	BEAKS
BATCHING	BATOONS	BAUDEKINS	BAYBERRY	BEAM
BATE	BATRACHIA	BAUDRIC	BAYE	BEAMED
BATEAU	BATS	BAUDRICK	BAYED	BEAMER
BATEAUX	BATSMAN	BAUDRICKE	BAYES	BEAMERS
BATED	BATSMEN	BAUDRICKES	BAYING	BEAMIER
BATELESS	BATSWING	BAUDRICKS	BAYLE	BEAMIEST
BATELEUR	BATSWINGS	BAUDRICS	BAYLES	BEAMILY
BATELEURS	BATT	BAUDS	BAYONET	BEAMINESS
BATEMENT	BATTA	BAUERA	BAYONETED	BEAMINESSES
BATEMENTS	BATTALIA	BAUERAS	BAYONETING	BEAMING
BATES	BATTALIAS	BAUHINIA	BAYONETS	BEAMINGLY
BATH	BATTALION	BAUHINIAS	BAYOU	BEAMINGS
BATHCUBE	BATTALIONS	BAUK	BAYOUS	BEAMISH
BATHCUBES,	BATTAS	BAUKED	BAYS	BEAMLESS

BEAMS	BEATINGS	BECK	BEDEAFENING	BEDRIDDEN
BEAMY	BEATITUDE	BECKE	BEDEAFENS	BEDRIGHT
BEAN	BEATITUDES	BECKED	BEDECK	BEDRIGHTS
BEANED	BEATNIK	BECKES	BEDECKED	BEDRITE
BEANFEAST	BEATNIKS	BECKET	BEDECKING	BEDRITES
BEANFEASTS	BEATS	BECKETS	BEDECKS	BEDROCK
BEANIE	BEAU	BECKING	BEDEGUAR	BEDROCKS
BEANIES	BEAUFET	BECKON	BEDEGUARS	BEDROOM
BEANING	BEAUFETS	BECKONED	BEDEL	BEDROOMS
BEANO	BEAUFFET	BECKONING	BEDELL	BEDROP
BEANOS	BEAUFFETS	BECKONS	BEDELLS	BEDROPPED
BEANPOLE	BEAUFIN	BECKS	BEDELS	BEDROPPING
BEANPOLES	BEAUFINS	BECLOUD	BEDELSHIP	BEDROPS
BEANS	BEAUISH	BECLOUDED	BEDELSHIPS	BEDROPT
BEANSTALK	BEAUT	BECLOUDING	BEDEMAN	BEDS
BEANSTALKS	BEAUTEOUS	BECLOUDS	BEDEMEN	BEDSIDE
BEAR	BEAUTIED	BECOME	BEDERAL	BEDSIDES
BEARABLE	BEAUTIES	BECOMES	BEDERALS	BEDSOCKS
BEARABLY	BEAUTIFIED	BECOMING	BEDES	BEDSORE
BEARBINE	BEAUTIFIES	BECQUEREL	BEDESMAN	BEDSORES
BEARBINES	BEAUTIFUL	BECQUERELS	BEDESMEN	BEDSPREAD
BEARD	BEAUTIFY	BECURL	BEDEVIL	BEDSPREADS
BEARDED	BEAUTIFYING	BECURLED	BEDEVILLED	BEDSTEAD
BEARDIE	BEAUTS	BECURLING	BEDEVILLING	BEDSTEADS
BEARDIES	BEAUTY	BECURLS	BEDEVILS	BEDSTRAW
BEARDING	BEAUIYING	BED	BEDEW	BEDSTRAWS
BEARDLESS	BEAUX	BEDABBLE	BEDEWED	BEDTICK
BEARDS	BEAUXITE	BEDABBLED	BEDEWING	BEDTICKS
BEARE	BEAUXITES	BEDABBLES	BEDEWS	BEDTIME
BEARED	BEAVER	BEDABBLING	BEDFAST	BEDTIMES
BEARER	BEAVERED	BEDAD	BEDFELLOW	BEDUCK
BEARERS	BEAVERIES	BEDAGGLE	BEDFELLOWS	BEDUCKED
BEARES	BEAVERS	BEDAGGLED	BEDIDE	BEDUCKING
BEARING	BEAVERY	BEDAGGLES	BEDIGHT	BEDUCKS
BEARINGS	BEBEERINE	BEDAGGLING	BEDIGHTING	BEDUIN
BEARISH	BEBEERINES	BEDARKEN	BEDIGHTS	BEDUINS
BÉARNAISE	BEBEERU	BEDARKENED	BEDIM	BEDUNG
BÉARNAISES	BEBEERUS	BEDARKENING	BEDIMMED	BEDUNGED
BEARS	BEBOP	BEDARKENS	BEDIMMING	BEDUNGING
BEARSKIN	BEBOPPED	BEDASH	BEDIMMINGS	BEDUNGS
BEARSKINS	BEBOPPING	BEDASHED	BEDIMS	BEDUST
BEARWARD	BEBOPS	BEDASHES	BEDIZEN	BEDUSTED
BEARWARDS	BEBUNG	BEDASHING	BEDIZENED	BEDUSTING
BEAST	BEBUNGS	BEDAUB	BEDIZENING	BEDUSTS
BEASTHOOD	BECALL	BEDAUBED	BEDIZENS	BEDWARD
BEASTHOODS	BECALLED	BEDAUBING	BEDLAM	BEDWARDS
BEASTIE	BECALLING	BEDAUBS	BEDLAMISM	BEDWARF
BEASTIES	BECALLS	BEDAWIN	BEDLAMISMS	BEDWARFED
BEASTILY	BECALM	BEDAWINS	BEDLAMITE	BEDWARFING
BEASTINGS	BECALMED	BEDAZE	BEDLAMITES	BEDWARFS
BEASTLIER	BECALMING	BEDAZED	BEDLAMS	BEDYDE
BEASTLIEST	BECALMS	BEDAZES	BEDMAKER	BEDYE
BEASTLIKE	BECAME	BEDAZING	BEDMAKERS	BEDYED
BEASTLY	BÉCASSE	BEDAZZLE	BEDOUIN	BEDYEING
BEASTS	BÉCASSES	BEDAZZLED	BEDOUINS	BEDYES
BEAT	BECAUSE	BEDAZZLES	BEDPAN	BEE
BEATABLE	BECCACCIA	BEDAZZLING	BEDPANS	BEECH
BEATEN	BECCACCIAS	BEDBUG	BEDPOST	BEECHEN
BEATER	BECCAFICO	BEDBUGS	BEDPOSTS	BEECHES
BEATERS	BECCAFICOS	BEDCOVER	BEDRAGGLE	BEEF
BEATH	BÉCHAMEL	BEDCOVERS	BEDRAGGLED	BEEFALO
BEATHED	BÉCHAMELS	BEDDABLE	BEDRAGGLES	BEEFALOES
BEATHING	BECHANCE	BEDDED	BEDRAGGLING	BEEFALOS
BEATHS	BECHANCED	BEDDER	BEDRAL	BEEFCAKE
BEATIFIC	BECHANCES	BEDDERS	BEDRALS	BEEFCAKES
BEATIFIED	BECHANCING	BEDDING	BEDRENCH	BEEFEATER
BEATIFIES	BECHARM	BEDDINGS	BEDRENCHED	BEEFEATERS
BEATIFY	BECHARMED	BEDE	BEDRENCHES	BEEFED
BEATIFYING	BECHARMING	BEDEAFEN	BEDRENCHING	BEEFIER
BEATING	BECHARMS	BEDEAFENED	BEDRID	BEEFIEST

BEEFING
BEEFS
BEEFSTEAK
BEEFSTEAKS
BEEFTEA
BEEFTEAS
BEEFY
BEEGAH
BEEGAHS
BEEHIVE
BEEHIVES
BEEKEEPER
BEEKEEPERS
BEEN
BEENAH
BEENAHS
BEEP
BEEPED
BEEPER
BEEPERS
BEEPING
BEEPS
BEER
BEERHALL
BEERHALLS
BEERIER
BEERIEST
BEERINESS
BEERINESSES
BEERS
BEERY
BEES
BEESOME
BEESTINGS
BEESWAX
BEESWAXED
BEESWAXES
BEESWAXING
BEESWING
BEESWINGED
BEESWINGS
BEET
BEETED
BEETING
BEETLE
BEETLED
BEETLES
BEETLING
BEETROOT
BEETROOTS
BEETS
BEEVES
BEFALL
BEFALLEN
BEFALLING
BEFALLS
BEFANA
BEFANAS
BEFELD
BEFELL
BEFFANA
BEFFANAS
BEFIT
BEFITS
BEFITTED
BEFITTING
BEFLOWER
BEFLOWERED
BEFLOWERING
BEFLOWERS

BEFLUM
BEFLUMMED
BEFLUMMING
BEFLUMS
BEFOAM
BEFOAMED
BEFOAMING
BEFOAMS
BEFOG
BEFOGGED
BEFOGGING
BEFOGS
BEFOOL
BEFOOLED
BEFOOLING
BEFOOLS
BEFORE
BEFORTUNE
BEFORTUNED
BEFORTUNES
BEFORTUNING
BEFOUL
BEFOULED
BEFOULING
BEFOULS
BEFRIEND
BEFRIENDED
BEFRIENDING
BEFRIENDS
BEFRINGE
BEFRINGED
BEFRINGES
BEFRINGING
BEFUDDLE
BEFUDDLED
BEFUDDLES
BEFUDDLING
BEG
BEGAD
BEGAN
BEGAR
BEGARS
BEGAT
BEGEM
BEGEMMED
BEGEMMING
BEGEMS
BEGET
BEGETS
BEGETTER
BEGETTERS
BEGETTING
BEGGAR
BEGGARDOM
BEGGARDOMS
BEGGARED
BEGGARIES
BEGGARING
BEGGARLY
BEGGARS
BEGGARY
BEGGED
BEGGING
BEGGINGLY
BEGGINGS
BEGHARD
BEGHARDS
BEGIFT
BEGIFTED
BEGIFTING

BEGIFTS
BEGILD
BEGILDED
BEGILDING
BEGILDS
BEGIN
BEGINNE
BEGINNER
BEGINNERS
BEGINNES
BEGINNING
BEGINNINGS
BEGINS
BEGIRD
BEGIRDED
BEGIRDING
BEGIRDS
BEGIRT
BEGLAMOUR
BEGLAMOURED
BEGLAMOURING
BEGLAMOURS
BEGLERBEG
BEGLERBEGS
BEGLOOM
BEGLOOMED
BEGLOOMING
BEGLOOMS
BEGNAW
BEGNAWED
BEGNAWING
BEGNAWS
BEGO
BEGOES
BEGOING
BEGONE
BEGONIA
BEGONIAS
BEGORED
BEGORRA
BEGORRAH
BEGOT
BEGOTTEN
BEGRIME
BEGRIMED
BEGRIMES
BEGRIMING
BEGRUDGE
BEGRUDGED
BEGRUDGES
BEGRUDGING
BEGS
BEGUILE
BEGUILED
BEGUILER
BEGUILERS
BEGUILES
BEGUILING
BEGUIN
BEGUINAGE
BEGUINAGES
BEGUINE
BEGUINES
BEGUINS
BEGUM
BEGUMS
BEGUN
BEGUNK
BEGUNKED
BEGUNKING

BEGUNKS
BEHALF
BEHALVES
BEHAPPEN
BEHAPPENED
BEHAPPENING
BEHAPPENS
BEHATTED
BEHAVE
BEHAVED
BEHAVES
BEHAVING
BEHAVIOR
BEHAVIORS
BEHAVIOUR
BEHAVIOURS
BEHEAD
BEHEADAL
BEHEADALS
BEHEADED
BEHEADING
BEHEADINGS
BEHEADS
BEHELD
BEHEMOTH
BEHEMOTHS
BEHEST
BEHESTS
BEHIGHT
BEHIGHTING
BEHIGHTS
BEHIND
BEHINDS
BEHOLD
BEHOLDEN
BEHOLDER
BEHOLDERS
BEHOLDING
BEHOLDINGS
BEHOLDS
BEHOOF
BEHOOFS
BEHOOVE
BEHOOVED
BEHOOVES
BEHOOVING
BEHOTE
BEHOTES
BEHOTING
BEHOVE
BEHOVED
BEHOVEFUL
BEHOVELY
BEHOVES
BEHOVING
BEHOWL
BEHOWLED
BEHOWLING
BEHOWLS
BEIGE
BEIGEL
BEIGELS
BEIGES
BEIGNET
BEIGNETS
BEIN
BEING
BEINGLESS
BEINGNESS
BEINGNESSES

BEINGS
BEINKED
BEINNESS
BEINNESSES
BEJABERS
BEJADE
BEJADED
BEJADES
BEJADING
BEJANT
BEJANTS
BEJESUIT
BEJESUITED
BEJESUITING
BEJESUITS
BEJEWEL
BEJEWELLED
BEJEWELLING
BEJEWELS
BEKAH
BEKAHS
BEKISS
BEKISSED
BEKISSES
BEKISSING
BEKNAVE
BEKNAVED
BEKNAVES
BEKNAVING
BEKNOWN
BEL
BELABOUR
BELABOURED
BELABOURING
BELABOURS
BELACE
BELACED
BELACES
BELACING
BELAH
BELAHS
BELAID
BELAMIES
BELAMOURE
BELAMOURES
BELAMY
BELATE
BELATED
BELATES
BELATING
BELAUD
BELAUDED
BELAUDING
BELAUDS
BELAY
BELAYING
BELAYS
BELCH
BELCHED
BELCHER
BELCHERS
BELCHES
BELCHING
BELDAM
BELDAME
BELDAMES
BELDAMS
BELEAGUER
BELEAGUERED
BELEAGUERING

BELEAGUERS
BELEE
BELEED
BELEEING
BELEES
BELEMNITE
BELEMNITES
BELFRIED
BELFRIES
BELFRY
BELGA
BELGARD
BELGARDS
BELGAS
BELIE
BELIED
BELIEF
BELIEFS
BELIER
BELIERS
BELIES
BELIEVE
BELIEVED
BELIEVER
BELIEVERS
BELIEVES
BELIEVING
BELIKE
BELITTLE
BELITTLED
BELITTLES
BELITTLING
BELIVE
BELL
BELLBIND
BELLBINDS
BELLCOTE
BELLCOTES
BELLE
BELLED
BELLES
BELLETER
BELLETERS
BELLHOP
BELLHOPS
BELLIBONE
BELLIBONES
BELLICOSE
BELLIED
BELLIES
BELLING
BELLMAN
BELLMEN
BELLOW
BELLOWED
BELLOWER
BELLOWERS
BELLOWING
BELLOWS
BELLPUSH
BELLPUSHES
BELLS
BELLWORT
BELLWORTS
BELLY
BELLYFUL
BELLYFULS
BELLYING
BELLYINGS
BELOMANCIES

BELOMANCY
BELONG
BELONGED
BELONGER
BELONGERS
BELONGING
BELONGINGS
BELONGS
BELOVE
BELOVED
BELOVEDS
BELOVES
BELOVING
BELOW
BELS
BELT
BELTED
BELTER
BELTERS
BELTING
BELTINGS
BELTS
BELTWAY
BELTWAYS
BELUGA
BELUGAS
BELVEDERE
BELVEDERES
BELYING
BEMA
BEMAD
BEMADDED
BEMADDING
BEMADS
BEMAS
BEMATA
BEMAUL
BEMAULED
BEMAULING
BEMAULS
BEMAZED
BEMEAN
BEMEANED
BEMEANING
BEMEANS
BEMEDAL
BEMEDALLED
BEMEDALLING
BEMEDALS
BEMETE
BEMETED
BEMETES
BEMETING
BEMIRE
BEMIRED
BEMIRES
BEMIRING
BEMOAN
BEMOANED
BEMOANERS
BEMOANING
BEMOANINGS
BEMOANS
BEMOCK
BEMOCKED
BEMOCKING
BEMOCKS
BEMOIL
BEMOILED

BEMOILING
BEMOILS
BEMONSTER
BEMONSTERED
BEMONSTERING
BEMONSTERS
BEMOUTH
BEMOUTHED
BEMOUTHING
BEMOUTHS
BEMUD
BEMUDDED
BEMUDDING
BEMUDDLE
BEMUDDLED
BEMUDDLES
BEMUDDLING
BEMUDS
BEMUFFLE
BEMUFFLED
BEMUFFLES
BEMUFFLING
BEMUSE
BEMUSED
BEMUSES
BEMUSING
BEN
BENAME
BENAMED
BENAMES
BENAMING
BENCH
BENCHED
BENCHER
BENCHERS
BENCHES
BENCHING
BEND
BENDED
BENDER
BENDERS
BENDING
BENDINGLY
BENDINGS
BENDLET
BENDLETS
BENDS
BENDWISE
BENDY
BENE
BENEATH
BENEDICT
BENEDIGHT
BENEFACT
BENEFACTED
BENEFACTING
BENEFACTS
BENEFIC
BENEFICE
BENEFICED
BENEFICES
BENEFIT
BENEFITED
BENEFITING
BENEFITS
BENEMPT
BENES
BENET
BENETS
BENETTED

BENETTING
BENGALINE
BENGALINES
BENI
BENIGHT
BENIGHTED
BENIGHTEN
BENIGHTENED
BENIGHTENING
BENIGHTENINGS
BENIGHTENS
BENIGHTER
BENIGHTERS
BENIGHTING
BENIGHTINGS
BENIGHTS
BENIGN
BENIGNACIES
BENIGNACY
BENIGNANT
BENIGNER
BENIGNEST
BENIGNITIES
BENIGNITY
BENIGNLY
BENIS
BENISEED
BENISEEDS
BENISON
BENISONS
BENITIER
BENITIERS
BENJ
BENJAMIN
BENJAMINS
BENJES
BENNE
BENNES
BENNET
BENNETS
BENNI
BENNIES
BENNIS
BENNY
BENS
BENT
BENTHIC
BENTHOAL
BENTHONIC
BENTHOS
BENTHOSES
BENTIER
BENTIEST
BENTONITE
BENTONITES
BENTS
BENTWOOD
BENTWOODS
BENTY
BENUMB
BENUMBED
BENUMBING
BENUMBS
BENZAL
BENZALS
BENZENE
BENZENES
BENZIDINE
BENZIDINES
BENZIL

BENZILS
BENZINE
BENZINES
BENZOATE
BENZOATES
BENZOIC
BENZOIN
BENZOINS
BENZOL
BENZOLE
BENZOLES
BENZOLINE
BENZOLINES
BENZOLS
BENZOYL
BENZOYLS
BENZYL
BENZYLS
BEPAINT
BEPAINTED
BEPAINTING
BEPAINTS
BEPAT
BEPATCHED
BEPATS
BEPATTED
BEPATTING
BEPEARL
BEPEARLED
BEPEARLING
BEPEARLS
BEPELT
BEPELTED
BEPELTING
BEPELTS
BEPEPPER
BEPEPPERED
BEPEPPERING
BEPEPPERS
BEPESTER
BEPESTERED
BEPESTERING
BEPESTERS
BEPITIED
BEPITIES
BEPITY
BEPITYING
BEPLASTER
BEPLASTERED
BEPLASTERING
BEPLASTERS
BEPLUMED
BEPOMMEL
BEPOMMELED
BEPOMMELING
BEPOMMELLED
BEPOMMELLING
BEPOMMELS
BEPOWDER
BEPOWDERED
BEPOWDERING
BEPOWDERS
BEPRAISE
BEPRAISED
BEPRAISES
BEPRAISING
BEPROSE
BEPROSED
BEPROSES
BEPROSING

BEPUFF	BERLINE	BESEEKES	BESMEARING	BESPOUTED
BEPUFFED	BERLINES	BESEEKING	BESMEARS	BESPOUTING
BEPUFFING	BERLINS	BESEEM	BESMIRCH	BESPOUTS
BEPUFFS	BERM	BESEEMED	BESMIRCHED	BESPREAD
BEQUEATH	BERMS	BESEEMING	BESMIRCHES	BESPREADING
BEQUEATHED	BEROB	BESEEMINGS	BESMIRCHING	BESPREADS
BEQUEATHING	BEROBBED	BESEEMLY	BESMUT	BESPRENT
BEQUEATHS	BEROBBING	BESEEMS	BESMUTCH	BEST
BEQUEST	BEROBS	BESEEN	BESMUTCHED	BESTAD
BEQUESTS	BERRET	BESEES	BESMUTCHES	BESTADDE
BERATE	BERRETS	BESET	BESMUTCHING	BESTAIN
BERATED	BERRIED	BESETMENT	BESMUTS	BESTAINED
BERATES	BERRIES	BESETMENTS	BESMUTTED	BESTAINING
BERATING	BERRY	BESETS	BESMUTTING	BESTAINS
BERAY	BERRYING	BESETTER	BESOGNIO	BESTAR
BERAYED	BERRYINGS	BESETTERS	BESOGNIOS	BESTARRED
BERAYING	BERSERK	BESETTING	BESOIN	BESTARRING
BERAYS	BERSERKER	BESHADOW	BESOINS	BESTARS
BERBERINE	BERSERKERS	BESHADOWED	BESOM	BESTEAD
BERBERINES	BERSERKEST	BESHADOWING	BESOMS	BESTEADED
BERBERIS	BERSERKLY	BESHADOWS	BESORT	BESTEADING
BERBERISES	BERSERKS	BESHAME	BESORTED	BESTEADS
BERCEAU	BERTH	BESHAMED	BESORTING	BESTED
BERCEAUX	BERTHA	BESHAMES	BESORTS	BESTIAL
BERCEUSE	BERTHAGE	BESHAMING	BESOT	BESTIALS
BERCEUSES	BERTHAGES	BESHINE	BESOTS	BESTIARIES
BERDACHE	BERTHAS	BESHINES	BESOTTED	BESTIARY
BERDACHES	BERTHE	BESHINING	BESOTTING	BESTICK
BERE	BERTHED	BESHONE	BESOUGHT	BESTICKING
BEREAVE	BERTHES	BESHREW	BESOULED	BESTICKS
BEREAVED	BERTHING	BESHREWED	BESPAKE	BESTILL
BEREAVEN	BERTHS	BESHREWING	BESPANGLE	BESTILLED
BEREAVES	BERYL	BESHREWS	BESPANGLED	BESTILLING
BEREAVING	BERYLLIA	BESIDE	BESPANGLES	BESTILLS
BEREFT	BERYLLIAS	BESIDES	BESPANGLING	BESTING
BERES	BERYLLIUM	BESIEGE	BESPAT	BESTIR
BERET	BERYLLIUMS	BESIEGED	BESPATE	BESTIRRED
BERETS	BERYLS	BESIEGER	BESPATTER	BESTIRRING
BERG	BESAINT	BESIEGERS	BESPATTERED	BESTIRS
BERGAMA	BESAINTED	BESIEGES	BESPATTERING	BESTORM
BERGAMAS	BESAINTING	BESIEGING	BESPATTERS	BESTORMED
BERGAMASK	BESAINTS	BESIEGINGS	BESPEAK	BESTORMING
BERGAMOT	BESANG	BESIGH	BESPEAKING	BESTORMS
BERGAMOTS	BESAT	BESIGHED	BESPEAKS	BESTOW
BERGANDER	BESAW	BESIGHING	BESPECKLE	BESTOWAL
BERGANDERS	BESCATTER	BESIGHS	BESPECKLED	BESTOWALS
BERGENIA	BESCATTERED	BESING	BESPECKLES	BESTOWED
BERGENIAS	BESCATTERING	BESINGING	BESPECKLING	BESTOWER
BERGÈRE	BESCATTERS	BESINGS	BESPED	BESTOWERS
BERGFALL	BESCRAWL	BESIT	BESPEED	BESTOWING
BERGFALLS	BESCRAWLED	BESITS	BESPEEDING	BESTOWS
BERGHAAN	BESCRAWLING	BESITTING	BESPEEDS	BESTREAK
BERGHAANS	BESCRAWLS	BESLAVE	BESPICE	BESTREAKED
BERGMEHL	BESCREEN	BESLAVED	BESPICED	BESTREAKING
BERGMEHLS	BESCREENED	BESLAVER	BESPICES	BESTREAKS
BERGOMASK	BESCREENING	BESLAVERED	BESPICING	BESTREW
BERGOMASKS	BESCREENS	BESLAVERING	BESPIT	BESTREWED
BERGS	BESCRIBBLE	BESLAVERS	BESPITS	BESTREWING
BERGYLT	BESCRIBBLED	BESLAVES	BESPITTING	BESTREWN
BERGYLTS	BESCRIBBLES	BESLAVING	BESPOKE	BESTREWS
BERIBERI	BESCRIBBLING	BESLOBBER	BESPOKEN	BESTRID
BERIBERIS	BESEE	BESLOBBERED	BESPORT	BESTRIDDEN
BERK	BESEECH	BESLOBBERING	BESPORTED	BESTRIDE
BERKELIUM	BESEECHED	BESLOBBERS	BESPORTING	BESTRIDES
BERKELIUMS	BESEECHER	BESLUBBER	BESPORTS	BESTRIDING
BERKS	BESEECHERS	BESLUBBERED	BESPOT	BESTRODE
BERLEY	BESEECHES	BESLUBBERING	BESPOTS	BESTROWN
BERLEYS	BESEECHING	BESLUBBERS	BESPOTTED	BESTS
BERLIN	BESEEKE	BESMEAR	BESPOTTING	BESTSELL
		BESMEARED	BESPOUT	BESTSELLING

BESTSELLS
BESTSOLD
BESTUCK
BESTUD
BESTUDDED
BESTUDDING
BESTUDS
BESUNG
BET
BETA
BETACISM
BETACISMS
BETAINE
BETAINES
BETAKE
BETAKEN
BETAKES
BETAKING
BETAS
BETATRON
BETATRONS
BÊTE
BETE
BETED
BETEEM
BETEEME
BETEEMED
BETEEMES
BETEEMING
BETEEMS
BETEL
BETELS
BÊTES
BETES
BETH
BETHANKIT
BETHEL
BETHELS
BETHESDA
BETHESDAS
BETHINK
BETHINKING
BETHINKS
BETHOUGHT
BETHRALL
BETHRALLED
BETHRALLING
BETHRALLS
BETHS
BETHUMB
BETHUMBED
BETHUMBING
BETHUMBS
BETHUMP
BETHUMPED
BETHUMPING
BETHUMPS
BETHWACK
BETHWACKED
BETHWACKING
BETHWACKS
BETID
BETIDE
BETIDED
BETIDES
BETIDING
BETIGHT
BETIME
BETIMED
BETIMES

BETIMING
BETING
BÊTISE
BÊTISES
BETITLE
BETITLED
BETITLES
BETITLING
BETOIL
BETOILED
BETOILING
BETOILS
BETOKEN
BETOKENED
BETOKENING
BETOKENS
BÉTON
BETONIES
BÉTONS
BETONY
BETOOK
BETOSS
BETOSSED
BETOSSES
BETOSSING
BETRAY
BETRAYAL
BETRAYALS
BETRAYED
BETRAYER
BETRAYERS
BETRAYING
BETRAYS
BETREAD
BETREADING
BETREADS
BETRIM
BETRIMMED
BETRIMMING
BETRIMS
BETROD
BETRODDEN
BETROTH
BETROTHAL
BETROTHALS
BETROTHED
BETROTHEDS
BETROTHING
BETROTHS
BETS
BETTED
BETTER
BETTERED
BETTERING
BETTERINGS
BETTERS
BETTIES
BETTING
BETTINGS
BETTOR
BETTORS
BETTY
BETUMBLED
BETWEEN
BETWEENS
BETWIXT
BEURRÉ
BEURRE
BEURRÉS
BEURRES

BEVATRON
BEVATRONS
BEVEL
BEVELLED
BEVELLER
BEVELLERS
BEVELLING
BEVELLINGS
BEVELMENT
BEVELMENTS
BEVELS
BEVER
BEVERAGE
BEVERAGES
BEVERS
BEVIES
BEVUE
BEVUES
BEVVIED
BEVVIES
BEVVY
BEVY
BEWAIL
BEWAILED
BEWAILING
BEWAILINGS
BEWAILS
BEWARE
BEWARED
BEWARES
BEWARING
BEWEEP
BEWEEPING
BEWEEPS
BEWEPT
BEWET
BEWETS
BEWETTED
BEWETTING
BEWHORE
BEWHORED
BEWHORES
BEWHORING
BEWIG
BEWIGGED
BEWIGGING
BEWIGS
BEWILDER
BEWILDERED
BEWILDERING
BEWILDERS
BEWITCH
BEWITCHED
BEWITCHES
BEWITCHING
BEWRAY
BEWRAYED
BEWRAYING
BEWRAYS
BEY
BEYOND
BEYONDS
BEYS
BEZ
BEZANT
BEZANTS
BEZAZZ
BEZAZZES
BEZEL
BEZELS

BEZES
BEZIQUE
BEZIQUES
BEZOAR
BEZOARDIC
BEZOARS
BEZONIAN
BEZONIANS
BEZZES
BEZZLE
BEZZLED
BEZZLES
BEZZLING
BHAJAN
BHAJANS
BHAKTI
BHAKTIS
BHANG
BHANGS
BHARAL
BHARALS
BHEESTIE
BHEESTIES
BHEESTY
BHEL
BHELS
BHINDI
BHINDIS
BHISTEE
BHISTEES
BHISTI
BHISTIS
BIANNUAL
BIAS
BIASED
BIASES
BIASING
BIASINGS
BIASSED
BIASSES
BIASSING
BIATHLON
BIATHLONS
BIAXAL
BIAXIAL
BIB
BIBACIOUS
BIBATION
BIBATIONS
BIBBED
BIBBER
BIBBERS
BIBBING
BIBCOCK
BIBCOCKS
BIBELOT
BIBELOTS
BIBFUL
BIBFULS
BIBLE
BIBLES
BIBLICAL
BIBLICISM
BIBLICISMS
BIBLICIST
BIBLICISTS
BIBLIST
BIBLISTS
BIBS
BIBULOUS

BICAMERAL
BICARB
BICARBS
BICE
BICEPS
BICEPSES
BICES
BICHORD
BICIPITAL
BICKER
BICKERED
BICKERING
BICKERS
BICONCAVE
BICONVEX
BICUSPID
BICUSPIDS
BICYCLE
BICYCLED
BICYCLES
BICYCLING
BICYCLIST
BICYCLISTS
BID
BIDDABLE
BIDDEN
BIDDER
BIDDERS
BIDDIES
BIDDING
BIDDINGS
BIDDY
BIDE
BIDED
BIDENT
BIDENTAL
BIDENTALS
BIDENTATE
BIDENTS
BIDES
BIDET
BIDETS
BIDING
BIDINGS
BIDON
BIDONS
BIDS
BIELD
BIELDIER
BIELDIEST
BIELDS
BIELDY
BIEN
BIENNIAL
BIENNIALS
BIER
BIERS
BIESTINGS
BIFACIAL
BIFARIOUS
BIFF
BIFFED
BIFFIN
BIFFING
BIFFINS
BIFFS
BIFID
BIFILAR
BIFOCAL
BIFOCALS

BIFOLD
BIFOLIATE
BIFORM
BIFURCATE
BIFURCATED
BIFURCATES
BIFURCATING
BIG
BIGA
BIGAE
BIGAMIES
BIGAMIST
BIGAMISTS
BIGAMOUS
BIGAMY
BIGENER
BIGENERIC
BIGENERS
BIGG
BIGGED
BIGGER
BIGGEST
BIGGIE
BIGGIES
BIGGIN
BIGGING
BIGGINS
BIGGISH
BIGGS
BIGGY
BIGHA
BIGHAS
BIGHEADED
BIGHORN
BIGHORNS
BIGHT
BIGHTS
BIGNESS
BIGNESSES
BIGOT
BIGOTED
BIGOTRIES
BIGOTRY
BIGOTS
BIGS
BIGWIG
BIGWIGS
BIJOU
BIJOUX
BIJWONER
BIJWONERS
BIKE
BIKED
BIKER
BIKERS
BIKES
BIKIE
BIKIES
BIKING
BIKINGS
BIKINI
BIKINIS
BILABIAL
BILABIALS
BILABIATE
BILANDER
BILANDERS
BILATERAL
BILBERRIES
BILBERRY

BILBO
BILBOES
BILBOS
BILE
BILES
BILGE
BILGED
BILGES
BILGIER
BILGIEST
BILGING
BILGY
BILHARZIA
BILHARZIAS
BILIAN
BILIANS
BILIARIES
BILIARY
BILIMBI
BILIMBING
BILIMBINGS
BILIMBIS
BILINGUAL
BILIOUS
BILIOUSLY
BILIRUBIN
BILIRUBINS
BILITERAL
BILK
BILKED
BILKER
BILKERS
BILKING
BILKS
BILL
BILLABONG
BILLABONGS
BILLBOARD
BILLBOARDS
BILLBOOK
BILLBOOKS
BILLED
BILLET
BILLETED
BILLETING
BILLETS
BILLHEAD
BILLHEADS
BILLHOOK
BILLHOOKS
BILLIARD
BILLIARDS
BILLIE
BILLIES
BILLING
BILLINGS
BILLION
BILLIONS
BILLIONTH
BILLIONTHS
BILLMAN
BILLMEN
BILLON
BILLONS
BILLOW
BILLOWED
BILLOWIER
BILLOWIEST
BILLOWING
BILLOWS

BILLOWY
BILLS
BILLY
BILLYBOY
BILLYBOYS
BILLYCOCK
BILLYCOCKS
BILOBAR
BILOBATE
BILOBED
BILOBULAR
BILOCULAR
BILTONG
BILTONGS
BIMANAL
BIMANOUS
BIMBASHI
BIMBASHIS
BIMBO
BIMBOS
BIMONTHLY
BIN
BINARIES
BINARY
BINATE
BINAURAL
BIND
BINDER
BINDERIES
BINDERS
BINDERY
BINDING
BINDINGS
BINDS
BINDWEED
BINDWEEDS
BINE
BINERVATE
BINES
BING
BINGE
BINGED
BINGEING
BINGER
BINGERS
BINGES
BINGING
BINGLE
BINGLED
BINGLES
BINGLING
BINGO
BINGOS
BINGS
BINK
BINKS
BINNACLE
BINNACLES
BINNED
BINNING
BINOCLE
BINOCLES
BINOCULAR
BINOCULARS
BINOMIAL
BINOMIALS
BINOMINAL
BINS
BINT
BINTS

BINTURONG
BINTURONGS
BIO
BIOASSAY
BIOASSAYS
BIOBLAST
BIOBLASTS
BIOCIDAL
BIOCIDE
BIOCIDES
BIODATA
BIOETHICS
BIOG
BIOGAS
BIOGASES
BIOGEN
BIOGENIC
BIOGENIES
BIOGENOUS
BIOGENS
BIOGENY
BIOGRAPH
BIOGRAPHIES
BIOGRAPHS
BIOGRAPHY
BIOGS
BIOHAZARD
BIOHAZARDS
BIOLOGIES
BIOLOGIST
BIOLOGISTS
BIOLOGY
BIOMASS
BIOMASSES
BIOME
BIOMES
BIOMETRIC
BIOMETRICS
BIOMETRIES
BIOMETRY
BIOMORPH
BIOMORPHS
BIONIC
BIONICS
BIONOMIC
BIONOMICS
BIONT
BIONTIC
BIONTS
BIOPARENT
BIOPARENTS
BIOPHOR
BIOPHORE
BIOPHORES
BIOPHORS
BIOPIC
BIOPICS
BIOPLASM
BIOPLASMS
BIOPLAST
BIOPLASTS
BIOPSIES
BIOPSY
BIOS
BIOSCOPE
BIOSCOPES
BIOSPHERE
BIOSPHERES
BIOSTABLE
BIOTA

BIOTAS
BIOTIC
BIOTIN
BIOTINS
BIOTITE
BIOTITES
BIOTYPE
BIOTYPES
BIPAROUS
BIPARTITE
BIPED
BIPEDAL
BIPEDS
BIPHENYL
BIPHENYLS
BIPINNATE
BIPLANE
BIPLANES
BIPOD
BIPODS
BIPOLAR
BIPYRAMID
BIPYRAMIDS
BIRCH
BIRCHED
BIRCHEN
BIRCHES
BIRCHING
BIRD
BIRDBATH
BIRDBATHS
BIRDCAGE
BIRDCAGES
BIRDCALL
BIRDCALLS
BIRDED
BIRDER
BIRDERS
BIRDIE
BIRDIED
BIRDIEING
BIRDIES
BIRDING
BIRDINGS
BIRDMAN
BIRDMEN
BIRDS
BIRDSEED
BIRDSEEDS
BIRDSHOT
BIRDSHOTS
BIRDWING
BIRDWINGS
BIREME
BIREMES
BIRETTA
BIRETTAS
BIRIYANI
BIRIYANIS
BIRK
BIRKEN
BIRKIE
BIRKIES
BIRKS
BIRL
BIRLE
BIRLED
BIRLER
BIRLERS
BIRLES

BIRLIEMAN	BISSON	BIVALENCE	BLACKHEADS	BLAMED
BIRLIEMEN	BISTABLE	BIVALENCES	BLACKING	BLAMEFUL
BIRLING	BISTER	BIVALENCIES	BLACKINGS	BLAMELESS
BIRLINGS	BISTERS	BIVALENCY	BLACKISH	BLAMES
BIRLINN	BISTORT	BIVALENT	BLACKJACK	BLAMING
BIRLINNS	BISTORTS	BIVALENTS	BLACKJACKS	BLANCH
BIRLS	BISTOURIES	BIVALVE	BLACKLEAD	BLANCHED
BIRR	BISTOURY	BIVALVES	BLACKLEADS	BLANCHES
BIRRS	BISTRE	BIVARIANT	BLACKLEG	BLANCHING
BIRSE	BISTRED	BIVARIANTS	BLACKLEGGED	BLANCO
BIRSES	BISTRES	BIVARIATE	BLACKLEGGING	BLANCOED
BIRSLE	BISTRO	BIVARIATES	BLACKLEGS	BLANCOES
BIRSLED	BISTROS	BIVIOUS	BLACKLIST	BLANCOING
BIRSLES	BISULCATE	BIVIUM	BLACKLISTED	BLAND
BIRSLING	BIT	BIVIUMS	BLACKLISTING	BLANDER
BIRSY	BITCH	BIVOUAC	BLACKLISTINGS	BLANDEST
BIRTH	BITCHED	BIVOUACKED	BLACKLISTS	BLANDISH
BIRTHDAY	BITCHERIES	BIVOUACKING	BLACKMAIL	BLANDISHED
BIRTHDAYS	BITCHERY	BIVOUACS	BLACKMAILED	BLANDISHES
BIRTHDOM	BITCHES	BIVVIED	BLACKMAILING	BLANDISHING
BIRTHDOMS	BITCHIER	BIVVIES	BLACKMAILS	BLANDLY
BIRTHMARK	BITCHIEST	BIVVY	BLACKNESS	BLANDNESS
BIRTHMARKS	BITCHILY	BIVVYING	BLACKNESSES	BLANDNESSES
BIRTHS	BITCHING	BIZ	BLACKOUT	BLANDS
BIRTHWORT	BITCHY	BIZARRE	BLACKOUTS	BLANK
BIRTHWORTS	BITE	BIZAZZ	BLACKS	BLANKED
BIRYANI	BITER	BIZAZZES	BLACKTOP	BLANKER
BIRYANIS	BITERS	BIZCACHA	BLACKTOPS	BLANKEST
BIS	BITES	BIZCACHAS	BLACKWASH	BLANKET
BISCACHA	BITING	BIZONAL	BLACKWASHES	BLANKETED
BISCACHAS	BITINGS	BIZONE	BLACKWOOD	BLANKETIES
BISCUIT	BITO	BIZONES	BLACKWOODS	BLANKETING
BISCUITS	BITONAL	BIZZES	BLAD	BLANKETINGS
BISCUITY	BITOS	BLAB	BLADDED	BLANKETS
BISE	BITS	BLABBED	BLADDER	BLANKETY
BISECT	BITSIER	BLABBER	BLADDERED	BLANKIES
BISECTED	BITSIEST	BLABBERS	BLADDERS	BLANKING
BISECTING	BITSY	BLABBING	BLADDERY	BLANKLY
BISECTION	BITT	BLABBINGS	BLADDING	BLANKNESS
BISECTIONS	BITTACLE	BLABS	BLADE	BLANKNESSES
BISECTOR	BITTACLES	BLACK	BLADED	BLANKS
BISECTORS	BITTE	BLACKBALL	BLADES	BLANKY
BISECTS	BITTED	BLACKBALLED	BLADS	BLANQUET
BISERIAL	BITTEN	BLACKBALLING	BLAE	BLANQUETS
BISERRATE	BITTER	BLACKBALLINGS	BLAEBERRIES	BLARE
BISES	BITTERER	BLACKBALLS	BLAEBERRY	BLARED
BISEXUAL	BITTEREST	BLACKBAND	BLAER	BLARES
BISH	BITTERISH	BLACKBANDS	BLAES	BLARING
BISHES	BITTERLY	BLACKBIRD	BLAEST	BLARNEY
BISHOP	BITTERN	BLACKBIRDS	BLAG	BLARNEYED
BISHOPDOM	BITTERNS	BLACKBOY	BLAGGED	BLARNEYING
BISHOPDOMS	BITTERS	BLACKBOYS	BLAGGING	BLARNEYS
BISHOPED	BITTIE	BLACKBUCK	BLAGS	BLASÉ
BISHOPESS	BITTIER	BLACKBUCKS	BLAGUE	BLASH
BISHOPESSES	BITTIES	BLACKCAP	BLAGUES	BLASHES
BISHOPING	BITTIEST	BLACKCAPS	BLAGUEUR	BLASHY
BISHOPRIC	BITTING	BLACKCOCK	BLAGUEURS	BLASPHEME
BISHOPRICS	BITTOCK	BLACKCOCKS	BLAH	BLASPHEMED
BISHOPS	BITTOCKS	BLACKED	BLAHED	BLASPHEMES
BISK	BITTOR	BLACKEN	BLAHING	BLASPHEMIES
BISKS	BITTORS	BLACKENED	BLAHS	BLASPHEMING
BISMAR	BITTOUR	BLACKENING	BLAIN	BLASPHEMY
BISMARS	BITTOURS	BLACKENS	BLAINS	BLAST
BISMILLAH	BITTS	BLACKER	BLAISE	BLASTED
BISMUTH	BITTUR	BLACKEST	BLAIZE	BLASTEMA
BISMUTHS	BITTURS	BLACKFISH	BLAMABLE	BLASTEMAS
BISON	BITTY	BLACKFISHES	BLAMABLY	BLASTER
BISONS	BITUMED	BLACKGAME	BLAME	BLASTERS
BISQUE	BITUMEN	BLACKGAMES	BLAMEABLE	BLASTING
BISQUES	BITUMENS	BLACKHEAD	BLAMEABLY	BLASTINGS

BLASTMENT	BLEAKNESS	BLETHER	BLINS	BLOKE
BLASTMENTS	BLEAKNESSES	BLETHERED	BLINTZ	BLOKES
BLASTOID	BLEAKS	BLETHERING	BLINTZE	BLONCKET
BLASTOIDS	BLEAKY	BLETHERINGS	BLINTZES	BLOND
BLASTS	BLEAR	BLETHERS	BLIP	BLONDE
BLASTULA	BLEARED	BLETS	BLIPPED	BLONDER
BLASTULAE	BLEARER	BLETTED	BLIPPING	BLONDES
BLASTULAR	BLEAREST	BLETTING	BLIPS	BLONDEST
BLASTULAS	BLEAREYED	BLEUÂTRE	BLISS	BLONDS
BLAT	BLEARIER	BLEW	BLISSES	BLOOD
BLATANT	BLEARIEST	BLEWART	BLISSFUL	BLOODED
BLATANTER	BLEARING	BLEWARTS	BLISSLESS	BLOODHEAT
BLATANTEST	BLEARS	BLEWITS	BLIST	BLOODHEATS
BLATANTLY	BLEARY	BLEWITSES	BLISTER	BLOODIED
BLATE	BLEAT	BLEWS	BLISTERED	BLOODIER
BLATER	BLEATED	BLEY	BLISTERING	BLOODIES
BLATEST	BLEATER	BLEYS	BLISTERS	BLOODIEST
BLATHER	BLEATERS	BLIGHT	BLISTERY	BLOODILY
BLATHERED	BLEATING	BLIGHTED	BLITE	BLOODING
BLATHERING	BLEATINGS	BLIGHTER	BLITES	BLOODLESS
BLATHERS	BLEATS	BLIGHTERS	BLITHE	BLOODLUST
BLATS	BLEB	BLIGHTIES	BLITHELY	BLOODLUSTS
BLATT	BLEBS	BLIGHTING	BLITHER	BLOODROOT
BLATTANT	BLED	BLIGHTINGS	BLITHERED	BLOODROOTS
BLATTED	BLEE	BLIGHTS	BLITHERING	BLOODS
BLATTER	BLEED	BLIGHTY	BLITHERS	BLOODSHED
BLATTERED	BLEEDER	BLIMBING	BLITHEST	BLOODSHEDS
BLATTERING	BLEEDERS	BLIMBINGS	BLITZ	BLOODSHOT
BLATTERS	BLEEDING	BLIMEY	BLITZED	BLOODWOOD
BLATTING	BLEEDINGS	BLIMP	BLITZES	BLOODWOODS
BLATTS	BLEEDS	BLIMPISH	BLITZING	BLOODY
BLAUBOK	BLEEP	BLIMPS	BLIVE	BLOODYING
BLAUBOKS	BLEEPED	BLIMY	BLIZZARD	BLOOM
BLAUD	BLEEPER	BLIN	BLIZZARDS	BLOOMED
BLAUDED	BLEEPERS	BLIND	BLOAT	BLOOMER
BLAUDING	BLEEPING	BLINDAGE	BLOATED	BLOOMERIES
BLAUDS	BLEEPS	BLINDAGES	BLOATER	BLOOMERS
BLAWORT	BLEES	BLINDED	BLOATERS	BLOOMERY
BLAWORTS	BLEMISH	BLINDER	BLOATING	BLOOMIER
BLAY	BLEMISHED	BLINDERS	BLOATINGS	BLOOMIEST
BLAYS	BLEMISHES	BLINDEST	BLOATS	BLOOMING
BLAZE	BLEMISHING	BLINDFISH	BLOB	BLOOMLESS
BLAZED	BLENCH	BLINDFISHES	BLOBBED	BLOOMS
BLAZER	BLENCHED	BLINDFOLD	BLOBBING	BLOOMY
BLAZERS	BLENCHES	BLINDFOLDED	BLOBS	BLOOP
BLAZES	BLENCHING	BLINDFOLDING	BLOC	BLOOPED
BLAZING	BLEND	BLINDFOLDS	BLOCK	BLOOPER
BLAZON	BLENDE	BLINDING	BLOCKADE	BLOOPERS
BLAZONED	BLENDED	BLINDINGS	BLOCKADED	BLOOPING
BLAZONER	BLENDER	BLINDLESS	BLOCKADES	BLOOPS
BLAZONERS	BLENDERS	BLINDLY	BLOCKADING	BLOOSME
BLAZONING	BLENDES	BLINDNESS	BLOCKAGE	BLOOSMED
BLAZONRIES	BLENDING	BLINDNESSES	BLOCKAGES	BLOOSMES
BLAZONRY	BLENDINGS	BLINDS	BLOCKED	BLOOSMING
BLAZONS	BLENDS	BLINDWORM	BLOCKER	BLORE
BLEACH	BLENNIES	BLINDWORMS	BLOCKERS	BLORES
BLEACHED	BLENNY	BLINI	BLOCKHEAD	BLOSSOM
BLEACHER	BLENT	BLINIS	BLOCKHEADS	BLOSSOMED
BLEACHERIES	BLESBOK	BLINK	BLOCKHOLE	BLOSSOMING
BLEACHERS	BLESBOKS	BLINKARD	BLOCKHOLES	BLOSSOMINGS
BLEACHERY	BLESS	BLINKARDS	BLOCKIER	BLOSSOMS
BLEACHES	BLESSED	BLINKED	BLOCKIEST	BLOSSOMY
BLEACHING	BLESSEDER	BLINKER	BLOCKING	BLOT
BLEACHINGS	BLESSEDEST	BLINKERED	BLOCKINGS	BLOTCH
BLEAK	BLESSEDLY	BLINKERING	BLOCKISH	BLOTCHED
BLEAKER	BLESSES	BLINKERS	BLOCKS	BLOTCHES
BLEAKEST	BLESSING	BLINKING	BLOCKWORK	BLOTCHIER
BLEAKIER	BLESSINGS	BLINKS	BLOCKWORKS	BLOTCHIEST
BLEAKIEST	BLEST	BLINNED	BLOCKY	BLOTCHING
BLEAKLY	BLET	BLINNING	BLOCS	BLOTCHINGS

BLOTCHY
BLOTS
BLOTTED
BLOTTER
BLOTTERS
BLOTTIER
BLOTTIEST
BLOTTING
BLOTTINGS
BLOTTO
BLOTTY
BLOUBOK
BLOUBOKS
BLOUSE
BLOUSED
BLOUSES
BLOUSING
BLOUSON
BLOUSONS
BLOW
BLOWBALL
BLOWBALLS
BLOWDOWN
BLOWDOWNS
BLOWED
BLOWER
BLOWERS
BLOWFLIES
BLOWFLY
BLOWGUN
BLOWGUNS
BLOWHARD
BLOWHARDS
BLOWHOLE
BLOWHOLES
BLOWIER
BLOWIEST
BLOWING
BLOWLAMP
BLOWLAMPS
BLOWN
BLOWPIPE
BLOWPIPES
BLOWS
BLOWSE
BLOWSED
BLOWSES
BLOWSIER
BLOWSIEST
BLOWSY
BLOWTORCH
BLOWTORCHES
BLOWY
BLOWZE
BLOWZED
BLOWZES
BLOWZIER
BLOWZIEST
BLOWZY
BLUB
BLUBBED
BLUBBER
BLUBBERED
BLUBBERING
BLUBBERS
BLUBBING
BLUBS
BLUCHER
BLUCHERS
BLUDE

BLUDES
BLUDGE
BLUDGED
BLUDGEON
BLUDGEONED
BLUDGEONING
BLUDGEONS
BLUDGER
BLUDGERS
BLUDGES
BLUDGING
BLUDIE
BLUDIER
BLUDIEST
BLUDY
BLUE
BLUEBACK
BLUEBACKS
BLUEBEARD
BLUEBEARDS
BLUEBELL
BLUEBELLS
BLUEBERRIES
BLUEBERRY
BLUEBIRD
BLUEBIRDS
BLUEBUCK
BLUEBUCKS
BLUECAP
BLUECAPS
BLUECOAT
BLUECOATS
BLUED
BLUEFISH
BLUEFISHES
BLUEGOWN
BLUEGOWNS
BLUEGRASS
BLUEGRASSES
BLUEING
BLUEINGS
BLUENESS
BLUENESSES
BLUENOSE
BLUENOSES
BLUEPRINT
BLUEPRINTED
BLUEPRINTING
BLUEPRINTS
BLUER
BLUES
BLUESIER
BLUESIEST
BLUEST
BLUESTONE
BLUESTONES
BLUESY
BLUETTE
BLUETTES
BLUEWEED
BLUEWEEDS
BLUEWING
BLUEWINGS
BLUEY
BLUEYS
BLUFF
BLUFFED
BLUFFER
BLUFFERS
BLUFFEST

BLUFFING
BLUFFLY
BLUFFNESS
BLUFFNESSES
BLUFFS
BLUGGY
BLUID
BLUIDIER
BLUIDIEST
BLUIDS
BLUIDY
BLUING
BLUINGS
BLUISH
BLUNDER
BLUNDERED
BLUNDERER
BLUNDERERS
BLUNDERING
BLUNDERINGS
BLUNDERS
BLUNGE
BLUNGED
BLUNGER
BLUNGERS
BLUNGES
BLUNGING
BLUNK
BLUNKED
BLUNKER
BLUNKERS
BLUNKING
BLUNKS
BLUNT
BLUNTED
BLUNTER
BLUNTEST
BLUNTING
BLUNTISH
BLUNTLY
BLUNTNESS
BLUNTNESSES
BLUNTS
BLUR
BLURB
BLURBS
BLURRED
BLURRING
BLURS
BLURT
BLURTED
BLURTING
BLURTINGS
BLURTS
BLUSH
BLUSHED
BLUSHER
BLUSHERS
BLUSHES
BLUSHET
BLUSHETS
BLUSHFUL
BLUSHING
BLUSHINGS
BLUSHLESS
BLUSTER
BLUSTERED
BLUSTERER
BLUSTERERS
BLUSTERIER

BLUSTERIEST
BLUSTERING
BLUSTERS
BLUSTERY
BLUSTROUS
BLUTWURST
BLUTWURSTS
BO
BOA
BOAR
BOARD
BOARDED
BOARDER
BOARDERS
BOARDING
BOARDINGS
BOARDROOM
BOARDROOMS
BOARDS
BOARDWALK
BOARDWALKS
BOARFISH
BOARFISHES
BOARISH
BOARS
BOART
BOARTS
BOAS
BOAST
BOASTED
BOASTER
BOASTERS
BOASTFUL
BOASTING
BOASTINGS
BOASTLESS
BOASTS
BOAT
BOATBILL
BOATBILLS
BOATED
BOATEL
BOATELS
BOATER
BOATERS
BOATHOUSE
BOATHOUSES
BOATING
BOATINGS
BOATMAN
BOATMEN
BOATRACE
BOATRACES
BOATS
BOATSWAIN
BOATSWAINS
BOATTAIL
BOATTAILS
BOB
BOBA
BOBAC
BOBACS
BOBAK
BOBAKS
BOBAS
BOBBED
BOBBERIES
BOBBERY
BOBBIES
BOBBIN

BOBBINET
BOBBINETS
BOBBING
BOBBINS
BOBBISH
BOBBLE
BOBBLED
BOBBLES
BOBBLING
BOBBY
BOBBYSOCK
BOBBYSOCKS
BOBCAT
BOBCATS
BOBOLINK
BOBOLINKS
BOBS
BOBSLED
BOBSLEDS
BOBSLEIGH
BOBSLEIGHS
BOBSTAYS
BOBTAIL
BOBTAILED
BOBTAILING
BOBTAILS
BOBWHEEL
BOBWHEELS
BOBWIG
BOBWIGS
BOCAGE
BOCAGES
BOCCA
BOCCAS
BOCHE
BOCHES
BOCK
BOCKED
BOCKING
BOCKS
BOD
BODACH
BODACHS
BODDLE
BODDLES
BODE
BODED
BODEFUL
BODEGA
BODEGAS
BODEGUERO
BODEGUEROS
BODEMENT
BODEMENTS
BODES
BODGE
BODGED
BODGER
BODGERS
BODGES
BODGIE
BODGIES
BODGING
BODICE
BODICES
BODIED
BODIES
BODIKIN
BODIKINS
BODILESS

BODILY
BODING
BODINGS
BODKIN
BODKINS
BODLE
BODLES
BODRAG
BODRAGS
BODS
BODY
BODYGUARD
BODYGUARDS
BODYING
BODYSHELL
BODYSHELLS
BODYWORK
BODYWORKS
BOEREWORS
BOFF
BOFFED
BOFFIN
BOFFING
BOFFINS
BOFFS
BOG
BOGAN
BOGANS
BOGBEAN
BOGBEANS
BOGEY
BOGEYISM
BOGEYISMS
BOGEYS
BOGGARD
BOGGARDS
BOGGART
BOGGARTS
BOGGED
BOGGIER
BOGGIEST
BOGGINESS
BOGGINESSES
BOGGING
BOGGLE
BOGGLED
BOGGLER
BOGGLERS
BOGGLES
BOGGLING
BOGGY
BOGIE
BOGIES
BOGLAND
BOGLANDS
BOGLE
BOGLES
BOGOAK
BOGOAKS
BOGONG
BOGONGS
BOGS
BOGUS
BOGY
BOGYISM
BOGYISMS
BOH
BOHEA
BOHEAS
BOHUNK

BOHUNKS
BOIL
BOILED
BOILER
BOILERIES
BOILERS
BOILERY
BOILING
BOILINGS
BOILS
BOING
BOINGED
BOINGING
BOINGS
BOINK
BOINKED
BOINKING
BOINKS
BOK
BOKE
BOKED
BOKES
BOKING
BOKO
BOKOS
BOKS
BOLA
BOLD
BOLDEN
BOLDENED
BOLDENING
BOLDENS
BOLDER
BOLDEST
BOLDLY
BOLDNESS
BOLDNESSES
BOLE
BOLECTION
BOLECTIONS
BOLERO
BOLEROS
BOLES
BOLETI
BOLETUS
BOLETUSES
BOLIDE
BOLIDES
BOLIVAR
BOLIVARES
BOLIVARS
BOLIVIANO
BOLIVIANOS
BOLIX
BOLIXED
BOLIXES
BOLIXING
BOLL
BOLLARD
BOLLARDS
BOLLED
BOLLEN
BOLLETRIE
BOLLETRIES
BOLLING
BOLLIX
BOLLIXED
BOLLIXES
BOLLIXING
BOLLOCK

BOLLOCKED
BOLLOCKING
BOLLOCKINGS
BOLLOCKS
BOLLOCKSED
BOLLOCKSES
BOLLOCKSING
BOLLS
BOLO
BOLOMETER
BOLOMETERS
BOLOMETRIES
BOLOMETRY
BOLONEY
BOLONEYS
BOLOS
BOLSHEVIK
BOLSHEVIKS
BOLSHIE
BOLSHIER
BOLSHIES
BOLSHIEST
BOLSHY
BOLSTER
BOLSTERED
BOLSTERING
BOLSTERINGS
BOLSTERS
BOLT
BOLTED
BOLTER
BOLTERS
BOLTHEAD
BOLTHEADS
BOLTHOLE
BOLTHOLES
BOLTING
BOLTINGS
BOLTS
BOLUS
BOLUSES
BOMA
BOMAS
BOMB
BOMBARD
BOMBARDED
BOMBARDING
BOMBARDON
BOMBARDONS
BOMBARDS
BOMBASINE
BOMBASINES
BOMBAST
BOMBASTED
BOMBASTIC
BOMBASTING
BOMBASTS
BOMBAX
BOMBAXES
BOMBAZINE
BOMBAZINES
BOMBE
BOMBÉ
BOMBED
BOMBER
BOMBERS
BOMBES
BOMBILATE
BOMBILATED
BOMBILATES

BOMBILATING
BOMBINATE
BOMBINATED
BOMBINATES
BOMBINATING
BOMBING
BOMBO
BOMBORA
BOMBORAS
BOMBOS
BOMBPROOF
BOMBS
BOMBSHELL
BOMBSHELLS
BOMBSITE
BOMBSITES
BOMBYCID
BOMBYCIDS
BON
BONA
BONAMANI
BONAMANO
BONANZA
BONANZAS
BONASSUS
BONASSUSES
BONASUS
BONASUSES
BONBON
BONBONS
BONCE
BONCES
BOND
BONDAGE
BONDAGER
BONDAGERS
BONDAGES
BONDED
BONDER
BONDERS
BONDING
BONDINGS
BONDMAID
BONDMAIDS
BONDMAN
BONDMEN
BONDS
BONDSMAN
BONDSMEN
BONDSTONE
BONDSTONES
BONDUC
BONDUCS
BONE
BONED
BONEHEAD
BONEHEADS
BONELESS
BONER
BONERS
BONES
BONESET
BONESETS
BONEYARD
BONEYARDS
BONFIRE
BONFIRES
BONG
BONGED
BONGING

BONGO
BONGOS
BONGRACE
BONGRACES
BONGS
BONHOMIE
BONHOMIES
BONHOMMIE
BONHOMMIES
BONHOMOUS
BONIBELL
BONIBELLS
BONIE
BONIER
BONIEST
BONIFACE
BONIFACES
BONILASSE
BONILASSES
BONINESS
BONINESSES
BONING
BONINGS
BONISM
BONISMS
BONIST
BONISTS
BONITO
BONITOS
BONJOUR
BONK
BONKED
BONKERS
BONKING
BONKS
BONNE
BONNES
BONNET
BONNETED
BONNETING
BONNETS
BONNIBELL
BONNIBELLS
BONNIE
BONNIER
BONNIES
BONNIEST
BONNILY
BONNINESS
BONNINESSES
BONNY
BONSAI
BONSOIR
BONSPIEL
BONSPIELS
BONTEBOK
BONTEBOKS
BONUS
BONUSES
BONXIE
BONXIES
BONY
BONZE
BONZER
BONZES
BOO
BOOB
BOOBED
BOOBIES
BOOBING

BOOBOO	BOOKSY	BOOTLICKS	BOREEN	BOSK
BOOBOOK	BOOKWORK	BOOTMAKER	BOREENS	BOSKER
BOOBOOKS	BOOKWORKS	BOOTMAKERS	BOREES	BOSKET
BOOBOOS	BOOKWORM	BOOTS	BOREHOLE	BOSKETS
BOOBS	BOOKWORMS	BOOTTREE	BOREHOLES	BOSKIER
BOOBY	BOOKY	BOOTTREES	BOREL	BOSKIEST
BOOBYISH	BOOM	BOOTY	BORER	BOSKINESS
BOOBYISM	BOOMED	BOOZE	BORERS	BOSKINESSES
BOOBYISMS	BOOMER	BOOZED	BORES	BOSKS
BOODIE	BOOMERANG	BOOZER	BORGHETTO	BOSKY
BOODIED	BOOMERANGED	BOOZERS	BORGHETTOS	BOSOM
BOODIES	BOOMERANGING	BOOZES	BORGO	BOSOMED
BOODLE	BOOMERANGS	BOOZEY	BORGOS	BOSOMING
BOODLES	BOOMERS	BOOZIER	BORIC	BOSOMS
BOODY	BOOMING	BOOZIEST	BORIDE	BOSOMY
BOODYING	BOOMINGS	BOOZILY	BORIDES	BOSON
BOOED	BOOMS	BOOZING	BORING	BOSONS
BOOGIE	BOOMSLANG	BOOZY	BORINGS	BOSS
BOOGIES	BOOMSLANGS	BOP	BORN	BOSSED
BOOH	BOON	BOPPED	BORNE	BOSSER
BOOHED	BOONDOCKS	BOPPER	BORNÉ	BOSSES
BOOHING	BOONG	BOPPERS	BORNITE	BOSSEST
BOOHS	BOONGS	BOPPING	BORNITES	BOSSIER
BOOING	BOONS	BOPS	BORON	BOSSIEST
BOOK	BOOR	BOR	BORONIA	BOSSILY
BOOKABLE	BOORD	BORA	BORONIAS	BOSSINESS
BOOKCASE	BOORDE	BORACHIO	BORONS	BOSSINESSES
BOOKCASES	BOORDES	BORACHIOS	BOROUGH	BOSSING
BOOKED	BOORDS	BORACIC	BOROUGHS	BOSSY
BOOKFUL	BOORISH	BORACITE	BORREL	BOSTANGI
BOOKIE	BOORISHLY	BORACITES	BORRELL	BOSTANGIS
BOOKIER	BOORS	BORAGE	BORROW	BOSTON
BOOKIES	BOOS	BORAGES	BORROWED	BOSTONS
BOOKIEST	BOOSE	BORANE	BORROWER	BOSTRYX
BOOKING	BOOSED	BORANES	BORROWERS	BOSTRYXES
BOOKINGS	BOOSES	BORAS	BORROWING	BOSUN
BOOKISH	BOOSING	BORATE	BORROWINGS	BOSUNS
BOOKLAND	BOOST	BORATES	BORROWS	BOT
BOOKLANDS	BOOSTED	BORAX	BORS	BOTANIC
BOOKLESS	BOOSTER	BORAXES	BORSCH	BOTANICAL
BOOKLET	BOOSTERS	BORAZON	BORSCHES	BOTANISE
BOOKLETS	BOOSTING	BORAZONS	BORSCHT	BOTANISED
BOOKLICE	BOOSTS	BORD	BORSCHTS	BOTANISES
BOOKLORE	BOOT	BORDAR	BORSTAL	BOTANISING
BOOKLORES	BOOTBLACK	BORDARS	BORSTALL	BOTANIST
BOOKLOUSE	BOOTBLACKS	BORDE	BORSTALLS	BOTANISTS
BOOKMAKER	BOOTED	BORDEL	BORSTALS	BOTANIZE
BOOKMAKERS	BOOTEE	BORDELLO	BORT	BOTANIZED
BOOKMAN	BOOTEES	BORDELLOS	BORTS	BOTANIZES
BOOKMARK	BOOTH	BORDELS	BORTSCH	BOTANIZING
BOOKMARKS	BOOTHOSE	BORDER	BORTSCHES	BOTANY
BOOKMEN	BOOTHS	BORDEREAU	BORTSCHT	BOTARGO
BOOKPLATE	BOOTIES	BORDEREAUX	BORZOI	BOTARGOES
BOOKPLATES	BOOTIKIN	BORDERED	BORZOIS	BOTARGOS
BOOKREST	BOOTIKINS	BORDERER	BOS	BOTCH
BOOKRESTS	BOOTING	BORDERERS	BOSBOK	BOTCHED
BOOKS	BOOTLACE	BORDERING	BOSBOKS	BOTCHER
BOOKSHELF	BOOTLACES	BORDERS	BOSCAGE	BOTCHERIES
BOOKSHELVES	BOOTLAST	BORDES	BOSCAGES	BOTCHERS
BOOKSHOP	BOOTLASTS	BORDS	BOSCHBOK	BOTCHERY
BOOKSHOPS	BOOTLEG	BORDURE	BOSCHBOKS	BOTCHES
BOOKSIE	BOOTLEGGED	BORDURES	BOSCHE	BOTCHIER
BOOKSIER	BOOTLEGGING	BORE	BOSCHES	BOTCHIEST
BOOKSIEST	BOOTLEGGINGS	BOREAL	BOSCHVELD	BOTCHING
BOOKSTALL	BOOTLEGS	BORECOLE	BOSCHVELDS	BOTCHINGS
BOOKSTALLS	BOOTLESS	BORECOLES	BOSH	BOTCHY
BOOKSTAND	BOOTLICK	BORED	BOSHES	BOTEL
BOOKSTANDS	BOOTLICKED	BOREDOM	BOSHTA	BOTELS
BOOKSTORE	BOOTLICKING	BOREDOMS	BOSHTER	BOTFLIES
BOOKSTORES	BOOTLICKINGS	BOREE		

BOTFLY
BOTH
BOTHAN
BOTHANS
BOTHER
BOTHERED
BOTHERING
BOTHERS
BOTHIE
BOTHIES
BOTHOLE
BOTHOLES
BOTHY
BOTHYMAN
BOTHYMEN
BOTONÉ
BOTRYOID
BOTRYOSE
BOTS
BOTT
BOTTE
BOTTEGA
BOTTEGAS
BOTTES
BOTTIES
BOTTINE
BOTTINES
BOTTLE
BOTTLED
BOTTLEFUL
BOTTLEFULS
BOTTLER
BOTTLERS
BOTTLES
BOTTLING
BOTTOM
BOTTOMED
BOTTOMING
BOTTOMS
BOTTONY
BOTTS
BOTTY
BOTULISM
BOTULISMS
BOUCHE
BOUCHÉ
BOUCHES
BOUCHÉS
BOUCLÉ
BOUCLÉS
BOUDERIE
BOUDERIES
BOUDOIR
BOUDOIRS
BOUFFANT
BOUGE
BOUGED
BOUGES
BOUGET
BOUGETS
BOUGH
BOUGHPOT
BOUGHPOTS
BOUGHS
BOUGHT
BOUGHTEN
BOUGHTS
BOUGIE
BOUGIES
BOUGING

BOUILLI
BOUILLIS
BOUILLON
BOUILLONS
BOUK
BOUKS
BOULDER
BOULDERS
BOULE
BOULES
BOULEVARD
BOULEVARDS
BOULLE
BOULLES
BOULT
BOULTED
BOULTER
BOULTERS
BOULTING
BOULTINGS
BOULTS
BOUN
BOUNCE
BOUNCED
BOUNCER
BOUNCERS
BOUNCES
BOUNCIER
BOUNCIEST
BOUNCILY
BOUNCING
BOUNCY
BOUND
BOUNDARIES
BOUNDARY
BOUNDED
BOUNDEN
BOUNDER
BOUNDERS
BOUNDING
BOUNDLESS
BOUNDS
BOUNED
BOUNING
BOUNS
BOUNTEOUS
BOUNTIES
BOUNTIFUL
BOUNTREE
BOUNTREES
BOUNTY
BOUNTYHED
BOUNTYHEDS
BOUQUET
BOUQUETS
BOURASQUE
BOURASQUES
BOURBON
BOURBONS
BOURD
BOURDER
BOURDERS
BOURDON
BOURDONS
BOURDS
BOURG
BOURGEOIS
BOURGEON
BOURGEONED
BOURGEONING

BOURGEONS
BOURGS
BOURKHA
BOURKHAS
BOURLAW
BOURLAWS
BOURN
BOURNE
BOURNES
BOURNS
BOURREE
BOURREES
BOURSE
BOURSES
BOURSIER
BOURSIERS
BOURTREE
BOURTREES
BOUSE
BOUSED
BOUSES
BOUSIER
BOUSIEST
BOUSING
BOUSY
BOUT
BOUTADE
BOUTADES
BOUTIQUE
BOUTIQUES
BOUTON
BOUTONNÉ
BOUTONNÉE
BOUTONS
BOUTS
BOUZOUKI
BOUZOUKIS
BOVATE
BOVATES
BOVINE
BOVVER
BOVVERS
BOW
BOWAT
BOWATS
BOWBENT
BOWED
BOWEL
BOWELLED
BOWELLING
BOWELS
BOWER
BOWERED
BOWERIES
BOWERING
BOWERS
BOWERY
BOWES
BOWET
BOWETS
BOWFIN
BOWFINS
BOWGET
BOWGETS
BOWHEAD
BOWHEADS
BOWING
BOWL
BOWLDER
BOWLDERS

BOWLED
BOWLER
BOWLERED
BOWLERING
BOWLERS
BOWLINE
BOWLINES
BOWLING
BOWLINGS
BOWLS
BOWMAN
BOWMEN
BOWNE
BOWNED
BOWNES
BOWNING
BOWPOT
BOWPOTS
BOWR
BOWRS
BOWS
BOWSE
BOWSED
BOWSER
BOWSERS
BOWSES
BOWSHOT
BOWSHOTS
BOWSING
BOWSPRIT
BOWSPRITS
BOWSTRING
BOWSTRINGED
BOWSTRINGING
BOWSTRINGS
BOWSTRUNG
BOWWOW
BOWWOWS
BOWYER
BOWYERS
BOX
BOXCAR
BOXCARS
BOXED
BOXEN
BOXER
BOXERS
BOXES
BOXFUL
BOXFULS
BOXIER
BOXIEST
BOXINESS
BOXINESSES
BOXING
BOXINGS
BOXKEEPER
BOXKEEPERS
BOXROOM
BOXROOMS
BOXWALLAH
BOXWALLAHS
BOXWOOD
BOXWOODS
BOXY
BOY
BOYAR
BOYARS
BOYAU
BOYAUX

BOYCOTT
BOYCOTTED
BOYCOTTING
BOYCOTTS
BOYED
BOYFRIEND
BOYFRIENDS
BOYG
BOYGS
BOYHOOD
BOYHOODS
BOYING
BOYISH
BOYISHLY
BOYO
BOYOS
BOYS
BOZZETTI
BOZZETTO
BRA
BRABBLE
BRABBLED
BRABBLES
BRABBLING
BRACCATE
BRACCIA
BRACCIO
BRACE
BRACED
BRACELET
BRACELETS
BRACER
BRACERS
BRACES
BRACH
BRACHES
BRACHET
BRACHETS
BRACHIAL
BRACING
BRACK
BRACKEN
BRACKENS
BRACKET
BRACKETED
BRACKETING
BRACKETS
BRACKISH
BRACKS
BRACT
BRACTEAL
BRACTEATE
BRACTEATES
BRACTEOLE
BRACTEOLES
BRACTLESS
BRACTLET
BRACTLETS
BRACTS
BRAD
BRADAWL
BRADAWLS
BRADS
BRAE
BRAES
BRAG
BRAGGART
BRAGGARTS
BRAGGED
BRAGGING

BRAGLY
BRAGS
BRAID
BRAIDE
BRAIDED
BRAIDER
BRAIDEST
BRAIDING
BRAIDINGS
BRAIDS
BRAIL
BRAILED
BRAILING
BRAILS
BRAIN
BRAINCASE
BRAINCASES
BRAINED
BRAINIER
BRAINIEST
BRAINING
BRAINISH
BRAINLESS
BRAINPAN
BRAINPANS
BRAINS
BRAINSICK
BRAINWASH
BRAINWASHED
BRAINWASHES
BRAINWASHING
BRAINWASHINGS
BRAINY
BRAIRD
BRAIRDED
BRAIRDING
BRAIRDS
BRAISE
BRAISED
BRAISES
BRAISING
BRAIZE
BRAIZES
BRAKE
BRAKED
BRAKELESS
BRAKEMAN
BRAKEMEN
BRAKES
BRAKIER
BRAKIEST
BRAKING
BRAKY
BRALESS
BRAMBLE
BRAMBLES
BRAMBLIER
BRAMBLIEST
BRAMBLING
BRAMBLINGS
BRAMBLY
BRAME
BRAMES
BRAN
BRANCARD
BRANCARDS
BRANCH
BRANCHED
BRANCHER
BRANCHERIES

BRANCHERS
BRANCHERY
BRANCHES
BRANCHIA
BRANCHIAE
BRANCHIAL
BRANCHIER
BRANCHIEST
BRANCHING
BRANCHINGS
BRANCHLET
BRANCHLETS
BRANCHY
BRAND
BRANDADE
BRANDADES
BRANDED
BRANDER
BRANDERED
BRANDERING
BRANDERS
BRANDIED
BRANDIES
BRANDING
BRANDISE
BRANDISES
BRANDISH
BRANDISHED
BRANDISHES
BRANDISHING
BRANDLING
BRANDLINGS
BRANDRETH
BRANDRETHS
BRANDS
BRANDY
BRANGLE
BRANGLED
BRANGLES
BRANGLING
BRANGLINGS
BRANK
BRANKED
BRANKIER
BRANKIEST
BRANKING
BRANKS
BRANKY
BRANLE
BRANLES
BRANNIER
BRANNIEST
BRANNY
BRANS
BRANSLE
BRANSLES
BRANTLE
BRANTLES
BRAS
BRASERO
BRASEROS
BRASES
BRASH
BRASHED
BRASHER
BRASHES
BRASHEST
BRASHIER
BRASHIEST
BRASHING

BRASHY
BRASIER
BRASIERS
BRASS
BRASSARD
BRASSARDS
BRASSART
BRASSARTS
BRASSERIE
BRASSERIES
BRASSES
BRASSET
BRASSETS
BRASSICA
BRASSICAS
BRASSIE
BRASSIER
BRASSIÈRE
BRASSIÈRES
BRASSIES
BRASSIEST
BRASSILY
BRASSY
BRAST
BRASTING
BRASTS
BRAT
BRATCHET
BRATCHETS
BRATLING
BRATLINGS
BRATS
BRATTICE
BRATTICED
BRATTICES
BRATTICING
BRATTICINGS
BRATTIER
BRATTIEST
BRATTISH
BRATTISHED
BRATTISHES
BRATTISHING
BRATTISHINGS
BRATTLE
BRATTLED
BRATTLES
BRATTLING
BRATTLINGS
BRATTY
BRATWURST
BRATWURSTS
BRAUNCH
BRAUNCHED
BRAUNCHING
BRAUNCHS
BRAVA
BRAVADO
BRAVADOED
BRAVADOES
BRAVADOING
BRAVADOS
BRAVE
BRAVED
BRAVELY
BRAVER
BRAVERIES
BRAVERY
BRAVES
BRAVEST

BRAVI
BRAVING
BRAVO
BRAVOES
BRAVOS
BRAVURA
BRAVURAS
BRAW
BRAWER
BRAWEST
BRAWL
BRAWLED
BRAWLER
BRAWLERS
BRAWLIER
BRAWLIEST
BRAWLING
BRAWLINGS
BRAWLS
BRAWLY
BRAWN
BRAWNED
BRAWNIER
BRAWNIEST
BRAWNS
BRAWNY
BRAWS
BRAXIES
BRAXY
BRAY
BRAYED
BRAYER
BRAYERS
BRAYING
BRAYS
BRAZE
BRAZED
BRAZELESS
BRAZEN
BRAZENED
BRAZENING
BRAZENLY
BRAZENRIES
BRAZENRY
BRAZENS
BRAZES
BRAZIER
BRAZIERS
BRAZIL
BRAZILS
BRAZING
BREACH
BREACHED
BREACHES
BREACHING
BREAD
BREADED
BREADHEAD
BREADHEADS
BREADING
BREADLINE
BREADLINES
BREADNUT
BREADNUTS
BREADROOM
BREADROOMS
BREADROOT
BREADROOTS
BREADS
BREADTH

BREADTHS
BREAK
BREAKABLE
BREAKABLES
BREAKAGE
BREAKAGES
BREAKAWAY
BREAKAWAYS
BREAKBACK
BREAKDOWN
BREAKDOWNS
BREAKER
BREAKERS
BREAKFAST
BREAKFASTED
BREAKFASTING
BREAKFASTS
BREAKING
BREAKINGS
BREAKNECK
BREAKS
BREAM
BREAMED
BREAMING
BREAMS
BREARE
BREARES
BREASKIT
BREASKITS
BREAST
BREASTED
BREASTING
BREASTPIN
BREASTPINS
BREASTS
BREATH
BREATHE
BREATHED
BREATHER
BREATHERS
BREATHES
BREATHFUL
BREATHIER
BREATHIEST
BREATHILY
BREATHING
BREATHINGS
BREATHS
BREATHY
BRECCIA
BRECCIAS
BRECHAM
BRECHAMS
BRED
BREDE
BREDED
BREDES
BREDING
BREE
BREECH
BREECHED
BREECHES
BREECHING
BREECHINGS
BREED
BREEDER
BREEDERS
BREEDING
BREEDINGS
BREEDS

BREEKS
BREEM
BREER
BREERED
BREERING
BREERS
BREES
BREESE
BREESES
BREEZE
BREEZED
BREEZES
BREEZIER
BREEZIEST
BREEZILY
BREEZING
BREEZY
BREGMA
BREGMATA
BREGMATIC
BREHON
BREHONS
BRELOQUE
BRELOQUES
BREME
BREN
BRENNE
BRENNES
BRENNING
BRENS
BRENT
BRENTER
BRENTEST
BRER
BRERE
BRERES
BRERS
BRETASCHE
BRETASCHES
BRETESSE
BRETESSES
BRETHREN
BRETON
BRETONS
BRETTICE
BRETTICED
BRETTICES
BRETTICING
BREVE
BREVES
BREVET
BREVETÉ
BREVETED
BREVETING
BREVETS
BREVETTED
BREVETTING
BREVIARIES
BREVIARY
BREVIATE
BREVIATES
BREVIER
BREVIERS
BREVITIES
BREVITY
BREW
BREWAGE
BREWAGES
BREWED
BREWER

BREWERIES
BREWERS
BREWERY
BREWING
BREWINGS
BREWIS
BREWISES
BREWS
BREWSTER
BREWSTERS
BRIAR
BRIARED
BRIARS
BRIBE
BRIBED
BRIBER
BRIBERIES
BRIBERS
BRIBERY
BRIBES
BRIBING
BRICABRAC
BRICABRACS
BRICK
BRICKBAT
BRICKBATS
BRICKCLAY
BRICKCLAYS
BRICKED
BRICKEN
BRICKIE
BRICKIER
BRICKIES
BRICKIEST
BRICKING
BRICKINGS
BRICKLE
BRICKLER
BRICKLEST
BRICKS
BRICKWALL
BRICKWALLS
BRICKWORK
BRICKWORKS
BRICKY
BRICKYARD
BRICKYARDS
BRICOLE
BRICOLES
BRIDAL
BRIDALS
BRIDE
BRIDECAKE
BRIDECAKES
BRIDED
BRIDEMAID
BRIDEMAIDS
BRIDEMAN
BRIDEMEN
BRIDES
BRIDESMAN
BRIDESMEN
BRIDEWELL
BRIDEWELLS
BRIDGE
BRIDGED
BRIDGES
BRIDGING
BRIDGINGS
BRIDIE

BRIDIES
BRIDING
BRIDLE
BRIDLED
BRIDLER
BRIDLERS
BRIDLES
BRIDLING
BRIDOON
BRIDOONS
BRIEF
BRIEFED
BRIEFER
BRIEFEST
BRIEFING
BRIEFINGS
BRIEFLESS
BRIEFLY
BRIEFNESS
BRIEFNESSES
BRIEFS
BRIER
BRIERED
BRIERS
BRIERY
BRIG
BRIGADE
BRIGADED
BRIGADES
BRIGADIER
BRIGADIERS
BRIGADING
BRIGAND
BRIGANDRIES
BRIGANDRY
BRIGANDS
BRIGHT
BRIGHTEN
BRIGHTENED
BRIGHTENING
BRIGHTENS
BRIGHTER
BRIGHTEST
BRIGHTLY
BRIGS
BRIGUE
BRIGUED
BRIGUES
BRIGUING
BRIGUINGS
BRILL
BRILLIANT
BRILLIANTED
BRILLIANTING
BRILLIANTS
BRILLS
BRIM
BRIMFUL
BRIMING
BRIMINGS
BRIMLESS
BRIMMED
BRIMMER
BRIMMERS
BRIMMING
BRIMS
BRIMSTONE
BRIMSTONES
BRIMSTONY
BRINDED

BRINDISI
BRINDISIS
BRINDLE
BRINDLED
BRINDLES
BRINE
BRINED
BRINES
BRING
BRINGER
BRINGERS
BRINGING
BRINGINGS
BRINGS
BRINIER
BRINIES
BRINIEST
BRINING
BRINISH
BRINJAL
BRINJALS
BRINJARRIES
BRINJARRY
BRINK
BRINKMAN
BRINKMEN
BRINKS
BRINY
BRIO
BRIOCHE
BRIOCHES
BRIONIES
BRIONY
BRIOS
BRIQUET
BRIQUETS
BRIQUETTE
BRIQUETTES
BRISÉ
BRISÉS
BRISK
BRISKED
BRISKEN
BRISKENED
BRISKENING
BRISKENS
BRISKER
BRISKEST
BRISKET
BRISKETS
BRISKING
BRISKISH
BRISKLY
BRISKNESS
BRISKNESSES
BRISKS
BRISKY
BRISLING
BRISLINGS
BRISTLE
BRISTLED
BRISTLES
BRISTLIER
BRISTLIEST
BRISTLING
BRISTLY
BRISTOLS
BRISURE
BRISURES
BRIT

BRITCHES
BRITS
BRITSCHKA
BRITSCHKAS
BRITSKA
BRITSKAS
BRITTLE
BRITTLER
BRITTLEST
BRITZKA
BRITZKAS
BRITZSKA
BRITZSKAS
BRIZE
BRIZES
BRO
BROACH
BROACHED
BROACHER
BROACHERS
BROACHES
BROACHING
BROAD
BROADBAND
BROADCAST
BROADCASTED
BROADCASTING
BROADCASTS
BROADEN
BROADENED
BROADENING
BROADENS
BROADER
BROADEST
BROADISH
BROADLOOM
BROADLY
BROADNESS
BROADNESSES
BROADS
BROADSIDE
BROADSIDES
BROADTAIL
BROADTAILS
BROADWAY
BROADWAYS
BROADWISE
BROCADE
BROCADED
BROCADES
BROCAGE
BROCAGES
BROCARD
BROCARDS
BROCATEL
BROCATELS
BROCCOLI
BROCCOLIS
BROCH
BROCHAN
BROCHANS
BROCHÉ
BROCHÉS
BROCHS
BROCHURE
BROCHURES
BROCK
BROCKAGE
BROCKAGES
BROCKED

BROCKET
BROCKETS
BROCKIT
BROCKRAM
BROCKRAMS
BROCKS
BROD
BRODDED
BRODDING
BRODEKIN
BRODEKINS
BRODKIN
BRODKINS
BRODS
BROG
BROGAN
BROGANS
BROGGED
BROGGING
BROGH
BROGHS
BROGS
BROGUE
BROGUES
BROIDER
BROIDERED
BROIDERER
BROIDERERS
BROIDERIES
BROIDERING
BROIDERINGS
BROIDERS
BROIDERY
BROIL
BROILED
BROILER
BROILERS
BROILING
BROILS
BROKAGE
BROKAGES
BROKE
BROKED
BROKEN
BROKENLY
BROKER
BROKERAGE
BROKERAGES
BROKERIES
BROKERS
BROKERY
BROKES
BROKING
BROLGA
BROLGAS
BROLLIES
BROLLY
BROMATE
BROMATES
BROMELIA
BROMELIAD
BROMELIADS
BROMELIAS
BROMIC
BROMIDE
BROMIDES
BROMIDIC
BROMINE
BROMINES
BROMMER

BROMMERS
BROMOFORM
BROMOFORMS
BRONCHI
BRONCHIA
BRONCHIAL
BRONCHO
BRONCHOS
BRONCHUS
BRONCO
BRONCOS
BROND
BRONDS
BRONDYRON
BRONDYRONS
BRONZE
BRONZED
BRONZEN
BRONZES
BRONZIER
BRONZIEST
BRONZIFIED
BRONZIFIES
BRONZIFY
BRONZIFYING
BRONZING
BRONZINGS
BRONZITE
BRONZITES
BRONZY
BROO
BROOCH
BROOCHED
BROOCHES
BROOCHING
BROOD
BROODED
BROODER
BROODERS
BROODIER
BROODIEST
BROODING
BROODMARE
BROODMARES
BROODS
BROODY
BROOK
BROOKED
BROOKING
BROOKITE
BROOKITES
BROOKLET
BROOKLETS
BROOKLIME
BROOKLIMES
BROOKS
BROOKWEED
BROOKWEEDS
BROOL
BROOLS
BROOM
BROOMBALL
BROOMBALLS
BROOMED
BROOMIER
BROOMIEST
BROOMING
BROOMRAPE
BROOMRAPES
BROOMS

BROOMY
BROOS
BROOSE
BROOSES
BROS
BROSE
BROSES
BROTH
BROTHEL
BROTHELS
BROTHER
BROTHERLY
BROTHERS
BROTHS
BROUGH
BROUGHAM
BROUGHAMS
BROUGHS
BROUGHT
BROUHAHA
BROUHAHAS
BROUZE
BROUZES
BROW
BROWBEAT
BROWBEATEN
BROWBEATING
BROWBEATS
BROWLESS
BROWN
BROWNED
BROWNER
BROWNEST
BROWNIE
BROWNIER
BROWNIES
BROWNIEST
BROWNING
BROWNINGS
BROWNISH
BROWNNESS
BROWNNESSES
BROWNOUT
BROWNOUTS
BROWNS
BROWNY
BROWS
BROWSE
BROWSED
BROWSES
BROWSING
BROWSINGS
BROWST
BROWSTS
BRUCHID
BRUCHIDS
BRUCINE
BRUCINES
BRUCITE
BRUCITES
BRUCKLE
BRUHAHA
BRUHAHAS
BRUILZIE
BRUILZIES
BRUISE
BRUISED
BRUISER
BRUISERS
BRUISES

BRUISING
BRUISINGS
BRUIT
BRUITED
BRUITING
BRUITS
BRÛLÉ
BRULYIE
BRULYIES
BRULZIE
BRULZIES
BRUMAL
BRUMBIES
BRUMBY
BRUME
BRUMES
BRUMMER
BRUMMERS
BRUMOUS
BRUNCH
BRUNCHES
BRUNET
BRUNETS
BRUNETTE
BRUNETTES
BRUNT
BRUNTED
BRUNTING
BRUNTS
BRUSH
BRUSHED
BRUSHER
BRUSHERS
BRUSHES
BRUSHIER
BRUSHIEST
BRUSHING
BRUSHINGS
BRUSHWOOD
BRUSHWOODS
BRUSHWORK
BRUSHWORKS
BRUSHY
BRUSQUE
BRUSQUELY
BRUSQUER
BRUSQUEST
BRUST
BRUSTED
BRUSTING
BRUSTS
BRUT
BRUTAL
BRUTALISE
BRUTALISED
BRUTALISES
BRUTALISING
BRUTALISM
BRUTALISMS
BRUTALIST
BRUTALISTS
BRUTALITIES
BRUTALITY
BRUTALIZE
BRUTALIZED
BRUTALIZES
BRUTALIZING
BRUTALLY
BRUTE
BRUTED

BRUTENESS
BRUTENESSES
BRUTES
BRUTIFIED
BRUTIFIES
BRUTIFY
BRUTIFYING
BRUTING
BRUTISH
BRUTISHLY
BRUXISM
BRUXISMS
BRYOLOGIES
BRYOLOGY
BRYONIES
BRYONY
BRYOPHYTE
BRYOPHYTES
BUAT
BUATS
BUAZE
BUAZES
BUB
BUBA
BUBAL
BUBALINE
BUBALIS
BUBALISES
BUBALS
BUBAS
BUBBIES
BUBBLE
BUBBLED
BUBBLES
BUBBLIER
BUBBLIES
BUBBLIEST
BUBBLING
BUBBLY
BUBBY
BUBINGA
BUBINGAS
BUBO
BUBOES
BUBONIC
BUBS
BUBUKLE
BUBUKLES
BUCCAL
BUCCANEER
BUCCANEERED
BUCCANEERING
BUCCANEERINGS
BUCCANEERS
BUCCANIER
BUCCANIERED
BUCCANIERING
BUCCANIERS
BUCCINA
BUCCINAS
BUCELLAS
BUCELLASES
BUCHU
BUCHUS
BUCK
BUCKAROO
BUCKAROOS
BUCKAYRO
BUCKAYROS
BUCKBEAN

BUCKBEANS
BUCKBOARD
BUCKBOARDS
BUCKCART
BUCKCARTS
BUCKED
BUCKEEN
BUCKEENS
BUCKER
BUCKEROO
BUCKEROOS
BUCKERS
BUCKET
BUCKETED
BUCKETFUL
BUCKETFULS
BUCKETING
BUCKETINGS
BUCKETS
BUCKHORN
BUCKHORNS
BUCKHOUND
BUCKHOUNDS
BUCKIE
BUCKIES
BUCKING
BUCKINGS
BUCKISH
BUCKLE
BUCKLED
BUCKLER
BUCKLERS
BUCKLES
BUCKLING
BUCKLINGS
BUCKO
BUCKOES
BUCKRA
BUCKRAM
BUCKRAMED
BUCKRAMING
BUCKRAMS
BUCKRAS
BUCKS
BUCKSAW
BUCKSAWS
BUCKSHEE
BUCKSHEES
BUCKSHISH
BUCKSHISHES
BUCKSHOT
BUCKSHOTS
BUCKSKIN
BUCKSKINS
BUCKSOM
BUCKTEETH
BUCKTHORN
BUCKTHORNS
BUCKTOOTH
BUCKU
BUCKUS
BUCKWHEAT
BUCKWHEATS
BUCOLIC
BUCOLICAL
BUCOLICS
BUD
BUDDED
BUDDIER
BUDDIES

BUDDIEST
BUDDING
BUDDINGS
BUDDLE
BUDDLED
BUDDLEIA
BUDDLEIAS
BUDDLES
BUDDLING
BUDDY
BUDGE
BUDGED
BUDGER
BUDGEREE
BUDGERO
BUDGEROS
BUDGEROW
BUDGEROWS
BUDGERS
BUDGES
BUDGET
BUDGETARY
BUDGETED
BUDGETING
BUDGETS
BUDGIE
BUDGIES
BUDGING
BUDLESS
BUDMASH
BUDMASHES
BUDO
BUDOS
BUDS
BUFF
BUFFA
BUFFALO
BUFFALOED
BUFFALOES
BUFFALOING
BUFFE
BUFFED
BUFFER
BUFFERED
BUFFERING
BUFFERS
BUFFET
BUFFETED
BUFFETING
BUFFETINGS
BUFFETS
BUFFI
BUFFING
BUFFO
BUFFOON
BUFFOONS
BUFFS
BUFO
BUFOS
BUG
BUGABOO
BUGABOOS
BUGBANE
BUGBANES
BUGBEAR
BUGBEARS
BUGGAN
BUGGANE
BUGGANES
BUGGANS

BUGGED
BUGGER
BUGGERED
BUGGERIES
BUGGERING
BUGGERS
BUGGERY
BUGGIES
BUGGIN
BUGGING
BUGGINGS
BUGGINS
BUGGY
BUGHOUSE
BUGHOUSES
BUGLE
BUGLED
BUGLER
BUGLERS
BUGLES
BUGLET
BUGLETS
BUGLING
BUGLOSS
BUGLOSSES
BUGONG
BUGONGS
BUGS
BUGWORT
BUGWORTS
BUHL
BUHLS
BUHRSTONE
BUHRSTONES
BUIK
BUIKS
BUILD
BUILDED
BUILDER
BUILDERS
BUILDING
BUILDINGS
BUILDS
BUILT
BUIRDLIER
BUIRDLIEST
BUIRDLY
BUIST
BUISTED
BUISTING
BUISTS
BUKE
BUKES
BUKSHEE
BUKSHEES
BUKSHI
BUKSHIS
BULB
BULBAR
BULBED
BULBIL
BULBILS
BULBING
BULBOUS
BULBS
BULBUL
BULBULS
BULGE
BULGED
BULGER

BULGERS
BULGES
BULGIER
BULGIEST
BULGINE
BULGINES
BULGINESS
BULGINESSES
BULGING
BULGY
BULIMIA
BULIMIAS
BULIMIC
BULIMICS
BULIMIES
BULIMUS
BULIMUSES
BULIMY
BULK
BULKED
BULKER
BULKERS
BULKHEAD
BULKHEADS
BULKIER
BULKIEST
BULKILY
BULKINESS
BULKINESSES
BULKING
BULKS
BULKY
BULL
BULLA
BULLACE
BULLACES
BULLAE
BULLARIES
BULLARY
BULLAS
BULLATE
BULLBAT
BULLBATS
BULLDOG
BULLDOGGED
BULLDOGGING
BULLDOGS
BULLDOZE
BULLDOZED
BULLDOZER
BULLDOZERS
BULLDOZES
BULLDOZING
BULLDUST
BULLDUSTS
BULLED
BULLER
BULLERED
BULLERING
BULLERS
BULLET
BULLETIN
BULLETINS
BULLETRIE
BULLETRIES
BULLETS
BULLFIGHT
BULLFIGHTS
BULLFINCH
BULLFINCHES

BULLFROG
BULLFROGS
BULLGINE
BULLGINES
BULLHEAD
BULLHEADS
BULLIED
BULLIES
BULLING
BULLION
BULLIONS
BULLISH
BULLISHLY
BULLOCK
BULLOCKS
BULLS
BULLSHIT
BULLSHITS
BULLSHITTED
BULLSHITTING
BULLWHACK
BULLWHACKED
BULLWHACKING
BULLWHACKS
BULLY
BULLYING
BULLYISM
BULLYISMS
BULLYRAG
BULLYRAGGED
BULLYRAGGING
BULLYRAGS
BULRUSH
BULRUSHES
BULRUSHY
BULSE
BULSES
BULWARK
BULWARKED
BULWARKING
BULWARKS
BUM
BUMALO
BUMBAZE
BUMBAZED
BUMBAZES
BUMBAZING
BUMBLE
BUMBLED
BUMBLES
BUMBLING
BUMBO
BUMBOS
BUMF
BUMFS
BUMKIN
BUMKINS
BUMMALO
BUMMALOTI
BUMMALOTIS
BUMMAREE
BUMMAREES
BUMMED
BUMMEL
BUMMELS
BUMMER
BUMMERS
BUMMING
BUMMLE
BUMMLED

BUMMLES
BUMMLING
BUMMOCK
BUMMOCKS
BUMP
BUMPED
BUMPER
BUMPERED
BUMPERING
BUMPERS
BUMPH
BUMPHS
BUMPIER
BUMPIEST
BUMPINESS
BUMPINESSES
BUMPING
BUMPKIN
BUMPKINS
BUMPOLOGIES
BUMPOLOGY
BUMPS
BUMPTIOUS
BUMPY
BUMS
BUN
BUNA
BUNAS
BUNCE
BUNCED
BUNCES
BUNCH
BUNCHED
BUNCHES
BUNCHIER
BUNCHIEST
BUNCHING
BUNCHINGS
BUNCHY
BUNCING
BUNCO
BUNCOED
BUNCOING
BUNCOMBE
BUNCOMBES
BUNCOS
BUND
BUNDED
BUNDING
BUNDLE
BUNDLED
BUNDLES
BUNDLING
BUNDLINGS
BUNDOBUST
BUNDOBUSTS
BUNDOOK
BUNDOOKS
BUNDS
BUNDU
BUNDUS
BUNG
BUNGALOID
BUNGALOIDS
BUNGALOW
BUNGALOWS
BUNGED
BUNGEE
BUNGEES
BUNGIE

BUNGIES
BUNGING
BUNGLE
BUNGLED
BUNGLER
BUNGLERS
BUNGLES
BUNGLING
BUNGLINGS
BUNGS
BUNGY
BUNIA
BUNIAS
BUNION
BUNIONS
BUNJE
BUNJEE
BUNJEES
BUNJES
BUNJIE
BUNJIES
BUNJY
BUNK
BUNKED
BUNKER
BUNKERED
BUNKERING
BUNKERS
BUNKHOUSE
BUNKHOUSES
BUNKING
BUNKO
BUNKOED
BUNKOING
BUNKOS
BUNKS
BUNKUM
BUNKUMS
BUNNIA
BUNNIAS
BUNNIES
BUNNY
BUNODONT
BUNRAKU
BUNRAKUS
BUNS
BUNT
BUNTED
BUNTER
BUNTERS
BUNTIER
BUNTIEST
BUNTING
BUNTINGS
BUNTLINE
BUNTLINES
BUNTS
BUNTY
BUNYA
BUNYAS
BUNYIP
BUNYIPS
BUONAMANI
BUONAMANO
BUOY
BUOYAGE
BUOYAGES
BUOYANCE
BUOYANCES
BUOYANCIES

BUOYANCY
BUOYANT
BUOYED
BUOYING
BUOYS
BUPLEVER
BUPLEVERS
BUR
BURAN
BURANS
BURBLE
BURBLED
BURBLES
BURBLING
BURBLINGS
BURBOT
BURBOTS
BURD
BURDASH
BURDASHES
BURDEN
BURDENED
BURDENING
BURDENOUS
BURDENS
BURDIE
BURDIES
BURDOCK
BURDOCKS
BURDS
BUREAU
BUREAUS
BUREAUX
BURETTE
BURETTES
BURG
BURGAGE
BURGAGES
BURGANET
BURGANETS
BURGEE
BURGEES
BURGEON
BURGEONING
BURGEONS
BURGER
BURGERS
BURGESS
BURGESSES
BURGH
BURGHAL
BURGHER
BURGHERS
BURGHS
BURGLAR
BURGLARED
BURGLARIES
BURGLARING
BURGLARS
BURGLARY
BURGLE
BURGLED
BURGLES
BURGLING
BURGONET
BURGONETS
BURGOO
BURGOOS
BURGRAVE

BURGRAVES
BURGS
BURGUNDIES
BURGUNDY
BURHEL
BURHELS
BURIAL
BURIALS
BURIED
BURIES
BURIN
BURINIST
BURINISTS
BURINS
BURITI
BURITIS
BURK
BURKA
BURKAS
BURKE
BURKED
BURKES
BURKHA
BURKHAS
BURKING
BURKS
BURL
BURLAP
BURLAPS
BURLED
BURLER
BURLERS
BURLESQUE
BURLESQUED
BURLESQUES
BURLESQUING
BURLETTA
BURLETTAS
BURLEY
BURLEYS
BURLIER
BURLIEST
BURLINESS
BURLINESSES
BURLING
BURLS
BURLY
BURN
BURNED
BURNER
BURNERS
BURNET
BURNETS
BURNING
BURNINGS
BURNISH
BURNISHED
BURNISHER
BURNISHERS
BURNISHES
BURNISHING
BURNISHINGS
BURNOUS
BURNOUSE
BURNOUSES
BURNS
BURNSIDE
BURNSIDES
BURNT
BUROO

BUROOS
BURP
BURPED
BURPING
BURPS
BURQA
BURQAS
BURR
BURRED
BURREL
BURRELL
BURRELLS
BURRELS
BURRHEL
BURRHELS
BURRIER
BURRIEST
BURRING
BURRO
BURROS
BURROW
BURROWED
BURROWING
BURROWS
BURRS
BURRSTONE
BURRSTONES
BURRY
BURS
BURSA
BURSAE
BURSAL
BURSAR
BURSARIAL
BURSARIES
BURSARS
BURSARY
BURSE
BURSES
BURSIFORM
BURSITIS
BURSITISES
BURST
BURSTEN
BURSTEN
BURSTER
BURSTERS
BURSTING
BURSTS
BURTHEN
BURTHENED
BURTHENING
BURTHENS
BURTON
BURTONS
BURWEED
BURWEEDS
BURY
BURYING
BUS
BUSBIES
BUSBOY
BUSBOYS
BUSBY
BUSED
BUSES
BUSGIRL
BUSGIRLS
BUSH
BUSHCRAFT

BUSHCRAFTS
BUSHED
BUSHEL
BUSHELLED
BUSHELLER
BUSHELLERS
BUSHELLING
BUSHELLINGS
BUSHELS
BUSHES
BUSHFIRE
BUSHFIRES
BUSHIDO
BUSHIDOS
BUSHIER
BUSHIES
BUSHIEST
BUSHINESS
BUSHINESSES
BUSHING
BUSHMAN
BUSHMEN
BUSHVELD
BUSHVELDS
BUSHWALK
BUSHWALKED
BUSHWALKING
BUSHWALKINGS
BUSHWALKS
BUSHWHACK
BUSHWHACKED
BUSHWHACKING
BUSHWHACKINGS
BUSHWHACKS
BUSHY
BUSIED
BUSIER
BUSIES
BUSIEST
BUSILY
BUSINESS
BUSINESSES
BUSING
BUSINGS
BUSK
BUSKED
BUSKER
BUSKERS
BUSKET
BUSKETS
BUSKIN
BUSKINED
BUSKING
BUSKINGS
BUSKINS
BUSKS

BUSKY
BUSMAN
BUSMEN
BUSS
BUSSED
BUSSES
BUSSING
BUSSINGS
BUSSU
BUSSUS
BUST
BUSTARD
BUSTARDS
BUSTED
BUSTEE
BUSTEES
BUSTER
BUSTERS
BUSTIER
BUSTIERS
BUSTIEST
BUSTING
BUSTLE
BUSTLED
BUSTLER
BUSTLERS
BUSTLES
BUSTLING
BUSTS
BUSTY
BUSY
BUSYBODIES
BUSYBODY
BUSYING
BUSYNESS
BUSYNESSES
BUT
BUTADIENE
BUTADIENES
BUTANE
BUTANES
BUTANOL
BUTANOLS
BUTCH
BUTCHER
BUTCHERED
BUTCHERIES
BUTCHERING
BUTCHERINGS
BUTCHERLY
BUTCHERS
BUTCHERY
BUTCHES
BUTCHEST
BUTCHING
BUTCHINGS

BUTE
BUTENE
BUTENES
BUTES
BUTLER
BUTLERAGE
BUTLERAGES
BUTLERED
BUTLERIES
BUTLERING
BUTLERS
BUTLERY
BUTMENT
BUTMENTS
BUTS
BUTT
BUTTE
BUTTED
BUTTER
BUTTERBUR
BUTTERBURS
BUTTERCUP
BUTTERCUPS
BUTTERED
BUTTERFLIES
BUTTERFLY
BUTTERIER
BUTTERIES
BUTTERIEST
BUTTERINE
BUTTERINES
BUTTERING
BUTTERNUT
BUTTERNUTS
BUTTERS
BUTTERY
BUTTES
BUTTIES
BUTTING
BUTTLE
BUTTLED
BUTTLES
BUTTLING
BUTTOCK
BUTTOCKED
BUTTOCKING
BUTTOCKS
BUTTON
BUTTONED
BUTTONING
BUTTONS
BUTTONSES
BUTTONY
BUTTRESS
BUTTRESSED
BUTTRESSES

BUTTRESSING
BUTTS
BUTTY
BUTTYMAN
BUTTYMEN
BUTYL
BUTYLENE
BUTYLENES
BUTYLS
BUTYRATE
BUTYRATES
BUTYRIC
BUVETTE
BUVETTES
BUXOM
BUXOMER
BUXOMEST
BUXOMNESS
BUXOMNESSES
BUY
BUYABLE
BUYABLES
BUYER
BUYERS
BUYING
BUYS
BUZZ
BUZZARD
BUZZARDS
BUZZED
BUZZER
BUZZERS
BUZZES
BUZZIER
BUZZIEST
BUZZING
BUZZINGLY
BUZZINGS
BUZZY
BWANA
BWANAS
BWAZI
BWAZIS
BY
BYCATCH
BYCATCHES
BYCOKET
BYCOKETS
BYE
BYES
BYGOING
BYGOINGS
BYGONE
BYGONES
BYKE
BYKED

BYKES
BYKING
BYLANDER
BYLANDERS
BYLAW
BYLAWS
BYLINE
BYLINES
BYLIVE
BYNEMPT
BYPASS
BYPASSED
BYPASSES
BYPASSING
BYPATH
BYPATHS
BYPLACE
BYPLACES
BYRE
BYREMAN
BYREMEN
BYRES
BYREWOMAN
BYREWOMEN
BYRLADY
BYRLAKIN
BYRLAW
BYRLAWS
BYRNIE
BYRNIES
BYROAD
BYROADS
BYROOM
BYROOMS
BYS
BYSSAL
BYSSINE
BYSSOID
BYSSUS
BYSSUSES
BYSTANDER
BYSTANDERS
BYTE
BYTES
BYTOWNITE
BYTOWNITES
BYWAY
BYWAYS
BYWONER
BYWONERS
BYWORD
BYWORDS
BYWORK
BYWORKS
BYZANT
BYZANTS

C

CAATINGA
CAATINGAS
CAB
CABA
CABAL
CABALA
CABALAS
CABALETTA
CABALETTAS
CABALETTE
CABALISM
CABALISMS
CABALIST
CABALISTS
CABALLED
CABALLER
CABALLERO
CABALLEROS
CABALLERS
CABALLINE
CABALLING
CABALS
CABANA
CABANAS
CABARET
CABARETS
CABAS
CABASES
CABBAGE
CABBAGED
CABBAGES
CABBAGING
CABBAGY
CABBALA
CABBALAS
CABBALISM
CABBALISMS
CABBALIST
CABBALISTS
CABBIE
CABBIES
CABBY
CABER
CABERS
CABIN
CABINED
CABINET
CABINETS
CABINING
CABINS
CABLE
CABLED
CABLEGRAM
CABLEGRAMS
CABLES
CABLEWAY
CABLEWAYS
CABLING
CABLINGS
CABMAN
CABMEN
CABOB
CABOBS
CABOC

CABOCEER
CABOCEERS
CABOCHED
CABOCHON
CABOCHONS
CABOCS
CABOODLE
CABOODLES
CABOOSE
CABOOSES
CABOSHED
CABOTAGE
CABOTAGES
CABRÉ
CABRIE
CABRIES
CABRIOLE
CABRIOLES
CABRIOLET
CABRIOLETS
CABRIT
CABRITS
CABS
CACAFOGO
CACAFOGOS
CACAFUEGO
CACAFUEGOS
CACAO
CACAOS
CACHAEMIA
CACHAEMIAS
CACHAEMIC
CACHALOT
CACHALOTS
CACHE
CACHECTIC
CACHED
CACHES
CACHET
CACHETS
CACHEXIA
CACHEXIAS
CACHEXIES
CACHEXY
CACHING
CACHOLONG
CACHOLONGS
CACHOLOT
CACHOLOTS
CACHOU
CACHOUS
CACHUCHA
CACHUCHAS
CACIQUE
CACIQUES
CACIQUISM
CACIQUISMS
CACKLE
CACKLED
CACKLER
CACKLERS
CACKLES
CACKLING
CACODEMON

CACODEMONS
CACODOXIES
CACODOXY
CACODYL
CACODYLIC
CACODYLS
CACOEPIES
CACOEPY
CACOETHES
CACOLET
CACOLETS
CACOLOGIES
CACOLOGY
CACOMIXL
CACOMIXLS
CACOON
CACOONS
CACOPHONIES
CACOPHONY
CACOTOPIA
CACOTOPIAS
CACTI
CACTIFORM
CACTUS
CACTUSES
CACUMEN
CACUMENS
CACUMINAL
CAD
CADASTRAL
CADASTRE
CADASTRES
CADAVER
CADAVERIC
CADAVERS
CADDICE
CADDICES
CADDIE
CADDIED
CADDIES
CADDIS
CADDISES
CADDISH
CADDY
CADDYING
CADDYSS
CADDYSSES
CADE
CADEAU
CADEAUX
CADENCE
CADENCED
CADENCES
CADENCIES
CADENCY
CADENT
CADENTIAL
CADENZA
CADENZAS
CADES
CADET
CADETS
CADETSHIP
CADETSHIPS

CADGE
CADGED
CADGER
CADGERS
CADGES
CADGING
CADGY
CADI
CADIE
CADIES
CADIS
CADMIUM
CADMIUMS
CADRANS
CADRANSES
CADRE
CADRES
CADS
CADUAC
CADUACS
CADUCEAN
CADUCEI
CADUCEUS
CADUCITIES
CADUCITY
CADUCOUS
CAECA
CAECAL
CAECILIAN
CAECILIANS
CAECUM
CAERULE
CAERULEAN
CAESAR
CAESARS
CAESE
CAESIOUS
CAESIUM
CAESIUMS
CAESTUS
CAESTUSES
CAESURA
CAESURAL
CAESURAS
CAFARD
CAFARDS
CAFÉ
CAFÉS
CAFETERIA
CAFETERIAS
CAFF
CAFFEINE
CAFFEINES
CAFFEISM
CAFFEISMS
CAFFILA
CAFFILAS
CAFFS
CAFILA
CAFILAS
CAFTAN
CAFTANS
CAGE
CAGEBIRD

CAGEBIRDS
CAGED
CAGELING
CAGELINGS
CAGES
CAGEWORK
CAGEWORKS
CAGEY
CAGEYNESS
CAGEYNESSES
CAGIER
CAGIEST
CAGILY
CAGINESS
CAGINESSES
CAGING
CAGOT
CAGOTS
CAGOUL
CAGOULE
CAGOULES
CAGOULS
CAGY
CAGYNESS
CAGYNESSES
CAHIER
CAHIERS
CAHOOT
CAHOOTS
CAILLACH
CAILLACHS
CAILLEACH
CAILLEACHS
CAILLIACH
CAILLIACHS
CAIMAC
CAIMACAM
CAIMACAMS
CAIMACS
CAIMAN
CAIMANS
CAIN
CAINS
CAIQUE
CAIQUE
CAÏQUES
CAIQUES
CAIRD
CAIRDS
CAIRN
CAIRNED
CAIRNGORM
CAIRNGORMS
CAIRNS
CAISSON
CAISSONS
CAITIFF
CAITIFFS
CAITIVE
CAITIVES
CAJEPUT
CAJEPUTS
CAJOLE
CAJOLED

CAJOLER
CAJOLERIES
CAJOLERS
CAJOLERY
CAJOLES
CAJOLING
CAJUN
CAJUPUT
CAJUPUTS
CAKE
CAKED
CAKES
CAKEWALK
CAKEWALKED
CAKEWALKING
CAKEWALKS
CAKIER
CAKIEST
CAKING
CAKINGS
CAKY
CALABASH
CALABASHES
CALABOOSE
CALABOOSES
CALABRESE
CALABRESES
CALAMANCO
CALAMANCOS
CALAMARIES
CALAMARY
CALAMI
CALAMINE
CALAMINES
CALAMINT
CALAMINTS
CALAMITE
CALAMITES
CALAMITIES
CALAMITY
CALAMUS
CALANDO
CALANDRIA
CALANDRIAS
CALANTHE
CALANTHES
CALASH
CALASHES
CALAVANCE
CALAVANCES
CALCANEAL
CALCANEAN
CALCANEUM
CALCANEUMS
CALCAR
CALCARATE
CALCARINE
CALCARS
CALCEATE
CALCEATED
CALCEATES
CALCEATING
CALCED
CALCEDONIES
CALCEDONY
CALCES
CALCIC
CALCICOLE
CALCIFIC
CALCIFIED

CALCIFIES
CALCIFUGE
CALCIFY
CALCIFYING
CALCINE
CALCINED
CALCINES
CALCINING
CALCITE
CALCITES
CALCIUM
CALCIUMS
CALCSPAR
CALCSPARS
CALCULAR
CALCULARY
CALCULATE
CALCULATED
CALCULATES
CALCULATING
CALCULI
CALCULOSE
CALCULOUS
CALCULUS
CALCULUSES
CALDARIUM
CALDARIUMS
CALDERA
CALDERAS
CALDRON
CALDRONS
CALEFIED
CALEFIES
CALEFY
CALEFYING
CALEMBOUR
CALEMBOURS
CALENDAR
CALENDARED
CALENDARING
CALENDARS
CALENDER
CALENDERED
CALENDERING
CALENDERS
CALENDRER
CALENDRERS
CALENDRIES
CALENDRY
CALENDS
CALENDULA
CALENDULAS
CALENTURE
CALENTURES
CALF
CALFDOZER
CALFDOZERS
CALFLESS
CALFSKIN
CALFSKINS
CALIATOUR
CALIATOURS
CALIBER
CALIBERED
CALIBERS
CALIBRATE
CALIBRATED
CALIBRATES
CALIBRATING
CALIBRE

CALIBRED
CALIBRES
CALICES
CALICHE
CALICHES
CALICO
CALICOES
CALICOS
CALID
CALIDITIES
CALIDITY
CALIF
CALIFS
CALIGO
CALIGOES
CALIGOS
CALIOLOGIES
CALIOLOGY
CALIPASH
CALIPASHES
CALIPEE
CALIPEES
CALIPERS
CALIPH
CALIPHAL
CALIPHATE
CALIPHATES
CALIPHS
CALISAYA
CALISAYAS
CALIVER
CALIVERS
CALIX
CALK
CALKED
CALKER
CALKERS
CALKIN
CALKING
CALKINS
CALKS
CALL
CALLA
CALLANT
CALLANTS
CALLAS
CALLED
CALLER
CALLERS
CALLET
CALLETS
CALLID
CALLIDITIES
CALLIDITY
CALLIGRAM
CALLIGRAMS
CALLING
CALLINGS
CALLIOPE
CALLIOPES
CALLIPER
CALLIPERED
CALLIPERING
CALLIPERS
CALLOSITIES
CALLOSITY
CALLOUS
CALLOUSLY
CALLOW
CALLOWER

CALLOWEST
CALLOWS
CALLS
CALLUS
CALLUSES
CALM
CALMANT
CALMANTS
CALMATIVE
CALMATIVES
CALMED
CALMER
CALMEST
CALMING
CALMLY
CALMNESS
CALMNESSES
CALMS
CALMSTANE
CALMSTANES
CALMSTONE
CALMSTONES
CALMY
CALOMEL
CALOMELS
CALORIC
CALORICS
CALORIE
CALORIES
CALORIFIC
CALORIST
CALORISTS
CALOTTE
CALOTTES
CALOTYPE
CALOTYPES
CALOYER
CALOYERS
CALP
CALPA
CALPAC
CALPACK
CALPACKS
CALPACS
CALPAS
CALPS
CALQUE
CALQUED
CALQUES
CALQUING
CALTHA
CALTHAS
CALTHROP
CALTHROPS
CALTRAP
CALTRAPS
CALTROP
CALTROPS
CALUMBA
CALUMBAS
CALUMET
CALUMETS
CALUMNIES
CALUMNY
CALVE
CALVED
CALVER
CALVERED
CALVERING
CALVERS

CALVES
CALVING
CALVITIES
CALX
CALXES
CALYCES
CALYCINAL
CALYCINE
CALYCLE
CALYCLED
CALYCLES
CALYCOID
CALYCULE
CALYCULES
CALYPSO
CALYPSOS
CALYPTRA
CALYPTRAS
CALYX
CALYXES
CALZONE
CALZONES
CALZONI
CAM
CAMAIEU
CAMAIEUS
CAMAIEUX
CAMAN
CAMANACHD
CAMANACHDS
CAMANS
CAMARILLA
CAMARILLAS
CAMARON
CAMARONS
CAMAS
CAMASES
CAMASH
CAMASHES
CAMASS
CAMASSES
CAMBER
CAMBERED
CAMBERING
CAMBERS
CAMBIAL
CAMBIFORM
CAMBISM
CAMBISMS
CAMBIST
CAMBISTRIES
CAMBISTRY
CAMBISTS
CAMBIUM
CAMBIUMS
CAMBOGE
CAMBOGES
CAMBREL
CAMBRELS
CAMBRIC
CAMBRICS
CAMCORDER
CAMCORDERS
CAME
CAMEL
CAMELBACK
CAMELBACKS
CAMELEER
CAMELEERS
CAMELEON

CAMELEONS
CAMELID
CAMELIDS
CAMELINE
CAMELINES
CAMELISH
CAMELLIA
CAMELLIAS
CAMELOID
CAMELOIDS
CAMELOT
CAMELOTS
CAMELRIES
CAMELRY
CAMELS
CAMEO
CAMEOS
CAMERA
CAMERAL
CAMERAMAN
CAMERAMEN
CAMERAS
CAMERATED
CAMES
CAMESE
CAMESES
CAMION
CAMIONS
CAMIS
CAMISADE
CAMISADES
CAMISADO
CAMISADOS
CAMISARD
CAMISARDS
CAMISE
CAMISES
CAMISOLE
CAMISOLES
CAMLET
CAMLETS
CAMMED
CAMMING
CAMOMILE
CAMOMILES
CAMOUFLET
CAMOUFLETS
CAMP
CAMPAGNA
CAMPAGNAS
CAMPAIGN
CAMPAIGNED
CAMPAIGNING
CAMPAIGNS
CAMPANA
CAMPANAS
CAMPANERO
CAMPANEROS
CAMPANILE
CAMPANILES
CAMPANILI
CAMPANIST
CAMPANISTS
CAMPEADOR
CAMPEADORS
CAMPED
CAMPER
CAMPERS
CAMPESINO
CAMPESINOS

CAMPEST
CAMPHANE
CAMPHANES
CAMPHENE
CAMPHENES
CAMPHINE
CAMPHINES
CAMPHIRE
CAMPHIRES
CAMPHOR
CAMPHORIC
CAMPHORS
CAMPIER
CAMPIEST
CAMPING
CAMPION
CAMPIONS
CAMPLE
CAMPLED
CAMPLES
CAMPLING
CAMPS
CAMPSITE
CAMPSITES
CAMPUS
CAMPUSES
CAMPY
CAMS
CAMSHAFT
CAMSHAFTS
CAMSHEUGH
CAMSHO
CAMSHOCH
CAMSTAIRY
CAMSTANE
CAMSTANES
CAMSTEARY
CAMSTONE
CAMSTONES
CAMUS
CAMUSES
CAN
CAÑADA
CAÑADAS
CANAIGRE
CANAIGRES
CANAILLE
CANAILLES
CANAKIN
CANAKINS
CANAL
CANALISE
CANALISED
CANALISES
CANALISING
CANALIZE
CANALIZED
CANALIZES
CANALIZING
CANALS
CANAPÉ
CANAPÉS
CANARD
CANARDS
CANARIED
CANARIES
CANARY
CANARYING
CANASTA
CANASTAS

CANASTER
CANASTERS
CANCAN
CANCANS
CANCEL
CANCELEER
CANCELEERED
CANCELEERING
CANCELEERS
CANCELIER
CANCELIERED
CANCELIERING
CANCELIERS
CANCELLED
CANCELLI
CANCELLING
CANCELS
CANCER
CANCERATE
CANCERATED
CANCERATES
CANCERATING
CANCEROUS
CANCERS
CANCRINE
CANCROID
CANCROIDS
CANDELA
CANDELAS
CANDENT
CANDID
CANDIDA
CANDIDACIES
CANDIDACY
CANDIDAS
CANDIDATE
CANDIDATES
CANDIDER
CANDIDEST
CANDIDLY
CANDIE
CANDIED
CANDIES
CANDLE
CANDLED
CANDLES
CANDLING
CANDOCK
CANDOCKS
CANDOR
CANDORS
CANDOUR
CANDOURS
CANDY
CANDYING
CANDYTUFT
CANDYTUFTS
CANE
CANED
CANEFRUIT
CANEFRUITS
CANEH
CANEHS
CANELLA
CANELLAS
CANEPHOR
CANEPHORA
CANEPHORAS
CANEPHORE
CANEPHORES

CANEPHORS
CANES
CANESCENT
CANFUL
CANFULS
CANG
CANGLE
CANGLED
CANGLES
CANGLING
CANGS
CANGUE
CANGUES
CANICULAR
CANID
CANIDS
CANIER
CANIEST
CANIKIN
CANIKINS
CANINE
CANINES
CANING
CANINGS
CANINITIES
CANINITY
CANISTER
CANISTERED
CANISTERING
CANISTERS
CANITIES
CANKER
CANKERED
CANKERING
CANKEROUS
CANKERS
CANKERY
CANN
CANNA
CANNABIC
CANNABIN
CANNABINS
CANNABIS
CANNABISES
CANNACH
CANNACHS
CANNAE
CANNAS
CANNED
CANNEL
CANNELS
CANNELURE
CANNELURES
CANNER
CANNERIES
CANNERS
CANNERY
CANNIBAL
CANNIBALS
CANNIER
CANNIEST
CANNIKIN
CANNIKINS
CANNILY
CANNINESS
CANNINESSES
CANNING
CANNON
CANNONADE
CANNONADED

CANNONADES
CANNONADING
CANNONED
CANNONEER
CANNONEERS
CANNONIER
CANNONIERS
CANNONING
CANNONRIES
CANNONRY
CANNONS
CANNOT
CANNS
CANNULA
CANNULAE
CANNULAS
CANNULATE
CANNY
CANOE
CANOED
CANOEING
CANOEINGS
CANOEIST
CANOEISTS
CANOES
CANON
CAÑON
CANONESS
CANONESSES
CANONIC
CANONICAL
CANONICALS
CANONISE
CANONISED
CANONISES
CANONISING
CANONIST
CANONISTS
CANONIZE
CANONIZED
CANONIZES
CANONIZING
CANONRIES
CANONRY
CANONS
CAÑONS
CANOODLE
CANOODLED
CANOODLES
CANOODLING
CANOPIED
CANOPIES
CANOPY
CANOPYING
CANOROUS
CANS
CANST
CANSTICK
CANSTICKS
CANT
CANTABANK
CANTABANKS
CANTABILE
CANTABILES
CANTALOUP
CANTALOUPS
CANTAR
CANTARS
CANTATA
CANTATAS

CANTATE	CANTUS	CAPITANS	CAPRIOLED	CAPUCCIO
CANTATES	CANTY	CAPITATE	CAPRIOLES	CAPUCCIOS
CANTDOG	CANUCK	CAPITAYN	CAPRIOLING	CAPUCHE
CANTDOGS	CANUCKS	CAPITAYNS	CAPROATE	CAPUCHES
CANTED	CANVAS	CAPITELLA	CAPROATES	CAPUCHIN
CANTEEN	CANVASED	CAPITULA	CAPROIC	CAPUCHINS
CANTEENS	CANVASES	CAPITULAR	CAPRYLATE	CAPUL
CANTER	CANVASING	CAPITULARS	CAPRYLATES	CAPULS
CANTERED	CANVASS	CAPITULUM	CAPRYLIC	CAPUT
CANTERING	CANVASSED	CAPLE	CAPS	CAPYBARA
CANTERS	CANVASSER	CAPLES	CAPSAICIN	CAPYBARAS
CANTEST	CANVASSERS	CAPLIN	CAPSAICINS	CAR
CANTHARI	CANVASSES	CAPLINS	CAPSICUM	CARABIN
CANTHARID	CANVASSING	CAPO	CAPSICUMS	CARABINE
CANTHARIDES	CANY	CAPOCCHIA	CAPSID	CARABINES
CANTHARIDS	CANYON	CAPOCCHIAS	CAPSIDS	CARABINS
CANTHARIS	CANYONS	CAPON	CAPSIZAL	CARACAL
CANTHARUS	CANZONA	CAPONIER	CAPSIZALS	CARACALS
CANTHI	CANZONAS	CAPONIERE	CAPSIZE	CARACARA
CANTHOOK	CANZONE	CAPONIERES	CAPSIZED	CARACARAS
CANTHOOKS	CANZONET	CAPONIERS	CAPSIZES	CARACK
CANTHUS	CANZONETS	CAPONISE	CAPSIZING	CARACKS
CANTICLE	CANZONI	CAPONISED	CAPSTAN	CARACOL
CANTICLES	CAP	CAPONISES	CAPSTANS	CARACOLE
CANTICO	CAPA	CAPONISING	CAPSTONE	CARACOLED
CANTICOED	CAPABLE	CAPONIZE	CAPSTONES	CARACOLES
CANTICOING	CAPABLER	CAPONIZED	CAPSULAR	CARACOLING
CANTICOS	CAPABLEST	CAPONIZES	CAPSULARY	CARACOLLED
CANTICOY	CAPACIOUS	CAPONIZING	CAPSULATE	CARACOLLING
CANTICOYED	CAPACITIES	CAPONS	CAPSULE	CARACOLS
CANTICOYING	CAPACITOR	CAPORAL	CAPSULES	CARACT
CANTICOYS	CAPACITORS	CAPORALS	CAPSULISE	CARACTS
CANTICUM	CAPACITY	CAPOS	CAPSULISED	CARACUL
CANTICUMS	CAPARISON	CAPOT	CAPSULISES	CARACULS
CANTIER	CAPARISONED	CAPOTAINE	CAPSULISING	CARAFE
CANTIEST	CAPARISONING	CAPOTASTO	CAPSULIZE	CARAFES
CANTILENA	CAPARISONS	CAPOTASTOS	CAPSULIZED	CARAMBA
CANTILENAS	CAPAS	CAPOTE	CAPSULIZES	CARAMBOLA
CANTINA	CAPE	CAPOTED	CAPSULIZING	CARAMBOLAS
CANTINAS	CAPED	CAPOTES	CAPTAIN	CARAMBOLE
CANTINESS	CAPELET	CAPOTING	CAPTAINCIES	CARAMBOLED
CANTINESSES	CAPELETS	CAPOTS	CAPTAINCY	CARAMBOLES
CANTING	CAPELIN	CAPPED	CAPTAINED	CARAMBOLING
CANTINGS	CAPELINE	CAPPER	CAPTAINING	CARAMEL
CANTION	CAPELINES	CAPPERS	CAPTAINRIES	CARAMELLED
CANTIONS	CAPELINS	CAPPING	CAPTAINRY	CARAMELLING
CANTLE	CAPELLET	CAPPINGS	CAPTAINS	CARAMELS
CANTLED	CAPELLETS	CAPRATE	CAPTAN	CARANGID
CANTLES	CAPELLINE	CAPRATES	CAPTANS	CARANGIDS
CANTLET	CAPELLINES	CAPRIC	CAPTION	CARANGOID
CANTLETS	CAPER	CAPRICCI	CAPTIONED	CARANNA
CANTLING	CAPERED	CAPRICCIO	CAPTIONING	CARANNAS
CANTO	CAPERER	CAPRICCIOS	CAPTIONS	CARANX
CANTON	CAPERERS	CAPRICE	CAPTIOUS	CARAP
CANTONAL	CAPERING	CAPRICES	CAPTIVATE	CARAPACE
CANTONED	CAPERS	CAPRID	CAPTIVATED	CARAPACES
CANTONING	CAPES	CAPRIDS	CAPTIVATES	CARAPS
CANTONS	CAPIAS	CAPRIFIED	CAPTIVATING	CARAT
CANTOR	CAPIASES	CAPRIFIES	CAPTIVE	CARATS
CANTORIAL	CAPILLARIES	CAPRIFIG	CAPTIVED	CARAUNA
CANTORIS	CAPILLARY	CAPRIFIGS	CAPTIVES	CARAUNAS
CANTORS	CAPING	CAPRIFOIL	CAPTIVING	CARAVAN
CANTOS	CAPITA	CAPRIFOILS	CAPTIVITIES	CARAVANCE
CANTRED	CAPITAL	CAPRIFOLE	CAPTIVITY	CARAVANCES
CANTREDS	CAPITALLY	CAPRIFOLES	CAPTOR	CARAVANED
CANTREF	CAPITALS	CAPRIFORM	CAPTORS	CARAVANER
CANTREFS	CAPITAN	CAPRIFY	CAPTURE	CARAVANERS
CANTRIP	CAPITANI	CAPRIFYING	CAPTURED	CARAVANING
CANTRIPS	CAPITANO	CAPRINE	CAPTURES	CARAVANNED
CANTS	CAPITANOS	CAPRIOLE	CAPTURING	CARAVANNING

CARAVANS
CARAVEL
CARAVELS
CARAWAY
CARAWAYS
CARB
CARBAMATE
CARBAMATES
CARBAMIDE
CARBAMIDES
CARBARYL
CARBARYLS
CARBIDE
CARBIDES
CARBINE
CARBINEER
CARBINEERS
CARBINES
CARBINIER
CARBINIERS
CARBOLIC
CARBOLICS
CARBON
CARBONADE
CARBONADES
CARBONADO
CARBONADOED
CARBONADOES
CARBONADOING
CARBONADOS
CARBONATE
CARBONATED
CARBONATES
CARBONATING
CARBONIC
CARBONISE
CARBONISED
CARBONISES
CARBONISING
CARBONIZE
CARBONIZED
CARBONIZES
CARBONIZING
CARBONS
CARBONYL
CARBONYLS
CARBOXYL
CARBOXYLS
CARBOY
CARBOYS
CARBS
CARBUNCLE
CARBUNCLES
CARBURATE
CARBURATED
CARBURATES
CARBURATING
CARBURET
CARBURETS
CARBURETTED
CARBURETTING
CARBURISE
CARBURISED
CARBURISES
CARBURISING
CARBURIZE
CARBURIZED
CARBURIZES
CARBURIZING
CARCAJOU

CARCAJOUS
CARCAKE
CARCAKES
CARCANET
CARCANETS
CARCASE
CARCASED
CARCASES
CARCASING
CARCASS
CARCASSED
CARCASSES
CARCASSING
CARCINOMA
CARCINOMAS
CARCINOMATA
CARD
CARDAMINE
CARDAMINES
CARDAMOM
CARDAMOMS
CARDAMON
CARDAMONS
CARDAMUM
CARDAMUMS
CARDBOARD
CARDBOARDS
CARDECU
CARDECUE
CARDECUES
CARDECUS
CARDED
CARDER
CARDERS
CARDI
CARDIAC
CARDIACAL
CARDIACS
CARDIALGIES
CARDIALGY
CARDIES
CARDIGAN
CARDIGANS
CARDINAL
CARDINALS
CARDING
CARDIOID
CARDIOIDS
CARDIS
CARDITIS
CARDITISES
CARDOON
CARDOONS
CARDPUNCH
CARDPUNCHES
CARDS
CARDUUS
CARDUUSES
CARDY
CARE
CARED
CAREEN
CAREENAGE
CAREENAGES
CAREENED
CAREENING
CAREENS
CAREER
CAREERED
CAREERING

CAREERISM
CAREERISMS
CAREERIST
CAREERISTS
CAREERS
CAREFREE
CAREFUL
CAREFULLY
CARELESS
CARÊME
CARÊMES
CARER
CARERS
CARES
CARESS
CARESSED
CARESSES
CARESSING
CARESSINGS
CARET
CARETAKE
CARETAKER
CARETAKERS
CARETAKES
CARETAKING
CARETOOK
CARETS
CAREWORN
CAREX
CARFAX
CARFAXES
CARFOX
CARFOXES
CARFUFFLE
CARFUFFLED
CARFUFFLES
CARFUFFLING
CARGEESE
CARGO
CARGOED
CARGOES
CARGOING
CARGOOSE
CARIACOU
CARIACOUS
CARIAMA
CARIAMAS
CARIBE
CARIBES
CARIBOU
CARIBOUS
CARICES
CARIERE
CARIERES
CARIES
CARILLON
CARILLONNED
CARILLONNING
CARILLONS
CARINA
CARINAS
CARINATE
CARING
CARIOCA
CARIOCAS
CARIOLE
CARIOLES
CARIOUS
CARITAS
CARJACOU

CARJACOUS
CARK
CARKED
CARKING
CARKS
CARL
CARLINE
CARLINES
CARLISH
CARLOAD
CARLOADS
CARLOCK
CARLOCKS
CARLOT
CARLOTS
CARLS
CARMAN
CARMELITE
CARMELITES
CARMEN
CARMINE
CARMINES
CARNAGE
CARNAGES
CARNAHUBA
CARNAHUBAS
CARNAL
CARNALISE
CARNALISED
CARNALISES
CARNALISING
CARNALISM
CARNALISMS
CARNALIST
CARNALISTS
CARNALITIES
CARNALITY
CARNALIZE
CARNALIZED
CARNALIZES
CARNALIZING
CARNALLED
CARNALLING
CARNALLY
CARNALS
CARNATION
CARNATIONS
CARNAUBA
CARNAUBAS
CARNELIAN
CARNELIANS
CARNEOUS
CARNET
CARNETS
CARNEY
CARNEYED
CARNEYING
CARNEYS
CARNIED
CARNIES
CARNIFEX
CARNIFEXES
CARNIVAL
CARNIVALS
CARNIVORE
CARNIVORES
CARNOSE
CARNOSITIES
CARNOSITY
CARNOTITE

CARNOTITES
CARNY
CARNYING
CAROB
CAROBS
CAROCHE
CAROCHES
CAROL
CAROLLED
CAROLLER
CAROLLERS
CAROLLING
CAROLS
CAROM
CAROMED
CAROMEL
CAROMELLED
CAROMELLING
CAROMELS
CAROMING
CAROMS
CAROTENE
CAROTENES
CAROTID
CAROTIN
CAROTINS
CAROUSAL
CAROUSALS
CAROUSE
CAROUSED
CAROUSEL
CAROUSELS
CAROUSER
CAROUSERS
CAROUSES
CAROUSING
CARP
CARPAL
CARPALS
CARPARK
CARPARKS
CARPED
CARPEL
CARPELS
CARPENTER
CARPENTERED
CARPENTERING
CARPENTERS
CARPENTRIES
CARPENTRY
CARPER
CARPERS
CARPET
CARPETED
CARPETING
CARPETINGS
CARPETS
CARPING
CARPINGLY
CARPINGS
CARPORT
CARPORTS
CARPS
CARPUS
CARPUSES
CARR
CARRACK
CARRACKS
CARRACT
CARRACTS

CARRAGEEN	CARTON	CASEATION	CASSIMERE	CASUALTIES
CARRAGEENS	CARTONAGE	CASEATIONS	CASSIMERES	CASUALTY
CARRAT	CARTONAGES	CASEBOOK	CASSINO	CASUARINA
CARRATS	CARTONED	CASEBOOKS	CASSINOS	CASUARINAS
CARRAWAY	CARTONING	CASED	CASSIS	CASUIST
CARRAWAYS	CARTONS	CASEIN	CASSISES	CASUISTIC
CARRECT	CARTOON	CASEINS	CASSOCK	CASUISTRIES
CARRECTS	CARTOONED	CASEMAKER	CASSOCKED	CASUISTRY
CARREL	CARTOONING	CASEMAKERS	CASSOCKS	CASUISTS
CARRELL	CARTOONS	CASEMAN	CASSONADE	CAT
CARRELLS	CARTOUCH	CASEMATE	CASSONADES	CATACLASM
CARRELS	CARTOUCHE	CASEMATED	CASSONE	CATACLASMS
CARRIAGE	CARTOUCHES	CASEMATES	CASSONES	CATACLYSM
CARRIAGES	CARTRIDGE	CASEMEN	CASSOULET	CATACLYSMS
CARRIED	CARTRIDGES	CASEMENT	CASSOULETS	CATACOMB
CARRIER	CARTROAD	CASEMENTS	CASSOWARIES	CATACOMBS
CARRIERS	CARTROADS	CASEOUS	CASSOWARY	CATAFALCO
CARRIES	CARTS	CASERN	CAST	CATAFALCOES
CARRIOLE	CARTULARIES	CASERNE	CASTANETS	CATALASE
CARRIOLES	CARTULARY	CASERNES	CASTAWAY	CATALASES
CARRION	CARTWAY	CASERNS	CASTAWAYS	CATALEPSIES
CARRIONS	CARTWAYS	CASES	CASTE	CATALEPSY
CARRITCH	CARTWHEEL	CASH	CASTED	CATALEXES
CARRITCHES	CARTWHEELED	CASHAW	CASTELESS	CATALEXIS
CARRONADE	CARTWHEELING	CASHAWS	CASTELLAN	CATALO
CARRONADES	CARTWHEELS	CASHED	CASTELLANS	CATALOES
CARROT	CARUCAGE	CASHES	CASTELLUM	CATALOG
CARROTS	CARUCAGES	CASHEW	CASTELLUMS	CATALOGED
CARROTY	CARUCATE	CASHEWS	CASTER	CATALOGER
CARROUSEL	CARUCATES	CASHIER	CASTERS	CATALOGERS
CARROUSELS	CARUNCLE	CASHIERED	CASTES	CATALOGING
CARRS	CARUNCLES	CASHIERER	CASTIGATE	CATALOGS
CARRY	CARVACROL	CASHIERERS	CASTIGATED	CATALOGUE
CARRYCOT	CARVACROLS	CASHIERING	CASTIGATES	CATALOGUED
CARRYCOTS	CARVE	CASHIERINGS	CASTIGATING	CATALOGUES
CARRYING	CARVED	CASHIERS	CASTING	CATALOGUING
CARRYTALE	CARVEL	CASHING	CASTINGS	CATALOS
CARRYTALES	CARVELS	CASHLESS	CASTLE	CATALPA
CARS	CARVEN	CASHMERE	CASTLED	CATALPAS
CARSE	CARVER	CASHMERES	CASTLES	CATALYSE
CARSES	CARVERS	CASING	CASTLING	CATALYSED
CART	CARVES	CASINGS	CASTOCK	CATALYSER
CARTA	CARVIES	CASINO	CASTOCKS	CATALYSERS
CARTAGE	CARVING	CASINOS	CASTOR	CATALYSES
CARTAGES	CARVINGS	CASK	CASTOREUM	CATALYSING
CARTAS	CARVY	CASKED	CASTOREUMS	CATALYSIS
CARTE	CARYATIC	CASKET	CASTORIES	CATALYST
CARTED	CARYATID	CASKETS	CASTORS	CATALYSTS
CARTEL	CARYATIDES	CASKING	CASTORY	CATALYTIC
CARTELISE	CARYATIDS	CASKS	CASTRAL	CATALYZE
CARTELISED	CARYOPSES	CASQUE	CASTRATE	CATALYZED
CARTELISES	CARYOPSIDES	CASQUES	CASTRATED	CATALYZER
CARTELISING	CARYOPSIS	CASSAREEP	CASTRATES	CATALYZERS
CARTELIZE	CASA	CASSAREEPS	CASTRATI	CATALYZES
CARTELIZED	CASAS	CASSARIPE	CASTRATING	CATALYZING
CARTELIZES	CASBAH	CASSARIPES	CASTRATO	CATAMARAN
CARTELIZING	CASBAHS	CASSATA	CASTS	CATAMARANS
CARTELS	CASCABEL	CASSATAS	CASUAL	CATAMENIA
CARTER	CASCABELS	CASSATION	CASUALISE	CATAMITE
CARTERS	CASCADE	CASSATIONS	CASUALISED	CATAMITES
CARTES	CASCADED	CASSAVA	CASUALISES	CATAMOUNT
CARTILAGE	CASCADES	CASSAVAS	CASUALISING	CATAMOUNTS
CARTILAGES	CASCADING	CASSEROLE	CASUALISM	CATAPAN
CARTING	CASCARA	CASSEROLED	CASUALISMS	CATAPANS
CARTLOAD	CASCARAS	CASSEROLES	CASUALIZE	CATAPHYLL
CARTLOADS	CASCHROM	CASSEROLING	CASUALIZED	CATAPHYLLS
CARTOGRAM	CASCHROMS	CASSETTE	CASUALIZES	CATAPLASM
CARTOGRAMS	CASCO	CASSETTES	CASUALIZING	CATAPLASMS
CARTOLOGIES	CASCOS	CASSIA	CASUALLY	CATAPLEXIES
CARTOLOGY	CASE	CASSIAS	CASUALS	CATAPLEXY

CATAPULT
CATAPULTED
CATAPULTING
CATAPULTS
CATARACT
CATARACTS
CATARHINE
CATARRH
CATARRHAL
CATARRHS
CATASTA
CATASTAS
CATATONIA
CATATONIAS
CATATONIC
CATATONICS
CATATONIES
CATATONY
CATAWBA
CATAWBAS
CATBIRD
CATBIRDS
CATBOAT
CATBOATS
CATCALL
CATCALLED
CATCALLING
CATCALLS
CATCH
CATCHABLE
CATCHED
CATCHEN
CATCHER
CATCHERS
CATCHES
CATCHFLIES
CATCHFLY
CATCHIER
CATCHIEST
CATCHING
CATCHINGS
CATCHMENT
CATCHMENTS
CATCHPOLE
CATCHPOLES
CATCHPOLL
CATCHPOLLS
CATCHT
CATCHUP
CATCHUPS
CATCHWEED
CATCHWEEDS
CATCHWORD
CATCHWORDS
CATCHY
CATE
CATECHISE
CATECHISED
CATECHISES
CATECHISING
CATECHISINGS
CATECHISM
CATECHISMS
CATECHIST
CATECHISTS
CATECHIZE
CATECHIZED
CATECHIZES
CATECHIZING
CATECHIZINGS

CATECHOL
CATECHOLS
CATECHU
CATECHUS
CATEGORIES
CATEGORY
CATELOG
CATELOGS
CATENA
CATENAE
CATENARIES
CATENARY
CATENAS
CATENATE
CATENATED
CATENATES
CATENATING
CATER
CATERAN
CATERANS
CATERED
CATERER
CATERERS
CATERESS
CATERESSES
CATERING
CATERINGS
CATERS
CATERWAUL
CATERWAULED
CATERWAULING
CATERWAULINGS
CATERWAULS
CATES
CATFISH
CATFISHES
CATGUT
CATGUTS
CATHARISE
CATHARISED
CATHARISES
CATHARISING
CATHARIZE
CATHARIZED
CATHARIZES
CATHARIZING
CATHARSES
CATHARSIS
CATHARTIC
CATHARTICS
CATHEAD
CATHEADS
CATHECTIC
CATHEDRA
CATHEDRAL
CATHEDRALS
CATHEDRAS
CATHETER
CATHETERS
CATHETUS
CATHETUSES
CATHEXES
CATHEXIS
CATHISMA
CATHISMAS
CATHODAL
CATHODE
CATHODES
CATHODIC
CATHOLIC

CATHOOD
CATHOODS
CATHOUSE
CATHOUSES
CATION
CATIONS
CATKIN
CATKINS
CATLING
CATLINGS
CATMINT
CATMINTS
CATNAP
CATNAPS
CATNEP
CATNEPS
CATNIP
CATNIPS
CATOPTRIC
CATOPTRICS
CATS
CATSKIN
CATSKINS
CATSUIT
CATSUITS
CATSUP
CATSUPS
CATTABU
CATTABUS
CATTALO
CATTALOES
CATTALOS
CATTED
CATTERIES
CATTERY
CATTIER
CATTIES
CATTIEST
CATTILY
CATTINESS
CATTINESSES
CATTING
CATTISH
CATTISHLY
CATTLE
CATTLEMAN
CATTLEMEN
CATTY
CAUCHEMAR
CAUCHEMARS
CAUCUS
CAUCUSED
CAUCUSES
CAUCUSING
CAUDAD
CAUDAL
CAUDATE
CAUDATED
CAUDEX
CAUDEXES
CAUDICLE
CAUDICLES
CAUDILLO
CAUDILLOS
CAUDLE
CAUDLED
CAUDLES
CAUDLING
CAUDRON

CAUDRONS
CAUF
CAUGHT
CAUK
CAUKER
CAUKERS
CAUKS
CAUL
CAULD
CAULDER
CAULDEST
CAULDRIFE
CAULDRON
CAULDRONS
CAULDS
CAULES
CAULICLE
CAULICLES
CAULIFORM
CAULINARY
CAULINE
CAULIS
CAULK
CAULKED
CAULKER
CAULKERS
CAULKING
CAULKINGS
CAULKS
CAULOME
CAULOMES
CAULS
CAUM
CAUMED
CAUMING
CAUMS
CAUMSTANE
CAUMSTANES
CAUMSTONE
CAUMSTONES
CAUP
CAUPS
CAUSAL
CAUSALITIES
CAUSALITY
CAUSALLY
CAUSATION
CAUSATIONS
CAUSATIVE
CAUSATIVES
CAUSE
CAUSED
CAUSELESS
CAUSEN
CAUSER
CAUSERIE
CAUSERIES
CAUSERS
CAUSES
CAUSEWAY
CAUSEWAYED
CAUSEWAYING
CAUSEWAYS
CAUSEY
CAUSEYED
CAUSEYING
CAUSEYS
CAUSING
CAUSTIC
CAUSTICS

CAUTEL
CAUTELOUS
CAUTELS
CAUTER
CAUTERANT
CAUTERANTS
CAUTERIES
CAUTERISE
CAUTERISED
CAUTERISES
CAUTERISING
CAUTERISM
CAUTERISMS
CAUTERIZE
CAUTERIZED
CAUTERIZES
CAUTERIZING
CAUTERS
CAUTERY
CAUTION
CAUTIONED
CAUTIONER
CAUTIONERS
CAUTIONING
CAUTIONRIES
CAUTIONRY
CAUTIONS
CAUTIOUS
CAUVES
CAVALCADE
CAVALCADED
CAVALCADES
CAVALCADING
CAVALIER
CAVALIERED
CAVALIERING
CAVALIERO
CAVALIEROS
CAVALIERS
CAVALLA
CAVALLAS
CAVALLIES
CAVALLY
CAVALRIES
CAVALRY
CAVASS
CAVASSES
CAVATINA
CAVATINAS
CAVE
CAVEAT
CAVEATS
CAVED
CAVEL
CAVELS
CAVEMAN
CAVEMEN
CAVENDISH
CAVENDISHES
CAVER
CAVERN
CAVERNED
CAVERNING
CAVERNOUS
CAVERNS
CAVERS
CAVES
CAVESSON
CAVESSONS
CAVETTI

CAVETTO
CAVIAR
CAVIARE
CAVIARES
CAVIARIE
CAVIARIES
CAVIARS
CAVICORN
CAVICORNS
CAVIE
CAVIER
CAVIERS
CAVIES
CAVIL
CAVILLED
CAVILLER
CAVILLERS
CAVILLING
CAVILLINGS
CAVILS
CAVING
CAVINGS
CAVITATE
CAVITATED
CAVITATES
CAVITATING
CAVITIED
CAVITIES
CAVITY
CAVORT
CAVORTED
CAVORTING
CAVORTS
CAVY
CAW
CAWED
CAWING
CAWINGS
CAWK
CAWKER
CAWKERS
CAWKS
CAWS
CAXON
CAXONS
CAY
CAYENNE
CAYENNED
CAYENNES
CAYMAN
CAYMANS
CAYS
CAYUSE
CAYUSES
CAZIQUE
CAZIQUES
CEAS
CEASE
CEASED
CEASELESS
CEASES
CEASING
CEASINGS
CEAZE
CEAZED
CEAZES
CEAZING
CEBADILLA
CEBADILLAS
CECA

CECILS
CECITIES
CECITY
CECUM
CEDAR
CEDARED
CEDARN
CEDARS
CEDARWOOD
CEDARWOODS
CEDE
CEDED
CEDES
CEDI
CEDILLA
CEDILLAS
CEDING
CEDIS
CEDRATE
CEDRATES
CEDRINE
CEDULA
CEDULAS
CEE
CEES
CEIL
CEILED
CEILI
CEILIDH
CEILIDHS
CEILING
CEILINGED
CEILINGS
CEILIS
CEILS
CEINTURE
CEINTURES
CEL
CELADON
CELADONS
CELANDINE
CELANDINES
CELEBRANT
CELEBRANTS
CELEBRATE
CELEBRATED
CELEBRATES
CELEBRATING
CELEBRITIES
CELEBRITY
CELERIAC
CELERIACS
CELERIES
CELERITIES
CELERITY
CELERY
CELESTA
CELESTAS
CELESTE
CELESTES
CELESTIAL
CELESTIALS
CELESTINE
CELESTINES
CELIAC
CELIBACIES
CELIBACY
CELIBATE
CELIBATES
CELL

CELLA
CELLAE
CELLAR
CELLARAGE
CELLARAGES
CELLARED
CELLARER
CELLARERS
CELLARET
CELLARETS
CELLARING
CELLARIST
CELLARISTS
CELLARMAN
CELLARMEN
CELLAROUS
CELLARS
CELLED
CELLIST
CELLISTS
CELLO
CELLOS
CELLPHONE
CELLPHONES
CELLS
CELLULAR
CELLULE
CELLULES
CELLULITE
CELLULITES
CELLULOID
CELLULOIDS
CELLULOSE
CELLULOSES
CELOM
CELOMS
CELS
CELSITUDE
CELSITUDES
CELT
CELTS
CEMBALIST
CEMBALISTS
CEMBALO
CEMBALOS
CEMBRA
CEMBRAS
CEMENT
CEMENTA
CEMENTED
CEMENTING
CEMENTITE
CEMENTITES
CEMENTS
CEMENTUM
CEMETERIES
CEMETERY
CEMITARE
CEMITARES
CENACLE
CENACLES
CENDRÉ
CENOBITE
CENOBITES
CENOTAPH
CENOTAPHS
CENOTE
CENOTES
CENSE
CENSED

CENSER
CENSERS
CENSES
CENSING
CENSOR
CENSORED
CENSORIAL
CENSORIAN
CENSORING
CENSORS
CENSUAL
CENSURE
CENSURED
CENSURES
CENSURING
CENSUS
CENSUSED
CENSUSES
CENSUSING
CENT
CENTAGE
CENTAGES
CENTAL
CENTALS
CENTAUR
CENTAURIES
CENTAURS
CENTAURY
CENTAVO
CENTAVOS
CENTENARIES
CENTENARY
CENTENIER
CENTENIERS
CENTER
CENTERED
CENTERING
CENTERINGS
CENTERS
CENTESES
CENTESIS
CENTIARE
CENTIARES
CENTIGRAM
CENTIGRAMS
CENTIME
CENTIMES
CENTINEL
CENTINELL
CENTINELLS
CENTINELS
CENTIPEDE
CENTIPEDES
CENTNER
CENTNERS
CENTO
CENTOIST
CENTOISTS
CENTONATE
CENTONEL
CENTONELL
CENTONELLS
CENTONELS
CENTONIST
CENTONISTS
CENTOS
CENTRAL
CENTRALLY
CENTRE
CENTRED

CENTREING
CENTREINGS
CENTRES
CENTRIC
CENTRICAL
CENTRIES
CENTRING
CENTRINGS
CENTRISM
CENTRISMS
CENTRIST
CENTRISTS
CENTRODE
CENTRODES
CENTROID
CENTROIDS
CENTRUM
CENTRUMS
CENTRY
CENTS
CENTUM
CENTUMS
CENTUMVIR
CENTUMVIRI
CENTUPLE
CENTUPLED
CENTUPLES
CENTUPLING
CENTURIAL
CENTURIES
CENTURION
CENTURIONS
CENTURY
CEORL
CEORLS
CEP
CEPHALAD
CEPHALATE
CEPHALIC
CEPHALICS
CEPHALOUS
CEPHEID
CEPHEIDS
CEPS
CERACEOUS
CERAMET
CERAMETS
CERAMIC
CERAMICS
CERAMIST
CERAMISTS
CERASIN
CERASINS
CERASTES
CERATE
CERATED
CERATES
CERATITIS
CERATITISES
CERATODUS
CERATODUSES
CERATOID
CERBERIAN
CERCAL
CERCARIA
CERCARIAE
CERCARIAN
CERCARIAS
CERCI
CERCUS

CERCUSES
CERE
CEREAL
CEREALIST
CEREALISTS
CEREALS
CEREBELLA
CEREBRAL
CEREBRATE
CEREBRATED
CEREBRATES
CEREBRATING
CEREBRIC
CEREBRUM
CEREBRUMS
CERED
CEREMENT
CEREMENTS
CEREMONIES
CEREMONY
CEREOUS
CERES
CERESIN
CERESINE
CERESINES
CERESINS
CERGE
CERGES
CERIA
CERIAS
CERING
CERIPH
CERIPHS
CERISE
CERISES
CERITE
CERITES
CERIUM
CERIUMS
CERMET
CERMETS
CERNE
CERNED
CERNES
CERNING
CERNUOUS
CEROGRAPH
CEROGRAPHS
CEROMANCIES
CEROMANCY
CEROON
CEROONS
CERRIAL
CERRIS
CERRISES
CERT
CERTAIN
CERTAINLY
CERTAINTIES
CERTAINTY
CERTES
CERTIFIED
CERTIFIER
CERTIFIERS
CERTIFIES
CERTIFY
CERTIFYING
CERTITUDE
CERTITUDES
CERTS

CERULEAN
CERULEIN
CERULEINS
CERULEOUS
CERUMEN
CERUMENS
CERUSE
CERUSES
CERUSITE
CERUSITES
CERUSSITE
CERUSSITES
CERVELAT
CERVELATS
CERVICAL
CERVINE
CERVIX
CERVIXES
CESAREVNA
CESAREVNAS
CESIUM
CESIUMS
CESPITOSE
CESS
CESSATION
CESSATIONS
CESSE
CESSED
CESSER
CESSERS
CESSES
CESSING
CESSION
CESSIONS
CESSPIT
CESSPITS
CESSPOOL
CESSPOOLS
CESTODE
CESTODES
CESTOID
CESTOIDS
CESTOS
CESTUI
CESTUIS
CESTUS
CESTUSES
CESURA
CESURAS
CESURE
CESURES
CETACEAN
CETACEANS
CETACEOUS
CETANE
CETANES
CETE
CETERACH
CETERACHS
CETES
CETOLOGIES
CETOLOGY
CETYL
CETYLS
CETYWALL
CETYWALLS
CEVADILLA
CEVADILLAS
CEYLANITE
CEYLANITES
CEYLONITE

CEYLONITES
CH
CHA
CHABAZITE
CHABAZITES
CHABOUK
CHABOUKS
CHACE
CHACED
CHACES
CHACING
CHACK
CHACKED
CHACKING
CHACKS
CHACMA
CHACMAS
CHACO
CHACOES
CHACONNE
CHACONNES
CHACOS
CHAD
CHADAR
CHADARS
CHADDAR
CHADDARS
CHADOR
CHADORS
CHADS
CHAETA
CHAETAE
CHAETODON
CHAETODONS
CHAETOPOD
CHAETOPODS
CHAFE
CHAFED
CHAFER
CHAFERS
CHAFF
CHAFFED
CHAFFER
CHAFFERED
CHAFFERER
CHAFFERERS
CHAFFERIES
CHAFFERING
CHAFFERS
CHAFFERY
CHAFFIER
CHAFFIEST
CHAFFINCH
CHAFFINCHES
CHAFFING
CHAFFINGS
CHAFFLESS
CHAFFRON
CHAFFRONS
CHAFFS
CHAFFY
CHAFING
CHAFT
CHAFTS
CHAGAN
CHAGANS
CHAGRIN
CHAGRINED
CHAGRINING

CHAGRINS
CHAI
CHAIN
CHAINED
CHAINING
CHAINLESS
CHAINLET
CHAINLETS
CHAINS
CHAINSAW
CHAINSAWS
CHAINWORK
CHAINWORKS
CHAIR
CHAIRDAYS
CHAIRED
CHAIRING
CHAIRLIFT
CHAIRLIFTS
CHAIRMAN
CHAIRMEN
CHAIRS
CHAIS
CHAISE
CHAISES
CHAKRA
CHAKRAS
CHAL
CHALAN
CHALANED
CHALANING
CHALANS
CHALAZA
CHALAZAE
CHALAZAS
CHALDAISM
CHALDAISMS
CHALDER
CHALDERS
CHALDRON
CHALDRONS
CHALET
CHALETS
CHALICE
CHALICED
CHALICES
CHALK
CHALKED
CHALKFACE
CHALKFACES
CHALKIER
CHALKIEST
CHALKING
CHALKPIT
CHALKPITS
CHALKS
CHALKY
CHALLAN
CHALLANED
CHALLANING
CHALLANS
CHALLENGE
CHALLENGED
CHALLENGES
CHALLENGING
CHALLIS
CHALLISES
CHALONE
CHALONES
CHALONIC

CHALS
CHALUMEAU
CHALUMEAUX
CHALYBITE
CHALYBITES
CHAM
CHAMADE
CHAMADES
CHAMBER
CHAMBERED
CHAMBERER
CHAMBERERS
CHAMBERING
CHAMBERINGS
CHAMBERS
CHAMBRÉ
CHAMELEON
CHAMELEONS
CHAMELOT
CHAMELOTS
CHAMFER
CHAMFERED
CHAMFERING
CHAMFERS
CHAMFRAIN
CHAMFRAINS
CHAMFRON
CHAMFRONS
CHAMISAL
CHAMISALS
CHAMISE
CHAMISES
CHAMISO
CHAMISOS
CHAMLET
CHAMLETS
CHAMOIS
CHAMOMILE
CHAMOMILES
CHAMP
CHAMPAC
CHAMPACS
CHAMPAGNE
CHAMPAGNES
CHAMPAIGN
CHAMPAIGNS
CHAMPAK
CHAMPAKS
CHAMPART
CHAMPARTS
CHAMPED
CHAMPERS
CHAMPERTIES
CHAMPERTY
CHAMPING
CHAMPION
CHAMPIONED
CHAMPIONING
CHAMPIONS
CHAMPLEVÉ
CHAMPLEVÉS
CHAMPS
CHAMS
CHANCE
CHANCED
CHANCEFUL
CHANCEL
CHANCELS
CHANCER
CHANCERS

CHANCES
CHANCIER
CHANCIEST
CHANCING
CHANCRE
CHANCRES
CHANCROID
CHANCROIDS
CHANCROUS
CHANCY
CHANDLER
CHANDLERIES
CHANDLERS
CHANDLERY
CHANGE
CHANGED
CHANGEFUL
CHANGER
CHANGERS
CHANGES
CHANGING
CHANK
CHANKS
CHANNEL
CHANNELLED
CHANNELLING
CHANNELS
CHANOYU
CHANOYUS
CHANSON
CHANSONS
CHANT
CHANTAGE
CHANTAGES
CHANTED
CHANTER
CHANTERS
CHANTEUSE
CHANTEUSES
CHANTEY
CHANTEYS
CHANTIE
CHANTIES
CHANTING
CHANTOR
CHANTORS
CHANTRESS
CHANTRESSES
CHANTRIES
CHANTRY
CHANTS
CHANTY
CHAOS
CHAOSES
CHAOTIC
CHAP
CHAPARRAL
CHAPARRALS
CHAPATI
CHAPATIS
CHAPATTI
CHAPATTIS
CHAPBOOK
CHAPBOOKS
CHAPE
CHAPEAU
CHAPEAUS
CHAPEL
CHAPELESS
CHAPELRIES

CHAPELRY
CHAPELS
CHAPERON
CHAPERONE
CHAPERONED
CHAPERONES
CHAPERONING
CHAPERONS
CHAPES
CHAPESS
CHAPESSES
CHAPITER
CHAPITERS
CHAPKA
CHAPKAS
CHAPLAIN
CHAPLAINS
CHAPLESS
CHAPLET
CHAPLETED
CHAPLETS
CHAPMAN
CHAPMEN
CHAPPED
CHAPPESS
CHAPPESSES
CHAPPIE
CHAPPIER
CHAPPIES
CHAPPIEST
CHAPPING
CHAPPY
CHAPRASSI
CHAPRASSIS
CHAPS
CHAPTER
CHAPTERED
CHAPTERING
CHAPTERS
CHAPTREL
CHAPTRELS
CHAR
CHARA
CHARABANC
CHARABANCS
CHARACIN
CHARACINS
CHARACT
CHARACTER
CHARACTERED
CHARACTERING
CHARACTERS
CHARACTS
CHARADE
CHARADES
CHARAS
CHARASES
CHARCOAL
CHARCOALS
CHARD
CHARDS
CHARE
CHARED
CHARES
CHARET
CHARETS
CHARGE
CHARGED
CHARGEFUL
CHARGER

CHARGERS
CHARGES
CHARGING
CHARIER
CHARIEST
CHARILY
CHARINESS
CHARINESSES
CHARING
CHARIOT
CHARIOTED
CHARIOTING
CHARIOTS
CHARISM
CHARISMA
CHARISMAS
CHARISMS
CHARITIES
CHARITY
CHARIVARI
CHARIVARIS
CHARK
CHARKED
CHARKING
CHARKS
CHARLADIES
CHARLADY
CHARLATAN
CHARLATANS
CHARLEY
CHARLEYS
CHARLIE
CHARLIES
CHARLOCK
CHARLOCKS
CHARLOTTE
CHARLOTTES
CHARM
CHARMED
CHARMER
CHARMERS
CHARMEUSE
CHARMEUSES
CHARMFUL
CHARMING
CHARMLESS
CHARMS
CHARNECO
CHARNECOS
CHARNEL
CHARNELS
CHAROSET
CHAROSETH
CHAROSETHS
CHAROSETS
CHARPIE
CHARPIES
CHARPOY
CHARPOYS
CHARQUI
CHARQUIS
CHARR
CHARRED
CHARRING
CHARRS
CHARRY
CHARS
CHART
CHARTA
CHARTAS

CHARTED
CHARTER
CHARTERED
CHARTERER
CHARTERERS
CHARTERING
CHARTERS
CHARTING
CHARTISM
CHARTISMS
CHARTIST
CHARTISTS
CHARTLESS
CHARTS
CHARWOMAN
CHARWOMEN
CHARY
CHAS
CHASE
CHASED
CHASER
CHASERS
CHASES
CHASING
CHASINGS
CHASM
CHASMED
CHASMIC
CHASMIER
CHASMIEST
CHASMS
CHASMY
CHASSÉ
CHASSE
CHASSÉED
CHASSÉING
CHASSÉS
CHASSES
CHASSEUR
CHASSEURS
CHASSIS
CHASTE
CHASTELY
CHASTEN
CHASTENED
CHASTENER
CHASTENERS
CHASTENING
CHASTENS
CHASTER
CHASTEST
CHASTISE
CHASTISED
CHASTISES
CHASTISING
CHASTITIES
CHASTITY
CHASUBLE
CHASUBLES
CHAT
CHÂTEAU
CHÂTEAUX
CHÂTELAIN
CHÂTELAINS
CHATON
CHATONS
CHATOYANT
CHATS
CHATTA
CHATTAS

CHATTED
CHATTEL
CHATTELS
CHATTER
CHATTERED
CHATTERER
CHATTERERS
CHATTERING
CHATTERINGS
CHATTERS
CHATTIER
CHATTIES
CHATTIEST
CHATTING
CHATTY
CHAUFE
CHAUFED
CHAUFES
CHAUFF
CHAUFFED
CHAUFFER
CHAUFFERS
CHAUFFEUR
CHAUFFEURED
CHAUFFEURING
CHAUFFEURS
CHAUFFING
CHAUFFS
CHAUFING
CHAUMER
CHAUMERS
CHAUNCE
CHAUNCED
CHAUNCES
CHAUNCING
CHAUNGE
CHAUNGED
CHAUNGES
CHAUNGING
CHAUNT
CHAUNTED
CHAUNTER
CHAUNTERS
CHAUNTING
CHAUNTRIES
CHAUNTRY
CHAUNTS
CHAUSSES
CHAUSSURE
CHAUSSURES
CHAUVIN
CHAUVINS
CHAVE
CHAVENDER
CHAVENDERS
CHAW
CHAWDRON
CHAWDRONS
CHAWED
CHAWING
CHAWS
CHAY
CHAYA
CHAYAS
CHAYOTE
CHAYOTES
CHAYS
CHE
CHEAP
CHEAPEN

CHEAPENED
CHEAPENER
CHEAPENERS
CHEAPENING
CHEAPENS
CHEAPER
CHEAPEST
CHEAPIE
CHEAPIES
CHEAPLY
CHEAPNESS
CHEAPNESSES
CHEAPO
CHEAPS
CHEAPY
CHEAT
CHEATED
CHEATER
CHEATERIES
CHEATERS
CHEATERY
CHEATING
CHEATS
CHECHAKO
CHECHAKOES
CHECHAKOS
CHECHAQUA
CHECHAQUAS
CHECHAQUO
CHECHAQUOS
CHECHIA
CHECHIAS
CHECK
CHECKED
CHECKER
CHECKERED
CHECKERS
CHECKIER
CHECKIEST
CHECKING
CHECKLIST
CHECKLISTS
CHECKMATE
CHECKMATED
CHECKMATES
CHECKMATING
CHECKROOM
CHECKROOMS
CHECKS
CHECKY
CHEECHAKO
CHEECHAKOES
CHEECHAKOS
CHEEK
CHEEKED
CHEEKIER
CHEEKIEST
CHEEKILY
CHEEKING
CHEEKS
CHEEKY
CHEEP
CHEEPED
CHEEPER
CHEEPERS
CHEEPING
CHEEPS
CHEER
CHEERED
CHEERER

CHEERERS
CHEERFUL
CHEERFULLER
CHEERFULLEST
CHEERIER
CHEERIEST
CHEERILY
CHEERING
CHEERIO
CHEERIOS
CHEERLESS
CHEERLY
CHEERO
CHEEROS
CHEERS
CHEERY
CHEESE
CHEESED
CHEESES
CHEESIER
CHEESIEST
CHEESING
CHEESY
CHEETAH
CHEETAHS
CHEEWINK
CHEEWINKS
CHEF
CHEFS
CHEKA
CHEKAS
CHEKIST
CHEKISTS
CHELA
CHELAE
CHELAS
CHELASHIP
CHELASHIPS
CHELATE
CHELATED
CHELATES
CHELATING
CHELATION
CHELATIONS
CHELATOR
CHELATORS
CHELICERA
CHELICERAE
CHELIPED
CHELIPEDS
CHELOID
CHELOIDAL
CHELOIDS
CHELONIAN
CHELONIANS
CHEMIC
CHEMICAL
CHEMICALS
CHEMICKED
CHEMICKING
CHEMICS
CHEMISE
CHEMISES
CHEMISM
CHEMISMS
CHEMIST
CHEMISTRIES
CHEMISTRY
CHEMISTS
CHEMITYPE

CHEMITYPES
CHEMITYPIES
CHEMITYPY
CHEMMIES
CHEMMY
CHEMOSTAT
CHEMOSTATS
CHEMURGIC
CHEMURGIES
CHEMURGY
CHENAR
CHENARS
CHENET
CHENETS
CHENILLE
CHENILLES
CHENIX
CHENIXES
CHEQUE
CHEQUER
CHEQUERED
CHEQUERING
CHEQUERS
CHEQUES
CHEQUIER
CHEQUIEST
CHEQUY
CHER
CHERALITE
CHERALITES
CHÈRE
CHERIMOYA
CHERIMOYAS
CHERISH
CHERISHED
CHERISHES
CHERISHING
CHERNOZEM
CHERNOZEMS
CHEROOT
CHEROOTS
CHERRIED
CHERRIER
CHERRIES
CHERRIEST
CHERRY
CHERRYING
CHERT
CHERTIER
CHERTIEST
CHERTS
CHERTY
CHERUB
CHERUBIC
CHERUBIM
CHERUBIMS
CHERUBIN
CHERUBINS
CHERUBS
CHERUP
CHERUPED
CHERUPING
CHERUPS
CHERVIL
CHERVILS
CHESIL
CHESILS
CHESNUT
CHESNUTS
CHESS

CHESSEL
CHESSELS
CHESSES
CHESSMAN
CHESSMEN
CHEST
CHESTED
CHESTFUL
CHESTFULS
CHESTIER
CHESTIEST
CHESTNUT
CHESTNUTS
CHESTS
CHESTY
CHEVALET
CHEVALETS
CHEVALIER
CHEVALIERS
CHEVELURE
CHEVELURES
CHEVEN
CHEVENS
CHEVEREL
CHEVERELS
CHEVERIL
CHEVERILS
CHEVERON
CHEVERONS
CHEVERYE
CHEVERYES
CHEVIED
CHEVIES
CHEVILLE
CHEVILLES
CHEVIN
CHEVINS
CHEVRETTE
CHEVRETTES
CHEVRON
CHEVRONED
CHEVRONS
CHEVRONY
CHEVY
CHEVYING
CHEW
CHEWED
CHEWET
CHEWETS
CHEWIER
CHEWIEST
CHEWING
CHEWINK
CHEWINKS
CHEWS
CHEWY
CHEZ
CHI
CHIACK
CHIACKED
CHIACKING
CHIACKINGS
CHIACKS
CHIAO
CHIASM
CHIASMA
CHIASMAS
CHIASMS
CHIASMUS
CHIASMUSES

CHIASTIC
CHIAUS
CHIAUSED
CHIAUSES
CHIAUSING
CHIBOL
CHIBOLS
CHIBOUK
CHIBOUKS
CHIBOUQUE
CHIBOUQUES
CHIC
CHICA
CHICANE
CHICANED
CHICANER
CHICANERIES
CHICANERS
CHICANERY
CHICANES
CHICANING
CHICANINGS
CHICANO
CHICANOS
CHICAS
CHICCORIES
CHICCORY
CHICER
CHICEST
CHICH
CHICHA
CHICHAS
CHICHES
CHICHI
CHICHIS
CHICK
CHICKADEE
CHICKADEES
CHICKAREE
CHICKAREES
CHICKEN
CHICKENED
CHICKENING
CHICKENO
CHICKLING
CHICKLINGS
CHICKS
CHICKWEED
CHICKWEEDS
CHICLE
CHICLES
CHICLY
CHICON
CHICONS
CHICORIES
CHICORY
CHICS
CHID
CHIDDEN
CHIDE
CHIDED
CHIDER
CHIDERS
CHIDES
CHIDING
CHIDINGS
CHIDLINGS
CHIEF
CHIEFDOM
CHIEFDOMS

CHIEFER	CHILIASMS	CHINES	CHIRMED	CHIVIED
CHIEFERIES	CHILIAST	CHINING	CHIRMING	CHIVIES
CHIEFERY	CHILIASTS	CHINK	CHIRMS	CHIVING
CHIEFESS	CHILIS	CHINKAPIN	CHIROLOGIES	CHIVS
CHIEFESSES	CHILL	CHINKAPINS	CHIROLOGY	CHIVVED
CHIEFEST	CHILLED	CHINKARA	CHIRONOMIES	CHIVVIED
CHIEFLESS	CHILLER	CHINKARAS	CHIRONOMY	CHIVVIES
CHIEFLING	CHILLERS	CHINKED	CHIROPODIES	CHIVVING
CHIEFLINGS	CHILLEST	CHINKIER	CHIROPODY	CHIVVY
CHIEFLY	CHILLI	CHINKIEST	CHIRP	CHIVVYING
CHIEFRIES	CHILLIER	CHINKING	CHIRPED	CHIVY
CHIEFRY	CHILLIES	CHINKS	CHIRPER	CHIVYING
CHIEFS	CHILLIEST	CHINKY	CHIRPERS	CHLAMYDES
CHIEFSHIP	CHILLILY	CHINLESS	CHIRPIER	CHLAMYDIA
CHIEFSHIPS	CHILLING	CHINO	CHIRPIEST	CHLAMYDIAS
CHIEFTAIN	CHILLINGS	CHINOOK	CHIRPILY	CHLAMYS
CHIEFTAINS	CHILLIS	CHINOOKS	CHIRPING	CHLOASMA
CHIEL	CHILLNESS	CHINOS	CHIRPS	CHLOASMAS
CHIELD	CHILLNESSES	CHINOVNIK	CHIRPY	CHLORACNE
CHIELDS	CHILLS	CHINOVNIKS	CHIRR	CHLORACNES
CHIELS	CHILLUM	CHINS	CHIRRED	CHLORAL
CHIFFON	CHILLUMS	CHINSTRAP	CHIRRING	CHLORALS
CHIFFONS	CHILLY	CHINSTRAPS	CHIRRS	CHLORATE
CHIGGER	CHIMAERA	CHINTZ	CHIRRUP	CHLORATES
CHIGGERS	CHIMAERAS	CHINTZES	CHIRRUPED	CHLORDAN
CHIGNON	CHIMAERID	CHINTZIER	CHIRRUPING	CHLORDANE
CHIGNONS	CHIMAERIDS	CHINTZIEST	CHIRRUPS	CHLORDANES
CHIGOE	CHIMB	CHINTZY	CHIRRUPY	CHLORDANS
CHIGOES	CHIMBS	CHINWAG	CHIRT	CHLORIC
CHIGRE	CHIME	CHINWAGGED	CHIRTED	CHLORIDE
CHIGRES	CHIMED	CHINWAGGING	CHIRTING	CHLORIDES
CHIHUAHUA	CHIMER	CHINWAGS	CHIRTS	CHLORINE
CHIHUAHUAS	CHIMERA	CHIP	CHIS	CHLORINES
CHIK	CHIMERAS	CHIPBOARD	CHISEL	CHLORITE
CHIKARA	CHIMERE	CHIPBOARDS	CHISELLED	CHLORITES
CHIKARAS	CHIMERES	CHIPMUCK	CHISELLING	CHLORITIC
CHIKHOR	CHIMERIC	CHIPMUCKS	CHISELLINGS	CHLOROSES
CHIKHORS	CHIMERS	CHIPMUNK	CHISELS	CHLOROSIS
CHIKOR	CHIMES	CHIPMUNKS	CHIT	CHLOROTIC
CHIKORS	CHIMING	CHIPOCHIA	CHITAL	CHLOROUS
CHIKS	CHIMLEY	CHIPOCHIAS	CHITALS	CHOBDAR
CHILBLAIN	CHIMLEYED	CHIPOLATA	CHITCHAT	CHOBDARS
CHILBLAINS	CHIMLEYING	CHIPOLATAS	CHITCHATS	CHOC
CHILD	CHIMLEYS	CHIPPED	CHITCHATTED	CHOCHO
CHILDBED	CHIMNEY	CHIPPER	CHITCHATTING	CHOCHOS
CHILDBEDS	CHIMNEYED	CHIPPIE	CHITIN	CHOCK
CHILDE	CHIMNEYING	CHIPPIER	CHITINOUS	CHOCKED
CHILDED	CHIMNEYS	CHIPPIES	CHITINS	CHOCKER
CHILDER	CHIMP	CHIPPIEST	CHITLINGS	CHOCKING
CHILDHOOD	CHIMPS	CHIPPING	CHITON	CHOCKS
CHILDHOODS	CHIN	CHIPPINGS	CHITONS	CHOCOLATE
CHILDING	CHINA	CHIPPY	CHITS	CHOCOLATES
CHILDISH	CHINAMPA	CHIPS	CHITTED	CHOCS
CHILDLESS	CHINAMPAS	CHIRAGRA	CHITTER	CHOCTAW
CHILDLIKE	CHINAR	CHIRAGRAS	CHITTERED	CHOCTAWS
CHILDLY	CHINAROOT	CHIRAGRIC	CHITTERING	CHODE
CHILDNESS	CHINAROOTS	CHIRAL	CHITTERINGS	CHOENIX
CHILDNESSES	CHINARS	CHIRALITIES	CHITTERS	CHOENIXES
CHILDREN	CHINAS	CHIRALITY	CHITTIER	CHOICE
CHILDS	CHINCAPIN	CHIRIMOYA	CHITTIES	CHOICEFUL
CHILE	CHINCAPINS	CHIRIMOYAS	CHITTIEST	CHOICELY
CHILES	CHINCH	CHIRK	CHITTING	CHOICER
CHILI	CHINCHES	CHIRKED	CHITTY	CHOICES
CHILIAD	CHINCOUGH	CHIRKING	CHIV	CHOICEST
CHILIADS	CHINCOUGHS	CHIRKS	CHIVALRIC	CHOIR
CHILIAGON	CHINDIT	CHIRL	CHIVALRIES	CHOIRBOY
CHILIAGONS	CHINDITS	CHIRLED	CHIVALRY	CHOIRBOYS
CHILIARCH	CHINÉ	CHIRLING	CHIVE	CHOIRED
CHILIARCHS	CHINE	CHIRLS	CHIVED	CHOIRING
CHILIASM	CHINED	CHIRM	CHIVES	CHOIRMAN

CHOIRMEN	CHOOSERS	CHOROLOGY	CHROMITE	CHUMMAGE
CHOIRS	CHOOSES	CHORTLE	CHROMITES	CHUMMAGES
CHOKE	CHOOSEY	CHORTLED	CHROMIUM	CHUMMED
CHOKEBORE	CHOOSIER	CHORTLES	CHROMIUMS	CHUMMIER
CHOKEBORES	CHOOSIEST	CHORTLING	CHROMO	CHUMMIES
CHOKED	CHOOSING	CHORUS	CHROMOS	CHUMMIEST
CHOKEDAMP	CHOOSY	CHORUSED	CHRONIC	CHUMMING
CHOKEDAMPS	CHOP	CHORUSES	CHRONICAL	CHUMMY
CHOKER	CHOPIN	CHORUSING	CHRONICLE	CHUMP
CHOKERS	CHOPINE	CHOSE	CHRONICLED	CHUMPS
CHOKES	CHOPINES	CHOSEN	CHRONICLES	CHUMS
CHOKEY	CHOPINS	CHOSES	CHRONICLING	CHUNDER
CHOKEYS	CHOPPED	CHOU	CHRONICS	CHUNDERED
CHOKIDAR	CHOPPER	CHOUGH	CHRONON	CHUNDERING
CHOKIDARS	CHOPPERS	CHOUGHS	CHRONONS	CHUNDERS
CHOKIER	CHOPPIER	CHOULTRIES	CHRYSALID	CHUNK
CHOKIES	CHOPPIEST	CHOULTRY	CHRYSALIDES	CHUNKIER
CHOKIEST	CHOPPING	CHOUNTER	CHRYSALIDS	CHUNKIEST
CHOKING	CHOPPINGS	CHOUNTERED	CHRYSALIS	CHUNKS
CHOKY	CHOPPY	CHOUNTERING	CHRYSALISES	CHUNKY
CHOLAEMIA	CHOPS	CHOUNTERS	CHRYSANTH	CHUNNEL
CHOLAEMIAS	CHORAGI	CHOUSE	CHRYSANTHS	CHUNNELS
CHOLAEMIC	CHORAGIC	CHOUSED	CHTHONIAN	CHUNNER
CHOLECYST	CHORAGUS	CHOUSES	CHTHONIC	CHUNNERED
CHOLECYSTS	CHORAGUSES	CHOUSING	CHUB	CHUNNERING
CHOLELITH	CHORAL	CHOUT	CHUBBED	CHUNNERS
CHOLELITHS	CHORALE	CHOUTS	CHUBBIER	CHUNTER
CHOLER	CHORALES	CHOUX	CHUBBIEST	CHUNTERED
CHOLERA	CHORALLY	CHOW	CHUBBY	CHUNTERING
CHOLERAIC	CHORALS	CHOWDER	CHUBS	CHUNTERS
CHOLERAS	CHORD	CHOWDERS	CHUCK	CHUPATI
CHOLERIC	CHORDAL	CHOWKIDAR	CHUCKED	CHUPATIS
CHOLERS	CHORDATE	CHOWKIDARS	CHUCKIE	CHUPATTI
CHOLI	CHORDATES	CHOWRI	CHUCKIES	CHUPATTIS
CHOLIAMB	CHORDS	CHOWRIES	CHUCKING	CHUPRASSIES
CHOLIAMBS	CHORE	CHOWRIS	CHUCKLE	CHUPRASSY
CHOLIC	CHOREA	CHOWRY	CHUCKLED	CHURCH
CHOLINE	CHOREAS	CHOWS	CHUCKLES	CHURCHED
CHOLINES	CHOREE	CHRISM	CHUCKLING	CHURCHES
CHOLIS	CHOREES	CHRISMAL	CHUCKLINGS	CHURCHIER
CHOLTRIES	CHOREGI	CHRISMALS	CHUCKS	CHURCHIEST
CHOLTRY	CHOREGIC	CHRISMS	CHUDDAH	CHURCHING
CHOMP	CHOREGUS	CHRISOM	CHUDDAHS	CHURCHINGS
CHOMPED	CHOREGUSES	CHRISOMS	CHUDDAR	CHURCHISM
CHOMPING	CHORES	CHRISTEN	CHUDDARS	CHURCHISMS
CHOMPS	CHOREUS	CHRISTENED	CHUFA	CHURCHLY
CHONDRAL	CHOREUSES	CHRISTENING	CHUFAS	CHURCHMAN
CHONDRE	CHORIA	CHRISTENINGS	CHUFF	CHURCHMEN
CHONDRES	CHORIAMB	CHRISTENS	CHUFFED	CHURCHWAY
CHONDRI	CHORIAMBS	CHRISTIE	CHUFFIER	CHURCHWAYS
CHONDRIFIED	CHORIC	CHRISTIES	CHUFFIEST	CHURCHY
CHONDRIFIES	CHORINE	CHRISTOM	CHUFFS	CHURINGA
CHONDRIFY	CHORINES	CHRISTOMS	CHUFFY	CHURINGAS
CHONDRIFYING	CHORIOID	CHRISTY	CHUG	CHURL
CHONDRIN	CHORIOIDS	CHROMA	CHUGGED	CHURLISH
CHONDRINS	CHORION	CHROMAKEY	CHUGGING	CHURLS
CHONDRITE	CHORIONIC	CHROMAKEYS	CHUGS	CHURN
CHONDRITES	CHORISES	CHROMAS	CHUKAR	CHURNED
CHONDROID	CHORISIS	CHROMATE	CHUKARS	CHURNING
CHONDRULE	CHORIST	CHROMATES	CHUKKA	CHURNINGS
CHONDRULES	CHORISTER	CHROMATIC	CHUKKAS	CHURNS
CHONDRUS	CHORISTERS	CHROMATICS	CHUKKER	CHURR
CHOOK	CHORISTS	CHROMATIN	CHUKKERS	CHURRED
CHOOKIE	CHORIZO	CHROMATINS	CHUKOR	CHURRING
CHOOKIES	CHORIZONT	CHROME	CHUKORS	CHURRS
CHOOKS	CHORIZONTS	CHROMED	CHUM	CHURRUS
CHOOM	CHORIZOS	CHROMES	CHUMLEY	CHURRUSES
CHOOMS	CHOROID	CHROMIC	CHUMLEYED	CHUSE
CHOOSE	CHOROIDS	CHROMIDIA	CHUMLEYING	CHUSES
CHOOSER	CHOROLOGIES	CHROMING	CHUMLEYS	CHUSING

CHUT	CICLATON	CINCTURING	CIRCUITING	CITATIONS
CHUTE	CICLATONS	CINDER	CIRCUITRIES	CITATORY
CHUTES	CICLATOUN	CINDERS	CIRCUITRY	CITE
CHUTIST	CICLATOUNS	CINDERY	CIRCUITS	CITED
CHUTISTS	CICUTA	CINEAST	CIRCUITY	CITER
CHUTNEY	CICUTAS	CINEASTE	CIRCULAR	CITERS
CHUTNEYS	CIDARIS	CINÉASTE	CIRCULARS	CITES
CHUTZPAH	CIDARISES	CINEASTES	CIRCULATE	CITESS
CHUTZPAHS	CIDE	CINÉASTES	CIRCULATED	CITESSES
CHYACK	CIDED	CINEASTS	CIRCULATES	CITHARA
CHYACKED	CIDER	CINEMA	CIRCULATING	CITHARAS
CHYACKING	CIDERKIN	CINEMAS	CIRCULATINGS	CITHARIST
CHYACKS	CIDERKINS	CINEMATIC	CIRCUS	CITHARISTS
CHYLDE	CIDERS	CINEOL	CIRCUSES	CITHER
CHYLE	CIDERY	CINEOLE	CIRCUSSY	CITHERN
CHYLES	CIDES	CINEOLES	CIRCUSY	CITHERNS
CHYLURIA	CIDING	CINEOLS	CIRÉ	CITHERS
CHYLURIAS	CIEL	CINERAMIC	CIRÉS	CITIES
CHYME	CIELED	CINERARIA	CIRL	CITIFIED
CHYMES	CIELING	CINERARIAS	CIRLS	CITIFIES
CHYMIFIED	CIELINGS	CINERARY	CIRQUE	CITIFY
CHYMIFIES	CIELS	CINERATOR	CIRQUES	CITIFYING
CHYMIFY	CIERGE	CINERATORS	CIRRATE	CITIGRADE
CHYMIFYING	CIERGES	CINEREA	CIRRHOPOD	CITING
CHYMISTRIES	CIG	CINEREAL	CIRRHOPODS	CITIZEN
CHYMISTRY	CIGAR	CINEREAS	CIRRHOSES	CITIZENRIES
CHYMOUS	CIGARETTE	CINEREOUS	CIRRHOSIS	CITIZENRY
CHYND	CIGARETTES	CINGULUM	CIRRHOTIC	CITIZENS
CHYPRE	CIGARILLO	CINGULUMS	CIRRI	CITO
CHYPRES	CIGARILLOS	CINNABAR	CIRRIFORM	CITOLE
CIAO	CIGARS	CINNABARS	CIRRIPED	CITOLES
CIAOS	CIGGIE	CINNAMIC	CIRRIPEDE	CITRANGE
CIBATION	CIGGIES	CINNAMON	CIRRIPEDES	CITRANGES
CIBATIONS	CIGGY	CINNAMONS	CIRRIPEDS	CITRATE
CIBOL	CIGS	CINQUAIN	CIRROSE	CITRATES
CIBOLS	CILIA	CINQUAINS	CIRROUS	CITREOUS
CIBORIA	CILIARY	CINQUE	CIRRUS	CITRIC
CIBORIUM	CILIATE	CINQUES	CISCO	CITRIN
CICADA	CILIATED	CION	CISCOES	CITRINE
CICADAS	CILICE	CIONS	CISCOS	CITRINES
CICALA	CILICES	CIPHER	CISELEUR	CITRINS
CICALAS	CILICIOUS	CIPHERED	CISELEURS	CITRON
CICATRICE	CILIOLATE	CIPHERING	CISELURE	CITRONS
CICATRICES	CILIUM	CIPHERINGS	CISELURES	CITROUS
CICATRISE	CILL	CIPHERS	CISLUNAR	CITRUS
CICATRISED	CILLS	CIPOLIN	CISSIER	CITRUSES
CICATRISES	CIMAR	CIPOLINS	CISSIES	CITS
CICATRISING	CIMARS	CIPOLLINO	CISSIEST	CITTERN
CICATRIX	CIMELIA	CIPOLLINOS	CISSOID	CITTERNS
CICATRIXES	CIMEX	CIPPI	CISSOIDS	CITY
CICATRIZE	CIMICES	CIPPUS	CISSY	CITYSCAPE
CICATRIZED	CIMIER	CIRCA	CIST	CITYSCAPES
CICATRIZES	CIMIERS	CIRCADIAN	CISTED	CIVE
CICATRIZING	CIMINITE	CIRCAR	CISTERN	CIVES
CICELIES	CIMINITES	CIRCARS	CISTERNS	CIVET
CICELY	CIMOLITE	CIRCINATE	CISTIC	CIVETS
CICERO	CIMOLITES	CIRCITER	CISTRON	CIVIC
CICERONE	CINCH	CIRCLE	CISTRONS	CIVICALLY
CICERONED	CINCHED	CIRCLED	CISTS	CIVICS
CICERONES	CINCHES	CIRCLER	CISTUS	CIVIL
CICERONI	CINCHING	CIRCLERS	CISTUSES	CIVILIAN
CICERONING	CINCHONA	CIRCLES	CISTVAEN	CIVILIANS
CICEROS	CINCHONAS	CIRCLET	CISTVAENS	CIVILISE
CICHLID	CINCHONIC	CIRCLETS	CIT	CIVILISED
CICHLIDS	CINCINNUS	CIRCLING	CITABLE	CIVILISER
CICHLOID	CINCINNUSES	CIRCLINGS	CITADEL	CIVILISERS
CICINNUS	CINCT	CIRCS	CITADELS	CIVILISES
CICINNUSES	CINCTURE	CIRCUIT	CITAL	CIVILISING
CICISBEI	CINCTURED	CIRCUITED	CITALS	CIVILIST
CICISBEO	CINCTURES	CIRCUITIES	CITATION	CIVILISTS

CIVILITIES
CIVILITY
CIVILIZE
CIVILIZED
CIVILIZER
CIVILIZERS
CIVILIZES
CIVILIZING
CIVILLER
CIVILLEST
CIVILLY
CIVISM
CIVISMS
CIVVIES
CIVVY
CIZERS
CLABBER
CLABBERS
CLACHAN
CLACHANS
CLACK
CLACKBOX
CLACKBOXES
CLACKDISH
CLACKDISHES
CLACKED
CLACKER
CLACKERS
CLACKING
CLACKS
CLAD
CLADDED
CLADDING
CLADDINGS
CLADE
CLADES
CLADISM
CLADISMS
CLADIST
CLADISTIC
CLADISTICS
CLADISTS
CLADODE
CLADODES
CLADOGRAM
CLADOGRAMS
CLADS
CLAES
CLAG
CLAGGED
CLAGGING
CLAGGY
CLAGS
CLAIM
CLAIMABLE
CLAIMANT
CLAIMANTS
CLAIMED
CLAIMER
CLAIMERS
CLAIMING
CLAIMS
CLAM
CLAMANCIES
CLAMANCY
CLAMANT
CLAMANTLY
CLAMBAKE
CLAMBAKES
CLAMBE

CLAMBER
CLAMBERED
CLAMBERING
CLAMBERS
CLAME
CLAMED
CLAMES
CLAMING
CLAMMED
CLAMMIER
CLAMMIEST
CLAMMILY
CLAMMING
CLAMMY
CLAMOR
CLAMORED
CLAMORING
CLAMOROUS
CLAMORS
CLAMOUR
CLAMOURED
CLAMOURER
CLAMOURERS
CLAMOURING
CLAMOURS
CLAMP
CLAMPDOWN
CLAMPDOWNS
CLAMPED
CLAMPER
CLAMPERED
CLAMPERING
CLAMPERS
CLAMPING
CLAMPS
CLAMS
CLAN
CLANG
CLANGED
CLANGER
CLANGERS
CLANGING
CLANGINGS
CLANGOR
CLANGORED
CLANGORING
CLANGORS
CLANGOUR
CLANGOURED
CLANGOURING
CLANGOURS
CLANGS
CLANK
CLANKED
CLANKING
CLANKINGS
CLANKLESS
CLANKS
CLANNISH
CLANS
CLANSHIP
CLANSHIPS
CLANSMAN
CLANSMEN
CLAP
CLAPBOARD
CLAPBOARDS
CLAPBREAD
CLAPBREADS
CLAPDISH

CLAPDISHES
CLAPNET
CLAPNETS
CLAPPED
CLAPPER
CLAPPERED
CLAPPERING
CLAPPERINGS
CLAPPERS
CLAPPING
CLAPPINGS
CLAPS
CLAPTRAP
CLAPTRAPS
CLAQUE
CLAQUES
CLAQUEUR
CLAQUEURS
CLARENCE
CLARENCES
CLARENDON
CLARENDONS
CLARET
CLARETED
CLARETING
CLARETS
CLARIES
CLARIFIED
CLARIFIER
CLARIFIERS
CLARIFIES
CLARIFY
CLARIFYING
CLARINET
CLARINETS
CLARINI
CLARINO
CLARINOS
CLARION
CLARIONET
CLARIONETS
CLARIONS
CLARITIES
CLARITY
CLARKIA
CLARKIAS
CLARSACH
CLARSACHS
CLART
CLARTED
CLARTIER
CLARTIEST
CLARTING
CLARTS
CLARTY
CLARY
CLASH
CLASHED
CLASHES
CLASHING
CLASHINGS
CLASP
CLASPED
CLASPER
CLASPERS
CLASPING
CLASPINGS
CLASPS
CLASS
CLASSABLE

CLASSED
CLASSES
CLASSIBLE
CLASSIC
CLASSICAL
CLASSICS
CLASSIER
CLASSIEST
CLASSIFIC
CLASSIFIED
CLASSIFIES
CLASSIFY
CLASSIFYING
CLASSING
CLASSIS
CLASSLESS
CLASSMAN
CLASSMATE
CLASSMATES
CLASSMEN
CLASSROOM
CLASSROOMS
CLASSY
CLASTIC
CLAT
CLATCH
CLATCHED
CLATCHES
CLATCHING
CLATHRATE
CLATS
CLATTED
CLATTER
CLATTERED
CLATTERER
CLATTERERS
CLATTERING
CLATTERS
CLATTING
CLAUCHT
CLAUCHTED
CLAUCHTING
CLAUGHT
CLAUGHTED
CLAUGHTING
CLAUGHTS
CLAUSAL
CLAUSE
CLAUSES
CLAUSTRA
CLAUSTRAL
CLAUSTRUM
CLAUSULA
CLAUSULAE
CLAUSULAR
CLAUT
CLAUTED
CLAUTING
CLAUTS
CLAVATE
CLAVATED
CLAVATION
CLAVATIONS
CLAVE
CLAVECIN
CLAVECINS
CLAVER
CLAVERED
CLAVERING

CLAVERS
CLAVES
CLAVICLE
CLAVICLES
CLAVICORN
CLAVICORNS
CLAVICULA
CLAVICULAS
CLAVIE
CLAVIER
CLAVIERS
CLAVIES
CLAVIFORM
CLAVIGER
CLAVIGERS
CLAVIS
CLAVULATE
CLAW
CLAWBACK
CLAWBACKS
CLAWED
CLAWING
CLAWLESS
CLAWS
CLAY
CLAYED
CLAYEY
CLAYIER
CLAYIEST
CLAYING
CLAYISH
CLAYMORE
CLAYMORES
CLAYS
CLEAN
CLEANED
CLEANER
CLEANERS
CLEANEST
CLEANING
CLEANINGS
CLEANLIER
CLEANLIEST
CLEANLY
CLEANNESS
CLEANNESSES
CLEANS
CLEANSE
CLEANSED
CLEANSER
CLEANSERS
CLEANSES
CLEANSING
CLEANSINGS
CLEAR
CLEARAGE
CLEARAGES
CLEARANCE
CLEARANCES
CLEARCOLE
CLEARCOLES
CLEARED
CLEARER
CLEARERS
CLEAREST
CLEARING
CLEARINGS
CLEARLY
CLEARNESS
CLEARNESSES

CLEARS
CLEARWAY
CLEARWAYS
CLEARWING
CLEARWINGS
CLEAT
CLEATED
CLEATING
CLEATS
CLEAVABLE
CLEAVAGE
CLEAVAGES
CLEAVE
CLEAVED
CLEAVER
CLEAVERS
CLEAVES
CLEAVING
CLEAVINGS
CLECHÉ
CLECK
CLECKED
CLECKING
CLECKINGS
CLECKS
CLEEK
CLEEKED
CLEEKING
CLEEKIT
CLEEKS
CLEEP
CLEEPING
CLEEPS
CLEEVE
CLEEVES
CLEF
CLEFS
CLEFT
CLEFTS
CLEG
CLEGS
CLEITHRAL
CLEM
CLEMATIS
CLEMATISES
CLEMENCE
CLEMENCES
CLEMENCIES
CLEMENCY
CLEMENT
CLEMENTLY
CLEMMED
CLEMMING
CLEMS
CLENCH
CLENCHED
CLENCHES
CLENCHING
CLEPE
CLEPES
CLEPING
CLEPSYDRA
CLEPSYDRAS
CLERECOLE
CLERECOLES
CLERGIES
CLERGY
CLERGYMAN
CLERGYMEN
CLERIC

CLERICAL
CLERICALS
CLERICATE
CLERICATES
CLERICITIES
CLERICITY
CLERICS
CLERIHEW
CLERIHEWS
CLERISIES
CLERISY
CLERK
CLERKDOM
CLERKDOMS
CLERKED
CLERKESS
CLERKESSES
CLERKING
CLERKISH
CLERKLESS
CLERKLIER
CLERKLIEST
CLERKLING
CLERKLINGS
CLERKLY
CLERKS
CLERKSHIP
CLERKSHIPS
CLERUCH
CLERUCHIA
CLERUCHIAS
CLERUCHIES
CLERUCHS
CLERUCHY
CLEUCH
CLEUCHS
CLEUGH
CLEUGHS
CLEVE
CLEVEITE
CLEVEITES
CLEVER
CLEVERER
CLEVEREST
CLEVERISH
CLEVERLY
CLEVES
CLEVIS
CLEVISES
CLEW
CLEWED
CLEWING
CLEWS
CLIANTHUS
CLIANTHUSES
CLICHÉ
CLICHÉD
CLICHÉS
CLICK
CLICKED
CLICKER
CLICKERS
CLICKET
CLICKETED
CLICKETING
CLICKETS
CLICKING
CLICKINGS
CLICKS
CLIED

CLIENT
CLIENTAGE
CLIENTAGES
CLIENTAL
CLIENTÈLE
CLIENTÈLES
CLIENTS
CLIES
CLIFF
CLIFFED
CLIFFHANG
CLIFFHANGING
CLIFFHANGS
CLIFFHUNG
CLIFFIER
CLIFFIEST
CLIFFS
CLIFFY
CLIFT
CLIFTED
CLIFTS
CLIFTY
CLIMACTIC
CLIMATAL
CLIMATE
CLIMATED
CLIMATES
CLIMATIC
CLIMATING
CLIMATISE
CLIMATISED
CLIMATISES
CLIMATISING
CLIMATIZE
CLIMATIZED
CLIMATIZES
CLIMATIZING
CLIMATURE
CLIMATURES
CLIMAX
CLIMAXED
CLIMAXES
CLIMAXING
CLIMB
CLIMBABLE
CLIMBED
CLIMBER
CLIMBERS
CLIMBING
CLIMBINGS
CLIMBS
CLIME
CLIMES
CLINAMEN
CLINAMENS
CLINCH
CLINCHED
CLINCHER
CLINCHERS
CLINCHES
CLINCHING
CLINE
CLINES
CLING
CLINGER
CLINGERS
CLINGIER
CLINGIEST
CLINGING
CLINGS

CLINGY
CLINIC
CLINICAL
CLINICIAN
CLINICIANS
CLINICS
CLINIQUE
CLINIQUES
CLINK
CLINKED
CLINKER
CLINKERS
CLINKING
CLINKS
CLINOAXES
CLINOAXIS
CLINQUANT
CLINQUANTS
CLINT
CLINTS
CLIP
CLIPBOARD
CLIPBOARDS
CLIPE
CLIPED
CLIPES
CLIPING
CLIPPED
CLIPPER
CLIPPERS
CLIPPIE
CLIPPIES
CLIPPING
CLIPPINGS
CLIPS
CLIPT
CLIQUE
CLIQUES
CLIQUEY
CLIQUIER
CLIQUIEST
CLIQUISH
CLIQUISM
CLIQUISMS
CLIQUY
CLITELLA
CLITELLAR
CLITELLUM
CLITHRAL
CLITIC
CLITICS
CLITORAL
CLITORIS
CLITORISES
CLITTER
CLITTERED
CLITTERING
CLITTERS
CLIVERS
CLOACA
CLOACAE
CLOACAL
CLOACALIN
CLOACINAL
CLOAK
CLOAKED
CLOAKING
CLOAKROOM
CLOAKROOMS
CLOAKS

CLOAM
CLOAMS
CLOBBER
CLOBBERED
CLOBBERING
CLOBBERS
CLOCHARD
CLOCHARDS
CLOCHE
CLOCHES
CLOCK
CLOCKED
CLOCKER
CLOCKERS
CLOCKING
CLOCKS
CLOCKWISE
CLOCKWORK
CLOCKWORKS
CLOD
CLODDED
CLODDIER
CLODDIEST
CLODDING
CLODDISH
CLODDY
CLODLY
CLODPATE
CLODPATED
CLODPATES
CLODPOLE
CLODPOLES
CLODPOLL
CLODPOLLS
CLODS
CLOFF
CLOFFS
CLOG
CLOGDANCE
CLOGDANCES
CLOGGED
CLOGGER
CLOGGERS
CLOGGIER
CLOGGIEST
CLOGGING
CLOGGY
CLOGS
CLOISON
CLOISONNÉ
CLOISONNÉS
CLOISONS
CLOISTER
CLOISTERED
CLOISTERING
CLOISTERS
CLOISTRAL
CLOKE
CLOKED
CLOKES
CLOKING
CLOMB
CLONAL
CLONE
CLONED
CLONES
CLONIC
CLONING
CLONK
CLONKED

CLONKING
CLONKS
CLONUS
CLONUSES
CLOOP
CLOOPS
CLOOT
CLOOTS
CLOP
CLOPPED
CLOPPING
CLOPS
CLOQUÉ
CLOQUÉS
CLOSE
CLOSED
CLOSELY
CLOSENESS
CLOSENESSES
CLOSER
CLOSERS
CLOSES
CLOSEST
CLOSET
CLOSETED
CLOSETING
CLOSETS
CLOSING
CLOSINGS
CLOSURE
CLOSURED
CLOSURES
CLOSURING
CLOT
CLOTBUR
CLOTBURS
CLOTE
CLOTEBUR
CLOTEBURS
CLOTES
CLOTH
CLOTHE
CLOTHED
CLOTHES
CLOTHIER
CLOTHIERS
CLOTHING
CLOTHINGS
CLOTHS
CLOTPOLL
CLOTPOLLS
CLOTS
CLOTTED
CLOTTER
CLOTTERED
CLOTTERING
CLOTTERS
CLOTTIER
CLOTTIEST
CLOTTING
CLOTTINGS
CLOTTY
CLOTURE
CLOTURED
CLOTURES
CLOTURING
CLOU
CLOUD
CLOUDAGE
CLOUDAGES

CLOUDED
CLOUDIER
CLOUDIEST
CLOUDILY
CLOUDING
CLOUDINGS
CLOUDLAND
CLOUDLANDS
CLOUDLESS
CLOUDLET
CLOUDLETS
CLOUDS
CLOUDY
CLOUGH
CLOUGHS
CLOUR
CLOURED
CLOURING
CLOURS
CLOUS
CLOUT
CLOUTED
CLOUTERLY
CLOUTING
CLOUTS
CLOVE
CLOVEN
CLOVER
CLOVERED
CLOVERS
CLOVERY
CLOVES
CLOW
CLOWDER
CLOWDERS
CLOWN
CLOWNED
CLOWNERIES
CLOWNERY
CLOWNING
CLOWNINGS
CLOWNISH
CLOWNO
CLOWNSHIP
CLOWNSHIPS
CLOWS
CLOY
CLOYE
CLOYED
CLOYES
CLOYING
CLOYLESS
CLOYMENT
CLOYMENTS
CLOYS
CLOYSOME
CLOZE
CLUB
CLUBABLE
CLUBBABLE
CLUBBED
CLUBBING
CLUBBINGS
CLUBBISH
CLUBBISM
CLUBBISMS
CLUBBIST
CLUBBISTS
CLUBHOUSE
CLUBHOUSES

CLUBLAND
CLUBLANDS
CLUBMAN
CLUBMEN
CLUBROOM
CLUBROOMS
CLUBROOT
CLUBROOTS
CLUBS
CLUBWOMAN
CLUBWOMEN
CLUCK
CLUCKED
CLUCKING
CLUCKS
CLUCKY
CLUDGIE
CLUDGIES
CLUE
CLUED
CLUEING
CLUELESS
CLUES
CLUMBER
CLUMBERS
CLUMP
CLUMPED
CLUMPIER
CLUMPIEST
CLUMPING
CLUMPS
CLUMPY
CLUMSIER
CLUMSIEST
CLUMSILY
CLUMSY
CLUNCH
CLUNCHES
CLUNG
CLUNK
CLUNKED
CLUNKING
CLUNKO
CLUPEID
CLUPEIDS
CLUPEOID
CLUPEOIDS
CLUSIA
CLUSIAS
CLUSTER
CLUSTERED
CLUSTERING
CLUSTERS
CLUSTERY
CLUTCH
CLUTCHED
CLUTCHES
CLUTCHING
CLUTTER
CLUTTERED
CLUTTERING
CLUTTERS
CLY
CLYING
CLYPE
CLYPEAL
CLYPEATE
CLYPED
CLYPEI
CLYPES

CLYPEUS
CLYPING
CLYSTER
CLYSTERS
CNIDA
CNIDAE
CNIDARIA
COACH
COACHDOG
COACHDOGS
COACHED
COACHEE
COACHEES
COACHER
COACHERS
COACHES
COACHIES
COACHING
COACHINGS
COACHMAN
COACHMEN
COACHWHIP
COACHWHIPS
COACHWORK
COACHWORKS
COACTLY
COACT
COACTED
COACTING
COACTION
COACTIONS
COACTIVE
COACTS
COADJUTOR
COADJUTORS
COADUNATE
COADUNATED
COADUNATES
COADUNATING
COAGULANT
COAGULANTS
COAGULATE
COAGULATED
COAGULATES
COAGULATING
COAGULUM
COAGULUMS
COAITA
COAITAS
COAL
COALBALL
COALBALLS
COALED
COALER
COALERS
COALESCE
COALESCED
COALESCES
COALESCING
COALFIELD
COALFIELDS
COALFISH
COALFISHES
COALIER
COALIEST
COALING
COALISE
COALISED
COALISES
COALISING

COALITION
COALITIONS
COALIZE
COALIZED
COALIZES
COALIZING
COALMAN
COALMEN
COALS
COALY
COAMING
COAMINGS
COAPT
COAPTED
COAPTING
COAPTS
COARB
COARBS
COARCTATE
COARSE
COARSELY
COARSEN
COARSENED
COARSENING
COARSENS
COARSER
COARSEST
COARSISH
COAST
COASTAL
COASTED
COASTER
COASTERS
COASTING
COASTINGS
COASTLINE
COASTLINES
COASTS
COASTWARD
COASTWARDS
COASTWISE
COAT
COATE
COATED
COATEE
COATEES
COATER
COATERS
COATES
COATI
COATING
COATINGS
COATIS
COATLESS
COATRACK
COATRACKS
COATS
COATSTAND
COATSTANDS
COAX
COAXED
COAXER
COAXERS
COAXES
COAXIAL
COAXIALLY
COAXING
COAXINGLY
COB
COBALT

COBALTIC
COBALTITE
COBALTITES
COBALTS
COBB
COBBED
COBBER
COBBERS
COBBIER
COBBIEST
COBBING
COBBLE
COBBLED
COBBLER
COBBLERIES
COBBLERS
COBBLERY
COBBLES
COBBLING
COBBLINGS
COBBS
COBBY
COBIA
COBIAS
COBLE
COBLES
COBLOAF
COBLOAVES
COBNUT
COBNUTS
COBRA
COBRAS
COBRIC
COBRIFORM
COBS
COBURG
COBURGS
COBWEB
COBWEBBED
COBWEBBIER
COBWEBBIEST
COBWEBBING
COBWEBBY
COBWEBS
COCA
COCAINE
COCAINES
COCAINISE
COCAINISED
COCAINISES
COCAINISING
COCAINISM
COCAINISMS
COCAINIST
COCAINISTS
COCAINIZE
COCAINIZED
COCAINIZES
COCAINIZING
COCAS
COCCAL
COCCI
COCCID
COCCIDIA
COCCIDIUM
COCCIDS
COCCO
COCCOID
COCCOLITE
COCCOLITES

COCCOLITH
COCCOLITHS
COCCOS
COCCUS
COCCYGEAL
COCCYGES
COCCYGIAN
COCCYX
COCH
COCHES
COCHINEAL
COCHINEALS
COCHLEA
COCHLEAE
COCHLEAR
COCHLEARE
COCHLEARES
COCHLEARS
COCHLEAS
COCHLEATE
COCK
COCKADE
COCKADES
COCKATEEL
COCKATEELS
COCKATIEL
COCKATIELS
COCKATOO
COCKATOOS
COCKBIRD
COCKBIRDS
COCKBOAT
COCKBOATS
COCKED
COCKER
COCKERED
COCKEREL
COCKERELS
COCKERING
COCKERS
COCKET
COCKETS
COCKEYE
COCKEYED
COCKEYES
COCKFIGHT
COCKFIGHTS
COCKHORSE
COCKHORSES
COCKIER
COCKIES
COCKIEST
COCKILY
COCKINESS
COCKINESSES
COCKING
COCKLAIRD
COCKLAIRDS
COCKLE
COCKLED
COCKLES
COCKLING
COCKLOFT
COCKLOFTS
COCKMATCH
COCKMATCHES
COCKNEY
COCKNEYFIED
COCKNEYFIES
COCKNEYFY

COCKNEYFYING
COCKNEYS
COCKPIT
COCKPITS
COCKROACH
COCKROACHES
COCKS
COCKSCOMB
COCKSCOMBS
COCKSFOOT
COCKSFOOTS
COCKSHIES
COCKSHOOT
COCKSHOOTS
COCKSHOT
COCKSHOTS
COCKSHUT
COCKSHUTS
COCKSHY
COCKSIER
COCKSIEST
COCKSPUR
COCKSPURS
COCKSURE
COCKSWAIN
COCKSWAINED
COCKSWAINING
COCKSWAINS
COCKSY
COCKTAIL
COCKTAILS
COCKY
COCKYOLLIES
COCKYOLLY
COCO
COCOA
COCOANUT
COCOANUTS
COCOAS
COCONUT
COCONUTS
COCOON
COCOONED
COCOONERIES
COCOONERY
COCOONING
COCOONS
COCOPLUM
COCOPLUMS
COCOS
COCOTTE
COCOTTES
COCTILE
COCTION
COCTIONS
COD
CODA
CODAS
CODDED
CODDING
CODDLE
CODDLED
CODDLES
CODDLING
CODE
CODED
CODEINE
CODEINES
CODES
CODEX

CODFISH
CODFISHES
CODGER
CODGERS
CODICES
CODICIL
CODICILS
CODIFIED
CODIFIER
CODIFIERS
CODIFIES
CODIFY
CODIFYING
CODILLA
CODILLAS
CODILLE
CODILLES
CODING
CODINGS
CODIST
CODISTS
CODLIN
CODLING
CODLINGS
CODLINS
CODON
CODONS
CODS
COED
COEDS
COEHORN
COEHORNS
COELIAC
COELOM
COELOMATE
COELOMATES
COELOME
COELOMES
COELOMIC
COELOMS
COELOSTAT
COELOSTATS
COEMPTION
COEMPTIONS
COENOBIA
COENOBITE
COENOBITES
COENOBIUM
COENOSARC
COENOSARCS
COENZYME
COENZYMES
COEQUAL
COEQUALLY
COEQUALS
COERCE
COERCED
COERCES
COERCIBLE
COERCIBLY
COERCING
COERCION
COERCIONS
COERCIVE
COEVAL
COEVALS
COFF
COFFEE
COFFEES
COFFER

COFFERED
COFFERING
COFFERS
COFFIN
COFFINED
COFFING
COFFINING
COFFINITE
COFFINITES
COFFINS
COFFLE
COFFLES
COFFRET
COFFRETS
COFFS
COFT
COG
COGENCE
COGENCES
COGENCIES
COGENCY
COGENER
COGENERS
COGENT
COGENTER
COGENTEST
COGENTLY
COGGED
COGGER
COGGERS
COGGIE
COGGIES
COGGING
COGGLE
COGGLED
COGGLES
COGGLIER
COGGLIEST
COGGLING
COGGLY
COGIE
COGIES
COGITABLE
COGITATE
COGITATED
COGITATES
COGITATING
COGNATE
COGNATES
COGNATION
COGNATIONS
COGNISANT
COGNISE
COGNISED
COGNISES
COGNISING
COGNITION
COGNITIONS
COGNITIVE
COGNIZANT
COGNIZE
COGNIZED
COGNIZES
COGNIZING
COGNOMEN
COGNOMENS
COGNOMINA
COGNOSCE
COGNOSCED
COGNOSCES

COGNOSCING	COINCIDE	COLIC	COLLIERIES	COLONIAL
COGNOVIT	COINCIDED	COLICKY	COLLIERS	COLONIALS
COGNOVITS	COINCIDES	COLICS	COLLIERY	COLONIC
COGS	COINCIDING	COLIFORM	COLLIES	COLONICS
COGUE	COINED	COLIFORMS	COLLIGATE	COLONIES
COGUES	COINER	COLIN	COLLIGATED	COLONISE
COHABIT	COINERS	COLINS	COLLIGATES	COLONISED
COHABITED	COINING	COLISEUM	COLLIGATING	COLONISES
COHABITEE	COININGS	COLISEUMS	COLLIMATE	COLONISING
COHABITEES	COINS	COLITIS	COLLIMATED	COLONIST
COHABITING	COIR	COLITISES	COLLIMATES	COLONISTS
COHABITS	COIRS	COLL	COLLIMATING	COLONIZE
COHERE	COISTREL	COLLAGE	COLLINEAR	COLONIZED
COHERED	COISTRELS	COLLAGEN	COLLING	COLONIZES
COHERENCE	COISTRIL	COLLAGENS	COLLINGS	COLONIZING
COHERENCES	COISTRILS	COLLAGES	COLLISION	COLONNADE
COHERENCIES	COITAL	COLLAGIST	COLLISIONS	COLONNADES
COHERENCY	COITION	COLLAGISTS	COLLOCATE	COLONS
COHERENT	COITIONS	COLLAPSE	COLLOCATED	COLONY
COHERER	COITUS	COLLAPSED	COLLOCATES	COLOPHON
COHERERS	COITUSES	COLLAPSES	COLLOCATING	COLOPHONIES
COHERES	COJOIN	COLLAPSING	COLLODION	COLOPHONS
COHERING	COJOINED	COLLAR	COLLODIONS	COLOPHONY
COHERITOR	COJOINING	COLLARD	COLLOGUE	COLOR
COHERITORS	COJOINS	COLLARDS	COLLOGUED	COLORANT
COHESIBLE	COKE	COLLARED	COLLOGUES	COLORANTS
COHESION	COKED	COLLARING	COLLOGUING	COLORED
COHESIONS	COKERNUT	COLLARS	COLLOID	COLORIFIC
COHESIVE	COKERNUTS	COLLATE	COLLOIDAL	COLORING
COHIBIT	COKES	COLLATED	COLLOIDS	COLORS
COHIBITED	COKIER	COLLATES	COLLOP	COLOSSAL
COHIBITING	COKIEST	COLLATING	COLLOPS	COLOSSEUM
COHIBITS	COKING	COLLATION	COLLOQUE	COLOSSEUMS
COHO	COKY	COLLATIONS	COLLOQUED	COLOSSI
COHOE	COL	COLLATIVE	COLLOQUES	COLOSSUS
COHOES	COLA	COLLATOR	COLLOQUIA	COLOSSUSES
COHOG	COLANDER	COLLATORS	COLLOQUIED	COLOSTOMIES
COHOGS	COLANDERS	COLLEAGUE	COLLOQUIES	COLOSTOMY
COHORN	COLAS	COLLEAGUED	COLLOQUING	COLOSTRIC
COHORNS	COLATION	COLLEAGUES	COLLOQUY	COLOSTRUM
COHORT	COLATIONS	COLLEAGUING	COLLOQUYING	COLOSTRUMS
COHORTS	COLATURE	COLLECT	COLLOTYPE	COLOTOMIES
COHOS	COLATURES	COLLECTED	COLLOTYPES	COLOTOMY
COHUNE	COLCANNON	COLLECTING	COLLS	COLOUR
COHUNES	COLCANNONS	COLLECTINGS	COLLUDE	COLOURANT
COIF	COLCHICA	COLLECTOR	COLLUDED	COLOURANTS
COIFED	COLCHICUM	COLLECTORS	COLLUDER	COLOURED
COIFFEUR	COLCHICUMS	COLLECTS	COLLUDERS	COLOUREDS
COIFFEURS	COLCOTHAR	COLLED	COLLUDES	COLOURFUL
COIFFEUSE	COLCOTHARS	COLLEEN	COLLUDING	COLOURING
COIFFEUSES	COLD	COLLEENS	COLLUSION	COLOURINGS
COIFFURE	COLDBLOOD	COLLEGE	COLLUSIONS	COLOURIST
COIFFURED	COLDBLOODS	COLLEGER	COLLUSIVE	COLOURISTS
COIFFURES	COLDER	COLLEGERS	COLLUVIES	COLOURMAN
COIFFURING	COLDEST	COLLEGES	COLLY	COLOURMEN
COIFING	COLDHOUSE	COLLEGIA	COLLYING	COLOURS
COIFS	COLDHOUSES	COLLEGIAL	COLLYRIA	COLOURY
COIGN	COLDISH	COLLEGIAN	COLLYRIUM	COLS
COIGNE	COLDLY	COLLEGIANS	COLLYRIUMS	COLT
COIGNED	COLDNESS	COLLEGIUM	COLOBI	COLTED
COIGNES	COLDNESSES	COLLEGIUMS	COLOBUS	COLTER
COIGNING	COLDS	COLLET	COLOBUSES	COLTERS
COIGNS	COLE	COLLETS	COLOCYNTH	COLTING
COIL	COLES	COLLIDE	COLOCYNTHS	COLTISH
COILED	COLEUS	COLLIDED	COLON	COLTS
COILING	COLEUSES	COLLIDES	COLONEL	COLTSFOOT
COILS	COLEY	COLLIDING	COLONELCIES	COLTSFOOTS
COIN	COLEYS	COLLIE	COLONELCY	COLTWOOD
COINAGE	COLIBRI	COLLIED	COLONELS	COLTWOODS
COINAGES	COLIBRIS	COLLIER	COLONES	COLUBER

COLUBERS	COMBRETUM	COMMANDS	COMMON	COMPACTORS
COLUBRIAD	COMBRETUMS	COMMAS	COMMONAGE	COMPACTS
COLUBRIADS	COMBS	COMMENCE	COMMONAGES	COMPAGE
COLUBRINE	COMBUST	COMMENCED	COMMONED	COMPAGES
COLUGO	COMBUSTED	COMMENCES	COMMONER	COMPANDER
COLUGOS	COMBUSTING	COMMENCING	COMMONERS	COMPANDERS
COLUMBARIES	COMBUSTS	COMMEND	COMMONEST	COMPANDOR
COLUMBARY	COMBWISE	COMMENDAM	COMMONEY	COMPANDORS
COLUMBATE	COMBY	COMMENDAMS	COMMONEYS	COMPANIED
COLUMBATES	COME	COMMENDED	COMMONING	COMPANIES
COLUMBIC	COMEDIAN	COMMENDING	COMMONLY	COMPANING
COLUMBINE	COMEDIANS	COMMENDS	COMMONS	COMPANION
COLUMBINES	COMEDIC	COMMENSAL	COMMORANT	COMPANIONED
COLUMBITE	COMEDIES	COMMENSALS	COMMORANTS	COMPANIONING
COLUMBITES	COMEDO	COMMENT	COMMOS	COMPANIONS
COLUMBIUM	COMEDOS	COMMENTED	COMMOT	COMPANY
COLUMBIUMS	COMEDOWN	COMMENTER	COMMOTE	COMPANYING
COLUMEL	COMEDOWNS	COMMENTERS	COMMOTES	COMPARE
COLUMELLA	COMEDY	COMMENTING	COMMOTION	COMPARED
COLUMELLAE	COMELIER	COMMENTOR	COMMOTIONS	COMPARES
COLUMELS	COMELIEST	COMMENTORS	COMMOTS	COMPARING
COLUMN	COMELY	COMMENTS	COMMOVE	COMPART
COLUMNAL	COMER	COMMER	COMMOVED	COMPARTED
COLUMNAR	COMERS	COMMERCE	COMMOVES	COMPARTING
COLUMNED	COMES	COMMERCED	COMMOVING	COMPARTS
COLUMNIST	COMET	COMMERCES	COMMUNAL	COMPASS
COLUMNISTS	COMETARY	COMMERCING	COMMUNARD	COMPASSED
COLUMNS	COMETHER	COMMÈRE	COMMUNARDS	COMPASSES
COLURE	COMETHERS	COMMÈRES	COMMUNE	COMPASSING
COLURES	COMETIC	COMMERGE	COMMUNED	COMPASSINGS
COLZA	COMETS	COMMERGED	COMMUNES	COMPAST
COLZAS	COMFIER	COMMERGES	COMMUNING	COMPEAR
COMA	COMFIEST	COMMERGING	COMMUNINGS	COMPEARED
COMAE	COMFIT	COMMERS	COMMUNION	COMPEARING
COMAL	COMFITS	COMMIE	COMMUNIONS	COMPEARS
COMARB	COMFITURE	COMMIES	COMMUNISE	COMPEER
COMARBS	COMFITURES	COMMINATE	COMMUNISED	COMPEERED
COMART	COMFORT	COMMINATED	COMMUNISES	COMPEERING
COMARTS	COMFORTED	COMMINATES	COMMUNISING	COMPEERS
COMAS	COMFORTER	COMMINATING	COMMUNISM	COMPEL
COMATE	COMFORTERS	COMMINGLE	COMMUNISMS	COMPELLED
COMATES	COMFORTING	COMMINGLED	COMMUNIST	COMPELLING
COMATOSE	COMFORTS	COMMINGLES	COMMUNISTS	COMPELS
COMB	COMFREY	COMMINGLING	COMMUNITIES	COMPEND
COMBAT	COMFREYS	COMMINUTE	COMMUNITY	COMPENDIA
COMBATANT	COMFY	COMMINUTED	COMMUNIZE	COMPENDS
COMBATANTS	COMIC	COMMINUTES	COMMUNIZED	COMPERE
COMBATED	COMICAL	COMMINUTING	COMMUNIZES	COMPERED
COMBATING	COMICALLY	COMMIS	COMMUNIZING	COMPERES
COMBATIVE	COMICS	COMMISSAR	COMMUTATE	COMPERING
COMBATS	COMING	COMMISSARS	COMMUTATED	COMPESCE
COMBE	COMINGS	COMMIT	COMMUTATES	COMPESCED
COMBED	COMIQUE	COMMITS	COMMUTATING	COMPESCES
COMBER	COMIQUES	COMMITTAL	COMMUTE	COMPESCING
COMBERS	COMITADJI	COMMITTALS	COMMUTED	COMPETE
COMBES	COMITADJIS	COMMITTED	COMMUTER	COMPETED
COMBIER	COMITAL	COMMITTEE	COMMUTERS	COMPETENT
COMBIEST	COMITATUS	COMMITTEES	COMMUTES	COMPETES
COMBINATE	COMITATUSES	COMMITTING	COMMUTING	COMPETING
COMBINE	COMITIA	COMMIX	COMMUTUAL	COMPILE
COMBINED	COMITIES	COMMIXED	COMOSE	COMPILED
COMBINES	COMITY	COMMIXES	COMOUS	COMPILER
COMBING	COMMA	COMMIXING	COMP	COMPILERS
COMBINGS	COMMAND	COMMO	COMPACT	COMPILES
COMBINING	COMMANDED	COMMODE	COMPACTED	COMPILING
COMBLE	COMMANDER	COMMODES	COMPACTER	COMPITAL
COMBLES	COMMANDERS	COMMODITIES	COMPACTEST	COMPLAIN
COMBLESS	COMMANDING	COMMODITY	COMPACTING	COMPLAINED
COMBO	COMMANDO	COMMODORE	COMPACTLY	COMPLAINING
COMBOS	COMMANDOS	COMMODORES	COMPACTOR	COMPLAININGS

COMPLAINS	COMPOSURE	CONATIONS	CONCHITIS	CONDEMN
COMPLAINT	COMPOSURES	CONATIVE	CONCHITISES	CONDEMNED
COMPLAINTS	COMPOT	CONATUS	CONCHOID	CONDEMNING
COMPLEAT	COMPOTE	CONCAUSE	CONCHOIDS	CONDEMNS
COMPLECT	COMPOTES	CONCAUSES	CONCHS	CONDENSE
COMPLECTED	COMPOTIER	CONCAVE	CONCHY	CONDENSED
COMPLECTING	COMPOTIERS	CONCAVED	CONCIERGE	CONDENSER
COMPLECTS	COMPOTS	CONCAVELY	CONCIERGES	CONDENSERS
COMPLETE	COMPOUND	CONCAVES	CONCILIAR	CONDENSES
COMPLETED	COMPOUNDED	CONCAVING	CONCISE	CONDENSING
COMPLETER	COMPOUNDING	CONCAVITIES	CONCISED	CONDER
COMPLETES	COMPOUNDS	CONCAVITY	CONCISELY	CONDERS
COMPLETEST	COMPRADOR	CONCEAL	CONCISER	CONDIDDLE
COMPLETING	COMPRADORS	CONCEALED	CONCISES	CONDIDDLED
COMPLEX	COMPRESS	CONCEALING	CONCISEST	CONDIDDLES
COMPLEXED	COMPRESSED	CONCEALS	CONCISING	CONDIDDLING
COMPLEXER	COMPRESSES	CONCEDE	CONCISION	CONDIGN
COMPLEXES	COMPRESSING	CONCEDED	CONCISIONS	CONDIGNLY
COMPLEXEST	COMPRINT	CONCEDER	CONCLAVE	CONDIMENT
COMPLEXING	COMPRINTED	CONCEDERS	CONCLAVES	CONDIMENTED
COMPLEXLY	COMPRINTING	CONCEDES	CONCLUDE	CONDIMENTING
COMPLEXUS	COMPRINTS	CONCEDING	CONCLUDED	CONDIMENTS
COMPLEXUSES	COMPRISAL	CONCEIT	CONCLUDES	CONDITION
COMPLIANT	COMPRISALS	CONCEITED	CONCLUDING	CONDITIONED
COMPLICE	COMPRISE	CONCEITING	CONCOCT	CONDITIONING
COMPLICES	COMPRISED	CONCEITS	CONCOCTED	CONDITIONINGS
COMPLIED	COMPRISES	CONCEITY	CONCOCTER	CONDITIONS
COMPLIER	COMPRISING	CONCEIVE	CONCOCTERS	CONDOLE
COMPLIERS	COMPS	CONCEIVED	CONCOCTING	CONDOLED
COMPLIES	COMPT	CONCEIVES	CONCOCTOR	CONDOLENT
COMPLIN	COMPTABLE	CONCEIVING	CONCOCTORS	CONDOLES
COMPLINE	COMPTED	CONCENT	CONCOCTS	CONDOLING
COMPLINES	COMPTER	CONCENTED	CONCOLOR	CONDOM
COMPLINS	COMPTERS	CONCENTER	CONCORD	CONDOMS
COMPLISH	COMPTIBLE	CONCENTERED	CONCORDAT	CONDONE
COMPLISHED	COMPTING	CONCENTERING	CONCORDATS	CONDONED
COMPLISHES	COMPTROLL	CONCENTERS	CONCORDED	CONDONES
COMPLISHING	COMPTROLLED	CONCENTING	CONCORDING	CONDONING
COMPLOT	COMPTROLLING	CONCENTRE	CONCORDS	CONDOR
COMPLOTS	COMPTROLLS	CONCENTRED	CONCOURS	CONDORS
COMPLOTTED	COMPTS	CONCENTRES	CONCOURSE	CONDUCE
COMPLOTTING	COMPULSE	CONCENTRING	CONCOURSES	CONDUCED
COMPLY	COMPULSED	CONCENTS	CONCREATE	CONDUCES
COMPLYING	COMPULSES	CONCEPT	CONCREATED	CONDUCING
COMPO	COMPULSING	CONCEPTI	CONCREATES	CONDUCIVE
COMPONÉ	COMPUTANT	CONCEPTS	CONCREATING	CONDUCT
COMPONENT	COMPUTANTS	CONCEPTUS	CONCRETE	CONDUCTED
COMPONENTS	COMPUTE	CONCEPTUSES	CONCRETED	CONDUCTI
COMPONY	COMPUTED	CONCERN	CONCRETER	CONDUCTING
COMPORT	COMPUTER	CONCERNED	CONCRETES	CONDUCTOR
COMPORTED	COMPUTERS	CONCERNING	CONCRETEST	CONDUCTORS
COMPORTING	COMPUTES	CONCERNS	CONCRETING	CONDUCTS
COMPORTS	COMPUTING	CONCERT	CONCREW	CONDUCTUS
COMPOS	COMPUTIST	CONCERTED	CONCREWED	CONDUIT
COMPOSE	COMPUTISTS	CONCERTING	CONCREWING	CONDUITS
COMPOSED	COMRADE	CONCERTO	CONCREWS	CONDYLAR
COMPOSER	COMRADELY	CONCERTOS	CONCUBINE	CONDYLE
COMPOSERS	COMRADES	CONCERTS	CONCUBINES	CONDYLES
COMPOSES	COMS	CONCETTI	CONCUPIES	CONDYLOID
COMPOSING	COMUS	CONCETTO	CONCUPY	CONDYLOMA
COMPOSITE	COMUSES	CONCH	CONCUR	CONDYLOMATA
COMPOSITED	CON	CONCHA	CONCURRED	CONE
COMPOSITES	CONACRE	CONCHAE	CONCURRING	CONED
COMPOSITING	CONACRED	CONCHATE	CONCURS	CONES
COMPOST	CONACRES	CONCHE	CONCUSS	CONEY
COMPOSTED	CONACRING	CONCHED	CONCUSSED	CONEYS
COMPOSTER	CONARIA	CONCHES	CONCUSSES	CONFAB
COMPOSTERS	CONARIAL	CONCHIE	CONCUSSING	CONFABBED
COMPOSTING	CONARIUM	CONCHIES	CONCYCLIC	CONFABBING
COMPOSTS	CONATION	CONCHING	COND	CONFABS

CONFECT
CONFECTED
CONFECTING
CONFECTS
CONFER
CONFEREE
CONFEREES
CONFERRED
CONFERRER
CONFERRERS
CONFERRING
CONFERS
CONFERVA
CONFERVAE
CONFESS
CONFESSED
CONFESSES
CONFESSING
CONFESSOR
CONFESSORS
CONFEST
CONFESTLY
CONFETTI
CONFIDANT
CONFIDANTS
CONFIDE
CONFIDED
CONFIDENT
CONFIDENTS
CONFIDER
CONFIDERS
CONFIDES
CONFIDING
CONFIGURE
CONFIGURED
CONFIGURES
CONFIGURING
CONFINE
CONFINED
CONFINER
CONFINERS
CONFINES
CONFINING
CONFIRM
CONFIRMED
CONFIRMEE
CONFIRMEES
CONFIRMER
CONFIRMERS
CONFIRMING
CONFIRMINGS
CONFIRMOR
CONFIRMORS
CONFIRMS
CONFISEUR
CONFISEURS
CONFIT
CONFITEOR
CONFITEORS
CONFITS
CONFITURE
CONFITURES
CONFIX
CONFIXED
CONFIXES
CONFIXING
CONFLATE
CONFLATED
CONFLATES
CONFLATING

CONFLICT
CONFLICTED
CONFLICTING
CONFLICTS
CONFLUENT
CONFLUENTS
CONFLUX
CONFLUXES
CONFORM
CONFORMAL
CONFORMED
CONFORMER
CONFORMERS
CONFORMING
CONFORMS
CONFOUND
CONFOUNDED
CONFOUNDING
CONFOUNDS
CONFRÈRE
CONFRÈRES
CONFRÉRIE
CONFRÉRIES
CONFRONT
CONFRONTÉ
CONFRONTED
CONFRONTING
CONFRONTS
CONFUSE
CONFUSED
CONFUSES
CONFUSING
CONFUSION
CONFUSIONS
CONFUTE
CONFUTED
CONFUTES
CONFUTING
CONGA
CONGAED
CONGAING
CONGAS
CONGÉ
CONGEAL
CONGEALED
CONGEALING
CONGEALS
CONGÉD
CONGEE
CONGEED
CONGEEING
CONGEES
CONGÉING
CONGENER
CONGENERS
CONGENIAL
CONGER
CONGERIES
CONGERS
CONGERY
CONGÉS
CONGEST
CONGESTED
CONGESTING
CONGESTS
CONGIARIES
CONGIARY
CONGLOBE
CONGLOBED
CONGLOBES

CONGLOBING
CONGO
CONGOS
CONGOU
CONGOUS
CONGREE
CONGREED
CONGREEING
CONGREES
CONGREET
CONGREETED
CONGREETING
CONGREETS
CONGRESS
CONGRESSED
CONGRESSES
CONGRESSING
CONGRUE
CONGRUED
CONGRUENT
CONGRUES
CONGRUING
CONGRUITIES
CONGRUITY
CONGRUOUS
CONIA
CONIAS
CONIC
CONICAL
CONICALLY
CONICALS
CONICS
CONIDIA
CONIDIAL
CONIDIUM
CONIES
CONIFER
CONIFERS
CONIFORM
CONIINE
CONIINES
CONIMA
CONIMAS
CONINE
CONINES
CONING
CONJECT
CONJECTED
CONJECTING
CONJECTS
CONJEE
CONJEED
CONJEEING
CONJEES
CONJOIN
CONJOINED
CONJOINING
CONJOINS
CONJOINT
CONJUGAL
CONJUGANT
CONJUGANTS
CONJUGATE
CONJUGATED
CONJUGATES
CONJUGATING
CONJUGATINGS
CONJUNCT
CONJURE
CONJURED

CONJURER
CONJURERS
CONJURES
CONJURIES
CONJURING
CONJURINGS
CONJUROR
CONJURORS
CONJURY
CONK
CONKED
CONKER
CONKERS
CONKIES
CONKING
CONKS
CONKY
CONN
CONNATE
CONNATION
CONNATIONS
CONNATURE
CONNATURES
CONNE
CONNECT
CONNECTED
CONNECTER
CONNECTERS
CONNECTING
CONNECTOR
CONNECTORS
CONNECTS
CONNED
CONNER
CONNERS
CONNES
CONNEXION
CONNEXIONS
CONNEXIVE
CONNING
CONNINGS
CONNIVE
CONNIVED
CONNIVENT
CONNIVER
CONNIVERS
CONNIVES
CONNIVING
CONNOTATE
CONNOTATED
CONNOTATES
CONNOTATING
CONNOTE
CONNOTED
CONNOTES
CONNOTING
CONNOTIVE
CONNS
CONNUBIAL
CONODONT
CONODONTS
CONOID
CONOIDAL
CONOIDIC
CONOIDS
CONQUER
CONQUERED
CONQUERING
CONQUEROR
CONQUERORS

CONQUERS
CONQUEST
CONQUESTS
CONS
CONSCIENT
CONSCIOUS
CONSCIOUSES
CONSCRIBE
CONSCRIBED
CONSCRIBES
CONSCRIBING
CONSCRIPT
CONSCRIPTED
CONSCRIPTING
CONSCRIPTS
CONSEIL
CONSEILS
CONSENSUS
CONSENSUSES
CONSENT
CONSENTED
CONSENTING
CONSENTS
CONSERVE
CONSERVED
CONSERVER
CONSERVERS
CONSERVES
CONSERVING
CONSIDER
CONSIDERED
CONSIDERING
CONSIDERINGS
CONSIDERS
CONSIGN
CONSIGNED
CONSIGNEE
CONSIGNEES
CONSIGNER
CONSIGNERS
CONSIGNING
CONSIGNOR
CONSIGNORS
CONSIGNS
CONSIST
CONSISTED
CONSISTING
CONSISTS
CONSOLATE
CONSOLATED
CONSOLATES
CONSOLATING
CONSOLE
CONSOLED
CONSOLER
CONSOLERS
CONSOLES
CONSOLING
CONSOLS
CONSOMMÉ
CONSOMMÉS
CONSONANT
CONSONANTS
CONSONOUS
CONSORT
CONSORTED
CONSORTER
CONSORTERS
CONSORTIA
CONSORTING

CONSORTS
CONSPIRE
CONSPIRED
CONSPIRER
CONSPIRERS
CONSPIRES
CONSPIRING
CONSTABLE
CONSTABLES
CONSTANCIES
CONSTANCY
CONSTANT
CONSTANTS
CONSTATE
CONSTATED
CONSTATES
CONSTATING
CONSTER
CONSTERED
CONSTERING
CONSTERS
CONSTRAIN
CONSTRAINED
CONSTRAINING
CONSTRAINS
CONSTRICT
CONSTRICTED
CONSTRICTING
CONSTRICTS
CONSTRUCT
CONSTRUCTED
CONSTRUCTING
CONSTRUCTS
CONSTRUE
CONSTRUED
CONSTRUER
CONSTRUERS
CONSTRUES
CONSTRUING
CONSUL
CONSULAGE
CONSULAGES
CONSULAR
CONSULARS
CONSULATE
CONSULATES
CONSULS
CONSULT
CONSULTA
CONSULTAS
CONSULTED
CONSULTEE
CONSULTEES
CONSULTER
CONSULTERS
CONSULTING
CONSULTOR
CONSULTORS
CONSULTS
CONSUME
CONSUMED
CONSUMER
CONSUMERS
CONSUMES
CONSUMING
CONSUMINGS
CONSUMPT
CONSUMPTS
CONTACT
CONTACTED

CONTACTING
CONTACTOR
CONTACTORS
CONTACTS
CONTADINA
CONTADINAS
CONTADINE
CONTADINI
CONTADINO
CONTAGION
CONTAGIONS
CONTAGIUM
CONTAGIUMS
CONTAIN
CONTAINED
CONTAINER
CONTAINERS
CONTAINING
CONTAINS
CONTANGO
CONTANGOED
CONTANGOING
CONTANGOS
CONTE
CONTECK
CONTECKS
CONTEMN
CONTEMNED
CONTEMNER
CONTEMNERS
CONTEMNING
CONTEMNOR
CONTEMNORS
CONTEMNS
CONTEMPER
CONTEMPERED
CONTEMPERING
CONTEMPERS
CONTEMPT
CONTEMPTS
CONTEND
CONTENDED
CONTENDER
CONTENDERS
CONTENDING
CONTENDINGS
CONTENDS
CONTENT
CONTENTED
CONTENTING
CONTENTS
CONTES
CONTEST
CONTESTED
CONTESTER
CONTESTERS
CONTESTING
CONTESTS
CONTEXT
CONTEXTS
CONTICENT
CONTINENT
CONTINENTS
CONTINUA
CONTINUAL
CONTINUE
CONTINUED
CONTINUER
CONTINUERS
CONTINUES

CONTINUING
CONTINUO
CONTINUOS
CONTINUUM
CONTLINE
CONTLINES
CONTO
CONTORNO
CONTORNOS
CONTORT
CONTORTED
CONTORTING
CONTORTS
CONTOS
CONTOUR
CONTOURED
CONTOURING
CONTOURS
CONTRA
CONTRACT
CONTRACTED
CONTRACTING
CONTRACTS
CONTRAIL
CONTRAILS
CONTRAIR
CONTRALTI
CONTRALTO
CONTRALTOS
CONTRARIED
CONTRARIES
CONTRARY
CONTRARYING
CONTRAS
CONTRAST
CONTRASTED
CONTRASTING
CONTRASTS
CONTRASTY
CONTRATE
CONTRIST
CONTRISTED
CONTRISTING
CONTRISTS
CONTRITE
CONTRIVE
CONTRIVED
CONTRIVER
CONTRIVERS
CONTRIVES
CONTRIVING
CONTROL
CONTROLLED
CONTROLLING
CONTROLS
CONTROUL
CONTROULED
CONTROULING
CONTROULS
CONTUMACIES
CONTUMACY
CONTUMELIES
CONTUMELY
CONTUND
CONTUNDED
CONTUNDING
CONTUNDS
CONTUSE
CONTUSED
CONTUSES

CONTUSING
CONTUSION
CONTUSIONS
CONTUSIVE
CONUNDRUM
CONUNDRUMS
CONURBAN
CONURBIA
CONURBIAS
CONVECTOR
CONVECTORS
CONVENE
CONVENED
CONVENER
CONVENERS
CONVENES
CONVENING
CONVENOR
CONVENORS
CONVENT
CONVENTED
CONVENTING
CONVENTS
CONVERGE
CONVERGED
CONVERGES
CONVERGING
CONVERSE
CONVERSED
CONVERSES
CONVERSING
CONVERT
CONVERTED
CONVERTER
CONVERTERS
CONVERTING
CONVERTOR
CONVERTORS
CONVERTS
CONVEX
CONVEXED
CONVEXES
CONVEXITIES
CONVEXITY
CONVEXLY
CONVEY
CONVEYAL
CONVEYALS
CONVEYED
CONVEYER
CONVEYERS
CONVEYING
CONVEYOR
CONVEYORS
CONVEYS
CONVICT
CONVICTED
CONVICTING
CONVICTS
CONVINCE
CONVINCED
CONVINCES
CONVINCING
CONVIVE
CONVIVED
CONVIVES
CONVIVIAL
CONVIVING
CONVOCATE
CONVOCATED

CONVOCATES
CONVOCATING
CONVOKE
CONVOKED
CONVOKES
CONVOKING
CONVOLUTE
CONVOLUTED
CONVOLVE
CONVOLVED
CONVOLVES
CONVOLVING
CONVOY
CONVOYED
CONVOYING
CONVOYS
CONVULSE
CONVULSED
CONVULSES
CONVULSING
CONY
COO
COOED
COOEE
COOEED
COOEEING
COOEES
COOEY
COOEYED
COOEYING
COOEYS
COOF
COOFS
COOING
COOINGLY
COOINGS
COOK
COOKABLE
COOKED
COOKER
COOKERIES
COOKERS
COOKERY
COOKHOUSE
COOKHOUSES
COOKIE
COOKIES
COOKING
COOKMAID
COOKMAIDS
COOKOUT
COOKOUTS
COOKROOM
COOKROOMS
COOKS
COOKSHOP
COOKSHOPS
COOKWARE
COOKWARES
COOKY
COOL
COOLABAH
COOLABAHS
COOLAMON
COOLAMONS
COOLANT
COOLANTS
COOLED
COOLER
COOLERS

COOLEST
COOLIBAH
COOLIBAHS
COOLIBAR
COOLIBARS
COOLIE
COOLIES
COOLING
COOLISH
COOLLY
COOLNESS
COOLNESSES
COOLS
COOLTH
COOLTHS
COOLY
COOM
COOMB
COOMBS
COOMED
COOMIER
COOMIEST
COOMING
COOMS
COOMY
COON
COONS
COONTIE
COONTIES
COONTY
COOP
COOPED
COOPER
COOPERAGE
COOPERAGES
COOPERANT
COOPERATE
COOPERATED
COOPERATES
COOPERATING
COOPERED
COOPERIES
COOPERING
COOPERINGS
COOPERS
COOPERY
COOPING
COOPS
COOS
COOSEN
COOSENS
COOSER
COOSERS
COOSIN
COOSINED
COOSINING
COOSINS
COOST
COOT
COOTIKIN
COOTIKINS
COOTS
COP
COPACETIC
COPAIBA
COPAIBAS
COPAIVA
COPAIVAS
COPAL
COPALS

COPARTNER
COPARTNERS
COPATAINE
COPATRIOT
COPATRIOTS
COPE
COPECK
COPECKS
COPED
COPEPOD
COPEPODS
COPER
COPERED
COPERING
COPERS
COPES
COPIED
COPIER
COPIERS
COPIES
COPILOT
COPILOTS
COPING
COPINGS
COPIOUS
COPIOUSLY
COPITA
COPITAS
COPPED
COPPER
COPPERAS
COPPERASES
COPPERED
COPPERING
COPPERINGS
COPPERISH
COPPERS
COPPERY
COPPICE
COPPICED
COPPICES
COPPICING
COPPICINGS
COPPIES
COPPIN
COPPING
COPPINS
COPPLE
COPPLES
COPPY
COPRA
COPRAS
COPRESENT
COPROLITE
COPROLITES
COPROLOGIES
COPROLOGY
COPS
COPSE
COPSED
COPSES
COPSEWOOD
COPSEWOODS
COPSIER
COPSIEST
COPSING
COPSY
COPULA
COPULAR
COPULAS

COPULATE
COPULATED
COPULATES
COPULATING
COPY
COPYBOOK
COPYBOOKS
COPYHOLD
COPYHOLDS
COPYING
COPYISM
COPYISMS
COPYIST
COPYISTS
COPYRIGHT
COPYRIGHTED
COPYRIGHTING
COPYRIGHTS
COQUET
COQUETRIES
COQUETRY
COQUETS
COQUETTE
COQUETTED
COQUETTES
COQUETTING
COQUILLA
COQUILLAS
COQUILLE
COQUILLES
COQUITO
COQUITOS
COR
CORACLE
CORACLES
CORACOID
CORACOIDS
CORAGGIO
CORAGGIOS
CORAL
CORALLA
CORALLINE
CORALLINES
CORALLITE
CORALLITES
CORALLOID
CORALLUM
CORALS
CORAMINE
CORAMINES
CORANACH
CORANACHS
CORANTO
CORANTOES
CORANTOS
CORBAN
CORBANS
CORBE
CORBEAU
CORBEAUS
CORBEIL
CORBEILLE
CORBEILLES
CORBEILS
CORBEL
CORBELLED
CORBELS
CORBES
CORBICULA
CORBICULAE

CORBIE
CORBIES
CORCASS
CORCASSES
CORD
CORDAGE
CORDAGES
CORDATE
CORDED
CORDIAL
CORDIALLY
CORDIALS
CORDIFORM
CORDINER
CORDINERS
CORDING
CORDINGS
CORDITE
CORDITES
CORDLESS
CÓRDOBA
CÓRDOBAS
CORDON
CORDONED
CORDONING
CORDONS
CORDOTOMIES
CORDOTOMY
CORDOVAN
CORDOVANS
CORDS
CORDUROY
CORDUROYS
CORDWAIN
CORDWAINS
CORDYLINE
CORDYLINES
CORE
CORED
CORELESS
CORELLA
CORELLAS
COREOPSIS
COREOPSISES
CORER
CORERS
CORES
CORF
CORGI
CORGIS
CORIA
CORIANDER
CORIANDERS
CORING
CORIOUS
CORIUM
CORIUMS
CORK
CORKAGE
CORKAGES
CORKED
CORKER
CORKERS
CORKIER
CORKIEST
CORKINESS
CORKINESSES
CORKING
CORKIR
CORKIRS

CORKS
CORKWING
CORKWINGS
CORKWOOD
CORKWOODS
CORKY
CORM
CORMORANT
CORMORANTS
CORMOUS
CORMS
CORMUS
CORMUSES
CORN
CORNACRE
CORNACRED
CORNACRES
CORNACRING
CORNAGE
CORNAGES
CORNBRASH
CORNBRASHES
CORNCRAKE
CORNCRAKES
CORNEA
CORNEAL
CORNEAS
CORNED
CORNEL
CORNELIAN
CORNELIANS
CORNELS
CORNEMUSE
CORNEMUSES
CORNEOUS
CORNER
CORNERED
CORNERING
CORNERS
CORNET
CORNETCIES
CORNETCY
CORNETIST
CORNETISTS
CORNETS
CORNETT
CORNETTI
CORNETTO
CORNETTS
CORNFIELD
CORNFIELDS
CORNFLIES
CORNFLOUR
CORNFLOURS
CORNFLY
CORNHUSK
CORNHUSKS
CORNI
CORNICE
CORNICED
CORNICES
CORNICHE
CORNICHES
CORNICING
CORNICLE
CORNICLES
CORNIER
CORNIEST
CORNIFIC
CORNIFORM

COWFEEDERS	COXINESSES	CRACKLIEST	CRAMPONS	CRASHES
COWFISH	COXING	CRACKLING	CRAMPS	CRASHING
COWFISHES	COXSWAIN	CRACKLINGS	CRAMPY	CRASHPAD
COWGIRL	COXSWAINED	CRACKLY	CRAMS	CRASHPADS
COWGIRLS	COXSWAINING	CRACKNEL	CRAN	CRASIS
COWGRASS	COXSWAINS	CRACKNELS	CRANAGE	CRASS
COWGRASSES	COXY	CRACKPOT	CRANAGES	CRASSER
COWHAGE	COY	CRACKPOTS	CRANBERRIES	CRASSEST
COWHAGES	COYED	CRACKS	CRANBERRY	CRASSLY
COWHAND	COYER	CRACKSMAN	CRANCH	CRASSNESS
COWHANDS	COYEST	CRACKSMEN	CRANCHED	CRASSNESSES
COWHEARD	COYING	CRACOWE	CRANCHES	CRATCH
COWHEARDS	COYISH	CRACOWES	CRANCHING	CRATCHES
COWHEEL	COYISHLY	CRADLE	CRANE	CRATE
COWHEELS	COYLY	CRADLED	CRANED	CRATED
COWHERD	COYNESS	CRADLES	CRANES	CRATER
COWHERDS	COYNESSES	CRADLING	CRANIA	CRATEROUS
COWHIDE	COYOTE	CRADLINGS	CRANIAL	CRATERS
COWHIDED	COYOTES	CRAFT	CRANING	CRATES
COWHIDES	COYPU	CRAFTED	CRANIUM	CRATING
COWHIDING	COYPUS	CRAFTIER	CRANIUMS	CRATON
COWHOUSE	COYS	CRAFTIEST	CRANK	CRATONS
COWHOUSES	COYSTREL	CRAFTILY	CRANKCASE	CRATUR
COWING	COYSTRELS	CRAFTING	CRANKCASES	CRATURS
COWISH	COYSTRIL	CRAFTLESS	CRANKED	CRAUNCH
COWITCH	COYSTRILS	CRAFTS	CRANKER	CRAUNCHED
COWITCHES	COZ	CRAFTSMAN	CRANKEST	CRAUNCHES
COWL	COZE	CRAFTSMEN	CRANKIER	CRAUNCHING
COWLED	COZED	CRAFTWORK	CRANKIEST	CRAVAT
COWLICK	COZEN	CRAFTWORKS	CRANKILY	CRAVATS
COWLICKS	COZENAGE	CRAFTY	CRANKING	CRAVATTED
COWLING	COZENAGES	CRAG	CRANKLE	CRAVATTING
COWLINGS	COZENED	CRAGFAST	CRANKLED	CRAVE
COWLS	COZENER	CRAGGED	CRANKLES	CRAVED
COWMAN	COZENERS	CRAGGIER	CRANKLING	CRAVEN
COWMEN	COZENING	CRAGGIEST	CRANKNESS	CRAVENLY
COWP	COZENS	CRAGGY	CRANKNESSES	CRAVENS
COWPAT	COZES	CRAGS	CRANKS	CRAVER
COWPATS	COZIER	CRAGSMAN	CRANKY	CRAVERS
COWPED	COZIERS	CRAGSMEN	CRANNIED	CRAVES
COWPING	COZIES	CRAIG	CRANNIES	CRAVING
COWPOKE	COZIEST	CRAIGS	CRANNOG	CRAVINGS
COWPOKES	COZING	CRAKE	CRANNOGS	CRAW
COWPOX	COZY	CRAKED	CRANNY	CRAWFISH
COWPOXES	COZZES	CRAKES	CRANNYING	CRAWFISHES
COWPS	CRAB	CRAKING	CRANREUCH	CRAWL
COWRIE	CRABBED	CRAM	CRANREUCHS	CRAWLED
COWRIES	CRABBEDLY	CRAMBO	CRANS	CRAWLER
COWRY	CRABBIER	CRAMBOES	CRANTS	CRAWLERS
COWS	CRABBIEST	CRAME	CRANTSES	CRAWLIER
COWSHED	CRABBILY	CRAMES	CRAP	CRAWLIEST
COWSHEDS	CRABBING	CRAMESIES	CRAPE	CRAWLING
COWSLIP	CRABBY	CRAMESY	CRAPED	CRAWLINGS
COWSLIPS	CRABLIKE	CRAMMABLE	CRAPES	CRAWLS
COX	CRABS	CRAMMED	CRAPIER	CRAWLY
COXA	CRABSTICK	CRAMMER	CRAPIEST	CRAWS
COXAE	CRABSTICKS	CRAMMERS	CRAPING	CRAYER
COXAL	CRABWISE	CRAMMING	CRAPLE	CRAYERS
COXALGIA	CRACK	CRAMOISIES	CRAPLES	CRAYFISH
COXALGIAS	CRACKDOWN	CRAMOISY	CRAPPED	CRAYFISHES
COXCOMB	CRACKDOWNS	CRAMP	CRAPPING	CRAYON
COXCOMBIC	CRACKED	CRAMPED	CRAPS	CRAYONED
COXCOMBRIES	CRACKER	CRAMPET	CRAPULENT	CRAYONING
COXCOMBRY	CRACKERS	CRAMPETS	CRAPULOUS	CRAYONS
COXCOMBS	CRACKING	CRAMPIER	CRAPY	CRAZE
COXED	CRACKJAW	CRAMPIEST	CRARE	CRAZED
COXES	CRACKLE	CRAMPING	CRARES	CRAZES
COXIER	CRACKLED	CRAMPIT	CRASES	CRAZIER
COXIEST	CRACKLES	CRAMPITS	CRASH	CRAZIES
COXINESS	CRACKLIER	CRAMPON	CRASHED	CRAZIEST

CRAZILY	CREDENZA	CREMORNES	CRESSY	CRICOID
CRAZINESS	CREDENZAS	CREMORS	CREST	CRICOIDS
CRAZINESSES	CREDIBLE	CREMOSIN	CRESTED	CRIED
CRAZING	CREDIBLY	CREMSIN	CRESTING	CRIER
CRAZY	CREDIT	CRENA	CRESTLESS	CRIERS
CREACH	CREDITED	CRENAS	CRESTS	CRIES
CREACHS	CREDITING	CRENATE	CRETIC	CRIKEY
CREAGH	CREDITOR	CRENATED	CRETICS	CRIME
CREAGHS	CREDITORS	CRENATION	CRETIN	CRIMED
CREAK	CREDITS	CRENATIONS	CRETINISM	CRIMEFUL
CREAKED	CREDO	CRENATURE	CRETINISMS	CRIMELESS
CREAKIER	CREDOS	CRENATURES	CRETINOID	CRIMES
CREAKIEST	CREDULITIES	CRENEL	CRETINOUS	CRIMINAL
CREAKILY	CREDULITY	CRENELATE	CRETINS	CRIMINALS
CREAKING	CREDULOUS	CRENELATED	CRETISM	CRIMINATE
CREAKS	CREE	CRENELATES	CRETISMS	CRIMINATED
CREAKY	CREED	CRENELATING	CRETONNE	CRIMINATES
CREAM	CREEDAL	CRENELLED	CRETONNES	CRIMINATING
CREAMED	CREEDS	CRENELLING	CREUTZER	CRIMINE
CREAMER	CREEING	CRENELS	CREUTZERS	CRIMING
CREAMERIES	CREEK	CRENULATE	CREVASSE	CRIMINI
CREAMERS	CREEKIER	CRENULATED	CREVASSED	CRIMINOUS
CREAMERY	CREEKIEST	CREODONT	CREVASSES	CRIMMER
CREAMIER	CREEKS	CREODONTS	CREVASSING	CRIMMERS
CREAMIEST	CREEKY	CREOLE	CREVICE	CRIMP
CREAMING	CREEL	CREOLES	CREVICES	CRIMPED
CREAMS	CREELS	CREOLIAN	CREW	CRIMPER
CREAMY	CREEP	CREOLIANS	CREWE	CRIMPERS
CREANCE	CREEPER	CREOLIST	CREWED	CRIMPIER
CREANCES	CREEPERED	CREOLISTS	CREWEL	CRIMPIEST
CREANT	CREEPERS	CREOSOTE	CREWELIST	CRIMPING
CREASE	CREEPIE	CREOSOTED	CREWELISTS	CRIMPLE
CREASED	CREEPIER	CREOSOTES	CREWELLED	CRIMPLED
CREASES	CREEPIES	CREOSOTING	CREWELLING	CRIMPLES
CREASIER	CREEPIEST	CREPANCE	CREWELS	CRIMPLING
CREASIEST	CREEPING	CREPANCES	CREWES	CRIMPS
CREASING	CREEPS	CRÊPE	CREWING	CRIMPY
CREASOTE	CREEPY	CRÊPED	CREWS	CRIMSON
CREASOTED	CREES	CRÊPES	CRIANT	CRIMSONED
CREASOTES	CREESE	CRÊPING	CRIB	CRIMSONING
CREASOTING	CREESED	CREPITANT	CRIBBAGE	CRIMSONS
CREASY	CREESES	CREPITATE	CRIBBAGES	CRINAL
CREATABLE	CREESH	CREPITATED	CRIBBED	CRINATE
CREATE	CREESHED	CREPITATES	CRIBBING	CRINATED
CREATED	CREESHES	CREPITATING	CRIBBLE	CRINE
CREATES	CREESHING	CREPITUS	CRIBBLED	CRINED
CREATIC	CREESHY	CREPITUSES	CRIBBLES	CRINES
CREATINE	CREESING	CREPOLINE	CRIBBLING	CRINGE
CREATINES	CREMASTER	CREPOLINES	CRIBELLA	CRINGED
CREATING	CREMASTERS	CREPON	CRIBELLAR	CRINGER
CREATION	CREMATE	CREPONS	CRIBELLUM	CRINGERS
CREATIONS	CREMATED	CREPT	CRIBLÉ	CRINGES
CREATIVE	CREMATES	CREPUSCLE	CRIBRATE	CRINGING
CREATOR	CREMATING	CREPUSCLES	CRIBROSE	CRINGINGS
CREATORS	CREMATION	CRÊPY	CRIBS	CRINGLE
CREATRESS	CREMATIONS	CRESCENDO	CRIBWORK	CRINGLES
CREATRESSES	CREMATOR	CRESCENDOED	CRIBWORKS	CRINING
CREATRIX	CREMATORIES	CRESCENDOING	CRICK	CRINITE
CREATRIXES	CREMATORS	CRESCENDOS	CRICKED	CRINITES
CREATURAL	CREMATORY	CRESCENT	CRICKET	CRINKLE
CREATURE	CRÈME	CRESCENTS	CRICKETED	CRINKLED
CREATURES	CRÊME	CRESCIVE	CRICKETER	CRINKLES
CRÈCHE	CRÈMES	CRESOL	CRICKETERS	CRINKLIER
CRÈCHES	CRÊMES	CRESOLS	CRICKETING	CRINKLIES
CREDAL	CREMOCARP	CRESS	CRICKETINGS	CRINKLIEST
CREDENCE	CREMOCARPS	CRESSES	CRICKETS	CRINKLING
CREDENCES	CREMONA	CRESSET	CRICKEY	CRINKLY
CREDENDA	CREMONAS	CRESSETS	CRICKING	CRINOID
CREDENDUM	CREMOR	CRESSIER	CRICKS	CRINOIDAL
CREDENT	CREMORNE	CRESSIEST	CRICKY	CRINOIDS

CRINOLINE
CRINOLINES
CRINOSE
CRINUM
CRINUMS
CRIOLLO
CRIOLLOS
CRIPES
CRIPPLE
CRIPPLED
CRIPPLES
CRIPPLING
CRIPPLINGS
CRISE
CRISES
CRISIS
CRISP
CRISPATE
CRISPATED
CRISPED
CRISPER
CRISPERS
CRISPEST
CRISPIER
CRISPIEST
CRISPIN
CRISPING
CRISPINS
CRISPLY
CRISPNESS
CRISPNESSES
CRISPS
CRISPY
CRISSA
CRISSUM
CRISTA
CRISTAE
CRISTATE
CRIT
CRITERIA
CRITERION
CRITH
CRITHS
CRITIC
CRITICAL
CRITICISE
CRITICISED
CRITICISES
CRITICISING
CRITICISM
CRITICISMS
CRITICIZE
CRITICIZED
CRITICIZES
CRITICIZING
CRITICS
CRITIQUE
CRITIQUES
CRITS
CRITTER
CRITTERS
CRITTUR
CRITTURS
CRIVENS
CRIVVENS
CROAK
CROAKED
CROAKER
CROAKERS
CROAKIER

CROAKIEST
CROAKILY
CROAKING
CROAKINGS
CROAKS
CROAKY
CROC
CROCEATE
CROCEOUS
CROCHE
CROCHES
CROCHET
CROCHETED
CROCHETING
CROCHETINGS
CROCHETS
CROCK
CROCKED
CROCKERIES
CROCKERY
CROCKET
CROCKETS
CROCKING
CROCKS
CROCODILE
CROCODILES
CROCOITE
CROCOITES
CROCS
CROCUS
CROCUSES
CROFT
CROFTER
CROFTERS
CROFTING
CROFTINGS
CROFTS
CROISSANT
CROISSANTS
CROMACK
CROMACKS
CROMB
CROMBED
CROMBING
CROMBS
CROME
CROMED
CROMES
CROMING
CROMLECH
CROMLECHS
CROMORNA
CROMORNAS
CROMORNE
CROMORNES
CRONE
CRONES
CRONET
CRONETS
CRONIES
CRONK
CRONKER
CRONKEST
CRONY
CRONYISM
CRONYISMS
CROODLE
CROODLED
CROODLES
CROODLING

CROOK
CROOKBACK
CROOKBACKED
CROOKBACKS
CROOKED
CROOKEDER
CROOKEDEST
CROOKEDLY
CROOKER
CROOKEST
CROOKING
CROOKS
CROON
CROONED
CROONER
CROONERS
CROONING
CROONINGS
CROONS
CROP
CROPBOUND
CROPFUL
CROPFULL
CROPFULS
CROPLAND
CROPLANDS
CROPPED
CROPPER
CROPPERS
CROPPIES
CROPPING
CROPPINGS
CROPPY
CROPS
CROPSICK
CROQUET
CROQUETED
CROQUETING
CROQUETS
CROQUETTE
CROQUETTES
CROQUIS
CRORE
CRORES
CROSIER
CROSIERED
CROSIERS
CROSS
CROSSBAND
CROSSBANDS
CROSSBAR
CROSSBARS
CROSSBEAM
CROSSBEAMS
CROSSBILL
CROSSBILLS
CROSSBIT
CROSSBITE
CROSSBITES
CROSSBITING
CROSSBITTEN
CROSSBOW
CROSSBOWS
CROSSBRED
CROSSCUT
CROSSCUTS
CROSSCUTTING
CROSSCUTTINGS
CROSSE
CROSSED

CROSSER
CROSSES
CROSSEST
CROSSETTE
CROSSETTES
CROSSFALL
CROSSFALLS
CROSSFIRE
CROSSFIRES
CROSSFISH
CROSSFISHES
CROSSING
CROSSINGS
CROSSISH
CROSSJACK
CROSSJACKS
CROSSLET
CROSSLETS
CROSSLY
CROSSNESS
CROSSNESSES
CROSSOVER
CROSSOVERS
CROSSROAD
CROSSROADS
CROSSTREE
CROSSTREES
CROSSWALK
CROSSWALKS
CROSSWAY
CROSSWAYS
CROSSWIND
CROSSWINDS
CROSSWISE
CROSSWORD
CROSSWORDS
CROSSWORT
CROSSWORTS
CROST
CROTAL
CROTALA
CROTALINE
CROTALISM
CROTALISMS
CROTALS
CROTALUM
CROTCH
CROTCHED
CROTCHES
CROTCHET
CROTCHETS
CROTCHETY
CROTON
CROTONS
CROTTLE
CROTTLES
CROUCH
CROUCHED
CROUCHES
CROUCHING
CROUP
CROUPADE
CROUPADES
CROUPE
CROUPED
CROUPER
CROUPES
CROUPIER
CROUPIERS

CROUPIEST
CROUPING
CROUPON
CROUPONS
CROUPOUS
CROUPS
CROUPY
CROUSE
CROUSELY
CROUSTADE
CROUSTADES
CROUT
CROÛTE
CROÛTES
CROÛTON
CROÛTONS
CROUTS
CROW
CROWD
CROWDED
CROWDER
CROWDERS
CROWDIE
CROWDIES
CROWDING
CROWDS
CROWED
CROWFOOT
CROWFOOTS
CROWING
CROWN
CROWNED
CROWNER
CROWNERS
CROWNET
CROWNETS
CROWNING
CROWNINGS
CROWNLESS
CROWNLET
CROWNLETS
CROWNS
CROWNWORK
CROWNWORKS
CROWS
CROZE
CROZES
CROZIER
CROZIERS
CRU
CRUBEEN
CRUBEENS
CRUCES
CRUCIAL
CRUCIAN
CRUCIANS
CRUCIATE
CRUCIATED
CRUCIATES
CRUCIATING
CRUCIBLE
CRUCIBLES
CRUCIFER
CRUCIFERS
CRUCIFIED
CRUCIFIER
CRUCIFIERS
CRUCIFIES
CRUCIFIX
CRUCIFIXES

CRUCIFORM
CRUCIFY
CRUCIFYING
CRUCK
CRUCKS
CRUD
CRUDDIER
CRUDDIEST
CRUDDLE
CRUDDLED
CRUDDLES
CRUDDLING
CRUDDY
CRUDE
CRUDELY
CRUDENESS
CRUDENESSES
CRUDER
CRUDES
CRUDEST
CRUDITÉS
CRUDITIES
CRUDITY
CRUDS
CRUDY
CRUE
CRUEL
CRUELLER
CRUELLEST
CRUELLS
CRUELLY
CRUELNESS
CRUELNESSES
CRUELS
CRUELTIES
CRUELTY
CRUES
CRUET
CRUETS
CRUISE
CRUISED
CRUISER
CRUISERS
CRUISES
CRUISEWAY
CRUISEWAYS
CRUISIE
CRUISIES
CRUISING
CRUIVE
CRUIVES
CRULLER
CRULLERS
CRUMB
CRUMBED
CRUMBIER
CRUMBIEST
CRUMBING
CRUMBLE
CRUMBLED
CRUMBLES
CRUMBLIER
CRUMBLIES
CRUMBLIEST
CRUMBLING
CRUMBLY
CRUMBS
CRUMBY
CRUMEN
CRUMENAL

CRUMENALS
CRUMENS
CRUMHORN
CRUMHORNS
CRUMMACK
CRUMMACKS
CRUMMIER
CRUMMIES
CRUMMIEST
CRUMMOCK
CRUMMOCKS
CRUMMY
CRUMP
CRUMPED
CRUMPER
CRUMPEST
CRUMPET
CRUMPETS
CRUMPING
CRUMPLE
CRUMPLED
CRUMPLES
CRUMPLING
CRUMPLINGS
CRUMPS
CRUMPY
CRUNCH
CRUNCHED
CRUNCHES
CRUNCHIER
CRUNCHIEST
CRUNCHING
CRUNCHY
CRUNKLE
CRUNKLED
CRUNKLES
CRUNKLING
CRUOR
CRUORS
CRUPPER
CRUPPERS
CRURAL
CRUS
CRUSADE
CRUSADED
CRUSADER
CRUSADERS
CRUSADES
CRUSADING
CRUSADO
CRUSADOS
CRUSE
CRUSES
CRUSET
CRUSETS
CRUSH
CRUSHABLE
CRUSHED
CRUSHER
CRUSHERS
CRUSHES
CRUSHING
CRUSIAN
CRUSIANS
CRUSIE
CRUSIES
CRUST
CRUSTA
CRUSTAE
CRUSTAL

CRUSTATE
CRUSTATED
CRUSTED
CRUSTIER
CRUSTIEST
CRUSTILY
CRUSTING
CRUSTLESS
CRUSTS
CRUSTY
CRUSY
CRUTCH
CRUTCHED
CRUTCHES
CRUTCHING
CRUVE
CRUVES
CRUX
CRUXES
CRUZEIRO
CRUZEIROS
CRWTH
CRWTHS
CRY
CRYING
CRYINGS
CRYOGEN
CRYOGENIC
CRYOGENICS
CRYOGENIES
CRYOGENS
CRYOGENY
CRYOLITE
CRYOLITES
CRYOMETER
CRYOMETERS
CRYONIC
CRYONICS
CRYOPROBE
CRYOPROBES
CRYOSCOPE
CRYOSCOPES
CRYOSCOPIES
CRYOSCOPY
CRYOSTAT
CRYOSTATS
CRYOTRON
CRYOTRONS
CRYPT
CRYPTADIA
CRYPTAL
CRYPTIC
CRYPTICAL
CRYPTO
CRYPTOGAM
CRYPTOGAMS
CRYPTON
CRYPTONS
CRYPTONYM
CRYPTONYMS
CRYPTOS
CRYPTS
CRYSTAL
CRYSTALS
CSÁRDÁS
CSÁRDÁSES
CTENE
CTENES
CTENIFORM
CTENOID

CUB
CUBAGE
CUBAGES
CUBATURE
CUBATURES
CUBBED
CUBBIES
CUBBING
CUBBINGS
CUBBISH
CUBBY
CUBE
CUBEB
CUBEBS
CUBED
CUBES
CUBHOOD
CUBHOODS
CUBIC
CUBICA
CUBICAL
CUBICALLY
CUBICAS
CUBICLE
CUBICLES
CUBIFORM
CUBING
CUBISM
CUBISMS
CUBIST
CUBISTS
CUBIT
CUBITAL
CUBITS
CUBITUS
CUBITUSES
CUBLESS
CUBOID
CUBOIDAL
CUBOIDS
CUBS
CUCKOLD
CUCKOLDED
CUCKOLDING
CUCKOLDLY
CUCKOLDOM
CUCKOLDOMS
CUCKOLDRIES
CUCKOLDRY
CUCKOLDS
CUCKOLDY
CUCKOO
CUCKOOS
CUCULLATE
CUCUMBER
CUCUMBERS
CUCURBIT
CUCURBITS
CUD
CUDBEAR
CUDBEARS
CUDDEEHIH
CUDDEEHIHS
CUDDEN
CUDDENS
CUDDIE
CUDDIES
CUDDIN
CUDDINS
CUDDLE

CUDDLED
CUDDLES
CUDDLIER
CUDDLIEST
CUDDLING
CUDDLY
CUDDY
CUDGEL
CUDGELLED
CUDGELLER
CUDGELLERS
CUDGELLING
CUDGELLINGS
CUDGELS
CUDS
CUDWEED
CUDWEEDS
CUE
CUED
CUEING
CUEIST
CUEISTS
CUES
CUESTA
CUESTAS
CUFF
CUFFED
CUFFIN
CUFFING
CUFFINS
CUFFLE
CUFFLED
CUFFLES
CUFFLING
CUFFO
CUFFS
CUIF
CUIFS
CUING
CUIRASS
CUIRASSED
CUIRASSES
CUIRASSING
CUISH
CUISHES
CUISINE
CUISINES
CUISINIER
CUISINIERS
CUISSE
CUISSER
CUISSERS
CUISSES
CUIT
CUITER
CUITERED
CUITERING
CUITERS
CUITIKIN
CUITIKINS
CUITS
CUITTLE
CUITTLED
CUITTLES
CUITTLING
CULCH
CULCHES
CULET
CULETS
CULEX

CULICES
CULICID
CULICIDS
CULICINE
CULINARY
CULL
CULLED
CULLENDER
CULLENDERS
CULLER
CULLERS
CULLET
CULLETS
CULLIED
CULLIES
CULLING
CULLINGS
CULLION
CULLIONLY
CULLIONS
CULLIS
CULLISES
CULLS
CULLY
CULLYING
CULLYISM
CULLYISMS
CULM
CULMED
CULMEN
CULMENS
CULMINANT
CULMINATE
CULMINATED
CULMINATES
CULMINATING
CULMING
CULMS
CULOTTE
CULOTTES
CULPABLE
CULPABLY
CULPATORY
CULPRIT
CULPRITS
CULT
CULTCH
CULTCHES
CULTER
CULTERS
CULTIC
CULTIGEN
CULTIGENS
CULTISH
CULTISM
CULTISMS
CULTIST
CULTISTS
CULTIVAR
CULTIVARS
CULTIVATE
CULTIVATED
CULTIVATES
CULTIVATING
CULTORIST
CULTORISTS
CULTRATE
CULTRATED
CULTS
CULTURAL

CULTURE
CULTURED
CULTURES
CULTURING
CULTURIST
CULTURISTS
CULTUS
CULTUSES
CULVER
CULVERIN
CULVERINS
CULVERS
CULVERT
CULVERTS
CUM
CUMARIN
CUMARINS
CUMBENT
CUMBER
CUMBERED
CUMBERER
CUMBERERS
CUMBERING
CUMBERS
CUMBRANCE
CUMBRANCES
CUMBROUS
CUMEC
CUMECS
CUMIN
CUMINS
CUMMER
CUMMERS
CUMMIN
CUMMINS
CUMQUAT
CUMQUATS
CUMSHAW
CUMSHAWS
CUMULATE
CUMULATED
CUMULATES
CUMULATING
CUMULI
CUMULOSE
CUMULUS
CUNABULA
CUNCTATOR
CUNCTATORS
CUNEAL
CUNEATE
CUNEATIC
CUNEIFORM
CUNEIFORMS
CUNETTE
CUNETTES
CUNJEVOI
CUNJEVOIS
CUNNER
CUNNERS
CUNNING
CUNNINGLY
CUNNINGS
CUNT
CUNTS
CUP
CUPBEARER
CUPBEARERS
CUPBOARD
CUPBOARDED

CUPBOARDING
CUPBOARDS
CUPEL
CUPELLED
CUPELLING
CUPELS
CUPFUL
CUPFULS
CUPGALL
CUPGALLS
CUPHEAD
CUPHEADS
CUPID
CUPIDITIES
CUPIDITY
CUPIDS
CUPMAN
CUPMEN
CUPOLA
CUPOLAED
CUPOLAING
CUPOLAR
CUPOLAS
CUPOLATED
CUPPA
CUPPAS
CUPPED
CUPPER
CUPPERS
CUPPING
CUPPINGS
CUPREOUS
CUPRIC
CUPRITE
CUPRITES
CUPROUS
CUPS
CUPULAR
CUPULATE
CUPULE
CUPULES
CUR
CURABLE
CURAÇAO
CURAÇAOS
CURACIES
CURAÇOA
CURAÇOAS
CURACY
CURARA
CURARAS
CURARE
CURARES
CURARI
CURARINE
CURARINES
CURARIS
CURARISE
CURARISED
CURARISES
CURARISING
CURARIZE
CURARIZED
CURARIZES
CURARIZING
CURASSOW
CURASSOWS
CURAT
CURATE
CURATES

CURATIVE
CURATOR
CURATORS
CURATORY
CURATRIX
CURATRIXES
CURATS
CURB
CURBABLE
CURBED
CURBING
CURBLESS
CURBS
CURCH
CURCHES
CURCULIO
CURCULIOS
CURCUMA
CURCUMAS
CURCUMINE
CURCUMINES
CURD
CURDED
CURDIER
CURDIEST
CURDINESS
CURDINESSES
CURDING
CURDLE
CURDLED
CURDLES
CURDLING
CURDS
CURDY
CURE
CURÉ
CURED
CURELESS
CURER
CURERS
CURES
CURÉS
CURETTAGE
CURETTAGES
CURETTE
CURETTED
CURETTES
CURETTING
CURFEW
CURFEWS
CURFUFFLE
CURFUFFLED
CURFUFFLES
CURFUFFLING
CURIA
CURIAE
CURIALISM
CURIALISMS
CURIALIST
CURIALISTS
CURIAS
CURIE
CURIES
CURIET
CURIETS
CURING
CURIO
CURIOS
CURIOSA
CURIOSITIES

CURIOSITY
CURIOUS
CURIOUSER
CURIOUSLY
CURIUM
CURIUMS
CURL
CURLED
CURLER
CURLERS
CURLEW
CURLEWS
CURLICUE
CURLICUES
CURLIER
CURLIEST
CURLINESS
CURLINESSES
CURLING
CURLINGS
CURLS
CURLY
CURN
CURNEY
CURNIER
CURNIEST
CURNS
CURNY
CURPEL
CURPELS
CURR
CURRACH
CURRACHS
CURRAGH
CURRAGHS
CURRAJONG
CURRAJONGS
CURRANT
CURRANTS
CURRANTY
CURRAWONG
CURRAWONGS
CURRED
CURRENCIES
CURRENCY
CURRENT
CURRENTLY
CURRENTS
CURRICLE
CURRICLES
CURRICULA
CURRIE
CURRIED
CURRIER
CURRIERS
CURRIES
CURRING
CURRISH
CURRISHLY
CURRS
CURRY
CURRYING
CURRYINGS
CURS
CURSAL
CURSE
CURSED
CURSEDLY
CURSENARY
CURSER

CURSERS	CURVETTED	CUSTOMIZE	CUTTINGS	CYCLEWAYS
CURSES	CURVETTING	CUSTOMIZED	CUTTLE	CYCLIC
CURSING	CURVIER	CUSTOMIZES	CUTTLES	CYCLICAL
CURSINGS	CURVIEST	CUSTOMIZING	CUTTO	CYCLICISM
CURSITOR	CURVIFORM	CUSTOMS	CUTTOE	CYCLICISMS
CURSITORS	CURVING	CUSTOS	CUTTOES	CYCLICITIES
CURSITORY	CURVITAL	CUSTREL	CUTTY	CYCLICITY
CURSIVE	CURVITIES	CUSTRELS	CUTWORM	CYCLING
CURSIVELY	CURVITY	CUSTUMARIES	CUTWORMS	CYCLINGS
CURSOR	CURVY	CUSTUMARY	CUVÉE	CYCLIST
CURSORARY	CUSCUS	CUT	CUVÉES	CYCLISTS
CURSORES	CUSCUSES	CUTANEOUS	CUVETTE	CYCLO
CURSORIAL	CUSEC	CUTAWAY	CUVETTES	CYCLOID
CURSORILY	CUSECS	CUTAWAYS	CUZ	CYCLOIDAL
CURSORS	CUSH	CUTBACK	CUZZES	CYCLOIDS
CURSORY	CUSHAT	CUTBACKS	CWM	CYCLOLITH
CURST	CUSHATS	CUTCH	CWMS	CYCLOLITHS
CURSTNESS	CUSHES	CUTCHA	CYAN	CYCLONE
CURSTNESSES	CUSHIER	CUTCHERIES	CYANAMIDE	CYCLONES
CURSUS	CUSHIEST	CUTCHERRIES	CYANAMIDES	CYCLONIC
CURSUSES	CUSHION	CUTCHERRY	CYANATE	CYCLOPEAN
CURT	CUSHIONED	CUTCHERY	CYANATES	CYCLOPES
CURTAIL	CUSHIONET	CUTCHES	CYANIC	CYCLOPIAN
CURTAILED	CUSHIONETS	CUTE	CYANIDE	CYCLOPIC
CURTAILING	CUSHIONING	CUTER	CYANIDED	CYCLOPS
CURTAILS	CUSHIONS	CUTES	CYANIDES	CYCLORAMA
CURTAIN	CUSHIONY	CUTESIER	CYANIDING	CYCLORAMAS
CURTAINED	CUSHY	CUTESIEST	CYANIDINGS	CYCLOS
CURTAINING	CUSK	CUTEST	CYANIN	CYCLOSES
CURTAINS	CUSKS	CUTESY	CYANINE	CYCLOSIS
CURTAL	CUSP	CUTEY	CYANINES	CYCLOTRON
CURTALS	CUSPATE	CUTEYS	CYANINS	CYCLOTRONS
CURTANA	CUSPED	CUTICLE	CYANISE	CYCLUS
CURTANAS	CUSPID	CUTICLES	CYANISED	CYCLUSES
CURTATE	CUSPIDAL	CUTICULAR	CYANISES	CYDER
CURTATION	CUSPIDATE	CUTIE	CYANISING	CYDERS
CURTATIONS	CUSPIDOR	CUTIES	CYANITE	CYESES
CURTAXE	CUSPIDORE	CUTIKIN	CYANITES	CYESIS
CURTAXES	CUSPIDORES	CUTIKINS	CYANIZE	CYGNET
CURTER	CUSPIDORS	CUTIN	CYANIZED	CYGNETS
CURTEST	CUSPS	CUTINISE	CYANIZES	CYLICES
CURTILAGE	CUSS	CUTINISED	CYANIZING	CYLINDER
CURTILAGES	CUSSED	CUTINISES	CYANOGEN	CYLINDERS
CURTLY	CUSSER	CUTINISING	CYANOGENS	CYLINDRIC
CURTNESS	CUSSERS	CUTINIZE	CYANOSED	CYLIX
CURTNESSES	CUSSES	CUTINIZED	CYANOSES	CYMA
CURTSEY	CUSSING	CUTINIZES	CYANOSIS	CYMAGRAPH
CURTSEYED	CUSTARD	CUTINIZING	CYANOTIC	CYMAGRAPHS
CURTSEYING	CUSTARDS	CUTINS	CYANOTYPE	CYMAR
CURTSEYS	CUSTOCK	CUTIS	CYANOTYPES	CYMARS
CURTSIED	CUSTOCKS	CUTISES	CYANS	CYMAS
CURTSIES	CUSTODE	CUTLASS	CYANURET	CYMATIUM
CURTSY	CUSTODES	CUTLASSES	CYANURETS	CYMATIUMS
CURTSYING	CUSTODIAL	CUTLER	CYATHI	CYMBAL
CURULE	CUSTODIAN	CUTLERIES	CYATHIA	CYMBALIST
CURVATE	CUSTODIANS	CUTLERS	CYATHIUM	CYMBALISTS
CURVATED	CUSTODIER	CUTLERY	CYATHUS	CYMBALO
CURVATION	CUSTODIERS	CUTLET	CYATHUSES	CYMBALOES
CURVATIONS	CUSTODIES	CUTLETS	CYCAD	CYMBALOS
CURVATIVE	CUSTODY	CUTLINE	CYCADS	CYMBALS
CURVATURE	CUSTOM	CUTLINES	CYCLAMATE	CYMBIDIA
CURVATURES	CUSTOMARIES	CUTPURSE	CYCLAMATES	CYMBIDIUM
CURVE	CUSTOMARY	CUTPURSES	CYCLAMEN	CYMBIDIUMS
CURVED	CUSTOMED	CUTS	CYCLAMENS	CYMBIFORM
CURVES	CUSTOMER	CUTTER	CYCLE	CYME
CURVESOME	CUSTOMERS	CUTTERS	CYCLED	CYMES
CURVET	CUSTOMISE	CUTTIER	CYCLER	CYMOGRAPH
CURVETED	CUSTOMISED	CUTTIES	CYCLERS	CYMOGRAPHS
CURVETING	CUSTOMISES	CUTTIEST	CYCLES	CYMOID
CURVETS	CUSTOMISING	CUTTING	CYCLEWAY	CYMOPHANE

CYMOPHANES
CYMOSE
CYMOUS
CYNANCHE
CYNANCHES
CYNEGETIC
CYNIC
CYNICAL
CYNICALLY
CYNICISM
CYNICISMS
CYNICS
CYNOMOLGI
CYNOSURE
CYNOSURES
CYPHER
CYPHERED
CYPHERING
CYPHERS
CYPRESS

CYPRESSES
CYPRIAN
CYPRIANS
CYPRID
CYPRIDES
CYPRIDS
CYPRINE
CYPRINOID
CYPRIS
CYPRUS
CYPRUSES
CYST
CYSTIC
CYSTID
CYSTIDEAN
CYSTIDEANS
CYSTIDS
CYSTIFORM
CYSTITIS
CYSTITISES

CYSTOCARP
CYSTOCARPS
CYSTOCELE
CYSTOCELES
CYSTOID
CYSTOIDS
CYSTOLITH
CYSTOLITHS
CYSTOTOMIES
CYSTOTOMY
CYSTS
CYTASE
CYTASES
CYTE
CYTES
CYTISI
CYTISINE
CYTISINES
CYTISUS
CYTODE

CYTODES
CYTOID
CYTOKININ
CYTOKININS
CYTOLOGIES
CYTOLOGY
CYTOLYSES
CYTOLYSIS
CYTON
CYTONS
CYTOPLASM
CYTOPLASMS
CYTOSINE
CYTOSINES
CYTOTOXIC
CYTOTOXIN
CYTOTOXINS
CZAPKA
CZAPKAS
CZAR

CZARDAS
CZARDASES
CZARDOM
CZARDOMS
CZAREVICH
CZAREVICHES
CZAREVNA
CZAREVNAS
CZARINA
CZARINAS
CZARISM
CZARISMS
CZARIST
CZARISTS
CZARITZA
CZARITZAS
CZARS

D

DA
DAB
DABBED
DABBER
DABBERS
DABBING
DABBITIES
DABBITY
DABBLE
DABBLED
DABBLER
DABBLERS
DABBLES
DABBLING
DABBLINGS
DABCHICK
DABCHICKS
DABS
DABSTER
DABSTERS
DACE
DACES
DACHA
DACHAS
DACHSHUND
DACHSHUNDS
DACITE
DACITES
DACKER
DACKERED
DACKERING
DACKERS
DACOIT
DACOITAGE
DACOITAGES
DACOITIES
DACOITS
DACOITY
DACTYL
DACTYLAR
DACTYLIC
DACTYLIST
DACTYLISTS
DACTYLS
DAD
DADDED
DADDIES
DADDING
DADDLE
DADDLED
DADDLES
DADDLING
DADDOCK
DADDOCKS
DADDY
DADO
DADOED
DADOES
DADOING
DADOS
DADS
DAEDAL
DAEDALE
DAEDALIC

DAEMON
DAEMONIC
DAEMONS
DAFF
DAFFED
DAFFIER
DAFFIES
DAFFIEST
DAFFING
DAFFINGS
DAFFODIL
DAFFODILS
DAFFS
DAFFY
DAFT
DAFTAR
DAFTARS
DAFTER
DAFTEST
DAFTIE
DAFTIES
DAFTLY
DAFTNESS
DAFTNESSES
DAG
DAGABA
DAGABAS
DAGGA
DAGGAS
DAGGED
DAGGER
DAGGERS
DAGGING
DAGGLE
DAGGLED
DAGGLES
DAGGLING
DAGLOCK
DAGLOCKS
DAGO
DAGOBA
DAGOBAS
DAGOES
DAGS
DAGWOOD
DAGWOODS
DAH
DAHABEEAH
DAHABEEAHS
DAHABIEH
DAHABIEHS
DAHABIYAH
DAHABIYAHS
DAHABIYEH
DAHABIYEHS
DAHL
DAHLIA
DAHLIAS
DAHLS
DAHS
DAIDLE
DAIDLED
DAIDLES
DAIDLING

DAIKER
DAIKERED
DAIKERING
DAIKERS
DAIKON
DAIKONS
DAILIES
DAILY
DAIMEN
DAIMIO
DAIMIOS
DAIMON
DAIMONIC
DAIMONS
DAINE
DAINED
DAINES
DAINING
DAINT
DAINTIER
DAINTIES
DAINTIEST
DAINTILY
DAINTY
DAIQUIRI
DAIQUIRIS
DAIRIES
DAIRY
DAIRYING
DAIRYINGS
DAIRYMAID
DAIRYMAIDS
DAIRYMAN
DAIRYMEN
DAIS
DAISES
DAISIED
DAISIES
DAISY
DAK
DAKER
DAKERED
DAKERING
DAKERS
DAKOIT
DAKOITI
DAKOITIS
DAKOITS
DAKS
DAL
DALE
DALES
DALESMAN
DALESMEN
DALI
DALIS
DALLE
DALLES
DALLIANCE
DALLIANCES
DALLIED
DALLIER
DALLIERS
DALLIES

DALLOP
DALLOPS
DALLY
DALLYING
DALMAHOY
DALMAHOYS
DALMATIC
DALMATICS
DALS
DALT
DALTON
DALTONS
DALTS
DAM
DAMAGE
DAMAGED
DAMAGES
DAMAGING
DAMAN
DAMANS
DAMAR
DAMARS
DAMASCENE
DAMASCENED
DAMASCENES
DAMASCENING
DAMASCENINGS
DAMASK
DAMASKED
DAMASKEEN
DAMASKEENED
DAMASKEENING
DAMASKEENS
DAMASKIN
DAMASKINED
DAMASKING
DAMASKINING
DAMASKINS
DAMASKS
DAMASQUIN
DAMASQUINED
DAMASQUINING
DAMASQUINS
DAMASSIN
DAMASSINS
DAMBOARD
DAMBOARDS
DAMBROD
DAMBRODS
DAME
DAMES
DAMFOOL
DAMMAR
DAMMARS
DAMME
DAMMED
DAMMER
DAMMERS
DAMMING
DAMMIT
DAMN
DAMNABLE
DAMNABLY
DAMNATION

DAMNATIONS
DAMNATORY
DAMNED
DAMNEDER
DAMNEDEST
DAMNIFIED
DAMNIFIES
DAMNIFY
DAMNIFYING
DAMNING
DAMNS
DAMOISEL
DAMOISELS
DAMOSEL
DAMOSELS
DAMOZEL
DAMOZELS
DAMP
DAMPED
DAMPEN
DAMPENED
DAMPENING
DAMPENS
DAMPER
DAMPERS
DAMPEST
DAMPIER
DAMPIEST
DAMPING
DAMPINGS
DAMPISH
DAMPLY
DAMPNESS
DAMPNESSES
DAMPS
DAMPY
DAMSEL
DAMSELFLIES
DAMSELFLY
DAMSELS
DAMSON
DAMSONS
DAN
DANCE
DANCEABLE
DANCED
DANCER
DANCERS
DANCES
DANCETTE
DANCETTÉ
DANCETTEE
DANCETTES
DANCETTY
DANCING
DANCINGS
DANDELION
DANDELIONS
DANDER
DANDERED
DANDERING
DANDERS
DANDIACAL

DANDIER
DANDIES
DANDIEST
DANDIFIED
DANDIFIES
DANDIFY
DANDIFYING
DANDILY
DANDIPRAT
DANDIPRATS
DANDLE
DANDLED
DANDLER
DANDLERS
DANDLES
DANDLING
DANDRIFF
DANDRIFFS
DANDRUFF
DANDRUFFS
DANDY
DANDYFUNK
DANDYFUNKS
DANDYISH
DANDYISM
DANDYISMS
DANDYPRAT
DANDYPRATS
DANEGELD
DANEGELDS
DANEGELT
DANEGELTS
DANELAGH
DANELAGHS
DANELAW
DANELAWS
DANG
DANGED
DANGER
DANGERED
DANGERING
DANGEROUS
DANGERS
DANGING
DANGLE
DANGLED
DANGLER
DANGLERS
DANGLES
DANGLING
DANGLINGS
DANGS
DANIO
DANIOS
DANK
DANKER
DANKEST
DANKISH
DANKNESS
DANKNESSES
DANKS
DANNEBROG
DANNEBROGS
DANS
DANSEUR
DANSEURS
DANSEUSE
DANSEUSES
DANT
DANTED

DANTING
DANTON
DANTONED
DANTONING
DANTONS
DANTS
DAP
DAPHNE
DAPHNES
DAPHNID
DAPHNIDS
DAPPED
DAPPER
DAPPERER
DAPPEREST
DAPPERLY
DAPPERS
DAPPING
DAPPLE
DAPPLED
DAPPLES
DAPPLING
DAPS
DAPSONE
DAPSONES
DARAF
DARAFS
DARBIES
DARE
DARED
DAREFUL
DARES
DARG
DARGA
DARGAS
DARGLE
DARGLES
DARGS
DARI
DARIC
DARICS
DARING
DARINGLY
DARINGS
DARIOLE
DARIOLES
DARIS
DARK
DARKEN
DARKENED
DARKENING
DARKENS
DARKER
DARKEST
DARKEY
DARKEYS
DARKIE
DARKIES
DARKISH
DARKLE
DARKLED
DARKLES
DARKLING
DARKLINGS
DARKLY
DARKMANS
DARKNESS
DARKNESSES
DARKROOM
DARKROOMS

DARKS
DARKSOME
DARKY
DARLING
DARLINGS
DARN
DARNED
DARNEDER
DARNEDEST
DARNEL
DARNELS
DARNER
DARNERS
DARNING
DARNINGS
DARNS
DARRAIGN
DARRAIGNE
DARRAIGNED
DARRAIGNES
DARRAIGNING
DARRAIGNS
DARRAIN
DARRAINE
DARRAINED
DARRAINES
DARRAINING
DARRAINS
DARRAYN
DARRAYNED
DARRAYNING
DARRAYNS
DARRE
DARRED
DARRES
DARRING
DARSHAN
DARSHANS
DART
DARTED
DARTER
DARTERS
DARTING
DARTINGLY
DARTLE
DARTLED
DARTLES
DARTLING
DARTRE
DARTRES
DARTROUS
DARTS
DARZI
DARZIS
DAS
DASH
DASHBOARD
DASHBOARDS
DASHED
DASHEEN
DASHEENS
DASHEKI
DASHEKIS
DASHER
DASHERS
DASHES
DASHIKI
DASHIKIS
DASHING
DASHINGLY

DASSIE
DASSIES
DASTARD
DASTARDIES
DASTARDLY
DASTARDS
DASTARDY
DASYPOD
DASYPODS
DASYURE
DASYURES
DATA
DATABANK
DATABANKS
DATABASE
DATABASES
DATABLE
DATABUS
DATABUSES
DATABUSSES
DATAL
DATALLER
DATALLERS
DATARIA
DATARIAS
DATARIES
DATARY
DATE
DATEABLE
DATED
DATELESS
DATER
DATERS
DATES
DATING
DATINGS
DATIVAL
DATIVE
DATIVES
DATOLITE
DATOLITES
DATUM
DATURA
DATURAS
DATURINE
DATURINES
DAUB
DAUBE
DAUBED
DAUBER
DAUBERIES
DAUBERS
DAUBERY
DAUBES
DAUBIER
DAUBIEST
DAUBING
DAUBINGS
DAUBS
DAUBY
DAUD
DAUDED
DAUDING
DAUDS
DAUGHTER
DAUGHTERS
DAULT
DAULTS
DAUNDER
DAUNDERED

DAUNDERING
DAUNDERS
DAUNER
DAUNERED
DAUNERING
DAUNERS
DAUNT
DAUNTED
DAUNTER
DAUNTERS
DAUNTING
DAUNTLESS
DAUNTON
DAUNTONED
DAUNTONING
DAUNTONS
DAUNTS
DAUPHIN
DAUPHINE
DAUPHINES
DAUPHINS
DAUR
DAURED
DAURING
DAURS
DAUT
DAUTED
DAUTIE
DAUTIES
DAUTING
DAUTS
DAVENPORT
DAVENPORTS
DAVIT
DAVITS
DAW
DAWBRIES
DAWBRY
DAWCOCK
DAWCOCKS
DAWD
DAWDED
DAWDING
DAWDLE
DAWDLED
DAWDLER
DAWDLERS
DAWDLES
DAWDLING
DAWDS
DAWED
DAWING
DAWISH
DAWK
DAWKS
DAWN
DAWNED
DAWNER
DAWNERED
DAWNERING
DAWNERS
DAWNING
DAWNINGS
DAWNS
DAWS
DAWT
DAWTED
DAWTIE
DAWTIES
DAWTING

DAWTS
DAY
DAYBREAK
DAYBREAKS
DAYDREAM
DAYDREAMED
DAYDREAMING
DAYDREAMS
DAYDREAMT
DAYGLO
DAYLIGHT
DAYLIGHTS
DAYLONG
DAYMARK
DAYMARKS
DAYNT
DAYS
DAYSMAN
DAYSMEN
DAYSPRING
DAYSPRINGS
DAYSTAR
DAYSTARS
DAYTALE
DAYTALER
DAYTALERS
DAYTALES
DAYTIME
DAYTIMES
DAZE
DAZED
DAZEDLY
DAZES
DAZING
DAZZLE
DAZZLED
DAZZLER
DAZZLERS
DAZZLES
DAZZLING
DAZZLINGS
DEACON
DEACONESS
DEACONESSES
DEACONRIES
DEACONRY
DEACONS
DEAD
DEADED
DEADEN
DEADENED
DEADENER
DEADENERS
DEADENING
DEADENINGS
DEADENS
DEADER
DEADERS
DEADEST
DEADHOUSE
DEADHOUSES
DEADING
DEADLIER
DEADLIEST
DEADLINE
DEADLINES
DEADLOCK
DEADLOCKED
DEADLOCKING
DEADLOCKS

DEADLY
DEADNESS
DEADNESSES
DEADPAN
DEADPANS
DEADS
DEAF
DEAFEN
DEAFENED
DEAFENING
DEAFENINGS
DEAFENS
DEAFER
DEAFEST
DEAFLY
DEAFNESS
DEAFNESSES
DEAL
DEALBATE
DEALER
DEALERS
DEALFISH
DEALFISHES
DEALING
DEALINGS
DEALS
DEALT
DEAN
DEANER
DEANERIES
DEANERS
DEANERY
DEANS
DEANSHIP
DEANSHIPS
DEAR
DEARE
DEARED
DEARER
DEARES
DEAREST
DEARIE
DEARIES
DEARING
DEARLING
DEARLINGS
DEARLY
DEARN
DEARNESS
DEARNESSES
DEARNFUL
DEARNLY
DEARNS
DEARS
DEARTH
DEARTHS
DEARY
DEASIL
DEASILS
DEASIUL
DEASIULS
DEASOIL
DEASOILS
DEATH
DEATHFUL
DEATHLESS
DEATHLIER
DEATHLIEST
DEATHLIKE
DEATHLY

DEATHS
DEATHSMAN
DEATHSMEN
DEATHWARD
DEATHWARDS
DEATHY
DEAVE
DEAVED
DEAVES
DEAVING
DEAW
DEAWIE
DEAWS
DEAWY
DEB
DEBACLE
DÉBÂCLE
DEBACLES
DÉBÂCLES
DEBAG
DEBAGGED
DEBAGGING
DEBAGGINGS
DEBAGS
DEBAR
DEBARK
DEBARKED
DEBARKING
DEBARKS
DEBARMENT
DEBARMENTS
DEBARRASS
DEBARRASSED
DEBARRASSES
DEBARRASSING
DEBARRED
DEBARRING
DEBARS
DEBASE
DEBASED
DEBASER
DEBASERS
DEBASES
DEBASING
DEBATABLE
DEBATE
DEBATED
DEBATEFUL
DEBATER
DEBATERS
DEBATES
DEBATING
DEBAUCH
DEBAUCHED
DEBAUCHEE
DEBAUCHEES
DEBAUCHER
DEBAUCHERS
DEBAUCHES
DEBAUCHING
DEBBIES
DEBBY
DEBEL
DEBELLED
DEBELLING
DEBELS
DEBENTURE
DEBENTURES
DEBILE
DEBILITIES

DEBILITY
DEBIT
DEBITED
DEBITING
DEBITOR
DEBITORS
DEBITS
DEBONAIR
DEBOSH
DEBOSHED
DEBOSHES
DEBOSHING
DEBOUCH
DÉBOUCHÉ
DEBOUCHED
DÉBOUCHÉS
DEBOUCHES
DEBOUCHING
DEBRIDE
DEBRIDED
DEBRIDES
DEBRIDING
DEBRIEF
DEBRIEFED
DEBRIEFING
DEBRIEFS
DEBRIS
DEBRUISED
DEBS
DEBT
DEBTED
DEBTEE
DEBTEES
DEBTOR
DEBTORS
DEBTS
DEBUG
DEBUGGED
DEBUGGING
DEBUGS
DEBUNK
DEBUNKED
DEBUNKING
DEBUNKS
DEBUS
DEBUSES
DEBUSSED
DEBUSSES
DEBUSSING
DÉBUT
DÉBUTANT
DEBUTANTE
DÉBUTANTES
DÉBUTANTS
DÉBUTS
DECACHORD
DECACHORDS
DECAD
DECADAL
DECADE
DECADENCE
DECADENCES
DECADENCIES
DECADENCY
DECADENT
DECADENTS
DECADES
DECADS
DECAGON
DECAGONAL

DECAGONS
DECAGRAM
DECAGRAMS
DECAL
DECALCIFIED
DECALCIFIES
DECALCIFY
DECALCIFYING
DECALITRE
DECALITRES
DECALOGUE
DECALOGUES
DECALS
DECAMETRE
DECAMETRES
DECAMP
DECAMPED
DECAMPING
DECAMPS
DECANAL
DECANE
DECANES
DECANI
DECANT
DECANTATE
DECANTATED
DECANTATES
DECANTATING
DECANTED
DECANTER
DECANTERS
DECANTING
DECANTS
DECAPOD
DECAPODAL
DECAPODAN
DECAPODS
DECARB
DECARBED
DECARBING
DECARBS
DECARE
DECARES
DECASTERE
DECASTERES
DECASTICH
DECASTICHS
DECASTYLE
DECASTYLES
DECATHLON
DECATHLONS
DECAUDATE
DECAUDATED
DECAUDATES
DECAUDATING
DECAY
DECAYED
DECAYING
DECAYS
DECCIE
DECCIES
DECEASE
DECEASED
DECEASES
DECEASING
DECEDENT
DECEDENTS
DECEIT
DECEITFUL
DECEITS

DECEIVE
DECEIVED
DECEIVER
DECEIVERS
DECEIVES
DECEIVING
DECEMVIR
DECEMVIRI
DECEMVIRS
DECENCIES
DECENCY
DECENNARIES
DECENNARY
DECENNIA
DECENNIAL
DECENNIUM
DECENNIUMS
DECENT
DECENTLY
DECEPTION
DECEPTIONS
DECEPTIVE
DECEPTORY
DECERN
DECERNED
DECERNING
DECERNS
DECESSION
DECESSIONS
DÉCHÉANCE
DÉCHÉANCES
DECIARE
DECIARES
DECIBEL
DECIBELS
DECIDABLE
DECIDE
DECIDED
DECIDEDLY
DECIDER
DECIDERS
DECIDES
DECIDING
DECIDUA
DECIDUAL
DECIDUAS
DECIDUATE
DECIDUOUS
DECIGRAM
DECIGRAMS
DECILITRE
DECILITRES
DECILLION
DECILLIONS
DECIMAL
DECIMALLY
DECIMALS
DECIMATE
DECIMATED
DECIMATES
DECIMATING
DECIMATOR
DECIMATORS
DÉCIME
DÉCIMES
DECIMETRE
DECIMETRES
DECIPHER
DECIPHERED
DECIPHERING

DECIPHERS
DECISION
DECISIONS
DECISIVE
DECISORY
DECISTERE
DECISTERES
DECK
DECKCHAIR
DECKCHAIRS
DECKED
DECKER
DECKERS
DECKING
DECKINGS
DECKLE
DECKLED
DECKLES
DECKO
DECKOED
DECKOING
DECKOS
DECKS
DECLAIM
DECLAIMED
DECLAIMER
DECLAIMERS
DECLAIMING
DECLAIMS
DECLARANT
DECLARANTS
DECLARE
DECLARED
DECLARER
DECLARERS
DECLARES
DECLARING
DECLASS
DÉCLASSÉ
DECLASSED
DÉCLASSÉE
DECLASSES
DECLASSING
DECLINAL
DECLINANT
DECLINATE
DECLINE
DECLINED
DECLINES
DECLINING
DECLIVITIES
DECLIVITY
DECLIVOUS
DECLUTCH
DECLUTCHED
DECLUTCHES
DECLUTCHING
DECO
DECOCT
DECOCTED
DECOCTING
DECOCTION
DECOCTIONS
DECOCTIVE
DECOCTS
DECOCTURE
DECOCTURES
DECODE
DECODED
DECODER

DECODERS
DECODES
DECODING
DECOHERER
DECOHERERS
DECOKE
DECOKED
DECOKES
DECOKING
DECOLLATE
DECOLLATED
DECOLLATES
DECOLLATING
DÉCOLLETÉ
DECOLOR
DECOLORED
DECOLORING
DECOLORS
DECOLOUR
DECOLOURED
DECOLOURING
DECOLOURS
DECOMPLEX
DECOMPOSE
DECOMPOSED
DECOMPOSES
DECOMPOSING
DECONGEST
DECONGESTED
DECONGESTING
DECONGESTS
DECONTROL
DECONTROLLED
DECONTROLLING
DECONTROLS
DÉCOR
DECORATE
DECORATED
DECORATES
DECORATING
DECORATOR
DECORATORS
DECOROUS
DÉCORS
DECORUM
DECORUMS
DECOUPAGE
DECOUPAGES
DECOUPLE
DECOUPLED
DECOUPLES
DECOUPLING
DECOUPLINGS
DECOY
DECOYED
DECOYING
DECOYS
DECREASE
DECREASED
DECREASES
DECREASING
DECREE
DECREED
DECREEING
DECREES
DECREET
DECREETS
DECREMENT
DECREMENTED
DECREMENTING

DECREMENTS
DECREPIT
DECRETAL
DECRETALS
DECRETIST
DECRETISTS
DECRETIVE
DECRETORY
DECREW
DECREWED
DECREWING
DECREWS
DECRIAL
DECRIALS
DECRIED
DECRIER
DECRIERS
DECRIES
DECROWN
DECROWNED
DECROWNING
DECROWNS
DECRY
DECRYING
DECRYPT
DECRYPTED
DECRYPTING
DECRYPTS
DECTET
DECTETS
DECUBITI
DECUBITUS
DECUMAN
DECUMANS
DECUMBENT
DECUPLE
DECUPLED
DECUPLES
DECUPLING
DECURIA
DECURIAS
DECURIES
DECURION
DECURIONS
DECURRENT
DECURSION
DECURSIONS
DECURSIVE
DECURVE
DECURVED
DECURVES
DECURVING
DECURY
DECUSSATE
DECUSSATED
DECUSSATES
DECUSSATING
DEDAL
DEDALIAN
DEDANS
DEDICANT
DEDICANTS
DEDICATE
DEDICATED
DEDICATEE
DEDICATEES
DEDICATES
DEDICATING
DEDICATOR
DEDICATORS

DEDIMUS
DEDIMUSES
DEDUCE
DEDUCED
DEDUCES
DEDUCIBLE
DEDUCING
DEDUCT
DEDUCTED
DEDUCTING
DEDUCTION
DEDUCTIONS
DEDUCTIVE
DEDUCTS
DEE
DEED
DEEDED
DEEDER
DEEDEST
DEEDFUL
DEEDIER
DEEDIEST
DEEDILY
DEEDING
DEEDLESS
DEEDS
DEEDY
DEEING
DEEJAY
DEEJAYED
DEEJAYING
DEEJAYS
DEEM
DEEMED
DEEMING
DEEMS
DEEMSTER
DEEMSTERS
DEEN
DEENS
DEEP
DEEPEN
DEEPENED
DEEPENING
DEEPENS
DEEPER
DEEPEST
DEEPFELT
DEEPIE
DEEPIES
DEEPLY
DEEPMOST
DEEPNESS
DEEPNESSES
DEEPS
DEER
DEERBERRIES
DEERBERRY
DEERE
DEERHORN
DEERHORNS
DEERLET
DEERLETS
DEERSKIN
DEERSKINS
DEES
DEEV
DEEVE
DEEVED
DEEVES

DEEVING	DEFENSE	DEFLEXING	DEFROZEN	DEHORNING
DEEVS	DEFENSES	DEFLEXION	DEFT	DEHORNS
DEFACE	DEFENSIVE	DEFLEXIONS	DEFTER	DEHORT
DEFACED	DEFENSIVES	DEFLEXURE	DEFTEST	DEHORTED
DEFACER	DEFER	DEFLEXURES	DEFTLY	DEHORTER
DEFACERS	DEFERABLE	DEFLORATE	DEFTNESS	DEHORTERS
DEFACES	DEFERENCE	DEFLORATED	DEFTNESSES	DEHORTING
DEFACING	DEFERENCES	DEFLORATES	DEFUNCT	DEHORTS
DEFAECATE	DEFERENT	DEFLORATING	DEFUNCTS	DEHYDRATE
DEFAECATED	DEFERENTS	DEFLOWER	DEFUSE	DEHYDRATED
DEFAECATES	DEFERMENT	DEFLOWERED	DEFUSED	DEHYDRATES
DEFAECATING	DEFERMENTS	DEFLOWERING	DEFUSES	DEHYDRATING
DEFALCATE	DEFERRAL	DEFLOWERS	DEFUSING	DEI
DEFALCATED	DEFERRALS	DEFLUENT	DEFUZE	DEICIDAL
DEFALCATES	DEFERRED	DEFLUXION	DEFUZED	DEICIDE
DEFALCATING	DEFERRER	DEFLUXIONS	DEFUZES	DEICIDES
DEFAME	DEFERRERS	DEFOLIANT	DEFUZING	DEICTIC
DEFAMED	DEFERRING	DEFOLIANTS	DEFY	DEICTICS
DEFAMES	DEFERS	DEFOLIATE	DEFYING	DEID
DEFAMING	DEFFLY	DEFOLIATED	DÉGAGÉ	DEIDER
DEFAMINGS	DEFIANCE	DEFOLIATES	DEGARNISH	DEIDEST
DEFAST	DEFIANCES	DEFOLIATING	DEGARNISHED	DEIDS
DEFASTE	DEFIANT	DEFORCE	DEGARNISHES	DEIFIC
DEFAT	DEFIANTLY	DEFORCED	DEGARNISHING	DEIFICAL
DEFATS	DEFICIENT	DEFORCES	DEGAS	DEIFIED
DEFATTED	DEFICIENTS	DEFORCING	DEGASES	DEIFIER
DEFATTING	DEFICIT	DEFOREST	DEGASSED	DEIFIERS
DEFAULT	DEFICITS	DEFORESTED	DEGASSING	DEIFIES
DEFAULTED	DEFIED	DEFORESTING	DEGAUSS	DEIFORM
DEFAULTER	DEFIER	DEFORESTS	DEGAUSSED	DEIFY
DEFAULTERS	DEFIERS	DEFORM	DEGAUSSES	DEIFYING
DEFAULTING	DEFIES	DEFORMED	DEGAUSSING	DEIGN
DEFAULTS	DEFILADE	DEFORMER	DEGENDER	DEIGNED
DEFEAT	DEFILADED	DEFORMERS	DEGENDERED	DEIGNING
DEFEATED	DEFILADES	DEFORMING	DEGENDERING	DEIGNS
DEFEATING	DEFILADING	DEFORMITIES	DEGENDERS	DEIL
DEFEATISM	DEFILE	DEFORMITY	DÉGOÛT	DEILED
DEFEATISMS	DEFILED	DEFORMS	DÉGOÛTS	DEILING
DEFEATIST	DEFILER	DEFOUL	DEGRADE	DEILS
DEFEATISTS	DEFILERS	DEFOULED	DEGRADED	DEINOSAUR
DEFEATS	DEFILES	DEFOULING	DEGRADES	DEINOSAURS
DEFEATURE	DEFILING	DEFOULS	DEGRADING	DEIPAROUS
DEFEATURES	DEFINABLE	DEFRAUD	DEGRAS	DEISEAL
DEFECATE	DEFINABLY	DEFRAUDED	DEGREASE	DEISEALS
DEFECATED	DEFINE	DEFRAUDER	DEGREASED	DEISHEAL
DEFECATES	DEFINED	DEFRAUDERS	DEGREASES	DEISHEALS
DEFECATING	DEFINER	DEFRAUDING	DEGREASING	DEISM
DEFECATOR	DEFINERS	DEFRAUDS	DEGREE	DEISMS
DEFECATORS	DEFINES	DEFRAY	DEGREES	DEIST
DEFECT	DEFINING	DEFRAYAL	DEGUM	DEISTIC
DEFECTED	DEFINITE	DEFRAYALS	DEGUMMED	DEISTICAL
DEFECTING	DEFLATE	DEFRAYED	DEGUMMING	DEISTS
DEFECTION	DEFLATED	DEFRAYER	DEGUMS	DEITIES
DEFECTIONS	DEFLATER	DEFRAYERS	DEGUST	DEITY
DEFECTIVE	DEFLATERS	DEFRAYING	DEGUSTATE	DEIXES
DEFECTIVES	DEFLATES	DEFRAYS	DEGUSTATED	DEIXIS
DEFECTOR	DEFLATING	DEFREEZE	DEGUSTATES	DEJECT
DEFECTORS	DEFLATION	DEFREEZES	DEGUSTATING	DEJECTA
DEFECTS	DEFLATIONS	DEFREEZING	DEGUSTED	DEJECTED
DEFENCE	DEFLATOR	DEFROCK	DEGUSTING	DEJECTING
DEFENCED	DEFLATORS	DEFROCKED	DEGUSTS	DEJECTION
DEFENCES	DEFLECT	DEFROCKING	DEHISCE	DEJECTIONS
DEFEND	DEFLECTED	DEFROCKS	DEHISCED	DEJECTORY
DEFENDANT	DEFLECTING	DEFROST	DEHISCENT	DEJECTS
DEFENDANTS	DEFLECTOR	DEFROSTED	DEHISCES	DEJEUNE
DEFENDED	DEFLECTORS	DEFROSTER	DEHISCING	DÉJEUNER
DEFENDER	DEFLECTS	DEFROSTERS	DEHORN	DÉJEUNERS
DEFENDERS	DEFLEX	DEFROSTING	DEHORNED	DEJEUNES
DEFENDING	DEFLEXED	DEFROSTS	DEHORNER	DEKALOGIES
DEFENDS	DEFLEXES	DEFROZE	DEHORNERS	DEKALOGY

DEKKO
DEKKOED
DEKKOING
DEKKOS
DEL
DELAINE
DELAINES
DELAPSE
DELAPSED
DELAPSES
DELAPSING
DELAPSION
DELAPSIONS
DELATE
DELATED
DELATES
DELATING
DELATION
DELATIONS
DELATOR
DELATORS
DELAY
DELAYED
DELAYER
DELAYERS
DELAYING
DELAYS
DELE
DELEBLE
DELED
DELEGABLE
DELEGACIES
DELEGACY
DELEGATE
DELEGATED
DELEGATES
DELEGATING
DELEING
DELENDA
DELES
DELETE
DELETED
DELETES
DELETING
DELETION
DELETIONS
DELETIVE
DELETORY
DELF
DELFS
DELFT
DELFTS
DELI
DELIBATE
DELIBATED
DELIBATES
DELIBATING
DELIBLE
DELICACIES
DELICACY
DELICATE
DELICATES
DELICE
DELICES
DELICIOUS
DELICT
DELICTS
DELIGHT
DELIGHTED
DELIGHTING
DELIGHTS

DELIMIT
DELIMITED
DELIMITING
DELIMITS
DELINEATE
DELINEATED
DELINEATES
DELINEATING
DELIQUIUM
DELIQUIUMS
DELIRIA
DELIRIANT
DELIRIANTS
DELIRIOUS
DELIRIUM
DELIRIUMS
DELIS
DELIVER
DELIVERED
DELIVERER
DELIVERERS
DELIVERIES
DELIVERING
DELIVERLY
DELIVERS
DELIVERY
DELL
DELLS
DELOUSE
DELOUSED
DELOUSES
DELOUSING
DELPH
DELPHIAN
DELPHIC
DELPHIN
DELPHINIA
DELPHS
DELS
DELTA
DELTAIC
DELTAS
DELTOID
DELUBRUM
DELUBRUMS
DELUDABLE
DELUDE
DELUDED
DELUDER
DELUDERS
DELUDES
DELUDING
DELUGE
DELUGED
DELUGES
DELUGING
DELUNDUNG
DELUNDUNGS
DELUSION
DELUSIONS
DELUSIVE
DELUSORY
DELVE
DELVED
DELVER
DELVERS
DELVES
DELVING
DEMAGOGIC
DEMAGOGIES
DEMAGOGUE

DEMAGOGUES
DEMAGOGY
DEMAIN
DEMAINE
DEMAINES
DEMAINS
DEMAN
DEMAND
DEMANDANT
DEMANDANTS
DEMANDED
DEMANDER
DEMANDERS
DEMANDING
DEMANDS
DEMANNED
DEMANNING
DEMANNINGS
DEMANS
DEMARCATE
DEMARCATED
DEMARCATES
DEMARCATING
DÉMARCHE
DÉMARCHES
DEMARK
DEMARKED
DEMARKING
DEMARKS
DEMAYNE
DEMAYNES
DEME
DEMEAN
DEMEANE
DEMEANED
DEMEANES
DEMEANING
DEMEANOR
DEMEANORS
DEMEANOUR
DEMEANOURS
DEMEANS
DEMENT
DEMENTATE
DEMENTATED
DEMENTATES
DEMENTATING
DEMENTED
DÉMENTI
DEMENTIA
DEMENTIAS
DEMENTING
DÉMENTIS
DEMENTS
DEMERARA
DEMERARAS
DEMERGE
DEMERGED
DEMERGER
DEMERGERS
DEMERGES
DEMERGING
DEMERIT
DEMERITS
DEMERSAL
DEMERSE
DEMERSED
DEMERSES
DEMERSING
DEMERSION

DEMERSIONS
DEMES
DEMESNE
DEMESNES
DEMIC
DEMIES
DEMIGOD
DEMIGODS
DEMIJOHN
DEMIJOHNS
DEMIPIQUE
DEMIPIQUES
DEMIREP
DEMIREPS
DEMISABLE
DEMISE
DEMISED
DEMISES
DEMISING
DEMISS
DEMISSION
DEMISSIONS
DEMISSIVE
DEMISSLY
DEMIST
DEMISTED
DEMISTER
DEMISTERS
DEMISTING
DEMISTS
DEMIT
DEMITASSE
DEMITASSES
DEMITS
DEMITTED
DEMITTING
DEMIURGE
DEMIURGES
DEMIURGIC
DEMIURGUS
DEMIURGUSES
DEMO
DEMOB
DEMOBBED
DEMOBBING
DEMOBS
DEMOCRACIES
DEMOCRACY
DEMOCRAT
DEMOCRATIES
DEMOCRATS
DEMOCRATY
DÉMODÉ
DEMODED
DEMOLISH
DEMOLISHED
DEMOLISHES
DEMOLISHING
DEMOLOGIES
DEMOLOGY
DEMON
DEMONESS
DEMONESSES
DEMONIAC
DEMONIACS
DEMONIAN
DEMONIC
DEMONISE
DEMONISED
DEMONISES

DEMONISING
DEMONISM
DEMONISMS
DEMONIST
DEMONISTS
DEMONIZE
DEMONIZED
DEMONIZES
DEMONIZING
DEMONRIES
DEMONRY
DEMONS
DEMOS
DEMOSES
DEMOTE
DEMOTED
DEMOTES
DEMOTIC
DEMOTING
DEMOTION
DEMOTIONS
DEMOTIST
DEMOTISTS
DEMOUNT
DEMOUNTED
DEMOUNTING
DEMOUNTS
DEMPSTER
DEMPSTERS
DEMPT
DEMULCENT
DEMULCENTS
DEMULSIFIED
DEMULSIFIES
DEMULSIFY
DEMULSIFYING
DEMUR
DEMURE
DEMURED
DEMURELY
DEMURER
DEMURES
DEMUREST
DEMURING
DEMURRAGE
DEMURRAGES
DEMURRAL
DEMURRALS
DEMURRED
DEMURRER
DEMURRERS
DEMURRING
DEMURS
DEMY
DEMYSHIP
DEMYSHIPS
DEMYSTIFIED
DEMYSTIFIES
DEMYSTIFY
DEMYSTIFYING
DEN
DENARIES
DENARII
DENARIUS
DENARY
DENATURE
DENATURED
DENATURES
DENATURING
DENAY

DENAYED	DENSIFIER	DEODORISING	DEPILATORS	DEPREHENDING
DENAYING	DENSIFIERS	DEODORIZE	DEPLANE	DEPREHENDS
DENAYS	DENSIFIES	DEODORIZED	DEPLANED	DEPRESS
DENAZIFIED	DENSIFY	DEODORIZES	DEPLANES	DEPRESSED
DENAZIFIES	DENSIFYING	DEODORIZING	DEPLANING	DEPRESSES
DENAZIFY	DENSITIES	DEONTIC	DEPLETE	DEPRESSING
DENAZIFYING	DENSITY	DEONTICS	DEPLETED	DEPRESSOR
DENDRITE	DENT	DEOXIDATE	DEPLETES	DEPRESSORS
DENDRITES	DENTAL	DEOXIDATED	DEPLETING	DEPRIVAL
DENDRITIC	DENTALIA	DEOXIDATES	DEPLETION	DEPRIVALS
DENDROID	DENTALIUM	DEOXIDATING	DEPLETIONS	DEPRIVE
DENDRON	DENTALIUMS	DEOXIDISE	DEPLETIVE	DEPRIVED
DENDRONS	DENTALS	DEOXIDISED	DEPLETORY	DEPRIVES
DENE	DENTARIA	DEOXIDISES	DEPLORE	DEPRIVING
DENES	DENTARIAS	DEOXIDISING	DEPLORED	DEPROGRAM
DENGUE	DENTARIES	DEOXIDIZE	DEPLORES	DEPROGRAMMED
DENGUES	DENTARY	DEOXIDIZED	DEPLORING	DEPROGRAMMING
DENIABLE	DENTATE	DEOXIDIZES	DEPLOY	DEPROGRAMS
DENIABLY	DENTATED	DEOXIDIZING	DEPLOYED	DEPSIDE
DENIAL	DENTATION	DEPAINT	DEPLOYING	DEPSIDES
DENIALS	DENTATIONS	DEPAINTED	DEPLOYS	DEPTH
DENIED	DENTED	DEPAINTING	DEPLUME	DEPTHLESS
DENIER	DENTEL	DEPAINTS	DEPLUMED	DEPTHS
DENIERS	DENTELLE	DEPART	DEPLUMES	DEPURANT
DENIES	DENTELLES	DEPARTED	DEPLUMING	DEPURANTS
DENIGRATE	DENTELS	DEPARTER	DEPONE	DEPURATE
DENIGRATED	DENTEX	DEPARTERS	DEPONED	DEPURATED
DENIGRATES	DENTEXES	DEPARTING	DEPONENT	DEPURATES
DENIGRATING	DENTICLE	DEPARTINGS	DEPONENTS	DEPURATING
DENIM	DENTICLES	DEPARTS	DEPONES	DEPURATOR
DENIMS	DENTIFORM	DEPARTURE	DEPONING	DEPURATORS
DENITRATE	DENTIL	DEPARTURES	DEPORT	DEPUTE
DENITRATED	DENTILS	DEPASTURE	DEPORTED	DEPUTED
DENITRATES	DENTIN	DEPASTURED	DEPORTEE	DEPUTES
DENITRATING	DENTINE	DEPASTURES	DEPORTEES	DEPUTIES
DENITRIFIED	DENTINES	DEPASTURING	DEPORTING	DEPUTING
DENITRIFIES	DENTING	DÉPÊCHE	DEPORTS	DEPUTISE
DENITRIFY	DENTINS	DÉPÊCHES	DEPOSABLE	DEPUTISED
DENITRIFYING	DENTIST	DEPEINCT	DEPOSAL	DEPUTISES
DENIZEN	DENTISTRIES	DEPEINCTED	DEPOSALS	DEPUTISING
DENIZENED	DENTISTRY	DEPEINCTING	DEPOSE	DEPUTIZE
DENIZENING	DENTISTS	DEPEINCTS	DEPOSED	DEPUTIZED
DENIZENS	DENTITION	DEPEND	DEPOSER	DEPUTIZES
DENNED	DENTITIONS	DEPENDANT	DEPOSERS	DEPUTIZING
DENNET	DENTOID	DEPENDANTS	DEPOSES	DEPUTY
DENNETS	DENTS	DEPENDED	DEPOSING	DÉRACINÉ
DENNING	DENTURE	DEPENDENT	DEPOSIT	DERAIGN
DENOTABLE	DENTURES	DEPENDENTS	DEPOSITED	DERAIGNED
DENOTATE	DENUDATE	DEPENDING	DEPOSITING	DERAIGNING
DENOTATED	DENUDATED	DEPENDS	DEPOSITOR	DERAIGNS
DENOTATES	DENUDATES	DEPICT	DEPOSITORS	DERAIL
DENOTATING	DENUDATING	DEPICTED	DEPOSITS	DERAILED
DENOTE	DENUDE	DEPICTER	DEPOT	DERAILER
DENOTED	DENUDED	DEPICTERS	DEPOTS	DERAILERS
DENOTES	DENUDES	DEPICTING	DEPRAVE	DERAILING
DENOTING	DENUDING	DEPICTION	DEPRAVED	DERAILS
DENOUNCE	DENY	DEPICTIONS	DEPRAVES	DERANGE
DENOUNCED	DENYING	DEPICTIVE	DEPRAVING	DERANGED
DENOUNCER	DENYINGLY	DEPICTOR	DEPRAVITIES	DERANGES
DENOUNCERS	DEODAND	DEPICTORS	DEPRAVITY	DERANGING
DENOUNCES	DEODANDS	DEPICTS	DEPRECATE	DERATE
DENOUNCING	DEODAR	DEPICTURE	DEPRECATED	DERATED
DENS	DEODARS	DEPICTURED	DEPRECATES	DERATES
DENSE	DEODATE	DEPICTURES	DEPRECATING	DERATING
DENSELY	DEODATES	DEPICTURING	DEPREDATE	DERATINGS
DENSENESS	DEODORANT	DEPILATE	DEPREDATED	DERATION
DENSENESSES	DEODORANTS	DEPILATED	DEPREDATES	DERATIONED
DENSER	DEODORISE	DEPILATES	DEPREDATING	DERATIONING
DENSEST	DEODORISED	DEPILATING	DEPREHEND	DERATIONS
DENSIFIED	DEODORISES	DEPILATOR	DEPREHENDED	DERAY

DERAYED	DERVISH	DESICCANT	DESOLATOR	DESTINING
DERAYING	DERVISHES	DESICCANTS	DESOLATORS	DESTINY
DERAYS	DERVS	DESICCATE	DESORB	DESTITUTE
DERBIES	DESALT	DESICCATED	DESORBED	DESTITUTED
DERBY	DESALTED	DESICCATES	DESORBING	DESTITUTES
DERE	DESALTING	DESICCATING	DESORBS	DESTITUTING
DERED	DESALTINGS	DESIGN	DESPAIR	DESTRIER
DERELICT	DESALTS	DESIGNATE	DESPAIRED	DESTRIERS
DERELICTS	DESCALE	DESIGNATED	DESPAIRING	DESTROY
DERES	DESCALED	DESIGNATES	DESPAIRS	DESTROYED
DERHAM	DESCALES	DESIGNATING	DESPATCH	DESTROYER
DERHAMS	DESCALING	DESIGNED	DESPATCHED	DESTROYERS
DERIDE	DESCANT	DESIGNER	DESPATCHES	DESTROYING
DERIDED	DESCANTED	DESIGNERS	DESPATCHING	DESTROYS
DERIDER	DESCANTING	DESIGNFUL	DESPERADO	DESTRUCT
DERIDERS	DESCANTS	DESIGNING	DESPERADOES	DESTRUCTED
DERIDES	DESCEND	DESIGNINGS	DESPERADOS	DESTRUCTING
DERIDING	DESCENDED	DESIGNS	DESPERATE	DESTRUCTS
DERING	DESCENDER	DESILVER	DESPIGHT	DESUETUDE
DERISIBLE	DESCENDERS	DESILVERED	DESPIGHTS	DESUETUDES
DERISION	DESCENDING	DESILVERING	DESPISAL	DESULPHUR
DERISIONS	DESCENDINGS	DESILVERS	DESPISALS	DESULPHURED
DERISIVE	DESCENDS	DESINE	DESPISE	DESULPHURING
DERISORY	DESCENT	DESINED	DESPISED	DESULPHURS
DERIVABLE	DESCENTS	DESINENCE	DESPISER	DESULTORY
DERIVABLY	DESCHOOL	DESINENCES	DESPISERS	DESYATIN
DERIVATE	DESCHOOLED	DESINENT	DESPISES	DESYATINS
DERIVATES	DESCHOOLING	DESINES	DESPISING	DESYNE
DERIVE	DESCHOOLINGS	DESINING	DESPITE	DESYNED
DERIVED	DESCHOOLS	DESIPIENT	DESPITES	DESYNES
DERIVES	DESCRIBE	DESIRABLE	DESPOIL	DESYNING
DERIVING	DESCRIBED	DESIRABLES	DESPOILED	DETACH
DERM	DESCRIBER	DESIRABLY	DESPOILER	DETACHED
DERMA	DESCRIBERS	DESIRE	DESPOILERS	DETACHES
DERMAL	DESCRIBES	DESIRED	DESPOILING	DETACHING
DERMAS	DESCRIBING	DESIRER	DESPOILS	DETAIL
DERMATIC	DESCRIED	DESIRERS	DESPOND	DETAILED
DERMATOID	DESCRIES	DESIRES	DESPONDED	DETAILING
DERMATOME	DESCRIVE	DESIRING	DESPONDING	DETAILS
DERMATOMES	DESCRIVED	DESIROUS	DESPONDINGS	DETAIN
DERMIC	DESCRIVES	DESIST	DESPONDS	DETAINED
DERMIS	DESCRIVING	DESISTED	DESPOT	DETAINEE
DERMISES	DESCRY	DESISTING	DESPOTAT	DETAINEES
DERMOID	DESCRYING	DESISTS	DESPOTATE	DETAINER
DERMOIDS	DESECRATE	DESK	DESPOTATES	DETAINERS
DERMO	DESECRATED	DESKBOUND	DESPOTATO	DETAINING
DERN	DESECRATES	DESKILL	DESPOTIC	DETAINS
DERNFUL	DESECRATING	DESKILLED	DESPOTISM	DETECT
DERNIER	DESELECT	DESKILLING	DESPOTISMS	DETECTED
DERNLY	DESELECTED	DESKILLS	DESPOTS	DETECTING
DERNS	DESELECTING	DESKS	DESPUMATE	DETECTION
DEROGATE	DESELECTS	DESKTOP	DESPUMATED	DETECTIONS
DEROGATED	DESERT	DESMAN	DESPUMATES	DETECTIVE
DEROGATES	DESERTED	DESMANS	DESPUMATING	DETECTIVES
DEROGATING	DESERTER	DESMID	DESSE	DETECTOR
DERRICK	DESERTERS	DESMIDS	DESSERT	DETECTORS
DERRICKED	DESERTING	DESMINE	DESSERTS	DETECTS
DERRICKING	DESERTION	DESMINES	DESSES	DETENT
DERRICKS	DESERTIONS	DESMODIUM	DESTEMPER	DÉTENTE
DERRIÈRE	DESERTS	DESMODIUMS	DESTEMPERED	DÉTENTES
DERRIÈRES	DESERVE	DESMOID	DESTEMPERING	DETENTION
DERRIES	DESERVED	DESMOSOME	DESTEMPERS	DETENTIONS
DERRINGER	DESERVER	DESMOSOMES	DESTINATE	DETENTS
DERRINGERS	DESERVERS	DÉSOEUVRÉ	DESTINATED	DÉTENU
DERRIS	DESERVES	DESOLATE	DESTINATES	DÉTENUE
DERRISES	DESERVING	DESOLATED	DESTINATING	DÉTENUES
DERRY	DESEX	DESOLATER	DESTINE	DÉTENUS
DERTH	DESEXED	DESOLATERS	DESTINED	DETER
DERTHS	DESEXES	DESOLATES	DESTINES	DETERGE
DERV	DESEXING	DESOLATING	DESTINIES	DETERGED

DETERGENT	DETRIMENTS	DEVIATE	DEVONPORTS	DEXTRORSE
DETERGENTS	DETRITAL	DEVIATED	DÉVOT	DEXTROSE
DETERGES	DETRITION	DEVIATES	DEVOTE	DEXTROSES
DETERGING	DETRITIONS	DEVIATING	DEVOTED	DEXTROUS
DETERMENT	DETRITUS	DEVIATION	DEVOTEDLY	DEY
DETERMENTS	DETRUDE	DEVIATIONS	DEVOTEE	DEYS
DETERMINE	DETRUDED	DEVIATOR	DEVOTEES	DHAK
DETERMINED	DETRUDES	DEVIATORS	DEVOTES	DHAKS
DETERMINES	DETRUDING	DEVIATORY	DEVOTING	DHAL
DETERMINING	DETRUSION	DEVICE	DEVOTION	DHALS
DETERRED	DETRUSIONS	DEVICEFUL	DEVOTIONS	DHARMA
DETERRENT	DEUCE	DEVICES	DÉVOTS	DHARMAS
DETERRENTS	DEUCED	DEVIL	DEVOUR	DHARMSALA
DETERRING	DEUCEDLY	DEVILDOM	DEVOURED	DHARMSALAS
DETERS	DEUCES	DEVILDOMS	DEVOURER	DHARNA
DETERSION	DEUDDARN	DEVILESS	DEVOURERS	DHARNAS
DETERSIONS	DEUDDARNS	DEVILESSES	DEVOURING	DHOBI
DETERSIVE	DEUS	DEVILET	DEVOURS	DHOBIS
DETERSIVES	DEUTERATE	DEVILETS	DEVOUT	DHOLE
DETEST	DEUTERATED	DEVILING	DEVOUTER	DHOLES
DETESTED	DEUTERATES	DEVILINGS	DEVOUTEST	DHOLL
DETESTING	DEUTERATING	DEVILISH	DEVOUTLY	DHOLLS
DETESTS	DEUTERIDE	DEVILISM	DEVVEL	DHOOLIES
DETHRONE	DEUTERIDES	DEVILISMS	DEVVELLED	DHOOLY
DETHRONED	DEUTERIUM	DEVILKIN	DEVVELLING	DHOOTI
DETHRONER	DEUTERIUMS	DEVILKINS	DEVVELS	DHOOTIS
DETHRONERS	DEUTERON	DEVILLED	DEW	DHOTI
DETHRONES	DEUTERONS	DEVILLING	DEWAN	DHOTIS
DETHRONING	DEUTON	DEVILMENT	DEWANI	DHOW
DETHRONINGS	DEUTONS	DEVILMENTS	DEWANIS	DHOWS
DETINUE	DEVA	DEVILRIES	DEWANNIES	DHURRA
DETINUES	DEVALL	DEVILRY	DEWANNY	DHURRAS
DETONATE	DEVALLED	DEVILS	DEWANS	DHURRIE
DETONATED	DEVALLING	DEVILSHIP	DEWATER	DHURRIES
DETONATES	DEVALLS	DEVILSHIPS	DEWATERED	DI
DETONATING	DEVALUATE	DEVILTRIES	DEWATERING	DIABASE
DETONATOR	DEVALUATED	DEVILTRY	DEWATERS	DIABASES
DETONATORS	DEVALUATES	DEVIOUS	DEWED	DIABASIC
DETORSION	DEVALUATING	DEVIOUSLY	DEWFULL	DIABETES
DETORSIONS	DEVALUE	DEVISABLE	DEWIER	DIABETIC
DETORT	DEVALUED	DEVISAL	DEWIEST	DIABETICS
DETORTED	DEVALUES	DEVISALS	DEWILY	DIABLERIE
DETORTING	DEVALUING	DEVISE	DEWINESS	DIABLERIES
DETORTION	DEVAS	DEVISED	DEWINESSES	DIABLERY
DETORTIONS	DEVASTATE	DEVISEE	DEWING	DIABOLIC
DETORTS	DEVASTATED	DEVISEES	DEWITT	DIABOLISE
DETOUR	DEVASTATES	DEVISER	DEWITTED	DIABOLISED
DETOURED	DEVASTATING	DEVISERS	DEWITTING	DIABOLISES
DETOURING	DEVEL	DEVISES	DEWITTS	DIABOLISING
DETOURS	DEVELLED	DEVISING	DEWLAP	DIABOLISM
DETOXIFIED	DEVELLING	DEVISOR	DEWLAPPED	DIABOLISMS
DETOXIFIES	DEVELOP	DEVISORS	DEWLAPS	DIABOLIZE
DETOXIFY	DEVELOPE	DEVITRIFIED	DEWLAPT	DIABOLIZED
DETOXIFYING	DEVELOPED	DEVITRIFIES	DEWPOINT	DIABOLIZES
DETRACT	DEVELOPER	DEVITRIFY	DEWPOINTS	DIABOLIZING
DETRACTED	DEVELOPERS	DEVITRIFYING	DEWS	DIABOLO
DETRACTING	DEVELOPES	DEVLING	DEWY	DIABOLOGIES
DETRACTINGS	DEVELOPING	DEVLINGS	DEXTER	DIABOLOGY
DETRACTOR	DEVELOPS	DEVOICE	DEXTERITIES	DIABOLOS
DETRACTORS	DEVELS	DEVOICED	DEXTERITY	DIACHYLON
DETRACTS	DEVEST	DEVOICES	DEXTEROUS	DIACHYLONS
DETRAIN	DEVESTED	DEVOICING	DEXTERS	DIACHYLUM
DETRAINED	DEVESTING	DEVOID	DEXTRAL	DIACHYLUMS
DETRAINING	DEVESTS	DEVOIR	DEXTRALLY	DIACID
DETRAINS	DEVIANCE	DEVOIRS	DEXTRAN	DIACODION
DÉTRAQUÉ	DEVIANCES	DEVOLVE	DEXTRANS	DIACODIONS
DÉTRAQUÉE	DEVIANCIES	DEVOLVED	DEXTRIN	DIACODIUM
DÉTRAQUÉES	DEVIANCY	DEVOLVES	DEXTRINE	DIACODIUMS
DÉTRAQUÉS	DEVIANT	DEVOLVING	DEXTRINES	DIACONAL
DETRIMENT	DEVIANTS	DEVONPORT	DEXTRINS	DIACONATE

DIACONATES	DIALYSES	DIARIST	DIBBLES	DICROTISMS
DIACRITIC	DIALYSING	DIARISTS	DIBBLING	DICROTOUS
DIACRITICS	DIALYSIS	DIARIZE	DIBBS	DICT
DIACT	DIALYTIC	DIARIZED	DIBS	DICTA
DIACTINAL	DIALYZE	DIARIZES	DIBUTYL	DICTATE
DIACTINE	DIALYZED	DIARIZING	DICACIOUS	DICTATED
DIACTINIC	DIALYZER	DIARRHEA	DICACITIES	DICTATES
DIADEM	DIALYZERS	DIARRHEAL	DICACITY	DICTATING
DIADEMED	DIALYZES	DIARRHEAS	DICAST	DICTATION
DIADEMS	DIALYZING	DIARRHEIC	DICASTERIES	DICTATIONS
DIADOCHI	DIAMAGNET	DIARRHOEA	DICASTERY	DICTATOR
DIADROM	DIAMAGNETS	DIARRHOEAS	DICASTIC	DICTATORS
DIADROMS	DIAMANTÉ	DIARY	DICASTS	DICTATORY
DIAERESES	DIAMANTÉS	DIASCOPE	DICE	DICTATRIX
DIAERESIS	DIAMETER	DIASCOPES	DICED	DICTATRIXES
DIAGLYPH	DIAMETERS	DIASPORA	DICENTRA	DICTATURE
DIAGLYPHS	DIAMETRAL	DIASPORAS	DICENTRAS	DICTATURES
DIAGNOSE	DIAMETRIC	DIASPORE	DICER	DICTED
DIAGNOSED	DIAMOND	DIASPORES	DICERS	DICTING
DIAGNOSES	DIAMONDED	DIASTASE	DICES	DICTION
DIAGNOSING	DIAMONDS	DIASTASES	DICEY	DICTIONS
DIAGNOSIS	DIAMYL	DIASTASIC	DICH	DICTS
DIAGONAL	DIANDRIES	DIASTASIS	DICHASIA	DICTUM
DIAGONALS	DIANDROUS	DIASTATIC	DICHASIAL	DICTY
DIAGRAM	DIANDRY	DIASTEMA	DICHASIUM	DICTYOGEN
DIAGRAMS	DIANETICS®	DIASTEMATA	DICHOGAMIES	DICTYOGENS
DIAGRAPH	DIANODAL	DIASTER	DICHOGAMY	DICYCLIC
DIAGRAPHS	DIANOETIC	DIASTERS	DICHORD	DID
DIAGRID	DIANTHUS	DIASTOLE	DICHORDS	DIDACTIC
DIAGRIDS	DIANTHUSES	DIASTOLES	DICHOTOMIES	DIDACTICS
DIAL	DIAPASE	DIASTOLIC	DICHOTOMY	DIDACTYL
DIALECT	DIAPASES	DIASTYLE	DICHROIC	DIDACTYLS
DIALECTAL	DIAPASON	DIASTYLES	DICHROISM	DIDAKAI
DIALECTIC	DIAPASONS	DIATHERMIES	DICHROISMS	DIDAKAIS
DIALECTICS	DIAPAUSE	DIATHERMY	DICHROITE	DIDAKEI
DIALECTS	DIAPAUSES	DIATHESES	DICHROITES	DIDAKEIS
DIALIST	DIAPENTE	DIATHESIS	DICHROMAT	DIDAPPER
DIALISTS	DIAPENTES	DIATHETIC	DICHROMATS	DIDAPPERS
DIALLAGE	DIAPER	DIATOM	DICHROMIC	DIDDER
DIALLAGES	DIAPERED	DIATOMIC	DICHT	DIDDERED
DIALLAGIC	DIAPERING	DIATOMIST	DICHTED	DIDDERING
DIALLED	DIAPERINGS	DIATOMISTS	DICHTING	DIDDERS
DIALLER	DIAPERS	DIATOMITE	DICHTS	DIDDICOI
DIALLERS	DIAPHONE	DIATOMITES	DICIER	DIDDICOIS
DIALLING	DIAPHONES	DIATOMS	DICIEST	DIDDICOY
DIALLINGS	DIAPHRAGM	DIATONIC	DICING	DIDDIOOYO
DIALOG	DIAPHRAGMS	DIATRETUM	DICINGS	DIDDLE
DIALOGIC	DIAPHYSES	DIATRETUMS	DICK	DIDDLED
DIALOGISE	DIAPHYSIS	DIATRIBE	DICKENS	DIDDLER
DIALOGISED	DIAPIR	DIATRIBES	DICKENSES	DIDDLERS
DIALOGISES	DIAPIRIC	DIATROPIC	DICKER	DIDDLES
DIALOGISING	DIAPIRISM	DIAXON	DICKERED	DIDDLING
DIALOGIST	DIAPIRISMS	DIAXONS	DICKERING	DIDDYCOY
DIALOGISTS	DIAPIRS	DIAZEPAM	DICKERS	DIDDYCOYS
DIALOGITE	DIAPYESES	DIAZEPAMS	DICKEY	DIDELPHIC
DIALOGITES	DIAPYESIS	DIAZEUXES	DICKEYS	DIDELPHID
DIALOGIZE	DIAPYETIC	DIAZEUXIS	DICKIE	DIDELPHIDS
DIALOGIZED	DIAPYETICS	DIAZO	DICKIER	DIDICOI
DIALOGIZES	DIARCH	DIAZOES	DICKIES	DIDICOIS
DIALOGIZING	DIARCHAL	DIAZOS	DICKIEST	DIDICOY
DIALOGS	DIARCHIC	DIB	DICKS	DIDICOYS
DIALOGUE	DIARCHIES	DIBASIC	DICKTY	DIDO
DIALOGUED	DIARCHY	DIBBED	DICKY	DIDOES
DIALOGUES	DIARIAL	DIBBER	DICLINISM	DIDOS
DIALOGUING	DIARIAN	DIBBERS	DICLINISMS	DIDRACHM
DIALS	DIARIES	DIBBING	DICLINOUS	DIDRACHMA
DIALYSE	DIARISE	DIBBLE	DICOT	DIDRACHMAS
DIALYSED	DIARISED	DIBBLED	DICOTS	DIDRACHMS
DIALYSER	DIARISES	DIBBLER	DICROTIC	DIDST
DIALYSERS	DIARISING	DIBBLERS	DICROTISM	DIDYMIUM

DIDYMIUMS	DIFFRACTS	DIGNIFYING	DILLS	DIMMING
DIDYMOUS	DIFFUSE	DIGNITARIES	DILLY	DIMMISH
DIE	DIFFUSED	DIGNITARY	DILUENT	DIMNESS
DIEB	DIFFUSELY	DIGNITIES	DILUENTS	DIMNESSES
DIEBACK	DIFFUSER	DIGNITY	DILUTABLE	DIMORPH
DIEBACKS	DIFFUSERS	DIGONAL	DILUTABLES	DIMORPHIC
DIEBS	DIFFUSES	DIGRAPH	DILUTE	DIMORPHS
DIED	DIFFUSEST	DIGRAPHS	DILUTED	DIMPLE
DIEDRAL	DIFFUSING	DIGRESS	DILUTEE	DIMPLED
DIEDRALS	DIFFUSION	DIGRESSED	DILUTEES	DIMPLES
DIÈDRE	DIFFUSIONS	DIGRESSES	DILUTER	DIMPLIER
DIÈDRES	DIFFUSIVE	DIGRESSING	DILUTERS	DIMPLIEST
DIEGESES	DIG	DIGS	DILUTES	DIMPLING
DIEGESIS	DIGAMIES	DIGYNIAN	DILUTING	DIMPLY
DIELDRIN	DIGAMIST	DIGYNOUS	DILUTION	DIMS
DIELDRINS	DIGAMISTS	DIHEDRAL	DILUTIONS	DIMWIT
DIELYTRA	DIGAMMA	DIHEDRALS	DILUTOR	DIMWITS
DIELYTRAS	DIGAMMAS	DIHEDRON	DILUTORS	DIMYARIAN
DIENE	DIGAMOUS	DIHEDRONS	DILUVIA	DIN
DIENES	DIGAMY	DIHYBRID	DILUVIAL	DINAR
DIERESES	DIGASTRIC	DIHYBRIDS	DILUVIAN	DINARCHIES
DIERESIS	DIGEST	DIHYDRIC	DILUVION	DINARCHY
DIES	DIGESTED	DIKA	DILUVIONS	DINARS
DIESEL	DIGESTER	DIKAS	DILUVIUM	DINDLE
DIESELISE	DIGESTERS	DIKAST	DILUVIUMS	DINDLED
DIESELISED	DIGESTING	DIKASTS	DIM	DINDLES
DIESELISES	DIGESTION	DIKE	DIMBLE	DINDLING
DIESELISING	DIGESTIONS	DIKED	DIMBLES	DINE
DIESELIZE	DIGESTIVE	DIKER	DIME	DINED
DIESELIZED	DIGESTIVES	DIKERS	DIMENSION	DINER
DIESELIZES	DIGESTS	DIKES	DIMENSIONED	DINERS
DIESELIZING	DIGGABLE	DIKEY	DIMENSIONING	DINES
DIESELS	DIGGED	DIKIER	DIMENSIONS	DINETTE
DIESES	DIGGER	DIKIEST	DIMER	DINETTES
DIESIS	DIGGERS	DIKING	DIMERIC	DINFUL
DIESTRUS	DIGGING	DIKTAT	DIMERISE	DING
DIESTRUSES	DIGGINGS	DIKTATS	DIMERISED	DINGBAT
DIET	DIGHT	DILATABLE	DIMERISES	DINGBATS
DIETARIAN	DIGHTED	DILATANCIES	DIMERISING	DINGE
DIETARIANS	DIGHTING	DILATANCY	DIMERISM	DINGED
DIETARY	DIGHTS	DILATANT	DIMERISMS	DINGER
DIETED	DIGIT	DILATATOR	DIMERIZE	DINGERS
DIETER	DIGITAL	DILATATORS	DIMERIZED	DINGES
DIETERS	DIGITALIN	DILATE	DIMERIZES	DINGESES
DIETETIC	DIGITALINS	DILATED	DIMERIZING	DINGEY
DIETETICS	DIGITALIS	DILATER	DIMEROUS	DINGEYS
DIETHYL	DIGITALISES	DILATERS	DIMERS	DINGHIES
DIETICIAN	DIGITALS	DILATES	DIMES	DINGHY
DIETICIANS	DIGITATE	DILATING	DIMETER	DINGIER
DIETINE	DIGITATED	DILATION	DIMETERS	DINGIES
DIETINES	DIGITISE	DILATIONS	DIMETHYL	DINGIEST
DIETING	DIGITISED	DILATIVE	DIMETHYLS	DINGINESS
DIETIST	DIGITISER	DILATOR	DIMETRIC	DINGINESSES
DIETISTS	DIGITISERS	DILATORS	DIMIDIATE	DINGING
DIETITIAN	DIGITISES	DILATORY	DIMIDIATED	DINGLE
DIETITIANS	DIGITISING	DILDO	DIMIDIATES	DINGLES
DIETS	DIGITIZE	DILDOE	DIMIDIATING	DINGO
DIFFER	DIGITIZED	DILDOES	DIMINISH	DINGOES
DIFFERED	DIGITIZER	DILDOS	DIMINISHED	DINGS
DIFFERENT	DIGITIZERS	DILEMMA	DIMINISHES	DINGUS
DIFFERING	DIGITIZES	DILEMMAS	DIMINISHING	DINGUSES
DIFFERS	DIGITIZING	DILIGENCE	DIMINISHINGS	DINGY
DIFFICILE	DIGITS	DILIGENCES	DIMISSORY	DINIC
DIFFICULT	DIGLOT	DILIGENT	DIMITIES	DINICS
DIFFIDENT	DIGLOTS	DILL	DIMITY	DINING
DIFFLUENT	DIGLYPH	DILLI	DIMLY	DINK
DIFFORM	DIGLYPHS	DILLIES	DIMMED	DINKED
DIFFRACT	DIGNIFIED	DILLING	DIMMER	DINKER
DIFFRACTED	DIGNIFIES	DILLINGS	DIMMERS	DINKEST
DIFFRACTING	DIGNIFY	DILLIS	DIMMEST	DINKIER

DINKIEST
DINKING
DINKS
DINKUM
DINKY
DINMONT
DINMONTS
DINNED
DINNER
DINNERED
DINNERING
DINNERS
DINNING
DINNLE
DINNLED
DINNLES
DINNLING
DINOSAUR
DINOSAURS
DINS
DINT
DINTED
DINTING
DINTS
DIOCESAN
DIOCESANS
DIOCESE
DIOCESES
DIODE
DIODES
DIOECIOUS
DIOECISM
DIOECISMS
DIOESTRUS
DIOESTRUSES
DIOPSIDE
DIOPSIDES
DIOPTASE
DIOPTASES
DIOPTER
DIOPTERS
DIOPTRATE
DIOPTRE
DIOPTRES
DIOPTRIC
DIOPTRICS
DIORAMA
DIORAMAS
DIORAMIC
DIORISM
DIORISMS
DIORISTIC
DIORITE
DIORITES
DIORITIC
DIOSGENIN
DIOSGENINS
DIOTA
DIOTAS
DIOXAN
DIOXANE
DIOXANES
DIOXANS
DIOXIDE
DIOXIDES
DIOXIN
DIOXINS
DIP
DIPCHICK
DIPCHICKS

DIPEPTIDE
DIPEPTIDES
DIPHENYL
DIPHENYLS
DIPHONE
DIPHONES
DIPHTHONG
DIPHTHONGS
DIPHYSITE
DIPHYSITES
DIPLEX
DIPLOE
DIPLOES
DIPLOGEN
DIPLOGENS
DIPLOID
DIPLOIDIES
DIPLOIDY
DIPLOMA
DIPLOMACIES
DIPLOMACY
DIPLOMAED
DIPLOMAING
DIPLOMAS
DIPLOMAT
DIPLOMATE
DIPLOMATED
DIPLOMATES
DIPLOMATING
DIPLOMATS
DIPLON
DIPLONS
DIPLONT
DIPLONTS
DIPLOPIA
DIPLOPIAS
DIPNOAN
DIPNOANS
DIPNOOUS
DIPODIES
DIPODY
DIPOLAR
DIPOLE
DIPOLES
DIPPED
DIPPER
DIPPERS
DIPPIER
DIPPIEST
DIPPING
DIPPINGS
DIPPY
DIPS
DIPSADES
DIPSAS
DIPSO
DIPSOS
DIPTERAL
DIPTERAN
DIPTERANS
DIPTERIST
DIPTERISTS
DIPTEROI
DIPTEROS
DIPTEROSES
DIPTEROUS
DIPTYCH
DIPTYCHS
DIRDAM
DIRDAMS

DIRDUM
DIRDUMS
DIRE
DIRECT
DIRECTED
DIRECTER
DIRECTEST
DIRECTING
DIRECTION
DIRECTIONS
DIRECTIVE
DIRECTIVES
DIRECTLY
DIRECTOR
DIRECTORIES
DIRECTORS
DIRECTORY
DIRECTRICES
DIRECTRIX
DIRECTRIXES
DIRECTS
DIREFUL
DIREFULLY
DIREMPT
DIREMPTED
DIREMPTING
DIREMPTS
DIRER
DIREST
DIRGE
DIRGES
DIRHAM
DIRHAMS
DIRHEM
DIRHEMS
DIRIGE
DIRIGENT
DIRIGES
DIRIGIBLE
DIRIGIBLES
DIRIGISM
DIRIGISME
DIRIGISMES
DIRIGISMS
DIRIGISTE
DIRIMENT
DIRK
DIRKE
DIRKED
DIRKES
DIRKING
DIRKS
DIRL
DIRLED
DIRLING
DIRLS
DIRNDL
DIRNDLS
DIRT
DIRTED
DIRTIED
DIRTIER
DIRTIES
DIRTIEST
DIRTILY
DIRTINESS
DIRTINESSES
DIRTING
DIRTS
DIRTY

DIRTYING
DISA
DISABLE
DISABLED
DISABLES
DISABLING
DISABUSE
DISABUSED
DISABUSES
DISABUSING
DISACCORD
DISACCORDED
DISACCORDING
DISACCORDS
DISADORN
DISADORNED
DISADORNING
DISADORNS
DISAFFECT
DISAFFECTED
DISAFFECTING
DISAFFECTS
DISAFFIRM
DISAFFIRMED
DISAFFIRMING
DISAFFIRMS
DISAGREE
DISAGREED
DISAGREEING
DISAGREES
DISALLIED
DISALLIES
DISALLOW
DISALLOWED
DISALLOWING
DISALLOWS
DISALLY
DISALLYING
DISANCHOR
DISANCHORED
DISANCHORING
DISANCHORS
DISANNEX
DISANNEXED
DISANNEXES
DISANNEXING
DISANNUL
DISANNULLED
DISANNULLING
DISANNULS
DISANOINT
DISANOINTED
DISANOINTING
DISANOINTS
DISAPPEAR
DISAPPEARED
DISAPPEARING
DISAPPEARS
DISAPPLIED
DISAPPLIES
DISAPPLY
DISAPPLYING
DISARM
DISARMED
DISARMER
DISARMERS
DISARMING
DISARMS
DISARRAY
DISARRAYED

DISARRAYING
DISARRAYS
DISAS
DISASTER
DISASTERS
DISATTIRE
DISATTIRED
DISATTIRES
DISATTIRING
DISATTUNE
DISATTUNED
DISATTUNES
DISATTUNING
DISAVOUCH
DISAVOUCHED
DISAVOUCHES
DISAVOUCHING
DISAVOW
DISAVOWAL
DISAVOWALS
DISAVOWED
DISAVOWING
DISAVOWS
DISBAND
DISBANDED
DISBANDING
DISBANDS
DISBAR
DISBARK
DISBARKED
DISBARKING
DISBARKS
DISBARRED
DISBARRING
DISBARS
DISBELIEF
DISBELIEFS
DISBENCH
DISBENCHED
DISBENCHES
DISBENCHING
DISBODIED
DISBOSOM
DISBOSOMED
DISBOSOMING
DISBODOMS
DISBOWEL
DISBOWELLED
DISBOWELLING
DISBOWELS
DISBRANCH
DISBRANCHED
DISBRANCHES
DISBRANCHING
DISBUD
DISBUDDED
DISBUDDING
DISBUDS
DISBURDEN
DISBURDENED
DISBURDENING
DISBURDENS
DISBURSAL
DISBURSALS
DISBURSE
DISBURSED
DISBURSES
DISBURSING
DISC
DISCAGE

DISCAGED
DISCAGES
DISCAGING
DISCAL
DISCALCED
DISCANDIE
DISCANDIED
DISCANDIES
DISCANDY
DISCANDYING
DISCANT
DISCANTED
DISCANTING
DISCANTS
DISCARD
DISCARDED
DISCARDING
DISCARDS
DISCASE
DISCASED
DISCASES
DISCASING
DISCED
DISCEPT
DISCEPTED
DISCEPTING
DISCEPTS
DISCERN
DISCERNED
DISCERNER
DISCERNERS
DISCERNING
DISCERNS
DISCERP
DISCERPED
DISCERPING
DISCERPS
DISCHARGE
DISCHARGED
DISCHARGES
DISCHARGING
DISCHURCH
DISCHURCHED
DISCHURCHES
DISCHURCHING
DISCIDE
DISCIDED
DISCIDES
DISCIDING
DISCINCT
DISCING
DISCIPLE
DISCIPLED
DISCIPLES
DISCIPLING
DISCLAIM
DISCLAIMED
DISCLAIMING
DISCLAIMS
DISCLOSE
DISCLOSED
DISCLOSES
DISCLOSING
DISCLOST
DISCO
DISCOER
DISCOERS
DISCOID
DISCOIDAL
DISCOLOUR

DISCOLOURED
DISCOLOURING
DISCOLOURS
DISCOMFIT
DISCOMFITED
DISCOMFITING
DISCOMFITS
DISCOMMON
DISCOMMONED
DISCOMMONING
DISCOMMONS
DISCORD
DISCORDED
DISCORDING
DISCORDS
DISCOS
DISCOUNT
DISCOUNTED
DISCOUNTING
DISCOUNTS
DISCOURE
DISCOURED
DISCOURES
DISCOURING
DISCOURSE
DISCOURSED
DISCOURSES
DISCOURSING
DISCOVER
DISCOVERED
DISCOVERIES
DISCOVERING
DISCOVERS
DISCOVERT
DISCOVERY
DISCREDIT
DISCREDITED
DISCREDITING
DISCREDITS
DISCREET
DISCREETER
DISCREETEST
DISCRETE
DISCRETER
DISCRETEST
DISCROWN
DISCROWNED
DISCROWNING
DISCROWNS
DISCS
DISCUMBER
DISCUMBERED
DISCUMBERING
DISCUMBERS
DISCURE
DISCURED
DISCURES
DISCURING
DISCURSUS
DISCURSUSES
DISCUS
DISCUSES
DISCUSS
DISCUSSED
DISCUSSES
DISCUSSING
DISDAIN
DISDAINED
DISDAINING
DISDAINS

DISEASE
DISEASED
DISEASES
DISEASING
DISEDGE
DISEDGED
DISEDGES
DISEDGING
DISEMBARK
DISEMBARKED
DISEMBARKING
DISEMBARKS
DISEMBODIED
DISEMBODIES
DISEMBODY
DISEMBODYING
DISEMPLOY
DISEMPLOYED
DISEMPLOYING
DISEMPLOYS
DISENABLE
DISENABLED
DISENABLES
DISENABLING
DISENDOW
DISENDOWED
DISENDOWING
DISENDOWS
DISENGAGE
DISENGAGED
DISENGAGES
DISENGAGING
DISENROL
DISENROLLED
DISENROLLING
DISENROLS
DISENTAIL
DISENTAILED
DISENTAILING
DISENTAILS
DISENTOMB
DISENTOMBED
DISENTOMBING
DISENTOMBS
DISESTEEM
DISESTEEMED
DISESTEEMING
DISESTEEMS
DISEUR
DISEURS
DISEUSE
DISEUSES
DISFAME
DISFAMES
DISFAVOR
DISFAVORED
DISFAVORING
DISFAVORS
DISFAVOUR
DISFAVOURED
DISFAVOURING
DISFAVOURS
DISFIGURE
DISFIGURED
DISFIGURES
DISFIGURING
DISFLESH
DISFLESHED
DISFLESHES
DISFLESHING

DISFLUENT
DISFOREST
DISFORESTED
DISFORESTING
DISFORESTS
DISFORM
DISFORMED
DISFORMING
DISFORMS
DISFROCK
DISFROCKED
DISFROCKING
DISFROCKS
DISGAVEL
DISGAVELLED
DISGAVELLING
DISGAVELS
DISGEST
DISGESTED
DISGESTING
DISGESTS
DISGODDED
DISGORGE
DISGORGED
DISGORGES
DISGORGING
DISGOWN
DISGOWNED
DISGOWNING
DISGOWNS
DISGRACE
DISGRACED
DISGRACER
DISGRACERS
DISGRACES
DISGRACING
DISGRADE
DISGRADED
DISGRADES
DISGRADING
DISGUISE
DISGUISED
DISGUISER
DISGUISERS
DISGUISES
DISGUISING
DISGUISINGS
DISGUST
DISGUSTED
DISGUSTING
DISGUSTS
DISH
DISHABIT
DISHABITED
DISHABITING
DISHABITS
DISHABLE
DISHABLED
DISHABLES
DISHABLING
DISHALLOW
DISHALLOWED
DISHALLOWING
DISHALLOWS
DISHED
DISHELM
DISHELMED
DISHELMING
DISHELMS
DISHERIT

DISHERITED
DISHERITING
DISHERITS
DISHES
DISHEVEL
DISHEVELLED
DISHEVELLING
DISHEVELS
DISHFUL
DISHFULS
DISHIER
DISHIEST
DISHING
DISHINGS
DISHOME
DISHOMED
DISHOMES
DISHOMING
DISHONEST
DISHONOR
DISHONORED
DISHONORING
DISHONORS
DISHONOUR
DISHONOURED
DISHONOURING
DISHONOURS
DISHORN
DISHORNED
DISHORNING
DISHORNS
DISHORSE
DISHORSED
DISHORSES
DISHORSING
DISHOUSE
DISHOUSED
DISHOUSES
DISHOUSING
DISHUMOUR
DISHUMOURED
DISHUMOURING
DISHUMOURS
DISHY
DISILLUDE
DISILLUDED
DISILLUDES
DISILLUDING
DISIMMURE
DISIMMURED
DISIMMURES
DISIMMURING
DISINFECT
DISINFECTED
DISINFECTING
DISINFECTS
DISINFEST
DISINFESTED
DISINFESTING
DISINFESTS
DISINHUME
DISINHUMED
DISINHUMES
DISINHUMING
DISINTER
DISINTERRED
DISINTERRING
DISINTERS
DISINURE
DISINURED

DISINURES
DISINURING
DISINVEST
DISINVESTED
DISINVESTING
DISINVESTS
DISJASKIT
DISJECT
DISJECTED
DISJECTING
DISJECTS
DISJOIN
DISJOINED
DISJOINING
DISJOINS
DISJOINT
DISJOINTED
DISJOINTING
DISJOINTS
DISJUNCT
DISJUNCTS
DISJUNE
DISJUNES
DISK
DISKED
DISKETTE
DISKETTES
DISKING
DISKS
DISLEAF
DISLEAFED
DISLEAFING
DISLEAFS
DISLEAL
DISLEAVE
DISLEAVED
DISLEAVES
DISLEAVING
DISLIKE
DISLIKED
DISLIKEN
DISLIKENED
DISLIKENING
DISLIKENS
DISLIKES
DISLIKING
DISLIMB
DISLIMBED
DISLIMBING
DISLIMBS
DISLIMN
DISLIMNED
DISLIMNING
DISLIMNS
DISLINK
DISLINKED
DISLINKING
DISLINKS
DISLOAD
DISLOADED
DISLOADING
DISLOADS
DISLOCATE
DISLOCATED
DISLOCATES
DISLOCATING
DISLODGE
DISLODGED
DISLODGES
DISLODGING

DISLOIGN
DISLOIGNED
DISLOIGNING
DISLOIGNS
DISLOYAL
DISLOYALLER
DISLOYALLEST
DISLUSTRE
DISLUSTRED
DISLUSTRES
DISLUSTRING
DISMAL
DISMALITIES
DISMALITY
DISMALLER
DISMALLEST
DISMALLY
DISMALS
DISMAN
DISMANNED
DISMANNING
DISMANS
DISMANTLE
DISMANTLED
DISMANTLES
DISMANTLING
DISMASK
DISMASKED
DISMASKING
DISMASKS
DISMAST
DISMASTED
DISMASTING
DISMASTS
DISMAY
DISMAYD
DISMAYED
DISMAYFUL
DISMAYING
DISMAYL
DISMAYLED
DISMAYLING
DISMAYLS
DISMAYS
DISME
DISMEMBER
DISMEMBERED
DISMEMBERING
DISMEMBERS
DISMES
DISMISS
DISMISSAL
DISMISSALS
DISMISSED
DISMISSES
DISMISSING
DISMODED
DISMOUNT
DISMOUNTED
DISMOUNTING
DISMOUNTS
DISNEST
DISNESTED
DISNESTING
DISNESTS
DISOBEY
DISOBEYED
DISOBEYING
DISOBEYS
DISOBLIGE

DISOBLIGED
DISOBLIGES
DISOBLIGING
DISORBED
DISORDER
DISORDERED
DISORDERING
DISORDERS
DISORIENT
DISORIENTED
DISORIENTING
DISORIENTS
DISOWN
DISOWNED
DISOWNING
DISOWNS
DISPACE
DISPACED
DISPACES
DISPACING
DISPARAGE
DISPARAGED
DISPARAGES
DISPARAGING
DISPARATE
DISPARATES
DISPARITIES
DISPARITY
DISPARK
DISPARKED
DISPARKING
DISPARKS
DISPART
DISPARTED
DISPARTING
DISPARTS
DISPATCH
DISPATCHED
DISPATCHES
DISPATCHING
DISPATHIES
DISPATHY
DISPAUPER
DISPAUPERED
DISPAUPERING
DISPAUPERS
DISPEACE
DISPEACES
DISPEL
DISPELLED
DISPELLING
DISPELS
DISPENCE
DISPENCED
DISPENCES
DISPENCING
DISPEND
DISPENDED
DISPENDING
DISPENDS
DISPENSE
DISPENSED
DISPENSER
DISPENSERS
DISPENSES
DISPENSING
DISPEOPLE
DISPEOPLED
DISPEOPLES
DISPEOPLING

DISPERSAL
DISPERSALS
DISPERSE
DISPERSED
DISPERSER
DISPERSERS
DISPERSES
DISPERSING
DISPIRIT
DISPIRITED
DISPIRITING
DISPIRITS
DISPLACE
DISPLACED
DISPLACES
DISPLACING
DISPLANT
DISPLANTED
DISPLANTING
DISPLANTS
DISPLAY
DISPLAYED
DISPLAYER
DISPLAYERS
DISPLAYING
DISPLAYS
DISPLE
DISPLEASE
DISPLEASED
DISPLEASES
DISPLEASING
DISPLED
DISPLES
DISPLING
DISPLODE
DISPLODED
DISPLODES
DISPLODING
DISPLUME
DISPLUMED
DISPLUMES
DISPLUMING
DISPONDEE
DISPONDEES
DISPONE
DISPONED
DISPONEE
DISPONEES
DISPONER
DISPONERS
DISPONES
DISPONGE
DISPONGED
DISPONGES
DISPONGING
DISPONING
DISPORT
DISPORTED
DISPORTING
DISPORTS
DISPOSAL
DISPOSALS
DISPOSE
DISPOSED
DISPOSER
DISPOSERS
DISPOSES
DISPOSING
DISPOSINGS
DISPOST

DISPOSTED
DISPOSTING
DISPOSTS
DISPOSURE
DISPOSURES
DISPRAD
DISPRAISE
DISPRAISED
DISPRAISES
DISPRAISING
DISPREAD
DISPREADING
DISPREADS
DISPRED
DISPREDDEN
DISPREDS
DISPRISON
DISPRISONED
DISPRISONING
DISPRISONS
DISPRIZE
DISPRIZED
DISPRIZES
DISPRIZING
DISPROFIT
DISPROFITS
DISPROOF
DISPROOFS
DISPROOVE
DISPROOVED
DISPROOVES
DISPROOVING
DISPROVAL
DISPROVALS
DISPROVE
DISPROVED
DISPROVEN
DISPROVES
DISPROVING
DISPUNGE
DISPUNGED
DISPUNGES
DISPUNGING
DISPURSE
DISPURSED
DISPURSES
DISPURSING
DISPURVEY
DISPURVEYED
DISPURVEYING
DISPURVEYS
DISPUTANT
DISPUTANTS
DISPUTE
DISPUTED
DISPUTER
DISPUTERS
DISPUTES
DISPUTING
DISQUIET
DISQUIETED
DISQUIETING
DISQUIETS
DISRANK
DISRANKED
DISRANKING
DISRANKS
DISRATE
DISRATED
DISRATES

DISRATING	DISSERTED	DISTENT	DISUNITY	DITTIT
DISREGARD	DISSERTING	DISTHENE	DISUSAGE	DITTO
DISREGARDED	DISSERTS	DISTHENES	DISUSAGES	DITTOED
DISREGARDING	DISSERVE	DISTHRONE	DISUSE	DITTOING
DISREGARDS	DISSERVED	DISTHRONED	DISUSED	DITTOLOGIES
DISRELISH	DISSERVES	DISTHRONES	DISUSES	DITTOLOGY
DISRELISHED	DISSERVING	DISTHRONING	DISUSING	DITTOS
DISRELISHES	DISSES	DISTICH	DISVALUE	DITTS
DISRELISHING	DISSEVER	DISTICHAL	DISVALUED	DITTY
DISREPAIR	DISSEVERED	DISTICHS	DISVALUES	DITTYING
DISREPAIRS	DISSEVERING	DISTIL	DISVALUING	DIURESES
DISREPUTE	DISSEVERS	DISTILL	DISVOUCH	DIURESIS
DISREPUTES	DISSHIVER	DISTILLED	DISVOUCHED	DIURETIC
DISROBE	DISSHIVERED	DISTILLER	DISVOUCHES	DIURETICS
DISROBED	DISSHIVERING	DISTILLERS	DISVOUCHING	DIURNAL
DISROBES	DISSHIVERS	DISTILLING	DISYOKE	DIURNALLY
DISROBING	DISSIDENT	DISTILLINGS	DISYOKED	DIURNALS
DISROOT	DISSIDENTS	DISTILLS	DISYOKES	DIUTURNAL
DISROOTED	DISSIGHT	DISTILS	DISYOKING	DIV
DISROOTING	DISSIGHTS	DISTINCT	DIT	DIVA
DISROOTS	DISSIMILE	DISTINCTER	DITA	DIVAGATE
DISRUPT	DISSIMILES	DISTINCTEST	DITAL	DIVAGATED
DISRUPTED	DISSIPATE	DISTINGUÉ	DITALS	DIVAGATES
DISRUPTER	DISSIPATED	DISTORT	DITAS	DIVAGATING
DISRUPTERS	DISSIPATES	DISTORTED	DITCH	DIVALENT
DISRUPTING	DISSIPATING	DISTORTING	DITCHED	DIVALENTS
DISRUPTOR	DISSOCIAL	DISTORTS	DITCHER	DIVAN
DISRUPTORS	DISSOLUTE	DISTRACT	DITCHERS	DIVANS
DISRUPTS	DISSOLUTES	DISTRACTED	DITCHES	DIVAS
DISS	DISSOLVE	DISTRACTING	DITCHING	DIVE
DISSEAT	DISSOLVED	DISTRACTS	DITE	DIVED
DISSEATED	DISSOLVES	DISTRAIN	DITED	DIVELLENT
DISSEATING	DISSOLVING	DISTRAINED	DITES	DIVER
DISSEATS	DISSONANT	DISTRAINING	DITHECAL	DIVERGE
DISSECT	DISSUADE	DISTRAINS	DITHECOUS	DIVERGED
DISSECTED	DISSUADED	DISTRAINT	DITHEISM	DIVERGENT
DISSECTING	DISSUADER	DISTRAINTS	DITHEISMS	DIVERGES
DISSECTINGS	DISSUADERS	DISTRAIT	DITHEIST	DIVERGING
DISSECTOR	DISSUADES	DISTRAITE	DITHEISTS	DIVERS
DISSECTORS	DISSUADING	DISTRESS	DITHELETE	DIVERSE
DISSECTS	DISSUNDER	DISTRESSED	DITHELETES	DIVERSED
DISSEISE	DISSUNDERED	DISTRESSES	DITHELISM	DIVERSELY
DISSEISED	DISSUNDERING	DISTRESSING	DITHELISMS	DIVERSES
DISSEISES	DISSUNDERS	DISTRICT	DITHER	DIVERSIFIED
DISSEISIN	DISTAFF	DISTRICTED	DITHERED	DIVERSIFIES
DISSEISING	DISTAFFS	DISTRICTING	DITHERER	DIVERSIFY
DISSEISINS	DISTAIN	DISTRICTS	DITHERERS	DIVERSIFYING
DISSEISOR	DISTAINED	DISTRUST	DITHERING	DIVERSING
DISSEISORS	DISTAINING	DISTRUSTED	DITHERS	DIVERSION
DISSEIZE	DISTAINS	DISTRUSTING	DITHERY	DIVERSIONS
DISSEIZED	DISTAL	DISTRUSTS	DITHYRAMB	DIVERSITIES
DISSEIZES	DISTALLY	DISTUNE	DITHYRAMBS	DIVERSITY
DISSEIZIN	DISTANCE	DISTUNED	DITING	DIVERSLY
DISSEIZING	DISTANCED	DISTUNES	DITOKOUS	DIVERT
DISSEIZINS	DISTANCES	DISTUNING	DITONE	DIVERTED
DISSEIZOR	DISTANCING	DISTURB	DITONES	DIVERTING
DISSEIZORS	DISTANT	DISTURBED	DITROCHEE	DIVERTIVE
DISSEMBLE	DISTANTLY	DISTURBER	DITROCHEES	DIVERTS
DISSEMBLED	DISTASTE	DISTURBERS	DITS	DIVES
DISSEMBLES	DISTASTED	DISTURBING	DITT	DIVEST
DISSEMBLIES	DISTASTES	DISTURBS	DITTANDER	DIVESTED
DISSEMBLING	DISTASTING	DISTYLE	DITTANDERS	DIVESTING
DISSEMBLY	DISTEMPER	DISTYLES	DITTANIES	DIVESTS
DISSENT	DISTEMPERED	DISUNION	DITTANY	DIVI
DISSENTED	DISTEMPERING	DISUNIONS	DITTAY	DIVIDABLE
DISSENTER	DISTEMPERS	DISUNITE	DITTAYS	DIVIDANT
DISSENTERS	DISTEND	DISUNITED	DITTED	DIVIDE
DISSENTING	DISTENDED	DISUNITES	DITTIED	DIVIDED
DISSENTS	DISTENDING	DISUNITIES	DITTIES	DIVIDEDLY
DISSERT	DISTENDS	DISUNITING	DITTING	DIVIDEND

DIVIDENDS	DIVVY	DOCILER	DODDERERS	DOGES
DIVIDER	DIVVYING	DOCILEST	DODDERIER	DOGESHIP
DIVIDERS	DIWAN	DOCILITIES	DODDERIEST	DOGESHIPS
DIVIDES	DIWANS	DOCILITY	DODDERING	DOGFIGHT
DIVIDING	DIXI	DOCIMASIES	DODDERS	DOGFIGHTS
DIVIDINGS	DIXIE	DOCIMASY	DODDERY	DOGFISH
DIVIDIVI	DIXIES	DOCK	DODDIER	DOGFISHES
DIVIDIVIS	DIXY	DOCKAGE	DODDIES	DOGFOX
DIVIDUAL	DIZAIN	DOCKAGES	DODDIEST	DOGFOXES
DIVIDUOUS	DIZAINS	DOCKED	DODDING	DOGGED
DIVINATOR	DIZEN	DOCKEN	DODDIPOLL	DOGGEDER
DIVINATORS	DIZENED	DOCKENS	DODDIPOLLS	DOGGEDEST
DIVINE	DIZENING	DOCKER	DODDLE	DOGGEDLY
DIVINED	DIZENS	DOCKERS	DODDLES	DOGGER
DIVINELY	DIZYGOTIC	DOCKET	DODDY	DOGGEREL
DIVINER	DIZZARD	DOCKETED	DODDYPOLL	DOGGERELS
DIVINERS	DIZZARDS	DOCKETING	DODDYPOLLS	DOGGERIES
DIVINES	DIZZIED	DOCKETS	DODECAGON	DOGGERMAN
DIVINEST	DIZZIER	DOCKING	DODECAGONS	DOGGERMEN
DIVING	DIZZIES	DOCKINGS	DODGE	DOGGERS
DIVINGS	DIZZIEST	DOCKISE	DODGED	DOGGERY
DIVINIFIED	DIZZILY	DOCKISED	DODGEM	DOGGESS
DIVINIFIES	DIZZINESS	DOCKISES	DODGEMS	DOGGESSES
DIVINIFY	DIZZINESSES	DOCKISING	DODGER	DOGGIE
DIVINIFYING	DIZZY	DOCKIZE	DODGERIES	DOGGIER
DIVINING	DIZZYING	DOCKIZED	DODGERS	DOGGIES
DIVINISE	DJEBEL	DOCKIZES	DODGERY	DOGGIEST
DIVINISED	DJEBELS	DOCKIZING	DODGES	DOGGINESS
DIVINISES	DJELLABA	DOCKLAND	DODGIER	DOGGINESSES
DIVINISING	DJELLABAH	DOCKLANDS	DODGIEST	DOGGING
DIVINITIES	DJELLABAHS	DOCKS	DODGING	DOGGINGS
DIVINITY	DJELLABAS	DOCKYARD	DODGY	DOGGISH
DIVINIZE	DJIBBAH	DOCKYARDS	DODKIN	DOGGISHLY
DIVINIZED	DJIBBAHS	DOCQUET	DODKINS	DOGGO
DIVINIZES	DJINN	DOCQUETED	DODMAN	DOGGONE
DIVINIZING	DJINNI	DOCQUETING	DODMANS	DOGGONED
DIVIS	DO	DOCQUETS	DODO	DOGGREL
DIVISIBLE	DOAB	DOCS	DODOES	DOGGRELS
DIVISIBLY	DOABLE	DOCTOR	DODOS	DOGGY
DIVISIM	DOABS	DOCTORAL	DODS	DOGHOLE
DIVISION	DOAT	DOCTORAND	DOE	DOGHOLES
DIVISIONS	DOATED	DOCTORANDS	DOEN	DOGIE
DIVISIVE	DOATER	DOCTORATE	DOER	DOGIES
DIVISOR	DOATERS	DOCTORATED	DOERS	DOGMA
DIVISORS	DOATING	DOCTORATES	DOES	DOGMAS
DIVORCE	DOATINGS	DOCTORATING	DOEST	DOGMATIC
DIVORCED	DOATS	DOCTORED	DOETH	DOGMATICS
DIVORCEE	DOB	DOCTORESS	DOFF	DOGMATISE
DIVORCEES	DOBBED	DOCTORESSES	DOFFED	DOGMATISED
DIVORCER	DOBBER	DOCTORIAL	DOFFER	DOGMATISES
DIVORCERS	DOBBERS	DOCTORING	DOFFERS	DOGMATISING
DIVORCES	DOBBIE	DOCTORLY	DOFFING	DOGMATISM
DIVORCING	DOBBIES	DOCTORS	DOFFS	DOGMATISMS
DIVORCIVE	DOBBIN	DOCTRESS	DOG	DOGMATIST
DIVOT	DOBBING	DOCTRESSES	DOGARESSA	DOGMATISTS
DIVOTS	DOBBINS	DOCTRINAL	DOGARESSAS	DOGMATIZE
DIVS	DOBBY	DOCTRINE	DOGATE	DOGMATIZED
DIVULGATE	DOBCHICK	DOCTRINES	DOGATES	DOGMATIZES
DIVULGATED	DOBCHICKS	DOCUDRAMA	DOGBANE	DOGMATIZING
DIVULGATES	DOBHASH	DOCUDRAMAS	DOGBANES	DOGMATORY
DIVULGATING	DOBHASHES	DOCUMENT	DOGBERRIES	DOGS
DIVULGE	DOBS	DOCUMENTED	DOGBERRY	DOGSBODIES
DIVULGED	DOC	DOCUMENTING	DOGBOLT	DOGSBODY
DIVULGES	DOCHMIAC	DOCUMENTS	DOGBOLTS	DOGSHIP
DIVULGING	DOCHMII	DOD	DOGCART	DOGSHIPS
DIVULSION	DOCHMIUS	DODDARD	DOGCARTS	DOGSHORES
DIVULSIONS	DOCHMIUSES	DODDED	DOGDAYS	DOGSKIN
DIVULSIVE	DOCHT	DODDER	DOGE	DOGSKINS
DIVVIED	DOCIBLE	DODDERED	DOGEATE	DOGSLEEP
DIVVIES	DOCILE	DODDERER	DOGEATES	DOGSLEEPS

DOGTEETH
DOGTOOTH
DOGTOWN
DOGTOWNS
DOGTROT
DOGTROTS
DOGVANE
DOGVANES
DOGWOOD
DOGWOODS
DOGY
DOH
DOHS
DOILED
DOILEDER
DOILEDEST
DOILIES
DOILT
DOILTER
DOILTEST
DOILY
DOING
DOINGS
DOIT
DOITED
DOITIT
DOITKIN
DOITKINS
DOITS
DOJO
DOJOS
DOLCE
DOLCES
DOLDRUMS
DOLE
DOLED
DOLEFUL
DOLEFULLY
DOLENT
DOLERITE
DOLERITES
DOLERITIC
DOLES
DOLESOME
DOLIA
DOLICHOS
DOLICHOSES
DOLING
DOLIUM
DOLL
DOLLAR
DOLLARED
DOLLARS
DOLLDOM
DOLLDOMS
DOLLED
DOLLHOOD
DOLLHOODS
DOLLIED
DOLLIER
DOLLIERS
DOLLIES
DOLLINESS
DOLLINESSES
DOLLING
DOLLISH
DOLLOP
DOLLOPS
DOLLS
DOLLY

DOLLYING
DOLMA
DOLMADES
DOLMAN
DOLMANS
DOLMAS
DOLMEN
DOLMENS
DOLOMITE
DOLOMITES
DOLOMITIC
DOLORIFIC
DOLOROSO
DOLOROUS
DOLOUR
DOLOURS
DOLPHIN
DOLPHINET
DOLPHINETS
DOLPHINS
DOLT
DOLTISH
DOLTISHLY
DOLTS
DOMAIN
DOMAINAL
DOMAINS
DOMAL
DOMANIAL
DOMATIA
DOMATIUM
DOME
DOMED
DOMES
DOMESTIC
DOMESTICS
DOMETT
DOMETTS
DOMICAL
DOMICIL
DOMICILE
DOMICILED
DOMICILES
DOMICILING
DOMICILS
DOMIER
DOMIEST
DOMINANCE
DOMINANCES
DOMINANCIES
DOMINANCY
DOMINANT
DOMINANTS
DOMINATE
DOMINATED
DOMINATES
DOMINATING
DOMINATOR
DOMINATORS
DOMINEER
DOMINEERED
DOMINEERING
DOMINEERS
DOMING
DOMINICAL
DOMINIE
DOMINIES
DOMINION
DOMINIONS
DOMINO

DOMINOES
DOMINOS
DOMY
DON
DONA
DONAH
DONAHS
DONARIES
DONARY
DONAS
DONATARIES
DONATARY
DONATE
DONATED
DONATES
DONATING
DONATION
DONATIONS
DONATISM
DONATISMS
DONATIVE
DONATIVES
DONATOR
DONATORIES
DONATORS
DONATORY
DONE
DONEE
DONEES
DONENESS
DONENESSES
DONG
DONGA
DONGAS
DONGED
DONGING
DONGLE
DONGLES
DONGS
DONING
DONINGS
DONJON
DONJONS
DONKEY
DONKEYS
DONNARD
DONNAT
DONNATS
DONNÉ
DONNE
DONNED
DONNÉE
DONNÉES
DONNERD
DONNERED
DONNERT
DONNÉS
DONNING
DONNISH
DONNISM
DONNISMS
DONNOT
DONNOTS
DONOR
DONORS
DONS
DONSHIP
DONSHIPS
DONSIE

DONUT
DONUTS
DONZEL
DONZELS
DOO
DOOB
DOOBS
DOOCOT
DOOCOTS
DOODAD
DOODADS
DOODAH
DOODAHS
DOODLE
DOODLEBUG
DOODLEBUGS
DOODLED
DOODLER
DOODLERS
DOODLES
DOODLING
DOOK
DOOKED
DOOKET
DOOKETS
DOOKING
DOOKS
DOOL
DOOLE
DOOLES
DOOLIE
DOOLIES
DOOLS
DOOM
DOOMED
DOOMFUL
DOOMIER
DOOMIEST
DOOMING
DOOMS
DOOMSDAY
DOOMSDAYS
DOOMSMAN
DOOMSMEN
DOOMSTER
DOOMSTERS
DOOMWATCH
DOOMWATCHED
DOOMWATCHES
DOOMWATCHING
DOOMWATCHINGS
DOOMY
DOOR
DOORBELL
DOORBELLS
DOORKNOB
DOORKNOBS
DOORKNOCK
DOORKNOCKED
DOORKNOCKING
DOORKNOCKS
DOORMAT
DOORMATS
DOORN
DOORNAIL
DOORNAILS
DOORNS
DOORPOST
DOORPOSTS
DOORS

DOORSTEP
DOORSTEPPED
DOORSTEPPING
DOORSTEPS
DOORSTONE
DOORSTONES
DOORSTOP
DOORSTOPS
DOORWAY
DOORWAYS
DOOS
DOP
DOPA
DOPAMINE
DOPAMINES
DOPANT
DOPANTS
DOPAS
DOPE
DOPED
DOPER
DOPERS
DOPES
DOPEY
DOPIER
DOPIEST
DOPING
DOPINGS
DOPPED
DOPPER
DOPPERS
DOPPIE
DOPPIES
DOPPING
DOPPINGS
DOPS
DOPY
DOR
DORAD
DORADO
DORADOS
DORADS
DOREE
DOREES
DORHAWK
DORHAWKS
DORIDOID
DORIDOIDS
DORIES
DORISE
DORISED
DORISES
DORISING
DORIZE
DORIZED
DORIZES
DORIZING
DORLACH
DORLACHS
DORM
DORMANCIES
DORMANCY
DORMANT
DORMANTS
DORMER
DORMERS
DORMICE
DORMIE
DORMIENT
DORMITION

DORMITIONS
DORMITIVE
DORMITIVES
DORMITORIES
DORMITORY
DORMOUSE
DORMS
DORMY
DORNICK
DORNICKS
DORP
DORPS
DORR
DORRED
DORRING
DORRS
DORS
DORSA
DORSAL
DORSALLY
DORSALS
DORSE
DORSEL
DORSELS
DORSER
DORSERS
DORSES
DORSIFLEX
DORSUM
DORT
DORTED
DORTER
DORTERS
DORTING
DORTOUR
DORTOURS
DORTS
DORTY
DORY
DOS
DOSAGE
DOSAGES
DOSE
DOSED
DOSEH
DOSEHS
DOSES
DOSIMETER
DOSIMETERS
DOSIMETRIES
DOSIMETRY
DOSING
DOSIOLOGIES
DOSIOLOGY
DOSOLOGIES
DOSOLOGY
DOSS
DOSSAL
DOSSALS
DOSSED
DOSSEL
DOSSELS
DOSSER
DOSSERS
DOSSES
DOSSIER
DOSSIERS
DOSSIL
DOSSILS
DOSSING

DOST
DOT
DOTAGE
DOTAGES
DOTAL
DOTANT
DOTANTS
DOTARD
DOTARDS
DOTATION
DOTATIONS
DOTE
DOTED
DOTER
DOTERS
DOTES
DOTH
DOTIER
DOTIEST
DOTING
DOTINGS
DOTISH
DOTS
DOTTED
DOTTEREL
DOTTERELS
DOTTIER
DOTTIEST
DOTTINESS
DOTTINESSES
DOTTING
DOTTIPOLL
DOTTIPOLLS
DOTTLE
DOTTLED
DOTTLER
DOTTLES
DOTTLEST
DOTTREL
DOTTRELS
DOTTY
DOTY
DOUANE
DOUANES
DOUANIER
DOUANIERO
DOUAR
DOUARS
DOUBLE
DOUBLED
DOUBLER
DOUBLERS
DOUBLES
DOUBLET
DOUBLETON
DOUBLETONS
DOUBLETS
DOUBLING
DOUBLINGS
DOUBLOON
DOUBLOONS
DOUBLY
DOUBT
DOUBTABLE
DOUBTED
DOUBTER
DOUBTERS
DOUBIFUL
DOUBTFULS
DOUBTING

DOUBTINGS
DOUBTLESS
DOUBTS
DOUC
DOUCE
DOUCELY
DOUCENESS
DOUCENESSES
DOUCEPERE
DOUCEPERES
DOUCER
DOUCEST
DOUCET
DOUCETS
DOUCEUR
DOUCEURS
DOUCHE
DOUCHED
DOUCHES
DOUCHING
DOUCINE
DOUCINES
DOUCS
DOUGH
DOUGHIER
DOUGHIEST
DOUGHNUT
DOUGHNUTS
DOUGHS
DOUGHT
DOUGHTIER
DOUGHTIEST
DOUGHTILY
DOUGHTY
DOUGHY
DOULEIA
DOULEIAS
DOUMA
DOUMAS
DOUP
DOUPS
DOUR
DOURA
DOURAS
DOURER
DOUREST
DOURINE
DOURINES
DOURNESS
DOURNESSES
DOUSE
DOUSED
DOUSER
DOUSERS
DOUSES
DOUSING
DOUT
DOUTED
DOUTER
DOUTERS
DOUTING
DOUTS
DOUZEPER
DOUZEPERS
DOVE
DOVECOT
DOVECOTE
DOVECOTES
DOVECOTS
DOVED

DOVEISH
DOVEKIE
DOVEKIES
DOVELET
DOVELETS
DOVER
DOVERED
DOVERING
DOVERS
DOVES
DOVETAIL
DOVETAILED
DOVETAILING
DOVETAILINGS
DOVETAILS
DOVIE
DOVIER
DOVIEST
DOVING
DOVISH
DOW
DOWABLE
DOWAGER
DOWAGERS
DOWAR
DOWARS
DOWD
DOWDIER
DOWDIES
DOWDIEST
DOWDILY
DOWDINESS
DOWDINESSES
DOWDS
DOWDY
DOWDYISH
DOWDYISM
DOWDYISMS
DOWED
DOWEL
DOWELLED
DOWELLING
DOWELLINGS
DOWELS
DOWER
DOWERED
DOWERING
DOWERLESS
DOWERS
DOWF
DOWFNESS
DOWFNESSES
DOWIE
DOWIER
DOWIEST
DOWING
DOWL
DOWLAS
DOWLASES
DOWLE
DOWLES
DOWLNE
DOWLNES
DOWLNEY
DOWLNEYS
DOWLS
DOWN
DOWNA
DOWNBEAT
DOWNBEATS

DOWNBOW
DOWNBOWS
DOWNCAST
DOWNCASTS
DOWNED
DOWNER
DOWNERS
DOWNFALL
DOWNFALLS
DOWNFLOW
DOWNFLOWS
DOWNFORCE
DOWNFORCES
DOWNGRADE
DOWNGRADED
DOWNGRADES
DOWNGRADING
DOWNHILL
DOWNHILLS
DOWNIER
DOWNIEST
DOWNINESS
DOWNINESSES
DOWNING
DOWNLAND
DOWNLANDS
DOWNMOST
DOWNPIPE
DOWNPIPES
DOWNPOUR
DOWNPOURS
DOWNRIGHT
DOWNRUSH
DOWNRUSHES
DOWNS
DOWNSTAGE
DOWNSTAIR
DOWNSTAIRS
DOWNSWING
DOWNSWINGS
DOWNTIME
DOWNTIMES
DOWNTREND
DOWNTRENDS
DOWNTURN
DOWNTURNS
DOWNWARD
DOWNWARDS
DOWNWIND
DOWNY
DOWP
DOWPS
DOWRIES
DOWRY
DOWS
DOWSE
DOWSED
DOWSER
DOWSERS
DOWSES
DOWSET
DOWSETS
DOWSING
DOWT
DOWTS
DOXIES
DOXOLOGIES
DOXOLOGY
DOXY
DOYEN

DOYENNE	DRAFT	DRAISENE	DRAUGHTS	DREARING
DOYENNES	DRAFTED	DRAISENES	DRAUGHTY	DREARINGS
DOYENS	DRAFTEE	DRAISINE	DRAUNT	DREARS
DOYLEY	DRAFTEES	DRAISINES	DRAUNTED	DREARY
DOYLEYS	DRAFTER	DRAKE	DRAUNTING	DRECK
DOYLIES	DRAFTERS	DRAKES	DRAUNTS	DRECKS
DOYLY	DRAFTING	DRAM	DRAVE	DREDGE
DOZE	DRAFTS	DRAMA	DRAW	DREDGED
DOZED	DRAFTSMAN	DRAMAS	DRAWABLE	DREDGER
DOZEN	DRAFTSMEN	DRAMATIC	DRAWBACK	DREDGERS
DOZENED	DRAG	DRAMATICS	DRAWBACKS	DREDGES
DOZENING	DRAGÉE	DRAMATISE	DRAWEE	DREDGING
DOZENS	DRAGÉES	DRAMATISED	DRAWEES	DREE
DOZENTH	DRAGGED	DRAMATISES	DRAWER	DREED
DOZENTHS	DRAGGIER	DRAMATISING	DRAWERS	DREEING
DOZER	DRAGGIEST	DRAMATIST	DRAWING	DREES
DOZERS	DRAGGING	DRAMATISTS	DRAWINGS	DREGGIER
DOZES	DRAGGLE	DRAMATIZE	DRAWL	DREGGIEST
DOZIER	DRAGGLED	DRAMATIZED	DRAWLED	DREGGY
DOZIEST	DRAGGLES	DRAMATIZES	DRAWLER	DREGS
DOZINESS	DRAGGLING	DRAMATIZING	DRAWLERS	DREICH
DOZINESSES	DRAGGY	DRAMATURG	DRAWLING	DREICHER
DOZING	DRAGHOUND	DRAMATURGE	DRAWLS	DREICHEST
DOZINGS	DRAGHOUNDS	DRAMATURGS	DRAWN	DRENCH
DOZY	DRAGLINE	DRAMMACH	DRAWS	DRENCHED
DRAB	DRAGLINES	DRAMMACHS	DRAY	DRENCHER
DRABBED	DRAGOMAN	DRAMMED	DRAYAGE	DRENCHERS
DRABBER	DRAGOMANS	DRAMMING	DRAYAGES	DRENCHES
DRABBERS	DRAGON	DRAMMOCK	DRAYMAN	DRENCHING
DRABBEST	DRAGONESS	DRAMMOCKS	DRAYMEN	DRENT
DRABBET	DRAGONESSES	DRAMS	DRAYS	DREPANIUM
DRABBETS	DRAGONET	DRANK	DRAZEL	DREPANIUMS
DRABBIER	DRAGONETS	DRANT	DRAZELS	DRERE
DRABBIEST	DRAGONFLIES	DRANTED	DREAD	DRERES
DRABBING	DRAGONFLY	DRANTING	DREADED	DRERYHEAD
DRABBISH	DRAGONISE	DRANTS	DREADER	DRERYHEADS
DRABBLE	DRAGONISED	DRAP	DREADERS	DRESS
DRABBLED	DRAGONISES	DRAPE	DREADFUL	DRESSAGE
DRABBLER	DRAGONISH	DRAPED	DREADING	DRESSAGES
DRABBLERS	DRAGONISING	DRAPER	DREADLESS	DRESSED
DRABBLES	DRAGONISM	DRAPERIED	DREADLY	DRESSER
DRABBLING	DRAGONISMS	DRAPERIES	DREADS	DRESSERS
DRABBLINGS	DRAGONIZE	DRAPERS	DREAM	DRESSES
DRABBY	DRAGONIZED	DRAPERY	DREAMBOAT	DRESSIER
DRABETTE	DRAGONIZES	DRAPERYING	DREAMBOATS	DRESSIEST
DRABETTES	DRAGONIZING	DRAPES	DREAMED	DRESSING
DRABLER	DRAGONNÉ	DRAPET	DREAMER	DRESSINGS
DRABLERS	DRAGONS	DRAPETS	DREAMERIES	DRESSY
DRABLY	DRAGOON	DRAPIER	DREAMERS	DREST
DRABNESS	DRAGOONED	DRAPIERS	DREAMERY	DREVILL
DRABNESSES	DRAGOONING	DRAPING	DREAMFUL	DREVILLS
DRABS	DRAGOONS	DRAPPED	DREAMHOLE	DREW
DRACHM	DRAGS	DRAPPIE	DREAMHOLES	DREY
DRACHMA	DRAGSMAN	DRAPPIES	DREAMIER	DREYS
DRACHMAE	DRAGSMEN	DRAPPING	DREAMIEST	DRIB
DRACHMAI	DRAGSTER	DRAPPY	DREAMILY	DRIBBED
DRACHMAS	DRAGSTERS	DRAPS	DREAMING	DRIBBER
DRACHMS	DRAIL	DRASTIC	DREAMINGS	DRIBBERS
DRACONE	DRAILED	DRASTICS	DREAMLESS	DRIBBING
DRACONES	DRAILING	DRAT	DREAMS	DRIBBLE
DRACONIAN	DRAILS	DRATCHELL	DREAMT	DRIBBLED
DRACONIC	DRAIN	DRATCHELLS	DREAMY	DRIBBLER
DRACONISM	DRAINABLE	DRATTED	DREAR	DRIBBLERS
DRACONISMS	DRAINAGE	DRAUGHT	DREARE	DRIBBLES
DRACONTIC	DRAINAGES	DRAUGHTED	DREARER	DRIBBLET
DRAD	DRAINED	DRAUGHTER	DREARES	DRIBBLETS
DRAFF	DRAINER	DRAUGHTERS	DREAREST	DRIBBLIER
DRAFFISH	DRAINERS	DRAUGHTIER	DREARIER	DRIBBLIEST
DRAFFS	DRAINING	DRAUGHTIEST	DREARIEST	DRIBBLING
DRAFFY	DRAINS	DRAUGHTING	DREARILY	DRIBBLY

DRIBLET	DRIZZLY	DROOLING	DROWNER	DRUMS
DRIBLETS	DROGER	DROOLS	DROWNERS	DRUMSTICK
DRIBS	DROGERS	DROOME	DROWNING	DRUMSTICKS
DRICKSIE	DROGHER	DROOMES	DROWNINGS	DRUNK
DRIED	DROGHERS	DROOP	DROWNS	DRUNKARD
DRIER	DROGUE	DROOPED	DROWS	DRUNKARDS
DRIERS	DROGUES	DROOPIER	DROWSE	DRUNKEN
DRIES	DROGUET	DROOPIEST	DROWSED	DRUNKENLY
DRIEST	DROGUETS	DROOPILY	DROWSES	DRUNKER
DRIFT	DROICH	DROOPING	DROWSIER	DRUNKEST
DRIFTAGE	DROICHS	DROOPS	DROWSIEST	DRUNKS
DRIFTAGES	DROICHY	DROOPY	DROWSIHED	DRUPE
DRIFTED	DROIL	DROP	DROWSIHEDS	DRUPEL
DRIFTER	DROILED	DROPFLIES	DROWSILY	DRUPELET
DRIFTERS	DROILING	DROPFLY	DROWSING	DRUPELETS
DRIFTIER	DROILS	DROPLET	DROWSY	DRUPELS
DRIFTIEST	DROIT	DROPLETS	DRUB	DRUPES
DRIFTING	DROITS	DROPPED	DRUBBED	DRUSE
DRIFTLESS	DRÔLE	DROPPER	DRUBBING	DRUSES
DRIFTPIN	DRÔLER	DROPPERS	DRUBBINGS	DRUSY
DRIFTPINS	DRÔLES	DROPPING	DRUBS	DRUXY
DRIFTS	DRÔLEST	DROPPINGS	DRUCKEN	DRY
DRIFTY	DROLL	DROPPLE	DRUDGE	DRYAD
DRILL	DROLLED	DROPPLES	DRUDGED	DRYADES
DRILLED	DROLLER	DROPS	DRUDGER	DRYADS
DRILLER	DROLLERIES	DROPSICAL	DRUDGERIES	DRYBEAT
DRILLERS	DROLLERY	DROPSIED	DRUDGERS	DRYBEATEN
DRILLING	DROLLEST	DROPSIES	DRUDGERY	DRYBEATING
DRILLINGS	DROLLING	DROPSTONE	DRUDGES	DRYBEATS
DRILLS	DROLLINGS	DROPSTONES	DRUDGING	DRYER
DRILY	DROLLISH	DROPSY	DRUDGISM	DRYERS
DRINK	DROLLNESS	DROPWISE	DRUDGISMS	DRYING
DRINKABLE	DROLLNESSES	DROSERA	DRUG	DRYINGS
DRINKER	DROLLS	DROSERAS	DRUGGED	DRYISH
DRINKERS	DROLLY	DROSHKIES	DRUGGER	DRYLY
DRINKING	DROME	DROSHKY	DRUGGERS	DRYNESS
DRINKINGS	DROMEDARE	DROSKIES	DRUGGET	DRYNESSES
DRINKS	DROMEDARES	DROSKY	DRUGGETS	DRYSALTER
DRIP	DROMEDARIES	DROSS	DRUGGING	DRYSALTERS
DRIPPED	DROMEDARY	DROSSES	DRUGGIST	DSO
DRIPPIER	DROMES	DROSSIER	DRUGGISTS	DSOBO
DRIPPIEST	DROMIC	DROSSIEST	DRUGS	DSOBOS
DRIPPING	DROMICAL	DROSSY	DRUIDIC	DSOMO
DRIPPINGS	DROMOI	DROSTDIES	DRUIDICAL	DSOMOS
DRIPPY	DROMON	DROSTDY	DRUIDISM	DSOS
DRIPS	DROMOND	DROSTDYS	DRUIDISMS	DUAD
DRISHEEN	DROMONDS	DROUGHT	DRUM	DUADS
DRISHEENS	DROMONS	DROUGHTIER	DRUMBEAT	DUAL
DRIVABLE	DROMOS	DROUGHTIEST	DRUMBEATS	DUALIN
DRIVE	DRONE	DROUGHTS	DRUMBLE	DUALINS
DRIVEABLE	DRONED	DROUGHTY	DRUMBLED	DUALISM
DRIVEL	DRONES	DROUK	DRUMBLES	DUALISMS
DRIVELLED	DRONGO	DROUKED	DRUMBLING	DUALIST
DRIVELLER	DRONGOES	DROUKING	DRUMFIRE	DUALISTIC
DRIVELLERS	DRONGOS	DROUKINGS	DRUMFIRES	DUALISTS
DRIVELLING	DRONIER	DROUKIT	DRUMFISH	DUALITIES
DRIVELS	DRONIEST	DROUKS	DRUMFISHES	DUALITY
DRIVEN	DRONING	DROUTH	DRUMHEAD	DUALLY
DRIVER	DRONINGLY	DROUTHIER	DRUMHEADS	DUALS
DRIVERS	DRONISH	DROUTHIEST	DRUMLIER	DUAN
DRIVES	DRONISHLY	DROUTHS	DRUMLIEST	DUANS
DRIVEWAY	DRONY	DROUTHY	DRUMLIN	DUAR
DRIVEWAYS	DROOK	DROVE	DRUMLINS	DUARCHIES
DRIVING	DROOKED	DROVER	DRUMLY	DUARCHY
DRIZZLE	DROOKING	DROVERS	DRUMMED	DUARS
DRIZZLED	DROOKINGS	DROVES	DRUMMER	DUB
DRIZZLES	DROOKIT	DROW	DRUMMERS	DUBBED
DRIZZLIER	DROOKS	DROWN	DRUMMING	DUBBIN
DRIZZLIEST	DROOL	DROWNDED	DRUMMOCK	DUBBING
DRIZZLING	DROOLED	DROWNED	DRUMMOCKS	DUBBINGS

DUBBINS
DUBIETIES
DUBIETY
DUBIOSITIES
DUBIOSITY
DUBIOUS
DUBIOUSLY
DUBITABLE
DUBITABLY
DUBITANCIES
DUBITANCY
DUBITATE
DUBITATED
DUBITATES
DUBITATING
DUBS
DUCAL
DUCALLY
DUCAT
DUCATOON
DUCATOONS
DUCATS
DUCDAME
DUCE
DUCES
DUCHESS
DUCHESSE
DUCHESSES
DUCHIES
DUCHY
DUCK
DUCKBILL
DUCKBILLS
DUCKED
DUCKER
DUCKERS
DUCKIER
DUCKIES
DUCKIEST
DUCKING
DUCKINGS
DUCKLING
DUCKLINGS
DUCKMOLE
DUCKMOLES
DUCKS
DUCKSES
DUCKSHOVE
DUCKSHOVED
DUCKSHOVES
DUCKSHOVING
DUCKWEED
DUCKWEEDS
DUCKY
DUCT
DUCTED
DUCTILE
DUCTILITIES
DUCTILITY
DUCTING
DUCTLESS
DUCTS
DUD
DUDDER
DUDDERIES
DUDDERS
DUDDERY
DUDDIE
DUDDIER
DUDDIEST

DUDE
DUDEEN
DUDEENS
DUDES
DUDGEON
DUDGEONS
DUDHEEN
DUDHEENS
DUDISH
DUDISM
DUDISMS
DUDS
DUE
DUED
DUEFUL
DUEL
DUELLED
DUELLER
DUELLERS
DUELLING
DUELLINGS
DUELLIST
DUELLISTS
DUELLO
DUELLOS
DUELS
DUELSOME
DUENNA
DUENNAS
DUES
DUET
DUETS
DUETT
DUETTED
DUETTI
DUETTING
DUETTINO
DUETTINOS
DUETTIST
DUETTISTS
DUETTO
DUETTOS
DUETTS
DUFF
DUFFED
DUFFEL
DUFFELS
DUFFER
DUFFERDOM
DUFFERDOMS
DUFFERISM
DUFFERISMS
DUFFERS
DUFFEST
DUFFING
DUFFINGS
DUFFLE
DUFFLES
DUFFS
DUG
DUGONG
DUGONGS
DUGOUT
DUGOUTS
DUGS
DUIKER
DUIKERS
DUING
DUKE
DUKED

DUKEDOM
DUKEDOMS
DUKELING
DUKELINGS
DUKERIES
DUKERY
DUKES
DUKESHIP
DUKESHIPS
DUKING
DULCAMARA
DULCAMARAS
DULCET
DULCIAN
DULCIANA
DULCIANAS
DULCIANS
DULCIFIED
DULCIFIES
DULCIFY
DULCIFYING
DULCIMER
DULCIMERS
DULCITE
DULCITES
DULCITOL
DULCITOLS
DULCITUDE
DULCITUDES
DULCOSE
DULCOSES
DULE
DULES
DULIA
DULIAS
DULL
DULLARD
DULLARDS
DULLED
DULLER
DULLEST
DULLIER
DULLIEST
DULLING
DULLISH
DULLNESS
DULLNESSES
DULLS
DULLY
DULNESS
DULNESSES
DULOCRACIES
DULOCRACY
DULOSES
DULOSIS
DULOTIC
DULSE
DULSES
DULY
DUMA
DUMAIST
DUMAISTS
DUMAS
DUMB
DUMBED
DUMBER
DUMBEST
DUMBFOUND
DUMBFOUNDED
DUMBFOUNDING

DUMBFOUNDS
DUMBING
DUMBLY
DUMBNESS
DUMBNESSES
DUMBS
DUMDUM
DUMDUMS
DUMFOUND
DUMFOUNDED
DUMFOUNDING
DUMFOUNDS
DUMKA
DUMKY
DUMMERER
DUMMERERS
DUMMIED
DUMMIER
DUMMIES
DUMMIEST
DUMMINESS
DUMMINESSES
DUMMY
DUMMYING
DUMOSE
DUMOSITIES
DUMOSITY
DUMOUS
DUMP
DUMPED
DUMPER
DUMPERS
DUMPIER
DUMPIES
DUMPIEST
DUMPINESS
DUMPINESSES
DUMPING
DUMPISH
DUMPISHLY
DUMPLE
DUMPLED
DUMPLES
DUMPLING
DUMPLINGS
DUMPS
DUMPY
DUN
DUNCE
DUNCEDOM
DUNCEDOMS
DUNCERIES
DUNCERY
DUNCES
DUNCH
DUNCHED
DUNCHES
DUNCHING
DUNDER
DUNDERS
DUNE
DUNES
DUNG
DUNGAREE
DUNGAREES
DUNGED
DUNGEON
DUNGEONED
DUNGEONER
DUNGEONERS

DUNGEONING
DUNGEONS
DUNGIER
DUNGIEST
DUNGING
DUNGMERE
DUNGMERES
DUNGS
DUNGY
DUNITE
DUNITES
DUNK
DUNKED
DUNKING
DUNKS
DUNLIN
DUNLINS
DUNNAGE
DUNNAGES
DUNNAKIN
DUNNAKINS
DUNNED
DUNNER
DUNNEST
DUNNIES
DUNNING
DUNNINGS
DUNNISH
DUNNITE
DUNNITES
DUNNO
DUNNOCK
DUNNOCKS
DUNNY
DUNS
DUNSH
DUNSHED
DUNSHES
DUNSHING
DUNT
DUNTED
DUNTING
DUNTS
DUO
DUODECIMO
DUODECIMOS
DUODENA
DUODENAL
DUODENARY
DUODENUM
DUOLOGUE
DUOLOGUES
DUOMI
DUOMO
DUOMOS
DUOPOLIES
DUOPOLY
DUOS
DUOTONE
DUOTONES
DUP
DUPABLE
DUPE
DUPED
DUPER
DUPERIES
DUPERS
DUPERY
DUPES
DUPING

DUPION
DUPIONS
DUPLE
DUPLET
DUPLETS
DUPLEX
DUPLEXES
DUPLICAND
DUPLICANDS
DUPLICATE
DUPLICATED
DUPLICATES
DUPLICATING
DUPLICITIES
DUPLICITY
DUPLIED
DUPLIES
DUPLY
DUPLYING
DUPONDII
DUPONDIUS
DUPPED
DUPPIES
DUPPING
DUPPY
DUPS
DURA
DURABLE
DURABLES
DURABLY
DURAL
DURALS
DURALUMIN
DURALUMINS
DURAMEN
DURAMENS
DURANCE
DURANCES
DURANT
DURANTS
DURAS
DURATION
DURATIONS
DURBAR
DURDANS
DURDUM
DURDUMS
DURE
DURED
DUREFUL
DURES
DURESS
DURESSE
DURESSES
DURGAN
DURGANS
DURGY
DURIAN
DURIANS
DURING
DURION
DURIONS
DURMAST
DURMASTS
DURN
DURNS
DURO
DUROS
DUROY
DUROYS

DURRA
DURRAS
DURRIE
DURRIES
DURST
DURUKULI
DURUKULIS
DURUM
DURUMS
DUSH
DUSHED
DUSHES
DUSHING
DUSK
DUSKED
DUSKEN
DUSKENED
DUSKENING
DUSKENS
DUSKER
DUSKEST
DUSKIER
DUSKIEST
DUSKILY
DUSKINESS
DUSKINESSES
DUSKING
DUSKISH
DUSKISHLY
DUSKLY
DUSKNESS
DUSKNESSES
DUSKS
DUSKY
DUST
DUSTBIN
DUSTBINS
DUSTED
DUSTER
DUSTERS
DUSTIER
DUSTIEST
DUSTILY
DUSTINESS
DUSTINESSES
DUSTING
DUSTLESS
DUSTMAN
DUSTMEN
DUSTPROOF
DUSTS
DUSTY
DUTCH
DUTCHES
DUTEOUS
DUTEOUSLY
DUTIABLE
DUTIED
DUTIES
DUTIFUL
DUTIFULLY
DUTY
DUUMVIR
DUUMVIRAL
DUUMVIRI
DUUMVIRS
DUVET
DUVETINE
DUVETINES
DUVETS

DUVETYN
DUVETYNE
DUVETYNES
DUVETYNS
DUX
DUXELLES
DUXES
DUYKER
DUYKERS
DVANDVA
DVANDVAS
DVORNIK
DVORNIKS
DWALE
DWALES
DWALM
DWALMED
DWALMING
DWALMS
DWAM
DWAMMED
DWAMMMING
DWAMS
DWARF
DWARFED
DWARFING
DWARFISH
DWARFISM
DWARFISMS
DWARFS
DWARVES
DWAUM
DWAUMED
DWAUMING
DWAUMS
DWELL
DWELLED
DWELLER
DWELLERS
DWELLING
DWELLINGS
DWELLS
DWELT
DWINDLE
DWINDLED
DWINDLES
DWINDLING
DWINE
DWINED
DWINES
DWINING
DYABLE
DYAD
DYADIC
DYADS
DYARCHIES
DYARCHY
DYBBUK
DYBBUKS
DYE
DYEABLE
DYED
DYEING
DYEINGS
DYELINE
DYELINES
DYER
DYERS
DYES
DYESTER

DYESTERS
DYESTUFF
DYESTUFFS
DYING
DYINGLY
DYINGNESS
DYINGNESSES
DYINGS
DYKE
DYKED
DYKES
DYKEY
DYKIER
DYKIEST
DYKING
DYNAMIC
DYNAMICAL
DYNAMICS
DYNAMISE
DYNAMISED
DYNAMISES
DYNAMISING
DYNAMISM
DYNAMISMS
DYNAMIST
DYNAMISTS
DYNAMITE
DYNAMITED
DYNAMITER
DYNAMITERS
DYNAMITES
DYNAMITING
DYNAMIZE
DYNAMIZED
DYNAMIZES
DYNAMIZING
DYNAMO
DYNAMOS
DYNAMOTOR
DYNAMOTORS
DYNAST
DYNASTIC
DYNASTIES
DYNASTS
DYNASTY
DYNATRON
DYNATRONS
DYNE
DYNES
DYNODE
DYNODES
DYSCHROA
DYSCHROAS
DYSCHROIA
DYSCHROIAS
DYSCRASIA
DYSCRASIAS
DYSENTERIES
DYSENTERY
DYSGENIC
DYSGENICS
DYSLECTIC
DYSLECTICS
DYSLEXIA
DYSLEXIAS
DYSLEXIC
DYSLEXICS
DYSLOGIES
DYSLOGY
DYSMELIA

DYSMELIAS
DYSMELIC
DYSODIL
DYSODILE
DYSODILES
DYSODILS
DYSODYLE
DYSODYLES
DYSPATHIES
DYSPATHY
DYSPEPSIA
DYSPEPSIAS
DYSPEPSIES
DYSPEPSY
DYSPEPTIC
DYSPEPTICS
DYSPHAGIA
DYSPHAGIAS
DYSPHAGIC
DYSPHAGIES
DYSPHAGY
DYSPHASIA
DYSPHASIAS
DYSPHONIA
DYSPHONIAS
DYSPHONIC
DYSPHORIA
DYSPHORIAS
DYSPHORIC
DYSPLASIA
DYSPLASIAS
DYSPNEA
DYSPNEAL
DYSPNEAS
DYSPNEIC
DYSPNOEA
DYSPNOEAL
DYSPNOEAS
DYSPNOEIC
DYSPRAXIA
DYSPRAXIAS
DYSTECTIC
DYSTHESIA
DYSTHESIAS
DYSTHETIC
DYSTHYMIA
DYSTHYMIAS
DYSTHYMIC
DYSTOPIA
DYSTOPIAN
DYSTOPIAS
DYSTROPHIES
DYSTROPHY
DYSURIA
DYSURIAS
DYSURIC
DYSURIES
DYSURY
DYTISCID
DYTISCIDS
DYVOUR
DYVOURIES
DYVOURS
DYVOURY
DZEREN
DZERENS
DZIGGETAI
DZIGGETAIS
DZO
DZOS

E

EA	EARLS	EARWIGGING	EAVESDRIP	ECBOLES
EACH	EARLY	EARWIGGY	EAVESDRIPS	ECBOLIC
EACHWHERE	EARMARK	EARWIGS	EAVESDROP	ECBOLICS
EADISH	EARMARKED	EAS	EAVESDROPPED	ECCE
EADISHES	EARMARKING	EASE	EAVESDROPPING	ECCENTRIC
EAGER	EARMARKS	EASED	EAVESDROPS	ECCENTRICS
EAGERLY	EARMUFFS	EASEFUL	ÉBAUCHE	ECCLESIA
EAGERNESS	EARN	EASEL	ÉBAUCHES	ECCLESIAL
EAGERNESSES	EARNED	EASELS	EBB	ECCLESIAS
EAGERS	EARNER	EASEMENT	EBBED	ECCO
EAGLE	EARNERS	EASEMENTS	EBBING	ECCRINE
EAGLES	EARNEST	EASES	EBBLESS	ECCRISES
EAGLET	EARNESTLY	EASIER	EBBS	ECCRISIS
EAGLETS	EARNESTS	EASIEST	EBBTIDE	ECCRITIC
EAGLEWOOD	EARNING	EASILY	EBBTIDES	ECCRITICS
EAGLEWOODS	EARNINGS	EASINESS	EBENEZER	ECDYSES
EAGRE	EARNS	EASINESSES	EBENEZERS	ECDYSIAST
EAGRES	EARPHONE	EASING	ÉBÉNISTE	ECDYSIASTS
EALDORMAN	EARPHONES	EASLE	ÉBÉNISTES	ECDYSIS
EALDORMEN	EARPICK	EASLES	EBIONISE	ECH
EALE	EARPICKS	EASSEL	EBIONISED	ÉCHAPPÉ
EALES	EARPIECE	EASSIL	EBIONISES	ÉCHAPPÉS
EAN	EARPIECES	EAST	EBIONISING	ECHE
EANED	EARPLUG	EASTED	EBIONISM	ECHED
EANING	EARPLUGS	EASTER	EBIONISMS	ECHELON
EANLING	EARRING	EASTERLIES	EBIONITIC	ECHELONS
EANLINGS	EARRINGS	EASTERLY	EBIONIZE	ECHES
EANS	EARS	EASTERN	EBIONIZED	ECHIDNA
EAR	EARST	EASTERNER	EBIONIZES	ECHIDNAS
EARACHE	EARTH	EASTERNERS	EBIONIZING	ECHIDNINE
EARACHES	EARTHBORN	EASTING	EBON	ECHIDNINES
EARBASH	EARTHED	EASTINGS	EBONIES	ECHINATE
EARBASHED	EARTHEN	EASTLAND	EBONISE	ECHINATED
EARBASHES	EARTHFALL	EASTLANDS	EBONISED	ECHING
EARBASHING	EARTHFALLS	EASTLIN	EBONISES	ECHINI
EARBOB	EARTHFAST	EASTLING	EBONISING	ECHINOID
EARBOBS	EARTHFLAX	EASTLINGS	EBONIST	ECHINOIDS
EARD	EARTHFLAXES	EASTLINS	EBONISTS	ECHINUS
EARDED	EARTHIER	EASTMOST	EBONITE	ECHINUSES
EARDING	EARTHIEST	EASTS	EBONITES	ECHO
EARDROP	EARTHING	EASTWARD	EBONIZE	ECHOED
EARDROPS	EARTHLIER	EASTWARDS	EBONIZED	ECHOER
EARDRUM	EARTHLIES	EASY	EBONIZES	ECHOERS
EARDRUMS	EARTHLIEST	EAT	EBONIZING	ECHOES
EARDS	EARTHLING	EATABLE	EBONS	ECHOGRAM
EARED	EARTHLINGS	EATABLES	EBONY	ECHOGRAMS
EARFLAP	EARTHLY	EATAGE	EBRIATE	ECHOIC
EARFLAPS	EARTHMAN	EATAGES	EBRIATED	ECHOING
EARFUL	EARTHMEN	EATCHE	EBRIETIES	ECHOISE
EARFULS	EARTHS	EATCHES	EBRIETY	ECHOISED
EARING	EARTHWARD	EATEN	EBRILLADE	ECHOISES
EARINGS	EARTHWAX	EATER	EBRILLADES	ECHOISING
EARL	EARTHWAXES	EATERIES	EBRIOSE	ECHOISM
EARLAP	EARTHWOLF	EATERS	EBRIOSITIES	ECHOISMS
EARLAPS	EARTHWOLVES	EATERY	EBRIOSITY	ECHOIST
EARLDOM	EARTHWORK	EATH	EBULLIENT	ECHOISTS
EARLDOMS	EARTHWORKS	EATHE	EBURNEAN	ECHOIZE
EARLESS	EARTHWORM	EATHLY	EBURNEOUS	ECHOIZED
EARLIER	EARTHWORMS	EATING	ECAD	ECHOIZES
EARLIEST	EARTHY	EATINGS	ECADS	ECHOIZING
EARLINESS	EARWAX	EATS	ÉCARTÉ	ECHOLALIA
EARLINESSES	EARWAXES	EAU	ÉCARTÉS	ECHOLALIAS
EARLOCK	EARWIG	EAUS	ECAUDATE	ECHOLESS
EARLOCKS	EARWIGGED	EAVES	ECBOLE	ECHS

ECHT	ÉCRITOIRE	ECUS	EDITORS	EFFACES
ÉCLAIR	ÉCRITOIRES	ECZEMA	EDITRESS	EFFACING
ÉCLAIRS	ECRU	ECZEMAS	EDITRESSES	EFFECT
ECLAMPSIA	ECRUS	EDACIOUS	EDITS	EFFECTED
ECLAMPSIAS	ECSTASES	EDACITIES	EDUCABLE	EFFECTER
ECLAMPSIES	ECSTASIED	EDACITY	EDUCATE	EFFECTERS
ECLAMPSY	ECSTASIES	EDAPHIC	EDUCATED	EFFECTING
ECLAMPTIC	ECSTASIS	EDDIED	EDUCATES	EFFECTIVE
ÉCLAT	ECSTASISE	EDDIES	EDUCATING	EFFECTIVES
ÉCLATS	ECSTASISED	EDDISH	EDUCATION	EFFECTOR
ECLECTIC	ECSTASISES	EDDISHES	EDUCATIONS	EFFECTORS
ECLECTICS	ECSTASISING	EDDO	EDUCATIVE	EFFECTS
ECLIPSE	ECSTASIZE	EDDOES	EDUCATOR	EFFECTUAL
ECLIPSED	ECSTASIZED	EDDY	EDUCATORS	EFFED
ECLIPSES	ECSTASIZES	EDDYING	EDUCATORY	EFFEIR
ECLIPSING	ECSTASIZING	EDELWEISS	EDUCE	EFFEIRED
ECLIPTIC	ECSTASY	EDELWEISSES	EDUCED	EFFEIRING
ECLIPTICS	ECSTASYING	EDEMA	EDUCEMENT	EFFEIRS
ECLOGITE	ECSTATIC	EDEMAS	EDUCEMENTS	EFFENDI
ECLOGITES	ECSTATICS	EDEMATOSE	EDUCES	EFFENDIS
ECLOGUE	ECTASES	EDEMATOUS	EDUCIBLE	EFFERE
ECLOGUES	ECTASIS	EDENTAL	EDUCING	EFFERED
ECLOSE	ECTHYMA	EDENTATE	EDUCT	EFFERENCE
ECLOSED	ECTHYMAS	EDENTATES	EDUCTION	EFFERENCES
ECLOSES	ECTOBLAST	EDGE	EDUCTIONS	EFFERENT
ECLOSING	ECTOBLASTS	EDGEBONE	EDUCTOR	EFFERES
ECLOSION	ECTOCRINE	EDGEBONES	EDUCTORS	EFFERING
ECLOSIONS	ECTOCRINES	EDGED	EDUCIS	EFFETE
ECOCIDE	ECTODERM	EDGELESS	EDUSKUNTA	EFFETELY
ECOCIDES	ECTODERMS	EDGER	EDUSKUNTAS	EFFETER
ECOFREAK	ECTOGENIC	EDGERS	EE	EFFETEST
ECOFREAKS	ECTOGENIES	EDGES	EECH	EFFICACIES
ECOLOGIC	ECTOGENY	EDGEWAYS	EECHED	EFFICACY
ECOLOGIES	ECTOMORPH	EDGEWISE	EECHES	EFFICIENT
ECOLOGIST	ECTOMORPHS	EDGIER	EECHING	EFFICIENTS
ECOLOGISTS	ECTOPHYTE	EDGIEST	EEK	EFFIERCE
ECOLOGY	ECTOPHYTES	EDGINESS	EEL	EFFIERCED
ECONOMIC	ECTOPIA	EDGINESSES	EELFARE	EFFIERCES
ECONOMICS	ECTOPIAS	EDGING	EELFARES	EFFIERCING
ECONOMIES	ECTOPIC	EDGINGS	EELGRASS	EFFIGIES
ECONOMISE	ECTOPIES	EDGY	EELGRASSES	EFFIGY
ECONOMISED	ECTOPLASM	EDH	EELIEST	EFFING
ECONOMISES	ECTOPLASMS	EDHS	EELPOUT	EFFLUENCE
ECONOMISING	ECTOPY	EDIBILITIES	EELPOUTS	EFFLUENCES
ECONOMISM	ECTOSARC	EDIBILITY	EELS	EFFLUENT
ECONOMISMS	ECTOSARCS	EDIBLE	EELS	EFFLUENTS
ECONOMIST	ECTOTHERM	EDIBLES	EELWORM	EFFLUVIA
ECONOMISTS	ECTOTHERMS	EDICT	EELWORMS	EFFLUVIAL
ECONOMIZE	ECTOZOA	EDICIAL	EELWRACK	EFFLUVIUM
ECONOMIZED	ECTOZOAN	EDICTALLY	EELWRACKS	EFFLUX
ECONOMIZES	ECTOZOANS	EDICTS	EELY	EFFLUXES
ECONOMIZING	ECTOZOIC	EDIFICE	EEN	EFFLUXION
ECONOMY	ECTOZOON	EDIFICES	EERIE	EFFLUXIONS
ECONUT	ECTROPIC	EDIFICIAL	EERIER	EFFORCE
ECONUTS	ECTROPION	EDIFIED	EERIEST	EFFORCED
ECOPHOBIA	ECTROPIONS	EDIFIER	EERILY	EFFORCES
ECOPHOBIAS	ECTROPIUM	EDIFIERS	EERINESS	EFFORCING
ÉCORCHÉ	ECTROPIUMS	EDIFIES	EERINESSES	EFFORT
ÉCORCHÉS	ECTYPAL	EDIFY	EERY	EFFORTFUL
ECOSPHERE	ECTYPE	EDIFYING	EEVEN	EFFORTS
ECOSPHERES	ECTYPES	EDILE	EEVENS	EFFRAIDE
ÉCOSSAISE	ECU	EDILES	EEVN	EFFRAY
ÉCOSSAISES	ÉCUELLE	EDIT	EEVNING	EFFRAYED
ECOSTATE	ÉCUELLES	EDITED	EEVNINGS	EFFRAYING
ECOSYSTEM	ECUMENIC	EDITING	EEVNS	EFFRAYS
ECOSYSTEMS	ECUMENICS	EDITION	EF	EFFS
ECOTYPE	ECUMENISM	EDITIONS	EFF	EFFULGE
ECOTYPES	ECUMENISMS	EDITOR	EFFABLE	EFFULGED
ÉCRASEUR	ÉCURIE	EDITORIAL	EFFACE	EFFULGENT
ÉCRASEURS	ÉCURIES	EDITORIALS	EFFACED	EFFULGES

EFFULGING
EFFUSE
EFFUSED
EFFUSES
EFFUSING
EFFUSION
EFFUSIONS
EFFUSIVE
EFS
EFT
EFTEST
EFTS
EFTSOONS
EGAD
EGAL
EGALITIES
EGALITY
EGALLY
EGAREMENT
EGAREMENTS
EGENCE
EGENCES
EGENCIES
EGENCY
EGER
EGERS
EGEST
EGESTA
EGESTED
EGESTING
EGESTION
EGESTIONS
EGESTIVE
EGESTS
EGG
EGGAR
EGGARS
EGGCUP
EGGCUPS
EGGED
EGGER
EGGERIES
EGGERS
EGGERY
EGGHEAD
EGGHEADS
EGGIER
EGGIEST
EGGING
EGGLER
EGGLERS
EGGMASS
EGGMASSES
EGGNOG
EGGNOGS
EGGS
EGGSHELL
EGGSHELLS
EGGY
EGIS
EGISES
EGLANTINE
EGLANTINES
EGLATERE
EGLATERES
EGMA
EGMAS
EGO
EGOISM
EGOISMS

EGOIST
EGOISTIC
EGOISTS
EGOITIES
EGOITY
EGOMANIA
EGOMANIAC
EGOMANIACS
EGOMANIAS
EGOS
EGOTHEISM
EGOTHEISMS
EGOTISE
EGOTISED
EGOTISES
EGOTISING
EGOTISM
EGOTISMS
EGOTIST
EGOTISTIC
EGOTISTS
EGOTIZE
EGOTIZED
EGOTIZES
EGOTIZING
EGREGIOUS
EGRESS
EGRESSES
EGRESSION
EGRESSIONS
EGRET
EGRETS
EH
EHED
EHING
EHS
EIDENT
EIDER
EIDERDOWN
EIDERDOWNS
EIDERS
EIDETIC
EIDETICS
EIDOGRAPH
EIDOGRAPHS
EIDOLA
EIDOLON
EIGENTONE
EIGENTONES
EIGHT
EIGHTEEN
EIGHTEENS
EIGHTFOIL
EIGHTFOILS
EIGHTFOLD
EIGHTFOOT
EIGHTH
EIGHTHLY
EIGHTHS
EIGHTIES
EIGHTIETH
EIGHTIETHS
EIGHTS
EIGHTSMAN
EIGHTSMEN
EIGHTSOME
EIGHTSOMES
EIGHTVO
EIGHTVOS
EIGHTY

EIGNE
EIK
EIKED
EIKING
EIKON
EIKONS
EIKS
EILD
EILDING
EILDINGS
EILDS
EINE
EIRACK
EIRACKS
EIRENIC
EIRENICON
EIRENICONS
EISEL
EISELL
EISELLS
EISELS
EITHER
EJACULATE
EJACULATED
EJACULATES
EJACULATING
EJECT
EJECTA
EJECTED
EJECTING
EJECTION
EJECTIONS
EJECTIVE
EJECTMENT
EJECTMENTS
EJECTOR
EJECTORS
EJECTS
EKE
EKED
EKES
EKING
EKISTIC
EKISTICS
EKKA
EKKAS
EKLOGITE
EKLOGITES
EKPWELE
EKPWELES
EKUELE
EL
ELABORATE
ELABORATED
ELABORATES
ELABORATING
ELAEOLITE
ELAEOLITES
ÉLAN
ELANCE
ELANCED
ELANCES
ELANCING
ELAND
ELANDS
ELANET
ELANETS
ÉLANS
ELAPHINE
ELAPSE

ELAPSED
ELAPSES
ELAPSING
ELASTANCE
ELASTANCES
ELASTASE
ELASTASES
ELASTIC
ELASTICS
ELASTIN
ELASTINS
ELASTOMER
ELASTOMERS
ELATE
ELATED
ELATEDLY
ELATER
ELATERIN
ELATERINS
ELATERITE
ELATERITES
ELATERIUM
ELATERIUMS
ELATERS
ELATES
ELATING
ELATION
ELATIONS
ELATIVE
ELATIVES
ELBOW
ELBOWED
ELBOWING
ELBOWS
ELCHEE
ELCHEES
ELCHI
ELCHIS
ELD
ELDER
ELDERLY
ELDERS
ELDERSHIP
ELDERSHIPS
ELDEST
ELDIN
ELDING
ELDINGS
ELDINS
ELDRITCH
ELDS
ELECT
ELECTABLE
ELECTED
ELECTING
ELECTION
ELECTIONS
ELECTIVE
ELECTIVES
ELECTOR
ELECTORAL
ELECTORS
ELECTRESS
ELECTRESSES
ELECTRET
ELECTRETS
ELECTRIC
ELECTRICS
ELECTRIFIED
ELECTRIFIES

ELECTRIFY
ELECTRIFYING
ELECTRISE
ELECTRISED
ELECTRISES
ELECTRISING
ELECTRIZE
ELECTRIZED
ELECTRIZES
ELECTRIZING
ELECTRO
ELECTRODE
ELECTRODES
ELECTRON
ELECTRONS
ELECTROS
ELECTRUM
ELECTRUMS
ELECTS
ELECTUARIES
ELECTUARY
ELEGANCE
ELEGANCES
ELEGANCIES
ELEGANCY
ELEGANT
ELEGANTLY
ELEGIAC
ELEGIACAL
ELEGIACS
ELEGIAST
ELEGIASTS
ELEGIES
ELEGISE
ELEGISED
ELEGISES
ELEGISING
ELEGIST
ELEGISTS
ELEGIT
ELEGITS
ELEGIZE
ELEGIZED
ELEGIZES
ELEGIZING
ELEGY
ELEMENT
ELEMENTAL
ELEMENTALS
ELEMENTS
ELEMI
ELEMIS
ELENCH
ELENCHI
ELENCHS
ELENCHUS
ELENCTIC
ELEPHANT
ELEPHANTS
ELEUTHERI
ELEVATE
ELEVATED
ELEVATES
ELEVATING
ELEVATION
ELEVATIONS
ELEVATOR
ELEVATORS
ELEVATORY
ELEVEN

ELEVENS
ELEVENSES
ELEVENTH
ELEVENTHS
ELEVON
ELEVONS
ELF
ELFED
ELFHOOD
ELFHOODS
ELFIN
ELFING
ELFINS
ELFISH
ELFLAND
ELFLANDS
ELFLOCKS
ELFS
ELIAD
ELIADS
ELICIT
ELICITED
ELICITING
ELICITOR
ELICITORS
ELICITS
ELIDE
ELIDED
ELIDES
ELIDING
ELIGIBLE
ELIGIBLES
ELIGIBLY
ELIMINANT
ELIMINANTS
ELIMINATE
ELIMINATED
ELIMINATES
ELIMINATING
ELISION
ELISIONS
ÉLITE
ÉLITES
ELITISM
ELITISMO
ELITIST
ELITISTS
ELIXIR
ELIXIRS
ELK
ELKHOUND
ELKHOUNDS
ELKS
ELL
ELLAGIC
ELLIPSE
ELLIPSES
ELLIPSIS
ELLIPSOID
ELLIPSOIDS
ELLIPTIC
ELLOPS
ELLOPSES
ELLS
ELLWAND
ELLWANDS
ELM
ELMEN
ELMIER
ELMIEST

ELMS
ELMWOOD
ELMWOODS
ELMY
ELOCUTE
ELOCUTED
ELOCUTES
ELOCUTING
ELOCUTION
ELOCUTIONS
ELOCUTORY
ÉLOGE
ÉLOGES
ELOGIES
ELOGIST
ELOGISTS
ELOGIUM
ELOGIUMS
ELOGY
ELOIGN
ELOIGNED
ELOIGNER
ELOIGNERS
ELOIGNING
ELOIGNS
ELOIN
ELOINED
ELOINER
ELOINERS
ELOINING
ELOINMENT
ELOINMENTS
ELOINS
ELONGATE
ELONGATED
ELONGATES
ELONGATING
ELOPE
ELOPED
ELOPEMENT
ELOPEMENTS
ELOPER
ELOPERS
ELOPES
ELOPING
ELOPS
ELOPSES
ELOQUENCE
ELOQUENCES
ELOQUENT
ELPEE
ELPEES
ELS
ELSE
ELSEWHERE
ELSEWISE
ELSHIN
ELSHINS
ELSIN
ELSINS
ELT
ELTCHI
ELTCHIS
ELTS
ELUANT
ELUANTS
ELUATE
ELUATES
ELUCIDATE
ELUCIDATED

ELUCIDATES
ELUCIDATING
ELUDE
ELUDED
ELUDER
ELUDERS
ELUDES
ELUDIBLE
ELUDING
ELUENT
ELUENTS
ELUSION
ELUSIONS
ELUSIVE
ELUSIVELY
ELUSORY
ELUTE
ELUTED
ELUTES
ELUTING
ELUTION
ELUTIONS
ELUTOR
ELUTORS
ELUTRIATE
ELUTRIATED
ELUTRIATES
ELUTRIATING
ELUVIA
ELUVIAL
ELUVIUM
ELUVIUMS
ELVAN
ELVANITE
ELVANITES
ELVANS
ELVER
ELVERS
ELVES
ELVISH
ELYTRA
ELYTRAL
ELYTRON
ELYTRONS
ELYTRUM
EM
EMACIATE
EMACIATED
EMACIATES
EMACIATING
EMALANGENI
EMANANT
EMANATE
EMANATED
EMANATES
EMANATING
EMANATION
EMANATIONS
EMANATIST
EMANATISTS
EMANATIVE
EMANATORY
EMBACE
EMBACED
EMBACES
EMBACING
EMBAIL
EMBAILED
EMBAILING
EMBAILS

EMBALE
EMBALED
EMBALES
EMBALING
EMBALL
EMBALLED
EMBALLING
EMBALLINGS
EMBALLS
EMBALM
EMBALMED
EMBALMER
EMBALMERS
EMBALMING
EMBALMINGS
EMBALMS
EMBANK
EMBANKED
EMBANKER
EMBANKERS
EMBANKING
EMBANKS
EMBAR
EMBARGO
EMBARGOED
EMBARGOES
EMBARGOING
EMBARGOS
EMBARK
EMBARKED
EMBARKING
EMBARKS
EMBARRASS
EMBARRASSED
EMBARRASSES
EMBARRASSING
EMBARRED
EMBARRING
EMBARRINGS
EMBARS
EMBASE
EMBASED
EMBASES
EMBASING
EMBASSADE
EMBASSADES
EMBASSAGE
EMBASSAGES
EMBASSIES
EMBASSY
EMBASTE
EMBATHE
EMBATHED
EMBATHES
EMBATHING
EMBATTLE
EMBATTLED
EMBATTLES
EMBATTLING
EMBAY
EMBAYED
EMBAYING
EMBAYLD
EMBAYMENT
EMBAYMENTS
EMBAYS
EMBED
EMBEDDED
EMBEDDING
EMBEDMENT

EMBEDMENTS
EMBEDS
EMBELLISH
EMBELLISHED
EMBELLISHES
EMBELLISHING
EMBER
EMBERS
EMBEZZLE
EMBEZZLED
EMBEZZLER
EMBEZZLERS
EMBEZZLES
EMBEZZLING
EMBITTER
EMBITTERED
EMBITTERING
EMBITTERINGS
EMBITTERS
EMBLAZE
EMBLAZED
EMBLAZES
EMBLAZING
EMBLAZON
EMBLAZONED
EMBLAZONING
EMBLAZONS
EMBLEM
EMBLEMA
EMBLEMATA
EMBLEMED
EMBLEMING
EMBLEMISE
EMBLEMISED
EMBLEMISES
EMBLEMISING
EMBLEMIZE
EMBLEMIZED
EMBLEMIZES
EMBLEMIZING
EMBLEMS
EMBLIC
EMBLICS
EMBLOOM
EMBLOOMED
EMBLOOMING
EMBLOOMS
EMBLOSSOM
EMBLOSSOMED
EMBLOSSOMING
EMBLOSSOMS
EMBODIED
EMBODIES
EMBODY
EMBODYING
EMBOG
EMBOGGED
EMBOGGING
EMBOGS
EMBOGUE
EMBOGUED
EMBOGUEING
EMBOGUES
EMBOGUING
EMBOIL
EMBOILED
EMBOILING
EMBOILS
EMBOLDEN
EMBOLDENED

EMBOLDENING
EMBOLDENS
EMBOLI
EMBOLIC
EMBOLIES
EMBOLISM
EMBOLISMS
EMBOLUS
EMBOLUSES
EMBOLY
EMBORDER
EMBORDERED
EMBORDERING
EMBORDERS
EMBOSCATA
EMBOSCATAS
EMBOSOM
EMBOSOMED
EMBOSOMING
EMBOSOMS
EMBOSS
EMBOSSED
EMBOSSER
EMBOSSERS
EMBOSSES
EMBOSSING
EMBOST
EMBOUND
EMBOUNDED
EMBOUNDING
EMBOUNDS
EMBOW
EMBOWED
EMBOWEL
EMBOWELLED
EMBOWELLING
EMBOWELS
EMBOWER
EMBOWERED
EMBOWERING
EMBOWERS
EMBOWING
EMBOWS
EMBOX
EMBOXED
EMBOXES
EMBOXING
EMBRACE
EMBRACED
EMBRACEOR
EMBRACEORS
EMBRACER
EMBRACERIES
EMBRACERS
EMBRACERY
EMBRACES
EMBRACING
EMBRACIVE
EMBRAID
EMBRAIDED
EMBRAIDING
EMBRAIDS
EMBRANGLE
EMBRANGLED
EMBRANGLES
EMBRANGLING
EMBRASOR
EMBRASORS
EMBRASURE
EMBRASURES

EMBRAVE
EMBRAVED
EMBRAVES
EMBRAVING
EMBRAZURE
EMBRAZURES
EMBREAD
EMBREADED
EMBREADING
EMBREADS
EMBREATHE
EMBREATHED
EMBREATHES
EMBREATHING
EMBREWE
EMBREWED
EMBREWES
EMBREWING
EMBRITTLE
EMBRITTLED
EMBRITTLES
EMBRITTLING
EMBROCATE
EMBROCATED
EMBROCATES
EMBROCATING
EMBROGLIO
EMBROGLIOS
EMBROIDER
EMBROIDERED
EMBROIDERING
EMBROIDERS
EMBROIL
EMBROILED
EMBROILING
EMBROILS
EMBROWN
EMBROWNED
EMBROWNING
EMBROWNS
EMBRUE
EMBRUED
EMBRUEING
EMBRUES
EMBRUING
EMBRUTE
EMBRUTED
EMBRUTES
EMBRUTING
EMBRYO
EMBRYON
EMBRYONAL
EMBRYONIC
EMBRYONS
EMBRYOS
EMBRYOTIC
EMBUS
EMBUSIED
EMBUSIES
EMBUSQUÉ
EMBUSQUÉS
EMBUSSED
EMBUSSES
EMBUSSING
EMBUSY
EMBUSYING
EMCEE
EMCEED
EMCEEING
EMCEES

EME
EMEER
EMEERS
EMEND
EMENDABLE
EMENDALS
EMENDATE
EMENDATED
EMENDATES
EMENDATING
EMENDATOR
EMENDATORS
EMENDED
EMENDING
EMENDS
EMERALD
EMERALDS
EMERAUDE
EMERAUDES
EMERGE
EMERGED
EMERGENCE
EMERGENCES
EMERGENCIES
EMERGENCY
EMERGENT
EMERGES
EMERGING
EMERIED
EMERIES
EMERITI
EMERITUS
EMERODS
EMERSED
EMERSION
EMERSIONS
EMERY
EMERYING
EMES
EMESES
EMESIS
EMETIC
EMETICAL
EMETICS
EMETIN
EMETINE
EMETINES
EMETINS
EMEU
EMEUS
ÉMEUTE
ÉMEUTES
EMICANT
EMICATE
EMICATED
EMICATES
EMICATING
EMICATION
EMICATIONS
EMICTION
EMICTIONS
EMICTORY
EMIGRANT
EMIGRANTS
EMIGRATE
EMIGRATED
EMIGRATES
EMIGRATING
ÉMIGRÉ
ÉMIGRÉS

EMINENCE
EMINENCES
EMINENCIES
EMINENCY
EMINENT
EMINENTLY
EMIR
EMIRATE
EMIRATES
EMIRS
EMISSARIES
EMISSARY
EMISSILE
EMISSION
EMISSIONS
EMISSIVE
EMIT
EMITS
EMITTED
EMITTING
EMMA
EMMARBLE
EMMARBLED
EMMARBLES
EMMARBLING
EMMAS
EMMER
EMMERS
EMMESH
EMMESHED
EMMESHES
EMMESHING
EMMET
EMMETROPE
EMMETROPES
EMMETS
EMMEW
EMMEWED
EMMEWING
EMMEWS
EMMOVE
EMMOVED
EMMOVES
EMMOVING
EMOLLIATE
EMOLLIATED
EMOLLIATES
EMOLLIATING
EMOLLIENT
EMOLLIENTS
EMOLUMENT
EMOLUMENTS
EMONG
EMONGES
EMONGST
EMONGST
EMOTE
EMOTED
EMOTES
EMOTING
EMOTION
EMOTIONAL
EMOTIONS
EMOTIVE
EMOVE
EMOVED
EMOVES
EMOVING
EMPACKET
EMPACKETED

EMPACKETING
EMPACKETS
EMPAESTIC
EMPAIRE
EMPAIRED
EMPAIRES
EMPAIRING
EMPALE
EMPALED
EMPALES
EMPALING
EMPANEL
EMPANELLED
EMPANELLING
EMPANELS
EMPANOPLIED
EMPANOPLIES
EMPANOPLY
EMPANOPLYING
EMPARE
EMPARED
EMPARES
EMPARING
EMPART
EMPARTED
EMPARTING
EMPARTS
EMPATHIC
EMPATHIES
EMPATHISE
EMPATHISED
EMPATHISES
EMPATHISING
EMPATHIZE
EMPATHIZED
EMPATHIZES
EMPATHIZING
EMPATHY
EMPATRON
EMPATRONED
EMPATRONING
EMPATRONS
EMPAYRE
EMPAYRED
EMPAYRES
EMPAYRING
EMPEACH
EMPEACHED
EMPEACHES
EMPEACHING
EMPENNAGE
EMPENNAGES
EMPEOPLE
EMPEOPLED
EMPEOPLES
EMPEOPLING
EMPERCE
EMPERCED
EMPERCES
EMPERCING
EMPERIES
EMPERISE
EMPERISED
EMPERISES
EMPERISH
EMPERISHED
EMPERISHES
EMPERISHING
EMPERISING
EMPERIZE

EMPERIZED	EMPOLDERED	EMULOUS	ENARCHING	ENCHEASONS
EMPERIZES	EMPOLDERING	EMULOUSLY	ENARM	ENCHEER
EMPERIZING	EMPOLDERS	EMULSIFIED	ENARMED	ENCHEERED
EMPEROR	EMPORIA	EMULSIFIES	ENARMING	ENCHEERING
EMPERORS	EMPORIUM	EMULSIFY	ENARMS	ENCHEERS
EMPERY	EMPORIUMS	EMULSIFYING	ENATE	ENCHILADA
EMPHASES	EMPOWER	EMULSIN	ENATION	ENCHILADAS
EMPHASIS	EMPOWERED	EMULSINS	ENATIONS	ENCHORIAL
EMPHASISE	EMPOWERING	EMULSION	ENAUNTER	ENCHORIC
EMPHASISED	EMPOWERS	EMULSIONS	ENCAENIA	ENCIPHER
EMPHASISES	EMPRESS	EMULSIVE	ENCAENIAS	ENCIPHERED
EMPHASISING	EMPRESSE	EMULSOID	ENCAGE	ENCIPHERING
EMPHASIZE	EMPRESSES	EMULSOIDS	ENCAGED	ENCIPHERS
EMPHASIZED	EMPRISE	EMULSOR	ENCAGES	ENCIRCLE
EMPHASIZES	EMPRISES	EMULSORS	ENCAGING	ENCIRCLED
EMPHASIZING	EMPTIED	EMUNCTORIES	ENCALM	ENCIRCLES
EMPHATIC	EMPTIER	EMUNCTORY	ENCALMED	ENCIRCLING
EMPHLYSES	EMPTIERS	EMUNGE	ENCALMING	ENCIRCLINGS
EMPHLYSIS	EMPTIES	EMUNGED	ENCALMS	ENCLASP
EMPHYSEMA	EMPTIEST	EMUNGES	ENCAMP	ENCLASPED
EMPHYSEMAS	EMPTILY	EMUNGING	ENCAMPED	ENCLASPING
EMPIERCE	EMPTINESS	EMURE	ENCAMPING	ENCLASPS
EMPIERCED	EMPTINESSES	EMURED	ENCAMPS	ENCLAVE
EMPIERCES	EMPTION	EMURES	ENCANTHIS	ENCLAVED
EMPIERCING	EMPTIONAL	EMURING	ENCANTHISES	ENCLAVES
EMPIGHT	EMPTIONS	EMUS	ENCARPUS	ENCLAVING
EMPIRE	EMPTY	EMYDES	ENCARPUSES	ENCLISES
EMPIRES	EMPTYING	EMYS	ENCASE	ENCLISIS
EMPIRIC	EMPTYINGS	EN	ENCASED	ENCLITIC
EMPIRICAL	EMPTYSES	ENABLE	ENCASES	ENCLITICS
EMPIRICS	EMPTYSIS	ENABLED	ENCASH	ENCLOSE
EMPLACE	EMPURPLE	ENABLER	ENCASHED	ENCLOSED
EMPLACED	EMPURPLED	ENABLERS	ENCASHES	ENCLOSER
EMPLACES	EMPURPLES	ENABLES	ENCASHING	ENCLOSERS
EMPLACING	EMPURPLING	ENABLING	ENCASING	ENCLOSES
EMPLANE	EMPUSA	ENACT	ENCAUSTIC	ENCLOSING
EMPLANED	EMPUSAS	ENACTED	ENCAUSTICS	ENCLOSURE
EMPLANES	EMPUSE	ENACTING	ENCAVE	ENCLOSURES
EMPLANING	EMPUSES	ENACTION	ENCAVED	ENCLOTHE
EMPLASTER	EMPYEMA	ENACTIONS	ENCAVES	ENCLOTHED
EMPLASTERED	EMPYEMAS	ENACTIVE	ENCAVING	ENCLOTHES
EMPLASTERING	EMPYESES	ENACTMENT	ENCEINTE	ENCLOTHING
EMPLASTERS	EMPYESIS	ENACTMENTS	ENCEINTES	ENCLOUD
EMPLASTIC	EMPYREAL	ENACTOR	ENCHAFE	ENCLOUDED
EMPLASTICS	EMPYREAN	ENACTORS	ENCHAFED	ENCLOUDING
EMPLECTON	EMPYREANS	ENACTS	ENCHAFES	ENCLOUDS
EMPLECTONS	EMPYREUMA	ENACTURE	ENCHAFING	ENCODE
EMPLECTUM	EMPYREUMATA	ENACTURES	ENCHAIN	ENCODED
EMPLECTUMS	EMS	ENALLAGE	ENCHAINED	ENCODES
EMPLONGE	EMU	ENALLAGES	ENCHAINING	ENCODING
EMPLONGED	EMULATE	ENAMEL	ENCHAINS	ENCOLOUR
EMPLONGES	EMULATED	ENAMELLED	ENCHANT	ENCOLOURED
EMPLONGING	EMULATES	ENAMELLER	ENCHANTED	ENCOLOURING
EMPLOY	EMULATING	ENAMELLERS	ENCHANTER	ENCOLOURS
EMPLOYED	EMULATION	ENAMELLING	ENCHANTERS	ENCOLPION
EMPLOYEE	EMULATIONS	ENAMELLINGS	ENCHANTING	ENCOLPIONS
EMPLOYEES	EMULATIVE	ENAMELS	ENCHANTS	ENCOLPIUM
EMPLOYER	EMULATOR	ENAMOR	ENCHARGE	ENCOLPIUMS
EMPLOYERS	EMULATORS	ENAMORADO	ENCHARGED	ENCOLURE
EMPLOYING	EMULE	ENAMORADOS	ENCHARGES	ENCOLURES
EMPLOYS	EMULED	ENAMORED	ENCHARGING	ENCOMIA
EMPLUME	EMULES	ENAMORING	ENCHARM	ENCOMIAST
EMPLUMED	EMULGE	ENAMORS	ENCHARMED	ENCOMIASTS
EMPLUMES	EMULGED	ENAMOUR	ENCHARMING	ENCOMION
EMPLUMING	EMULGENCE	ENAMOURED	ENCHARMS	ENCOMIONS
EMPOISON	EMULGENCES	ENAMOURING	ENCHASE	ENCOMIUM
EMPOISONED	EMULGENT	ENAMOURS	ENCHASED	ENCOMIUMS
EMPOISONING	EMULGES	ENARCH	ENCHASES	ENCOMPASS
EMPOISONS	EMULGING	ENARCHED	ENCHASING	ENCOMPASSED
EMPOLDER	EMULING	ENARCHES	ENCHEASON	ENCOMPASSES

ENCOMPASSING	ENDART	ENDOLYMPH	ENDURED	ENFILADE
ENCORE	ENDARTED	ENDOLYMPHS	ENDURER	ENFILADED
ENCORED	ENDARTING	ENDOMIXES	ENDURERS	ENFILADES
ENCORES	ENDARTS	ENDOMIXIS	ENDURES	ENFILADING
ENCORING	ENDEAR	ENDOMIXISES	ENDURING	ENFILED
ENCOUNTER	ENDEARED	ENDOMORPH	ENDWAYS	ENFIRE
ENCOUNTERED	ENDEARING	ENDOMORPHS	ENDWISE	ENFIRED
ENCOUNTERING	ENDEARS	ENDOPHAGIES	ENE	ENFIRES
ENCOUNTERS	ENDEAVOUR	ENDOPHAGY	ENEMA	ENFIRING
ENCOURAGE	ENDEAVOURED	ENDOPHYTE	ENEMAS	ENFIX
ENCOURAGED	ENDEAVOURING	ENDOPHYTES	ENEMATA	ENFIXED
ENCOURAGES	ENDEAVOURS	ENDOPLASM	ENEMIES	ENFIXES
ENCOURAGING	ENDECAGON	ENDOPLASMS	ENEMY	ENFIXING
ENCOURAGINGS	ENDECAGONS	ENDORPHIN	ENERGETIC	ENFLESH
ENCRADLE	ENDED	ENDORPHINS	ENERGETICS	ENFLESHED
ENCRADLED	ENDEICTIC	ENDORSE	ENERGIC	ENFLESHES
ENCRADLES	ENDEIXES	ENDORSED	ENERGID	ENFLESHING
ENCRADLING	ENDEIXIS	ENDORSEE	ENERGIDS	ENFLOWER
ENCRATIES	ENDEIXISES	ENDORSEES	ENERGIES	ENFLOWERED
ENCRATY	ENDEMIAL	ENDORSER	ENERGISE	ENFLOWERING
ENCREASE	ENDEMIC	ENDORSERS	ENERGISED	ENFLOWERS
ENCREASED	ENDEMICAL	ENDORSES	ENERGISES	ENFOLD
ENCREASES	ENDEMICS	ENDORSING	ENERGISING	ENFOLDED
ENCREASING	ENDEMISM	ENDOSARC	ENERGIZE	ENFOLDING
ENCRIMSON	ENDEMISMS	ENDOSARCS	ENERGIZED	ENFOLDS
ENCRIMSONED	ENDENIZEN	ENDOSCOPE	ENERGIZES	ENFORCE
ENCRIMSONING	ENDENIZENED	ENDOSCOPES	ENERGIZING	ENFORCED
ENCRIMSONS	ENDENIZENING	ENDOSCOPIES	ENERGUMEN	ENFORCES
ENCRINAL	ENDENIZENS	ENDOSCOPY	ENERGUMENS	ENFORCING
ENCRINIC	ENDERMIC	ENDOSMOSE	ENERGY	ENFOREST
ENCRINITE	ENDERON	ENDOSMOSES	ENERVATE	ENFORESTED
ENCRINITES	ENDERONS	ENDOSPERM	ENERVATED	ENFORESTING
ENCROACH	ENDEW	ENDOSPERMS	ENERVATES	ENFORESTS
ENCROACHED	ENDEWED	ENDOSPORE	ENERVATING	ENFORM
ENCROACHES	ENDEWING	ENDOSPORES	ENERVE	ENFORMED
ENCROACHING	ENDEWS	ENDOSS	ENERVED	ENFORMING
ENCRUST	ENDGAME	ENDOSSED	ENERVES	ENFORMS
ENCRUSTED	ENDGAMES	ENDOSSES	ENERVING	ENFRAME
ENCRUSTING	ENDING	ENDOSSING	ENES	ENFRAMED
ENCRUSTS	ENDINGS	ENDOSTEAL	ENEW	ENFRAMES
ENCRYPT	ENDIRON	ENDOSTEUM	ENEWED	ENFRAMING
ENCRYPTED	ENDIRONS	ENDOSTEUMS	ENEWING	ENFREE
ENCRYPTING	ENDITE	ENDOW	ENEWS	ENFREED
ENCRYPTS	ENDITED	ENDOWED	ENFACE	ENFREEDOM
ENCUMBER	ENDITES	ENDOWER	ENFACED	ENFREEDOMED
ENCUMBERED	ENDITING	ENDOWERS	ENFACES	ENFREEDOMING
ENCUMBERING	ENDIVE	ENDOWING	ENFACING	ENFREEDOMS
ENCUMBERS	ENDIVES	ENDOWMENT	ENFANT	ENFREEING
ENCURTAIN	ENDLANG	ENDOWMENTS	ENFANTS	ENFREES
ENCURTAINED	ENDLESS	ENDOWS	ENFEEBLE	ENFREEZE
ENCURTAINING	ENDLESSLY	ENDOZOA	ENFEEBLED	ENFREEZES
ENCURTAINS	ENDLONG	ENDOZOIC	ENFEEBLES	ENFREEZING
ENCYCLIC	ENDMOST	ENDOZOON	ENFEEBLING	ENFROSEN
ENCYCLICS	ENDOBLAST	ENDS	ENFELON	ENFROZE
ENCYST	ENDOBLASTS	ENDSHIP	ENFELONED	ENFROZEN
ENCYSTED	ENDOCARP	ENDSHIPS	ENFELONING	ENG
ENCYSTING	ENDOCARPS	ENDUE	ENFELONS	ENGAGÉ
ENCYSTS	ENDOCRINE	ENDUED	ENFEOFF	ENGAGE
END	ENDOCRINES	ENDUEING	ENFEOFFED	ENGAGED
ENDAMAGE	ENDODERM	ENDUES	ENFEOFFING	ENGAGER
ENDAMAGED	ENDODERMS	ENDUING	ENFEOFFS	ENGAGERS
ENDAMAGES	ENDODYNE	ENDUNGEON	ENFESTED	ENGAGES
ENDAMAGING	ENDOGAMIC	ENDUNGEONED	ENFETTER	ENGAGING
ENDAMOEBA	ENDOGAMIES	ENDUNGEONING	ENFETTERED	ENGAOL
ENDAMOEBAE	ENDOGAMY	ENDUNGEONS	ENFETTERING	ENGAOLED
ENDANGER	ENDOGEN	ENDURABLE	ENFETTERS	ENGAOLING
ENDANGERED	ENDOGENIC	ENDURABLY	ENFIERCE	ENGAOLS
ENDANGERING	ENDOGENIES	ENDURANCE	ENFIERCED	ENGARLAND
ENDANGERS	ENDOGENS	ENDURANCES	ENFIERCES	ENGARLANDED
ENDARCH	ENDOGENY	ENDURE	ENFIERCING	ENGARLANDING

ENGARLANDS	ENGRAFTS	ENHEARSE	ENLARGES	ENOSES
ENGENDER	ENGRAIL	ENHEARSED	ENLARGING	ENOSIS
ENGENDERED	ENGRAILED	ENHEARSES	ENLEVÉ	ENOUGH
ENGENDERING	ENGRAILING	ENHEARSING	ENLIGHT	ENOUGHS
ENGENDERS	ENGRAILS	ENHEARTEN	ENLIGHTED	ENOUNCE
ENGENDURE	ENGRAIN	ENHEARTENED	ENLIGHTEN	ENOUNCED
ENGENDURES	ENGRAINED	ENHEARTENING	ENLIGHTENED	ENOUNCES
ENGILD	ENGRAINER	ENHEARTENS	ENLIGHTENING	ENOUNCING
ENGILDED	ENGRAINERS	ENHUNGER	ENLIGHTENS	ENOW
ENGILDING	ENGRAINING	ENHUNGERED	ENLIGHTING	ENPRINT
ENGILDS	ENGRAINS	ENHUNGERING	ENLIGHTS	ENPRINTS
ENGINE	ENGRAM	ENHUNGERS	ENLINK	ENQUIRE
ENGINED	ENGRAMMA	ENHYDRITE	ENLINKED	ENQUIRED
ENGINEER	ENGRAMMAS	ENHYDRITES	ENLINKING	ENQUIRER
ENGINEERED	ENGRAMS	ENHYDROS	ENLINKS	ENQUIRERS
ENGINEERING	ENGRASP	ENHYDROSES	ENLIST	ENQUIRES
ENGINEERINGS	ENGRASPED	ENHYDROUS	ENLISTED	ENQUIRIES
ENGINEERS	ENGRASPING	ENIAC	ENLISTING	ENQUIRING
ENGINER	ENGRASPS	ENIACS	ENLISTS	ENQUIRY
ENGINERIES	ENGRAVE	ENIGMA	ENLIVEN	ENRACE
ENGINERS	ENGRAVED	ENIGMAS	ENLIVENED	ENRACED
ENGINERY	ENGRAVEN	ENIGMATIC	ENLIVENER	ENRACES
ENGINES	ENGRAVER	ENISLE	ENLIVENERS	ENRACING
ENGINING	ENGRAVERIES	ENISLED	ENLIVENING	ENRAGÉ
ENGIRD	ENGRAVERS	ENISLES	ENLIVENS	ENRAGE
ENGIRDING	ENGRAVERY	ENISLING	ENLOCK	ENRAGED
ENGIRDLE	ENGRAVES	ENJAMB	ENLOCKED	ENRAGES
ENGIRDLED	ENGRAVING	ENJAMBED	ENLOCKING	ENRAGING
ENGIRDLES	ENGRAVINGS	ENJAMBING	ENLOCKS	ENRANCKLE
ENGIRDLING	ENGRENAGE	ENJAMBS	ENLUMINE	ENRANCKLED
ENGIRDS	ENGRENAGES	ENJOIN	ENLUMINED	ENRANCKLES
ENGIRT	ENGRIEVE	ENJOINED	ENLUMINES	ENRANCKLING
ENGISCOPE	ENGRIEVED	ENJOINER	ENLUMINING	ENRANGE
ENGISCOPES	ENGRIEVES	ENJOINERS	ENMESH	ENRANGED
ENGLOBE	ENGRIEVING	ENJOINING	ENMESHED	ENRANGES
ENGLOBED	ENGROOVE	ENJOINS	ENMESHES	ENRANGING
ENGLOBES	ENGROOVED	ENJOY	ENMESHING	ENRANK
ENGLOBING	ENGROOVES	ENJOYABLE	ENMEW	ENRANKED
ENGLOOM	ENGROOVING	ENJOYABLY	ENMEWED	ENRANKING
ENGLOOMED	ENGROSS	ENJOYED	ENMEWING	ENRANKS
ENGLOOMING	ENGROSSED	ENJOYER	ENMEWS	ENRAPT
ENGLOOMS	ENGROSSER	ENJOYERS	ENMITIES	ENRAPTURE
ENGLUT	ENGROSSERS	ENJOYING	ENMITY	ENRAPTURED
ENGLUTS	ENGROSSES	ENJOYMENT	ENMOSSED	ENRAPTURES
ENGLUTTED	ENGROSSING	ENJOYMENTS	ENMOVE	ENRAPTURING
ENGLUTTING	ENGS	ENJOYS	ENMOVED	ENRAUNGE
ENGOBE	ENGUARD	ENKERNEL	ENMOVES	ENRAUNGED
ENGOBES	ENGUARDED	ENKERNELLED	ENMOVING	ENRAUNGES
ENGORE	ENGUARDING	ENKERNELLING	ENNEAD	ENRAUNGING
ENGORED	ENGUARDS	ENKERNELS	ENNEADIC	ENRAVISH
ENGORES	ENGULF	ENKINDLE	ENNEADS	ENRAVISHED
ENGORGE	ENGULFED	ENKINDLED	ENNEAGON	ENRAVISHES
ENGORGED	ENGULFING	ENKINDLES	ENNEAGONS	ENRAVISHING
ENGORGES	ENGULFS	ENKINDLING	ENNOBLE	ENRHEUM
ENGORGING	ENGULPH	ENLACE	ENNOBLED	ENRHEUMED
ENGORING	ENGULPHED	ENLACED	ENNOBLES	ENRHEUMING
ENGOULED	ENGULPHING	ENLACES	ENNOBLING	ENRHEUMS
ENGOÛMENT	ENGULPHS	ENLACING	ENNUI	ENRICH
ENGOÛMENTS	ENGYSCOPE	ENLARD	ENNUIED	ENRICHED
ENGRACE	ENGYSCOPES	ENLARDED	ENNUIS	ENRICHES
ENGRACED	ENHALO	ENLARDING	ENNUYÉ	ENRICHING
ENGRACES	ENHALOED	ENLARDS	ENNUYED	ENRIDGED
ENGRACING	ENHALOES	ENLARGE	ENNUYING	ENRING
ENGRAFF	ENHALOING	ENLARGED	ENODAL	ENRINGED
ENGRAFFED	ENHALOS	ENLARGEN	ENOMOTIES	ENRINGING
ENGRAFFING	ENHANCE	ENLARGENED	ENOMOTY	ENRINGS
ENGRAFFS	ENHANCED	ENLARGENING	ENORM	ENRIVEN
ENGRAFT	ENHANCES	ENLARGENS	ENORMITIES	ENROBE
ENGRAFTED	ENHANCING	ENLARGER	ENORMITY	ENROBED
ENGRAFTING	ENHANCIVE	ENLARGERS	ENORMOUS	ENROBES

ENROBING	ENSHRINED	ENSURE	ENTERTAKING	ENTRAILS
ENROL	ENSHRINES	ENSURED	ENTERTOOK	ENTRAIN
ENROLL	ENSHRINING	ENSURER	ENTÊTÉ	ENTRAINED
ENROLLED	ENSHROUD	ENSURERS	ENTÊTÉE	ENTRAINING
ENROLLER	ENSHROUDED	ENSURES	ENTHALPIES	ENTRAINS
ENROLLERS	ENSHROUDING	ENSURING	ENTHALPY	ENTRALL
ENROLLING	ENSHROUDS	ENSWATHE	ENTHETIC	ENTRALLES
ENROLLS	ENSIFORM	ENSWATHED	ENTHRAL	ENTRAMMEL
ENROLMENT	ENSIGN	ENSWATHES	ENTHRALL	ENTRAMMELLED
ENROLMENTS	ENSIGNCIES	ENSWATHING	ENTHRALLED	ENTRAMMELLING
ENROLS	ENSIGNCY	ENSWEEP	ENTHRALLING	ENTRAMMELS
ENROOT	ENSIGNED	ENSWEEPING	ENTHRALLS	ENTRANCE
ENROOTED	ENSIGNING	ENSWEEPS	ENTHRALS	ENTRANCED
ENROOTING	ENSIGNS	ENSWEPT	ENTHRONE	ENTRANCES
ENROOTS	ENSILAGE	ENTAIL	ENTHRONED	ENTRANCING
ENROUGH	ENSILAGED	ENTAILED	ENTHRONES	ENTRANT
ENROUGHED	ENSILAGES	ENTAILER	ENTHRONING	ENTRANTS
ENROUGHING	ENSILAGING	ENTAILERS	ENTHUSE	ENTRAP
ENROUGHS	ENSILE	ENTAILING	ENTHUSED	ENTRAPPED
ENROUND	ENSILED	ENTAILS	ENTHUSES	ENTRAPPER
ENROUNDED	ENSILES	ENTAME	ENTHUSING	ENTRAPPERS
ENROUNDING	ENSILING	ENTAMED	ENTHYMEME	ENTRAPPING
ENROUNDS	ENSKIED	ENTAMES	ENTHYMEMES	ENTRAPS
ENS	ENSKIES	ENTAMING	ENTIA	ENTREAT
ENSAMPLE	ENSKY	ENTAMOEBA	ENTICE	ENTREATED
ENSAMPLED	ENSKYING	ENTAMOEBAE	ENTICED	ENTREATIES
ENSAMPLES	ENSLAVE	ENTANGLE	ENTICER	ENTREATING
ENSAMPLING	ENSLAVED	ENTANGLED	ENTICERS	ENTREATS
ENSATE	ENSLAVER	ENTANGLES	ENTICES	ENTREATY
ENSCONCE	ENSLAVERS	ENTANGLING	ENTICING	ENTRECHAT
ENSCONCED	ENSLAVES	ENTASES	ENTICINGS	ENTRECHATS
ENSCONCES	ENSLAVING	ENTASIS	ENTIRE	ENTRECÔTE
ENSCONCING	ENSNARE	ENTAYLE	ENTIRELY	ENTRECÔTES
ENSEAL	ENSNARED	ENTAYLED	ENTIRES	ENTRÉE
ENSEALED	ENSNARES	ENTAYLES	ENTIRETIES	ENTRÉES
ENSEALING	ENSNARING	ENTAYLING	ENTIRETY	ENTREMES
ENSEALS	ENSNARL	ENTELECHIES	ENTITIES	ENTREMETS
ENSEAM	ENSNARLED	ENTELECHY	ENTITLE	ENTRENCH
ENSEAMED	ENSNARLING	ENTELLUS	ENTITLED	ENTRENCHED
ENSEAMING	ENSNARLS	ENTELLUSES	ENTITLES	ENTRENCHES
ENSEAMS	ENSORCELL	ENTENDER	ENTITLING	ENTRENCHING
ENSEAR	ENSORCELLED	ENTENDERED	ENTITY	ENTREPOT
ENSEARED	ENSORCELLING	ENTENDERING	ENTOBLAST	ENTREPOTS
ENSEARING	ENSORCELLS	ENTENDERS	ENTOBLASTS	ENTRESOL
ENSEARS	ENSOUL	ENTENTE	ENTODERM	ENTRESOLS
ENSEMBLE	ENSOULED	ENTENTES	ENTODERMS	ENTREZ
ENSEMBLES	ENSOULING	ENTER	ENTOIL	ENTRIES
ENSEW	ENSOULS	ENTERA	ENTOILED	ENTRISM
ENSEWED	ENSPHERE	ENTERABLE	ENTOILING	ENTRISMS
ENSEWING	ENSPHERED	ENTERAL	ENTOILS	ENTRIST
ENSEWS	ENSPHERES	ENTERATE	ENTOMB	ENTRISTS
ENSHEATH	ENSPHERING	ENTERED	ENTOMBED	ENTROLD
ENSHEATHE	ENSTAMP	ENTERER	ENTOMBING	ENTROPIES
ENSHEATHED	ENSTAMPED	ENTERERS	ENTOMBS	ENTROPION
ENSHEATHES	ENSTAMPING	ENTERIC	ENTOMIC	ENTROPIONS
ENSHEATHING	ENSTAMPS	ENTERICS	ENTOPHYTE	ENTROPIUM
ENSHEATHS	ENSTATITE	ENTERING	ENTOPHYTES	ENTROPIUMS
ENSHELL	ENSTATITES	ENTERINGS	ENTOPIC	ENTROPY
ENSHELLED	ENSTEEP	ENTERITIS	ENTOPTIC	ENTRUST
ENSHELLING	ENSTEEPED	ENTERITISES	ENTOPTICS	ENTRUSTED
ENSHELLS	ENSTEEPING	ENTERON	ENTOTIC	ENTRUSTING
ENSHELTER	ENSTEEPS	ENTERS	ENTOURAGE	ENTRUSTS
ENSHELTERED	ENSTYLE	ENTERTAIN	ENTOURAGES	ENTRY
ENSHELTERING	ENSTYLED	ENTERTAINED	ENTOZOA	ENTRYISM
ENSHELTERS	ENSTYLES	ENTERTAINING	ENTOZOAL	ENTRYISMS
ENSHIELD	ENSTYLING	ENTERTAININGS	ENTOZOIC	ENTRYIST
ENSHIELDED	ENSUE	ENTERTAINS	ENTOZOON	ENTRYISTS
ENSHIELDING	ENSUED	ENTERTAKE	ENTRAIL	ENTWINE
ENSHIELDS	ENSUES	ENTERTAKEN	ENTRAILED	ENTWINED
ENSHRINE	ENSUING	ENTERTAKES	ENTRAILING	ENTWINES

ENTWINING	ENVISIONS	EPACRIS	EPIBLAST	EPIGEOUS
ENTWIST	ENVOI	EPACRISES	EPIBLASTS	EPIGON
ENTWISTED	ENVOIS	EPACT	EPIC	EPIGONE
ENTWISTING	ENVOY	EPACTS	EPICAL	EPIGONES
ENTWISTS	ENVOYS	EPAENETIC	EPICALLY	EPIGONI
ENUCLEATE	ENVOYSHIP	EPAGOGE	EPICALYCES	EPIGONS
ENUCLEATED	ENVOYSHIPS	EPAGOGES	EPICALYX	EPIGRAM
ENUCLEATES	ENVY	EPAGOGIC	EPICALYXES	EPIGRAMS
ENUCLEATING	ENVYING	EPAINETIC	EPICARP	EPIGRAPH
ENUMERATE	ENVYINGS	EPANODOS	EPICARPS	EPIGRAPHED
ENUMERATED	ENWALL	EPANODOSES	EPICEDE	EPIGRAPHIES
ENUMERATES	ENWALLED	EPARCH	EPICEDES	EPIGRAPHING
ENUMERATING	ENWALLING	ÉPARCHATE	EPICEDIA	EPIGRAPHS
ENUNCIATE	ENWALLOW	EPARCHATES	EPICEDIAL	EPIGRAPHY
ENUNCIATED	ENWALLOWED	EPARCHIES	EPICEDIAN	EPIGYNIES
ENUNCIATES	ENWALLOWING	EPARCHS	EPICEDIUM	EPIGYNOUS
ENUNCIATING	ENWALLOWS	EPARCHY	EPICENE	EPIGYNY
ENURE	ENWALLS	ÉPATANT	EPICENES	EPILATE
ENURED	ENWHEEL	EPAULE	EPICENTRE	EPILATED
ENURES	ENWHEELED	EPAULES	EPICENTRES	EPILATES
ENURESES	ENWHEELING	EPAULET	ÉPICIER	EPILATING
ENURESIS	ENWHEELS	EPAULETS	ÉPICIERS	EPILATION
ENURETIC	ENWIND	EPAULETTE	EPICISM	EPILATIONS
ENURETICS	ENWINDING	EPAULETTES	EPICISMS	EPILATOR
ENURING	ENWINDS	EPAXIAL	EPICIST	EPILATORS
ENVASSAL	ENWOMB	EPEDAPHIC	EPICISTS	EPILEPSIES
ENVASSALLED	ENWOMBED	ÉPÉE	EPICLESES	EPILEPSY
ENVASSALLING	ENWOMBING	ÉPÉES	EPICLESIS	EPILEPTIC
ENVASSALS	ENWOMBS	EPEIRA	EPICOTYL	EPILEPTICS
ENVAULT	ENWOUND	EPEIRAS	EPICOTYLS	EPILOBIUM
ENVAULTED	ENWRAP	EPEIRID	EPICRITIC	EPILOBIUMS
ENVAULTING	ENWRAPPED	EPEIRIDS	EPICS	EPILOGIC
ENVAULTS	ENWRAPPING	EPEOLATRIES	EPICURE	EPILOGISE
ENVEIGLE	ENWRAPPINGS	EPEOLATRY	EPICUREAN	EPILOGISED
ENVEIGLED	ENWRAPS	ÉPERDU	EPICUREANS	EPILOGISES
ENVEIGLES	ENWREATHE	ÉPERDUE	EPICURES	EPILOGISING
ENVEIGLING	ENWREATHED	EPERGNE	EPICURISE	EPILOGIZE
ENVELOP	ENWREATHES	EPERGNES	EPICURISED	EPILOGIZED
ENVELOPE	ENWREATHING	EPHA	EPICURISES	EPILOGIZES
ENVELOPED	ENZIAN	EPHAH	EPICURISING	EPILOGIZING
ENVELOPES	ENZIANS	EPHAHS	EPICURISM	EPILOGUE
ENVELOPING	ENZONE	EPHAS	EPICURISMS	EPILOGUES
ENVELOPS	ENZONED	EPHEBE	EPICURIZE	EPIMER
ENVENOM	ENZONES	EPHEBI	EPICURIZED	EPIMERIC
ENVENOMED	ENZONING	EPHEBIC	EPICURIZES	EPIMERS
ENVENOMING	ENZOOTIC	EPHEBOS	EPICURIZING	EPINASTIC
ENVENOMS	ENZOOTICS	EPHEBUS	EPICYCLE	EPINASTIES
ENVERMEIL	ENZYMATIC	EPHEDRA	EPICYCLES	EPINASTY
ENVERMEILED	ENZYME	EPHEDRAS	EPICYCLIC	EPINICIAN
ENVERMEILING	ENZYMES	EPHEDRINE	EPIDEMIC	EPINICION
ENVERMEILS	ENZYMIC	EPHEDRINES	EPIDEMICS	EPINICIONS
ENVIABLE	EOAN	EPHELIDES	EPIDERMAL	EPINIKIAN
ENVIABLY	ÉOLIENNE	EPHELIS	EPIDERMIC	EPINIKION
ENVIED	ÉOLIENNES	EPHEMERA	EPIDERMIS	EPINIKIONS
ENVIER	EOLIPILE	EPHEMERAE	EPIDERMISES	EPINOSIC
ENVIERS	EOLIPILES	EPHEMERAL	EPIDOSITE	EPIPHANIC
ENVIES	EOLITH	EPHEMERALS	EPIDOSITES	EPIPHRAGM
ENVIOUS	EOLITHIC	EPHEMERAS	EPIDOTE	EPIPHRAGMS
ENVIOUSLY	EOLITHS	EPHEMERID	EPIDOTES	EPIPHYSES
ENVIRON	EON	EPHEMERIDES	EPIDOTIC	EPIPHYSIS
ENVIRONED	EONISM	EPHEMERIDS	EPIDURAL	EPIPHYTAL
ENVIRONING	EONISMS	EPHEMERIS	EPIDURALS	EPIPHYTE
ENVIRONS	EONS	EPHEMERON	EPIFOCAL	EPIPHYTES
ENVISAGE	EORL	EPHIALTES	EPIGAEAL	EPIPHYTIC
ENVISAGED	EORLS	EPHOD	EPIGAEAN	EPIPLOIC
ENVISAGES	EOSIN	EPHODS	EPIGAEOUS	EPIPLOON
ENVISAGING	EOSINS	EPHOR	EPIGAMIC	EPIPLOONS
ENVISION	EOTHEN	EPHORALTIES	EPIGEAL	EPIPOLIC
ENVISIONED	EPACRID	EPHORALTY	EPIGEAN	EPIPOLISM
ENVISIONING	EPACRIDS	EPHORS	EPIGENE	EPIPOLISMS

EPIRRHEMA	EPITOMISED	EQUABLY	EQUIVOKES	ERGATE
EPIRRHEMAS	EPITOMISES	EQUAL	EQUIVOQUE	ERGATES
EPISCOPAL	EPITOMISING	EQUALISE	EQUIVOQUES	ERGATOID
EPISCOPE	EPITOMIST	EQUALISED	ER —	ERGO
EPISCOPES	EPITOMISTS	EQUALISER	ERA	ERGODIC
EPISCOPIES	EPITOMIZE	EQUALISERS	ERADIATE	ERGOGRAM
EPISCOPY	EPITOMIZED	EQUALISES	ERADIATED	ERGOGRAMS
EPISEMON	EPITOMIZES	EQUALISING	ERADIATES	ERGOGRAPH
EPISEMONS	EPITOMIZING	EQUALITIES	ERADIATING	ERGOGRAPHS
EPISODAL	EPITONIC	EQUALITY	ERADICATE	ERGOMETER
EPISODE	EPITRITE	EQUALIZE	ERADICATED	ERGOMETERS
EPISODES	EPITRITES	EQUALIZED	ERADICATES	ERGON
EPISODIAL	EPIZEUXES	EQUALIZER	ERADICATING	ERGONOMIC
EPISODIC	EPIZEUXIS	EQUALIZERS	ERAS	ERGONOMICS
EPISOME	EPIZEUXISES	EQUALIZES	ERASABLE	ERGONS
EPISOMES	EPIZOA	EQUALIZING	ERASE	ERGOT
EPISPERM	EPIZOAN	EQUALLED	ERASED	ERGOTISE
EPISPERMS	EPIZOANS	EQUALLING	ERASEMENT	ERGOTISED
EPISPORE	EPIZOIC	EQUALLY	ERASEMENTS	ERGOTISES
EPISPORES	EPIZOON	EQUALNESS	ERASER	ERGOTISING
EPISTASES	EPIZOOTIC	EQUALNESSES	ERASERS	ERGOTISM
EPISTASIS	EPIZOOTICS	EQUALS	ERASES	ERGOTISMS
EPISTATIC	EPOCH	EQUANT	ERASING	ERGOTIZE
EPISTAXES	EPOCHA	EQUANTS	ERASION	ERGOTIZED
EPISTAXIS	EPOCHAL	EQUATE	ERASIONS	ERGOTIZES
EPISTAXISES	EPOCHAS	EQUATED	ERASURE	ERGOTIZING
EPISTEMIC	EPOCHS	EQUATES	ERASURES	ERGOTS
EPISTEMICS	EPODE	EQUATING	ERATHEM	ERGS
EPISTLE	EPODES	EQUATION	ERATHEMS	ERIACH
EPISTLED	EPODIC	EQUATIONS	ERBIA	ERIACHS
EPISTLER	EPONYM	EQUATOR	ERBIAS	ERIC
EPISTLERS	EPONYMOUS	EQUATORS	ERBIUM	ERICA
EPISTLES	EPONYMS	EQUERRIES	ERBIUMS	ERICAS
EPISTLING	EPOPEE	EQUERRY	ERE	ERICK
EPISTOLER	EPOPEES	EQUINAL	ERECT	ERICKS
EPISTOLERS	EPOPOEIA	EQUINE	ERECTED	ERICOID
EPISTOLET	EPOPOEIAS	EQUINIA	ERECTER	ERICS
EPISTOLETS	EPOPT	EQUINIAS	ERECTERS	ERIGERON
EPISTOLIC	EPOPTS	EQUINITIES	ERECTILE	ERIGERONS
EPISTYLE	EPOS	EQUINITY	ERECTING	ERING
EPISTYLES	EPOSES	EQUINOX	ERECTION	ERINGO
EPITAPH	EPOXIDE	EQUINOXES	ERECTIONS	ERINGOES
EPITAPHED	EPOXIDES	EQUIP	ERECTIVE	ERINGOS
EPITAPHER	EPOXIES	EQUIPAGE	ERECTLY	ERINITE
EPITAPHERS	EPOXY	EQUIPAGED	ERECTNESS	ERINITES
EPITAPHIC	ÉPRIS	EQUIPAGES	ERECTNESSES	ERIOMETER
EPITAPHING	ÉPRISE	EQUIPAGING	ERECTOR	ERIOMETERS
EPITAPHS	EPSILON	ÉQUIPE	ERECTORS	ERIONITE
EPITASES	EPSILONS	ÉQUIPES	ERECTS	ERIONITES
EPITASIS	EPSOMITE	EQUIPMENT	ERED	ERISTIC
EPITAXIAL	EPSOMITES	EQUIPMENTS	ERELONG	ERISTICAL
EPITAXIES	ÉPUISÉ	EQUIPOISE	EREMIC	ERK
EPITAXY	ÉPUISÉE	EQUIPOISED	EREMITAL	ERKS
EPITHEM	EPULARY	EQUIPOISES	EREMITE	ERMELIN
EPITHEMA	EPULATION	EQUIPOISING	EREMITES	ERMELINS
EPITHEMATA	EPULATIONS	EQUIPPED	EREMITIC	ERMINE
EPITHEMS	EPULIDES	EQUIPPING	EREMITISM	ERMINED
EPITHESES	EPULIS	EQUIPS	EREMITISMS	ERMINES
EPITHESIS	EPULISES	EQUISETA	ERENOW	ERN
EPITHET	EPULOTIC	EQUISETIC	EREPSIN	ERNE
EPITHETED	EPULOTICS	EQUISETUM	EREPSINS	ERNED
EPITHETIC	EPURATE	EQUISETUMS	ERES	ERNES
EPITHETING	EPURATED	EQUITABLE	ERETHISM	ERNING
EPITHETON	EPURATES	EQUITABLY	ERETHISMS	ERNS
EPITHETONS	EPURATING	EQUITANT	ERETHITIC	ERODE
EPITHETS	EPURATION	EQUITIES	EREWHILE	ERODED
EPITOME	EPURATIONS	EQUITY	ERF	ERODENT
EPITOMES	EPYLLION	EQUIVALVE	ERG	ERODENTS
EPITOMIC	EPYLLIONS	EQUIVOCAL	ERGATANER	ERODES
EPITOMISE	EQUABLE	EQUIVOKE	ERGATANERS	ERODING

ERODIUM	ERUDITES	ESCARPED	ESLOYNING	ESSENTIAL
ERODIUMS	ERUDITION	ESCARPING	ESNE	ESSENTIALS
EROGENIC	ERUDITIONS	ESCARPS	ESNECIES	ESSES
EROGENOUS	ERUPT	ESCHALOT	ESNECY	ESSIVE
EROSE	ERUPTED	ESCHALOTS	ESNES	ESSIVES
EROSION	ERUPTING	ESCHAR	ESOPHAGI	ESSOIN
EROSIONS	ERUPTION	ESCHARS	ESOPHAGUS	ESSOINER
EROSIVE	ERUPTIONS	ESCHEAT	ESOTERIC	ESSOINERS
EROSTRATE	ERUPTIVE	ESCHEATED	ESOTERICA	ESSOINS
EROTEMA	ERUPTS	ESCHEATING	ESOTERIES	ESSONITE
EROTEMAS	ERVALENTA	ESCHEATOR	ESOTERISM	ESSONITES
EROTEME	ERVALENTAS	ESCHEATORS	ESOTERISMS	ESSOYNE
EROTEMES	ERVEN	ESCHEATS	ESOTERY	ESSOYNES
EROTESES	ERYNGIUM	ESCHEW	ESPADA	ESTABLISH
EROTESIS	ERYNGIUMS	ESCHEWED	ESPADAS	ESTABLISHED
EROTETIC	ERYNGO	ESCHEWING	ESPAGNOLE	ESTABLISHES
EROTIC	ERYNGOES	ESCHEWS	ESPAGNOLES	ESTABLISHING
EROTICA	ERYNGOS	ESCLANDRE	ESPALIER	ESTACADE
EROTICAL	ERYTHEMA	ESCLANDRES	ESPALIERED	ESTACADES
EROTICALS	ERYTHEMAL	ESCOLAR	ESPALIERING	ESTAFETTE
EROTICISM	ERYTHEMAS	ESCOLARS	ESPALIERS	ESTAFETTES
EROTICISMS	ERYTHRINA	ESCOPETTE	ESPARTO	ESTAMINET
EROTICIST	ERYTHRINAS	ESCOPETTES	ESPARTOS	ESTAMINETS
EROTICISTS	ERYTHRISM	ESCORT	ESPECIAL	ESTANCIA
EROTICS	ERYTHRISMS	ESCORTAGE	ESPERANCE	ESTANCIAS
EROTISM	ERYTHRITE	ESCORTAGES	ESPERANCES	ESTATE
EROTISMS	ERYTHRITES	ESCORTED	ESPIAL	ESTATED
ERR	ES	ESCORTING	ESPIALS	ESTATES
ERRABLE	ESCALADE	ESCORTS	ESPIED	ESTATING
ERRAND	ESCALADED	ESCOT	ESPIÈGLE	ESTEEM
ERRANDS	ESCALADES	ESCOTS	ESPIES	ESTEEMED
ERRANT	ESCALADING	ESCOTTED	ESPIONAGE	ESTEEMING
ERRANTLY	ESCALADO	ESCOTTING	ESPIONAGES	ESTEEMS
ERRANTRIES	ESCALADOES	ESCRIBANO	ESPLANADE	ESTER
ERRANTRY	ESCALATE	ESCRIBANOS	ESPLANADES	ESTERIFIED
ERRANTS	ESCALATED	ESCRIBE	ESPOUSAL	ESTERIFIES
ERRATA	ESCALATES	ESCRIBED	ESPOUSALS	ESTERIFY
ERRATIC	ESCALATING	ESCRIBES	ESPOUSE	ESTERIFYING
ERRATICAL	ESCALATOR	ESCRIBING	ESPOUSED	ESTERS
ERRATICS	ESCALATORS	ESCROC	ESPOUSER	ESTHESES
ERRATUM	ESCALIER	ESCROCS	ESPOUSERS	ESTHESIA
ERRED	ESCALIERS	ESCROL	ESPOUSES	ESTHESIAS
ERRHINE	ESCALLOP	ESCROLL	ESPOUSING	ESTHESIS
ERRHINES	ESCALLOPS	ESCROLLS	ESPRESSO	ESTHETE
ERRING	ESCALOP	ESCROLS	ESPRESSOS	ESTHETES
ERRINGLY	ESCALOPE	ESCROW	ESPRIT	ESTHETIC
ERRINGS	ESCALOPES	ESCROWS	ESPRITS	ESTHETICS
ERRONEOUS	ESCALOPS	ESCUAGE	ESPUMOSO	ESTIMABLE
ERROR	ESCAPABLE	ESCUAGES	ESPUMOSOS	ESTIMABLY
ERRORIST	ESCAPADE	ESCUDO	ESPY	ESTIMATE
ERRORISTS	ESCAPADES	ESCUDOS	ESPYING	ESTIMATED
ERRORS	ESCAPADO	ESCULENT	ESQUIRE	ESTIMATES
ERRS	ESCAPADOES	ESCULENTS	ESQUIRES	ESTIMATING
ERS	ESCAPE	ESEMPLASIES	ESQUISSE	ESTIMATOR
ERSATZ	ESCAPED	ESEMPLASY	ESQUISSES	ESTIMATORS
ERSATZES	ESCAPEE	ESILE	ESS	ESTIVAL
ERSES	ESCAPEES	ESILES	ESSAY	ESTIVATE
ERST	ESCAPER	ESKAR	ESSAYED	ESTIVATED
ERSTWHILE	ESCAPERS	ESKARS	ESSAYER	ESTIVATES
ERUCIFORM	ESCAPES	ESKER	ESSAYERS	ESTIVATING
ERUCT	ESCAPING	ESKERS	ESSAYETTE	ESTOC
ERUCTATE	ESCAPISM	ESKIES	ESSAYETTES	ESTOCS
ERUCTATED	ESCAPISMS	ESKY	ESSAYING	ESTOILE
ERUCTATES	ESCAPIST	ESLOIN	ESSAYISH	ESTOILES
ERUCTATING	ESCAPISTS	ESLOINED	ESSAYIST	ESTOP
ERUCTED	ESCARGOT	ESLOINING	ESSAYISTS	ESTOPPAGE
ERUCTING	ESCARGOTS	ESLOINS	ESSAYS	ESTOPPAGES
ERUCTS	ESCAROLE	ESLOYNE	ESSE	ESTOPPED
ERUDITE	ESCAROLES	ESLOYNED	ESSENCE	ESTOPPEL
ERUDITELY	ESCARP	ESLOYNES	ESSENCES	ESTOPPELS

ESTOPPING	ÉTATISMES	ETHICISM	ETTIN	EUK
ESTOPS	ÉTATISTE	ETHICISMS	ETTINS	EUKARYON
ESTOVER	ÉTATISTES	ETHICIST	ETTLE	EUKARYONS
ESTOVERS	ÉTATS	ETHICISTS	ETTLED	EUKARYOT
ESTRADE	ETCH	ETHICIZE	ETTLES	EUKARYOTE
ESTRADES	ETCHANT	ETHICIZED	ETTLING	EUKARYOTES
ESTRAL	ETCHANTS	ETHICIZES	ÉTUDE	EUKARYOTS
ESTRANGE	ETCHED	ETHICIZING	ÉTUDES	EUKED
ESTRANGED	ETCHER	ETHICS	ETUI	EUKING
ESTRANGER	ETCHERS	ETHIOPS	ETUIS	EUKS
ESTRANGERS	ETCHES	ETHIOPSES	ETWEE	EULACHON
ESTRANGES	ETCHING	ETHMOID	ETWEES	EULACHONS
ESTRANGING	ETCHINGS	ETHMOIDAL	ETYMA	EULOGIA
ESTRAPADE	ETEN	ETHNARCH	ETYMIC	EULOGIES
ESTRAPADES	ETENS	ETHNARCHIES	ETYMOLOGIES	EULOGISE
ESTRAY	ETERNAL	ETHNARCHS	ETYMOLOGY	EULOGISED
ESTRAYED	ETERNALLY	ETHNARCHY	ETYMON	EULOGISES
ESTRAYING	ETERNE	ETHNIC	ETYMONS	EULOGISING
ESTRAYS	ETERNISE	ETHNICAL	ETYPIC	EULOGIST
ESTREAT	ETERNISED	ETHNICISM	ETYPICAL	EULOGISTS
ESTREATED	ETERNISES	ETHNICISMS	EUCAIN	EULOGIUM
ESTREATING	ETERNISING	ETHNICITIES	EUCAINE	EULOGIUMS
ESTREATS	ETERNITIES	ETHNICITY	EUCAINES	EULOGIZE
ESTREPE	ETERNITY	ETHNICS	EUCAINS	EULOGIZED
ESTREPED	ETERNIZE	ETHNOCIDE	EUCALYPT	EULOGIZES
ESTREPES	ETERNIZED	ETHNOCIDES	EUCALYPTI	EULOGIZING
ESTREPING	ETERNIZES	ETHNOLOGIES	EUCALYPTS	EULOGY
ESTRICH	ETERNIZING	ETHNOLOGY	EUCARYON	EUMELANIN
ESTRICHES	ETESIAN	ETHOLOGIC	EUCARYONS	EUMELANINS
ESTRIDGE	ETH	ETHOLOGIES	EUCARYOT	EUMERISM
ESTRIDGES	ETHAL	ETHOLOGY	EUCARYOTE	EUMERISMS
ESTRILDID	ETHALS	ETHOS	EUCARYOTES	EUNUCH
ESTRILDIDS	ETHANE	ETHOSES	EUCARYOTS	EUNUCHISE
ESTRO	ETHANES	ETHS	EUCHARIS	EUNUCHISED
ESTROGEN	ETHANOL	ETHYL	EUCHARISES	EUNUCHISES
ESTROGENS	ETHANOLS	ETHYLATE	EUCHLORIC	EUNUCHISING
ESTROS	ETHE	ETHYLATED	EUCHOLOGIES	EUNUCHISM
ESTROUS	ETHENE	ETHYLATES	EUCHOLOGY	EUNUCHISMS
ESTRUM	ETHENES	ETHYLATING	EUCHRE	EUNUCHIZE
ESTRUMS	ETHER	ETHYLENE	EUCHRED	EUNUCHIZED
ESTRUS	ETHERCAP	ETHYLENES	EUCHRES	EUNUCHIZES
ESTRUSES	ETHERCAPS	ETHYLS	EUCHRING	EUNUCHIZING
ESTUARIAL	ETHEREAL	ETHYNE	EUCLASE	EUNUCHOID
ESTUARIAN	ETHEREOUS	ETHYNES	EUCLASES	EUNUCHOIDS
ESTUARIES	ETHERIAL	ETIOLATE	EUCRITE	EUNUCHS
ESTUARINE	ETHERIC	ETIOLATED	EUCRITES	EUOI
ESTUARY	ETHERICAL	ETIOLATES	EUCRITIC	EUONYMIN
ESURIENCE	ETHERION	ETIOLATING	EUCYCLIC	EUONYMINS
ESURIENCES	ETHERIONS	ETIOLIN	EUDAEMONIES	EUONYMUS
ESURIENCIES	ETHERISE	ETIOLINS	EUDAEMONY	EUONYMUSES
ESURIENCY	ETHERISED	ETIOLOGIES	EUDEMONIA	EUOUAE
ESURIENT	ETHERISES	ETIOLOGY	EUDEMONIAS	EUOUAES
ETA	ETHERISING	ETIQUETTE	EUDEMONIC	EUPAD
ETACISM	ETHERISM	ETIQUETTES	EUDEMONICS	EUPADS
ETACISMS	ETHERISMS	ETNA	EUDEMONIES	EUPATRID
ETAERIO	ETHERIST	ETNAS	EUDEMONY	EUPATRIDAE
ETAERIOS	ETHERISTS	ÉTOILE	EUDIALYTE	EUPATRIDS
ÉTAGE	ETHERIZE	ÉTOILES	EUDIALYTES	EUPEPSIA
ÉTAGÈRE	ETHERIZED	ÉTOURDI	EUGE	EUPEPSIAS
ÉTAGÈRES	ETHERIZES	ÉTOURDIE	EUGENIC	EUPEPSIES
ÉTAGES	ETHERIZING	ÉTRANGER	EUGENICS	EUPEPSY
ÉTALAGE	ETHERS	ÉTRANGÈRE	EUGENISM	EUPEPTIC
ÉTALAGES	ETHIC	ÉTRANGÈRES	EUGENISMS	EUPHAUSID
ETALON	ETHICAL	ÉTRANGERS	EUGENIST	EUPHAUSIDS
ETALONS	ETHICALLY	ÉTRENNE	EUGENISTS	EUPHEMISE
ÉTAPE	ETHICALS	ÉTRENNES	EUGENOL	EUPHEMISED
ÉTAPES	ETHICISE	ÉTRIER	EUGENOLS	EUPHEMISES
ETAS	ETHICISED	ÉTRIERS	EUGH	EUPHEMISING
ÉTAT	ETHICISES	ETTERCAP	EUGHEN	EUPHEMISM
ÉTATISME	ETHICISING	ETTERCAPS	EUGHS	EUPHEMISMS

EUPHEMIZE	EUSTYLES	EVAPORATE	EVICT	EVOLVED
EUPHEMIZED	EUTAXIES	EVAPORATED	EVICTED	EVOLVENT
EUPHEMIZES	EUTAXITE	EVAPORATES	EVICTING	EVOLVES
EUPHEMIZING	EUTAXITES	EVAPORATING	EVICTION	EVOLVING
EUPHENICS	EUTAXITIC	EVAPORITE	EVICTIONS	EVOVAE
EUPHOBIA	EUTAXY	EVAPORITES	EVICTOR	EVOVAES
EUPHOBIAS	EUTECTIC	EVASIBLE	EVICTORS	EVULGATE
EUPHON	EUTECTICS	EVASION	EVICTS	EVULGATED
EUPHONIA	EUTECTOID	EVASIONS	EVIDENCE	EVULGATES
EUPHONIAS	EUTECTOIDS	EVASIVE	EVIDENCED	EVULGATING
EUPHONIC	EUTEXIA	EVASIVELY	EVIDENCES	EVULSE
EUPHONIES	EUTEXIAS	EVE	EVIDENCING	EVULSED
EUPHONISE	EUTHANASIES	EVECTION	EVIDENT	EVULSES
EUPHONISED	EUTHANASY	EVECTIONS	EVIDENTLY	EVULSING
EUPHONISES	EUTHENICS	EVEJAR	EVIDENTS	EVULSION
EUPHONISING	EUTHENIST	EVEJARS	EVIL	EVULSIONS
EUPHONIUM	EUTHENISTS	EVEN	EVILLER	EVZONE
EUPHONIUMS	EUTHERIAN	EVENED	EVILLEST	EVZONES
EUPHONIZE	EUTHERIANS	ÉVÉNEMENT	EVILLY	EWE
EUPHONIZED	EUTRAPELIES	ÉVÉNEMENTS	EVILNESS	EWER
EUPHONIZES	EUTRAPELY	EVENER	EVILNESSES	EWERS
EUPHONIZING	EUTROPHIC	EVENEST	EVILS	EWES
EUPHONS	EUTROPHIES	EVENFALL	EVINCE	EWEST
EUPHONY	EUTROPHY	EVENFALLS	EVINCED	EWFTES
EUPHORBIA	EUTROPIC	EVENING	EVINCES	EWGHEN
EUPHORBIAS	EUTROPIES	EVENINGS	EVINCIBLE	EWHOW
EUPHORIA	EUTROPOUS	EVENLY	EVINCIBLY	EWK
EUPHORIAS	EUTROPY	EVENNESS	EVINCING	EWKED
EUPHORIC	EUXENITE	EVENNESSES	EVINCIVE	EWKING
EUPHORIES	EUXENITES	EVENS	EVIRATE	EWKS
EUPHORY	EVACUANT	EVENSONG	EVIRATED	EWT
EUPHRASIES	EVACUANTS	EVENSONGS	EVIRATES	EWTS
EUPHRASY	EVACUATE	EVENT	EVIRATING	EX
EUPHROE	EVACUATED	EVENTER	EVITABLE	EXACT
EUPHROES	EVACUATES	EVENTERS	EVITATE	EXACTED
EUPHUISE	EVACUATING	EVENTFUL	EVITATED	EXACTER
EUPHUISED	EVACUATOR	EVENTIDE	EVITATES	EXACTERS
EUPHUISES	EVACUATORS	EVENTIDES	EVITATING	EXACTEST
EUPHUISING	EVACUEE	EVENTING	EVITATION	EXACTING
EUPHUISM	EVACUEES	EVENTINGS	EVITATIONS	EXACTION
EUPHUISMS	EVADABLE	EVENTS	EVITE	EXACTIONS
EUPHUIST	EVADE	EVENTUAL	EVITED	EXACTLY
EUPHUISTS	EVADED	EVENTUATE	EVITERNAL	EXACTMENT
EUPHUIZE	EVADES	EVENTUATED	EVITES	EXACTMENTS
EUPHUIZED	EVADING	EVENTUATES	EVITING	EXACTNESS
EUPHUIZES	EVAGATION	EVENTUATING	EVOCATE	EXACTNESSES
EUPHUIZING	EVAGATIONS	EVER	EVOCATED	EXACTOR
EUREKA	EVAGINATE	EVERGLADE	EVOCATES	EXACTORS
EUREKAS	EVAGINATED	EVERGLADES	EVOCATING	EXACTRESS
EURHYTHMIES	EVAGINATES	EVERGREEN	EVOCATION	EXACTRESSES
EURHYTHMY	EVAGINATING	EVERGREENS	EVOCATIONS	EXACTS
EURIPI	EVALUATE	EVERMORE	EVOCATIVE	EXALT
EURIPUS	EVALUATED	EVERSIBLE	EVOCATORY	EXALTED
EURIPUSES	EVALUATES	EVERSION	EVOE	EXALTING
EURO	EVALUATING	EVERSIONS	EVOHE	EXALTS
EUROPIUM	EVANESCE	EVERT	EVOKE	EXAM
EUROPIUMS	EVANESCED	EVERTED	EVOKED	EXAMEN
EUROS	EVANESCES	EVERTING	EVOKES	EXAMENS
EURYTHERM	EVANESCING	EVERTS	EVOKING	EXAMINANT
EURYTHERMS	EVANGEL	EVERY	ÉVOLUÉ	EXAMINANTS
EURYTHMIES	EVANGELIC	EVERYBODY	ÉVOLUÉS	EXAMINATE
EURYTHMY	EVANGELIES	EVERYDAY	EVOLUTE	EXAMINATES
EUSOL	EVANGELS	EVERYDAYS	EVOLUTED	EXAMINE
EUSOLS	EVANGELY	EVERYONE	EVOLUTES	EXAMINED
EUSTACIES	EVANISH	EVERYWAY	EVOLUTING	EXAMINEE
EUSTACY	EVANISHED	EVERYWHEN	EVOLUTION	EXAMINEES
EUSTASIES	EVANISHES	EVES	EVOLUTIONS	EXAMINER
EUSTASY	EVANISHING	EVET	EVOLUTIVE	EXAMINERS
EUSTATIC	EVANITION	EVETS	EVOLVABLE	EXAMINES
EUSTYLE	EVANITIONS	EVHOE	EVOLVE	EXAMINING

EXAMPLAR
EXAMPLARS
EXAMPLE
EXAMPLED
EXAMPLES
EXAMPLING
EXAMS
EXANIMATE
EXANTHEM
EXANTHEMA
EXANTHEMATA
EXANTHEMS
EXARATE
EXARATION
EXARATIONS
EXARCH
EXARCHATE
EXARCHATES
EXARCHIES
EXARCHIST
EXARCHISTS
EXARCHS
EXARCHY
EXCAMB
EXCAMBED
EXCAMBING
EXCAMBION
EXCAMBIONS
EXCAMBIUM
EXCAMBIUMS
EXCAMBS
EXCARNATE
EXCARNATED
EXCARNATES
EXCARNATING
EXCAUDATE
EXCAVATE
EXCAVATED
EXCAVATES
EXCAVATING
EXCAVATOR
EXCAVATORS
EXCEED
EXCEEDED
EXCEEDING
EXCEEDS
EXCEL
EXCELLED
EXCELLENT
EXCELLING
EXCELS
EXCELSIOR
EXCELSIORS
EXCENTRIC
EXCENTRICS
EXCEPT
EXCEPTANT
EXCEPTANTS
EXCEPTED
EXCEPTING
EXCEPTION
EXCEPTIONS
EXCEPTIVE
EXCEPTOR
EXCEPTORS
EXCEPTS
EXCERPT
EXCERPTA
EXCERPTED
EXCERPTING

EXCERPTINGS
EXCERPTOR
EXCERPTORS
EXCERPTS
EXCERPTUM
EXCESS
EXCESSES
EXCESSIVE
EXCHANGE
EXCHANGED
EXCHANGER
EXCHANGERS
EXCHANGES
EXCHANGING
EXCHEAT
EXCHEATS
EXCHEQUER
EXCHEQUERED
EXCHEQUERING
EXCHEQUERS
EXCIDE
EXCIDED
EXCIDES
EXCIDING
EXCIPIENT
EXCIPIENTS
EXCISABLE
EXCISE
EXCISED
EXCISEMAN
EXCISEMEN
EXCISES
EXCISING
EXCISION
EXCISIONS
EXCITABLE
EXCITANCIES
EXCITANCY
EXCITANT
EXCITANTS
EXCITE
EXCITED
EXCITER
EXCITERS
EXCITES
EXCITING
EXCITON
EXCITONS
EXCITOR
EXCITORS
EXCLAIM
EXCLAIMED
EXCLAIMING
EXCLAIMS
EXCLAVE
EXCLAVES
EXCLOSURE
EXCLOSURES
EXCLUDE
EXCLUDED
EXCLUDEE
EXCLUDEES
EXCLUDES
EXCLUDING
EXCLUSION
EXCLUSIONS
EXCLUSIVE
EXCLUSIVES
EXCLUSORY
EXCORIATE

EXCORIATED
EXCORIATES
EXCORIATING
EXCREMENT
EXCREMENTS
EXCRETA
EXCRETE
EXCRETED
EXCRETES
EXCRETING
EXCRETION
EXCRETIONS
EXCRETIVE
EXCRETORIES
EXCRETORY
EXCUBANT
EXCUDIT
EXCULPATE
EXCULPATED
EXCULPATES
EXCULPATING
EXCURRENT
EXCURSE
EXCURSED
EXCURSES
EXCURSING
EXCURSION
EXCURSIONED
EXCURSIONING
EXCURSIONS
EXCURSIVE
EXCURSUS
EXCURSUSES
EXCUSABLE
EXCUSABLY
EXCUSAL
EXCUSALS
EXCUSE
EXCUSED
EXCUSER
EXCUSERS
EXCUSES
EXCUSING
EXCUSIVE
EXEAT
EXEATS
EXECRABLE
EXECRABLY
EXECRATE
EXECRATED
EXECRATES
EXECRATING
EXECUTANT
EXECUTANTS
EXECUTE
EXECUTED
EXECUTER
EXECUTERS
EXECUTES
EXECUTING
EXECUTION
EXECUTIONS
EXECUTIVE
EXECUTIVES
EXECUTOR
EXECUTORS
EXECUTORY
EXECUTRICES
EXECUTRIES
EXECUTRIX

EXECUTRIXES
EXECUTRY
EXEDRA
EXEDRAE
EXEEM
EXEEMED
EXEEMING
EXEEMS
EXEGESES
EXEGESIS
EXEGETE
EXEGETES
EXEGETIC
EXEGETICS
EXEGETIST
EXEGETISTS
EXEME
EXEMED
EXEMES
EXEMING
EXEMPLA
EXEMPLAR
EXEMPLARS
EXEMPLARY
EXEMPLE
EXEMPLES
EXEMPLIFIED
EXEMPLIFIES
EXEMPLIFY
EXEMPLIFYING
EXEMPLUM
EXEMPT
EXEMPTED
EXEMPTING
EXEMPTION
EXEMPTIONS
EXEMPTS
EXEQUATUR
EXEQUATURS
EXEQUIAL
EXEQUIES
EXEQUY
EXERCISE
EXERCISED
EXERCISER
EXERCISERS
EXERCISES
EXERCISING
EXERGUAL
EXERGUE
EXERGUES
EXERT
EXERTED
EXERTING
EXERTION
EXERTIONS
EXERTIVE
EXERTS
EXES
EXEUNT
EXFOLIATE
EXFOLIATED
EXFOLIATES
EXFOLIATING
EXHALABLE
EXHALANT
EXHALANTS
EXHALE
EXHALED
EXHALES

EXHALING
EXHAUST
EXHAUSTED
EXHAUSTER
EXHAUSTERS
EXHAUSTING
EXHAUSTS
EXHEDRA
EXHEDRAE
EXHIBIT
EXHIBITED
EXHIBITER
EXHIBITERS
EXHIBITING
EXHIBITOR
EXHIBITORS
EXHIBITS
EXHORT
EXHORTED
EXHORTER
EXHORTERS
EXHORTING
EXHORTS
EXHUMATE
EXHUMATED
EXHUMATES
EXHUMATING
EXHUME
EXHUMED
EXHUMER
EXHUMERS
EXHUMES
EXHUMING
EXIES
EXIGEANT
EXIGEANTE
EXIGENCE
EXIGENCES
EXIGENCIES
EXIGENCY
EXIGENT
EXIGENTS
EXIGIBLE
EXIGUITIES
EXIGUITY
EXIGUOUS
EXILE
EXILED
EXILEMENT
EXILEMENTS
EXILES
EXILIAN
EXILIC
EXILING
EXILITIES
EXILITY
EXIMIOUS
EXINE
EXINES
EXIST
EXISTED
EXISTENCE
EXISTENCES
EXISTENT
EXISTING
EXISTS
EXIT
EXITANCE
EXITANCES
EXITED

EXITING
EXITS
EXOCARP
EXOCARPS
EXOCRINE
EXOCRINES
EXODE
EXODERM
EXODERMAL
EXODERMIS
EXODERMISES
EXODERMS
EXODES
EXODIC
EXODIST
EXODISTS
EXODUS
EXODUSES
EXOENZYME
EXOENZYMES
EXOERGIC
EXOGAMIC
EXOGAMIES
EXOGAMOUS
EXOGAMY
EXOGEN
EXOGENOUS
EXOGENS
EXOMION
EXOMIONS
EXOMIS
EXOMISES
EXON
EXONERATE
EXONERATED
EXONERATES
EXONERATING
EXONS
EXONYM
EXONYMS
EXOPHAGIES
EXOPHAGY
EXOPLASM
EXOPLASMS
EXOPOD
EXOPODITE
EXOPODITES
EXOPODS
EXORABLE
EXORATION
EXORATIONS
EXORCISE
EXORCISED
EXORCISER
EXORCISERS
EXORCISES
EXORCISING
EXORCISM
EXORCISMS
EXORCIST
EXORCISTS
EXORCIZE
EXORCIZED
EXORCIZER
EXORCIZERS
EXORCIZES
EXORCIZING
EXORDIA
EXORDIAL
EXORDIUM

EXORDIUMS
EXOSMOSE
EXOSMOSES
EXOSMOSIS
EXOSMOTIC
EXOSPHERE
EXOSPHERES
EXOSPORAL
EXOSPORE
EXOSPORES
EXOSTOSES
EXOSTOSIS
EXOTERIC
EXOTIC
EXOTICA
EXOTICISM
EXOTICISMS
EXOTICS
EXOTOXIC
EXOTOXIN
EXOTOXINS
EXPAND
EXPANDED
EXPANDER
EXPANDERS
EXPANDING
EXPANDOR
EXPANDORS
EXPANDS
EXPANSE
EXPANSES
EXPANSILE
EXPANSION
EXPANSIONS
EXPANSIVE
EXPAT
EXPATIATE
EXPATIATED
EXPATIATES
EXPATIATING
EXPATS
EXPECT
EXPECTANT
EXPECTANTS
EXPECTED
EXPECTER
EXPECTERS
EXPECTING
EXPECTINGS
EXPECTS
EXPEDIENT
EXPEDIENTS
EXPEDITE
EXPEDITED
EXPEDITES
EXPEDITING
EXPEL
EXPELLANT
EXPELLANTS
EXPELLED
EXPELLEE
EXPELLEES
EXPELLENT
EXPELLENTS
EXPELLING
EXPELS
EXPEND
EXPENDED
EXPENDER
EXPENDERS

EXPENDING
EXPENDS
EXPENSE
EXPENSES
EXPENSIVE
EXPERT
EXPERTED
EXPERTING
EXPERTISE
EXPERTISED
EXPERTISES
EXPERTISING
EXPERTIZE
EXPERTIZED
EXPERTIZES
EXPERTIZING
EXPERTLY
EXPERTS
EXPIABLE
EXPIATE
EXPIATED
EXPIATES
EXPIATING
EXPIATION
EXPIATIONS
EXPIATOR
EXPIATORS
EXPIATORY
EXPIRABLE
EXPIRANT
EXPIRANTS
EXPIRE
EXPIRED
EXPIRES
EXPIRIES
EXPIRING
EXPIRY
EXPISCATE
EXPISCATED
EXPISCATES
EXPISCATING
EXPLAIN
EXPLAINED
EXPLAINER
EXPLAINERS
EXPLAINING
EXPLAINS
EXPLANT
EXPLANTED
EXPLANTING
EXPLANTS
EXPLETIVE
EXPLETIVES
EXPLETORY
EXPLICATE
EXPLICATED
EXPLICATES
EXPLICATING
EXPLICIT
EXPLICITS
EXPLODE
EXPLODED
EXPLODER
EXPLODERS
EXPLODES
EXPLODING
EXPLOIT
EXPLOITED
EXPLOITER
EXPLOITERS

EXPLOITING
EXPLOITS
EXPLORE
EXPLORED
EXPLORER
EXPLORERS
EXPLORES
EXPLORING
EXPLOSION
EXPLOSIONS
EXPLOSIVE
EXPLOSIVES
EXPO
EXPONENT
EXPONENTS
EXPONIBLE
EXPORT
EXPORTED
EXPORTER
EXPORTERS
EXPORTING
EXPORTS
EXPOS
EXPOSAL
EXPOSALS
EXPOSE
EXPOSÉ
EXPOSED
EXPOSER
EXPOSERS
EXPOSÉS
EXPOSES
EXPOSING
EXPOSITOR
EXPOSITORS
EXPOSTURE
EXPOSTURES
EXPOSURE
EXPOSURES
EXPOUND
EXPOUNDED
EXPOUNDER
EXPOUNDERS
EXPOUNDING
EXPOUNDS
EXPRESS
EXPRESSED
EXPRESSES
EXPRESSING
EXPRESSLY
EXPRESSO
EXPRESSOS
EXPUGN
EXPUGNED
EXPUGNING
EXPUGNS
EXPULSE
EXPULSED
EXPULSES
EXPULSING
EXPULSION
EXPULSIONS
EXPULSIVE
EXPUNCT
EXPUNCTED
EXPUNCTING
EXPUNCTS
EXPUNGE
EXPUNGED
EXPUNGER

EXPUNGERS
EXPUNGES
EXPUNGING
EXPURGATE
EXPURGATED
EXPURGATES
EXPURGATING
EXPURGE
EXPURGED
EXPURGES
EXPURGING
EXQUISITE
EXQUISITES
EXSCIND
EXSCINDED
EXSCINDING
EXSCINDS
EXSECT
EXSECTED
EXSECTING
EXSECTION
EXSECTIONS
EXSECTS
EXSERT
EXSERTED
EXSERTILE
EXSERTING
EXSERTION
EXSERTIONS
EXSERTS
EXSICCANT
EXSICCATE
EXSICCATED
EXSICCATES
EXSICCATING
EXSUCCOUS
EXTANT
EXTASIES
EXTASY
EXTATIC
EXTATICS
EXTEMPORE
EXTEMPORES
EXTEND
EXTENDANT
EXTENDED
EXTENDER
EXTENDERS
EXTENDING
EXTENDS
EXTENSE
EXTENSILE
EXTENSION
EXTENSIONS
EXTENSITIES
EXTENSITY
EXTENSIVE
EXTENSOR
EXTENSORS
EXTENT
EXTENTS
EXTENUATE
EXTENUATED
EXTENUATES
EXTENUATING
EXTENUATINGS
EXTERIOR
EXTERIORS
EXTERMINE
EXTERMINED

EXTERMINES
EXTERMINING
EXTERN
EXTERNAL
EXTERNALS
EXTERNAT
EXTERNATS
EXTERNE
EXTERNES
EXTERNS
EXTINCT
EXTINCTED
EXTINE
EXTINES
EXTIRP
EXTIRPATE
EXTIRPATED
EXTIRPATES
EXTIRPATING
EXTIRPED
EXTIRPING
EXTIRPS
EXTOL
EXTOLD
EXTOLLED
EXTOLLER
EXTOLLERS
EXTOLLING
EXTOLMENT
EXTOLMENTS
EXTOLS
EXTORSIVE
EXTORT
EXTORTED
EXTORTING
EXTORTION
EXTORTIONS
EXTORTIVE
EXTORTS

EXTRA
EXTRACT
EXTRACTED
EXTRACTING
EXTRACTOR
EXTRACTORS
EXTRACTS
EXTRADITE
EXTRADITED
EXTRADITES
EXTRADITING
EXTRADOS
EXTRADOSES
EXTRAIT
EXTRAITS
EXTRAS
EXTRAUGHT
EXTRAVERT
EXTRAVERTED
EXTRAVERTING
EXTRAVERTS
EXTREAT
EXTREATS
EXTREME
EXTREMELY
EXTREMER
EXTREMES
EXTREMEST
EXTREMISM
EXTREMISMS
EXTREMIST
EXTREMISTS
EXTREMITIES
EXTREMITY
EXTRICATE
EXTRICATED
EXTRICATES
EXTRICATING
EXTRINSIC

EXTRORSE
EXTROVERT
EXTROVERTED
EXTROVERTING
EXTROVERTS
EXTRUDE
EXTRUDED
EXTRUDER
EXTRUDERS
EXTRUDES
EXTRUDING
EXTRUSION
EXTRUSIONS
EXTRUSIVE
EXTRUSORY
EXUBERANT
EXUBERATE
EXUBERATED
EXUBERATES
EXUBERATING
EXUDATE
EXUDATES
EXUDATION
EXUDATIONS
EXUDATIVE
EXUDE
EXUDED
EXUDES
EXUDING
EXUL
EXULS
EXULT
EXULTANCE
EXULTANCES
EXULTANCIES
EXULTANCY
EXULTANT
EXULTED
EXULTING

EXULTS
EXURB
EXURBAN
EXURBIA
EXURBIAS
EXURBS
EXUVIAE
EXUVIAL
EXUVIATE
EXUVIATED
EXUVIATES
EXUVIATING
EYALET
EYALETS
EYAS
EYASES
EYE
EYEBALL
EYEBALLED
EYEBALLING
EYEBALLS
EYEBOLT
EYEBOLTS
EYEBRIGHT
EYEBRIGHTS
EYEBROW
EYEBROWED
EYEBROWING
EYEBROWS
EYED
EYEFUL
EYEFULS
EYEGLASS
EYEGLASSES
EYEHOOK
EYEHOOKS
EYEING
EYELASH
EYELASHES

EYELESS
EYELET
EYELETED
EYELETING
EYELETS
EYELIAD
EYELIADS
EYELID
EYELIDS
EYELINER
EYELINERS
EYES
EYESHADE
EYESHADES
EYESIGHT
EYESIGHTS
EYESORE
EYESORES
EYESTALK
EYESTALKS
EYESTRAIN
EYESTRAINS
EYING
EYLIAD
EYLIADS
EYNE
EYOT
EYOTS
EYRA
EYRAS
EYRE
EYRES
EYRIE
EYRIES
EYRY

F

FA
FAB
FABACEOUS
FABBER
FABBEST
FABLE
FABLED
FABLER
FABLERS
FABLES
FABLIAU
FABLIAUX
FABLING
FABLINGS
FABRIC
FABRICANT
FABRICANTS
FABRICATE
FABRICATED
FABRICATES
FABRICATING
FABRICKED
FABRICKING
FABRICS
FABULAR
FABULISE
FABULISED
FABULISES
FABULISING
FABULIST
FABULISTS
FABULIZE
FABULIZED
FABULIZES
FABULIZING
FABULOUS
FABURDEN
FABURDENS
FAÇADE
FAÇADES
FACE
FACED
FACELESS
FACEMAN
FACEMEN
FACER
FACERS
FACES
FACET
FACETE
FACETED
FACETIAE
FACETING
FACETIOUS
FACETS
FACIA
FACIAL
FACIALLY
FACIALS
FACIAS
FACIES
FACIESES
FACILE
FACILELY

FACILITIES
FACILITY
FACING
FACINGS
FAÇONNÉ
FAÇONNÉS
FACSIMILE
FACSIMILED
FACSIMILEING
FACSIMILES
FACT
FACTION
FACTIONAL
FACTIONS
FACTIOUS
FACTITIVE
FACTIVE
FACTOID
FACTOIDS
FACTOR
FACTORAGE
FACTORAGES
FACTORED
FACTORIAL
FACTORIALS
FACTORIES
FACTORING
FACTORINGS
FACTORISE
FACTORISED
FACTORISES
FACTORISING
FACTORIZE
FACTORIZED
FACTORIZES
FACTORIZING
FACTORS
FACTORY
FACTOTUM
FACTOTUMS
FACTS
FACTUAL
FACTUM
FACTUMS
FACTURE
FACTURES
FACULA
FACULAE
FACULAR
FACULTIES
FACULTY
FACUNDITIES
FACUNDITY
FAD
FADABLE
FADAISE
FADAISES
FADDIER
FADDIEST
FADDINESS
FADDINESSES
FADDISH
FADDISM
FADDISMS

FADDIST
FADDISTS
FADDLE
FADDLED
FADDLES
FADDLING
FADDY
FADE
FADED
FADEDLY
FADEDNESS
FADEDNESSES
FADELESS
FADES
FADEUR
FADEURS
FADGE
FADGED
FADGES
FADGING
FADIER
FADIEST
FADING
FADINGS
FADO
FADOS
FADS
FADY
FAECAL
FAECES
FAERIE
FAERIES
FAERY
FAFF
FAFFED
FAFFING
FAFFS
FAG
FAGACEOUS
FAGGED
FAGGERIES
FAGGERY
FAGGING
FAGGINGS
FAGGOT
FAGGOTED
FAGGOTING
FAGGOTINGS
FAGGOTS
FAGOT
FAGOTED
FAGOTING
FAGOTINGS
FAGOTS
FAGOTTI
FAGOTTIST
FAGOTTISTS
FAGOTTO
FAGS
FAH
FAHLBAND
FAHLBANDS
FAHLERZ
FAHLERZES

FAHLORE
FAHLORES
FAHS
FAIBLE
FAIBLES
FAÏENCE
FAIENCE
FAÏENCES
FAIENCES
FAIK
FAIKED
FAIKES
FAIKING
FAIKS
FAIL
FAILED
FAILING
FAILINGS
FAILLE
FAILLES
FAILS
FAILURE
FAILURES
FAIN
FAINE
FAINÉANCE
FAINÉANCES
FAINÉANCIES
FAINÉANCY
FAINÉANT
FAINÉANTS
FAINED
FAINER
FAINES
FAINEST
FAINING
FAINITES
FAINLY
FAINNESS
FAINNESSES
FAINS
FAINT
FAINTED
FAINTER
FAINTEST
FAINTIER
FAINTIEST
FAINTING
FAINTINGS
FAINTISH
FAINTLY
FAINTNESS
FAINTNESSES
FAINTS
FAINTY
FAIR
FAIRED
FAIRER
FAIREST
FAIRIES
FAIRILY
FAIRING
FAIRINGS
FAIRISH

FAIRLY
FAIRNESS
FAIRNESSES
FAIRS
FAIRWAY
FAIRWAYS
FAIRY
FAIRYDOM
FAIRYDOMS
FAIRYHOOD
FAIRYHOODS
FAIRYISM
FAIRYISMS
FAIRYLAND
FAIRYLANDS
FAIRYLIKE
FAITH
FAITHED
FAITHFUL
FAITHING
FAITHLESS
FAITHS
FAITOR
FAITORS
FAITOUR
FAITOURS
FAIX
FAKE
FAKED
FAKEMENT
FAKEMENTS
FAKER
FAKERIES
FAKERS
FAKERY
FAKES
FAKING
FAKIR
FAKIRISM
FAKIRISMS
FAKIRS
FALAFEL
FALAFELS
FALAJ
FALANGISM
FALANGISMS
FALANGIST
FALANGISTS
FALBALA
FALBALAS
FALCADE
FALCADES
FALCATE
FALCATED
FALCATION
FALCATIONS
FALCES
FALCHION
FALCHIONS
FALCIFORM
FALCON
FALCONER
FALCONERS
FALCONET

FALCONETS
FALCONINE
FALCONRIES
FALCONRY
FALCONS
FALCULA
FALCULAS
FALCULATE
FALDAGE
FALDAGES
FALDERAL
FALDERALS
FALDETTA
FALDETTAS
FALDSTOOL
FALDSTOOLS
FALL
FALLACIES
FALLACY
FALLAL
FALLALERIES
FALLALERY
FALLALS
FALLEN
FALLIBLE
FALLIBLY
FALLING
FALLINGS
FALLOW
FALLOWED
FALLOWER
FALLOWEST
FALLOWING
FALLOWS
FALLS
FALSE
FALSED
FALSEHOOD
FALSEHOODS
FALSELY
FALSENESS
FALSENESSES
FALSER
FALSERS
FALSES
FALSEST
FALSETTO
FALSETTOS
FALSEWORK
FALSEWORKS
FALSIE
FALSIES
FALSIFIED
FALSIFIER
FALSIFIERS
FALSIFIES
FALSIFY
FALSIFYING
FALSING
FALSISH
FALSISM
FALSISMS
FALSITIES
FALSITY
FALTBOAT
FALTBOATS
FALTER
FALTERED
FALTERING
FALTERINGS

FALTERS
FALX
FAME
FAMED
FAMELESS
FAMES
FAMILIAL
FAMILIAR
FAMILIARS
FAMILIES
FAMILISM
FAMILISMS
FAMILY
FAMINE
FAMINES
FAMING
FAMISH
FAMISHED
FAMISHES
FAMISHING
FAMOUS
FAMOUSED
FAMOUSES
FAMOUSING
FAMOUSLY
FAMULUS
FAMULUSES
FAN
FANAL
FANALS
FANATIC
FANATICAL
FANATICS
FANCIED
FANCIER
FANCIERS
FANCIES
FANCIEST
FANCIFUL
FANCILESS
FANCY
FANCYING
FANCYWORK
FANCYWORKS
FAND
FANDANGLE
FANDANGLES
FANDANGO
FANDANGOS
FANDED
FANDING
FANDOM
FANDOMS
FANDS
FANE
FANES
FANFARADE
FANFARADES
FANFARE
FANFARED
FANFARES
FANFARING
FANFARON
FANFARONA
FANFARONAS
FANFARONS
FANFOLD
FANG
FANGED
FANGING

FANGLE
FANGLED
FANGLES
FANGLESS
FANGLING
FANGO
FANGOS
FANGS
FANION
FANIONS
FANK
FANKLE
FANKLED
FANKLES
FANKLING
FANKS
FANLIGHT
FANLIGHTS
FANNED
FANNEL
FANNELL
FANNELLS
FANNELS
FANNER
FANNERS
FANNIES
FANNING
FANNINGS
FANNY
FANON
FANONS
FANS
FANTAD
FANTADS
FANTAIL
FANTAILED
FANTAILS
FANTASIA
FANTASIAS
FANTASIED
FANTASIES
FANTASISE
FANTASISED
FANTASISES
FANTASISING
FANTASIST
FANTASISTS
FANTASIZE
FANTASIZED
FANTASIZES
FANTASIZING
FANTASM
FANTASMS
FANTASQUE
FANTASQUES
FANTAST
FANTASTIC
FANTASTICS
FANTASTRIES
FANTASTRY
FANTASTS
FANTASY
FANTASYING
FANTEEG
FANTEEGS
FANTIGUE
FANTIGUES
FANTOD
FANTODS
FANTOM

FANTOMS
FANTOOSH
FANZINE
FANZINES
FAP
FAQUIR
FAQUIRS
FAR
FARAD
FARADAY
FARADAYS
FARADIC
FARADISE
FARADISED
FARADISES
FARADISING
FARADISM
FARADISMS
FARADIZE
FARADIZED
FARADIZES
FARADIZING
FARADS
FARAND
FARANDINE
FARANDINES
FARANDOLE
FARANDOLES
FARAWAY
FARAWAYS
FARCE
FARCED
FARCES
FARCEUR
FARCEURS
FARCEUSE
FARCEUSES
FARCI
FARCICAL
FARCIED
FARCIES
FARCIFIED
FARCIFIES
FARCIFY
FARCIFYING
FARCIN
FARCING
FARCINGS
FARCINS
FARCY
FARD
FARDAGE
FARDAGES
FARDED
FARDEL
FARDELS
FARDEN
FARDENS
FARDING
FARDINGS
FARDS
FARE
FARED
FARES
FAREWELL
FAREWELLS
FARFET
FARINA
FARINAS
FARING

FARINOSE
FARL
FARLE
FARLES
FARLS
FARM
FARMED
FARMER
FARMERESS
FARMERESSES
FARMERIES
FARMERS
FARMERY
FARMHOUSE
FARMHOUSES
FARMING
FARMINGS
FARMOST
FARMS
FARMSTEAD
FARMSTEADS
FARMYARD
FARMYARDS
FARNESOL
FARNESOLS
FARNESS
FARNESSES
FARO
FAROS
FAROUCHE
FARRAGO
FARRAGOES
FARRAND
FARRANT
FARRED
FARREN
FARRENS
FARRIER
FARRIERIES
FARRIERS
FARRIERY
FARRING
FARROW
FARROWED
FARROWING
FARROWS
FARRUCA
FARRUCAS
FARS
FARSE
FARSED
FARSES
FARSING
FART
FARTED
FARTHEL
FARTHELS
FARTHER
FARTHEST
FARTHING
FARTHINGS
FARTING
FARTS
FAS
FASCES
FASCI
FASCIA
FASCIAL
FASCIAS
FASCIATE

FASCIATED
FASCICLE
FASCICLED
FASCICLES
FASCICULE
FASCICULES
FASCICULI
FASCINATE
FASCINATED
FASCINATES
FASCINATING
FASCINE
FASCINES
FASCIO
FASCIOLA
FASCIOLAS
FASCIOLE
FASCIOLES
FASCISM
FASCISMI
FASCISMO
FASCISMS
FASCIST
FASCISTA
FASCISTI
FASCISTIC
FASCISTS
FASH
FASHED
FASHERIES
FASHERY
FASHES
FASHING
FASHION
FASHIONED
FASHIONER
FASHIONERS
FASHIONING
FASHIONS
FASHIOUS
FAST
FASTBACK
FASTBACKS
FASTED
FASTEN
FASTENED
FASTENER
FASTENERS
FASTENING
FASTENINGS
FASTENS
FASTER
FASTERS
FASTEST
FASTI
FASTIGIUM
FASTIGIUMS
FASTING
FASTINGS
FASTISH
FASTLY
FASTNESS
FASTNESSES
FASTS
FASTUOUS
FAT
FATAL
FATALISM
FATALISMS
FATALIST

FATALISTS
FATALITIES
FATALITY
FATALLY
FATE
FATED
FATEFUL
FATEFULLY
FATES
FATHER
FATHERED
FATHERING
FATHERLY
FATHERS
FATHOM
FATHOMED
FATHOMING
FATHOMS
FATIDICAL
FATIGABLE
FATIGATE
FATIGATED
FATIGATES
FATIGATING
FATIGUE
FATIGUED
FATIGUES
FATIGUING
FATISCENT
FATLING
FATLINGS
FATLY
FATNESS
FATNESSES
FATS
FATSO
FATSOES
FATSOS
FATSTOCK
FATTED
FATTEN
FATTENED
FATTENER
FATTENERS
FATTENING
FATTENINGS
FATTENS
FATTER
FATTEST
FATTIER
FATTIES
FATTIEST
FATTINESS
FATTINESSES
FATTING
FATTISH
FATTRELS
FATTY
FATUITIES
FATUITOUS
FATUITY
FATUOUS
FAUBOURG
FAUBOURGS
FAUCAL
FAUCES
FAUCET
FAUCETS
FAUCHION
FAUCHIONS

FAUCHON
FAUCHONS
FAUCIAL
FAUGH
FAULCHIN
FAULCHINS
FAULCHION
FAULCHIONS
FAULT
FAULTED
FAULTFUL
FAULTIER
FAULTIEST
FAULTILY
FAULTING
FAULTLESS
FAULTS
FAULTY
FAUN
FAUNA
FAUNAE
FAUNAL
FAUNAS
FAUNIST
FAUNISTIC
FAUNISTS
FAUNS
FAURD
FAUSTIAN
FAUTEUIL
FAUTEUILS
FAUTOR
FAUTORS
FAUVETTE
FAUVETTES
FAUX
FAVEL
FAVELA
FAVELAS
FAVELL
FAVEOLATE
FAVISM
FAVISMS
FAVOR
FAVORED
FAVORING
FAVORS
FAVOSE
FAVOUR
FAVOURED
FAVOURER
FAVOURERS
FAVOURING
FAVOURITE
FAVOURITES
FAVOURS
FAVOUS
FAVRILE
FAVRILES
FAVUS
FAVUSES
FAW
FAWN
FAWNED
FAWNER
FAWNERS
FAWNING
FAWNINGLY
FAWNINGS
FAWNS

FAWS
FAX
FAXED
FAXES
FAXING
FAY
FAYALITE
FAYALITES
FAYED
FAYENCE
FAYENCES
FAYER
FAYEST
FAYING
FAYNE
FAYNED
FAYNES
FAYNING
FAYS
FAZE
FAZED
FAZES
FAZING
FEAGUE
FEAGUED
FEAGUEING
FEAGUES
FFAGUING
FEAL
FEALED
FEALING
FEALS
FEALTIES
FEALTY
FEAR
FEARE
FEARED
FEARES
FEARFUL
FEARFULLY
FEARING
FEARLESS
FEARS
FEARSOME
FEARSOMER
FEARSOMEST
FEASIBLE
FEASIBLY
FEAST
FEASTED
FEASTER
FEASTERS
FEASTFUL
FEASTING
FEASTINGS
FEASTS
FEAT
FEATED
FEATEOUS
FEATHER
FEATHERED
FEATHERING
FEATHERINGS
FEATHERS
FEATHERY
FEATING
FEATLY
FEATOUS
FEATS
FEATUOUS

FEATURE
FEATURED
FEATURELY
FEATURES
FEATURING
FEBLESSE
FEBLESSES
FEBRICITIES
FEBRICITY
FEBRICULA
FEBRICULAS
FEBRICULE
FEBRICULES
FEBRIFIC
FEBRIFUGE
FEBRIFUGES
FEBRILE
FEBRILITIES
FEBRILITY
FECAL
FECES
FECHT
FECHTER
FECHTERS
FECHTING
FECHTS
FECIAL
FECIT
FECK
FECKLESS
FECKLY
FECKS
FECULA
FECULAS
FECULENCE
FECULENCES
FECULENCIES
FECULENCY
FECULENT
FECUND
FECUNDATE
FECUNDATED
FECUNDATES
FECUNDATING
FECUNDITIES
FECUNDITY
FED
FEDARIE
FEDARIES
FEDAYEE
FEDAYEEN
FEDELINI
FEDELINIS
FEDERACIES
FEDERACY
FEDERAL
FEDERALS
FEDERARIE
FEDERARIES
FEDERARY
FEDERATE
FEDERATED
FEDERATES
FEDERATING
FEDORA
FEDORAS
FEDS
FEE
FÉE
FEEBLE

FEEBLED
FEEBLER
FEEBLES
FEEBLEST
FEEBLING
FEEBLISH
FEEBLY
FEED
FEEDBACK
FEEDBACKS
FEEDER
FEEDERS
FEEDING
FEEDINGS
FEEDLOT
FEEDLOTS
FEEDS
FEEDSTOCK
FEEDSTOCKS
FEEDSTUFF
FEEDSTUFFS
FEEING
FEEL
FEELER
FEELERS
FEELING
FEELINGLY
FEELINGS
FEELS
FEER
FEERED
FÉERIE
FÉERIES
FEERIN
FEERING
FEERINGS
FEERINS
FEERS
FEES
FFFT
FEETLESS
FEEZE
FEEZED
FEEZES
FEEZING
FEGARIES
FEGARY
FEGS
FEHM
FEHME
FEHMIC
FEIGN
FEIGNED
FEIGNEDLY
FEIGNING
FEIGNINGS
FEIGNS
FEINT
FEINTED
FEINTER
FEINTEST
FEINTING
FEINTS
FEIS
FEISEANNA
FEISTIER
FEISTIEST
FEISTY
FELAFEL
FELAFELS

FELDGRAU
FELDGRAUS
FELDSHER
FELDSHERS
FELDSPAR
FELDSPARS
FELDSPATH
FELDSPATHS
FELICIFIC
FELICITER
FELICITIES
FELICITY
FELINE
FELINES
FELINITIES
FELINITY
FELL
FELLA
FELLABLE
FELLAH
FELLAHÎN
FELLAHS
FELLAS
FELLATE
FELLATED
FELLATES
FELLATING
FELLATIO
FELLATION
FELLATIONS
FELLATIOS
FELLED
FELLER
FELLERS
FELLEST
FELLIER
FELLIES
FELLIEST
FELLING
FELLNESS
FELLNESSES
FELLOE
FELLOES
FELLOW
FELLOWLY
FELLOWS
FELLS
FELLY
FELON
FELONIES
FELONIOUS
FELONOUS
FELONRIES
FELONRY
FELONS
FELONY
FELSITE
FELSITES
FELSITIC
FELSPAR
FELSPARS
FELSTONE
FELSTONES
FELT
FELTED
FELTER
FELTERED
FELTERING
FELTERS
FELTING

FELTINGS
FELTS
FELUCCA
FELUCCAS
FELWORT
FELWORTS
FEMAL
FEMALE
FEMALES
FEMALITIES
FEMALITY
FEMALS
FEME
FEMERALL
FEMERALLS
FEMES
FEMETARIES
FEMETARY
FEMINAL
FEMINEITIES
FEMINEITY
FEMININE
FEMININES
FEMINISE
FEMINISED
FEMINISES
FEMINISING
FEMINISM
FEMINISMS
FEMINIST
FEMINISTS
FEMINITIES
FEMINITY
FEMINIZE
FEMINIZED
FEMINIZES
FEMINIZING
FEMITER
FEMITERS
FEMME
FEMMES
FEMORA
FEMORAL
FEMUR
FEMURS
FEN
FENCE
FENCED
FENCELESS
FENCER
FENCERS
FENCES
FENCIBLE
FENCIBLES
FENCING
FENCINGS
FEND
FENDED
FENDER
FENDERS
FENDIER
FENDIEST
FENDING
FENDS
FENDY
FENESTRA
FENESTRAL
FENESTRALS
FENESTRAS
FENITAR

FENITARS
FENKS
FENLAND
FENLANDS
FENMAN
FENMEN
FENNEC
FENNECS
FENNEL
FENNELS
FENNIER
FENNIEST
FENNISH
FENNY
FENS
FENT
FENTS
FENUGREEK
FENUGREEKS
FEOD
FEODAL
FEODARIES
FEODARY
FEODS
FEOFF
FEOFFED
FEOFFEE
FEOFFEES
FEOFFER
FEOFFERS
FEOFFING
FEOFFMENT
FEOFFMENTS
FEOFFOR
FEOFFORS
FEOFFS
FERACIOUS
FERACITIES
FERACITY
FERAL
FERALISED
FERALIZED
FERE
FERER
FERES
FEREST
FERETORIES
FERETORY
FERIAL
FERINE
FERITIES
FERITY
FERLIED
FERLIES
FERLY
FERLYING
FERM
FERMATA
FERMATAS
FERMENT
FERMENTED
FERMENTING
FERMENTS
FERMI
FERMION
FERMIONS
FERMIS
FERMIUM
FERMIUMS
FERMS

FERN
FERNBIRD
FERNBIRDS
FERNERIES
FERNERY
FERNIER
FERNIEST
FERNING
FERNINGS
FERNS
FERNSHAW
FERNSHAWS
FERNTICLE
FERNTICLES
FERNY
FEROCIOUS
FEROCITIES
FEROCITY
FERRATE
FERRATES
FERREL
FERRELS
FERREOUS
FERRET
FERRETED
FERRETER
FERRETERS
FERRETING
FERRETS
FERRETY
FERRIAGE
FERRIAGES
FERRIC
FERRIED
FERRIES
FERRITE
FERRITES
FERRITIC
FERROGRAM
FERROGRAMS
FERROTYPE
FERROTYPES
FERROUS
FERRUGO
FERRUGOS
FERRULE
FERRULES
FERRY
FERRYING
FERRYMAN
FERRYMEN
FERTILE
FERTILELY
FERTILER
FERTILEST
FERTILISE
FERTILISED
FERTILISES
FERTILISING
FERTILITIES
FERTILITY
FERTILIZE
FERTILIZED
FERTILIZES
FERTILIZING
FERULA
FERULAS
FERULE
FERULES
FERVENCIES

FERVENCY	FETICHIZE	FEUDALISMS	FIAT	FICTIONAL
FERVENT	FETICHIZED	FEUDALIST	FIATED	FICTIONS
FERVENTER	FETICHIZES	FEUDALISTS	FIATING	FICTIVE
FERVENTEST	FETICHIZING	FEUDALITIES	FIATS	FICTOR
FERVENTLY	FETICIDAL	FEUDALITY	FIAUNT	FICTORS
FERVID	FETICIDE	FEUDALIZE	FIAUNTS	FID
FERVIDER	FETICIDES	FEUDALIZED	FIB	FIDDIOUS
FERVIDEST	FETID	FEUDALIZES	FIBBED	FIDDIOUSED
FERVIDITIES	FETIDER	FEUDALIZING	FIBBER	FIDDIOUSES
FERVIDITY	FETIDEST	FEUDALLY	FIBBERIES	FIDDIOUSING
FERVIDLY	FETIDNESS	FEUDARIES	FIBBERS	FIDDLE
FERVOROUS	FETIDNESSES	FEUDARY	FIBBERY	FIDDLED
FERVOUR	FÊTING	FEUDATORIES	FIBBING	FIDDLER
FERVOURS	FETISH	FEUDATORY	FIBER	FIDDLERS
FESCUE	FETISHES	FEUDED	FIBERS	FIDDLES
FESCUES	FETISHISE	FEUDING	FIBRE	FIDDLEY
FESS	FETISHISED	FEUDINGS	FIBRED	FIDDLEYS
FESSE	FETISHISES	FEUDIST	FIBRELESS	FIDDLIER
FESSES	FETISHISING	FEUDISTS	FIBRES	FIDDLIEST
FESTA	FETISHISM	FEUDS	FIBRIFORM	FIDDLING
FESTAL	FETISHISMS	FEUED	FIBRIL	FIDDLY
FESTALLY	FETISHIST	FEUILLETÉ	FIBRILLA	FIDEISM
FESTALS	FETISHISTS	FEUILLETÉS	FIBRILLAE	FIDEISMS
FESTAS	FETISHIZE	FEUING	FIBRILLAR	FIDEISTIC
FESTER	FETISHIZED	FEUS	FIBRILS	FIDELITIES
FESTERED	FETISHIZES	FEUTRE	FIBRIN	FIDELITY
FESTERING	FETISHIZING	FEUTRED	FIBRINOUS	FIDGE
FESTERS	FETLOCK	FEUTRES	FIBRINS	FIDGED
FESTILOGIES	FETLOCKED	FEUTRING	FIBRO	FIDGES
FESTILOGY	FETLOCKS	FEVER	FIBROCYTE	FIDGET
FESTINATE	FETOR	FEVERED	FIBROCYTES	FIDGETED
FESTINATED	FETORS	FEVERFEW	FIBROID	FIDGETING
FESTINATES	FETOSCOPIES	FEVERFEWS	FIBROIDS	FIDGETS
FESTINATING	FETOSCOPY	FEVERING	FIBROIN	FIDGETY
FESTIVAL	FETS	FEVERISH	FIBROINS	FIDGING
FESTIVALS	FETT	FEVEROUS	FIBROLINE	FIDIBUS
FESTIVE	FETTA	FEVERS	FIBROLINES	FIDIBUSES
FESTIVELY	FETTAS	FEW	FIBROLITE	FIDS
FESTIVITIES	FETTED	FEWER	FIBROLITES	FIDUCIAL
FESTIVITY	FETTER	FEWEST	FIBROMA	FIDUCIARIES
FESTIVOUS	FETTERED	FEWMET	FIBROMATA	FIDUCIARY
FESTOLOGIES	FETTERING	FEWMETS	FIBROS	FIE
FESTOLOGY	FETTERS	FEWNESS	FIBROSE	FIEF
FESTOON	FETTING	FEWNESSES	FIBROSED	FIEFS
FESTOONED	FETTLE	FEWTER	FIBROSES	FIELD
FESTOONING	FETTLED	FEWTERED	FIBROSING	FIELDED
FESTOONS	FETTLER	FEWTERING	FIBROSIS	FIELDER
FET	FETTLERS	FEWTERS	FIBROTIC	FIELDERS
FETA	FETTLES	FEWTRILS	FIBROUS	FIELDFARE
FETAL	FETTLING	FEY	FIBS	FIELDFARES
FETAS	FETTLINGS	FEYED	FIBSTER	FIELDING
FETCH	FETTS	FEYER	FIBSTERS	FIELDINGS
FETCHED	FETTUCINE	FEYEST	FIBULA	FIELDMICE
FETCHES	FETTUCINES	FEYING	FIBULAR	FIELDS
FETCHING	FETTUCINI	FEYS	FIBULAS	FIELDSMAN
FÊTE	FETTUCINIS	FEZ	FICHE	FIELDSMEN
FÊTED	FETUS	FEZES	FICHES	FIELDWARD
FÊTES	FETUSES	FEZZED	FICHU	FIELDWORK
FETIAL	FETWA	FEZZES	FICHUS	FIELDWORKS
FETICH	FETWAS	FIACRE	FICKLE	FIEND
FETICHE	FEU	FIACRES	FICKLED	FIENDISH
FETICHES	FEUAR	FIANCÉ	FICKLER	FIENDS
FETICHISE	FEUARS	FIANCÉE	FICKLES	FIENT
FETICHISED	FEUD	FIANCÉES	FICKLEST	FIENTS
FETICHISES	FEUDAL	FIANCÉS	FICKLING	FIERCE
FETICHISING	FEUDALISE	FIAR	FICO	FIERCELY
FETICHISM	FEUDALISED	FIARS	FICOES	FIERCER
FETICHISMS	FEUDALISES	FIASCO	FICOS	FIERCEST
FETICHIST	FEUDALISING	FIASCOES	FICTILE	FIERE
FETICHISTS	FEUDALISM	FIASCOS	FICTION	FIERES

FIERIER
FIERIEST
FIERILY
FIERINESS
FIERINESSES
FIERY
FIESTA
FIESTAS
FIFE
FIFED
FIFER
FIFERS
FIFES
FIFING
FIFTEEN
FIFTEENER
FIFTEENERS
FIFTEENS
FIFTEENTH
FIFTEENTHS
FIFTH
FIFTHLY
FIFTHS
FIFTIES
FIFTIETH
FIFTIETHS
FIFTY
FIFTYISH
FIG
FIGGED
FIGGERIES
FIGGERY
FIGGING
FIGHT
FIGHTABLE
FIGHTBACK
FIGHTBACKS
FIGHTER
FIGHTERS
FIGHTING
FIGHTINGS
FIGHTS
FIGMENT
FIGMENTS
FIGO
FIGOS
FIGS
FIGULINE
FIGULINES
FIGURABLE
FIGURAL
FIGURANT
FIGURANTE
FIGURANTES
FIGURANTS
FIGURATE
FIGURE
FIGURED
FIGURES
FIGURINE
FIGURINES
FIGURING
FIGURIST
FIGURISTS
FIGWORT
FIGWORTS
FIKE
FIKED
FIKERIES
FIKERY

FIKES
FIKIER
FIKIEST
FIKING
FIKISH
FIKY
FIL
FILABEG
FILABEGS
FILACEOUS
FILACER
FILACERS
FILAGREE
FILAGREES
FILAMENT
FILAMENTS
FILANDER
FILANDERS
FILAR
FILARIA
FILARIAL
FILARIAS
FILASSE
FILASSES
FILATORIES
FILATORY
FILATURE
FILATURES
FILAZER
FILAZERS
FILBERD
FILBERDS
FILBERT
FILBERTS
FILCH
FILCHED
FILCHER
FILCHERS
FILCHES
FILCHING
FILCHINGS
FILE
FILED
FILEMOT
FILEMOTS
FILER
FILERS
FILES
FILET
FILETS
FILFOT
FILFOTS
FILIAL
FILIALLY
FILIATE
FILIATED
FILIATES
FILIATING
FILIATION
FILIATIONS
FILIBEG
FILIBEGS
FILICIDE
FILICIDES
FILIFORM
FILIGRAIN
FILIGRAINS
FILIGRANE
FILIGRANES
FILIGREE

FILIGREED
FILIGREES
FILING
FILINGS
FILIOQUE
FILIOQUES
FILL
FILLE
FILLED
FILLER
FILLERS
FILLES
FILLET
FILLETED
FILLETING
FILLETS
FILLIBEG
FILLIBEGS
FILLIES
FILLING
FILLINGS
FILLIP
FILLIPED
FILLIPEEN
FILLIPEENS
FILLIPING
FILLIPS
FILLISTER
FILLISTERS
FILLS
FILLY
FILM
FILMABLE
FILMDOM
FILMDOMS
FILMED
FILMGOER
FILMGOERS
FILMIC
FILMIER
FILMIEST
FILMINESS
FILMINESSES
FILMING
FILMISH
FILMLAND
FILMLANDS
FILMS
FILMSET
FILMSETS
FILMSETTING
FILMSETTINGS
FILMY
FILOPLUME
FILOPLUMES
FILOPODIA
FILOSE
FILOSELLE
FILOSELLES
FILS
FILTER
FILTERED
FILTERING
FILTERS
FILTH
FILTHIER
FILTHIEST
FILTHILY
FILTHS
FILTHY

FILTRABLE
FILTRATE
FILTRATED
FILTRATES
FILTRATING
FIMBLE
FIMBLES
FIMBRIA
FIMBRIAS
FIMBRIATE
FIMBRIATED
FIMBRIATES
FIMBRIATING
FIN
FINABLE
FINAGLE
FINAGLED
FINAGLES
FINAGLING
FINAL
FINALE
FINALES
FINALISE
FINALISED
FINALISES
FINALISING
FINALISM
FINALISMS
FINALIST
FINALISTS
FINALITIES
FINALITY
FINALIZE
FINALIZED
FINALIZES
FINALIZING
FINALLY
FINALS
FINANCE
FINANCED
FINANCES
FINANCIAL
FINANCIER
FINANCIERED
FINANCIERING
FINANCIERS
FINANCING
FINBACK
FINBACKS
FINCH
FINCHED
FINCHES
FIND
FINDER
FINDERS
FINDING
FINDINGS
FINDRAM
FINDRAMS
FINDS
FINE
FINED
FINEER
FINEERED
FINEERING
FINEERS
FINEISH
FINELESS
FINELY
FINENESS

FINENESSES
FINER
FINERIES
FINERS
FINERY
FINES
FINESSE
FINESSED
FINESSER
FINESSERS
FINESSES
FINESSING
FINESSINGS
FINEST
FINGAN
FINGANS
FINGER
FINGERED
FINGERING
FINGERINGS
FINGERS
FINGERTIP
FINGERTIPS
FINIAL
FINIALS
FINICAL
FINICALLY
FINICKING
FINICKINGS
FINICKY
FINIKIN
FINING
FININGS
FINIS
FINISES
FINISH
FINISHED
FINISHER
FINISHERS
FINISHES
FINISHING
FINISHINGS
FINITE
FINITELY
FINITUDE
FINITUDES
FINJAN
FINJANS
FINK
FINKED
FINKING
FINKS
FINLESS
FINNAC
FINNACK
FINNACKS
FINNACS
FINNAN
FINNANS
FINNED
FINNER
FINNERS
FINNESKO
FINNIER
FINNIEST
FINNOCHIO
FINNOCHIOS
FINNOCK
FINNOCKS
FINNSKO

FINNY
FINO
FINOCCHIO
FINOCCHIOS
FINOCHIO
FINOCHIOS
FINOS
FINSKO
FINS
FIORD
FIORDS
FIORIN
FIORINS
FIORITURA
FIORITURE
FIPPENCE
FIPPENCES
FIPPLE
FIPPLES
FIR
FIRE
FIREARM
FIREARMS
FIREBALL
FIREBALLS
FIREBRAND
FIREBRANDS
FIREBRAT
FIREBRATS
FIREBRICK
FIREBRICKS
FIREBUG
FIREBUGS
FIRECREST
FIRECRESTS
FIRED
FIREDAMP
FIREDAMPS
FIREDOG
FIREDOGS
FIREFLIES
FIREFLOAT
FIREFLOATS
FIREFLY
FIREGUARD
FIREGUARDS
FIREHOUSE
FIREHOUSES
FIRELESS
FIRELIGHT
FIRELIGHTS
FIRELOCK
FIRELOCKS
FIREMAN
FIREMARK
FIREMARKS
FIREMEN
FIREPAN
FIREPANS
FIREPLACE
FIREPLACES
FIREPOT
FIREPOTS
FIREPROOF
FIREPROOFED
FIREPROOFING
FIREPROOFINGS
FIREPROOFS
FIRER
FIRERS

FIRES
FIRESHIP
FIRESHIPS
FIRESIDE
FIRESIDES
FIRESTONE
FIRESTONES
FIRETHORN
FIRETHORNS
FIREWEED
FIREWEEDS
FIREWOMAN
FIREWOMEN
FIREWOOD
FIREWOODS
FIREWORK
FIREWORKS
FIREWORM
FIREWORMS
FIRING
FIRINGS
FIRK
FIRKED
FIRKIN
FIRKING
FIRKINS
FIRKS
FIRLOT
FIRLOTS
FIRM
FIRMAMENT
FIRMAMENTS
FIRMAN
FIRMANS
FIRMED
FIRMER
FIRMERS
FIRMEST
FIRMING
FIRMLESS
FIRMLY
FIRMNESS
FIRMNESSES
FIRMS
FIRMWARE
FIRMWARES
FIRN
FIRNS
FIRRIER
FIRRIEST
FIRRING
FIRRINGS
FIRRY
FIRS
FIRST
FIRSTLING
FIRSTLINGS
FIRSTLY
FIRSTS
FIRTH
FIRTHS
FISC
FISCAL
FISCALS
FISCS
FISGIG
FISGIGS
FISH
FISHABLE
FISHBALL

FISHBALLS
FISHCAKE
FISHCAKES
FISHED
FISHER
FISHERIES
FISHERMAN
FISHERMEN
FISHERS
FISHERY
FISHES
FISHEYE
FISHEYES
FISHFUL
FISHGIG
FISHGIGS
FISHIER
FISHIEST
FISHIFIED
FISHIFIES
FISHIFY
FISHIFYING
FISHINESS
FISHINESSES
FISHING
FISHINGS
FISHSKIN
FISHSKINS
FISHWIFE
FISHWIVES
FISHY
FISHYBACK
FISHYBACKS
FISK
FISKED
FISKING
FISKS
FISNOMIE
FISNOMIES
FISSILE
FISSILITIES
FISSION
FISSIONS
FISSIPED
FISSIPEDE
FISSIPEDES
FISSIPEDS
FISSIVE
FISSLE
FISSLED
FISSLES
FISSLING
FISSURE
FISSURED
FISSURES
FISSURING
FIST
FISTED
FISTFUL
FISTFULS
FISTIANA
FISTIANAS
FISTIC
FISTICAL
FISTICUFF
FISTICUFFS
FISTIER
FISTIEST
FISTING

FISTMELE
FISTMELES
FISTS
FISTULA
FISTULAE
FISTULAR
FISTULAS
FISTULOSE
FISTULOUS
FISTY
FIT
FITCH
FITCHÉ
FITCHÉE
FITCHES
FITCHET
FITCHETS
FITCHEW
FITCHEWS
FITCHY
FITFUL
FITFULLY
FITLIER
FITLIEST
FITLY
FITMENT
FITMENTS
FITNESS
FITNESSES
FITS
FITT
FITTE
FITTED
FITTER
FITTERS
FITTES
FITTEST
FITTING
FITTINGLY
FITTINGS
FITTS
FIVE
FIVEFOLD
FIVEPENCE
FIVEPENCES
FIVEPENNY
FIVEPIN
FIVEPINS
FIVER
FIVERS
FIVES
FIX
FIXABLE
FIXATE
FIXATED
FIXATES
FIXATING
FIXATION
FIXATIONS
FIXATIVE
FIXATIVES
FIXATURE
FIXATURES
FIXED
FIXEDLY
FIXEDNESS
FIXEDNESSES
FIXER
FIXERS
FIXES

FIXING
FIXINGS
FIXITIES
FIXITY
FIXIVE
FIXTURE
FIXTURES
FIXURE
FIXURES
FIZ
FIZGIG
FIZGIGS
FIZZ
FIZZED
FIZZEN
FIZZENS
FIZZER
FIZZERS
FIZZES
FIZZGIG
FIZZGIGS
FIZZIER
FIZZIEST
FIZZING
FIZZINGS
FIZZLE
FIZZLED
FIZZLES
FIZZLING
FIZZY
FJORD
FJORDS
FLAB
FLABBIER
FLABBIEST
FLABBY
FLABELLA
FLABELLUM
FLABELLUMS
FLABS
FLACCID
FLACCIDER
FLACCIDEST
FLACCIDLY
FLACK
FLACKERED
FLACKERING
FLACKERS
FLACKET
FLACKETS
FLACKS
FLACON
FLACONS
FLAFF
FLAFFED
FLAFFER
FLAFFERED
FLAFFERING
FLAFFERS
FLAFFING
FLAFFS
FLAG
FLAGELLA
FLAGELLUM
FLAGEOLET
FLAGEOLETS
FLAGGED
FLAGGIER
FLAGGIEST

FLAGGING	FLAMMED	FLASHING	FLAUNT	FLEDGES
FLAGGINGS	FLAMMING	FLASHINGS	FLAUNTED	FLEDGIER
FLAGGY	FLAMMS	FLASHY	FLAUNTER	FLEDGIEST
FLAGITATE	FLAMMULE	FLASK	FLAUNTERS	FLEDGING
FLAGITATED	FLAMMULES	FLASKET	FLAUNTIER	FLEDGLING
FLAGITATES	FLAMS	FLASKETS	FLAUNTIEST	FLEDGLINGS
FLAGITATING	FLAMY	FLASKS	FLAUNTING	FLEDGY
FLAGON	FLAN	FLAT	FLAUNTS	FLEE
FLAGONS	FLANCH	FLATBACK	FLAUNTY	FLEECE
FLAGPOLE	FLANCHED	FLATBACKS	FLAUTIST	FLEECED
FLAGPOLES	FLANCHES	FLATBOAT	FLAUTISTS	FLEECER
FLAGRANCE	FLANCHING	FLATBOATS	FLAVIN	FLEECERS
FLAGRANCES	FLANCHINGS	FLATFISH	FLAVINE	FLEECES
FLAGRANCIES	FLÂNERIE	FLATFISHES	FLAVINES	FLEECH
FLAGRANCY	FLÂNERIES	FLATHEAD	FLAVINS	FLEECHED
FLAGRANT	FLÂNEUR	FLATHEADS	FLAVONE	FLEECHES
FLAGS	FLÂNEURS	FLATIRON	FLAVONES	FLEECHING
FLAGSHIP	FLANGE	FLATIRONS	FLAVOROUS	FLEECHINGS
FLAGSHIPS	FLANGED	FLATLET	FLAVOUR	FLEECIER
FLAGSTAFF	FLANGES	FLATLETS	FLAVOURED	FLEECIEST
FLAGSTAFFS	FLANGING	FLATLING	FLAVOURING	FLEECING
FLAGSTICK	FLANK	FLATLINGS	FLAVOURINGS	FLEECY
FLAGSTICKS	FLANKED	FLATLONG	FLAVOURS	FLEEING
FLAGSTONE	FLANKER	FLATLY	FLAW	FLEER
FLAGSTONES	FLANKERED	FLATMATE	FLAWED	FLEERED
FLAIL	FLANKERING	FLATMATES	FLAWIER	FLEERER
FLAILED	FLANKERS	FLATNESS	FLAWIEST	FLEERERS
FLAILING	FLANKING	FLATNESSES	FLAWING	FLEERING
FLAILS	FLANKS	FLATS	FLAWLESS	FLEERINGS
FLAIR	FLANNEL	FLATTED	FLAWN	FLEERS
FLAIRS	FLANNELLED	FLATTEN	FLAWNS	FLEES
FLAK	FLANNELLING	FLATTENED	FLAWS	FLEET
FLAKE	FLANNELLY	FLATTENING	FLAWY	FLEETED
FLAKED	FLANNELS	FLATTENS	FLAX	FLEETER
FLAKES	FLANNEN	FLATTER	FLAXEN	FLEETEST
FLAKIER	FLANNENS	FLATTERED	FLAXES	FLEETING
FLAKIEST	FLANS	FLATTERER	FLAXIER	FLEETLIER
FLAKINESS	FLAP	FLATTERERS	FLAXIEST	FLEETLIEST
FLAKINESSES	FLAPJACK	FLATTERIES	FLAXY	FLEETLY
FLAKING	FLAPJACKS	FLATTERING	FLAY	FLEETNESS
FLAKS	FLAPPABLE	FLATTERS	FLAYED	FLEETNESSES
FLAKY	FLAPPED	FLATTERY	FLAYER	FLEETS
FLAM	FLAPPER	FLATTEST	FLAYERS	FLEG
FLAMBÉ	FLAPPERS	FLATTING	FLAYING	FLEGGED
FLAMBEAU	FLAPPING	FLATTINGS	FLAYS	FLEGGING
FLAMBEAUS	FLAPPINGS	FLATTISH	FLEA	FLEGS
FLAMBEAUX	FLAPS	FLATULENT	FLEAM	FLEME
FLAMBÉED	FLAPTRACK	FLATUOUS	FLEAMS	FLEMES
FLAME	FLAPTRACKS	FLATUS	FLEAS	FLEMING
FLAMED	FLARE	FLATUSES	FLEASOME	FLEMISH
FLAMELESS	FLARED	FLATWARE	FLÈCHE	FLEMISHED
FLAMELET	FLARES	FLATWARES	FLÈCHES	FLEMISHES
FLAMELETS	FLARIER	FLATWAYS	FLECHETTE	FLEMISHING
FLAMEN	FLARIEST	FLATWISE	FLÉCHETTE	FLEMIT
FLAMENCO	FLARING	FLATWORM	FLECHETTES	FLENCH
FLAMENCOS	FLARINGLY	FLATWORMS	FLÉCHETTES	FLENCHED
FLAMENS	FLARY	FLAUGHT	FLECK	FLENCHES
FLAMES	FLASER	FLAUGHTED	FLECKED	FLENCHING
FLAMFEW	FLASERS	FLAUGHTER	FLECKER	FLENSE
FLAMFEWS	FLASH	FLAUGHTERED	FLECKERED	FLENSED
FLAMIER	FLASHCUBE	FLAUGHTERING	FLECKERING	FLENSES
FLAMIEST	FLASHCUBES	FLAUGHTERS	FLECKERS	FLENSING
FLAMINES	FLASHED	FLAUGHTING	FLECKING	FLESH
FLAMING	FLASHER	FLAUGHTS	FLECKLESS	FLESHED
FLAMINGLY	FLASHERS	FLAUNCH	FLECKS	FLESHER
FLAMINGO	FLASHES	FLAUNCHED	FLECTION	FLESHERS
FLAMINGOES	FLASHEST	FLAUNCHES	FLECTIONS	FLESHES
FLAMINGOS	FLASHIER	FLAUNCHING	FLED	FLESHIER
FLAMM	FLASHIEST	FLAUNE	FLEDGE	FLESHIEST
FLAMMABLE	FLASHILY	FLAUNES	FLEDGED	FLESHING

FLESHINGS
FLESHLESS
FLESHLIER
FLESHLIEST
FLESHLING
FLESHLINGS
FLESHLY
FLESHMENT
FLESHMENTS
FLESHWORM
FLESHWORMS
FLESHY
FLETCH
FLETCHED
FLETCHER
FLETCHERS
FLETCHES
FLETCHING
FLETTON
FLETTONS
FLEURET
FLEURETS
FLEURETTE
FLEURETTES
FLEURON
FLEURONS
FLEURY
FLEW
FLEWED
FLEWS
FLEX
FLEXED
FLEXES
FLEXIBLE
FLEXIBLY
FLEXILE
FLEXING
FLEXION
FLEXIONS
FLEXITIME
FLEXITIMES
FLEXOR
FLEXORS
FLEXUOSE
FLEXUOUS
FLEXURAL
FLEXURE
FLEXURES
FLEY
FLEYED
FLEYING
FLEYS
FLIC
FLICHTER
FLICHTERED
FLICHTERING
FLICHTERS
FLICK
FLICKED
FLICKER
FLICKERED
FLICKERING
FLICKERS
FLICKING
FLICKS
FLICS
FLIER
FLIERS
FLIES
FLIEST

FLIGHT
FLIGHTED
FLIGHTIER
FLIGHTIEST
FLIGHTILY
FLIGHTING
FLIGHTS
FLIGHTY
FLIMP
FLIMPED
FLIMPING
FLIMPS
FLIMSIER
FLIMSIES
FLIMSIEST
FLIMSILY
FLIMSY
FLINCH
FLINCHED
FLINCHER
FLINCHERS
FLINCHES
FLINCHING
FLINCHINGS
FLINDER
FLINDERS
FLING
FLINGER
FLINGERS
FLINGING
FLINGS
FLINT
FLINTIER
FLINTIEST
FLINTIFIED
FLINTIFIES
FLINTIFY
FLINTIFYING
FLINTILY
FLINTLOCK
FLINTLOCKS
FLINTS
FLINTY
FLIP
FLIPFLOP
FLIPFLOPS
FLIPPANCIES
FLIPPANCY
FLIPPANT
FLIPPED
FLIPPER
FLIPPERS
FLIPPEST
FLIPPING
FLIPS
FLIRT
FLIRTED
FLIRTIER
FLIRTIEST
FLIRTING
FLIRTINGS
FLIRTISH
FLIRTS
FLIRTY
FLISK
FLISKED
FLISKIER
FLISKIEST
FLISKING
FLISKS

FLISKY
FLIT
FLITCH
FLITCHES
FLITE
FLITED
FLITES
FLITING
FLITS
FLITT
FLITTER
FLITTERED
FLITTERING
FLITTERN
FLITTERNS
FLITTERS
FLITTING
FLITTINGS
FLIVVER
FLIVVERS
FLIX
FLIXED
FLIXES
FLIXING
FLOAT
FLOATABLE
FLOATAGE
FLOATAGES
FLOATANT
FLOATANTS
FLOATED
FLOATEL
FLOATELS
FLOATER
FLOATERS
FLOATIER
FLOATIEST
FLOATING
FLOATINGS
FLOATS
FLOATY
FLOCCI
FLOCCOSE
FLOCCULAR
FLOCCULE
FLOCCULES
FLOCCULI
FLOCCULUS
FLOCCUS
FLOCK
FLOCKED
FLOCKING
FLOCKS
FLOE
FLOES
FLOG
FLOGGED
FLOGGING
FLOGGINGS
FLOGS
FLONG
FLONGS
FLOOD
FLOODED
FLOODGATE
FLOODGATES
FLOODING
FLOODINGS
FLOODLIT

FLOODMARK
FLOODMARKS
FLOODS
FLOODTIDE
FLOODTIDES
FLOODWALL
FLOODWALLS
FLOODWAY
FLOODWAYS
FLOOR
FLOORED
FLOORER
FLOORERS
FLOORHEAD
FLOORHEADS
FLOORING
FLOORINGS
FLOORS
FLOOSIE
FLOOSIES
FLOOSY
FLOOZIE
FLOOZIES
FLOOZY
FLOP
FLOPHOUSE
FLOPHOUSES
FLOPPED
FLOPPIER
FLOPPIEST
FLOPPILY
FLOPPING
FLOPPY
FLOPS
FLOR
FLORA
FLORAE
FLORAL
FLORALLY
FLORAS
FLOREAT
FLOREATED
FLORENCE
FLORENCES
FLORET
FLORETS
FLORIATED
FLORID
FLORIDEAN
FLORIDEANS
FLORIDER
FLORIDEST
FLORIDITIES
FLORIDITY
FLORIDLY
FLORIER
FLORIEST
FLORIFORM
FLORIGEN
FLORIGENS
FLORIN
FLORINS
FLORIST
FLORISTIC
FLORISTICS
FLORISTRIES
FLORISTRY
FLORISTS
FLORS
FLORUIT

FLORUITS
FLORY
FLOSCULAR
FLOSCULE
FLOSCULES
FLOSH
FLOSHES
FLOSS
FLOSSES
FLOSSIER
FLOSSIEST
FLOSSY
FLOTA
FLOTAGE
FLOTAGES
FLOTANT
FLOTAS
FLOTATION
FLOTATIONS
FLOTE
FLOTEL
FLOTELS
FLOTES
FLOTILLA
FLOTILLAS
FLOTSAM
FLOTSAMS
FLOUNCE
FLOUNCED
FLOUNCES
FLOUNCING
FLOUNCINGS
FLOUNDER
FLOUNDERED
FLOUNDERING
FLOUNDERS
FLOUR
FLOURED
FLOURIER
FLOURIEST
FLOURING
FLOURISH
FLOURISHED
FLOURISHES
FLOURISHING
FLOURISHY
FLOURS
FLOURY
FLOUSE
FLOUSED
FLOUSES
FLOUSH
FLOUSHED
FLOUSHES
FLOUSHING
FLOUSING
FLOUT
FLOUTED
FLOUTING
FLOUTS
FLOW
FLOWAGE
FLOWAGES
FLOWED
FLOWER
FLOWERAGE
FLOWERAGES
FLOWERED
FLOWERER
FLOWERERS

FLOWERET
FLOWERETS
FLOWERING
FLOWERINGS
FLOWERPOT
FLOWERPOTS
FLOWERS
FLOWERY
FLOWING
FLOWINGLY
FLOWMETER
FLOWMETERS
FLOWN
FLOWS
FLU
FLUATE
FLUATES
FLUB
FLUBBED
FLUBBING
FLUBS
FLUCTUANT
FLUCTUATE
FLUCTUATED
FLUCTUATES
FLUCTUATING
FLUE
FLUELLIN
FLUELLINS
FLUENCE
FLUENCES
FLUENCIES
FLUENCY
FLUENT
FLUENTLY
FLUENTS
FLUES
FLUEWORK
FLUEWORKS
FLUEY
FLUFF
FLUFFED
FLUFFIER
FLUFFIEST
FLUFFING
FLUFFS
FLUFFY
FLUGEL
FLUGELMAN
FLUGELMEN
FLUGELS
FLUID
FLUIDAL
FLUIDER
FLUIDEST
FLUIDIC
FLUIDICS
FLUIDIFIED
FLUIDIFIES
FLUIDIFY
FLUIDIFYING
FLUIDISE
FLUIDISED
FLUIDISES
FLUIDISING
FLUIDITIES
FLUIDITY
FLUIDIZE
FLUIDIZED
FLUIDIZES

FLUIDIZING
FLUIDNESS
FLUIDNESSES
FLUIDS
FLUIER
FLUIEST
FLUKE
FLUKED
FLUKES
FLUKEY
FLUKIER
FLUKIEST
FLUKING
FLUKY
FLUME
FLUMES
FLUMMERIES
FLUMMERY
FLUMMOX
FLUMMOXED
FLUMMOXES
FLUMMOXING
FLUMP
FLUMPED
FLUMPING
FLUMPS
FLUNG
FLUNK
FLUNKED
FLUNKEY
FLUNKEYS
FLUNKIES
FLUNKING
FLUNKS
FLUNKY
FLUOR
FLUORESCE
FLUORESCED
FLUORESCES
FLUORESCING
FLUORIC
FLUORIDE
FLUORIDES
FLUORINE
FLUORINES
FLUORITE
FLUORITES
FLUOROSES
FLUOROSIS
FLUORS
FLUORSPAR
FLUORSPARS
FLURR
FLURRED
FLURRIED
FLURRIES
FLURRING
FLURRS
FLURRY
FLURRYING
FLUS
FLUSH
FLUSHED
FLUSHER
FLUSHERS
FLUSHES
FLUSHEST
FLUSHIER
FLUSHIEST
FLUSHING

FLUSHINGS
FLUSHNESS
FLUSHNESSES
FLUSHY
FLUSTER
FLUSTERED
FLUSTERING
FLUSTERS
FLUSTERY
FLUSTRATE
FLUSTRATED
FLUSTRATES
FLUSTRATING
FLUTE
FLUTED
FLUTER
FLUTERS
FLUTES
FLUTIER
FLUTIEST
FLUTINA
FLUTINAS
FLUTING
FLUTINGS
FLUTIST
FLUTISTS
FLUTTER
FLUTTERED
FLUTTERING
FLUTTERS
FLUTY
FLUVIAL
FLUVIATIC
FLUX
FLUXED
FLUXES
FLUXING
FLUXION
FLUXIONAL
FLUXIONS
FLUXIVE
FLY
FLYABLE
FLYAWAY
FLYBANE
FLYBANES
FLYBELT
FLYBELTS
FLYBLOW
FLYBLOWS
FLYBOAT
FLYBOATS
FLYBOOK
FLYBOOKS
FLYER
FLYERS
FLYEST
FLYING
FLYINGS
FLYLEAF
FLYLEAVES
FLYMAKER
FLYMAKERS
FLYOVER
FLYOVERS
FLYPAPER
FLYPAPERS
FLYPE
FLYPED
FLYPES

FLYPING
FLYTE
FLYTED
FLYTES
FLYTING
FLYTINGS
FLYTRAP
FLYTRAPS
FLYWEIGHT
FLYWEIGHTS
FLYWHEEL
FLYWHEELS
FOAL
FOALED
FOALFOOT
FOALFOOTS
FOALING
FOALS
FOAM
FOAMED
FOAMIER
FOAMIEST
FOAMILY
FOAMINESS
FOAMINESSES
FOAMING
FOAMINGLY
FOAMINGS
FOAMLESS
FOAMS
FOAMY
FOB
FOBBED
FOBBING
FOBS
FOCAL
FOCALISE
FOCALISED
FOCALISES
FOCALISING
FOCALIZE
FOCALIZED
FOCALIZES
FOCALIZING
FOCALLY
FOCI
FOCIMETER
FOCIMETERS
FOCUS
FOCUSED
FOCUSES
FOCUSING
FOCUSSED
FOCUSSING
FODDER
FODDERED
FODDERER
FODDERERS
FODDERING
FODDERINGS
FODDERS
FOE
FOEDARIE
FOEDARIES
FOEDERATI
FOEHN
FOEHNS
FOEMAN
FOEMEN
FOEN

FOES
FOETAL
FOETICIDE
FOETICIDES
FOETID
FOETIDER
FOETIDEST
FOETOR
FOETORS
FOETUS
FOETUSES
FOG
FOGASH
FOGASHES
FOGBOUND
FOGEY
FOGEYS
FOGGAGE
FOGGAGED
FOGGAGES
FOGGAGING
FOGGED
FOGGER
FOGGERS
FOGGIER
FOGGIEST
FOGGILY
FOGGINESS
FOGGINESSES
FOGGING
FOGGY
FOGHORN
FOGHORNS
FOGIES
FOGLE
FOGLES
FOGLESS
FOGMAN
FOGMEN
FOGRAM
FOGRAMITE
FOGRAMITES
FOGRAMITIES
FOGRAMITY
FOGRAMS
FOGS
FOGY
FOGYDOM
FOGYDOMS
FOGYISH
FOGYISM
FOGYISMS
FOH
FÖHN
FÖHNS
FOIBLE
FOIBLES
FOIL
FOILED
FOILING
FOILINGS
FOILS
FOIN
FOINED
FOINING
FOININGLY
FOINS
FOISON
FOISONS
FOIST

FOISTED	FOLLOWINGS	FOOLPROOF	FOOTRULE	FORBODE
FOISTER	FOLLOWS	FOOLS	FOOTRULES	FORBODES
FOISTERS	FOLLY	FOOLSCAP	FOOTS	FORBORE
FOISTING	FOLLYING	FOOLSCAPS	FOOTSLOG	FORBORNE
FOISTS	FOMENT	FOOT	FOOTSLOGGED	FORBY
FOLACIN	FOMENTED	FOOTAGE	FOOTSLOGGING	FORBYE
FOLACINS	FOMENTER	FOOTAGES	FOOTSLOGGINGS	FORÇAT
FOLD	FOMENTERS	FOOTBALL	FOOTSLOGS	FORÇATS
FOLDABLE	FOMENTING	FOOTBALLS	FOOTSORE	FORCE
FOLDAWAY	FOMENTS	FOOTBAR	FOOTSTALK	FORCED
FOLDBOAT	FOMES	FOOTBARS	FOOTSTALKS	FORCEDLY
FOLDBOATS	FOMITES	FOOTBOARD	FOOTSTEP	FORCEFUL
FOLDED	FON	FOOTBOARDS	FOOTSTEPS	FORCELESS
FOLDER	FOND	FOOTBOY	FOOTSTOOL	FORCEMEAT
FOLDEROL	FONDA	FOOTBOYS	FOOTSTOOLS	FORCEMEATS
FOLDEROLS	FONDANT	FOOTCLOTH	FOOTWAY	FORCEPS
FOLDERS	FONDANTS	FOOTCLOTHS	FOOTWAYS	FORCEPSES
FOLDING	FONDAS	FOOTED	FOOTWEAR	FORCER
FOLDINGS	FONDED	FOOTER	FOOTWORK	FORCERS
FOLDS	FONDER	FOOTERS	FOOTWORKS	FORCES
FOLIA	FONDEST	FOOTFALL	FOOTWORN	FORCIBLE
FOLIAGE	FONDING	FOOTFALLS	FOOTY	FORCIBLY
FOLIAGED	FONDLE	FOOTFAULT	FOOZLE	FORCING
FOLIAGES	FONDLED	FOOTFAULTED	FOOZLED	FORCIPES
FOLIAR	FONDLER	FOOTFAULTING	FOOZLER	FORD
FOLIATE	FONDLERS	FOOTFAULTS	FOOZLERS	FORDABLE
FOLIATED	FONDLES	FOOTGEAR	FOOZLES	FORDED
FOLIATES	FONDLING	FOOTHILL	FOOZLING	FORDID
FOLIATING	FONDLINGS	FOOTHILLS	FOOZLINGS	FORDING
FOLIATION	FONDLY	FOOTHOLD	FOP	FORDO
FOLIATIONS	FONDNESS	FOOTHOLDS	FOPLING	FORDOES
FOLIATURE	FONDNESSES	FOOTING	FOPLINGS	FORDOING
FOLIATURES	FONDS	FOOTINGS	FOPPERIES	FORDONE
FOLIE	FONDUE	FOOTLE	FOPPERY	FORDS
FOLIES	FONDUES	FOOTLED	FOPPISH	FORE
FOLIO	FONE	FOOTLES	FOPPISHLY	FOREANENT
FOLIOED	FONLY	FOOTLESS	FOPS	FOREARM
FOLIOING	FONNED	FOOTLIGHT	FOR	FOREARMED
FOLIOLATE	FONNING	FOOTLIGHTS	FORA	FOREARMING
FOLIOLE	FONS	FOOTLING	FORAGE	FOREARMS
FOLIOLES	FONT	FOOTLINGS	FORAGED	FOREBEAR
FOLIOLOSE	FONTAL	FOOTLOOSE	FORAGER	FOREBEARS
FOLIOS	FONTANEL	FOOTMAN	FORAGERS	FOREBITT
FOLIOSE	FONTANELS	FOOTMARK	FORAGES	FOREBITTS
FOLIUM	FONTANGE	FOOTMARKS	FORAGING	FOREBODE
FOLK	FONTANGES	FOOTMEN	FORAMEN	FOREBODED
FOLKLAND	FONTLET	FOOTMUFF	FORAMINA	FOREBODER
FOLKLANDS	FONTLETS	FOOTMUFFS	FORAMINAL	FOREBODERS
FOLKLORE	FONTS	FOOTNOTE	FORANE	FOREBODES
FOLKLORES	FOOD	FOOTNOTES	FORASMUCH	FOREBODING
FOLKLORIC	FOODED	FOOTPACE	FORAY	FOREBODINGS
FOLKMOOT	FOODFUL	FOOTPACES	FORAYED	FOREBY
FOLKMOOTS	FOODIE	FOOTPAD	FORAYER	FORECABIN
FOLKROCK	FOODIES	FOOTPADS	FORAYERS	FORECABINS
FOLKROCKS	FOODING	FOOTPAGE	FORAYING	FORECAR
FOLKS	FOODLESS	FOOTPAGES	FORAYS	FORECARS
FOLKSIER	FOODS	FOOTPATH	FORBAD	FORECAST
FOLKSIEST	FOODSTUFF	FOOTPATHS	FORBADE	FORECASTED
FOLKSY	FOODSTUFFS	FOOTPLATE	FORBEAR	FORECASTING
FOLKWAY	FOOL	FOOTPLATES	FORBEARING	FORECASTS
FOLKWAYS	FOOLED	FOOTPOST	FORBEARS	FORECLOSE
FOLLICLE	FOOLERIES	FOOTPOSTS	FORBID	FORECLOSED
FOLLICLES	FOOLERY	FOOTPRINT	FORBIDDAL	FORECLOSES
FOLLIED	FOOLHARDY	FOOTPRINTS	FORBIDDALS	FORECLOSING
FOLLIES	FOOLING	FOOTRA	FORBIDDEN	FORECLOTH
FOLLOW	FOOLINGS	FOOTRAS	FORBIDDER	FORECLOTHS
FOLLOWED	FOOLISH	FOOTREST	FORBIDDERS	FORECOURT
FOLLOWER	FOOLISHER	FOOTRESTS	FORBIDDING	FORECOURTS
FOLLOWERS	FOOLISHEST	FOOTROT	FORBIDDINGS	FOREDATE
FOLLOWING	FOOLISHLY	FOOTROTS	FORBIDS	FOREDATED

FOREDATES	FORELOCK	FORESHOCK	FORETHINKS	FORGERS
FOREDATING	FORELOCKS	FORESHOCKS	FORETHOUGHT	FORGERY
FOREDECK	FORELS	FORESHORE	FORETIME	FORGES
FOREDECKS	FORELYING	FORESHORES	FORETIMES	FORGET
FOREDOOM	FOREMAN	FORESHOW	FORETOKEN	FORGETFUL
FOREDOOMED	FOREMAST	FORESHOWED	FORETOKENED	FORGETIVE
FOREDOOMING	FOREMASTS	FORESHOWING	FORETOKENING	FORGETS
FOREDOOMS	FOREMEAN	FORESHOWN	FORETOKENINGS	FORGETTER
FOREFEEL	FOREMEANING	FORESHOWS	FORETOKENS	FORGETTERS
FOREFEELING	FOREMEANS	FORESIDE	FORETOLD	FORGETTING
FOREFEELS	FOREMEANT	FORESIDES	FORETOOTH	FORGETTINGS
FOREFEET	FOREMEN	FORESIGHT	FORETOP	FORGING
FOREFELT	FOREMOST	FORESIGHTS	FORETOPS	FORGINGS
FOREFOOT	FORENAME	FORESKIN	FOREVER	FORGIVE
FOREFRONT	FORENAMED	FORESKINS	FOREVERS	FORGIVEN
FOREFRONTS	FORENAMES	FORESKIRT	FOREWARD	FORGIVES
FOREGLEAM	FORENIGHT	FORESKIRTS	FOREWARDS	FORGIVING
FOREGLEAMS	FORENIGHTS	FORESLACK	FOREWARN	FORGO
FOREGO	FORENOON	FORESLACKED	FOREWARNED	FORGOES
FOREGOER	FORENOONS	FORESLACKING	FOREWARNING	FORGOING
FOREGOERS	FORENSIC	FORESLACKS	FOREWARNINGS	FORGONE
FOREGOES	FORENSICS	FORESLOW	FOREWARNS	FORGOT
FOREGOING	FOREPART	FORESLOWED	FOREWEIGH	FORGOTTEN
FOREGOINGS	FOREPARTS	FORESLOWING	FOREWEIGHED	FORHAILE
FOREGONE	FOREPAST	FORESLOWS	FOREWEIGHING	FORHAILED
FOREGUT	FOREPAW	FORESPEAK	FOREWEIGHS	FORHAILES
FOREGUTS	FOREPAWS	FORESPEAKING	FOREWENT	FORHAILING
FOREHAND	FOREPEAK	FORESPEAKS	FOREWIND	FORHENT
FOREHANDS	FOREPEAKS	FORESPEND	FOREWINDS	FORHENTED
FOREHEAD	FOREPLAN	FORESPENDING	FOREWING	FORHENTING
FOREHEADS	FOREPLANNED	FORESPENDS	FOREWINGS	FORHENTS
FOREHENT	FOREPLANNING	FORESPENT	FOREWOMAN	FORHOO
FOREHENTED	FOREPLANS	FORESPOKE	FOREWOMEN	FORHOOED
FOREHENTING	FOREPLAY	FORESPOKEN	FOREWORD	FORHOOIE
FOREHENTS	FOREPLAYS	FOREST	FOREWORDS	FORHOOIED
FOREIGN	FOREPOINT	FORESTAGE	FORFAIR	FORHOOIEING
FOREIGNER	FOREPOINTED	FORESTAGES	FORFAIRED	FORHOOIES
FOREIGNERS	FOREPOINTING	FORESTAIR	FORFAIRING	FORHOOING
FOREJUDGE	FOREPOINTS	FORESTAIRS	FORFAIRN	FORHOOS
FOREJUDGED	FORERAN	FORESTAL	FORFAIRS	FORHOW
FOREJUDGES	FOREREACH	FORESTALL	FORFAULT	FORHOWED
FOREJUDGING	FOREREACHED	FORESTALLED	FORFAULTED	FORHOWING
FOREKING	FOREREACHES	FORESTALLING	FORFAULTING	FORHOWS
FOREKINGS	FOREREACHING	FORESTALLINGS	FORFAULTS	FORINSEC
FOREKNEW	FOREREAD	FORESTALLS	FORFEIT	FORINT
FOREKNOW	FOREREADING	FORESTAY	FORFEITED	FORINTS
FOREKNOWING	FOREREADINGS	FORESTAYS	FORFEITER	FORJASKIT
FOREKNOWN	FOREREADS	FORESTEAL	FORFEITERS	FORJESKIT
FOREKNOWS	FORERUN	FORESTED	FORFEITING	FORJUDGE
FOREL	FORERUNNING	FORESTER	FORFEITS	FORJUDGED
FORELAID	FORERUNS	FORESTERS	FORFEND	FORJUDGES
FORELAND	FORES	FORESTINE	FORFENDED	FORJUDGING
FORELANDS	FORESAID	FORESTING	FORFENDING	FORK
FORELAY	FORESAIL	FORESTRIES	FORFENDS	FORKED
FORELAYING	FORESAILS	FORESTRY	FORFEX	FORKEDLY
FORELAYS	FORESAW	FORESTS	FORFEXES	FORKER
FORELEG	FORESAY	FORETASTE	FORFICATE	FORKERS
FORELEGS	FORESAYING	FORETASTED	FORGAT	FORKHEAD
FORELEND	FORESAYS	FORETASTES	FORGATHER	FORKHEADS
FORELENDING	FORESEE	FORETASTING	FORGATHERED	FORKIER
FORELENDS	FORESEEING	FORETAUGHT	FORGATHERING	FORKIEST
FORELENT	FORESEEN	FORETEACH	FORGATHERS	FORKINESS
FORELIE	FORESEES	FORETEACHES	FORGAVE	FORKINESSES
FORELIES	FORESHEW	FORETEACHING	FORGE	FORKING
FORELIFT	FORESHEWED	FORETEETH	FORGEABLE	FORKS
FORELIFTED	FORESHEWING	FORETELL	FORGED	FORKTAIL
FORELIFTING	FORESHEWN	FORETELLING	FORGEMAN	FORKTAILS
FORELIFTS	FORESHEWS	FORETELLS	FORGEMEN	FORKY
FORELIMB	FORESHIP	FORETHINK	FORGER	FORLANA
FORELIMBS	FORESHIPS	FORETHINKING	FORGERIES	FORLANAS

FORLEND	FORMULAE	FORSOOK	FORTUNED	FOSSILS
FORLENDING	FORMULAIC	FORSOOTH	FORTUNES	FOSSOR
FORLENDS	FORMULAR	FORSPEAK	FORTUNING	FOSSORIAL
FORLENT	FORMULARIES	FORSPEAKING	FORTUNIZE	FOSSORS
FORLESE	FORMULARY	FORSPEAKS	FORTUNIZED	FOSSULA
FORLESED	FORMULAS	FORSPEND	FORTUNIZES	FOSSULAS
FORLESES	FORMULATE	FORSPENDING	FORTUNIZING	FOSSULATE
FORLESING	FORMULATED	FORSPENDS	FORTY	FOSTER
FORLORE	FORMULATES	FORSPENT	FORTYISH	FOSTERAGE
FORLORN	FORMULATING	FORSPOKE	FORUM	FOSTERAGES
FORLORNER	FORMULISE	FORSPOKEN	FORUMS	FOSTERED
FORLORNEST	FORMULISED	FORSWATT	FORWANDER	FOSTERER
FORLORNLY	FORMULISES	FORSWEAR	FORWANDERED	FOSTERERS
FORLORNS	FORMULISING	FORSWEARING	FORWANDERING	FOSTERING
FORM	FORMULISM	FORSWEARS	FORWANDERS	FOSTERINGS
FORMABLE	FORMULISMS	FORSWINK	FORWARD	FOSTERS
FORMAL	FORMULIST	FORSWINKED	FORWARDED	FOSTRESS
FORMALIN	FORMULISTS	FORSWINKING	FORWARDER	FOSTRESSES
FORMALINS	FORMULIZE	FORSWINKS	FORWARDERS	FOTHER
FORMALISE	FORMULIZED	FORSWONCK	FORWARDEST	FOTHERED
FORMALISED	FORMULIZES	FORSWORE	FORWARDING	FOTHERING
FORMALISES	FORMULIZING	FORSWORN	FORWARDINGS	FOTHERS
FORMALISING	FORMWORK	FORSWUNK	FORWARDLY	FOU
FORMALISM	FORMWORKS	FORSYTHIA	FORWARDS	FOUAT
FORMALISMS	FORNENST	FORSYTHIAS	FORWARN	FOUATS
FORMALIST	FORNENT	FORT	FORWARNED	FOUD
FORMALISTS	FORNICAL	FORTALICE	FORWARNING	FOUDRIE
FORMALITIES	FORNICATE	FORTALICES	FORWARNS	FOUDRIES
FORMALITY	FORNICATED	FORTE	FORWASTE	FOUDS
FORMALIZE	FORNICATES	FORTED	FORWASTED	FOUER
FORMALIZED	FORNICATING	FORTES	FORWASTES	FOUEST
FORMALIZES	FORNIX	FORTH	FORWASTING	FOUET
FORMALIZING	FORNIXES	FORTHCAME	FORWEARIED	FOUETS
FORMALLY	FORPET	FORTHCOME	FORWEARIES	FOUETTÉ
FORMANT	FORPETS	FORTHCOMES	FORWEARY	FOUETTÉS
FORMANTS	FORPINE	FORTHCOMING	FORWEARYING	FOUGADE
FORMAT	FORPINED	FORTHINK	FORWENT	FOUGADES
FORMATE	FORPINES	FORTHINKING	FORWHY	FOUGASSE
FORMATED	FORPINING	FORTHINKS	FORWORN	FOUGASSES
FORMATES	FORPIT	FORTHOUGHT	FORZANDI	FOUGHT
FORMATING	FORPITS	FORTHWITH	FORZANDO	FOUGHTEN
FORMATION	FORRAD	FORTHY	FORZANDOS	FOUGHTY
FORMATIONS	FORRADEN	FORTIES	FORZATI	FOUL
FORMATIVE	FORRAY	FORTIETH	FORZATO	FOULARD
FORMATIVES	FORRAYED	FORTIETHS	FORZATOS	FOULARDS
FORMATS	FORRAYING	FORTIFIED	FOSS	FOULDER
FORMATTED	FORRAYS	FORTIFIER	FOSSA	FOULDERED
FORMATTER	FORREN	FORTIFIERS	FOSSAE	FOULDERING
FORMATTERS	FORRIT	FORTIFIES	FOSSAS	FOULDERS
FORMATTING	FORSAID	FORTIFY	FOSSE	FOULE
FORME	FORSAKE	FORTIFYING	FOSSED	FOULED
FORMED	FORSAKEN	FORTILAGE	FOSSES	FOULER
FORMER	FORSAKES	FORTILAGES	FOSSETTE	FOULÉS
FORMERLY	FORSAKING	FORTING	FOSSETTES	FOULEST
FORMERS	FORSAKINGS	FORTIS	FOSSICK	FOULING
FORMES	FORSAY	FORTITUDE	FOSSICKED	FOULLY
FORMIATE	FORSAYING	FORTITUDES	FOSSICKER	FOULMART
FORMIATES	FORSAYS	FORTLET	FOSSICKERS	FOULMARTS
FORMIC	FORSLACK	FORTLETS	FOSSICKING	FOULNESS
FORMICANT	FORSLACKED	FORTNIGHT	FOSSICKINGS	FOULNESSES
FORMICARIES	FORSLACKING	FORTNIGHTS	FOSSICKS	FOULS
FORMICARY	FORSLACKS	FORTRESS	FOSSIL	FOUMART
FORMICATE	FORSLOE	FORTRESSED	FOSSILISE	FOUMARTS
FORMING	FORSLOED	FORTRESSES	FOSSILISED	FOUND
FORMINGS	FORSLOEING	FORTRESSING	FOSSILISES	FOUNDED
FORMLESS	FORSLOES	FORTS	FOSSILISING	FOUNDER
FORMOL	FORSLOW	FORTUITIES	FOSSILIZE	FOUNDERED
FORMOLS	FORSLOWED	FORTUITY	FOSSILIZED	FOUNDERING
FORMS	FORSLOWING	FORTUNATE	FOSSILIZES	FOUNDERS
FORMULA	FORSLOWS	FORTUNE	FOSSILIZING	FOUNDING

FOUNDINGS	FOXHOUND	FRAGRANCED	FRAPPED	FREE
FOUNDLING	FOXHOUNDS	FRAGRANCES	FRAPPÉE	FREEBEE
FOUNDLINGS	FOXIER	FRAGRANCIES	FRAPPING	FREEBEES
FOUNDRESS	FOXIEST	FRAGRANCING	FRAPS	FREEBIE
FOUNDRESSES	FOXINESS	FRAGRANCY	FRAS	FREEBIES
FOUNDRIES	FOXINESSES	FRAGRANT	FRASS	FREEBOOTIES
FOUNDRY	FOXING	FRAÎCHEUR	FRASSES	FREEBOOTY
FOUNDS	FOXINGS	FRAÎCHEURS	FRATCH	FREEBORN
FOUNT	FOXSHARK	FRAIL	FRATCHES	FREED
FOUNTAIN	FOXSHARKS	FRAILER	FRATCHETY	FREEDMAN
FOUNTAINED	FOXSHIP	FRAILEST	FRATCHING	FREEDMEN
FOUNTAINING	FOXSHIPS	FRAILISH	FRATCHY	FREEDOM
FOUNTAINS	FOXTROT	FRAILLY	FRATE	FREEDOMS
FOUNTFUL	FOXTROTS	FRAILNESS	FRATER	FREEHOLD
FOUNTS	FOXTROTTED	FRAILNESSES	FRATERIES	FREEHOLDS
FOUR	FOXTROTTING	FRAILS	FRATERNAL	FREEING
FOURFOLD	FOXY	FRAILTEE	FRATERS	FREELOAD
FOURGON	FOY	FRAILTEES	FRATERY	FREELOADED
FOURGONS	FOYER	FRAILTIES	FRATI	FREELOADING
FOURPENCE	FOYERS	FRAILTY	FRATRIES	FREELOADINGS
FOURPENCES	FOYLE	FRAIM	FRATRY	FREELOADS
FOURPENNIES	FOYLED	FRAIMS	FRAU	FREELY
FOURPENNY	FOYLES	FRAISE	FRAUD	FREEMAN
FOURS	FOYLING	FRAISED	FRAUDFUL	FREEMASON
FOURSCORE	FOYNE	FRAISES	FRAUDS	FREEMASONS
FOURSES	FOYNED	FRAISING	FRAUDSMAN	FREEMEN
FOURSOME	FOYNES	FRAME	FRAUDSMEN	FREENESS
FOURSOMES	FOYNING	FRAMED	FRAUDSTER	FREENESSES
FOURTEEN	FOYS	FRAMER	FRAUDSTERS	FREER
FOURTEENS	FOZIER	FRAMERS	FRAUGHT	FREERS
FOURTH	FOZIEST	FRAMES	FRAUGHTED	FREES
FOURTHLY	FOZINESS	FRAMEWORK	FRAUGHTER	FREESHEET
FOURTHS	FOZINESSES	FRAMEWORKS	FRAUGHTEST	FREESHEETS
FOUS	FOZY	FRAMING	FRAUGHTING	FREESIA
FOUSSA	FRA	FRAMINGS	FRAUGHTS	FREESIAS
FOUSSAS	FRAB	FRAMPAL	FRÄULEIN	FREEST
FOUTER	FRABBED	FRAMPLER	FRÄULEINS	FREESTONE
FOUTERS	FRABBING	FRAMPLERS	FRAUS	FREESTONES
FOUTH	FRABBIT	FRAMPOLD	FRAUTAGE	FREESTYLE
FOUTHS	FRABJOUS	FRANC	FRAUTAGES	FREESTYLES
FOUTRA	FRABS	FRANCHISE	FRAY	FREET
FOUTRAS	FRACAS	FRANCHISED	FRAYED	FREETIER
FOUTRE	FRACK	FRANCHISES	FRAYING	FREETIEST
FOUTRES	FRACT	FRANCHISING	FRAYINGS	FREETS
FOVEA	FRACTED	FRANCIUM	FRAYS	FREETY
FOVEAE	FRACTING	FRANCIUMS	FRAZIL	FREEWAY
FOVEAL	FRACTION	FRANCO	FRAZILS	FREEWAYS
FOVEATE	FRACTIONS	FRANCOLIN	FRAZZLE	FREEWOMAN
FOVEOLA	FRACTIOUS	FRANCOLINS	FRAZZLED	FREEWOMEN
FOVEOLAS	FRACTS	FRANCS	FRAZZLES	FREEZABLE
FOVEOLE	FRACTURE	FRANGIBLE	FRAZZLING	FREEZE
FOVEOLES	FRACTURED	FRANION	FREAK	FREEZER
FOWL	FRACTURES	FRANIONS	FREAKED	FREEZERS
FOWLED	FRACTURING	FRANK	FREAKFUL	FREEZES
FOWLER	FRAE	FRANKED	FREAKIER	FREEZING
FOWLERS	FRAENA	FRANKER	FREAKIEST	FREEZINGS
FOWLING	FRAENUM	FRANKEST	FREAKING	FREIGHT
FOWLINGS	FRAGILE	FRANKING	FREAKISH	FREIGHTED
FOWLS	FRAGILELY	FRANKLIN	FREAKS	FREIGHTER
FOWTH	FRAGILER	FRANKLINS	FREAKY	FREIGHTERS
FOWTHS	FRAGILEST	FRANKLY	FRECKLE	FREIGHTING
FOX	FRAGILITIES	FRANKNESS	FRECKLED	FREIGHTS
FOXBERRIES	FRAGILITY	FRANKNESSES	FRECKLES	FREIT
FOXBERRY	FRAGMENT	FRANKS	FRECKLIER	FREITIER
FOXED	FRAGMENTED	FRANTIC	FRECKLIEST	FREITIEST
FOXES	FRAGMENTING	FRANTICLY	FRECKLING	FREITS
FOXGLOVE	FRAGMENTS	FRANZY	FRECKLINGS	FREITY
FOXGLOVES	FRAGOR	FRAP	FRECKLY	FREMD
FOXHOLE	FRAGORS	FRAPPANT	FREDAINE	FREMDS
FOXHOLES	FRAGRANCE	FRAPPÉ	FREDAINES	FREMIT

FREMITS
FREMITUS
FREMITUSES
FRENA
FRENCH
FRENETIC
FRENETICS
FRENNE
FRENNES
FRENUM
FRENZICAL
FRENZIED
FRENZIES
FRENZY
FRENZYING
FREON
FREONS
FREQUENCE
FREQUENCES
FREQUENCIES
FREQUENCY
FREQUENT
FREQUENTED
FREQUENTER
FREQUENTEST
FREQUENTING
FREQUENTS
FRÈRE
FRÈRES
FRESCADE
FRESCADES
FRESCO
FRESCOED
FRESCOER
FRESCOERS
FRESCOES
FRESCOING
FRESCOINGS
FRESCOIST
FRESCOISTS
FRESCOS
FRESH
FRESHED
FRESHEN
FRESHENED
FRESHENER
FRESHENERS
FRESHENING
FRESHENS
FRESHER
FRESHERS
FRESHES
FRESHEST
FRESHET
FRESHETS
FRESHING
FRESHISH
FRESHLY
FRESHMAN
FRESHMEN
FRESHNESS
FRESHNESSES
FRET
FRETFUL
FRETFULLY
FRETS
FRETSAW
FRETSAWS
FRETTED
FRETTIER

FRETTIEST
FRETTING
FRETTINGS
FRETTY
FRETWORK
FRETWORKS
FRIABLE
FRIAND
FRIANDE
FRIANDES
FRIANDS
FRIAR
FRIARBIRD
FRIARBIRDS
FRIARIES
FRIARLY
FRIARS
FRIARY
FRIBBLE
FRIBBLED
FRIBBLER
FRIBBLERS
FRIBBLES
FRIBBLING
FRIBBLISH
FRICADEL
FRICADELS
FRICASSEE
FRICASSEED
FRICASSEEING
FRICASSEES
FRICATIVE
FRICATIVES
FRICHT
FRICHTED
FRICHTING
FRICHTS
FRICTION
FRICTIONS
FRIDGE
FRIDGED
FRIDGES
FRIDGING
FRIED
FRIEDCAKE
FRIEDCAKES
FRIEND
FRIENDED
FRIENDING
FRIENDINGS
FRIENDLIER
FRIENDLIES
FRIENDLIEST
FRIENDLY
FRIENDS
FRIER
FRIERS
FRIES
FRIEZE
FRIEZED
FRIEZES
FRIEZING
FRIG
FRIGATE
FRIGATES
FRIGATOON
FRIGATOONS
FRIGES
FRIGGED
FRIGGER

FRIGGERS
FRIGGING
FRIGGINGS
FRIGHT
FRIGHTED
FRIGHTEN
FRIGHTENED
FRIGHTENING
FRIGHTENS
FRIGHTFUL
FRIGHTING
FRIGHTS
FRIGID
FRIGIDER
FRIGIDEST
FRIGIDITIES
FRIGIDITY
FRIGIDLY
FRIGOT
FRIGOTS
FRIGS
FRIJOL
FRIJOLE
FRIJOLES
FRIKKADEL
FRIKKADELS
FRILL
FRILLED
FRILLIER
FRILLIES
FRILLIEST
FRILLING
FRILLINGS
FRILLS
FRILLY
FRINGE
FRINGED
FRINGES
FRINGIER
FRINGIEST
FRINGING
FRINGY
FRIPON
FRIPONS
FRIPPER
FRIPPERER
FRIPPERERS
FRIPPERIES
FRIPPERS
FRIPPERY
FRIS
FRISES
FRISETTE
FRISETTES
FRISEUR
FRISEURS
FRISK
FRISKA
FRISKAS
FRISKED
FRISKER
FRISKERS
FRISKET
FRISKETS
FRISKFUL
FRISKIER
FRISKIEST
FRISKILY
FRISKING
FRISKINGS

FRISKS
FRISKY
FRISSON
FRISSONS
FRIST
FRISTED
FRISTING
FRISTS
FRISURE
FRISURES
FRIT
FRITFLIES
FRITFLY
FRITH
FRITHBORH
FRITHBORHS
FRITHGILD
FRITHGILDS
FRITHS
FRITS
FRITTED
FRITTER
FRITTERED
FRITTERER
FRITTERERS
FRITTERING
FRITTERS
FRITTING
FRITURE
FRITURES
FRIVOL
FRIVOLITIES
FRIVOLITY
FRIVOLLED
FRIVOLLING
FRIVOLOUS
FRIVOLS
FRIZ
FRIZE
FRIZES
FRIZING
FRIZZ
FRIZZANTE
FRIZZED
FRIZZES
FRIZZIER
FRIZZIEST
FRIZZING
FRIZZLE
FRIZZLED
FRIZZLES
FRIZZLIER
FRIZZLIEST
FRIZZLING
FRIZZLY
FRIZZY
FRO
FROCK
FROCKED
FROCKING
FROCKINGS
FROCKLESS
FROCKS
FROG
FROGBIT
FROGBITS
FROGGED
FROGGERIES
FROGGERY
FROGGIER

FROGGIEST
FROGGING
FROGGINGS
FROGGY
FROGLET
FROGLETS
FROGLING
FROGLINGS
FROGMAN
FROGMEN
FROGMOUTH
FROGMOUTHS
FROGS
FROISE
FROISES
FROLIC
FROLICKED
FROLICKING
FROLICS
FROM
FROMENTIES
FROMENTY
FROND
FRONDAGE
FRONDAGES
FRONDED
FRONDENT
FRONDEUR
FRONDEURS
FRONDOSE
FRONDS
FRONT
FRONTAGE
FRONTAGER
FRONTAGERS
FRONTAGES
FRONTAL
FRONTALS
FRONTED
FRONTIER
FRONTIERED
FRONTIERING
FRONTIERS
FRONTING
FRONTLESS
FRONTLET
FRONTLETS
FRONTMAN
FRONTMEN
FRONTON
FRONTONS
FRONTOON
FRONTOONS
FRONTS
FRONTWARD
FRONTWAYS
FRONTWISE
FRORE
FROREN
FRORN
FRORNE
FRORY
FROST
FROSTBIT
FROSTBITE
FROSTBITES
FROSTBITING
FROSTBITTEN
FROSTED
FROSTIER

FROSTIEST
FROSTILY
FROSTING
FROSTINGS
FROSTLESS
FROSTS
FROSTWORK
FROSTWORKS
FROSTY
FROTH
FROTHED
FROTHERIES
FROTHERY
FROTHIER
FROTHIEST
FROTHILY
FROTHING
FROTHLESS
FROTHS
FROTHY
FROTTAGE
FROTTAGES
FROTTEUR
FROTTEURS
FROUGHY
FROUNCE
FROUNCED
FROUNCES
FROUNCING
FROW
FROWARD
FROWARDLY
FROWARDS
FROWIE
FROWN
FROWNED
FROWNING
FROWNS
FROWS
FROWST
FROWSTED
FROWSTER
FROWSTERS
FROWSTIER
FROWSTIEST
FROWSTING
FROWSTS
FROWSTY
FROWSY
FROWY
FROWZY
FROZE
FROZEN
FRUCTED
FRUCTIFIED
FRUCTIFIES
FRUCTIFY
FRUCTIFYING
FRUCTOSE
FRUCTOSES
FRUCTUARIES
FRUCTUARY
FRUCTUATE
FRUCTUATED
FRUCTUATES
FRUCTUATING
FRUCTUOUS
FRUGAL
FRUGALIST
FRUGALISTS

FRUGALITIES
FRUGALITY
FRUGALLY
FRUICT
FRUICTED
FRUICTING
FRUICTS
FRUIT
FRUITAGE
FRUITAGES
FRUITED
FRUITER
FRUITERER
FRUITERERS
FRUITERIES
FRUITERS
FRUITERY
FRUITFUL
FRUITIER
FRUITIEST
FRUITING
FRUITINGS
FRUITION
FRUITIONS
FRUITIVE
FRUITLESS
FRUITLET
FRUITLETS
FRUITS
FRUITWOOD
FRUITWOODS
FRUITY
FRUMENTIES
FRUMENTY
FRUMP
FRUMPED
FRUMPIER
FRUMPIEST
FRUMPING
FRUMPISH
FRUMPLE
FRUMPLED
FRUMPLES
FRUMPLING
FRUMPS
FRUMPY
FRUSH
FRUSHED
FRUSHES
FRUSHING
FRUST
FRUSTA
FRUSTRATE
FRUSTRATED
FRUSTRATES
FRUSTRATING
FRUSTS
FRUSTULE
FRUSTULES
FRUSTUM
FRUSTUMS
FRUTEX
FRUTICES
FRUTICOSE
FRUTIFIED
FRUTIFIES
FRUTIFY
FRUTIFYING
FRY
FRYER

FRYERS
FRYING
FRYINGS
FUB
FUBBED
FUBBERIES
FUBBERY
FUBBING
FUBBY
FUBS
FUBSY
FUCHSIA
FUCHSIAS
FUCHSINE
FUCHSINES
FUCHSITE
FUCHSITES
FUCI
FUCK
FUCKED
FUCKER
FUCKERS
FUCKING
FUCKINGS
FUCKS
FUCOID
FUCOIDAL
FUCOIDS
FUCUS
FUCUSED
FUCUSES
FUD
FUDDLE
FUDDLED
FUDDLER
FUDDLERS
FUDDLES
FUDDLING
FUDDLINGS
FUDGE
FUDGED
FUDGES
FUDGING
FUDS
FUEL
FUELLED
FUELLER
FUELLERS
FUELLING
FUELS
FUERO
FUEROS
FUFF
FUFFED
FUFFIER
FUFFIEST
FUFFING
FUFFS
FUFFY
FUG
FUGACIOUS
FUGACITIES
FUGACITY
FUGAL
FUGALLY
FUGATO
FUGATOS
FUGGED
FUGGIER
FUGGIEST

FUGGING
FUGGY
FUGHETTA
FUGHETTAS
FUGIE
FUGIES
FUGITIVE
FUGITIVES
FUGLE
FUGLED
FUGLEMAN
FUGLEMEN
FUGLES
FUGLING
FUGS
FUGUE
FUGUES
FUGUIST
FUGUISTS
FULCRA
FULCRATE
FULCRUM
FULCRUMS
FULFIL
FULFILLED
FULFILLER
FULFILLERS
FULFILLING
FULFILLINGS
FULFILS
FULGENCIES
FULGENCY
FULGENT
FULGENTLY
FULGID
FULGIDER
FULGIDEST
FULGOR
FULGOROUS
FULGORS
FULGOUR
FULGOURS
FULGURAL
FULGURANT
FULGURATE
FULGURATED
FULGURATES
FULGURATING
FULGURITE
FULGURITES
FULGUROUS
FULHAM
FULHAMS
FULL
FULLAGE
FULLAGES
FULLAM
FULLAMS
FULLAN
FULLANS
FULLED
FULLER
FULLERS
FULLEST
FULLING
FULLISH
FULLNESS
FULLNESSES
FULLS
FULLY

FULMAR
FULMARS
FULMINANT
FULMINANTS
FULMINATE
FULMINATED
FULMINATES
FULMINATING
FULMINE
FULMINED
FULMINES
FULMINING
FULMINOUS
FULNESS
FULNESSES
FULSOME
FULSOMELY
FULSOMER
FULSOMEST
FULVID
FULVIDER
FULVIDEST
FULVOUS
FUM
FUMADO
FUMADOES
FUMADOS
FUMAGE
FUMAGES
FUMAROLE
FUMAROLES
FUMATORIA
FUMATORIES
FUMATORY
FUMBLE
FUMBLED
FUMBLER
FUMBLERS
FUMBLES
FUMBLING
FUME
FUMED
FUMEROLE
FUMEROLES
FUMES
FUMET
FUMETS
FUMETTE
FUMETTES
FUMETTI
FUMETTO
FUMIER
FUMIEST
FUMIGANT
FUMIGANTS
FUMIGATE
FUMIGATED
FUMIGATES
FUMIGATING
FUMIGATOR
FUMIGATORS
FUMING
FUMITORIES
FUMITORY
FUMOSITIES
FUMOSITY
FUMOUS
FUMS
FUMY
FUN

FUNCTION
FUNCTIONED
FUNCTIONING
FUNCTIONS
FUND
FUNDABLE
FUNDAMENT
FUNDAMENTS
FUNDED
FUNDER
FUNDERS
FUNDI
FUNDING
FUNDINGS
FUNDIS
FUNDLESS
FUNDS
FUNDUS
FUNEBRAL
FUNÈBRE
FUNEBRIAL
FUNERAL
FUNERALS
FUNERARY
FUNEREAL
FUNEST
FUNFAIR
FUNFAIRS
FUNG
FUNGAL
FUNGI
FUNGIBLES
FUNGICIDE
FUNGICIDES
FUNGIFORM
FUNGOID
FUNGOIDAL
FUNGOSITIES
FUNGOSITY
FUNGOUS
FUNGS
FUNGUS
FUNGUSES
FUNICLE
FUNICLES
FUNICULAR
FUNICULI
FUNICULUS
FUNK
FUNKED
FUNKHOLE
FUNKHOLES
FUNKIA
FUNKIAS
FUNKIER
FUNKIEST
FUNKINESS
FUNKINESSES
FUNKING
FUNKS
FUNKY
FUNNED
FUNNEL
FUNNELLED
FUNNELLING
FUNNELS
FUNNIER
FUNNIES

FUNNIEST
FUNNILY
FUNNINESS
FUNNINESSES
FUNNING
FUNNY
FUNS
FUR
FURACIOUS
FURACITIES
FURACITY
FURAL
FURALS
FURAN
FURANE
FURANES
FURANS
FURBELOW
FURBELOWED
FURBELOWING
FURBELOWS
FURBISH
FURBISHED
FURBISHER
FURBISHERS
FURBISHES
FURBISHING
FURCAL
FURCATE
FURCATED
FURCATION
FURCATIONS
FURCULA
FURCULAR
FURCULAS
FURDER
FUREUR
FUREURS
FURFAIR
FURFAIRS
FURFUR
FURFURAL
FURFURALS
FURFURAN
FURFURANS
FURFUROL
FURFUROLE
FURFUROLES
FURFUROLS
FURFUROUS
FURFURS
FURIBUND
FURIES
FURIOSITIES
FURIOSITY
FURIOSO
FURIOSOS
FURIOUS
FURIOUSLY
FURL
FURLANA
FURLANAS
FURLED
FURLING
FURLONG
FURLONGS
FURLOUGH
FURLOUGHED

FURLOUGHING
FURLOUGHS
FURLS
FURMENTIES
FURMENTY
FURMETIES
FURMETY
FURMITIES
FURMITY
FURNACE
FURNACED
FURNACES
FURNACING
FURNIMENT
FURNIMENTS
FURNISH
FURNISHED
FURNISHER
FURNISHERS
FURNISHES
FURNISHING
FURNISHINGS
FURNITURE
FURNITURES
FUROL
FUROLE
FUROLES
FUROLS
FUROR
FURORE
FURORES
FURORS
FURPHIES
FURPHY
FURR
FURRED
FURRIER
FURRIERIES
FURRIERS
FURRIERY
FURRIEST
FURRING
FURRINGS
FURROW
FURROWED
FURROWING
FURROWS
FURROWY
FURRS
FURRY
FURS
FURTH
FURTHER
FURTHERED
FURTHERER
FURTHERERS
FURTHERING
FURTHERS
FURTHEST
FURTIVE
FURTIVELY
FURTIVER
FURTIVEST
FURUNCLE
FURUNCLES
FURY
FURZE
FURZES

FURZIER
FURZIEST
FURZY
FUSAIN
FUSAINS
FUSAROL
FUSAROLE
FUSAROLES
FUSAROLS
FUSC
FUSCOUS
FUSE
FUSED
FUSEE
FUSEES
FUSELAGE
FUSELAGES
FUSES
FUSHION
FUSHIONS
FUSIBLE
FUSIFORM
FUSIL
FUSILE
FUSILEER
FUSILEERS
FUSILIER
FUSILIERS
FUSILLADE
FUSILLADES
FUSILS
FUSING
FUSION
FUSIONISM
FUSIONISMS
FUSIONIST
FUSIONISTS
FUSIONS
FUSS
FUSSED
FUSSER
FUSSERS
FUSSES
FUSSIER
FUSSIEST
FUSSILY
FUSSINESS
FUSSINESSES
FUSSING
FUSSY
FUST
FUSTED
FUSTET
FUSTETS
FUSTIAN
FUSTIANS
FUSTIC
FUSTICS
FUSTIER
FUSTIEST
FUSTIGATE
FUSTIGATED
FUSTIGATES
FUSTIGATING
FUSTILUGS
FUSTILY
FUSTINESS
FUSTINESSES

FUSTING
FUSTOC
FUSTOCS
FUSTS
FUSTY
FUTCHEL
FUTCHELS
FUTHARK
FUTHARKS
FUTHORC
FUTHORCS
FUTHORK
FUTHORKS
FUTILE
FUTILELY
FUTILER
FUTILEST
FUTILITIES
FUTILITY
FUTON
FUTONS
FUTTOCK
FUTTOCKS
FUTURE
FUTURES
FUTURISM
FUTURISMS
FUTURIST
FUTURISTS
FUTURITIES
FUTURITY
FUZE
FUZEE
FUZEES
FUZES
FUZZ
FUZZED
FUZZES
FUZZIER
FUZZIEST
FUZZILY
FUZZINESS
FUZZINESSES
FUZZING
FUZZLE
FUZZLED
FUZZLES
FUZZLING
FUZZY
FY
FYKE
FYKED
FYKES
FYKING
FYLE
FYLES
FYLFOT
FYLFOTS
FYNBOS
FYNBOSES
FYRD
FYRDS
FYTTE
FYTTES

G

GAB
GABARDINE
GABARDINES
GABBARD
GABBARDS
GABBART
GABBARTS
GABBED
GABBER
GABBERS
GABBIER
GABBIEST
GABBING
GABBLE
GABBLED
GABBLER
GABBLERS
GABBLES
GABBLING
GABBLINGS
GABBRO
GABBROIC
GABBROID
GABBROS
GABBY
GABELLE
GABELLER
GABELLERS
GABELLES
GABERDINE
GABERDINES
GABFEST
GABFESTS
GABIES
GABION
GABIONADE
GABIONADES
GABIONAGE
GABIONED
GABIONS
GABLE
GABLED
GABLES
GABLET
GABLETS
GABNASH
GABNASHES
GABS
GABY
GAD
GADABOUT
GADABOUTS
GADDED
GADDER
GADDERS
GADDING
GADE
GADES
GADFLIES
GADFLY
GADGE
GADGES
GADGET
GADGETEER

GADGETEERS
GADGETRIES
GADGETRY
GADGETS
GADGIE
GADGIES
GADI
GADIS
GADJE
GADJES
GADLING
GADLINGS
GADOID
GADOIDS
GADROON
GADROONED
GADROONS
GADS
GADSMAN
GADSMEN
GADSO
GADSOS
GADWALL
GADWALLS
GADZOOKS
GAE
GAED
GAEING
GAELICISE
GAELICISED
GAELICISES
GAELICISING
GAELICISM
GAELICISMS
GAELICIZE
GAELICIZED
GAELICIZES
GAELICIZING
GAES
GAFF
GAFFE
GAFFED
GAFFER
GAFFERS
GAFFES
GAFFING
GAFFINGS
GAFFS
GAG
GAGA
GAGAKU
GAGAKUS
GAGE
GAGED
GAGES
GAGGED
GAGGER
GAGGERS
GAGGING
GAGGLE
GAGGLED
GAGGLES
GAGGLING
GAGGLINGS

GAGING
GAGMAN
GAGMEN
GAGS
GAGSTER
GAGSTERS
GAHNITE
GAHNITES
GAID
GAIDS
GAIETIES
GAIETY
GAILLARD
GAILLARDS
GAILY
GAIN
GAINABLE
GAINED
GAINER
GAINERS
GAINEST
GAINFUL
GAINFULLY
GAINING
GAININGS
GAINLESS
GAINLY
GAINS
GAINSAID
GAINSAY
GAINSAYER
GAINSAYERS
GAINSAYING
GAINSAYINGS
GAINSAYS
GAINST
GAIR
GAIRFOWL
GAIRFOWLS
GAIRS
GAIT
GAITED
GAITER
GAITERS
GAITS
GAITT
GAITTS
GAJO
GAJOS
GAL
GALA
GALABEA
GALABEAH
GALABEAHS
GALABEAS
GALABIA
GALABIAH
GALABIAHS
GALABIAS
GALABIEH
GALABIYA
GALABIYAH
GALABIYAHS

GALABIYAS
GALABIYEH
GALABIYEHS
GALACTIC
GALACTOSE
GALACTOSES
GALAGE
GALAGES
GALAH
GALAHS
GALANGA
GALANGAL
GALANGALS
GALANGAS
GALANT
GALANTINE
GALANTINES
GALAPAGO
GALAPAGOS
GALAS
GALATEA
GALATEAS
GALAXIES
GALAXY
GALBANUM
GALBANUMS
GALDRAGON
GALDRAGONS
GALE
GALEA
GALEAS
GALEATE
GALEATED
GALENA
GALENAS
GALENGALE
GALENGALES
GALENITE
GALENITES
GALENOID
GALÈRE
GALÈRES
GALES
GALILEE
GALILEES
GALINGALE
GALINGALES
GALIONGEE
GALIONGEES
GALIOT
GALIOTS
GALIPOT
GALIPOTS
GALL
GALLABEA
GALLABEAH
GALLABEAHS
GALLABEAS
GALLABIA
GALLABIAH
GALLABIAHS
GALLABIAS
GALLABIEH
GALLABIEHS

GALLABIYA
GALLABIYAS
GALLANT
GALLANTER
GALLANTEST
GALLANTLY
GALLANTRIES
GALLANTRY
GALLANTS
GALLATE
GALLATES
GALLEASS
GALLEASSES
GALLED
GALLEON
GALLEONS
GALLERIED
GALLERIES
GALLERY
GALLERYING
GALLET
GALLETED
GALLETING
GALLETS
GALLEY
GALLEYS
GALLIARD
GALLIARDS
GALLIASS
GALLIASSES
GALLICISE
GALLICISED
GALLICISES
GALLICISING
GALLICISM
GALLICISMS
GALLICIZE
GALLICIZED
GALLICIZES
GALLICIZING
GALLIED
GALLIES
GALLINAZO
GALLINAZOS
GALLING
GALLINGLY
GALLINULE
GALLINULES
GALLIOT
GALLIOTS
GALLIPOT
GALLIPOTS
GALLISE
GALLISED
GALLISES
GALLISING
GALLISISE
GALLISISED
GALLISISES
GALLISISING
GALLISIZE
GALLISIZED
GALLISIZES
GALLISIZING

GALLIUM
GALLIUMS
GALLIVANT
GALLIVANTED
GALLIVANTING
GALLIVANTS
GALLIVAT
GALLIVATS
GALLIWASP
GALLIWASPS
GALLIZE
GALLIZED
GALLIZES
GALLIZING
GALLON
GALLONAGE
GALLONAGES
GALLONS
GALLOON
GALLOONED
GALLOONS
GALLOP
GALLOPADE
GALLOPADED
GALLOPADES
GALLOPADING
GALLOPED
GALLOPER
GALLOPERS
GALLOPHIL
GALLOPHILS
GALLOPING
GALLOPS
GALLOW
GALLOWED
GALLOWING
GALLOWS
GALLOWSES
GALLS
GALLUMPH
GALLUMPHED
GALLUMPHING
GALLUMPHS
GALLUS
GALLUSES
GALLY
GALLYING
GALOCHE
GALOCHED
GALOCHES
GALOCHING
GALOOT
GALOOTS
GALOP
GALOPED
GALOPIN
GALOPING
GALOPINS
GALOPPED
GALOPPING
GALOPS
GALORE
GALOSH
GALOSHED
GALOSHES
GALOSHING
GALOWSES
GALRAVAGE
GALRAVAGED
GALRAVAGES

GALRAVAGING
GALS
GALTONIA
GALTONIAS
GALUMPH
GALUMPHED
GALUMPHER
GALUMPHERS
GALUMPHING
GALUMPHS
GALUT
GALUTH
GALUTHS
GALUTS
GALVANIC
GALVANISE
GALVANISED
GALVANISES
GALVANISING
GALVANISM
GALVANISMS
GALVANIST
GALVANISTS
GALVANIZE
GALVANIZED
GALVANIZES
GALVANIZING
GAM
GAMASH
GAMASHES
GAMB
GAMBA
GAMBADO
GAMBADOES
GAMBADOS
GAMBAS
GAMBESON
GAMBESONS
GAMBET
GAMBETS
GAMBIER
GAMBIERS
GAMBIR
GAMBIRS
GAMBIST
GAMBISTS
GAMBIT
GAMBITED
GAMBITING
GAMBITS
GAMBLE
GAMBLED
GAMBLER
GAMBLERS
GAMBLES
GAMBLING
GAMBLINGS
GAMBOGE
GAMBOGES
GAMBOGIAN
GAMBOGIC
GAMBOL
GAMBOLLED
GAMBOLLING
GAMBOLS
GAMBREL
GAMBRELS
GAMBROON
GAMBROONS
GAMBS

GAME
GAMED
GAMELAN
GAMELANS
GAMELY
GAMENESS
GAMENESSES
GAMER
GAMESIER
GAMESIEST
GAMESOME
GAMEST
GAMESTER
GAMESTERS
GAMESY
GAMETAL
GAMETE
GAMETES
GAMETIC
GAMIC
GAMIER
GAMIEST
GAMIN
GAMINE
GAMINERIE
GAMINERIES
GAMINES
GAMING
GAMINGS
GAMINS
GAMMA
GAMMADION
GAMMADIONS
GAMMAS
GAMMATION
GAMMATIONS
GAMME
GAMMED
GAMMER
GAMMERS
GAMMES
GAMMIER
GAMMIEST
GAMMING
GAMMOCK
GAMMOCKED
GAMMOCKING
GAMMOCKS
GAMMON
GAMMONED
GAMMONER
GAMMONERS
GAMMONING
GAMMONINGS
GAMMONS
GAMMY
GAMP
GAMPISH
GAMPS
GAMS
GAMUT
GAMUTS
GAMY
GAN
GANCH
GANCHED
GANCHES
GANCHING
GANDER

GANDERISM
GANDERISMS
GANDERS
GANE
GANG
GANGBOARD
GANGBOARDS
GANGED
GANGER
GANGERS
GANGING
GANGINGS
GANGLAND
GANGLANDS
GANGLIA
GANGLIAR
GANGLIATE
GANGLIER
GANGLIEST
GANGLING
GANGLION
GANGLIONS
GANGLY
GANGPLANK
GANGPLANKS
GANGREL
GANGRELS
GANGRENE
GANGRENED
GANGRENES
GANGRENING
GANGS
GANGSMAN
GANGSMEN
GANGSTER
GANGSTERS
GANGUE
GANGUES
GANGWAY
GANGWAYS
GANISTER
GANISTERS
GANJA
GANJAS
GANNET
GANNETRIES
GANNETRY
GANNETS
GANNISTER
GANNISTERS
GANOID
GANOIDS
GANOIN
GANOINS
GANT
GANTED
GANTING
GANTLET
GANTLETS
GANTLINE
GANTLINES
GANTLOPE
GANTLOPES
GANTRIES
GANTRY
GANTS
GAOL
GAOLED
GAOLER
GAOLERESS

GAOLERESSES
GAOLERS
GAOLING
GAOLS
GAP
GAPE
GAPED
GAPER
GAPERS
GAPES
GAPESEED
GAPESEEDS
GAPEWORM
GAPEWORMS
GAPING
GAPINGLY
GAPINGS
GAPÓ
GAPÓS
GAPPED
GAPPIER
GAPPIEST
GAPPING
GAPPY
GAPS
GAR
GARAGE
GARAGED
GARAGES
GARAGING
GARAGINGS
GARB
GARBAGE
GARBAGES
GARBANZO
GARBANZOS
GARBE
GARBED
GARBES
GARBING
GARBLE
GARBLED
GARBLER
GARBLERS
GARBLES
GARBLING
GARBLINGS
GARBO
GARBOARD
GARBOARDS
GARBOIL
GARBOILS
GARBOS
GARBS
GARÇON
GARÇONS
GARDA
GARDAI
GARDANT
GARDANTS
GARDEN
GARDENED
GARDENER
GARDENERS
GARDENIA
GARDENIAS
GARDENING
GARDENINGS
GARDENS
GARDEROBE

GARDEROBES	GARNISHINGS	GASAHOL	GASPY	GAUCIE
GARDYLOO	GARNISHRIES	GASAHOLS	GASSED	GAUCIER
GARDYLOOS	GARNISHRY	GASALIER	GASSES	GAUCIEST
GARE	GARNITURE	GASALIERS	GASSIER	GAUCY
GAREFOWL	GARNITURES	GASCON	GASSIEST	GAUD
GAREFOWLS	GAROTTE	GASCONADE	GASSINESS	GAUDEAMUS
GARFISH	GAROTTED	GASCONADED	GASSINESSES	GAUDEAMUSES
GARFISHES	GAROTTER	GASCONADES	GASSING	GAUDED
GARGANEY	GAROTTERS	GASCONADING	GASSINGS	GAUDERIES
GARGANEYS	GAROTTES	GASCONISM	GASSY	GAUDERY
GARGARISE	GAROTTING	GASCONISMS	GAST	GAUDGIE
GARGARISED	GAROTTINGS	GASCONS	GASTED	GAUDGIES
GARGARISES	GARPIKE	GASEITIES	GASTFULL	GAUDIER
GARGARISING	GARPIKES	GASEITY	GASTING	GAUDIES
GARGARISM	GARRAN	GASELIER	GASTNESS	GAUDIEST
GARGARISMS	GARRANS	GASELIERS	GASTNESSE	GAUDILY
GARGARIZE	GARRE	GASEOUS	GASTNESSES	GAUDINESS
GARGARIZED	GARRED	GASES	GASTRAEA	GAUDINESSES
GARGARIZES	GARRES	GASFIELD	GASTRAEAS	GAUDING
GARGARIZING	GARRET	GASFIELDS	GASTRAEUM	GAUDS
GARGET	GARRETED	GASH	GASTRAEUMS	GAUDY
GARGETS	GARRETEER	GASHED	GASTRIC	GAUFER
GARGLE	GARRETEERS	GASHES	GASTRIN	GAUFERS
GARGLED	GARRETS	GASHFUL	GASTRINS	GAUFRE
GARGLES	GARRIGUE	GASHING	GASTRITIS	GAUFRES
GARGLING	GARRIGUES	GASHLY	GASTRITISES	GAUGE
GARGOYLE	GARRING	GASIFIED	GASTROPOD	GAUGEABLE
GARGOYLES	GARRISON	GASIFIER	GASTROPODS	GAUGED
GARIAL	GARRISONED	GASIFIERS	GASTRULA	GAUGER
GARIALS	GARRISONING	GASIFIES	GASTRULAE	GAUGERS
GARIBALDI	GARRISONS	GASIFORM	GASTRULAS	GAUGES
GARIBALDIS	GARRON	GASIFY	GASTS	GAUGING
GARIGUE	GARRONS	GASIFYING	GAT	GAUGINGS
GARIGUES	GARROT	GASKET	GATE	GAUJE
GARISH	GARROTE	GASKETS	GÂTEAU	GAUJES
GARISHED	GARROTED	GASKIN	GÂTEAUS	GAULEITER
GARISHES	GARROTES	GASKINS	GÂTEAUX	GAULEITERS
GARISHING	GARROTING	GASLIGHT	GATECRASH	GAULT
GARISHLY	GARROTS	GASLIGHTS	GATECRASHED	GAULTER
GARJAN	GARROTTE	GASLIT	GATECRASHES	GAULTERS
GARJANS	GARROTTED	GASMAN	GATECRASHING	GAULTS
GARLAND	GARROTTER	GASMEN	GATED	GAUM
GARLANDED	GARROTTERS	GASOGENE	GATEFOLD	GAUMED
GARLANDING	GARROTTES	GASOGENES	GATEFOLDS	GAUMIER
GARLANDRY	GARROTTING	GASOHOL	GATELEG	GAUMIEST
GARLANDS	GARROTTINGS	GASOHOLS	GATELESS	GAUMING
GARLIC	GARRULITIES	GASOLENE	GATES	GAUMLESS
GARLICKY	GARRULITY	GASOLENES	GATEWAY	GAUMS
GARLICS	GARRULOUS	GASOLIER	GATEWAYS	GAUMY
GARMENT	GARRYA	GASOLIERS	GATH	GAUN
GARMENTED	GARRYAS	GASOLINE	GATHER	GAUNCH
GARMENTING	GARRYOWEN	GASOLINES	GATHERED	GAUNCHED
GARMENTS	GARRYOWENS	GASOMETER	GATHERER	GAUNCHES
GARNER	GARS	GASOMETERS	GATHERERS	GAUNCHING
GARNERED	GART	GASOMETRIES	GATHERING	GAUNT
GARNERING	GARTER	GASOMETRY	GATHERINGS	GAUNTED
GARNERS	GARTERED	GASP	GATHERS	GAUNTER
GARNET	GARTERING	GASPED	GATHS	GAUNTEST
GARNETS	GARTERS	GASPER	GATING	GAUNTING
GARNI	GARTH	GASPEREAU	GATINGS	GAUNTLET
GARNISH	GARTHS	GASPEREAUS	GATS	GAUNTLETS
GARNISHED	GARUDA	GASPERS	GAU	GAUNTLY
GARNISHEE	GARUDAS	GASPIER	GAUCHE	GAUNTNESS
GARNISHEED	GARUM	GASPIEST	GAUCHER	GAUNTNESSES
GARNISHEEING	GARUMS	GASPINESS	GAUCHERIE	GAUNTREE
GARNISHEES	GARVIE	GASPINESSES	GAUCHERIES	GAUNTREES
GARNISHER	GARVIES	GASPING	GAUCHESCO	GAUNTRIES
GARNISHERS	GARVOCK	GASPINGLY	GAUCHEST	GAUNTRY
GARNISHES	GARVOCKS	GASPINGS	GAUCHO	GAUNTS
GARNISHING	GAS	GASPS	GAUCHOS	GAUP

GAUPED
GAUPER
GAUPERS
GAUPING
GAUPS
GAUPUS
GAUPUSES
GAUR
GAURS
GAUS
GAUSS
GAUSSES
GAUSSIAN
GAUZE
GAUZES
GAUZIER
GAUZIEST
GAUZINESS
GAUZINESSES
GAUZY
GAVAGE
GAVAGES
GAVE
GAVEL
GAVELKIND
GAVELKINDS
GAVELMAN
GAVELMEN
GAVELOCK
GAVELOCKS
GAVELS
GAVIAL
GAVIALS
GAVOTTE
GAVOTTES
GAWCIER
GAWCIEST
GAWCY
GAWD
GAWDS
GAWK
GAWKED
GAWKER
GAWKERS
GAWKIER
GAWKIES
GAWKIEST
GAWKIHOOD
GAWKIHOODS
GAWKINESS
GAWKINESSES
GAWKING
GAWKS
GAWKY
GAWP
GAWPED
GAWPER
GAWPERS
GAWPING
GAWPS
GAWPUS
GAWPUSES
GAWSIER
GAWSIEST
GAWSY
GAY
GAYAL
GAYALS
GAYER
GAYEST

GAYNESS
GAYNESSES
GAYS
GAYSOME
GAZAL
GAZALS
GAZE
GAZEBO
GAZEBOES
GAZEBOS
GAZED
GAZEFUL
GAZEL
GAZELLE
GAZELLES
GAZELS
GAZEMENT
GAZEMENTS
GAZER
GAZERS
GAZES
GAZETTE
GAZETTED
GAZETTEER
GAZETTEERED
GAZETTEERING
GAZETTEERS
GAZETTES
GAZETTING
GAZIER
GAZIEST
GAZING
GAZOGENE
GAZOGENES
GAZON
GAZONS
GAZOO
GAZOOKA
GAZOOKAS
GAZOON
GAZOONS
GAZOOS
GAZPACHO
GAZPACHOS
GAZUMP
GAZUMPED
GAZUMPING
GAZUMPS
GAZY
GEAL
GEALED
GEALING
GEALOUS
GEALOUSIES
GEALOUSY
GEALS
GEAN
GEANS
GEAR
GEARBOX
GEARBOXES
GEARE
GEARED
GEARES
GEARING
GEARINGS
GEARLESS
GEARS
GEASON
GEAT

GEATS
GEBUR
GEBURS
GECK
GECKED
GECKING
GECKO
GECKOES
GECKOS
GECKS
GED
GEDS
GEE
GEEBUNG
GEEBUNGS
GEED
GEEING
GEES
GEESE
GEEZER
GEFZERS
GEFUFFLE
GEFUFFLED
GEFUFFLES
GEFUFFLING
GEISHA
GEISHAS
GEIST
GEISTS
GEIT
GEITS
GEL
GELADA
GELADAS
GELASTIC
GELATI
GELATIN
GELATINE
GELATINES
GELATINS
GELATION
GELATIONS
GELATO
GELD
GELDED
GELDER
GELDERS
GELDING
GELDINGS
GELDS
GELID
GELIDER
GELIDEST
GELIDITIES
GELIDITY
GELIDLY
GELIDNESS
GELIDNESSES
GELIGNITE
GELIGNITES
GELLED
GELLING
GELLY
GELOSIES
GELOSY
GELS
GELSEMINE
GELSEMINES
GELSEMIUM
GELSEMIUMS

GELT
GELTED
GELTING
GELTS
GEM
GEMATRIA
GEMATRIAS
GEMEL
GEMELS
GEMINATE
GEMINATED
GEMINATES
GEMINATING
GEMINI
GEMINIES
GEMINIS
GEMINOUS
GEMINY
GEMMA
GEMMAE
GEMMAN
GEMMATE
GEMMATED
GEMMATES
GEMMATING
GEMMATION
GEMMATIONS
GEMMATIVE
GEMMED
GEMMEN
GEMMEOUS
GEMMERY
GEMMIER
GEMMIEST
GEMMING
GEMMOLOGIES
GEMMOLOGY
GEMMULE
GEMMULES
GEMMY
GEMOLOGIES
GEMOLOGY
GEMONIES
GEMONY
GEMOT
GEMOTS
GEMS
GEMSBOK
GEMSBOKS
GEMSTONE
GEMSTONES
GEMÜTLICH
GEN
GENA
GENAL
GENAPPE
GENAPPES
GENAS
GENDARME
GENDARMES
GENDER
GENDERED
GENDERING
GENDERS
GENE
GENEALOGIES
GENEALOGY
GENERA
GENERABLE
GENERAL

GENERALE
GENERALIA
GENERALLED
GENERALLING
GENERALLY
GENERALS
GENERANT
GENERANTS
GENERATE
GENERATED
GENERATES
GENERATING
GENERATOR
GENERATORS
GENERIC
GENERICAL
GENERICS
GENEROUS
GENES
GENESES
GENESIS
GENET
GENETIC
GENETICAL
GENETICS
GENETRICES
GENETRIX
GENETRIXES
GENETS
GENETTE
GENETTES
GENEVA
GENEVAS
GENIAL
GENIALISE
GENIALISED
GENIALISES
GENIALISING
GENIALITIES
GENIALITY
GENIALIZE
GENIALIZED
GENIALIZES
GENIALIZING
GENIALLY
GENIC
GENIE
GENIES
GENII
GENIP
GENIPAP
GENIPAPS
GENIPS
GENISTA
GENISTAS
GENITAL
GENITALIA
GENITALS
GENITIVAL
GENITIVE
GENITIVES
GENITOR
GENITORS
GENITRICES
GENITRIX
GENITRIXES
GENITURE
GENITURES
GENIUS
GENIUSES

GENIZAH
GENIZAHS
GENNET
GENNETS
GENOA
GENOAS
GENOCIDAL
GENOCIDE
GENOCIDES
GENOM
GENOME
GENOMES
GENOMS
GENOTYPE
GENOTYPES
GENOTYPIC
GENRE
GENRES
GENS
GENSDARMES
GENT
GENTEEL
GENTEELER
GENTEELEST
GENTEELLY
GENTES
GENTIAN
GENTIANS
GENTIER
GENTIEST
GENTILE
GENTILES
GENTILIC
GENTILISE
GENTILISED
GENTILISES
GENTILISH
GENTILISING
GENTILISM
GENTILISMS
GENTILITIES
GENTILITY
GENTILIZE
GENTILIZED
GENTILIZES
GENTILIZING
GENTLE
GENTLED
GENTLEMAN
GENTLEMEN
GENTLER
GENTLES
GENTLEST
GENTLING
GENTLY
GENTOO
GENTOOS
GENTRICE
GENTRICES
GENTRIES
GENTRIFIED
GENTRIFIES
GENTRIFY
GENTRIFYING
GENTRY
GENTS
GENTY
GENU
GENUFLECT
GENUFLECTED

GENUFLECTING
GENUFLECTS
GENUINE
GENUINELY
GENUS
GENUSES
GEO
GEOCARPIC
GEOCARPIES
GEOCARPY
GEODE
GEODES
GEODESIC
GEODESIES
GEODESIST
GEODESISTS
GEODESY
GEODETIC
GEODETICS
GEODIC
GEOGENIES
GEOGENY
GEOGNOSES
GEOGNOSIES
GEOGNOSIS
GEOGNOST
GEOGNOSTS
GEOGNOSY
GEOGONIC
GEOGONIES
GEOGONY
GEOGRAPHIES
GEOGRAPHY
GEOID
GEOIDAL
GEOIDS
GEOLATRIES
GEOLATRY
GEOLOGER
GEOLOGERS
GEOLOGIAN
GEOLOGIANS
GEOLOGIC
GEOLOGIES
GEOLOGISE
GEOLOGISED
GEOLOGISES
GEOLOGISING
GEOLOGIST
GEOLOGISTS
GEOLOGIZE
GEOLOGIZED
GEOLOGIZES
GEOLOGIZING
GEOLOGY
GEOMANCER
GEOMANCERS
GEOMANCIES
GEOMANCY
GEOMANTIC
GEOMETER
GEOMETERS
GEOMETRIC
GEOMETRID
GEOMETRIDS
GEOMETRIES
GEOMETRY
GEOMYOID
GEOPHAGIES
GEOPHAGY

GEOPHILIC
GEOPHONE
GEOPHONES
GEOPHYTE
GEOPHYTES
GEOPHYTIC
GEOPONIC
GEOPONICS
GEORDIE
GEORDIES
GEORGETTE
GEORGETTES
GEORGIC
GEORGICS
GEOS
GEOSPHERE
GEOSPHERES
GEOSTATIC
GEOSTATICS
GEOTACTIC
GEOTAXES
GEOTAXIS
GEOTROPIC
GERAH
GERAHS
GERANIOL
GERANIOLS
GERANIUM
GERANIUMS
GERBE
GERBERA
GERBERAS
GERBES
GERBIL
GERBILLE
GERBILLES
GERBILS
GERE
GERENT
GERENTS
GERENUK
GERENUKS
GERES
GERFALCON
GERFALCONS
GERIATRIC
GERIATRICS
GERIATRIES
GERIATRY
GERLE
GERLES
GERM
GERMAIN
GERMAINE
GERMAINES
GERMAINS
GERMAN
GERMANDER
GERMANDERS
GERMANE
GERMANELY
GERMANER
GERMANEST
GERMANIUM
GERMANIUMS
GERMANS
GERMED
GERMEN
GERMENS
GERMICIDE

GERMICIDES
GERMIN
GERMINAL
GERMINANT
GERMINATE
GERMINATED
GERMINATES
GERMINATING
GERMING
GERMINS
GERMS
GERNE
GERNED
GERNES
GERNING
GERONTIC
GEROPIGA
GEROPIGAS
GERUND
GERUNDIAL
GERUNDIVE
GERUNDIVES
GERUNDS
GESNERIA
GESNERIAS
GESSAMINE
GESSAMINES
GESSE
GESSED
GESSES
GESSING
GESSO
GESSOES
GEST
GESTALT
GESTALTS
GESTANT
GESTATE
GESTATED
GESTATES
GESTATING
GESTATION
GESTATIONS
GESTATIVE
GESTATORY
GESTE
GESTES
GESTIC
GESTS
GESTURAL
GESTURE
GESTURED
GESTURES
GESTURING
GET
GETA
GETAS
GETAWAY
GETAWAYS
GETS
GETTABLE
GETTER
GETTERED
GETTERING
GETTERINGS
GETTERS
GETTING
GETTINGS
GEUM
GEUMS

GEWGAW
GEWGAWS
GEY
GEYAN
GEYER
GEYEST
GEYSER
GEYSERITE
GEYSERITES
GEYSERS
GHARIAL
GHARIALS
GHARRI
GHARRIES
GHARRIS
GHARRY
GHAST
GHASTED
GHASTFUL
GHASTFULL
GHASTING
GHASTLIER
GHASTLIEST
GHASTLY
GHASTNESS
GHASTNESSES
GHASTS
GHAT
GHATS
GHAUT
GHAUTS
GHAZAL
GHAZALS
GHAZEL
GHAZELS
GHAZI
GHAZIS
GHEE
GHEES
GHERAO
GHERAOED
GHERAOING
GHERAOS
GHERKIN
GHERKINS
GHESSE
GHESSED
GHESSES
GHESSING
GHEST
GHETTO
GHETTOES
GHETTOISE
GHETTOISED
GHETTOISES
GHETTOISING
GHETTOIZE
GHETTOIZED
GHETTOIZES
GHETTOIZING
GHETTOS
GHI
GHILGAI
GHILGAIS
GHILLIE
GHILLIED
GHILLIES
GHILLYING
GHIS
GHOST

GHOSTED
GHOSTIER
GHOSTIEST
GHOSTING
GHOSTLIER
GHOSTLIEST
GHOSTLY
GHOSTS
GHOSTY
GHOUL
GHOULISH
GHOULS
GHYLL
GHYLLS
GI
GIAMBEUX
GIANT
GIANTESS
GIANTESSES
GIANTHOOD
GIANTHOODS
GIANTISM
GIANTISMS
GIANTLIER
GIANTLIEST
GIANTLY
GIANTRIES
GIANTRY
GIANTS
GIANTSHIP
GIANTSHIPO
GIAOUR
GIAOURS
GIB
GIBBED
GIBBER
GIBBERED
GIBBERING
GIBBERISH
GIBBERISHES
GIBBERS
GIBBET
GIBBETED
GIBBETING
GIBBETS
GIBBING
GIBBON
GIBBONS
GIBBOSE
GIBBOSITIES
GIBBOSITY
GIBBOUS
GIBBOUSLY
GIBBSITE
GIBBSITES
GIBE
GIBED
GIBEL
GIBELS
GIBER
GIBERS
GIBES
GIBING
GIBINGLY
GIBLET
GIBLETS
GIBS
GIBUS
GIBUSES
GID

GIDDIED
GIDDIER
GIDDIES
GIDDIEST
GIDDILY
GIDDINESS
GIDDINESSES
GIDDY
GIDDYING
GIDGEE
GIDGEES
GIDJEE
GIDJEES
GIDS
GIE
GIED
GIEN
GIES
GIF
GIFT
GIFTED
GIFTEDLY
GIFTING
GIFTS
GIG
GIGA
GIGAHERTZ
GIGAHERTZES
GIGANTEAN
GIGANTIC
GIGANTISM
GIGANTISMS
GIGAS
GIGAWATT
GIGAWATTS
GIGGED
GIGGING
GIGGIT
GIGGITED
GIGGITING
GIGGITS
GIGGLE
GIGGLED
GIGGLER
GIGGLERS
GIGGLES
GIGGLIER
GIGGLIEST
GIGGLING
GIGGLINGS
GIGGLY
GIGLET
GIGLETS
GIGLOT
GIGLOTS
GIGMAN
GIGMANITIES
GIGMANITY
GIGMEN
GIGOLO
GIGOLOS
GIGOT
GIGOTS
GIGS
GIGUE
GIGUES
GILA
GILAS
GILBERT
GILBERTS

GILCUP
GILCUPS
GILD
GILDED
GILDEN
GILDER
GILDERS
GILDING
GILDINGS
GILDS
GILET
GILETS
GILGAI
GILGAIS
GILGIE
GILGIES
GILL
GILLAROO
GILLAROOS
GILLED
GILLET
GILLETS
GILLFLIRT
GILLFLIRTS
GILLIE
GILLIED
GILLIES
GILLING
GILLION
GILLIONS
GILLS
GILLY
GILLYING
GILLYVOR
GILLYVORS
GILPEY
GILPEYS
GILPIES
GILPY
GILRAVAGE
GILRAVAGED
GILRAVAGES
GILRAVAGING
GILT
GILTCUP
GILTCUPS
GILTS
GILTWOOD
GIMBAL
GIMBALS
GIMCRACK
GIMCRACKS
GIMLET
GIMLETED
GIMLETING
GIMLETS
GIMMAL
GIMMALLED
GIMMALS
GIMME
GIMMER
GIMMERS
GIMMES
GIMMICK
GIMMICKRIES
GIMMICKRY
GIMMICKS
GIMMICKY
GIMMOR
GIMMORS

GIMP
GIMPED
GIMPING
GIMPS
GIN
GING
GINGAL
GINGALL
GINGALLS
GINGALS
GINGELLIES
GINGELLY
GINGER
GINGERADE
GINGERADES
GINGERED
GINGERING
GINGERLY
GINGEROUS
GINGERS
GINGERY
GINGHAM
GINGHAMS
GINGILI
GINGILIS
GINGIVAL
GINGKO
GINGKOES
GINGLE
GINGLED
GINGLES
GINGLING
GINGLYMI
GINGLYMUS
GINGS
GINHOUSE
GINHOUSES
GINK
GINKGO
GINKGOES
GINKS
GINN
GINNED
GINNEL
GINNELS
GINNER
GINNERIED
GINNERS
GINNERY
GINNING
GINS
GINSENG
GINSENGS
GINSHOP
GINSHOPS
GIO
GIOCOSO
GIOS
GIP
GIPPIES
GIPPO
GIPPOS
GIPPY
GIPS
GIPSEN
GIPSENS
GIPSIED
GIPSIES
GIPSY
GIPSYING

GIRAFFE
GIRAFFES
GIRAFFID
GIRAFFINE
GIRAFFOID
GIRANDOLA
GIRANDOLAS
GIRANDOLE
GIRANDOLES
GIRASOL
GIRASOLE
GIRASOLES
GIRASOLS
GIRD
GIRDED
GIRDER
GIRDERS
GIRDING
GIRDINGS
GIRDLE
GIRDLED
GIRDLER
GIRDLERS
GIRDLES
GIRDLING
GIRDS
GIRKIN
GIRKINS
GIRL
GIRLHOOD
GIRLHOODS
GIRLIE
GIRLIES
GIRLISH
GIRLISHLY
GIRLOND
GIRLONDS
GIRLS
GIRLY
GIRN
GIRNED
GIRNEL
GIRNELS
GIRNIE
GIRNIER
GIRNIEST
GIRNING
GIRNS
GIRO
GIRON
GIRONS
GIROS
GIROSOL
GIROSOLS
GIRR
GIRRS
GIRT
GIRTED
GIRTH
GIRTHED
GIRTHING
GIRTHLINE
GIRTHLINES
GIRTHS
GIRTING
GIRTLINE
GIRTLINES
GIRTS
GIS
GISARME

GISARMES
GISM
GISMO
GISMOS
GISMS
GIST
GISTS
GIT
GITANA
GITANAS
GITANO
GITANOS
GITE
GITES
GITS
GITTERN
GITTERNED
GITTERNING
GITTERNS
GIUST
GIUSTED
GIUSTING
GIUSTO
GIUSTS
GIVE
GIVEAWAY
GIVEAWAYS
GIVED
GIVEN
GIVENNESS
GIVENNESSES
GIVER
GIVERS
GIVES
GIVING
GIVINGS
GIZMO
GIZMOS
GIZZ
GIZZARD
GIZZARDS
GIZZEN
GIZZENED
GIZZENING
GIZZENS
GIZZES
GJU
GJUS
GLABELLA
GLABELLAE
GLABELLAR
GLABRATE
GLABROUS
GLACÉ
GLACÉED
GLACÉING
GLACÉS
GLACIAL
GLACIALS
GLACIATE
GLACIATED
GLACIATES
GLACIATING
GLACIER
GLACIERS
GLACIS
GLACISES
GLAD
GLADDED
GLADDEN

GLADDENED
GLADDENING
GLADDENS
GLADDER
GLADDEST
GLADDIE
GLADDIES
GLADDING
GLADDON
GLADDONS
GLADE
GLADES
GLADFUL
GLADIATE
GLADIATOR
GLADIATORS
GLADIER
GLADIEST
GLADIOLE
GLADIOLES
GLADIOLI
GLADIOLUS
GLADIOLUSES
GLADIUS
GLADIUSES
GLADLY
GLADNESS
GLADNESSES
GLADS
GLADSOME
GLADSOMER
GLADSOMEST
GLADY
GLAIK
GLAIKET
GLAIKIT
GLAIKS
GLAIR
GLAIRED
GLAIREOUS
GLAIRIER
GLAIRIEST
GLAIRIN
GLAIRING
GLAIRINS
GLAIRS
GLAIRY
GLAIVE
GLAIVED
GLAIVES
GLAM
GLAMOR
GLAMORED
GLAMORING
GLAMORISE
GLAMORISED
GLAMORISES
GLAMORISING
GLAMORIZE
GLAMORIZED
GLAMORIZES
GLAMORIZING
GLAMOROUS
GLAMORS
GLAMOUR
GLAMOURED
GLAMOURING
GLAMOURS
GLANCE
GLANCED

GLANCES
GLANCING
GLANCINGS
GLAND
GLANDERED
GLANDERS
GLANDES
GLANDS
GLANDULAR
GLANDULE
GLANDULES
GLANS
GLARE
GLAREAL
GLARED
GLAREOUS
GLARES
GLARIER
GLARIEST
GLARING
GLARINGLY
GLARY
GLASNOST
GLASNOSTS
GLASS
GLASSED
GLASSEN
GLASSES
GLASSFUL
GLASSFULS
GLASSIER
GLASSIEST
GLASSIFIED
GLASSIFIES
GLASSIFY
GLASSIFYING
GLASSILY
GLASSINE
GLASSINES
GLASSING
GLASSLIKE
GLASSMAN
GLASSMEN
GLASSWARE
GLASSWARES
GLASSWORK
GLASSWORKS
GLASSWORT
GLASSWORTS
GLASSY
GLAUCOMA
GLAUCOMAS
GLAUCOUS
GLAUM
GLAUMED
GLAUMING
GLAUMS
GLAUR
GLAURIER
GLAURIEST
GLAURS
GLAURY
GLAZE
GLAZED
GLAZEN
GLAZER
GLAZERS
GLAZES
GLAZIER
GLAZIERS

GLAZIEST
GLAZING
GLAZINGS
GLAZY
GLEAM
GLEAMED
GLEAMIER
GLEAMIEST
GLEAMING
GLEAMINGS
GLEAMS
GLEAMY
GLEAN
GLEANED
GLEANER
GLEANERS
GLEANING
GLEANINGS
GLEANS
GLEAVE
GLEAVES
GLEBE
GLEBES
GLEBOUS
GLEBY
GLED
GLEDE
GLEDES
GLEDGE
GLEDGED
GLEDGES
GLEDGING
GLEDS
GLEE
GLEED
GLEEDED
GLEEDING
GLEEDS
GLEEFUL
GLEEING
GLEEK
GLEEKED
GLEEKING
GLEEKS
GLEEMAN
GLEEMEN
GLEES
GLEESOME
GLEET
GLEETED
GLEETIER
GLEETIEST
GLEETING
GLEETS
GLEETY
GLEG
GLEGGER
GLEGGEST
GLEI
GLEIS
GLEN
GLENGARRIES
GLENGARRY
GLENOID
GLENOIDAL
GLENOIDS
GLENS
GLENT
GLENTED
GLENTING

GLENTS
GLEY
GLEYED
GLEYING
GLEYS
GLIA
GLIADIN
GLIADINE
GLIADINES
GLIADINS
GLIAL
GLIAS
GLIB
GLIBBED
GLIBBER
GLIBBERY
GLIBBEST
GLIBBING
GLIBLY
GLIBNESS
GLIBNESSES
GLIBS
GLID
GLIDDER
GLIDDERY
GLIDDEST
GLIDE
GLIDED
GLIDER
GLIDERS
GLIDES
GLIDING
GLIDINGLY
GLIDINGS
GLIFF
GLIFFING
GLIFFINGS
GLIFFS
GLIFT
GLIFTS
GLIKE
GLIKES
GLIM
GLIMMER
GLIMMERED
GLIMMERING
GLIMMERINGS
GLIMMERS
GLIMMERY
GLIMPSE
GLIMPSED
GLIMPSES
GLIMPSING
GLIMS
GLINT
GLINTED
GLINTING
GLINTS
GLIOMA
GLIOMAS
GLIOMATA
GLIOSES
GLIOSIS
GLISK
GLISKS
GLISSADE
GLISSADED
GLISSADES
GLISSADING
GLISSANDO

GLISSANDOS
GLISTEN
GLISTENED
GLISTENING
GLISTENS
GLISTER
GLISTERED
GLISTERING
GLISTERS
GLIT
GLITCH
GLITCHES
GLITS
GLITTER
GLITTERED
GLITTERING
GLITTERINGS
GLITTERS
GLITTERY
GLITZ
GLITZES
GLITZIER
GLITZIEST
GLITZY
GLOAMING
GLOAMINGS
GLOAT
GLOATED
GLOATING
GLOATS
GLOB
GLOBAL
GLOBALISE
GLOBALISED
GLOBALISES
GLOBALISING
GLOBALIZE
GLOBALIZED
GLOBALIZES
GLOBALIZING
GLOBALLY
GLOBATE
GLOBATED
GLOBE
GLODED
GLOBES
GLOBIN
GLOBING
GLOBINS
GLOBOID
GLOBOIDS
GLOBOSE
GLOBOSES
GLOBOSITIES
GLOBOSITY
GLOBOUS
GLOBS
GLOBULAR
GLOBULE
GLOBULES
GLOBULET
GLOBULETS
GLOBULIN
GLOBULINS
GLOBULITE
GLOBULITES
GLOBULOUS
GLOBY
GLODE
GLOGG

GLOGGS
GLOIRE
GLOIRES
GLOM
GLOMERATE
GLOMERATED
GLOMERATES
GLOMERATING
GLOMERULE
GLOMERULES
GLOMERULI
GLOMMED
GLOMMING
GLOMS
GLONOIN
GLONOINS
GLOOM
GLOOMED
GLOOMFUL
GLOOMIER
GLOOMIEST
GLOOMILY
GLOOMING
GLOOMINGS
GLOOMS
GLOOMY
GLORIA
GLORIAS
GLORIED
GLORIES
GLORIFIED
GLORIFIES
GLORIFY
GLORIFYING
GLORIOLE
GLORIOLES
GLORIOSA
GLORIOSAS
GLORIOUS
GLORY
GLORYBOX
GLORYBOXES
GLORYING
GLOSS
GLOSSA
GLOSSAE
GLOSSAL
GLOSSARIES
GLOSSARY
GLOSSAS
GLOSSATOR
GLOSSATORS
GLOSSED
GLOSSEME
GLOSSEMES
GLOSSER
GLOSSERS
GLOSSES
GLOSSIER
GLOSSIES
GLOSSIEST
GLOSSILY
GLOSSINA
GLOSSINAS
GLOSSING
GLOSSITIS
GLOSSITISES
GLOSSY
GLOTTAL
GLOTTIC

GLOTTIDES
GLOTTIS
GLOTTISES
GLOUT
GLOUTED
GLOUTING
GLOUTS
GLOVE
GLOVED
GLOVER
GLOVERS
GLOVES
GLOVING
GLOW
GLOWED
GLOWER
GLOWERED
GLOWERING
GLOWERS
GLOWING
GLOWINGLY
GLOWLAMP
GLOWLAMPS
GLOWS
GLOXINIA
GLOXINIAS
GLOZE
GLOZED
GLOZES
GLOZING
GLOZINGS
GLUCAGON
GLUCAGONS
GLUCINA
GLUCINAS
GLUCINIUM
GLUCINIUMS
GLUCINUM
GLUCINUMS
GLUCOSE
GLUCOSES
GLUCOSIDE
GLUCOSIDES
GLUE
GLUED
GLUER
GLUERS
GLUES
GLUEY
GLUEYNESS
GLUEYNESSES
GLUG
GLUGGED
GLUGGING
GLUGS
GLÜHWEIN
GLÜHWEINS
GLUIER
GLUIEST
GLUING
GLUISH
GLUM
GLUME
GLUMELLA
GLUMELLAS
GLUMES
GLUMLY
GLUMMER
GLUMMEST
GLUMNESS

GLUMNESSES
GLUMPISH
GLUMPS
GLUMPY
GLUON
GLUONS
GLUT
GLUTAEAL
GLUTAEI
GLUTAEUS
GLUTAMATE
GLUTAMATES
GLUTAMINE
GLUTAMINES
GLUTEAL
GLUTEI
GLUTELIN
GLUTELINS
GLUTEN
GLUTENOUS
GLUTENS
GLUTEUS
GLUTINOUS
GLUTS
GLUTTED
GLUTTING
GLUTTON
GLUTTONIES
GLUTTONS
GLUTTONY
GLYCERIC
GLYCERIDE
GLYCERIDES
GLYCERIN
GLYCERINE
GLYCERINES
GLYCERINS
GLYCEROL
GLYCEROLS
GLYCERYL
GLYCERYLS
GLYCIN
GLYCINE
GLYCINES
GLYCINS
GLYCOCOLL
GLYCOCOLLS
GLYCOGEN
GLYCOGENS
GLYCOL
GLYCOLIC
GLYCOLLIC
GLYCOLS
GLYCONIC
GLYCONICS
GLYCOSE
GLYCOSES
GLYCOSIDE
GLYCOSIDES
GLYCOSYL
GLYCOSYLS
GLYPH
GLYPHIC
GLYPHS
GLYPTIC
GLYPTICS
GMELINITE
GMELINITES
GNAR
GNARL

GNARLED
GNARLIER
GNARLIEST
GNARLING
GNARLS
GNARLY
GNARR
GNARRED
GNARRING
GNARRS
GNARS
GNASH
GNASHED
GNASHER
GNASHERS
GNASHES
GNASHING
GNAT
GNATHAL
GNATHIC
GNATHITE
GNATHITES
GNATHONIC
GNATLING
GNATLINGS
GNATS
GNAW
GNAWED
GNAWER
GNAWERS
GNAWING
GNAWN
GNAWS
GNEISS
GNEISSES
GNEISSIC
GNEISSOID
GNEISSOSE
GNOCCHI
GNOCCHIS
GNOMAE
GNOME
GNOMES
GNOMIC
GNOMISH
GNOMIST
GNOMISTS
GNOMON
GNOMONIC
GNOMONICS
GNOMONS
GNOSES
GNOSIS
GNOSTIC
GNOSTICAL
GNU
GNUS
GO
GOA
GOAD
GOADED
GOADING
GOADS
GOADSMAN
GOADSMEN
GOADSTER
GOADSTERS
GOAF
GOAFS
GOAL

GOALED
GOALIE
GOALIES
GOALING
GOALLESS
GOALMOUTH
GOALMOUTHS
GOALPOST
GOALPOSTS
GOALS
GOANNA
GOANNAS
GOARY
GOAS
GOAT
GOATEE
GOATEED
GOATEES
GOATFISH
GOATFISHES
GOATHERD
GOATHERDS
GOATIER
GOATIEST
GOATISH
GOATLING
GOATLINGS
GOATS
GOATSKIN
GOATSKINS
GOATWEED
GOATWEEDS
GOATY
GOB
GOBANG
GOBANGS
GOBBELINE
GOBBELINES
GOBBET
GOBBETS
GOBBI
GOBBLE
GOBBLED
GOBBLER
GOBBLERS
GOBBLES
GOBBLING
GOBBO
GOBIES
GOBIOID
GOBLET
GOBLETS
GOBLIN
GOBLINS
GOBO
GOBOES
GOBONY
GOBOS
GOBS
GOBURRA
GOBURRAS
GOBY
GOD
GODCHILD
GODCHILDREN
GODDAM
GODDAMN
GODDAMNED
GODDED
GODDESS

GODDESSES
GODDING
GODET
GODETIA
GODETIAS
GODETS
GODFATHER
GODFATHERS
GODHEAD
GODHEADS
GODHOOD
GODHOODS
GODLESS
GODLESSLY
GODLIER
GODLIEST
GODLIKE
GODLILY
GODLINESS
GODLINESSES
GODLING
GODLINGS
GODLY
GODMOTHER
GODMOTHERS
GODOWN
GODOWNS
GODPARENT
GODPARENTS
GODROON
GODROONS
GODS
GODSEND
GODSENDS
GODSHIP
GODSHIPS
GODSO
GODSON
GODSONS
GODSOS
GODSPEED
GODSPEEDS
GODWARD
GODWARDS
GODWIT
GODWITS
GOE
GOEIER
GOEIEST
GOEL
GOELS
GOER
GOERS
GOES
GOETHITE
GOETHITES
GOETIC
GOETIES
GOETY
GOEY
GOFER
GOFERS
GOFF
GOFFED
GOFFER
GOFFERED
GOFFERING
GOFFERINGS
GOFFERS
GOFFING

GOFFS
GOG
GOGGLE
GOGGLED
GOGGLER
GOGGLERS
GOGGLES
GOGGLIER
GOGGLIEST
GOGGLING
GOGGLINGS
GOGGLY
GOGLET
GOGLETS
GOGO
GOGS
GOING
GOINGS
GOITER
GOITERS
GOITRE
GOITRED
GOITRES
GOITROUS
GOLD
GOLDARN
GOLDCREST
GOLDCRESTS
GOLDEN
GOLDENED
GOLDENER
GOLDENEST
GOLDENING
GOLDENLY
GOLDENROD
GOLDENRODS
GOLDENS
GOLDER
GOLDEST
GOLDEYE
GOLDEYES
GOLDFIELD
GOLDFIELDS
GOLDFINCH
GOLDFINCHES
GOLDFINNIES
GOLDFINNY
GOLDFISH
GOLDFISHES
GOLDIER
GOLDIEST
GOLDISH
GOLDLESS
GOLDS
GOLDSINNIES
GOLDSINNY
GOLDSIZE
GOLDSIZES
GOLDSMITH
GOLDSMITHS
GOLDSPINK
GOLDSPINKS
GOLDSTICK
GOLDSTICKS
GOLDSTONE
GOLDSTONES
GOLDY
GOLE
GOLEM
GOLEMS

GOLES
GOLF
GOLFED
GOLFER
GOLFERS
GOLFIANA
GOLFIANAS
GOLFING
GOLFINGS
GOLFS
GOLIARD
GOLIARDIC
GOLIARDIES
GOLIARDS
GOLIARDY
GOLIAS
GOLIASED
GOLIASES
GOLIASING
GOLLAN
GOLLAND
GOLLANDS
GOLLANS
GOLLAR
GOLLARED
GOLLARING
GOLLARS
GOLLIES
GOLLIWOG
GOLLIWOGS
GOLLOP
GOLLOPED
GOLLOPING
GOLLOPS
GOLLY
GOLLYWOG
GOLLYWOGS
GOLOMYNKA
GOLOMYNKAS
GOLOSH
GOLOSHED
GOLOSHES
GOLOSHING
GOLP
GOLPE
GOLPES
GOLPS
GOMBEEN
GOMBEENS
GOMBO
GOMBOS
GOMBRO
GOMBROS
GOMERAL
GOMERALS
GOMERIL
GOMERILS
GOMOKU
GOMOKUS
GOMPA
GOMPAS
GOMPHOSES
GOMPHOSIS
GOMUTI
GOMUTIS
GOMUTO
GOMUTOS
GON
GONAD
GONADIAL

GONADIC
GONADS
GONDELAY
GONDELAYS
GONDOLA
GONDOLAS
GONDOLIER
GONDOLIERS
GONE
GONENESS
GONENESSES
GONER
GONERS
GONFALON
GONFALONS
GONFANON
GONFANONS
GONG
GONGED
GONGING
GONGS
GONGSTER
GONGSTERS
GONIA
GONIATITE
GONIATITES
GONIDIA
GONIDIAL
GONIDIC
GONIDIUM
GONION
GONK
GONKS
GONNA
GONOCOCCI
GONOCYTE
GONOCYTES
GONOPHORE
GONOPHORES
GONORRHEA
GONORRHEAS
GONS
GOO
GOOBER
GOOBERS
GOOD
GOODFACED
GOODIER
GOODIES
GOODIEST
GOODINESS
GOODINESSES
GOODISH
GOODLIER
GOODLIEST
GOODLY
GOODMAN
GOODMEN
GOODNESS
GOODNESSES
GOODNIGHT
GOODNIGHTS
GOODS
GOODSIRE
GOODSIRES
GOODTIME
GOODWIFE
GOODWILL
GOODWILLS
GOODWIVES

GOODY	GOOSY	GORSEDD	GOUACHE	GOWF
GOODYEAR	GOPAK	GORSEDDS	GOUACHES	GOWFED
GOODYEARS	GOPAKS	GORSES	GOUGE	GOWFER
GOOEY	GOPHER	GORSIER	GOUGED	GOWFERS
GOOF	GOPHERED	GORSIEST	GOUGÈRE	GOWFING
GOOFBALL	GOPHERING	GORSOON	GOUGÈRES	GOWFS
GOOFBALLS	GOPHERS	GORSOONS	GOUGES	GOWK
GOOFED	GOPURA	GORSY	GOUGING	GOWKS
GOOFIER	GOPURAM	GORY	GOUJEERS	GOWL
GOOFIEST	GOPURAMS	GOS	GOUJONS	GOWLAND
GOOFILY	GOPURAS	GOSH	GOUK	GOWLANDS
GOOFINESS	GORAL	GOSHAWK	GOUKS	GOWLED
GOOFINESSES	GORALS	GOSHAWKS	GOULASH	GOWLING
GOOFING	GORAMIES	GOSLARITE	GOULASHES	GOWLS
GOOFS	GORAMY	GOSLARITES	GOURAMI	GOWN
GOOFY	GORBLIMEY	GOSLET	GOURAMIS	GOWNBOY
GOOGLE	GORBLIMY	GOSLETS	GOURD	GOWNBOYS
GOOGLED	GORCOCK	GOSLING	GOURDE	GOWNED
GOOGLES	GORCOCKS	GOSLINGS	GOURDES	GOWNING
GOOGLIES	GORCROW	GOSPEL	GOURDS	GOWNMAN
GOOGLING	GORCROWS	GOSPELISE	GOURDY	GOWNMEN
GOOGLY	GORE	GOSPELISED	GOURMAND	GOWNS
GOOGOL	GORED	GOSPELISES	GOURMANDS	GOWNSMAN
GOOGOLS	GORES	GOSPELISING	GOURMET	GOWNSMEN
GOOIER	GORGE	GOSPELIZE	GOURMETS	GOWPEN
GOOIEST	GORGED	GOSPELIZED	GOUSTIER	GOWPENFUL
GOOK	GORGEOUS	GOSPELIZES	GOUSTIEST	GOWPENFULS
GOOKS	GORGERIN	GOSPELIZING	GOUSTROUS	GOWPENS
GOOL	GORGERINS	GOSPELLED	GOUSTY	GOY
GOOLD	GORGES	GOSPELLER	GOUT	GOYIM
GOOLDS	GORGET	GOSPELLERS	GOUTFLIES	GOYISCH
GOOLEY	GORGETS	GOSPELLING	GOUTFLY	GOYISH
GOOLEYS	GORGIA	GOSPELS	GOUTIER	GOZZAN
GOOLIE	GORGIAS	GOSPODAR	GOUTIEST	GOZZANS
GOOLIES	GORGING	GOSPODARS	GOUTINESS	GRAAL
GOOLS	GORGIO	GOSSAMER	GOUTINESSES	GRAALS
GOOLY	GORGIOS	GOSSAMERS	GOUTS	GRAB
GOON	GORGON	GOSSAMERY	GOUTTE	GRABBED
GOONEY	GORGONEIA	GOSSAN	GOUTTES	GRABBER
GOONEYS	GORGONIAN	GOSSANS	GOUTWEED	GRABBERS
GOONS	GORGONIANS	GOSSE	GOUTWEEDS	GRABBING
GOOP	GORGONISE	GOSSES	GOUTWORT	GRABBLE
GOOPS	GORGONISED	GOSSIB	GOUTWORTS	GRABBLED
GOOPY	GORGONISES	GOSSIBS	GOUTY	GRABBLER
GOOR	GORGONISING	GOSSIP	GOV	GRABBLERS
GOOROO	GORGONIZE	GOSSIPED	GOVERN	GRABBLES
GOOROOS	GORGONIZED	GOSSIPING	GOVERNALL	GRABBLING
GOORS	GORGONIZES	GOSSIPINGS	GOVERNALLS	GRABEN
GOOS	GORGONIZING	GOSSIPRIES	GOVERNED	GRABENS
GOOSANDER	GORGONS	GOSSIPRY	GOVERNESS	GRABS
GOOSANDERS	GORIER	GOSSIPY	GOVERNESSED	GRACE
GOOSE	GORIEST	GOSSOON	GOVERNESSES	GRACED
GOOSED	GORILLA	GOSSOONS	GOVERNESSING	GRACEFUL
GOOSEFOOT	GORILLAS	GOSSYPINE	GOVERNING	GRACELESS
GOOSEFOOTS	GORILLIAN	GOSSYPOL	GOVERNOR	GRACES
GOOSEGOB	GORILLINE	GOSSYPOLS	GOVERNORS	GRACILE
GOOSEGOBS	GORILY	GOT	GOVERNS	GRACILITIES
GOOSEGOG	GORING	GOTHICISE	GOVS	GRACILITY
GOOSEGOGS	GORINGS	GOTHICISED	GOWAN	GRACING
GOOSEHERD	GORM	GOTHICISES	GOWANED	GRACIOSO
GOOSEHERDS	GORMAND	GOTHICISING	GOWANS	GRACIOSOS
GOOSERIES	GORMANDS	GOTHICIZE	GOWANY	GRACIOUS
GOOSERY	GORMED	GOTHICIZED	GOWD	GRACKLE
GOOSES	GORMIER	GOTHICIZES	GOWDED	GRACKLES
GOOSEY	GORMIEST	GOTHICIZING	GOWDER	GRADABLE
GOOSEYS	GORMING	GÖTHITE	GOWDEST	GRADABLES
GOOSIER	GORMLESS	GÖTHITES	GOWDING	GRADATE
GOOSIES	GORMS	GOTTA	GOWDS	GRADATED
GOOSIEST	GORMY	GOTTEN	GOWDSPINK	GRADATES
GOOSING	GORSE		GOWDSPINKS	GRADATIM

GRADATING
GRADATION
GRADATIONS
GRADATORY
GRADDAN
GRADDANED
GRADDANING
GRADDANS
GRADE
GRADED
GRADELY
GRADER
GRADERS
GRADES
GRADIENT
GRADIENTS
GRADIN
GRADINE
GRADINES
GRADING
GRADINI
GRADINO
GRADINOS
GRADINS
GRADUAL
GRADUALLY
GRADUALS
GRADUAND
GRADUANDS
GRADUATE
GRADUATED
GRADUATES
GRADUATING
GRADUATOR
GRADUATORS
GRADUS
GRADUSES
GRAFF
GRAFFED
GRAFFING
GRAFFITI
GRAFFITIS
GRAFFITO
GRAFFS
GRAFT
GRAFTED
GRAFTER
GRAFTERS
GRAFTING
GRAFTINGS
GRAFTS
GRAIL
GRAILE
GRAILES
GRAILS
GRAIN
GRAINAGE
GRAINAGES
GRAINE
GRAINED
GRAINER
GRAINERS
GRAINES
GRAINIER
GRAINIEST
GRAINING
GRAININGS
GRAINS
GRAINY
GRAIP

GRAIPS
GRAITH
GRAITHED
GRAITHING
GRAITHLY
GRAITHS
GRAKLE
GRAKLES
GRALLOCH
GRALLOCHED
GRALLOCHING
GRALLOCHS
GRAM
GRAMA
GRAMARIES
GRAMARY
GRAMARYE
GRAMARYES
GRAMAS
GRAMASH
GRAMASHES
GRAME
GRAMERCIES
GRAMERCY
GRAMES
GRAMMAR
GRAMMARS
GRAMMATIC
GRAMME
GRAMMES
GRAMOCHE
GRAMOCHES
GRAMPUS
GRAMPUSES
GRAMS
GRAN
GRANARIES
GRANARY
GRAND
GRANDAD
GRANDADDIES
GRANDADDY
GRANDADS
GRANDAM
GRANDAMS
GRANDDAD
GRANDDADS
GRANDE
GRANDEE
GRANDEES
GRANDER
GRANDEST
GRANDEUR
GRANDEURS
GRANDIOSE
GRANDLY
GRANDMA
GRANDMAMA
GRANDMAMAS
GRANDMAS
GRANDNESS
GRANDNESSES
GRANDPA
GRANDPAPA
GRANDPAPAS
GRANDPAS
GRANDS
GRANDSIRE
GRANDSIRES
GRANDSON

GRANDSONS
GRANFER
GRANFERS
GRANGE
GRANGER
GRANGERS
GRANGES
GRANITE
GRANITES
GRANITIC
GRANITISE
GRANITISED
GRANITISES
GRANITISING
GRANITITE
GRANITITES
GRANITIZE
GRANITIZED
GRANITIZES
GRANITIZING
GRANITOID
GRANIVORE
GRANIVORES
GRANNAM
GRANNAMS
GRANNIE
GRANNIES
GRANNY
GRANS
GRANT
GRANTABLE
GRANTED
GRANTEE
GRANTEES
GRANTER
GRANTERS
GRANTING
GRANTOR
GRANTORS
GRANTS
GRANULAR
GRANULARY
GRANULATE
GRANULATED
GRANULATES
GRANULATING
GRANULE
GRANULES
GRANULITE
GRANULITES
GRANULOMA
GRANULOMAS
GRANULOMATA
GRANULOSE
GRANULOUS
GRAPE
GRAPED
GRAPELESS
GRAPERIES
GRAPERY
GRAPES
GRAPESEED
GRAPESEEDS
GRAPESHOT
GRAPESHOTS
GRAPETREE
GRAPETREES
GRAPEVINE
GRAPEVINES
GRAPEY

GRAPH
GRAPHED
GRAPHEME
GRAPHEMES
GRAPHEMIC
GRAPHEMICS
GRAPHIC
GRAPHICAL
GRAPHICLY
GRAPHICS
GRAPHING
GRAPHITE
GRAPHITES
GRAPHITIC
GRAPHIUM
GRAPHIUMS
GRAPHS
GRAPIER
GRAPIEST
GRAPING
GRAPLE
GRAPLED
GRAPLES
GRAPLING
GRAPNEL
GRAPNELS
GRAPPA
GRAPPAS
GRAPPLE
GRAPPLED
GRAPPLES
GRAPPLING
GRAPY
GRASP
GRASPABLE
GRASPED
GRASPER
GRASPERS
GRASPING
GRASPLESS
GRASPS
GRASS
GRASSED
GRASSER
GRASSERS
GRASSES
GRASSHOOK
GRASSHOOKS
GRASSIER
GRASSIEST
GRASSING
GRASSINGS
GRASSLAND
GRASSLANDS
GRASSUM
GRASSUMS
GRASSY
GRASTE
GRAT
GRATE
GRATED
GRATEFUL
GRATER
GRATERS
GRATES
GRATICULE
GRATICULES
GRATIFIED
GRATIFIER
GRATIFIERS

GRATIFIES
GRATIFY
GRATIFYING
GRATING
GRATINGLY
GRATINGS
GRATIS
GRATITUDE
GRATITUDES
GRATTOIR
GRATTOIRS
GRATUITIES
GRATUITY
GRATULANT
GRATULATE
GRATULATED
GRATULATES
GRATULATING
GRAUPEL
GRAUPELS
GRAVAMEN
GRAVAMINA
GRAVE
GRAVED
GRAVEL
GRAVELESS
GRAVELLED
GRAVELLING
GRAVELLY
GRAVELS
GRAVELY
GRAVEN
GRAVENESS
GRAVENESSES
GRAVER
GRAVERS
GRAVES
GRAVEST
GRAVEYARD
GRAVEYARDS
GRAVID
GRAVIDITIES
GRAVIDITY
GRAVIES
GRAVING
GRAVINGS
GRAVITAS
GRAVITASES
GRAVITATE
GRAVITATED
GRAVITATES
GRAVITATING
GRAVITIES
GRAVITON
GRAVITONS
GRAVITY
GRAVURE
GRAVURES
GRAVY
GRAY
GRAYED
GRAYER
GRAYEST
GRAYFLIES
GRAYFLY
GRAYING
GRAYLE
GRAYLES
GRAYLING
GRAYLINGS

GRAYS
GRAYWACKE
GRAYWACKES
GRAZE
GRAZED
GRAZER
GRAZERS
GRAZES
GRAZIER
GRAZIERS
GRAZING
GRAZINGS
GRAZIOSO
GREASE
GREASED
GREASER
GREASERS
GREASES
GREASIER
GREASIEST
GREASILY
GREASING
GREASY
GREAT
GREATCOAT
GREATCOATS
GREATEN
GREATENED
GREATENING
GREATENS
GREATER
GREATEST
GREATLY
GREATNESS
GREATNESSES
GREATS
GREAVE
GREAVED
GREAVES
GREAVING
GREBE
GREBES
GRECE
GRECES
GRECIAN
GRECIANS
GRECQUE
GRECQUES
GREE
GREECE
GREECES
GREED
GREEDIER
GREEDIEST
GREEDILY
GREEDS
GREEDY
GREEGREE
GREFGREES
GREEING
GREEN
GREENBACK
GREENBACKS
GREENED
GREENER
GREENERIES
GREENERY
GREENEST
GREENFLIES
GREENFLY

GREENGAGE
GREENGAGES
GREENHAND
GREENHANDS
GREENHORN
GREENHORNS
GREENIER
GREENIEST
GREENING
GREENINGS
GREENISH
GREENLET
GREENLETS
GREENLY
GREENMAIL
GREENMAILS
GREENNESS
GREENNESSES
GREENROOM
GREENROOMS
GREENS
GREENSAND
GREENSANDS
GREENTH
GREENTHS
GREENWEED
GREENWEEDS
GREENWOOD
GREENWOODS
GREENY
GREES
GREESE
GREESES
GREESING
GREESINGS
GREET
GREETE
GREETED
GREETES
GREETING
GREETINGS
GREETS
GREFFIER
GREFFIERS
GREGALE
GREGALES
GREGARIAN
GREGARINE
GREGARINES
GREGATIM
GRÈGE
GREGO
GREGORIES
GREGORY
GREGOS
GREIGE
GREIN
GREINED
GREINING
GREINS
GREISEN
GREISENS
GREISLY
GREMIAL
GREMIALS
GREMLIN
GREMLINS
GREN
GRENADE
GRENADES

GRENADIER
GRENADIERS
GRENADINE
GRENADINES
GRENNED
GRENNING
GRENS
GRESE
GRESES
GRESSING
GRESSINGS
GREVE
GREVES
GREW
GREWED
GREWHOUND
GREWHOUNDS
GREWING
GREWS
GREY
GREYBEARD
GREYBEARDS
GREYED
GREYER
GREYEST
GREYHEN
GREYHENS
GREYHOUND
GREYHOUNDS
GREYING
GREYISH
GREYLY
GREYNESS
GREYNESSES
GREYS
GREYWACKE
GREYWACKES
GRIBBLE
GRIBBLES
GRICE
GRICER
GRICERS
GRICES
GRICING
GRICINGS
GHID
GRIDDLE
GRIDDLES
GRIDE
GRIDED
GRIDELIN
GRIDELINS
GRIDES
GRIDING
GRIDIRON
GRIDIRONED
GRIDIRONING
GRIDIRONS
GRIDLOCK
GRIDLOCKS
GRIDS
GRIECE
GRIECED
GRIECES
GRIEF
GRIEFFUL
GRIEFLESS
GRIEFS
GRIESIE
GRIESLY

GRIESY
GRIEVANCE
GRIEVANCES
GRIEVE
GRIEVED
GRIEVER
GRIEVERS
GRIEVES
GRIEVING
GRIEVOUS
GRIFF
GRIFFE
GRIFFES
GRIFFIN
GRIFFINS
GRIFFON
GRIFFONS
GRIFFS
GRIFT
GRIFTED
GRIFTER
GRIFTERS
GRIFTING
GRIFTS
GRIG
GRIGGED
GRIGGING
GRIGRI
GRIGRIS
GRIGS
GRIKE
GRIKES
GRILL
GRILLADE
GRILLADES
GRILLAGE
GRILLAGES
GRILLE
GRILLED
GRILLES
GRILLING
GRILLINGS
GRILLS
GRILSE
GRILSES
GRIM
GRIMACE
GRIMACED
GRIMACES
GRIMACING
GRIMALKIN
GRIMALKINS
GRIME
GRIMED
GRIMES
GRIMIER
GRIMIEST
GRIMILY
GRIMINESS
GRIMINESSES
GRIMING
GRIMLY
GRIMMER
GRIMMEST
GRIMNESS
GRIMNESSES
GRIMOIRE
GRIMOIRES
GRIMY
GRIN

GRIND
GRINDED
GRINDER
GRINDERIES
GRINDERS
GRINDERY
GRINDING
GRINDINGS
GRINDS
GRINGO
GRINGOS
GRINNED
GRINNER
GRINNERS
GRINNING
GRINS
GRIOT
GRIOTS
GRIP
GRIPE
GRIPED
GRIPER
GRIPERS
GRIPES
GRIPING
GRIPINGLY
GRIPLE
GRIPLES
GRIPPE
GRIPPED
GRIPPER
GRIPPERS
GRIPPES
GRIPPIER
GRIPPIEST
GRIPPING
GRIPPLE
GRIPPLES
GRIPPY
GRIPS
GRIPSACK
GRIPSACKS
GRIS
GRISAILLE
GRISAILLES
GRISE
GRISELY
GRISEOUS
GRISES
GRISETTE
GRISETTES
GRISGRIS
GRISING
GRISKIN
GRISKINS
GRISLED
GRISLIER
GRISLIEST
GRISLY
GRISON
GRISONS
GRIST
GRISTLE
GRISTLES
GRISTLIER
GRISTLIEST
GRISTLY
GRISTS
GRISY

GRIT	GRONEFULL	GROUCHY	GROWLS	GRUMOSE
GRITH	GRONES	GROUF	GROWLY	GRUMOUS
GRITHS	GRONING	GROUFS	GROWN	GRUMPH
GRITS	GROOF	GROUND	GROWS	GRUMPHED
GRITSTONE	GROOFS	GROUNDAGE	GROWTH	GRUMPHIE
GRITSTONES	GROOLY	GROUNDAGES	GROWTHIST	GRUMPHIES
GRITTED	GROOM	GROUNDED	GROWTHISTS	GRUMPHING
GRITTER	GROOMED	GROUNDEN	GROWTHS	GRUMPHS
GRITTERS	GROOMING	GROUNDER	GROYNE	GRUMPIER
GRITTEST	GROOMS	GROUNDERS	GROYNES	GRUMPIEST
GRITTIER	GROOMSMAN	GROUNDING	GRUB	GRUMPILY
GRITTIEST	GROOMSMEN	GROUNDINGS	GRUBBED	GRUMPY
GRITTING	GROOVE	GROUNDMAN	GRUBBER	GRUNGIER
GRITTY	GROOVED	GROUNDMEN	GRUBBERS	GRUNGIEST
GRIVET	GROOVES	GROUNDS	GRUBBIER	GRUNGY
GRIVETS	GROOVIER	GROUNDSEL	GRUBBIEST	GRUNION
GRIZE	GROOVIEST	GROUNDSELS	GRUBBING	GRUNIONS
GRIZES	GROOVING	GROUP	GRUBBLE	GRUNT
GRIZZLE	GROOVY	GROUPAGE	GRUBBLED	GRUNTED
GRIZZLED	GROPE	GROUPAGES	GRUBBLES	GRUNTER
GRIZZLER	GROPED	GROUPED	GRUBBLING	GRUNTERS
GRIZZLERS	GROPER	GROUPER	GRUBBY	GRUNTING
GRIZZLES	GROPERS	GROUPERS	GRUBS	GRUNTINGS
GRIZZLIER	GROPES	GROUPIE	GRUDGE	GRUNTLE
GRIZZLIES	GROPING	GROUPIES	GRUDGED	GRUNTLED
GRIZZLIEST	GROPINGLY	GROUPING	GRUDGEFUL	GRUNTLES
GRIZZLING	GROSBEAK	GROUPINGS	GRUDGES	GRUNTLING
GRIZZLY	GROSBEAKS	GROUPIST	GRUDGING	GRUNTS
GROAN	GROSCHEN	GROUPISTS	GRUDGINGS	GRUPPETTI
GROANED	GROSCHENS	GROUPLET	GRUE	GRUPPETTO
GROANER	GROSER	GROUPLETS	GRUED	GRUTCH
GROANERS	GROSERS	GROUPS	GRUEING	GRUTCHED
GROANFUL	GROSERT	GROUPY	GRUEL	GRUTCHES
GROANING	GROSERTS	GROUSE	GRUELLED	GRUTCHING
GROANINGS	GROSET	GROUSED	GRUELLING	GRUTTEN
GROANS	GROSETS	GROUSER	GRUELLINGS	GRYCE
GROAT	GROSGRAIN	GROUSERS	GRUELS	GRYCES
GROATS	GROSGRAINS	GROUSES	GRUES	GRYDE
GROCER	GROSS	GROUSING	GRUESOME	GRYDED
GROCERIES	GROSSART	GROUT	GRUESOMER	GRYDES
GROCERS	GROSSARTS	GROUTED	GRUESOMEST	GRYDING
GROCERY	GROSSED	GROUTIER	GRUFF	GRYESLY
GROCKLE	GROSSER	GROUTIEST	GRUFFER	GRYESY
GROCKLES	GROSSES	GROUTING	GRUFFEST	GRYFON
GROG	GROSSEST	GROUTINGS	GRUFFISH	GRYFONS
GROGGED	GROSSING	GROUTS	GRUFFLY	GRYKE
GROGGERIES	GROSSLY	GROUTY	GRUFFNESS	GRYKES
GROGGERY	GROSSNESS	GROVE	GRUFFNESSES	GRYPE
GROGGIER	GROSSNESSES	GROVEL	GRUFTED	GRYPES
GROGGIEST	GROSSULAR	GROVELLED	GRUING	GRYPHON
GROGGING	GROSSULARS	GROVELLER	GRUM	GRYPHONS
GROGGY	GROT	GROVELLERS	GRUMBLE	GRYPT
GROGRAM	GROTESQUE	GROVELLING	GRUMBLED	GRYSBOK
GROGRAMS	GROTESQUER	GROVELS	GRUMBLER	GRYSBOKS
GROGS	GROTESQUES	GROVES	GRUMBLERS	GRYSELY
GROIN	GROTESQUEST	GROW	GRUMBLES	GRYSIE
GROINED	GROTS	GROWER	GRUMBLIER	GU
GROINING	GROTTIER	GROWERS	GRUMBLIEST	GUACAMOLE
GROININGS	GROTTIEST	GROWING	GRUMBLING	GUACAMOLES
GROINS	GROTTO	GROWINGS	GRUMBLINGS	GUACHARO
GROMA	GROTTOES	GROWL	GRUMBLY	GUACHAROS
GROMAS	GROTTOS	GROWLED	GRUME	GUACO
GROMET	GROTTY	GROWLER	GRUMES	GUACOS
GROMETS	GROUCH	GROWLERIES	GRUMLY	GUAIACUM
GROMMET	GROUCHED	GROWLERS	GRUMMER	GUAIACUMS
GROMMETS	GROUCHES	GROWLERY	GRUMMEST	GUAN
GROMWELL	GROUCHIER	GROWLIER	GRUMMET	GUANA
GROMWELLS	GROUCHIEST	GROWLIEST	GRUMMETS	GUANACO
GRONE	GROUCHILY	GROWLING	GRUMNESS	GUANACOS
GRONED	GROUCHING	GROWLINGS	GRUMNESSES	GUANAS

GUANAZOLO
GUANAZOLOS
GUANIN
GUANINE
GUANINES
GUANINS
GUANO
GUANOS
GUANS
GUAR
GUARANÁ
GUARANÁS
GUARANI
GUARANIES
GUARANTEE
GUARANTEED
GUARANTEEING
GUARANTEES
GUARANTIED
GUARANTIES
GUARANTOR
GUARANTORS
GUARANTY
GUARANTYING
GUARD
GUARDABLE
GUARDAGE
GUARDAGES
GUARDANT
GUARDANTS
GUARDED
GUARDEDLY
GUARDEE
GUARDEES
GUARDIAN
GUARDIANS
GUARDING
GUARDLESS
GUARDS
GUARDSMAN
GUARDSMEN
GUARISH
GUARISHED
GUARISHES
GUARISHING
GUARS
GUAVA
GUAVAS
GUAYULE
GUAYULES
GUB
GUBBAH
GUBBAHS
GUBBINS
GUBS
GUCK
GUCKIER
GUCKIEST
GUCKS
GUCKY
GUDDLE
GUDDLED
GUDDLES
GUDDLING
GUDE
GUDEMAN
GUDEMEN
GUDESIRE
GUDESIRES
GUDEWIFE

GUDEWIVES
GUDGEON
GUDGEONED
GUDGEONING
GUDGEONS
GUE
GUENON
GUENONS
GUERDON
GUERDONED
GUERDONING
GUERDONS
GUEREZA
GUEREZAS
GUÉRIDON
GUÉRIDONS
GUERILLA
GUERILLAS
GUERNSEY
GUERNSEYS
GUERRILLA
GUERRILLAS
GUES
GUESS
GUESSABLE
GUESSED
GUESSER
GUESSERS
GUESSES
GUESSING
GUESSINGS
GUEST
GUESTED
GUESTEN
GUESTENED
GUESTENING
GUESTENS
GUESTING
GUESTS
GUESTWISE
GUFF
GUFFAW
GUFFAWED
GUFFAWING
GUFFAWS
GUFFS
GUGGLE
GUGGLED
GUGGLES
GUGGLING
GUICHET
GUICHETS
GUID
GUIDABLE
GUIDAGE
GUIDAGES
GUIDANCE
GUIDANCES
GUIDE
GUIDED
GUIDELESS
GUIDELINE
GUIDELINES
GUIDER
GUIDERS
GUIDES
GUIDESHIP
GUIDESHIPS
GUIDING
GUIDINGS

GUIDON
GUIDONS
GUILD
GUILDER
GUILDERS
GUILDHALL
GUILDHALLS
GUILDRIES
GUILDRY
GUILDS
GUILE
GUILED
GUILEFUL
GUILELESS
GUILER
GUILERS
GUILES
GUILING
GUILLEMOT
GUILLEMOTS
GUILLOCHE
GUILLOCHED
GUILLOCHES
GUILLOCHING
GUILT
GUILTIER
GUILTIEST
GUILTILY
GUILTLESS
GUILTS
GUILTY
GUIMBARD
GUIMBARDS
GUIMP
GUIMPE
GUIMPED
GUIMPES
GUIMPING
GUIMPS
GUINEA
GUINEAS
GUIPURE
GUIPURES
GUIRO
GUIROS
GUISARD
GUISARDS
GUISE
GUISED
GUISER
GUISERS
GUISES
GUISING
GUITAR
GUITARIST
GUITARISTS
GUITARS
GUIZER
GUIZERS
GULA
GULAG
GULAGS
GULAR
GULAS
GULCH
GULCHED
GULCHES
GULCHING
GULDEN
GULDENS

GULE
GULES
GULF
GULFED
GULFIER
GULFIEST
GULFING
GULFS
GULFWEED
GULFWEEDS
GULFY
GULL
GULLABLE
GULLED
GULLER
GULLERIES
GULLERS
GULLERY
GULLET
GULLETS
GULLEY
GULLEYED
GULLEYING
GULLEYS
GULLIBLE
GULLIED
GULLIES
GULLING
GULLISH
GULLS
GULLY
GULLYING
GULOSITIES
GULOSITY
GULP
GULPED
GULPER
GULPERS
GULPH
GULPHED
GULPHING
GULPHS
GULPING
GULPS
GULY
GUM
GUMBO
GUMBOIL
GUMBOILS
GUMBOOT
GUMBOOTS
GUMBOS
GUMDROP
GUMDROPS
GUMMA
GUMMATA
GUMMATOUS
GUMMED
GUMMIER
GUMMIEST
GUMMINESS
GUMMINESSES
GUMMING
GUMMINGS
GUMMITE
GUMMITES
GUMMOSES
GUMMOSIS
GUMMOSITIES
GUMMOSITY

GUMMOUS
GUMMY
GUMP
GUMPED
GUMPHION
GUMPHIONS
GUMPING
GUMPS
GUMPTION
GUMPTIONS
GUMPTIOUS
GUMS
GUMSHIELD
GUMSHIELDS
GUMSHOE
GUMSHOED
GUMSHOEING
GUMSHOES
GUN
GUNBOAT
GUNBOATS
GUNCOTTON
GUNCOTTONS
GUNDIES
GUNDY
GUNFIGHT
GUNFIGHTING
GUNFIGHTS
GUNFIRE
GUNFIRES
GUNFLINT
GUNFLINTS
GUNFOUGHT
GUNGE
GUNGES
GUNGIER
GUNGIEST
GUNGY
GUNITE
GUNITES
GUNK
GUNKS
GUNLAYER
GUNLAYERS
GUNMAKER
GUNMAKERS
GUNMAN
GUNMEN
GUNMETAL
GUNMETALS
GUNNAGE
GUNNAGES
GUNNED
GUNNEL
GUNNELS
GUNNER
GUNNERA
GUNNERAS
GUNNERIES
GUNNERS
GUNNERY
GUNNIES
GUNNING
GUNNINGS
GUNNY
GUNPLAY
GUNPLAYS
GUNPORT
GUNPORTS
GUNPOWDER

GUNPOWDERS
GUNROOM
GUNROOMS
GUNRUNNER
GUNRUNNERS
GUNS
GUNSEL
GUNSELS
GUNSHIP
GUNSHIPS
GUNSHOT
GUNSHOTS
GUNSMITH
GUNSMITHS
GUNSTICK
GUNSTICKS
GUNSTOCK
GUNSTOCKS
GUNSTONE
GUNSTONES
GUNTER
GUNTERS
GUNWALE
GUNWALES
GUNYAH
GUNYAHS
GUP
GUPPIES
GUPPY
GUPS
GUR
GURAMI
GURAMIS
GURDWARA
GURDWARAS
GURGE
GURGES
GURGLE
GURGLED
GURGLES
GURGLING
GURGOYLE
GURGOYLES
GURJUN
GURJUNS
GURL
GURLED
GURLET
GURLETS
GURLIER
GURLIEST
GURLING
GURLS
GURLY
GURN
GURNARD
GURNARDS
GURNED
GURNET
GURNETS
GURNEY

GURNEYS
GURNING
GURNS
GURRAH
GURRAHS
GURRIES
GURRY
GURS
GURU
GURUDOM
GURUDOMS
GURUISM
GURUISMS
GURUS
GURUSHIP
GURUSHIPS
GUS
GUSH
GUSHED
GUSHER
GUSHERS
GUSHES
GUSHIER
GUSHIEST
GUSHING
GUSHINGLY
GUSHY
GUSLA
GUSLAR
GUSLARS
GUSLAS
GUSLE
GUSLES
GUSLI
GUSLIS
GUSSET
GUSSETED
GUSSETING
GUSSETS
GUST
GUSTABLE
GUSTABLES
GUSTATION
GUSTATIONS
GUSTATIVE
GUSTATORY
GUSTED
GUSTFUL
GUSTIER
GUSTIEST
GUSTINESS
GUSTINESSES
GUSTING
GUSTO
GUSTOS
GUSTS
GUSTY
GUT
GUTBUCKET
GUTBUCKETS
GUTCHER

GUTCHERS
GUTLESS
GUTS
GUTSIER
GUTSIEST
GUTSINESS
GUTSINESSES
GUTSY
GUTTA
GUTTAE
GUTTAS
GUTTATE
GUTTATED
GUTTATES
GUTTATING
GUTTATION
GUTTATIONS
GUTTED
GUTTER
GUTTERED
GUTTERING
GUTTERINGS
GUTTERS
GUTTIES
GUTTING
GUTTLE
GUTTLED
GUTTLES
GUTTLING
GUTTURAL
GUTTURALS
GUTTY
GUY
GUYED
GUYING
GUYLE
GUYLER
GUYLERS
GUYLES
GUYOT
GUYOTS
GUYS
GUYSE
GUYSES
GUZZLE
GUZZLED
GUZZLER
GUZZLERS
GUZZLES
GUZZLING
GWINIAD
GWINIADS
GWYNIAD
GWYNIADS
GYAL
GYALS
GYBE
GYBED
GYBES
GYBING
GYELD

GYELDS
GYLDEN
GYM
GYMBAL
GYMBALS
GYMKHANA
GYMKHANAS
GYMMAL
GYMMALS
GYMNASIA
GYMNASIAL
GYMNASIC
GYMNASIEN
GYMNASIUM
GYMNASIUMS
GYMNAST
GYMNASTIC
GYMNASTICS
GYMNASTS
GYMNIC
GYMNOSOPH
GYMNOSOPHS
GYMP
GYMPED
GYMPING
GYMPS
GYMS
GYNAE
GYNAECEUM
GYNAECEUMS
GYNAECOID
GYNAES
GYNANDRIES
GYNANDRY
GYNECIUM
GYNECIUMS
GYNIES
GYNNEY
GYNNY
GYNOCRACIES
GYNOCRACY
GYNOECIUM
GYNOECIUMS
GYNOPHORE
GYNOPHORES
GYNY
GYP
GYPPED
GYPPIE
GYPPIES
GYPPING
GYPPO
GYPPOS
GYPPY
GYPS
GYPSEOUS
GYPSIED
GYPSIES
GYPSUM
GYPSUMS
GYPSY

GYPSYDOM
GYPSYDOMS
GYPSYING
GYPSYISM
GYPSYISMS
GYPSYWORT
GYPSYWORTS
GYRAL
GYRALLY
GYRANT
GYRATE
GYRATED
GYRATES
GYRATING
GYRATION
GYRATIONS
GYRATORY
GYRE
GYRED
GYRES
GYRFALCON
GYRFALCONS
GYRI
GYRING
GYRO
GYROCAR
GYROCARS
GYRODYNE
GYRODYNES
GYROIDAL
GYROMANCIES
GYROMANCY
GYRON
GYRONNY
GYRONS
GYROPLANE
GYROPLANES
GYROS
GYROSCOPE
GYROSCOPES
GYROSE
GYROSTAT
GYROSTATS
GYROUS
GYROVAGUE
GYROVAGUES
GYRUS
GYRUSES
GYTE
GYTER
GYTES
GYTEST
GYTRASH
GYTRASHES
GYVE
GYVED
GYVES
GYVING

H

HA
HAAF
HAAFS
HAANEPOOT
HAANEPOOTS
HAAR
HAARS
HABANERA
HABANERAS
HABDABS
HABERDINE
HABERDINES
HABERGEON
HABERGEONS
HABILABLE
HABILE
HABIT
HABITABLE
HABITABLY
HABITANS
HABITANT
HABITANTS
HABITAT
HABITATS
HABITED
HABITING
HABITS
HABITUAL
HABITUALS
HABITUATE
HABITUATED
HABITUATES
HABITUATING
HABITUDE
HABITUDES
HABITUÉ
HABITUÉS
HABITUS
HABLE
HABOOB
HABOOBS
HACEK
HACEKS
HACHIS
HACHURE
HACHURED
HACHURES
HACHURING
HACIENDA
HACIENDAS
HACK
HACKAMORE
HACKAMORES
HACKBERRIES
HACKBERRY
HACKBOLT
HACKBOLTS
HACKBUT
HACKBUTS
HACKED
HACKEE
HACKEES
HACKER
HACKERIES

HACKERS
HACKERY
HACKETTE
HACKETTES
HACKING
HACKINGS
HACKLE
HACKLED
HACKLER
HACKLERS
HACKLES
HACKLET
HACKLETS
HACKLIER
HACKLIEST
HACKLING
HACKLY
HACKNEY
HACKNEYED
HACKNEYING
HACKNEYS
HACKS
HACQUETON
HACQUETONS
HAD
HADAL
HADDEN
HADDIE
HADDIES
HADDING
HADDOCK
HADDOCKS
HADE
HADED
HADES
HADING
HADITH
HADITHS
HADJ
HADJES
HADJI
HADJIS
HADROME
HADROMES
HADRON
HADRONIC
HADRONS
HADROSAUR
HADROSAURS
HADS
HADST
HAE
HAECCEITIES
HAECCEITY
HAEM
HAEMAL
HAEMATIC
HAEMATIN
HAEMATINS
HAEMATITE
HAEMATITES
HAEMATOID
HAEMATOMA
HAEMATOMAS

HAEMIC
HAEMIN
HAEMINS
HAEMOCYTE
HAEMOCYTES
HAEMONIES
HAEMONY
HAEMOSTAT
HAEMOSTATS
HAEMS
HAET
HAETS
HAFF
HAFFET
HAFFETS
HAFFIT
HAFFITS
HAFFLIN
HAFFLINS
HAFFS
HAFNIUM
HAFNIUMS
HAFT
HAFTED
HAFTING
HAFTS
HAG
HAGBERRIES
HAGBERRY
HAGBOLT
HAGBOLTS
HAGBUT
HAGBUTS
HAGDEN
HAGDENS
HAGDON
HAGDONS
HAGDOWN
HAGDOWNS
HAGFISH
HAGFISHES
HAGG
HAGGARD
HAGGARDLY
HAGGARDS
HAGGED
HAGGING
HAGGIS
HAGGISES
HAGGISH
HAGGISHLY
HAGGLE
HAGGLED
HAGGLER
HAGGLERS
HAGGLES
HAGGLING
HAGGS
HAGIARCHIES
HAGIARCHY
HAGIOLOGIES
HAGIOLOGY
HAGLET
HAGLETS

HAGS
HAH
HAHNIUM
HAHNIUMS
HAICK
HAICKS
HAIDUK
HAIDUKS
HAIK
HAIKAI
HAIKS
HAIKU
HAIL
HAILED
HAILER
HAILERS
HAILIER
HAILIEST
HAILING
HAILS
HAILSHOT
HAILSHOTS
HAILSTONE
HAILSTONES
HAILY
HAIN
HAINCH
HAINCHED
HAINCHES
HAINCHING
HAINED
HAINING
HAININGS
HAINS
HAIQUE
HAIQUES
HAIR
HAIRBELL
HAIRBELLS
HAIRCLOTH
HAIRCLOTHS
HAIRCUT
HAIRCUTS
HAIRED
HAIRIER
HAIRIEST
HAIRINESS
HAIRINESSES
HAIRING
HAIRLESS
HAIRLIKE
HAIRLINE
HAIRLINES
HAIRPIN
HAIRPINS
HAIRS
HAIRST
HAIRSTED
HAIRSTING
HAIRSTS
HAIRSTYLE
HAIRSTYLES
HAIRY
HAITH

HAJ
HAJES
HAJI
HAJIS
HAJJ
HAJJES
HAJJI
HAJJIS
HAKA
HAKAM
HAKAMS
HAKAS
HAKE
HAKES
HAKIM
HAKIMS
HALAL
HALALLED
HALALLING
HALALS
HALATION
HALATIONS
HALAVAH
HALAVAHS
HALBERD
HALBERDS
HALBERT
HALBERTS
HALCYON
HALCYONS
HALE
HALED
HALENESS
HALENESSES
HALER
HALERS
HALES
HALEST
HALF
HALFA
HALFAS
HALFEN
HALFLIN
HALFLING
HALFLINGS
HALFLINS
HALFPACE
HALFPACES
HALFPENCE
HALFPENNIES
HALFPENNY
HALFWAY
HALIBUT
HALIBUTS
HALICORE
HALICORES
HALIDE
HALIDES
HALIDOM
HALIDOMS
HALIEUTIC
HALIEUTICS
HALIMOT
HALIMOTE

HALIMOTES
HALIMOTS
HALING
HALIOTIS
HALITE
HALITES
HALITOSES
HALITOSIS
HALITOUS
HALITUS
HALITUSES
HALL
HALLAL
HALLALI
HALLALIS
HALLALLED
HALLALLING
HALLALOO
HALLALOOS
HALLALS
HALLAN
HALLANS
HALLIAN
HALLIANS
HALLIARD
HALLIARDS
HALLING
HALLINGS
HALLION
HALLIONS
HALLMARK
HALLMARKED
HALLMARKING
HALLMARKS
HALLO
HALLOA
HALLOAED
HALLOAING
HALLOAS
HALLOED
HALLOES
HALLOING
HALLOO
HALLOOED
HALLOOING
HALLOOS
HALLOS
HALLOW
HALLOWED
HALLOWING
HALLOWS
HALLS
HALLSTAND
HALLSTANDS
HALLUCES
HALLUX
HALLWAY
HALLWAYS
HALLYON
HALLYONS
HALM
HALMA
HALMAS
HALMS
HALO
HALOBIONT
HALOBIONTS
HALOED
HALOES
HALOGEN

HALOGENS
HALOID
HALOIDS
HALOING
HALOPHILE
HALOPHILIES
HALOPHILY
HALOPHOBE
HALOPHOBES
HALOPHYTE
HALOPHYTES
HALOS
HALOTHANE
HALOTHANES
HALSE
HALSED
HALSER
HALSERS
HALSES
HALSING
HALT
HALTED
HALTER
HALTERED
HALTERES
HALTERING
HALTERS
HALTING
HALTINGLY
HALTINGS
HALTS
HALVA
HALVAH
HALVAHS
HALVAS
HALVE
HALVED
HALVER
HALVERS
HALVES
HALVING
HALYARD
HALYARDS
HAM
HAMADRYAD
HAMADRYADES
HAMADRYADS
HAMAL
HAMALS
HAMARTIA
HAMARTIAS
HAMATE
HAMBLE
HAMBLED
HAMBLES
HAMBLING
HAMBURGER
HAMBURGERS
HAME
HAMED
HAMES
HAMEWITH
HAMFATTER
HAMFATTERED
HAMFATTERING
HAMFATTERS
HAMING
HAMLET
HAMLETS
HAMMAL

HAMMALS
HAMMAM
HAMMAMS
HAMMED
HAMMER
HAMMERED
HAMMERER
HAMMERERS
HAMMERING
HAMMERINGS
HAMMERKOP
HAMMERKOPS
HAMMERMAN
HAMMERMEN
HAMMERS
HAMMIER
HAMMIEST
HAMMILY
HAMMING
HAMMOCK
HAMMOCKS
HAMMY
HAMOSE
HAMOUS
HAMPER
HAMPERED
HAMPERING
HAMPERS
HAMPSTER
HAMPSTERS
HAMS
HAMSTER
HAMSTERS
HAMSTRING
HAMSTRINGED
HAMSTRINGING
HAMSTRINGS
HAMSTRUNG
HAMULAR
HAMULATE
HAMULI
HAMULUS
HAMZA
HAMZAH
HAMZAHS
HAMZAS
HAN
HANAP
HANAPER
HANAPERS
HANAPS
HANCE
HANCES
HANCH
HANCHED
HANCHES
HANCHING
HAND
HANDBAG
HANDBAGS
HANDBALL
HANDBALLS
HANDBELL
HANDBELLS
HANDBILL
HANDBILLS
HANDBOOK
HANDBOOKS
HANDCAR
HANDCARS

HANDCLAP
HANDCLAPS
HANDCLASP
HANDCLASPS
HANDCRAFT
HANDCRAFTS
HANDCUFF
HANDCUFFED
HANDCUFFING
HANDCUFFS
HANDED
HANDER
HANDERS
HANDFAST
HANDFASTED
HANDFASTING
HANDFASTINGS
HANDFASTS
HANDFUL
HANDFULS
HANDGRIP
HANDGRIPS
HANDHOLD
HANDHOLDS
HANDICAP
HANDICAPPED
HANDICAPPING
HANDICAPS
HANDIER
HANDIEST
HANDILY
HANDINESS
HANDINESSES
HANDING
HANDIWORK
HANDIWORKS
HANDJAR
HANDJARS
HANDLE
HANDLEBAR
HANDLEBARS
HANDLED
HANDLER
HANDLERS
HANDLES
HANDLESS
HANDLING
HANDLINGS
HANDLIST
HANDLISTS
HANDMADE
HANDMAID
HANDMAIDS
HANDOUT
HANDOUTS
HANDOVER
HANDOVERS
HANDPLAY
HANDPLAYS
HANDRAIL
HANDRAILS
HANDS
HANDSAW
HANDSAWS
HANDSEL
HANDSELLED
HANDSELLING
HANDSELS
HANDSET
HANDSETS

HANDSHAKE
HANDSHAKES
HANDSOME
HANDSOMER
HANDSOMEST
HANDSPIKE
HANDSPIKES
HANDSTAFF
HANDSTAFFS
HANDSTAND
HANDSTANDS
HANDSTAVES
HANDSTURN
HANDSTURNS
HANDTOWEL
HANDTOWELS
HANDWORK
HANDWORKS
HANDY
HANDYMAN
HANDYMEN
HANDYWORK
HANDYWORKS
HANEPOOT
HANEPOOTS
HANG
HANGABLE
HANGAR
HANGARS
HANGBIRD
HANGBIRDS
HANGDOG
HANGDOGS
HANGED
HANGER
HANGERS
HANGFIRE
HANGFIRES
HANGING
HANGINGS
HANGMAN
HANGMEN
HANGNAIL
HANGNAILS
HANGNEST
HANGNESTS
HANGOUT
HANGOUTS
HANGOVER
HANGOVERS
HANGS
HANJAR
HANJARS
HANK
HANKED
HANKER
HANKERED
HANKERING
HANKERINGS
HANKERS
HANKIE
HANKIES
HANKING
HANKS
HANKY
HANSEL
HANSELLED
HANSELLING
HANSELS
HANSOM

HANSOMS
HANTLE
HANTLES
HANUMAN
HANUMANS
HAOMA
HAOMAS
HAP
HAPHAZARD
HAPHAZARDS
HAPLESS
HAPLESSLY
HAPLOID
HAPLOIDIES
HAPLOIDY
HAPLOLOGIES
HAPLOLOGY
HAPLY
HAPPED
HAPPEN
HAPPENED
HAPPENING
HAPPENINGS
HAPPENS
HAPPIED
HAPPIER
HAPPIES
HAPPIEST
HAPPILY
HAPPINESS
HAPPINESSES
HAPPING
HAPPY
HAPPYING
HAPS
HAPTERON
HAPTERONS
HAPTIC
HAPTICS
HAQUETON
HAQUETONS
HARAM
HARAMS
HARANGUE
HARANGUED
HARANGUER
HARANGUERS
HARANGUES
HARANGUING
HARASS
HARASSED
HARASSER
HARASSERS
HARASSES
HARASSING
HARASSINGS
HARBINGER
HARBINGERED
HARBINGERING
HARBINGERS
HARBOR
HARBORED
HARBORING
HARBORS
HARBOUR
HARBOURED
HARBOURER
HARBOURERS
HARBOURING
HARBOURS

HARD
HARDBACK
HARDBACKS
HARDBAKE
HARDBAKES
HARDBEAM
HARDBEAMS
HARDBOARD
HARDBOARDS
HARDCORE
HARDCORES
HARDEN
HARDENED
HARDENER
HARDENERS
HARDENING
HARDENINGS
HARDENS
HARDER
HARDEST
HARDFACE
HARDFACES
HARDGRASS
HARDGRASSES
HARDHACK
HARDHACKS
HARDHEAD
HARDHEADS
HARDIER
HARDIEST
HARDIHEAD
HARDIHEADS
HARDIHOOD
HARDIHOODS
HARDILY
HARDIMENT
HARDIMENTS
HARDINESS
HARDINESSES
HARDISH
HARDLINE
HARDLINER
HARDLINERS
HARDLY
HARDNESS
HARDNESSES
HARDNOSED
HARDOKE
HARDOKES
HARDPARTS
HARDS
HARDSHELL
HARDSHIP
HARDSHIPS
HARDTACK
HARDTACKS
HARDWARE
HARDWARES
HARDWOOD
HARDWOODS
HARDY
HARE
HAREBELL
HAREBELLS
HARED
HAREEM
HAREEMS
HARELD
HARELDS
HAREM

HAREMS
HARES
HAREWOOD
HAREWOODS
HARICOT
HARICOTS
HARIGALDS
HARIGALS
HARIM
HARIMS
HARING
HARIOLATE
HARIOLATED
HARIOLATES
HARIOLATING
HARISH
HARK
HARKED
HARKEN
HARKENED
HARKENING
HARKENS
HARKING
HARKS
HARL
HARLED
HARLEQUIN
HARLEQUINED
HARLEQUINING
HARLEQUINS
HARLING
HARLINGS
HARLOT
HARLOTRIES
HARLOTRY
HARLOTS
HARLS
HARM
HARMALA
HARMALAS
HARMALIN
HARMALINE
HARMALINES
HARMALINS
HARMAN
HARMANS
HARMATTAN
HARMATTANS
HARMED
HARMEL
HARMELS
HARMFUL
HARMFULLY
HARMIN
HARMINE
HARMINES
HARMING
HARMINS
HARMLESS
HARMONIC
HARMONICA
HARMONICAS
HARMONICS
HARMONIES
HARMONISE
HARMONISED
HARMONISES
HARMONISING
HARMONIST
HARMONISTS

HARMONIUM
HARMONIUMS
HARMONIZE
HARMONIZED
HARMONIZES
HARMONIZING
HARMONY
HARMOST
HARMOSTIES
HARMOSTS
HARMOSTY
HARMOTOME
HARMOTOMES
HARMS
HARN
HARNESS
HARNESSED
HARNESSES
HARNESSING
HARNS
HARO
HAROS
HAROSET
HAROSETH
HAROSETHS
HAROSETS
HARP
HARPED
HARPER
HARPERS
HARPIES
HARPING
HARPINGS
HARPIST
HARPISTS
HARPOON
HARPOONED
HARPOONER
HARPOONERS
HARPOONING
HARPOONS
HARPS
HARPY
HARQUEBUS
HARQUEBUSES
HARRIDAN
HARRIDANS
HARRIED
HARRIER
HARRIERS
HARRIES
HARROW
HARROWED
HARROWING
HARROWS
HARRUMPH
HARRUMPHED
HARRUMPHING
HARRUMPHS
HARRY
HARRYING
HARSH
HARSHEN
HARSHENED
HARSHENING
HARSHENS
HARSHER
HARSHEST
HARSHLY
HARSHNESS

HARSHNESSES
HARSLET
HARSLETS
HART
HARTAL
HARTALS
HARTBEES
HARTBEESES
HARTELY
HARTEN
HARTENED
HARTENING
HARTENS
HARTLESSE
HARTS
HARTSHORN
HARTSHORNS
HARUSPEX
HARUSPICES
HARUSPICIES
HARUSPICY
HARVEST
HARVESTED
HARVESTER
HARVESTERS
HARVESTING
HARVESTS
HAS
HASH
HASHED
HASHEESH
HASHEESHES
HASHES
HASHIER
HASHIEST
HASHING
HASHISH
HASHISHES
HASHY
HASK
HASKS
HASLET
HASLETS
HASP
HASPED
HASPING
HASPS
HASSAR
HASSARS
HASSLE
HASSLED
HASSLES
HASSLING
HASSOCK
HASSOCKS
HASSOCKY
HAST
HASTA
HASTATE
HASTATED
HASTE
HASTED
HASTEN
HASTENED
HASTENER
HASTENERS
HASTENING
HASTENS
HASTES
HASTIER

HASTIEST	HATTERED	HAVENING	HAWTHORN	HEADACHY
HASTILY	HATTERING	HAVENS	HAWTHORNS	HEADBAND
HASTINESS	HATTERS	HAVEOUR	HAY	HEADBANDS
HASTINESSES	HATTING	HAVEOURS	HAYBAND	HEADBOARD
HASTING	HATTINGS	HAVER	HAYBANDS	HEADBOARDS
HASTINGS	HATTOCK	HAVERED	HAYBOX	HEADCHAIR
HASTY	HATTOCKS	HAVEREL	HAYBOXES	HEADCHAIRS
HAT	HAUBERK	HAVERELS	HAYCOCK	HEADCLOTH
HATABLE	HAUBERKS	HAVERING	HAYCOCKS	HEADCLOTHS
HATBAND	HAUD	HAVERINGS	HAYED	HEADED
HATBANDS	HAUDING	HAVERS	HAYFIELD	HEADER
HATBOX	HAUDS	HAVERSACK	HAYFIELDS	HEADERS
HATBOXES	HAUGH	HAVERSACKS	HAYFORK	HEADFAST
HATBRUSH	HAUGHS	HAVERSINE	HAYFORKS	HEADFASTS
HATBRUSHES	HAUGHT	HAVERSINES	HAYING	HEADFRAME
HATCH	HAUGHTIER	HAVES	HAYINGS	HEADFRAMES
HATCHBACK	HAUGHTIEST	HAVILDAR	HAYLE	HEADGEAR
HATCHBACKS	HAUGHTILY	HAVILDARS	HAYLES	HEADGEARS
HATCHED	HAUGHTY	HAVING	HAYLOFT	HEADHUNT
HATCHEL	HAUL	HAVINGS	HAYLOFTS	HEADHUNTED
HATCHELLED	HAULAGE	HAVIOUR	HAYMAKER	HEADHUNTING
HATCHELLING	HAULAGES	HAVIOURS	HAYMAKERS	HEADHUNTINGS
HATCHELS	HAULD	HAVOC	HAYMAKING	HEADHUNTS
HATCHER	HAULDS	HAVOCKED	HAYMAKINGS	HEADIER
HATCHERIES	HAULED	HAVOCKING	HAYMOW	HEADIEST
HATCHERS	HAULER	HAVOCS	HAYMOWS	HEADILY
HATCHERY	HAULERS	HAW	HAYRICK	HEADINESS
HATCHES	HAULIER	HAWBUCK	HAYRICKS	HEADINESSES
HATCHET	HAULIERS	HAWBUCKS	HAYS	HEADING
HATCHETS	HAULING	HAWED	HAYSEED	HEADINGS
HATCHETY	HAULM	HAWFINCH	HAYSEEDS	HEADLAMP
HATCHING	HAULMS	HAWFINCHES	HAYSEL	HEADLAMPS
HATCHINGS	HAULS	HAWING	HAYSELS	HEADLAND
HATCHLING	HAULST	HAWK	HAYSTACK	HEADLANDS
HATCHLINGS	HAULT	HAWKBELL	HAYSTACKS	HEADLESS
HATCHMENT	HAUNCH	HAWKBELLS	HAYWARD	HEADLIGHT
HATCHMENTS	HAUNCHED	HAWKBIT	HAYWARDS	HEADLIGHTS
HATCHWAY	HAUNCHES	HAWKBITS	HAYWIRE	HEADLINE
HATCHWAYS	HAUNCHING	HAWKED	HAYWIRES	HEADLINED
HATE	HAUNT	HAWKER	HAZARD	HEADLINER
HATEABLE	HAUNTED	HAWKERS	HAZARDED	HEADLINERS
HATED	HAUNTER	HAWKEY	HAZARDING	HEADLINES
HATEFUL	HAUNTERS	HAWKEYS	HAZARDIZE	HEADLINING
HATEFULLY	HAUNTING	HAWKIE	HAZARDIZES	HEADLOCK
HATELESS	HAUNTINGS	HAWKIES	HAZARDOUS	HEADLOCKS
HATER	HAUNTS	HAWKING	HAZARDRIES	HEADLONG
HATERENT	HAURIANT	HAWKINGS	HAZARDRY	HEADMAN
HATERENTS	HAURIENT	HAWKISH	HAZARDS	HEADMARK
HATERS	HAUSE	HAWKISHLY	HAZE	HEADMARKS
HATES	HAUSED	HAWKIT	HAZED	HEADMEN
HATFUL	HAUSES	HAWKS	HAZEL	HEADMOST
HATFULS	HAUSFRAU	HAWKSBILL	HAZELLY	HEADNOTE
HATGUARD	HAUSFRAUS	HAWKSBILLS	HAZELNUT	HEADNOTES
HATGUARDS	HAUSING	HAWKWEED	HAZELNUTS	HEADPEACE
HATH	HAUSTELLA	HAWKWEEDS	HAZELS	HEADPEACES
HATING	HAUSTORIA	HAWM	HAZER	HEADPHONE
HATLESS	HAUT	HAWMED	HAZERS	HEADPHONES
HATPEG	HAUTBOIS	HAWMING	HAZES	HEADPIECE
HATPEGS	HAUTBOY	HAWMS	HAZIER	HEADPIECES
HATPIN	HAUTBOYS	HAWS	HAZIEST	HEADRACE
HATPINS	HAUTE	HAWSE	HAZILY	HEADRACES
HATRACK	HAUTEUR	HAWSED	HAZINESS	HEADRAIL
HATRACKS	HAUTEURS	HAWSEHOLE	HAZINESSES	HEADRAILS
HATRED	HAÜYNE	HAWSEHOLES	HAZING	HEADREACH
HATREDS	HAÜYNES	HAWSEPIPE	HAZINGS	HEADREACHED
HATS	HAVE	HAWSEPIPES	HAZY	HEADREACHES
HATSTAND	HAVELOCK	HAWSER	HE	HEADREACHING
HATSTANDS	HAVELOCKS	HAWSERS	HEAD	HEADREST
HATTED	HAVEN	HAWSES	HEADACHE	HEADRESTS
HATTER	HAVENED	HAWSING	HEADACHES	HEADRIG

153

HEADRIGS
HEADRING
HEADRINGS
HEADROOM
HEADROOMS
HEADROPE
HEADROPES
HEADS
HEADSCARF
HEADSCARVES
HEADSET
HEADSETS
HEADSHAKE
HEADSHAKES
HEADSHIP
HEADSHIPS
HEADSMAN
HEADSMEN
HEADSTALL
HEADSTALLS
HEADSTICK
HEADSTICKS
HEADSTOCK
HEADSTOCKS
HEADSTONE
HEADSTONES
HEADWAY
HEADWAYS
HEADWORD
HEADWORDS
HEADWORK
HEADWORKS
HEADY
HEAL
HEALABLE
HEALD
HEALDED
HEALDING
HEALDS
HEALED
HEALER
HEALERS
HEALING
HEALINGLY
HEALINGS
HEALS
HEALSOME
HEALTH
HEALTHFUL
HEALTHIER
HEALTHIEST
HEALTHILY
HEALTHS
HEALTHY
HEAME
HEAP
HEAPED
HEAPIER
HEAPIEST
HEAPING
HEAPS
HEAPSTEAD
HEAPSTEADS
HEAPY
HEAR
HEARD
HEARDS
HEARE
HEARER
HEARERS

HEARES
HEARIE
HEARING
HEARINGS
HEARKEN
HEARKENED
HEARKENER
HEARKENERS
HEARKENING
HEARKENS
HEARS
HEARSAY
HEARSAYS
HEARSE
HEARSED
HEARSES
HEARSIER
HEARSIEST
HEARSING
HEARSY
HEART
HEARTACHE
HEARTACHES
HEARTBURN
HEARTBURNS
HEARTED
HEARTEN
HEARTENED
HEARTENING
HEARTENS
HEARTFELT
HEARTH
HEARTHS
HEARTIER
HEARTIES
HEARTIEST
HEARTIKIN
HEARTIKINS
HEARTILY
HEARTING
HEARTLAND
HEARTLANDS
HEARTLESS
HEARTLET
HEARTLETS
HEARTLING
HEARTLINGS
HEARTLY
HEARTPEA
HEARTPEAS
HEARTS
HEARTSEED
HEARTSEEDS
HEARTSOME
HEARTWOOD
HEARTWOODS
HEARTY
HEAST
HEASTE
HEASTES
HEASTS
HEAT
HEATED
HEATER
HEATERS
HEATH
HEATHBIRD
HEATHBIRDS
HEATHCOCK
HEATHCOCKS

HEATHEN
HEATHENRIES
HEATHENRY
HEATHENS
HEATHER
HEATHERS
HEATHERY
HEATHIER
HEATHIEST
HEATHS
HEATHY
HEATING
HEATINGS
HEATS
HEATSPOT
HEATSPOTS
HEAUME
HEAUMES
HEAVE
HEAVED
HEAVEN
HEAVENLIER
HEAVENLIEST
HEAVENLY
HEAVENS
HEAVER
HEAVERS
HEAVES
HEAVIER
HEAVIES
HEAVIEST
HEAVILY
HEAVINESS
HEAVINESSES
HEAVING
HEAVINGS
HEAVY
HEBDOMAD
HEBDOMADS
HEBE
HEBEN
HEBENON
HEBENONS
HEBENS
HERES
HEBETANT
HEBETATE
HEBETATED
HEBETATES
HEBETATING
HEBETUDE
HEBETUDES
HEBONA
HEBONAS
HECATOMB
HECATOMBS
HECH
HECHT
HECHTING
HECHTS
HECK
HECKLE
HECKLED
HECKLER
HECKLERS
HECKLES
HECKLING
HECKLINGS
HECKS
HECOGENIN

HECOGENINS
HECTARE
HECTARES
HECTIC
HECTICAL
HECTICS
HECTOGRAM
HECTOGRAMS
HECTOR
HECTORED
HECTORER
HECTORERS
HECTORING
HECTORINGS
HECTORISM
HECTORISMS
HECTORLY
HECTORS
HEDDLE
HEDDLED
HEDDLES
HEDDLING
HEDERAL
HEDERATED
HEDGE
HEDGEBILL
HEDGEBILLS
HEDGED
HEDGEHOG
HEDGEHOGS
HEDGEPIG
HEDGEPIGS
HEDGER
HEDGEROW
HEDGEROWS
HEDGERS
HEDGES
HEDGIER
HEDGIEST
HEDGING
HEDGINGS
HEDGY
HEDONIC
HEDONICS
HEDONISM
HEDONISMS
HEDONIST
HEDONISTS
HEDYPHANE
HEDYPHANES
HEED
HEEDED
HEEDFUL
HEEDFULLY
HEEDINESS
HEEDINESSES
HEEDING
HEEDLESS
HEEDS
HEEDY
HEEHAW
HEEHAWED
HEEHAWING
HEEHAWS
HEEL
HEELED
HEELER
HEELERS
HEELING
HEELINGS

HEELS
HEEZE
HEEZED
HEEZES
HEEZIE
HEEZIES
HEEZING
HEFT
HEFTE
HEFTED
HEFTIER
HEFTIEST
HEFTING
HEFTS
HEFTY
HEGEMONIC
HEGEMONIES
HEGEMONY
HEGIRA
HEGIRAS
HEID
HEIDS
HEIFER
HEIFERS
HEIGH
HEIGHT
HEIGHTEN
HEIGHTENED
HEIGHTENING
HEIGHTENS
HEIGHTS
HEIL
HEINOUS
HEINOUSLY
HEIR
HEIRDOM
HEIRDOMS
HEIRED
HEIRESS
HEIRESSES
HEIRING
HEIRLESS
HEIRLOOM
HEIRLOOMS
HEIRS
HEIRSHIP
HEIRSHIPS
HEIST
HEISTED
HEISTER
HEISTERS
HEISTING
HEISTS
HEJAB
HEJABS
HEJIRA
HEJIRAS
HEJRA
HEJRAS
HELCOID
HELD
HELE
HELED
HELES
HELIAC
HELIACAL
HELIBUS
HELIBUSES
HELICAL
HELICALLY

HELICES	HELLUVA	HEMIOPIC	HEP	HERBIEST
HELICOID	HELLWARD	HEMIOPSIA	HEPAR	HERBIST
HELICTITE	HELLWARDS	HEMIOPSIAS	HEPARIN	HERBISTS
HELICTITES	HELM	HEMISPACE	HEPARINS	HERBIVORA
HELIDROME	HELMED	HEMISPACES	HEPARS	HERBIVORE
HELIDROMES	HELMET	HEMISTICH	HEPATIC	HERBIVORES
HELIMAN	HELMETED	HEMISTICHS	HEPATICAL	HERBIVORIES
HELIMEN	HELMETS	HEMITROPE	HEPATICS	HERBIVORY
HELING	HELMING	HEMITROPES	HEPATISE	HERBLESS
HELIODOR	HELMINTH	HEMLOCK	HEPATISED	HERBLET
HELIODORS	HELMINTHS	HEMLOCKS	HEPATISES	HERBLETS
HELIOLOGIES	HELMLESS	HEMMED	HEPATISING	HERBORISE
HELIOLOGY	HELMS	HEMMING	HEPATITE	HERBORISED
HELIOSES	HELMSMAN	HEMP	HEPATITES	HERBORISES
HELIOSIS	HELMSMEN	HEMPBUSH	HEPATITIS	HERBORISING
HELIOSTAT	HELOT	HEMPBUSHES	HEPATITISES	HERBORIST
HELIOSTATS	HELOTAGE	HEMPEN	HEPATIZE	HERBORISTS
HELIOTYPE	HELOTAGES	HEMPIER	HEPATIZED	HERBORIZE
HELIOTYPES	HELOTISM	HEMPIES	HEPATIZES	HERBORIZED
HELIOTYPIES	HELOTISMS	HEMPIEST	HEPATIZING	HERBORIZES
HELIOTYPY	HELOTRIES	HEMPS	HEPPER	HERBORIZING
HELIOZOAN	HELOTRY	HEMPY	HEPPEST	HERBOSE
HELIOZOANS	HELOTS	HEMS	HEPS	HERBOUS
HELIOZOIC	HELP	HEN	HEPSTER	HERBS
HELIPAD	HELPABLE	HENBANE	HEPSTERS	HERBY
HELIPADS	HELPED	HENBANES	HEPT	HERCOGAMIES
HELIPILOT	HELPER	HENCE	HEPTAD	HERCOGAMY
HELIPILOTS	HELPERS	HENCHMAN	HEPTADS	HERCULEAN
HELIPORT	HELPFUL	HENCHMEN	HEPTAGLOT	HERCYNITE
HELIPORTS	HELPING	HEND	HEPTAGLOTS	HERCYNITES
HELISCOOP	HELPINGS	HENDED	HEPTAGON	HERD
HELISCOOPS	HELPLESS	HENDIADYS	HEPTAGONS	HERDBOY
HELISTOP	HELPLINE	HENDIADYSES	HEPTANE	HERDBOYS
HELISTOPS	HELPLINES	HENDING	HEPTANES	HERDED
HELIUM	HELPMATE	HENDS	HEPTAPODIES	HERDEN
HELIUMS	HELPMATES	HENEQUEN	HEPTAPODY	HERDENS
HELIX	HELPMEET	HENEQUENS	HEPTARCH	HERDESS
HELIXES	HELPMEETS	HENEQUIN	HEPTARCHIES	HERDESSES
HELL	HELPS	HENEQUINS	HEPTARCHS	HERDIC
HELLEBORE	HELVE	HENGE	HEPTARCHY	HERDICS
HELLEBORES	HELVED	HENGES	HER	HERDING
HELLED	HELVES	HENIQUIN	HERALD	HERDMAN
HELLENISE	HELVETIUM	HENIQUINS	HERALDED	HERDMEN
HELLENISED	HELVETIUMS	HENNA	HERALDIC	HERDS
HELLENISES	HELVING	HENNAED	HERALDING	HERDSMAN
HELLENISING	HEM	HENNAS	HERALDRIES	HERDSMEN
HELLENIZE	HEMAL	HENNED	HERALDRY	HERDWICK
HELLENIZED	HEMATITE	HENNER	HERALDS	HERDWICKS
HELLENIZES	HEMATITES	HENNERIES	HERB	HERE
HELLENIZING	HEME	HENNERS	HERBAGE	HEREABOUT
HELLER	HEMES	HENNERY	HERBAGED	HEREAFTER
HELLERS	HEMIALGIA	HENNIER	HERBAGES	HEREAFTERS
HELLHOUND	HEMIALGIAS	HENNIES	HERBAL	HEREAT
HELLHOUNDS	HEMICYCLE	HENNIEST	HERBALIST	HEREAWAY
HELLICAT	HEMICYCLES	HENNIN	HERBALISTS	HEREBY
HELLICATS	HEMIHEDRIES	HENNING	HERBALS	HEREDITIES
HELLIER	HEMIHEDRY	HENNINS	HERBAR	HEREDITY
HELLIERS	HEMINA	HENNY	HERBARIA	HEREFROM
HELLING	HEMINAS	HENOTIC	HERBARIAN	HEREIN
HELLION	HEMIOLA	HENPECK	HERBARIANS	HERENESS
HELLIONS	HEMIOLAS	HENPECKED	HERBARIES	HERENESSES
HELLISH	HEMIOLIA	HENPECKING	HERBARIUM	HEREOF
HELLISHLY	HEMIOLIAS	HENPECKS	HERBARIUMS	HEREON
HELLO	HEMIOLIC	HENRIES	HERBARS	HERESIES
HELLOED	HEMIONE	HENRY	HERBARY	HERESY
HELLOES	HEMIONES	HENRYS	HERBELET	HERETIC
HELLOING	HEMIONUS	HENS	HERBELETS	HERETICAL
HELLOS	HEMIONUSES	HENT	HERBICIDE	HERETICS
HELLOVA	HEMIOPIA	HENTING	HERBICIDES	HERETO
HELLS	HEMIOPIAS	HENTS	HERBIER	HEREUNDER

HEREUNTO	HERON	HETAERAE	HEXAGON	HICCOUGH
HEREUPON	HERONRIES	HETAERAS	HEXAGONAL	HICCOUGHED
HEREWITH	HERONRY	HETAERIA	HEXAGONS	HICCOUGHING
HERIED	HERONS	HETAERIAS	HEXAGRAM	HICCOUGHS
HERIES	HERONSEW	HETAERISM	HEXAGRAMS	HICCUP
HERIOT	HERONSEWS	HETAERISMS	HEXAHEDRA	HICCUPED
HERIOTS	HERONSHAW	HETAERIST	HEXAMETER	HICCUPING
HÉRISSÉ	HERONSHAWS	HETAERISTS	HEXAMETERS	HICCUPS
HERISSON	HEROON	HETAIRA	HEXANE	HICCUPY
HERISSONS	HEROONS	HETAIRAI	HEXANES	HICK
HERITABLE	HEROSHIP	HETAIRIA	HEXAPLA	HICKEY
HERITABLY	HEROSHIPS	HETAIRIAS	HEXAPLAR	HICKEYS
HERITAGE	HERPES	HETAIRISM	HEXAPLAS	HICKORIES
HERITAGES	HERPETIC	HETAIRISMS	HEXAPLOID	HICKORY
HERITOR	HERPETOID	HETAIRIST	HEXAPLOIDS	HICKS
HERITORS	HERRIED	HETAIRISTS	HEXAPOD	HICKWALL
HERITRESS	HERRIES	HETE	HEXAPODIES	HICKWALLS
HERITRESSES	HERRIMENT	HETERODOX	HEXAPODS	HID
HERITRICES	HERRIMENTS	HETERONYM	HEXAPODY	HIDAGE
HERITRIX	HERRING	HETERONYMS	HEXARCH	HIDAGES
HERITRIXES	HERRINGER	HETEROPOD	HEXASTICH	HIDALGA
HERKOGAMIES	HERRINGERS	HETEROPODS	HEXASTICHS	HIDALGAS
HERKOGAMY	HERRINGS	HETEROSES	HEXASTYLE	HIDALGO
HERL	HERRY	HETEROSIS	HEXASTYLES	HIDALGOS
HERLING	HERRYING	HETEROTIC	HEXED	HIDDEN
HERLINGS	HERRYMENT	HETES	HEXENE	HIDDENITE
HERLS	HERRYMENTS	HETHER	HEXENES	HIDDENITES
HERM	HERS	HETING	HEXES	HIDDENLY
HERMA	HERSALL	HETMAN	HEXING	HIDDER
HERMAE	HERSALLS	HETMANATE	HEXINGS	HIDDERS
HERMANDAD	HERSE	HETMANATES	HEXOSE	HIDE
HERMANDADS	HERSED	HETMANS	HEXOSES	HIDED
HERMETIC	HERSELF	HETS	HEXPLARIC	HIDEOSITIES
HERMETICS	HERSES	HETTED	HEXYLENE	HIDEOSITY
HERMIT	HERSHIP	HETTING	HEXYLENES	HIDEOUS
HERMITAGE	HERSHIPS	HEUCH	HEY	HIDEOUSLY
HERMITAGES	HERTZ	HEUCHS	HEYDAY	HIDEOUT
HERMITESS	HERTZES	HEUGH	HEYDAYS	HIDEOUTS
HERMITESSES	HERY	HEUGHS	HEYDUCK	HIDES
HERMITS	HERYE	HEUREKA	HEYDUCKS	HIDING
HERMS	HERYED	HEUREKAS	HEYED	HIDINGS
HERN	HERYES	HEURETIC	HEYING	HIDLING
HERNIA	HERYING	HEURETICS	HEYS	HIDLINGS
HERNIAL	HES	HEURISM	HI	HIDLINS
HERNIAS	HESITANCE	HEURISMS	HIANT	HIDROSES
HERNIATED	HESITANCES	HEURISTIC	HIATUS	HIDROSIS
HERNS	HESITANCIES	HEURISTICS	HIATUSES	HIDROTIC
HERNSHAW	HESITANCY	HEVEA	HIBACHI	HIDROTICS
HERNSHAWS	HESITANT	HEVEAS	HIBACHIS	HIE
HERO	HESITATE	HEW	HIBAKUSHA	HIED
HEROE	HESITATED	HEWED	HIBERNAL	HIEING
HEROES	HESITATES	HEWEDS	HIBERNATE	HIELAMAN
HEROIC	HESITATING	HEWER	HIBERNATED	HIELAMANS
HEROICAL	HESITATOR	HEWERS	HIBERNATES	HIEMAL
HEROICLY	HESITATORS	HEWGH	HIBERNATING	HIEMS
HEROICS	HESP	HEWING	HIBERNISE	HIERACIUM
HEROIN	HESPED	HEWINGS	HIBERNISED	HIERACIUMS
HEROINE	HESPERID	HEWN	HIBERNISES	HIERARCH
HEROINES	HESPERIDS	HEWS	HIBERNISING	HIERARCHIES
HEROINS	HESPING	HEX	HIBERNIZE	HIERARCHS
HEROISE	HESPS	HEXACHORD	HIBERNIZED	HIERARCHY
HEROISED	HESSIAN	HEXACHORDS	HIBERNIZES	HIERATIC
HEROISES	HESSIANS	HEXACT	HIBERNIZING	HIERATICA
HEROISING	HESSONITE	HEXACTS	HIBISCUS	HIERATICAS
HEROISM	HESSONITES	HEXAD	HIBISCUSES	HIEROCRAT
HEROISMS	HEST	HEXADIC	HIC	HIEROCRATS
HEROIZE	HESTERNAL	HEXADS	HICATEE	HIERODULE
HEROIZED	HESTS	HEXAFOIL	HICATEES	HIERODULES
HEROIZES	HET	HEXAFOILS	HICCATEE	HIEROGRAM
HEROIZING	HETAERA	HEXAGLOT	HICCATEES	HIEROGRAMS

HIEROLOGIES	HIKE	HINDLEGS	HIRELINGS	HISTORIFIES
HIEROLOGY	HIKED	HINDMOST	HIRER	HISTORIFY
HIERURGIES	HIKER	HINDRANCE	HIRERS	HISTORIFYING
HIERURGY	HIKERS	HINDRANCES	HIRES	HISTORISM
HIES	HIKES	HINDS	HIRING	HISTORISMS
HIGGLE	HIKING	HINDSIGHT	HIRINGS	HISTORY
HIGGLED	HILA	HINDSIGHTS	HIRLING	HISTORYING
HIGGLER	HILAR	HINDWARD	HIRLINGS	HISTRIO
HIGGLERS	HILARIOUS	HING	HIRPLE	HISTRION
HIGGLES	HILARITIES	HINGE	HIRPLED	HISTRIONS
HIGGLING	HILARITY	HINGED	HIRPLES	HISTRIOS
HIGGLINGS	HILCH	HINGES	HIRPLING	HISTS
HIGH	HILCHED	HINGING	HIRRIENT	HIT
HIGHBALL	HILCHES	HINGS	HIRRIENTS	HITCH
HIGHBALLED	HILCHING	HINNIED	HIRSEL	HITCHED
HIGHBALLING	HILD	HINNIES	HIRSELLED	HITCHER
HIGHBALLS	HILDING	HINNY	HIRSELLING	HITCHERS
HIGHBOY	HILDINGS	HINNYING	HIRSELS	HITCHES
HIGHBOYS	HILI	HINS	HIRSLE	HITCHIER
HIGHBROW	HILL	HINT	HIRSLED	HITCHIEST
HIGHBROWS	HILLED	HINTED	HIRSLES	HITCHILY
HIGHED	HILLFOLK	HINTING	HIRSLING	HITCHING
HIGHER	HILLFOLKS	HINTINGLY	HIRSTIE	HITCHY
HIGHERED	HILLIER	HINTS	HIRSUTE	HITHE
HIGHERING	HILLIEST	HIP	HIRSUTER	HITHER
HIGHERS	HILLINESS	HIPPARCH	HIRSUTEST	HITHERED
HIGHEST	HILLINESSES	HIPPARCHS	HIRUDIN	HITHERING
HIGHING	HILLING	HIPPED	HIRUDINS	HITHERS
HIGHISH	HILLMEN	HIPPER	HIRUNDINE	HITHERTO
HIGHJACK	HILLO	HIPPEST	HIS	HITHES
HIGHJACKED	HILLOCK	HIPPIATRIES	HISH	HITS
HIGHJACKING	HILLOCKS	HIPPIATRY	HISHED	HITTER
HIGHJACKS	HILLOCKY	HIPPIC	HISHES	HITTERS
HIGHLAND	HILLOED	HIPPIE	HISHING	HITTING
HIGHLANDS	HILLOING	HIPPIEDOM	HISN	HIVE
HIGHLIGHT	HILLOS	HIPPIEDOMS	HISPID	HIVED
HIGHLIGHTED	HILLS	HIPPIER	HISPIDITIES	HIVELESS
HIGHLIGHTING	HILLSIDE	HIPPIES	HISPIDITY	HIVELIKE
HIGHLIGHTS	HILLSIDES	HIPPIEST	HISS	HIVER
HIGHLY	HILLTOP	HIPPING	HISSED	HIVERS
HIGHMAN	HILLTOPS	HIPPINGS	HISSES	HIVES
HIGHMEN	HILLY	HIPPISH	HISSING	HIVEWARD
HIGHMOST	HILT	HIPPO	HISSINGLY	HIVEWARDS
HIGHNESS	HILTED	HIPPOCRAS	HISSINGS	HIVING
HIGHNESSES	HILTING	HIPPOCRASES	HIST	HIYA
HIGHROAD	HILTS	HIPPODAME	HISTAMINE	HIZEN
HIGHROADS	HILUM	HIPPODAMES	HISTAMINES	HIZENS
HIGHS	HILUS	HIPPOLOGIES	HISTED	HIZZ
HIGHT	HIM	HIPPOLOGY	HISTIDINE	HIZZED
HIGHTAIL	HIMATIA	HIPPOS	HISTIDINES	HIZZES
HIGHTAILED	HIMATION	HIPPURIC	HISTIE	HIZZING
HIGHTAILING	HIMATIONS	HIPPURITE	HISTING	HO
HIGHTAILS	HIMSEEMED	HIPPURITES	HISTIOID	HOA
HIGHTH	HIMSEEMS	HIPPUS	HISTOGEN	HOACTZIN
HIGHTHS	HIMSELF	HIPPUSES	HISTOGENIES	HOACTZINS
HIGHTING	HIN	HIPPY	HISTOGENS	HOAED
HIGHTS	HIND	HIPPYDOM	HISTOGENY	HOAING
HIGHWAY	HINDBERRIES	HIPPYDOMS	HISTOGRAM	HOAR
HIGHWAYS	HINDBERRY	HIPS	HISTOGRAMS	HOARD
HIJACK	HINDER	HIPSTER	HISTOID	HOARDED
HIJACKED	HINDERED	HIPSTERS	HISTOLOGIES	HOARDER
HIJACKER	HINDERER	HIPT	HISTOLOGY	HOARDERS
HIJACKERS	HINDERERS	HIRABLE	HISTONE	HOARDING
HIJACKING	HINDERING	HIRCINE	HISTONES	HOARDINGS
HIJACKS	HINDERS	HIRCOSITIES	HISTORIAN	HOARDS
HIJINKS	HINDFEET	HIRCOSITY	HISTORIANS	HOARED
HIJRA	HINDFOOT	HIRE	HISTORIC	HOARHEAD
HIJRAH	HINDHEAD	HIREABLE	HISTORIED	HOARHEADS
HIJRAHS	HINDHEADS	HIRED	HISTORIES	HOARHOUND
HIJRAS	HINDLEG	HIRELING	HISTORIFIED	HOARHOUNDS

HOARIER
HOARIEST
HOARILY
HOARINESS
HOARINESSES
HOARING
HOARS
HOARSE
HOARSELY
HOARSEN
HOARSENED
HOARSENING
HOARSENS
HOARSER
HOARSEST
HOARY
HOAS
HOAST
HOASTED
HOASTING
HOASTMAN
HOASTMEN
HOASTS
HOATZIN
HOATZINS
HOAX
HOAXED
HOAXER
HOAXERS
HOAXES
HOAXING
HOB
HOBBIES
HOBBISH
HOBBIT
HOBBITRIES
HOBBITRY
HOBBITS
HOBBLE
HOBBLED
HOBBLER
HOBBLERS
HOBBLES
HOBBLING
HOBBLINGS
HOBBY
HOBBYISM
HOBBYISMO
HOBBYIST
HOBBYISTS
HOBBYLESS
HOBDAY
HOBDAYED
HOBDAYING
HOBDAYS
HOBGOBLIN
HOBGOBLINS
HOBJOB
HOBJOBBED
HOBJOBBER
HOBJOBBERS
HOBJOBBING
HOBJOBBINGS
HOBJOBS
HOBNAIL
HOBNAILED
HOBNAILING
HOBNAILS
HOBNOB
HOBNOBBED

HOBNOBBING
HOBNOBBINGS
HOBNOBBY
HOBNOBS
HOBO
HOBODOM
HOBODOMS
HOBOED
HOBOES
HOBOING
HOBOISM
HOBOISMS
HOBS
HOC
HOCK
HOCKED
HOCKER
HOCKERS
HOCKEY
HOCKEYS
HOCKING
HOCKS
HOCUS
HOCUSED
HOCUSES
HOCUSING
HOCUSSED
HOCUSSES
HOCUSSING
HOD
HODDED
HODDEN
HODDENS
HODDING
HODDLE
HODDLED
HODDLES
HODDLING
HODIERNAL
HODJA
HODJAS
HODMAN
HODMANDOD
HODMANDODS
HODMEN
HODOGRAPH
HODOGRAPHS
HODOMETER
HODOMETERS
HODOMETRIES
HODOMETRY
HODOSCOPE
HODOSCOPES
HODS
HOE
HOED
HOEDOWN
HOEDOWNS
HOEING
HOER
HOERS
HOES
HOG
HOGAN
HOGANS
HOGBACK
HOGBACKS
HOGEN
HOGENS
HOGG

HOGGED
HOGGER
HOGGEREL
HOGGERELS
HOGGERIES
HOGGERS
HOGGERY
HOGGET
HOGGETS
HOGGIN
HOGGING
HOGGINGS
HOGGINS
HOGGISH
HOGGISHLY
HOGGS
HOGH
HOGHOOD
HOGHOODS
HOGHS
HOGS
HOGSHEAD
HOGSHEADS
HOGTIE
HOGTIED
HOGTIES
HOGTYING
HOGWARD
HOGWARDS
HOGWASH
HOGWASHES
HOGWEED
HOGWEEDS
HOH
HOHED
HOHING
HOHS
HOI
HOICK
HOICKED
HOICKING
HOICKS
HOICKSED
HOICKSES
HOICKSING
HOIDEN
HOIDENS
HOIK
HOIKED
HOIKING
HOIKS
HOING
HOISE
HOISED
HOISES
HOISING
HOIST
HOISTED
HOISTER
HOISTERS
HOISTING
HOISTMAN
HOISTMEN
HOISTS
HOISTWAY
HOISTWAYS
HOKE
HOKED
HOKES
HOKEY

HOKIER
HOKIEST
HOKING
HOKKU
HOKUM
HOKUMS
HOLD
HOLDBACK
HOLDBACKS
HOLDEN
HOLDER
HOLDERBAT
HOLDERBATS
HOLDERS
HOLDFAST
HOLDFASTS
HOLDING
HOLDINGS
HOLDOVER
HOLDOVERS
HOLDS
HOLE
HOLED
HOLES
HOLESOM
HOLESOME
HOLEY
HOLIBUT
HOLIBUTS
HOLIDAY
HOLIDAYED
HOLIDAYING
HOLIDAYS
HOLIER
HOLIES
HOLIEST
HOLILY
HOLINESS
HOLINESSES
HOLING
HOLINGS
HOLISM
HOLISMS
HOLIST
HOLISTIC
HOLISTS
HOLLA
HOLLAND
HOLLANDS
HOLLAS
HOLLER
HOLLERED
HOLLERING
HOLLERS
HOLLIDAM
HOLLIDAMS
HOLLIES
HOLLO
HOLLOA
HOLLOAED
HOLLOAING
HOLLOAS
HOLLOED
HOLLOES
HOLLOING
HOLLOS
HOLLOW
HOLLOWARE
HOLLOWARES
HOLLOWED

HOLLOWER
HOLLOWEST
HOLLOWING
HOLLOWLY
HOLLOWS
HOLLY
HOLLYHOCK
HOLLYHOCKS
HOLM
HOLMIA
HOLMIAS
HOLMIC
HOLMIUM
HOLMIUMS
HOLMS
HOLOCAUST
HOLOCAUSTS
HOLOCRINE
HOLOGRAM
HOLOGRAMS
HOLOGRAPH
HOLOGRAPHED
HOLOGRAPHING
HOLOGRAPHS
HOLOPHOTE
HOLOPHOTES
HOLOPHYTE
HOLOPHYTES
HOLOPTIC
HOLOTYPE
HOLOTYPES
HOLOTYPIC
HOLOZOIC
HOLP
HOLPEN
HOLS
HOLSTER
HOLSTERED
HOLSTERS
HOLT
HOLTS
HOLY
HOLYDAM
HOLYDAME
HOLYDAMES
HOLYDAMS
HOLYSTONE
HOLYSTONED
HOLYSTONES
HOLYSTONING
HOMAGE
HOMAGED
HOMAGER
HOMAGERS
HOMAGES
HOMAGING
HOMALOID
HOMALOIDS
HOMBRE
HOMBRES
HOME
HOMEBOUND
HOMECRAFT
HOMECRAFTS
HOMED
HOMEFELT
HOMELAND
HOMELANDS
HOMELESS
HOMELIER

HOMELIEST
HOMELIKE
HOMELILY
HOMELY
HOMELYN
HOMELYNS
HOMEMAKER
HOMEMAKERS
HOMEOMERIES
HOMEOMERY
HOMEOPATH
HOMEOPATHS
HOMEOSES
HOMEOSIS
HOMER
HOMERS
HOMES
HOMESICK
HOMESPUN
HOMESPUNS
HOMESTALL
HOMESTALLS
HOMESTEAD
HOMESTEADS
HOMEWARD
HOMEWARDS
HOMEWORK
HOMEWORKS
HOMEY
HOMICIDAL
HOMICIDE
HOMICIDES
HOMIER
HOMIEST
HOMILETIC
HOMILETICS
HOMILIES
HOMILIST
HOMILISTS
HOMILY
HOMING
HOMINGS
HOMINID
HOMINIDS
HOMINIES
HOMINOID
HOMINOIDS
HOMINY
HOMME
HOMMES
HOMMOCK
HOMMOCKS
HOMO
HOMODONT
HOMODYNE
HOMOEOSES
HOMOEOSIS
HOMOGAMIC
HOMOGAMIES
HOMOGAMY
HOMOGENIES
HOMOGENY
HOMOGRAFT
HOMOGRAFTS
HOMOGRAPH
HOMOGRAPHS
HOMOLOG
HOMOLOGIES
HOMOLOGS
HOMOLOGUE

HOMOLOGUES
HOMOLOGY
HOMOMORPH
HOMOMORPHS
HOMONYM
HOMONYMIC
HOMONYMIES
HOMONYMS
HOMONYMY
HOMOPHILE
HOMOPHILES
HOMOPHOBE
HOMOPHOBES
HOMOPHONE
HOMOPHONES
HOMOPHONIES
HOMOPHONY
HOMOPHYLIES
HOMOPHYLY
HOMOPLASIES
HOMOPLASY
HOMOPOLAR
HOMOS
HOMOTAXES
HOMOTAXIC
HOMOTAXIS
HOMOTONIC
HOMOTONIES
HOMOTONY
HOMOTYPAL
HOMOTYPE
HOMOTYPES
HOMOTYPIC
HOMOTYPIES
HOMOTYPY
HOMOUSIAN
HOMOUSIANS
HOMUNCLE
HOMUNCLES
HOMUNCULE
HOMUNCULES
HOMUNCULI
HOMY
HON
HOND
HONDS
HONE
HONED
HONES
HONEST
HONESTER
HONESTEST
HONESTIES
HONESTLY
HONESTY
HONEY
HONEYBUN
HONEYBUNS
HONEYCOMB
HONEYCOMBED
HONEYCOMBING
HONEYCOMBS
HONEYED
HONEYING
HONEYLESS
HONEYMOON
HONEYMOONED
HONEYMOONING
HONEYMOONS
HONEYPOT

HONEYPOTS
HONEYS
HONEYSEED
HONEYSEEDS
HONG
HONGING
HONGS
HONIED
HONING
HONK
HONKED
HONKER
HONKERS
HONKIE
HONKIES
HONKING
HONKS
HONKY
HONOR
HONORAND
HONORANDS
HONORARIA
HONORARIES
HONORARY
HONORED
HONORIFIC
HONORIFICS
HONORING
HONORS
HONOUR
HONOURED
HONOURER
HONOURERS
HONOURING
HONOURS
HONS
HONYSEED
HONYSEEDS
HOO
HOOCH
HOOCHES
HOOD
HOODED
HOODING
HOODLESS
HOODLUM
HOODLUMS
HOODMAN
HOODMEN
HOODOO
HOODOOED
HOODOOING
HOODOOS
HOODS
HOODWINK
HOODWINKED
HOODWINKING
HOODWINKS
HOOEY
HOOEYS
HOOF
HOOFBEAT
HOOFBEATS
HOOFED
HOOFER
HOOFERS
HOOFING
HOOFLESS
HOOFPRINT
HOOFPRINTS

HOOFROT
HOOFROTS
HOOFS
HOOK
HOOKA
HOOKAH
HOOKAHS
HOOKAS
HOOKED
HOOKER
HOOKERS
HOOKEY
HOOKEYS
HOOKIER
HOOKIES
HOOKIEST
HOOKING
HOOKS
HOOKY
HOOLACHAN
HOOLACHANS
HOOLEY
HOOLEYS
HOOLICAN
HOOLICANS
HOOLIER
HOOLIEST
HOOLIGAN
HOOLIGANS
HOOLOCK
HOOLOCKS
HOOLY
HOOP
HOOPED
HOOPER
HOOPERS
HOOPING
HOOPOE
HOOPOES
HOOPS
HOORAH
HOORAHED
HOORAHING
HOORAHS
HOORAY
HOORAYED
HOORAYING
HOORAYS
HOORD
HOORDS
HOOROO
HOOSEGOW
HOOSEGOWS
HOOSGOW
HOOSGOWS
HOOSH
HOOSHED
HOOSHES
HOOSHING
HOOT
HOOTCH
HOOTCHES
HOOTED
HOOTER
HOOTERS
HOOTING
HOOTNANNIES
HOOTNANNY
HOOTS
HOOVE

HOOVED
HOOVEN
HOOVER
HOOVERED
HOOVERING
HOOVERS
HOOVES
HOOVING
HOP
HOPBIND
HOPBINDS
HOPBINE
HOPBINES
HOPDOG
HOPDOGS
HOPE
HOPED
HOPEFUL
HOPEFULLY
HOPEFULS
HOPELESS
HOPER
HOPERS
HOPES
HOPING
HOPINGLY
HOPLITE
HOPLITES
HOPLOLOGIES
HOPLOLOGY
HOPPED
HOPPER
HOPPERS
HOPPIER
HOPPIEST
HOPPING
HOPPINGS
HOPPLE
HOPPLED
HOPPLES
HOPPLING
HOPPY
HOPS
HOPSACK
HOPSACKS
HORAL
HORARY
HORDE
HORDED
HORDEIN
HORDEINS
HORDEOLUM
HORDEOLUMS
HORDES
HORDING
HORDOCK
HORDOCKS
HORE
HOREHOUND
HOREHOUNDS
HORIZON
HORIZONS
HORKEY
HORKEYS
HORME
HORMES
HORMONAL
HORMONE
HORMONES
HORMONIC

HORN	HORRID	HOSEPIPES	HOTHOUSE	HOUSETOPS
HORNBEAK	HORRIDER	HOSES	HOTHOUSES	HOUSEWIFE
HORNBEAKS	HORRIDEST	HOSIER	HOTLY	HOUSEWIVES
HORNBEAM	HORRIDLY	HOSIERIES	HOTNESS	HOUSEWORK
HORNBEAMS	HORRIFIC	HOSIERS	HOTNESSES	HOUSEWORKS
HORNBILL	HORRIFIED	HOSIERY	HOTPOT	HOUSING
HORNBILLS	HORRIFIES	HOSING	HOTPOTS	HOUSINGS
HORNBOOK	HORRIFY	HOSPICE	HOTS	HOUSLING
HORNBOOKS	HORRIFYING	HOSPICES	HOTSHOT	HOUT
HORNBUG	HORROR	HOSPITAGE	HOTSHOTS	HOUTS
HORNBUGS	HORRORS	HOSPITAGES	HOTTED	HOVE
HORNED	HORS	HOSPITAL	HOTTENTOT	HOVED
HORNER	HORSE	HOSPITALE	HOTTENTOTS	HOVEL
HORNERS	HORSEBACK	HOSPITALES	HOTTER	HOVELED
HORNET	HORSEBACKS	HOSPITALS	HOTTERED	HOVELLED
HORNETS	HORSECAR	HOSPITIA	HOTTERING	HOVELLER
HORNFELS	HORSECARS	HOSPITIUM	HOTTERS	HOVELLERS
HORNFELSES	HORSED	HOSPODAR	HOTTEST	HOVELLING
HORNFUL	HORSEFLIES	HOSPODARS	HOTTIE	HOVELS
HORNFULS	HORSEFLY	HOSS	HOTTIES	HOVEN
HORNGELD	HORSEHAIR	HOSSES	HOTTING	HOVER
HORNGELDS	HORSEHAIRS	HOST	HOTTISH	HOVERED
HORNIER	HORSEHIDE	HOSTA	HOUDAH	HOVERING
HORNIEST	HORSEHIDES	HOSTAGE	HOUDAHS	HOVERPORT
HORNINESS	HORSELESS	HOSTAGES	HOUDAN	HOVERPORTS
HORNINESSES	HORSEMAN	HOSTAS	HOUDANS	HOVERS
HORNING	HORSEMEAT	HOSTED	HOUF	HOVES
HORNINGS	HORSEMEATS	HOSTEL	HOUFED	HOVING
HORNISH	HORSEMEN	HOSTELER	HOUFF	HOW
HORNIST	HORSEMINT	HOSTELERS	HOUFFED	HOWBE
HORNISTS	HORSEMINTS	HOSTELLER	HOUFFING	HOWBEIT
HORNITO	HORSEPLAY	HOSTELLERS	HOUFFS	HOWDAH
HORNITOS	HORSEPLAYS	HOSTELRIES	HOUFING	HOWDAHS
HORNLESS	HORSEPOND	HOSTELRY	HOUFS	HOWDIE
HORNLET	HORSEPONDS	HOSTELS	HOUGH	HOWDIES
HORNLETS	HORSES	HOSTESS	HOUGHED	HOWDY
HORNPIPE	HORSESHOE	HOSTESSED	HOUGHING	HOWE
HORNPIPES	HORSESHOES	HOSTESSES	HOUGHS	HOWES
HORNS	HORSETAIL	HOSTESSING	HOUND	HOWEVER
HORNSTONE	HORSETAILS	HOSTILE	HOUNDED	HOWF
HORNSTONES	HORSEWAY	HOSTILELY	HOUNDING	HOWFED
HORNTAIL	HORSEWAYS	HOSTILITIES	HOUNDS	HOWFF
HORNTAILS	HORSEWHIP	HOSTILITY	HOUR	HOWFFED
HORNWORK	HORSEWHIPPED	HOSTING	HOURI	HOWFFING
HORNWORKS	HORSEWHIPPING	HOSTINGS	HOURIS	HOWFFS
HORNWORM	HORSEWHIPS	HOSTLER	HOURLONG	HOWFING
HORNWORMS	HORSIER	HOSTLERS	HOURLY	HOWFS
HORNWORT	HORSIEST	HOSTLESSE	HOURPLATE	HOWITZER
HORNWORTS	HORSINESS	HOSTRIES	HOURPLATES	HOWITZERS
HORNWRACK	HORSINESSES	HOSTRY	HOURS	HOWK
HORNWRACKS	HORSING	HOSTS	HOUSE	HOWKED
HORNY	HORSINGS	HOT	HOUSEBOY	HOWKER
HORNYHEAD	HORSON	HOTBED	HOUSEBOYS	HOWKERS
HORNYHEADS	HORSONS	HOTBEDS	HOUSED	HOWKING
HOROLOGE	HORST	HOTCH	HOUSEFUL	HOWKS
HOROLOGER	HORSTS	HOTCHED	HOUSEFULS	HOWL
HOROLOGERS	HORSY	HOTCHES	HOUSEHOLD	HOWLED
HOROLOGES	HORTATION	HOTCHING	HOUSEHOLDS	HOWLER
HOROLOGIC	HORTATIONS	HOTCHPOT	HOUSEL	HOWLERS
HOROLOGIES	HORTATIVE	HOTCHPOTS	HOUSELESS	HOWLET
HOROLOGY	HORTATORY	HOTE	HOUSELLED	HOWLETS
HOROMETRIES	HOS	HOTEL	HOUSELLING	HOWLING
HOROMETRY	HOSANNA	HOTELIER	HOUSELLINGS	HOWLINGS
HOROSCOPE	HOSANNAS	HOTELIERS	HOUSELS	HOWLS
HOROSCOPES	HOSE	HOTELS	HOUSEMAID	HOWRE
HOROSCOPIES	HOSED	HOTEN	HOUSEMAIDS	HOWRES
HOROSCOPY	HOSEMAN	HOTFOOT	HOUSEMAN	HOWS
HORRENT	HOSEMEN	HOTHEAD	HOUSEMEN	HOWSO
HORRIBLE	HOSEN	HOTHEADED	HOUSES	HOWSOEVER
HORRIBLY	HOSEPIPE	HOTHEADS	HOUSETOP	HOWTOWDIE

HOWTOWDIES	HUGELY	HUMAS	HUMILIATED	HUMUS
HOWZAT	HUGENESS	HUMBLE	HUMILIATES	HUMUSES
HOX	HUGENESSES	HUMBLED	HUMILIATING	HUMUSY
HOXED	HUGEOUS	HUMBLER	HUMILITIES	HUNCH
HOXES	HUGEOUSLY	HUMBLES	HUMILITY	HUNCHBACK
HOXING	HUGER	HUMBLESSE	HUMITE	HUNCHBACKS
HOY	HUGEST	HUMBLESSES	HUMITES	HUNCHED
HOYA	HUGGABLE	HUMBLEST	HUMLIE	HUNCHES
HOYAS	HUGGED	HUMBLING	HUMLIES	HUNCHING
HOYDEN	HUGGING	HUMBLINGS	HUMMABLE	HUNDRED
HOYDENISH	HUGS	HUMBLY	HUMMAUM	HUNDREDER
HOYDENISM	HUGY	HUMBUG	HUMMAUMS	HUNDREDERS
HOYDENISMS	HUH	HUMBUGGED	HUMMED	HUNDREDOR
HOYDENS	HUIA	HUMBUGGER	HUMMEL	HUNDREDORS
HOYED	HUIAS	HUMBUGGERS	HUMMELLED	HUNDREDS
HOYING	HUISSIER	HUMBUGGING	HUMMELLER	HUNDREDTH
HOYS	HUISSIERS	HUMBUGS	HUMMELLERS	HUNDREDTHS
HUANACO	HUITAIN	HUMBUZZ	HUMMELLING	HUNG
HUANACOS	HUITAINS	HUMBUZZES	HUMMELS	HUNGER
HUB	HULA	HUMDINGER	HUMMER	HUNGERED
HUBBIES	HULAS	HUMDINGERS	HUMMERS	HUNGERFUL
HUBBUB	HULE	HUMDRUM	HUMMING	HUNGERING
HUBBUBOO	HULES	HUMDRUMS	HUMMINGS	HUNGERLY
HUBBUBOOS	HULK	HUMECT	HUMMOCK	HUNGERS
HUBBUBS	HULKIER	HUMECTANT	HUMMOCKED	HUNGRIER
HUBBY	HULKIEST	HUMECTANTS	HUMMOCKS	HUNGRIEST
HUBRIS	HULKING	HUMECTATE	HUMMOCKY	HUNGRILY
HUBRISES	HULKS	HUMECTATED	HUMMUM	HUNGRY
HUBRISTIC	HULKY	HUMECTATES	HUMMUMS	HUNK
HUBS	HULL	HUMECTATING	HUMMUS	HUNKER
HUCK	HULLED	HUMECTED	HUMMUSES	HUNKERED
HUCKABACK	HULLIER	HUMECTING	HUMOGEN	HUNKERING
HUCKABACKS	HULLIEST	HUMECTIVE	HUMOGENS	HUNKERS
HUCKLE	HULLING	HUMECTIVES	HUMOR	HUNKIER
HUCKLES	HULLO	HUMECTS	HUMORAL	HUNKIES
HUCKS	HULLOED	HUMEFIED	HUMORALLY	HUNKIEST
HUCKSTER	HULLOES	HUMEFIES	HUMORED	HUNKS
HUCKSTERED	HULLOING	HUMEFY	HUMORESK	HUNKSES
HUCKSTERIES	HULLOS	HUMEFYING	HUMORESKS	HUNKY
HUCKSTERING	HULLS	HUMERAL	HUMORING	HUNT
HUCKSTERS	HULLY	HUMERALS	HUMORIST	HUNTED
HUCKSTERY	HUM	HUMERI	HUMORISTS	HUNTER
HUDDEN	HUMA	HUMERUS	HUMOROUS	HUNTERS
HUDDLE	HUMAN	HUMF	HUMORS	HUNTING
HUDDLED	HUMANE	HUMFED	HUMOUR	HUNTINGS
HUDDLES	HUMANELY	HUMFING	HUMOURED	HUNTRESS
HUDDLING	HUMANER	HUMFS	HUMOURING	HUNTRESSES
HUDDUP	HUMANEST	HUMHUM	HUMOURS	HUNTS
HUE	HUMANISE	HUMHUMS	HUMOUS	HUNTSMAN
HUED	HUMANISED	HUMIC	HUMP	HUNTSMEN
HUELESS	HUMANISES	HUMID	HUMPBACK	HUP
HUER	HUMANISING	HUMIDER	HUMPBACKS	HUPPED
HUERS	HUMANISM	HUMIDEST	HUMPED	HUPPING
HUES	HUMANISMS	HUMIDIFIED	HUMPEN	HUPS
HUFF	HUMANIST	HUMIDIFIES	HUMPENS	HURCHEON
HUFFED	HUMANISTS	HUMIDIFY	HUMPH	HURCHEONS
HUFFIER	HUMANITIES	HUMIDIFYING	HUMPHED	HURDEN
HUFFIEST	HUMANITY	HUMIDITIES	HUMPHING	HURDENS
HUFFILY	HUMANIZE	HUMIDITY	HUMPHS	HURDIES
HUFFINESS	HUMANIZED	HUMIDLY	HUMPIER	HURDLE
HUFFINESSES	HUMANIZES	HUMIDNESS	HUMPIES	HURDLED
HUFFING	HUMANIZING	HUMIDNESSES	HUMPIEST	HURDLER
HUFFISH	HUMANKIND	HUMIDOR	HUMPING	HURDLERS
HUFFISHLY	HUMANLIKE	HUMIDORS	HUMPS	HURDLES
HUFFKIN	HUMANLY	HUMIFIED	HUMPTIES	HURDLING
HUFFKINS	HUMANNESS	HUMIFIES	HUMPTY	HURDLINGS
HUFFS	HUMANNESSES	HUMIFY	HUMPY	HURDS
HUFFY	HUMANOID	HUMIFYING	HUMS	HURL
HUG	HUMANOIDS	HUMILIANT	HUMSTRUM	HURLED
HUGE	HUMANS	HUMILIATE	HUMSTRUMS	HURLER

HURLERS	HUSKIER	HYALITES	HYDROLYSE	HYKE
HURLEY	HUSKIES	HYALOID	HYDROLYSED	HYKES
HURLEYS	HUSKIEST	HYALONEMA	HYDROLYSES	HYLDING
HURLIES	HUSKILY	HYALONEMAS	HYDROLYSING	HYLDINGS
HURLING	HUSKINESS	HYBRID	HYDROLYTE	HYLE
HURLINGS	HUSKINESSES	HYBRIDISE	HYDROLYTES	HYLEG
HURLS	HUSKING	HYBRIDISED	HYDROLYZE	HYLEGS
HURLY	HUSKINGS	HYBRIDISES	HYDROLYZED	HYLES
HURRA	HUSKS	HYBRIDISING	HYDROLYZES	HYLIC
HURRAED	HUSKY	HYBRIDISM	HYDROLYZING	HYLICISM
HURRAH	HUSO	HYBRIDISMS	HYDROMEL	HYLICISMS
HURRAHED	HUSOS	HYBRIDITIES	HYDROMELS	HYLICIST
HURRAHING	HUSS	HYBRIDITY	HYDRONAUT	HYLICISTS
HURRAHS	HUSSAR	HYBRIDIZE	HYDRONAUTS	HYLISM
HURRAING	HUSSARS	HYBRIDIZED	HYDROPIC	HYLISMS
HURRAS	HUSSES	HYBRIDIZES	HYDROPSIES	HYLIST
HURRAY	HUSSIES	HYBRIDIZING	HYDROPSY	HYLISTS
HURRAYED	HUSSIF	HYBRIDOMA	HYDROPTIC	HYLOBATE
HURRAYING	HUSSIFS	HYBRIDOMAS	HYDROPULT	HYLOBATES
HURRAYS	HUSSY	HYBRIDOUS	HYDROPULTS	HYLOIST
HURRICANE	HUSTINGS	HYBRIDS	HYDROS	HYLOISTS
HURRICANES	HUSTLE	HYBRIS	HYDROSKI	HYLOPHYTE
HURRICANO	HUSTLED	HYBRISES	HYDROSKIS	HYLOPHYTES
HURRICANOES	HUSTLER	HYDATHODE	HYDROSOMA	HYLOZOISM
HURRIED	HUSTLERS	HYDATHODES	HYDROSOMATA	HYLOZOISMS
HURRIEDLY	HUSTLES	HYDATID	HYDROSOME	HYLOZOIST
HURRIES	HUSTLING	HYDATIDS	HYDROSOMES	HYLOZOISTS
HURRY	HUSTLINGS	HYDATOID	HYDROSTAT	HYMEN
HURRYING	HUSWIFE	HYDRA	HYDROSTATS	HYMENAEAL
HURRYINGS	HUSWIVES	HYDRAEMIA	HYDROUS	HYMENAEAN
HURSI	HUT	HYDRAEMIAS	HYDROVANE	HYMENAL
HURSTS	HUTCH	HYDRANGEA	HYDROVANES	HYMENEAL
HURT	HUTCHED	HYDRANGEAS	HYDROXIDE	HYMENEALS
HURTER	HUTCHES	HYDRANT	HYDROXIDES	HYMENEAN
HURTERS	HUTCHING	HYDRANTH	HYDROXY	HYMENIA
HURTFUL	HUTIA	HYDRANTHS	HYDROXYL	HYMENIAL
HURTFULLY	HUTIAS	HYDRANTS	HYDROXYLS	HYMENIUM
HURTING	HUTMENT	HYDRAS	HYDROZOA	HYMENIUMS
HURTLE	HUTMENTS	HYDRATE	HYDROZOAN	HYMENS
HURTLED	HUTS	HYDRATED	HYDROZOANS	HYMN
HURTLES	HUTTED	HYDRATES	HYDROZOON	HYMNAL
HURTLESS	HUTTING	HYDRATING	HYDYNE	HYMNALS
HURTLING	HUTTINGS	HYDRATION	HYDYNES	HYMNARIES
HURTS	HUZOOR	HYDRATIONS	HYE	HYMNARY
HUSBAND	HUZOORS	HYDRAULIC	HYED	HYMNED
HUSBANDED	HUZZA	HYDRAULICKED	HYFING	HYMNIC
HUSBANDING	HUZZAED	HYDRAULICKING	HYEN	HYMNING
HUSBANDLY	HUZZAING	HYDRAULICS	HYENA	HYMNIST
HUSBANDRIES	HUZZAS	HYDRAZINE	HYENAS	HYMNISTS
HUSBANDRY	HUZZIES	HYDRAZINES	HYENS	HYMNODIES
HUSBANDS	HUZZY	HYDREMIA	HYES	HYMNODIST
HUSH	HWYL	HYDREMIAS	HYETAL	HYMNODISTS
HUSHABIED	HWYLS	HYDRIA	HYETOLOGIES	HYMNODY
HUSHABIES	HYACINE	HYDRIAE	HYETOLOGY	HYMNOLOGIES
HUSHABY	HYACINES	HYDRIAS	HYGIENE	HYMNOLOGY
HUSHABYING	HYACINTH	HYDRIC	HYGIENES	HYMNS
HUSHED	HYACINTHS	HYDRIDE	HYGIENIC	HYNDE
HUSHER	HYAENA	HYDRIDES	HYGIENICS	HYNDES
HUSHERED	HYAENAS	HYDRIODIC	HYGIENIST	HYOID
HUSHERING	HYALINE	HYDRO	HYGIENISTS	HYOSCINE
HUSHERS	HYALINES	HYDROCELE	HYGRISTOR	HYOSCINES
HUSHES	HYALINISE	HYDROCELES	HYGRISTORS	HYP
HUSHIER	HYALINISED	HYDROFOIL	HYGRODEIK	HYPALGIA
HUSHIEST	HYALINISES	HYDROFOILS	HYGRODEIKS	HYPALGIAS
HUSHING	HYALINISING	HYDROGEN	HYGROLOGIES	HYPALLAGE
HUSHY	HYALINIZE	HYDROGENS	HYGROLOGY	HYPALLAGES
HUSK	HYALINIZED	HYDROID	HYGROPHIL	HYPATE
HUSKED	HYALINIZES	HYDROIDS	HYGROSTAT	HYPATES
HUSKER	HYALINIZING	HYDROLOGIES	HYGROSTATS	HYPE
HUSKERS	HYALITE	HYDROLOGY	HYING	HYPED

HYPER
HYPERBOLA
HYPERBOLAS
HYPERBOLE
HYPERBOLES
HYPERCUBE
HYPERCUBES
HYPEREMIA
HYPEREMIAS
HYPERGAMIES
HYPERGAMY
HYPERMART
HYPERMARTS
HYPERON
HYPERONS
HYPEROPIA
HYPEROPIAS
HYPERS
HYPES
HYPHA
HYPHAE
HYPHAL
HYPHEN
HYPHENATE
HYPHENATED
HYPHENATEDS
HYPHENATES
HYPHENATING
HYPHENED
HYPHENIC
HYPHENING

HYPHENISE
HYPHENISED
HYPHENISES
HYPHENISING
HYPHENISM
HYPHENISMS
HYPHENIZE
HYPHENIZED
HYPHENIZES
HYPHENIZING
HYPHENS
HYPING
HYPINOSES
HYPINOSIS
HYPNA
HYPNIC
HYPNICS
HYPNOGENIES
HYPNOGENY
HYPNOID
HYPNOIDAL
HYPNOLOGIES
HYPNOLOGY
HYPNONE
HYPNONES
HYPNOSES
HYPNOSIS
HYPNOTEE
HYPNOTEES
HYPNOTIC
HYPNOTICS

HYPNOTISE
HYPNOTISED
HYPNOTISES
HYPNOTISING
HYPNOTISM
HYPNOTISMS
HYPNOTIST
HYPNOTISTS
HYPNOTIZE
HYPNOTIZED
HYPNOTIZES
HYPNOTIZING
HYPNOTOID
HYPNUM
HYPNUMS
HYPO
HYPOBLAST
HYPOBLASTS
HYPOBOLE
HYPOBOLES
HYPOCAUST
HYPOCAUSTS
HYPOCIST
HYPOCISTS
HYPOCOTYL
HYPOCOTYLS
HYPOCRISIES
HYPOCRISY
HYPOCRITE
HYPOCRITES
HYPODERM

HYPODERMA
HYPODERMAS
HYPODERMS
HYPOGAEA
HYPOGAEAL
HYPOGAEAN
HYPOGAEUM
HYPOGEA
HYPOGEAL
HYPOGEAN
HYPOGENE
HYPOGEOUS
HYPOGEUM
HYPOGYNIES
HYPOGYNY
HYPOID
HYPOMANIA
HYPOMANIAS
HYPOMANIC
HYPONASTIES
HYPONASTY
HYPONYM
HYPONYMS
HYPOS
HYPOSTYLE
HYPOSTYLES
HYPOTAXES
HYPOTAXIS
HYPOTHEC
HYPOTHECS
HYPOTONIA

HYPOTONIAS
HYPOTONIC
HYPOXEMIA
HYPOXEMIAS
HYPOXEMIC
HYPOXIA
HYPOXIAS
HYPOXIC
HYPPED
HYPPING
HYPS
HYPURAL
HYRACES
HYRACOID
HYRAX
HYRAXES
HYSON
HYSONS
HYSSOP
HYSSOPS
HYSTERIA
HYSTERIAS
HYSTERIC
HYSTERICS
HYSTEROID
HYTHE
HYTHES

I

IAIDO
IAIDOS
IAMB
IAMBI
IAMBIC
IAMBICS
IAMBIST
IAMBISTS
IAMBS
IAMBUS
IAMBUSES
IANTHINE
IATRIC
IATRICAL
IATROGENIES
IATROGENY
IBEX
IBEXES
IBICES
IBIDEM
IBIS
IBISES
IBUPROFEN
IBUPROFENS
ICE
ICEBERG
ICEBERGS
ICEBLINK
ICEBLINKS
ICEBOX
ICEBOXES
ICED
ICEMAN
ICEMEN
ICEPACK
ICEPACKS
ICEPLANT
ICEPLANTS
ICER
ICERS
ICES
ICH
ICHABOD
ICHED
ICHING
ICHNEUMON
ICHNEUMONS
ICHNITE
ICHNITES
ICHNOLITE
ICHNOLITES
ICHNOLOGIES
ICHNOLOGY
ICHOR
ICHOROUS
ICHORS
ICHTHIC
ICHTHYOID
ICHTHYOIDS
ICHTHYS
ICHTHYSES
ICICLE
ICICLES
ICIER

ICIEST
ICILY
ICINESS
ICINESSES
ICING
ICINGS
ICKER
ICKERS
ICKIER
ICKIEST
ICKY
ICON
ICONIC
ICONISE
ICONISED
ICONISES
ICONISING
ICONIZE
ICONIZED
ICONIZES
ICONIZING
ICONOLOGIES
ICONOLOGY
ICONOSIAS
ICONOSTASES
ICONS
ICTAL
ICTERIC
ICTERICAL
ICTERICALS
ICTERICS
ICTERINE
ICTERUS
ICTERUSES
ICTIC
ICTUS
ICTUSES
ICY
ID
IDANT
IDANTS
IDE
IDEA
IDEAED
IDEAL
IDEALESS
IDEALISE
IDEALISED
IDEALISER
IDEALISERS
IDEALISES
IDEALISING
IDEALISM
IDEALISMS
IDEALIST
IDEALISTS
IDEALITIES
IDEALITY
IDEALIZE
IDEALIZED
IDEALIZER
IDEALIZERS
IDEALIZES
IDEALIZING

IDEALLESS
IDEALLY
IDEALOGUE
IDEALOGUES
IDEALS
IDEAS
IDEATE
IDEATED
IDEATES
IDEATING
IDEATION
IDEATIONS
IDEATIVE
IDÉE
IDÉES
IDEM
IDENTIC
IDENTICAL
IDENTIFIED
IDENTIFIES
IDENTIFY
IDENTIFYING
IDENTIKIT
IDENTIKITS
IDENTITIES
IDENTITY
IDEOGRAM
IDEOGRAMS
IDEOGRAPH
IDEOGRAPHS
IDEOLOGIC
IDEOLOGIES
IDEOLOGUE
IDEOLOGUES
IDEOLOGY
IDEOPHONE
IDEOPHONES
IDES
IDIOBLAST
IDIOBLASTS
IDIOCIES
IDIOCY
IDIOGRAPH
IDIOGRAPHS
IDIOLECT
IDIOLECTS
IDIOM
IDIOMATIC
IDIOMS
IDIOPATHIES
IDIOPATHY
IDIOPHONE
IDIOPHONES
IDIOPLASM
IDIOPLASMS
IDIOT
IDIOTCIES
IDIOTCY
IDIOTIC
IDIOTICAL
IDIOTICON
IDIOTICONS
IDIOTISH
IDIOTISM

IDIOTISMS
IDIOTS
IDLE
IDLED
IDLEHOOD
IDLEHOODS
IDLENESS
IDLENESSES
IDLER
IDLERS
IDLES
IDLESSE
IDLESSES
IDLEST
IDLING
IDLY
IDOCRASE
IDOCRASES
IDOL
IDOLATER
IDOLATERS
IDOLATRIES
IDOLATRY
IDOLISE
IDOLISED
IDOLISER
IDOLISERS
IDOLISES
IDOLISING
IDOLISM
IDOLISMS
IDOLIST
IDOLISTS
IDOLIZE
IDOLIZED
IDOLIZER
IDOLIZERS
IDOLIZES
IDOLIZING
IDOLS
IDS
IDYL
IDYLL
IDYLLIAN
IDYLLIC
IDYLLIST
IDYLLISTS
IDYLLS
IDYLS
IF
IFF
IFFIER
IFFIEST
IFFY
IFS
IGAD
IGAPO
IGAPOS
IGARAPÉ
IGARAPÉS
IGLOO
IGLOOS
IGNARO
IGNAROES

IGNAROS
IGNEOUS
IGNESCENT
IGNESCENTS
IGNITABLE
IGNITE
IGNITED
IGNITER
IGNITERS
IGNITES
IGNITIBLE
IGNITING
IGNITION
IGNITIONS
IGNITRON
IGNITRONS
IGNOBLE
IGNOBLED
IGNOBLER
IGNOBLES
IGNOBLEST
IGNOBLING
IGNOBLY
IGNOMIES
IGNOMINIES
IGNOMINY
IGNOMY
IGNORABLE
IGNORAMUS
IGNORAMUSES
IGNORANCE
IGNORANCES
IGNORANT
IGNORANTS
IGNORE
IGNORED
IGNORER
IGNORERS
IGNORES
IGNORING
IGUANA
IGUANAS
IGUANID
IGUANIDS
IHRAM
IHRAMS
IKAT
IKATS
IKEBANA
IKEBANAS
IKON
IKONS
ILEA
ILEAC
ILEITIS
ILEITISES
ILEUM
ILEUS
ILEUSES
ILEX
ILEXES
ILIA
ILIAC
ILICES

ILIUM	IMAGELESS	IMBODY	IMITATION	IMMISSION
ILK	IMAGERIES	IMBODYING	IMITATIONS	IMMISSIONS
ILKA	IMAGERY	IMBORDER	IMITATIVE	IMMIT
ILKADAY	IMAGES	IMBORDERED	IMITATOR	IMMITS
ILKADAYS	IMAGINAL	IMBORDERING	IMITATORS	IMMITTED
ILKS	IMAGINARY	IMBORDERS	IMMANACLE	IMMITTING
ILL	IMAGINE	IMBOSK	IMMANACLED	IMMIX
ILLAPSE	IMAGINED	IMBOSKED	IMMANACLES	IMMIXED
ILLAPSED	IMAGINER	IMBOSKING	IMMANACLING	IMMIXES
ILLAPSES	IMAGINERS	IMBOSKS	IMMANE	IMMIXING
ILLAPSING	IMAGINES	IMBOSOM	IMMANELY	IMMOBILE
ILLATION	IMAGING	IMBOSOMED	IMMANENCE	IMMODEST
ILLATIONS	IMAGINGS	IMBOSOMING	IMMANENCES	IMMODESTIES
ILLATIVE	IMAGINING	IMBOSOMS	IMMANENCIES	IMMODESTY
ILLATIVES	IMAGININGS	IMBOSS	IMMANENCY	IMMOLATE
ILLEGAL	IMAGINIST	IMBOSSED	IMMANENT	IMMOLATED
ILLEGALLY	IMAGINISTS	IMBOSSES	IMMANITIES	IMMOLATES
ILLEGIBLE	IMAGISM	IMBOSSING	IMMANITY	IMMOLATING
ILLEGIBLY	IMAGISMS	IMBOWER	IMMANTLE	IMMOLATOR
ILLER	IMAGIST	IMBOWERED	IMMANTLED	IMMOLATORS
ILLEST	IMAGISTIC	IMBOWERING	IMMANTLES	IMMOMENT
ILLIAD	IMAGISTS	IMBOWERS	IMMANTLING	IMMORAL
ILLIADS	IMAGO	IMBRANGLE	IMMASK	IMMORALLY
ILLIBERAL	IMAGOES	IMBRANGLED	IMMASKED	IMMORTAL
ILLICIT	IMAGOS	IMBRANGLES	IMMASKING	IMMORTALS
ILLICITLY	IMAM	IMBRANGLING	IMMASKS	IMMOVABLE
ILLIMITED	IMAMATE	IMBRAST	IMMATURE	IMMOVABLY
ILLINIUM	IMAMATES	IMBREX	IMMATURED	IMMUNE
ILLINIUMS	IMAMS	IMBRICATE	IMMEDIACIES	IMMUNES
ILLIPE	IMARI	IMBRICATED	IMMEDIACY	IMMUNISE
ILLIPES	IMARIS	IMBRICATES	IMMEDIATE	IMMUNISED
ILLIQUID	IMAUM	IMBRICATING	IMMENSE	IMMUNISES
ILLISION	IMAUMS	IMBRICES	IMMENSELY	IMMUNISING
ILLISIONS	IMBALANCE	IMBROGLIO	IMMENSER	IMMUNITIES
ILLITE	IMBALANCES	IMBROGLIOS	IMMENSEST	IMMUNITY
ILLITES	IMBAR	IMBROWN	IMMENSITIES	IMMUNIZE
ILLNESS	IMBARK	IMBROWNED	IMMENSITY	IMMUNIZED
ILLNESSES	IMBARKED	IMBROWNING	IMMERGE	IMMUNIZES
ILLOGIC	IMBARKING	IMBROWNS	IMMERGED	IMMUNIZING
ILLOGICAL	IMBARKS	IMBRUE	IMMERGES	IMMUNOGEN
ILLOGICS	IMBARRED	IMBRUED	IMMERGING	IMMUNOGENS
ILLS	IMBARRING	IMBRUEING	IMMERSE	IMMURE
ILLTH	IMBARS	IMBRUES	IMMERSED	IMMURED
ILLTHS	IMBASE	IMBRUING	IMMERSES	IMMURES
ILLUDE	IMBASED	IMBRUTE	IMMERSING	IMMURING
ILLUDED	IMBASES	IMBRUTED	IMMERSION	IMMUTABLE
ILLUDES	IMBASING	IMBRUTES	IMMERSIONS	IMMUTABLY
ILLUDING	IMBATHE	IMBRUTING	IMMESH	IMP
ILLUME	IMBATHED	IMBUE	IMMESHED	IMPACABLE
ILLUMED	IMBATHES	IMBUED	IMMESHES	IMPACT
ILLUMES	IMBATHING	IMBUEING	IMMESHING	IMPACTED
ILLUMINE	IMBECILE	IMBUES	IMMEW	IMPACTING
ILLUMINED	IMBECILES	IMBUING	IMMEWED	IMPACTION
ILLUMINER	IMBECILIC	IMBURSE	IMMEWING	IMPACTIONS
ILLUMINERS	IMBED	IMBURSED	IMMEWS	IMPACTITE
ILLUMINES	IMBEDDED	IMBURSES	IMMIGRANT	IMPACTITES
ILLUMING	IMBEDDING	IMBURSING	IMMIGRANTS	IMPACTS
ILLUMINING	IMBEDS	IMIDE	IMMIGRATE	IMPAINT
ILLUPI	IMBIBE	IMIDES	IMMIGRATED	IMPAINTED
ILLUPIS	IMBIBED	IMINE	IMMIGRATES	IMPAINTING
ILLUSION	IMBIBER	IMINES	IMMIGRATING	IMPAINTS
ILLUSIONS	IMBIBERS	IMITABLE	IMMINENCE	IMPAIR
ILLUSIVE	IMBIBES	IMITANCIES	IMMINENCES	IMPAIRED
ILLUSORY	IMBIBING	IMITANCY	IMMINENCIES	IMPAIRING
ILLY	IMBITTER	IMITANT	IMMINENCY	IMPAIRS
ILMENITE	IMBITTERED	IMITANTS	IMMINENT	IMPALA
ILMENITES	IMBITTERING	IMITATE	IMMINGLE	IMPALAS
IMAGE	IMBITTERS	IMITATED	IMMINGLED	IMPALE
IMAGEABLE	IMBODIED	IMITATES	IMMINGLES	IMPALED
IMAGED	IMBODIES	IMITATING	IMMINGLING	IMPALES

IMPALING	IMPEDING	IMPLEADERS	IMPONENTS	IMPRINTED
IMPANATE	IMPEL	IMPLEADING	IMPONES	IMPRINTING
IMPANEL	IMPELLED	IMPLEADS	IMPONING	IMPRINTINGS
IMPANELLED	IMPELLENT	IMPLEDGE	IMPORT	IMPRINTS
IMPANELLING	IMPELLENTS	IMPLEDGED	IMPORTANT	IMPRISON
IMPANELS	IMPELLER	IMPLEDGES	IMPORTED	IMPRISONED
IMPANNEL	IMPELLERS	IMPLEDGING	IMPORTER	IMPRISONING
IMPANNELLED	IMPELLING	IMPLEMENT	IMPORTERS	IMPRISONS
IMPANNELLING	IMPELS	IMPLEMENTED	IMPORTING	IMPROBITIES
IMPANNELS	IMPEND	IMPLEMENTING	IMPORTS	IMPROBITY
IMPARITIES	IMPENDED	IMPLEMENTS	IMPORTUNE	IMPROMPTU
IMPARITY	IMPENDENT	IMPLETE	IMPORTUNED	IMPROMPTUS
IMPARK	IMPENDING	IMPLETED	IMPORTUNES	IMPROPER
IMPARKED	IMPENDS	IMPLETES	IMPORTUNING	IMPROVE
IMPARKING	IMPERATOR	IMPLETING	IMPORTUNINGS	IMPROVED
IMPARKS	IMPERATORS	IMPLETION	IMPOSABLE	IMPROVER
IMPARL	IMPERFECT	IMPLETIONS	IMPOSE	IMPROVERS
IMPARLED	IMPERFECTS	IMPLEX	IMPOSED	IMPROVES
IMPARLING	IMPERIAL	IMPLEXES	IMPOSER	IMPROVING
IMPARLS	IMPERIALS	IMPLEXION	IMPOSERS	IMPROVISE
IMPART	IMPERIL	IMPLEXIONS	IMPOSES	IMPROVISED
IMPARTED	IMPERILLED	IMPLICATE	IMPOSING	IMPROVISES
IMPARTER	IMPERILLING	IMPLICATED	IMPOST	IMPROVISING
IMPARTERS	IMPERILS	IMPLICATES	IMPOSTER	IMPRUDENT
IMPARTIAL	IMPERIOUS	IMPLICATING	IMPOSTERS	IMPS
IMPARTING	IMPERIUM	IMPLICIT	IMPOSTOR	IMPUDENCE
IMPARTS	IMPERIUMS	IMPLIED	IMPOSTORS	IMPUDENCES
IMPASSE	IMPETICOS	IMPLIEDLY	IMPOSTS	IMPUDENT
IMPASSES	IMPETICOSED	IMPLIES	IMPOSTUME	IMPUGN
IMPASSION	IMPETICOSES	IMPLODE	IMPOSTUMES	IMPUGNED
IMPASSIONED	IMPETICOSING	IMPLODED	IMPOSTURE	IMPUGNER
IMPASSIONING	IMPETIGINES	IMPLODENT	IMPOSTURES	IMPUGNERS
IMPASSIONS	IMPETIGO	IMPLODENTS	IMPOT	IMPUGNING
IMPASSIVE	IMPETIGOS	IMPLODES	IMPOTENCE	IMPUGNS
IMPASTE	IMPETRATE	IMPLODING	IMPOTENCES	IMPULSE
IMPASTED	IMPETRATED	IMPLORE	IMPOTENCIES	IMPULSES
IMPASTES	IMPETRATES	IMPLORED	IMPOTENCY	IMPULSION
IMPASTING	IMPETRATING	IMPLORER	IMPOTENT	IMPULSIONS
IMPASTO	IMPETUOUS	IMPLORERS	IMPOTS	IMPULSIVE
IMPASTOED	IMPETUS	IMPLORES	IMPOUND	IMPULSORY
IMPASTOS	IMPETUSES	IMPLORING	IMPOUNDED	IMPUNITIES
IMPATIENS	IMPI	IMPLOSION	IMPOUNDER	IMPUNITY
IMPATIENT	IMPIETIES	IMPLOSIONS	IMPOUNDERS	IMPURE
IMPAVE	IMPIETY	IMPLOSIVE	IMPOUNDING	IMPURELY
IMPAVED	IMPING	IMPLOSIVES	IMPOUNDS	IMPURER
IMPAVES	IMPINGE	IMPLUNGE	IMPRECATE	IMPUREST
IMPAVID	IMPINGED	IMPLUNGED	IMPRECATED	IMPURITIES
IMPAVIDLY	IMPINGENT	IMPLUNGES	IMPRECATES	IMPURITY
IMPAVING	IMPINGES	IMPLUNGING	IMPRECATING	IMPURPLE
IMPAWN	IMPINGING	IMPLUVIA	IMPRECISE	IMPURPLED
IMPAWNED	IMPIOUS	IMPLUVIUM	IMPREGN	IMPURPLES
IMPAWNING	IMPIOUSLY	IMPLY	IMPREGNED	IMPURPLING
IMPAWNS	IMPIS	IMPLYING	IMPREGNING	IMPUTABLE
IMPEACH	IMPISH	IMPOCKET	IMPREGNS	IMPUTABLY
IMPEACHED	IMPISHLY	IMPOCKETED	IMPRESA	IMPUTE
IMPEACHER	IMPLANT	IMPOCKETING	IMPRESARI	IMPUTED
IMPEACHERS	IMPLANTED	IMPOCKETS	IMPRESAS	IMPUTER
IMPEACHES	IMPLANTING	IMPOLDER	IMPRESE	IMPUTERS
IMPEACHING	IMPLANTS	IMPOLDERED	IMPRESES	IMPUTES
IMPEARL	IMPLATE	IMPOLDERING	IMPRESS	IMPUTING
IMPEARLED	IMPLATED	IMPOLDERS	IMPRESSE	IMSHI
IMPEARLING	IMPLATES	IMPOLICIES	IMPRESSED	IMSHY
IMPEARLS	IMPLATING	IMPOLICY	IMPRESSES	IN
IMPECCANT	IMPLEACH	IMPOLITE	IMPRESSING	INABILITIES
IMPED	IMPLEACHED	IMPOLITER	IMPREST	INABILITY
IMPEDANCE	IMPLEACHES	IMPOLITEST	IMPRESTED	INACTION
IMPEDANCES	IMPLEACHING	IMPOLITIC	IMPRESTING	INACTIONS
IMPEDE	IMPLEAD	IMPONE	IMPRESTS	INACTIVE
IMPEDED	IMPLEADED	IMPONED	IMPRIMIS	INAIDABLE
IMPEDES	IMPLEADER	IMPONENT	IMPRINT	INAMORATA

INAMORATAS	INCASE	INCISION	INCONY	INCURVED
INAMORATO	INCASED	INCISIONS	INCORPSE	INCURVES
INAMORATOS	INCASES	INCISIVE	INCORPSED	INCURVING
INANE	INCASING	INCISOR	INCORPSES	INCURVITIES
INANELY	INCAUTION	INCISORS	INCORPSING	INCURVITY
INANENESS	INCAUTIONS	INCISORY	INCORRECT	INCUS
INANENESSES	INCAVE	INCISURE	INCORRUPT	INCUSE
INANER	INCAVED	INCISURES	INCREASE	INCUSED
INANES	INCAVES	INCITANT	INCREASED	INCUSES
INANEST	INCAVI	INCITANTS	INCREASER	INCUSING
INANIMATE	INCAVING	INCITE	INCREASERS	INCUT
INANITIES	INCAVO	INCITED	INCREASES	INDABA
INANITION	INCAVOS	INCITER	INCREASING	INDABAS
INANITIONS	INCEDE	INCITERS	INCREASINGS	INDAGATE
INANITY	INCEDED	INCITES	INCREATE	INDAGATED
INAPT	INCEDES	INCITING	INCREMATE	INDAGATES
INAPTLY	INCEDING	INCIVIL	INCREMATED	INDAGATING
INAPTNESS	INCENSE	INCIVISM	INCREMATES	INDAGATOR
INAPTNESSES	INCENSED	INCIVISMS	INCREMATING	INDAGATORS
INARABLE	INCENSER	INCLASP	INCREMENT	INDART
INARCH	INCENSERS	INCLASPED	INCREMENTS	INDARTED
INARCHED	INCENSES	INCLASPING	INCROSS	INDARTING
INARCHES	INCENSING	INCLASPS	INCROSSED	INDARTS
INARCHING	INCENSOR	INCLE	INCROSSES	INDEBTED
INARM	INCENSORIES	INCLEMENT	INCROSSING	INDECENCIES
INARMED	INCENSORS	INCLES	INCRUST	INDECENCY
INARMING	INCENSORY	INCLINE	INCRUSTED	INDECENT
INARMS	INCENTIVE	INCLINED	INCRUSTING	INDECENTER
INAUDIBLE	INCENTIVES	INCLINES	INCRUSTS	INDECENTEST
INAUDIBLY	INCENTRE	INCLINING	INCUBATE	INDECORUM
INAUGURAL	INCENTRES	INCLININGS	INCUBATED	INDECORUMS
INAUGURALS	INCEPT	INCLIP	INCUBATES	INDEED
INAURATE	INCEPTED	INCLIPPED	INCUBATING	INDELIBLE
INBEING	INCEPTING	INCLIPPING	INCUBATOR	INDELIBLY
INBEINGS	INCEPTION	INCLIPS	INCUBATORS	INDEMNIFIED
INBENT	INCEPTIONS	INCLOSE	INCUBI	INDEMNIFIES
INBOARD	INCEPTIVE	INCLOSED	INCUBOUS	INDEMNIFY
INBORN	INCEPTIVES	INCLOSER	INCUBUS	INDEMNIFYING
INBREAK	INCEPTOR	INCLOSERS	INCUBUSES	INDEMNITIES
INBREAKS	INCEPTORS	INCLOSES	INCUDES	INDEMNITY
INBREATHE	INCEPTS	INCLOSING	INCULCATE	INDENE
INBREATHED	INCERTAIN	INCLOSURE	INCULCATED	INDENES
INBREATHES	INCESSANT	INCLOSURES	INCULCATES	INDENT
INBREATHING	INCEST	INCLUDE	INCULCATING	INDENTED
INBRED	INCESTS	INCLUDED	INCULPATE	INDENTER
INBREED	INCH	INCLUDES	INCULPATED	INDENTERS
INBREEDING	INCHASE	INCLUDING	INCULPATES	INDENTING
INBREEDINGS	INCHASED	INCLUSION	INCULPATING	INDENTION
INBREEDS	INCHASES	INCLUSIONS	INCULT	INDENTIONS
INBRING	INCHASING	INCLUSIVE	INCUMBENT	INDENTS
INBRINGING	INCHED	INCOGNITA	INCUMBENTS	INDENTURE
INBRINGINGS	INCHES	INCOGNITAS	INCUNABLE	INDENTURED
INBRINGS	INCHING	INCOGNITO	INCUNABLES	INDENTURES
INBROUGHT	INCHMEAL	INCOGNITOS	INCUR	INDENTURING
INBURNING	INCHOATE	INCOME	INCURABLE	INDEW
INBURST	INCHOATED	INCOMER	INCURABLES	INDEWED
INBURSTS	INCHOATES	INCOMERS	INCURABLY	INDEWING
INBY	INCHOATING	INCOMES	INCURIOUS	INDEWS
INBYE	INCHPIN	INCOMING	INCURRED	INDEX
INCAGE	INCHPINS	INCOMINGS	INCURRENT	INDEXED
INCAGED	INCIDENCE	INCOMMODE	INCURRING	INDEXER
INCAGES	INCIDENCES	INCOMMODED	INCURS	INDEXERS
INCAGING	INCIDENT	INCOMMODES	INCURSION	INDEXES
INCAPABLE	INCIDENTS	INCOMMODING	INCURSIONS	INDEXICAL
INCAPABLES	INCIPIENT	INCONDITE	INCURSIVE	INDEXING
INCAPABLY	INCIPIT	INCONIE	INCURVATE	INDEXINGS
INCARNATE	INCISE	INCONNU	INCURVATED	INDEXLESS
INCARNATED	INCISED	INCONNUE	INCURVATES	INDICAN
INCARNATES	INCISES	INCONNUES	INCURVATING	INDICANS
INCARNATING	INCISING	INCONNUS	INCURVE	INDICANT

INDICANTS	INDORSE	INDWELLINGS	INFANCY	INFILTERING
INDICATE	INDORSED	INDWELLS	INFANT	INFILTERS
INDICATED	INDORSES	INDWELT	INFANTA	INFINITE
INDICATES	INDORSING	INEARTH	INFANTAS	INFINITES
INDICATING	INDRAFT	INEARTHED	INFANTE	INFINITIES
INDICATOR	INDRAFTS	INEARTHING	INFANTED	INFINITY
INDICATORS	INDRAUGHT	INEARTHS	INFANTES	INFIRM
INDICES	INDRAUGHTS	INEBRIANT	INFANTILE	INFIRMARIES
INDICIA	INDRAWN	INEBRIANTS	INFANTINE	INFIRMARY
INDICIUM	INDRENCH	INEBRIATE	INFANTING	INFIRMER
INDICT	INDRENCHED	INEBRIATED	INFANTRIES	INFIRMEST
INDICTED	INDRENCHES	INEBRIATES	INFANTRY	INFIRMITIES
INDICTEE	INDRENCHING	INEBRIATING	INFANTS	INFIRMITY
INDICTEES	INDRI	INEBRIETIES	INFARCT	INFIRMLY
INDICTING	INDRIS	INEBRIETY	INFARCTS	INFIX
INDICTION	INDRISES	INEBRIOUS	INFARE	INFIXED
INDICTIONS	INDUBIOUS	INEDIBLE	INFARES	INFIXES
INDICTS	INDUCE	INEDITED	INFATUATE	INFIXING
INDIGENCE	INDUCED	INEFFABLE	INFATUATED	INFLAME
INDIGENCES	INDUCER	INEFFABLY	INFATUATES	INFLAMED
INDIGENCIES	INDUCERS	INELASTIC	INFATUATING	INFLAMER
INDIGENCY	INDUCES	INELEGANT	INFAUST	INFLAMERS
INDIGENE	INDUCIAE	INEPT	INFECT	INFLAMES
INDIGENES	INDUCIBLE	INEPTER	INFECTED	INFLAMING
INDIGENT	INDUCING	INEPTEST	INFECTING	INFLATE
INDIGEST	INDUCT	INEPTLY	INFECTION	INFLATED
INDIGESTS	INDUCTED	INEPTNESS	INFECTIONS	INFLATES
INDIGN	INDUCTILE	INEPTNESSES	INFECTIVE	INFLATING
INDIGNANT	INDUCTING	INEQUABLE	INFECTOR	INFLATION
INDIGNIFIED	INDUCTION	INEQUITIES	INFECTORS	INFLATIONS
INDIGNIFIES	INDUCTIONS	INEQUITY	INFECTS	INFLATIVE
INDIGNIFY	INDUCTIVE	INERM	INFECUND	INFLATOR
INDIGNIFYING	INDUCTOR	INERRABLE	INFEFT	INFLATORS
INDIGNITIES	INDUCTORS	INERRABLY	INFEFTED	INFLATUS
INDIGNITY	INDUCTS	INERRANCIES	INFEFTING	INFLATUSES
INDIGO	INDUE	INERRANCY	INFEFTS	INFLECT
INDIGOES	INDUED	INERRANT	INFELT	INFLECTED
INDIGOS	INDUEING	INERT	INFER	INFLECTING
INDIGOTIN	INDUES	INERTER	INFERABLE	INFLECTS
INDIGOTINS	INDUING	INERTEST	INFERE	INFLEXED
INDIRECT	INDULGE	INERTIA	INFERENCE	INFLEXION
INDIRECTER	INDULGED	INERTIAL	INFERENCES	INFLEXIONS
INDIRECTEST	INDULGENT	INERTIAS	INFERIAE	INFLEXURE
INDIRUBIN	INDULGER	INERTLY	INFERIOR	INFLEXURES
INDIRUBINS	INDULGERS	INERTNESS	INFERIORS	INFLICT
INDISPOSE	INDULGES	INERTNESSES	INFERNAL	INFLICTED
INDISPOSED	INDULGING	INERUDITE	INFERNO	INFLICTING
INDISPOSES	INDULINE	INESSIVE	INFERNOS	INFLICTS
INDISPOSING	INDULINES	INESSIVES	INFERRED	INFLOW
INDITE	INDULT	INEXACT	INFERRING	INFLOWING
INDITED	INDULTS	INEXACTLY	INFERS	INFLOWS
INDITER	INDUNA	INEXPERT	INFERTILE	INFLUENCE
INDITERS	INDUNAS	INFALL	INFEST	INFLUENCED
INDITES	INDURATE	INFALLS	INFESTED	INFLUENCES
INDITING	INDURATED	INFAME	INFESTING	INFLUENCING
INDIUM	INDURATES	INFAMED	INFESTS	INFLUENT
INDIUMS	INDURATING	INFAMES	INFICETE	INFLUENTS
INDOCIBLE	INDUSIA	INFAMIES	INFIDEL	INFLUENZA
INDOCILE	INDUSIAL	INFAMING	INFIDELS	INFLUENZAS
INDOL	INDUSIATE	INFAMISE	INFIELD	INFLUX
INDOLE	INDUSIUM	INFAMISED	INFIELDER	INFLUXES
INDOLENCE	INDUSTRIES	INFAMISES	INFIELDERS	INFLUXION
INDOLENCES	INDUSTRY	INFAMISING	INFIELDS	INFLUXIONS
INDOLENCIES	INDUVIAE	INFAMIZE	INFILL	INFO
INDOLENCY	INDUVIAL	INFAMIZED	INFILLED	INFOLD
INDOLENT	INDUVIATE	INFAMIZES	INFILLING	INFOLDED
INDOLES	INDWELL	INFAMIZING	INFILLINGS	INFOLDING
INDOLS	INDWELLER	INFAMOUS	INFILLS	INFOLDS
INDOOR	INDWELLERS	INFAMY	INFILTER	INFORCE
INDOORS	INDWELLING	INFANCIES	INFILTERED	INFORCED

INFORCES	INGLE	INHARMONY	INITIATED	INLACE
INFORCING	INGLES	INHAUST	INITIATES	INLACED
INFORM	INGLOBE	INHAUSTED	INITIATING	INLACES
INFORMAL	INGLOBED	INHAUSTING	INITIATOR	INLACING
INFORMANT	INGLOBES	INHAUSTS	INITIATORS	INLAID
INFORMANTS	INGLOBING	INHEARSE	INJECT	INLAND
INFORMED	INGLUVIAL	INHEARSED	INJECTED	INLANDER
INFORMER	INGLUVIES	INHEARSES	INJECTING	INLANDERS
INFORMERS	INGLUVIESES	INHEARSING	INJECTION	INLANDS
INFORMING	INGO	INHERCE	INJECTIONS	INLAY
INFORMS	INGOES	INHERCED	INJECTOR	INLAYER
INFORTUNE	INGOING	INHERCES	INJECTORS	INLAYERS
INFORTUNES	INGOINGS	INHERCING	INJECTS	INLAYING
INFOS	INGOT	INHERE	INJELLIED	INLAYINGS
INFRA	INGOTS	INHERED	INJELLIES	INLAYS
INFRACT	INGOWES	INHERENCE	INJELLY	INLET
INFRACTED	INGRAFT	INHERENCES	INJELLYING	INLETS
INFRACTING	INGRAFTED	INHERENCIES	INJOINT	INLIER
INFRACTOR	INGRAFTING	INHERENCY	INJOINTED	INLIERS
INFRACTORS	INGRAFTS	INHERENT	INJOINTING	INLIEST
INFRACTS	INGRAIN	INHERES	INJOINTS	INLOCK
INFRINGE	INGRAINED	INHERING	INJUNCT	INLOCKED
INFRINGED	INGRAINING	INHERIT	INJUNCTED	INLOCKING
INFRINGES	INGRAINS	INHERITED	INJUNCTING	INLOCKS
INFRINGING	INGRAM	INHERITING	INJUNCTS	INLY
INFULA	INGRATE	INHERITOR	INJURANT	INLYING
INFULAE	INGRATES	INHERITORS	INJURANTS	INMATE
INFURIATE	INGRESS	INHERITS	INJURE	INMATES
INFURIATED	INGRESSES	INHESION	INJURED	INMESH
INFURIATES	INGROOVE	INHESIONS	INJURER	INMESHED
INFURIATING	INGROOVED	INHIBIT	INJURERS	INMESHES
INFUSCATE	INGROOVES	INHIBITED	INJURES	INMESHING
INFUSE	INGROOVING	INHIBITING	INJURIES	INMOST
INFUSED	INGROSS	INHIBITOR	INJURING	INN
INFUSER	INGROSSED	INHIBITORS	INJURIOUS	INNARDS
INFUSERS	INGROSSES	INHIBITS	INJURY	INNATE
INFUSES	INGROSSING	INHOLDER	INJUSTICE	INNATELY
INFUSIBLE	INGROUP	INHOLDERS	INJUSTICES	INNATIVE
INFUSING	INGROUPS	INHOOP	INK	INNED
INFUSION	INGROWING	INHOOPED	INKBERRIES	INNER
INFUSIONS	INGROWN	INHOOPING	INKBERRY	INNERMOST
INFUSIVE	INGROWTH	INHOOPS	INKED	INNERS
INFUSORIA	INGROWTHS	INHUMAN	INKER	INNERVATE
INFUSORY	INGRUM	INHUMANE	INKERS	INNERVATED
INGAN	INGUINAL	INHUMANER	INKHOLDER	INNERVATES
INGANS	INGULF	INHUMANEST	INKHOLDERS	INNERVATING
INGATE	INGULFED	INHUMANLY	INKHORN	INNERVE
INGATES	INGULFING	INHUMATE	INKHORNS	INNERVED
INGENER	INGULFS	INHUMATED	INKIER	INNERVES
INGENERS	INGULPH	INHUMATES	INKIEST	INNERVING
INGENIOUS	INGULPHED	INHUMATING	INKINESS	INNHOLDER
INGENIUM	INGULPHING	INHUME	INKINESSES	INNHOLDERS
INGENIUMS	INGULPHS	INHUMED	INKING	INNING
INGÉNU	INHABIT	INHUMES	INKLE	INNINGS
INGÉNUE	INHABITED	INHUMING	INKLED	INNKEEPER
INGÉNUES	INHABITING	INIA	INKLES	INNKEEPERS
INGENUITIES	INHABITOR	INIMICAL	INKLING	INNOCENCE
INGENUITY	INHABITORS	INION	INKLINGS	INNOCENCES
INGENUOUS	INHABITS	INIQUITIES	INKPOT	INNOCENCIES
INGÉNUS	INHALANT	INIQUITY	INKPOTS	INNOCENCY
INGEST	INHALANTS	INISLE	INKS	INNOCENT
INGESTA	INHALATOR	INISLED	INKSPOT	INNOCENTS
INGESTED	INHALATORS	INISLES	INKSPOTS	INNOCUITIES
INGESTING	INHALE	INISLING	INKSTAND	INNOCUITY
INGESTION	INHALED	INITIAL	INKSTANDS	INNOCUOUS
INGESTIONS	INHALER	INITIALLED	INKSTONE	INNOVATE
INGESTIVE	INHALERS	INITIALLING	INKSTONES	INNOVATED
INGESTS	INHALES	INITIALLY	INKWELL	INNOVATES
INGINE	INHALING	INITIALS	INKWELLS	INNOVATING
INGINES	INHARMONIES	INITIATE	INKY	INNOVATOR

INNOVATORS	INRUSHING	INSETTING	INSOLVENT	INSTIGATED
INNOXIOUS	INRUSHINGS	INSHALLAH	INSOLVENTS	INSTIGATES
INNS	INS	INSHEATHE	INSOMNIA	INSTIGATING
INNUENDO	INSANE	INSHEATHED	INSOMNIAC	INSTIL
INNUENDOED	INSANELY	INSHEATHES	INSOMNIACS	INSTILL
INNUENDOES	INSANER	INSHEATHING	INSOMNIAS	INSTILLED
INNUENDOING	INSANEST	INSHELL	INSOMUCH	INSTILLING
INNUENDOS	INSANIE	INSHELLED	INSOOTH	INSTILLS
INNYARD	INSANIES	INSHELLING	INSOUL	INSTILS
INNYARDS	INSANITIES	INSHELLS	INSOULED	INSTINCT
INOCULATE	INSANITY	INSHELTER	INSOULING	INSTINCTS
INOCULATED	INSATIATE	INSHELTERED	INSOULS	INSTITUTE
INOCULATES	INSATIETIES	INSHELTERING	INSPAN	INSTITUTED
INOCULATING	INSATIETY	INSHELTERS	INSPANNED	INSTITUTES
INOCULUM	INSCAPE	INSHIP	INSPANNING	INSTITUTING
INOCULUMS	INSCAPES	INSHIPPED	INSPANS	INSTRESS
INODOROUS	INSCIENCE	INSHIPPING	INSPECT	INSTRESSED
INOPINATE	INSCIENCES	INSHIPS	INSPECTED	INSTRESSES
INORB	INSCIENT	INSHORE	INSPECTING	INSTRESSING
INORBED	INSCONCE	INSHRINE	INSPECTOR	INSTRUCT
INORBING	INSCONCED	INSHRINED	INSPECTORS	INSTRUCTED
INORBS	INSCONCES	INSHRINES	INSPECTS	INSTRUCTING
INORGANIC	INSCONCING	INSHRINING	INSPHEARE	INSTRUCTS
INORNATE	INSCRIBE	INSIDE	INSPHERE	INSUCKEN
INOSITOL	INSCRIBED	INSIDER	INSPHERED	INSULA
INOSITOLS	INSCRIBER	INSIDERS	INSPHERES	INSULAE
INOTROPIC	INSCRIBERS	INSIDES	INSPHERING	INSULANCE
INPAYMENT	INSCRIBES	INSIDIOUS	INSPIRE	INSULANCES
INPAYMENTS	INSCRIBING	INSIGHT	INSPIRED	INSULANT
INPHASE	INSCROLL	INSIGHTS	INSPIRER	INSULANTS
INPOURING	INSCROLLED	INSIGNE	INSPIRERS	INSULAR
INPOURINGS	INSCROLLING	INSIGNES	INSPIRES	INSULARLY
INPUT	INSCROLLS	INSIGNIA	INSPIRING	INSULAS
INPUTS	INSCULP	INSIGNIAS	INSPIRIT	INSULATE
INPUTTER	INSCULPED	INSINCERE	INSPIRITED	INSULATED
INPUTTERS	INSCULPING	INSINEW	INSPIRITING	INSULATES
INPUTTING	INSCULPS	INSINEWED	INSPIRITS	INSULATING
INQILAB	INSCULPT	INSINEWING	INSPYRE	INSULATOR
INQILABS	INSEAM	INSINEWS	INSPYRED	INSULATORS
INQUERE	INSEAMED	INSINUATE	INSPYRES	INSULIN
INQUERED	INSEAMING	INSINUATED	INSPYRING	INSULINS
INQUERES	INSEAMS	INSINUATES	INSTABLE	INSULSE
INQUERING	INSECT	INSINUATING	INSTAL	INSULSITIES
INQUEST	INSECTARIES	INSIPID	INSTALL	INSULSITY
INQUESTS	INSECTARY	INSIPIDER	INSTALLED	INSULT
INQUIET	INSECTILE	INSIPIDEST	INSTALLING	INSULTANT
INQUIETED	INSECTION	INSIPIDLY	INSTALLS	INSULTED
INQUIETING	INSECTIONS	INSIPIENT	INSTALS	INSULTER
INQUIETLY	INSECTS	INSIST	INSTANCE	INSULTERS
INQUIETS	INSECTY	INSISTED	INSTANCED	INSULTING
INQUILINE	INSECURE	INSISTENT	INSTANCES	INSULTS
INQUILINES	INSECURER	INSISTING	INSTANCIES	INSURABLE
INQUINATE	INSECUREST	INSISTS	INSTANCING	INSURANCE
INQUINATED	INSEEM	INSISTURE	INSTANCY	INSURANCES
INQUINATES	INSEEMED	INSISTURES	INSTANT	INSURANT
INQUINATING	INSEEMING	INSNARE	INSTANTER	INSURANTS
INQUIRE	INSEEMS	INSNARED	INSTANTLY	INSURE
INQUIRED	INSELBERG	INSNARES	INSTANTS	INSURED
INQUIRER	INSELBERGE	INSNARING	INSTAR	INSURER
INQUIRERS	INSENSATE	INSOLATE	INSTARRED	INSURERS
INQUIRES	INSERT	INSOLATED	INSTARRING	INSURES
INQUIRIES	INSERTED	INSOLATES	INSTARS	INSURGENT
INQUIRING	INSERTER	INSOLATING	INSTATE	INSURGENTS
INQUIRY	INSERTERS	INSOLE	INSTATED	INSURING
INQUORATE	INSERTING	INSOLENCE	INSTATES	INSWATHE
INRO	INSERTION	INSOLENCES	INSTATING	INSWATHED
INROAD	INSERTIONS	INSOLENT	INSTEAD	INSWATHES
INROADS	INSERTS	INSOLES	INSTEP	INSWATHING
INRUSH	INSET	INSOLUBLE	INSTEPS	INSWING
INRUSHES	INSETS	INSOLUBLY	INSTIGATE	INSWINGER

INSWINGERS	INTERACTED	INTERGROW	INTERNAL	INTERWINDING
INSWINGS	INTERACTING	INTERGROWING	INTERNALS	INTERWINDS
INTACT	INTERACTS	INTERGROWN	INTERNE	INTERWORK
INTAGLIO	INTERBANK	INTERGROWS	INTERNED	INTERWORKED
INTAGLIOED	INTERBRED	INTERIM	INTERNEE	INTERWORKING
INTAGLIOING	INTERCEDE	INTERIMS	INTERNEES	INTERWORKS
INTAGLIOS	INTERCEDED	INTERIOR	INTERNES	INTERWOUND
INTAKE	INTERCEDES	INTERIORS	INTERNING	INTERZONE
INTAKES	INTERCEDING	INTERJECT	INTERNIST	INTERZONES
INTARSI	INTERCEPT	INTERJECTED	INTERNISTS	INTESTACIES
INTARSIA	INTERCEPTED	INTERJECTING	INTERNODE	INTESTACY
INTARSIAS	INTERCEPTING	INTERJECTS	INTERNODES	INTESTATE
INTARSIO	INTERCEPTS	INTERJOIN	INTERNS	INTESTATES
INTARSIOS	INTERCITY	INTERJOINED	INTERPAGE	INTESTINE
INTEGER	INTERCOM	INTERJOINING	INTERPAGED	INTESTINES
INTEGERS	INTERCOMS	INTERJOINS	INTERPAGES	INTHRAL
INTEGRAL	INTERCROP	INTERKNIT	INTERPAGING	INTHRALL
INTEGRALS	INTERCROPPED	INTERKNITS	INTERPLAY	INTHRALLED
INTEGRAND	INTERCROPPING	INTERKNITTED	INTERPLAYS	INTHRALLING
INTEGRANDS	INTERCROPS	INTERKNITTING	INTERPONE	INTHRALLS
INTEGRANT	INTERCUT	INTERLACE	INTERPONED	INTHRALS
INTEGRATE	INTERCUTS	INTERLACED	INTERPONES	INTIL
INTEGRATED	INTERCUTTING	INTERLACES	INTERPONING	INTIMA
INTEGRATES	INTERDASH	INTERLACING	INTERPOSE	INTIMACIES
INTEGRATING	INTERDASHED	INTERLAID	INTERPOSED	INTIMACY
INTEGRITIES	INTERDASHES	INTERLARD	INTERPOSES	INTIMAE
INTEGRITY	INTERDASHING	INTERLARDED	INTERPOSING	INTIMATE
INTELLECT	INTERDEAL	INTERLARDING	INTERPRET	INTIMATED
INTELLECTS	INTERDEALING	INTERLARDS	INTERPRETED	INTIMATES
INTENABLE	INTERDEALS	INTERLAY	INTERPRETING	INTIMATING
INTEND	INTERDEALT	INTERLAYING	INTERPRETS	INTIME
INTENDANT	INTERDICT	INTERLAYS	INTERRED	INTIMISM
INTENDANTS	INTERDICTED	INTERLEAF	INTERREGES	INTIMISMS
INTENDED	INTERDICTING	INTERLEAVES	INTERREX	INTIMIST
INTENDEDS	INTERDICTS	INTERLINE	INTERRING	INTIMISTE
INTENDER	INTERDINE	INTERLINED	INTERRUPT	INTIMISTES
INTENDERED	INTERDINED	INTERLINES	INTERRUPTED	INTIMISTS
INTENDERING	INTERDINES	INTERLINING	INTERRUPTING	INTIMITIES
INTENDERS	INTERDINING	INTERLININGS	INTERRUPTS	INTIMITY
INTENDING	INTERESS	INTERLINK	INTERS	INTINE
INTENDS	INTERESSE	INTERLINKED	INTERSECT	INTINES
INTENIBLE	INTERESSED	INTERLINKING	INTERSECTED	INTIRE
INTENSATE	INTERESSES	INTERLINKS	INTERSECTING	INTITULE
INTENSATED	INTERESSING	INTERLOCK	INTERSECTS	INTITULED
INTENSATES	INTEREST	INTERLOCKED	INTERSERT	INTITULES
INTENSATING	INTERESTED	INTERLOCKING	INTERSERTED	INTITULING
INTENSE	INTERESTING	INTERLOCKS	INTERSERTING	INTO
INTENSELY	INTERESTS	INTERLOPE	INTERSERTS	INTOED
INTENSER	INTERFACE	INTERLOPED	INTERSEX	INTOMB
INTENSEST	INTERFACED	INTERLOPES	INTERSEXES	INTOMBED
INTENSIFIED	INTERFACES	INTERLOPING	INTERTIE	INTOMBING
INTENSIFIES	INTERFACING	INTERLUDE	INTERTIES	INTOMBS
INTENSIFY	INTERFACINGS	INTERLUDED	INTERVAL	INTONATE
INTENSIFYING	INTERFERE	INTERLUDES	INTERVALE	INTONATED
INTENSION	INTERFERED	INTERLUDING	INTERVALES	INTONATES
INTENSIONS	INTERFERES	INTERMENT	INTERVALS	INTONATING
INTENSITIES	INTERFERING	INTERMENTS	INTERVEIN	INTONATOR
INTENSITY	INTERFLOW	INTERMIT	INTERVEINED	INTONATORS
INTENSIVE	INTERFLOWED	INTERMITS	INTERVEINING	INTONE
INTENSIVES	INTERFLOWING	INTERMITTED	INTERVEINS	INTONED
INTENT	INTERFLOWS	INTERMITTING	INTERVENE	INTONER
INTENTER	INTERFOLD	INTERMIX	INTERVENED	INTONERS
INTENTEST	INTERFOLDED	INTERMIXED	INTERVENES	INTONES
INTENTION	INTERFOLDING	INTERMIXES	INTERVENING	INTONING
INTENTIONS	INTERFOLDS	INTERMIXING	INTERVIEW	INTONINGS
INTENTIVE	INTERFUSE	INTERMURE	INTERVIEWED	INTORSION
INTENTLY	INTERFUSED	INTERMURED	INTERVIEWING	INTORSIONS
INTENTS	INTERFUSES	INTERMURES	INTERVIEWS	INTORTED
INTER	INTERFUSING	INTERMURING	INTERWAR	INTORTION
INTERACT	INTERGREW	INTERN	INTERWIND	INTORTIONS

INTOWN
INTRA
INTRADOS
INTRADOSES
INTRANT
INTRANTS
INTREAT
INTREATED
INTREATING
INTREATS
INTRENCH
INTRENCHED
INTRENCHES
INTRENCHING
INTREPID
INTREPIDER
INTREPIDEST
INTRICACIES
INTRICACY
INTRICATE
INTRIGANT
INTRIGANTS
INTRIGUE
INTRIGUED
INTRIGUER
INTRIGUERS
INTRIGUES
INTRIGUING
INTRINCE
INTRINSIC
INTRO
INTRODUCE
INTRODUCED
INTRODUCES
INTRODUCING
INTROIT
INTROITS
INTROITUS
INTROITUSES
INTROJECT
INTROJECTED
INTROJECTING
INTROJECTS
INTROLD
INTROMIT
INTROMITS
INTROMITTED
INTROMITTING
INTRON
INTRONS
INTRORSE
INTROS
INTROVERT
INTROVERTED
INTROVERTING
INTROVERTS
INTRUDE
INTRUDED
INTRUDER
INTRUDERS
INTRUDES
INTRUDING
INTRUSION
INTRUSIONS
INTRUSIVE
INTRUSIVES
INTRUST
INTRUSTED
INTRUSTING
INTRUSTS

INTUBATE
INTUBATED
INTUBATES
INTUBATING
INTUIT
INTUITED
INTUITING
INTUITION
INTUITIONS
INTUITIVE
INTUITS
INTUMESCE
INTUMESCED
INTUMESCES
INTUMESCING
INTUSE
INTUSES
INTWINE
INTWINED
INTWINES
INTWINING
INTWIST
INTWISTED
INTWISTING
INTWISTS
INULA
INULAS
INULASE
INULASES
INULIN
INULINS
INUMBRATE
INUMBRATED
INUMBRATES
INUMBRATING
INUNCTION
INUNCTIONS
INUNDANT
INUNDATE
INUNDATED
INUNDATES
INUNDATING
INURBANE
INURE
INURED
INUREMENT
INUREMENTS
INURES
INURING
INURN
INURNED
INURNING
INURNS
INUSITATE
INUST
INUSTION
INUSTIONS
INUTILITIES
INUTILITY
INVADE
INVADED
INVADER
INVADERS
INVADES
INVADING
INVALID
INVALIDED
INVALIDING
INVALIDINGS
INVALIDLY

INVALIDS
INVARIANT
INVARIANTS
INVASION
INVASIONS
INVASIVE
INVEAGLE
INVEAGLED
INVEAGLES
INVEAGLING
INVECKED
INVECTED
INVECTIVE
INVECTIVES
INVEIGH
INVEIGHED
INVEIGHING
INVEIGHS
INVEIGLE
INVEIGLED
INVEIGLER
INVEIGLERS
INVEIGLES
INVEIGLING
INVENIT
INVENT
INVENTED
INVENTING
INVENTION
INVENTIONS
INVENTIVE
INVENTOR
INVENTORIED
INVENTORIES
INVENTORS
INVENTORY
INVENTORYING
INVENTS
INVERSE
INVERSED
INVERSELY
INVERSES
INVERSING
INVERSION
INVERSIONS
INVERSIVE
INVERT
INVERTASE
INVERTASES
INVERTED
INVERTER
INVERTERS
INVERTIN
INVERTING
INVERTINS
INVERTOR
INVERTORS
INVERTS
INVEST
INVESTED
INVESTING
INVESTOR
INVESTORS
INVESTS
INVEXED
INVIABLE
INVIDIOUS
INVIOLATE
INVIOUS
INVISIBLE

INVISIBLES
INVISIBLY
INVITE
INVITED
INVITEE
INVITEES
INVITER
INVITERS
INVITES
INVITING
INVITINGS
INVOCATE
INVOCATED
INVOCATES
INVOCATING
INVOICE
INVOICED
INVOICES
INVOICING
INVOKE
INVOKED
INVOKES
INVOKING
INVOLUCEL
INVOLUCELS
INVOLUCRE
INVOLUCRES
INVOLUTE
INVOLUTED
INVOLUTES
INVOLUTING
INVOLVE
INVOLVED
INVOLVES
INVOLVING
INWALL
INWALLED
INWALLING
INWALLS
INWARD
INWARDLY
INWARDS
INWEAVE
INWEAVES
INWEAVING
INWICK
INWICKED
INWICKING
INWICKS
INWIND
INWINDING
INWINDS
INWIT
INWITH
INWITS
INWORK
INWORKED
INWORKING
INWORKINGS
INWORKS
INWORN
INWOUND
INWOVE
INWOVEN
INWRAP
INWRAPPED
INWRAPPING
INWRAPS
INWREATHE
INWREATHED

INWREATHES
INWREATHING
INWROUGHT
INYALA
INYALAS
IO
IODATE
IODATES
IODIC
IODIDE
IODIDES
IODINE
IODINES
IODISE
IODISED
IODISES
IODISING
IODISM
IODISMS
IODIZE
IODIZED
IODIZES
IODIZING
IODOFORM
IODOFORMS
IODOPHILE
IODOUS
IODURET
IODURETS
IODYRITE
IODYRITES
IOLITE
IOLITES
ION
IONIC
IONISE
IONISED
IONISER
IONISERS
IONISES
IONISING
IONIUM
IONIUMS
IONIZE
IONIZED
IONIZER
IONIZERS
IONIZES
IONIZING
IONOMER
IONOMERS
IONONE
IONONES
IONOPAUSE
IONOPAUSES
IONS
IOS
IOTA
IOTACISM
IOTACISMS
IOTAS
IPECAC
IPECACS
IPOMOEA
IPOMOEAS
IRACUND
IRADE
IRADES
IRASCIBLE
IRASCIBLY

IRATE	IRONIES	ISAGOGE	ISOCHORE	ISOLINE
IRATELY	IRONING	ISAGOGES	ISOCHORES	ISOLINES
IRATER	IRONINGS	ISAGOGIC	ISOCHORIC	ISOLOGOUS
IRATEST	IRONISE	ISAGOGICS	ISOCHORS	ISOLOGUE
IRE	IRONISED	ISALLOBAR	ISOCHRONE	ISOLOGUES
IREFUL	IRONISES	ISALLOBARS	ISOCHRONES	ISOMER
IREFULLY	IRONISING	ISATIN	ISOCLINAL	ISOMERE
IRENIC	IRONIST	ISATINE	ISOCLINALS	ISOMERES
IRENICAL	IRONISTS	ISATINES	ISOCLINE	ISOMERIC
IRENICISM	IRONIZE	ISATINS	ISOCLINES	ISOMERISE
IRENICISMS	IRONIZED	ISCHAEMIA	ISOCLINIC	ISOMERISED
IRENICON	IRONIZES	ISCHAEMIAS	ISOCLINICS	ISOMERISES
IRENICONS	IRONIZING	ISCHAEMIC	ISOCRACIES	ISOMERISING
IRENICS	IRONS	ISCHEMIA	ISOCRACY	ISOMERISM
IRENOLOGIES	IRONSMITH	ISCHEMIAS	ISOCRATIC	ISOMERISMS
IRENOLOGY	IRONSMITHS	ISCHEMIC	ISOCRYMAL	ISOMERIZE
IRES	IRONSTONE	ISCHIA	ISOCRYMALS	ISOMERIZED
IRID	IRONSTONES	ISCHIADIC	ISOCRYME	ISOMERIZES
IRIDAL	IRONWARE	ISCHIAL	ISOCRYMES	ISOMERIZING
IRIDEAL	IRONWARES	ISCHIATIC	ISOCYCLIC	ISOMEROUS
IRIDES	IRONWOOD	ISCHIUM	ISODICON	ISOMERS
IRIDIAL	IRONWOODS	ISCHURIA	ISODICONS	ISOMETRIC
IRIDIAN	IRONWORK	ISCHURIAS	ISODOMA	ISOMETRICS
IRIDIC	IRONWORKS	ISENERGIC	ISODOMON	ISOMETRIES
IRIDISE	IRONY	ISH	ISODOMONS	ISOMETRY
IRIDISED	IRRADIANT	ISHES	ISODOMOUS	ISOMORPH
IRIDISES	IRRADIATE	ISINGLASS	ISODOMUM	ISOMORPHS
IRIDISING	IRRADIATED	ISINGLASSES	ISODONT	ISONIAZID
IRIDIUM	IRRADIATES	ISLAND	ISODONTAL	ISONIAZIDS
IRIDIUMS	IRRADIATING	ISLANDED	ISODONTS	ISONOMIC
IRIDIZE	IRREALITIES	ISLANDER	ISOETES	ISONOMIES
IRIDIZED	IRREALITY	ISLANDERS	ISOGAMETE	ISONOMOUS
IRIDIZES	IRREGULAR	ISLANDING	ISOGAMETES	ISONOMY
IRIDIZING	IRREGULARS	ISLANDS	ISOGAMIC	ISOPLETH
IRIDOLOGIES	IRRELATED	ISLE	ISOGAMIES	ISOPLETHS
IRIDOLOGY	IRRIGABLE	ISLED	ISOGAMOUS	ISOPOD
IRIDOTOMIES	IRRIGATE	ISLEMAN	ISOGAMY	ISOPODAN
IRIDOTOMY	IRRIGATED	ISLEMEN	ISOGENIES	ISOPODOUS
IRIDS	IRRIGATES	ISLES	ISOGENOUS	ISOPODS
IRIS	IRRIGATING	ISLESMAN	ISOGENY	ISOPOLITIES
IRISATE	IRRIGATOR	ISLESMEN	ISOGLOSS	ISOPOLITY
IRISATED	IRRIGATORS	ISLET	ISOGLOSSES	ISOPRENE
IRISATES	IRRIGUOUS	ISLETS	ISOGON	ISOPRENES
IRISATING	IRRISION	ISLING	ISOGONAL	ISOPROPYL
IRISATION	IRRISIONS	ISM	ISOGONALS	ISOPROPYLS
IRISATIONS	IRRISORY	ISMATIC	ISOGONIC	ISOSCELES
IRISCOPE	IRRITABLE	ISMATICAL	ISOGONICS	ISOSPIN
IRISCOPES	IRRITABLY	ISMS	ISOGONS	ISOSPINS
IRISED	IRRITANCIES	ISMY	ISOGRAM	ISOSPORIES
IRISES	IRRITANCY	ISOBAR	ISOGRAMS	ISOSPORY
IRISING	IRRITANT	ISOBARE	ISOHEL	ISOSTASIES
IRITIC	IRRITANTS	ISOBARES	ISOHELS	ISOSTASY
IRITIS	IRRITATE	ISOBARIC	ISOHYET	ISOSTATIC
IRITISES	IRRITATED	ISOBARS	ISOHYETAL	ISOSTERIC
IRK	IRRITATES	ISOBASE	ISOHYETALS	ISOTACTIC
IRKED	IRRITATING	ISOBASES	ISOHYETS	ISOTHERAL
IRKING	IRRITATOR	ISOBATH	ISOKONT	ISOTHERALS
IRKS	IRRITATORS	ISOBATHIC	ISOKONTAN	ISOTHERE
IRKSOME	IRRUPT	ISOBATHS	ISOKONTANS	ISOTHERES
IRKSOMELY	IRRUPTED	ISOBRONT	ISOKONTS	ISOTHERM
IROKO	IRRUPTING	ISOBRONTS	ISOLABLE	ISOTHERMS
IROKOS	IRRUPTION	ISOCHASM	ISOLATE	ISOTONE
IRON	IRRUPTIONS	ISOCHASMS	ISOLATED	ISOTONES
IRONBARK	IRRUPTIVE	ISOCHEIM	ISOLATES	ISOTONIC
IRONBARKS	IRRUPTS	ISOCHEIMS	ISOLATING	ISOTOPE
IRONED	IS	ISOCHIMAL	ISOLATION	ISOTOPES
IRONER	ISABEL	ISOCHIMALS	ISOLATIONS	ISOTOPIC
IRONERS	ISABELLA	ISOCHIME	ISOLATIVE	ISOTOPIES
IRONIC	ISABELLAS	ISOCHIMES	ISOLATOR	ISOTOPY
IRONICAL	ISABELS	ISOCHOR	ISOLATORS	ISOTRON

ISOTRONS
ISOTROPIC
ISOTROPIES
ISOTROPY
ISOTYPE
ISOTYPES
ISSEI
ISSEIS
ISSUABLE
ISSUABLY
ISSUANCE
ISSUANCES
ISSUANT
ISSUE
ISSUED
ISSUELESS
ISSUER
ISSUERS
ISSUES
ISSUING
ISTHMIAN
ISTHMUS

ISTHMUSES
ISTLE
ISTLES
IT
ITA
ITACISM
ITACISMS
ITALIC
ITALICISE
ITALICISED
ITALICISES
ITALICISING
ITALICIZE
ITALICIZED
ITALICIZES
ITALICIZING
ITALICS
ITAS
ITCH
ITCHED
ITCHES
ITCHIER

ITCHIEST
ITCHINESS
ITCHINESSES
ITCHING
ITCHWEED
ITCHWEEDS
ITCHY
ITEM
ITEMED
ITEMING
ITEMISE
ITEMISED
ITEMISES
ITEMISING
ITEMIZE
ITEMIZED
ITEMIZES
ITEMIZING
ITEMS
ITERANCE
ITERANCES
ITERANT

ITERATE
ITERATED
ITERATES
ITERATING
ITERATION
ITERATIONS
ITERATIVE
ITERUM
ITINERACIES
ITINERACY
ITINERANT
ITINERANTS
ITINERARIES
ITINERARY
ITINERATE
ITINERATED
ITINERATES
ITINERATING
ITS
ITSELF
IVIED
IVIES

IVORIED
IVORIES
IVORIST
IVORISTS
IVORY
IVRESSE
IVRESSES
IVY
IWIS
IXIA
IXIAS
IXTLE
IXTLES
IYNX
IYNXES
IZARD
IZARDS
IZZARD
IZZARDS
IZZET
IZZETS

J

JAB	JACKPOT	JAILER	JAMBOOLS	JANTIER
JABBED	JACKPOTS	JAILERESS	JAMBOREE	JANTIES
JABBER	JACKS	JAILERESSES	JAMBOREES	JANTIEST
JABBERED	JACKSIE	JAILERS	JAMBOS	JANTY
JABBERER	JACKSIES	JAILHOUSE	JAMBS	JAP
JABBERERS	JACKSMITH	JAILHOUSES	JAMBU	JAPAN
JABBERING	JACKSMITHS	JAILING	JAMBUL	JAPANNED
JABBERINGS	JACKSY	JAILOR	JAMBULS	JAPANNER
JABBERS	JACOBUS	JAILORESS	JAMBUS	JAPANNERS
JABBING	JACOBUSES	JAILORESSES	JAMDANI	JAPANNING
JABBLE	JACONET	JAILORS	JAMDANIS	JAPANS
JABBLED	JACONETS	JAILS	JAMES	JAPE
JABBLES	JACQUARD	JAK	JAMESES	JAPED
JABBLING	JACQUARDS	JAKE	JAMJAR	JAPES
JABERS	JACTATION	JAKES	JAMJARS	JAPING
JABIRU	JACTATIONS	JAKESES	JAMMED	JAPONICA
JABIRUS	JACULATE	JAKS	JAMMER	JAPONICAS
JABORANDI	JACULATED	JALAP	JAMMERS	JAPPED
JABORANDIS	JACULATES	JALAPIC	JAMMIER	JAPPING
JABOT	JACULATING	JALAPIN	JAMMIEST	JAPS
JABOTS	JACULATOR	JALAPINS	JAMMING	JAR
JABS	JACULATORS	JALAPS	JAMMY	JARARACA
JACAMAR	JACUZZI	JALOPIES	JAMPAN	JARARACAS
JACAMARS	JACUZZIS	JALOPPIES	JAMPANEE	JARARAKA
JACANA	JADE	JALOPPY	JAMPANEES	JARARAKAS
JAÇANA	JADED	JALOPY	JAMPANI	JARFUL
JACANAS	JADEDLY	JALOUSE	JAMPANIS	JARFULS
JAÇANAS	JADEITE	JALOUSED	JAMPANS	JARGON
JACARANDA	JADEITES	JALOUSES	JAMPOT	JARGONED
JACARANDAS	JADERIES	JALOUSIE	JAMPOTS	JARGONEER
JACCHUS	JADERY	JALOUSIED	JAMS	JARGONEERS
JACCHUSES	JADES	JALOUSIES	JANE	JARGONING
JACENT	JADING	JALOUSING	JANES	JARGONISE
JACINTH	JADISH	JAM	JANGLE	JARGONISED
JACINTHS	JAEGER	JAMADAR	JANGLED	JARGONISES
JACK	JAEGERS	JAMADARS	JANGLER	JARGONISING
JACKAL	JAG	JAMB	JANGLERS	JARGONIST
JACKALLED	JAGANNATH	JAMBE	JANGLES	JARGONISTS
JACKALLING	JAGANNATHS	JAMBEAU	JANGLIER	JARGONIZE
JACKALS	JÄGER	JAMBEAUX	JANGLIEST	JARGONIZED
JACKAROO	JÄGERS	JAMBEE	JANGLING	JARGONIZES
JACKAROOED	JAGGED	JAMBEES	JANGLINGS	JARGONIZING
JACKAROOING	JAGGEDLY	JAMBER	JANGLY	JARGONS
JACKAROOS	JAGGER	JAMBERS	JANISSARIES	JARGOON
JACKASS	JAGGERIES	JAMBES	JANISSARY	JARGOONS
JACKASSES	JAGGERS	JAMBEUX	JANITOR	JARK
JACKBOOT	JAGGERY	JAMBIER	JANITORS	JARKMAN
JACKBOOTED	JAGGIER	JAMBIERS	JANITRESS	JARKMEN
JACKBOOTING	JAGGIEST	JAMBIYA	JANITRESSES	JARKS
JACKBOOTS	JAGGING	JAMBIYAH	JANITRIX	JARL
JACKDAW	JAGGY	JAMBIYAHS	JANITRIXES	JARLS
JACKDAWS	JAGHIR	JAMBIYAS	JANIZAR	JAROOL
JACKED	JAGHIRDAR	JAMBO	JANIZARIES	JAROOLS
JACKEROO	JAGHIRDARS	JAMBOK	JANIZARS	JAROSITE
JACKEROOED	JAGHIRE	JAMBOKKED	JANIZARY	JAROSITES
JACKEROOING	JAGHIRES	JAMBOKKING	JANKER	JARRAH
JACKEROOS	JAGHIRS	JAMBOKS	JANKERS	JARRAHS
JACKET	JAGIR	JAMBOLAN	JANN	JARRED
JACKETED	JAGIRS	JAMBOLANA	JANNOCK	JARRING
JACKETING	JAGS	JAMBOLANAS	JANNOCKS	JARRINGLY
JACKETS	JAGUAR	JAMBOLANS	JANNS	JARRINGS
JACKING	JAGUARS	JAMBONE	JANSKIES	JARS
JACKMAN	JAIL	JAMBONES	JANSKY	JARTA
JACKMEN	JAILED	JAMBOOL	JANTEE	JARTAS

JARUL	JAWARIS	JEELY	JEOFAILS	JESTBOOK
JARULS	JAWBATION	JEELYING	JEOPARD	JESTBOOKS
JARVEY	JAWBATIONS	JEEP	JEOPARDED	JESTED
JARVEYS	JAWBONE	JEEPERS	JEOPARDER	JESTEE
JARVIE	JAWBONED	JEEPNEY	JEOPARDERS	JESTEES
JARVIES	JAWBONES	JEEPNEYS	JEOPARDIED	JESTER
JASEY	JAWBONING	JEEPS	JEOPARDIES	JESTERS
JASEYS	JAWBONINGS	JEER	JEOPARDING	JESTFUL
JASIES	JAWBOX	JEERED	JEOPARDS	JESTING
JASMINE	JAWBOXES	JEERER	JEOPARDY	JESTINGLY
JASMINES	JAWED	JEERERS	JEOPARDYING	JESTINGS
JASP	JAWFALL	JEERING	JEQUIRITIES	JESTS
JASPÉ	JAWFALLS	JEERINGLY	JEQUIRITY	JÉSUS
JASPER	JAWHOLE	JEERINGS	JERBIL	JET
JASPERISE	JAWHOLES	JEERS	JERBILS	JETÉ
JASPERISED	JAWING	JEES	JERBOA	JETÉS
JASPERISES	JAWINGS	JEFF	JERBOAS	JETFOIL
JASPERISING	JAWS	JEFFED	JEREED	JETFOILS
JASPERIZE	JAY	JEFFING	JEREEDS	JETLINER
JASPERIZED	JAYS	JEFFS	JEREMIAD	JETLINERS
JASPERIZES	JAYWALK	JEHAD	JEREMIADS	JETON
JASPERIZING	JAYWALKED	JEHADS	JERFALCON	JETONS
JASPEROUS	JAYWALKER	JEJUNA	JERFALCONS	JETPLANE
JASPERS	JAYWALKERS	JEJUNE	JERID	JETPLANES
JASPERY	JAYWALKING	JEJUNELY	JERIDS	JETS
JASPES	JAYWALKINGS	JEJUNITIES	JERK	JETSAM
JASPIDEAN	JAYWALKS	JEJUNITY	JERKED	JETSAMS
JASPIS	JAZERANT	JEJUNUM	JERKER	JETSOM
JASPISES	JAZERANTS	JELAB	JERKERS	JETSOMS
JASPS	JAZIES	JELABS	JERKIER	JETSON
JASY	JAZY	JELL	JERKIES	JETSONS
JATAKA	JAZZ	JELLABA	JERKIEST	JETSTREAM
JATAKAS	JAZZED	JELLABAS	JERKIN	JETSTREAMS
JATO	JAZZES	JELLED	JERKINESS	JETTATURA
JATOS	JAZZIER	JELLIED	JERKINESSES	JETTATURAS
JAUNCE	JAZZIEST	JELLIES	JERKING	JETTED
JAUNCED	JAZZILY	JELLIFIED	JERKINGS	JETTIES
JAUNCES	JAZZINESS	JELLIFIES	JERKINS	JETTINESS
JAUNCING	JAZZINESSES	JELLIFORM	JERKS	JETTINESSES
JAUNDICE	JAZZING	JELLIFY	JERKY	JETTING
JAUNDICED	JAZZMAN	JELLIFYING	JEROBOAM	JETTISON
JAUNDICES	JAZZMEN	JELLING	JEROBOAMS	JETTISONED
JAUNDICING	JAZZY	JELLO	JERQUE	JETTISONING
JAUNSE	JEALOUS	JELLOS	JERQUED	JETTISONS
JAUNSED	JEALOUSE	JELLS	JERQUER	JETTON
JAUNSES	JEALOUSED	JELLY	JERQUERS	JETTONS
JAUNSING	JEALOUSES	JELLYBEAN	JERQUES	JETTY
JAUNT	JEALOUSIES	JELLYBEANS	JERQUING	JEU
JAUNTED	JEALOUSING	JELLYFISH	JERQUINGS	JEUNE
JAUNTEE	JEALOUSLY	JELLYFISHES	JERRICAN	JEUX
JAUNTIE	JEALOUSY	JELLYING	JERRICANS	JEWEL
JAUNTIER	JEAN	JELUTONG	JERRIES	JEWELFISH
JAUNTIES	JEANETTE	JELUTONGS	JERRY	JEWELFISHES
JAUNTIEST	JEANETTES	JEMADAR	JERRYCAN	JEWELLED
JAUNTILY	JEANS	JEMADARS	JERRYCANS	JEWELLER
JAUNTING	JEAT	JEMIDAR	JERSEY	JEWELLERIES
JAUNTS	JEATS	JEMIDARS	JERSEYS	JEWELLERS
JAUNTY	JEBEL	JEMIMA	JESS	JEWELLERY
JAUP	JEBELS	JEMIMAS	JESSAMIES	JEWELLING
JAUPED	JEE	JEMMIES	JESSAMINE	JEWELRIES
JAUPING	JEED	JEMMINESS	JESSAMINES	JEWELRY
JAUPS	JEEING	JEMMINESSES	JESSAMY	JEWELS
JAVEL	JEEL	JEMMY	JESSANT	JEWFISH
JAVELIN	JEELED	JENNET	JESSED	JEWFISHES
JAVELINS	JEELIE	JENNETING	JESSERANT	JEZAIL
JAVELS	JEELIED	JENNETINGS	JESSERANTS	JEZAILS
JAW	JEELIEING	JENNETS	JESSES	JHALA
JAWAN	JEELIES	JENNIES	JESSIE	JHALAS
JAWANS	JEELING	JENNY	JESSIES	JIAO
JAWARI	JEELS	JEOFAIL	JEST	JIAOS

JIB
JIBBAH
JIBBAHS
JIBBED
JIBBER
JIBBERED
JIBBERING
JIBBERS
JIBBING
JIBBINGS
JIBE
JIBED
JIBER
JIBERS
JIBES
JIBING
JIBS
JICKAJOG
JICKAJOGS
JIFF
JIFFIES
JIFFS
JIFFY
JIG
JIGAJIG
JIGAJIGS
JIGAJOG
JIGAJOGS
JIGAMAREE
JIGAMAREES
JIGGED
JIGGER
JIGGERED
JIGGERING
JIGGERS
JIGGING
JIGGINGS
JIGGISH
JIGGLE
JIGGLED
JIGGLES
JIGGLING
JIGGUMBOB
JIGGUMBOBS
JIGJIG
JIGJIGS
JIGOT
JIGOTS
JIGS
JIGSAW
JIGSAWED
JIGSAWING
JIGSAWN
JIGSAWS
JIHAD
JIHADS
JILGIE
JILGIES
JILL
JILLAROO
JILLAROOS
JILLET
JILLETS
JILLFLIRT
JILLFLIRTS
JILLS
JILT
JILTED
JILTING
JILTS

JIMCRACK
JIMCRACKS
JIMINIES
JIMINY
JIMJAM
JIMJAMS
JIMMIES
JIMMY
JIMP
JIMPER
JIMPEST
JIMPIER
JIMPIEST
JIMPLY
JIMPNESS
JIMPNESSES
JIMPY
JINGAL
JINGALS
JINGBANG
JINGBANGS
JINGLE
JINGLED
JINGLER
JINGLERS
JINGLES
JINGLET
JINGLETS
JINGLIER
JINGLIEST
JINGLING
JINGLINGS
JINGLY
JINGO
JINGOES
JINGOISH
JINGOISM
JINGOISMS
JINGOIST
JINGOISTS
JINJILI
JINJILIS
JINK
JINKED
JINKER
JINKERS
JINKING
JINKS
JINN
JINNEE
JINNI
JINNS
JINX
JINXED
JINXES
JIRBLE
JIRBLED
JIRBLES
JIRBLING
JIRD
JIRDS
JIRGA
JIRGAS
JIRKINET
JIRKINETS
JISM
JISMS
JISSOM
JISSOMS
JITNEY

JITNEYS
JITTER
JITTERBUG
JITTERBUGGED
JITTERBUGGING
JITTERBUGS
JITTERED
JITTERING
JITTERS
JITTERY
JIVE
JIVED
JIVER
JIVERS
JIVES
JIVING
JIZ
JIZZ
JIZZES
JO
JOANNA
JOANNAS
JOANNES
JOANNESES
JOB
JOBATION
JOBATIONS
JOBBED
JOBBER
JOBBERIES
JOBBERS
JOBBERY
JOBBING
JOBBINGS
JOBCENTRE
JOBCENTRES
JOBE
JOBED
JOBERNOWL
JOBERNOWLS
JOBES
JOBING
JOBLESS
JOBS
JOBSWORTH
JOBSWORTHS
JOCK
JOCKETTE
JOCKETTES
JOCKEY
JOCKEYED
JOCKEYING
JOCKEYISM
JOCKEYISMS
JOCKEYS
JOCKO
JOCKOS
JOCKS
JOCKSTRAP
JOCKSTRAPS
JOCKTELEG
JOCKTELEGS
JOCO
JOCOROUS
JOCOSE
JOCOSELY
JOCOSITIES
JOCOSITY
JOCULAR
JOCULARLY

JOCULATOR
JOCULATORS
JOCUND
JOCUNDITIES
JOCUNDITY
JOCUNDLY
JODEL
JODELLED
JODELLING
JODELS
JODHPURS
JOE
JOES
JOEY
JOEYS
JOG
JOGGED
JOGGER
JOGGERS
JOGGING
JOGGINGS
JOGGLE
JOGGLED
JOGGLES
JOGGLING
JOGS
JOGTROT
JOGTROTS
JOHANNES
JOHANNESES
JOHN
JOHNNIE
JOHNNIES
JOHNNY
JOHNS
JOIN
JOINDER
JOINDERS
JOINED
JOINER
JOINERIES
JOINERS
JOINERY
JOINING
JOININGS
JOINS
JOINT
JOINTED
JOINTER
JOINTERS
JOINTING
JOINTLESS
JOINTLY
JOINTNESS
JOINTNESSES
JOINTRESS
JOINTRESSES
JOINTS
JOINTURE
JOINTURED
JOINTURES
JOINTURING
JOIST
JOISTED
JOISTING
JOISTS
JOJOBA
JOJOBAS
JOKE
JOKED

JOKER
JOKERS
JOKES
JOKESMITH
JOKESMITHS
JOKESOME
JOKEY
JOKIER
JOKIEST
JOKING
JOKINGLY
JOKOL
JOKY
JOLE
JOLED
JOLES
JOLING
JOLL
JOLLED
JOLLIED
JOLLIER
JOLLIES
JOLLIEST
JOLLIFIED
JOLLIFIES
JOLLIFY
JOLLIFYING
JOLLILY
JOLLIMENT
JOLLIMENTS
JOLLINESS
JOLLINESSES
JOLLING
JOLLITIES
JOLLITY
JOLLS
JOLLY
JOLLYBOAT
JOLLYBOATS
JOLLYHEAD
JOLLYHEADS
JOLLYING
JOLT
JOLTED
JOLTER
JOLTERS
JOLTHEAD
JOLTHEADS
JOLTIER
JOLTIEST
JOLTING
JOLTINGLY
JOLTS
JOLTY
JOMO
JOMOS
JONCANOE
JONCANOES
JONGLEUR
JONGLEURS
JONQUIL
JONQUILS
JONTIES
JONTY
JOOK
JOOKED
JOOKERIES
JOOKERY
JOOKING
JOOKS

JOR	JOURNO	JUDGEMENT	JUKE	JUNGLIER
JORAM	JOURNOS	JUDGEMENTS	JUKED	JUNGLIEST
JORAMS	JOURS	JUDGES	JUKES	JUNGLIS
JORDAN	JOUST	JUDGESHIP	JUKING	JUNGLY
JORDANS	JOUSTED	JUDGESHIPS	JULEP	JUNIOR
JORDELOO	JOUSTER	JUDGING	JULEPS	JUNIORITIES
JORDELOOS	JOUSTERS	JUDGMENT	JULIENNE	JUNIORITY
JORS	JOUSTING	JUDGMENTS	JULIENNES	JUNIORS
JORUM	JOUSTS	JUDICABLE	JUMAR	JUNIPER
JORUMS	JOUYSANCE	JUDICATOR	JUMARED	JUNIPERS
JOSEPH	JOUYSANCES	JUDICATORS	JUMARING	JUNK
JOSEPHS	JOVIAL	JUDICIAL	JUMARS	JUNKANOO
JOSH	JOVIALITIES	JUDICIARIES	JUMART	JUNKANOOS
JOSHED	JOVIALITY	JUDICIARY	JUMARTS	JUNKED
JOSHER	JOVIALLY	JUDICIOUS	JUMBAL	JUNKER
JOSHERS	JOW	JUDIES	JUMBALS	JUNKERDOM
JOSHES	JOWAR	JUDO	JUMBIE	JUNKERDOMS
JOSHING	JOWARI	JUDOGI	JUMBIES	JUNKERISM
JOSKIN	JOWARIS	JUDOGIS	JUMBLE	JUNKERISMS
JOSKINS	JOWARS	JUDOIST	JUMBLED	JUNKERS
JOSS	JOWED	JUDOISTS	JUMBLER	JUNKET
JOSSER	JOWING	JUDOKA	JUMBLERS	JUNKETED
JOSSERS	JOWL	JUDOKAS	JUMBLES	JUNKETING
JOSSES	JOWLED	JUDOS	JUMBLIER	JUNKETINGS
JOSTLE	JOWLER	JUDS	JUMBLIEST	JUNKETS
JOSTLED	JOWLERS	JUDY	JUMBLING	JUNKIE
JOSTLES	JOWLING	JUG	JUMBLY	JUNKIER
JOSTLING	JOWLS	JUGA	JUMBO	JUNKIES
JOSTLINGS	JOWS	JUGAL	JUMBOISE	JUNKIEST
JOT	JOY	JUGALS	JUMBOISED	JUNKING
JOTA	JOYANCE	JUGATE	JUMBOISES	JUNKMAN
JOTAS	JOYANCES	JUGFUL	JUMBOISING	JUNKMEN
JOTS	JOYED	JUGFULS	JUMBOIZE	JUNKS
JOTTED	JOYFUL	JUGGED	JUMBOIZED	JUNKY
JOTTER	JOYFULLER	JUGGING	JUMBOIZES	JUNTA
JOTTERS	JOYFULLEST	JUGGINS	JUMBOIZING	JUNTAS
JOTTING	JOYFULLY	JUGGINSES	JUMBOS	JUNTO
JOTTINGS	JOYING	JUGGLE	JUMBUCK	JUNTOS
JOTUN	JOYLESS	JUGGLED	JUMBUCKS	JUPATI
JÖTUNN	JOYLESSLY	JUGGLER	JUMBY	JUPATIS
JÖTUNNS	JOYOUS	JUGGLERIES	JUMELLE	JUPON
JOTUNS	JOYOUSLY	JUGGLERS	JUMELLES	JUPONS
JOUGS	JOYS	JUGGLERY	JUMP	JURA
JOUISANCE	JUDA	JUGGLES	JUMPED	JURAL
JOUISANCES	JUBAS	JUGGLING	JUMPER	JURALLY
JOUK	JUBATE	JUGGLINGO	JUMPERS	JURANT
JOUKED	JUBBAH	JUGS	JUMPIER	JURANTS
JOUKERIES	JUBBAHS	JUGULAR	JUMPIEST	JURAT
JOUKERY	JUBE	JUGULARS	JUMPILY	JURATORY
JOUKING	JUBES	JUGULATE	JUMPINESS	JURATS
JOUKS	JUBILANCE	JUGULATED	JUMPINESSES	JURE
JOULE	JUBILANCES	JUGULATES	JUMPING	JURIDIC
JOULED	JUBILANCIES	JUGULATING	JUMPS	JURIDICAL
JOULES	JUBILANCY	JUGUM	JUMPY	JURIES
JOULING	JUBILANT	JUICE	JUNCATE	JURIST
JOUNCE	JUBILATE	JUICED	JUNCATES	JURISTIC
JOUNCED	JUBILATED	JUICELESS	JUNCO	JURISTS
JOUNCES	JUBILATES	JUICER	JUNCOES	JUROR
JOUNCING	JUBILATING	JUICERS	JUNCOS	JURORS
JOUR	JUBILEE	JUICES	JUNCTION	JURY
JOURNAL	JUBILEES	JUICIER	JUNCTIONS	JURYMAN
JOURNALLED	JUD	JUICIEST	JUNCTURE	JURYMAST
JOURNALLING	JUDAS	JUICINESS	JUNCTURES	JURYMASTS
JOURNALS	JUDASES	JUICINESSES	JUNCUS	JURYMEN
JOURNEY	JUDDER	JUICING	JUNCUSES	JURYWOMAN
JOURNEYED	JUDDERED	JUICY	JUNEATING	JURYWOMEN
JOURNEYER	JUDDERING	JUJU	JUNEATINGS	JUS
JOURNEYERS	JUDDERS	JUJUBE	JUNGLE	JUSSIVE
JOURNEYING	JUDGE	JUJUBES	JUNGLES	JUSSIVES
JOURNEYS	JUDGED	JUJUS	JUNGLI	JUST

JUSTED
JUSTER
JUSTEST
JUSTICE
JUSTICER
JUSTICERS
JUSTICES
JUSTICIAR
JUSTICIARS
JUSTIFIED

JUSTIFIER
JUSTIFIERS
JUSTIFIES
JUSTIFY
JUSTIFYING
JUSTING
JUSTLE
JUSTLED
JUSTLES
JUSTLING

JUSTLY
JUSTNESS
JUSTNESSES
JUSTS
JUT
JUTE
JUTES
JUTS
JUTTED
JUTTIED

JUTTIES
JUTTING
JUTTINGLY
JUTTY
JUTTYING
JUVENAL
JUVENALS
JUVENILE
JUVENILES
JUVENILIA

JUXTAPOSE
JUXTAPOSED
JUXTAPOSES
JUXTAPOSING
JYMOLD
JYNX
JYNXES

K

KA
KAAMA
KAAMAS
KABAB
KABABS
KABALA
KABALAS
KABAYA
KABAYAS
KABBALA
KABBALAH
KABBALAHS
KABBALAS
KABELE
KABELES
KABELJOU
KABELJOUS
KABELJOUW
KABELJOUWS
KABOB
KABOBS
KABUKI
KABUKIS
KACCHA
KACCHAS
KACHA
KACHAHRI
KACHAHRIS
KACHCHA
KACHERI
KACHERIS
KACHINA
KACHINAS
KADE
KADES
KADI
KADIS
KAE
KAED
KAEING
KAES
KAFFIYEH
KAFFIYEHS
KAFILA
KAFILAS
KAFTAN
KAFTANS
KAGO
KAGOOL
KAGOOLS
KAGOS
KAGOUL
KAGOULE
KAGOULES
KAGOULS
KAHAL
KAHALS
KAI
KAIAK
KAIAKS
KAID
KAIDS
KAIE
KAIES

KAIF
KAIFS
KAIKAI
KAIKAIED
KAIKAIING
KAIKAIS
KAIL
KAILS
KAILYAIRD
KAILYAIRDS
KAILYARD
KAILYARDS
KAIM
KAIMAKAM
KAIMAKAMS
KAIMS
KAIN
KAING
KAINITE
KAINITES
KAINS
KAIS
KAISER
KAISERDOM
KAISERDOMS
KAISERIN
KAISERINS
KAISERISM
KAISERISMS
KAISERS
KAJAWAH
KAJAWAHS
KAKA
KAKAPO
KAKAPOS
KAKAS
KAKEMONO
KAKEMONOS
KAKI
KAKIS
KAKODYL
KAKODYLS
KALAMDAN
KALAMDANS
KALAMKARI
KALAMKARIS
KALE
KALENDAR
KALENDARED
KALENDARING
KALENDARS
KALENDS
KALES
KALI
KALIAN
KALIANS
KALIF
KALIFS
KALINITE
KALINITES
KALIS
KALIUM
KALIUMS
KALLITYPE

KALLITYPES
KALMIA
KALMIAS
KALONG
KALONGS
KALOTYPE
KALOTYPES
KALPA
KALPAK
KALPAKS
KALPAS
KALPIS
KALPISES
KALUMPIT
KALUMPITS
KALYPTRA
KALYPTRAS
KAM
KAMACITE
KAMACITES
KAMALA
KAMALAS
KAME
KAMEES
KAMEESES
KAMELA
KAMELAS
KAMERAD
KAMERADED
KAMERADING
KAMERADS
KAMES
KAMI
KAMICHI
KAMICHIS
KAMIK
KAMIKAZE
KAMIKAZES
KAMIKS
KAMILA
KAMILAS
KAMIS
KAMISES
KAMME
KAMPONG
KAMPONGS
KAMSEEN
KAMSEENS
KAMSIN
KAMSINS
KANA
KANAKA
KANAKAS
KANAS
KANDIES
KANDY
KANEH
KANEHS
KANG
KANGA
KANGAROO
KANGAROOS
KANGAS
KANGHA

KANGHAS
KANGS
KANS
KANSES
KANT
KANTAR
KANTARS
KANTED
KANTELA
KANTELAS
KANTELE
KANTELES
KANTEN
KANTENS
KANTHA
KANTHAS
KANTICOY
KANTICOYED
KANTICOYING
KANTICOYS
KANTIKOY
KANTIKOYED
KANTIKOYING
KANTIKOYS
KANTING
KANTS
KANZU
KANZUS
KAOLIANG
KAOLIANGS
KAOLIN
KAOLINE
KAOLINES
KAOLINISE
KAOLINISED
KAOLINISES
KAOLINISING
KAOLINITE
KAOLINITES
KAOLINIZE
KAOLINIZED
KAOLINIZES
KAOLINIZING
KAOLINS
KAON
KAONS
KAPOK
KAPOKS
KAPPA
KAPPAS
KAPUT
KAPUTT
KARA
KARABINER
KARABINERS
KARAIT
KARAITS
KARAKA
KARAKAS
KARAKUL
KARAKULS
KARAS
KARAT
KARATE

KARATEIST
KARATEISTS
KARATEKA
KARATEKAS
KARATES
KARATS
KARITE
KARITES
KARMA
KARMAS
KARMIC
KAROSS
KAROSSES
KARRI
KARRIS
KARSEY
KARSEYS
KARSIES
KARST
KARSTS
KARSY
KART
KARTING
KARTINGS
KARTS
KARYOLOGIES
KARYOLOGY
KARYOSOME
KARYOSOMES
KARZIES
KARZY
KAS
KASBA
KASBAH
KASBAHS
KASBAS
KAT
KATABASES
KATABASIS
KATABATIC
KATABOLIC
KATAKANA
KATAKANAS
KATHAK
KATHAKALI
KATHAKALIS
KATHAKS
KATHARSES
KATHARSIS
KATHODE
KATHODES
KATI
KATION
KATIONS
KATIS
KATORGA
KATORGAS
KATS
KATTI
KATTIS
KATYDID
KATYDIDS
KAUGH
KAUGHS

KAURI
KAURIS
KAVA
KAVAS
KAVASS
KAVASSES
KAW
KAWED
KAWING
KAWS
KAY
KAYAK
KAYAKS
KAYLE
KAYLES
KAYO
KAYOE
KAYOED
KAYOEING
KAYOES
KAYOING
KAYOS
KAYS
KAZATZKA
KAZATZKAS
KAZI
KAZIS
KAZOO
KAZOOS
KEA
KEAS
KEASAR
KEASARS
KEB
KEBAB
KEBABS
KEBBED
KEBBIE
KEBBIES
KEBBING
KEBBOCK
KEBBOCKS
KEBBUCK
KEBBUCKS
KEBELE
KEBELES
KEBLAH
KEBLAHS
KEBOB
KEBOBS
KEBS
KECK
KECKED
KECKING
KECKLE
KECKLED
KECKLES
KECKLING
KECKLINGS
KECKS
KECKSES
KECKSIES
KECKSY
KED
KEDDAH
KEDDAHS
KEDGE
KEDGED
KEDGER
KEDGEREE

KEDGEREES
KEDGERS
KEDGES
KEDGING
KEDGY
KEDS
KEECH
KEECHES
KEEK
KEEKED
KEEKER
KEEKERS
KEEKING
KEEKS
KEEL
KEELAGE
KEELAGES
KEELBOAT
KEELBOATS
KEELED
KEELER
KEELERS
KEELHAUL
KEELHAULED
KEELHAULING
KEELHAULINGS
KEELHAULS
KEELIE
KEELIES
KEELING
KEELINGS
KEELIVINE
KEELIVINES
KEELMAN
KEELMEN
KEELS
KEELSON
KEELSONS
KEELYVINE
KEELYVINES
KEEN
KEENED
KEENER
KEENERS
KEENEST
KEENING
KEENINGS
KEENLY
KEENNESS
KEENNESSES
KEENS
KEEP
KEEPER
KEEPERS
KEEPING
KEEPINGS
KEEPNET
KEEPNETS
KEEPS
KEEPSAKE
KEEPSAKES
KEEPSAKY
KEESHOND
KEESHONDS
KEEVE
KEEVES
KEF
KEFFEL
KEFFELS
KEFFIYEH

KEFFIYEHS
KEFIR
KEFIRS
KEFS
KEFUFFLE
KEFUFFLED
KEFUFFLES
KEFUFFLING
KEG
KEGS
KEIGHT
KEIR
KEIRS
KEITLOA
KEITLOAS
KEKSYE
KEKSYES
KELIM
KELIMS
KELL
KELLAUT
KELLAUTS
KELLIES
KELLS
KELLY
KELOID
KELOIDAL
KELOIDS
KELP
KELPER
KELPERS
KELPIE
KELPIES
KELPS
KELPY
KELSON
KELSONS
KELT
KELTER
KELTERS
KELTIE
KELTIES
KELTS
KELTY
KELVIN
KELVINS
KEMB
KEMBED
KEMBING
KEMBO
KEMBOED
KEMBOING
KEMBOS
KEMBS
KEMP
KEMPED
KEMPER
KEMPERS
KEMPING
KEMPINGS
KEMPLE
KEMPLES
KEMPS
KEMPT
KEN
KENAF
KENAFS
KENDO
KENDOS
KENNED

KENNEL
KENNELLED
KENNELLING
KENNELS
KENNER
KENNERS
KENNET
KENNETS
KENNING
KENNINGS
KENOSES
KENOSIS
KENOTIC
KENS
KENSPECK
KENT
KENTED
KENTING
KENTLEDGE
KENTLEDGES
KENTS
KEP
KEPHALIC
KEPHALICS
KEPHIR
KEPHIRS
KEPI
KEPIS
KEPPING
KEPPIT
KEPS
KEPT
KERAMIC
KERATIN
KERATINS
KERATITIS
KERATITISES
KERATOID
KERATOSE
KERATOSES
KERATOSIS
KERB
KERBS
KERBSIDE
KERBSIDES
KERBSTONE
KERBSTONES
KERCHIEF
KERCHIEFED
KERCHIEFING
KERCHIEFS
KERF
KERFS
KERFUFFLE
KERFUFFLED
KERFUFFLES
KERFUFFLING
KERMES
KERMESES
KERMESITE
KERMESITES
KERMESS
KERMESSE
KERMESSES
KERMIS
KERMISES
KERN
KERNE
KERNED
KERNEL

KERNELLED
KERNELLING
KERNELLY
KERNELS
KERNES
KERNING
KERNISH
KERNITE
KERNITES
KERNS
KEROGEN
KEROGENS
KEROSENE
KEROSENES
KEROSINE
KEROSINES
KERRIA
KERRIAS
KERSEY
KERSEYS
KERVE
KERVED
KERVES
KERVING
KERYGMA
KERYGMAS
KESAR
KESARS
KESH
KESHES
KEST
KESTING
KESTREL
KESTRELS
KESTS
KET
KETA
KETAS
KETCH
KETCHES
KETCHING
KETCHUP
KETCHUPS
KETONE
KETONES
KETOSE
KETOSES
KETOSIS
KETS
KETTLE
KETTLEFUL
KETTLEFULS
KETTLES
KEVEL
KEVELS
KEX
KEXES
KEY
KEYBOARD
KEYBOARDED
KEYBOARDING
KEYBOARDS
KEYBUGLE
KEYBUGLES
KEYED
KEYHOLE
KEYHOLES
KEYING
KEYLESS
KEYNOTE

KEYNOTED	KHOJA	KIDDYWINK	KILLOGIE	KINDLED
KEYNOTES	KHOJAS	KIDDYWINKS	KILLOGIES	KINDLER
KEYNOTING	KHOR	KIDEL	KILLS	KINDLERS
KEYS	KHORS	KIDELS	KILLUT	KINDLES
KEYSTONE	KHOTBAH	KIDGE	KILLUTS	KINDLESS
KEYSTONED	KHOTBAHS	KIDLING	KILN	KINDLIER
KEYSTONES	KHOTBEH	KIDLINGS	KILNED	KINDLIEST
KEYSTONING	KHOTBEHS	KIDNAP	KILNING	KINDLILY
KEYSTROKE	KHUD	KIDNAPPED	KILNS	KINDLING
KEYSTROKES	KHUDS	KIDNAPPER	KILO	KINDLINGS
KGOTLA	KHURTA	KIDNAPPERS	KILOBAR	KINDLY
KGOTLAS	KHURTAS	KIDNAPPING	KILOBARS	KINDNESS
KHADDAR	KHUSKHUS	KIDNAPPINGS	KILOBIT	KINDNESSES
KHADDARS	KHUSKHUSES	KIDNAPS	KILOBITS	KINDRED
KHADI	KHUTBAH	KIDNEY	KILOBYTE	KINDREDS
KHADIS	KHUTBAHS	KIDNEYS	KILOBYTES	KINDS
KHAKI	KIANG	KIDOLOGIES	KILOGRAM	KINE
KHAKIS	KIANGS	KIDOLOGY	KILOGRAMS	KINEMA
KHALAT	KIAUGH	KIDS	KILOHERTZ	KINEMAS
KHALATS	KIAUGHS	KIER	KILOHERTZES	KINEMATIC
KHALIF	KIBBLE	KIERIE	KILOJOULE	KINEMATICS
KHALIFA	KIBBLED	KIERIES	KILOJOULES	KINESES
KHALIFAH	KIBBLES	KIERS	KILOMETRE	KINESICS
KHALIFAHS	KIBBLING	KIESERITE	KILOMETRES	KINESIS
KHALIFAS	KIBBUTZ	KIESERITES	KILOS	KINETIC
KHALIFAT	KIBBUTZIM	KIEVE	KILOTON	KINETICAL
KHALIFATE	KIBE	KIEVES	KILOTONNE	KINETICS
KHALIFATES	KIBES	KIF	KILOTONNES	KINFOLK
KHALIFATS	KIBITKA	KIFS	KILOTONS	KINFOLKS
KHALIFS	KIBITKAS	KIGHT	KILOVOLT	KING
KHAMSIN	KIBITZ	KIGHTS	KILOVOLTS	KINGCRAFT
KHAMSINS	KIBITZED	KIKE	KILOWATT	KINGCRAFTS
KHAN	KIBITZER	KIKES	KILOWATTS	KINGCUP
KHANATE	KIBITZERS	KIKUMON	KILP	KINGCUPS
KHANATES	KIBITZES	KIKUMONS	KILPS	KINGDOM
KHANGA	KIBITZING	KIKUYU	KILT	KINGDOMED
KHANGAS	KIBLAH	KIKUYUS	KILTED	KINGDOMS
KHANJAR	KIBLAHS	KILD	KILTER	KINGED
KHANJARS	KIBOSH	KILDERKIN	KILTERS	KINGFISH
KHANS	KIBOSHED	KILDERKINS	KILTIE	KINGFISHES
KHANSAMA	KIBOSHES	KILERG	KILTIES	KINGHOOD
KHANSAMAH	KIBOSHING	KILERGS	KILTING	KINGHOODS
KHANSAMAHS	KICK	KILEY	KILTS	KINGING
KHANSAMAS	KICKABLE	KILEYS	KILTY	KINGLE
KHANUM	KICKBACK	KILIM	KIMBO	KINGLES
KHANUMS	KICKBACKS	KILIMS	KIMBOED	KINGLESS
KHARIF	KICKDOWN	KILL	KIMBOING	KINGLET
KHARIFS	KICKDOWNS	KILLADAR	KIMBOS	KINGLETS
KHAT	KICKED	KILLADARS	KIMMER	KINGLIER
KHATS	KICKER	KILLAS	KIMMERS	KINGLIEST
KHAYA	KICKERS	KILLASES	KIMONO	KINGLING
KHAYAS	KICKING	KILLCOW	KIMONOS	KINGLINGS
KHEDA	KICKS	KILLCOWS	KIN	KINGLY
KHEDAS	KICKSHAW	KILLCROP	KINA	KINGMAKER
KHEDIVA	KICKSHAWS	KILLCROPS	KINAKINA	KINGMAKERS
KHEDIVAL	KID	KILLDEE	KINAKINAS	KINGPOST
KHEDIVAS	KIDDED	KILLDEER	KINAS	KINGPOSTS
KHEDIVATE	KIDDER	KILLDEERS	KINASE	KINGS
• KHEDIVATES	KIDDERS	KILLDEES	KINASES	KINGSHIP
KHEDIVE	KIDDIED	KILLED	KINCHIN	KINGSHIPS
KHEDIVES	KIDDIER	KILLER	KINCHINS	KINGWOOD
KHEDIVIAL	KIDDIERS	KILLERS	KINCOB	KINGWOODS
KHILAFAT	KIDDIES	KILLICK	KINCOBS	KININ
KHILAFATS	KIDDING	KILLICKS	KIND	KININS
KHILAT	KIDDLE	KILLING	KINDA	KINK
KHILATS	KIDDLES	KILLINGS	KINDED	KINKAJOU
KHILIM	KIDDUSH	KILLJOY	KINDER	KINKAJOUS
KHILIMS	KIDDUSHES	KILLJOYS	KINDEST	KINKED
KHODJA	KIDDY	KILLOCK	KINDING	KINKIER
KHODJAS	KIDDYING	KILLOCKS	KINDLE	KINKIEST

KINKING
KINKLE
KINKLES
KINKS
KINKY
KINLESS
KINO
KINONE
KINONES
KINOS
KINRED
KINREDS
KINS
KINSFOLK
KINSFOLKS
KINSHIP
KINSHIPS
KINSMAN
KINSMEN
KINSWOMAN
KINSWOMEN
KINTLEDGE
KINTLEDGES
KIOSK
KIOSKS
KIP
KIPE
KIPES
KIPP
KIPPAGE
KIPPAGES
KIPPED
KIPPER
KIPPERED
KIPPERER
KIPPERERS
KIPPERING
KIPPERS
KIPPING
KIPPS
KIPS
KIR
KIRBEH
KIRBEHS
KIRBIGRIP
KIRBIGRIPS
KIRI
KIRIMON
KIRIMONS
KIRIS
KIRK
KIRKED
KIRKING
KIRKINGS
KIRKS
KIRKTON
KIRKTONS
KIRKTOWN
KIRKTOWNS
KIRKWARD
KIRKYAIRD
KIRKYAIRDS
KIRKYARD
KIRKYARDS
KIRMESS
KIRMESSES
KIRN
KIRNS
KIRPAN
KIRPANS

KIRS
KIRSCH
KIRSCHES
KIRTLE
KIRTLED
KIRTLES
KISAN
KISANS
KISH
KISHES
KISMET
KISMETS
KISS
KISSABLE
KISSED
KISSER
KISSERS
KISSES
KISSING
KIST
KISTED
KISTING
KISTS
KISTVAEN
KISTVAENS
KIT
KITCHEN
KITCHENED
KITCHENER
KITCHENERS
KITCHENING
KITCHENS
KITE
KITED
KITES
KITH
KITHARA
KITHARAS
KITHE
KITHED
KITHES
KITHING
KITHS
KITING
KITLING
KITLINGS
KITS
KITSCH
KITSCHES
KITSCHIER
KITSCHIEST
KITSCHLY
KITSCHY
KITTED
KITTEN
KITTENED
KITTENING
KITTENISH
KITTENS
KITTENY
KITTIES
KITTING
KITTIWAKE
KITTIWAKES
KITTLE
KITTLED
KITTLER
KITTLES
KITTLEST
KITTLIER

KITTLIEST
KITTLING
KITTLY
KITTUL
KITTULS
KITTY
KIWI
KIWIS
KLANG
KLANGS
KLAVIER
KLAVIERS
KLAXON
KLAXONS
KLENDUSIC
KLEPHT
KLEPHTIC
KLEPHTISM
KLEPHTISMS
KLEPHTS
KLINKER
KLINKERS
KLINOSTAT
KLINOSTATS
KLIPDAS
KLIPDASES
KLONDIKE
KLONDIKED
KLONDIKES
KLONDIKING
KLONDYKE
KLONDYKED
KLONDYKER
KLONDYKERS
KLONDYKES
KLONDYKING
KLOOF
KLOOFS
KLUDGE
KLUDGES
KLUTZ
KLUTZES
KLYSTRON
KLYSTRONS
KNACK
KNACKER
KNACKERED
KNACKERIES
KNACKERING
KNACKERS
KNACKERY
KNACKIER
KNACKIEST
KNACKISH
KNACKS
KNACKY
KNAG
KNAGGIER
KNAGGIEST
KNAGGY
KNAGS
KNAP
KNAPPED
KNAPPER
KNAPPERS
KNAPPING
KNAPPLE
KNAPPLED
KNAPPLES
KNAPPLING

KNAPS
KNAPSACK
KNAPSACKS
KNAPSCAL
KNAPSCALS
KNAPSCULL
KNAPSCULLS
KNAPSKULL
KNAPSKULLS
KNAPWEED
KNAPWEEDS
KNAR
KNARL
KNARLS
KNARRED
KNARRING
KNARS
KNAVE
KNAVERIES
KNAVERY
KNAVES
KNAVESHIP
KNAVESHIPS
KNAVISH
KNAVISHLY
KNAWEL
KNAWELS
KNEAD
KNEADED
KNEADER
KNEADERS
KNEADING
KNEADS
KNEE
KNEED
KNEEHOLE
KNEEHOLES
KNEEING
KNEEL
KNEELED
KNEELER
KNEELERS
KNEELING
KNEELS
KNEES
KNELL
KNELLED
KNELLING
KNELLS
KNELT
KNEVELL
KNEVELLED
KNEVELLING
KNEVELLS
KNEW
KNICKER
KNICKERED
KNICKERS
KNICKS
KNIFE
KNIFED
KNIFELESS
KNIFES
KNIFING
KNIFINGS
KNIGHT
KNIGHTAGE
KNIGHTAGES
KNIGHTED
KNIGHTING

KNIGHTLIER
KNIGHTLIEST
KNIGHTLY
KNIGHTS
KNISH
KNISHES
KNIT
KNITCH
KNITCHES
KNITS
KNITTED
KNITTER
KNITTERS
KNITTING
KNITTINGS
KNITTLE
KNITTLES
KNITWEAR
KNITWEARS
KNIVE
KNIVED
KNIVES
KNIVING
KNOB
KNOBBED
KNOBBER
KNOBBERS
KNOBBIER
KNOBBIEST
KNOBBLE
KNOBBLED
KNOBBLES
KNOBBLIER
KNOBBLIEST
KNOBBLING
KNOBBLY
KNOBBY
KNOBS
KNOCK
KNOCKED
KNOCKER
KNOCKERS
KNOCKING
KNOCKINGS
KNOCKOUT
KNOCKOUTS
KNOCKS
KNOLL
KNOLLED
KNOLLING
KNOLLS
KNOP
KNOPS
KNOSP
KNOSPS
KNOT
KNOTGRASS
KNOTGRASSES
KNOTLESS
KNOTS
KNOTTED
KNOTTER
KNOTTERS
KNOTTIER
KNOTTIEST
KNOTTING
KNOTTINGS
KNOTTY
KNOTWEED
KNOTWEEDS

KNOTWORK
KNOTWORKS
KNOUT
KNOUTED
KNOUTING
KNOUTS
KNOW
KNOWABLE
KNOWE
KNOWER
KNOWERS
KNOWES
KNOWING
KNOWINGLY
KNOWLEDGE
KNOWLEDGED
KNOWLEDGES
KNOWLEDGING
KNOWN
KNOWS
KNUB
KNUBBIER
KNUBBIEST
KNUBBLE
KNUBBLED
KNUBBLES
KNUBBLIER
KNUBBLIEST
KNUDDLING
KNUBBLY
KNUBBY
KNUBS
KNUCKLE
KNUCKLED
KNUCKLES
KNUCKLING
KNUR
KNURL
KNURLED
KNURLIER
KNURLIEST
KNURLING
KNURLINGS
KNURLS
KNURLY
KNURR
KNURRS
KNURS
KNUT
KNUTS
KO
KOA
KOALA
KOALAS
KOAN
KOANS
KOAS
KOB
KOBAN
KOBANG
KOBANGS
KOBANS
KOBOLD
KOBOLDS
KOBS
KOFF
KOFFS
KOFTA
KOFTAS
KOFTGAR
KOFTGARI

KOFTGARIS
KOFTGARS
KOFTWORK
KOFTWORKS
KOHL
KOHLRABI
KOHLRABIS
KOHLS
KOINE
KOINES
KOKRA
KOKRAS
KOKUM
KOKUMS
KOLA
KOLAS
KOLINSKIES
KOLINSKY
KOLKHOZ
KOLKHOZES
KOLO
KOLOS
KOMISSAR
KOMISSARS
KOMITAJI
KOMITAJIS
KON
KOND
KONFYT
KONFYTS
KONIMETER
KONIMETERS
KONIOLOGIES
KONIOLOGY
KONISCOPE
KONISCOPES
KONK
KONKED
KONKING
KONKS
KONNING
KONS
KOODOO
KOODOOS
KOOK
KOOKED
KOOKIE
KOOKIER
KOOKIEST
KOOKING
KOOKS
KOOKY
KOOLAH
KOOLAHS
KOP
KOPECK
KOPECKS
KOPJE
KOPJES
KOPPA
KOPPAS
KOPPIE
KOPPIES
KOPS
KORA
KORAS
KORFBALL
KORFBALLS
KORKIR
KORKIRS

KORMA
KORMAS
KORORA
KOROORAS
KORUNA
KORUNAS
KOS
KOSES
KOSHER
KOSHERS
KOSMOS
KOSMOSES
KOSS
KOSSES
KOTO
KOTOS
KOTOW
KOTOWED
KOTOWING
KOTOWS
KOTTABOS
KOTTABOSES
KOTWAL
KOTWALS
KOULAN
KOULANS
KOUMISS
KOUMISSES
KOURBASH
KOURBASHED
KOURBASHES
KOURBASHING
KOUSKOUS
KOUSKOUSES
KOW
KOWHAI
KOWHAIS
KOWS
KOWTOW
KOWTOWED
KOWTOWING
KOWTOWS
KRAAL
KRAALED
KRAALING
KRAALS
KRAB
KRAFTS
KRAIT
KRAITS
KRAKEN
KRAKENS
KRAKOWIAK
KRAKOWIAKS
KRAMERIA
KRAMERIAS
KRANG
KRANGS
KRANS
KRANSES
KRANTZ
KRANTZES
KRANZ
KRANZES
KRAUT
KRAUTS
KREASOTE
KREASOTED
KREASOTES
KREASOTING

KREATINE
KREATINES
KREESE
KREESED
KREESES
KREESING
KREMLIN
KREMLINS
KRENG
KRENGS
KREOSOTE
KREOSOTED
KREOSOTES
KREOSOTING
KREPLACH
KREUTZER
KREUTZERS
KRILL
KRILLS
KRIMMER
KRIMMERS
KRIS
KRISED
KRISES
KRISING
KROMESKIES
KROMESKY
KRONA
KRONE
KRONEN
KRONER
KRONOR
KRONUR
KRUMHORN
KRUMHORNS
KRUMMHORN
KRUMMHORNS
KRYOMETER
KRYOMETERS
KRYPSES
KRYPSIS
KRYPTON
KRYPTONS
KSAR
KSARS
KUCHCHA
KUDOS
KUDOSES
KUDU
KUDUS
KUDZU
KUDZUS
KUFFIAH
KUFFIAHS
KUFFIEH
KUFFIEHS
KUFFIYEH
KUFFIYEHS
KUFIAH
KUFIAHS
KUFIYA
KUFIYAH
KUFIYAHS
KUFIYAS
KUKRI
KUKRIS
KUKU
KUKUS
KULAK
KULAKS

KULAN
KULANS
KUMARA
KUMARAS
KUMARI
KUMARIS
KUMISS
KUMISSES
KÜMMEL
KÜMMELS
KUMQUAT
KUMQUATS
KUNKAR
KUNKARS
KUNKUR
KUNKURS
KURBASH
KURBASHED
KURBASHES
KURBASHING
KURGAN
KURGANS
KURRAJONG
KURRAJONGS
KURRE
KURRES
KURSAAL
KURSAALS
KURTA
KURTAS
KURTOSES
KURTOSIS
KURVEY
KURVEYED
KURVEYING
KURVEYOR
KURVEYORS
KURVEYS
KUTCH
KUTCHA
KUTCHES
KVASS
KVASSES
KVETCH
KVETCHED
KVETCHER
KVETCHERS
KVETCHES
KVETCHING
KWACHA
KWACHAS
KWELA
KWELAS
KY
KYANG
KYANGS
KYANISE
KYANISED
KYANISES
KYANISING
KYANITE
KYANITES
KYANIZE
KYANIZED
KYANIZES
KYANIZING
KYAT
KYATS
KYBOSH
KYBOSHED

KYBOSHES	KYLICES	KYLOE	KYNDED	KYRIELLE
KYBOSHING	KYLIE	KYLOES	KYNDES	KYRIELLES
KYDST	KYLIES	KYMOGRAM	KYNDING	KYTE
KYE	KYLIN	KYMOGRAMS	KYNDS	KYTES
KYLE	KYLINS	KYMOGRAPH	KYNE	KYTHE
KYLES	KYLIX	KYMOGRAPHS	KYPHOSES	KYTHED
KYLEY	KYLLOSES	KYND	KYPHOSIS	KYTHES
KYLEYS	KYLLOSIS	KYNDE	KYPHOTIC	KYTHING

L

LA
LAAGER
LAAGERED
LAAGERING
LAAGERS
LAB
LABARA
LABARUM
LABARUMS
LABDA
LABDACISM
LABDACISMS
LABDANUM
LABDANUMS
LABDAS
LABEL
LABELLA
LABELLED
LABELLING
LABELLOID
LABELLUM
LABELS
LABIA
LABIAL
LABIALISE
LABIALISED
LABIALISES
LABIALISING
LABIALISM
LABIALISMS
LABIALIZE
LABIALIZED
LABIALIZES
LABIALIZING
LABIALLY
LABIALS
LABIATE
LABIATES
LABILE
LABILITIES
LABILITY
LABIS
LABISES
LABIUM
LABLAB
LABLABS
LABOR
LABORED
LABORING
LABORIOUS
LABORS
LABOUR
LABOURED
LABOURER
LABOURERS
LABOURING
LABOURISM
LABOURISMS
LABOURIST
LABOURISTS
LABOURS
LABRA
LABRET
LABRETS

LABRID
LABRIDS
LABROID
LABROIDS
LABROSE
LABRUM
LABRYS
LABRYSES
LABS
LABURNUM
LABURNUMS
LABYRINTH
LABYRINTHS
LAC
LACCOLITE
LACCOLITES
LACCOLITH
LACCOLITHS
LACE
LACEBARK
LACEBARKS
LACED
LACERABLE
LACERANT
LACERATE
LACERATED
LACERATES
LACERATING
LACERTIAN
LACERTINE
LACES
LACET
LACETS
LACEY
LACHES
LACHESES
LACHRYMAL
LACHRYMALS
LACIER
LACIEST
LACING
LACINGS
LACINIA
LACINIAE
LACINIATE
LACINIATED
LACK
LACKADAY
LACKED
LACKER
LACKERED
LACKERING
LACKERS
LACKEY
LACKEYED
LACKEYING
LACKEYS
LACKING
LACKLAND
LACKLANDS
LACKS
LACMUS
LACMUSES
LACONIC

LACONICAL
LACONISM
LACONISMS
LACQUER
LACQUERED
LACQUERER
LACQUERERS
LACQUERING
LACQUERS
LACQUEY
LACQUEYED
LACQUEYING
LACQUEYS
LACRIMAL
LACRIMALS
LACROSSE
LACROSSES
LACRYMAL
LACRYMALS
LACS
LACTASE
LACTASES
LACTASESD
LACTATE
LACTATED
LACTATES
LACTATING
LACTATION
LACTATIONS
LACTEAL
LACTEALS
LACTEOUS
LACTIC
LACTIFIC
LACTOSE
LACTOSES
LACUNA
LACUNAE
LACUNAL
LACUNAR
LACUNARIA
LACUNARS
LACUNARY
LACUNATE
LACUNOSE
LACY
LAD
LADANUM
LADANUMS
LADDER
LADDERED
LADDERING
LADDERS
LADDERY
LADDIE
LADDIES
LADE
LADED
LADEN
LADES
LADIES
LADIFIED
LADIFIES
LADIFY

LADIFYING
LADING
LADINGS
LADLE
LADLED
LADLEFUL
LADLEFULS
LADLES
LADLING
LADRONE
LADRONES
LADS
LADY
LADYBIRD
LADYBIRDS
LADYBUG
LADYBUGS
LADYCOW
LADYCOWS
LADYFIED
LADYFIES
LADYFLIES
LADYFLY
LADYFY
LADYFYING
LADYHOOD
LADYHOODS
LADYISH
LADYISM
LADYISMS
LADYKIN
LADYKINS
LADYLIKE
LADYSHIP
LADYSHIPS
LAER
LAESIE
LAETARE
LAETARES
LAEVIGATE
LAEVIGATED
LAEVIGATES
LAEVIGATING
LAEVULOSE
LAEVULOSES
LAG
LAGAN
LAGANS
LAGENA
LAGENAS
LAGER
LAGERS
LAGGARD
LAGGARDS
LAGGED
LAGGEN
LAGGENS
LAGGER
LAGGERS
LAGGIN
LAGGING
LAGGINGLY
LAGGINGS
LAGGINS

LAGNIAPPE
LAGNIAPPES
LAGOMORPH
LAGOMORPHS
LAGOON
LAGOONAL
LAGOONS
LAGRIMOSO
LAGS
LAGUNE
LAGUNES
LAH
LAHAR
LAHARS
LAHS
LAIC
LAICAL
LAICISE
LAICISED
LAICISES
LAICISING
LAICITIES
LAICITY
LAICIZE
LAICIZED
LAICIZES
LAICIZING
LAICS
LAID
LAIDED
LAIDEN
LAIDING
LAIDLY
LAIDS
LAIGH
LAIGHER
LAIGHEST
LAIGHS
LAIK
LAIKA
LAIKAS
LAIKED
LAIKING
LAIKS
LAIN
LAIR
LAIRAGE
LAIRAGES
LAIRD
LAIRDS
LAIRDSHIP
LAIRDSHIPS
LAIRED
LAIRIER
LAIRIEST
LAIRING
LAIRISE
LAIRISED
LAIRISES
LAIRISING
LAIRIZE
LAIRIZED
LAIRIZES
LAIRIZING

LAIRS
LAIRY
LAISSE
LAISSES
LAITANCE
LAITANCES
LAITH
LAITIES
LAITY
LAKE
LAKED
LAKELET
LAKELETS
LAKER
LAKERS
LAKES
LAKH
LAKHS
LAKIER
LAKIEST
LAKIN
LAKING
LAKINS
LAKISH
LAKY
LALANG
LALANGS
LALDIE
LALDIES
LALDY
LALLAN
LALLANS
LALLATION
LALLATIONS
LALLING
LALLINGS
LALLYGAG
LALLYGAGGED
LALLYGAGGING
LALLYGAGS
LAM
LAMA
LAMAISTIC
LAMANTIN
LAMANTINS
LAMAS
LAMASERAI
LAMASERAIS
LAMASERIES
LAMASERY
LAMB
LAMBAST
LAMBASTE
LAMBASTED
LAMBASTES
LAMBASTING
LAMBASTS
LAMBDA
LAMBDAS
LAMBDOID
LAMBED
LAMBENCIES
LAMBENCY
LAMBENT
LAMBENTLY
LAMBER
LAMBERS
LAMBERT
LAMBERTS
LAMBIE

LAMBIES
LAMBING
LAMBITIVE
LAMBITIVES
LAMBKIN
LAMBKINS
LAMBLING
LAMBLINGS
LAMBOYS
LAMBS
LAMBSKIN
LAMBSKINS
LAME
LAMED
LAMELLA
LAMELLAE
LAMELLAR
LAMELLATE
LAMELLATED
LAMELLOID
LAMELLOSE
LAMELY
LAMENESS
LAMENESSES
LAMENT
LAMENTED
LAMENTING
LAMENTINGS
LAMENTS
LAMER
LAMES
LAMEST
LAMETER
LAMETERS
LAMIA
LAMIAE
LAMIAS
LAMIGER
LAMIGERS
LAMINA
LAMINABLE
LAMINAE
LAMINAR
LAMINARY
LAMINATE
LAMINATED
LAMINATES
LAMINATING
LAMINATOR
LAMINATORS
LAMING
LAMINGTON
LAMINGTONS
LAMINITIS
LAMINITISES
LAMISH
LAMITER
LAMITERS
LAMMED
LAMMER
LAMMERS
LAMMIE
LAMMIES
LAMMIGER
LAMMIGERS
LAMMING
LAMMINGS
LAMMY
LAMP
LAMPAD

LAMPADARIES
LAMPADARY
LAMPADIST
LAMPADISTS
LAMPADS
LAMPAS
LAMPASES
LAMPASSE
LAMPASSES
LAMPED
LAMPERN
LAMPERNS
LAMPHOLE
LAMPHOLES
LAMPING
LAMPION
LAMPIONS
LAMPLIGHT
LAMPLIGHTS
LAMPOON
LAMPOONED
LAMPOONER
LAMPOONERS
LAMPOONING
LAMPOONS
LAMPPOST
LAMPPOSTS
LAMPREY
LAMPREYS
LAMPS
LAMPSHADE
LAMPSHADES
LAMPUKA
LAMPUKAS
LAMPUKI
LAMPUKIS
LAMS
LANA
LANAS
LANATE
LANCE
LANCED
LANCEGAY
LANCEGAYS
LANCELET
LANCELETS
LANCEOLAR
LANCER
LANCERS
LANCES
LANCET
LANCETED
LANCETS
LANCH
LANCHED
LANCHES
LANCHING
LANCIFORM
LANCINATE
LANCINATED
LANCINATES
LANCINATING
LANCING
LAND
LANDAMMAN
LANDAMMANS
LANDAU
LANDAULET
LANDAULETS
LANDAULETTE

LANDAULETTES
LANDAUS
LANDDAMNE
LANDDAMNED
LANDDAMNES
LANDDAMNING
LANDDROS
LANDDROSES
LANDDROST
LANDDROSTS
LANDE
LANDED
LANDER
LANDERS
LANDES
LANDFALL
LANDFALLS
LANDFILL
LANDFILLS
LANDFORCE
LANDFORCES
LANDFORM
LANDFORMS
LANDGRAVE
LANDGRAVES
LANDING
LANDINGS
LANDLADIES
LANDLADY
LÄNDLER
LÄNDLERS
LANDLESS
LANDLOPER
LANDLOPERS
LANDLORD
LANDLORDS
LANDMAN
LANDMARK
LANDMARKS
LANDMASS
LANDMASSES
LANDMEN
LANDOWNER
LANDOWNERS
LANDRACE
LANDRACES
LANDRAIL
LANDRAILS
LANDS
LANDSCAPE
LANDSCAPED
LANDSCAPES
LANDSCAPING
LANDSKIP
LANDSKIPS
LANDSLIDE
LANDSLIDES
LANDSLIP
LANDSLIPS
LANDSMAN
LANDSMEN
LANDWARD
LANDWARDS
LANDWIND
LANDWINDS
LANE
LANES
LANEWAY
LANEWAYS
LANG

LANGAHA
LANGAHAS
LANGER
LANGEST
LANGLAUF
LANGLAUFS
LANGOUSTE
LANGOUSTES
LANGRAGE
LANGRAGES
LANGREL
LANGRELS
LANGRIDGE
LANGRIDGES
LANGSPEL
LANGSPELS
LANGSPIEL
LANGSPIELS
LANGUAGE
LANGUAGED
LANGUAGES
LANGUAGING
LANGUE
LANGUED
LANGUES
LANGUET
LANGUETS
LANGUETTE
LANGUETTES
LANGUID
LANGUIDER
LANGUIDEST
LANGUIDLY
LANGUISH
LANGUISHED
LANGUISHES
LANGUISHING
LANGUOR
LANGUORS
LANGUR
LANGURS
LANIARD
LANIARDS
LANIARY
LANK
LANKED
LANKER
LANKEST
LANKIER
LANKIEST
LANKINESS
LANKINESSES
LANKING
LANKLY
LANKNESS
LANKNESSES
LANKS
LANKY
LANNER
LANNERET
LANNERETS
LANNERS
LANOLIN
LANOLINE
LANOLINES
LANOLINS
LANOSE
LANT
LANTANA
LANTANAS

LANTERLOO
LANTERLOOS
LANTERN
LANTERNED
LANTERNING
LANTERNS
LANTHANUM
LANTHANUMS
LANTHORN
LANTHORNS
LANTS
LANTSKIP
LANTSKIPS
LANUGO
LANUGOS
LANX
LANYARD
LANYARDS
LAP
LAPDOG
LAPDOGS
LAPEL
LAPELLED
LAPELS
LAPFUL
LAPFULS
LAPIDARIES
LAPIDARY
LAPIDATE
LAPIDATED
LAPIDATES
LAPIDATING
LAPIDEOUS
LAPIDIFIC
LAPIDIFIED
LAPIDIFIES
LAPIDIFY
LAPIDIFYING
LAPILLI
LAPIS
LAPISES
LAPJE
LAPJES
LAPPED
LAPPER
LAPPER
LAPPERS
LAPPET
LAPPETED
LAPPETS
LAPPIE
LAPPIES
LAPPING
LAPPINGS
LAPS
LAPSABLE
LAPSANG
LAPSANGS
LAPSE
LAPSED
LAPSES
LAPSING
LAPSTONE
LAPSTONES
LAPSTREAK
LAPSTREAKS
LAPSUS
LAPSUSES
LAPTOP

LAPTOPS
LAPWING
LAPWINGS
LAPWORK
LAPWORKS
LAQUEARIA
LAR
LARBOARD
LARBOARDS
LARCENER
LARCENERS
LARCENIES
LARCENIST
LARCENISTS
LARCENOUS
LARCENY
LARCH
LARCHEN
LARCHES
LARD
LARDALITE
LARDALITES
LARDED
LARDER
LARDERER
LARDERERS
LARDERS
LARDIER
LARDIEST
LARDING
LARDON
LARDONS
LARDOON
LARDOONS
LARDS
LARDY
LARE
LARES
LARGE
LARGELY
LARGEN
LARGENED
LARGENESS
LARGENESSES
LARGENING
LARGENS
LARGER
LARGES
LARGESS
LARGESSE
LARGESSES
LARGEST
LARGHETTO
LARGHETTOS
LARGISH
LARGITION
LARGITIONS
LARGO
LARGOS
LARIAT
LARIATS
LARINE
LARK
LARKED
LARKER
LARKERS
LARKIER
LARKIEST
LARKINESS
LARKINESSES

LARKING
LARKISH
LARKS
LARKSPUR
LARKSPURS
LARKY
LARMIER
LARMIERS
LARN
LARNAKES
LARNAX
LARNED
LARNING
LARNS
LAROID
LARRIGAN
LARRIGANS
LARRIKIN
LARRIKINS
LARRUP
LARRUPED
LARRUPING
LARRUPS
LARUM
LARUMS
LARVA
LARVAE
LARVAL
LARVATE
LARVATED
LARVICIDE
LARVICIDES
LARVIFORM
LARVIKITE
LARVIKITES
LARYNGAL
LARYNGEAL
LARYNGES
LARYNX
LARYNXES
LAS
LASAGNA
LASAGNAS
LASAGNE
LASAGNES
LASCAR
LASCARS
LASE
LASED
LASER
LASERS
LASERWORT
LASERWORTS
LASES
LASH
LASHED
LASHER
LASHERS
LASHES
LASHING
LASHINGS
LASHKAR
LASHKARS
LASING
LASINGS
LASKET
LASKETS
LASQUE
LASQUES
LASS

LASSES
LASSIE
LASSIES
LASSITUDE
LASSITUDES
LASSLORN
LASSO
LASSOCK
LASSOCKS
LASSOED
LASSOES
LASSOING
LASSOS
LASSU
LASSUS
LAST
LASTAGE
LASTAGES
LASTED
LASTER
LASTERS
LASTING
LASTINGLY
LASTINGS
LASTLY
LASTS
LAT
LATCH
LATCHED
LATCHES
LATCHET
LATCHETS
LATCHING
LATCHKEY
LATCHKEYS
LATE
LATED
LATEEN
LATELY
LATEN
LATENCE
LATENCES
LATENCIES
LATENCY
LATENED
LATENESS
LATENESSES
LATENING
LATENS
LATENT
LATENTLY
LATER
LATERAL
LATERALLY
LATERALS
LATERITE
LATERITES
LATESCENT
LATEST
LATESTS
LATEWAKE
LATEWAKES
LATEX
LATEXES
LATH
LATHE
LATHED
LATHEE
LATHEES
LATHEN

LATHER
LATHERED
LATHERING
LATHERS
LATHERY
LATHES
LATHI
LATHIER
LATHIEST
LATHING
LATHINGS
LATHIS
LATHS
LATHY
LATHYRISM
LATHYRISMS
LATHYRUS
LATHYRUSES
LATICES
LATICLAVE
LATICLAVES
LATIFONDI
LATISH
LATITANCIES
LATITANCY
LATITANT
LATITAT
LATITATS
LATITUDE
LATITUDES
LATKE
LATKES
LATRANT
LATRATION
LATRATIONS
LATRIA
LATRIAS
LATRINE
LATRINES
LATROCINIES
LATROCINY
LATRON
LATRONS
LATS
LATTEN
LATTENS
LATTER
LATTERLY
LATTICE
LATTICED
LATTICES
LATTICING
LATTICINI
LATTICINO
LAUCH
LAUCHING
LAUCHS
LAUD
LAUDABLE
LAUDABLY
LAUDANUM
LAUDANUMS
LAUDATION
LAUDATIONS
LAUDATIVE
LAUDATIVES
LAUDATORIES
LAUDATORY
LAUDED
LAUDER

LAUDERS
LAUDING
LAUDS
LAUF
LAUFS
LAUGH
LAUGHABLE
LAUGHABLY
LAUGHED
LAUGHER
LAUGHERS
LAUGHFUL
LAUGHING
LAUGHINGS
LAUGHS
LAUGHSOME
LAUGHTER
LAUGHTERS
LAUGHY
LAUNCE
LAUNCED
LAUNCES
LAUNCH
LAUNCHED
LAUNCHER
LAUNCHERS
LAUNCHES
LAUNCHING
LAUNCING
LAUND
LAUNDER
LAUNDERED
LAUNDERER
LAUNDERERS
LAUNDERING
LAUNDERS
LAUNDRESS
LAUNDRESSES
LAUNDRIES
LAUNDRY
LAUNDS
LAURA
LAURAS
LAUREATE
LAUREATED
LAUREATES
LAUREATING
LAUREL
LAURELLED
LAURELS
LAUWINE
LAUWINES
LAV
LAVA
LAVABO
LAVABOES
LAVABOS
LAVAFORM
LAVAGE
LAVAGES
LAVALIERE
LAVALIERES
LAVAS
LAVATERA
LAVATERAS
LAVATION
LAVATIONS
LAVATORIES
LAVATORY
LAVE

LAVED
LAVEER
LAVEERED
LAVEERING
LAVEERS
LAVEMENT
LAVEMENTS
LAVENDER
LAVENDERED
LAVENDERING
LAVENDERS
LAVER
LAVEROCK
LAVEROCKED
LAVEROCKING
LAVEROCKS
LAVERS
LAVES
LAVING
LAVISH
LAVISHED
LAVISHER
LAVISHES
LAVISHEST
LAVISHING
LAVISHLY
LAVOLT
LAVOLTA
LAVOLTAS
LAVOLTED
LAVOLTING
LAVOLTS
LAVRA
LAVRAS
LAVS
LAW
LAWED
LAWER
LAWEST
LAWFUL
LAWFULLY
LAWING
LAWINGS
LAWK
LAWKS
LAWLAND
LAWLANDS
LAWLESS
LAWLESSLY
LAWMAN
LAWMEN
LAWMONGER
LAWMONGERS
LAWN
LAWNS
LAWNY
LAWS
LAWSUIT
LAWSUITS
LAWYER
LAWYERLY
LAWYERS
LAX
LAXATIVE
LAXATIVES
LAXATOR
LAXATORS
LAXER
LAXES
LAXEST

LAXISM
LAXISMS
LAXIST
LAXISTS
LAXITIES
LAXITY
LAXLY
LAXNESS
LAXNESSES
LAY
LAYABOUT
LAYABOUTS
LAYAWAY
LAYAWAYS
LAYBACK
LAYBACKED
LAYBACKING
LAYBACKS
LAYER
LAYERED
LAYERING
LAYERINGS
LAYERS
LAYETTE
LAYETTES
LAYING
LAYINGS
LAYLOCK
LAYLOCKS
LAYMAN
LAYMEN
LAYPERSON
LAYPERSONS
LAYS
LAYSTALL
LAYSTALLS
LAYTIME
LAYTIMES
LAZAR
LAZARET
LAZARETS
LAZARETTO
LAZARETTOS
LAZARS
LAZE
LAZED
LAZES
LAZIER
LAZIEST
LAZILY
LAZINESS
LAZINESSES
LAZING
LAZULITE
LAZULITES
LAZURITE
LAZURITES
LAZY
LAZZARONE
LAZZARONI
LAZZI
LAZZO
LEA
LEACH
LEACHATE
LEACHATES
LEACHED
LEACHES
LEACHIER
LEACHIEST

LEACHING
LEACHINGS
LEACHOUR
LEACHOURS
LEACHY
LEAD
LEADED
LEADEN
LEADENED
LEADENING
LEADENLY
LEADENS
LEADER
LEADERS
LEADIER
LEADIEST
LEADING
LEADINGS
LEADLESS
LEADS
LEADSMAN
LEADSMEN
LEADY
LEAF
LEAFAGE
LEAFAGES
LEAFBUD
LEAFBUDS
LEAFED
LEAFERIES
LEAFERY
LEAFIER
LEAFIEST
LEAFINESS
LEAFINESSES
LEAFING
LEAFLESS
LEAFLET
LEAFLETED
LEAFLETING
LEAFLETS
LEAFLETTED
LEAFLETTING
LEAFS
LEAFY
LEAGUE
LEAGUED
LEAGUER
LEAGUERED
LEAGUERING
LEAGUERS
LEAGUES
LEAGUING
LEAK
LEAKAGE
LEAKAGES
LEAKED
LEAKER
LEAKERS
LEAKIER
LEAKIEST
LEAKINESS
LEAKINESSES
LEAKING
LEAKS
LEAKY
LEAL
LEALTIES
LEALTY
LEAM

LEAMED
LEAMING
LEAMS
LEAN
LEANED
LEANER
LEANEST
LEANING
LEANINGS
LEANLY
LEANNESS
LEANNESSES
LEANS
LEANT
LEANY
LEAP
LEAPED
LEAPER
LEAPEROUS
LEAPERS
LEAPING
LEAPOROUS
LEAPROUS
LEAPS
LEAPT
LEAR
LEARE
LEARED
LEARES
LEARIER
LEARIEST
LEARING
LEARN
LEARNABLE
LEARNED
LEARNEDLY
LEARNER
LEARNERS
LEARNING
LEARNINGS
LEARNS
LEARNT
LEARS
LEARY
LEAS
LEASABLE
LEASE
LEASEBACK
LEASEBACKS
LEASED
LEASEHOLD
LEASEHOLDS
LEASER
LEASERS
LEASES
LEASH
LEASHED
LEASHES
LEASHING
LEASING
LEASINGS
LEASOW
LEASOWE
LEASOWED
LEASOWES
LEASOWING
LEASOWS
LEAST
LEASTS
LEASTWAYS

LEASTWISE
LEASURE
LEASURES
LEAT
LEATHER
LEATHERED
LEATHERING
LEATHERINGS
LEATHERN
LEATHERS
LEATHERY
LEATS
LEAVE
LEAVED
LEAVEN
LEAVENED
LEAVENING
LEAVENINGS
LEAVENOUS
LEAVENS
LEAVES
LEAVIER
LEAVIEST
LEAVING
LEAVINGS
LEAVY
LEAZE
LEAZES
LEBBEK
LEBBEKS
LECANORA
LECANORAS
LECH
LECHED
LECHER
LECHERED
LECHERIES
LECHERING
LECHEROUS
LECHERS
LECHERY
LECHES
LECHING
LECHWE
LECHWES
LECITHIN
LECITHINS
LECTERN
LECTERNS
LECTIN
LECTINS
LECTION
LECTIONS
LECTOR
LECTORATE
LECTORATES
LECTORS
LECTRESS
LECTRESSES
LECTURE
LECTURED
LECTURER
LECTURERS
LECTURES
LECTURING
LECTURN
LECTURNS
LECYTHI
LECYTHUS
LED

LEDDEN
LEDDENS
LEDGE
LEDGER
LEDGERED
LEDGERING
LEDGERS
LEDGES
LEDGIER
LEDGIEST
LEDGY
LEDUM
LEDUMS
LEE
LEEAR
LEEARS
LEECH
LEECHDOM
LEECHDOMS
LEECHED
LEECHEE
LEECHEES
LEECHES
LEECHING
LEED
LEEING
LEEK
LEEKS
LEEP
LEEPED
LEEPING
LEEPS
LEER
LEERED
LEERIER
LEERIEST
LEERING
LEERINGLY
LEERINGS
LEERS
LEERY
LEES
LEESE
LEESES
LEESING
LEET
LEETLE
LEETS
LEEWARD
LEEWARDS
LEEWAY
LEEWAYS
LEEZE
LEFT
LEFTE
LEFTIE
LEFTIES
LEFTISM
LEFTISMS
LEFTIST
LEFTISTS
LEFTS
LEFTWARD
LEFTWARDS
LEFTY
LEG
LEGACIES
LEGACY
LEGAL
LEGALESE

LEGALESES
LEGALISE
LEGALISED
LEGALISES
LEGALISING
LEGALISM
LEGALISMS
LEGALIST
LEGALISTS
LEGALITIES
LEGALITY
LEGALIZE
LEGALIZED
LEGALIZES
LEGALIZING
LEGALLY
LEGATARIES
LEGATARY
LEGATE
LEGATEE
LEGATEES
LEGATES
LEGATINE
LEGATION
LEGATIONS
LEGATO
LEGATOR
LEGATORS
LEGATOS
LEGEND
LEGENDARIES
LEGENDARY
LEGENDIST
LEGENDISTS
LEGENDRIES
LEGENDRY
LEGENDS
LEGER
LEGERING
LEGERINGS
LEGERITIES
LEGERITY
LEGERS
LEGGE
LEGGED
LEGGER
LEGGERS
LEGGES
LEGGIER
LEGGIEST
LEGGINESS
LEGGINESSES
LEGGING
LEGGINGS
LEGGISM
LEGGISMS
LEGGY
LEGHORN
LEGHORNS
LEGIBLE
LEGIBLY
LEGION
LEGIONARIES
LEGIONARY
LEGIONED
LEGIONS
LEGISLATE
LEGISLATED
LEGISLATES
LEGISLATING

LEGIST
LEGISTS
LEGIT
LEGITIM
LEGITIMS
LEGLAN
LEGLANS
LEGLEN
LEGLENS
LEGLESS
LEGLET
LEGLETS
LEGLIN
LEGLINS
LEGROOM
LEGROOMS
LEGS
LEGUME
LEGUMES
LEGUMIN
LEGUMINS
LEGWORK
LEGWORKS
LEHR
LEHREJAHRE
LEHRS
LEI
LEIDGER
LEIDGERS
LEIGER
LEIGERS
LEIPOA
LEIPOAS
LEIR
LEIRED
LEIRING
LEIRS
LEIS
LEISH
LEISHER
LEISHEST
LEISLER
LEISLERS
LEISTER
LEISTERED
LEISTERING
LEISTERS
LEISURE
LEISURED
LEISURELY
LEISURES
LEISURING
LEITMOTIF
LEITMOTIFS
LEITMOTIV
LEITMOTIVS
LEK
LEKE
LEKKED
LEKKING
LEKKINGS
LEKS
LEKYTHOI
LEKYTHOS
LEMAN
LEMANS
LEME
LEMED
LEMEL

LEMELS
LEMES
LEMING
LEMMA
LEMMAS
LEMMATA
LEMMING
LEMMINGS
LEMON
LEMONADE
LEMONADES
LEMONED
LEMONING
LEMONS
LEMONY
LEMPIRA
LEMPIRAS
LEMUR
LEMURES
LEMURIAN
LEMURIANS
LEMURINE
LEMURINES
LEMUROID
LEMUROIDS
LEMURS
LEND
LENDER
LENDERS
LENDING
LENDINGS
LENDS
LENES
LENG
LENGED
LENGER
LENGEST
LENGING
LENGS
LENGTH
LENGTHEN
LENGTHENED
LENGTHENING
LENGTHENS
LENGTHFUL
LENGTHIER
LENGTHIEST
LENGTHILY
LENGTHS
LENGTHY
LENIENCE
LENIENCES
LENIENCIES
LENIENCY
LENIENT
LENIENTLY
LENIENTS
LENIFIED
LENIFIES
LENIFY
LENIFYING
LENIS
LENITIES
LENITION
LENITIONS
LENITIVE
LENITIVES
LENITY
LENO

LENOS	LESBIAN	LEUCOCYTE	LEVULOSES	LIBATORY
LENS	LESBIANS	LEUCOCYTES	LEVY	LIBBARD
LENSES	LESBIC	LEUCOMA	LEVYING	LIBBARDS
LENT	LESES	LEUCOMAS	LEW	LIBBED
LENTANDO	LESION	LEUCOTOME	LEWD	LIBBER
LENTEN	LESIONS	LEUCOTOMES	LEWDER	LIBBERS
LENTI	LESS	LEUCOTOMIES	LEWDEST	LIBBING
LENTIC	LESSEE	LEUCOTOMY	LEWDLY	LIBECCHIO
LENTICEL	LESSEES	LEUGH	LEWDNESS	LIBECCHIOS
LENTICELS	LESSEN	LEUGHEN	LEWDNESSES	LIBECCIO
LENTICLE	LESSENED	LEUKAEMIA	LEWDSBIES	LIBECCIOS
LENTICLES	LESSENING	LEUKAEMIAS	LEWDSBY	LIBEL
LENTIFORM	LESSENS	LEV	LEWDSTER	LIBELLANT
LENTIGINES	LESSER	LEVA	LEWDSTERS	LIBELLANTS
LENTIGO	LESSES	LEVANT	LEWIS	LIBELLED
LENTIL	LESSON	LEVANTED	LEWISES	LIBELLEE
LENTILS	LESSONED	LEVANTER	LEWISITE	LIBELLEES
LENTISK	LESSONING	LEVANTERS	LEWISITES	LIBELLER
LENTISKS	LESSONINGS	LEVANTINE	LEWISSON	LIBELLERS
LENTO	LESSONS	LEVANTINES	LEWISSONS	LIBELLING
LENTOID	LESSOR	LEVANTING	LEX	LIBELLINGS
LENTOR	LESSORS	LEVANTS	LEXEME	LIBELLOUS
LENTORS	LEST	LEVATOR	LEXEMES	LIBELS
LENTOS	LET	LEVATORS	LEXES	LIBER
LENTOUS	LETCH	LEVE	LEXICAL	LIBERAL
LENVOY	LETCHED	LEVEE	LEXICALLY	LIBERALLY
LENVOYS	LETCHES	LEVEED	LEXICON	LIBERALS
LEONE	LETCHING	LEVEEING	LEXICONS	LIBERATE
LEONES	LETHAL	LEVEES	LEXIGRAM	LIBERATED
LEONINE	LETHALITIES	LEVEL	LEXIGRAMS	LIBERATES
LEOPARD	LETHALITY	LEVELLED	LEXIS	LIBERATING
LEOPARDS	LETHALLY	LEVELLER	LEXISES	LIBERATOR
LEOTARD	LETHARGIC	LEVELLERS	LEY	LIBERATORS
LEOTARDS	LETHARGIES	LEVELLEST	LEYS	LIBERS
LEP	LETHARGY	LEVELLING	LEZ	LIBERTIES
LEPER	LETHEAN	LEVELS	LEZES	LIBERTINE
LEPERS	LETHEE	LEVER	LEZZ	LIBERTINES
LEPID	LETHEES	LEVERAGE	LEZZES	LIBERTY
LEPIDOTE	LETHIED	LEVERAGES	LEZZIES	LIBIDINAL
LEPORINE	LETS	LEVERED	LEZZY	LIBIDO
LEPPED	LETTABLE	LEVERET	LI	LIBIDOS
LEPPING	LETTED	LEVERETS	LIABILITIES	LIBKEN
LEPRA	LETTER	LEVERING	LIABILITY	LIBKENS
LEPRAS	LETTERED	LEVERS	LIABLE	LIBRA
LEPROSE	LETTERER	LEVIABLE	LIAISE	LIBRAIRE
LEPROSERIES	LETTERERS	LEVIATHAN	LIAISED	LIBRAIRES
LEPROSERY	LETTERING	LEVIATHANS	LIAISES	LIBRAIRIE
LEPROSIES	LETTERINGS	LEVIED	LIAISING	LIBRARIAN
LEPROSITIES	LETTERN	LEVIES	LIAISON	LIBRARIANS
LEPROSITY	LETTERNS	LEVIGABLE	LIAISONS	LIBRARIES
LEPROSY	LETTERS	LEVIGATE	LIANA	LIBRARY
LEPROUS	LETTING	LEVIGATED	LIANAS	LIBRAS
LEPS	LETTINGS	LEVIGATES	LIANE	LIBRATE
LEPTA	LETTRE	LEVIGATING	LIANES	LIBRATED
LEPTOME	LETTRES	LEVIN	LIANG	LIBRATES
LEPTOMES	LETTUCE	LEVINS	LIANGS	LIBRATING
LEPTON	LETTUCES	LEVIRATE	LIANOID	LIBRATION
LEPTONIC	LEU	LEVIRATES	LIAR	LIBRATIONS
LEPTONS	LEUCAEMIA	LEVIS	LIARD	LIBRATORY
LEPTOSOME	LEUCAEMIAS	LEVITATE	LIARDS	LIBRETTI
LEPTOSOMES	LEUCAEMIC	LEVITATED	LIARS	LIBRETTO
LEPTOTENE	LEUCH	LEVITATES	LIART	LIBRETTOS
LEPTOTENES	LEUCHEN	LEVITATING	LIB	LIBS
LERE	LEUCIN	LEVITE	LIBANT	LICE
LERED	LEUCINE	LEVITES	LIBATE	LICENCE
LERES	LEUCINES	LEVITIC	LIBATED	LICENCED
LERING	LEUCINS	LEVITICAL	LIBATES	LICENCES
LERNAEAN	LEUCITE	LEVITIES	LIBATING	LICENCING
LERNEAN	LEUCITES	LEVITY	LIBATION	LICENSE
LES	LEUCITIC	LEVULOSE	LIBATIONS	LICENSED

LICENSEE
LICENSEES
LICENSER
LICENSERS
LICENSES
LICENSING
LICENSOR
LICENSORS
LICENSURE
LICENSURES
LICH
LICHANOS
LICHANOSES
LICHED
LICHEE
LICHEES
LICHEN
LICHENED
LICHENIN
LICHENINS
LICHENISM
LICHENISMS
LICHENIST
LICHENISTS
LICHENOID
LICHENOSE
LICHENOUS
LICHENS
LICHES
LICHGATE
LICHGATES
LICHI
LICHING
LICHIS
LICHT
LICHTED
LICHTER
LICHTEST
LICHTING
LICHTLIED
LICHTLIES
LICHTLY
LICHTLYING
LICHTS
LICHWAKE
LICHWAKES
LICHWAY
LICHWAYS
LICIT
LICITLY
LICK
LICKED
LICKER
LICKERISH
LICKERS
LICKING
LICKINGS
LICKPENNIES
LICKPENNY
LICKS
LICORICE
LICORICES
LICTOR
LICTORS
LID
LIDDED
LIDGER
LIDGERS
LIDLESS
LIDO

LIDOCAINE
LIDOCAINES
LIDOS
LIDS
LIE
LIED
LIEDER
LIEF
LIEFER
LIEFEST
LIEFS
LIEGE
LIEGEDOM
LIEGEDOMS
LIEGELESS
LIEGEMAN
LIEGEMEN
LIEGER
LIEGERS
LIEGES
LIEN
LIENAL
LIENS
LIENTERIC
LIENTERIES
LIENTERY
LIER
LIERNE
LIERNES
LIERS
LIES
LIEU
LIEUS
LIEVE
LIEVER
LIEVEST
LIFE
LIFEBELT
LIFEBELTS
LIFEBOAT
LIFEBOATS
LIFEFUL
LIFEGUARD
LIFEGUARDS
LIFEHOLD
LIFELESS
LIFELIKE
LIFELONG
LIFER
LIFERS
LIFESOME
LIFESPAN
LIFESPANS
LIFETIME
LIFETIMES
LIFT
LIFTABLE
LIFTED
LIFTER
LIFTERS
LIFTING
LIFTS
LIFULL
LIG
LIGAMENT
LIGAMENTS
LIGAN
LIGAND
LIGANDS
LIGANS

LIGATE
LIGATED
LIGATES
LIGATING
LIGATION
LIGATIONS
LIGATURE
LIGATURES
LIGER
LIGERS
LIGGE
LIGGED
LIGGEING
LIGGEN
LIGGER
LIGGERS
LIGGES
LIGGING
LIGGINGS
LIGHT
LIGHTED
LIGHTEN
LIGHTENED
LIGHTENING
LIGHTENS
LIGHTER
LIGHTERS
LIGHTEST
LIGHTFAST
LIGHTFUL
LIGHTING
LIGHTINGS
LIGHTISH
LIGHTLESS
LIGHTLIED
LIGHTLIES
LIGHTLY
LIGHTLYING
LIGHTNESS
LIGHTNESSES
LIGHTNING
LIGHTNINGS
LIGHTS
LIGHTSHIP
LIGHTSHIPS
LIGHTSOME
LIGNAGE
LIGNAGES
LIGNALOES
LIGNE
LIGNEOUS
LIGNES
LIGNIFIED
LIGNIFIES
LIGNIFORM
LIGNIFY
LIGNIFYING
LIGNIN
LIGNINS
LIGNITE
LIGNITES
LIGNITIC
LIGNUM
LIGNUMS
LIGROIN
LIGROINS
LIGS
LIGULA
LIGULAE
LIGULAR

LIGULAS
LIGULATE
LIGULE
LIGULES
LIGULOID
LIGURE
LIGURES
LIKABLE
LIKE
LIKEABLE
LIKED
LIKELIER
LIKELIEST
LIKELY
LIKEN
LIKENED
LIKENESS
LIKENESSES
LIKENING
LIKENS
LIKER
LIKERS
LIKES
LIKEWAKE
LIKEWAKES
LIKEWALK
LIKEWALKS
LIKEWISE
LIKIN
LIKING
LIKINGS
LIKINS
LILAC
LILACS
LILANGENI
LILIED
LILIES
LILL
LILLED
LILLING
LILLS
LILO
LILOS
LILT
LILTED
LILTING
LILTS
LILY
LIMA
LIMACEL
LIMACELS
LIMACEOUS
LIMACES
LIMACINE
LIMAÇON
LIMAÇONS
LIMAIL
LIMAILS
LIMAS
LIMATION
LIMATIONS
LIMAX
LIMB
LIMBATE
LIMBEC
LIMBECK
LIMBECKS
LIMBECS
LIMBED
LIMBER

LIMBERED
LIMBERING
LIMBERS
LIMBIC
LIMBING
LIMBLESS
LIMBMEAL
LIMBO
LIMBOS
LIMBOUS
LIMBS
LIME
LIMED
LIMEKILN
LIMEKILNS
LIMELIGHT
LIMELIGHTED
LIMELIGHTING
LIMELIGHTS
LIMELIT
LIMEN
LIMENS
LIMEPIT
LIMEPITS
LIMERICK
LIMERICKS
LIMES
LIMESTONE
LIMESTONES
LIMEWASH
LIMEWASHES
LIMEWATER
LIMEWATERS
LIMEY
LIMEYS
LIMIER
LIMIEST
LIMINAL
LIMINESS
LIMINESSES
LIMING
LIMINGS
LIMIT
LIMITABLE
LIMITARY
LIMITED
LIMITEDLY
LIMITEDS
LIMITER
LIMITERS
LIMITES
LIMITING
LIMITINGS
LIMITLESS
LIMITS
LIMMA
LIMMAS
LIMMER
LIMMERS
LIMN
LIMNAEID
LIMNAEIDS
LIMNED
LIMNER
LIMNERS
LIMNETIC
LIMNING
LIMNOLOGIES
LIMNOLOGY
LIMNS

LIMONITE	LINEATION	LINKED	LIONIZES	LIQUIDATED
LIMONITES	LINEATIONS	LINKING	LIONIZING	LIQUIDATES
LIMONITIC	LINED	LINKMAN	LIONLY	LIQUIDATING
LIMOSES	LINEMAN	LINKMEN	LIONS	LIQUIDER
LIMOSIS	LINEMEN	LINKS	LIP	LIQUIDEST
LIMOSISES	LINEN	LINKSTER	LIPARITE	LIQUIDISE
LIMOUS	LINENS	LINKSTERS	LIPARITES	LIQUIDISED
LIMOUSINE	LINEOLATE	LINKWORK	LIPASE	LIQUIDISES
LIMOUSINES	LINER	LINKWORKS	LIPASES	LIQUIDISING
LIMP	LINERS	LINN	LIPECTOMIES	LIQUIDITIES
LIMPED	LINES	LINNED	LIPECTOMY	LIQUIDITY
LIMPER	LINESMAN	LINNET	LIPGLOSS	LIQUIDIZE
LIMPEST	LINESMEN	LINNETS	LIPGLOSSES	LIQUIDIZED
LIMPET	LINEY	LINNIES	LIPID	LIQUIDIZES
LIMPETS	LING	LINNING	LIPIDE	LIQUIDIZING
LIMPID	LINGA	LINNS	LIPIDES	LIQUIDLY
LIMPIDITIES	LINGAM	LINNY	LIPIDS	LIQUIDS
LIMPIDITY	LINGAMS	LINO	LIPLESS	LIQUIDUS
LIMPIDLY	LINGAS	LINOCUT	LIPOGRAM	LIQUIDUSES
LIMPING	LINGEL	LINOCUTS	LIPOGRAMS	LIQUIFIED
LIMPINGLY	LINGELS	LINOLEUM	LIPOID	LIQUOR
LIMPINGS	LINGER	LINOLEUMS	LIPOIDS	LIQUORED
LIMPKIN	LINGERED	LINOS	LIPOMA	LIQUORICE
LIMPKINS	LINGERER	LINS	LIPOMATA	LIQUORICES
LIMPS	LINGERERS	LINSANG	LIPOSOMAL	LIQUORING
LIMULI	LINGERIE	LINSANGS	LIPOSOME	LIQUORISH
LIMULUS	LINGERIES	LINSEED	LIPOSOMES	LIQUORS
LIMULUSES	LINGERING	LINSEEDS	LIPPED	LIRA
LIMY	LINGERINGS	LINSEY	LIPPEN	LIRAS
LIN	LINGERS	LINSEYS	LIPPENED	LIRE
LINAC	LINGIER	LINSTOCK	LIPPENING	LIRIPIPE
LINAGE	LINGIEST	LINSTOCKS	LIPPENS	LIRIPIPES
LINAGES	LINGLE	LINT	LIPPIE	LIRIPOOP
LINALOOL	LINGLES	LINTEL	LIPPIER	LIRIPOOPS
LINALOOLS	LINGO	LINTELLED	LIPPIES	LIRK
LINCH	LINGOES	LINTELS	LIPPIEST	LIRKED
LINCHES	LINGOT	LINTER	LIPPING	LIRKING
LINCHET	LINGOTS	LINTERS	LIPPITUDE	LIRKS
LINCHETS	LINGS	LINTIE	LIPPITUDES	LIS
LINCHPIN	LINGSTER	LINTIER	LIPPY	LISK
LINCHPINS	LINGSTERS	LINTIES	LIPS	LISKS
LINCRUSTA	LINGUA	LINTIEST	LIPSALVE	LISLE
LINCRUSTAS	LINGUAE	LINTS	LIPSALVES	LISLES
LINCTURE	LINGUAL	LINTSEED	LIPSTICK	LISP
LINCTURES	LINGUALLY	LINTSEEDS	LIPSTICKED	LISPED
LINCTUS	LINGUAS	LINTSTOCK	LIPSTICKING	LISPER
LINCTUSES	LINGUINI	LINTSTOCKS	LIPSTICKS	LISPERS
LIND	LINGUIST	LINTWHITE	LIQUABLE	LISPING
LINDANE	LINGUISTS	LINTWHITES	LIQUATE	LISPINGLY
LINDANES	LINGULA	LINTY	LIQUATED	LISPINGS
LINDEN	LINGULAE	LINY	LIQUATES	LISPOUND
LINDENS	LINGULAR	LION	LIQUATING	LISPOUNDS
LINDS	LINGULAS	LIONCEL	LIQUATION	LISPS
LINDWORM	LINGULATE	LIONCELLE	LIQUATIONS	LISPUND
LINDWORMS	LINGY	LIONCELLES	LIQUEFIED	LISPUNDS
LINE	LINHAY	LIONCELS	LIQUEFIER	LISSES
LINEAGE	LINHAYS	LIONEL	LIQUEFIERS	LISSOM
LINEAGES	LINIER	LIONELS	LIQUEFIES	LISSOME
LINEAL	LINIEST	LIONESS	LIQUEFY	LISSOMER
LINEALITIES	LINIMENT	LIONESSES	LIQUEFYING	LISSOMEST
LINEALITY	LINIMENTS	LIONET	LIQUESCE	LIST
LINEALLY	LININ	LIONETS	LIQUESCED	LISTED
LINEAMENT	LINING	LIONISE	LIQUESCES	LISTEL
LINEAMENTS	LININGS	LIONISED	LIQUESCING	LISTELS
LINEAR	LININS	LIONISES	LIQUEUR	LISTEN
LINEARITIES	LINK	LIONISING	LIQUEURED	LISTENED
LINEARITY	LINKAGE	LIONISM	LIQUEURING	LISTENER
LINEARLY	LINKAGES	LIONISMS	LIQUEURS	LISTENERS
LINEATE	LINKBOY	LIONIZE	LIQUID	LISTENING
LINEATED	LINKBOYS	LIONIZED	LIQUIDATE	LISTENS

LISTER
LISTERS
LISTETH
LISTFUL
LISTING
LISTINGS
LISTLESS
LISTS
LIT
LITANIES
LITANY
LITCHI
LITCHIS
LITE
LITER
LITERACIES
LITERACY
LITERAL
LITERALLY
LITERALS
LITERARY
LITERATE
LITERATES
LITERATI
LITERATIM
LITERATO
LITERATOR
LITERATORS
LITERATUS
LITEROSE
LITERS
LITES
LITH
LITHARGE
LITHARGES
LITHATE
LITHATES
LITHE
LITHED
LITHELY
LITHENESS
LITHENESSES
LITHER
LITHERLY
LITHES
LITHESOME
LITHEST
LITHIA
LITHIAS
LITHIASES
LITHIASIS
LITHIC
LITHING
LITHISTID
LITHISTIDS
LITHITE
LITHITES
LITHIUM
LITHIUMS
LITHO
LITHOCYST
LITHOCYSTS
LITHOID
LITHOIDAL
LITHOLOGIES
LITHOLOGY
LITHOPONE
LITHOPONES
LITHOS
LITHOTOME

LITHOTOMES
LITHOTOMIES
LITHOTOMY
LITHS
LITIGABLE
LITIGANT
LITIGANTS
LITIGATE
LITIGATED
LITIGATES
LITIGATING
LITIGIOUS
LITMUS
LITMUSES
LITOTES
LITRE
LITRES
LITTEN
LITTER
LITTERED
LITTERING
LITTERS
LITTERY
LITTLE
LITTLEANE
LITTLEANES
LITTLER
LITTLEST
LITTLIN
LITTLING
LITTLINGS
LITTLINS
LITTORAL
LITTORALS
LITURGIC
LITURGICS
LITURGIES
LITURGIST
LITURGISTS
LITURGY
LITUUS
LITUUSES
LIVABLE
LIVE
LIVEABLE
LIVED
LIVELIER
LIVELIEST
LIVELILY
LIVELOD
LIVELODS
LIVELONG
LIVELONGS
LIVELOOD
LIVELOODS
LIVELY
LIVEN
LIVENED
LIVENING
LIVENS
LIVER
LIVERED
LIVERIED
LIVERIES
LIVERISH
LIVERS
LIVERWORT
LIVERWORTS
LIVERY

LIVERYMAN
LIVERYMEN
LIVES
LIVESTOCK
LIVESTOCKS
LIVEWARE
LIVEWARES
LIVID
LIVIDER
LIVIDEST
LIVIDITIES
LIVIDITY
LIVIDNESS
LIVIDNESSES
LIVING
LIVINGS
LIVOR
LIVORS
LIVRAISON
LIVRAISONS
LIVRE
LIVRES
LIXIVIAL
LIXIVIATE
LIXIVIATED
LIXIVIATES
LIXIVIATING
LIXIVIOUS
LIXIVIUM
LIXIVIUMS
LIZARD
LIZARDS
LLAMA
LLAMAS
LLANERO
LLANEROS
LLANO
LLANOS
LO
LOACH
LOACHES
LOAD
LOADED
LOADEN
LOADENED
LOADENING
LOADENS
LOADER
LOADERS
LOADING
LOADINGS
LOADS
LOADSTAR
LOADSTARS
LOADSTONE
LOADSTONES
LOAF
LOAFED
LOAFER
LOAFERISH
LOAFERS
LOAFING
LOAFINGS
LOAFS
LOAM
LOAMED
LOAMIER
LOAMIEST
LOAMINESS
LOAMINESSES

LOAMING
LOAMS
LOAMY
LOAN
LOANABLE
LOANED
LOANING
LOANINGS
LOANS
LOAST
LOATH
LOATHE
LOATHED
LOATHEING
LOATHER
LOATHERS
LOATHES
LOATHEST
LOATHFUL
LOATHING
LOATHINGS
LOATHLY
LOATHSOME
LOATHSOMER
LOATHSOMEST
LOATHY
LOAVE
LOAVED
LOAVES
LOAVING
LOB
LOBAR
LOBATE
LOBATION
LOBATIONS
LOBBED
LOBBIED
LOBBIES
LOBBING
LOBBY
LOBBYER
LOBBYERS
LOBBYING
LOBBYINGS
LOBBYIST
LOBBYISTS
LOBE
LOBECTOMIES
LOBECTOMY
LOBED
LOBELET
LOBELETS
LOBELIA
LOBELIAS
LOBELINE
LOBELINES
LOBES
LOBI
LOBING
LOBINGS
LOBIPED
LOBLOLLIES
LOBLOLLY
LOBO
LOBOS
LOBOSE
LOBOTOMIES
LOBOTOMY
LOBS
LOBSCOUSE

LOBSCOUSES
LOBSTER
LOBSTERS
LOBULAR
LOBULATE
LOBULATED
LOBULE
LOBULES
LOBULI
LOBULUS
LOBUS
LOBWORM
LOBWORMS
LOCAL
LOCALE
LOCALES
LOCALISE
LOCALISED
LOCALISER
LOCALISERS
LOCALISES
LOCALISING
LOCALISM
LOCALISMS
LOCALIST
LOCALISTS
LOCALITIES
LOCALITY
LOCALIZE
LOCALIZED
LOCALIZER
LOCALIZERS
LOCALIZES
LOCALIZING
LOCALLY
LOCALS
LOCATE
LOCATED
LOCATES
LOCATING
LOCATION
LOCATIONS
LOCATIVE
LOCATIVES
LOCELLATE
LOCH
LOCHAN
LOCHANS
LOCHIA
LOCHIAL
LOCHS
LOCI
LOCK
LOCKAGE
LOCKAGES
LOCKAWAY
LOCKAWAYS
LOCKED
LOCKER
LOCKERS
LOCKET
LOCKETS
LOCKFAST
LOCKFUL
LOCKFULS
LOCKHOUSE
LOCKHOUSES
LOCKING
LOCKMAN
LOCKMEN

LOCKOUT
LOCKOUTS
LOCKPICK
LOCKPICKS
LOCKRAM
LOCKRAMS
LOCKS.
LOCKSMAN
LOCKSMEN
LOCKSMITH
LOCKSMITHS
LOCKSTEP
LOCKSTEPS
LOCO
LOCOED
LOCOES
LOCOFOCO
LOCOFOCOS
LOCOMAN
LOCOMEN
LOCOMOTE
LOCOMOTED
LOCOMOTES
LOCOMOTING
LOCOMOTOR
LOCOMOTORS
LOCOS
LOCULAR
LOCULATE
LOCULE
LOCULES
LOCULI
LOCULUS
LOCUM
LOCUMS
LOCUPLETE
LOCUS
LOCUST
LOCUSTA
LOCUSTAE
LOCUSTED
LOCUSTING
LOCUSTS
LOCUTION
LOCUTIONS
LOCUTORIES
LOCUTORY
LODE
LODEN
LODENS
LODES
LODESMAN
LODESMEN
LODESTAR
LODESTARS
LODESTONE
LODESTONES
LODGE
LODGED
LODGEMENT
LODGEMENTS
LODGEPOLE
LODGEPOLES
LODGER
LODGERS
LODGES
LODGING
LODGINGS
LODGMENT
LODGMENTS

LODICULA
LODICULAE
LODICULE
LODICULES
LOESS
LOESSES
LOFT
LOFTED
LOFTER
LOFTERS
LOFTIER
LOFTIEST
LOFTILY
LOFTINESS
LOFTINESSES
LOFTING
LOFTS
LOFTY
LOG
LOGAN
LOGANS
LOGAOEDIC
LOGARITHM
LOGARITHMS
LOGBOARD
LOGBOARDS
LOGE
LOGES
LOGGAT
LOGGATS
LOGGED
LOGGER
LOGGERS
LOGGIA
LOGGIAS
LOGGIE
LOGGING
LOGGINGS
LOGIA
LOGIC
LOGICAL
LOGICALLY
LOGICIAN
LOGICIANS
LOGICISE
LOGICISED
LOGICISES
LOGICISING
LOGICIZE
LOGICIZED
LOGICIZES
LOGICIZING
LOGICS
LOGIE
LOGIES
LOGION
LOGISTIC
LOGISTICS
LOGJUICE
LOGJUICES
LOGLINE
LOGLINES
LOGLOG
LOGLOGS
LOGO
LOGOGRAM
LOGOGRAMS
LOGOGRAPH
LOGOGRAPHS
LOGOGRIPH

LOGOGRIPHS
LOGOMACHIES
LOGOMACHY
LOGORRHEA
LOGORRHEAS
LOGOS
LOGOTHETE
LOGOTHETES
LOGOTYPE
LOGOTYPES
LOGS
LOGWOOD
LOGWOODS
LOID
LOIDED
LOIDING
LOIDS
LOIN
LOINS
LOIPE
LOIPES
LOIR
LOIRS
LOITER
LOITERED
LOITERER
LOITERERS
LOITERING
LOITERINGS
LOITERS
LOKE
LOKES
LOKSHEN
LOLL
LOLLED
LOLLER
LOLLERS
LOLLIES
LOLLING
LOLLINGLY
LOLLIPOP
LOLLIPOPS
LOLLOP
LOLLOPED
LOLLOPING
LOLLOPS
LOLLS
LOLLY
LOLLYGAG
LOLLYGAGGED
LOLLYGAGGING
LOLLYGAGS
LOLOG
LOLOGS
LOMA
LOMAS
LOME
LOMED
LOMENT
LOMENTA
LOMENTS
LOMENTUM
LOMES
LOMING
LOMPISH
LONE
LONELIER
LONELIEST
LONELY
LONENESS

LONENESSES
LONER
LONERS
LONESOME
LONESOMER
LONESOMEST
LONG
LONGA
LONGAEVAL
LONGAN
LONGANS
LONGAS
LONGBOAT
LONGBOATS
LONGBOW
LONGBOWS
LONGCLOTH
LONGCLOTHES
LONGCOATS
LONGE
LONGED
LONGEING
LONGER
LONGERON
LONGERONS
LONGES
LONGEST
LONGEVAL
LONGEVITIES
LONGEVITY
LONGEVOUS
LONGHAND
LONGHANDS
LONGHORN
LONGHORNS
LONGICORN
LONGICORNS
LONGING
LONGINGLY
LONGINGS
LONGISH
LONGITUDE
LONGITUDES
LONGLY
LONGNESS
LONGNESSES
LONGS
LONGSHIP
LONGSHIPS
LONGSHORE
LONGSOME
LONGTAIL
LONGTAILS
LONGUEUR
LONGUEURS
LONGWALL
LONGWALLS
LONGWAYS
LONGWISE
LONICERA
LONICERAS
LOO
LOOBIES
LOOBILY
LOOBY
LOOED
LOOF
LOOFA
LOOFAH
LOOFAHS

LOOFAS
LOOFED
LOOFFUL
LOOFFULS
LOOFING
LOOFS
LOOING
LOOK
LOOKED
LOOKER
LOOKERS
LOOKING
LOOKINGS
LOOKOUT
LOOKOUTS
LOOKS
LOOM
LOOMED
LOOMING
LOOMS
LOON
LOONIE
LOONIER
LOONIES
LOONIEST
LOONING
LOONINGS
LOONS
LOONY
LOOP
LOOPED
LOOPER
LOOPERS
LOOPHOLE
LOOPHOLED
LOOPHOLES
LOOPHOLING
LOOPIER
LOOPIEST
LOOPING
LOOPINGS
LOOPS
LOOPY
LOOR
LOORD
LOORDS
LOOS
LOOSE
LOOSED
LOOSELY
LOOSEN
LOOSENED
LOOSENER
LOOSENERS
LOOSENESS
LOOSENESSES
LOOSENING
LOOSENS
LOOSER
LOOSES
LOOSEST
LOOSING
LOOT
LOOTED
LOOTEN
LOOTER
LOOTERS
LOOTING
LOOTS
LOOVES

LOP	LORINER	LOUDLY	LOVE	LOWNESSES
LOPE	LORINERS	LOUDMOUTH	LOVEABLE	LOWNING
LOPED	LORING	LOUDMOUTHS	LOVEBIRD	LOWNS
LOPER	LORINGS	LOUDNESS	LOVEBIRDS	LOWS
LOPERS	LORIOT	LOUDNESSES	LOVEBITE	LOWSE
LOPES	LORIOTS	LOUGH	LOVEBITES	LOWSER
LOPGRASS	LORIS	LOUGHS	LOVED	LOWSES
LOPGRASSES	LORISES	LOUIS	LOVELESS	LOWSEST
LOPHODONT	LORN	LOUN	LOVELIER	LOWSING
LOPING	LORRELL	LOUND	LOVELIES	LOWSIT
LOPPED	LORRELLS	LOUNDED	LOVELIEST	LOWT
LOPPER	LORRIES	LOUNDERED	LOVELIGHT	LOWTED
LOPPERS	LORRY	LOUNDERING	LOVELIGHTS	LOWTING
LOPPING	LORY	LOUNDERS	LOVELILY	LOWTS
LOPPINGS	LOS	LOUNDING	LOVELOCK	LOWVELD
LOPS	LOSABLE	LOUNDS	LOVELOCKS	LOWVELDS
LOQUACITIES	LOSE	LOUNED	LOVELORN	LOX
LOQUACITY	LOSEL	LOUNGE	LOVELY	LOXES
LOQUAT	LOSELS	LOUNGED	LOVER	LOXODROME
LOQUATS	LOSEN	LOUNGER	LOVERED	LOXODROMES
LOQUITUR	LOSER	LOUNGERS	LOVERLESS	LOXODROMIES
LOR	LOSERS	LOUNGES	LOVERLY	LOXODROMY
LORAL	LOSES	LOUNGING	LOVERS	LOXYGEN
LORAN	LOSH	LOUNGINGS	LOVES	LOXYGENS
LORANS	LOSING	LOUNING	LOVESICK	LOY
LORATE	LOSINGLY	LOUNS	LOVESOME	LOYAL
LORCHA	LOSINGS	LOUP	LOVEY	LOYALIST
LORCHAS	LOSS	LOUPE	LOVEYS	LOYALISTS
LORD	LOSSES	LOUPED	LOVING	LOYALLER
LORDED	LOSSIER	LOUPEN	LOVINGLY	LOYALLEST
LORDING	LOSSIEST	LOUPES	LOVINGS	LOYALLY
LORDINGS	LOSSY	LOUPING	LOW	LOYALTIES
LORDKIN	LOST	LOUPIT	LOWAN	LOYALTY
LORDKINS	LOT	LOUPS	LOWANS	LOYS
LORDLESS	LOTA	LOUR	LOWBOY	LOZELL
LORDLIER	LOTAH	LOURE	LOWBOYS	LOZELLS
LORDLIEST	LOTAHS	LOURED	LOWE	LOZEN
LORDLING	LOTAS	LOURES	LOWED	LOZENGE
LORDLINGS	LOTE	LOURING	LOWER	LOZENGED
LORDLY	LOTES	LOURINGLY	LOWERED	LOZENGES
LORDOSES	LOTH	LOURINGS	LOWERING	LOZENGY
LORDOSIS	LOTHEFULL	LOURS	LOWERINGS	LOZENS
LORDOTIC	LOTHER	LOURY	LOWERMOST	LUAU
LORDS	LOTHEST	LOUSE	LOWERS	LUAUS
LORDSHIP	LOTHFULL	LOUSED	LOWERY	LUBBARD
LORDSHIPS	LOTIC	LOUSES	LOWES	LUDDARDS
LORDY	LOTION	LOUSIER	LOWEST	LUBBER
LORE	LOTIONS	LOUSIEST	LOWING	LUBBERLY
LOREL	LOTO	LOUSILY	LOWINGS	LUBBERS
LORELS	LOTOS	LOUSINESS	LOWLAND	LUBFISH
LORES	LOTOSES	LOUSINESSES	LOWLANDER	LUBFISHES
LORETTE	LOTS	LOUSING	LOWLANDERS	LUBRA
LORETTES	LOTTED	LOUSY	LOWLANDS	LUBRAS
LORGNETTE	LOTTERIES	LOUT	LOWLIER	LUBRIC
LORGNETTES	LOTTERY	LOUTED	LOWLIEST	LUBRICAL
LORGNON	LOTTING	LOUTING	LOWLIHEAD	LUBRICANT
LORGNONS	LOTTO	LOUTISH	LOWLIHEADS	LUBRICANTS
LORIC	LOTTOS	LOUTISHLY	LOWLILY	LUBRICATE
LORICA	LOTUS	LOUTS	LOWLINESS	LUBRICATED
LORICATE	LOTUSES	LOUVER	LOWLINESSES	LUBRICATES
LORICATED	LOUCHE	LOUVERED	LOWLY	LUBRICATING
LORICATES	LOUCHELY	LOUVERS	LOWN	LUBRICITIES
LORICATING	LOUD	LOUVRE	LOWND	LUBRICITY
LORICS	LOUDEN	LOUVRED	LOWNDED	LUBRICOUS
LORIES	LOUDENED	LOUVRES	LOWNDING	LUCARNE
LORIKEET	LOUDENING	LOVABLE	LOWNDS	LUCARNES
LORIKEETS	LOUDENS	LOVAGE	LOWNE	LUCE
LORIMER	LOUDER	LOVAGES	LOWNED	LUCENCIES
LORIMERS	LOUDEST	LOVAT	LOWNES	LUCENCY
	LOUDISH	LOVATS	LOWNESS	LUCENT

LUCERN	LUGGAGES	LUMINIST	LUNGIE	LURRY
LUCERNE	LUGGED	LUMINISTS	LUNGIES	LURS
LUCERNES	LUGGER	LUMINOUS	LUNGING	LUSCIOUS
LUCERNS	LUGGERS	LUMME	LUNGIS	LUSH
LUCES	LUGGIE	LUMMOX	LUNGS	LUSHED
LUCID	LUGGIES	LUMMOXES	LUNGWORT	LUSHER
LUCIDER	LUGGING	LUMMY	LUNGWORTS	LUSHERS
LUCIDEST	LUGING	LUMP	LUNISOLAR	LUSHES
LUCIDITY	LUGINGS	LUMPED	LUNITIDAL	LUSHEST
LUCIDLY	LUGS	LUMPEN	LUNKER	LUSHING
LUCIDNESS	LUGSAIL	LUMPENLY	LUNKERS	LUSHLY
LUCIFER	LUGSAILS	LUMPER	LUNKHEAD	LUSHNESS
LUCIFERIN	LUGWORM	LUMPERS	LUNKHEADS	LUSHNESSES
LUCIFERINS	LUGWORMS	LUMPFISH	LUNT	LUSHY
LUCIFERS	LUIT	LUMPFISHES	LUNTED	LUSK
LUCIGEN	LUITEN	LUMPIER	LUNTING	LUSKED
LUCIGENS	LUKE	LUMPIEST	LUNTS	LUSKING
LUCK	LUKEWARM	LUMPILY	LUNULA	LUSKISH
LUCKEN	LULL	LUMPINESS	LUNULAR	LUSKS
LUCKIE	LULLABIED	LUMPINESSES	LUNULAS	LUST
LUCKIER	LULLABIES	LUMPING	LUNULATE	LUSTED
LUCKIES	LULLABY	LUMPISH	LUNULATED	LUSTER
LUCKIEST	LULLABYING	LUMPISHLY	LUNULE	LUSTERED
LUCKILY	LULLED	LUMPKIN	LUNULES	LUSTERING
LUCKINESS	LULLING	LUMPKINS	LUNYIE	LUSTERS
LUCKINESSES	LULLS	LUMPS	LUNYIES	LUSTFUL
LUCKLESS	LULU	LUMPY	LUPIN	LUSTFULLY
LUCKS	LULUS	LUMS	LUPINE	LUSTICK
LUCKY	LUM	LUNACIES	LUPINES	LUSTIER
LUCRATIVE	LUMBAGO	LUNACY	LUPINS	LUSTIEST
LUCRE	LUMBAGOS	LUNANAUT	LUPPEN	LUSTIHEAD
LUCRES	LUMBANG	LUNANAUTS	LUPULIN	LUSTIHEADS
LUCTATION	LUMBANGS	LUNAR	LUPULINE	LUSTIHOOD
LUCTATIONS	LUMBAR	LUNARIAN	LUPULINIC	LUSTIHOODS
LUCUBRATE	LUMBER	LUNARIANS	LUPULINS	LUSTILY
LUCUBRATED	LUMBERED	LUNARIES	LUPUS	LUSTINESS
LUCUBRATES	LUMBERER	LUNARIST	LUPUSES	LUSTINESSES
LUCUBRATING	LUMBERERS	LUNARISTS	LUR	LUSTING
LUCULENT	LUMBERING	LUNARNAUT	LURCH	LUSTIQUE
LUCUMA	LUMBERINGS	LUNARNAUTS	LURCHED	LUSTLESS
LUCUMAS	LUMBERLY	LUNARS	LURCHER	LUSTRA
LUCUMO	LUMBERMAN	LUNARY	LURCHERS	LUSTRAL
LUCUMONES	LUMBERMEN	LUNATE	LURCHES	LUSTRATE
LUCUMOS	LUMBERS	LUNATED	LURCHING	LUSTRATED
LUD	LUMBRICAL	LUNATIC	LURDAN	LUSTRATES
LUDIC	LUMBRICALS	LUNATICS	LURDANE	LUSTRATING
LUDICROUS	LUMBRICI	LUNATION	LURDANES	LUSTRE
LUDO	LUMBRICUS	LUNATIONS	LURDANS	LUSTRED
LUDOS	LUMBRICUSES	LUNCH	LURDEN	LUSTRES
LUDS	LUMEN	LUNCHED	LURDENS	LUSTRINE
LUDSHIP	LUMENAL	LUNCHEON	LURE	LUSTRINES
LUDSHIPS	LUMENS	LUNCHEONED	LURED	LUSTRING
LUES	LUMINA	LUNCHEONING	LURES	LUSTRINGS
LUESES	LUMINAIRE	LUNCHEONS	LURGIES	LUSTROUS
LUETIC	LUMINAIRES	LUNCHER	LURGY	LUSTRUM
LUFF	LUMINAL	LUNCHERS	LURID	LUSTRUMS
LUFFA	LUMINANCE	LUNCHES	LURIDER	LUSTS
LUFFAS	LUMINANCES	LUNCHING	LURIDEST	LUSTY
LUFFED	LUMINANT	LUNE	LURIDLY	LUTANIST
LUFFING	LUMINANTS	LUNES	LURIDNESS	LUTANISTS
LUFFS	LUMINARIES	LUNETTE	LURIDNESSES	LUTE
LUFTWAFFE	LUMINARY	LUNETTES	LURING	LUTEAL
LUFTWAFFES	LUMINE	LUNG	LURK	LUTECIUM
LUG	LUMINED	LUNGE	LURKED	LUTECIUMS
LUGE	LUMINES	LUNGED	LURKER	LUTED
LUGED	LUMINESCE	LUNGEING	LURKERS	LUTEIN
LUGEING	LUMINESCED	LUNGES	LURKING	LUTEINISE
LUGEINGS	LUMINESCES	LUNGFUL	LURKINGS	LUTEINISED
LUGES	LUMINESCING	LUNGFULS	LURKS	LUTEINISES
LUGGAGE	LUMINING	LUNGI	LURRIES	LUTEINISING

LUTEINIZE
LUTEINIZED
LUTEINIZES
LUTEINIZING
LUTEINS
LUTENIST
LUTENISTS
LUTEOLIN
LUTEOLINS
LUTEOLOUS
LUTEOUS
LUTER
LUTERS
LUTES
LUTESCENT
LUTETIUM
LUTETIUMS
LUTHERN
LUTHERNS
LUTHIER
LUTHIERS
LUTING
LUTINGS
LUTIST
LUTISTS
LUTTEN
LUTZ
LUTZES
LUX
LUXATE
LUXATED
LUXATES
LUXATING

LUXATION
LUXATIONS
LUXES
LUXMETER
LUXMETERS
LUXURIANT
LUXURIATE
LUXURIATED
LUXURIATES
LUXURIATING
LUXURIES
LUXURIOUS
LUXURIST
LUXURISTS
LUXURY
LUZ
LUZERN
LUZERNS
LUZZES
LYAM
LYAMS
LYART
LYCÉE
LYCÉES
LYCEUM
LYCEUMS
LYCHEE
LYCHEES
LYCHGATE
LYCHGATES
LYCHNIS
LYCHNISES
LYCOPOD

LYCOPODS
LYDDITE
LYDDITES
LYE
LYES
LYFULL
LYING
LYINGLY
LYINGS
LYKEWAKE
LYKEWAKES
LYKEWALK
LYKEWALKS
LYM
LYME
LYMES
LYMITER
LYMITERS
LYMPH
LYMPHAD
LYMPHADS
LYMPHATIC
LYMPHATICS
LYMPHOID
LYMPHOMA
LYMPHOMAS
LYMPHS
LYMS
LYNAGE
LYNAGES
LYNCEAN
LYNCH
LYNCHED

LYNCHES
LYNCHET
LYNCHETS
LYNCHING
LYNCHPIN
LYNCHPINS
LYNE
LYNES
LYNX
LYNXES
LYOMEROUS
LYOPHIL
LYOPHILE
LYOPHILIC
LYOPHOBE
LYOPHOBIC
LYRATE
LYRATED
LYRE
LYRES
LYRIC
LYRICAL
LYRICALLY
LYRICISM
LYRICISMS
LYRICIST
LYRICISTS
LYRICS
LYRIFORM
LYRISM
LYRISMS
LYRIST
LYRISTS

LYSE
LYSED
LYSERGIDE
LYSERGIDES
LYSES
LYSIGENIC
LYSIMETER
LYSIMETERS
LYSIN
LYSINE
LYSINES
LYSING
LYSINS
LYSIS
LYSOL
LYSOLS
LYSOSOME
LYSOSOMES
LYSOZYME
LYSOZYMES
LYSSA
LYSSAS
LYTE
LYTED
LYTES
LYTHE
LYTHES
LYTING
LYTTA
LYTTAS

M

MA
MAAR
MAARS
MAC
MACABRE
MACACO
MACACOS
MACADAM
MACADAMIA
MACADAMIAS
MACADAMS
MACAHUBA
MACAHUBAS
MACAQUE
MACAQUES
MACARISE
MACARISED
MACARISES
MACARISING
MACARISM
MACARISMS
MACARIZE
MACARIZED
MACARIZES
MACARIZING
MACARONI
MACARONIC
MACARONICS
MACARONIES
MACARONIS
MACAROON
MACAROONS
MACAW
MACAWS
MACCHIE
MACE
MACÉDOINE
MACÉDOINES
MACER
MACERATE
MACERATED
MACERATES
MACERATING
MACERATOR
MACERATORS
MACERS
MACES
MACHAIR
MACHAIRS
MACHAN
MACHANS
MACHETE
MACHETES
MACHINATE
MACHINATED
MACHINATES
MACHINATING
MACHINE
MACHINED
MACHINERIES
MACHINERY
MACHINES
MACHINING
MACHINIST

MACHINISTS
MACHISMO
MACHISMOES
MACHISMOS
MACHMETER
MACHMETERS
MACHO
MACHOS
MACHREE
MACHREES
MACHZOR
MACHZORIM
MACINTOSH
MACINTOSHES
MACK
MACKEREL
MACKERELS
MACKINAW
MACKINAWS
MACKLE
MACKLED
MACKLES
MACKLING
MACKS
MACLE
MACLED
MACLES
MACOYA
MACOYAS
MACRAMÉ
MACRAMÉS
MACRAMI
MACRAMIS
MACRO
MACROBIAN
MACROCODE
MACROCODES
MACROCOPIES
MACROCOPY
MACROCOSM
MACROCOSMS
MACROCYTE
MACROCYTES
MACRODOME
MACRODOMES
MACROLOGIES
MACROLOGY
MACRON
MACRONS
MACROPOD
MACROPODS
MACROS
MACRURAL
MACRUROUS
MACS
MACTATION
MACTATIONS
MACULA
MACULAE
MACULAR
MACULATE
MACULATED
MACULATES
MACULATING

MACULE
MACULES
MACULOSE
MAD
MADAM
MADAME
MADAMED
MADAMING
MADAMS
MADAROSES
MADAROSIS
MADBRAIN
MADBRAINED
MADCAP
MADCAPS
MADDED
MADDEN
MADDENED
MADDENING
MADDENS
MADDER
MADDERS
MADDEST
MADDING
MADDINGLY
MADE
MADEFIED
MADEFIES
MADEFY
MADEFYING
MADELEINE
MADELEINES
MADERISE
MADERISED
MADERISES
MADERISING
MADERIZE
MADERIZED
MADERIZES
MADERIZING
MADGE
MADGES
MADHOUSE
MADHOUSES
MADID
MADLING
MADLINGS
MADLY
MADMAN
MADMEN
MADNESS
MADNESSES
MADOQUA
MADOQUAS
MADRAS
MADRASA
MADRASAH
MADRASAHS
MADRASAS
MADRASES
MADRASSA
MADRASSAH
MADRASSAHS
MADRASSAS

MADREPORE
MADREPORES
MADRIGAL
MADRIGALS
MADROÑA
MADROÑAS
MADROÑO
MADROÑOS
MADS
MADWOMAN
MADWOMEN
MADWORT
MADWORTS
MADZOON
MADZOONS
MAE
MAELSTROM
MAELSTROMS
MAENAD
MAENADIC
MAENADS
MAESTOSO
MAESTRI
MAESTRO
MAESTROS
MAFFIA
MAFFIAS
MAFFICK
MAFFICKED
MAFFICKER
MAFFICKERS
MAFFICKING
MAFFICKINGS
MAFFICKS
MAFFLED
MAFFLIN
MAFFLING
MAFFLINGS
MAFFLINS
MAFIA
MAFIAS
MAFIOSI
MAFIOSO
MAG
MAGAZINE
MAGAZINES
MAGDALEN
MAGDALENE
MAGDALENES
MAGDALENS
MAGE
MAGENTA
MAGENTAS
MAGES
MAGESHIP
MAGESHIPS
MAGG
MAGGED
MAGGING
MAGGOT
MAGGOTS
MAGGOTY
MAGGS
MAGI

MAGIC
MAGICAL
MAGICALLY
MAGICIAN
MAGICIANS
MAGICKED
MAGICKING
MAGICS
MAGILP
MAGILPS
MAGISTER
MAGISTERIES
MAGISTERS
MAGISTERY
MAGISTRAL
MAGISTRALS
MAGLEV
MAGMA
MAGMAS
MAGMATA
MAGMATIC
MAGNALIUM
MAGNALIUMS
MAGNATE
MAGNATES
MAGNES
MAGNESES
MAGNESIA
MAGNESIAN
MAGNESIAS
MAGNESITE
MAGNESITES
MAGNESIUM
MAGNESIUMS
MAGNET
MAGNETIC
MAGNETICS
MAGNETISE
MAGNETISED
MAGNETISES
MAGNETISING
MAGNETISM
MAGNETISMS
MAGNETIST
MAGNETISTS
MAGNETITE
MAGNETITES
MAGNETIZE
MAGNETIZED
MAGNETIZES
MAGNETIZING
MAGNETO
MAGNETON
MAGNETONS
MAGNETOS
MAGNETRON
MAGNETRONS
MAGNETS
MAGNIFIC
MAGNIFICO
MAGNIFICOES
MAGNIFIED
MAGNIFIER
MAGNIFIERS

MAGNIFIES	MAIDLESS	MAINSTAYS	MALACHITES	MALIGN
MAGNIFY	MAIDS	MAINTAIN	MALACIA	MALIGNANT
MAGNIFYING	MAIEUTIC	MAINTAINED	MALACIAS	MALIGNANTS
MAGNITUDE	MAIEUTICS	MAINTAINING	MALADIES	MALIGNED
MAGNITUDES	MAIGRE	MAINTAINS	MALADROIT	MALIGNER
MAGNOLIA	MAIGRES	MAINTOP	MALADY	MALIGNERS
MAGNOLIAS	MAIK	MAINTOPS	MALAGUEÑA	MALIGNING
MAGNOX	MAIKO	MAINYARD	MALAGUEÑAS	MALIGNITIES
MAGNOXES	MAIKOS	MAINYARDS	MALAISE	MALIGNITY
MAGNUM	MAIKS	MAIOLICA	MALAISES	MALIGNLY
MAGNUMS	MAIL	MAIOLICAS	MALAMUTE	MALIGNS
MAGOT	MAILABLE	MAIRE	MALAMUTES	MALINGER
MAGOTS	MAILE	MAIRES	MALANDER	MALINGERED
MAGPIE	MAILED	MAISE	MALANDERS	MALINGERIES
MAGPIES	MAILER	MAISES	MALAPERT	MALINGERING
MAGS	MAILERS	MAIST	MALAR	MALINGERS
MAGSMAN	MAILES	MAISTER	MALARIA	MALINGERY
MAGSMEN	MAILING	MAISTERED	MALARIAL	MALIS
MAGUEY	MAILINGS	MAISTERING	MALARIAN	MALISON
MAGUEYS	MAILLOT	MAISTERS	MALARIAS	MALISONS
MAGUS	MAILLOTS	MAISTRIES	MALARIOUS	MALIST
MAGYAR	MAILMAN	MAISTRING	MALARKEY	MALKIN
MAHARAJA	MAILMEN	MAISTRINGS	MALARKEYS	MALKINS
MAHARAJAH	MAILMERGE	MAISTRY	MALARKIES	MALL
MAHARAJAHS	MAILMERGED	MAIZE	MALARKY	MALLAM
MAHARAJAS	MAILMERGES	MAIZES	MALARS	MALLAMS
MAHARANEE	MAILMERGING	MAJESTIC	MALATE	MALLANDER
MAHARANEES	MAILS	MAJESTIES	MALATES	MALLANDERS
MAHARANI	MAIM	MAJESTY	MALAX	MALLARD
MAHARANIS	MAIMED	MAJOLICA	MALAXAGE	MALLARDS
MAHARISHI	MAIMING	MAJOLICAS	MALAXAGES	MALLEABLE
MAHARISHIS	MAIMINGS	MAJOR	MALAXATE	MALLEATE
MAHATMA	MAIMS	MAJORAT	MALAXATED	MALLEATED
MAHATMAS	MAIN	MAJORATS	MALAXATES	MALLEATES
MAHLSTICK	MAINBOOM	MAJORED	MALAXATING	MALLEATING
MAHLSTICKS	MAINBOOMS	MAJORETTE	MALAXATOR	MALLECHO
MAHMAL	MAINBRACE	MAJORETTES	MALAXATORS	MALLECHOES
MAHMALS	MAINBRACES	MAJORING	MALAXED	MALLECHOS
MAHOE	MAINDOOR	MAJORITIES	MALAXES	MALLED
MAHOES	MAINDOORS	MAJORITY	MALAXING	MALLEE
MAHOGANIES	MAINED	MAJORS	MALE	MALLEES
MAHOGANY	MAINER	MAJORSHIP	MALEATE	MALLEI
MAHONIA	MAINEST	MAJORSHIPS	MALEATES	MALLEMUCK
MAHONIAS	MAINFRAME	MAJUSCULE	MALEDICT	MALLEMUCKS
MAHOUT	MAINFRAMES	MAJUSCULES	MALEDICTED	MALLENDER
MAHOUTS	MAINING	MAK	MALEDICTING	MALLENDERS
MAHSEER	MAINLAND	MAKABLE	MALEDICTS	MALLEOLAR
MAHSEERS	MAINLANDS	MAKAR	MALEFIC	MALLEOLI
MAHSIR	MAINLINE	MAKARS	MALEFICE	MALLEOLUS
MAHSIRS	MAINLINED	MAKE	MALEFICES	MALLEOLUSES
MAHUA	MAINLINER	MAKEABLE	MALEIC	MALLET
MAHUAS	MAINLINERS	MAKEBATE	MALEMUTE	MALLETS
MAHWA	MAINLINES	MAKEBATES	MALEMUTES	MALLEUS
MAHWAS	MAINLINING	MAKELESS	MALENGINE	MALLEUSES
MAHZOR	MAINLININGS	MAKER	MALENGINES	MALLING
MAHZORIM	MAINLY	MAKERS	MALES	MALLOW
MAID	MAINMAST	MAKES	MALFORMED	MALLOWS
MAIDAN	MAINMASTS	MAKESHIFT	MALGRADO	MALLS
MAIDANS	MAINOR	MAKESHIFTS	MALGRE	MALM
MAIDED	MAINORS	MAKIMONO	MALGRES	MALMAG
MAIDEN	MAINOUR	MAKIMONOS	MALI	MALMAGS
MAIDENISH	MAINOURS	MAKING	MALIC	MALMS
MAIDENLY	MAINPRISE	MAKINGS	MALICE	MALMSEY
MAIDENS	MAINPRISES	MAKO	MALICED	MALMSEYS
MAIDHOOD	MAINS	MAKOMAKO	MALICES	MALODOUR
MAIDHOODS	MAINSAIL	MAKOMAKOS	MALICHO	MALODOURS
MAIDING	MAINSAILS	MAKOS	MALICHOES	MALONATE
MAIDISH	MAINSHEET	MAKS	MALICHOS	MALONATES
MAIDISM	MAINSHEETS	MAL	MALICING	MALS
MAIDISMS	MAINSTAY	MALACHITE	MALICIOUS	MALSTICK

MALSTICKS	MAMMETRIES	MANDARINE	MANFULLY	MANIFESTING
MALT	MAMMETRY	MANDARINES	MANGABEY	MANIFESTO
MALTALENT	MAMMETS	MANDARINS	MANGABEYS	MANIFESTOED
MALTALENTS	MAMMIES	MANDATARIES	MANGAL	MANIFESTOES
MALTASE	MAMMIFER	MANDATARY	MANGALS	MANIFESTOING
MALTASES	MAMMIFERS	MANDATE	MANGANATE	MANIFESTOS
MALTED	MAMMIFORM	MANDATED	MANGANATES	MANIFESTS
MALTHA	MAMMILLA	MANDATES	MANGANESE	MANIFOLD
MALTHAS	MAMMILLAE	MANDATING	MANGANESES	MANIFOLDED
MALTIER	MAMMOCK	MANDATOR	MANGANIC	MANIFOLDING
MALTIEST	MAMMOCKED	MANDATORIES	MANGANIN	MANIFOLDS
MALTING	MAMMOCKING	MANDATORS	MANGANITE	MANIFORM
MALTINGS	MAMMOCKS	MANDATORY	MANGANITES	MANIHOC
MALTMAN	MAMMOGRAM	MANDIBLE	MANGANOUS	MANIHOCS
MALTMEN	MAMMOGRAMS	MANDIBLES	MANGE	MANIKIN
MALTOSE	MAMMON	MANDILION	MANGEL	MANIKINS
MALTOSES	MAMMONISH	MANDILIONS	MANGELS	MANILA
MALTREAT	MAMMONISM	MANDIOC	MANGER	MANILAS
MALTREATED	MAMMONISMS	MANDIOCA	MANGERS	MANILLA
MALTREATING	MAMMONIST	MANDIOCAS	MANGES	MANILLAS
MALTREATS	MAMMONISTS	MANDIOCCA	MANGETOUT	MANILLE
MALTS	MAMMONITE	MANDIOCCAS	MANGETOUTS	MANILLES
MALTSTER	MAMMONITES	MANDIOCS	MANGEY	MANIOC
MALTSTERS	MAMMONS	MANDIR	MANGIER	MANIOCS
MALTWORM	MAMMOTH	MANDIRA	MANGIEST	MANIPLE
MALTWORMS	MAMMOTHS	MANDIRAS	MANGINESS	MANIPLES
MALTY	MAMMY	MANDIRS	MANGINESSES	MANIPLIES
MALVA	MAMS	MANDOLA	MANGLE	MANIPULAR
MALVAS	MAMSELLE	MANDOLAS	MANGLED	MANIPULARS
MALVASIA	MAMSELLES	MANDOLIN	MANGLER	MANITO
MALVASIAS	MAN	MANDOLINE	MANGLERS	MANITOS
MALVESIE	MANA	MANDOLINES	MANGLES	MANITOU
MALVESIES	MANACLE	MANDOLINS	MANGLING	MANITOUS
MALVOISIE	MANACLED	MANDOM	MANGO	MANJACK
MALVOISIES	MANACLES	MANDOMS	MANGOES	MANJACKS
MAM	MANACLING	MANDORA	MANGOLD	MANKIER
MAMA	MANAGE	MANDORAS	MANGOLDS	MANKIEST
MAMAS	MANAGED	MANDORLA	MANGONEL	MANKIND
MAMBA	MANAGER	MANDORLAS	MANGONELS	MANKY
MAMBAS	MANAGERS	MANDRAKE	MANGOSTAN	MANLIER
MAMBO	MANAGES	MANDRAKES	MANGOSTANS	MANLIEST
MAMBOED	MANAGING	MANDREL	MANGOUSTE	MANLINESS
MAMBOING	MANAKIN	MANDRELS	MANGOUSTES	MANLINESSES
MAMBOS	MANAKINS	MANDRIL	MANGROVE	MANLY
MAMELON	MAÑANA	MANDRILL	MANGROVES	MANNA
MAMELONS	MAÑANAS	MANDRILLS	MANGY	MANNAS
MAMELUCO	MANAS	MANDRILS	MANHANDLE	MANNED
MAMELUCOS	MANATEE	MANDUCATE	MANHANDLED	MANNEQUIN
MAMILLA	MANATEES	MANDUCATED	MANHANDLES	MANNEQUINS
MAMILLAE	MANATI	MANDUCATES	MANHANDLING	MANNER
MAMILLAR	MANATIS	MANDUCATING	MANHOLE	MANNERED
MAMILLARY	MANCANDO	MANDYLION	MANHOLES	MANNERISM
MAMILLATE	MANCHE	MANDYLIONS	MANHOOD	MANNERISMS
MAMMA	MANCHES	MANE	MANHOODS	MANNERIST
MAMMAE	MANCHET	MANED	MANHUNT	MANNERISTS
MAMMAL	MANCHETS	MANÈGE	MANHUNTS	MANNERLY
MAMMALIAN	MANCIPATE	MANÈGED	MANIA	MANNERS
MAMMALOGIES	MANCIPATED	MANÈGES	MANIAC	MANNIKIN
MAMMALOGY	MANCIPATES	MANÈGING	MANIACAL	MANNIKINS
MAMMALS	MANCIPATING	MANEH	MANIACS	MANNING
MAMMARY	MANCIPLE	MANEHS	MANIAS	MANNISH
MAMMAS	MANCIPLES	MANELESS	MANIC	MANNITE
MAMMATE	MANCUS	MANENT	MANICALLY	MANNITES
MAMMEE	MANCUSES	MANES	MANICURE	MANNITOL
MAMMEES	MAND	MANET	MANICURED	MANNITOLS
MAMMER	MANDALA	MANEUVER	MANICURES	MANNOSE
MAMMERED	MANDALAS	MANEUVERED	MANICURING	MANNOSES
MAMMERING	MANDAMUS	MANEUVERING	MANIES	MANOAO
MAMMERS	MANDAMUSES	MANEUVERS	MANIFEST	MANOAOS
MAMMET	MANDARIN	MANFUL	MANIFESTED	MANOEUVRE

MANOEUVRED	MANTRAM	MARABOUTS	MARESCHAL	MARIPOSAS
MANOEUVRES	MANTRAMS	MARACA	MARESCHALLED	MARISCHAL
MANOEUVRING	MANTRAP	MARACAS	MARESCHALLING	MARISCHALLED
MANOMETER	MANTRAPS	MARAGING	MARESCHALS	MARISCHALLING
MANOMETERS	MANTRAS	MARAGINGS	MARG	MARISCHALS
MANOMETRIES	MANTUA	MARAH	MARGARIC	MARISH
MANOMETRY	MANTUAS	MARAHS	MARGARIN	MARISHES
MANOR	MANTY	MARAS	MARGARINE	MARITAGE
MANORIAL	MANUAL	MARASMIC	MARGARINES	MARITAGES
MANORS	MANUALLY	MARASMUS	MARGARINS	MARITAL
MANPACK	MANUALS	MARASMUSES	MARGARITA	MARITALLY
MANPACKS	MANUBRIA	MARATHON	MARGARITAS	MARITIME
MANPOWER	MANUBRIAL	MARATHONS	MARGARITE	MARJORAM
MANPOWERS	MANUBRIUM	MARAUD	MARGARITES	MARJORAMS
MANQUÉ	MANUKA	MARAUDED	MARGAY	MARK
MANRED	MANUKAS	MARAUDER	MARGAYS	MARKED
MANREDS	MANUL	MARAUDERS	MARGE	MARKEDLY
MANRENT	MANULS	MARAUDING	MARGENT	MARKER
MANRENTS	MANUMIT	MARAUDS	MARGENTED	MARKERS
MANRIDER	MANUMITS	MARAVEDI	MARGENTING	MARKET
MANRIDERS	MANUMITTED	MARAVEDIS	MARGENTS	MARKETED
MANS	MANUMITTING	MARBLE	MARGES	MARKETEER
MANSARD	MANURANCE	MARBLED	MARGIN	MARKETEERS
MANSARDS	MANURANCES	MARBLER	MARGINAL	MARKETER
MANSE	MANURE	MARBLERS	MARGINALS	MARKETERS
MANSES	MANURED	MARBLES	MARGINATE	MARKETING
MANSHIFT	MANURER	MARBLIER	MARGINATED	MARKETINGS
MANSHIFTS	MANURERS	MARBLIEST	MARGINED	MARKETS
MANSION	MANURES	MARBLING	MARGINING	MARKHOR
MANSIONS	MANURIAL	MARBLINGS	MARGINS	MARKHORS
MANSONRIES	MANURING	MARBLY	MARGOSA	MARKING
MANSONRY	MANURINGS	MARC	MARGOSAS	MARKINGS
MANSUETE	MANUS	MARCASITE	MARGRAVE	MARKKA
MANSWORN	MANY	MARCASITES	MARGRAVES	MARKKAA
MANTA	MANYFOLD	MARCATO	MARGS	MARKKAS
MANTAS	MANYPLIES	MARCEL	MARIA	MARKMAN
MANTEAU	MANZANITA	MARCELLA	MARIACHI	MARKMEN
MANTEAUS	MANZANITAS	MARCELLAS	MARIACHIS	MARKS
MANTEAUX	MANZELLO	MARCELLED	MARIALITE	MARKSMAN
MANTEEL	MANZELLOS	MARCELLING	MARIALITES	MARKSMEN
MANTEELS	MAORMOR	MARCELS	MARID	MARL
MANTEL	MAORMORS	MARCH	MARIDS	MARLE
MANTELET	MAP	MARCHED	MARIGOLD	MARLED
MANTELETS	MAPLE	MARCHER	MARIGOLDS	MARLES
MANTLETS	MAPLES	MARCHERS	MARIGRAM	MARLIER
MANTIC	MAPPED	MARCHES	MARIGRAMS	MARLIEST
MANTICORA	MAPPEMOND	MARCHESA	MARIGRAPH	MARLIN
MANTICORAS	MAPPEMONDS	MARCHESAS	MARIGRAPHS	MARLINE
MANTICORE	MAPPER	MARCHESE	MARIHUANA	MARLINES
MANTICORES	MAPPERIES	MARCHESES	MARIHUANAS	MARLING
MANTID	MAPPERS	MARCHESI	MARIJUANA	MARLINGS
MANTIDS	MAPPERY	MARCHING	MARIJUANAS	MARLINS
MANTIES	MAPPING	MARCHMAN	MARIMBA	MARLS
MANTILLA	MAPPIST	MARCHMEN	MARIMBAS	MARLSTONE
MANTILLAS	MAPPISTS	MARCHPANE	MARINA	MARLSTONES
MANTIS	MAPS	MARCHPANES	MARINADE	MARLY
MANTISES	MAPSTICK	MARCONI	MARINADED	MARM
MANTISSA	MAPSTICKS	MARCONIED	MARINADES	MARMALADE
MANTISSAS	MAPWISE	MARCONIES	MARINADING	MARMALADES
MANTLE	MAQUETTE	MARCONIING	MARINAS	MARMARISE
MANTLED	MAQUETTES	MARCS	MARINATE	MARMARISED
MANTLES	MAQUI	MARD	MARINATED	MARMARISES
MANTLET	MAQUIS	MARDIED	MARINATES	MARMARISING
MANTLETS	MAQUISARD	MARDIES	MARINATING	MARMARIZE
MANTLING	MAQUISARDS	MARDY	MARINE	MARMARIZED
MANTLINGS	MAR	MARDYING	MARINER	MARMARIZES
MANTO	MARA	MARE	MARINERS	MARMARIZING
MANTOES	MARABOU	MAREMMA	MARINES	MARMITE
MANTOS	MARABOUS	MAREMMAS	MARINIÈRE	MARMITES
MANTRA	MARABOUT	MARES	MARIPOSA	MARMOREAL

MARMOSE
MARMOSES
MARMOSET
MARMOSETS
MARMOT
MARMOTS
MARMS
MAROCAIN
MAROCAINS
MAROON
MAROONED
MAROONER
MAROONERS
MAROONING
MAROONINGS
MAROONS
MAROQUIN
MAROQUINS
MAROR
MARORS
MARPLOT
MARPLOTS
MARQUE
MARQUEE
MARQUEES
MARQUES
MARQUESS
MARQUESSES
MARQUETRIES
MARQUETRY
MARQUIS
MARQUISE
MARQUISES
MARRAM
MARRAMS
MARRED
MARRELS
MARRIAGE
MARRIAGES
MARRIED
MARRIER
MARRIERS
MARRIES
MARRING
MARROW
MARROWED
MARROWFAT
MARROWFATS
MARROWING
MARROWISH
MARROWS
MARROWSKIED
MARROWSKIES
MARROWSKY
MARROWSKYING
MARROWY
MARRUM
MARRUMS
MARRY
MARRYING
MARRYINGS
MARS
MARSH
MARSHAL
MARSHALCIES
MARSHALCY
MARSHALLED
MARSHALLING
MARSHALS
MARSHES

MARSHIER
MARSHIEST
MARSHLAND
MARSHLANDS
MARSHWORT
MARSHWORTS
MARSHY
MARSUPIA
MARSUPIAL
MARSUPIALS
MARSUPIUM
MARSUPIUMS
MART
MARTAGON
MARTAGONS
MARTED
MARTEL
MARTELLED
MARTELLING
MARTELLO
MARTELLOS
MARTELS
MARTEN
MARTENOT
MARTENOTS
MARTENS
MARTIAL
MARTIALLY
MARTIN
MARTINET
MARTINETS
MARTING
MARTINI
MARTINIS
MARTINS
MARTLET
MARTLETS
MARTS
MARTYR
MARTYRDOM
MARTYRDOMS
MARTYRED
MARTYRIES
MARTYRING
MARTYRISE
MARTYRISED
MARTYRISES
MARTYRISING
MARTYRIZE
MARTYRIZED
MARTYRIZES
MARTYRIZING
MARTYRS
MARTYRY
MARVEL
MARVELLED
MARVELLING
MARVELS
MARYBUD
MARYBUDS
MARZIPAN
MARZIPANS
MAS
MASCARA
MASCARAS
MASCARON
MASCARONS
MASCLE
MASCLED
MASCLES

MASCON
MASCONS
MASCOT
MASCOTS
MASCULINE
MASCULINES
MASCULY
MASE
MASED
MASER
MASERS
MASES
MASH
MASHALLAH
MASHED
MASHER
MASHERS
MASHES
MASHIE
MASHIER
MASHIES
MASHIEST
MASHING
MASHINGS
MASHLAM
MASHLAMS
MASHLIM
MASHLIMS
MASHLIN
MASHLINS
MASHLOCH
MASHLOCHS
MASHLUM
MASHLUMS
MASHMAN
MASHMEN
MASHY
MASING
MASJID
MASJIDS
MASK
MASKED
MASKER
MASKERS
MASKING
MASKS
MASLIN
MASLINS
MASOCHISM
MASOCHISMS
MASOCHIST
MASOCHISTS
MASON
MASONED
MASONIC
MASONING
MASONRIED
MASONRIES
MASONRY
MASONS
MASOOLAH
MASOOLAHS
MASQUE
MASQUER
MASQUERS
MASQUES
MASS
MASSA
MASSACRE
MASSACRED

MASSACRES
MASSACRING
MASSAGE
MASSAGED
MASSAGES
MASSAGING
MASSAGIST
MASSAGISTS
MASSAS
MASSÉ
MASSED
MASSES
MASSÉS
MASSETER
MASSETERS
MASSEUR
MASSEURS
MASSEUSE
MASSEUSES
MASSICOT
MASSICOTS
MASSIER
MASSIEST
MASSIF
MASSIFS
MASSINESS
MASSINESSES
MASSING
MASSIVE
MASSIVELY
MASSOOLA
MASSOOLAS
MASSY
MASSYMORE
MASSYMORES
MAST
MASTABA
MASTABAS
MASTED
MASTER
MASTERATE
MASTERATES
MASTERDOM
MASTERDOMS
MASTERED
MASTERFUL
MASTERIES
MASTERING
MASTERINGS
MASTERLY
MASTERS
MASTERY
MASTFUL
MASTHEAD
MASTHEADED
MASTHEADING
MASTHEADS
MASTHOUSE
MASTHOUSES
MASTIC
MASTICATE
MASTICATED
MASTICATES
MASTICATING
MASTICH
MASTICHS
MASTICOT
MASTICOTS
MASTICS
MASTIFF

MASTIFFS
MASTING
MASTITIS
MASTITISES
MASTLESS
MASTODON
MASTODONS
MASTOID
MASTOIDAL
MASTOIDS
MASTS
MASTY
MASU
MASULA
MASULAS
MASURIUM
MASURIUMS
MASUS
MAT
MATACHIN
MATACHINS
MATADOR
MATADORE
MATADORES
MATADORS
MATAMATA
MATAMATAS
MATCH
MATCHABLE
MATCHBOX
MATCHBOXES
MATCHED
MATCHER
MATCHERS
MATCHES
MATCHING
MATCHLESS
MATCHLOCK
MATCHLOCKS
MATCHWOOD
MATCHWOODS
MATE
MATÉ
MATED
MATELASSÉ
MATELASSÉS
MATELESS
MATELOT
MATELOTE
MATELOTES
MATELOTS
MATER
MATERIAL
MATERIALS
MATÉRIEL
MATÉRIELS
MATERNAL
MATERNITIES
MATERNITY
MATERS
MATES
MATÉS
MATEY
MATFELON
MATFELONS
MATGRASS
MATGRASSES
MATH
MATHESES
MATHESIS

MATHESISES
MATHS
MATICO
MATICOS
MATIER
MATIEST
MATIN
MATINAL
MATINEE
MATINÉE
MATINEES
MATINÉES
MATING
MATINS
MATLO
MATLOS
MATLOW
MATLOWS
MATRASS
MATRASSES
MATRIARCH
MATRIARCHS
MATRIC
MATRICE
MATRICES
MATRICIDE
MATRICIDES
MATRICS
MATRICULA
MATRICULAS
MATRILINIES
MATRILINY
MATRIMONIES
MATRIMONY
MATRIX
MATRIXES
MATRON
MATRONAGE
MATRONAGES
MATRONAL
MATRONISE
MATRONISED
MATRONISES
MATRONISING
MATRONIZE
MATRONIZED
MATRONIZES
MATRONIZING
MATRONLY
MATRONS
MATROSS
MATROSSES
MATS
MATT
MATTAMORE
MATTAMORES
MATTE
MATTED
MATTER
MATTERED
MATTERFUL
MATTERING
MATTERS
MATTERY
MATTES
MATTIE
MATTIES
MATTING
MATTINGS
MATTINS

MATTOCK
MATTOCKS
MATTOID
MATTOIDS
MATTRESS
MATTRESSES
MATURABLE
MATURATE
MATURATED
MATURATES
MATURATING
MATURE
MATURED
MATURELY
MATURER
MATURES
MATUREST
MATURING
MATURITIES
MATURITY
MATUTINAL
MATUTINE
MATWEED
MATWEEDS
MATY
MATZA
MATZAH
MATZAHS
MATZAS
MATZO
MATZOH
MATZOON
MATZOONS
MATZOS
MATZOT
MATZOTH
MAUD
MAUDLIN
MAUDS
MAUGRE
MAUGRES
MAUL
MAULED
MAULERS
MAULGRE
MAULGRES
MAULING
MAULS
MAULSTICK
MAULSTICKS
MAULVI
MAULVIS
MAUMET
MAUMETRIES
MAUMETRY
MAUMETS
MAUN
MAUND
MAUNDED
MAUNDER
MAUNDERED
MAUNDERER
MAUNDERERS
MAUNDERING
MAUNDERINGS
MAUNDERS
MAUNDIES
MAUNDING
MAUNDS
MAUNDY

MAUNNA
MAUSOLEAN
MAUSOLEUM
MAUSOLEUMS
MAUTHER
MAUTHERS
MAUVAIS
MAUVAISE
MAUVE
MAUVEIN
MAUVEINE
MAUVEINES
MAUVEINS
MAUVER
MAUVES
MAUVEST
MAUVIN
MAUVINE
MAUVINES
MAUVINS
MAVERICK
MAVERICKED
MAVERICKING
MAVERICKS
MAVIN
MAVINS
MAVIS
MAVISES
MAW
MAWBOUND
MAWK
MAWKIN
MAWKINS
MAWKISH
MAWKISHLY
MAWKS
MAWKY
MAWMET
MAWMETRIES
MAWMETRY
MAWMETS
MAWPUS
MAWPUSES
MAWR
MAWRS
MAWS
MAWSEED
MAWSEEDS
MAWTHER
MAWTHERS
MAX
MAXES
MAXI
MAXILLA
MAXILLAE
MAXILLARY
MAXILLULA
MAXILLULAE
MAXILLULAS
MAXIM
MAXIMA
MAXIMAL
MAXIMALLY
MAXIMIN
MAXIMINS
MAXIMISE
MAXIMISED
MAXIMISES
MAXIMISING
MAXIMIST

MAXIMISTS
MAXIMIZE
MAXIMIZED
MAXIMIZES
MAXIMIZING
MAXIMS
MAXIMUM
MAXIS
MAXIXE
MAXIXES
MAXWELL
MAXWELLS
MAY
MAYA
MAYAS
MAYBE
MAYBES
MAYDAY
MAYDAYS
MAYED
MAYEST
MAYFLIES
MAYFLOWER
MAYFLOWERS
MAYFLY
MAYHAP
MAYHEM
MAYHEMS
MAYING
MAYINGS
MAYOR
MAYORAL
MAYORALTIES
MAYORALTY
MAYORESS
MAYORESSES
MAYORS
MAYORSHIP
MAYORSHIPS
MAYPOLE
MAYPOLES
MAYS
MAYST
MAYSTER
MAYSTERS
MAYWEED
MAYWEEDS
MAZARD
MAZARDS
MAZARINE
MAZARINES
MAZE
MAZED
MAZEFUL
MAZEMENT
MAZEMENTS
MAZER
MAZERS
MAZES
MAZHBI
MAZHBIS
MAZIER
MAZIEST
MAZILY
MAZINESS
MAZINESSES
MAZING
MAZOUT
MAZOUTS
MAZUMA

MAZUMAS
MAZURKA
MAZURKAS
MAZUT
MAZUTS
MAZY
MAZZARD
MAZZARDS
ME
MEACOCK
MEACOCKS
MEAD
MEADOW
MEADOWS
MEADOWY
MEADS
MEAGRE
MEAGRELY
MEAGRER
MEAGRES
MEAGREST
MEAL
MEALED
MEALER
MEALERS
MEALIE
MEALIER
MEALIES
MEALIEST
MEALINESS
MEALINESSES
MEALING
MEALS
MEALY
MEAN
MEANDER
MEANDERED
MEANDERING
MEANDERS
MEANDRIAN
MEANDROUS
MEANE
MEANED
MEANER
MEANES
MEANEST
MEANIE
MEANIES
MEANING
MEANINGLY
MEANINGS
MEANLY
MEANNESS
MEANNESSES
MEANS
MEANT
MEANTIME
MEANTIMES
MEANWHILE
MEANWHILES
MEANY
MEARE
MEARES
MEASE
MEASED
MEASES
MEASING
MEASLE
MEASLED
MEASLES

MEASLIER
MEASLIEST
MEASLING
MEASLY
MEASURE
MEASURED
MEASURER
MEASURERS
MEASURES
MEASURING
MEASURINGS
MEAT
MEATAL
MEATH
MEATHE
MEATHEAD
MEATHEADS
MEATHES
MEATHS
MEATIER
MEATIEST
MEATINESS
MEATINESSES
MEATLESS
MEATS
MEATUS
MEATUSES
MEATY
MEAWES
MEAWESS
MEAZEL
MEAZELS
MEBOS
MEBOSES
MECHANIC
MECHANICS
MECHANISE
MECHANISED
MECHANISES
MECHANISING
MECHANISM
MECHANISMS
MECHANIST
MECHANISTS
MECHANIZE
MECHANIZED
MECHANIZES
MECHANIZING
MECONATE
MECONATES
MECONIC
MECONIN
MECONINS
MECONIUM
MECONIUMS
MEDAEWART
MEDAEWARTS
MEDAL
MEDALET
MEDALETS
MEDALLED
MEDALLIC
MEDALLING
MEDALLION
MEDALLIONED
MEDALLIONING
MEDALLIONS
MEDALLIST
MEDALLISTS
MEDALS

MEDDLE
MEDDLED
MEDDLER
MEDDLERS
MEDDLES
MEDDLING
MEDDLINGS
MEDIA
MEDIACIES
MEDIACY
MEDIAE
MEDIAEVAL
MEDIAL
MEDIALLY
MEDIALS
MEDIAN
MEDIANS
MEDIANT
MEDIANTS
MEDIATE
MEDIATED
MEDIATELY
MEDIATES
MEDIATING
MEDIATION
MEDIATIONS
MEDIATISE
MEDIATISED
MEDIATISES
MEDIATISING
MEDIATIVE
MEDIATIZE
MEDIATIZED
MEDIATIZES
MEDIATIZING
MEDIATOR
MEDIATORS
MEDIATORY
MEDIATRICES
MEDIATRIX
MEDIC
MEDICABLE
MEDICAID
MEDICAIDS
MEDICAL
MEDICALLY
MEDICALS
MEDICARE
MEDICARES
MEDICATE
MEDICATED
MEDICATES
MEDICATING
MEDICINAL
MEDICINE
MEDICINED
MEDICINER
MEDICINERS
MEDICINES
MEDICINING
MEDICK
MEDICKS
MEDICO
MEDICOS
MEDICS
MEDIEVAL
MEDII
MEDINA
MEDINAS
MEDIOCRE

MEDITATE
MEDITATED
MEDITATES
MEDITATING
MEDIUM
MEDIUMS
MEDIUS
MEDIUSES
MEDLAR
MEDLARS
MEDLE
MEDLED
MEDLES
MEDLEY
MEDLEYS
MEDLING
MEDRESSEH
MEDRESSEHS
MEDULLA
MEDULLAE
MEDULLAR
MEDULLARY
MEDULLAS
MEDULLATE
MEDUSA
MEDUSAE
MEDUSAN
MEDUSANS
MEDUSAS
MEDUSOID
MEDUSOIDS
MEED
MEEDS
MEEK
MEEKEN
MEEKENED
MEEKENING
MEEKENS
MEEKER
MEEKEST
MEEKLY
MEEKNESS
MEEKNESSES
MEER
MEERCAT
MEERCATS
MEERKAT
MEERKATS
MEERS
MEET
MEETER
MEETEST
MEETING
MEETINGS
MEETLY
MEETNESS
MEETNESSES
MEETS
MEGABAR
MEGABARS
MEGABIT
MEGABITS
MEGABYTE
MEGABYTES
MEGACURIE
MEGACURIES
MEGACYCLE
MEGACYCLES
MEGADEATH
MEGADEATHS

MEGADYNE
MEGADYNES
MEGAFARAD
MEGAFARADS
MEGAFAUNA
MEGAFLORA
MEGAFOG
MEGAFOGS
MEGAGAUSS
MEGAGAUSSES
MEGAHERTZ
MEGAHERTZES
MEGAJOULE
MEGAJOULES
MEGALITH
MEGALITHS
MEGAPHONE
MEGAPHONED
MEGAPHONES
MEGAPHONING
MEGAPODE
MEGAPODES
MEGARA
MEGARAD
MEGARADS
MEGARON
MEGARONS
MEGASCOPE
MEGASCOPES
MEGASPORE
MEGASPORES
MEGASS
MEGASSE
MEGASSES
MEGASTORE
MEGASTORES
MEGATON
MEGATONNE
MEGATONNES
MEGATONS
MEGAVOLT
MEGAVOLTS
MEGAWATT
MEGAWATTS
MEGILP
MEGILPS
MEGOHM
MEGOHMS
MEGRIM
MEGRIMS
MEIN
MEINED
MEINEY
MEINEYS
MEINIE
MEINIES
MEINING
MEINS
MEINT
MEINY
MEIOFAUNA
MEIONITE
MEIONITES
MEIOSES
MEIOSIS
MEIOTIC
MEITH
MEITHS
MEKOMETER
MEKOMETERS

MEL
MELAMINE
MELAMINES
MELAMPODE
MELAMPODES
MÉLANGE
MÉLANGES
MELANIC
MELANIN
MELANINS
MELANISM
MELANISMS
MELANITE
MELANITES
MELANO
MELANOMA
MELANOMAS
MELANOMATA
MELANOS
MELANOSIS
MELANOSISES
MELANOTIC
MELANOUS
MELANURIA
MELANURIAS
MELANURIC
MELAPHYRE
MELAPHYRES
MELATONIN
MELATONINS
MELD
MELDED
MELDER
MELDERS
MELDING
MELDS
MÊLÉE
MÊLÉES
MELIC
MELICS
MELILITE
MELILITES
MELILOT
MELILOTS
MELINITE
MELINITES
MELIORATE
MELIORATED
MELIORATES
MELIORATING
MELIORISM
MELIORISMS
MELIORIST
MELIORISTS
MELIORITIES
MELIORITY
MELISMA
MELISMAS
MELISMATA
MELL
MELLAY
MELLAYS
MELLED
MELLING
MELLITE
MELLITES
MELLITIC
MELLOW
MELLOWED
MELLOWER

MELLOWEST
MELLOWING
MELLOWLY
MELLOWS
MELLOWY
MELLS
MELOCOTON
MELOCOTONS
MELODEON
MELODEONS
MELODIC
MELODICS
MELODIES
MELODION
MELODIONS
MELODIOUS
MELODISE
MELODISED
MELODISES
MELODISING
MELODIST
MELODISTS
MELODIZE
MELODIZED
MELODIZES
MELODIZING
MELODRAMA
MELODRAMAS
MELODRAME
MELODRAMES
MELODY
MELOMANIA
MELOMANIAS
MELOMANIC
MELON
MELONS
MELS
MELT
MELTDOWN
MELTDOWNS
MELTED
MELTING
MELTINGLY
MELTINGS
MELTITH
MELTITHS
MELTON
MELTONS
MELTS
MEMBER
MEMBERED
MEMBERS
MEMBRAL
MEMBRANE
MEMBRANES
MEMENTO
MEMENTOES
MEMENTOS
MEMO
MEMOIR
MEMOIRISM
MEMOIRISMS
MEMOIRIST
MEMOIRISTS
MEMOIRS
MEMORABLE
MEMORABLY
MEMORANDA
MEMORIAL
MEMORIALS

MEMORIES
MEMORISE
MEMORISED
MEMORISES
MEMORISING
MEMORITER
MEMORIZE
MEMORIZED
MEMORIZES
MEMORIZING
MEMORY
MEMOS
MEN
MENACE
MENACED
MENACER
MENACERS
MENACES
MENACING
MENADIONE
MENADIONES
MÉNAGE
MENAGERIE
MENAGERIES
MÉNAGES
MENARCHE
MENARCHES
MEND
MENDACITIES
MENDACITY
MENDED
MENDER
MENDERS
MENDICANT
MENDICANTS
MENDICITIES
MENDICITY
MENDING
MENDINGS
MENDS
MENE
MENED
MENEER
MENEERS
MENES
MENFOLK
MENFOLKS
MENG
MENGE
MENGED
MENGES
MENGING
MENGS
MENHADEN
MENHADENS
MENHIR
MENHIRS
MENIAL
MENIALS
MENING
MENINGEAL
MENINGES
MENINX
MENISCI
MENISCOID
MENISCUS
MENISCUSES
MENOLOGIES
MENOLOGY
MENOMINEE

MENOMINEES
MENOPAUSE
MENOPAUSES
MENOPOME
MENOPOMES
MENORAH
MENORAHS
MENORRHEA
MENORRHEAS
MENSAL
MENSCH
MENSCHES
MENSE
MENSED
MENSEFUL
MENSELESS
MENSES
MENSH
MENSHED
MENSHES
MENSHING
MENSING
MENSTRUA
MENSTRUAL
MENSTRUUM
MENSTRUUMS
MENSUAL
MENSURAL
MENSWEAR
MENSWEARS
MENT
MENTAL
MENTALISM
MENTALISMS
MENTALIST
MENTALISTS
MENTALITIES
MENTALITY
MENTALLY
MENTATION
MENTATIONS
MENTHOL
MENTHOLS
MENTICIDE
MENTICIDES
MENTION
MENTIONED
MENTIONING
MENTIONS
MENTOR
MENTORIAL
MENTORING
MENTORINGS
MENTORS
MENTUM
MENTUMS
MENU
MENUS
MEOW
MEOWED
MEOWING
MEOWS
MEPACRINE
MEPACRINES
MEPHITIC
MEPHITIS
MEPHITISES
MEPHITISM
MEPHITISMS
MERC

MERCAPTAN
MERCAPTANS
MERCAT
MERCATS
MERCENARIES
MERCENARY
MERCER
MERCERIES
MERCERISE
MERCERISED
MERCERISES
MERCERISING
MERCERIZE
MERCERIZED
MERCERIZES
MERCERIZING
MERCERS
MERCERY
MERCHANT
MERCHANTED
MERCHANTING
MERCHANTS
MERCHET
MERCHETS
MERCHILD
MERCHILDREN
MERCIABLE
MERCIES
MERCIFIDE
MERCIFIED
MERCIFIES
MERCIFUL
MERCIFY
MERCIFYING
MERCILESS
MERCS
MERCURATE
MERCURATED
MERCURATES
MERCURATING
MERCURIAL
MERCURIC
MERCURIES
MERCUROUS
MERCURY
MERCY
MERE
MERED
MEREL
MERELL
MERELLS
MERELS
MERELY
MERER
MERES
MERESMAN
MERESMEN
MEREST
MERESTONE
MERESTONES
MERFOLK
MERFOLKS
MERGANSER
MERGANSERS
MERGE
MERGED
MERGENCE
MERGENCES
MERGER
MERGERS

MERGES
MERGING
MERI
MERICARP
MERICARPS
MERIDIAN
MERIDIANS
MERIL
MERILS
MERIMAKE
MERIMAKES
MERING
MERINGUE
MERINGUES
MERINO
MERINOS
MERIS
MERISM
MERISMS
MERISTEM
MERISTEMS
MERISTIC
MERIT
MERITED
MERITING
MERITS
MERK
MERKIN
MERKINS
MERKS
MERL
MERLE
MERLES
MERLIN
MERLING
MERLINGS
MERLINS
MERLON
MERLONS
MERLS
MERMAID
MERMAIDEN
MERMAIDENS
MERMAIDS
MERMAN
MERMEN
MEROGONIES
MEROGONY
MEROISTIC
MEROME
MEROMES
MEROPIDAN
MEROPIDANS
MEROSOME
MEROSOMES
MEROZOITE
MEROZOITES
MERPEOPLE
MERRIER
MERRIES
MERRIEST
MERRILY
MERRIMENT
MERRIMENTS
MERRINESS
MERRINESSES
MERRY
MERRYMADE
MERRYMAKER
MERRYMAKERS

MERRYMAKING	MESODERM	METALLING	METHANES	METRICATING
MERRYMAKINGS	MESODERMS	METALLINGS	METHANOL	METRICIAN
MERRYMAN	MESOGLOEA	METALLISE	METHANOLS	METRICIANS
MERRYMEN	MESOGLOEAS	METALLISED	METHEGLIN	METRICISE
MERSALYL	MESOLITE	METALLISES	METHEGLINS	METRICISED
MERSALYLS	MESOLITES	METALLISING	METHINK	METRICISES
MERSE	MESOMORPH	METALLIST	METHINKS	METRICISING
MERSES	MESOMORPHS	METALLISTS	METHOD	METRICIST
MERSION	MESON	METALLIZE	METHODIC	METRICISTS
MERSIONS	MESONIC	METALLIZED	METHODISE	METRICIZE
MERYCISM	MESONS	METALLIZES	METHODISED	METRICIZED
MERYCISMS	MESOPHYLL	METALLIZING	METHODISES	METRICIZES
MES	MESOPHYLLS	METALLOID	METHODISING	METRICIZING
MESA	MESOPHYTE	METALLOIDS	METHODIST	METRICS
MESAIL	MESOPHYTES	METALLY	METHODISTS	METRIFIER
MESAILS	MESOTRON	METALS	METHODIZE	METRIFIERS
MESAL	MESOTRONS	METAMER	METHODIZED	METRING
MESALLY	MESPRISE	METAMERE	METHODIZES	METRIST
MESARAIC	MESPRISES	METAMERES	METHODIZING	METRISTS
MESARCH	MESPRIZE	METAMERIC	METHODS	METRITIS
MESAS	MESPRIZES	METAMERS	METHOUGHT	METRITISES
MESCAL	MESQUIN	METANOIA	METHS	METRO
MESCALIN	MESQUINE	METANOIAS	METHYL	MÉTRO
MESCALINS	MESQUIT	METAPHASE	METHYLATE	METROLOGIES
MESCALISM	MESQUITE	METAPHASES	METHYLATED	METROLOGY
MESCALISMS	MESQUITES	METAPHOR	METHYLATES	METRONOME
MESCALS	MESQUITS	METAPHORS	METHYLATING	METRONOMES
MESDAMES	MESS	METAPLASM	METHYLENE	METROS
MESE	MESSAGE	METAPLASMS	METHYLENES	MÉTROS
MESEEMED	MESSAGED	MÉTAYAGE	METHYLIC	METTLE
MESEEMS	MESSAGES	MÉTAYAGES	METHYLS	METTLED
MESEL	MESSAGING	MÉTAYER	METHYSES	METTLES
MESELED	MESSAN	MÉTAYERS	METHYSIS	MEU
MESELS	MESSANS	METAZOA	METHYSTIC	MEUNIÈRE
MESENTERIES	MESSED	METAZOAN	METIC	MEUS
MESENTERY	MESSENGER	METAZOANS	METICAL	MEUSE
MESES	MESSENGERS	METAZOIC	METICALS	MEUSED
MESH	MESSES	METAZOON	METICS	MEUSES
MESHED	MESSIER	METCAST	MÉTIER	MEUSING
MESHES	MESSIEST	METCASTS	MÉTIERS	MEVE
MESHIER	MESSIEURS	METE	METIF	MEVED
MESHIEST	MESSILY	METED	METIFS	MEVES
MESHING	MESSINESS	METEOR	METING	MEVING
MESHINGS	MESSINESSES	METEORIC	MÉTIS	MEW
MESHUGA	MESSING	METEORISM	MÉTISSE	MEWED
MESHUGGA	MESSMATE	METEORISMS	MÉTISSES	MEWING
MESHUGGE	MESSMATES	METEORIST	METOL	MEWL
MESHY	MESSUAGE	METEORISTS	METOLS	MEWLED
MESIAL	MESSUAGES	METEORITE	METONYM	MEWLING
MESIALLY	MESSY	METEORITES	METONYMIC	MEWLS
MESIAN	MESTEE	METEOROID	METONYMIES	MEWS
MESIC	MESTEES	METEOROIDS	METONYMS	MEWSED
MESMERIC	MESTIZA	METEOROUS	METONYMY	MEWSES
MESMERISE	MESTIZAS	METEORS	METOPE	MEWSING
MESMERISED	MESTIZO	METER	METOPES	MEYNT
MESMERISES	MESTIZOS	METERED	METOPIC	MEZAIL
MESMERISING	MESTO	METERING	METOPISM	MEZAILS
MESMERISM	MET	METERS	METOPISMS	MÉZÉ
MESMERISMS	METABASES	METES	METOPON	MEZE
MESMERIST	METABASIS	METESTICK	METOPONS	MEZEREON
MESMERISTS	METABATIC	METESTICKS	METOPRYL	MEZEREONS
MESMERIZE	METABOLIC	METEWAND	METOPRYLS	MEZEREUM
MESMERIZED	METAGE	METEWANDS	METRE	MEZEREUMS
MESMERIZES	METAGES	METEYARD	METRED	MÉZÉS
MESMERIZING	MÉTAIRIE	METEYARDS	METRES	MEZES
MESNE	MÉTAIRIES	METHADON	METRIC	MEZUZA
MESOBLAST	METAL	METHADONE	METRICAL	MEZUZAH
MESOBLASTS	METALLED	METHADONES	METRICATE	MEZUZAHS
MESOCARP	METALLIC	METHADONS	METRICATED	MEZUZOTH
MESOCARPS	METALLINE	METHANE	METRICATES	MEZZANINE

MEZZANINES	MICROCHIPS	MIDFIELDS	MIGNONNE	MILITATE
MEZZO	MICROCODE	MIDGE	MIGRAINE	MILITATED
MEZZOS	MICROCODES	MIDGES	MIGRAINES	MILITATES
MEZZOTINT	MICROCOPIES	MIDGET	MIGRANT	MILITATING
MEZZOTINTS	MICROCOPY	MIDGETS	MIGRANTS	MILITIA
MGANGA	MICROCOSM	MIDI	MIGRATE	MILITIAS
MGANGAS	MICROCOSMS	MIDINETTE	MIGRATED	MILK
MHO	MICROCYTE	MIDINETTES	MIGRATES	MILKED
MHORR	MICROCYTES	MIDIRON	MIGRATING	MILKEN
MHORRS	MICRODOT	MIDIRONS	MIGRATION	MILKER
MHOS	MICRODOTS	MIDIS	MIGRATIONS	MILKERS
MI	MICROFILM	MIDLAND	MIGRATOR	MILKFISH
MIAOW	MICROFILMED	MIDLANDS	MIGRATORS	MILKFISHES
MIAOWED	MICROFILMING	MIDMOST	MIGRATORY	MILKIER
MIAOWING	MICROFILMS	MIDMOSTS	MIHRAB	MILKIEST
MIAOWS	MICROFORM	MIDNIGHT	MIHRABS	MILKILY
MIASM	MICROFORMS	MIDNIGHTS	MIKADO	MILKINESS
MIASMA	MICROGRAM	MIDNOON	MIKADOS	MILKINESSES
MIASMAL	MICROGRAMS	MIDNOONS	MIKE	MILKING
MIASMAS	MICROLITE	MIDRIB	MIKES	MILKINGS
MIASMATA	MICROLITES	MIDRIBS	MIKRON	MILKLESS
MIASMATIC	MICROLITH	MIDRIFF	MIKRONS	MILKLIKE
MIASMIC	MICROLITHS	MIDRIFFS	MIL	MILKMAID
MIASMOUS	MICROLOGIES	MIDS	MILADI	MILKMAIDS
MIASMS	MICROLOGY	MIDSHIP	MILADIES	MILKMAN
MIAUL	MICRON	MIDSHIPS	MILADIS	MILKMEN
MIAULED	MICRONS	MIDST	MILADY	MILKS
MIAULING	MICROPSIA	MIDSTREAM	MILAGE	MILKWOOD
MIAULS	MICROPSIAS	MIDSTREAMS	MILAGES	MILKWOODS
MICA	MICROPYLE	MIDSTS	MILCH	MILKWORT
MICACEOUS	MICROPYLES	MIDSUMMER	MILD	MILKWORTS
MICAS	MICROS	MIDSUMMERS	MILDEN	MILKY
MICATE	MICROSOME	MIDWAY	MILDENED	MILL
MICATED	MICROSOMES	MIDWAYS	MILDENING	MILLDAM
MICATES	MICROTOME	MIDWIFE	MILDENS	MILLDAMS
MICATING	MICROTOMES	MIDWIFED	MILDER	MILLE
MICE	MICROTOMIES	MIDWIFERIES	MILDEST	MILLED
MICELLA	MICROTOMY	MIDWIFERY	MILDEW	MILLENARIES
MICELLAR	MICROTONE	MIDWIFES	MILDEWED	MILLENARY
MICELLAS	MICROTONES	MIDWIFING	MILDEWING	MILLENNIA
MICELLE	MICROWAVE	MIDWIVE	MILDEWS	MILLEPED
MICELLES	MICROWAVES	MIDWIVED	MILDEWY	MILLEPEDE
MICHE	MICROWIRE	MIDWIVES	MILDLY	MILLEPEDES
MICHED	MICROWIRES	MIDWIVING	MILDNESS	MILLEPEDS
MICHER	MICRURGIES	MIEN	MILDNESSES	MILLEPORE
MICHERS	MICRURGY	MIENS	MILDS	MILLEPORES
MICHES	MICTION	MIEVE	MILE	MILLER
MICHING	MICTIONS	MIEVED	MILEAGE	MILLERITE
MICHINGS	MICTURATE	MIEVES	MILEAGES	MILLERITES
MICK	MICTURATED	MIEVING	MILER	MILLERS
MICKEY	MICTURATES	MIFF	MILERS	MILLES
MICKEYS	MICTURATING	MIFFED	MILES	MILLET
MICKIES	MID	MIFFIER	MILESTONE	MILLETS
MICKLE	MIDBRAIN	MIFFIEST	MILESTONES	MILLIARD
MICKLES	MIDBRAINS	MIFFINESS	MILFOIL	MILLIARDS
MICKS	MIDDAY	MIFFINESSES	MILFOILS	MILLIARE
MICKY	MIDDAYS	MIFFING	MILIARIA	MILLIARES
MICO	MIDDEN	MIFFS	MILIARIAS	MILLIARIES
MICOS	MIDDENS	MIFFY	MILIARY	MILLIARY
MICRO	MIDDEST	MIFTY	MILIEU	MILLIBAR
MICROBAR	MIDDIES	MIGHT	MILIEUS	MILLIBARS
MICROBARS	MIDDLE	MIGHTEST	MILIEUX	MILLIÈME
MICROBE	MIDDLED	MIGHTFUL	MILITANCIES	MILLIÈMES
MICROBES	MIDDLEMAN	MIGHTIER	MILITANCY	MILLIME
MICROBIAL	MIDDLEMEN	MIGHTIEST	MILITANT	MILLIMES
MICROBIAN	MIDDLES	MIGHTILY	MILITANTS	MILLINER
MICROBIC	MIDDLING	MIGHTS	MILITAR	MILLINERIES
MICROCARD	MIDDLINGS	MIGHTST	MILITARIA	MILLINERS
MICROCARDS	MIDDY	MIGHTY	MILITARIES	MILLINERY
MICROCHIP	MIDFIELD	MIGNON	MILITARY	MILLING

MILLINGS	MIMING	MINGLES	MINK	MINYANS
MILLION	MIMMER	MINGLING	MINKE	MIOSES
MILLIONS	MIMMEST	MINGLINGS	MINKES	MIOSIS
MILLIONTH	MIMMICK	MINGS	MINKS	MIR
MILLIONTHS	MIMMICKED	MINGY	MINNEOLA	MIRABELLE
MILLIPED	MIMMICKING	MINI	MINNEOLAS	MIRABELLES
MILLIPEDE	MIMMICKS	MINIATE	MINNICK	MIRABILIA
MILLIPEDES	MIMOSA	MINIATED	MINNICKED	MIRABILIS
MILLIPEDS	MIMOSAS	MINIATES	MINNICKING	MIRABILISES
MILLOCRAT	MIMULUS	MINIATING	MINNICKS	MIRABLE
MILLOCRATS	MIMULUSES	MINIATION	MINNIE	MIRACLE
MILLPOND	MINA	MINIATIONS	MINNIES	MIRACLES
MILLPONDS	MINACIOUS	MINIATURE	MINNOCK	MIRADOR
MILLRACE	MINACITIES	MINIATURED	MINNOCKED	MIRADORS
MILLRACES	MINACITY	MINIATURES	MINNOCKING	MIRAGE
MILLRIND	MINAE	MINIATURING	MINNOCKS	MIRAGES
MILLRINDS	MINAR	MINIBUS	MINNOW	MIRBANE
MILLS	MINARET	MINIBUSES	MINNOWS	MIRE
MILLSTONE	MINARETS	MINIFIED	MINO	MIRED
MILLSTONES	MINARS	MINIFIES	MINOR	MIREPOIX
MILLTAIL	MINAS	MINIFY	MINORESS	MIRES
MILLTAILS	MINATORY	MINIFYING	MINORESSES	MIRIER
MILO	MINBAR	MINIKIN	MINORITE	MIRIEST
MILOMETER	MINBARS	MINIKINS	MINORITES	MIRIFIC
MILOMETERS	MINCE	MINIM	MINORITIES	MIRIFICAL
MILOR	MINCED	MINIMA	MINORITY	MIRINESS
MILORD	MINCEMEAT	MINIMAL	MINORS	MIRINESSES
MILORDS	MINCEMEATS	MINIMENT	MINORSHIP	MIRING
MILORS	MINCER	MINIMENTS	MINORSHIPS	MIRITI
MILOS	MINCERS	MINIMISE	MINOS	MIRITIS
MILREIS	MINCES	MINIMISED	MINSTER	MIRK
MILS	MINCING	MINIMISES	MINSTERS	MIRKER
MILSEY	MINCINGLY	MINIMISING	MINSTREL	MIRKEST
MILSEYS	MINCINGS	MINIMISM	MINSTRELS	MIRKIER
MILT	MIND	MINIMISMS	MINT	MIRKIEST
MILTED	MINDED	MINIMIST	MINTAGE	MIRKS
MILTER	MINDER	MINIMISTS	MINTAGES	MIRKSOME
MILTERS	MINDERS	MINIMIZE	MINTED	MIRKY
MILTING	MINDFUL	MINIMIZED	MINTER	MIRLIGOES
MILTONIA	MINDFULLY	MINIMIZES	MINTERS	MIRLITON
MILTONIAS	MINDING	MINIMIZING	MINTIER	MIRLITONS
MILTS	MINDINGS	MINIMS	MINTIEST	MIRLY
MILTZ	MINDLESS	MINIMUM	MINTING	MIRROR
MILTZES	MINDS	MINIMUS	MINTS	MIRRORED
MILVINE	MINDSET	MINIMUSES	MINTY	MIRRORING
MIM	MINDSETS	MINING	MINUEND	MIRRORS
MIMBAR	MINE	MININGS	MINUENDS	MIRS
MIMBARS	MINED	MINION	MINUET	MIRTH
MIME	MINEOLA	MINIONS	MINUETS	MIRTHFUL
MIMED	MINEOLAS	MINIPILL	MINUS	MIRTHLESS
MIMER	MINER	MINIPILLS	MINUSCULE	MIRTHS
MIMERS	MINERAL	MINIS	MINUSCULES	MIRY
MIMES	MINERALS	MINISCULE	MINUSES	MIS
MIMESES	MINERS	MINISCULES	MINUTE	MISADVISE
MIMESIS	MINES	MINISH	MINUTED	MISADVISED
MIMESTER	MINETTE	MINISHED	MINUTELY	MISADVISES
MIMESTERS	MINETTES	MINISHES	MINUTEMAN	MISADVISING
MIMETIC	MINEVER	MINISHING	MINUTEMEN	MISAIM
MIMETICAL	MINEVERS	MINISTER	MINUTER	MISAIMED
MIMETITE	MING	MINISTERED	MINUTES	MISAIMING
MIMETITES	MINGED	MINISTERING	MINUTEST	MISAIMS
MIMIC	MINGIER	MINISTERS	MINUTIA	MISALLEGE
MIMICAL	MINGIEST	MINISTRIES	MINUTIAE	MISALLEGED
MIMICKED	MINGINESS	MINISTRY	MINUTING	MISALLEGES
MIMICKER	MINGINESSES	MINIUM	MINUTIOSE	MISALLEGING
MIMICKERS	MINGING	MINIUMS	MINX	MISALLIED
MIMICKING	MINGLE	MINIVER	MINXES	MISALLOT
MIMICRIES	MINGLED	MINIVERS	MINY	MISALLOTS
MIMICRY	MINGLER	MINIVET	MINYAN	MISALLOTTED
MIMICS	MINGLERS	MINIVETS	MINYANIM	MISALLOTTING

MISANDRIES
MISANDRY
MISAPPLIED
MISAPPLIES
MISAPPLY
MISAPPLYING
MISARRAY
MISARRAYS
MISASSIGN
MISASSIGNED
MISASSIGNING
MISASSIGNS
MISAUNTER
MISAUNTERS
MISAVISED
MISBECAME
MISBECOME
MISBECOMES
MISBECOMING
MISBEGOT
MISBEHAVE
MISBEHAVED
MISBEHAVES
MISBEHAVING
MISBELIEF
MISBELIEFS
MISBESEEM
MISBESEEMED
MISBESEEMING
MISBESEEMS
MISBESTOW
MISBESTOWED
MISBESTOWING
MISBESTOWS
MISBIRTH
MISBIRTHS
MISBORN
MISCALL
MISCALLED
MISCALLING
MISCALLS
MISCARRIED
MISCARRIES
MISCARRY
MISCARRYING
MISCAST
MISCASTED
MISCASTING
MISCASTS
MISCEGEN
MISCEGENE
MISCEGENES
MISCEGENS
MISCEGINE
MISCEGINES
MISCHANCE
MISCHANCED
MISCHANCES
MISCHANCING
MISCHANCY
MISCHARGE
MISCHARGED
MISCHARGES
MISCHARGING
MISCHIEF
MISCHIEFED
MISCHIEFING
MISCHIEFS
MISCIBLE
MISCOLOUR

MISCOLOURED
MISCOLOURING
MISCOLOURS
MISCOPIED
MISCOPIES
MISCOPY
MISCOPYING
MISCOUNT
MISCOUNTED
MISCOUNTING
MISCOUNTS
MISCREANT
MISCREANTS
MISCREATE
MISCREDIT
MISCREDITED
MISCREDITING
MISCREDITS
MISCREED
MISCREEDS
MISCUE
MISCUED
MISCUEING
MISCUES
MISCUING
MISDATE
MISDATED
MISDATES
MISDATING
MISDEAL
MISDEALING
MISDEALS
MISDEALT
MISDEED
MISDEEDS
MISDEEM
MISDEEMED
MISDEEMING
MISDEEMINGS
MISDEEMS
MISDEMEAN
MISDEMEANED
MISDEMEANING
MISDEMEANS
MISDEMPT
MISDESERT
MISDOCENTS
MISDID
MISDIET
MISDIETS
MISDIGHT
MISDIRECT
MISDIRECTED
MISDIRECTING
MISDIRECTS
MISDO
MISDOER
MISDOERS
MISDOES
MISDOING
MISDOINGS
MISDONE
MISDONNE
MISDOUBT
MISDOUBTED
MISDOUBTING
MISDOUBTS
MISDRAW
MISDRAWING
MISDRAWINGS

MISDRAWN
MISDRAWS
MISDREAD
MISDREADS
MISDREW
MISE
MISEASE
MISEASES
MISED
MISEMPLOY
MISEMPLOYED
MISEMPLOYING
MISEMPLOYS
MISENTRIES
MISENTRY
MISER
MISERABLE
MISERABLES
MISERABLY
MISERE
MISÈRE
MISERERE
MISERERES
MISÈRES
MISERIES
MISERLY
MISERS
MISERY
MISES
MISESTEEM
MISESTEEMED
MISESTEEMING
MISESTEEMS
MISFAITH
MISFAITHS
MISFALL
MISFALLEN
MISFALLING
MISFALLS
MISFALNE
MISFARE
MISFARED
MISFARES
MISFARING
MISFARINGS
MISFEASOR
MISFEASORS
MISFEIGN
MISFEIGNED
MISFEIGNING
MISFEIGNS
MISFELL
MISFILE
MISFILED
MISFILES
MISFILING
MISFIRE
MISFIRED
MISFIRES
MISFIRING
MISFIT
MISFITS
MISFITTED
MISFITTING
MISFORM
MISFORMED
MISFORMING
MISFORMS
MISGAVE
MISGIVE

MISGIVEN
MISGIVES
MISGIVING
MISGIVINGS
MISGO
MISGOES
MISGOING
MISGONE
MISGOTTEN
MISGOVERN
MISGOVERNED
MISGOVERNING
MISGOVERNS
MISGRAFF
MISGRAFFED
MISGRAFFING
MISGRAFFS
MISGRAFT
MISGROWTH
MISGROWTHS
MISGUGGLE
MISGUGGLED
MISGUGGLES
MISGUGGLING
MISGUIDE
MISGUIDED
MISGUIDER
MISGUIDERS
MISGUIDES
MISGUIDING
MISHANDLE
MISHANDLED
MISHANDLES
MISHANDLING
MISHANTER
MISHANTERS
MISHAP
MISHAPPED
MISHAPPEN
MISHAPPENED
MISHAPPENING
MISHAPPENS
MISHAPPING
MISHAPS
MISHAPT
MISHEAR
MISHEARD
MISHEARING
MISHEARS
MISHIT
MISHITS
MISHITTING
MISHMASH
MISHMASHES
MISHMEE
MISHMEES
MISHMI
MISHMIS
MISINFORM
MISINFORMED
MISINFORMING
MISINFORMS
MISING
MISINTEND
MISINTENDED
MISINTENDING
MISINTENDS
MISJOIN
MISJOINED
MISJOINING

MISJOINS
MISJUDGE
MISJUDGED
MISJUDGES
MISJUDGING
MISKEN
MISKENNED
MISKENNING
MISKENS
MISKENT
MISKNEW
MISKNOW
MISKNOWING
MISKNOWN
MISKNOWS
MISLAID
MISLAY
MISLAYING
MISLAYS
MISLEAD
MISLEADER
MISLEADERS
MISLEADING
MISLEADS
MISLEARED
MISLED
MISLEEKE
MISLEEKED
MISLEEKES
MISLEEKING
MISLETOE
MISLETOES
MISLIGHT
MISLIGHTING
MISLIGHTS
MISLIKE
MISLIKED
MISLIKER
MISLIKERS
MISLIKES
MISLIKING
MISLIKINGS
MISLIPPEN
MISLIPPENED
MISLIPPENING
MISLIPPENS
MISLIT
MISLIVE
MISLIVED
MISLIVES
MISLIVING
MISLUCK
MISLUCKED
MISLUCKING
MISLUCKS
MISMADE
MISMAKE
MISMAKES
MISMAKING
MISMANAGE
MISMANAGED
MISMANAGES
MISMANAGING
MISMARRIED
MISMARRIES
MISMARRY
MISMARRYING
MISMATCH
MISMATCHED
MISMATCHES

MISMATCHING
MISMATE
MISMATED
MISMATES
MISMATING
MISMETRE
MISMETRED
MISMETRES
MISMETRING
MISNAME
MISNAMED
MISNAMES
MISNAMING
MISNOMER
MISNOMERED
MISNOMERING
MISNOMERS
MISO
MISOCLERE
MISOGAMIES
MISOGAMY
MISOGYNIES
MISOGYNY
MISOLOGIES
MISOLOGY
MISONEISM
MISONEISMS
MISONEIST
MISONEISTS
MISORDER
MISORDERED
MISORDERING
MISORDERS
MISOS
MISPICKEL
MISPICKELS
MISPLACE
MISPLACED
MISPLACES
MISPLACING
MISPLAY
MISPLAYED
MISPLAYING
MISPLAYS
MISPLEAD
MISPLEADED
MISPLEADING
MISPLEADINGS
MISPLEADS
MISPLEASE
MISPLEASED
MISPLEASES
MISPLEASING
MISPLED
MISPOINT
MISPOINTED
MISPOINTING
MISPOINTS
MISPRAISE
MISPRAISED
MISPRAISES
MISPRAISING
MISPRINT
MISPRINTED
MISPRINTING
MISPRINTS
MISPRISE
MISPRISED
MISPRISES
MISPRISING

MISPRIZE
MISPRIZED
MISPRIZES
MISPRIZING
MISPROUD
MISQUOTE
MISQUOTED
MISQUOTES
MISQUOTING
MISRATE
MISRATED
MISRATES
MISRATING
MISREAD
MISREADING
MISREADINGS
MISREADS
MISRECKON
MISRECKONED
MISRECKONING
MISRECKONINGS
MISRECKONS
MISREGARD
MISREGARDS
MISRELATE
MISRELATED
MISRELATES
MISRELATING
MISREPORT
MISREPORTED
MISREPORTING
MISREPORTS
MISRULE
MISRULED
MISRULES
MISRULING
MISS
MISSA
MISSABLE
MISSAID
MISSAL
MISSALS
MISSAS
MISSAW
MISSAY
MISSAYING
MISSAYINGS
MISSAYS
MISSED
MISSEE
MISSEEING
MISSEEM
MISSEEMED
MISSEEMING
MISSEEMINGS
MISSEEMS
MISSEEN
MISSEES
MISSEL
MISSELS
MISSEND
MISSENDING
MISSENDS
MISSENT
MISSES
MISSET
MISSETS
MISSETTING
MISSHAPE
MISSHAPED

MISSHAPEN
MISSHAPES
MISSHAPING
MISSHOOD
MISSHOODS
MISSIES
MISSILE
MISSILERIES
MISSILERY
MISSILES
MISSILRIES
MISSILRY
MISSING
MISSINGLY
MISSION
MISSIONED
MISSIONER
MISSIONERS
MISSIONING
MISSIONS
MISSIS
MISSISES
MISSISH
MISSIVE
MISSIVES
MISSPEAK
MISSPEAKING
MISSPEAKS
MISSPELL
MISSPELLED
MISSPELLING
MISSPELLINGS
MISSPELLS
MISSPELT
MISSPEND
MISSPENDING
MISSPENDS
MISSPENT
MISSPOKE
MISSPOKEN
MISSTATE
MISSTATED
MISSTATES
MISSTATING
MISSTEP
MISSTEPPED
MISSTEPPING
MISSTEPS
MISSUIT
MISSUITED
MISSUITING
MISSUITS
MISSUS
MISSUSES
MISSY
MIST
MISTAKE
MISTAKEN
MISTAKES
MISTAKING
MISTAKINGS
MISTAUGHT
MISTEACH
MISTEACHES
MISTEACHING
MISTED
MISTELL
MISTELLING
MISTELLS
MISTEMPER

MISTEMPERED
MISTEMPERING
MISTEMPERS
MISTER
MISTERED
MISTERIES
MISTERING
MISTERM
MISTERMED
MISTERMING
MISTERMS
MISTERS
MISTERY
MISTFUL
MISTHINK
MISTHINKING
MISTHINKS
MISTHOUGHT
MISTHOUGHTS
MISTICO
MISTICOS
MISTIER
MISTIEST
MISTIGRIS
MISTIGRISES
MISTILY
MISTIME
MISTIMED
MISTIMES
MISTIMING
MISTINESS
MISTINESSES
MISTING
MISTINGS
MISTITLE
MISTITLED
MISTITLES
MISTITLING
MISTLE
MISTLED
MISTLES
MISTLETOE
MISTLETOES
MISTLING
MISTOLD
MISTOOK
MISTRAL
MISTRALS
MISTREAT
MISTREATED
MISTREATING
MISTREATS
MISTRESS
MISTRESSED
MISTRESSES
MISTRESSING
MISTRIAL
MISTRIALS
MISTRUST
MISTRUSTED
MISTRUSTING
MISTRUSTS
MISTRYST
MISTRYSTED
MISTRYSTING
MISTRYSTS
MISTS
MISTUNE
MISTUNED
MISTUNES

MISTUNING
MISTY
MISUSAGE
MISUSAGES
MISUSE
MISUSED
MISUSER
MISUSERS
MISUSES
MISUSING
MISUST
MISWEEN
MISWEENED
MISWEENING
MISWEENS
MISWEND
MISWENDING
MISWENDS
MISWENT
MISWORD
MISWORDED
MISWORDING
MISWORDINGS
MISWORDS
MISWRITE
MISWRITES
MISWRITING
MISWRITTEN
MISWROTE
MISYOKE
MISYOKED
MISYOKES
MISYOKING
MITCH
MITCHED
MITCHES
MITCHING
MITE
MITER
MITERED
MITERING
MITERS
MITES
MITHER
MITHERED
MITHERING
MITHERS
MITICIDAL
MITICIDE
MITICIDES
MITIER
MITIEST
MITIGABLE
MITIGANT
MITIGATE
MITIGATED
MITIGATES
MITIGATING
MITIGATOR
MITIGATORS
MITOGEN
MITOGENIC
MITOGENS
MITOSES
MITOSIS
MITOTIC
MITRAILLE
MITRAILLES
MITRAL
MITRE

MITRED
MITRES
MITRIFORM
MITRING
MITT
MITTEN
MITTENED
MITTENS
MITTIMUS
MITTIMUSES
MITTS
MITY
MITZVAH
MITZVAHS
MITZVOTH
MIURUS
MIURUSES
MIX
MIXABLE
MIXED
MIXEDLY
MIXEDNESS
MIXEDNESSES
MIXEN
MIXENS
MIXER
MIXERS
MIXES
MIXIER
MIXIEST
MIXING
MIXT
MIXTION
MIXTIONS
MIXTURE
MIXTURES
MIXY
MIZ
MIZEN
MIZENS
MIZES
MIZMAZE
MIZMAZES
MIZZ
MIZZEN
MIZZENS
MIZZES
MIZZLE
MIZZLED
MIZZLES
MIZZLIER
MIZZLIEST
MIZZLING
MIZZLINGS
MIZZLY
MIZZONITE
MIZZONITES
MNA
MNAS
MNEME
MNEMES
MNEMIC
MNEMON
MNEMONIC
MNEMONICS
MNEMONIST
MNEMONISTS
MNEMONS
MO
MOA

MOAN
MOANED
MOANER
MOANERS
MOANFUL
MOANFULLY
MOANING
MOANS
MOAS
MOAT
MOATED
MOATING
MOATS
MOB
MOBBED
MOBBIE
MOBBIES
MOBBING
MOBBISH
MOBBLE
MOBBLED
MOBBLES
MOBBLING
MOBBY
MOBILE
MOBILES
MOBILISE
MOBILISED
MOBILISES
MOBILISING
MOBILITIES
MOBILITY
MOBILIZE
MOBILIZED
MOBILIZES
MOBILIZING
MOBLE
MOBLED
MOBLES
MOBLING
MOBOCRACIES
MOBOCRACY
MOBOCRAT
MOBOCRATS
MOBS
MOBSMAN
MOBSMEN
MOBSTER
MOBSTERS
MOCASSIN
MOCASSINS
MOCCASIN
MOCCASINS
MOCHA
MOCHAS
MOCHELL
MOCHELLS
MOCK
MOCKABLE
MOCKADO
MOCKADOES
MOCKAGE
MOCKAGES
MOCKED
MOCKER
MOCKERIES
MOCKERS
MOCKERY
MOCKING
MOCKINGLY

MOCKINGS
MOCKS
MOCOCK
MOCOCKS
MOCUCK
MOCUCKS
MOCUDDUM
MOCUDDUMS
MOD
MODAL
MODALISM
MODALISMS
MODALIST
MODALISTS
MODALITIES
MODALITY
MODALLY
MODE
MODEL
MODELLED
MODELLER
MODELLERS
MODELLING
MODELLINGS
MODELS
MODEM
MODEMS
MODENA
MODENAS
MODERATE
MODERATED
MODERATES
MODERATING
MODERATO
MODERATOR
MODERATORS
MODERN
MODERNER
MODERNEST
MODERNISE
MODERNISED
MODERNISES
MODERNISING
MODERNISM
MODERNISMS
MODERNIST
MODERNISTS
MODERNITIES
MODERNITY
MODERNIZE
MODERNIZED
MODERNIZES
MODERNIZING
MODERNLY
MODERNS
MODES
MODEST
MODESTER
MODESTEST
MODESTIES
MODESTLY
MODESTY
MODI
MODICUM
MODICUMS
MODIFIED
MODIFIER
MODIFIERS
MODIFIES
MODIFY

MODIFYING
MODII
MODILLION
MODILLIONS
MODIOLAR
MODIOLI
MODIOLUS
MODIOLUSES
MODISH
MODISHLY
MODIST
MODISTE
MODISTES
MODISTS
MODIUS
MODIWORT
MODIWORTS
MODS
MODULAR
MODULATE
MODULATED
MODULATES
MODULATING
MODULATOR
MODULATORS
MODULE
MODULES
MODULI
MODULO
MODULUS
MODUS
MOE
MOED
MOEING
MOELLON
MOELLONS
MOES
MOFETTE
MOFETTES
MOFUSSIL
MOFUSSILS
MOG
MOGGAN
MOGGANS
MOGGIE
MOGGIES
MOGGY
MOGS
MOGUL
MOGULS
MOHAIR
MOHAIRS
MOHAWK
MOHAWKS
MOHEL
MOHELS
MOHR
MOHRS
MOHUR
MOHURS
MOIDER
MOIDERED
MOIDERING
MOIDERS
MOIDORE
MOIDORES
MOIETIES
MOIETY
MOIL
MOILED

MOILER
MOILERS
MOILING
MOILS
MOINEAU
MOINEAUS
MOIRE
MOIRÉ
MOIRES
MOIRÉS
MOIST
MOISTED
MOISTEN
MOISTENED
MOISTENING
MOISTENS
MOISTER
MOISTEST
MOISTIFIED
MOISTIFIES
MOISTIFY
MOISTIFYING
MOISTING
MOISTLY
MOISTNESS
MOISTNESSES
MOISTS
MOISTURE
MOISTURES
MOIT
MOITHER
MOITHERED
MOITHERING
MOITHERS
MOITS
MOKADDAM
MOKADDAMS
MOKE
MOKES
MOKO
MOKOS
MOLAL
MOLALITIES
MOLALITY
MOLAR
MOLARITIES
MOLARITY
MOLARS
MOLASSES
MOLD
MOLDED
MOLDING
MOLDS
MOLDWARP
MOLDWARPS
MOLE
MOLECAST
MOLECASTS
MOLECULAR
MOLECULE
MOLECULES
MOLEHILL
MOLEHILLS
MOLERAT
MOLERATS
MOLES
MOLESKIN
MOLESKINS
MOLEST
MOLESTED

MOLESTER
MOLESTERS
MOLESTFUL
MOLESTING
MOLESTS
MOLIES
MOLIMEN
MOLIMENS
MOLINE
MOLINES
MOLL
MOLLA
MOLLAH
MOLLAHS
MOLLAS
MOLLIE
MOLLIES
MOLLIFIED
MOLLIFIER
MOLLIFIERS
MOLLIFIES
MOLLIFY
MOLLIFYING
MOLLITIES
MOLLS
MOLLUSC
MOLLUSCAN
MOLLUSCS
MOLLUSK
MOLLUSKS
MOLLY
MOLLYMAWK
MOLLYMAWKS
MOLOCH
MOLOCHISE
MOLOCHISED
MOLOCHISES
MOLOCHISING
MOLOCHIZE
MOLOCHIZED
MOLOCHIZES
MOLOCHIZING
MOLOCHS
MOLOSSI
MOLOSSUS
MOLT
MOLTED
MOLTEN
MOLTENLY
MOLTING
MOLTO
MOLTS
MOLY
MOLYBDATE
MOLYBDATES
MOLYBDIC
MOLYBDOUS
MOM
MOME
MOMENT
MOMENTA
MOMENTANIES
MOMENTANY
MOMENTARY
MOMENTLY
MOMENTOUS
MOMENTS
MOMENTUM
MOMES
MOMMA

MOMMAS
MOMMET
MOMMETS
MOMMIES
MOMMY
MOMS
MONA
MONACHAL
MONACHISM
MONACHISMS
MONACHIST
MONACID
MONACT
MONACTINE
MONAD
MONADES
MONADIC
MONADICAL
MONADISM
MONADISMS
MONADS
MONAL
MONALS
MONANDRIES
MONANDRY
MONARCH
MONARCHAL
MONARCHIC
MONARCHIES
MONARCHS
MONARCHY
MONARDA
MONARDAS
MONAS
MONASES
MONASTERIES
MONASTERY
MONASTIC
MONASTICS
MONATOMIC
MONAUL
MONAULS
MONAURAL
MONAXIAL
MONAXON
MONAXONIC
MONAXONS
MONAZITE
MONAZITES
MONDAIN
MONDAINE
MONDAINES
MONDAINS
MONDIAL
MONECIOUS
MONER
MONERA
MONERGISM
MONERGISMS
MONERON
MONERONS
MONETARY
MONETH
MONETHS
MONETISE
MONETISED
MONETISES
MONETISING
MONETIZE
MONETIZED

MONETIZES
MONETIZING
MONEY
MONEYED
MONEYER
MONEYERS
MONEYLESS
MONEYS
MONEYWORT
MONEYWORTS
MONG
MONGCORN
MONGCORNS
MONGER
MONGERIES
MONGERING
MONGERINGS
MONGERS
MONGERY
MONGOL
MONGOLISM
MONGOLISMS
MONGOLOID
MONGOLOIDS
MONGOLS
MONGOOSE
MONGOOSES
MONGREL
MONGRELLY
MONGRELS
MONGS
MONIAL
MONIALS
MONICKER
MONICKERS
MONIED
MONIES
MONIKER
MONIKERS
MONILIA
MONILIAS
MONIMENT
MONIMENTS
MONIPLIES
MONISM
MONISMS
MONIST
MONISTIC
MONISTS
MONITION
MONITIONS
MONITIVE
MONITOR
MONITORED
MONITORING
MONITORS
MONITORY
MONITRESS
MONITRESSES
MONK
MONKERIES
MONKERY
MONKEY
MONKEYED
MONKEYING
MONKEYISH
MONKEYISM
MONKEYISMS
MONKEYS
MONKFISH

MONKFISHES
MONKHOOD
MONKHOODS
MONKISH
MONKS
MONKSHOOD
MONKSHOODS
MONO
MONOACID
MONOAMINE
MONOAMINES
MONOBASIC
MONOCARP
MONOCARPS
MONOCEROS
MONOCEROSES
MONOCHORD
MONOCHORDS
MONOCLE
MONOCLED
MONOCLES
MONOCLINE
MONOCLINES
MONOCOQUE
MONOCOQUES
MONOCOT
MONOCOTS
MONOCRACIES
MONOCRACY
MONOCRAT
MONOCRATS
MONOCULAR
MONOCYTE
MONOCYTES
MONODIC
MONODICAL
MONODIES
MONODIST
MONODISTS
MONODONT
MONODRAMA
MONODRAMAS
MONODY
MONOECISM
MONOECISMS
MONOFIL
MONOFILS
MONOGAMIC
MONOGAMIES
MONOGAMY
MONOGENIES
MONOGENY
MONOGLOT
MONOGLOTS
MONOGONIES
MONOGONY
MONOGRAM
MONOGRAMS
MONOGRAPH
MONOGRAPHS
MONOGYNIES
MONOGYNY
MONOHULL
MONOHULLS
MONOLATER
MONOLATERS
MONOLATRIES
MONOLATRY
MONOLITH
MONOLITHS

MONOLOGIC
MONOLOGIES
MONOLOGUE
MONOLOGUES
MONOLOGY
MONOMACHIES
MONOMACHY
MONOMANIA
MONOMANIAS
MONOMARK
MONOMARKS
MONOMER
MONOMERIC
MONOMERS
MONOMETER
MONOMETERS
MONOMIAL
MONOMIALS
MONOMODE
MONOPHAGIES
MONOPHAGY
MONOPHASE
MONOPHONIES
MONOPHONY
MONOPITCH
MONOPLANE
MONOPLANES
MONOPODE
MONOPODES
MONOPOLE
MONOPOLES
MONOPOLIES
MONOPOLY
MONOPSONIES
MONOPSONY
MONOPTOTE
MONOPTOTES
MONORAIL
MONORAILS
MONORCHID
MONORHINE
MONORHYME
MONORHYMES
MONOS
MONOSES
MONOSIES
MONOSIS
MONOSTICH
MONOSTICHES
MONOSTICHS
MONOSTYLE
MONOSY
MONOTINT
MONOTINTS
MONOTONE
MONOTONED
MONOTONES
MONOTONIC
MONOTONIES
MONOTONING
MONOTONY
MONOTREME
MONOTREMES
MONOTROCH
MONOTROCHS
MONOTYPE
MONOTYPES
MONOTYPIC
MONOXIDE
MONOXIDES

MONOXYLON	MOOI	MOOPED	MOPPED	MORBUSES
MONOXYLONS	MOOING	MOOPING	MOPPER	MORCEAU
MONSIEUR	MOOKTAR	MOOPS	MOPPERS	MORCEAUX
MONSOON	MOOKTARS	MOOR	MOPPET	MORDACITIES
MONSOONAL	MOOL	MOORAGE	MOPPETS	MORDACITY
MONSOONS	MOOLA	MOORAGES	MOPPIER	MORDANCIES
MONSTER	MOOLAH	MOORCOCK	MOPPIEST	MORDANCY
MONSTERA	MOOLAHS	MOORCOCKS	MOPPING	MORDANT
MONSTERAS	MOOLAS	MOORED	MOPPY	MORDANTED
MONSTERS	MOOLED	MOORFOWL	MOPS	MORDANTING
MONSTROUS	MOOLEY	MOORFOWLS	MOPSIES	MORDANTLY
MONTAGE	MOOLEYS	MOORHEN	MOPSTICK	MORDANTS
MONTAGES	MOOLI	MOORHENS	MOPSTICKS	MORDENT
MONTANE	MOOLIES	MOORIER	MOPSY	MORDENTS
MONTANT	MOOLING	MOORIEST	MOPUS	MORE
MONTANTO	MOOLIS	MOORILL	MOPUSES	MOREEN
MONTANTOES	MOOLS	MOORILLS	MOPY	MOREENS
MONTANTOS	MOOLY	MOORING	MOQUETTE	MOREISH
MONTANTS	MOON	MOORINGS	MOQUETTES	MOREL
MONTARIA	MOONBEAM	MOORISH	MOR	MORELLO
MONTARIAS	MOONBEAMS	MOORLAND	MORA	MORELLOS
MONTE	MOONBLIND	MOORLANDS	MORACEOUS	MORELS
MONTEITH	MOONCALF	MOORLOG	MORAINAL	MORENDO
MONTEITHS	MOONCALVES	MOORLOGS	MORAINE	MOREOVER
MONTEM	MOONED	MOORMAN	MORAINES	MOREPORK
MONTEMS	MOONER	MOORMEN	MORAINIC	MOREPORKS
MONTERO	MOONERS	MOORS	MORAL	MORES
MONTEROS	MOONEYE	MOORVA	MORALE	MORGANITE
MONTES	MOONEYES	MOORVAS	MORALES	MORGANITES
MONTH	MOONFACE	MOORY	MORALISE	MORGAY
MONTHLIES	MOONFACES	MOOS	MORALISED	MORGAYS
MONTHLING	MOONIER	MOOSE	MORALISER	MORGEN
MONTHLINGS	MOONIES	MOOSEYARD	MORALISERS	MORGENS
MONTHLY	MOONIEST	MOOSEYARDS	MORALISES	MORGUE
MONTHS	MOONING	MOOT	MORALISING	MORGUES
MONTICLE	MOONISH	MOOTABLE	MORALISM	MORIA
MONTICLES	MOONLESS	MOOTED	MORALISMS	MORIAS
MONTICULE	MOONLET	MOOTER	MORALIST	MORIBUND
MONTICULES	MOONLETS	MOOTERS	MORALISTS	MORICHE
MONTRE	MOONLIGHT	MOOTEST	MORALITIES	MORICHES
MONTRES	MOONLIGHTS	MOOTING	MORALITY	MORION
MONTURE	MOONLIT	MOOTINGS	MORALIZE	MORIONS
MONTURES	MOONQUAKE	MOOTMAN	MORALIZED	MORISCO
MONUMENT	MOONQUAKES	MOOTMEN	MORALIZES	MORISCOES
MONUMENTED	MOONRAKER	MOOTS	MORALIZING	MORISCOS
MONUMENTING	MOONRAKERS	MOOVE	MORALL	MORISH
MONUMENTS	MOONRISE	MOOVED	MORALLED	MORKIN
MONY	MOONRISES	MOOVES	MORALLER	MORKINS
MONYPLIES	MOONS	MOOVING	MORALLERS	MORLING
MONZONITE	MOONSAIL	MOP	MORALLING	MORLINGS
MONZONITES	MOONSAILS	MOPANE	MORALLS	MORMAOR
MOO	MOONSCAPE	MOPANES	MORALLY	MORMAORS
MOOCH	MOONSCAPES	MOPBOARD	MORALS	MORN
MOOCHED	MOONSEED	MOPBOARDS	MORAS	MORNAY
MOOCHER	MOONSEEDS	MOPE	MORASS	MORNAYS
MOOCHERS	MOONSET	MOPED	MORASSES	MORNE
MOOCHES	MOONSETS	MOPEDS	MORASSY	MORNÉ
MOOCHING	MOONSHEE	MOPEHAWK	MORAT	MORNED
MOOD	MOONSHEES	MOPEHAWKS	MORATORIA	MORNES
MOODIED	MOONSHINE	MOPER	MORATORY	MORNING
MOODIER	MOONSHINES	MOPERS	MORATS	MORNINGS
MOODIES	MOONSHINY	MOPES	MORAY	MORNS
MOODIEST	MOONSHOT	MOPIER	MORAYS	MOROCCO
MOODILY	MOONSHOTS	MOPIEST	MORBID	MOROCCOS
MOODINESS	MOONSTONE	MOPING	MORBIDITIES	MORON
MOODINESSES	MOONSTONES	MOPINGLY	MORBIDITY	MORONIC
MOODS	MOONWORT	MOPISH	MORBIDLY	MORONS
MOODY	MOONWORTS	MOPISHLY	MORBIFIC	MOROSE
MOODYING	MOONY	MOPOKE	MORBILLI	MOROSELY
MOOED	MOOP	MOPOKES	MORBUS	MOROSER

MOROSEST
MOROSITIES
MOROSITY
MORPH
MORPHEAN
MORPHEME
MORPHEMES
MORPHEMIC
MORPHETIC
MORPHEW
MORPHEWS
MORPHIA
MORPHIAS
MORPHIC
MORPHINE
MORPHINES
MORPHO
MORPHOS
MORPHOSES
MORPHOSIS
MORPHOTIC
MORPHS
MORRA
MORRAS
MORRHUA
MORRHUAS
MORRICE
MORRICES
MORRION
MORRIONS
MORRIS
MORRISED
MORRISES
MORRISING
MORRO
MORROS
MORROW
MORROWS
MORS
MORSAL
MORSE
MORSEL
MORSELLED
MORSELLING
MORSELS
MORSES
MORSURE
MORSURES
MORT
MORTAL
MORTALISE
MORTALISED
MORTALISES
MORTALISING
MORTALITIES
MORTALITY
MORTALIZE
MORTALIZED
MORTALIZES
MORTALIZING
MORTALLY
MORTALS
MORTAR
MORTARED
MORTARING
MORTARS
MORTBELL
MORTBELLS
MORTCLOTH
MORTCLOTHS

MORTGAGE
MORTGAGED
MORTGAGEE
MORTGAGEES
MORTGAGER
MORTGAGERS
MORTGAGES
MORTGAGING
MORTGAGOR
MORTGAGORS
MORTICE
MORTICED
MORTICER
MORTICERS
MORTICES
MORTICIAN
MORTICIANS
MORTICING
MORTIFIC
MORTIFIED
MORTIFIER
MORTIFIERS
MORTIFIES
MORTIFY
MORTIFYING
MORTIFYINGS
MORTISE
MORTISED
MORTISER
MORTISERS
MORTISES
MORTISING
MORTLING
MORTLINGS
MORTMAIN
MORTMAINS
MORTS
MORTUARIES
MORTUARY
MORULA
MORULAR
MORULAS
MORWONG
MORWONGS
MOSAIC
MOSAICISM
MOSAICISMS
MOSAICIST
MOSAICISTS
MOSAICS
MOSCHATEL
MOSCHATELS
MOSE
MOSED
MOSES
MOSEY
MOSEYED
MOSEYING
MOSEYS
MOSHAV
MOSHAVIM
MOSING
MOSKONFYT
MOSKONFYTS
MOSLINGS
MOSQUE
MOSQUES
MOSQUITO
MOSQUITOES
MOSQUITOS

MOSS
MOSSED
MOSSES
MOSSIE
MOSSIER
MOSSIES
MOSSIEST
MOSSINESS
MOSSINESSES
MOSSING
MOSSLAND
MOSSLANDS
MOSSPLANT
MOSSPLANTS
MOSSY
MOST
MOSTLY
MOSTS
MOSTWHAT
MOT
MOTE
MOTED
MOTEL
MOTELIER
MOTELIERS
MOTELS
MOTEN
MOTES
MOTET
MOTETS
MOTETT
MOTETTIST
MOTETTISTS
MOTETTS
MOTEY
MOTH
MOTHBALL
MOTHBALLED
MOTHBALLING
MOTHBALLS
MOTHED
MOTHER
MOTHERED
MOTHERING
MOTHERINGS
MOTHERLY
MOTHERS
MOTHERY
MOTHIER
MOTHIEST
MOTHS
MOTHY
MOTIF
MOTIFS
MOTILE
MOTILES
MOTILITIES
MOTILITY
MOTION
MOTIONAL
MOTIONED
MOTIONING
MOTIONIST
MOTIONISTS
MOTIONS
MOTIVATE
MOTIVATED
MOTIVATES
MOTIVATING
MOTIVE

MOTIVED
MOTIVES
MOTIVIC
MOTIVING
MOTIVITIES
MOTIVITY
MOTLEY
MOTLEYER
MOTLEYEST
MOTLEYS
MOTLIER
MOTLIEST
MOTMOT
MOTMOTS
MOTOCROSS
MOTOCROSSES
MOTOR
MOTORABLE
MOTORAIL
MOTORAILS
MOTORCADE
MOTORCADES
MOTORED
MOTORIAL
MOTORING
MOTORISE
MOTORISED
MOTORISES
MOTORISING
MOTORIST
MOTORISTS
MOTORIUM
MOTORIUMS
MOTORIZE
MOTORIZED
MOTORIZES
MOTORIZING
MOTORMAN
MOTORMEN
MOTORS
MOTORWAY
MOTORWAYS
MOTORY
MOTOSCAFI
MOTOSCAFO
MOTS
MOTSER
MOTSERS
MOTT
MOTTE
MOTTES
MOTTLE
MOTTLED
MOTTLES
MOTTLING
MOTTLINGS
MOTTO
MOTTOED
MOTTOES
MOTTS
MOTTY
MOTUCA
MOTUCAS
MOTZA
MOTZAS
MOU
MOUCH
MOUCHARD
MOUCHARDS
MOUCHED

MOUCHER
MOUCHERS
MOUCHES
MOUCHING
MOUCHOIR
MOUCHOIRS
MOUDIWART
MOUDIWARTS
MOUDIWORT
MOUDIWORTS
MOUE
MOUES
MOUFFLON
MOUFFLONS
MOUFLON
MOUFLONS
MOUGHT
MOUILLÉ
MOUJIK
MOUJIKS
MOULAGE
MOULAGES
MOULD
MOULDABLE
MOULDED
MOULDER
MOULDERED
MOULDERING
MOULDERS
MOULDIER
MOULDIEST
MOULDING
MOULDINGS
MOULDS
MOULDWARP
MOULDWARPS
MOULDY
MOULIN
MOULINET
MOULINETS
MOULINS
MOULS
MOULT
MOULTED
MOULTEN
MOULTING
MOULTINGS
MOULTS
MOUND
MOUNDED
MOUNDING
MOUNDS
MOUNSEER
MOUNSEERS
MOUNT
MOUNTAIN
MOUNTAINS
MOUNTANT
MOUNTANTS
MOUNTED
MOUNTER
MOUNTERS
MOUNTIE
MOUNTIES
MOUNTING
MOUNTINGS
MOUNTS
MOUNTY
MOUP
MOUPED

MOUPING	MOUTHWASH	MOZZETTA	MUDDIED	MUGGED
MOUPS	MOUTHWASHES	MOZZETTAS	MUDDIER	MUGGER
MOURN	MOUTHY	MOZZIE	MUDDIES	MUGGERS
MOURNED	MOUTON	MOZZIES	MUDDIEST	MUGGIER
MOURNER	MOUTONS	MOZZLE	MUDDILY	MUGGIEST
MOURNERS	MOVABLE	MOZZLES	MUDDINESS	MUGGINESS
MOURNFUL	MOVABLES	MPRET	MUDDINESSES	MUGGINESSES
MOURNING	MOVABLY	MPRETS	MUDDING	MUGGING
MOURNINGS	MOVE	MRIDAMGAM	MUDDLE	MUGGINGS
MOURNIVAL	MOVEABLE	MRIDAMGAMS	MUDDLED	MUGGINS
MOURNIVALS	MOVEABLES	MRIDANGAM	MUDDLER	MUGGINSES
MOURNS	MOVEABLY	MRIDANGAMS	MUDDLERS	MUGGISH
MOUS	MOVED	MU	MUDDLES	MUGGY
MOUSAKA	MOVELESS	MUCATE	MUDDLING	MUGS
MOUSAKAS	MOVEMENT	MUCATES	MUDDY	MUGSHOT
MOUSE	MOVEMENTS	MUCH	MUDDYING	MUGSHOTS
MOUSED	MOVER	MUCHEL	MUDÉJAR	MUGWORT
MOUSEKIN	MOVERS	MUCHELL	MUDÉJARES	MUGWORTS
MOUSEKINS	MOVES	MUCHELLS	MUDIR	MUGWUMP
MOUSER	MOVIE	MUCHELS	MUDIRIA	MUGWUMPS
MOUSERIES	MOVIES	MUCHES	MUDIRIAS	MUID
MOUSERS	MOVING	MUCHLY	MUDIRIEH	MUIDS
MOUSERY	MOVINGLY	MUCHNESS	MUDIRIEHS	MUIL
MOUSES	MOVY	MUCHNESSES	MUDIRS	MUILS
MOUSEY	MOW	MUCIC	MUDLARK	MUIR
MOUSIE	MOWA	MUCID	MUDLARKED	MUIRS
MOUSIER	MOWAS	MUCIGEN	MUDLARKING	MUIST
MOUSIES	MOWBURN	MUCIGENS	MUDLARKS	MUISTED
MOUSIEST	MOWBURNED	MUCILAGE	MUDPACK	MUISTING
MOUSING	MOWBURNING	MUCILAGES	MUDPACKS	MUISTS
MOUSINGS	MOWBURNS	MUCIN	MUDRA	MUJAHEDIN
MOUSLE	MOWBURNT	MUCINS	MUDRAS	MUJAHIDIN
MOUSLED	MOWDIWART	MUCK	MUDS	MUJIK
MOUSLES	MOWDIWARTS	MUCKED	MUDSCOW	MUJIKS
MOUSLING	MOWDIWORT	MUCKENDER	MUDSCOWS	MUKHTAR
MOUSMÉ	MOWDIWORTS	MUCKENDERS	MUDSTONE	MUKHTARS
MOUSMEE	MOWED	MUCKER	MUDSTONES	MUKLUK
MOUSMEES	MOWER	MUCKERED	MUDWORT	MUKLUKS
MOUSMÉS	MOWERS	MUCKERING	MUDWORTS	MULATTA
MOUSSAKA	MOWING	MUCKERS	MUEDDIN	MULATTAS
MOUSSAKAS	MOWINGS	MUCKIER	MUEDDINS	MULATTO
MOUSSE	MOWN	MUCKIEST	MUESLI	MULATTOS
MOUSSES	MOWRA	MUCKINESS	MUESLIS	MULBERRIES
MOUST	MOWRAS	MUCKINESSES	MUEZZIN	MULBERRY
MOUSTACHE	MOWS	MUCKING	MUEZZINS	MULCH
MOUSTACHES	MOXA	MUCKLE	MUFF	MULCHED
MOUSTED	MOXAS	MUCKLES	MUFFED	MULCHES
MOUSTING	MOXIE	MUCKLUCK	MUFFETTEE	MULCHING
MOUSTS	MOXIES	MUCKLUCKS	MUFFETTEES	MULCT
MOUSY	MOY	MUCKS	MUFFIN	MULCTED
MOUTAN	MOYA	MUCKY	MUFFINEER	MULCTING
MOUTANS	MOYAS	MUCLUC	MUFFINEERS	MULCTS
MOUTER	MOYGASHEL	MUCLUCS	MUFFING	MULE
MOUTERED	MOYGASHELS	MUCOID	MUFFINS	MULES
MOUTERER	MOYITIES	MUCOR	MUFFLE	MULETEER
MOUTERERS	MOYITY	MUCORS	MUFFLED	MULETEERS
MOUTERING	MOYL	MUCOSA	MUFFLER	MULEY
MOUTERS	MOYLE	MUCOSAE	MUFFLERS	MULEYS
MOUTH	MOYLES	MUCOSITIES	MUFFLES	MULGA
MOUTHABLE	MOYLS	MUCOSITY	MUFFLING	MULGAS
MOUTHED	MOYS	MUCOUS	MUFFS	MULISH
MOUTHER	MOZ	MUCRO	MUFLON	MULISHLY
MOUTHERS	MOZE	MUCRONATE	MUFLONS	MULL
MOUTHFUL	MOZED	MUCRONES	MUFTI	MULLAH
MOUTHFULS	MOZES	MUCROS	MUFTIS	MULLAHS
MOUTHIER	MOZETTA	MUCULENT	MUG	MULLED
MOUTHIEST	MOZETTAS	MUCUS	MUGEARITE	MULLEIN
MOUTHING	MOZING	MUCUSES	MUGEARITES	MULLEINS
MOUTHLESS	MOZZ	MUD	MUGFUL	MULLER
MOUTHS	MOZZES	MUDDED	MUGFULS	MULLERS

MULLET	MUMBLES	MUNIMENT	MURING	MURVAS
MULLETS	MUMBLING	MUNIMENTS	MURK	MUS
MULLEY	MUMBLINGS	MUNITE	MURKER	MUSACEOUS
MULLEYS	MUMCHANCE	MUNITED	MURKEST	MUSANG
MULLIGAN	MUMCHANCES	MUNITES	MURKIER	MUSANGS
MULLIGANS	MUMM	MUNITING	MURKIEST	MUSCADEL
MULLING	MUMMED	MUNITION	MURKILY	MUSCADELS
MULLION	MUMMER	MUNITIONED	MURKINESS	MUSCADIN
MULLIONED	MUMMERIES	MUNITIONING	MURKINESSES	MUSCADINE
MULLIONS	MUMMERS	MUNITIONS	MURKISH	MUSCADINES
MULLOCK	MUMMERY	MUNNION	MURKS	MUSCADINS
MULLOCKS	MUMMIA	MUNNIONS	MURKSOME	MUSCARINE
MULLOWAY	MUMMIAS	MUNSHI	MURKY	MUSCARINES
MULLOWAYS	MUMMIED	MUNSHIS	MURL	MUSCAT
MULLS	MUMMIES	MUNSTER	MURLAIN	MUSCATEL
MULMUL	MUMMIFIED	MUNSTERS	MURLAINS	MUSCATELS
MULMULL	MUMMIFIES	MUNTIN	MURLAN	MUSCATS
MULMULLS	MUMMIFORM	MUNTING	MURLANS	MUSCID
MULMULS	MUMMIFY	MUNTINGS	MURLED	MUSCIDS
MULSE	MUMMIFYING	MUNTINS	MURLIER	MUSCLE
MULSES	MUMMING	MUNTJAC	MURLIEST	MUSCLED
MULSH	MUMMINGS	MUNTJACS	MURLIN	MUSCLES
MULSHED	MUMMOCK	MUNTJAK	MURLING	MUSCLING
MULSHES	MUMMOCKS	MUNTJAKS	MURLINS	MUSCLINGS
MULSHING	MUMMS	MUON	MURLS	MUSCOID
MULTEITIES	MUMMY	MUONIC	MURLY	MUSCOLOGIES
MULTEITY	MUMMYING	MUONIUM	MURMUR	MUSCOLOGY
MULTIFID	MUMP	MUONIUMS	MURMURED	MUSCOSE
MULTIFIL	MUMPED	MUONS	MURMURER	MUSCOVADO
MULTIFILS	MUMPER	MUQADDAM	MURMURERS	MUSCOVADOS
MULTIFOIL	MUMPERS	MUQADDAMS	MURMURING	MUSCOVITE
MULTIFOILS	MUMPING	MURAENA	MURMURINGS	MUSCOVITES
MULTIFORM	MUMPISH	MURAENAS	MURMUROUS	MUSCULAR
MULTIFORMS	MUMPISHLY	MURAGE	MURMURS	MUSCULOUS
MULTIHULL	MUMPS	MURAGES	MURPHIES	MUSE
MULTIHULLS	MUMPSIMUS	MURAL	MURPHY	MUSED
MULTIPARA	MUMPSIMUSES	MURALIST	MURRA	MUSEFUL
MULTIPARAE	MUMS	MURALISTS	MURRAIN	MUSEFULLY
MULTIPARAS	MUN	MURALS	MURRAINED	MUSEOLOGIES
MULTIPED	MUNCH	MURDER	MURRAINS	MUSEOLOGY
MULTIPEDE	MUNCHED	MURDERED	MURRAM	MUSER
MULTIPEDES	MUNCHER	MURDERER	MURRAMS	MUSERS
MULTIPEDS	MUNCHERS	MURDERERS	MURRAS	MUSES
MULTIPLE	MUNCHES	MURDERESS	MURRAY	MUSET
MULTIPLES	MUNCHING	MURDERESSES	MURRAYS	MUSETS
MULTIPLET	MUNDANE	MURDERING	MURRE	MUSETTE
MULTIPLETS	MUNDANELY	MURDEROUS	MURRELET	MUSETTES
MULTIPLEX	MUNDANER	MURDERS	MURRELETS	MUSEUM
MULTIPLEXED	MUNDANEST	MURE	MURREN	MUSEUMS
MULTIPLEXES	MUNDANITIES	MURED	MURRENS	MUSH
MULTIPLEXING	MUNDANITY	MURENA	MURRES	MUSHA
MULTIPLIED	MUNDIC	MURENAS	MURREY	MUSHED
MULTIPLIES	MUNDICS	MURES	MURREYS	MUSHER
MULTIPLY	MUNDIFIED	MUREX	MURRHA	MUSHERS
MULTIPLYING	MUNDIFIES	MUREXES	MURRHAS	MUSHES
MULTITUDE	MUNDIFY	MUREXS	MURRHINE	MUSHIER
MULTITUDES	MUNDIFYING	MURGEON	MURRIES	MUSHIEST
MULTUM	MUNDUNGUS	MURGEONED	MURRIN	MUSHILY
MULTUMS	MUNDUNGUSES	MURGEONING	MURRINE	MUSHINESS
MULTURE	MUNGCORN	MURGEONS	MURRINS	MUSHINESSES
MULTURED	MUNGCORNS	MURIATE	MURRION	MUSHING
MULTURER	MUNGO	MURIATED	MURRIONS	MUSHROOM
MULTURERS	MUNGOOSE	MURIATES	MURRY	MUSHROOMED
MULTURES	MUNGOOSES	MURIATIC	MURTHER	MUSHROOMING
MULTURING	MUNGOS	MURICATE	MURTHERED	MUSHROOMS
MUM	MUNICIPAL	MURICATED	MURTHERER	MUSHY
MUMBLE	MUNIFIED	MURICES	MURTHERERS	MUSIC
MUMBLED	MUNIFIES	MURIFORM	MURTHERING	MUSICAL
MUMBLER	MUNIFY	MURINE	MURTHERS	MUSICALE
MUMBLERS	MUNIFYING	MURINES	MURVA	MUSICALES

MUSICALLY
MUSICALS
MUSICIAN
MUSICIANS
MUSICKED
MUSICKER
MUSICKERS
MUSICKING
MUSICS
MUSIMON
MUSIMONS
MUSING
MUSINGLY
MUSINGS
MUSIT
MUSITS
MUSIVE
MUSK
MUSKED
MUSKEG
MUSKEGS
MUSKET
MUSKETEER
MUSKETEERS
MUSKETOON
MUSKETOONS
MUSKETRIES
MUSKETRY
MUSKETS
MUSKIER
MUSKIEST
MUSKILY
MUSKINESS
MUSKINESSES
MUSKING
MUSKLE
MUSKLES
MUSKONE
MUSKONES
MUSKS
MUSKY
MUSLIN
MUSLINED
MUSLINET
MUSLINETS
MUSLINS
MUOMON
MUSMONS
MUSQUASH
MUSQUASHES
MUSROL
MUSROLS
MUSS
MUSSE
MUSSED
MUSSEL
MUSSELLED
MUSSELS
MUSSES
MUSSIER
MUSSIEST
MUSSINESS
MUSSINESSES
MUSSING
MUSSITATE
MUSSITATED
MUSSITATES
MUSSITATING
MUSSY
MUST

MUSTACHE
MUSTACHES
MUSTACHIO
MUSTACHIOS
MUSTANG
MUSTANGS
MUSTARD
MUSTARDS
MUSTED
MUSTEE
MUSTEES
MUSTELINE
MUSTELINES
MUSTER
MUSTERED
MUSTERING
MUSTERS
MUSTH
MUSTHS
MUSTIER
MUSTIEST
MUSTING
MUSTS
MUSTY
MUTABLE
MUTABLY
MUTAGEN
MUTAGENIC
MUTAGENS
MUTANDA
MUTANDUM
MUTANT
MUTANTS
MUTATE
MUTATED
MUTATES
MUTATING
MUTATION
MUTATIONS
MUTATIVE
MUTATORY
MUTCH
MUTCHES
MUTCHKIN
MUTCHKINS
MUTE
MUTED
MUTELY
MUTENESS
MUTENESSES
MUTER
MUTES
MUTEST
MUTICOUS
MUTILATE
MUTILATED
MUTILATES
MUTILATING
MUTILATOR
MUTILATORS
MUTINE
MUTINED
MUTINEER
MUTINEERED
MUTINEERING
MUTINEERS
MUTINES
MUTING
MUTINIED
MUTINIES

MUTINING
MUTINOUS
MUTINY
MUTINYING
MUTISM
MUTISMS
MUTON
MUTONS
MUTOSCOPE
MUTOSCOPES
MUTT
MUTTER
MUTTERED
MUTTERER
MUTTERERS
MUTTERING
MUTTERINGS
MUTTERS
MUTTON
MUTTONS
MUTTONY
MUTTS
MUTUAL
MUTUALISE
MUTUALISED
MUTUALISES
MUTUALISING
MUTUALISM
MUTUALISMS
MUTUALITIES
MUTUALITY
MUTUALIZE
MUTUALIZED
MUTUALIZES
MUTUALIZING
MUTUALLY
MUTUCA
MUTUCAS
MUTULE
MUTULES
MUTUUM
MUTUUMS
MUX
MUXED
MUXES
MUXING
MUZHIK
MUZHIKS
MUZZIER
MUZZIEST
MUZZILY
MUZZINESS
MUZZINESSES
MUZZLE
MUZZLED
MUZZLER
MUZZLERS
MUZZLES
MUZZLING
MUZZY
MVULE
MVULES
MY
MYAL
MYALGIA
MYALGIAS
MYALGIC
MYALISM
MYALISMS
MYALL

MYALLS
MYCELIA
MYCELIAL
MYCELIUM
MYCETES
MYCETOMA
MYCETOMAS
MYCOLOGIC
MYCOLOGIES
MYCOLOGY
MYCOPHAGIES
MYCOPHAGY
MYCORHIZA
MYCORHIZAS
MYCOSES
MYCOSIS
MYCOTIC
MYCOTOXIN
MYCOTOXINS
MYDRIASES
MYDRIASIS
MYDRIATIC
MYDRIATICS
MYELIN
MYELINS
MYELITES
MYELITIS
MYELOID
MYELOMA
MYELOMAS
MYELON
MYELONS
MYGALE
MYGALES
MYIASES
MYIASIS
MYLODON
MYLODONS
MYLODONT
MYLODONTS
MYLOHYOID
MYLOHYOIDS
MYLONITE
MYLONITES
MYLONITIC
MYNA
MYNAH
MYNAHS
MYNAS
MYNHEER
MYNHEERS
MYOBLAST
MYOBLASTS
MYOFIBRIL
MYOFIBRILS
MYOGEN
MYOGENIC
MYOGENS
MYOGLOBIN
MYOGLOBINS
MYOGRAM
MYOGRAMS
MYOGRAPH
MYOGRAPHIES
MYOGRAPHS
MYOGRAPHY
MYOID
MYOLOGIES
MYOLOGIST
MYOLOGISTS

MYOLOGY
MYOMA
MYOMANCIES
MYOMANCY
MYOMANTIC
MYOMAS
MYOPE
MYOPES
MYOPIA
MYOPIAS
MYOPIC
MYOPICS
MYOPS
MYOPSES
MYOSES
MYOSIN
MYOSINS
MYOSIS
MYOSITES
MYOSITIC
MYOSITICS
MYOSITIS
MYOSOTE
MYOSOTES
MYOSOTIS
MYOSOTISES
MYOTIC
MYOTICS
MYOTUBE
MYOTUBES
MYRBANE
MYRIAD
MYRIADS
MYRIADTH
MYRIADTHS
MYRIAPOD
MYRIAPODS
MYRINGA
MYRINGAS
MYRIOPOD
MYRIOPODS
MYRIORAMA
MYRIORAMAS
MYRISTIC
MYRMECOID
MYRMIDON
MYRMIDONS
MYROBALAN
MYROBALANS
MYRRH
MYRRHIC
MYRRHINE
MYRRHOL
MYRRHOLS
MYRRHS
MYRTLE
MYRTLES
MYSELF
MYSTAGOGIES
MYSTAGOGY
MYSTERIES
MYSTERY
MYSTIC
MYSTICAL
MYSTICISM
MYSTICISMS
MYSTICS
MYSTIFIED
MYSTIFIER
MYSTIFIERS

MYSTIFIES	MYTHICISING	MYTHISES	MYTHOLOGY	MYXEDEMA
MYSTIFY	MYTHICISM	MYTHISING	MYTHOMANE	MYXEDEMAS
MYSTIFYING	MYTHICISMS	MYTHISM	MYTHOMANES	MYXOEDEMA
MYSTIQUE	MYTHICIST	MYTHISMS	MYTHOPOET	MYXOEDEMAS
MYSTIQUES	MYTHICISTS	MYTHIST	MYTHOPOETS	MYXOMA
MYTH	MYTHICIZE	MYTHISTS	MYTHOS	MYXOMATA
MYTHIC	MYTHICIZED	MYTHIZE	MYTHOSES	MYXOVIRUS
MYTHICAL	MYTHICIZES	MYTHIZED	MYTHS	MYXOVIRUSES
MYTHICISE	MYTHICIZING	MYTHIZES	MYTHUS	MZUNGU
MYTHICISED	MYTHISE	MYTHIZING	MYTHUSES	MZUNGUS
MYTHICISES	MYTHISED	MYTHOLOGIES	MYTILOID	

N

NA	NAGGER	NAMABLE	NAPIFORM	NARGILIES
NAAM	NAGGERS	NAMASKAR	NAPKIN	NARGILLIES
NAAMS	NAGGIER	NAMASKARS	NAPKINS	NARGILLY
NAAN	NAGGIEST	NAMASTE	NAPLESS	NARGILY
NAANS	NAGGING	NAMASTES	NAPOLEON	NARIAL
NAARTJE	NAGGY	NAME	NAPOLEONS	NARICORN
NAARTJES	NAGMAAL	NAMEABLE	NAPOO	NARICORNS
NAB	NAGMAALS	NAMED	NAPOOED	NARINE
NABBED	NAGOR	NAMELESS	NAPOOING	NARK
NABBER	NAGORS	NAMELY	NAPOOS	NARKED
NABBERS	NAGS	NAMER	NAPPA	NARKIER
NABBING	NAHAL	NAMERS	NAPPAS	NARKIEST
NABK	NAHALS	NAMES	NAPPE	NARKING
NABKS	NAIAD	NAMESAKE	NAPPED	NARKS
NABLA	NAIADES	NAMESAKES	NAPPER	NARKY
NABLAS	NAIADS	NAMING	NAPPERS	NARQUOIS
NABOB	NAIANT	NAMINGS	NAPPES	NARRAS
NABOBS	NAÏF	NAMS	NAPPIER	NARRASES
NABS	NAÏFER	NAN	NAPPIES	NARRATE
NABSES	NAÏFEST	NANA	NAPPIEST	NARRATED
NACARAT	NAIK	NANAS	NAPPINESS	NARRATES
NACANATO	NAIICO	NANCE	NAPPINESSES	NARRATING
NACELLE	NAIL	NANCES	NAPPING	NARRATION
NACELLES	NAILED	NANCIES	NAPPY	NARRATIONS
NACH	NAILER	NANCY	NAPRON	NARRATIVE
NACHE	NAILERIES	NANDINE	NAPRONS	NARRATIVES
NACHES	NAILERS	NANDINES	NAPS	NARRATOR
NACHTMAAL	NAILERY	NANDOO	NARAS	NARRATORS
NACHTMAALS	NAILING	NANDOOS	NARASES	NARRATORY
NACKET	NAILINGS	NANDU	NARCISSI	NARRE
NACKETS	NAILS	NANDUS	NARCISSUS	NARROW
NACRE	NAIN	NANISM	NARCISSUSES	NARROWED
NACREOUS	NAINSELL	NANISMS	NARCOSES	NARROWER
NACRES	NAINSELLS	NANKEEN	NARCOSIS	NARROWEST
NACRITE	NAINSOOK	NANKEENS	NARCOTIC	NARROWING
NACRITES	NAINSOOKS	NANKIN	NARCOTICS	NARROWINGS
NACROUS	NAIRA	NANKINS	NARCOTINE	NARROWLY
NADA	NAIRAS	NANNA	NARCOTINES	NARROWS
NADAS	NAISSANT	NANNAS	NARCOTISE	NARTHEX
NADIR	NAÏVE	NANNIED	NARCOTISED	NARTHEXES
NADIRS	NAIVELY	NANNIES	NARCOTISES	NARTJIE
NAE	NAÏVER	NANNY	NARCOTISING	NARTJIES
NAEBODIES	NAÏVEST	NANNYING	NARCOTISM	NARWHAL
NAEBODY	NAÏVETÉ	NANNYISH	NARCOTISMS	NARWHALS
NAETHING	NAÏVETÉS	NANOGRAM	NARCOTIST	NARY
NAETHINGS	NAÏVETIES	NANOGRAMS	NARCOTISTS	NAS
NAEVE	NAÏVETY	NANOMETRE	NARD	NASAL
NAEVES	NAKED	NANOMETRES	NARDED	NASALISE
NAEVI	NAKEDER	NANS	NARDING	NASALISED
NAEVOID	NAKEDEST	NAOS	NARDOO	NASALISES
NAEVUS	NAKEDLY	NAOSES	NARDOOS	NASALISING
NAFF	NAKEDNESS	NAP	NARDS	NASALITIES
NAFFING	NAKEDNESSES	NAPA	NARE	NASALITY
NAFFS	NAKER	NAPALM	NARES	NASALIZE
NAG	NAKERS	NAPALMS	NARGHILE	NASALIZED
NAGA	NALA	NAPAS	NARGHILES	NASALIZES
NAGANA	NALAS	NAPE	NARGHILIES	NASALIZING
NAGANAS	NALLA	NAPERIES	NARGHILLIES	NASALLY
NAGAPIE	NALLAH	NAPERY	NARGHILLY	NASALS
NAGAPIES	NALLAHS	NAPES	NARGHILY	NASARD
NAGARI	NALLAS	NAPHTHA	NARGILE	NASARDS
NAGARIS	NALOXONE	NAPHTHAS	NARGILEH	NASCENCE
NAGAS	NALOXONES	NAPHTHOL	NARGILEHS	NASCENCES
NAGGED	NAM	NAPHTHOLS	NARGILES	NASCENCIES

NASCENCY	NATURALLY	NAVICULARS	NEBBICHES	NECKWEEDS
NASCENT	NATURALS	NAVICULAS	NEBBING	NECROLOGIES
NASEBERRIES	NATURE	NAVIES	NEBBISH	NECROLOGY
NASEBERRY	NATURED	NAVIGABLE	NEBBISHE	NECROPSIES
NASHGAB	NATURES	NAVIGATE	NEBBISHER	NECROPSY
NASHGABS	NATURING	NAVIGATED	NEBBISHERS	NECROSE
NASION	NATURISM	NAVIGATES	NEBBISHES	NECROSED
NASIONS	NATURISMS	NAVIGATING	NEBBUK	NECROSES
NASTALIK	NATURIST	NAVIGATOR	NEBBUKS	NECROSING
NASTALIKS	NATURISTS	NAVIGATORS	NEBECK	NECROSIS
NASTIC	NAUGHT	NAVVIED	NEBECKS	NECROTIC
NASTIER	NAUGHTIER	NAVVIES	NEBEK	NECROTISE
NASTIES	NAUGHTIEST	NAVVY	NEBEKS	NECROTISED
NASTIEST	NAUGHTILY	NAVVYING	NEBEL	NECROTISES
NASTILY	NAUGHTS	NAVVY	NEBELS	NECROTISING
NASTINESS	NAUGHTY	NAWAB	NEBISH	NECROTIZE
NASTINESSES	NAUMACHIA	NAWABS	NEBISHES	NECROTIZED
NASTY	NAUMACHIAE	NAY	NEBRIS	NECROTIZES
NASUTE	NAUMACHIAS	NAYS	NEBRISES	NECROTIZING
NASUTES	NAUMACHIES	NAYTHLES	NEBS	NECROTOMIES
NAT	NAUMACHY	NAYWARD	NEBULA	NECROTOMY
NATAL	NAUNT	NAYWARDS	NEBULAE	NECTAR
NATALITIES	NAUNTS	NAYWORD	NEBULAR	NECTAREAL
NATALITY	NAUPLII	NAYWORDS	NEBULE	NECTAREAN
NATANT	NAUPLIOID	NAZE	NEBULÉ	NECTARED
NATATION	NAUPLIUS	NAZES	NEBULES	NECTARIAL
NATATIONS	NAUSEA	NAZIR	NEBULISE	NECTARIES
NATATORY	NAUSEANT	NAZIRS	NEBULISED	NECTARINE
NATCH	NAUSEANTS	NE	NEBULISER	NECTARINES
NATCHES	NAUSEAS	NEAFE	NEBULISERS	NECTAROUS
NATES	NAUSEATE	NEAFES	NEBULISES	NECTARS
NATHELESS	NAUSEATED	NEAFFE	NEBULISING	NECTARY
NATHEMO	NAUSEATES	NEAFFES	NEBULIUM	NED
NATHEMORE	NAUSEATING	NEAL	NEBULIUMS	NEDDIES
NATHLESS	NAUSEOUS	NEALED	NEBULIZE	NEDDY
NATIFORM	NAUTCH	NEALING	NEBULIZED	NEDS
NATION	NAUTCHES	NEALS	NEBULIZER	NÉE
NATIONAL	NAUTIC	NEANIC	NEBULIZERS	NEED
NATIONALS	NAUTICAL	NEAP	NEBULIZES	NEEDED
NATIONS	NAUTICS	NEAPED	NEBULIZING	NEEDER
NATIVE	NAUTILI	NEAPING	NEBULOUS	NEEDERS
NATIVELY	NAUTILUS	NEAPS	NEBULY	NEEDFUL
NATIVES	NAUTILUSES	NEAPTIDE	NECESSARIES	NEEDFULLY
NATIVISM	NAVAID	NEAPTIDES	NECESSARY	NEEDIER
NATIVISMS	NAVAIDS	NEAR	NECESSITIES	NEEDIEST
NATIVIST	NAVAL	NEARED	NECESSITY	NEEDILY
NATIVISTS	NAVALISM	NEARER	NECK	NEEDINESS
NATIVITIES	NAVALISMS	NEAREST	NECKATEE	NEEDINESSES
NATIVITY	NAVARCH	NEARING	NECKATEES	NEEDING
NATRIUM	NAVARCHIES	NEARLY	NECKBEEF	NEEDLE
NATRIUMS	NAVARCHS	NEARNESS	NECKBEEFS	NEEDLED
NATROLITE	NAVARCHY	NEARNESSES	NECKED	NEEDLEFUL
NATROLITES	NAVARHO	NEARS	NECKGEAR	NEEDLEFULS
NATRON	NAVARHOS	NEARSIDE	NECKGEARS	NEEDLER
NATRONS	NAVARIN	NEARSIDES	NECKING	NEEDLERS
NATS	NAVARINS	NEAT	NECKINGS	NEEDLES
NATTER	NAVE	NEATEN	NECKLACE	NEEDLESS
NATTERED	NAVEL	NEATENED	NECKLACES	NEEDLIER
NATTERING	NAVELS	NEATENING	NECKLET	NEEDLIEST
NATTERS	NAVELWORT	NEATENS	NECKLETS	NEEDLING
NATTERY	NAVELWORTS	NEATER	NECKLINE	NEEDLY
NATTIER	NAVES	NEATEST	NECKLINES	NEEDMENT
NATTIEST	NAVETTE	NEATH	NECKS	NEEDMENTS
NATTILY	NAVETTES	NEATLY	NECKTIE	NEEDS
NATTINESS	NAVEW	NEATNESS	NECKTIES	NEEDY
NATTINESSES	NAVEWS	NEATNESSES	NECKVERSE	NEELD
NATTY	NAVICERT	NEATS	NECKVERSES	NEELDS
NATURA	NAVICERTS	NEB	NECKWEAR	NEELE
NATURAE	NAVICULA	NEBBED	NECKWEARS	NEELES
NATURAL	NAVICULAR	NEBBICH	NECKWEED	NEEM

NEEMS
NEEP
NEEPS
NEESBERRIES
NEESBERRY
NEESE
NEESED
NEESES
NEESING
NEEZE
NEEZED
NEEZES
NEEZING
NEF
NEFANDOUS
NEFARIOUS
NEFAST
NEFS
NEGATE
NEGATED
NEGATES
NEGATING
NEGATION
NEGATIONS
NEGATIVE
NEGATIVED
NEGATIVES
NEGATIVING
NEGATORY
NEGATRON
NEGATRONS
NEGLECT
NEGLECTED
NEGLECTER
NEGLECTERS
NEGLECTING
NEGLECTS
NÉGLIGÉ
NEGLIGEE
NEGLIGEES
NEGLIGENT
NÉGLIGÉS
NÉGOCIANT
NÉGOCIANTS
NEGOTIATE
NEGOTIATED
NEGOTIATES
NEGOTIATING
NEGRESS
NEGRESSES
NEGRITUDE
NEGRITUDES
NEGRO
NEGROES
NEGROHEAD
NEGROHEADS
NEGROID
NEGROIDAL
NEGROIDS
NEGROISM
NEGROISMS
NEGROPHIL
NEGROPHILS
NEGUS
NEGUSES
NEIF
NEIFS
NEIGH
NEIGHBOUR
NEIGHBOURED

NEIGHBOURING
NEIGHBOURS
NEIGHED
NEIGHING
NEIGHS
NEIST
NEITHER
NEIVE
NEIVES
NEK
NEKS
NEKTON
NEKTONS
NELIES
NELIS
NELLIE
NELLIES
NELLY
NELSON
NELSONS
NELUMBIUM
NELUMBIUMS
NELUMBO
NELUMBOS
NEMATIC
NEMATODE
NEMATODES
NEMATOID
NEMERTEAN
NEMERTEANS
NEMERTIAN
NEMERTIANS
NEMERTINE
NEMERTINES
NEMESES
NEMESIA
NEMESIAS
NEMESIS
NEMN
NEMNED
NEMNING
NEMNS
NEMOPHILA
NEMOPHILAS
NEMORAL
NEMOROUS
NEMPT
NENE
NENES
NENUPHAR
NENUPHARS
NEOBLAST
NEOBLASTS
NEODYMIUM
NEODYMIUMS
NEOLITH
NEOLITHS
NEOLOGIAN
NEOLOGIANS
NEOLOGIC
NEOLOGIES
NEOLOGISE
NEOLOGISED
NEOLOGISES
NEOLOGISING
NEOLOGISM
NEOLOGISMS
NEOLOGIST
NEOLOGISTS
NEOLOGIZE

NEOLOGIZED
NEOLOGIZES
NEOLOGIZING
NEOLOGY
NEOMYCIN
NEOMYCINS
NEON
NEONATAL
NEONATE
NEONATES
NEONOMIAN
NEONOMIANS
NEONS
NEOPAGAN
NEOPAGANS
NEOPHILE
NEOPHILES
NEOPHILIA
NEOPHILIAS
NEOPHOBIA
NEOPHOBIAS
NEOPHYTE
NEOPHYTES
NEOPHYTIC
NEOPLASM
NEOPLASMS
NEOPRENE
NEOPHENES
NEOTEINIA
NEOTEINIAS
NEOTEINIC
NEOTENIC
NEOTENIES
NEOTENOUS
NEOTENY
NEOTERIC
NEOTERISE
NEOTERISED
NEOTERISES
NEOTERISING
NEOTERISM
NEOTERISMS
NEOTERIST
NEOTERISTS
NEOTORIZE
NEOTORIZED
NEOTORIZES
NEOTORIZING
NEP
NEPENTHE
NEPENTHES
NEPER
NEPERS
NEPHALISM
NEPHALISMS
NEPHALIST
NEPHALISTS
NEPHELINE
NEPHELINES
NEPHELITE
NEPHELITES
NEPHEW
NEPHEWS
NEPHOGRAM
NEPHOGRAMS
NEPHOLOGIES
NEPHOLOGY
NEPHRALGIES
NEPHRALGY
NEPHRIC

NEPHRITE
NEPHRITES
NEPHRITIC
NEPHRITIS
NEPHROID
NEPHRON
NEPHRONS
NEPHROSES
NEPHROSIS
NEPHROTIC
NEPIONIC
NEPIT
NEPITS
NEPOTIC
NEPOTISM
NEPOTISMS
NEPOTIST
NEPOTISTS
NEPS
NEPTUNIUM
NEPTUNIUMS
NERD
NERDS
NEREID
NEREIDS
NERINE
NERINES
NERITE
NERITES
NERITIC
NERKA
NERKAS
NEROLI
NEROLIS
NERVAL
NERVATE
NERVATION
NERVATIONS
NERVATURE
NERVATURES
NERVE
NERVED
NERVELESS
NERVELET
NERVELETS
NERVER
NERVERS
NERVES
NERVIER
NERVIEST
NERVINE
NERVINES
NERVINESS
NERVINESSES
NERVING
NERVOUS
NERVOUSLY
NERVULAR
NERVULE
NERVULES
NERVURE
NERVURES
NERVY
NESCIENCE
NESCIENCES
NESCIENT
NESH
NESHNESS
NESHNESSES
NESS

NESSES
NEST
NESTED
NESTER
NESTERS
NESTING
NESTLE
NESTLED
NESTLES
NESTLING
NESTLINGS
NESTS
NET
NETBALL
NETBALLS
NETE
NETES
NETFUL
NETFULS
NETHELESS
NETHER
NETS
NETSUKE
NETSUKES
NETT
NETTED
NETTIER
NETTIEST
NETTING
NETTINGS
NETTLE
NETTLED
NETTLES
NETTLING
NETTS
NETTY
NETWORK
NETWORKED
NETWORKING
NETWORKS
NEUK
NEUKS
NEUM
NEUME
NEUMES
NEUMS
NEURAL
NEURALGIA
NEURALGIAS
NEURALGIC
NEURATION
NEURATIONS
NEURILITIES
NEURILITY
NEURINE
NEURINES
NEURISM
NEURISMS
NEURITE
NEURITES
NEURITIC
NEURITICS
NEURITIS
NEUROGLIA
NEUROGLIAS
NEUROGRAM
NEUROGRAMS
NEUROLOGIES
NEUROLOGY
NEUROMA

NEUROMAS
NEURON
NEURONAL
NEURONE
NEURONES
NEURONS
NEUROPATH
NEUROPATHS
NEUROSES
NEUROSIS
NEUROTIC
NEUROTICS
NEUROTOMIES
NEUROTOMY
NEUSTON
NEUSTONS
NEUTER
NEUTERED
NEUTERING
NEUTERS
NEUTRAL
NEUTRALLY
NEUTRALS
NEUTRETTO
NEUTRETTOS
NEUTRINO
NEUTRINOS
NEUTRON
NEUTRONS
NÉVÉ
NEVEL
NEVELLED
NEVELLING
NEVELS
NEVER
NEVERMORE
NÉVÉS
NEW
NEWBORN
NEWCOME
NEWCOMER
NEWCOMERS
NEWED
NEWEL
NEWELL
NEWELLED
NEWELLS
NEWELS
NEWER
NEWEST
NEWFANGLE
NEWFANGLED
NEWING
NEWISH
NEWLY
NEWMARKET
NEWMARKETS
NEWNESS
NEWNESSES
NEWS
NEWSAGENT
NEWSAGENTS
NEWSBOY
NEWSBOYS
NEWSCAST
NEWSCASTS
NEWSED
NEWSES
NEWSFLASH
NEWSFLASHES

NEWSGIRL
NEWSGIRLS
NEWSHAWK
NEWSHAWKS
NEWSHOUND
NEWSHOUNDS
NEWSIER
NEWSIES
NEWSIEST
NEWSINESS
NEWSINESSES
NEWSING
NEWSMAN
NEWSMEN
NEWSPAPER
NEWSPAPERS
NEWSPEAK
NEWSPEAKS
NEWSPRINT
NEWSPRINTS
NEWSREEL
NEWSREELS
NEWSROOM
NEWSROOMS
NEWSTRADE
NEWSTRADES
NEWSWOMAN
NEWSWOMEN
NEWSY
NEWT
NEWTON
NEWTONS
NEWTS
NEXT
NEXTLY
NEXTNESS
NEXTNESSES
NEXUS
NEXUSES
NGAIO
NGAIOS
NGWEE
NIACIN
NIACINS
NIB
NIBBED
NIBBING
NIBBLE
NIBBLED
NIBBLER
NIBBLERS
NIBBLES
NIBBLING
NIBBLINGS
NIBLICK
NIBLICKS
NIBS
NICCOLITE
NICCOLITES
NICE
NICEISH
NICELY
NICENESS
NICENESSES
NICER
NICEST
NICETIES
NICETY
NICHE
NICHED

NICHER
NICHERED
NICHERING
NICHERS
NICHES
NICHING
NICK
NICKAR
NICKARS
NICKED
NICKEL
NICKELIC
NICKELINE
NICKELINES
NICKELISE
NICKELISED
NICKELISES
NICKELISING
NICKELIZE
NICKELIZED
NICKELIZES
NICKELIZING
NICKELLED
NICKELLING
NICKELOUS
NICKELS
NICKER
NICKERED
NICKERING
NICKERS
NICKING
NICKNAME
NICKNAMED
NICKNAMES
NICKNAMING
NICKS
NICKSTICK
NICKSTICKS
NICKUM
NICKUMS
NICOL
NICOLS
NICOMPOOP
NICOMPOOPS
NICOTIAN
NICOTIANA
NICOTIANAS
NICOTIANS
NICOTINE
NICOTINES
NICOTINIC
NICTATE
NICTATED
NICTATES
NICTATING
NICTATION
NICTATIONS
NICTITATE
NICTITATED
NICTITATES
NICTITATING
NID
NIDAL
NIDATION
NIDATIONS
NIDDERING
NIDE
NIDERING
NIDERLING
NIDES

NIDGET
NIDGETS
NIDI
NIDIFIED
NIDIFIES
NIDIFY
NIDIFYING
NIDING
NIDOR
NIDOROUS
NIDORS
NIDS
NIDUS
NIE
NIECE
NIECES
NIEF
NIEFS
NIELLATED
NIELLI
NIELLIST
NIELLISTS
NIELLO
NIELLOED
NIELLOING
NIELLOS
NIEVE
NIEVEFUL
NIEVEFULS
NIEVES
NIFE
NIFES
NIFF
NIFFER
NIFFERED
NIFFERING
NIFFERS
NIFFIER
NIFFIEST
NIFFNAFF
NIFFNAFFED
NIFFNAFFING
NIFFNAFFS
NIFFS
NIFFY
NIFTIER
NIFTIEST
NIFTINESS
NIFTINESSES
NIFTY
NIGELLA
NIGELLAS
NIGER
NIGERS
NIGGARD
NIGGARDED
NIGGARDING
NIGGARDLY
NIGGARDS
NIGGER
NIGGERDOM
NIGGERDOMS
NIGGERED
NIGGERING
NIGGERISH
NIGGERISM
NIGGERISMS
NIGGERS
NIGGERY
NIGGLE

NIGGLED
NIGGLER
NIGGLERS
NIGGLES
NIGGLIER
NIGGLIEST
NIGGLING
NIGGLINGS
NIGGLY
NIGH
NIGHED
NIGHING
NIGHLY
NIGHNESS
NIGHNESSES
NIGHS
NIGHT
NIGHTCAP
NIGHTCAPS
NIGHTED
NIGHTFALL
NIGHTFALLS
NIGHTFIRE
NIGHTFIRES
NIGHTGEAR
NIGHTGEARS
NIGHTGOWN
NIGHTGOWNS
NIGHTHAWK
NIGHTHAWKS
NIGHTIE
NIGHTIES
NIGHTJAR
NIGHTJARS
NIGHTLESS
NIGHTLONG
NIGHTLY
NIGHTMARE
NIGHTMARES
NIGHTMARY
NIGHTS
NIGHTSPOT
NIGHTSPOTS
NIGHTWARD
NIGHTWEAR
NIGHTWEARS
NIGHTY
NIGRICANT
NIGRIFIED
NIGRIFIES
NIGRIFY
NIGRIFYING
NIGRITUDE
NIGRITUDES
NIGROSINE
NIGROSINES
NIHIL
NIHILISM
NIHILISMS
NIHILIST
NIHILISTS
NIHILITIES
NIHILITY
NIHILS
NIL
NILGAI
NILGAIS
NILGAU
NILGAUS
NILL

NILLED	NIPPERS	NITROXYL	NOCKING	NOGAKU
NILLING	NIPPIER	NITROXYLS	NOCKS	NOGGIN
NILLS	NIPPIEST	NITRY	NOCTILUCA	NOGGING
NILS	NIPPING	NITRYL	NOCTILUCAS	NOGGINGS
NIM	NIPPINGLY	NITRYLS	NOCTUA	NOGGINS
NIMBED	NIPPLE	NITS	NOCTUARIES	NOGS
NIMBI	NIPPLED	NITTIER	NOCTUARY	NOH
NIMBLE	NIPPLES	NITTIEST	NOCTUAS	NOHOW
NIMBLER	NIPPLING	NITTY	NOCTUID	NOHOWISH
NIMBLESSE	NIPPY	NITWIT	NOCTUIDS	NOIL
NIMBLESSES	NIPS	NITWITS	NOCTULE	NOILS
NIMBLEST	NIPTER	NITWITTED	NOCTULES	NOINT
NIMBLY	NIPTERS	NIVAL	NOCTURN	NOINTED
NIMBUS	NIRL	NIVEOUS	NOCTURNAL	NOINTING
NIMBUSED	NIRLED	NIX	NOCTURNALS	NOINTS
NIMBUSES	NIRLIE	NIXES	NOCTURNE	NOISE
NIMIETIES	NIRLIER	NIXIE	NOCTURNES	NOISED
NIMIETY	NIRLIEST	NIXIES	NOCTURNS	NOISEFUL
NIMIOUS	NIRLING	NIXY	NOCUOUS	NOISELESS
NIMMED	NIRLIT	NIZAM	NOCUOUSLY	NOISES
NIMMER	NIRLS	NIZAMS	NOD	NOISETTE
NIMMERS	NIRLY	NO	NODAL	NOISETTES
NIMMING	NIRVANA	NOB	NODALISE	NOISIER
NIMONIC	NIRVANAS	NOBBIER	NODALISED	NOISIEST
NIMS	NIS	NOBBIEST	NODALISES	NOISILY
NINCOM	NISBERRIES	NOBBILY	NODALISING	NOISINESS
NINCOMS	NISBERRY	NOBBINESS	NODALITIES	NOISINESSES
NINCUM	NISEI	NOBBINESSES	NODALITY	NOISING
NINCUMS	NISEIS	NOBBLE	NODALIZE	NOISOME
NINE	NISES	NOBBLED	NODALIZED	NOISOMELY
NINEFOLD	NISI	NOBBLER	NODALIZES	NOISY
NINEHOLES	NISSE	NOBBLERS	NODALIZING	NOLE
NINEPENCE	NISSES	NOBBLES	NODATED	NOLES
NINEPENCES	NISUS	NOBBLING	NODATION	NOLITION
NINEPENNIES	NIT	NOBBUT	NODATIONS	NOLITIONS
NINEPENNY	NITERIE	NOBBY	NODDED	NOLL
NINEPINS	NITERIES	NOBELIUM	NODDER	NOLLS
NINES	NITERY	NOBELIUMS	NODDERS	NOM
NINESCORE	NITHING	NOBILESSE	NODDIES	NOMA
NINESCORES	NITHINGS	NOBILESSES	NODDING	NOMAD
NINETEEN	NITID	NOBILIARY	NODDINGS	NOMADE
NINETEENS	NITON	NOBILITIES	NODDLE	NOMADES
NINETIES	NITONS	NOBILITY	NODDLED	NOMADIC
NINETIETH	NITRATE	NOBLE	NODDLES	NOMADIES
NINETIETHS	NITRATED	NOBLEMAN	NODDLING	NOMADISE
NINETY	NITRATES	NOBLEMEN	NODDY	NOMADISED
NINJA	NITRATINE	NOBLENESS	NODE	NOMADISES
NINJAS	NITRATINES	NOBLENESSES	NODES	NOMADISING
NINNIES	NITRATING	NOBLER	NODI	NOMADISM
NINNY	NITRATION	NOBLES	NODICAL	NOMADISMS
NINON	NITRATIONS	NOBLESSE	NODOSE	NOMADIZE
NINONS	NITRE	NOBLESSES	NODOSITIES	NOMADIZED
NINTH	NITRES	NOBLEST	NODOSITY	NOMADIZES
NINTHLY	NITRIC	NOBLY	NODOUS	NOMADIZING
NINTHS	NITRIDE	NOBODIES	NODS	NOMADS
NIOBATE	NITRIDED	NOBODY	NODULAR	NOMADY
NIOBATES	NITRIDES	NOBS	NODULATED	NOMARCH
NIOBIC	NITRIDING	NOCAKE	NODULE	NOMARCHIES
NIOBITE	NITRIDINGS	NOCAKES	NODULED	NOMARCHS
NIOBITES	NITRIFIED	NOCENT	NODULES	NOMARCHY
NIOBIUM	NITRIFIES	NOCENTLY	NODULOSE	NOMAS
NIOBIUMS	NITRIFY	NOCENTS	NODULOUS	NOMBRIL
NIOBOUS	NITRIFYING	NOCHEL	NODUS	NOMBRILS
NIP	NITRILE	NOCHELLED	NOEL	NOME
NIPPED	NITRILES	NOCHELLING	NOELS	NOMEN
NIPPER	NITRITE	NOCHELS	NOES	NOMES
NIPPERED	NITRITES	NOCK	NOESES	NOMIC
NIPPERING	NITROGEN	NOCKED	NOESIS	NOMINA
NIPPERKIN	NITROGENS	NOCKET	NOETIC	NOMINABLE
NIPPERKINS	NITROUS	NOCKETS	NOG	NOMINAL

NOMINALLY	NONSENSES	NORMALITIES	NOSTOC	NOTICED
NOMINALS	NONSUCH	NORMALITY	NOSTOCS	NOTICES
NOMINATE	NONSUCHES	NORMALIZE	NOSTOI	NOTICING
NOMINATED	NONSUIT	NORMALIZED	NOSTOLOGIES	NOTIFIED
NOMINATES	NONSUITED	NORMALIZES	NOSTOLOGY	NOTIFIER
NOMINATING	NONSUITING	NORMALIZING	NOSTOS	NOTIFIERS
NOMINATOR	NONSUITS	NORMALLY	NOSTRIL	NOTIFIES
NOMINATORS	NONUPLE	NORMALS	NOSTRILS	NOTIFY
NOMINEE	NONUPLET	NORMAN	NOSTRUM	NOTIFYING
NOMINEES	NONUPLETS	NORMANS	NOSTRUMS	NOTING
NOMISM	NOODLE	NORMAS	NOSY	NOTION
NOMISMS	NOODLED	NORMATIVE	NOT	NOTIONAL
NOMISTIC	NOODLEDOM	NORMS	NOTABILIA	NOTIONIST
NOMOCRACIES	NOODLEDOMS	NORSEL	NOTABLE	NOTIONISTS
NOMOCRACY	NOODLES	NORSELLED	NOTABLES	NOTIONS
NOMOGENIES	NOODLING	NORSELLER	NOTABLY	NOTITIA
NOMOGENY	NOOK	NORSELLERS	NOTAEUM	NOTITIAS
NOMOGRAM	NOOKIE	NORSELLING	NOTAEUMS	NOTOCHORD
NOMOGRAMS	NOOKIER	NORSELS	NOTAL	NOTOCHORDS
NOMOGRAPH	NOOKIES	NORTH	NOTANDA	NOTORIETIES
NOMOGRAPHS	NOOKIEST	NORTHED	NOTANDUM	NOTORIETY
NOMOI	NOOKS	NORTHER	NOTAPHILIES	NOTORIOUS
NOMOLOGIES	NOOKY	NORTHERED	NOTAPHILY	NOTORNIS
NOMOLOGY	NOOLOGIES	NORTHERING	NOTARIAL	NOTORNISES
NOMOS	NOOLOGY	NORTHERLY	NOTARIES	NOTOUR
NOMOTHETE	NOOMETRIES	NORTHERN	NOTARISE	NOTT
NOMOTHETES	NOOMETRY	NORTHERNS	NOTARISED	NOTUM
NOMS	NOON	NORTHERS	NOTARISES	NOTUMS
NON	NOONDAY	NORTHING	NOTARISING	NOUGAT
NONAGE	NOONDAYS	NORTHINGS	NOTARIZE	NOUGATS
NONAGED	NOONED	NORTHLAND	NOTARIZED	NOUGHT
NONAGES	NOONING	NORTHLANDS	NOTARIZES	NOUGHTS
NONAGON	NOONINGS	NORTHMOST	NOTARIZING	NOUL
NONAGONS	NOONS	NORTHS	NOTARY	NOULD
NONANE	NOONTIDE	NORTHWARD	NOTATE	NOULDE
NONANES	NOONTIDES	NORWARD	NOTATED	NOULE
NONARY	NOOP	NORWARDS	NOTATES	NOULES
NONCE	NOOPS	NOSE	NOTATING	NOULS
NONCES	NOOSE	NOSEAN	NOTATION	NOUMENA
NONE	NOOSED	NOSEANS	NOTATIONS	NOUMENAL
NONENTITIES	NOOSES	NOSEBAG	NOTCH	NOUMENON
NONENTITY	NOOSING	NOSEBAGS	NOTCHBACK	NOUN
NONES	NOOSPHERE	NOSED	NOTCHBACKS	NOUNAL
NONESUCH	NOOSPHERES	NOSEGAY	NOTCHED	NOUNS
NONESUCHES	NOPAL	NOSEGAYS	NOTCHEL	NOUNY
NONET	NOPALS	NOSELESS	NOTCHELLED	NOUP
NONETS	NOPE	NOSELITE	NOTCHELLING	NOUPS
NONETTE	NOPES	NOSELITES	NOTCHELS	NOURICE
NONETTES	NOR	NOSER	NOTCHES	NOURICES
NONETTI	NORI	NOSERS	NOTCHING	NOURISH
NONETTO	NORIA	NOSES	NOTCHINGS	NOURISHED
NONETTOS	NORIAS	NOSEY	NOTCHY	NOURISHER
NONG	NORIMON	NOSEYS	NOTE	NOURISHERS
NONGS	NORIMONS	NOSH	NOTEBOOK	NOURISHES
NONILLION	NORIS	NOSHED	NOTEBOOKS	NOURISHING
NONILLIONS	NORITE	NOSHES	NOTED	NOURITURE
NONJURING	NORITES	NOSHING	NOTEDLY	NOURITURES
NONJUROR	NORK	NOSIER	NOTEDNESS	NOURSLE
NONJURORS	NORKS	NOSIES	NOTEDNESSES	NOURSLED
NONNIES	NORLAND	NOSIEST	NOTELESS	NOURSLES
NONNY	NORLANDS	NOSILY	NOTELET	NOURSLING
NONPAREIL	NORM	NOSINESS	NOTELETS	NOUS
NONPAREILS	NORMA	NOSINESSES	NOTEPAPER	NOUSELL
NONPAROUS	NORMAL	NOSING	NOTEPAPERS	NOUSES
NONPLUS	NORMALCIES	NOSINGS	NOTER	NOUSLE
NONPLUSSED	NORMALCY	NOSOLOGIES	NOTERS	NOUSLED
NONPLUSSES	NORMALISE	NOSOLOGY	NOTES	NOUSLES
NONPLUSSING	NORMALISED	NOSTALGIA	NOTHING	NOUSLING
NONPOLAR	NORMALISES	NOSTALGIAS	NOTHINGS	NOUT
NONSENSE	NORMALISING	NOSTALGIC	NOTICE	NOUVEAU

NOUVELLE	NOWLS	NUCLEATE	NULLING	NUNCLE
NOUVELLES	NOWN	NUCLEATED	NULLINGS	NUNCLES
NOVA	NOWNESS	NUCLEATES	NULLIPARA	NUNCUPATE
NOVAE	NOWNESSES	NUCLEATING	NULLIPARAE	NUNCUPATED
NOVALIA	NOWS	NUCLEI	NULLIPARAS	NUNCUPATES
NOVAS	NOWT	NUCLEIDE	NULLIPORE	NUNCUPATING
NOVATION	NOWTS	NUCLEIDES	NULLIPORES	NUNDINAL
NOVATIONS	NOWY	NUCLEIN	NULLITIES	NUNDINE
NOVEL	NOXAL	NUCLEINS	NULLITY	NUNDINES
NOVELDOM	NOXIOUS	NUCLEOLAR	NULLNESS	NUNHOOD
NOVELDOMS	NOXIOUSLY	NUCLEOLE	NULLNESSES	NUNHOODS
NOVELESE	NOY	NUCLEOLES	NULLS	NUNNATION
NOVELESES	NOYADE	NUCLEOLI	NUMB	NUNNATIONS
NOVELETTE	NOYADES	NUCLEOLUS	NUMBAT	NUNNERIES
NOVELETTES	NOYANCE	NUCLEON	NUMBATS	NUNNERY
NOVELISE	NOYANCES	NUCLEONS	NUMBED	NUNNISH
NOVELISED	NOYAU	NUCLEUS	NUMBER	NUNS
NOVELISER	NOYAUS	NUCLIDE	NUMBERED	NUNSHIP
NOVELISERS	NOYED	NUCLIDES	NUMBERER	NUNSHIPS
NOVELISES	NOYES	NUCULE	NUMBERERS	NUPTIAL
NOVELISH	NOYESES	NUCULES	NUMBERING	NUPTIALS
NOVELISING	NOYING	NUDATION	NUMBERS	NUR
NOVELISM	NOYOUS	NUDATIONS	NUMBEST	NURAGHE
NOVELISMS	NOYS	NUDE	NUMBING	NURAGHI
NOVELIST	NOYSOME	NUDELY	NUMBLES	NURAGHIC
NOVELISTS	NOZZLE	NUDENESS	NUMBS	NURHAG
NOVELIZE	NOZZLES	NUDENESSES	NUMBSKULL	NURHAGS
NOVELIZED	NTH	NUDER	NUMBSKULLS	NURL
NOVELIZER	NU	NUDES	NUMDAH	NURLED
NOVELIZERS	NUANCE	NUDEST	NUMDAHS	NURLING
NOVELIZES	NUANCED	NUDGE	NUMEN	NURLS
NOVELIZING	NUANCES	NUDGED	NUMERABLE	NURR
NOVELLA	NUANCING	NUDGES	NUMERABLY	NURRS
NOVELLAE	NUB	NUDGING	NUMERACIES	NURS
NOVELLAS	NUBBED	NUDICAUL	NUMERACY	NURSE
NOVELLE	NUBBIER	NUDIE	NUMERAIRE	NURSED
NOVELS	NUBBIEST	NUDIES	NUMERAIRES	NURSELIKE
NOVELTIES	NUBBIN	NUDISM	NUMERAL	NURSELING
NOVELTY	NUBBING	NUDISMS	NUMERALLY	NURSELINGS
NOVENA	NUBBINS	NUDIST	NUMERALS	NURSEMAID
NOVENARIES	NUBBLE	NUDISTS	NUMERARY	NURSEMAIDS
NOVENARY	NUBBLED	NUDITIES	NUMERATE	NURSER
NOVENAS	NUBBLES	NUDITY	NUMERATED	NURSERIES
NOVENNIAL	NUBBLIER	NUGAE	NUMERATES	NURSERS
NOVERCAL	NUBBLIEST	NUGATORY	NUMERATING	NURSERY
NOVERINT	NUBBLING	NUGGAR	NUMERATOR	NURSES
NOVERINTS	NUBBLY	NUGGARS	NUMERATORS	NURSING
NOVICE	NUBBY	NUGGET	NUMERIC	NURSLE
NOVICES	NUBECULA	NUGGETS	NUMERICAL	NURSLING
NOVICIATE	NUBECULAE	NUGGETY	NUMEROUS	NURSLINGS
NOVICIATES	NUBIA	NUISANCE	NUMINA	NURTURAL
NOVITIATE	NUBIAS	NUISANCER	NUMINOUS	NURTURANT
NOVITIATES	NUBIFORM	NUISANCERS	NUMMARY	NURTURE
NOVITIES	NUBILE	NUISANCES	NUMMULAR	NURTURED
NOVITY	NUBILITIES	NUKE	NUMMULARY	NURTURER
NOVODAMUS	NUBILITY	NUKED	NUMMULINE	NURTURERS
NOVODAMUSES	NUBILOUS	NUKES	NUMMULITE	NURTURES
NOVUM	NUBS	NUKING	NUMMULITES	NURTURING
NOVUMS	NUCELLAR	NULL	NUMNAH	NUS
NOW	NUCELLI	NULLA	NUMNAHS	NUT
NOWADAYS	NUCELLUS	NULLAH	NUMSKULL	NUTANT
NOWAY	NUCELLUSES	NULLAHS	NUMSKULLS	NUTARIAN
NOWAYS	NUCHA	NULLAS	NUN	NUTARIANS
NOWED	NUCHAL	NULLED	NUNATAK	NUTATE
NOWHENCE	NUCHAS	NULLIFIED	NUNATAKER	NUTATED
NOWHERE	NUCLEAL	NULLIFIER	NUNATAKS	NUTATES
NOWHERES	NUCLEAR	NULLIFIERS	NUNCHEON	NUTATING
NOWHITHER	NUCLEARY	NULLIFIES	NUNCHEONS	NUTATION
NOWISE	NUCLEASE	NULLIFY	NUNCIO	NUTATIONS
NOWL	NUCLEASES	NULLIFYING	NUNCIOS	NUTCASE

NUTCASES
NUTHATCH
NUTHATCHES
NUTJOBBER
NUTJOBBERS
NUTLET
NUTLETS
NUTMEAL
NUTMEALS
NUTMEG
NUTMEGGED
NUTMEGGY
NUTMEGS
NUTPECKER
NUTPECKERS
NUTRIA
NUTRIAS
NUTRIENT

NUTRIENTS
NUTRIMENT
NUTRIMENTS
NUTRITION
NUTRITIONS
NUTRITIVE
NUTS
NUTSHELL
NUTSHELLS
NUTTED
NUTTER
NUTTERIES
NUTTERS
NUTTERY
NUTTIER
NUTTIEST
NUTTINESS
NUTTINESSES

NUTTING
NUTTINGS
NUTTY
NUZZER
NUZZERS
NUZZLE
NUZZLED
NUZZLES
NUZZLING
NY
NYAFF
NYAFFED
NYAFFING
NYAFFS
NYALA
NYALAS
NYANZA
NYANZAS

NYAS
NYASES
NYCTALOPES
NYCTALOPS
NYE
NYES
NYING
NYLGHAU
NYLGHAUS
NYLON
NYLONS
NYMPH
NYMPHAE
NYMPHAEA
NYMPHAEUM
NYMPHAEUMS
NYMPHAL
NYMPHALID

NYMPHALIDS
NYMPHEAN
NYMPHET
NYMPHETS
NYMPHIC
NYMPHICAL
NYMPHISH
NYMPHLY
NYMPHO
NYMPHOS
NYMPHS
NYS
NYSTAGMIC
NYSTAGMUS
NYSTAGMUSES

O

OAF
OAFISH
OAFS
OAK
OAKEN
OAKENSHAW
OAKENSHAWS
OAKER
OAKERS
OAKIER
OAKIEST
OAKLING
OAKLINGS
OAKS
OAKUM
OAKUMS
OAKY
OAR
OARAGE
OARAGES
OARED
OARING
OARLESS
OARS
OARSMAN
OARSMEN
OARSWOMAN
OARSWOMEN
OARWEED
OARWEEDS
OARY
OASES
OASIS
OAST
OASTS
OAT
OATCAKE
OATCAKES
OATEN
OATH
OATHABLE
OATHS
OATMEAL
OATMEALS
OATS
OAVES
OB
OBANG
OBANGS
OBBLIGATI
OBBLIGATO
OBBLIGATOS
OBCONIC
OBCONICAL
OBCORDATE
OBDURACIES
OBDURACY
OBDURATE
OBDURATED
OBDURATES
OBDURATING
OBDURE
OBDURED
OBDURES

OBDURING
OBEAH
OBEAHED
OBEAHING
OBEAHISM
OBEAHISMS
OBEAHS
OBECHE
OBECHES
OBEDIENCE
OBEDIENCES
OBEDIENT
OBEISANCE
OBEISANCES
OBEISANT
OBEISM
OBEISMS
OBELI
OBELION
OBELIONS
OBELISCAL
OBELISE
OBELISED
OBELISES
OBELISING
OBELISK
OBELISKS
OBELIZE
OBELIZED
OBELIZES
OBELIZING
OBELUS
OBESE
OBESENESS
OBESENESSES
OBESER
OBESEST
OBESITIES
OBESITY
OBEY
OBEYED
OBEYER
OBEYERS
OBEYING
OBEYS
OBFUSCATE
OBFUSCATED
OBFUSCATES
OBFUSCATING
OBI
OBIA
OBIAS
OBIED
OBIING
OBIISM
OBIISMS
OBIIT
OBIS
OBIT
OBITAL
OBITER
OBITS
OBITUAL
OBITUARIES

OBITUARY
OBJECT
OBJECTED
OBJECTIFIED
OBJECTIFIES
OBJECTIFY
OBJECTIFYING
OBJECTING
OBJECTION
OBJECTIONS
OBJECTIVE
OBJECTIVES
OBJECTOR
OBJECTORS
OBJECTS
OBJET
OBJETS
OBJURE
OBJURED
OBJURES
OBJURGATE
OBJURGATED
OBJURGATES
OBJURGATING
OBJURING
OBLAST
OBLASTS
OBLATE
OBLATES
OBLATION
OBLATIONS
OBLATORY
OBLIGANT
OBLIGANTS
OBLIGATE
OBLIGATED
OBLIGATES
OBLIGATING
OBLIGE
OBLIGED
OBLIGEE
OBLIGEES
OBLIGES
OBLIGING
OBLIGOR
OBLIGORS
OBLIQUE
OBLIQUED
OBLIQUELY
OBLIQUER
OBLIQUES
OBLIQUEST
OBLIQUID
OBLIQUING
OBLIQUITIES
OBLIQUITY
OBLIVION
OBLIVIONS
OBLIVIOUS
OBLONG
OBLONGS
OBLOQUIES
OBLOQUY
OBNOXIOUS

OBOE
OBOES
OBOIST
OBOISTS
OBOL
OBOLARY
OBOLI
OBOLS
OBOLUS
OBOVATE
OBOVATELY
OBOVOID
OBREPTION
OBREPTIONS
OBS
OBSCENE
OBSCENELY
OBSCENER
OBSCENEST
OBSCENITIES
OBSCENITY
OBSCURANT
OBSCURANTS
OBSCURE
OBSCURED
OBSCURELY
OBSCURER
OBSCURERS
OBSCURES
OBSCUREST
OBSCURING
OBSCURITIES
OBSCURITY
OBSECRATE
OBSECRATED
OBSECRATES
OBSECRATING
OBSEQUENT
OBSEQUIAL
OBSEQUIE
OBSEQUIES
OBSEQUY
OBSERVANT
OBSERVANTS
OBSERVE
OBSERVED
OBSERVER
OBSERVERS
OBSERVES
OBSERVING
OBSESS
OBSESSED
OBSESSES
OBSESSING
OBSESSION
OBSESSIONS
OBSESSIVE
OBSIDIAN
OBSIDIANS
OBSIGN
OBSIGNATE
OBSIGNATED
OBSIGNATES
OBSIGNATING

OBSIGNED
OBSIGNING
OBSIGNS
OBSOLESCE
OBSOLESCED
OBSOLESCES
OBSOLESCING
OBSOLETE
OBSTACLE
OBSTACLES
OBSTETRIC
OBSTETRICS
OBSTINACIES
OBSTINACY
OBSTINATE
OBSTRUCT
OBSTRUCTED
OBSTRUCTING
OBSTRUCTS
OBSTRUENT
OBSTRUENTS
OBTAIN
OBTAINED
OBTAINER
OBTAINERS
OBTAINING
OBTAINS
OBTECT
OBTECTED
OBTEMPER
OBTEMPERED
OBTEMPERING
OBTEMPERS
OBTEND
OBTENDED
OBTENDING
OBTENDS
OBTENTION
OBTENTIONS
OBTEST
OBTESTED
OBTESTING
OBTESTS
OBTRUDE
OBTRUDED
OBTRUDER
OBTRUDERS
OBTRUDES
OBTRUDING
OBTRUDINGS
OBTRUSION
OBTRUSIONS
OBTRUSIVE
OBTUND
OBTUNDED
OBTUNDENT
OBTUNDENTS
OBTUNDING
OBTUNDS
OBTURATE
OBTURATED
OBTURATES
OBTURATING
OBTURATOR

OBTURATORS	OCCULTS	OCOTILLOS	OCTUPLET	ODONTIST
OBTUSE	OCCUPANCE	OCREA	OCTUPLETS	ODONTISTS
OBTUSELY	OCCUPANCES	OCREAE	OCTUPLING	ODONTOID
OBTUSER	OCCUPANCIES	OCREATE	OCULAR	ODONTOMA
OBTUSEST	OCCUPANCY	OCTACHORD	OCULARIST	ODONTOMAS
OBTUSITIES	OCCUPANT	OCTACHORDS	OCULARISTS	ODONTOMATA
OBTUSITY	OCCUPANTS	OCTAD	OCULARLY	ODOR
OBUMBRATE	OCCUPATE	OCTADIC	OCULARS	ODORANT
OBUMBRATED	OCCUPATED	OCTADS	OCULATE	ODORATE
OBUMBRATES	OCCUPATES	OCTAGON	OCULATED	ODOROUS
OBUMBRATING	OCCUPATING	OCTAGONAL	OCULI	ODOROUSLY
OBVENTION	OCCUPIED	OCTAGONS	OCULIST	ODORS
OBVENTIONS	OCCUPIER	OCTAHEDRA	OCULISTS	ODOUR
OBVERSE	OCCUPIERS	OCTAL	OCULUS	ODOURED
OBVERSELY	OCCUPIES	OCTAMETER	OD	ODOURLESS
OBVERSES	OCCUPY	OCTAMETERS	ODA	ODOURS
OBVERSION	OCCUPYING	OCTANE	ODAL	ODS
OBVERSIONS	OCCUR	OCTANES	ODALIQUE	ODSO
OBVERT	OCCURRED	OCTANT	ODALIQUES	ODSOS
OBVERTED	OCCURRENT	OCTANTAL	ODALISK	ODYL
OBVERTING	OCCURRENTS	OCTANTS	ODALISKS	ODYLE
OBVERTS	OCCURRING	OCTAPLA	ODALISQUE	ODYLES
OBVIATE	OCCURS	OCTAPLOID	ODALISQUES	ODYLISM
OBVIATED	OCEAN	OCTAPLOIDS	ODALLER	ODYLISMS
OBVIATES	OCEANAUT	OCTAPODIC	ODALLERS	ODYLS
OBVIATING	OCEANAUTS	OCTAPODIES	ODALS	ODYSSEY
OBVIATION	OCEANIC	OCTAPODY	ODAS	ODYSSEYS
OBVIATIONS	OCEANID	OCTAROON	ODD	ODZOOKS
OBVIOUS	OCEANIDES	OCTAROONS	ODDBALL	OE
OBVIOUSLY	OCEANIDS	OCTASTICH	ODDBALLS	OECIST
OBVOLUTE	OCEANS	OCTASTICHS	ODDER	OECISTS
OBVOLUTED	OCELLAR	OCTASTYLE	ODDEST	OECOLOGIES
OBVOLVENT	OCELLATE	OCTASTYLES	ODDISH	OECOLOGY
OCA	OCELLATED	OCTAVAL	ODDITIES	OECUMENIC
OCARINA	OCELLI	OCTAVE	ODDITY	OEDEMA
OCARINAS	OCELLUS	OCTAVES	ODDLY	OEDEMAS
OCAS	OCELOID	OCTAVO	ODDMENT	OEILLADE
OCCAMIES	OCELOT	OCTAVOS	ODDMENTS	OEILLADES
OCCAMY	OCELOTS	OCTENNIAL	ODDNESS	OENANTHIC
OCCASION	OCH	OCTET	ODDNESSES	OENOLOGIES
OCCASIONED	OCHE	OCTETS	ODDS	OENOLOGY
OCCASIONING	OCHER	OCTETT	ODDSMAN	OENOMANCIES
OCCASIONS	OCHERED	OCTETTE	ODDSMEN	OENOMANCY
OCCIDENT	OCHERING	OCTETTES	ODE	OENOMANIA
OCCIDENTS	OCHEROUS	OCTETTS	ODEA	OENOMANIAS
OCCIPITAL	OCHERS	OCTILLION	ODEON	OENOMEL
OCCIPITALS	OCHERY	OCTILLIONS	ODEONS	OENOMELS
OCCIPUT	OCHES	OCTOFID	ODES	OENOMETER
OCCIPUTS	OCHIDORE	OCTONARIES	ODEUM	OENOMETERS
OCCLUDE	OCHIDORES	OCTONARII	ODEUMS	OENOPHIL
OCCLUDED	OCHLOCRAT	OCTONARY	ODIC	OENOPHILE
OCCLUDENT	OCHLOCRATS	OCTOPI	ODIOUS	OENOPHILES
OCCLUDENTS	OCHONE	OCTOPLOID	ODIOUSLY	OENOPHILIES
OCCLUDES	OCHRE	OCTOPLOIDS	ODISM	OENOPHILS
OCCLUDING	OCHREA	OCTOPOD	ODISMS	OENOPHILY
OCCLUSAL	OCHREAE	OCTOPODES	ODIST	OERLIKON
OCCLUSION	OCHREATE	OCTOPODS	ODISTS	OERLIKONS
OCCLUSIONS	OCHRED	OCTOPUS	ODIUM	OERSTED
OCCLUSIVE	OCHREOUS	OCTOPUSES	ODIUMS	OERSTEDS
OCCLUSIVES	OCHRES	OCTOROON	ODOGRAPH	OES
OCCLUSOR	OCHREY	OCTOROONS	ODOGRAPHS	OESOPHAGI
OCCLUSORS	OCHRING	OCTOSTYLE	ODOMETER	OESTRAL
OCCULT	OCHROID	OCTOSTYLES	ODOMETERS	OESTROGEN
OCCULTED	OCHROUS	OCTROI	ODOMETRIES	OESTROGENS
OCCULTING	OCHRY	OCTROIS	ODOMETRY	OESTROUS
OCCULTISM	OCKER	OCTUOR	ODONATIST	OESTRUM
OCCULTISMS	OCKERISM	OCTUORS	ODONATISTS	OESTRUMS
OCCULTIST	OCKERISMS	OCTUPLE	ODONTALGIES	OESTRUS
OCCULTISTS	OCKERS	OCTUPLED	ODONTALGY	OESTRUSES
OCCULTLY	OCOTILLO	OCTUPLES	ODONTIC	OEUVRE

OEUVRES
OF
OFAY
OFAYS
OFF
OFFAL
OFFALS
OFFBEAT
OFFCUT
OFFCUTS
OFFED
OFFENCE
OFFENCES
OFFEND
OFFENDED
OFFENDER
OFFENDERS
OFFENDING
OFFENDRESS
OFFENDRESSES
OFFENDS
OFFENSE
OFFENSED
OFFENSES
OFFENSING
OFFENSIVE
OFFENSIVES
OFFER
OFFERABLE
OFFERED
OFFEREE
OFFEREES
OFFERER
OFFERERS
OFFERING
OFFERINGS
OFFEROR
OFFERORS
OFFERS
OFFERTORIES
OFFERTORY
OFFHAND
OFFHANDED
OFFICE
OFFICER
OFFICERED
OFFICERING
OFFICERS
OFFICES
OFFICIAL
OFFICIALS
OFFICIANT
OFFICIANTS
OFFICIATE
OFFICIATED
OFFICIATES
OFFICIATING
OFFICINAL
OFFICIOUS
OFFING
OFFINGS
OFFISH
OFFLOAD
OFFLOADED
OFFLOADING
OFFLOADS
OFFPEAK
OFFPRINT
OFFPRINTS
OFFPUT

OFFPUTS
OFFS
OFFSADDLE
OFFSADDLED
OFFSADDLES
OFFSADDLING
OFFSCUM
OFFSCUMS
OFFSEASON
OFFSEASONS
OFFSET
OFFSETS
OFFSETTING
OFFSHOOT
OFFSHOOTS
OFFSHORE
OFFSIDE
OFFSIDER
OFFSIDERS
OFFSIDES
OFFSPRING
OFFSPRINGS
OFFTAKE
OFFTAKES
OFLAG
OFLAGS
OFT
OFTEN
OFTENER
OFTENEST
OFTENNESS
OFTENNESSES
OFTTIMES
OGAM
OGAMIC
OGAMS
OGDOAD
OGDOADS
OGEE
OGEES
OGGIN
OGGINS
OGHAM
OGHAMIC
OGHAMS
OGIVAL
OGIVE
OGIVES
OGLE
OGLED
OGLER
OGLERS
OGLES
OGLING
OGLINGS
OGMIC
OGRE
OGREISH
OGRES
OGRESS
OGRESSES
OGRISH
OH
OHM
OHMIC
OHMMETER
OHMMETERS
OHMS
OHO
OHONE

OHOS
OI
OIDIA
OIDIUM
OIK
OIKIST
OIKISTS
OIKS
OIL
OILCAN
OILCANS
OILCLOTH
OILCLOTHS
OILED
OILER
OILERIES
OILERS
OILERY
OILIER
OILIEST
OILILY
OILINESS
OILINESSES
OILING
OILLET
OILLETS
OILNUT
OILNUTS
OILS
OILSKIN
OILSKINS
OILSTONE
OILSTONES
OILY
OINT
OINTED
OINTING
OINTMENT
OINTMENTS
OINTS
OITICICA
OITICICAS
OJIME
OJIMES
OKAPI
OKAPIS
OKAY
OKAYED
OKAYING
OKAYS
OKE
OKES
OKIMONO
OKIMONOS
OKRA
OKRAS
OLD
OLDEN
OLDENED
OLDENING
OLDENS
OLDER
OLDEST
OLDIE
OLDIES
OLDISH
OLDNESS
OLDNESSES
OLDS
OLDSQUAW

OLDSQUAWS
OLDSTER
OLDSTERS
OLDY
OLÉ
OLEACEOUS
OLEANDER
OLEANDERS
OLEARIA
OLEARIAS
OLEASTER
OLEASTERS
OLEATE
OLEATES
OLECRANAL
OLECRANON
OLECRANONS
OLEFIANT
OLEFIN
OLEFINE
OLEFINES
OLEFINS
OLEIC
OLEIN
OLEINS
OLENT
OLEO
OLEOGRAPH
OLEOGRAPHS
OLEOS
OLEPHILIC
OLEUM
OLEUMS
OLFACT
OLFACTED
OLFACTING
OLFACTION
OLFACTIONS
OLFACTIVE
OLFACTORY
OLFACTS
OLIBANUM
OLIBANUMS
OLID
OLIGAEMIA
OLIGAEMIAS
OLIGARCH
OLIGARCHIES
OLIGARCHS
OLIGARCHY
OLIGIST
OLIGISTS
OLIGOPOLIES
OLIGOPOLY
OLIO
OLIOS
OLIPHANT
OLIPHANTS
OLITORIES
OLITORY
OLIVARY
OLIVE
OLIVENITE
OLIVENITES
OLIVER
OLIVERS
OLIVES
OLIVET
OLIVETS
OLIVINE

OLIVINES
OLLA
OLLAMH
OLLAMHS
OLLAS
OLLAV
OLLAVS
OLM
OLMS
OLOGIES
OLOGY
OLOROSO
OLOROSOS
OLPAE
OLPE
OLPES
OLYCOOK
OLYCOOKS
OLYKOEK
OLYKOEKS
OLYMPIAD
OLYMPIADS
OLYMPICS
OM
OMADHAUN
OMADHAUNS
OMASA
OMASAL
OMASUM
OMBRE
OMBRÉ
OMBRELLA
OMBRELLAS
OMBRES
OMBROPHIL
OMBROPHILS
OMBU
OMBÚ
OMBUDSMAN
OMBUDSMEN
OMBUS
OMBUS
OMEGA
OMEGAS
OMELET
OMELETS
OMELETTE
OMELETTES
OMEN
OMENED
OMENING
OMENS
OMENTA
OMENTAL
OMENTUM
OMER
OMERS
OMERTA
OMERTAS
OMICRON
OMICRONS
OMINOUS
OMINOUSLY
OMISSIBLE
OMISSION
OMISSIONS
OMISSIVE
OMIT
OMITS
OMITTANCE

OMITTANCES
OMITTED
OMITTER
OMITTERS
OMITTING
OMLAH
OMLAHS
OMMATEA
OMMATEUM
OMMATIDIA
OMNEITIES
OMNEITY
OMNIANA
OMNIBUS
OMNIBUSES
OMNIETIES
OMNIETY
OMNIFIC
OMNIFIED
OMNIFIES
OMNIFORM
OMNIFY
OMNIFYING
OMNIUM
OMNIUMS
OMNIVORE
OMNIVORES
OMOHYOID
OMOHYOIDS
OMOPHAGIA
OMOPHAGIAS
OMOPHAGIC
OMOPHAGIES
OMOPHAGY
OMOPLATE
OMOPLATES
OMPHACITE
OMPHACITES
OMPHALIC
OMPHALOID
OMPHALOS
OMPHALOSES
OMRAH
OMRAHS
OMS
ON
ONAGER
ONAGERS
ONANISM
ONANISMS
ONANIST
ONANISTIC
ONANISTS
ONBOARD
ONCE
ONCER
ONCERS
ONCES
ONCIDIUM
ONCIDIUMS
ONCOGEN
ONCOGENE
ONCOGENES
ONCOGENIC
ONCOGENS
ONCOLOGIES
ONCOLOGY
ONCOME
ONCOMES
ONCOMETER

ONCOMETERS
ONCOMING
ONCOMINGS
ONCOST
ONCOSTMAN
ONCOSTMEN
ONCOSTS
ONCOTOMIES
ONCOTOMY
ONCUS
ONDATRA
ONDATRAS
ONDINE
ONDINES
ONDING
ONDINGS
ONE
ONEFOLD
ONEIRIC
ONELY
ONENESS
ONENESSES
ONER
ONEROUS
ONEROUSLY
ONERS
ONES
ONESELF
ONESTEP
ONESTEPPED
ONESTEPPING
ONESTEPS
ONEYER
ONEYERS
ONEYRE
ONEYRES
ONFALL
ONFALLS
ONFLOW
ONFLOWS
ONGOING
ONGOINGS
ONION
ONIONED
ONIONING
ONIONS
ONIONY
ONIRIC
ONISCOID
ONKUS
ONLOOKER
ONLOOKERS
ONLOOKING
ONLY
ONNED
ONNING
ONOMASTIC
ONOMASTICS
ONRUSH
ONRUSHES
ONS
ONSET
ONSETS
ONSETTER
ONSETTERS
ONSETTING
ONSETTINGS
ONSHORE
ONSIDE
ONSIDES

ONSLAUGHT ·
ONSLAUGHTS
ONST
ONSTEAD
ONSTEADS
ONTO
ONTOGENIC
ONTOGENIES
ONTOGENY
ONTOLOGIC
ONTOLOGIES
ONTOLOGY
ONUS
ONUSES
ONWARD
ONWARDLY
ONWARDS
ONYCHA
ONYCHAS
ONYCHIA
ONYCHIAS
ONYCHITE
ONYCHITES
ONYCHITIS
ONYCHIUM
ONYCHIUMS
ONYMOUS
ONYX
ONYXES
OO
OOBIT
OOBITS
OOCYTE
OOCYTES
OODLES
OODLINS
OOF
OOFS
OOFTISH
OOFTISHES
OOGAMIES
OOGAMOUS
OOGAMY
OOGENESES
OOGENESIS
OOGENETIC
OOGENIES
OOGENY
OOGONIA
OOGONIAL
OOGONIUM
OOH
OOHED
OOHING
OOHS
OOIDAL
OOLAKAN
OOLAKANS
OOLITE
OOLITES
OOLITIC
OOLOGIES
OOLOGIST
OOLOGISTS
OOLOGY
OOLONG
OOLONGS
OOM
OOMIAC
OOMIACK

OOMIACKS
OOMIACS
OOMIAK
OOMIAKS
OOMPAH
OOMPAHED
OOMPAHING
OOMPAHS
OOMPH
OOMPHS
OOMS
OON
OONS
OONT
OONTS
OOP
OOPED
OOPHORON
OOPHORONS
OOPHYTE
OOPHYTES
OOPING
OOPS
OOR
OORIAL
OORIALS
OORIE
OOS
OOSE
OOSES
OOSIER
OOSIEST
OOSPHERE
OOSPHERES
OOSPORE
OOSPORES
OOSY
OOZE
OOZED
OOZES
OOZIER
OOZIEST
OOZILY
OOZINESS
OOZINESSES
OOZING
OOZY
OP
OPACITIES
OPACITY
OPACOUS
OPAH
OPAHS
OPAL
OPALED
OPALINE
OPALINES
OPALISED
OPALIZED
OPALS
OPAQUE
OPAQUED
OPAQUELY
OPAQUER
OPAQUES
OPAQUEST
OPAQUING
OPE
OPED
OPEN

OPENABLE
OPENED
OPENER
OPENERS
OPENEST
OPENING
OPENINGS
OPENLY
OPENNESS
OPENNESSES
OPENS
OPERA
OPERABLE
OPERAND
OPERANDS
OPERANT
OPERANTS
OPERAS
OPERATE
OPERATED
OPERATES
OPERATIC
OPERATING
OPERATION
OPERATIONS
OPERATIVE
OPERATIVES
OPERATOR
OPERATORS
OPERCULA
OPERCULAR
OPERCULUM
OPERETTA
OPERETTAS
OPEROSE
OPEROSELY
OPEROSITIES
OPEROSITY
OPES
OPHIDIAN
OPHIDIANS
OPHIOLITE
OPHIOLITES
OPHIOLOGIES
OPHIOLOGY
OPHITE
OPHITES
OPHITIC
OPHIURAN
OPHIURANS
OPHIURID
OPHIURIDS
OPHIUROID
OPHIUROIDS
OPIATE
OPIATED
OPIATES
OPIATING
OPIFICER
OPIFICERS
OPINABLE
OPINE
OPINED
OPINES
OPING
OPINICUS
OPINICUSES
OPINING
OPINION
OPINIONED

OPINIONS
OPIOID
OPIUM
OPIUMS
OPOBALSAM
OPOBALSAMS
OPODELDOC
OPODELDOCS
OPOPANAX
OPOPANAXES
OPORICE
OPORICES
OPOSSUM
OPOSSUMS
OPPIDAN
OPPIDANS
OPPILATE
OPPILATED
OPPILATES
OPPILATING
OPPO
OPPONENCIES
OPPONENCY
OPPONENT
OPPONENTS
OPPORTUNE
OPPOSE
OPPOSABLE
OPPOSE
OPPOSED
OPPOSER
OPPOSERS
OPPOSES
OPPOSING
OPPOSITE
OPPOSITES
OPPRESS
OPPRESSED
OPPRESSES
OPPRESSING
OPPRESSOR
OPPRESSORS
OPPUGN
OPPUGNANT
OPPUGNANTS
OPPUGNED
OPPUGNER
OPPUGNERS
OPPUGNING
OPPUGNS
OPS
OPSIMATH
OPSIMATHIES
OPSIMATHS
OPSIMATHY
OPSOMANIA
OPSOMANIAS
OPSONIC
OPSONIN
OPSONINS
OPSONIUM
OPSONIUMS
OPT
OPTANT
OPTANTS
OPTATIVE
OPTATIVES
OPTED
OPTIC
OPTICAL

OPTICALLY
OPTICIAN
OPTICIANS
OPTICS
OPTIMA
OPTIMAL
OPTIMATE
OPTIMATES
OPTIME
OPTIMES
OPTIMISE
OPTIMISED
OPTIMISES
OPTIMISING
OPTIMISM
OPTIMISMS
OPTIMIST
OPTIMISTS
OPTIMIZE
OPTIMIZED
OPTIMIZES
OPTIMIZING
OPTIMUM
OPTING
OPTION
OPTIONAL
OPTIONS
OPTOLOGIES
OPTOLOGY
OPTOMETER
OPTOMETERS
OPTOMETRIES
OPTOMETRY
OPTOPHONE
OPTOPHONES
OPTS
OPULENCE
OPULENCES
OPULENT
OPULENTLY
OPULUS
OPULUSES
OPUNTIA
OPUNTIAS
OPUS
OPUSCLE
OPUSCLES
OPUSCULA
OPUSCULE
OPUSCULES
OPUSCULUM
OPUSES
OR
ORACH
ORACHE
ORACHES
ORACHS
ORACIES
ORACLE
ORACLED
ORACLES
ORACLING
ORACULAR
ORACULOUS
ORACY
ORAGIOUS
ORAL
ORALLY
ORALS
ORANG

ORANGE
ORANGEADE
ORANGEADES
ORANGER
ORANGERIES
ORANGERY
ORANGES
ORANGEST
ORANGS
ORANT
ORANTS
ORARIA
ORARIAN
ORARIANS
ORARION
ORARIONS
ORARIUM
ORARIUMS
ORATE
ORATED
ORATES
ORATING
ORATION
ORATIONS
ORATOR
ORATORIAL
ORATORIAN
ORATORIANS
ORATORIES
ORATORIO
ORATORIOS
ORATORS
ORATORY
ORATRESS
ORATRESSES
ORATRIX
ORATRIXES
ORB
ORBED
ORBICULAR
ORBIER
ORBIEST
ORBING
ORBIT
ORBITA
ORBITAL
ORBITALS
ORBITAS
ORBITED
ORBITER
ORBITERS
ORBITIES
ORBITING
ORBITS
ORBITY
ORBS
ORBY
ORC
ORCEIN
ORCEINS
ORCHARD
ORCHARDS
ORCHAT
ORCHATS
ORCHEL
ORCHELLA
ORCHELLAS
ORCHELS
ORCHESES
ORCHESIS

ORCHESTIC
ORCHESTRA
ORCHESTRAS
ORCHID
ORCHIDIST
ORCHIDISTS
ORCHIDS
ORCHIL
ORCHILLA
ORCHILLAS
ORCHILS
ORCHIS
ORCHISES
ORCHITIC
ORCHITIS
ORCHITISES
ORCIN
ORCINE
ORCINES
ORCINOL
ORCINOLS
ORCINS
ORCS
ORD
ORDAIN
ORDAINED
ORDAINER
ORDAINERS
ORDAINING
ORDAINS
ORDALIAN
ORDALIUM
ORDALIUMS
ORDEAL
ORDEALS
ORDER
ORDERED
ORDERER
ORDERERS
ORDERING
ORDERINGS
ORDERLESS
ORDERLIES
ORDERLY
ORDERS
ORDINAIRE
ORDINAIRES
ORDINAL
ORDINALS
ORDINANCE
ORDINANCES
ORDINAND
ORDINANDS
ORDINANT
ORDINANTS
ORDINAR
ORDINARIES
ORDINARS
ORDINARY
ORDINATE
ORDINATED
ORDINATES
ORDINATING
ORDINEE
ORDINEES
ORDNANCE
ORDNANCES
ORDS
ORDURE
ORDURES

ORDUROUS
ORE
OREAD
OREADES
OREADS
ORECROWE
ORECTIC
OREGANO
OREGANOS
OREIDE
OREIDES
OREOLOGIES
OREOLOGY
OREPEARCH
ORES
ORESTUNCK
OREWEED
OREWEEDS
OREXIS
OREXISES
ORF
ORFE
ORFES
ORFS
ORGAN
ORGANA
ORGANDIE
ORGANDIES
ORGANELLE
ORGANELLES
ORGANIC
ORGANICAL
ORGANISE
ORGANISED
ORGANISER
ORGANISERS
ORGANISES
ORGANISING
ORGANISM
ORGANISMS
ORGANIST
ORGANISTS
ORGANITIES
ORGANITY
ORGANIZE
ORGANIZED
ORGANIZER
ORGANIZERS
ORGANIZES
ORGANIZING
ORGANON
ORGANS
ORGANUM
ORGANZA
ORGANZAS
ORGANZINE
ORGANZINES
ORGASM
ORGASMED
ORGASMIC
ORGASMING
ORGASMS
ORGASTIC
ORGEAT
ORGEATS
ORGIA
ORGIAS
ORGIAST
ORGIASTIC
ORGIASTS

ORGIC
ORGIES
ORGILLOUS
ORGONE
ORGONES
ORGUE
ORGUES
ORGULOUS
ORGY
ORIBI
ORIBIS
ORICALCHE
ORICALCHES
ORICHALC
ORICHALCS
ORIEL
ORIELLED
ORIELS
ORIENCIES
ORIENCY
ORIENT
ORIENTAL
ORIENTALS
ORIENTATE
ORIENTATED
ORIENTATES
ORIENTATING
ORIENTED
ORIENTEER
ORIENTEERED
ORIENTEERING
ORIENTEERINGS
ORIENTEERS
ORIENTING
ORIENTS
ORIFEX
ORIFEXES
ORIFICE
ORIFICES
ORIFICIAL
ORIFLAMME
ORIFLAMMES
ORIGAMI
ORIGAMIS
ORIGAN
ORIGANE
ORIGANES
ORIGANS
ORIGANUM
ORIGANUMS
ORIGIN
ORIGINAL
ORIGINALS
ORIGINATE
ORIGINATED
ORIGINATES
ORIGINATING
ORIGINS
ORILLION
ORILLIONS
ORIOLE
ORIOLES
ORISON
ORISONS
ORLE
ORLEANS
ORLEANSES
ORLES
ORLOP
ORLOPS

ORMER
ORMERS
ORMOLU
ORMOLUS
ORNAMENT
ORNAMENTED
ORNAMENTING
ORNAMENTS
ORNATE
ORNATELY
ORNATER
ORNATEST
ORNERY
ORNIS
ORNISES
ORNITHIC
ORNITHOID
OROGENIC
OROGENIES
OROGENY
OROGRAPHIES
OROGRAPHY
OROIDE
OROIDES
OROLOGIES
OROLOGIST
OROLOGISTS
OROLOGY
OROPESA
OROPESAS
OROROTUND
OROTUND
ORPHAN
ORPHANAGE
ORPHANAGES
ORPHANED
ORPHANING
ORPHANISM
ORPHANISMS
ORPHANS
ORPHARION
ORPHARIONS
ORPHREY
ORPHREYS
ORPIMENT
ORPIMENTS
ORPIN
ORPINE
ORPINES
ORPINS
ORRA
ORRERIES
ORRERY
ORRIS
ORRISES
ORS
ORSEILLE
ORSEILLES
ORSELLIC
ORT
ORTANIQUE
ORTANIQUES
ORTHIAN
ORTHICON
ORTHICONS
ORTHO
ORTHOAXES
ORTHOAXIS
ORTHODOX
ORTHODOXIES

ORTHODOXY
ORTHOEPIC
ORTHOEPIES
ORTHOEPY
ORTHOPEDIES
ORTHOPEDY
ORTHOPOD
ORTHOPODS
ORTHOPTIC
ORTHOS
ORTHOSES
ORTHOSIS
ORTHOTIC
ORTHOTICS
ORTHOTIST
ORTHOTISTS
ORTHOTONE
ORTHROS
ORTHROSES
ORTOLAN
ORTOLANS
ORTS
ORVAL
ORVALS
ORYX
ORYXES
OS
OSCHEAL
OSCILLATE
OSCILLATED
OSCILLATES
OSCILLATING
OSCINE
OSCININE
OSCITANCIES
OSCITANCY
OSCITANT
OSCITATE
OSCITATED
OSCITATES
OSCITATING
OSCULA
OSCULANT
OSCULAR
OSCULATE
OSCULATED
OSCULATES
OSCULATING
OSCULE
OSCULES
OSCULUM
OSCULUMS
OSHAC
OSHACS
OSIER
OSIERED
OSIERIES
OSIERS
OSIERY
OSMATE
OSMATES
OSMETERIA
OSMIATE
OSMIATES
OSMIC
OSMIOUS
OSMIUM
OSMIUMS
OSMOMETER
OSMOMETERS

OSMOMETRIES
OSMOMETRY
OSMOSE
OSMOSED
OSMOSES
OSMOSING
OSMOSIS
OSMOTIC
OSMOUS
OSMUND
OSMUNDA
OSMUNDAS
OSMUNDS
OSNABURG
OSNABURGS
OSPREY
OSPREYS
OSSA
OSSARIUM
OSSARIUMS
OSSEIN
OSSEINS
OSSELET
OSSELETS
OSSEOUS
OSSETER
OSSETERS
OSSIA
OSSICLE
OSSICLES
OSSICULAR
OSSIFIC
OSSIFIED
OSSIFIES
OSSIFRAGA
OSSIFRAGAS
OSSIFRAGE
OSSIFRAGES
OSSIFY
OSSIFYING
OSSUARIES
OSSUARY
OSTEAL
OSTEITIS
OSTEITISES
OSTENSIVE
OSTENSORIES
OSTENSORY
OSTENT
OSTENTS
OSTEODERM
OSTEODERMS
OSTEOGENIES
OSTEOGENY
OSTEOID
OSTEOLOGIES
OSTEOLOGY
OSTEOMA
OSTEOMAS
OSTEOPATH
OSTEOPATHS
OSTEOTOME
OSTEOTOMES
OSTEOTOMIES
OSTEOTOMY
OSTIA
OSTIAL
OSTIARIES
OSTIARY
OSTIATE

OSTINATO
OSTINATOS
OSTIOLATE
OSTIOLE
OSTIOLES
OSTIUM
OSTLER
OSTLERESS
OSTLERESSES
OSTLERS
OSTRACA
OSTRACEAN
OSTRACISE
OSTRACISED
OSTRACISES
OSTRACISING
OSTRACISM
OSTRACISMS
OSTRACIZE
OSTRACIZED
OSTRACIZES
OSTRACIZING
OSTRACOD
OSTRACODS
OSTRACON
OSTRAKA
OSTRAKON
OSTREGER
OSTREGERS
OSTRICH
OSTRICHES
OTALGIA
OTALGIAS
OTALGIES
OTALGY
OTARIES
OTARINE
OTARY
OTHER
OTHERNESS
OTHERNESSES
OTHERS
OTHERWISE
OTIC
OTIOSE
OTIOSITIES
OTIOSITY
OTITIS
OTITISES
OTOCYST
OTOCYSTS
OTOLITH
OTOLITHS
OTOLOGIES
OTOLOGIST
OTOLOGISTS
OTOLOGY
OTORRHOEA
OTORRHOEAS
OTOSCOPE
OTOSCOPES
OTTAR
OTTARS
OTTAVA
OTTAVAS
OTTAVINO
OTTAVINOS
OTTER
OTTERED
OTTERING

OTTERS
OTTO
OTTOMAN
OTTOMANS
OTTOS
OTTRELITE
OTTRELITES
OU
OUABAIN
OUABAINS
OUBIT
OUBITS
OUBLIETTE
OUBLIETTES
OUCH
OUCHES
OUCHT
OUCHTS
OUGHLIED
OUGHLIES
OUGHLY
OUGHLYING
OUGHT
OUGHTNESS
OUGHTNESSES
OUGHTS
OUGLIE
OUGLIED
OUGLIEING
OUGLIES
OUIJA
OUIJAS
OUISTITI
OUISTITIS
OUK
OUKS
OULACHON
OULACHONS
OULAKAN
OULAKANS
OULK
OULKS
OULONG
OULONGS
OUNCE
OUNCES
OUNDY
OUP
OUPED
OUPH
OUPHE
OUPHES
OUPHS
OUPING
OUPS
OUR
OURALI
OURALIS
OURARI
OURARIS
OUREBI
OUREBIS
OURIE
OURN
OUROBOROS
OUROBOROSES
OUROLOGIES
OUROLOGY
OUROSCOPIES
OUROSCOPY

OURS
OURSELF
OURSELVES
OUSEL
OUSELS
OUST
OUSTED
OUSTER
OUSTERS
OUSTING
OUSTITI
OUSTITIS
OUSTS
OUT
OUTACT
OUTACTED
OUTACTING
OUTACTS
OUTAGE
OUTAGES
OUTATE
OUTBACK
OUTBACKER
OUTBACKERS
OUTBACKS
OUTBAR
OUTBARRED
OUTBARRING
OUTBARS
OUTBID
OUTBIDDING
OUTBIDS
OUTBOARD
OUTBOUND
OUTBOUNDS
OUTBOX
OUTBOXED
OUTBOXES
OUTBOXING
OUTBRAG
OUTBRAGGED
OUTBRAGGING
OUTBRAGS
OUTBRAVE
OUTBRAVED
OUTBRAVES
OUTBRAVING
OUTBREAK
OUTBREAKING
OUTBREAKS
OUTBRED
OUTBREED
OUTBREEDING
OUTBREEDS
OUTBROKE
OUTBROKEN
OUTBURN
OUTBURNED
OUTBURNING
OUTBURNS
OUTBURNT
OUTBURST
OUTBURSTING
OUTBURSTS
OUTBY
OUTBYE
OUTCAST
OUTCASTE
OUTCASTED
OUTCASTES

OUTCASTING
OUTCASTS
OUTCLASS
OUTCLASSED
OUTCLASSES
OUTCLASSING
OUTCOME
OUTCOMES
OUTCRAFTIED
OUTCRAFTIES
OUTCRAFTY
OUTCRAFTYING
OUTCRIED
OUTCRIES
OUTCROP
OUTCROPPED
OUTCROPPING
OUTCROPS
OUTCROSS
OUTCROSSED
OUTCROSSES
OUTCROSSING
OUTCRY
OUTCRYING
OUTDANCE
OUTDANCED
OUTDANCES
OUTDANCING
OUTDARE
OUTDARED
OUTDARES
OUTDARING
OUTDATE
OUTDATED
OUTDATES
OUTDATING
OUTDID
OUTDO
OUTDOES
OUTDOING
OUTDONE
OUTDOOR
OUTDOORS
OUTDOORSY
OUTDRANK
OUTDRINK
OUTDRINKING
OUTDRINKS
OUTDRIVE
OUTDRIVEN
OUTDRIVES
OUTDRIVING
OUTDROVE
OUTDRUNK
OUTDURE
OUTDURED
OUTDURES
OUTDURING
OUTDWELL
OUTDWELLED
OUTDWELLING
OUTDWELLS
OUTEAT
OUTEATEN
OUTEATING
OUTEATS
OUTED
OUTEDGE
OUTEDGES
OUTER

OUTERMOST
OUTERS
OUTERWEAR
OUTERWEARS
OUTFACE
OUTFACED
OUTFACES
OUTFACING
OUTFALL
OUTFALLS
OUTFIELD
OUTFIELDS
OUTFIGHT
OUTFIGHTING
OUTFIGHTS
OUTFIT
OUTFITS
OUTFITTED
OUTFITTER
OUTFITTERS
OUTFITTING
OUTFLANK
OUTFLANKED
OUTFLANKING
OUTFLANKS
OUTFLASH
OUTFLASHED
OUTFLASHES
OUTFLASHING
OUTFLEW
OUTFLIES
OUTFLING
OUTFLINGS
OUTFLOW
OUTFLOWED
OUTFLOWING
OUTFLOWN
OUTFLOWS
OUTFLUSH
OUTFLUSHED
OUTFLUSHES
OUTFLUSHING
OUTFLY
OUTFLYING
OUTFOOT
OUTFOOTED
OUTFOOTING
OUTFOOTS
OUTFOUGHT
OUTFOX
OUTFOXED
OUTFOXES
OUTFOXING
OUTFROWN
OUTFROWNED
OUTFROWNING
OUTFROWNS
OUTGAS
OUTGASES
OUTGASSED
OUTGASSING
OUTGATE
OUTGATES
OUTGAVE
OUTGIVE
OUTGIVEN
OUTGIVES
OUTGIVING
OUTGIVINGS
OUTGLARE

OUTGLARED
OUTGLARES
OUTGLARING
OUTGO
OUTGOER
OUTGOERS
OUTGOES
OUTGOING
OUTGOINGS
OUTGONE
OUTGREW
OUTGROW
OUTGROWING
OUTGROWN
OUTGROWS
OUTGROWTH
OUTGROWTHS
OUTGUARD
OUTGUARDS
OUTGUN
OUTGUNNED
OUTGUNNING
OUTGUNS
OUTGUSH
OUTGUSHED
OUTGUSHES
OUTGUSHING
OUTHAUL
OUTHAULER
OUTHAULERS
OUTHAULS
OUTHER
OUTHIRE
OUTHIRED
OUTHIRES
OUTHIRING
OUTHIT
OUTHITS
OUTHITTING
OUTHOUSE
OUTHOUSES
OUTHYRE
OUTING
OUTINGS
OUTJEST
OUTJESTED
OUTJESTING
OUTJESTS
OUTJET
OUTJETS
OUTJUMP
OUTJUMPED
OUTJUMPING
OUTJUMPS
OUTJUT
OUTJUTS
OUTLAID
OUTLAND
OUTLANDER
OUTLANDERS
OUTLANDS
OUTLASH
OUTLASHES
OUTLAST
OUTLASTED
OUTLASTING
OUTLASTS
OUTLAUNCE
OUTLAUNCH
OUTLAUNCHED

OUTLAUNCHES
OUTLAUNCHING
OUTLAW
OUTLAWED
OUTLAWING
OUTLAWRIES
OUTLAWRY
OUTLAWS
OUTLAY
OUTLAYING
OUTLAYS
OUTLEAP
OUTLEAPED
OUTLEAPING
OUTLEAPS
OUTLEAPT
OUTLEARN
OUTLEARNED
OUTLEARNING
OUTLEARNS
OUTLEARNT
OUTLER
OUTLERS
OUTLET
OUTLETS
OUTLIE
OUTLIED
OUTLIER
OUTLIERS
OUTLIES
OUTLINE
OUTLINEAR
OUTLINED
OUTLINES
OUTLINING
OUTLIVE
OUTLIVED
OUTLIVES
OUTLIVING
OUTLOOK
OUTLOOKED
OUTLOOKING
OUTLOOKS
OUTLUSTRE
OUTLUSTRED
OUTLUSTRES
OUTLUSTRING
OUTLYING
OUTMAN
OUTMANNED
OUTMANNING
OUTMANS
OUTMANTLE
OUTMANTLED
OUTMANTLES
OUTMANTLING
OUTMARCH
OUTMARCHED
OUTMARCHES
OUTMARCHING
OUTMATCH
OUTMATCHED
OUTMATCHES
OUTMATCHING
OUTMODE
OUTMODED
OUTMODES
OUTMODING
OUTMOST
OUTMOVE

OUTMOVED
OUTMOVES
OUTMOVING
OUTNAME
OUTNAMED
OUTNAMES
OUTNAMING
OUTNESS
OUTNESSES
OUTNIGHT
OUTNIGHTED
OUTNIGHTING
OUTNIGHTS
OUTNUMBER
OUTNUMBERED
OUTNUMBERING
OUTNUMBERS
OUTPACE
OUTPACED
OUTPACES
OUTPACING
OUTPART
OUTPARTS
OUTPEEP
OUTPEEPED
OUTPEEPING
OUTPEEPS
OUTPEER
OUTPEERED
OUTPEERING
OUTPEERS
OUTPLAY
OUTPLAYED
OUTPLAYING
OUTPLAYS
OUTPOINT
OUTPOINTED
OUTPOINTING
OUTPOINTS
OUTPORT
OUTPORTS
OUTPOST
OUTPOSTS
OUTPOUR
OUTPOURED
OUTPOURERS
OUTPOURING
OUTPOURS
OUTPOWER
OUTPOWERED
OUTPOWERING
OUTPOWERS
OUTPRAY
OUTPRAYED
OUTPRAYING
OUTPRAYS
OUTPRICE
OUTPRICED
OUTPRICES
OUTPRICING
OUTPRIZE
OUTPRIZED
OUTPRIZES
OUTPRIZING
OUTPUT
OUTPUTS
OUTPUTTED
OUTPUTTING
OUTRACE

OUTRACED
OUTRACES
OUTRACING
OUTRAGE
OUTRAGED
OUTRAGES
OUTRAGING
OUTRAIGNE
OUTRAN
OUTRANCE
OUTRANCES
OUTRANK
OUTRANKED
OUTRANKING
OUTRANKS
OUTRATE
OUTRATED
OUTRATES
OUTRATING
OUTRÉ
OUTREACH
OUTREACHED
OUTREACHES
OUTREACHING
OUTRED
OUTREDDED
OUTREDDEN
OUTREDDENED
OUTREDDENING
OUTREDDENS
OUTREDDING
OUTREDS
OUTREIGN
OUTREIGNED
OUTREIGNING
OUTREIGNS
OUTRELIEF
OUTRELIEFS
OUTREMER
OUTREMERS
OUTRIDDEN
OUTRIDE
OUTRIDER
OUTRIDERS
OUTRIDES
OUTRIDING
OUTRIGGER
OUTRIGGERS
OUTRIGHT
OUTRIVAL
OUTRIVALLED
OUTRIVALLING
OUTRIVALS
OUTROAR
OUTROARED
OUTROARING
OUTROARS
OUTRODE
OUTROOP
OUTROOPER
OUTROOPERS
OUTROOPS
OUTROOT
OUTROOTED
OUTROOTING
OUTROOTS
OUTROPE
OUTROPER
OUTROPERS
OUTROPES

OUTRUN
OUTRUNNER
OUTRUNNERS
OUTRUNNING
OUTRUNS
OUTRUSH
OUTRUSHED
OUTRUSHES
OUTRUSHING
OUTS
OUTSAIL
OUTSAILED
OUTSAILING
OUTSAILS
OUTSAT
OUTSCOLD
OUTSCOLDED
OUTSCOLDING
OUTSCOLDS
OUTSCORN
OUTSCORNED
OUTSCORNING
OUTSCORNS
OUTSELL
OUTSELLING
OUTSELLS
OUTSET
OUTSETS
OUTSHINE
OUTSHINES
OUTSHINING
OUTSHONE
OUTSHOOT
OUTSHOOTING
OUTSHOOTS
OUTSHOT
OUTSHOTS
OUTSIDE
OUTSIDER
OUTSIDERS
OUTSIDES
OUTSIGHT
OUTSIGHTS
OUTSIT
OUTSITS
OUTSITTING
OUTSIZE
OUTSIZED
OUTSIZES
OUTSKIRT
OUTSKIRTS
OUTSLEEP
OUTSLEEPING
OUTSLEEPS
OUTSLEPT
OUTSMART
OUTSMARTED
OUTSMARTING
OUTSMARTS
OUTSOAR
OUTSOARED
OUTSOARING
OUTSOARS
OUTSOLD
OUTSOLE
OUTSOLES
OUTSPAN
OUTSPANNED
OUTSPANNING
OUTSPANS

OUTSPEAK
OUTSPEAKING
OUTSPEAKS
OUTSPEND
OUTSPENDING
OUTSPENDS
OUTSPENT
OUTSPOKE
OUTSPOKEN
OUTSPORT
OUTSPORTED
OUTSPORTING
OUTSPORTS
OUTSPREAD
OUTSPREADING
OUTSPREADS
OUTSPRING
OUTSPRINGING
OUTSPRINGS
OUTSPRUNG
OUTSTAND
OUTSTANDING
OUTSTANDS
OUTSTARE
OUTSTARED
OUTSTARES
OUTSTARING
OUTSTAY
OUTSTAYED
OUTSTAYING
OUTSTAYS
OUTSTEP
OUTSTEPPED
OUTSTEPPING
OUTSTEPS
OUTSTOOD
OUTSTRAIN
OUTSTRAINED
OUTSTRAINING
OUTSTRAINS
OUTSTRIKE
OUTSTRIKES
OUTSTRIKING
OUTSTRIP
OUTSTRIPPED
OUTSTRIPPING
OUTSTRIPS
OUTSTRUCK
OUTSUM
OUTSUMMED
OUTSUMMING
OUTSUMS
OUTSWEAR
OUTSWEARING
OUTSWEARS
OUTSWELL
OUTSWELLED
OUTSWELLING
OUTSWELLS
OUTSWING
OUTSWINGS
OUTSWOLLEN
OUTSWORE
OUTSWORN
OUTTAKE
OUTTAKEN
OUTTAKES
OUTTAKING
OUTTALK
OUTTALKED

OUTTALKING
OUTTALKS
OUTTELL
OUTTELLING
OUTTELLS
OUTTHINK
OUTTHINKING
OUTTHINKS
OUTTHOUGHT
OUTTOLD
OUTTONGUE
OUTTONGUED
OUTTONGUES
OUTTONGUING
OUTTOOK
OUTTOP
OUTTOPPED
OUTTOPPING
OUTTOPS
OUTTRAVEL
OUTTRAVELLED
OUTTRAVELLING
OUTTRAVELS
OUTTURN
OUTTURNS
OUTVALUE
OUTVALUED
OUTVALUES
OUTVALUING
OUTVENOM
OUTVENOMED
OUTVENOMING
OUTVENOMS
OUTVIE
OUTVIED
OUTVIES
OUTVOICE
OUTVOICED
OUTVOICES
OUTVOICING
OUTVOTE
OUTVOTED
OUTVOTER
OUTVOTERS
OUTVOTES
OUTVOTING
OUTVYING
OUTWALK
OUTWALKED
OUTWALKING
OUTWALKS
OUTWARD
OUTWARDLY
OUTWARDS
OUTWATCH
OUTWATCHED
OUTWATCHES
OUTWATCHING
OUTWEAR
OUTWEARIED
OUTWEARIES
OUTWEARING
OUTWEARS
OUTWEARY
OUTWEARYING
OUTWEED
OUTWEEDED
OUTWEEDING
OUTWEEDS
OUTWEEP

OUTWEEPING
OUTWEEPS
OUTWEIGH
OUTWEIGHED
OUTWEIGHING
OUTWEIGHS
OUTWELL
OUTWELLED
OUTWELLING
OUTWELLS
OUTWENT
OUTWEPT
OUTWICK
OUTWICKED
OUTWICKING
OUTWICKS
OUTWIN
OUTWIND
OUTWINDING
OUTWINDS
OUTWING
OUTWINGED
OUTWINGING
OUTWINGS
OUTWINNING
OUTWINS
OUTWIT
OUTWITH
OUTWITS
OUTWITTED
OUTWITTING
OUTWON
OUTWORE
OUTWORK
OUTWORKED
OUTWORKER
OUTWORKERS
OUTWORKING
OUTWORKS
OUTWORN
OUTWORTH
OUTWORTHED
OUTWORTHING
OUTWORTHS
OUTWOUND
OUTWREST
OUTWRESTED
OUTWRESTING
OUTWRESTS
OUTWROUGHT
OUVERT
OUVERTE
OUVRAGE
OUVRAGES
OUVRIER
OUVRIÈRE
OUVRIÈRES
OUVRIERS
OUZEL
OUZELS
OUZO
OUZOS
OVA
OVAL
OVALBUMIN
OVALBUMINS
OVALLY
OVALS
OVARIAN
OVARIES

OVARIOLE
OVARIOLES
OVARIOUS
OVARITIS
OVARITISES
OVARY
OVATE
OVATED
OVATES
OVATING
OVATION
OVATIONS
OVATOR
OVATORS
OVEN
OVENS
OVENWARE
OVENWARES
OVENWOOD
OVENWOODS
OVER
OVERACT
OVERACTED
OVERACTING
OVERACTS
OVERALL
OVERALLED
OVERALLS
OVERARCH
OVERARCHED
OVERARCHES
OVERARCHING
OVERARM
OVERATE
OVERAWE
OVERAWED
OVERAWES
OVERAWING
OVERBEAR
OVERBEARING
OVERBEARS
OVERBEAT
OVERBEATEN
OVERBEATING
OVERBEATS
OVERBID
OVERBIDDING
OVERBIDS
OVERBITE
OVERBITES
OVERBLEW
OVERBLOW
OVERBLOWING
OVERBLOWN
OVERBLOWS
OVERBOARD
OVERBOIL
OVERBOILED
OVERBOILING
OVERBOILS
OVERBOLD
OVERBOOK
OVERBOOKED
OVERBOOKING
OVERBOOKS
OVERBORE
OVERBORNE
OVERBOUGHT
OVERBOUND
OVERBOUNDED

OVERBOUNDING
OVERBOUNDS
OVERBROW
OVERBROWED
OVERBROWING
OVERBROWS
OVERBUILD
OVERBUILDING
OVERBUILDS
OVERBUILT
OVERBULK
OVERBULKED
OVERBULKING
OVERBULKS
OVERBURN
OVERBURNED
OVERBURNING
OVERBURNS
OVERBURNT
OVERBUSIED
OVERBUSIES
OVERBUSY
OVERBUSYING
OVERBUY
OVERBUYING
OVERBUYS
OVERCALL
OVERCALLED
OVERCALLING
OVERCALLS
OVERCAME
OVERCARRIED
OVERCARRIES
OVERCARRY
OVERCARRYING
OVERCAST
OVERCASTING
OVERCASTS
OVERCATCH
OVERCATCHES
OVERCATCHING
OVERCAUGHT
OVERCHECK
OVERCHECKS
OVERCLAD
OVERCLOUD
OVERCLOUDED
OVERCLOUDING
OVERCLOUDS
OVERCLOY
OVERCLOYED
OVERCLOYING
OVERCLOYS
OVERCOAT
OVERCOATS
OVERCOME
OVERCOMES
OVERCOMING
OVERCOUNT
OVERCOUNTED
OVERCOUNTING
OVERCOUNTS
OVERCOVER
OVERCOVERED
OVERCOVERING
OVERCOVERS
OVERCROP
OVERCROPPED
OVERCROPPING

OVERCROPS
OVERCROW
OVERCROWD
OVERCROWDED
OVERCROWDING
OVERCROWDS
OVERCROWED
OVERCROWING
OVERCROWS
OVERDATED
OVERDID
OVERDIGHT
OVERDO
OVERDOER
OVERDOERS
OVERDOES
OVERDOING
OVERDONE
OVERDOSE
OVERDOSED
OVERDOSES
OVERDOSING
OVERDRAFT
OVERDRAFTS
OVERDRAW
OVERDRAWING
OVERDRAWN
OVERDRESS
OVERDRESSED
OVERDRESSES
OVERDRESSING
OVERDREW
OVERDRIVE
OVERDRIVEN
OVERDRIVES
OVERDRIVING
OVERDROVE
OVERDUE
OVERDUST
OVERDUSTED
OVERDUSTING
OVERDUSTS
OVERDYE
OVERDYED
OVERDYEING
OVERDYES
OVEREAT
OVEREATEN
OVEREATING
OVEREATS
OVERED
OVEREXERT
OVEREXERTED
OVEREXERTING
OVEREXERTS
OVEREYE
OVEREYED
OVEREYEING
OVEREYES
OVEREYING
OVERFALL
OVERFALLEN
OVERFALLING
OVERFALLS
OVERFAR
OVERFED
OVERFEED
OVERFEEDING
OVERFEEDS

OVERFELL
OVERFILL
OVERFILLED
OVERFILLING
OVERFILLS
OVERFINE
OVERFIRE
OVERFIRED
OVERFIRES
OVERFIRING
OVERFISH
OVERFISHED
OVERFISHES
OVERFISHING
OVERFLEW
OVERFLIES
OVERFLOW
OVERFLOWED
OVERFLOWING
OVERFLOWN
OVERFLOWS
OVERFLUSH
OVERFLUSHED
OVERFLUSHES
OVERFLUSHING
OVERFLY
OVERFLYING
OVERFOLD
OVERFOLDED
OVERFOLDING
OVERFOLDS
OVERFOND
OVERFREE
OVERFULL
OVERGALL
OVERGALLED
OVERGALLING
OVERGALLS
OVERGANG
OVERGANGED
OVERGANGING
OVERGANGS
OVERGAVE
OVERGET
OVERGETS
OVERGETTING
OVERGIVE
OVERGIVES
OVERGIVING
OVERGLAZE
OVERGLAZED
OVERGLAZES
OVERGLAZING
OVERGLOOM
OVERGLOOMED
OVERGLOOMING
OVERGLOOMS
OVERGO
OVERGOES
OVERGOING
OVERGOINGS
OVERGONE
OVERGORGE
OVERGORGED
OVERGORGES
OVERGORGING
OVERGOT
OVERGOTTEN
OVERGRAIN
OVERGRAINED

OVERGRAINING
OVERGRAINS
OVERGRASS
OVERGRASSED
OVERGRASSES
OVERGRASSING
OVERGRAZE
OVERGRAZED
OVERGRAZES
OVERGRAZING
OVERGREAT
OVERGREEN
OVERGREENED
OVERGREENING
OVERGREENS
OVERGREW
OVERGROW
OVERGROWING
OVERGROWN
OVERGROWS
OVERHAILE
OVERHAILED
OVERHAILES
OVERHAILING
OVERHAIR
OVERHAIRS
OVERHALE
OVERHALED
OVERHALES
OVERHALING
OVERHAND
OVERHANDED
OVERHANDING
OVERHANDS
OVERHANG
OVERHANGING
OVERHANGS
OVERHAPPY
OVERHASTE
OVERHASTES
OVERHASTY
OVERHAUL
OVERHAULED
OVERHAULING
OVERHAULS
OVERHEAD
OVERHEADS
OVERHEAR
OVERHEARD
OVERHFARING
OVERHEARS
OVERHEAT
OVERHEATED
OVERHEATING
OVERHEATS
OVERHELD
OVERHENT
OVERHENTED
OVERHENTING
OVERHENTS
OVERHIT
OVERHITS
OVERHITTING
OVERHOLD
OVERHOLDING
OVERHOLDS
OVERHUNG
OVERING
OVERINKED
OVERISSUE

OVERISSUED
OVERISSUES
OVERISSUING
OVERJOY
OVERJOYED
OVERJOYING
OVERJOYS
OVERJUMP
OVERJUMPED
OVERJUMPING
OVERJUMPS
OVERKEEP
OVERKEEPING
OVERKEEPS
OVERKEPT
OVERKEST
OVERKILL
OVERKILLS
OVERKIND
OVERKING
OVERKINGS
OVERKNEE
OVERLADE
OVERLADED
OVERLADEN
OVERLADES
OVERLADING
OVERLAID
OVERLAIN
OVERLAND
OVERLANDED
OVERLANDING
OVERLANDS
OVERLAP
OVERLAPPED
OVERLAPPING
OVERLAPS
OVERLARD
OVERLARDED
OVERLARDING
OVERLARDS
OVERLAY
OVERLAYING
OVERLAYS
OVERLEAF
OVERLEAP
OVERLEAPED
OVERLEAPING
OVERLEAPS
OVERLEAPT
OVERLEND
OVERLENDING
OVERLENDS
OVERLENT
OVERLIE
OVERLIER
OVERLIERS
OVERLIES
OVERLIVE
OVERLIVED
OVERLIVES
OVERLIVING
OVERLOAD
OVERLOADED
OVERLOADING
OVERLOADS
OVERLONG
OVERLOOK
OVERLOOKED
OVERLOOKING

OVERLOOKS
OVERLORD
OVERLORDED
OVERLORDING
OVERLORDS
OVERLUSTY
OVERLY
OVERLYING
OVERMAN
OVERMANNED
OVERMANNING
OVERMANS
OVERMAST
OVERMASTED
OVERMASTING
OVERMASTS
OVERMATCH
OVERMATCHED
OVERMATCHES
OVERMATCHING
OVERMEN
OVERMERRY
OVERMOUNT
OVERMOUNTED
OVERMOUNTING
OVERMOUNTS
OVERMUCH
OVERNAME
OVERNAMED
OVERNAMES
OVERNAMING
OVERNEAT
OVERNET
OVERNETS
OVERNETTED
OVERNETTING
OVERNICE
OVERNIGHT
OVERNIGHTS
OVERPAGE
OVERPAID
OVERPAINT
OVERPAINTED
OVERPAINTING
OVERPAINTS
OVERPART
OVERPARTED
OVERPARTING
OVERPARTS
OVERPASS
OVERPASSED
OVERPASSES
OVERPASSING
OVERPAST
OVERPAY
OVERPAYING
OVERPAYS
OVERPEDAL
OVERPEDALLED
OVERPEDALLING
OVERPEDALS
OVERPEER
OVERPEERED
OVERPEERING
OVERPEERS
OVERPERCH
OVERPERCHED
OVERPERCHES
OVERPERCHING
OVERPITCH

OVERPITCHED
OVERPITCHES
OVERPITCHING
OVERPLAST
OVERPLAY
OVERPLAYED
OVERPLAYING
OVERPLAYS
OVERPLIED
OVERPLIES
OVERPLUS
OVERPLUSES
OVERPLY
OVERPLYING
OVERPOISE
OVERPOISED
OVERPOISES
OVERPOISING
OVERPOST
OVERPOSTED
OVERPOSTING
OVERPOSTS
OVERPOWER
OVERPOWERED
OVERPOWERING
OVERPOWERS
OVERPRESS
OVERPRESSED
OVERPRESSES
OVERPRESSING
OVERPRINT
OVERPRINTED
OVERPRINTING
OVERPRINTS
OVERPRIZE
OVERPRIZED
OVERPRIZES
OVERPRIZING
OVERPROOF
OVERPROUD
OVERRACK
OVERRACKED
OVERRACKING
OVERRACKS
OVERRAKE
OVERRAKED
OVERRAKES
OVERRAKING
OVERRAN
OVERRANK
OVERRASH
OVERRATE
OVERRATED
OVERRATES
OVERRATING
OVERREACH
OVERREACHED
OVERREACHES
OVERREACHING
OVERREACT
OVERREACTED
OVERREACTING
OVERREACTS
OVERREAD
OVERREADING
OVERREADS
OVERRED
OVERREDDED
OVERREDDING
OVERREDS

OVERREN
OVERRENNED
OVERRENNING
OVERRENS
OVERRIDDEN
OVERRIDE
OVERRIDER
OVERRIDERS
OVERRIDES
OVERRIDING
OVERRIPE
OVERRIPEN
OVERRIPENED
OVERRIPENING
OVERRIPENS
OVERROAST
OVERROASTED
OVERROASTING
OVERROASTS
OVERRODE
OVERRUFF
OVERRUFFED
OVERRUFFING
OVERRUFFS
OVERRULE
OVERRULED
OVERRULER
OVERRULERS
OVERRULES
OVERRULING
OVERRUN
OVERRUNNING
OVERRUNS
OVERS
OVERSAIL
OVERSAILED
OVERSAILING
OVERSAILS
OVERSAW
OVERSCORE
OVERSCORED
OVERSCORES
OVERSCORING
OVERSEA
OVERSEAS
OVERSEE
OVERSEEING
OVERSEEN
OVERSEER
OVERSEERS
OVERSEES
OVERSELL
OVERSELLING
OVERSELLS
OVERSET
OVERSETS
OVERSETTING
OVERSEW
OVERSEWING
OVERSEWN
OVERSEWS
OVERSEXED
OVERSHADE
OVERSHADED
OVERSHADES
OVERSHADING
OVERSHINE
OVERSHINES
OVERSHINING
OVERSHIRT

OVERSHIRTS
OVERSHOE
OVERSHOES
OVERSHONE
OVERSHOOT
OVERSHOOTING
OVERSHOOTS
OVERSHOT
OVERSIDE
OVERSIGHT
OVERSIGHTS
OVERSIZE
OVERSIZED
OVERSIZES
OVERSIZING
OVERSKIP
OVERSKIPPED
OVERSKIPPING
OVERSKIPS
OVERSKIRT
OVERSKIRTS
OVERSLEEP
OVERSLEEPING
OVERSLEEPS
OVERSLEPT
OVERSLIP
OVERSLIPPED
OVERSLIPPING
OVERSLIPS
OVERSMAN
OVERSMEN
OVERSOLD
OVERSOUL
OVERSOULS
OVERSOW
OVERSOWED
OVERSOWING
OVERSOWN
OVERSOWS
OVERSPEND
OVERSPENDING
OVERSPENDS
OVERSPENT
OVERSPILL
OVERSPILLS
OVERSPIN
OVERSPINS
OVERSTAFF
OVERSTAFFED
OVERSTAFFING
OVERSTAFFS
OVERSTAIN
OVERSTAINED
OVERSTAINING
OVERSTAINS
OVERSTAND
OVERSTANDING
OVERSTANDS
OVERSTANK
OVERSTARE
OVERSTARED
OVERSTARES
OVERSTARING
OVERSTATE
OVERSTATED
OVERSTATES
OVERSTATING
OVERSTAY
OVERSTAYED
OVERSTAYING

OVERSTAYS
OVERSTEER
OVERSTEERED
OVERSTEERING
OVERSTEERS
OVERSTEP
OVERSTEPPED
OVERSTEPPING
OVERSTEPS
OVERSTINK
OVERSTINKING
OVERSTINKS
OVERSTOCK
OVERSTOCKED
OVERSTOCKING
OVERSTOCKS
OVERSTOOD
OVERSTREW
OVERSTREWING
OVERSTREWN
OVERSTREWS
OVERSTUDIED
OVERSTUDIES
OVERSTUDY
OVERSTUDYING
OVERSTUFF
OVERSTUFFED
OVERSTUFFING
OVERSTUFFS
OVERSTUNK
OVERSWAM
OVERSWAY
OVERSWAYED
OVERSWAYING
OVERSWAYS
OVERSWEAR
OVERSWEARING
OVERSWEARS
OVERSWELL
OVERSWELLED
OVERSWELLING
OVERSWELLS
OVERSWIM
OVERSWIMMING
OVERSWIMS
OVERSWORN
OVERSWUM
OVERT
OVERTAKE
OVERTAKEN
OVERTAKES
OVERTAKING
OVERTALK
OVERTALKED
OVERTALKING
OVERTALKS
OVERTASK
OVERTASKED
OVERTASKING
OVERTASKS
OVERTAX
OVERTAXED
OVERTAXES
OVERTAXING
OVERTEEM
OVERTEEMED
OVERTEEMING
OVERTEEMS
OVERTHROW

OVERTHROWING
OVERTHROWN
OVERTHROWS
OVERTIME
OVERTIMED
OVERTIMER
OVERTIMERS
OVERTIMES
OVERTIMING
OVERTIRE
OVERTIRED
OVERTIRES
OVERTIRING
OVERTLY
OVERTOIL
OVERTOILED
OVERTOILING
OVERTOILS
OVERTONE
OVERTONES
OVERTOOK
OVERTOP
OVERTOPPED
OVERTOPPING
OVERTOPS
OVERTOWER
OVERTOWERED
OVERTOWERING
OVERTOWERS
OVERTRAIN
OVERTRAINED
OVERTRAINING
OVERTRAINS
OVERTRICK
OVERTRICKS
OVERTRIP
OVERTRIPPED
OVERTRIPPING
OVERTRIPS
OVERTRUMP
OVERTRUMPED
OVERTRUMPING
OVERTRUMPS
OVERTRUST
OVERTRUSTED
OVERTRUSTING
OVERTRUSTS
OVERTURE
OVERTURED
OVERTURES
OVERTURING
OVERTURN
OVERTURNED
OVERTURNING
OVERTURNS
OVERUSE
OVERUSED
OVERUSES
OVERUSING
OVERVALUE
OVERVALUED
OVERVALUES
OVERVALUING
OVERVEIL
OVERVEILED
OVERVEILING
OVERVEILS
OVERVIEW
OVERVIEWS
OVERWASH

OVERWASHES
OVERWATCH
OVERWATCHED
OVERWATCHES
OVERWATCHING
OVERWEAR
OVERWEARIED
OVERWEARIES
OVERWEARING
OVERWEARS
OVERWEARY
OVERWEARYING
OVERWEEN
OVERWEENED
OVERWEENING
OVERWEENS
OVERWEIGH
OVERWEIGHED
OVERWEIGHING
OVERWEIGHS
OVERWENT
OVERWHELM
OVERWHELMED
OVERWHELMING
OVERWHELMS
OVERWIND
OVERWINDING
OVERWINDS
OVERWING
OVERWINGED
OVERWINGING
OVERWINGS
OVERWISE
OVERWORD
OVERWORDS
OVERWORE
OVERWORK
OVERWORKED
OVERWORKING
OVERWORKS
OVERWORN
OVERWOUND
OVERWREST
OVERWRESTED
OVERWRESTING
OVERWRITE
OVERWRITES
OVERWRITING
OVERWRITTEN
OVERWROUGHT
OVERYEAR
OVERYEARED
OVERYEARING
OVERYEARS
OVIBOS
OVIBOSES
OVIBOVINE
OVICIDE
OVICIDES
OVIDUCAL
OVIDUCT
OVIDUCTAL
OVIDUCTS
OVIFEROUS
OVIFORM
OVIGEROUS
OVINE
OVIPARITIES
OVIPARITY

OVIPAROUS
OVIPOSIT
OVIPOSITED
OVIPOSITING
OVIPOSITS
OVISAC
OVISACS
OVIST
OVISTS
OVOID
OVOIDAL
OVOIDS
OVOLI
OVOLO
OVOTESTES
OVOTESTIS
OVULAR
OVULATE
OVULATED
OVULATES
OVULATING
OVULATION
OVULATIONS
OVULE
OVULES
OVUM
OW
OWCHE
OWCHES
OWE
OWED
OWELTIES
OWELTY
OWER
OWERBY
OWERING
OWERLOUP
OWERLOUPED
OWERLOUPING
OWERLOUPS

OWERS
OWES
OWING
OWL
OWLED
OWLER
OWLERIES
OWLERS
OWLERY
OWLET
OWLETS
OWLING
OWLISH
OWLS
OWLY
OWN
OWNED
OWNER
OWNERLESS
OWNERS
OWNERSHIP
OWNERSHIPS
OWNING
OWNS
OWRE
OWRECOME
OWRECOMES
OWRED
OWRES
OWREWORD
OWREWORDS
OWRIE
OWRING
OWSEN
OWT
OWTS
OX
OXALATE
OXALATES
OXALIC

OXALIS
OXALISES
OXAZINE
OXAZINES
OXBLOOD
OXBLOODS
OXEN
OXER
OXERS
OXGANG
OXGANGS
OXGATE
OXGATES
OXHEAD
OXHEADS
OXIDANT
OXIDANTS
OXIDASE
OXIDASES
OXIDATE
OXIDATED
OXIDATES
OXIDATING
OXIDATION
OXIDATIONS
OXIDE
OXIDES
OXIDISE
OXIDISED
OXIDISER
OXIDISERS
OXIDISES
OXIDISING
OXIDIZE
OXIDIZED
OXIDIZER
OXIDIZERS
OXIDIZES
OXIDIZING
OXIME

OXIMES
OXIMETER
OXIMETERS
OXLAND
OXLANDS
OXLIP
OXLIPS
OXONIUM
OXONIUMS
OXSLIP
OXSLIPS
OXTAIL
OXTAILS
OXTER
OXTERED
OXTERING
OXTERS
OXYGEN
OXYGENATE
OXYGENATED
OXYGENATES
OXYGENATING
OXYGENISE
OXYGENISED
OXYGENISES
OXYGENISING
OXYGENIZE
OXYGENIZED
OXYGENIZES
OXYGENIZING
OXYGENOUS
OXYGENS
OXYMEL
OXYMELS
OXYMORON
OXYMORONS
OXYTOCIC
OXYTOCICS
OXYTOCIN
OXYTOCINS

OXYTONE
OXYTONES
OY
OYE
OYER
OYERS
OYES
OYESES
OYEZ
OYEZES
OYS
OYSTER
OYSTERS
OYSTRIGE
OYSTRIGES
OZAENA
OZAENAS
OZEKI
OZEKIS
OZOCERITE
OZOCERITES
OZOKERITE
OZOKERITES
OZONATION
OZONATIONS
OZONE
OZONES
OZONISE
OZONISED
OZONISER
OZONISERS
OZONISES
OZONISING
OZONIZE
OZONIZED
OZONIZER
OZONIZERS
OZONIZES
OZONIZING

P

PA
PABOUCHE
PABOUCHES
PABULAR
PABULOUS
PABULUM
PABULUMS
PACA
PACABLE
PACAS
PACATION
PACATIONS
PACE
PACED
PACEMAKER
PACEMAKERS
PACER
PACERS
PACES
PACEY
PACHA
PACHAK
PACHAKS
PACHALIC
PACHALICS
PACHAS
PACHINKO
PACHINKOS
PACHISI
PACHISIS
PACHYDERM
PACHYDERMS
PACIER
PACIEST
PACIFIC
PACIFICAL
PACIFIED
PACIFIER
PACIFIERS
PACIFIES
PACIFISM
PACIFISMS
PACIFIST
PACIFISTS
PACIFY
PACIFYING
PACING
PACK
PACKAGE
PACKAGED
PACKAGER
PACKAGERS
PACKAGES
PACKAGING
PACKAGINGS
PACKED
PACKER
PACKERS
PACKET
PACKETED
PACKETING
PACKETS
PACKFONG
PACKFONGS

PACKING
PACKINGS
PACKMAN
PACKMEN
PACKS
PACKSHEET
PACKSHEETS
PACKSTAFF
PACKSTAFFS
PACKWAY
PACKWAYS
PACO
PACOS
PACT
PACTA
PACTION
PACTIONAL
PACTIONED
PACTIONING
PACTIONS
PACTS
PACTUM
PACY
PAD
PADANG
PADANGS
PADAUK
PADAUKS
PADDED
PADDER
PADDERS
PADDIES
PADDING
PADDINGS
PADDLE
PADDLED
PADDLER
PADDLERS
PADDLES
PADDLING
PADDLINGS
PADDOCK
PADDOCKS
PADDY
PADELLA
PADELLAS
PADEMELON
PADEMELONS
PADERERO
PADEREROES
PADEREROS
PADISHAH
PADISHAHS
PADLE
PADLES
PADLOCK
PADLOCKED
PADLOCKING
PADLOCKS
PADMA
PADMAS
PADOUK
PADOUKS
PADRE

PADRES
PADRONE
PADRONI
PADS
PADUASOY
PADUASOYS
PADYMELON
PADYMELONS
PAEAN
PAEANS
PAEDERAST
PAEDERASTS
PAEDEUTIC
PAEDEUTICS
PAEDIATRIES
PAEDIATRY
PAEDOLOGIES
PAEDOLOGY
PAELLA
PAELLAS
PAENULA
PAENULAE
PAENULAS
PAEON
PAEONIC
PAEONICS
PAEONIES
PAEONS
PAEONY
PAGAN
PAGANISE
PAGANISED
PAGANISES
PAGANISH
PAGANISING
PAGANISM
PAGANISMS
PAGANIZE
PAGANIZED
PAGANIZES
PAGANIZING
PAGANS
PAGE
PAGEANT
PAGEANTRIES
PAGEANTRY
PAGEANTS
PAGED
PAGEHOOD
PAGEHOODS
PAGER
PAGERS
PAGES
PAGINAL
PAGINATE
PAGINATED
PAGINATES
PAGINATING
PAGING
PAGINGS
PAGLE
PAGLES
PAGOD
PAGODA

PAGODAS
PAGODS
PAGRI
PAGRIS
PAGURIAN
PAGURIANS
PAGURID
PAGURIDS
PAH
PAHOEHOE
PAHOEHOES
PAHS
PAID
PAIDEUTIC
PAIDEUTICS
PAIDLE
PAIDLES
PAIGLE
PAIGLES
PAIK
PAIKED
PAIKING
PAIKS
PAIL
PAILFUL
PAILFULS
PAILLASSE
PAILLASSES
PAILLETTE
PAILLETTES
PAILLON
PAILLONS
PAILS
PAIN
PAINED
PAINFUL
PAINFULLER
PAINFULLEST
PAINFULLY
PAINIM
PAINIMS
PAINING
PAINLESS
PAINS
PAINT
PAINTABLE
PAINTED
PAINTER
PAINTERLY
PAINTERS
PAINTIER
PAINTIEST
PAINTING
PAINTINGS
PAINTRESS
PAINTRESSES
PAINTS
PAINTURE
PAINTURES
PAINTY
PAIOCK
PAIOCKE
PAIOCKES
PAIOCKS

PAIR
PAIRE
PAIRED
PAIRIAL
PAIRIALS
PAIRING
PAIRINGS
PAIRS
PAIRWISE
PAIS
PAISA
PAISANO
PAISANOS
PAISAS
PAISE
PAISES
PAISLEY
PAISLEYS
PAITRICK
PAITRICKS
PAJAMAS
PAJOCK
PAJOCKE
PAJOCKES
PAJOCKS
PAKAPOO
PAKAPOOS
PAKEHA
PAKEHAS
PAKFONG
PAKFONGS
PAKKA
PAKORA
PAKORAS
PAKTONG
PAKTONGS
PAL
PALABRA
PALABRAS
PALACE
PALACES
PALADIN
PALADINS
PALAESTRA
PALAESTRAE
PALAESTRAS
PALAFITTE
PALAFITTES
PALAMA
PALAMAE
PALAMATE
PALAMINO
PALAMINOS
PALAMPORE
PALAMPORES
PALANKEEN
PALANKEENS
PALANQUIN
PALANQUINS
PALAS
PALASES
PALATABLE
PALATABLY
PALATAL

PALATALS	PALKEES	PALMHOUSES	PALTRIEST	PANDATIONS
PALATE	PALKI	PALMIER	PALTRILY	PANDECT
PALATED	PALKIS	PALMIES	PALTRY	PANDECTS
PALATES	PALL	PALMIEST	PALUDAL	PANDEMIA
PALATIAL	PALLA	PALMIET	PALUDIC	PANDEMIAN
PALATINE	PALLADIC	PALMIETS	PALUDINAL	PANDEMIAS
PALATINES	PALLADIUM	PALMING	PALUDINE	PANDEMIC
PALATING	PALLADIUMS	PALMIPED	PALUDISM	PANDEMICS
PALAVER	PALLADOUS	PALMIPEDE	PALUDISMS	PANDER
PALAVERED	PALLAE	PALMIPEDES	PALUDOSE	PANDERED
PALAVERER	PALLAH	PALMIPEDS	PALUDOUS	PANDERESS
PALAVERERS	PALLAHS	PALMIST	PALUSTRAL	PANDERESSES
PALAVERING	PALLED	PALMISTRIES	PALY	PANDERING
PALAVERS	PALLET	PALMISTRY	PAM	PANDERISM
PALAY	PALLETED	PALMISTS	PAMPA	PANDERISMS
PALAYS	PALLETISE	PALMITATE	PAMPAS .	PANDERLY
PALAZZI	PALLETISED	PALMITATES	PAMPEAN	PANDEROUS
PALAZZO	PALLETISES	PALMITIN	PAMPER	PANDERS
PALE	PALLETISING	PALMITINS	PAMPERED	PANDIED
PALEA	PALLETIZE	PALMS	PAMPERER	PANDIES
PALEAE	PALLETIZED	PALMY	PAMPERERS	PANDIT
PALEBUCK	PALLETIZES	PALMYRA	PAMPERING	PANDITS
PALEBUCKS	PALLETIZING	PALMYRAS	PAMPERO	PANDOOR
PALED	PALLETS	PALOLO	PAMPEROS	PANDOORS
PALEFACE	PALLIA	PALOLOS	PAMPERS	PANDORA
PALEFACES	PALLIAL	PALOMINO	PAMPHLET	PANDORAS
PALELY	PALLIARD	PALOMINOS	PAMPHLETS	PANDORE
PALEMPORE	PALLIARDS	PALOOKA	PAMS	PANDORES
PALEMPORES	PALLIASSE	PALOOKAS	PAN	PANDOUR
PALENESS	PALLIASSES	PALP	PANACEA	PANDOURS
PALENESSES	PALLIATE	PALPABLE	PANACEAN	PANDOWDIES
PALER	PALLIATED	PALPABLY	PANACEAS	PANDOWDY
PALES	PALLIATES	PALPAL	PANACHAEA	PANDS
PALEST	PALLIATING	PALPATE	PANACHAEAS	PANDURA
PALESTRA	PALLID	PALPATED	PANACHE	PANDURAS
PALESTRAE	PALLIDER	PALPATES	PANACHES	PANDURATE
PALESTRAS	PALLIDEST	PALPATING	PANADA	PANDY
PALET	PALLIDITIES	PALPATION	PANADAS	PANDYING
PALETOT	PALLIDITY	PALPATIONS	PANAMA	PANE
PALETOTS	PALLIDLY	PALPEBRAL	PANAMAS	PANED
PALETS	PALLIER	PALPED	PANARIES	PANEGOISM
PALETTE	PALLIEST	PALPI	PANARY	PANEGOISMS
PALETTES	PALLING	PALPING	PANATELLA	PANEGYRIC
PALEWISE	PALLIUM	PALPITANT	PANATELLAS	PANEGYRICS
PALFREY	PALLONE	PALPITATE	PANAX	PANEGYRIES
PALFREYED	PALLONES	PALPITATED	PANAXES	PANEGYRY
PALFREYS	PALLOR	PALPITATES	PANCAKE	PANEITIES
PALIER	PALLORS	PALPITATING	PANCAKED	PANEITY
PALIEST	PALLS	PALPS	PANCAKES	PANEL
PALIFORM	PALLY	PALPUS	PANCAKING	PANELLED
PALILALIA	PALM	PALS	PANCE	PANELLING
PALILALIAS	PALMAR	PALSGRAVE	PANCES	PANELLINGS
PALILLOGIES	PALMARIAN	PALSGRAVES	PANCHAX	PANELLIST
PALILLOGY	PALMARY	PALSIED	PANCHAXES	PANELLISTS
PALIMONIES	PALMATE	PALSIER	PANCHAYAT	PANELS
PALIMONY	PALMATED	PALSIES	PANCHAYATS	PANES
PALING	PALMATELY	PALSIEST	PANCHEON	PANETTONE
PALINGS	PALMATION	PALSTAFF	PANCHEONS	PANETTONI
PALINODE	PALMATIONS	PALSTAFFS	PANCHION	PANFUL
PALINODES	PALMED	PALSTAVE	PANCHIONS	PANFULS
PALINODIES	PALMER	PALSTAVES	PANCOSMIC	PANG
PALINODY	PALMERS	PALSY	PANCRATIC	PANGA
PALISADE	PALMETTE	PALSYING	PANCREAS	PANGAMIC
PALISADED	PALMETTES	PALTER	PANCREASES	PANGAMIES
PALISADES	PALMETTO	PALTERED	PAND	PANGAMY
PALISADING	PALMETTOES	PALTERER	PANDA	PANGAS
PALISADO	PALMETTOS	PALTERERS	PANDAR	PANGED
PALISADOES	PALMFUL	PALTERING	PANDARS	PANGEN
PALISH	PALMFULS	PALTERS	PANDAS	PANGENE
PALKEE	PALMHOUSE	PALTRIER	PANDATION	PANGENES

PANGENS	PANORAMAS	PANZER	PAPISHERS	PARADISAL
PANGING	PANORAMIC	PANZERS	PAPISHES	PARADISE
PANGLESS	PANS	PAOLI	PAPISM	PARADISES
PANGOLIN	PANSEXUAL	PAOLO	PAPISMS	PARADISIC
PANGOLINS	PANSIED	PAP	PAPIST	PARADOS
PANGRAM	PANSIES	PAPA	PAPISTIC	PARADOSES
PANGRAMS	PANSOPHIC	PAPABLE	PAPISTRIES	PARADOX
PANGS	PANSOPHIES	PAPACIES	PAPISTRY	PARADOXAL
PANHANDLE	PANSOPHY	PAPACY	PAPISTS	PARADOXER
PANHANDLED	PANSPERMIES	PAPAIN	PAPOOSE	PARADOXERS
PANHANDLES	PANSPERMY	PAPAINS	PAPOOSES	PARADOXES
PANHANDLING	PANSY	PAPAL	PAPPADOM	PARADOXIES
PANIC	PANT	PAPALISE	PAPPADOMS	PARADOXY
PANICK	PANTABLE	PAPALISED	PAPPED	PARADROP
PANICKED	PANTABLES	PAPALISES	PAPPIER	PARADROPS
PANICKING	PANTAGAMIES	PAPALISING	PAPPIES	PARAFFIN
PANICKS	PANTAGAMY	PAPALISM	PAPPIEST	PARAFFINE
PANICKY	PANTALEON	PAPALISMS	PAPPING	PARAFFINED
PANICLE	PANTALEONS	PAPALIST	PAPPOOSE	PARAFFINES
PANICLED	PANTALETS	PAPALISTS	PAPPOOSES	PARAFFINING
PANICLES	PANTALON	PAPALIZE	PAPPOSE	PARAFFINS
PANICS	PANTALONS	PAPALIZED	PAPPOUS	PARAFFINY
PANIM	PANTALOON	PAPALIZES	PAPPUS	PARAFFLE
PANIMS	PANTALOONS	PAPALIZING	PAPPUSES	PARAFFLES
PANING	PANTED	PAPALLY	PAPPY	PARAFLE
PANISC	PANTER	PAPARAZZI	PAPRIKA	PARAFLES
PANISCS	PANTERS	PAPARAZZO	PAPRIKAS	PARAFOIL
PANISK	PANTHEISM	PAPAS	PAPS	PARAFOILS
PANIOKO	PANTHEISMS	PAPAW	PAPULA	PARAGE
PANISLAM	PANTHEIST	PAPAWS	PAPULAE	PARAGES
PANISLAMS	PANTHEISTS	PAPAYA	PAPULAR	PARAGOGE
PANLOGISM	PANTHENOL	PAPAYAS	PAPULE	PARAGOGES
PANLOGISMS	PANTHENOLS	PAPE	PAPULES	PARAGOGIC
PANMICTIC	PANTHER	PAPER	PAPULOSE	PARAGOGUE
PANMIXIA	PANTHERS	PAPERBACK	PAPULOUS	PARAGOGUES
PANMIXIAS	PANTIES	PAPERBACKED	PAPYRI	PARAGON
PANMIXIS	PANTIHOSE	PAPERBACKING	PAPYRUS	PARAGONED
PANMIXISES	PANTILE	PAPERBACKS	PAR	PARAGONING
PANNAGE	PANTILED	PAPERED	PARA	PARAGONS
PANNAGES	PANTILES	PAPERER	PARABASES	PARAGRAM
PANNE	PANTILING	PAPERERS	PARABASIS	PARAGRAMS
PANNED	PANTILINGS	PAPERING	PARABEMA	PARAGRAPH
PANNELLED	PANTINE	PAPERINGS	PARABEMATA	PARAGRAPHED
PANNES	PANTINES	PAPERLESS	PARABLE	PARAGRAPHING
PANNICK	PANTING	PAPERS	PARABLED	PARAGRAPHS
PANNICKS	PANTINGLY	PAPERWARE	PARABLES	PARAKEET
PANNICLE	PANTINGS	PAPERWARES	PARABLING	PARAKEETS
PANNICLES	PANTLER	PAPERY	PARABOLA	PARALALIA
PANNIER	PANTLERS	PAPES	PARABOLAS	PARALALIAS
PANNIERED	PANTO	PAPETERIE	PARABOLE	PARALEGAL
PANNIERS	PANTOFFLE	PAPETERIES	PARABOLES	PARALEGALS
PANNIKEL	PANTOFFLES	PAPILIO	PARABOLIC	PARALEXIA
PANNIKELL	PANTOFLE	PAPILIOS	PARABRAKE	PARALEXIAS
PANNIKELLS	PANTOFLES	PAPILLA	PARABRAKES	PARALLAX
PANNIKELS	PANTOMIME	PAPILLAE	PARACHUTE	PARALLAXES
PANNIKIN	PANTOMIMES	PAPILLAR	PARACHUTED	PARALLEL
PANNIKINS	PANTON	PAPILLARY	PARACHUTES	PARALLELED
PANNING	PANTONS	PAPILLATE	PARACHUTING	PARALLELING
PANNINGS	PANTOS	PAPILLOMA	PARACLETE	PARALLELS
PANNOSE	PANTOUFLE	PAPILLOMAS	PARACLETES	PARALOGIA
PANNUS	PANTOUFLES	PAPILLON	PARACME	PARALOGIAS
PANNUSES	PANTOUM	PAPILLONS	PARACMES	PARALOGIES
PANOCHA	PANTOUMS	PAPILLOSE	PARACUSES	PARALOGY
PANOCHAS	PANTRIES	PAPILLOTE	PARACUSIS	PARALYSE
PANOISTIC	PANTRY	PAPILLOTES	PARADE	PARALYSED
PANOPLIED	PANTRYMAN	PAPILLOUS	PARADED	PARALYSER
PANOPLIES	PANTRYMEN	PAPILLULE	PARADES	PARALYSERS
PANOPLY	PANTS	PAPILLULES	PARADIGM	PARALYSES
PANOPTIC	PANTUN	PAPISH	PARADIGMS	PARALYSING
PANORAMA	PANTUNS	PAPISHER	PARADING	PARALYSIS

PARALYTIC	PARATAXES	PARECIOUS	PARITOR	PAROEMIAL
PARALYTICS	PARATAXIS	PARED	PARITORS	PAROEMIAS
PARALYZE	PARATHA	PAREGORIC	PARITY	PAROICOUS
PARALYZED	PARATHAS	PAREGORICS	PARK	PAROL
PARALYZER	PARATONIC	PAREIRA	PARKA	PAROLE
PARALYZERS	PARAVAIL	PAREIRAS	PARKAS	PAROLED
PARALYZES	PARAVANE	PARELLA	PARKED	PAROLEE
PARALYZING	PARAVANES	PARELLAS	PARKEE	PAROLEES
PARAMATTA	PARAVANT	PARELLE	PARKEES	PAROLES
PARAMATTAS	PARAVAUNT	PARELLES	PARKER	PAROLING
PARAMECIA	PARAZOA	PARENESES	PARKERS	PARONYM
PARAMEDIC	PARAZOAN	PARENESIS	PARKI	PARONYMIES
PARAMEDICS	PARAZOANS	PARENT	PARKIER	PARONYMS
PARAMENT	PARAZOON	PARENTAGE	PARKIEST	PARONYMY
PARAMENTS	PARBOIL	PARENTAGES	PARKIN	PAROQUET
PARAMESE	PARBOILED	PARENTAL	PARKING	PAROQUETS
PARAMESES	PARBOILING	PARENTED	PARKINGS	PAROTIC
PARAMETER	PARBOILS	PARENTING	PARKINS	PAROTID
PARAMETERS	PARBREAK	PARENTS	PARKIS	PAROTIDS
PARAMO	PARBREAKED	PARER	PARKISH	PAROTIS
PARAMORPH	PARBREAKING	PARERGA	PARKLAND	PAROTISES
PARAMORPHS	PARBREAKS	PARERGON	PARKLANDS	PAROTITIS
PARAMOS	PARBUCKLE	PARERS	PARKLIKE	PAROTITISES
PARAMOUNT	PARBUCKLED	PARES	PARKLY	PAROUSIA
PARAMOUNTS	PARBUCKLES	PARESES	PARKS	PAROUSIAS
PARAMOUR	PARBUCKLING	PARESIS	PARKWARD	PAROXYSM
PARAMOURS	PARCEL	PARETIC	PARKWARDS	PAROXYSMS
PARANETE	PARCELLED	PAREU	PARKWAY	PARPANE
PARANETES	PARCELLING	PAREUS	PARKWAYS	PARPANES
PARANG	PARCELS	PARFAIT	PARKY	PARPEN
PARANGS	PARCENARIES	PARFAITS	PARLAID	PARPEND
PARANOEA	PARCENARY	PARFLECHE	PARLANCE	PARPENDS
PARANOEAS	PARCENER	PARFLECHES	PARLANCES	PARPENS
PARANOEIC	PARCENERS	PARGANA	PARLANDO	PARPENT
PARANOEICS	PARCH	PARGANAS	PARLAY	PARPENTS
PARANOIA	PARCHED	PARGASITE	PARLAYING	PARPOINT
PARANOIAC	PARCHEDLY	PARGASITES	PARLAYS	PARPOINTS
PARANOIACS	PARCHES	PARGE	PARLE	PARQUET
PARANOIAS	PARCHESI	PARGED	PARLED	PARQUETED
PARANOIC	PARCHESIS	PARGES	PARLES	PARQUETING
PARANOICS	PARCHING	PARGET	PARLEY	PARQUETRIES
PARANOID	PARCHMENT	PARGETED	PARLEYED	PARQUETRY
PARANYM	PARCHMENTS	PARGETER	PARLEYING	PARQUETS
PARANYMPH	PARCIMONIES	PARGETERS	PARLEYS	PARQUETTED
PARANYMPHS	PARCIMONY	PARGETING	PARLEYVOO	PARR
PARANYMS	PARCLOSE	PARGETINGS	PARLEYVOOED	PARRAKEET
PARAPET	PARCLOSES	PARGETS	PARLEYVOOING	PARRAKEETS
PARAPETED	PARD	PARGING	PARLEYVOOS	PARRAL
PARAPETS	PARDAL	PARHELIA	PARLIES	PARRALS
PARAPH	PARDALE	PARHELIC	PARLING	PARREL
PARAPHED	PARDALES	PARHELION	PARLOUR	PARRELS
PARAPHING	PARDALIS	PARHYPATE	PARLOURS	PARRHESIA
PARAPHS	PARDALISES	PARHYPATES	PARLOUS	PARRHESIAS
PARAPODIA	PARDALS	PARIAH	PARLY	PARRICIDE
PARAQUAT	PARDED	PARIAHS	PAROCHIAL	PARRICIDES
PARAQUATS	PARDI	PARIAL	PAROCHIN	PARRIED
PARAQUITO	PARDIE	PARIALS	PAROCHINE	PARRIES
PARAQUITOS	PARDINE	PARIETAL	PAROCHINES	PARRITCH
PARARHYME	PARDNER	PARIETALS	PAROCHINS	PARRITCHES
PARARHYMES	PARDNERS	PARING	PARODIC	PARROCK
PARAS	PARDON	PARINGS	PARODICAL	PARROCKED
PARASANG	PARDONED	PARISCHAN	PARODIED	PARROCKING
PARASANGS	PARDONER	PARISCHANS	PARODIES	PARROCKS
PARASCEVE	PARDONERS	PARISH	PARODIST	PARROQUET
PARASCEVES	PARDONING	PARISHEN	PARODISTS	PARROQUETS
PARASITE	PARDONINGS	PARISHENS	PARODY	PARROT
PARASITES	PARDONS	PARISHES	PARODYING	PARROTED
PARASITIC	PARDS	PARISON	PAROEMIA	PARROTER
PARASOL	PARDY	PARISONS	PAROEMIAC	PARROTERS
PARASOLS	PARE	PARITIES	PAROEMIACS	PARROTING

PARROTRIES
PARROTRY
PARROTS
PARROTY
PARRS
PARRY
PARRYING
PARS
PARSE
PARSEC
PARSECS
PARSED
PARSER
PARSERS
PARSES
PARSIMONIES
PARSIMONY
PARSING
PARSINGS
PARSLEY
PARSLEYS
PARSNEP
PARSNEPS
PARSNIP
PARSNIPS
PARSON
PARSONAGE
PARSONAGES
PARSONIC
PARSONISH
PARSONS
PART
PARTAKE
PARTAKEN
PARTAKER
PARTAKERS
PARTAKES
PARTAKING
PARTAKINGS
PARTAN
PARTANS
PARTED
PARTER
PARTERRE
PARTERRES
PARTERS
PARTI
PARTIAL
PARTIALLY
PARTIALS
PARTIBLE
PARTICLE
PARTICLES
PARTIED
PARTIES
PARTIM
PARTING
PARTINGS
PARTIS
PARTISAN
PARTISANS
PARTITA
PARTITAS
PARTITE
PARTITION
PARTITIONED
PARTITIONING
PARTITIONS
PARTITIVE
PARTITIVES

PARTITUR
PARTITURA
PARTITURAS
PARTITURS
PARTIZAN
PARTIZANS
PARTLET
PARTLETS
PARTLY
PARTNER
PARTNERED
PARTNERING
PARTNERS
PARTON
PARTONS
PARTOOK
PARTRIDGE
PARTRIDGES
PARTS
PARTURE
PARTURES
PARTWORK
PARTWORKS
PARTY
PARTYING
PARTYISM
PARTYISMS
PARULIS
PARULISES
PARURE
PARURES
PARVENU
PARVENUS
PARVIS
PARVISE
PARVISES
PAS
PASCAL
PASCALS
PASCHAL
PASCUAL
PASEAR
PASEARED
PASEARING
PASEARS
PASEO
PASEOS
PASH
PASHA
PASHALIK
PASHALIKS
PASHAS
PASHED
PASHIM
PASHIMS
PASHING
PASHM
PASHMINA
PASHMINAS
PASHMS
PASPALUM
PASPALUMS
PASPIES
PASPY
PASQUILER
PASQUILERS
PASS
PASSABLE
PASSABLY

PASSADE
PASSADES
PASSADO
PASSADOES
PASSADOS
PASSAGE
PASSAGED
PASSAGES
PASSAGING
PASSAMENT
PASSAMENTED
PASSAMENTING
PASSAMENTS
PASSANT
PASSÉ
PASSED
PASSÉE
PASSEMENT
PASSEMENTED
PASSEMENTING
PASSEMENTS
PASSENGER
PASSENGERS
PASSEPIED
PASSEPIEDS
PASSER
PASSERINE
PASSERINES
PASSERS
PASSES
PASSIBLE
PASSIBLY
PASSIM
PASSING
PASSINGS
PASSION
PASSIONAL
PASSIONALS
PASSIONED
PASSIONING
PASSIONS
PASSIVE
PASSIVELY
PASSIVES
PASSIVISM
PASSIVISMS
PASSIVIST
PASSIVISTS
PASSIVITIES
PASSIVITY
PASSKEY
PASSKEYS
PASSLESS
PASSMAN
PASSMEN
PASSMENT
PASSMENTED
PASSMENTING
PASSMENTS
PASSOUT
PASSPORT
PASSPORTS
PASSUS
PASSUSES
PASSWORD
PASSWORDS
PAST
PASTA
PASTANCE
PASTANCES

PASTAS
PASTE
PASTED
PASTEL
PASTELS
PASTER
PASTERN
PASTERNS
PASTERS
PASTES
PASTICCI
PASTICCIO
PASTICHE
PASTICHES
PASTIER
PASTIES
PASTIEST
PASTIL
PASTILLE
PASTILLES
PASTILS
PASTIME
PASTIMES
PASTINESS
PASTINESSES
PASTING
PASTINGS
PASTIO
PASTISES
PASTOR
PASTORAL
PASTORALE
PASTORALES
PASTORALS
PASTORATE
PASTORATES
PASTORLY
PASTORS
PASTRAMI
PASTRAMIS
PASTRIES
PASTRY
PASTS
PASTURAGE
PASTURAGES
PASTURAL
PASTURE
PASTURED
PASTURES
PASTURING
PASTY
PAT
PATACA
PATACAS
PATAGIA
PATAGIAL
PATAGIUM
PATAMAR
PATAMARS
PATBALL
PATBALLS
PATCH
PATCHABLE
PATCHED
PATCHER
PATCHERIES
PATCHERS
PATCHERY
PATCHES
PATCHIER

PATCHIEST
PATCHILY
PATCHING
PATCHINGS
PATCHOCKE
PATCHOCKES
PATCHOULI
PATCHOULIES
PATCHOULIS
PATCHOULY
PATCHWORK
PATCHWORKS
PATCHY
PÂTÉ
PATE
PATED
PATELLA
PATELLAE
PATELLAR
PATELLAS
PATELLATE
PATEN
PATENCIES
PATENCY
PATENS
PATENT
PATENTED
PATENTEE
PATENTEES
PATENTING
PATENTLY
PATENTOR
PATENTORS
PATENTS
PATER
PATERA
PATERAE
PATERCOVE
PATERCOVES
PATERERO
PATEREROES
PATEREROS
PATERNAL
PATERNITIES
PATERNITY
PATEN
PATEO
PÂTÉS
PATH
PATHED
PATHETIC
PATHETICS
PATHIC
PATHICS
PATHING
PATHLESS
PATHOGEN
PATHOGENIES
PATHOGENS
PATHOGENY
PATHOLOGIES
PATHOLOGY
PATHOS
PATHOSES
PATHS
PATHWAY
PATHWAYS
PATIBLE
PATIENCE
PATIENCES

PATIENT
PATIENTED
PATIENTING
PATIENTLY
PATIENTS
PATIN
PATINA
PATINAS
PATINATED
PATINE
PATINED
PATINES
PATINS
PATIO
PATIOS
PATLY
PATNESS
PATNESSES
PATOIS
PATONCE
PATRERO
PATREROES
PATREROS
PATRIAL
PATRIALS
PATRIARCH
PATRIARCHS
PATRIATE
PATRIATED
PATRIATES
PATRIATING
PATRICIAN
PATRICIANS
PATRICIDE
PATRICIDES
PATRICK
PATRICKS
PATRICO
PATRICOES
PATRILINIES
PATRILINY
PATRIMONIES
PATRIMONY
PATRIOT
PATRIOTIC
PATRIOTS
PATRISTIC
PATROL
PATROLLED
PATROLLER
PATROLLERS
PATROLLING
PATROLMAN
PATROLMEN
PATROLOGIES
PATROLOGY
PATROLS
PATRON
PATRONAGE
PATRONAGED
PATRONAGES
PATRONAGING
PATRONAL
PATRONESS
PATRONESSES
PATRONISE
PATRONISED
PATRONISES
PATRONISING
PATRONIZE

PATRONIZED
PATRONIZES
PATRONIZING
PATRONNE
PATRONNES
PATRONS
PATROON
PATROONS
PATS
PATSIES
PATSY
PATTE
PATTÉ
PATTED
PATTÉE
PATTEN
PATTENED
PATTENING
PATTENS
PATTER
PATTERED
PATTERER
PATTERERS
PATTERING
PATTERN
PATTERNED
PATTERNING
PATTERNS
PATTERS
PATTES
PATTIES
PATTING
PATTLE
PATTLES
PATTY
PATULIN
PATULINS
PATULOUS
PATZER
PATZERS
PAUA
PAUAS
PAUCITIES
PAUCITY
PAUGHTY
PAUL
PAULDRON
PAULDRONS
PAULOWNIA
PAULOWNIAS
PAULS
PAUNCE
PAUNCES
PAUNCH
PAUNCHED
PAUNCHES
PAUNCHIER
PAUNCHIEST
PAUNCHING
PAUNCHY
PAUPER
PAUPERESS
PAUPERESSES
PAUPERISE
PAUPERISED
PAUPERISES
PAUPERISING
PAUPERISM
PAUPERISMS
PAUPERIZE

PAUPERIZED
PAUPERIZES
PAUPERIZING
PAUPERS
PAUSAL
PAUSE
PAUSED
PAUSEFUL
PAUSELESS
PAUSER
PAUSERS
PAUSES
PAUSING
PAUSINGLY
PAUSINGS
PAVAGE
PAVAGES
PAVAN
PAVANE
PAVANES
PAVANS
PAVE
PAVED
PAVEMENT
PAVEMENTED
PAVEMENTING
PAVEMENTS
PAVEN
PAVENS
PAVER
PAVERS
PAVES
PAVID
PAVILION
PAVILIONED
PAVILIONING
PAVILIONS
PAVIN
PAVING
PAVINGS
PAVINS
PAVIOR
PAVIORS
PAVIOUR
PAVIOURS
PAVIS
PAVISE
PAVISES
PAVLOVA
PAVLOVAS
PAVONAZZO
PAVONAZZOS
PAVONE
PAVONES
PAVONIAN
PAVONINE
PAW
PAWA
PAWAS
PAWAW
PAWAWS
PAWED
PAWING
PAWK
PAWKIER
PAWKIEST
PAWKILY
PAWKINESS
PAWKINESSES
PAWKS

PAWKY
PAWL
PAWLS
PAWN
PAWNCE
PAWNCES
PAWNED
PAWNEE
PAWNEES
PAWNER
PAWNERS
PAWNING
PAWNS
PAWNSHOP
PAWNSHOPS
PAWPAW
PAWPAWS
PAWS
PAX
PAXES
PAXIUBA
PAXIUBAS
PAXWAX
PAXWAXES
PAY
PAYABLE
PAYED
PAYEE
PAYEES
PAYER
PAYERS
PAYING
PAYINGS
PAYMASTER
PAYMASTERS
PAYMENT
PAYMENTS
PAYNIM
PAYNIMRIES
PAYNIMRY
PAYNIMS
PAYOLA
PAYOLAS
PAYS
PAYSAGE
PAYSAGES
PAYSAGIST
PAYSAGISTS
PAYSD
PAZAZZ
PAZAZZES
PEA
PEABERRIES
PEABERRY
PEACE
PEACEABLE
PEACEABLY
PEACED
PEACEFUL
PEACELESS
PEACENIK
PEACENIKS
PEACES
PEACETIME
PEACETIMES
PEACH
PEACHED
PEACHER
PEACHERS
PEACHES

PEACHIER
PEACHIEST
PEACHING
PEACHY
PEACING
PEACOCK
PEACOCKED
PEACOCKING
PEACOCKS
PEACOCKY
PEACOD
PEACODS
PEAG
PEAGS
PEAK
PEAKED
PEAKIER
PEAKIEST
PEAKING
PEAKS
PEAKY
PEAL
PEALED
PEALING
PEALS
PEAN
PEANED
PEANING
PEANS
PEANUT
PEANUTS
PEAR
PEARCE
PEARCED
PEARCES
PEARCING
PEARE
PEARES
PEARL
PEARLED
PEARLER
PEARLERS
PEARLIER
PEARLIES
PEARLIEST
PEARLIN
PEARLING
PEARLINGS
PEARLINS
PEARLISED
PEARLITE
PEARLITES
PEARLITIC
PEARLIZED
PEARLS
PEARLY
PEARMAIN
PEARMAINS
PEARS
PEARST
PEART
PEARTLY
PEAS
PEASANT
PEASANTRIES
PEASANTRY
PEASANTS
PEASANTY
PEASCOD
PEASCODS

PEASE
PEASECOD
PEASECODS
PEASED
PEASES
PEASEWEEP
PEASEWEEPS
PEASING
PEASON
PEAT
PEATARIES
PEATARY
PEATERIES
PEATERY
PEATIER
PEATIEST
PEATMAN
PEATMEN
PEATS
PEATSHIP
PEATSHIPS
PEATY
PEAVEY
PEAVEYS
PEAVIES
PEAVY
PEAZE
PEAZED
PEAZES
PEAZING
PEBA
PEBAS
PEBBLE
PEBBLED
PEBBLES
PEBBLIER
PEBBLIEST
PEBBLING
PEBBLINGS
PEBBLY
PÉBRINE
PÉBRINES
PEC
PECAN
PECANS
PECCABLE
PECCANCIES
PECCANCY
PECCANT
PECCANTLY
PECCARIES
PECCARY
PECCAVI
PECCAVIS
PECH
PECHED
PECHING
PECHS
PECK
PECKE
PECKED
PECKER
PECKERS
PECKES
PECKING
PECKINGS
PECKISH
PECKS
PECS
PECTEN

PECTIC
PECTIN
PECTINAL
PECTINATE
PECTINATED
PECTINEAL
PECTINES
PECTINS
PECTISE
PECTISED
PECTISES
PECTISING
PECTIZE
PECTIZED
PECTIZES
PECTIZING
PECTOLITE
PECTOLITES
PECTORAL
PECTORALS
PECTOSE
PECTOSES
PECULATE
PECULATED
PECULATES
PECULATING
PECULATOR
PECULATORS
PECULIAR
PECULIARS
PECULIUM
PECULIUMS
PECUNIARY
PECUNIOUS
PED
PEDAGOGIC
PEDAGOGIES
PEDAGOGUE
PEDAGOGUED
PEDAGOGUES
PEDAGOGUING
PEDAGOGY
PEDAL
PEDALIER
PEDALIERS
PEDALLED
PEDALLER
PEDALLERS
PEDALLING
PEDALLINGS
PEDALO
PEDALOES
PEDALOS
PEDALS
PEDANT
PEDANTIC
PEDANTISE
PEDANTISED
PEDANTISES
PEDANTISING
PEDANTISM
PEDANTISMS
PEDANTIZE
PEDANTIZED
PEDANTIZES
PEDANTIZING
PEDANTRIES
PEDANTRY
PEDANTS
PEDATE

PEDATELY
PEDATIFID
PEDDER
PEDDERS
PEDDLE
PEDDLED
PEDDLER
PEDDLERS
PEDDLES
PEDDLING
PEDDLINGS
PEDERERO
PEDEREROES
PEDEREROS
PEDESES
PEDESIS
PEDESTAL
PEDESTALLED
PEDESTALLING
PEDESTALS
PEDETIC
PEDICAB
PEDICABS
PEDICEL
PEDICELS
PEDICLE
PEDICLED
PEDICLES
PEDICULAR
PEDICULUS
PEDICULUSES
PEDICURE
PEDICURED
PEDICURES
PEDICURING
PEDIGREE
PEDIGREED
PEDIGREES
PEDIMENT
PEDIMENTS
PEDIPALP
PEDIPALPS
PEDLAR
PEDLARIES
PEDLARS
PEDLARY
PEDOLOGIES
PEDOLOGY
PEDOMETER
PEDOMETERS
PEDRAIL
PEDRAILS
PEDRERO
PEDREROES
PEDREROS
PEDRO
PEDROS
PEDS
PEDUNCLE
PEDUNCLES
PEE
PEECE
PEECES
PEED
PEEING
PEEK
PEEKABO
PEEKABOO
PEEKABOOS
PEEKABOS

PEEKED
PEEKING
PEEKS
PEEL
PEELED
PEELER
PEELERS
PEELING
PEELINGS
PEELS
PEEN
PEENED
PEENGE
PEENGED
PEENGEING
PEENGES
PEENING
PEENS
PEEOY
PEEOYS
PEEP
PEEPE
PEEPED
PEEPER
PEEPERS
PEEPES
PEEPING
PEEPO
PEEPUL
PEEPULS
PEER
PEERAGE
PEERAGES
PEERED
PEERESS
PEERESSES
PEERIE
PEERIER
PEERIES
PEERIEST
PEERING
PEERLESS
PEERS
PEERY
PEES
PEESWEEP
PEESWEEPS
PEETWEET
PEETWEETS
PEEVE
PEEVED
PEEVER
PEEVERS
PEEVES
PEEVING
PEEVISH
PEEVISHLY
PEEWEE
PEEWEES
PEEWIT
PEEWITS
PEG
PEGASUS
PEGASUSES
PEGBOARD
PEGBOARDS
PEGGED
PEGGIES
PEGGING
PEGGINGS

PEGGY
PEGH
PEGHED
PEGHING
PEGHS
PEGMATITE
PEGMATITES
PEGS
PEIGNOIR
PEIGNOIRS
PEIN
PEINCT
PEINCTS
PEINED
PEINING
PEINS
PEIRASTIC
PEISE
PEISED
PEISES
PEISHWA
PEISHWAH
PEISHWAHS
PEISHWAS
PEISING
PEIZE
PEIZED
PEIZES
PEIZING
PEJORATE
PEJORATED
PEJORATES
PEJORATING
PEKAN
PEKANS
PEKE
PEKES
PEKOE
PEKOES
PELA
PELAGE
PELAGES
PELAGIAN
PELAGIC
PELAS
PELE
PELERINE
PELERINES
PELES
PELF
PELFS
PELHAM
PELHAMS
PELICAN
PELICANS
PELISSE
PELISSES
PELITE
PELITES
PELITIC
PELL
PELLACH
PELLACHS
PELLACK
PELLACKS
PELLAGRA
PELLAGRAS
PELLAGRIN
PELLAGRINS
PELLET

PELLETED
PELLETIFIED
PELLETIFIES
PELLETIFY
PELLETIFYING
PELLETING
PELLETISE
PELLETISED
PELLETISES
PELLETISING
PELLETIZE
PELLETIZED
PELLETIZES
PELLETIZING
PELLETS
PELLICLE
PELLICLES
PELLITORIES
PELLITORY
PELLOCK
PELLOCKS
PELLS
PELLUCID
PELMA
PELMANISM
PELMANISMS
PELMAS
PELMATIC
PELMET
PELMETS
PELOID
PELOIDS
PELOLOGIES
PELOLOGY
PELORIA
PELORIAS
PELORIC
PELORIES
PELORISED
PELORISM
PELORISMS
PELORIZED
PELORUS
PELORUSES
PELORY
PELOTA
PELOTAS
PELT
PELTA
PELTAE
PELTAS
PELTAST
PELTASTS
PELTATE
PELTED
PELTER
PELTERED
PELTERING
PELTERS
PELTING
PELTINGLY
PELTINGS
PELTRIES
PELTRY
PELTS
PELVES
PELVIC
PELVIFORM
PELVIS
PELVISES

PEMBROKE
PEMBROKES
PEMICAN
PEMICANS
PEMMICAN
PEMMICANS
PEMOLINE
PEMOLINES
PEMPHIGUS
PEMPHIGUSES
PEN
PENAL
PENALISE
PENALISED
PENALISES
PENALISING
PENALIZE
PENALIZED
PENALIZES
PENALIZING
PENALLY
PENALTIES
PENALTY
PENANCE
PENANCED
PENANCES
PENANCING
PENATES
PENCE
PENCEL
PENCELS
PENCES
PENCHANT
PENCHANTS
PENCIL
PENCILLED
PENCILLER
PENCILLERS
PENCILLING
PENCILS
PENCRAFT
PENCRAFTS
PEND
PENDANT
PENDANTS
PENDED
PENDENCIES
PENDENCY
PENDENT
PENDENTLY
PENDENTS
PENDICLE
PENDICLER
PENDICLERS
PENDICLES
PENDING
PENDRAGON
PENDRAGONS
PENDS
PENDULAR
PENDULATE
PENDULATED
PENDULATES
PENDULATING
PENDULINE
PENDULOUS
PENDULUM
PENDULUMS
PENE
PENED

PENEPLAIN
PENEPLAINS
PENEPLANE
PENEPLANES
PENES
PENETRANT
PENETRANTS
PENETRATE
PENETRATED
PENETRATES
PENETRATING
PENFOLD
PENFOLDS
PENFUL
PENFULS
PENGUIN
PENGUINRIES
PENGUINRY
PENGUINS
PENHOLDER
PENHOLDERS
PENI
PENIAL
PENIE
PENIES
PENILE
PENILLION
PENING
PENINSULA
PENINSULAS
PENIS
PENISES
PENISTONE
PENISTONES
PENITENCE
PENITENCES
PENITENCIES
PENITENCY
PENITENT
PENITENTS
PENK
PENKNIFE
PENKNIVES
PENKS
PENLIGHT
PENLIGHTS
PENMAN
PENMEN
PENNA
PENNAE
PENNAL
PENNALISM
PENNALISMS
PENNALS
PENNANT
PENNANTS
PENNATE
PENNATULA
PENNATULAE
PENNATULAS
PENNE
PENNED
PENNEECH
PENNEECHES
PENNEECK
PENNEECKS
PENNER
PENNERS
PENNES
PENNIED

PENNIES
PENNIFORM
PENNILESS
PENNILL
PENNILLION
PENNINE
PENNINES
PENNING
PENNINITE
PENNINITES
PENNON
PENNONCEL
PENNONCELS
PENNONED
PENNONS
PENNY
PENNYLAND
PENNYLANDS
PENOLOGIES
PENOLOGY
PENONCEL
PENONCELS
PENS
PENSÉE
PENSÉES
PENSEL
PENSELS
PENSIL
PENSILE
PENSILITIES
PENSILITY
PENSILS
PENSION
PENSIONED
PENSIONER
PENSIONERS
PENSIONING
PENSIONS
PENSIVE
PENSIVELY
PENSTEMON
PENSTEMONS
PENSTOCK
PENSTOCKS
PENSUM
PENSUMS
PENT
PENTACLE
PENTACLES
PENTACT
PENTACTS
PENTAD
PENTADIC
PENTADS
PENTAGON
PENTAGONS
PENTAGRAM
PENTAGRAMS
PENTALOGIES
PENTALOGY
PENTALPHA
PENTALPHAS
PENTAMERIES
PENTAMERY
PENTANE
PENTANES
PENTANGLE
PENTANGLES
PENTAPODIES
PENTAPODY

PENTARCH
PENTARCHIES
PENTARCHS
PENTARCHY
PENTEL ®
PENTELS ®
PENTENE
PENTENES
PENTHIA
PENTHIAS
PENTHOUSE
PENTHOUSED
PENTHOUSES
PENTHOUSING
PENTICE
PENTICED
PENTICES
PENTICING
PENTISE
PENTISED
PENTISES
PENTISING
PENTODE
PENTODES
PENTOMIC
PENTOSAN
PENTOSANE
PENTOSANES
PENTOSANS
PENTOSE
PENTOSES
PENTOXIDE
PENTOXIDES
PENTROOF
PENTROOFS
PENTS
PENTYLENE
PENTYLENES
PENUCHE
PENUCHES
PENUCHI
PENUCHIS
PENUCHLE
PENUCHLES
PENULT
PENULTIMA
PENULTIMAS
PENULTS
PENUMBRA
PENUMBRAL
PENUMBRAS
PENURIES
PENURIOUS
PENURY
PENWOMAN
PENWOMEN
PEON
PEONAGE
PEONAGES
PEONIES
PEONISM
PEONISMS
PEONS
PEONY
PEOPLE
PEOPLED
PEOPLES
PEOPLING
PEP
PEPERINO

PEPERINOS
PEPEROMIA
PEPEROMIAS
PEPERONI
PEPERONIS
PEPFUL
PEPLOS
PEPLOSES
PEPLUM
PEPLUMS
PEPLUS
PEPLUSES
PEPO
PEPOS
PEPPED
PEPPER
PEPPERED
PEPPERER
PEPPERERS
PEPPERING
PEPPERINGS
PEPPERONI
PEPPERONIS
PEPPERS
PEPPERY
PEPPIER
PEPPIEST
PEPPING
PEPPY
PEPS
PEPSIN
PEPSINATE
PEPSINATED
PEPSINATES
PEPSINATING
PEPSINE
PEPSINES
PEPSINS
PEPTIC
PEPTICITIES
PEPTICITY
PEPTICS
PEPTIDE
PEPTIDES
PEPTISE
PEPTISED
PEPTISES
PEPTISING
PEPTIZE
PEPTIZED
PEPTIZES
PEPTIZING
PEPTONE
PEPTONES
PEPTONISE
PEPTONISED
PEPTONISES
PEPTONISING
PEPTONIZE
PEPTONIZED
PEPTONIZES
PEPTONIZING
PER
PERACUTE
PERAEA
PERAEON
PERAEONS
PERAEOPOD
PERAEOPODS
PERAI

PERAIS
PERCALE
PERCALES
PERCALINE
PERCALINES
PERCASE
PERCE
PERCEABLE
PERCEANT
PERCEIVE
PERCEIVED
PERCEIVER
PERCEIVERS
PERCEIVES
PERCEIVING
PERCEIVINGS
PERCEN
PERCENTAL
PERCEPT
PERCEPTS
PERCH
PERCHANCE
PERCHED
PERCHER
PERCHERONS
PERCHERS
PERCHES
PERCHING
PERCHINGS
PERCIFORM
PERCINE
PERCOCT
PERCOID
PERCOLATE
PERCOLATED
PERCOLATES
PERCOLATING
PERCOLIN
PERCOLINS
PERCUSS
PERCUSSED
PERCUSSES
PERCUSSING
PERCUSSOR
PERCUSSORS
PERDENDO
PERDIE
PERDITION
PERDITIONS
PERDU
PERDUE
PERDUES
PERDURE
PERDURED
PERDURES
PERDURING
PERDUS
PERDY
PÈRE
PEREGAL
PEREGALS
PEREGRINE
PEREGRINES
PEREIA
PEREION
PEREIOPOD
PEREIOPODS
PEREIRA
PEREIRAS

PERENNATE
PERENNATED
PERENNATES
PERENNATING
PERENNIAL
PERENNIALS
PERENNITIES
PERENNITY
PÈRES
PERFAY
PERFECT
PERFECTED
PERFECTER
PERFECTERS
PERFECTEST
PERFECTI
PERFECTING
PERFECTLY
PERFECTO
PERFECTOR
PERFECTORS
PERFECTOS
PERFECTS
PERFERVID
PERFERVOR
PERFERVORS
PERFET
PERFIDIES
PERFIDY
PERFORANS
PERFORANSES
PERFORANT
PERFORATE
PERFORATED
PERFORATES
PERFORATING
PERFORCE
PERFORM
PERFORMED
PERFORMER
PERFORMERS
PERFORMING
PERFORMINGS
PERFORMS
PERFUME
PERFUMED
PERFUMER
PERFUMERIES
PERFUMERS
PERFUMERY
PERFUMES
PERFUMING
PERFUMY
PERFUSATE
PERFUSATES
PERFUSE
PERFUSED
PERFUSES
PERFUSING
PERFUSION
PERFUSIONS
PERFUSIVE
PERGOLA
PERGOLAS
PERGUNNAH
PERGUNNAHS
PERHAPS
PERI
PERIAGUA
PERIAGUAS

PERIAKTOI
PERIAKTOS
PERIANTH
PERIANTHS
PERIAPT
PERIAPTS
PERIBLAST
PERIBLASTS
PERIBLEM
PERIBLEMS
PERIBOLI
PERIBOLOI
PERIBOLOS
PERIBOLUS
PERICARP
PERICARPS
PERICLASE
PERICLASES
PERICLINE
PERICLINES
PERICON
PERICONES
PERICOPE
PERICOPES
PERICRANIES
PERICRANY
PERICYCLE
PERICYCLES
PERIDERM
PERIDERMS
PERIDIA
PERIDIAL
PERIDINIA
PERIDIUM
PERIDIUMS
PERIDOT
PERIDOTE
PERIDOTES
PERIDOTIC
PERIDOTS
PERIDROME
PERIDROMES
PERIGEAL
PERIGEAN
PERIGEE
PERIGEES
PERIGON
PERIGONE
PERIGONES
PERIGONS
PERIGYNIES
PERIGYNY
PERIKARYA
PERIL
PERILLED
PERILLING
PERILOUS
PERILS
PERILUNE
PERILUNES
PERILYMPH
PERILYMPHS
PERIMETER
PERIMETERS
PERIMETRIES
PERIMETRY
PERIMORPH
PERIMORPHS
PERINAEAL
PERINAEUM

PERINAEUMS
PERINATAL
PERINEAL
PERINEUM
PERINEUMS
PERIOD
PERIODATE
PERIODATES
PERIODED
PERIODIC
PERIODING
PERIODS
PERIOST
PERIOSTS
PERIOTIC
PERIOTICS
PERIPATUS
PERIPATUSES
PERIPETIA
PERIPETIAS
PERIPETIES
PERIPETY
PERIPHERIES
PERIPHERY
PERIPLAST
PERIPLASTS
PERIPLUS
PERIPLUSES
PERIPROCT
PERIPROCTS
PERIPTERIES
PERIPTERY
PERIQUE
PERIQUES
PERIS
PERISARC
PERISARCS
PERISCIAN
PERISCIANS
PERISCOPE
PERISCOPES
PERISH
PERISHED
PERISHER
PERISHERS
PERISHES
PERISHING
PERISPERM
PERISPERMS
PERISTOME
PERISTOMES
PERISTYLE
PERISTYLES
PERITI
PERITRICH
PERITRICHA
PERITUS
PERIWIG
PERIWIGGED
PERIWIGGING
PERIWIGS
PERJINK
PERJINKER
PERJINKEST
PERJURE
PERJURED
PERJURER
PERJURERS
PERJURES
PERJURIES

PERJURING
PERJUROUS
PERJURY
PERK
PERKED
PERKIER
PERKIEST
PERKILY
PERKIN
PERKINESS
PERKINESSES
PERKING
PERKINS
PERKS
PERKY
PERLITE
PERLITES
PERLITIC
PERLOUS
PERM
PERMALLOY
PERMALLOYS
PERMANENT
PERMEABLE
PERMEABLY
PERMEANCE
PERMEANCES
PERMEASE
PERMEASES
PERMEATE
PERMEATED
PERMEATES
PERMEATING
PERMED
PERMING
PERMIT
PERMITS
PERMITTED
PERMITTER
PERMITTERS
PERMITTING
PERMS
PERMUTATE
PERMUTATED
PERMUTATES
PERMUTATING
PERMUTE
PERMUTED
PERMUTES
PERMUTING
PERN
PERNANCIES
PERNANCY
PERNS
PERONE
PERONEAL
PERONES
PERONEUS
PERONEUSES
PERORATE
PERORATED
PERORATES
PERORATING
PEROXIDE
PEROXIDED
PEROXIDES
PEROXIDING
PERPEND
PERPENDED
PERPENDING

PERPENDS
PERPENT
PERPENTS
PERPETUAL
PERPETUALS
PERPLEX
PERPLEXED
PERPLEXES
PERPLEXING
PERRADIAL
PERRADII
PERRADIUS
PERRIER
PERRIERS
PERRIES
PERRON
PERRONS
PERRUQUE
PERRUQUES
PERRY
PERSANT
PERSAUNT
PERSE
PERSECUTE
PERSECUTED
PERSECUTES
PERSECUTING
PERSED
PERSEITIES
PERSEITY
PERSELINE
PERSELINES
PERSES
PERSEVERE
PERSEVERED
PERSEVERES
PERSEVERING
PERSICO
PERSICOS
PERSICOT
PERSICOTS
PERSIENNE
PERSIENNES
PERSIMMON
PERSIMMONS
PERSING
PERSIST
PERSISTED
PERSISTING
PERSISTS
PERSON
PERSONA
PERSONAE
PERSONAGE
PERSONAGES
PERSONAL
PERSONAS
PERSONATE
PERSONATED
PERSONATES
PERSONATING
PERSONATINGS
PERSONIFIED
PERSONIFIES
PERSONIFY
PERSONIFYING
PERSONISE
PERSONISED
PERSONISES
PERSONISING

PERSONIZE
PERSONIZED
PERSONIZES
PERSONIZING
PERSONNEL
PERSONNELS
PERSONS
PERSPIRE
PERSPIRED
PERSPIRES
PERSPIRING
PERST
PERSUADE
PERSUADED
PERSUADER
PERSUADERS
PERSUADES
PERSUADING
PERSUE
PERSUES
PERSWADE
PERT
PERTAIN
PERTAINED
PERTAINING
PERTAINS
PERTAKE
PERTER
PERTEST
PERTHITE
PERTHITES
PERTHITIC
PERTINENT
PERTINENTS
PERTLY
PERTNESS
PERTNESSES
PERTS
PERTURB
PERTURBED
PERTURBER
PERTURBERS
PERTURBING
PERTURBS
PERTUSATE
PERTUSE
PERTUSED
PERTUSION
PERTUSIONS
PERTUSSAL
PERTUSSIS
PERTUSSISES
PERUKE
PERUKED
PERUKES
PERUSAL
PERUSALS
PERUSE
PERUSED
PERUSER
PERUSERS
PERUSES
PERUSING
PERV
PERVADE
PERVADED
PERVADES
PERVADING
PERVASION
PERVASIONS

PERVASIVE
PERVERSE
PERVERSER
PERVERSEST
PERVERT
PERVERTED
PERVERTER
PERVERTERS
PERVERTING
PERVERTS
PERVES
PERVIATE
PERVIATED
PERVIATES
PERVIATING
PERVICACIES
PERVICACY
PERVIOUS
PERVS
PESADE
PESADES
PESANT
PESANTE
PESANTS
PESAUNT
PESAUNTS
PESETA
PESETAS
PESEWA
PESEWAS
PESHWA
PESHWAS
PESKIER
PESKIEST
PESKILY
PESKY
PESO
PESOS
PESSARIES
PESSARY
PESSIMISM
PESSIMISMS
PESSIMIST
PESSIMISTS
PEST
PESTER
PESTERED
PESTERER
PESTERERS
PESTERING
PESTEROUS
PESTERS
PESTFUL
PESTHOUSE
PESTHOUSES
PESTICIDE
PESTICIDES
PESTILENT
PESTLE
PESTLED
PESTLES
PESTLING
PESTO
PESTOLOGIES
PESTOLOGY
PESTOS
PESTS
PET
PETAL
PETALINE

PETALISM
PETALISMS
PETALLED
PETALODIES
PETALODY
PETALOID
PETALOUS
PETALS
PÉTANQUE
PÉTANQUES
PETAR
PETARA
PETARAS
PETARD
PETARDS
PETARIES
PETARS
PETARY
PETASUS
PETASUSES
PETAURINE
PETAURIST
PETAURISTS
PETCHARIES
PETCHARY
PETCOCK
PETCOCKS
PETECHIA
PETECHIAE
PETECHIAL
PETER
PETERED
PETERING
PETERMAN
PETERMEN
PETERS
PETERSHAM
PETERSHAMS
PETHER
PETHERS
PETHIDINE
PETHIDINES
PÉTILLANT
PETIOLAR
PETIOLATE
PETIOLATED
PETIOLE
PETIOLED
PETIOLES
PETIOLULE
PETIOLULES
PETIT
PETITE
PETITION
PETITIONED
PETITIONING
PETITIONS
PETITORY
PETRARIES
PETRARY
PETRE
PETREL
PETRELS
PETRES
PETRIFIC
PETRIFIED
PETRIFIES
PETRIFY
PETRIFYING
PETROGRAM

PETROGRAMS
PETROL
PETROLAGE
PETROLAGES
PETROLEUM
PETROLEUMS
PETROLEUR
PETROLEURS
PETROLIC
PETROLLED
PETROLLING
PETROLOGIES
PETROLOGY
PETROLS
PETRONEL
PETRONELS
PETROSAL
PETROSALS
PETROUS
PETS
PETTED
PETTEDLY
PETTER
PETTERS
PETTICOAT
PETTICOATS
PETTIER
PETTIES
PETTIEST
PETTIFOG
PETTIFOGGED
PETTIFOGGING
PETTIFOGS
PETTILY
PETTINESS
PETTINESSES
PETTING
PETTINGS
PETTISH
PETTISHLY
PETTITOES
PETTLE
PETTLED
PETTLES
PETTLING
PETTY
PETULANCE
PETULANCES
PETULANCIES
PETULANCY
PETULANT
PETUNIA
PETUNIAS
PETUNTSE
PETUNTSES
PETUNTZE
PETUNTZES
PEW
PEWIT
PEWITS
PEWS
PEWTER
PEWTERER
PEWTERERS
PEWTERS
PEYOTE
PEYOTES
PEYOTISM
PEYOTISMS
PEYOTIST

PEYOTISTS
PEYSE
PEYSED
PEYSES
PEYSING
PEZANT
PEZANTS
PEZIZOID
PFENNIG
PFENNIGE
PFENNIGS
PFENNING
PFENNINGS
PHACOID
PHACOIDAL
PHACOLITE
PHACOLITES
PHACOLITH
PHACOLITHS
PHAEIC
PHAEISM
PHAEISMS
PHAENOGAM
PHAENOGAMS
PHAETON
PHAETONS
PHAGE
PHAGEDENA
PHAGEDENAS
PHAGES
PHAGOCYTE
PHAGOCYTES
PHALANGAL
PHALANGE
PHALANGER
PHALANGERS
PHALANGES
PHALANGID
PHALANGIDS
PHALANX
PHALANXES
PHALAROPE
PHALAROPES
PHALLI
PHALLIO
PHALLIN
PHALLISM
PHALLISMS
PHALLOID
PHALLUS
PHALLUSES
PHANG
PHANGS
PHANTASIES
PHANTASIM
PHANTASIMS
PHANTASM
PHANTASMA
PHANTASMATA
PHANTASMS
PHANTASY
PHANTOM
PHANTOMS
PHANTOMY
PHANTOSME
PHANTOSMES
PHARAONIC
PHARE
PHARES

PHARISAIC
PHARMACIES
PHARMACY
PHAROS
PHAROSES
PHARYNGAL
PHARYNGES
PHARYNX
PHARYNXES
PHASE
PHASED
PHASELESS
PHASES
PHASIC
PHASING
PHASIS
PHASMID
PHASMIDS
PHATIC
PHEASANT
PHEASANTS
PHEAZAR
PHEAZARS
PHEER
PHEERE
PHEERES
PHEERS
PHEESE
PHEESED
PHEESES
PHEESING
PHEEZE
PHEEZED
PHEEZES
PHEEZING
PHELLEM
PHELLEMS
PHELLOGEN
PHELLOGENS
PHELLOID
PHELONION
PHELONIONS
PHENACITE
PHENACITES
PHENAKISM
PHENAKISMS
PHENAKITE
PHENAKITES
PHENATE
PHENATES
PHENE
PHENES
PHENETIC
PHENETICS
PHENGITE
PHENGITES
PHENIC
PHENOGAM
PHENOGAMS
PHENOL
PHENOLATE
PHENOLATES
PHENOLIC
PHENOLOGIES
PHENOLOGY
PHENOLS
PHENOMENA
PHENOTYPE
PHENOTYPED
PHENOTYPES

PHENOTYPING
PHENYL
PHENYLIC
PHENYLS
PHEON
PHEONS
PHEROMONE
PHEROMONES
PHESE
PHESED
PHESES
PHESING
PHEW
PHI
PHIAL
PHIALLED
PHIALLING
PHIALS
PHILABEG
PHILABEGS
PHILAMOT
PHILAMOTS
PHILANDER
PHILANDERED
PHILANDERING
PHILANDERS
PHILATELIES
PHILATELY
PHILHORSE
PHILHORSES
PHILIBEG
PHILIBEGS
PHILIPPIC
PHILIPPICS
PHILISTER
PHILISTERS
PHILLABEG
PHILLABEGS
PHILLIBEG
PHILLIBEGS
PHILOGYNIES
PHILOGYNY
PHILOLOGIES
PHILOLOGY
PHILOMATH
PHILOMATHS
PHILOMOT
PHILOMOTS
PHILOPENA
PHILOPENAS
PHILTER
PHILTERS
PHILTRE
PHILTRES
PHIMOSES
PHIMOSIS
PHINNOCK
PHINNOCKS
PHIS
PHISNOMIES
PHISNOMY
PHIZ
PHIZOG
PHIZOGS
PHIZZES
PHLEBITIS
PHLEBITISES
PHLEGM
PHLEGMIER
PHLEGMIEST

PHLEGMON
PHLEGMONS
PHLEGMS
PHLEGMY
PHLOEM
PHLOEMS
PHLOX
PHLOXES
PHLYCTENA
PHLYCTENAE
PHO
PHOBIA
PHOBIAS
PHOBIC
PHOBISM
PHOBISMS
PHOBIST
PHOBISTS
PHOCA
PHOCAE
PHOCAS
PHOCINE
PHOEBE
PHOEBES
PHOENIX
PHOENIXES
PHOH
PHOLADES
PHOLAS
PHON
PHONAL
PHONATE
PHONATED
PHONATES
PHONATING
PHONATION
PHONATIONS
PHONATORY
PHONE
PHONECARD
PHONECARDS
PHONED
PHONEME
PHONEMES
PHONEMIC
PHONEMICS
PHONES
PHONETIC
PHONETICS
PHONETISM
PHONETISMS
PHONETIST
PHONETISTS
PHONEY
PHONEYED
PHONEYING
PHONEYS
PHONIC
PHONICS
PHONIED
PHONIER
PHONIES
PHONIEST
PHONINESS
PHONINESSES
PHONING
PHONMETER
PHONMETERS
PHONOGRAM
PHONOGRAMS

PHONOLITE	PHOTOPHIL	PHYLLARIES	PIANISTIC	PICKETING
PHONOLITES	PHOTOPHILS	PHYLLARY	PIANISTS	PICKETS
PHONOLOGIES	PHOTOPIA	PHYLLITE	PIANO	PICKIER
PHONOLOGY	PHOTOPIAS	PHYLLITES	PIANOS	PICKIEST
PHONON	PHOTOPIC	PHYLLO	PIARIST	PICKING
PHONONS	PHOTOPSIA	PHYLLODE	PIARISTS	PICKINGS
PHONOPORE	PHOTOPSIAS	PHYLLODES	PIAS	PICKLE
PHONOPORES	PHOTOPSIES	PHYLLODIES	PIASSABA	PICKLED
PHONOTYPE	PHOTOPSY	PHYLLODY	PIASSABAS	PICKLER
PHONOTYPED	PHOTOS	PHYLLOID	PIASSAVA	PICKLERS
PHONOTYPES	PHOTOTYPE	PHYLLOME	PIASSAVAS	PICKLES
PHONOTYPIES	PHOTOTYPED	PHYLLOMES	PIASTRE	PICKLING
PHONOTYPING	PHOTOTYPES	PHYLLOPOD	PIASTRES	PICKLOCK
PHONOTYPY	PHOTOTYPIES	PHYLLOPODS	PIAZZA	PICKLOCKS
PHONS	PHOTOTYPING	PHYLLOS	PIAZZAS	PICKMAW
PHONY	PHOTOTYPY	PHYLOGENIES	PIAZZIAN	PICKMAWS
PHONYING	PHOTS	PHYLOGENY	PIBROCH	PICKS
PHOOEY	PHRASAL	PHYLUM	PIBROCHS	PICKY
PHORMINGES	PHRASE	PHYSALIA	PIC	PICNIC
PHORMINX	PHRASED	PHYSALIAS	PICA	PICNICKED
PHORMIUM	PHRASEMAN	PHYSALIS	PICADOR	PICNICKER
PHORMIUMS	PHRASEMEN	PHYSALISES	PICADORS	PICNICKERS
PHOS	PHRASER	PHYSIC	PICAMAR	PICNICKING
PHOSGENE	PHRASERS	PHYSICAL	PICAMARS	PICNICKY
PHOSGENES	PHRASES	PHYSICALS	PICARIAN	PICNICS
PHOSPHATE	PHRASING	PHYSICIAN	PICARIANS	PICOT
PHOSPHATED	PHRASINGS	PHYSICIANS	PICAROON	PICOTÉ
PHOSPHATES	PHRASY	PHYSICISM	PICAROONS	PICOTED
PHOSPHATING	PHRATRIES	PHYSICISMS	PICAS	PICOTEE
PHOSPHENE	PHRATRY	PHYSICIST	PICAYUNE	PICOTEES
PHOSPHENES	PHREATIC	PHYSICISTS	PICAYUNES	PICOTING
PHOSPHIDE	PHRENESES	PHYSICKED	PICCADILL	PICOTITE
PHOSPHIDES	PHRENESIS	PHYSICKING	PICCADILLS	PICOTITES
PHOSPHINE	PHRENETIC	PHYSICKY	PICCANIN	PICOTS
PHOSPHINES	PHRENETICS	PHYSICS	PICCANINS	PICQUET
PHOSPHITE	PHRENIC	PHYSIO	PICCOLO	PICQUETED
PHOSPHITES	PHRENISM	PHYSIOS	PICCOLOS	PICQUETING
PHOSPHOR	PHRENISMS	PHYSIQUE	PICE	PICQUETS
PHOSPHORS	PHRENITIC	PHYSIQUES	PICENE	PICRA
PHOT	PHRENITIS	PHYTOGENIES	PICENES	PICRAS
PHOTIC	PHRENITISES	PHYTOGENY	PICEOUS	PICRATE
PHOTICS	PHRENSIES	PHYTOLOGIES	PICHURIM	PICRATES
PHOTISM	PHRENSY	PHYTOLOGY	PICHURIMS	PICRIC
PHOTISMS	PHRENTICK	PHYTON	PICINE	PICRITE
PHOTO	PHTHALATE	PHYTONS	PICK	PICRITES
PHOTOCALL	PHTHALATES	PHYTOSES	PICKABACK	PICS
PHOTOCALLS	PHTHALEIN	PHYTOSIS	PICKABACKS	PICTARNIE
PHOTOCELL	PHTHALEINS	PHYTOTOMIES	PICKAPACK	PICTARNIES
PHOTOCELLS	PHTHALIC	PHYTOTOMY	PICKAPACKS	PICTOGRAM
PHOTOCOPIED	PHTHALIN	PHYTOTRON	PICKAXE	PICTOGRAMS
PHOTOCOPIES	PHTHALINS	PHYTOTRONS	PICKAXES	PICTORIAL
PHOTOCOPY	PHTHISES	PI	PICKBACK	PICTORIALS
PHOTOCOPYING	PHTHISIC	PIA	PICKBACKS	PICTURAL
PHOTOED	PHTHISICS	PIACEVOLE	PICKED	PICTURALS
PHOTOGEN	PHTHISIS	PIACULAR	PICKEER	PICTURE
PHOTOGENE	PHUT	PIAFFE	PICKEERED	PICTURED
PHOTOGENES	PHUTS	PIAFFED	PICKEERER	PICTURES
PHOTOGENIES	PHYCOCYAN	PIAFFER	PICKEERERS	PICTURING
PHOTOGENS	PHYCOCYANS	PIAFFERS	PICKEERING	PICUL
PHOTOGENY	PHYCOLOGIES	PIAFFES	PICKEERS	PICULS
PHOTOGRAM	PHYCOLOGY	PIAFFING	PICKER	PIDDLE
PHOTOGRAMS	PIIYLA	PIANETTE	PICKEREL	PIDDLED
PHOTOING	PHYLAE	PIANETTES	PICKERELS	PIDDLER
PHOTOLYSE	PHYLARCH	PIANINO	PICKERIES	PIDDLERS
PHOTOLYSED	PHYLARCHIES	PIANINOS	PICKERS	PIDDLES
PHOTOLYSES	PHYLARCHS	PIANISM	PICKERY	PIDDLING
PHOTOLYSING	PHYLARCHY	PIANISMS	PICKET	PIDDOCK
PHOTON	PHYLE	PIANIST	PICKETED	PIDDOCKS
PHOTONICS	PHYLES	PIANISTE	PICKETER	PIDGEON
PHOTONS	PHYLETIC	PIANISTES	PICKETERS	PIDGEONS

PIDGIN	PIFFERO	PIGSNIES	PILFERERS	PILOTING
PIDGINS	PIFFEROS	PIGSNY	PILFERIES	PILOTLESS
PIE	PIFFLE	PIGSTIES	PILFERING	PILOTS
PIEBALD	PIFFLED	PIGSTY	PILFERINGS	PILOUS
PIEBALDS	PIFFLER	PIGSWILL	PILFERS	PILOW
PIECE	PIFFLERS	PIGSWILLS	PILFERY	PILOWS
PIECED	PIFFLES	PIGTAIL	PILGRIM	PILSENER
PIECELESS	PIFFLING	PIGTAILS	PILGRIMER	PILSENERS
PIECEMEAL	PIG	PIGWASH	PILGRIMERS	PILSNER
PIECEMEALED	PIGBOAT	PIGWASHES	PILGRIMS	PILSNERS
PIECEMEALING	PIGBOATS	PIGWEED	PILHORSE	PILULA
PIECEMEALS	PIGEON	PIGWEEDS	PILHORSES	PILULAR
PIECEN	PIGEONED	PIKA	PILI	PILULAS
PIECENED	PIGEONING	PIKADELL	PILIFORM	PILULE
PIECENER	PIGEONRIES	PIKADELLS	PILING	PILULES
PIECENERS	PIGEONRY	PIKAS	PILIS	PILUM
PIECENING	PIGEONS	PIKE	PILL	PILUS
PIECENS	PIGFEED	PIKED	PILLAGE	PIMENT
PIECER	PIGFEEDS	PIKELET	PILLAGED	PIMENTO
PIECERS	PIGGED	PIKELETS	PILLAGER	PIMENTOS
PIECES	PIGGERIES	PIKEMAN	PILLAGERS	PIMENTS
PIECING	PIGGERY	PIKEMEN	PILLAGES	PIMIENTO
PIECRUST	PIGGIE	PIKER	PILLAGING	PIMIENTOS
PIECRUSTS	PIGGIER	PIKERS	PILLAR	PIMP
PIED	PIGGIES	PIKES	PILLARIST	PIMPED
PIEDISH	PIGGIEST	PIKESTAFF	PILLARISTS	PIMPERNEL
PIEDISHES	PIGGIN	PIKESTAFFS	PILLARS	PIMPERNELS
PIEDMONT	PIGGING	PIKING	PILLAU	PIMPING
PIEDMONTS	PIGGINGS	PIKUL	PILLAUS	PIMPLE
PIEDNESS	PIGGINS	PIKULS	PILLED	PIMPLED
PIEDNESSES	PIGGISH	PILA	PILLHEAD	PIMPLES
PIEING	PIGGISHLY	PILAFF	PILLHEADS	PIMPLIER
PIEMAN	PIGGY	PILAFFS	PILLICOCK	PIMPLIEST
PIEMEN	PIGGYBACK	PILASTER	PILLICOCKS	PIMPLY
PIEND	PIGGYBACKS	PILASTERS	PILLING	PIMPS
PIENDS	PIGHEADED	PILAU	PILLION	PIN
PIEPOWDER	PIGHT	PILAUS	PILLIONED	PIÑA
PIEPOWDERS	PIGHTLE	PILAW	PILLIONING	PINACOID
PIER	PIGHTLES	PILAWS	PILLIONS	PINACOIDS
PIERAGE	PIGLET	PILCH	PILLOCK	PINAFORE
PIERAGES	PIGLETS	PILCHARD	PILLOCKS	PINAFORED
PIERCE	PIGLING	PILCHARDS	PILLORIED	PINAFORES
PIERCED	PIGLINGS	PILCHER	PILLORIES	PINAKOID
PIERCEN	PIGMEAN	PILCHERS	PILLORISE	PINAKOIDS
PIERCERS	PIGMEAT	PILCHES	PILLORISED	PIÑAS
PIERCES	PIGMEATS	PILCORN	PILLORISES	PINASTER
PIERCING	PIGMENT	PILCORNS	PILLORISING	PINASTERS
PIERID	PIGMENTAL	PILCROW	PILLORIZE	PINBALL
PIERIDINE	PIGMENTED	PILCROWS	PILLORIZED	PINBALLS
PIERIDS	PIGMENTS	PILE	PILLORIZES	PINCASE
PIERROT	PIGMIES	PILEA	PILLORIZING	PINCASES
PIERROTS	PIGMY	PILEATE	PILLORY	PINCER
PIERS	PIGNERATE	PILEATED	PILLORYING	PINCERED
PIERST	PIGNERATED	PILED	PILLOW	PINCERING
PIERT	PIGNERATES	PILEI	PILLOWED	PINCERS
PIES	PIGNERATING	PILEOUS	PILLOWING	PINCH
PIET	PIGNORATE	PILER	PILLOWS	PINCHBECK
PIETÀ	PIGNORATED	PILERS	PILLOWY	PINCHBECKS
PIETÀS	PIGNORATES	PILES	PILLS	PINCHCOCK
PIETIES	PIGNORATING	PILEUM	PILLWORM	PINCHCOCKS
PIETISM	PIGPEN	PILEUS	PILLWORMS	PINCHED
PIETISMS	PIGPENS	PILEWORK	PILLWORT	PINCHER
PIETIST	PIGS	PILEWORKS	PILLWORTS	PINCHERS
PIETISTIC	PIGSCONCE	PILEWORT	PILOSE	PINCHES
PIETISTS	PIGSCONCES	PILEWORTS	PILOSITIES	PINCHFIST
PIETS	PIGSKIN	PILFER	PILOSITY	PINCHFISTS
PIETY	PIGSKINS	PILFERAGE	PILOT	PINCHGUT
PIEZO	PIGSNEY	PILFERAGES	PILOTAGE	PINCHGUTS
PIFFERARI	PIGSNEYS	PILFERED	PILOTAGES	PINCHING
PIFFERARO	PIGSNIE	PILFERER	PILOTED	PINCHINGS

PINDAREE
PINDAREES
PINDARI
PINDARIS
PINDER
PINDERS
PINE
PINEAL
PINEAPPLE
PINEAPPLES
PINED
PINERIES
PINERY
PINES
PINETA
PINETUM
PINEY
PINFISH
PINFISHES
PINFOLD
PINFOLDED
PINFOLDING
PINFOLDS
PING
PINGED
PINGER
PINGERS
PINGING
PINGLE
PINGLED
PINGLER
PINGLERS
PINGLES
PINGLING
PINGO
PINGOES
PINGOS
PINGS
PINGUEFIED
PINGUEFIES
PINGUEFY
PINGUEFYING
PINGUID
PINGUIN
PINGUINS
PINHEAD
PINHEADS
PINHOLE
PINHOLES
PINIER
PINIES
PINIEST
PINING
PINION
PINIONED
PINIONING
PINIONS
PINITE
PINITES
PINK
PINKED
PINKER
PINKERTON
PINKERTONS
PINKEST
PINKIE
PINKIER
PINKIES
PINKIEST
PINKINESS

PINKINESSES
PINKING
PINKINGS
PINKISH
PINKNESS
PINKNESSES
PINKO
PINKOES
PINKOS
PINKROOT
PINKROOTS
PINKS
PINKY
PINNA
PINNACE
PINNACES
PINNACLE
PINNACLED
PINNACLES
PINNACLING
PINNAE
PINNATE
PINNATED
PINNATELY
PINNED
PINNER
PINNERS
PINNET
PINNETS
PINNIE
PINNIES
PINNING
PINNINGS
PINNIPED
PINNIPEDE
PINNIPEDES
PINNIPEDS
PINNOCK
PINNOCKS
PINNOED
PINNULA
PINNULAS
PINNULATE
PINNULE
PINNULES
PINNY
PINOCHLE
PINOCHLES
PINOCLE
PINOCLES
PINOLE
PINOLES
PIÑON
PIÑONS
PINOT
PINOTS
PINS
PINT
PINTA
PINTABLE
PINTABLES
PINTADO
PINTADOS
PINTAIL
PINTAILED
PINTAILS
PINTAS
PINTLE
PINTLES
PINTO

PINTOS
PINTS
PINXIT
PINY
PIOLET
PIOLETS
PION
PIONED
PIONEER
PIONEERED
PIONEERING
PIONEERS
PIONER
PIONERS
PIONEY
PIONEYS
PIONIES
PIONING
PIONINGS
PIONS
PIONY
PIOTED
PIOUS
PIOUSLY
PIOY
PIOYE
PIOYES
PIOYS
PIP
PIPA
PIPAGE
PIPAGES
PIPAL
PIPALS
PIPAS
PIPE
PIPECLAY
PIPECLAYED
PIPECLAYING
PIPECLAYS
PIPED
PIPEFISH
PIPEFISHES
PIPEFUL
PIPEFULS
PIPELESS
PIPELIKE
PIPELINE
PIPELINES
PIPER
PIPERIC
PIPERINE
PIPERINES
PIPERONAL
PIPERONALS
PIPERS
PIPES
PIPESTONE
PIPESTONES
PIPETTE
PIPETTED
PIPETTES
PIPETTING
PIPEWORK
PIPEWORKS
PIPEWORT
PIPEWORTS
PIPI
PIPIER
PIPIEST

PIPING
PIPINGS
PIPIS
PIPIT
PIPITS
PIPKIN
PIPKINS
PIPLESS
PIPPED
PIPPIER
PIPPIEST
PIPPIN
PIPPING
PIPPINS
PIPPY
PIPS
PIPSQUEAK
PIPSQUEAKS
PIPUL
PIPULS
PIPY
PIQUANCIES
PIQUANCY
PIQUANT
PIQUANTLY
PIQUE
PIQUED
PIQUES
PIQUET
PIQUETED
PIQUETING
PIQUETS
PIQUING
PIR
PIRACIES
PIRACY
PIRAGUA
PIRAGUAS
PIRAI
PIRAIS
PIRAÑA
PIRAÑAS
PIRANHA
PIRANHAS
PIRARUCU
PIRARUCUS
PIRATE
PIRATED
PIRATES
PIRATIC
PIRATICAL
PIRATING
PIRAYA
PIRAYAS
PIRL
PIRLICUE
PIRLICUED
PIRLICUES
PIRLICUING
PIRLS
PIRN
PIRNIE
PIRNIES
PIRNIT
PIRNS
PIROGUE
PIROGUES
PIROSHKI
PIROUETTE
PIROUETTED

PIROUETTES
PIROUETTING
PIROZHKI
PIRS
PIS
PISCARIES
PISCARY
PISCATOR
PISCATORS
PISCATORY
PISCATRIX
PISCATRIXES
PISCIFORM
PISCINA
PISCINAE
PISCINAS
PISCINE
PISCINES
PISÉ
PISÉS
PISH
PISHED
PISHES
PISHING
PISHOGUE
PISHOGUES
PISIFORM
PISIFORMS
PISKIES
PISKY
PISMIRE
PISMIRES
PISOLITE
PISOLITES
PISOLITIC
PISS
PISSED
PISSES
PISSING
PISSOIR
PISSOIRS
PISTACHIO
PISTACHIOS
PISTAREEN
PISTAREENS
PISTE
PISTES
PISTIL
PISTILS
PISTOL
PISTOLE
PISTOLEER
PISTOLEERS
PISTOLES
PISTOLET
PISTOLETS
PISTOLLED
PISTOLLING
PISTOLS
PISTON
PISTONS
PIT
PITA
PITAPAT
PITAPATS
PITAPATTED
PITAPATTING
PITARA
PITARAH
PITARAHS

PITARAS	PITTING	PLACCATS	PLAINER	PLANKTONS
PITAS	PITTINGS	PLACE	PLAINEST	PLANLESS
PITCH	PITTITE	PLACEBO	PLAINFUL	PLANNED
PITCHED	PITTITES	PLACEBOS	PLAINING	PLANNER
PITCHER	PITUITA	PLACED	PLAININGS	PLANNERS
PITCHERS	PITUITARY	PLACELESS	PLAINISH	PLANNING
PITCHES	PITUITAS	PLACEMAN	PLAINLY	PLANS
PITCHFORK	PITUITE	PLACEMEN	PLAINNESS	PLANT
PITCHFORKED	PITUITES	PLACEMENT	PLAINNESSES	PLANTA
PITCHFORKING	PITUITRIN	PLACEMENTS	PLAINS	PLANTABLE
PITCHFORKS	PITUITRINS	PLACENTA	PLAINSMAN	PLANTAGE
PITCHIER	PITURI	PLACENTAE	PLAINSMEN	PLANTAGES
PITCHIEST	PITURIS	PLACENTAL	PLAINSONG	PLANTAIN
PITCHING	PITY	PLACENTALS	PLAINSONGS	PLANTAINS
PITCHINGS	PITYING	PLACENTAS	PLAINT	PLANTAR
PITCHMAN	PITYINGLY	PLACER	PLAINTFUL	PLANTAS
PITCHMEN	PITYROID	PLACERS	PLAINTIFF	PLANTED
PITCHPINE	PIÙ	PLACES	PLAINTIFFS	PLANTER
PITCHPINES	PIUM	PLACET	PLAINTIVE	PLANTERS
PITCHPIPE	PIUMS	PLACETS	PLAINTS	PLANTING
PITCHPIPES	PIUPIU	PLACID	PLAINWORK	PLANTINGS
PITCHY	PIUPIUS	PLACIDER	PLAINWORKS	PLANTLESS
PITEOUS	PIVOT	PLACIDEST	PLAISTER	PLANTLET
PITEOUSLY	PIVOTAL	PLACIDITIES	PLAISTERS	PLANTLETS
PITFALL	PIVOTALLY	PLACIDITY	PLAIT	PLANTLING
PITFALLS	PIVOTED	PLACIDLY	PLAITED	PLANTLINGS
PITH	PIVOTER	PLACING	PLAITER	PLANTS
PITHBALL	PIVOTERS	PLACINGS	PLAITERS	PLANTSMAN
PITHBALLS	PIVOTING	PLACIT	PLAITING	PLANTSMEN
PITHEAD	PIVOTINGS	PLACITA	PLAITINGS	PLANTULE
PITHEADS	PIVOTS	PLACITORY	PLAITS	PLANTULES
PITHECOID	PIX	PLACITS	PLAN	PLANULA
PITHED	PIXED	PLACITUM	PLANAR	PLANULAE
PITHFUL	PIXEL	PLACK	PLANARIAN	PLANULAR
PITHIER	PIXELS	PLACKET	PLANARIANS	PLANULOID
PITHIEST	PIXES	PLACKETS	PLANATION	PLANURIA
PITHILY	PIXIE	PLACKLESS	PLANATIONS	PLANURIAS
PITHINESS	PIXIES	PLACKS	PLANCH	PLANURIES
PITHINESSES	PIXILATED	PLACODERM	PLANCHED	PLANURY
PITHING	PIXING	PLACODERMS	PLANCHES	PLANXTIES
PITHLESS	PIXY	PLACOID	PLANCHET	PLANXTY
PITHLIKE	PIZAZZ	PLAFOND	PLANCHETS	PLAP
PITHOI	PIZAZZES	PLAFONDS	PLANCHING	PLAPPED
PITHOS	PIZE	PLAGAL	PLANE	PLAPPING
PITHS	PIZES	PLAGE	PLANED	PLAPS
PITHY	PIZZA	PLAGES	PLANER	PLAQUE
PITIABLE	PIZZAIOLA	PLAGIARIES	PLANERS	PLAQUES
PITIABLY	PIZZAS	PLAGIARY	PLANES	PLAQUETTE
PITIED	PIZZERIA	PLAGIUM	PLANET	PLAQUETTES
PITIER	PIZZERIAS	PLAGIUMS	PLANETARY	PLASH
PITIERS	PIZZICATO	PLAGUE	PLANETIC	PLASHED
PITIES	PIZZICATOS	PLAGUED	PLANETOID	PLASHES
PITIFUL	PIZZLE	PLAGUES	PLANETOIDS	PLASHET
PITIFULLY	PIZZLES	PLAGUEY	PLANETS	PLASHETS
PITILESS	PLACABLE	PLAGUILY	PLANGENCIES	PLASHIER
PITMAN	PLACABLY	PLAGUING	PLANGENCY	PLASHIEST
PITMEN	PLACARD	PLAGUY	PLANGENT	PLASHING
PITON	PLACARDED	PLAICE	PLANING	PLASHINGS
PITONS	PLACARDING	PLAICES	PLANISH	PLASHY
PITS	PLACARDS	PLAID	PLANISHED	PLASM
PITTA	PLACATE	PLAIDED	PLANISHER	PLASMA
PITTANCE	PLACATED	PLAIDING	PLANISHERS	PLASMAS
PITTANCES	PLACATES	PLAIDINGS	PLANISHES	PLASMATIC
PITTAS	PLACATING	PLAIDMAN	PLANISHING	PLASMIC
PITTED	PLACATION	PLAIDMEN	PLANK	PLASMID
PITTEN	PLACATIONS	PLAIDS	PLANKED	PLASMIDS
PITTER	PLACATORY	PLAIN	PLANKING	PLASMIN
PITTERED	PLACCAT	PLAINANT	PLANKINGS	PLASMINS
PITTERING	PLACCATE	PLAINANTS	PLANKS	PLASMODIA
PITTERS	PLACCATES	PLAINED	PLANKTON	PLASMS

PLAST
PLASTE
PLASTER
PLASTERED
PLASTERER
PLASTERERS
PLASTERING
PLASTERINGS
PLASTERS
PLASTERY
PLASTIC
PLASTICS
PLASTID
PLASTIDS
PLASTIQUE
PLASTIQUES
PLASTISOL
PLASTISOLS
PLASTRAL
PLASTRON
PLASTRONS
PLAT
PLATAN
PLATANE
PLATANES
PLATANNA
PLATANNAS
PLATANS
PLATBAND
PLATBANDS
PLATE
PLATEASM
PLATEASMS
PLATEAU
PLATEAUED
PLATEAUING
PLATEAUS
PLATEAUX
PLATED
PLATEFUL
PLATEFULS
PLATELET
PLATELETS
PLATEMAN
PLATEMARK
PLATEMARKS
PLATEMEN
PLATEN
PLATENS
PLATER
PLATERS
PLATES
PLATFORM
PLATFORMED
PLATFORMING
PLATFORMINGS
PLATFORMS
PLATIER
PLATIEST
PLATINA
PLATINAS
PLATING
PLATINGS
PLATINIC
PLATINISE
PLATINISED
PLATINISES
PLATINISING
PLATINIZE
PLATINIZED

PLATINIZES
PLATINIZING
PLATINOID
PLATINOIDS
PLATINOUS
PLATINUM
PLATINUMS
PLATITUDE
PLATITUDES
PLATONIC
PLATONICS
PLATOON
PLATOONS
PLATS
PLATTED
PLATTER
PLATTERS
PLATTING
PLATTINGS
PLATY
PLATYPUS
PLATYPUSES
PLATYSMA
PLATYSMAS
PLAUDIT
PLAUDITE
PLAUDITS
PLAUSIBLE
PLAUSIBLY
PLAUSIVE
PLAUSTRAL
PLAY
PLAYA
PLAYABLE
PLAYAS
PLAYBACK
PLAYBACKS
PLAYBILL
PLAYBILLS
PLAYBOOK
PLAYBOOKS
PLAYBOY
PLAYBOYS
PLAYBUS
PLAYBUSES
PLAYED
PLAYER
PLAYERS
PLAYFUL
PLAYFULLER
PLAYFULLEST
PLAYFULLY
PLAYGIRL
PLAYGIRLS
PLAYGROUP
PLAYGROUPS
PLAYHOUSE
PLAYHOUSES
PLAYING
PLAYLET
PLAYLETS
PLAYMATE
PLAYMATES
PLAYROOM
PLAYROOMS
PLAYS
PLAYSOME
PLAYSUIT
PLAYSUITS
PLAYTHING

PLAYTHINGS
PLAYTIME
PLAYTIMES
PLAZA
PLAZAS
PLEA
PLEACH
PLEACHED
PLEACHES
PLEACHING
PLEAD
PLEADABLE
PLEADED
PLEADER
PLEADERS
PLEADING
PLEADINGS
PLEADS
PLEAED
PLEAING
PLEAS
PLEASANCE
PLEASANCES
PLEASANT
PLEASANTER
PLEASANTEST
PLEASE
PLEASED
PLEASEMAN
PLEASEMEN
PLEASER
PLEASERS
PLEASES
PLEASETH
PLEASING
PLEASINGS
PLEASURE
PLEASURED
PLEASURER
PLEASURERS
PLEASURES
PLEASURING
PLEAT
PLEATED
PLEATING
PLEATS
PLEB
PLEBBIER
PLEBBIEST
PLEBBY
PLEBEAN
PLEBEIAN
PLEBEIANS
PLEBIFIED
PLEBIFIES
PLEBIFY
PLEBIFYING
PLEBS
PLECTRA
PLECTRE
PLECTRES
PLECTRON
PLECTRONS
PLECTRUM
PLECTRUMS
PLED
PLEDGE
PLEDGED
PLEDGEE
PLEDGEES

PLEDGEOR
PLEDGEORS
PLEDGER
PLEDGERS
PLEDGES
PLEDGET
PLEDGETS
PLEDGING
PLEDGOR
PLEDGORS
PLEIOMERIES
PLEIOMERY
PLENARILY
PLENARTIES
PLENARTY
PLENARY
PLENILUNE
PLENILUNES
PLENIPO
PLENIPOES
PLENIPOS
PLENISH
PLENISHED
PLENISHES
PLENISHING
PLENISHINGS
PLENIST
PLENISTS
PLENITUDE
PLENITUDES
PLENTEOUS
PLENTIES
PLENTIFUL
PLENTY
PLENUM
PLENUMS
PLEON
PLEONASM
PLEONASMS
PLEONAST
PLEONASTE
PLEONASTES
PLEONASTS
PLEONEXIA
PLEONEXIAS
PLEONS
PLEOPOD
PLEOPODS
PLEROMA
PLEROMAS
PLEROME
PLEROMES
PLESH
PLESHES
PLESSOR
PLESSORS
PLETHORA
PLETHORAS
PLETHORIC
PLEUCH
PLEUCHS
PLEUGH
PLEUGHS
PLEURA
PLEURAE
PLEURAL
PLEURISIES
PLEURISY
PLEURITIC
PLEURITIS

PLEURITISES
PLEURON
PLEXIFORM
PLEXOR
PLEXORS
PLEXURE
PLEXURES
PLEXUS
PLEXUSES
PLIABLE
PLIABLY
PLIANCIES
PLIANCY
PLIANT
PLIANTLY
PLICA
PLICAE
PLICAL
PLICATE
PLICATED
PLICATELY
PLICATES
PLICATING
PLICATION
PLICATIONS
PLICATURE
PLICATURES
PLIÉ
PLIED
PLIER
PLIERS
PLIÉS
PLIES
PLIGHT
PLIGHTED
PLIGHTER
PLIGHTERS
PLIGHTFUL
PLIGHTING
PLIGHTS
PLIM
PLIMMED
PLIMMING
PLIMS
PLIMSOLE
PLIMSOLES
PLIMSOLL
PLIMSOLLS
PLINK
PLINKED
PLINKING
PLINKS
PLINTH
PLINTHS
PLISKIE
PLISKIES
PLISSÉ
PLOAT
PLOATED
PLOATING
PLOATS
PLOD
PLODDED
PLODDER
PLODDERS
PLODDING
PLODDINGS
PLODS
PLONG
PLONGD

PLONGE
PLONK
PLONKED
PLONKER
PLONKERS
PLONKING
PLONKS
PLOOK
PLOOKIE
PLOOKS
PLOP
PLOPPED
PLOPPING
PLOPS
PLOSION
PLOSIONS
PLOSIVE
PLOSIVES
PLOT
PLOTFUL
PLOTLESS
PLOTS
PLOTTED
PLOTTER
PLOTTERED
PLOTTERING
PLOTTERS
PLOTTIE
PLOTTIES
PLOTTING
PLOTTINGS
PLOTTY
PLOUGH
PLOUGHBOY
PLOUGHBOYS
PLOUGHED
PLOUGHER
PLOUGHERS
PLOUGHING
PLOUGHINGS
PLOUGHMAN
PLOUGHMEN
PLOUGHS
PLOUK
PLOUKIE
PLOUKS
PLOUTER
PLOUTERED
PLOUTERING
PLOUTERS
PLOVER
PLOVERS
PLOVERY
PLOW
PLOWED
PLOWING
PLOWS
PLOWTER
PLOWTERED
PLOWTERING
PLOWTERS
PLOY
PLOYS
PLUCK
PLUCKED
PLUCKER
PLUCKERS
PLUCKIER
PLUCKIEST
PLUCKILY

PLUCKING
PLUCKS
PLUCKY
PLUFF
PLUFFED
PLUFFING
PLUFFS
PLUFFY
PLUG
PLUGGED
PLUGGER
PLUGGERS
PLUGGING
PLUGGINGS
PLUGS
PLUM
PLUMAGE
PLUMAGED
PLUMAGES
PLUMATE
PLUMB
PLUMBAGO
PLUMBAGOS
PLUMBATE
PLUMBATES
PLUMBED
PLUMBEOUS
PLUMBER
PLUMBERIES
PLUMBERS
PLUMBERY
PLUMBIC
PLUMBING
PLUMBINGS
PLUMBISM
PLUMBISMS
PLUMBITE
PLUMBITES
PLUMBLESS
PLUMBOUS
PLUMBS
PLUMBUM
PLUMBUMS
PLUMCOT
PLUMCOTS
PLUMDAMAS
PLUMDAMASES
PLUME
PLUMED
PLUMELESS
PLUMELET
PLUMELETS
PLUMERIES
PLUMERY
PLUMES
PLUMIER
PLUMIEST
PLUMING
PLUMIPED
PLUMIST
PLUMISTS
PLUMMET
PLUMMETED
PLUMMETING
PLUMMETS
PLUMMIER
PLUMMIEST
PLUMMY
PLUMOSE
PLUMOUS

PLUMP
PLUMPED
PLUMPEN
PLUMPENED
PLUMPENING
PLUMPENS
PLUMPER
PLUMPERS
PLUMPEST
PLUMPIE
PLUMPING
PLUMPISH
PLUMPLY
PLUMPNESS
PLUMPNESSES
PLUMPS
PLUMPY
PLUMS
PLUMULA
PLUMULAE
PLUMULAR
PLUMULATE
PLUMULE
PLUMULES
PLUMULOSE
PLUMY
PLUNDER
PLUNDERED
PLUNDERER
PLUNDERERS
PLUNDERING
PLUNDERS
PLUNGE
PLUNGED
PLUNGER
PLUNGERS
PLUNGES
PLUNGING
PLUNGINGS
PLUNK
PLUNKED
PLUNKER
PLUNKERS
PLUNKING
PLUNKO
PLURAL
PLURALISE
PLURALISED
PLURALISES
PLURALISING
PLURALISM
PLURALISMS
PLURALIST
PLURALISTS
PLURALITIES
PLURALITY
PLURALIZE
PLURALIZED
PLURALIZES
PLURALIZING
PLURALLY
PLURALS
PLURIPARA
PLURIPARAE
PLURIPARAS
PLURISIE
PLURISIES
PLUS
PLUSAGE
PLUSAGES

PLUSES
PLUSH
PLUSHER
PLUSHES
PLUSHEST
PLUSHIER
PLUSHIEST
PLUSHY
PLUSSAGE
PLUSSAGES
PLUSSED
PLUSSES
PLUSSING
PLUTEAL
PLUTEUS
PLUTEUSES
PLUTOCRAT
PLUTOCRATS
PLUTOLOGIES
PLUTOLOGY
PLUTON
PLUTONIUM
PLUTONIUMS
PLUTONOMIES
PLUTONOMY
PLUTONS
PLUVIAL
PLUVIALS
PLUVIOSE
PLUVIOUS
PLY
PLYING
PLYWOOD
PLYWOODS
PNEUMA
PNEUMAS
PNEUMATIC
PNEUMATICS
PNEUMONIA
PNEUMONIAS
PNEUMONIC
PNEUMONICS
PO
POA
POACEOUS
POACH
POACHED
POACHER
POACHERS
POACHES
POACHIER
POACHIEST
POACHING
POACHINGS
POACHY
POAKA
POAKAS
POAKE
POAKES
POAS
POCAS
POCHARD
POCHARDS
POCHAY
POCHAYED
POCHAYING
POCHAYS
POCHETTE
POCHETTES
POCHOIR

POCHOIRS
POCK
POCKARD
POCKARDS
POCKED
POCKET
POCKETED
POCKETFUL
POCKETFULS
POCKETING
POCKETS
POCKIER
POCKIEST
POCKMANKIES
POCKMANKY
POCKMARK
POCKMARKS
POCKPIT
POCKPITS
POCKS
POCKY
POCO
POD
PODAGRA
PODAGRAL
PODAGRAS
PODAGRIC
PODAGROUS
PODAL
PODALIC
PODDED
PODDIER
PODDIEST
PODDING
PODDY
PODESTA
PODESTAS
PODEX
PODEXES
PODGE
PODGES
PODGIER
PODGIEST
PODGINESS
PODGINESSES
PODGY
PODIA
PODIAL
PODIATRIES
PODIATRY
PODITE
PODITES
PODIUM
PODLEY
PODLEYS
PODOLOGIES
PODOLOGY
PODS
PODSOL
PODSOLIC
PODSOLS
PODZOL
PODZOLS
POEM
POEMATIC
POEMS
POENOLOGIES
POENOLOGY
POESIED
POESIES

POESY	POINTELS	POLARONS	POLITIES	POLLYWIG
POESYING	POINTER	POLARS	POLITIQUE	POLLYWIGS
POET	POINTERS	POLDER	POLITIQUES	POLLYWOG
POETASTER	POINTES	POLDERED	POLITY	POLLYWOGS
POETASTERS	POINTIER	POLDERING	POLK	POLO
POETASTRIES	POINTIEST	POLDERS	POLKA	POLOIST
POETASTRY	POINTILLÉ	POLE	POLKAS	POLOISTS
POETESS	POINTING	POLECAT	POLKED	POLONAISE
POETESSES	POINTINGS	POLECATS	POLKING	POLONAISES
POETIC	POINTLESS	POLED	POLKS	POLONIE
POETICAL	POINTS	POLEMARCH	POLL	POLONIES
POETICISE	POINTSMAN	POLEMARCHS	POLLACK	POLONISE
POETICISED	POINTSMEN	POLEMIC	POLLACKS	POLONISED
POETICISES	POINTY	POLEMICAL	POLLAN	POLONISES
POETICISING	POIS	POLEMICS	POLLANS	POLONISING
POETICISM	POISE	POLEMISE	POLLARD	POLONISM
POETICISMS	POISED	POLEMISED	POLLARDED	POLONISMS
POETICIZE	POISER	POLEMISES	POLLARDING	POLONIUM
POETICIZED	POISERS	POLEMISING	POLLARDS	POLONIUMS
POETICIZES	POISES	POLEMIST	POLLED	POLONIZE
POETICIZING	POISING	POLEMISTS	POLLEN	POLONIZED
POETICS	POISON	POLEMIZE	POLLENED	POLONIZES
POETICULE	POISONED	POLEMIZED	POLLENING	POLONIZING
POETICULES	POISONER	POLEMIZES	POLLENS	POLONY
POETISE	POISONERS	POLEMIZING	POLLENT	POLOS
POETISED	POISONING	POLENTA	POLLER	POLT
POETISES	POISONOUS	POLENTAS	POLLERS	POLTED
POETISING	POISONS	POLES	POLLEX	POLTFEET
POETIZE	POISSON	POLEY	POLLICAL	POLTFOOT
POETIZED	POISSONS	POLEYN	POLLICES	POLTING
POETIZES	POITREL	POLEYNS	POLLICIE	POLTROON
POETIZING	POITRELS	POLIANITE	POLLICIES	POLTROONS
POETRESSE	POKAL	POLIANITES	POLLICY	POLTS
POETRESSES	POKALS	POLICE	POLLIES	POLVERINE
POETRIES	POKE	POLICED	POLLINATE	POLVERINES
POETRY	POKEBERRIES	POLICEMAN	POLLINATED	POLY
POETS	POKEBERRY	POLICEMEN	POLLINATES	POLYACID
POETSHIP	POKED	POLICES	POLLINATING	POLYACT
POETSHIPS	POKEFUL	POLICIES	POLLING	POLYAMIDE
POFFLE	POKEFULS	POLICING	POLLINGS	POLYAMIDES
POFFLES	POKER	POLICY	POLLINIA	POLYANDRIES
POGGE	POKERISH	POLING	POLLINIC	POLYANDRY
POGGES	POKERS	POLINGS	POLLINIUM	POLYARCH
POGROM	POKES	POLIO	POLLIWIG	POLYARCHIES
POGROMS	POKEWEED	POLIOS	POLLIWIGS	POLYARCHY
POH	POKEWEEDS	POLISH	POLLIWOG	POLYAXIAL
POI	POKIER	POLISHED	POLLIWOGS	POLYAXON
POIGNADO	POKIEST	POLISHER	POLLMAN	POLYAXONS
POIGNADOS	POKING	POLISHERS	POLLMEN	POLYBASIC
POIGNANCIES	POKY	POLISHES	POLLOCK	POLYCONIC
POIGNANCY	POLACCA	POLISHING	POLLOCKS	POLYESTER
POIGNANT	POLACCAS	POLISHINGS	POLLS	POLYESTERS
POILU	POLACRE	POLITE	POLLSTER	POLYGALA
POILUS	POLACRES	POLITELY	POLLSTERS	POLYGALAS
POINADO	POLAR	POLITER	POLLUSION	POLYGAM
POINADOS	POLARISE	POLITESSE	POLLUSIONS	POLYGAMIC
POINCIANA	POLARISED	POLITESSES	POLLUTANT	POLYGAMIES
POINCIANAS	POLARISER	POLITEST	POLLUTANTS	POLYGAMS
POIND	POLARISERS	POLITIC	POLLUTE	POLYGAMY
POINDED	POLARISES	POLITICAL	POLLUTED	POLYGENE
POINDER	POLARISING	POLITICK	POLLUTER	POLYGENES
POINDERS	POLARITIES	POLITICKED	POLLUTERS	POLYGENIC
POINDING	POLARITY	POLITICKING	POLLUTES	POLYGENIES
POINDINGS	POLARIZE	POLITICKINGS	POLLUTING	POLYGENY
POINDS	POLARIZED	POLITICKS	POLLUTION	POLYGLOT
POINT	POLARIZER	POLITICLY	POLLUTIONS	POLYGLOTS
POINTE	POLARIZERS	POLITICO	POLLUTIVE	POLYGLOTT
POINTED	POLARIZES	POLITICOES	POLLY	POLYGLOTTS
POINTEDLY	POLARIZING	POLITICOS	POLLYANNA	POLYGON
POINTEL	POLARON	POLITICS	POLLYANNAS	POLYGONAL

POLYGONIES
POLYGONS
POLYGONUM
POLYGONUMS
POLYGONY
POLYGRAPH
POLYGRAPHS
POLYGYNIES
POLYGYNY
POLYHEDRA
POLYLEMMA
POLYLEMMAS
POLYMASTIES
POLYMASTY
POLYMATH
POLYMATHIES
POLYMATHS
POLYMATHY
POLYMER
POLYMERIC
POLYMERIES
POLYMERS
POLYMERY
POLYMORPH
POLYMORPHS
POLYNIA
POLYNIAS
POLYNYA
POLYNYAS
POLYOMINO
POLYOMINOS
POLYONYM
POLYONYMIES
POLYONYMS
POLYONYMY
POLYP
POLYPARIES
POLYPARY
POLYPE
POLYPES
POLYPHAGIES
POLYPHAGY
POLYPHASE
POLYPHON
POLYPHONE
POLYPHONES
POLYPHONIES
POLYPHONS
POLYPHONY
POLYPI
POLYPIDE
POLYPIDES
POLYPIDOM
POLYPIDOMS
POLYPINE
POLYPITE
POLYPITES
POLYPLOID
POLYPOD
POLYPODIES
POLYPODS
POLYPODY
POLYPOID
POLYPOSES
POLYPOSIS
POLYPOUS
POLYPS
POLYPTYCH
POLYPTYCHS
POLYPUS

POLYS
POLYSEME
POLYSEMES
POLYSEMIES
POLYSEMY
POLYSOME
POLYSOMES
POLYSOMIES
POLYSOMY
POLYSTYLE
POLYTENE
POLYTHENE
POLYTHENES
POLYTONAL
POLYTYPIC
POLYURIA
POLYURIAS
POLYVINYL
POLYVINYLS
POLYWATER
POLYWATERS
POLYZOA
POLYZOAN
POLYZOANS
POLYZOARIES
POLYZOARY
POLYZOIC
POLYZONAL
POLYZOOID
POLYZOON
POLYZOONS
POM
POMACE
POMACEOUS
POMACES
POMADE
POMADED
POMADES
POMADING
POMANDER
POMANDERS
POMATO
POMATOES
POMATUM
POMATUMS
POMBE
POMBES
POME
POMELO
POMELOS
POMEROY
POMEROYS
POMES
POMFRET
POMFRETS
POMMEL
POMMELE
POMMELLED
POMMELLING
POMMELS
POMMETTY
POMMIES
POMMY
POMOERIUM
POMOERIUMS
POMOLOGIES
POMOLOGY
POMP
POMPADOUR
POMPADOURS

POMPANO
POMPANOS
POMPELO
POMPELOS
POMPEY
POMPEYED
POMPEYING
POMPEYS
POMPHOLYX
POMPHOLYXES
POMPIER
POMPION
POMPIONS
POMPOM
POMPOMS
POMPON
POMPONS
POMPOON
POMPOONS
POMPOSITIES
POMPOSITY
POMPOUS
POMPOUSLY
POMPS
POMROY
POMROYS
POMS
POMWATER
POMWATERS
PONCE
PONCEAU
PONCEAUS
PONCEAUX
PONCED
PONCES
PONCHO
PONCHOS
PONCING
POND
PONDAGE
PONDAGES
PONDED
PONDER
PONDERAL
PONDERATE
PONDERATED
PONDERATES
PONDERATING
PONDERED
PONDERER
PONDERERS
PONDERING
PONDEROUS
PONDERS
PONDING
PONDOK
PONDOKKIE
PONDOKKIES
PONDOKS
PONDS
PONDWEED
PONDWEEDS
PONE
PONENT
PONES
PONEY
PONEYED
PONEYING
PONEYS
PONG

PONGED
PONGEE
PONGEES
PONGID
PONGIDS
PONGIER
PONGIEST
PONGING
PONGO
PONGOES
PONGOS
PONGS
PONGY
PONIARD
PONIARDED
PONIARDING
PONIARDS
PONIED
PONIES
PONK
PONKED
PONKING
PONKS
PONS
PONTAGE
PONTAGES
PONTAL
PONTES
PONTIANAO
PONTIANACS
PONTIANAK
PONTIANAKS
PONTIC
PONTIE
PONTIES
PONTIFEX
PONTIFF
PONTIFFS
PONTIFIC
PONTIFICE
PONTIFICES
PONTIFIED
PONTIFIES
PONTIFY
PONTIFYING
PONTIL
PONTILE
PONTILS
PONTLEVIS
PONTLEVISES
PONTON
PONTONED
PONTONEER
PONTONEERS
PONTONIER
PONTONIERS
PONTONING
PONTONS
PONTOON
PONTOONED
PONTOONER
PONTOONERS
PONTOONING
PONTOONS
PONTY
PONY
PONYING
POO
POOCH
POOCHES

POOD
POODLE
POODLES
POODS
POOED
POOF
POOFS
POOFTAH
POOFTAHS
POOFTER
POOFTERS
POOGYE
POOGYEE
POOGYEES
POOGYES
POOH
POOING
POOJA
POOJAH
POOJAHS
POOJAS
POOK
POOKA
POOKAS
POOKED
POOKING
POOKIT
POOKS
POOL
POOLED
POOLING
POOLS
POOLSIDE
POOLSIDES
POON
POONAC
POONACS
POONS
POONTANG
POONTANGS
POOP
POOPED
POOPING
POOPS
POOR
POORER
POOREST
POORHOUSE
POORHOUSES
POORISH
POORLIER
POORLIEST
POORLY
POORNESS
POORNESSES
POORT
POORTITH
POORTITHS
POORTS
POORWILL
POORWILLS
POOS
POOT
POOTED
POOTER
POOTERS
POOTING
POOTS
POOVE
POOVERIES

POOVERY
POOVES
POOVIER
POOVIEST
POOVY
POP
POPADUM
POPADUMS
POPCORN
POPCORNS
POPE
POPEDOM
POPEDOMS
POPEHOOD
POPEHOODS
POPELING
POPELINGS
POPERIES
POPERIN
POPERINS
POPERY
POPES
POPESHIP
POPESHIPS
POPINJAY
POPINJAYS
POPISH
POPISHLY
POPJOY
POPJOYED
POPJOYING
POPJOYS
POPLAR
POPLARS
POPLIN
POPLINS
POPLITEAL
POPLITIC
POPOVER
POPOVERS
POPPA
POPPADUM
POPPADUMS
POPPAS
POPPED
POPPER
POPPERING
POPPERINGS
POPPERS
POPPET
POPPETS
POPPIED
POPPIES
POPPING
POPPIT
POPPITS
POPPLE
POPPLED
POPPLES
POPPLIER
POPPLIEST
POPPLING
POPPLY
POPPY
POPPYCOCK
POPPYCOCKS
POPRIN
POPRINS
POPS
POPSIES

POPSY
POPULACE
POPULACES
POPULAR
POPULARLY
POPULARS
POPULATE
POPULATED
POPULATES
POPULATING
POPULISM
POPULISMS
POPULIST
POPULISTS
POPULOUS
PORAL
PORBEAGLE
PORBEAGLES
PORCELAIN
PORCELAINS
PORCH
PORCHES
PORCINE
PORCPISCE
PORCPISCES
PORCUPINE
PORCUPINES
PORE
PORED
PORER
PORERS
PORES
PORGE
PORGED
PORGES
PORGIE
PORGIES
PORGING
PORGY
PORIFER
PORIFERAL
PORIFERAN
PORIFERS
PORINESS
PORINESSES
PORING
PORISM
PORISMS
PORISTIC
PORK
PORKER
PORKERS
PORKIER
PORKIEST
PORKLING
PORKLINGS
PORKS
PORKY
PORN
PORNO
PORNOMAG
PORNOMAGS
PORNOS
PORNS
POROGAMIC
POROGAMIES
POROGAMY
POROMERIC
POROSCOPE
POROSCOPES

POROSCOPIES
POROSCOPY
POROSE
POROSES
POROSIS
POROSITIES
POROSITY
POROUS
PORPESS
PORPESSE
PORPESSES
PORPHYRIA
PORPHYRIAS
PORPHYRIES
PORPHYRIO
PORPHYRIOS
PORPHYRY
PORPOISE
PORPOISED
PORPOISES
PORPOISING
PORPORATE
PORRECT
PORRECTED
PORRECTING
PORRECTS
PORRENGER
PORRENGERS
PORRIDGE
PORRIDGES
PORRIGO
PORRIGOS
PORRINGER
PORRINGERS
PORT
PORTA
PORTABLE
PORTABLES
PORTAGE
PORTAGES
PORTAGUE
PORTAGUES
PORTAL
PORTALS
PORTANCE
PORTANCES
PORTAS
PORTASES
PORTATE
PORTATILE
PORTATIVE
PORTATIVES
PORTED
PORTEND
PORTENDED
PORTENDING
PORTENDS
PORTENT
PORTENTS
PORTEOUS
PORTEOUSES
PORTER
PORTERAGE
PORTERAGES
PORTERESS
PORTERESSES
PORTERLY
PORTERS
PORTESS
PORTESSE

PORTESSES
PORTFOLIO
PORTFOLIOS
PORTHOLE
PORTHOLES
PORTHORS
PORTHORSES
PORTHOS
PORTHOSES
PORTHOUSE
PORTHOUSES
PORTICO
PORTICOED
PORTICOES
PORTICOS
PORTIÈRE
PORTIÈRES
PORTIGUE
PORTIGUES
PORTING
PORTION
PORTIONED
PORTIONER
PORTIONERS
PORTIONING
PORTIONS
PORTLAND
PORTLANDS
PORTLAST
PORTLASTS
PORTLIER
PORTLIEST
PORTLY
PORTMAN
PORTMEN
PORTOISE
PORTOISES
PORTOLAN
PORTOLANI
PORTOLANO
PORTOLANOS
PORTOLANS
PORTOUS
PORTOUSES
PORTRAIT
PORTRAITED
PORTRAITING
PORTRAITS
PORTRAY
PORTRAYAL
PORTRAYALS
PORTRAYED
PORTRAYER
PORTRAYERS
PORTRAYING
PORTRAYS
PORTREEVE
PORTREEVES
PORTRESS
PORTRESSES
PORTS
PORTULACA
PORTULACAS
PORTULAN
PORTULANS
PORTY
PORWIGGLE
PORWIGGLES
PORY
POS

POSADA
POSADAS
POSAUNE
POSAUNES
POSE
POSÉ
POSEABLE
POSED
POSER
POSERS
POSES
POSEUR
POSEURS
POSEUSE
POSEUSES
POSH
POSHED
POSHER
POSHES
POSHEST
POSHING
POSHLY
POSHNESS
POSHNESSES
POSHTEEN
POSHTEENS
POSIES
POSIGRADE
POSING
POSINGLY
POSINGS
POSIT
POSITED
POSITING
POSITION
POSITIONED
POSITIONING
POSITIONS
POSITIVE
POSITIVES
POSITON
POSITONS
POSITRON
POSITRONS
POSITS
POSNET
POSNETS
POSOLOGIES
POSOLOGY
POSS
POSSE
POSSED
POSSER
POSSERS
POSSES
POSSESS
POSSESSED
POSSESSES
POSSESSING
POSSESSOR
POSSESSORS
POSSET
POSSETED
POSSETING
POSSETS
POSSIBLE
POSSIBLES
POSSIBLY
POSSIE
POSSIES

POSSING
POSSUM
POSSUMED
POSSUMING
POSSUMS
POST
POSTAGE
POSTAGES
POSTAL
POSTALS
POSTCARD
POSTCARDED
POSTCARDING
POSTCARDS
POSTCODE
POSTCODED
POSTCODES
POSTCODING
POSTDATE
POSTDATED
POSTDATES
POSTDATING
POSTED
POSTEEN
POSTEENS
POSTER
POSTERED
POSTERING
POSTERIOR
POSTERIORS
POSTERITIES
POSTERITY
POSTERN
POSTERNS
POSTERS
POSTFACE
POSTFACES
POSTFIX
POSTFIXED
POSTFIXES
POSTFIXING
POSTHASTE
POSTHORSE
POSTHORSES
POSTHOUSE
POSTHOUSES
POSTICHE
POSTICHES
POSTICOUS
POSTIE
POSTIES
POSTIL
POSTILION
POSTILIONS
POSTILLED
POSTILLER
POSTILLERS
POSTILLING
POSTILS
POSTING
POSTINGS
POSTLUDE
POSTLUDES
POSTMAN
POSTMARK
POSTMARKS
POSTMEN
POSTPONE
POSTPONED
POSTPONER

POSTPONERS
POSTPONES
POSTPONING
POSTS
POSTULANT
POSTULANTS
POSTULATE
POSTULATED
POSTULATES
POSTULATING
POSTURAL
POSTURE
POSTURED
POSTURER
POSTURERS
POSTURES
POSTURING
POSTURIST
POSTURISTS
POSTWOMAN
POSTWOMEN
POSY
POT
POTABLE
POTABLES
POTAGE
POTAGES
POTAMIC
POTASH
POTASHED
POTASHES
POTASHING
POTASS
POTASSA
POTASSAS
POTASSES
POTASSIC
POTASSIUM
POTASSIUMS
POTATION
POTATIONS
POTATO
POTATOES
POTATORY
POTCH
POTCHE
POTCHED
POTCHER
POTCHERS
POTCHES
POTCHING
POTCHY
POTE
POTED
POTEEN
POTEENS
POTENCE
POTENCE
POTENCES
POTENCES
POTENCIES
POTENCY
POTENT
POTENTATE
POTENTATES
POTENTIAL
POTENTIALS
POTENTISE
POTENTISED
POTENTISES

POTENTISING
POTENTIZE
POTENTIZED
POTENTIZES
POTENTIZING
POTENTLY
POTENTS
POTES
POTFUL
POTFULS
POTGUN
POTGUNS
POTHECARIES
POTHECARY
POTHEEN
POTHEENS
POTHER
POTHERED
POTHERING
POTHERS
POTHERY
POTHOLE
POTHOLER
POTHOLERS
POTHOLES
POTHOLING
POTHOLINGS
POTHOOK
POTHOOKS
POTHOUSE
POTHOUSES
POTICARIES
POTICARY
POTICHE
POTICHES
POTIN
POTING
POTINS
POTION
POTIONS
POTLACH
POTLACHES
POTOMETER
POTOMETERS
POTOROO
POTOROOS
POTS
POTSHERD
POTSHERDS
POTSTONE
POTSTONES
POTT
POTTAGE
POTTAGES
POTTED
POTTER
POTTERED
POTTERER
POTTERERS
POTTERIES
POTTERING
POTTERINGS
POTTERS
POTTERY
POTTIER
POTTIES
POTTIEST
POTTINESS
POTTINESSES
POTTING

POTTINGAR
POTTINGARS
POTTINGER
POTTINGERS
POTTLE
POTTLES
POTTO
POTTOS
POTTS
POTTY
POUCH
POUCHED
POUCHES
POUCHFUL
POUCHFULS
POUCHIER
POUCHIEST
POUCHING
POUCHY
POUDER
POUDERS
POUDRE
POUDRES
POUF
POUFED
POUFFE
POUFFES
POUFS
POUFTAH
POUFTAHS
POUFTER
POUFTERS
POUK
POUKE
POUKED
POUKES
POUKING
POUKIT
POUKS
POULAINE
POULAINES
POULARD
POULARDS
POULDER
POULDERS
POULDRE
POULDRES
POULDRON
POULDRONS
POULE
POULES
POULP
POULPE
POULPES
POULPS
POULT
POULTER
POULTERER
POULTERERS
POULTERS
POULTICE
POULTICED
POULTICES
POULTICING
POULTRIES
POULTRY
POULTS
POUNCE
POUNCED
POUNCES

POUNCET
POUNCETS
POUNCING
POUND
POUNDAGE
POUNDAGES
POUNDAL
POUNDALS
POUNDED
POUNDER
POUNDERS
POUNDING
POUNDS
POUPE
POUPED
POUPES
POUPING
POUPT
POUR
POURABLE
POURBOIRE
POURBOIRES
POURED
POURER
POURERS
POURIE
POURIES
POURING
POURINGS
POURPOINT
POURPOINTS
POURS
POURSEW
POURSUE
POURSUIT
POURSUITS
POURSUITT
POURSUITTS
POURTRAY
POURTRAYD
POURTRAYED
POURTRAYING
POURTRAYS
POUSOWDIE
POUSOWDIES
POUSSE
POUSSES
POUSSETTE
POUSSETTED
POUSSETTES
POUSSETTING
POUSSIN
POUSSINS
POUT
POUTED
POUTER
POUTERS
POUTHER
POUTHERED
POUTHERING
POUTHERS
POUTIER
POUTIEST
POUTING
POUTINGLY
POUTINGS
POUTS
POUTY
POVERTIES
POVERTY

POW	POYSED	PRAISES	PRATTLED	PRECEPITS
POWAN	POYSES	PRAISING	PRATTLER	PRECEPT
POWANS	POYSING	PRAISINGS	PRATTLERS	PRECEPTOR
POWDER	POYSON	PRALINE	PRATTLES	PRECEPTORS
POWDERED	POYSONED	PRALINES	PRATTLING	PRECEPTS
POWDERING	POYSONING	PRAM	PRATY	PRECESS
POWDERS	POYSONS	PRAMS	PRAU	PRECESSED
POWDERY	POZ	PRANA	PRAUNCE	PRECESSES
POWELLISE	POZZ	PRANAS	PRAUS	PRECESSING
POWELLISED	POZZIES	PRANAYAMA	PRAVITIES	PRÉCIEUSE
POWELLISES	POZZOLANA	PRANAYAMAS	PRAVITY	PRÉCIEUSES
POWELLISING	POZZOLANAS	PRANCE	PRAWLE	PRECINCT
POWELLITE	POZZY	PRANCED	PRAWLES	PRECINCTS
POWELLITES	PRAAM	PRANCER	PRAWLIN	PRECIOUS
POWELLIZE	PRAAMS	PRANCERS	PRAWLINS	PRECIOUSES
POWELLIZED	PRABBLE	PRANCES	PRAWN	PRECIPICE
POWELLIZES	PRABBLES	PRANCING	PRAWNED	PRECIPICES
POWELLIZING	PRACTIC	PRANCINGS	PRAWNING	PRÉCIS
POWER	PRACTICAL	PRANCK	PRAWNS	PRECISE
POWERBOAT	PRACTICALS	PRANCKE	PRAXES	PRÉCISED
POWERBOATS	PRACTICE	PRANCKED	PRAXIS	PRECISELY
POWERED	PRACTICED	PRANCKES	PRAY	PRECISER
POWERFUL	PRACTICES	PRANCKING	PRAYED	PRÉCISES
POWERING	PRACTICING	PRANCKS	PRAYER	PRECISEST
POWERLESS	PRACTICK	PRANDIAL	PRAYERFUL	PRECISIAN
POWERPLAY	PRACTICKS	PRANG	PRAYERS	PRECISIANS
POWERPLAYS	PRACTICS	PRANGED	PRAYING	PRÉCISING
POWERS	PRACTICUM	PRANGING	PRAYINGLY	PRECISION
POWIN	PRACTICUMS	PRANGS	PRAYINGS	PRECISIONS
POWINS	PRACTIQUE	PRANK	PRAYS	PRECISIVE
POWN	PRACTIQUES	PRANKED	PRE	PRECLUDE
POWND	PRACTISE	PRANKFUL	PREACE	PRECLUDED
POWNEY	PRACTISED	PRANKIER	PREACH	PRECLUDES
POWNEYED	PRACTISER	PRANKIEST	PREACHED	PRECLUDING
POWNEYING	PRACTISERS	PRANKING	PREACHER	PRECOCIAL
POWNEYS	PRACTISES	PRANKINGS	PREACHERS	PRECOCITIES
POWNIE	PRACTISING	PRANKISH	PREACHES	PRECOCITY
POWNIED	PRACTIVE	PRANKLE	PREACHIER	PRECONISE
POWNIES	PRACTOLOL	PRANKLED	PREACHIEST	PRECONISED
POWNS	PRACTOLOLS	PRANKLES	PREACHIFIED	PRECONISES
POWNY	PRAD	PRANKLING	PREACHIFIES	PRECONISING
POWNYING	PRADS	PRANKS	PREACHIFY	PRECONIZE
POWRE	PRAEAMBLE	PRANKSOME	PREACHIFYING	PRECONIZED
POWS	PRAEAMBLES	PRANKSTER	PREACHILY	PRECONIZES
POWSOWDIES	PRAECOCES	PRANKSTERS	PREACHING	PRECONIZING
POWSOWDY	PRAEDIAL	PRANKY	PREACHINGS	PRECOOK
POWTER	PRAEDIALS	PRASE	PREACHY	PRECOOKED
POWTERED	PRAEFECT	PRASES	PREAMBLE	PRECOOKING
POWTERING	PRAEFECTS	PRAT	PREAMBLED	PRECOOKS
POWTERS	PRAENOMEN	PRATE	PREAMBLES	PRECURRER
POWWAW	PRAENOMENS	PRATED	PREAMBLING	PRECURRERS
POWWOW	PRAENOMINA	PRATER	PREASE	PRECURSE
POWWOWED	PRAESES	PRATERS	PREASSE	PRECURSES
POWWOWING	PRAESIDIA	PRATES	PREBEND	PRECURSOR
POWWOWS	PRAETOR	PRATFALL	PREBENDAL	PRECURSORS
POX	PRAETORS	PRATFALLEN	PREBENDS	PREDACITIES
POXED	PRAGMATIC	PRATFALLING	PREBIOTIC	PREDACITY
POXES	PRAGMATICS	PRATFALLS	PRECAST	PREDATE
POXIER	PRAHU	PRATFELL	PRECATIVE	PREDATED
POXIEST	PRAHUS	PRATIE	PRECATORY	PREDATES
POXING	PRAIRIE	PRATIES	PRECEDE	PREDATING
POXVIRUS	PRAIRIED	PRATING	PRECEDED	PREDATION
POXVIRUSES	PRAIRIES	PRATINGLY	PRECEDENT	PREDATIONS
POXY	PRAISE	PRATINGS	PRECEDENTS	PREDATIVE
POYNANT	PRAISEACH	PRATIQUE	PRECEDES	PREDATOR
POYNT	PRAISEACHS	PRATIQUES	PRECEDING	PREDATORS
POYNTED	PRAISED	PRATS	PRECEESE	PREDATORY
POYNTING	PRAISEFUL	PRATTED	PRECENTOR	PREDEFINE
POYNTS	PRAISER	PRATTING	PRECENTORS	PREDEFINED
POYSE	PRAISERS	PRATTLE	PRECEPIT	PREDEFINES

PREDEFINING	PREFERRING	PRELATISM	PREMY	PRESAGE
PREDELLA	PREFERS	PRELATISMS	PRENASAL	PRESAGED
PREDELLAS	PREFIGURE	PRELATIST	PRENASALS	PRESAGER
PREDESIGN	PREFIGURED	PRELATISTS	PRENATAL	PRESAGERS
PREDESIGNED	PREFIGURES	PRELATIZE	PRENOTION	PRESAGES
PREDESIGNING	PREFIGURING	PRELATIZED	PRENOTIONS	PRESAGING
PREDESIGNS	PREFIX	PRELATIZES	PRENT	PRESBYOPE
PREDEVOTE	PREFIXED	PRELATIZING	PRENTICE	PRESBYOPES
PREDIAL	PREFIXES	PRELATURE	PRENTICES	PRESBYOPIES
PREDIALS	PREFIXING	PRELATURES	PRENTS	PRESBYOPY
PREDICANT	PREFIXION	PRELATY	PRENUBILE	PRESBYTE
PREDICANTS	PREFIXIONS	PRELECT	PRENZIE	PRESBYTER
PREDICATE	PREFLIGHT	PRELECTED	PREOCCUPIED	PRESBYTERS
PREDICATED	PREFORM	PRELECTING	PREOCCUPIES	PRESBYTES
PREDICATES	PREFORMED	PRELECTOR	PREOCCUPY	PRESCHOOL
PREDICATING	PREFORMING	PRELECTORS	PREOCCUPYING	PRESCIENT
PREDICT	PREFORMS	PRELECTS	PREOPTION	PRESCIND
PREDICTED	PREGGERS	PRELIM	PREOPTIONS	PRESCINDED
PREDICTING	PREGNABLE	PRELIMS	PREORAL	PRESCINDING
PREDICTOR	PREGNANCE	PRELUDE	PREORALLY	PRESCINDS
PREDICTORS	PREGNANCES	PRELUDED	PREORDAIN	PRESCIOUS
PREDICTS	PREGNANCIES	PRELUDES	PREORDAINED	PRESCRIBE
PREDIED	PREGNANCY	PRELUDI	PREORDAINING	PRESCRIBED
PREDIES	PREGNANT	PRELUDIAL	PREORDAINS	PRESCRIBES
PREDIGEST	PREHALLUX	PRELUDING	PREORDER	PRESCRIBING
PREDIGESTED	PREHALLUXES	PRELUDIO	PREORDERED	PRESCRIPT
PREDIGESTING	PREHEAT	PRELUSION	PREORDERING	PRESCRIPTS
PREDIGESTS	PREHEATED	PRELUSIONS	PREORDERS	PRESCUTA
PREDIKANT	PREHEATING	PRELUSIVE	PREP	PRESCUTUM
PREDIKANTS	PREHEATS	PRELUSORY	PREPACK	PRESE
PREDILECT	PREHEND	PREMATURE	PREPACKED	PRESELECT
PREDOOM	PREHENDED	PREMED	PREPACKING	PRESELECTED
PREDOOMED	PREHENDING	PREMEDIC	PREPACKS	PRESELECTING
PREDOOMING	PREHENDS	PREMEDICS	PREPAID	PRESELECTS
PREDOOMS	PREHENSOR	PREMEDS	PREPARE	PRESENCE
PREDY	PREHENSORS	PREMIA	PREPARED	PRESENCES
PREDYING	PREHNITE	PREMIER	PREPARER	PRESENT
PREE	PREHNITES	PREMIÈRE	PREPARERS	PRESENTED
PREED	PREHUMAN	PREMIÈRED	PREPARES	PRESENTEE
PREEING	PREIF	PREMIÈRES	PREPARING	PRESENTEES
PREEMIE	PREIFE	PREMIÈRING	PREPAY	PRESENTER
PREEMIES	PREIFES	PREMIERS	PREPAYING	PRESENTERS
PREEN	PREIFS	PREMIES	PREPAYS	PRESENTING
PREENED	PREJINK	PREMISE	PREPENSE	PRESENTLY
PREENING	PREJUDGE	PREMISED	PREPENSED	PRESENTS
PREENS	PREJUDGED	PREMISES	PREPENSES	PRESERVE
PREES	PREJUDGES	PREMISING	PREPENSING	PRESERVED
PREEVE	PREJUDGING	PREMISS	PREPOLLEX	PRESERVER
PREEVED	PREJUDICE	PREMISSED	PREPOLLEXES	PRESERVERS
PREEVES	PREJUDICED	PREMISSES	PREPOTENT	PRESERVES
PREEVING	PREJUDICES	PREMIUM	PREPPED	PRESERVING
PREFAB	PREJUDICING	PREMIUMS	PREPPIER	PRESES
PREFABS	PREJUDIZE	PREMIX	PREPPIES	PRESET
PREFACE	PREJUDIZES	PREMIXED	PREPPIEST	PRESETS
PREFACED	PRELACIES	PREMIXES	PREPPING	PRESETTING
PREFACES	PRELACY	PREMIXING	PREPPY	PRESIDE
PREFACIAL	PRELATE	PREMOLAR	PREPS	PRESIDED
PREFACING	PRELATES	PREMOLARS	PREPUCE	PRESIDENT
PREFADE	PRELATESS	PREMONISH	PREPUCES	PRESIDENTS
PREFADED	PRELATESSES	PREMONISHED	PREPUTIAL	PRESIDES
PREFADES	PRELATIAL	PREMONISHES	PREQUEL	PRESIDIA
PREFADING	PRELATIC	PREMONISHING	PREQUELS	PRESIDIAL
PREFARD	PRELATIES	PREMORSE	PRERECORD	PRESIDING
PREFATORY	PRELATION	PREMOSAIC	PRERECORDED	PRESIDIO
PREFECT	PRELATIONS	PREMOTION	PRERECORDING	PRESIDIOS
PREFECTS	PRELATISE	PREMOTIONS	PRERECORDS	PRESIDIUM
PREFER	PRELATISED	PREMOVE	PREROSION	PRESIDIUMS
PREFERRED	PRELATISES	PREMOVED	PREROSIONS	PRESS
PREFERRER	PRELATISH	PREMOVES	PRERUPT	PRESSED
PREFERRERS	PRELATISING	PREMOVING	PRESA	PRESSER

PRESSERS	PREVAILING	PRICKLIEST	PRIMED	PRINCIPLE
PRESSES	PREVAILS	PRICKLING	PRIMELY	PRINCIPLED
PRESSFAT	PREVALENT	PRICKLINGS	PRIMENESS	PRINCIPLES
PRESSFATS	PREVE	PRICKLY	PRIMENESSES	PRINCIPLING
PRESSFUL	PREVENE	PRICKS	PRIMER	PRINCOCK
PRESSFULS	PREVENED	PRICKWOOD	PRIMERO	PRINCOCKS
PRESSING	PREVENES	PRICKWOODS	PRIMEROS	PRINCOX
PRESSINGS	PREVENING	PRICY	PRIMERS	PRINCOXES
PRESSION	PREVENT	PRIDE	PRIMES	PRINK
PRESSIONS	PREVENTED	PRIDED	PRIMEUR	PRINKED
PRESSMAN	PREVENTER	PRIDEFUL	PRIMEURS	PRINKING
PRESSMEN	PREVENTERS	PRIDELESS	PRIMEVAL	PRINKS
PRESSOR	PREVENTING	PRIDES	PRIMINE	PRINT
PRESSURE	PREVENTS	PRIDIAN	PRIMINES	PRINTABLE
PRESSURED	PREVERBAL	PRIDING	PRIMING	PRINTED
PRESSURES	PREVIEW	PRIED	PRIMINGS	PRINTER
PRESSURING	PREVIEWED	PRIEF	PRIMIPARA	PRINTERS
PREST	PREVIEWING	PRIEFE	PRIMIPARAE	PRINTING
PRESTED	PREVIEWS	PRIEFES	PRIMIPARAS	PRINTINGS
PRESTIGE	PREVIOUS	PRIEFS	PRIMITIAE	PRINTLESS
PRESTIGES	PREVISE	PRIER	PRIMITIAL	PRINTS
PRESTING	PREVISED	PRIERS	PRIMITIAS	PRION
PRESTO	PREVISES	PRIES	PRIMITIVE	PRIONS
PRESTOS	PREVISING	PRIEST	PRIMITIVES	PRIOR
PRESTS	PREVISION	PRIESTED	PRIMLY	PRIORATE
PRESUME	PREVISIONS	PRIESTESS	PRIMMED	PRIORATES
PRESUMED	PREWYN	PRIESTESSES	PRIMMER	PRIORESS
PRESUMER	PREWYNS	PRIESTING	PRIMMEST	PRIORESSES
PRESUMERS	PREX	PRIESTLY	PRIMMING	PRIORIES
PRESUMES	PREXES	PRIESTS	PRIMNESS	PRIORITIES
PRESUMING	PREXIES	PRIEVE	PRIMNESSES	PRIORITY
PRETENCE	PREXY	PRIEVED	PRIMO	PRIORS
PRETENCES	PREY	PRIEVES	PRIMOS	PRIORSHIP
PRETEND	PREYED	PRIEVING	PRIMP	PRIORSHIPS
PRETENDED	PREYFUL	PRIG	PRIMPED	PRIORY
PRETENDER	PREYING	PRIGGED	PRIMPING	PRISAGE
PRETENDERS	PREYS	PRIGGER	PRIMPS	PRISAGES
PRETENDING	PREZZIE	PRIGGERIES	PRIMROSE	PRISE
PRETENDS	PREZZIES	PRIGGERS	PRIMROSED	PRISED
PRETENSE	PRIAL	PRIGGERY	PRIMROSES	PRISER
PRETENSES	PRIALS	PRIGGING	PRIMROSING	PRISERS
PRETERIST	PRIAPIC	PRIGGINGS	PRIMROSY	PRISES
PRETERISTS	PRIAPISM	PRIGGISH	PRIMS	PRISING
PRETERIT	PRIAPISMS	PRIGGISM	PRIMSIE	PRISM
PRETERITE	PRIBBLE	PRIGGISMS	PRIMULA	PRISMATIC
PRETERITES	PRIBBLES	PRIGS	PRIMULAS	PRISMOID
PRETERITS	PRICE	PRILL	PRIMULINE	PRISMOIDS
PRETERM	PRICED	PRILLED	PRIMULINES	PRISMS
PRETERMIT	PRICELESS	PRILLING	PRIMUS	PRISMY
PRETERMITS	PRICER	PRILLS	PRIMUSES	PRISON
PRETERMITTED	PRICERS	PRIM	PRIMY	PRISONED
PRETERMITTING	PRICES	PRIMA	PRINCE	PRISONER
PRETEXT	PRICEY	PRIMACIES	PRINCED	PRISONERS
PRETEXTS	PRICIER	PRIMACY	PRINCEDOM	PRISONING
PRETTIER	PRICIEST	PRIMAEVAL	PRINCEDOMS	PRISONOUS
PRETTIES	PRICINESS	PRIMAGE	PRINCEKIN	PRISONS
PRETTIEST	PRICINESSES	PRIMAGES	PRINCEKINS	PRISSIER
PRETTIFIED	PRICING	PRIMAL	PRINCELET	PRISSIEST
PRETTIFIES	PRICK	PRIMALITIES	PRINCELETS	PRISSY
PRETTIFY	PRICKED	PRIMALITY	PRINCELIER	PRISTINE
PRETTIFYING	PRICKER	PRIMALLY	PRINCELIEST	PRITHEE
PRETTILY	PRICKERS	PRIMARIES	PRINCELY	PRIVACIES
PRETTY	PRICKET	PRIMARILY	PRINCES	PRIVACY
PRETTYISH	PRICKETS	PRIMARY	PRINCESS	PRIVADO
PRETTYISM	PRICKING	PRIMATAL	PRINCESSE	PRIVADOES
PRETTYISMS	PRICKINGS	PRIMATE	PRINCESSES	PRIVADOS
PRETZEL	PRICKLE	PRIMATES	PRINCING	PRIVATE
PRETZELS	PRICKLED	PRIMATIAL	PRINCIPAL	PRIVATEER
PREVAIL	PRICKLES	PRIMATIC	PRINCIPALS	PRIVATEERED
PREVAILED	PRICKLIER	PRIME	PRINCIPIA	PRIVATEERING

PRIVATEERS	PROCARYONS	PRODROME	PROFOUNDEST	PROLAPSED
PRIVATELY	PROCEDURE	PRODROMES	PROFOUNDS	PROLAPSES
PRIVATES	PROCEDURES	PRODROMI	PROFS	PROLAPSING
PRIVATION	PROCEED	PRODROMIC	PROFUSE	PROLAPSUS
PRIVATIONS	PROCEEDED	PRODROMUS	PROFUSELY	PROLAPSUSES
PRIVATISE	PROCEEDER	PRODS	PROFUSERS	PROLATE
PRIVATISED	PROCEEDERS	PRODUCE	PROFUSION	PROLATED
PRIVATISES	PROCEEDING	PRODUCED	PROFUSIONS	PROLATELY
PRIVATISING	PROCEEDINGS	PRODUCER	PROG	PROLATES
PRIVATIVE	PROCEEDS	PRODUCERS	PROGENIES	PROLATING
PRIVATIVES	PROCERITIES	PRODUCES	PROGENY	PROLATION
PRIVATIZE	PROCERITY	PRODUCING	PROGERIA	PROLATIONS
PRIVATIZED	PROCESS	PRODUCT	PROGERIAS	PROLATIVE
PRIVATIZES	PROCESSED	PRODUCTS	PROGESTIN	PROLE
PRIVATIZING	PROCESSES	PROEM	PROGESTINS	PROLEG
PRIVET	PROCESSING	PROEMBRYO	PROGGED	PROLEGS
PRIVETS	PROCESSOR	PROEMBRYOS	PROGGING	PROLEPSES
PRIVIES	PROCESSORS	PROEMIAL	PROGGINS	PROLEPSIS
PRIVILEGE	PROCIDENT	PROEMS	PROGGINSES	PROLEPTIC
PRIVILEGED	PROCINCT	PROENZYME	PROGNOSES	PROLER
PRIVILEGES	PROCINCTS	PROENZYMES	PROGNOSIS	PROLERS
PRIVILEGING	PROCLAIM	PROF	PROGRADE	PROLES
PRIVILY	PROCLAIMED	PROFACE	PROGRADED	PROLETARIES
PRIVITIES	PROCLAIMING	PROFANE	PROGRADES	PROLETARY
PRIVITY	PROCLAIMS	PROFANED	PROGRADING	PROLICIDE
PRIVY	PROCLISES	PROFANELY	PROGRAM	PROLICIDES
PRIZABLE	PROCLISIS	PROFANER	PROGRAMME	PROLIFIC
PRIZE	PROCLITIC	PROFANERS	PROGRAMMED	PROLINE
PRIZED	PROCLITICS	PROFANES	PROGRAMMES	PROLINES
PRIZER	PROCLIVE	PROFANEST	PROGRAMMING	PROLIX
PRIZERS	PROCONSUL	PROFANING	PROGRAMS	PROLIXITIES
PRIZES	PROCONSULS	PROFANITIES	PROGRESS	PROLIXITY
PRIZING	PROCREANT	PROFANITY	PROGRESSED	PROLIXLY
PRO	PROCREANTS	PROFESS	PROGRESSES	PROLL
PROA	PROCREATE	PROFESSED	PROGRESSING	PROLLER
PROAS	PROCREATED	PROFESSES	PROGS	PROLLERS
PROBABLE	PROCREATES	PROFESSING	PROHIBIT	PROLOGISE
PROBABLES	PROCREATING	PROFESSOR	PROHIBITED	PROLOGISED
PROBABLY	PROCTAL	PROFESSORS	PROHIBITING	PROLOGISES
PROBALL	PROCTITIS	PROFFER	PROHIBITS	PROLOGISING
PROBAND	PROCTITISES	PROFFERED	PROIGN	PROLOGIZE
PROBANDS	PROCTOR	PROFFERER	PROIGNS	PROLOGIZED
PROBANG	PROCTORS	PROFFERERS	PROIN	PROLOGIZES
PROBANGS	PROCURACIES	PROFFERING	PROINE	PROLOGIZING
PROBATE	PROCURACY	PROFFERS	PROINED	PROLOGUE
PROBATED	PROCURE	PROFILE	PROINES	PROLOGUED
PROBATES	PROCURED	PROFILED	PROINS	PROLOGUES
PROBATING	PROCURER	PROFILER	PROJECT	PROLOGUING
PROBATION	PROCURERS	PROFILERS	PROJECTED	PROLONG
PROBATIONS	PROCURES	PROFILES	PROJECTING	PROLONGE
PROBATIVE	PROCURESS	PROFILING	PROJECTINGS	PROLONGED
PROBATORY	PROCURESSES	PROFILIST	PROJECTOR	PROLONGER
PROBE	PROCUREUR	PROFILISTS	PROJECTORS	PROLONGERS
PROBED	PROCUREURS	PROFIT	PROJECTS	PROLONGES
PROBES	PROCURING	PROFITED	PROKARYON	PROLONGING
PROBING	PROD	PROFITEER	PROKARYONS	PROLONGS
PROBIT	PRODDED	PROFITEERED	PROKARYOT	PROLUSION
PROBITIES	PRODDING	PROFITEERING	PROKARYOTS	PROLUSIONS
PROBITS	PRODIGAL	PROFITEERINGS	PROKE	PROLUSORY
PROBITY	PRODIGALS	PROFITEERS	PROKED	PROM
PROBLEM	PRODIGIES	PROFITER	PROKER	PROMACHOS
PROBLEMS	PRODIGY	PROFITERS	PROKERS	PROMACHOSES
PROBOSCIDES	PRODITOR	PROFITING	PROKES	PROMENADE
PROBOSCIS	PRODITORS	PROFITINGS	PROKING	PROMENADED
PROBOSCISES	PRODITORY	PROFITS	PROLACTIN	PROMENADES
PROCACITIES	PRODNOSE	PROFLUENT	PROLACTINS	PROMENADING
PROCACITY	PRODNOSED	PROFORMA	PROLAMIN	PROMETAL
PROCAINE	PRODNOSES	PROFORMAS	PROLAMINE	PROMETALS
PROCAINES	PRODNOSING	PROFOUND	PROLAMINES	PROMINENT
PROCARYON	PRODROMAL	PROFOUNDER	PROLAMINS	PROMISE
			PROLAPSE	

PROMISED
PROMISEE
PROMISEES
PROMISER
PROMISERS
PROMISES
PROMISING
PROMISOR
PROMISORS
PROMISSOR
PROMISSORS
PROMMER
PROMMERS
PROMO
PROMOS
PROMOTE
PROMOTED
PROMOTER
PROMOTERS
PROMOTES
PROMOTING
PROMOTION
PROMOTIONS
PROMOTIVE
PROMOTOR
PROMOTORS
PROMPT
PROMPTED
PROMPTER
PROMPTERS
PROMPTEST
PROMPTING
PROMPTINGS
PROMPTLY
PROMPTS
PROMPTURE
PROMPTURES
PROMS
PROMULGE
PROMULGED
PROMULGES
PROMULGING
PROMUSCIS
PROMUSCISES
PRONAOI
PRONAOS
PRONATE
PRONATED
PRONATES
PRONATING
PRONATION
PRONATIONS
PRONATOR
PRONATORS
PRONE
PRONELY
PRONENESS
PRONENESSES
PRONER
PRONES
PRONEST
PRONEUR
PRONEURS
PRONG
PRONGBUCK
PRONGBUCKS
PRONGED
PRONGHORN
PRONGHORNS
PRONGING

PRONGS
PRONOTA
PRONOTAL
PRONOTUM
PRONOUN
PRONOUNCE
PRONOUNCED
PRONOUNCES
PRONOUNCING
PRONOUNCINGS
PRONOUNS
PRONTO
PRONUCLEI
PROO
PROOEMION
PROOEMIONS
PROOEMIUM
PROOEMIUMS
PROOF
PROOFED
PROOFING
PROOFINGS
PROOFLESS
PROOFS
PROOTIC
PROOTICS
PROP
PROPAGATE
PROPAGATED
PROPAGATES
PROPAGATING
PROPAGE
PROPAGED
PROPAGES
PROPAGING
PROPAGULE
PROPAGULES
PROPALE
PROPALED
PROPALES
PROPALING
PROPANE
PROPANES
PROPEL
PROPELLED
PROPELLER
PROPELLERS
PROPELLING
PROPELS
PROPEND
PROPENDED
PROPENDING
PROPENDS
PROPENE
PROPENES
PROPENSE
PROPER
PROPERDIN
PROPERDINS
PROPERLY
PROPERS
PROPERTIED
PROPERTIES
PROPERTY
PROPERTYING
PROPHASE
PROPHASES
PROPHECIES
PROPHECY
PROPHESIED

PROPHESIES
PROPHESY
PROPHESYING
PROPHET
PROPHETIC
PROPHETS
PROPHYLL
PROPHYLLS
PROPINE
PROPINED
PROPINES
PROPINING
PROPODEON
PROPODEONS
PROPODEUM
PROPODEUMS
PROPOLIS
PROPOLISES
PROPONE
PROPONED
PROPONENT
PROPONENTS
PROPONES
PROPONING
PROPOSAL
PROPOSALS
PROPOSE
PROPOSED
PROPOSER
PROPOSERS
PROPOSES
PROPOSING
PROPOUND
PROPOUNDED
PROPOUNDING
PROPOUNDS
PROPPED
PROPPING
PROPRIETIES
PROPRIETY
PROPS
PROPSES
PROPTOSES
PROPTOSIS
PROPYL
PROPYLA
PROPYLAEA
PROPYLENE
PROPYLENES
PROPYLIC
PROPYLITE
PROPYLITES
PROPYLON
PROPYLONS
PROPYLS
PRORATE
PRORATED
PRORATES
PRORATING
PRORATION
PRORATIONS
PRORE
PRORECTOR
PRORECTORS
PRORES
PROROGATE
PROROGATED
PROROGATES
PROROGATING
PROROGUE

PROROGUED
PROROGUES
PROROGUING
PROS
PROSAIC
PROSAICAL
PROSAISM
PROSAISMS
PROSAIST
PROSAISTS
PROSATEUR
PROSATEURS
PROSCRIBE
PROSCRIBED
PROSCRIBES
PROSCRIBING
PROSCRIPT
PROSCRIPTS
PROSE
PROSECTOR
PROSECTORS
PROSECUTE
PROSECUTED
PROSECUTES
PROSECUTING
PROSED
PROSELYTE
PROSELYTED
PROSELYTES
PROSELYTING
PROSEMAN
PROSEMEN
PROSER
PROSERS
PROSES
PROSEUCHA
PROSEUCHAE
PROSEUCHE
PROSIER
PROSIEST
PROSILY
PROSIMIAN
PROSIMIANS
PROSINESS
PROSINESSES
PROSING
PROSINGS
PROSIT
PROSODIAL
PROSODIAN
PROSODIANS
PROSODIC
PROSODIES
PROSODIST
PROSODISTS
PROSODY
PROSOPON
PROSOPONS
PROSPECT
PROSPECTED
PROSPECTING
PROSPECTINGS
PROSPECTS
PROSPER
PROSPERED
PROSPERING
PROSPERS
PROSTATE
PROSTATES
PROSTATIC

PROSTRATE
PROSTRATED
PROSTRATES
PROSTRATING
PROSTYLE
PROSTYLES
PROSY
PROTAMINE
PROTAMINES
PROTANDRIES
PROTANDRY
PROTANOPE
PROTANOPES
PROTASES
PROTASIS
PROTATIC
PROTEA
PROTEAN
PROTEAS
PROTEASE
PROTEASES
PROTECT
PROTECTED
PROTECTING
PROTECTOR
PROTECTORS
PROTECTS
PROTÉGÉ
PROTÉGÉE
PROTÉGÉES
PROTÉGÉS
PROTEID
PROTEIDS
PROTEIN
PROTEINIC
PROTEINS
PROTEND
PROTENDED
PROTENDING
PROTENDS
PROTENSE
PROTENSES
PROTEST
PROTESTED
PROTESTER
PROTESTERS
PROTESTING
PROTESTOR
PROTESTORS
PROTESTS
PROTEUS
PROTEUSES
PROTHALLI
PROTHESES
PROTHESIS
PROTHETIC
PROTHORACES
PROTHORAX
PROTHORAXES
PROTHYL
PROTHYLE
PROTHYLES
PROTHYLS
PROTIST
PROTISTIC
PROTISTS
PROTIUM
PROTIUMS
PROTOCOL
PROTOCOLLED

PROTOCOLLING
PROTOCOLS
PROTOGINE
PROTOGINES
PROTOGYNIES
PROTOGYNY
PROTON
PROTONEMA
PROTONEMATA
PROTONIC
PROTONS
PROTOSTAR
PROTOSTARS
PROTOTYPE
PROTOTYPED
PROTOTYPES
PROTOTYPING
PROTOXIDE
PROTOXIDES
PROTOZOA
PROTOZOAN
PROTOZOANS
PROTOZOIC
PROTOZOON
PROTRACT
PROTRACTED
PROTRACTING
PROTRACTS
PROTRUDE
PROTRUDED
PROTRUDES
PROTRUDING
PROTYL
PROTYLE
PROTYLES
PROTYLS
PROUD
PROUDER
PROUDEST
PROUDISH
PROUDLY
PROUDNESS
PROUDNESSES
PROUL
PROULED
PROULER
PROULERS
PROULING
PROULS
PROUSTITE
PROUSTITES
PROVABLE
PROVABLY
PROVAND
PROVANDS
PROVANT
PROVE
PROVEABLE
PROVEABLY
PROVED
PROVEDOR
PROVEDORE
PROVEDORES
PROVEDORS
PROVEN
PROVEND
PROVENDER
PROVENDERED
PROVENDERING
PROVENDERS

PROVENDS
PROVER
PROVERB
PROVERBED
PROVERBING
PROVERBS
PROVERS
PROVES
PROVIANT
PROVIANTS
PROVIDE
PROVIDED
PROVIDENT
PROVIDER
PROVIDERS
PROVIDES
PROVIDING
PROVIDOR
PROVIDORS
PROVINCE
PROVINCES
PROVINE
PROVINED
PROVINES
PROVING
PROVINING
PROVIRAL
PROVIRUS
PROVIRUSES
PROVISION
PROVISIONED
PROVISIONING
PROVISIONS
PROVISO
PROVISOES
PROVISOR
PROVISORS
PROVISORY
PROVISOS
PROVOCANT
PROVOCANTS
PROVOKE
PROVOKED
PROVOKER
PROVOKERS
PROVOKES
PROVOKING
PROVOST
PROVOSTRIES
PROVOSTRY
PROVOSTS
PROW
PROWESS
PROWESSED
PROWESSES
PROWEST
PROWL
PROWLED
PROWLER
PROWLERS
PROWLING
PROWLINGS
PROWLS
PROWS
PROXIES
PROXIMAL
PROXIMATE
PROXIMITIES
PROXIMITY
PROXIMO

PROXY
PROYN
PROYNE
PROYNES
PROYNS
PROZYMITE
PROZYMITES
PRUDE
PRUDENCE
PRUDENCES
PRUDENT
PRUDENTLY
PRUDERIES
PRUDERY
PRUDES
PRUDISH
PRUDISHLY
PRUH
PRUINA
PRUINAS
PRUINE
PRUINES
PRUINOSE
PRUNE
PRUNED
PRUNELLA
PRUNELLAS
PRUNELLE
PRUNELLES
PRUNELLO
PRUNELLOS
PRUNER
PRUNERS
PRUNES
PRUNING
PRUNINGS
PRUNT
PRUNTED
PRUNTS
PRURIENCE
PRURIENCES
PRURIENCIES
PRURIENCY
PRURIENT
PRURIGO
PRURIGOS
PRURITIC
PRURITUS
PRURITUSES
PRUSSIAN
PRUSSIANS
PRUSSIATE
PRUSSIATES
PRUSSIC
PRY
PRYER
PRYERS
PRYING
PRYINGLY
PRYINGS
PRYS
PRYSE
PRYSES
PRYTANEA
PRYTANEUM
PRYTHEE
PSALM
PSALMIST
PSALMISTS
PSALMODIC

PSALMODIES
PSALMODY
PSALMS
PSALTER
PSALTERIA
PSALTERIES
PSALTERS
PSALTERY
PSALTRESS
PSALTRESSES
PSAMMITE
PSAMMITES
PSAMMITIC
PSELLISM
PSELLISMS
PSEPHISM
PSEPHISMS
PSEPHITE
PSEPHITES
PSEPHITIC
PSEUD
PSEUDAXES
PSEUDAXIS
PSEUDERIES
PSEUDERY
PSEUDISH
PSEUDO
PSEUDONYM
PSEUDONYMS
PSEUDOPOD
PSEUDOPODS
PSEUDOS
PSEUDS
PSHAW
PSHAWED
PSHAWING
PSHAWS
PSI
PSILOSES
PSILOSIS
PSILOTIC
PSIONIC
PSIS
PSOAS
PSOASES
PSORA
PSORAS
PSORIASES
PSORIASIS
PSORIATIC
PSORIC
PSST
PST
PSYCH
PSYCHE
PSYCHED
PSYCHES
PSYCHIC
PSYCHICAL
PSYCHICS
PSYCHING
PSYCHISM
PSYCHISMS
PSYCHIST
PSYCHISTS
PSYCHO
PSYCHOGAS
PSYCHOGASES
PSYCHOID
PSYCHOIDS

PSYCHOS
PSYCHOSES
PSYCHOSIS
PSYCHOTIC
PSYCHOTICS
PSYCHS
PSYOP
PSYOPS
PSYWAR
PSYWARS
PTARMIC
PTARMICS
PTARMIGAN
PTARMIGANS
PTERIA
PTERIN
PTERINS
PTERION
PTEROPOD
PTEROPODS
PTEROSAUR
PTEROSAURS
PTERYGIA
PTERYGIAL
PTERYGIUM
PTERYGOID
PTERYGOIDS
PTERYLA
PTERYLAE
PTILOSES
PTILOSIS
PTISAN
PTISANS
PTOMAINE
PTOMAINES
PTOSES
PTOSIS
PTYALIN
PTYALINS
PTYALISE
PTYALISED
PTYALISES
PTYALISING
PTYALISM
PTYALISMS
PTYALIZE
PTYALIZED
PTYALIZES
PTYALIZING
PTYXES
PTYXIS
PTYXISES
PUB
PUBBED
PUBBING
PUBERAL
PUBERTAL
PUBERTIES
PUBERTY
PUBES
PUBESCENT
PUBIC
PUBIS
PUBISES
PUBLIC
PUBLICAN
PUBLICANS
PUBLICISE
PUBLICISED
PUBLICISES

PUBLICISING
PUBLICIST
PUBLICISTS
PUBLICITIES
PUBLICITY
PUBLICIZE
PUBLICIZED
PUBLICIZES
PUBLICIZING
PUBLICLY
PUBLICS
PUBLISH
PUBLISHED
PUBLISHER
PUBLISHERS
PUBLISHES
PUBLISHING
PUBS
PUCCOON
PUCCOONS
PUCE
PUCELAGE
PUCELAGES
PUCELLE
PUCELLES
PUCES
PUCK
PUCKA
PUCKER
PUCKERED
PUCKERING
PUCKERS
PUCKERY
PUCKFIST
PUCKFISTS
PUCKISH
PUCKS
PUD
PUDDED
PUDDEN
PUDDENING
PUDDENINGS
PUDDENS
PUDDER
PUDDERED
PUDDERING
PUDDERS
PUDDIES
PUDDING
PUDDINGS
PUDDINGY
PUDDLE
PUDDLED
PUDDLER
PUDDLERS
PUDDLES
PUDDLIER
PUDDLIEST
PUDDLING
PUDDLINGS
PUDDLY
PUDDOCK
PUDDOCKS
PUDDY
PUDENCIES
PUDENCY
PUDENDA
PUDENDAL
PUDENDOUS
PUDENDUM

PUDENT
PUDGE
PUDGES
PUDGIER
PUDGIEST
PUDGINESS
PUDGINESSES
PUDGY
PUDIBUND
PUDIC
PUDICITIES
PUDICITY
PUDOR
PUDORS
PUDS
PUDSEY
PUDSY
PUEBLO
PUEBLOS
PUER
PUERED
PUERILE
PUERILISM
PUERILISMS
PUERILITIES
PUERILITY
PUERING
PUERPERAL
PUERS
PUFF
PUFFBALL
PUFFBALLS
PUFFED
PUFFER
PUFFERIES
PUFFERS
PUFFERY
PUFFIER
PUFFIEST
PUFFILY
PUFFIN
PUFFINESS
PUFFINESSES
PUFFING
PUFFINGLY
PUFFINGS
PUFFINS
PUFFS
PUFFY
PUG
PUGGAREE
PUGGAREES
PUGGED
PUGGERIES
PUGGERY
PUGGIER
PUGGIES
PUGGIEST
PUGGING
PUGGINGS
PUGGISH
PUGGREE
PUGGREES
PUGGY
PUGH
PUGIL
PUGILISM
PUGILISMS
PUGILIST
PUGILISTS

PUGILS
PUGNACITIES
PUGNACITY
PUGS
PUH
PUIR
PUIRER
PUIREST
PUISNE
PUISNES
PUISNIES
PUISNY
PUISSANCE
PUISSANCES
PUISSANT
PUISSAUNT
PUJA
PUJAS
PUKE
PUKED
PUKER
PUKERS
PUKES
PUKING
PUKKA
PULDRON
PULDRONS
PULE
PULED
PULER
PULERS
PULES
PULICIDE
PULICIDES
PULING
PULINGLY
PULINGS
PULK
PULKA
PULKAS
PULKHA
PULKHAS
PULKS
PULL
PULLED
PULLER
PULLERS
PULLET
PULLETS
PULLEY
PULLEYS
PULLING
PULLOVER
PULLOVERS
PULLS
PULLULATE
PULLULATED
PULLULATES
PULLULATING
PULMO
PULMONARY
PULMONATE
PULMONATES
PULMONES
PULMONIC
PULMONICS
PULP
PULPBOARD
PULPBOARDS
PULPED

PULPER
PULPERS
PULPIER
PULPIEST
PULPIFIED
PULPIFIES
PULPIFY
PULPIFYING
PULPILY
PULPINESS
PULPINESSES
PULPING
PULPIT
PULPITED
PULPITEER
PULPITEERS
PULPITER
PULPITERS
PULPITRIES
PULPITRY
PULPITS
PULPITUM
PULPITUMS
PULPMILL
PULPMILLS
PULPOUS
PULPS
PULPSTONE
PULPSTONES
PULPWOOD
PULPWOODS
PULPY
PULQUE
PULQUES
PULSAR
PULSARS
PULSATE
PULSATED
PULSATES
PULSATILE
PULSATING
PULSATION
PULSATIONS
PULSATIVE
PULSATOR
PULSATORS
PULSATORY
PULSE
PULSED
PULSEJET
PULSEJETS
PULSELESS
PULSES
PULSIDGE
PULSIDGES
PULSIFIC
PULSING
PULSOJET
PULSOJETS
PULTAN
PULTANS
PULTON
PULTONS
PULTOON
PULTOONS
PULTUN
PULTUNS
PULTURE
PULTURES
PULU

PULUS
PULVER
PULVERED
PULVERINE
PULVERINES
PULVERING
PULVERISE
PULVERISED
PULVERISES
PULVERISING
PULVERIZE
PULVERIZED
PULVERIZES
PULVERIZING
PULVEROUS
PULVERS
PULVIL
PULVILIO
PULVILIOS
PULVILLAR
PULVILLE
PULVILLED
PULVILLES
PULVILLI
PULVILLING
PULVILLIO
PULVILLIOS
PULVILLUS
PULVILS
PULVINAR
PULVINATE
PULVINI
PULVINULE
PULVINULES
PULVINUS
PULWAR
PULWARS
PULY
PUMA
PUMAS
PUMELO
PUMELOS
PUMICATE
PUMICATED
PUMICATES
PUMICATING
PUMICE
PUMICED
PUMICEOUS
PUMICES
PUMICING
PUMIE
PUMIES
PUMMEL
PUMMELLED
PUMMELLING
PUMMELS
PUMP
PUMPED
PUMPER
PUMPERS
PUMPING
PUMPION
PUMPIONS
PUMPKIN
PUMPKINS
PUMPS
PUMY
PUN
PUNA

PUSSYFOOTS

PUNALUA
PUNALUAN
PUNALUAS
PUNAS
PUNCE
PUNCES
PUNCH
PUNCHED
PUNCHEON
PUNCHEONS
PUNCHER
PUNCHERS
PUNCHES
PUNCHIER
PUNCHIEST
PUNCHING
PUNCHY
PUNCTA
PUNCTATE
PUNCTATED
PUNCTATOR
PUNCTATORS
PUNCTILIO
PUNCTILIOS
PUNCTO
PUNCTOS
PUNCTUAL
PUNCTUATE
PUNCTUATED
PUNCTUATES
PUNCTUATING
PUNCTULE
PUNCTULES
PUNCTUM
PUNCTURE
PUNCTURED
PUNCTURES
PUNCTURING
PUNDIT
PUNDITRIES
PUNDITRY
PUNDITS
PUNDONOR
PUNDONORES
PUNGENCE
PUNGENCES
PUNGENCIES
PUNGENCY
PUNGENT
PUNGENTLY
PUNIER
PUNIEST
PUNILY
PUNINESS
PUNINESSES
PUNISH
PUNISHED
PUNISHER
PUNISHERS
PUNISHES
PUNISHING
PUNITION
PUNITIONS
PUNITIVE
PUNITORY
PUNK
PUNKA
PUNKAH
PUNKAHS
PUNKAS

PUNKINESS
PUNKINESSES
PUNKS
PUNNED
PUNNER
PUNNERS
PUNNET
PUNNETS
PUNNING
PUNNINGS
PUNS
PUNSTER
PUNSTERS
PUNT
PUNTED
PUNTEE
PUNTEES
PUNTER
PUNTERS
PUNTIES
PUNTING
PUNTO
PUNTOS
PUNTS
PUNTSMAN
PUNTSMEN
PUNTY
PUNY
PUP
PUPA
PUPAE
PUPAL
PUPARIA
PUPARIAL
PUPARIUM
PUPAS
PUPATE
PUPATED
PUPATES
PUPATING
PUPATION
PUPATIONS
PUPFISH
PUPFISHES
PUPIL
PUPILLAGE
PUPILLAGES
PUPILLARY
PUPILLATE
PUPILS
PUPPED
PUPPET
PUPPETEER
PUPPETEERS
PUPPETRIES
PUPPETRY
PUPPETS
PUPPIED
PUPPIES
PUPPING
PUPPODUM
PUPPODUMS
PUPPY
PUPPYDOM
PUPPYDOMS
PUPPYHOOD
PUPPYHOODS
PUPPYING
PUPPYISH
PUPPYISM

PUPPYISMS
PUPS
PUPUNHA
PUPUNHAS
PUR
PURBLIND
PURCHASE
PURCHASED
PURCHASER
PURCHASERS
PURCHASES
PURCHASING
PURDAH
PURDAHS
PURDONIUM
PURDONIUMS
PURE
PURED
PURÉE
PURÉED
PURÉEING
PURÉES
PURELY
PURENESS
PURENESSES
PURER
PURES
PUREST
PURFLE
PURFLED
PURFLES
PURFLING
PURFLINGS
PURFLY
PURGATION
PURGATIONS
PURGATIVE
PURGATIVES
PURGATORIES
PURGATORY
PURGE
PURGED
PURGER
PURGERS
PURGES
PURGING
PURGINGS
PURI
PURIFIED
PURIFIER
PURIFIERS
PURIFIES
PURIFY
PURIFYING
PURIM
PURIMS
PURIN
PURINE
PURINES
PURINS
PURIS
PURISM
PURISMS
PURIST
PURISTIC
PURISTS
PURITAN
PURITANIC
PURITANS

PURITIES
PURITY
PURL
PURLED
PURLER
PURLERS
PURLICUE
PURLICUED
PURLICUES
PURLICUING
PURLIEU
PURLIEUS
PURLIN
PURLINE
PURLINES
PURLING
PURLINGS
PURLINS
PURLOIN
PURLOINED
PURLOINER
PURLOINERS
PURLOINING
PURLOINS
PURLS
PURPIE
PURPIES
PURPLE
PURPLED
PURPLES
PURPLING
PURPLISH
PURPLY
PURPORT
PURPORTED
PURPORTING
PURPORTS
PURPOSE
PURPOSED
PURPOSELY
PURPOSES
PURPOSING
PURPOSIVE
PURPURA
PURPURAS
PURPURE
PURPUREAL
PURPURES
PURPURIC
PURPURIN
PURPURINS
PURPY
PURR
PURRED
PURRING
PURRINGLY
PURRINGS
PURRS
PURS
PURSE
PURSED
PURSEFUL
PURSEFULS
PURSER
PURSERS
PURSES
PURSEW
PURSIER
PURSIEST
PURSINESS

PURSINESSES
PURSING
PURSLAIN
PURSLAINS
PURSLANE
PURSLANES
PURSUABLE
PURSUAL
PURSUALS
PURSUANCE
PURSUANCES
PURSUANT
PURSUE
PURSUED
PURSUER
PURSUERS
PURSUES
PURSUING
PURSUINGS
PURSUIT
PURSUITS
PURSY
PURTRAID
PURTRAYD
PURTY
PURULENCE
PURULENCES
PURULENCIES
PURULENCY
PURULENT
PURVEY
PURVEYED
PURVEYING
PURVEYOR
PURVEYORS
PURVEYS
PURVIEW
PURVIEWS
PUS
PUSES
PUSH
PUSHED
PUSHER
PUSHERS
PUSHES
PUSHFUL
PUSHFULLY
PUSHIER
PUSHIEST
PUSHINESS
PUSHINESSES
PUSHING
PUSHINGLY
PUSHROD
PUSHRODS
PUSHY
PUSLE
PUSLED
PUSLES
PUSLING
PUSS
PUSSEL
PUSSELS
PUSSES
PUSSIES
PUSSY
PUSSYFOOT
PUSSYFOOTED
PUSSYFOOTING
PUSSYFOOTS

PUSTULANT
PUSTULANTS
PUSTULAR
PUSTULATE
PUSTULATED
PUSTULATES
PUSTULATING
PUSTULE
PUSTULES
PUSTULOUS
PUT
PUTAMEN
PUTAMINA
PUTATIVE
PUTCHER
PUTCHERS
PUTCHOCK
PUTCHOCKS
PUTCHUK
PUTCHUKS
PUTEAL
PUTEALS
PUTELI
PUTELIS
PUTID
PUTLOCK
PUTLOCKS
PUTLOG
PUTLOGS
PUTOIS
PUTOISES
PUTREFIED
PUTREFIES
PUTREFY
PUTREFYING
PUTRID
PUTRIDER
PUTRIDEST
PUTRIDITIES
PUTRIDITY
PUTRIDLY
PUTS
PUTSCH
PUTSCHES
PUTT
PUTTED
PUTTEE
PUTTEES
PUTTEN
PUTTER
PUTTERED
PUTTERING
PUTTERS
PUTTI
PUTTIE
PUTTIED
PUTTIER

PUTTIERS
PUTTIES
PUTTING
PUTTINGS
PUTTO
PUTTOCK
PUTTOCKS
PUTTS
PUTTY
PUTTYING
PUTURE
PUTURES
PUTZ
PUTZES
PUY
PUYS
PUZEL
PUZELS
PUZZEL
PUZZELS
PUZZLE
PUZZLED
PUZZLEDOM
PUZZLEDOMS
PUZZLER
PUZZLERS
PUZZLES
PUZZLING
PUZZOLANA
PUZZOLANAS
PYAEMIA
PYAEMIAS
PYAEMIC
PYAT
PYATS
PYCNIC
PYCNIDIA
PYCNIDIUM
PYCNIDIUMS
PYCNITE
PYCNITES
PYCNON
PYCNONS
PYE
PYEBALD
PYEBALDS
PYEING
PYELITIC
PYELITIS
PYELITISES
PYELOGRAM
PYELOGRAMS
PYEMIA
PYEMIAS
PYENGADU
PYENGADUS
PYES

PYET
PYETS
PYGAL
PYGALS
PYGARG
PYGARGS
PYGIDIA
PYGIDIAL
PYGIDIUM
PYGIDIUMS
PYGMAEAN
PYGMEAN
PYGMIES
PYGMOID
PYGMY
PYGOSTYLE
PYGOSTYLES
PYJAMAED
PYJAMAS
PYKNIC
PYKNOSOME
PYKNOSOMES
PYLON
PYLONS
PYLORIC
PYLORUS
PYLORUSES
PYNE
PYNED
PYNES
PYNING
PYOGENIC
PYOID
PYONER
PYONERS
PYONINGS
PYORRHOEA
PYORRHOEAS
PYOT
PYOTS
PYRACANTH
PYRACANTHS
PYRAL
PYRALID
PYRALIDS
PYRALIS
PYRALISES
PYRAMID
PYRAMIDAL
PYRAMIDED
PYRAMIDES
PYRAMIDIC
PYRAMIDING
PYRAMIDON
PYRAMIDONS
PYRAMIDS
PYRAMIS

PYRAMISES
PYRE
PYRENE
PYRENEITE
PYRENEITES
PYRENES
PYRENOID
PYRENOIDS
PYRES
PYRETHRIN
PYRETHRINS
PYRETHRUM
PYRETHRUMS
PYRETIC
PYREXIA
PYREXIAL
PYREXIAS
PYREXIC
PYRIDINE
PYRIDINES
PYRIDOXIN
PYRIDOXINS
PYRIFORM
PYRITE
PYRITES
PYRITESES
PYRITIC
PYRITICAL
PYRITISE
PYRITISED
PYRITISES
PYRITISING
PYRITIZE
PYRITIZED
PYRITIZES
PYRITIZING
PYRITOUS
PYRO
PYROCLAST
PYROCLASTS
PYROGEN
PYROGENIC
PYROGENS
PYROLATER
PYROLATERS
PYROLATRIES
PYROLATRY
PYROLYSE
PYROLYSED
PYROLYSES
PYROLYSING
PYROLYSIS
PYROLYTIC
PYROLYZE
PYROLYZED
PYROLYZES
PYROLYZING

PYROMANCIES
PYROMANCY
PYROMANIA
PYROMANIAS
PYROMETER
PYROMETERS
PYROMETRIES
PYROMETRY
PYROPE
PYROPES
PYROPHONE
PYROPHONES
PYROPUS
PYROPUSES
PYROS
PYROSCOPE
PYROSCOPES
PYROSES
PYROSIS
PYROSOME
PYROSOMES
PYROSTAT
PYROSTATS
PYROXENE
PYROXENES
PYROXENIC
PYROXYLE
PYROXYLES
PYROXYLIC
PYROXYLIN
PYROXYLINS
PYRRHIC
PYRRHICS
PYRRHOUS
PYRROLE
PYRROLES
PYRUVATE
PYRUVATES
PYTHIUM
PYTHIUMS
PYTHON
PYTHONESS
PYTHONESSES
PYTHONIC
PYTHONS
PYURIA
PYURIAS
PYX
PYXED
PYXES
PYXIDES
PYXIDIA
PYXIDIUM
PYXING
PYXIS
PZAZZ
PZAZZES

Q

QADI
QADIS
QALAMDAN
QALAMDANS
QANAT
QANATS
QAT
QATS
QIBLA
QIBLAS
QIGONG
QIGONGS
QINTAR
QINTARS
QUA
QUACK
QUACKED
QUACKERIES
QUACKERY
QUACKING
QUACKLE
QUACKLED
QUACKLES
QUACKLING
QUACKS
QUAD
QUADDED
QUADDING
QUADRANS
QUADRANT
QUADRANTES
QUADRANTS
QUADRAT
QUADRATE
QUADRATED
QUADRATES
QUADRATIC
QUADRATICS
QUADRATING
QUADRATS
QUADRATUS
QUADRATUSES
QUADRELLA
QUADRELLAS
QUADRIC
QUADRIFID
QUADRIGA
QUADRIGAE
QUADRILLE
QUADRILLED
QUADRILLES
QUADRILLING
QUADROON
QUADROONS
QUADRUMAN
QUADRUMANS
QUADRUPED
QUADRUPEDS
QUADRUPLE
QUADRUPLED
QUADRUPLES
QUADRUPLIES
QUADRUPLING
QUADRUPLY
QUADS
QUAERE

QUAERED
QUAERES
QUAERING
QUAERITUR
QUAESITUM
QUAESITUMS
QUAESTOR
QUAESTORS
QUAFF
QUAFFED
QUAFFER
QUAFFERS
QUAFFING
QUAFFS
QUAG
QUAGGA
QUAGGAS
QUAGGIER
QUAGGIEST
QUAGGY
QUAGMIRE
QUAGMIRED
QUAGMIRES
QUAGMIRIER
QUAGMIRIEST
QUAGMIRING
QUAGMIRY
QUAGS
QUAHAUG
QUAHAUGS
QUAHOG
QUAHOGS
QUAICH
QUAICHS
QUAIGH
QUAIGHS
QUAIL
QUAILED
QUAILING
QUAILINGS
QUAILS
QUAINT
QUAINTER
QUAINTEST
QUAINTLY
QUAIR
QUAIRS
QUAKE
QUAKED
QUAKES
QUAKIER
QUAKIEST
QUAKINESS
QUAKINESSES
QUAKING
QUAKINGLY
QUAKINGS
QUAKY
QUALAMDAN
QUALAMDANS
QUALE
QUALIA
QUALIFIED
QUALIFIER

QUALIFIERS
QUALIFIES
QUALIFY
QUALIFYING
QUALIFYINGS
QUALITIED
QUALITIES
QUALITY
QUALM
QUALMIER
QUALMIEST
QUALMING
QUALMISH
QUALMLESS
QUALMS
QUALMY
QUAMASH
QUAMASHES
QUANDANG
QUANDANGS
QUANDARIES
QUANDARY
QUANDONG
QUANDONGS
QUANGO
QUANGOS
QUANNET
QUANNETS
QUANT
QUANTA
QUANTAL
QUANTED
QUANTIC
QUANTICAL
QUANTICS
QUANTIFIED
QUANTIFIES
QUANTIFY
QUANTIFYING
QUANTING
QUANTISE
QUANTISED
QUANTISES
QUANTISING
QUANTITIES
QUANTITY
QUANTIZE
QUANTIZED
QUANTIZES
QUANTIZING
QUANTONG
QUANTONGS
QUANTS
QUANTUM
QUARENDEN
QUARENDENS
QUARENDER
QUARENDERS
QUARK
QUARKS
QUARLE
QUARLES
QUARREL
QUARRELLED

QUARRELLING
QUARRELLINGS
QUARRELS
QUARRIED
QUARRIER
QUARRIERS
QUARRIES
QUARRY
QUARRYING
QUARRYMAN
QUARRYMEN
QUART
QUARTAN
QUARTANS
QUARTE
QUARTER
QUARTERED
QUARTERING
QUARTERINGS
QUARTERLIES
QUARTERLY
QUARTERN
QUARTERNS
QUARTERS
QUARTES
QUARTET
QUARTETS
QUARTETT
QUARTETTE
QUARTETTES
QUARTETTI
QUARTETTO
QUARTETTS
QUARTIC
QUARTICS
QUARTIER
QUARTIERS
QUARTILE
QUARTILES
QUARTO
QUARTOS
QUARTS
QUARTZ
QUARTZES
QUARTZITE
QUARTZITES
QUARTZOSE
QUARTZY
QUASAR
QUASARS
QUASH
QUASHED
QUASHEE
QUASHEES
QUASHES
QUASHIE
QUASHIES
QUASHING
QUASI
QUASSIA
QUASSIAS
QUAT
QUATCH
QUATCHED

QUATCHES
QUATCHING
QUATORZE
QUATORZES
QUATRAIN
QUATRAINS
QUATS
QUAVER
QUAVERED
QUAVERER
QUAVERERS
QUAVERING
QUAVERINGS
QUAVERS
QUAVERY
QUAY
QUAYAGE
QUAYAGES
QUAYD
QUAYS
QUAYSIDE
QUAYSIDES
QUEACH
QUEACHES
QUEACHY
QUEAN
QUEANS
QUEASIER
QUEASIEST
QUEASILY
QUEASY
QUEAZIER
QUEAZIEST
QUEAZY
QUEBRACHO
QUEBRACHOS
QUEECHY
QUEEN
QUEENDOM
QUEENDOMS
QUEENED
QUEENHOOD
QUEENHOODS
QUEENING
QUEENINGS
QUEENITE
QUEENITES
QUEENLESS
QUEENLET
QUEENLETS
QUEENLIER
QUEENLIEST
QUEENLY
QUEENS
QUEENSHIP
QUEENSHIPS
QUEER
QUEERDOM
QUEERDOMS
QUEERED
QUEERER
QUEEREST
QUEERING
QUEERISH

QUEERITIES
QUEERITY
QUEERLY
QUEERNESS
QUEERNESSES
QUEERS
QUEEST
QUEESTS
QUEINT
QUELCH
QUELCHED
QUELCHES
QUELCHING
QUELEA
QUELEAS
QUELL
QUELLED
QUELLER
QUELLERS
QUELLING
QUELLS
QUEME
QUEMED
QUEMES
QUEMING
QUENA
QUENAS
QUENCH
QUENCHED
QUENCHER
QUENCHERS
QUENCHES
QUENCHING
QUENCHINGS
QUENELLE
QUENELLES
QUEP
QUERCETUM
QUERCETUMS
QUERIED
QUERIES
QUERIMONIES
QUERIMONY
QUERIST
QUERISTS
QUERN
QUERNS
QUERULOUS
QUERY
QUERYING
QUERYINGS
QUEST
QUESTANT
QUESTANTS
QUESTED
QUESTER
QUESTERS
QUESTING
QUESTINGS
QUESTION
QUESTIONED
QUESTIONING
QUESTIONS
QUESTOR
QUESTORS
QUESTRIST
QUESTRISTS
QUESTS
QUETCH
QUETCHED

QUETCHES
QUETCHING
QUETHE
QUETHES
QUETHING
QUETSCH
QUETSCHES
QUETZAL
QUETZALS
QUEUE
QUEUED
QUEUEING
QUEUEINGS
QUEUES
QUEUING
QUEUINGS
QUEY
QUEYN
QUEYNIE
QUEYNIES
QUEYNS
QUEYS
QUIBBLE
QUIBBLED
QUIBBLER
QUIBBLERS
QUIBBLES
QUIBBLING
QUIBBLINGS
QUIBLIN
QUIBLINS
QUICH
QUICHE
QUICHED
QUICHES
QUICHING
QUICK
QUICKBEAM
QUICKBEAMS
QUICKEN
QUICKENED
QUICKENER
QUICKENERS
QUICKENING
QUICKENINGS
QUICKENS
QUICKER
QUICKEST
QUICKIE
QUICKIES
QUICKLIME
QUICKLIMES
QUICKLY
QUICKNESS
QUICKNESSES
QUICKS
QUICKSAND
QUICKSANDS
QUICKSET
QUICKSETS
QUICKSTEP
QUICKSTEPPED
QUICKSTEPPING
QUICKSTEPS
QUID
QUIDAM
QUIDAMS
QUIDDANIES
QUIDDANY
QUIDDIT

QUIDDITIES
QUIDDITS
QUIDDITY
QUIDDLE
QUIDDLED
QUIDDLER
QUIDDLERS
QUIDDLES
QUIDDLING
QUIDNUNC
QUIDNUNCS
QUIDS
QUIESCE
QUIESCED
QUIESCENT
QUIESCES
QUIESCING
QUIET
QUIETED
QUIETEN
QUIETENED
QUIETENING
QUIETENINGS
QUIETENS
QUIETER
QUIETERS
QUIETEST
QUIETING
QUIETINGS
QUIETISM
QUIETISMS
QUIETIST
QUIETISTS
QUIETIVE
QUIETIVES
QUIETLY
QUIETNESS
QUIETNESSES
QUIETS
QUIETSOME
QUIETUDE
QUIETUDES
QUIETUS
QUIETUSES
QUIFF
QUIFFS
QUIGHT
QUILL
QUILLAI
QUILLAIA
QUILLAIAS
QUILLAIS
QUILLAJA
QUILLAJAS
QUILLED
QUILLET
QUILLETS
QUILLING
QUILLINGS
QUILLMAN
QUILLMEN
QUILLON
QUILLONS
QUILLS
QUILLWORT
QUILLWORTS
QUILT
QUILTED
QUILTER
QUILTERS

QUILTING
QUILTINGS
QUILTS
QUIM
QUIMS
QUIN
QUINA
QUINARY
QUINAS
QUINATE
QUINCE
QUINCES
QUINCHE
QUINCHED
QUINCHES
QUINCHING
QUINCUNX
QUINCUNXES
QUINE
QUINELLA
QUINELLAS
QUINES
QUINIC
QUINIDINE
QUINIDINES
QUINIE
QUINIES
QUININE
QUININES
QUINNAT
QUINNATS
QUINOA
QUINOAS
QUINOL
QUINOLINE
QUINOLINES
QUINOLS
QUINONE
QUINONES
QUINQUINA
QUINQUINAS
QUINS
QUINSIED
QUINSIES
QUINSY
QUINT
QUINTA
QUINTAIN
QUINTAINS
QUINTAL
QUINTALS
QUINTAN
QUINTAS
QUINTE
QUINTES
QUINTET
QUINTETS
QUINTETT
QUINTETTE
QUINTETTES
QUINTETTI
QUINTETTO
QUINTETTS
QUINTIC
QUINTILE
QUINTILES
QUINTROON
QUINTROONS
QUINTS
QUINTUPLE

QUINTUPLED
QUINTUPLES
QUINTUPLING
QUINZE
QUINZES
QUIP
QUIPO
QUIPOS
QUIPPED
QUIPPING
QUIPPISH
QUIPS
QUIPSTER
QUIPSTERS
QUIPU
QUIPUS
QUIRE
QUIRED
QUIRES
QUIRING
QUIRISTER
QUIRISTERS
QUIRK
QUIRKED
QUIRKIER
QUIRKIEST
QUIRKING
QUIRKISH
QUIRKS
QUIRKY
QUIRT
QUIRTED
QUIRTING
QUIRTS
QUISLING
QUISLINGS
QUIST
QUISTS
QUIT
QUITCH
QUITCHED
QUITCHES
QUITCHING
QUITE
QUITED
QUITES
QUITING
QUITS
QUITTAL
QUITTALS
QUITTANCE
QUITTANCED
QUITTANCES
QUITTANCING
QUITTED
QUITTER
QUITTERS
QUITTING
QUITTOR
QUITTORS
QUIVER
QUIVERED
QUIVERFUL
QUIVERFULS
QUIVERING
QUIVERINGS
QUIVERISH
QUIVERS
QUIVERY
QUIXOTIC

QUIXOTISM
QUIXOTISMS
QUIXOTRIES
QUIXOTRY
QUIZ
QUIZZED
QUIZZER
QUIZZERIES
QUIZZERS
QUIZZERY
QUIZZES
QUIZZICAL
QUIZZIFIED
QUIZZIFIES
QUIZZIFY
QUIZZIFYING
QUIZZING
QUIZZINGS

QUOAD
QUOD
QUODDED
QUODDING
QUODLIBET
QUODLIBETS
QUODLIN
QUODLINS
QUODS
QUOIF
QUOIFED
QUOIFING
QUOIFS
QUOIN
QUOINED
QUOINING
QUOINS
QUOIST

QUOISTS
QUOIT
QUOITED
QUOITER
QUOITERS
QUOITING
QUOITS
QUOKKA
QUOKKAS
QUOLL
QUOLLS
QUONDAM
QUONK
QUONKED
QUONKING
QUONKS
QUOOKE
QUOP

QUOPPED
QUOPPING
QUOPS
QUORATE
QUORUM
QUORUMS
QUOTA
QUOTABLE
QUOTABLY
QUOTAS
QUOTATION
QUOTATIONS
QUOTATIVE
QUOTATIVES
QUOTE
QUOTED
QUOTER
QUOTERS

QUOTES
QUOTH
QUOTHA
QUOTIDIAN
QUOTIDIANS
QUOTIENT
QUOTIENTS
QUOTING
QUOTITION
QUOTITIONS
QUOTUM
QUOTUMS
QUYTE
QWERTIES
QWERTY
QWERTYS

R

RABANNA	RACAHOUTS	RACISM	RADIALIZE	RADULA
RABANNAS	RACCAHOUT	RACISMS	RADIALIZED	RADULAE
RABAT	RACCAHOUTS	RACIST	RADIALIZES	RADULAR
RABATINE	RACCOON	RACISTS	RADIALIZING	RADULATE
RABATINES	RACCOONS	RACK	RADIALLY	RAFALE
RABATMENT	RACE	RACKED	RADIALS	RAFALES
RABATMENTS	RACED	RACKER	RADIAN	RAFF
RABATO	RACEGOER	RACKERS	RADIANCE	RAFFIA
RABATOES	RACEGOERS	RACKET	RADIANCES	RAFFIAS
RABATS	RACEGOING	RACKETED	RADIANCIES	RAFFINATE
RABATTE	RACEGOINGS	RACKETEER	RADIANCY	RAFFINATES
RABATTED	RACEHORSE	RACKETEERED	RADIANS	RAFFINOSE
RABATTES	RACEHORSES	RACKETEERING	RADIANT	RAFFINOSES
RABATTING	RACEMATE	RACKETEERS	RADIANTLY	RAFFISH
RABATTINGS	RACEMATES	RACKETER	RADIANTS	RAFFISHLY
RABBET	RACEME	RACKETERS	RADIATE	RAFFLE
RABBETED	RACEMED	RACKETING	RADIATED	RAFFLED
RABBETING	RACEMES	RACKETRIES	RADIATELY	RAFFLER
RABBETS	RACEMIC	RACKETRY	RADIATES	RAFFLERS
RABBI	RACEMISE	RACKETS	RADIATING	RAFFLES
RABBIN	RACEMISED	RACKETT	RADIATION	RAFFLING
RABBINATE	RACEMISES	RACKETTS	RADIATIONS	RAFFS
RABBINATES	RACEMISING	RACKETY	RADIATIVE	RAFT
RABBINIC	RACEMISM	RACKING	RADIATOR	RAFTED
RABBINISM	RACEMISMS	RACKINGS	RADIATORS	RAFTER
RABBINISMS	RACEMIZE	RACKS	RADIATORY	RAFTERED
RABBINIST	RACEMIZED	RACKWORK	RADICAL	RAFTERING
RABBINISTS	RACEMIZES	RACKWORKS	RADICALLY	RAFTERINGS
RABBINITE	RACEMIZING	RACLETTE	RADICALS	RAFTERS
RABBINITES	RACEMOSE	RACLETTES	RADICANT	RAFTING
RABBINS	RACER	RACLOIR	RADICATE	RAFTMAN
RABBIS	RACERS	RACLOIRS	RADICATED	RAFTMEN
RABBIT	RACES	RACON	RADICATES	RAFTS
RABBITED	RACEWAY	RACONS	RADICATING	RAFTSMAN
RABBITER	RACEWAYS	RACONTEUR	RADICEL	RAFTSMEN
RABBITERS	RACH	RACONTEURS	RADICELS	RAG
RABBITING	RACHE	RACOON	RADICES	RAGA
RABBITRIES	RACHES	RACOONS	RADICLE	RAGAS
RABBITRY	RACHIAL	RACQUET	RADICLES	RAGBOLT
RABBITS	RACHIDES	RACQUETED	RADICULAR	RAGBOLTS
RABBITY	RACHIDIAL	RACQUETING	RADICULE	RAGDE
RABBLE	RACHIDIAN	RACQUETS	RADICULES	RAGE
RABBLED	RACHILLA	RACY	RADII	RAGED
RABBLER	RACHILLAS	RAD	RADIO	RAGEFUL
RABBLERS	RACHIS	RADAR	RADIOED	RAGER
RABBLES	RACHISES	RADARS	RADIOGRAM	RAGERS
RABBLING	RACHITIC	RADDLE	RADIOGRAMS	RAGES
RABBLINGS	RACHITIS	RADDLED	RADIOING	RAGG
RABBONI	RACHITISES	RADDLEMAN	RADIOLOGIES	RAGGED
RABBONIS	RACIAL	RADDLEMEN	RADIOLOGY	RAGGEDER
RABI	RACIALISM	RADDLES	RADIONICS	RAGGEDEST
RABIC	RACIALISMS	RADDLING	RADIOS	RAGGEDLY
RABID	RACIALIST	RADDOCKE	RADISH	RAGGEDY
RABIDER	RACIALISTS	RADDOCKES	RADISHES	RAGGEE
RABIDEST	RACIALLY	RADE	RADIUM	RAGGEES
RABIDITIES	RACIATION	RADIAL	RADIUMS	RAGGERIES
RABIDITY	RACIATIONS	RADIALE	RADIUS	RAGGERY
RABIDLY	RACIER	RADIALIA	RADIUSES	RAGGIER
RABIDNESS	RACIEST	RADIALISE	RADIX	RAGGIES
RABIDNESSES	RACILY	RADIALISED	RADOME	RAGGIEST
RABIES	RACINESS	RADIALISES	RADOMES	RAGGING
RABIS	RACINESSES	RADIALISING	RADON	RAGGINGS
RACA	RACING	RADIALITIES	RADONS	RAGGLE
RACAHOUT	RACINGS	RADIALITY	RADS	RAGGLED

RAGGLES
RAGGLING
RAGGS
RAGGY
RAGI
RAGING
RAGINGLY
RAGINI
RAGINIS
RAGIS
RAGLAN
RAGLANS
RAGMAN
RAGMEN
RAGMENT
RAGMENTS
RAGOUT
RAGOUTED
RAGOUTING
RAGOUTS
RAGS
RAGSTONE
RAGSTONES
RAGTIME
RAGTIMER
RAGTIMERS
RAGTIMES
RAGULED
RAGULY
RAGWEED
RAGWEEDS
RAGWHEEL
RAGWHEELS
RAGWORK
RAGWORKS
RAGWORM
RAGWORMS
RAGWORT
RAGWORTS
RAH
RAHED
RAHING
RAHS
RAID
RAIDED
RAIDER
RAIDERS
RAIDING
RAIDS
RAIK
RAIKED
RAIKING
RAIKS
RAIL
RAILBUS
RAILBUSES
RAILBUSSES
RAILCARD
RAILCARDS
RAILE
RAILED
RAILER
RAILERS
RAILING
RAILINGLY
RAILINGS
RAILLERIES
RAILLERY
RAILLESS
RAILLIES

RAILLY
RAILMAN
RAILMEN
RAILROAD
RAILROADED
RAILROADING
RAILROADS
RAILS
RAILWAY
RAILWAYS
RAIMENT
RAIMENTS
RAIN
RAINBAND
RAINBANDS
RAINBOW
RAINBOWED
RAINBOWS
RAINBOWY
RAINCHECK
RAINCHECKS
RAINCOAT
RAINCOATS
RAINDROP
RAINDROPS
RAINE
RAINED
RAINES
RAINFALL
RAINFALLS
RAINIER
RAINIEST
RAININESS
RAININESSES
RAINING
RAINLESS
RAINPROOF
RAINPROOFED
RAINPROOFING
RAINPROOFS
RAINS
RAINSTORM
RAINSTORMS
RAINTIGHT
RAINY
RAIRD
RAIRDS
RAISABLE
RAISE
RAISEABLE
RAISED
RAISER
RAISERS
RAISES
RAISIN
RAISING
RAISINGS
RAISINS
RAISONNÉ
RAIT
RAITED
RAITING
RAITS
RAIYAT
RAIYATS
RAJ
RAJA
RAJAH
RAJAHS
RAJAHSHIP

RAJAHSHIPS
RAJAS
RAJASHIP
RAJASHIPS
RAJES
RAKE
RAKED
RAKEE
RAKEES
RAKEHELL
RAKEHELLS
RAKEHELLY
RAKER
RAKERIES
RAKERS
RAKERY
RAKES
RAKESHAME
RAKESHAMES
RAKI
RAKING
RAKINGS
RAKIS
RAKISH
RAKISHLY
RAKSHAS
RAKSHASA
RAKSHASAS
RAKSHASES
RALE
RÂLE
RALES
RÂLES
RALLIED
RALLIER
RALLIERS
RALLIES
RALLINE
RALLY
RALLYE
RALLYES
RALLYING
RALLYINGS
RALLYIST
RALLYISTS
RAM
RAMAKIN
RAMAKINS
RAMAL
RAMATE
RAMBLE
RAMBLED
RAMBLER
RAMBLERS
RAMBLES
RAMBLING
RAMBLINGS
RAMBUTAN
RAMBUTANS
RAMCAT
RAMCATS
RAMEAL
RAMEE
RAMEES
RAMEKIN
RAMEKINS
RAMENTA
RAMENTUM
RAMEOUS
RAMEQUIN

RAMEQUINS
RAMFEEZLE
RAMFEEZLED
RAMFEEZLES
RAMFEEZLING
RAMI
RAMIE
RAMIES
RAMIFIED
RAMIFIES
RAMIFORM
RAMIFY
RAMIFYING
RAMIS
RAMMED
RAMMER
RAMMERS
RAMMIES
RAMMING
RAMMISH
RAMMY
RAMOSE
RAMOUS
RAMP
RAMPAGE
RAMPAGED
RAMPAGES
RAMPAGING
RAMPANCIES
RAMPANCY
RAMPANT
RAMPANTLY
RAMPART
RAMPARTED
RAMPARTING
RAMPARTS
RAMPAUGE
RAMPAUGED
RAMPAUGES
RAMPAUGING
RAMPED
RAMPER
RAMPERS
RAMPICK
RAMPICKED
RAMPICKS
RAMPIKE
RAMPIKES
RAMPING
RAMPION
RAMPIONS
RAMPIRE
RAMPIRED
RAMPIRES
RAMPS
RAMPSMAN
RAMPSMEN
RAMROD
RAMRODS
RAMS
RAMSON
RAMSONS
RAMSTAM
RAMULAR
RAMULI
RAMULOSE
RAMULOUS
RAMULUS
RAMUS
RAN

RANA
RANARIAN
RANARIUM
RANARIUMS
RANAS
RANCE
RANCED
RANCEL
RANCELS
RANCES
RANCH
RANCHED
RANCHER
RANCHERIA
RANCHERIAS
RANCHERO
RANCHEROS
RANCHERS
RANCHES
RANCHING
RANCHINGS
RANCHMAN
RANCHMEN
RANCHO
RANCHOS
RANCID
RANCIDER
RANCIDEST
RANCIDITIES
RANCIDITY
RANCING
RANCOR
RANCOROUS
RANCORS
RANCOUR
RANCOURS
RAND
RANDAN
RANDANS
RANDED
RANDEM
RANDEMS
RANDIE
RANDIER
RANDIES
RANDIEST
RANDING
RANDOM
RANDOMISE
RANDOMISED
RANDOMISES
RANDOMISING
RANDOMIZE
RANDOMIZED
RANDOMIZES
RANDOMIZING
RANDOMLY
RANDOMS
RANDON
RANDONS
RANDS
RANDY
RANEE
RANEES
RANG
RANGE
RANGED
RANGELAND
RANGELANDS
RANGER

RANGERS
RANGES
RANGIER
RANGIEST
RANGINESS
RANGINESSES
RANGING
RANGY
RANI
RANIFORM
RANINE
RANIS
RANK
RANKE
RANKED
RANKER
RANKERS
RANKES
RANKEST
RANKING
RANKINGS
RANKLE
RANKLED
RANKLES
RANKLING
RANKLY
RANKNESS
RANKNESSES
RANKS
RANSACK
RANSACKED
RANSACKER
RANSACKERS
RANSACKING
RANSACKS
RANSEL
RANSELS
RANSHAKLE
RANSHAKLED
RANSHAKLES
RANSHAKLING
RANSOM
RANSOMED
RANSOMER
RANSOMERS
RANSOMING
RANSOMS
RANT
RANTED
RANTER
RANTERISM
RANTERISMS
RANTERS
RANTING
RANTINGLY
RANTIPOLE
RANTIPOLED
RANTIPOLES
RANTIPOLING
RANTS
RANULA
RANULAS
RANUNCULI
RANZEL
RANZELMAN
RANZELMEN
RANZELS
RAP
RAPACIOUS
RAPACITIES

RAPACITY
RAPE
RAPED
RAPER
RAPERS
RAPES
RAPHANIA
RAPHANIAS
RAPHE
RAPHES
RAPHIA
RAPHIAS
RAPHIDE
RAPHIDES
RAPHIS
RAPID
RAPIDER
RAPIDEST
RAPIDITIES
RAPIDITY
RAPIDLY
RAPIDNESS
RAPIDNESSES
RAPIDS
RAPIER
RAPIERS
RAPINE
RAPINES
RAPING
RAPIST
RAPISTS
RAPLOCH
RAPLOCHS
RAPPAREE
RAPPAREES
RAPPED
RAPPEE
RAPPEES
RAPPEL
RAPPELLED
RAPPELLING
RAPPELS
RAPPER
RAPPERS
RAPPING
RAPPINGS
RAPPORT
RAPPORTS
RAPS
RAPT
RAPTOR
RAPTORIAL
RAPTORS
RAPTURE
RAPTURED
RAPTURES
RAPTURING
RAPTURISE
RAPTURISED
RAPTURISES
RAPTURISING
RAPTURIST
RAPTURISTS
RAPTURIZE
RAPTURIZED
RAPTURIZES
RAPTURIZING
RAPTUROUS
RARE
RAREBIT

RAREBITS
RAREFIED
RAREFIES
RAREFY
RAREFYING
RARELY
RARENESS
RARENESSES
RARER
RAREST
RARING
RARITIES
RARITY
RAS
RASCAILLE
RASCAILLES
RASCAL
RASCALDOM
RASCALDOMS
RASCALISM
RASCALISMS
RASCALITIES
RASCALITY
RASCALLY
RASCALS
RASCHEL
RASCHELS
RASE
RASED
RASES
RASH
RASHED
RASHER
RASHERS
RASHES
RASHEST
RASHING
RASHLY
RASHNESS
RASHNESSES
RASING
RASORIAL
RASP
RASPATORIES
RASPATORY
RASPBERRIES
RASPBERRY
RASPED
RASPER
RASPERS
RASPIER
RASPIEST
RASPING
RASPINGLY
RASPINGS
RASPS
RASPY
RASSE
RASSES
RAST
RASTA
RASTAFARI
RASTER
RASTERS
RASTRUM
RASTRUMS
RASURE
RASURES
RAT
RATA

RATABLE
RATABLY
RATAFIA
RATAFIAS
RATAN
RATANS
RATAPLAN
RATAPLANS
RATAS
RATBAG
RATBAGS
RATCH
RATCHES
RATCHET
RATCHETS
RATE
RATEABLE
RATEABLY
RATED
RATEL
RATELS
RATEPAYER
RATEPAYERS
RATER
RATERS
RATES
RATFINK
RATFINKS
RATH
RATHE
RATHER
RATHEREST
RATHERIPE
RATHERIPES
RATHERISH
RATHEST
RATHRIPE
RATHRIPES
RATHS
RATIFIED
RATIFIER
RATIFIERS
RATIFIES
RATIFY
RATIFYING
RATINE
RATINES
RATING
RATINGS
RATIO
RATION
RATIONAL
RATIONALE
RATIONALES
RATIONALS
RATIONED
RATIONING
RATIONS
RATIOS
RATITE
RATLIN
RATLINE
RATLINES
RATLING
RATLINGS
RATLINS
RATOON
RATOONED
RATOONER
RATOONERS

RATOONING
RATOONS
RATPACK
RATPACKS
RATPROOF
RATS
RATSBANE
RATSBANES
RATTAN
RATTANS
RATTED
RATTEEN
RATTEENS
RATTEN
RATTENED
RATTENING
RATTENINGS
RATTENS
RATTER
RATTERIES
RATTERS
RATTERY
RATTIER
RATTIEST
RATTING
RATTINGS
RATTISH
RATTLE
RATTLEBAG
RATTLEBAGS
RATTLED
RATTLER
RATTLERS
RATTLES
RATTLIN
RATTLINE
RATTLINES
RATTLING
RATTLINGS
RATTLINS
RATTLY
RATTON
RATTONS
RATTY
RAUCID
RAUCLE
RAUCLER
RAUCLEST
RAUCOUS
RAUCOUSLY
RAUGHT
RAUN
RAUNCH
RAUNCHES
RAUNCHIER
RAUNCHIEST
RAUNCHY
RAUNGE
RAUNS
RAVAGE
RAVAGED
RAVAGER
RAVAGERS
RAVAGES
RAVAGING
RAVE
RAVED
RAVEL
RAVELIN
RAVELINS

RAVELLED
RAVELLING
RAVELLINGS
RAVELMENT
RAVELMENTS
RAVELS
RAVEN
RAVENED
RAVENER
RAVENERS
RAVENING
RAVENOUS
RAVENS
RAVER
RAVERS
RAVES
RAVIN
RAVINE
RAVINED
RAVINES
RAVING
RAVINGLY
RAVINGS
RAVINING
RAVINS
RAVIOLI
RAVIOLIS
RAVISH
RAVISHED
RAVISHER
RAVISHERS
RAVISHES
RAVISHING
RAW
RAWBONE
RAWBONED
RAWER
RAWEST
RAWHEAD
RAWHEADS
RAWHIDE
RAWHIDES
RAWING
RAWINGS
RAWISH
RAWLY
RAWN
RAWNESS
RAWNESSES
RAWNS
RAWS
RAX
RAXED
RAXES
RAXING
RAY
RAYAH
RAYAHS
RAYED
RAYING
RAYLE
RAYLES
RAYLESS
RAYLET
RAYLETS
RAYNE
RAYNES
RAYON
RAYONS
RAYS

RAZE
RAZED
RAZEE
RAZEED
RAZEEING
RAZEES
RAZES
RAZING
RAZMATAZ
RAZMATAZES
RAZMATAZZ
RAZMATAZZES
RAZOR
RAZORABLE
RAZORS
RAZURE
RAZURES
RAZZ
RAZZED
RAZZES
RAZZIA
RAZZIAS
RAZZING
RAZZLE
RAZZLES
RAZZMATAZ
RAZZMATAZES
RE
REABSORB
REABSORBED
REABSORBING
REABSORBS
REACH
REACHABLE
REACHED
REACHER
REACHERS
REACHES
REACHING
REACHLESS
REACQUIRE
REACQUIRED
REACQUIRES
REACQUIRING
REACT
REACTANCE
REACTANCES
REACTANT
REACTANTS
REACTED
REACTING
REACTION
REACTIONS
REACTIVE
REACTOR
REACTORS
REACTS
REACTUATE
REACTUATED
REACTUATES
REACTUATING
READ
READABLE
READABLY
READAPT
READAPTED
READAPTING
READAPTS
READDRESS
READDRESSED

READDRESSES
READDRESSING
READER
READERS
READIED
READIER
READIES
READIEST
READILY
READINESS
READINESSES
READING
READINGS
READJUST
READJUSTED
READJUSTING
READJUSTS
READMIT
READMITS
READMITTED
READMITTING
READOPT
READOPTED
READOPTING
READOPTS
READS
READVANCE
READVANCED
READVANCES
READVANCING
READVISE
READVISED
READVISES
READVISING
READY
READYING
REAEDIFIED
REAEDIFIES
REAEDIFY
REAEDIFYE
REAEDIFYING
REAFFIRM
REAFFIRMED
REAFFIRMING
REAFFIRMS
REAGENCIES
REAGENCY
REAGENT
REAGENTS
REAK
REAKS
REAL
REALER
REALEST
REALGAR
REALGARS
REALIA
REALIGN
REALIGNED
REALIGNING
REALIGNS
REALISE
REALISED
REALISER
REALISERS
REALISES
REALISING
REALISM
REALISMS
REALIST

REALISTIC
REALISTS
REALITIES
REALITY
REALIZE
REALIZED
REALIZER
REALIZERS
REALIZES
REALIZING
REALLIE
REALLIED
REALLIES
REALLOT
REALLOTS
REALLOTTED
REALLOTTING
REALLY
REALLYING
REALM
REALMLESS
REALMS
REALNESS
REALNESSES
REALS
REALTIE
REALTIES
REALTIME
REALTOR
REALTORS
REALTY
REAM
REAME
REAMED
REAMEND
REAMENDED
REAMENDING
REAMENDS
REAMER
REAMERS
REAMES
REAMIER
REAMIEST
REAMING
REAMS
REAMY
REAN
REANIMATE
REANIMATED
REANIMATES
REANIMATING
REANNEX
REANNEXED
REANNEXES
REANNEXING
REANS
REANSWER
REANSWERED
REANSWERING
REANSWERS
REAP
REAPED
REAPER
REAPERS
REAPING
REAPPAREL
REAPPARELLED
REAPPARELLING
REAPPARELS
REAPPEAR

REAPPEARED
REAPPEARING
REAPPEARS
REAPPLIED
REAPPLIES
REAPPLY
REAPPLYING
REAPPOINT
REAPPOINTED
REAPPOINTING
REAPPOINTS
REAPS
REAR
REARED
REARER
REARERS
REARHORSE
REARHORSES
REARING
REARISE
REARISEN
REARISES
REARISING
REARLY
REARM
REARMED
REARMICE
REARMING
REARMOST
REARMOUSE
REARMS
REAROSE
REAROUSAL
REAROUSALS
REAROUSE
REAROUSED
REAROUSES
REAROUSING
REARRANGE
REARRANGED
REARRANGES
REARRANGING
REARREST
REARRESTED
REARRESTING
REARRESTS
REARS
REARWARD
REARWARDS
REASCEND
REASCENDED
REASCENDING
REASCENDS
REASCENT
REASCENTS
REASON
REASONED
REASONER
REASONERS
REASONING
REASONINGS
REASONS
REASSERT
REASSERTED
REASSERTING
REASSERTS
REASSESS
REASSESSED
REASSESSES
REASSESSING

REASSIGN
REASSIGNED
REASSIGNING
REASSIGNS
REASSUME
REASSUMED
REASSUMES
REASSUMING
REASSURE
REASSURED
REASSURER
REASSURERS
REASSURES
REASSURING
REAST
REASTED
REASTIER
REASTIEST
REASTING
REASTS
REASTY
REATA
REATAS
REATE
REATES
REATTACH
REATTACHED
REATTACHES
REATTACHING
REATTAIN
REATTAINED
REATTAINING
REATTAINS
REATTEMPT
REATTEMPTED
REATTEMPTING
REATTEMPTS
REAVE
REAVER
REAVERS
REAVES
REAVING
REAWAKE
REAWAKED
REAWAKEN
REAWAKENED
REAWAKENING
REAWAKENINGS
REAWAKENS
REAWAKES
REAWAKING
REAWOKE
REAWOKEN
REBACK
REBACKED
REBACKING
REBACKS
REBAPTISE
REBAPTISED
REBAPTISES
REBAPTISING
REBAPTISM
REBAPTISMS
REBAPTIZE
REBAPTIZED
REBAPTIZES
REBAPTIZING
REBATE
REBATED
REBATER

REBATERS
REBATES
REBATING
REBATO
REBATOES
REBEC
REBECK
REBECKS
REBECS
REBEL
REBELDOM
REBELDOMS
REBELLED
REBELLER
REBELLERS
REBELLING
REBELLION
REBELLIONS
REBELLOW
REBELLOWED
REBELLOWING
REBELLOWS
REBELS
REBID
REBIDDING
REBIDS
REBIND
REBINDING
REBINDS
REBIRTH
REBIRTHS
REBIT
REBITE
REBITES
REBITING
REBITTEN
REBLOOM
REBLOOMED
REBLOOMING
REBLOOMS
REBLOSSOM
REBLOSSOMED
REBLOSSOMING
REBLOSSOMS
REBOANT
REBOATION
REBOATIONS
REBOIL
REBOILED
REBOILING
REBOILS
REBORE
REBORED
REBORES
REBORING
REBORN
REBOUND
REBOUNDED
REBOUNDING
REBOUNDS
REBRACE
REBRACED
REBRACES
REBRACING
REBUFF
REBUFFED
REBUFFING
REBUFFS
REBUILD
REBUILDING

REBUILDS
REBUILT
REBUKABLE
REBUKE
REBUKED
REBUKEFUL
REBUKER
REBUKERS
REBUKES
REBUKING
REBURIAL
REBURIALS
REBURIED
REBURIES
REBURY
REBURYING
REBUS
REBUSES
REBUT
REBUTMENT
REBUTMENTS
REBUTS
REBUTTAL
REBUTTALS
REBUTTED
REBUTTER
REBUTTERS
REBUTTING
REBUTTON
REBUTTONED
REBUTTONING
REBUTTONS
RECAL
RECALESCE
RECALESCED
RECALESCES
RECALESCING
RECALL
RECALLED
RECALLING
RECALLS
RECALMENT
RECALMENTS
RECALS
RECANT
RECANTED
RECANTER
RECANTERS
RECANTING
RECANTS
RECAP
RECAPPED
RECAPPING
RECAPS
RECAPTION
RECAPTIONS
RECAPTOR
RECAPTORS
RECAPTURE
RECAPTURED
RECAPTURES
RECAPTURING
RECAST
RECASTING
RECASTS
RECATCH
RECATCHES
RECATCHING
RECAUGHT
RECCE

RECCED
RECCEED
RECCEING
RECCES
RECCIED
RECCIES
RECCO
RECCOS
RECCY
RECCYING
RECEDE
RECEDED
RECEDES
RECEDING
RECEIPT
RECEIPTED
RECEIPTING
RECEIPTS
RECEIVAL
RECEIVALS
RECEIVE
RECEIVED
RECEIVER
RECEIVERS
RECEIVES
RECEIVING
RECEIVINGS
RECENCIES
RECENCY
RECENSE
RECENSED
RECENSES
RECENSING
RECENSION
RECENSIONS
RECENT
RECENTER
RECENTEST
RECENTLY
RECENTRE
RECENTRED
RECENTRES
RECENTRING
RECEPT
RECEPTION
RECEPTIONS
RECEPTIVE
RECEPTOR
RECEPTORS
RECEPTS
RECESS
RECESSED
RECESSES
RECESSING
RECESSION
RECESSIONS
RECESSIVE
RECHARGE
RECHARGED
RECHARGES
RECHARGING
RECHART
RECHARTED
RECHARTER
RECHARTERED
RECHARTERING
RECHARTERS
RECHARTING
RECHARTS
RECHATE

RECHATES
RÉCHAUFFÉ
RÉCHAUFFÉS
RECHEAT
RECHEATS
RECHECK
RECHECKED
RECHECKING
RECHECKS
RECHERCHÉ
RECHIE
RECHLESSE
RECIPE
RECIPES
RECIPIENT
RECIPIENTS
RECISION
RECISIONS
RÉCIT
RECITAL
RECITALS
RECITE
RECITED
RECITER
RECITERS
RECITES
RECITING
RÉCITS
RECK
RECKAN
RECKED
RECKING
RECKLESS
RECKLING
RECKLINGS
RECKON
RECKONED
RECKONER
RECKONERS
RECKONING
RECKONINGS
RECKONS
RECKS
RECLAIM
RECLAIMED
RECLAIMER
RECLAIMERS
RECLAIMING
RECLAIMS
RÉCLAME
RÉCLAMES
RECLIMB
RECLIMBED
RECLIMBING
RECLIMBS
RECLINATE
RECLINE
RECLINED
RECLINER
RECLINERS
RECLINES
RECLINING
RECLOSE
RECLOSED
RECLOSES
RECLOSING
RECLOTHE
RECLOTHED
RECLOTHES
RECLOTHING

RECLUSE
RECLUSELY
RECLUSES
RECLUSION
RECLUSIONS
RECLUSIVE
RECLUSORIES
RECLUSORY
RECOGNISE
RECOGNISED
RECOGNISES
RECOGNISING
RECOGNIZE
RECOGNIZED
RECOGNIZES
RECOGNIZING
RECOIL
RECOILED
RECOILER
RECOILERS
RECOILING
RECOILS
RECOINAGE
RECOINAGES
RECOLLECT
RECOLLECTED
RECOLLECTING
RECOLLECTS
RÉCOLLET
RÉCOLLETS
RECOMBINE
RECOMBINED
RECOMBINES
RECOMBINING
RECOMFORT
RECOMFORTED
RECOMFORTING
RECOMFORTS
RECOMMEND
RECOMMENDED
RECOMMENDING
RECOMMENDS
RECOMMIT
RECOMMITS
RECOMMITTED
RECOMMITTING
RECOMPACT
RECOMPACTED
RECOMPACTING
RECOMPACTS
RECOMPOSE
RECOMPOSED
RECOMPOSES
RECOMPOSING
RECONCILE
RECONCILED
RECONCILES
RECONCILING
RECONDITE
RECONFIRM
RECONFIRMED
RECONFIRMING
RECONFIRMS
RECONNECT
RECONNECTED
RECONNECTING
RECONNECTS
RECONQUER
RECONQUERED
RECONQUERING

RECONQUERS
RECONVENE
RECONVENED
RECONVENES
RECONVENING
RECONVERT
RECONVERTED
RECONVERTING
RECONVERTS
RECONVEY
RECONVEYED
RECONVEYING
RECONVEYS
RECORD
RECORDED
RECORDER
RECORDERS
RECORDING
RECORDINGS
RECORDIST
RECORDISTS
RECORDS
RECOUNT
RECOUNTAL
RECOUNTALS
RECOUNTED
RECOUNTING
RECOUNTS
RECOUP
RECOUPED
RECOUPING
RECOUPS
RECOURE
RECOURSE
RECOURSED
RECOURSES
RECOURSING
RECOVER
RECOVERED
RECOVEREE
RECOVEREES
RECOVERER
RECOVERERS
RECOVERIES
RECOVERING
RECOVEROR
RECOVERORS
RECOVERS
RECOVERY
RECOWER
RECOYLE
RECREANCE
RECREANCES
RECREANCIES
RECREANCY
RECREANT
RECREANTS
RECREATE
RECREATED
RECREATES
RECREATING
RECREMENT
RECREMENTS
RECROSS
RECROSSED
RECROSSES
RECROSSING
RECRUIT
RECRUITAL
RECRUITALS

RECRUITED
RECRUITER
RECRUITERS
RECRUITING
RECRUITS
RECTA
RECTAL
RECTALLY
RECTANGLE
RECTANGLES
RECTI
RECTIFIED
RECTIFIER
RECTIFIERS
RECTIFIES
RECTIFY
RECTIFYING
RECTION
RECTIONS
RECTITIC
RECTITIS
RECTITISES
RECTITUDE
RECTITUDES
RECTO
RECTOR
RECTORAL
RECTORATE
RECTORATES
RECTORESS
RECTORESSES
RECTORIAL
RECTORIALS
RECTORIES
RECTORS
RECTORY
RECTOS
RECTRESS
RECTRESSES
RECTRICES
RECTRIX
RECTUM
RECTUMS
RECTUS
RECUILE
RECULE
RECUMBENT
RECUR
RECURE
RECURED
RECURES
RECURING
RECURRED
RECURRENT
RECURRING
RECURS
RECURSION
RECURSIONS
RECURSIVE
RECURVE
RECURVED
RECURVES
RECURVING
RECUSANCE
RECUSANCES
RECUSANCIES
RECUSANCY
RECUSANT
RECUSANTS
RECUSE

RECUSED
RECUSES
RECUSING
RECYCLE
RECYCLED
RECYCLES
RECYCLING
RED
REDACT
REDACTED
REDACTING
REDACTION
REDACTIONS
REDACTOR
REDACTORS
REDACTS
REDAN
REDANS
REDARGUE
REDARGUED
REDARGUES
REDARGUING
REDBACK
REDBACKS
REDBREAST
REDBREASTS
REDBRICK
REDCOAT
REDCOATS
REDD
REDDED
REDDEN
REDDENDA
REDDENDO
REDDENDOS
REDDENDUM
REDDENED
REDDENING
REDDENS
REDDER
REDDERS
REDDEST
REDDIER
REDDIEST
REDDING
REDDINGS
REDDISH
REDDLE
REDDLED
REDDLEMAN
REDDLEMEN
REDDLES
REDDLING
REDDS
REDDY
REDE
REDEAL
REDEALING
REDEALS
REDEALT
REDECRAFT
REDECRAFTS
REDED
REDEEM
REDEEMED
REDEEMER
REDEEMERS
REDEEMING
REDEEMS
REDEFINE

REDEFINED
REDEFINES
REDEFINING
REDELESS
REDELIVER
REDELIVERED
REDELIVERING
REDELIVERS
REDEPLOY
REDEPLOYED
REDEPLOYING
REDEPLOYS
REDES
REDESCEND
REDESCENDED
REDESCENDING
REDESCENDS
REDESIGN
REDESIGNED
REDESIGNING
REDESIGNS
REDEVELOP
REDEVELOPED
REDEVELOPING
REDEVELOPS
REDEYE
REDEYES
REDFISH
REDFISHES
REDHANDED
REDIA
REDIAE
REDID
REDING
REDINGOTE
REDINGOTES
REDIP
REDIPPED
REDIPPING
REDIPS
REDIRECT
REDIRECTED
REDIRECTING
REDIRECTS
REDISTIL
REDISTILLED
REDISTILLING
REDISTILS
REDIVIDE
REDIVIDED
REDIVIDES
REDIVIDING
REDIVIVUS
REDLEG
REDLEGS
REDLY
REDNECK
REDNECKS
REDNESS
REDNESSES
REDO
REDOES
REDOING
REDOLENCE
REDOLENCES
REDOLENCIES
REDOLENCY
REDOLENT
REDONE
REDOUBLE

REDOUBLED
REDOUBLES
REDOUBLING
REDOUBT
REDOUBTED
REDOUBTING
REDOUBTS
REDOUND
REDOUNDED
REDOUNDING
REDOUNDINGS
REDOUNDS
REDOWA
REDOWAS
REDOX
REDPOLL
REDPOLLS
REDRAFT
REDRAFTED
REDRAFTING
REDRAFTS
REDRAW
REDRAWING
REDRAWN
REDRAWS
REDRESS
REDRESSED
REDRESSER
REDRESSERS
REDRESSES
REDRESSING
REDREW
REDRIVE
REDRIVEN
REDRIVES
REDRIVING
REDROVE
REDS
REDSEAR
REDSHANK
REDSHANKS
REDSHARE
REDSHIRE
REDSHORT
REDSKIN
REDSKINS
REDSTART
REDSTARTS
REDSTREAK
REDSTREAKS
REDTOP
REDTOPS
REDUCE
REDUCED
REDUCER
REDUCERS
REDUCES
REDUCIBLE
REDUCING
REDUCTANT
REDUCTANTS
REDUCTASE
REDUCTASES
REDUCTION
REDUCTIONS
REDUCTIVE
REDUIT
REDUITS
REDUNDANT
REDWING

REDWINGS
REDWOOD
REDWOODS
REE
REEBOK
REEBOKS
REECH
REECHED
REECHES
REECHIE
REECHIER
REECHIEST
REECHING
REECHY
REED
REEDE
REEDED
REEDEN
REEDER
REEDERS
REEDES
REEDIER
REEDIEST
REEDINESS
REEDINESSES
REEDING
REEDINGS
REEDLING
REEDLINGS
REEDS
REEDSTOP
REEDSTOPS
REEDY
REEF
REEFED
REEFER
REEFERS
REEFING
REEFINGS
REEFS
REEK
REEKED
REEKIE
REEKIER
REEKIEST
REEKING
REEKS
REEKY
REEL
REELED
REELER
REELERS
REELING
REELINGLY
REELINGS
REELMAN
REELMEN
REELS
REEN
REENS
REES
REEST
REESTED
REESTIER
REESTIEST
REESTING
REESTS
REESTY
REEVE
REEVED

REEVES
REEVING
REF
REFACE
REFACED
REFACES
REFACING
REFASHION
REFASHIONED
REFASHIONING
REFASHIONS
REFECT
REFECTED
REFECTING
REFECTION
REFECTIONS
REFECTORIES
REFECTORY
REFECTS
REFEL
REFELLED
REFELLING
REFELS
REFER
REFERABLE
REFEREE
REFEREED
REFEREEING
REFEREES
REFERENCE
REFERENCED
REFERENCES
REFERENCING
REFERENDA
REFERENT
REFERENTS
REFERRAL
REFERRALS
REFERRED
REFERRING
REFERS
REFFED
REFFING
REFFO
REFFOS
REFIGURE
REFIGURED
REFIGURES
REFIGURING
REFILL
REFILLED
REFILLING
REFILLS
REFINE
REFINED
REFINEDLY
REFINER
REFINERIES
REFINERS
REFINERY
REFINES
REFINING
REFININGS
REFIT
REFITMENT
REFITMENTS
REFITS
REFITTED
REFITTING
REFITTINGS

REFLATE
REFLATED
REFLATES
REFLATING
REFLATION
REFLATIONS
REFLECT
REFLECTED
REFLECTER
REFLECTERS
REFLECTING
REFLECTOR
REFLECTORS
REFLECTS
REFLET
REFLETS
REFLEX
REFLEXED
REFLEXES
REFLEXING
REFLEXION
REFLEXIONS
REFLEXIVE
REFLEXLY
REFLOAT
REFLOATED
REFLOATING
REFLOATS
REFLOW
REFLOWED
REFLOWER
REFLOWERED
REFLOWERING
REFLOWERS
REFLOWING
REFLOWINGS
REFLOWS
REFLUENCE
REFLUENCES
REFLUENT
REFLUX
REFLUXED
REFLUXES
REFLUXING
REFOOT
REFOOTED
REFOOTING
REFOOTS
REFORM
REFORMADE
REFORMADES
REFORMADO
REFORMADOES
REFORMADOS
REFORMED
REFORMER
REFORMERS
REFORMING
REFORMISM
REFORMISMS
REFORMIST
REFORMISTS
REFORMS
REFORTIFIED
REFORTIFIES
REFORTIFY
REFORTIFYING
REFOUND
REFOUNDED
REFOUNDER

REFOUNDERS
REFOUNDING
REFOUNDS
REFRACT
REFRACTED
REFRACTING
REFRACTOR
REFRACTORS
REFRACTS
REFRAIN
REFRAINED
REFRAINING
REFRAINS
REFRAME
REFRAMED
REFRAMES
REFRAMING
REFREEZE
REFREEZES
REFREEZING
REFRESH
REFRESHED
REFRESHEN
REFRESHENED
REFRESHENING
REFRESHENS
REFRESHER
REFRESHERS
REFRESHES
REFRESHING
REFRINGE
REFRINGED
REFRINGES
REFRINGING
REFROZE
REFROZEN
REFS
REFT
REFUEL
REFUELLED
REFUELLING
REFUELS
REFUGE
REFUGED
REFUGEE
REFUGEES
REFUGES
REFUGIA
REFUGING
REFUGIUM
REFULGENT
REFUND
REFUNDED
REFUNDER
REFUNDERS
REFUNDING
REFUNDS
REFURBISH
REFURBISHED
REFURBISHES
REFURBISHING
REFURNISH
REFURNISHED
REFURNISHES
REFURNISHING
REFUSABLE
REFUSAL
REFUSALS
REFUSE
REFUSED

REFUSENIK
REFUSENIKS
REFUSER
REFUSERS
REFUSES
REFUSING
REFUSION
REFUSIONS
REFUSNIK
REFUSNIKS
REFUTABLE
REFUTABLY
REFUTAL
REFUTALS
REFUTE
REFUTED
REFUTER
REFUTERS
REFUTES
REFUTING
REGAIN
REGAINED
REGAINER
REGAINERS
REGAINING
REGAINS
REGAL
REGALE
REGALED
REGALES
REGALIA
REGALIAN
REGALIAS
REGALING
REGALISM
REGALISMS
REGALIST
REGALISTS
REGALITIES
REGALITY
REGALLY
REGALS
REGAR
REGARD
REGARDANT
REGARDED
REGARDER
REGARDERS
REGARDFUL
REGARDING
REGARDS
REGARS
REGATHER
REGATHERED
REGATHERING
REGATHERS
REGATTA
REGATTAS
REGAVE
REGELATE
REGELATED
REGELATES
REGELATING
REGENCE
REGENCES
REGENCIES
REGENCY
REGENT
REGENTS
REGEST

REGESTS
REGGAE
REGGAES
REGICIDAL
REGICIDE
REGICIDES
RÉGIE
RÉGIES
RÉGIME
REGIMEN
REGIMENS
REGIMENT
REGIMENTED
REGIMENTING
REGIMENTS
RÉGIMES
REGIMINAL
REGINA
REGINAE
REGINAL
REGINAS
REGION
REGIONAL
REGIONARY
REGIONS
REGISSEUR
REGISSEURS
REGISTER
REGISTERED
REGISTERING
REGISTERS
REGISTRAR
REGISTRARS
REGISTRIES
REGISTRY
REGIUS
REGIVE
REGIVEN
REGIVES
REGIVING
REGLET
REGLETS
REGMA
REGMATA
REGNAL
REGNANT
REGOLITH
REGOLITHS
REGORGE
REGORGED
REGORGES
REGORGING
REGRADE
REGRADED
REGRADES
REGRADING
REGRANT
REGRANTED
REGRANTING
REGRANTS
REGRATE
REGRATED
REGRATER
REGRATERS
REGRATES
REGRATING
REGRATINGS
REGRATOR
REGRATORS
REGREDE

REGREDED
REGREDES
REGREDING
REGREET
REGREETED
REGREETING
REGREETS
REGRESS
REGRESSED
REGRESSES
REGRESSING
REGRET
REGRETFUL
REGRETS
REGRETTED
REGRETTING
REGRIND
REGRINDING
REGRINDS
REGROUND
REGROUP
REGROUPED
REGROUPING
REGROUPS
REGROWTH
REGROWTHS
REGUERDON
REGUERDONED
REGUERDONING
REGUERDONS
REGULA
REGULAE
REGULAR
REGULARLY
REGULARS
REGULATE
REGULATED
REGULATES
REGULATING
REGULATOR
REGULATORS
REGULINE
REGULISE
REGULISED
REGULISES
REGULISING
REGULIZE
REGULIZED
REGULIZES
REGULIZING
REGULO®
REGULOS®
REGULUS
REGULUSES
REGUR
REGURS
REH
REHANDLE
REHANDLED
REHANDLES
REHANDLING
REHANDLINGS
REHASH
REHASHED
REHASHES
REHASHING
REHEAR
REHEARD
REHEARING
REHEARINGS

REHEARS
REHEARSAL
REHEARSALS
REHEARSE
REHEARSED
REHEARSER
REHEARSERS
REHEARSES
REHEARSING
REHEARSINGS
REHEAT
REHEATED
REHEATER
REHEATERS
REHEATING
REHEATS
REHEEL
REHEELED
REHEELING
REHEELS
REHOBOAM
REHOBOAMS
REHOUSE
REHOUSED
REHOUSES
REHOUSING
REHOUSINGS
REHS
REIF
REIFIED
REIFIES
REIFS
REIFY
REIFYING
REIGN
REIGNED
REIGNING
REIGNS
REIK
REIKS
REILLUME
REILLUMED
REILLUMES
REILLUMING
REIMBURSE
REIMBURSED
REIMBURSES
REIMBURSING
REIMPLANT
REIMPLANTED
REIMPLANTING
REIMPLANTS
REIMPORT
REIMPORTED
REIMPORTING
REIMPORTS
REIMPOSE
REIMPOSED
REIMPOSES
REIMPOSING
REIN
REINDEER
REINDEERS
REINED
REINETTE
REINETTES
REINFORCE
REINFORCED
REINFORCES
REINFORCING

REINFORM
REINFORMED
REINFORMING
REINFORMS
REINFUND
REINFUNDED
REINFUNDING
REINFUNDS
REINFUSE
REINFUSED
REINFUSES
REINFUSING
REINHABIT
REINHABITED
REINHABITING
REINHABITS
REINING
REINLESS
REINS
REINSERT
REINSERTED
REINSERTING
REINSERTS
REINSMAN
REINSMEN
REINSPECT
REINSPECTED
REINSPECTING
REINSPECTS
REINSPIRE
REINSPIRED
REINSPIRES
REINSPIRING
REINSTALL
REINSTALLED
REINSTALLING
REINSTALLS
REINSTATE
REINSTATED
REINSTATES
REINSTATING
REINSURE
REINSURED
REINSURER
REINSURERS
REINSURES
REINSURING
REINTER
REINTERRED
REINTERRING
REINTERS
REINVEST
REINVESTED
REINVESTING
REINVESTS
REINVOLVE
REINVOLVED
REINVOLVES
REINVOLVING
REIRD
REIRDS
REIS
REISES
REISSUE
REISSUED
REISSUES
REISSUING
REIST
REISTAFEL
REISTAFELS

REISTED
REISTIER
REISTIEST
REISTING
REISTS
REISTY
REITER
REITERANT
REITERATE
REITERATED
REITERATES
REITERATING
REITERS
REIVE
REIVER
REIVERS
REIVES
REIVING
REJECT
REJECTED
REJECTER
REJECTERS
REJECTING
REJECTION
REJECTIONS
REJECTIVE
REJECTOR
REJECTORS
REJECTS
REJIG
REJIGGED
REJIGGER
REJIGGERED
REJIGGERING
REJIGGERS
REJIGGING
REJIGS
REJOICE
REJOICED
REJOICER
REJOICERS
REJOICES
REJOICING
REJOICINGS
REJOIN
REJOINDER
REJOINDERS
REJOINED
REJOINING
REJOINS
REJÓN
REJONEO
REJONEOS
REJONES
REJOURN
REJOURNED
REJOURNING
REJOURNS
REJUDGE
REJUDGED
REJUDGES
REJUDGING
REKE
REKED
REKES
REKINDLE
REKINDLED
REKINDLES
REKINDLING
REKING

RELÂCHE
RELÂCHES
RELAID
RELAPSE
RELAPSED
RELAPSER
RELAPSERS
RELAPSES
RELAPSING
RELATE
RELATED
RELATER
RELATERS
RELATES
RELATING
RELATION
RELATIONS
RELATIVAL
RELATIVE
RELATIVES
RELATOR
RELATORS
RELAX
RELAXANT
RELAXANTS
RELAXED
RELAXES
RELAXIN
RELAXING
RELAXINS
RELAY
RELAYED
RELAYING
RELAYS
RELEASE
RELEASED
RELEASEE
RELEASEES
RELEASER
RELEASERS
RELEASES
RELEASING
RELEASOR
RELEASORS
RELEGABLE
RELEGATE
RELEGATED
RELEGATES
RELEGATING
RELENT
RELENTED
RELENTING
RELENTINGS
RELENTS
RELET
RELETS
RELETTING
RELEVANCE
RELEVANCES
RELEVANCIES
RELEVANCY
RELEVANT
RELIABLE
RELIABLY
RELIANCE
RELIANCES
RELIANT
RELIC
RELICS
RELICT

RELICTS
RELIDE
RELIE
RELIED
RELIEF
RELIEFS
RELIER
RELIERS
RELIES
RELIEVE
RELIEVED
RELIEVER
RELIEVERS
RELIEVES
RELIEVING
RELIEVO
RELIEVOS
RELIGHT
RELIGHTING
RELIGHTS
RELIGION
RELIGIONS
RELIGIOSE
RELIGIOSO
RELIGIOUS
RELIGIOUSES
RELINE
RELINED
RELINES
RELINING
RELIQUARIES
RELIQUARY
RELIQUE
RELIQUES
RELIQUIAE
RELISH
RELISHED
RELISHES
RELISHING
RELIT
RELIVE
RELIVED
RELIVER
RELIVERED
RELIVERING
RELIVERS
RELIVES
RELIVING
RELLISH
RELLISHED
RELLISHES
RELLISHING
RELOAD
RELOADED
RELOADING
RELOADS
RELOCATE
RELOCATED
RELOCATES
RELOCATING
RELUCENT
RELUCT
RELUCTANT
RELUCTATE
RELUCTATED
RELUCTATES
RELUCTATING
RELUCTED
RELUCTING
RELUCTS

RELUME
RELUMED
RELUMES
RELUMINE
RELUMINED
RELUMINES
RELUMING
RELUMINING
RELY
RELYING
REM
REMADE
REMADES
REMAIN
REMAINDER
REMAINDERED
REMAINDERING
REMAINDERS
REMAINED
REMAINING
REMAINS
REMAKE
REMAKES
REMAKING
REMAN
REMAND
REMANDED
REMANDING
REMANDS
REMANENCE
REMANENCES
REMANENCIES
REMANENCY
REMANENT
REMANENTS
REMANET
REMANETS
REMANIÉ
REMANIÉS
REMANNED
REMANNING
REMANS
REMARK
REMARKED
REMARKER
REMARKERS
REMARKING
REMARKS
REMARQUÉ
REMARQUED
REMARQUÉS
REMARRIED
REMARRIES
REMARRY
REMARRYING
REMATCH
REMATCHED
REMATCHES
REMATCHING
REMBLAI
REMBLAIS
REMBLE
REMBLED
REMBLES
REMBLING
REMEAD
REMEADED
REMEADING
REMEADS
REMEASURE

REMEASURED
REMEASURES
REMEASURING
REMEDE
REMEDED
REMEDES
REMEDIAL
REMEDIAT
REMEDIATE
REMEDIED
REMEDIES
REMEDING
REMEDY
REMEDYING
REMEID
REMEIDED
REMEIDING
REMEIDS
REMEMBER
REMEMBERED
REMEMBERING
REMEMBERS
REMEN
REMENS
REMERCIED
REMERCIES
REMERCY
REMERCYING
REMERGE
REMERGED
REMERGES
REMERGING
REMEX
REMIGATE
REMIGATED
REMIGATES
REMIGATING
REMIGES
REMIGIAL
REMIGRATE
REMIGRATED
REMIGRATES
REMIGRATING
REMIND
REMINDED
REMINDER
REMINDERS
REMINDFUL
REMINDING
REMINDS
REMINISCE
REMINISCED
REMINISCES
REMINISCING
REMISE
REMISED
REMISES
REMISING
REMISS
REMISSION
REMISSIONS
REMISSIVE
REMISSLY
REMISSORY
REMIT
REMITMENT
REMITMENTS
REMITS
REMITTAL
REMITTALS

REMITTED
REMITTEE
REMITTEES
REMITTENT
REMITTER
REMITTERS
REMITTING
REMITTOR
REMITTORS
REMNANT
REMNANTS
REMODEL
REMODELLED
REMODELLING
REMODELS
REMODIFIED
REMODIFIES
REMODIFY
REMODIFYING
REMONTANT
REMONTANTS
REMORA
REMORAS
REMORSE
REMORSES
REMOTE
REMOTELY
REMOTER
REMOTES
REMOTEST
REMOTION
REMOTIONS
REMOUD
REMOULADE
RÉMOULADE
REMOULADES
RÉMOULADES
REMOULD
REMOULDED
REMOULDING
REMOULDS
REMOUNT
REMOUNTED
REMOUNTING
REMOUNTS
REMOVABLE
REMOVABLY
REMOVAL
REMOVALS
REMOVE
REMOVED
REMOVER
REMOVERS
REMOVES
REMOVING
REMS
REMUAGE
REMUAGES
REMUDA
REMUDAS
REMUEUR
REMUEURS
REMURMUR
REMURMURED
REMURMURING
REMURMURS
REN
RENAGUE
RENAGUED
RENAGUES

RENAGUING
RENAL
RENAME
RENAMED
RENAMES
RENAMING
RENASCENT
RENAY
RENAYED
RENAYING
RENAYS
RENCONTRE
RENCONTRED
RENCONTRES
RENCONTRING
REND
RENDER
RENDERED
RENDERER
RENDERERS
RENDERING
RENDERINGS
RENDERS
RENDING
RENDITION
RENDITIONS
RENDS
RENDZINA
RENDZINAS
RENEGADE
RENEGADED
RENEGADES
RENEGADING
RENEGADO
RENEGADOS
RENEGATE
RENEGATES
RENEGE
RENEGED
RENEGER
RENEGERS
RENEGES
RENEGING
RENEGUE
RENEGUED
RENEGUER
RENEGUERS
RENEGUES
RENEGUING
RENEW
RENEWABLE
RENEWAL
RENEWALS
RENEWED
RENEWER
RENEWERS
RENEWING
RENEWINGS
RENEWS
RENEY
RENEYED
RENEYING
RENEYS
RENFIERST
RENFORCE
RENFORCED
RENFORCING
RENFORST
RENGA

RENGAS
RENIED
RENIES
RENIFORM
RENIG
RENIGGED
RENIGGING
RENIGS
RENIN
RENINS
RENITENCIES
RENITENCY
RENITENT
RENMINBI
RENMINBIS
RENNE
RENNED
RENNES
RENNET
RENNETS
RENNIN
RENNING
RENNINGS
RENNINS
RENOUNCE
RENOUNCED
RENOUNCER
RENOUNCERS
RENOUNCES
RENOUNCING
RENOVATE
RENOVATED
RENOVATES
RENOVATING
RENOVATOR
RENOVATORS
RENOWN
RENOWNED
RENOWNER
RENOWNERS
RENOWNING
RENOWNS
RENS
RENT
RENTABLE
RENTAL
RENTALLER
RENTALLERS
RENTALS
RENTE
RENTED
RENTER
RENTERS
RENTES
RENTIER
RENTIERS
RENTING
RENTS
RENUMBER
RENUMBERED
RENUMBERING
RENUMBERS
RENVERSE
RENVERSED
RENVERSES
RENVERSING
RENVERST
RENVOI
RENVOIS
RENVOY

RENVOYS
RENY
RENYING
REOCCUPIED
REOCCUPIES
REOCCUPY
REOCCUPYING
REOFFEND
REOFFENDED
REOFFENDING
REOFFENDS
REOPEN
REOPENED
REOPENER
REOPENERS
REOPENING
REOPENS
REORDAIN
REORDAINED
REORDAINING
REORDAINS
REORDER
REORDERED
REORDERING
REORDERS
REORIENT
REORIENTED
REORIENTING
REORIENTS
REP
REPACK
REPACKED
REPACKING
REPACKS
REPAID
REPAINT
REPAINTED
REPAINTING
REPAINTINGS
REPAINTS
REPAIR
REPAIRED
REPAIRER
REPAIRERS
REPAIRING
REPAIRMAN
REPAIRMEN
REPAIRS
REPAND
REPAPER
REPAPERED
REPAPERING
REPAPERS
REPARABLE
REPARABLY
REPARTEE
REPARTEED
REPARTEEING
REPARTEES
REPASS
REPASSAGE
REPASSAGES
REPASSED
REPASSES
REPASSING
REPAST
REPASTED
REPASTING
REPASTS
REPASTURE

REPASTURES
REPAY
REPAYABLE
REPAYING
REPAYMENT
REPAYMENTS
REPAYS
REPEAL
REPEALED
REPEALER
REPEALERS
REPEALING
REPEALS
REPEAT
REPEATED
REPEATER
REPEATERS
REPEATING
REPEATINGS
REPEATS
REPECHAGE
REPEL
REPELLANT
REPELLANTS
REPELLED
REPELLENT
REPELLENTS
REPELLER
REPELLERS
REPELLING
REPELS
REPENT
REPENTANT
REPENTANTS
REPENTED
REPENTER
REPENTERS
REPENTING
REPENTS
REPEOPLE
REPEOPLED
REPEOPLES
REPEOPLING
REPERCUSS
REPERCUSSED
REPERCUSSES
REPERCUSSING
REPERTORIES
REPERTORY
REPERUSAL
REPERUSALS
REPERUSE
REPERUSED
REPERUSES
REPERUSING
REPETEND
REPETENDS
REPHRASE
REPHRASED
REPHRASES
REPHRASING
REPINE
REPINED
REPINER
REPINERS
REPINES
REPINING
REPININGS
REPIQUE
REPIQUED

REPIQUES	REPOS	REPRINTED	REPUGNS	REQUOYLE
REPIQUING	REPOSAL	REPRINTING	REPULP	RERADIATE
REPLA	REPOSALL	REPRINTS	REPULPED	RERADIATED
REPLACE	REPOSALLS	REPRISAL	REPULPING	RERADIATES
REPLACED	REPOSALS	REPRISALS	REPULPS	RERADIATING
REPLACER	REPOSE	REPRISE	REPULSE	RERAIL
REPLACERS	REPOSED	REPRISED	REPULSED	RERAILED
REPLACES	REPOSEDLY	REPRISES	REPULSES	RERAILING
REPLACING	REPOSEFUL	REPRISING	REPULSING	RERAILS
REPLAN	REPOSES	REPRIVE	REPULSION	RERAN
REPLANNED	REPOSING	REPRIZE	REPULSIONS	REREAD
REPLANNING	REPOSIT	REPRIZED	REPULSIVE	REREADING
REPLANS	REPOSITED	REPRIZES	REPURE	REREADS
REPLANT	REPOSITING	REPRIZING	REPURED	REREBRACE
REPLANTED	REPOSITOR	REPRO	REPURES	REREBRACES
REPLANTING	REPOSITORS	REPROACH	REPURIFIED	REREDORSE
REPLANTS	REPOSITS	REPROACHED	REPURIFIES	REREDORSES
REPLAY	REPOSSESS	REPROACHES	REPURIFY	REREDOS
REPLAYED	REPOSSESSED	REPROACHING	REPURIFYING	REREDOSES
REPLAYING	REPOSSESSES	REPROBACIES	REPURING	REREDOSSE
REPLAYS	REPOSSESSING	REPROBACY	REPUTABLE	REREDOSSES
REPLENISH	REPOST	REPROBATE	REPUTABLY	REREMICE
REPLENISHED	REPOSTED	REPROBATED	REPUTE	REREMOUSE
REPLENISHES	REPOSTING	REPROBATES	REPUTED	REREVISE
REPLENISHING	REPOSTS	REPROBATING	REPUTEDLY	REREVISED
REPLETE	REPOSURE	REPROCESS	REPUTES	REREVISES
REPLETED	REPOSURES	REPROCESSED	REPUTING	REREVISING
REPLETES	REPOT	REPROCESSES	REPUTINGS	REREWARD
REPLETING	REPOTS	REPROCESSING	REQUERE	REREWARDS
REPLETION	REPOTTED	REPRODUCE	REQUERED	REROUTE
REPLETIONS	REPOTTING	REPRODUCED	REQUERES	REROUTED
REPLEVIED	REPOTTINGS	REPRODUCES	REQUERING	REROUTES
REPLEVIES	REPOUSSÉ	REPRODUCING	REQUEST	REROUTING
REPLEVIN	REPOUSSÉS	REPROOF	REQUESTED	RERUN
REPLEVINED	REPP	REPROOFED	REQUESTER	RERUNNING
REPLEVINING	REPPED	REPROOFING	REQUESTERS	RERUNS
REPLEVINS	REPPING	REPROOFS	REQUESTING	RES
REPLEVY	REPPS	REPROS	REQUESTS	RESAID
REPLEVYING	REPREEVE	REPROVAL	REQUICKEN	RESALE
REPLICA	REPREHEND	REPROVALS	REQUICKENED	RESALES
REPLICAS	REPREHENDED	REPROVE	REQUICKENING	RESALGAR
REPLICATE	REPREHENDING	REPROVED	REQUICKENS	RESALGARS
REPLICATED	REPREHENDS	REPROVER	REQUIEM	RESALUTE
REPLICATES	REPRESENT	REPROVERS	REQUIEMS	RESALUTED
REPLICATING	REPRESENTED	REPROVES	REQUIGHT	RESALUTES
REPLIED	REPRESENTING	REPROVING	REQUIRE	RESALUTING
REPLIER	REPRESENTS	REPROVINGS	REQUIRED	RESAT
REPLIERS	REPRESS	REPRYVE	REQUIRER	RESAY
REPLIES	REPRESSED	REPS	REQUIRERS	RESAYING
REPLUM	REPRESSES	REPTANT	REQUIRES	RESAYS
REPLY	REPRESSING	REPTATION	REQUIRING	RESCALE
REPLYING	REPRESSOR	REPTATIONS	REQUIRINGS	RESCALED
REPO	REPRESSORS	REPTILE	REQUISITE	RESCALES
REPOINT	REPRIEFE	REPTILES	REQUISITES	RESCALING
REPOINTED	REPRIEFES	REPTILIAN	REQUIT	RESCIND
REPOINTING	REPRIEVAL	REPTILOID	REQUITAL	RESCINDED
REPOINTS	REPRIEVALS	REPUBLIC	REQUITALS	RESCINDING
REPONE	REPRIEVE	REPUBLICS	REQUITE	RESCINDS
REPONED	REPRIEVED	REPUBLISH	REQUITED	RESCORE
REPONES	REPRIEVES	REPUBLISHED	REQUITER	RESCORED
REPONING	REPRIEVING	REPUBLISHES	REQUITERS	RESCORES
REPORT	REPRIMAND	REPUBLISHING	REQUITES	RESCORING
REPORTAGE	REPRIMANDED	REPUDIATE	REQUITING	RESCRIPT
REPORTAGES	REPRIMANDING	REPUDIATED	REQUITS	RESCRIPTED
REPORTED	REPRIMANDS	REPUDIATES	REQUITTED	RESCRIPTING
REPORTER	REPRIME	REPUDIATING	REQUITTING	RESCRIPTS
REPORTERS	REPRIMED	REPUGN	REQUOTE	RESCUABLE
REPORTING	REPRIMES	REPUGNANT	REQUOTED	RESCUE
REPORTINGS	REPRIMING	REPUGNED	REQUOTES	RESCUED
REPORTS	REPRINT	REPUGNING	REQUOTING	RESCUER

RESCUERS
RESCUES
RESCUING
RESEAL
RESEALED
RESEALING
RESEALS
RESEARCH
RESEARCHED
RESEARCHES
RESEARCHING
RESEAT
RESEATED
RESEATING
RESEATS
RÉSEAU
RÉSEAUS
RÉSEAUX
RESECT
RESECTED
RESECTING
RESECTION
RESECTIONS
RESECTS
RESEDA
RESEDAS
RESEIZE
RESEIZED
RESEIZES
RESEIZING
RESELECT
RESELECTED
RESELECTING
RESELECTS
RESELL
RESELLING
RESELLS
RESEMBLE
RESEMBLED
RESEMBLER
RESEMBLERS
RESEMBLES
RESEMBLING
RESENT
RESENTED
RESENTER
RESENTERS
RESENTFUL
RESENTING
RESENTIVE
RESENTS
RESERPINE
RESERPINES
RESERVE
RESERVED
RESERVES
RESERVING
RESERVIST
RESERVISTS
RESERVOIR
RESERVOIRED
RESERVOIRING
RESERVOIRS
RESET
RESETS
RESETTER
RESETTERS
RESETTING
RESETTLE
RESETTLED

RESETTLES
RESETTLING
RESHAPE
RESHAPED
RESHAPES
RESHAPING
RESHIP
RESHIPPED
RESHIPPING
RESHIPS
RESHUFFLE
RESHUFFLED
RESHUFFLES
RESHUFFLING
RESIANCE
RESIANCES
RESIANT
RESIANTS
RESIDE
RESIDED
RESIDENCE
RESIDENCES
RESIDENCIES
RESIDENCY
RESIDENT
RESIDENTS
RESIDER
RESIDERS
RESIDES
RESIDING
RESIDUA
RESIDUAL
RESIDUALS
RESIDUARY
RESIDUE
RESIDUES
RESIDUOUS
RESIDUUM
RESIGN
RESIGNED
RESIGNER
RESIGNERS
RESIGNING
RESIGNS
RESILE
RESILED
RESILES
RESILIENT
RESILING
RESIN
RESINATA
RESINATAS
RESINATE
RESINATES
RESINED
RESINER
RESINERS
RESINIFIED
RESINIFIES
RESINIFY
RESINIFYING
RESINING
RESINISE
RESINISED
RESINISES
RESINISING
RESINIZE
RESINIZED
RESINIZES
RESINIZING

RESINOID
RESINOIDS
RESINOSES
RESINOSIS
RESINOUS
RESINS
RESIST
RESISTANT
RESISTANTS
RESISTED
RESISTENT
RESISTENTS
RESISTING
RESISTIVE
RESISTOR
RESISTORS
RESISTS
RESIT
RESITS
RESITTING
RESKEW
RESKUE
RESNATRON
RESNATRONS
RESOLD
RESOLE
RESOLED
RESOLES
RESOLING
RESOLUBLE
RESOLUTE
RESOLUTES
RESOLVE
RESOLVED
RESOLVENT
RESOLVENTS
RESOLVER
RESOLVERS
RESOLVES
RESOLVING
RESONANCE
RESONANCES
RESONANT
RESONATE
RESONATED
RESONATES
RESONATING
RESONATOR
RESONATORS
RESORB
RESORBED
RESORBENT
RESORBING
RESORBS
RESORCIN
RESORCINS
RESORT
RESORTED
RESORTER
RESORTERS
RESORTING
RESORTS
RESOUND
RESOUNDED
RESOUNDING
RESOUNDS
RESOURCE
RESOURCED
RESOURCES
RESOURCING

RESPEAK
RESPEAKING
RESPEAKS
RESPECT
RESPECTED
RESPECTER
RESPECTERS
RESPECTING
RESPECTS
RESPELL
RESPELLED
RESPELLING
RESPELLS
RESPELT
RESPIRE
RESPIRED
RESPIRES
RESPIRING
RESPITE
RESPITED
RESPITES
RESPITING
RESPLEND
RESPLENDED
RESPLENDING
RESPLENDS
RESPOKE
RESPOKEN
RESPOND
RESPONDED
RESPONDER
RESPONDERS
RESPONDING
RESPONDS
RESPONSA
RESPONSE
RESPONSER
RESPONSERS
RESPONSES
RESPONSOR
RESPONSORS
RESPONSUM
RESPONSUMS
RESPRAY
RESPRAYED
RESPRAYING
RESSALDAR
RESSALDARS
REST
RESTAFF
RESTAFFED
RESTAFFING
RESTAFFS
RESTAGE
RESTAGED
RESTAGES
RESTAGING
RESTART
RESTARTED
RESTARTER
RESTARTERS
RESTARTING
RESTARTS
RESTATE
RESTATED
RESTATES
RESTATING
RESTED
RESTEM

RESTEMMED
RESTEMMING
RESTEMS
RESTER
RESTERS
RESTFUL
RESTFULLER
RESTFULLEST
RESTFULLY
RESTIER
RESTIEST
RESTIFF
RESTIFORM
RESTING
RESTINGS
RESTITUTE
RESTITUTED
RESTITUTES
RESTITUTING
RESTIVE
RESTIVELY
RESTLESS
RESTOCK
RESTOCKED
RESTOCKING
RESTOCKS
RESTORE
RESTORED
RESTORER
RESTORERS
RESTORES
RESTORING
RESTRAIN
RESTRAINED
RESTRAINING
RESTRAININGS
RESTRAINS
RESTRAINT
RESTRAINTS
RESTRICT
RESTRICTED
RESTRICTING
RESTRICTS
RESTRING
RESTRINGE
RESTRINGED
RESTRINGEING
RESTRINGES
RESTRINGING
RESTRINGS
RESTRUNG
RESTS
RESTY
RESTYLE
RESTYLED
RESTYLES
RESTYLING
RESUBMIT
RESUBMITS
RESUBMITTED
RESUBMITTING
RESULT
RESULTANT
RESULTANTS
RESULTED
RESULTFUL
RESULTING
RESULTS
RESUMABLE
RESUME

RÉSUMÉ
RESUMED
RESUMES
RÉSUMÉS
RESUMING
RESUPINE
RESURGE
RESURGED
RESURGENT
RESURGES
RESURGING
RESURRECT
RESURRECTED
RESURRECTING
RESURRECTS
RESURVEY
RESURVEYED
RESURVEYING
RESURVEYS
RET
RETABLE
RETABLES
RETAIL
RETAILED
RETAILER
RETAILERS
RETAILING
RETAILS
RETAIN
RETAINED
RETAINER
RETAINERS
RETAINING
RETAINS
RETAKE
RETAKEN
RETAKER
RETAKERS
RETAKES
RETAKING
RETAKINGS
RETALIATE
RETALIATED
RETALIATES
RETALIATING
RETAMA
RETAMAS
RETARD
RETARDANT
RETARDANTS
RETARDATE
RETARDATES
RETARDED
RETARDER
RETARDERS
RETARDING
RETARDS
RETCH
RETCHED
RETCHES
RETCHING
RETCHLESS
RETE
RETELL
RETELLER
RETELLERS
RETELLING
RETELLS
RETENE
RETENES

RETENTION
RETENTIONS
RETENTIVE
RETES
RETEXTURE
RETEXTURED
RETEXTURES
RETEXTURING
RETHINK
RETHINKING
RETHINKS
RETHOUGHT
RETIAL
RETIARII
RETIARIUS
RETIARIUSES
RETIARY
RETICENCE
RETICENCES
RETICENCIES
RETICENCY
RETICENT
RETICLE
RETICLES
RETICULAR
RETICULE
RETICULES
RETICULUM
RETICULUMS
RETIE
RETIED
RETIES
RETIFORM
RETILE
RETILED
RETILES
RETILING
RETINA
RETINAE
RETINAL
RETINAS
RETINITE
RETINITES
RETINITIS
RETINITISES
RETINOL
RETINOLS
RETINUE
RETINUES
RETINULA
RETINULAE
RETINULAR
RETIRACIES
RETIRACY
RETIRAL
RETIRALS
RETIRE
RETIRED
RETIREDLY
RETIREE
RETIREES
RETIRER
RETIRERS
RETIRES
RETIRING
RETITLE
RETITLED
RETITLES
RETITLING
RETOLD

RETOOK
RETOOL
RETOOLED
RETOOLING
RETOOLS
RETORSION
RETORSIONS
RETORT
RETORTED
RETORTER
RETORTERS
RETORTING
RETORTION
RETORTIONS
RETORTIVE
RETORTS
RETOUCH
RETOUCHED
RETOUCHER
RETOUCHERS
RETOUCHES
RETOUCHING
RETOUR
RETOURED
RETOURING
RETOURS
RETRACE
RETRACED
RETRACES
RETRACING
RETRACT
RETRACTED
RETRACTING
RETRACTOR
RETRACTORS
RETRACTS
RETRAICT
RETRAIN
RETRAINED
RETRAINING
RETRAINS
RETRAIT
RETRAITE
RETRAITES
RETRAITS
RETRAITT
RETRAITTS
RETRAL
RETRALLY
RETRATE
RETRATES
RETREAD
RETREADED
RETREADING
RETREADS
RETREAT
RETREATED
RETREATING
RETREATS
RETREE
RETREES
RETRENCH
RETRENCHED
RETRENCHES
RETRENCHING
RETRIAL
RETRIALS
RETRIBUTE
RETRIBUTED
RETRIBUTES

RETRIBUTING
RETRIED
RETRIES
RETRIEVAL
RETRIEVALS
RETRIEVE
RETRIEVED
RETRIEVER
RETRIEVERS
RETRIEVES
RETRIEVING
RETRIEVINGS
RETRIM
RETRIMMED
RETRIMMING
RETRIMS
RETRO
RETROACT
RETROACTED
RETROACTING
RETROACTS
RETROCEDE
RETROCEDED
RETROCEDES
RETROCEDING
RETROD
RETRODDEN
RETROFIT
RETROFITS
RETROFITTED
RETROFITTING
RETROFLEX
RETROJECT
RETROJECTED
RETROJECTING
RETROJECTS
RETRORSE
RETROS
RETROUSSÉ
RETROVERT
RETROVERTED
RETROVERTING
RETROVERTS
RETRY
RETRYING
RETS
RETSINA
RETSINAS
RETTED
RETTERIES
RETTERY
RETTING
RETUND
RETUNDED
RETUNDING
RETUNDS
RETUNE
RETUNED
RETUNES
RETUNING
RETURF
RETURFED
RETURFING
RETURFS
RETURN
RETURNED
RETURNEE
RETURNEES
RETURNING
RETURNS

RETUSE
RETYING
REUNIFIED
REUNIFIES
REUNIFY
REUNIFYING
REUNION
REUNIONS
REUNITE
REUNITED
REUNITES
REUNITING
REURGE
REURGED
REURGES
REURGING
REUSABLE
REUSE
REUSED
REUSES
REUSING
REUTTER
REUTTERED
REUTTERING
REUTTERS
REV
REVALENTA
REVALENTAS
REVALUE
REVALUED
REVALUES
REVALUING
REVAMP
REVAMPED
REVAMPING
REVAMPS
REVANCHE
REVANCHES
REVEAL
REVEALED
REVEALER
REVEALERS
REVEALING
REVEALINGS
REVEALS
REVEILLE
REVEILLES
REVEL
REVELATOR
REVELATORS
REVELLED
REVELLER
REVELLERS
REVELLING
REVELLINGS
REVELRIES
REVELRY
REVELS
REVENANT
REVENANTS
REVENGE
REVENGED
REVENGER
REVENGERS
REVENGES
REVENGING
REVENGINGS
REVENGIVE
REVENUE
REVENUED

REVENUES
REVERABLE
REVERB
REVERBED
REVERBING
REVERBS
REVERE
REVERED
REVERENCE
REVERENCES
REVEREND
REVERENDS
REVERENT
REVERER
REVERERS
REVERES
REVERIE
REVERIES
REVERING
REVERIST
REVERISTS
REVERS
REVERSAL
REVERSALS
REVERSE
REVERSED
REVERSELY
REVERSER
REVERSERS
REVERSES
REVERSI
REVERSING
REVERSINGS
REVERSION
REVERSIONS
REVERSIS
REVERSO
REVERSOS
REVERT
REVERTED
REVERTING
REVERTIVE
REVERTS
REVERY
REVEST
REVESTED
REVESTING
REVESTRIES
REVESTRY
REVESTS
REVET
REVETMENT
REVETMENTS
REVETS
REVETTED
REVETTING
RÊVEUR
RÊVEURS
RÊVEUSE
RÊVEUSES
REVICTUAL
REVICTUALLED
REVICTUALLING
REVICTUALS
REVIE
REVIED
REVIES
REVIEW
REVIEWAL
REVIEWALS

REVIEWED
REVIEWER
REVIEWERS
REVIEWING
REVIEWS
REVILE
REVILED
REVILER
REVILERS
REVILES
REVILING
REVILINGS
REVISABLE
REVISAL
REVISALS
REVISE
REVISED
REVISER
REVISERS
REVISES
REVISING
REVISION
REVISIONS
REVISIT
REVISITED
REVISITING
REVISITS
REVISOR
REVISORS
REVISORY
REVIVABLE
REVIVABLY
REVIVAL
REVIVALS
REVIVE
REVIVED
REVIVER
REVIVERS
REVIVES
REVIVIFIED
REVIVIFIES
REVIVIFY
REVIVIFYING
REVIVING
REVIVINGS
REVIVOR
REVIVORS
REVOCABLE
REVOCABLY
REVOKE
REVOKED
REVOKES
REVOKING
REVOLT
REVOLTED
REVOLTER
REVOLTERS
REVOLTING
REVOLTS
REVOLUTE
REVOLVE
REVOLVED
REVOLVER
REVOLVERS
REVOLVES
REVOLVING
REVOLVINGS
REVS
REVUE
REVUES

REVULSION
REVULSIONS
REVULSIVE
REVVED
REVVING
REVYING
REW
REWARD
REWARDED
REWARDER
REWARDERS
REWARDFUL
REWARDING
REWARDS
REWAREWA
REWAREWAS
REWEIGH
REWEIGHED
REWEIGHING
REWEIGHS
REWIND
REWINDING
REWINDS
REWIRE
REWIRED
REWIRES
REWIRING
REWORD
REWORDED
REWORDING
REWORDS
REWORK
REWORKED
REWORKING
REWORKS
REWOUND
REWRAP
REWRAPPED
REWRAPPING
REWRAPS
REWRITE
REWRITES
REWRITING
REWRITTEN
REWROTE
REWS
REWTH
REWTHS
REX
REYNARD
REYNARDS
RHABDOID
RHABDOIDS
RHABDOM
RHABDOMS
RHABDUS
RHABDUSES
RHACHIDES
RHACHIS
RHACHISES
RHACHITIS
RHACHITISES
RHAMPHOID
RHAPHE
RHAPHES
RHAPHIDE
RHAPHIDES
RHAPHIS
RHAPONTIC
RHAPONTICS

RHAPSODE
RHAPSODES
RHAPSODIC
RHAPSODIES
RHAPSODY
RHATANIES
RHATANY
RHEA
RHEAS
RHEMATIC
RHENIUM
RHENIUMS
RHEOCHORD
RHEOCHORDS
RHEOCORD
RHEOCORDS
RHEOLOGIC
RHEOLOGIES
RHEOLOGY
RHEOMETER
RHEOMETERS
RHEOSTAT
RHEOSTATS
RHEOTAXIS
RHEOTAXISES
RHEOTOME
RHEOTOMES
RHEOTROPE
RHEOTROPES
RHESUS
RHESUSES
RHETOR
RHETORIC
RHETORICS
RHETORISE
RHETORISED
RHETORISES
RHETORISING
RHETORIZE
RHETORIZED
RHETORIZES
RHETORIZING
RHETORS
RHEUM
RHEUMATIC
RHEUMATICS
RHEUMATIZE
RHEUMATIZES
RHEUMED
RHEUMS
RHEUMY
RHEXES
RHEXIS
RHEXISES
RHIME
RHIMES
RHINAL
RHINE
RHINES
RHINITIS
RHINITISES
RHINO
RHINOLITH
RHINOLITHS
RHINOLOGIES
RHINOLOGY
RHINOS
RHIPIDATE
RHIPIDION
RHIPIDIONS

RHIPIDIUM
RHIPIDIUMS
RHIZIC
RHIZINE
RHIZINES
RHIZOBIA
RHIZOBIUM
RHIZOCARP
RHIZOCARPS
RHIZOCAUL
RHIZOCAULS
RHIZOID
RHIZOIDAL
RHIZOIDS
RHIZOME
RHIZOMES
RHIZOPI
RHIZOPOD
RHIZOPODS
RHIZOPUS
RHIZOPUSES
RHO
RHODAMINE
RHODAMINES
RHODANATE
RHODANATES
RHODANIC
RHODANISE
RHODANISED
RHODANISES
RHODANISING
RHODANIZE
RHODANIZED
RHODANIZES
RHODANIZING
RHODIC
RHODIUM
RHODIUMS
RHODOLITE
RHODOLITES
RHODONITE
RHODONITES
RHODOPSIN
RHODOPSINS
RHODORA
RHODORAS
RHODOUS
RHOEADINE
RHOEADINES
RHOMB
RHOMBI
RHOMBIC
RHOMBOI
RHOMBOID
RHOMBOIDS
RHOMBOS
RHOMBS
RHOMBUS
RHOMBUSES
RHONCHAL
RHONCHI
RHONCHIAL
RHONCHUS
RHONE
RHONES
RHOPALIC
RHOPALISM
RHOPALISMS
RHOS
RHOTACISE

RHOTACISED
RHOTACISES
RHOTACISING
RHOTACISM
RHOTACISMS
RHOTACIZE
RHOTACIZED
RHOTACIZES
RHOTACIZING
RHOTIC
RHUBARB
RHUBARBS
RHUBARBY
RHUMB
RHUMBA
RHUMBAS
RHUMBS
RHUS
RHUSES
RHY
RHYME
RHYMED
RHYMELESS
RHYMER
RHYMERS
RHYMES
RHYMESTER
RHYMESTERS
RHYMING
RHYMIST
RHYMISTS
RHYOLITE
RHYOLITES
RHYOLITIC
RHYS
RHYTA
RHYTHM
RHYTHMAL
RHYTHMED
RHYTHMI
RHYTHMIC
RHYTHMICS
RHYTHMING
RHYTHMISE
RHYTHMISED
RHYTHMISES
RHYTHMISING
RHYTHMIST
RHYTHMISTS
RHYTHMIZE
RHYTHMIZED
RHYTHMIZES
RHYTHMIZING
RHYTHMS
RHYTHMUS
RHYTHMUSES
RHYTINA
RHYTINAS
RHYTON
RIA
RIAL
RIALS
RIANCIES
RIANCY
RIANT
RIAS
RIATA
RIATAS
RIB
RIBALD

RIBALDRIES
RIBALDRY
RIBALDS
RIBAND
RIBANDED
RIBANDING
RIBANDS
RIBATTUTA
RIBATTUTAS
RIBAUD
RIBAUDRED
RIBAUDRIES
RIBAUDRY
RIBAUDS
RIBBAND
RIBBANDED
RIBBANDING
RIBBANDS
RIBBED
RIBBIER
RIBBIEST
RIBBING
RIBBINGS
RIBBON
RIBBONED
RIBBONING
RIBBONRIES
RIBBONRY
RIBBONS
RIBBONY
RIBBY
RIBCAGE
RIBCAGES
RIBIBE
RIBIBES
RIBIBLE
RIBIBLES
RIBLESS
RIBLIKE
RIBOSE
RIBOSES
RIBOSOME
RIBOSOMES
RIBS
RIBSTON
RIBSTONE
RIBSTONES
RIBSTONS
RIBWORK
RIBWORKS
RIBWORT
RIBWORTS
RICE
RICED
RICER
RICERCAR
RICERCARE
RICERCARES
RICERCARS
RICERCATA
RICERCATAS
RICERS
RICES
RICEY
RICH
RICHED
RICHEN
RICHENED
RICHENING
RICHENS

RICHER
RICHES
RICHESSE
RICHESSES
RICHEST
RICHING
RICHLY
RICHNESS
RICHNESSES
RICHT
RICHTED
RICHTER
RICHTEST
RICHTING
RICHTS
RICIER
RICIEST
RICIN
RICING
RICINS
RICK
RICKED
RICKER
RICKERS
RICKETILY
RICKETS
RICKETTY
RICKETY
RICKING
RICKLE
RICKLES
RICKLY
RICKS
RICKSHA
RICKSHAS
RICKSHAW
RICKSHAWS
RICKSTAND
RICKSTANDS
RICKSTICK
RICKSTICKS
RICKYARD
RICKYARDS
RICOCHET
RICOCHETED
RICOCHETING
RICOCHETS
RICOCHETTED
RICOCHETTING
RICOTTA
RICOTTAS
RICTAL
RICTUS
RICTUSES
RICY
RID
RIDABLE
RIDDANCE
RIDDANCES
RIDDED
RIDDEN
RIDDER
RIDDERS
RIDDING
RIDDLE
RIDDLED
RIDDLER
RIDDLERS
RIDDLES
RIDDLING

RIDDLINGS
RIDE
RIDEABLE
RIDENT
RIDER
RIDERED
RIDERLESS
RIDERS
RIDES
RIDGE
RIDGEBACK
RIDGEBACKS
RIDGED
RIDGEL
RIDGELS
RIDGES
RIDGEWAY
RIDGEWAYS
RIDGIER
RIDGIEST
RIDGIL
RIDGILS
RIDGING
RIDGINGS
RIDGLING
RIDGLINGS
RIDGY
RIDICULE
RIDICULED
RIDICULER
RIDICULERS
RIDICULES
RIDICULING
RIDING
RIDINGS
RIDOTTO
RIDOTTOS
RIDS
RIEL
RIELS
RIEM
RIEMPIE
RIEMPIES
RIEMS
RIEVE
RIEVER
RIEVERS
RIEVES
RIEVING
RIFE
RIFELY
RIFENESS
RIFENESSES
RIFER
RIFEST
RIFF
RIFFLE
RIFFLED
RIFFLER
RIFFLERS
RIFFLES
RIFFLING
RIFFS
RIFLE
RIFLED
RIFLEMAN
RIFLEMEN
RIFLER
RIFLERS
RIFLES

RIFLING
RIFLINGS
RIFT
RIFTE
RIFTED
RIFTING
RIFTLESS
RIFTS
RIFTY
RIG
RIGADOON
RIGADOONS
RIGG
RIGGALD
RIGGALDS
RIGGED
RIGGER
RIGGERS
RIGGING
RIGGINGS
RIGGISH
RIGGS
RIGHT
RIGHTABLE
RIGHTED
RIGHTEN
RIGHTENED
RIGHTENING
RIGHTENS
RIGHTEOUS
RIGHTER
RIGHTERS
RIGHTEST
RIGHTFUL
RIGHTING
RIGHTINGS
RIGHTIST
RIGHTISTS
RIGHTLESS
RIGHTLY
RIGHTNESS
RIGHTNESSES
RIGHTO
RIGHTOS
RIGHTS
RIGHTWARD
RIGHTWARDS
RIGID
RIGIDER
RIGIDEST
RIGIDIFIED
RIGIDIFIES
RIGIDIFY
RIGIDIFYING
RIGIDISE
RIGIDISED
RIGIDISES
RIGIDISING
RIGIDITIES
RIGIDITY
RIGIDIZE
RIGIDIZED
RIGIDIZES
RIGIDIZING
RIGIDLY
RIGIDNESS
RIGIDNESSES
RIGIDS
RIGLIN
RIGLING

RIGLINGS	RINDY	RIOTOUS	RISIBLE	RIVAGES
RIGLINS	RINE	RIOTOUSLY	RISING	RIVAL
RIGMAROLE	RINES	RIOTRIES	RISINGS	RIVALESS
RIGMAROLES	RING	RIOTRY	RISK	RIVALESSES
RIGOL	RINGBIT	RIOTS	RISKED	RIVALISE
RIGOLL	RINGBITS	RIP	RISKER	RIVALISED
RIGOLLS	RINGBONE	RIPARIAL	RISKERS	RIVALISES
RIGOLS	RINGBONES	RIPARIAN	RISKFUL	RIVALISING
RIGOR	RINGED	RIPARIANS	RISKIER	RIVALITIES
RIGORISM	RINGENT	RIPE	RISKIEST	RIVALITY
RIGORISMS	RINGER	RIPECK	RISKILY	RIVALIZE
RIGORIST	RINGERS	RIPECKS	RISKINESS	RIVALIZED
RIGORISTS	RINGGIT	RIPED	RISKINESSES	RIVALIZES
RIGOROUS	RINGGITS	RIPELY	RISKING	RIVALIZING
RIGORS	RINGHALS	RIPEN	RISKS	RIVALLED
RIGOUR	RINGHALSES	RIPENED	RISKY	RIVALLESS
RIGOURS	RINGING	RIPENESS	RISOLUTO	RIVALLING
RIGS	RINGINGLY	RIPENESSES	RISOTTO	RIVALRIES
RIGWIDDIE	RINGINGS	RIPENING	RISOTTOS	RIVALRY
RIGWIDDIES	RINGLESS	RIPENS	RISP	RIVALS
RIGWOODIE	RINGLET	RIPER	RISPED	RIVALSHIP
RIGWOODIES	RINGLETED	RIPERS	RISPETTI	RIVALSHIPS
RIJSTAFEL	RINGLETS	RIPES	RISPETTO	RIVAS
RIJSTAFELS	RINGMAN	RIPEST	RISPING	RIVE
RILE	RINGMEN	RIPIENI	RISPINGS	RIVED
RILED	RINGS	RIPIENIST	RISPS	RIVEL
RILES	RINGSIDE	RIPIENISTS	RISQUE	RIVELLED
RILEY	RINGSIDER	RIPIENO	RISQUÉ	RIVELLING
RILIEVI	RINGSIDERS	RIPIENOS	RISQUES	RIVELS
RILIEVO	RINGSIDES	RIPING	RISSOLE	RIVEN
RILING	RINGSTAND	RIPOSTE	RISSOLES	RIVER
RILL	RINGSTANDS	RIPOSTED	RISUS	RIVERAIN
RILLE	RINGSTER	RIPOSTES	RISUSES	RIVERAINS
RILLED	RINGSTERS	RIPOSTING	RIT	RIVERED
RILLES	RINGTAIL	RIPP	RITE	RIVERET
RILLET	RINGTAILS	RIPPED	RITELESS	RIVERETS
RILLETS	RINGWAY	RIPPER	RITENUTO	RIVERINE
RILLETTES	RINGWAYS	RIPPERS	RITENUTOS	RIVERLESS
RILLING	RINGWISE	RIPPIER	RITES	RIVERLIKE
RILLMARK	RINGWORK	RIPPIERS	RITORNEL	RIVERMAN
RILLMARKS	RINGWORKS	RIPPING	RITORNELL	RIVERMEN
RILLS	RINGWORM	RIPPINGLY	RITORNELLS	RIVERS
RIM	RINGWORMS	RIPPLE	RITS	RIVERSIDE
RIMA	RINK	RIPPLED	RITT	RIVERSIDES
RIMAE	RINKED	RIPPLER	RITTED	RIVERWAY
RIME	RINKHALS	RIPPLERS	RITTER	RIVERWAYS
RIMED	RINKHALSES	RIPPLES	RITTERS	RIVERWEED
RIMER	RINKING	RIPPLET	RITTING	RIVERWEEDS
RIMERS	RINKS	RIPPLETS	RITTS	RIVERY
RIMES	RINNING	RIPPLIER	RITUAL	RIVES
RIMIER	RINS	RIPPLIEST	RITUALISE	RIVET
RIMIEST	RINSABLE	RIPPLING	RITUALISED	RIVETED
RIMING	RINSE	RIPPLINGS	RITUALISES	RIVETER
RIMLESS	RINSED	RIPPLY	RITUALISING	RIVETERS
RIMMED	RINSER	RIPPS	RITUALISM	RIVETING
RIMMING	RINSERS	RIPRAP	RITUALISMS	RIVETINGS
RIMOSE	RINSES	RIPRAPS	RITUALIST	RIVETS
RIMOUS	RINSIBLE	RIPS	RITUALISTS	RIVETTED
RIMS	RINSING	RIPT	RITUALIZE	RIVETTING
RIMU	RINSINGS	RIPTIDE	RITUALIZED	RIVIERA
RIMUS	RIOT	RIPTIDES	RITUALIZES	RIVIERAS
RIMY	RIOTED	RISALDAR	RITUALIZING	RIVIÈRE
RIN	RIOTER	RISALDARS	RITUALLY	RIVIÈRES
RIND	RIOTERS	RISE	RITUALS	RIVING
RINDED	RIOTING	RISEN	RITZIER	RIVLIN
RINDIER	RIOTINGS	RISER	RITZIEST	RIVLINS
RINDIEST	RIOTISE	RISERS	RITZY	RIVO
RINDING	RIOTISES	RISES	RIVA	RIVOS
RINDLESS	RIOTIZE	RISHI	RIVAGE	RIVULET
RINDS	RIOTIZES	RISHIS	RIVAGE	RIVULETS

RIYAL	ROASTER	ROCKERY	ROESTONE	ROLLMOP
RIYALS	ROASTERS	ROCKET	ROESTONES	ROLLMOPS
RIZ	ROASTING	ROCKETED	ROGATION	ROLLOCK
RIZARD	ROASTINGS	ROCKETEER	ROGATIONS	ROLLOCKS
RIZARDS	ROASTS	ROCKETEERS	ROGATORY	ROLLS
RIZZAR	ROATE	ROCKETER	ROGER	ROM
RIZZARED	ROATED	ROCKETERS	ROGERED	ROMA
RIZZARING	ROATES	ROCKETING	ROGERING	ROMAGE
RIZZARS	ROATING	ROCKETRIES	ROGERS	ROMAGES
RIZZART	ROB	ROCKETRY	ROGUE	ROMAIKA
RIZZARTS	ROBALO	ROCKETS	ROGUED	ROMAIKAS
RIZZER	ROBALOS	ROCKIER	ROGUERIES	ROMAL
RIZZERED	ROBBED	ROCKIERS	ROGUERY	ROMALS
RIZZERING	ROBBER	ROCKIEST	ROGUES	ROMAN
RIZZERS	ROBBERIES	ROCKILY	ROGUESHIP	ROMANCE
RIZZOR	ROBBERS	ROCKINESS	ROGUESHIPS	ROMANCED
RIZZORED	ROBBERY	ROCKINESSES	ROGUING	ROMANCER
RIZZORING	ROBBING	ROCKING	ROGUISH	ROMANCERS
RIZZORS	ROBE	ROCKINGS	ROGUISHLY	ROMANCES
ROACH	ROBED	ROCKLAY	ROGUY	ROMANCING
ROACHED	ROBES	ROCKLAYS	ROIL	ROMANCINGS
ROACHES	ROBIN	ROCKLING	ROILED	ROMANS
ROACHING	ROBING	ROCKLINGS	ROILIER	ROMANTIC
ROAD	ROBINGS	ROCKS	ROILIEST	ROMANTICS
ROADBLOCK	ROBINIA	ROCKWATER	ROILING	ROMAS
ROADBLOCKS	ROBINIAS	ROCKWATERS	ROILS	ROMAUNT
ROADHOUSE	ROBINS	ROCKWEED	ROILY	ROMAUNTS
ROADHOUSES	ROBLE	ROCKWEEDS	ROIN	ROMNEYA
ROADIE	ROBLES	ROCKWORK	ROINISH	ROMNEYAS
ROADIES	ROBORANT	ROCKWORKS	ROINS	ROMP
ROADING	ROBORANTS	ROCKY	ROIST	ROMPED
ROADINGS	ROBOT	ROCOCO	ROISTED	ROMPER
ROADLESS	ROBOTIC	ROCOCOS	ROISTER	ROMPERS
ROADMAN	ROBOTICS	ROCQUET	ROISTERED	ROMPING
ROADMEN	ROBOTISE	ROCQUETS	ROISTERER	ROMPINGLY
ROADS	ROBOTISED	ROCS	ROISTERERS	ROMPISH
ROADSHOW	ROBOTISES	ROD	ROISTERING	ROMPISHLY
ROADSHOWS	ROBOTISING	RODDED	ROISTERS	ROMPS
ROADSIDE	ROBOTIZE	RODDING	ROISTING	RONCADOR
ROADSIDES	ROBOTIZED	RODE	ROISTS	RONCADORS
ROADSMAN	ROBOTIZES	RODED	ROK	RONDACHE
ROADSMEN	ROBOTIZING	RODENT	ROKE	RONDACHES
ROADSTEAD	ROBOTS	RODENTS	ROKED	RONDAVEL
ROADSTEADS	ROBS	RODEO	ROKELAY	RONDAVELS
ROADSTER	ROBURITE	RODEOS	ROKELAYS	RONDE
ROADSTERS	ROBURITES	RODES	ROKER	RONDEAU
ROADWAY	ROBUST	RODEWAY	ROKERS	RONDEAUX
ROADWAYS	ROBUSTA	RODEWAYS	ROKES	RONDEL
ROAM	ROBUSTAS	RODFISHER	ROKIER	RONDELS
ROAMED	ROBUSTER	RODFISHERS	ROKIEST	RONDES
ROAMER	ROBUSTEST	RODING	ROKING	RONDINO
ROAMERS	ROBUSTLY	RODINGS	ROKS	RONDINOS
ROAMING	ROC	RODLESS	ROKY	RONDO
ROAMS	ROCAILLE	RODLIKE	ROLAG	RONDOS
ROAN	ROCAILLES	RODMAN	ROLAGS	RONDURE
ROANS	ROCAMBOLE	RODMEN	RÔLE	RONDURES
ROAR	ROCAMBOLES	RODS	ROLE	RONE
ROARED	ROCH	RODSMAN	RÔLES	RONEO
ROARER	ROCHES	RODSMEN	ROLES	RONEOED
ROARERS	ROCHET	RODSTER	ROLL	RONEOING
ROARIE	ROCHETS	RODSTERS	ROLLABLE	RONEOS
ROARIER	ROCK	ROE	ROLLED	RONES
ROARIEST	ROCKAWAY	ROEBUCK	ROLLER	RONG
ROARING	ROCKAWAYS	ROEBUCKS	ROLLERS	RONGGENG
ROARINGLY	ROCKCRESS	ROED	ROLLICK	RONGGENGS
ROARINGS	ROCKCRESSES	ROEMER	ROLLICKED	RONNE
ROARS	ROCKED	ROEMERS	ROLLICKING	RONNING
ROARY	ROCKER	ROENTGEN	ROLLICKS	RONT
ROAST	ROCKERIES	ROENTGENS	ROLLING	RONTE
ROASTED	ROCKERS	ROES	ROLLINGS	RONTES

RÖNTGEN
RÖNTGENS
RONTS
RONYON
RONYONS
ROO
ROOD
ROODS
ROOF
ROOFED
ROOFER
ROOFERS
ROOFIER
ROOFIEST
ROOFING
ROOFINGS
ROOFLESS
ROOFS
ROOFY
ROOINEK
ROOINEKS
ROOK
ROOKED
ROOKERIES
ROOKERY
ROOKIE
ROOKIER
ROOKIES
ROOKIEST
ROOKING
ROOKISH
ROOKS
ROOKY
ROOM
ROOMED
ROOMER
ROOMERS
ROOMETTE
ROOMETTES
ROOMFUL
ROOMFULS
ROOMIER
ROOMIEST
ROOMILY
ROOMINESS
ROOMINESSES
ROOMING
ROOMS
ROOMSOME
ROOMY
ROON
ROONS
ROOP
ROOPED
ROOPIER
ROOPIEST
ROOPING
ROOPIT
ROOPS
ROOPY
ROOS
ROOSA
ROOSAS
ROOSE
ROOSED
ROOSES
ROOSING
ROOST
ROOSTED
ROOSTER

ROOSTERS
ROOSTING
ROOSTS
ROOT
ROOTAGE
ROOTAGES
ROOTED
ROOTEDLY
ROOTER
ROOTERS
ROOTHOLD
ROOTHOLDS
ROOTIER
ROOTIES
ROOTIEST
ROOTING
ROOTINGS
ROOTLE
ROOTLED
ROOTLES
ROOTLESS
ROOTLET
ROOTLETS
ROOTLIKE
ROOTLING
ROOTS
ROOTSTOCK
ROOTSTOCKS
ROOTY
ROPABLE
ROPE
ROPEABLE
ROPED
ROPER
ROPERIES
ROPERS
ROPERY
ROPES
ROPEWAY
ROPEWAYS
ROPEWORK
ROPEWORKS
ROPEY
ROPIER
ROPIEST
ROPILY
ROPINESS
ROPINESSES
ROPING
ROPINGS
ROPY
ROQUE
ROQUES
ROQUET
ROQUETED
ROQUETING
ROQUETS
ROQUETTE
ROQUETTES
RORAL
RORE
RORES
RORIC
RORID
RORIE
RORIER
RORIEST
RORQUAL
RORQUALS
RORT

RORTER
RORTERS
RORTIER
RORTIEST
RORTS
RORTY
RORY
ROSACE
ROSACEA
ROSACEAS
ROSACEOUS
ROSACES
ROSAKER
ROSAKERS
ROSALIA
ROSALIAS
ROSARIAN
ROSARIANS
ROSARIES
ROSARIUM
ROSARIUMS
ROSARY
ROSCID
ROSE
ROSÉ
ROSEAL
ROSEATE
ROSED
ROSEFISH
ROSEFISHES
ROSELESS
ROSELIKE
ROSELLA
ROSELLAS
ROSELLE
ROSELLES
ROSEMARIES
ROSEMARY
ROSEOLA
ROSEOLAS
ROSERIES
ROSERY
ROSES
ROSÉS
ROSET
ROSETED
ROSETING
ROSETS
ROSETTE
ROSETTED
ROSETTES
ROSETTY
ROSETY
ROSEWOOD
ROSEWOODS
ROSIED
ROSIER
ROSIERE
ROSIERES
ROSIERS
ROSIES
ROSIEST
ROSILY
ROSIN
ROSINATE
ROSINATES
ROSINED
ROSINESS
ROSINESSES
ROSING

ROSINING
ROSINS
ROSINY
ROSIT
ROSITED
ROSITING
ROSITS
ROSITTY
ROSITY
ROSMARINE
ROSMARINES
ROSOGLIO
ROSOGLIOS
ROSOLIO
ROSOLIOS
ROSSER
ROSSERS
ROST
ROSTED
ROSTELLAR
ROSTELLUM
ROSTELLUMS
ROSTER
ROSTERED
ROSTERING
ROSTERINGS
ROSTERS
ROSTING
ROSTRA
ROSTRAL
ROSTRATE
ROSTRATED
ROSTRUM
ROSTS
ROSULA
ROSULAS
ROSULATE
ROSY
ROSYING
ROT
ROTA
ROTAL
ROTAPLANE
ROTAPLANES
ROTARIES
ROTARY
ROTAS
ROTATABLE
ROTATE
ROTATED
ROTATES
ROTATING
ROTATION
ROTATIONS
ROTATIVE
ROTATOR
ROTATORS
ROTATORY
ROTAVATE
ROTAVATED
ROTAVATES
ROTAVATING
ROTAVATOR
ROTAVATORS
ROTAVIRUS
ROTAVIRUSES
ROTCH
ROTCHE
ROTCHES
ROTCHIE

ROTCHIES
ROTE
ROTED
ROTENONE
ROTENONES
ROTES
ROTGRASS
ROTGRASSES
ROTGUT
ROTGUTS
ROTHER
ROTHERS
ROTI
ROTIFER
ROTIFERAL
ROTIFERS
ROTING
ROTIS
ROTL
ROTLS
ROTOGRAPH
ROTOGRAPHED
ROTOGRAPHING
ROTOGRAPHS
ROTOLO
ROTOLOS
ROTOR
ROTORS
ROTOVATE
ROTOVATED
ROTOVATES
ROTOVATING
ROTOVATOR
ROTOVATORS
ROTS
ROTTAN
ROTTANS
ROTTED
ROTTEN
ROTTENER
ROTTENEST
ROTTENLY
ROTTENS
ROTTER
ROTTERS
ROTTING
ROTULA
ROTULAS
ROTUND
ROTUNDA
ROTUNDAS
ROTUNDATE
ROTUNDED
ROTUNDER
ROTUNDEST
ROTUNDING
ROTUNDITIES
ROTUNDITY
ROTUNDLY
ROTUNDS
ROTURIER
ROTURIERS
ROUBLE
ROUBLES
ROUCOU
ROUCOUS
ROUÉ
ROUÉS
ROUGE
ROUGED

ROUGES
ROUGH
ROUGHAGE
ROUGHAGES
ROUGHCAST
ROUGHCASTING
ROUGHCASTS
ROUGHED
ROUGHEN
ROUGHENED
ROUGHENING
ROUGHENS
ROUGHER
ROUGHERS
ROUGHEST
ROUGHIE
ROUGHIES
ROUGHING
ROUGHISH
ROUGHLY
ROUGHNECK
ROUGHNECKS
ROUGHNESS
ROUGHNESSES
ROUGHS
ROUGHT
ROUGHY
ROUGING
ROUL
ROULADE
ROULADES
ROULE
ROULEAU
ROULEAUS
ROULEAUX
ROULES
ROULETTE
ROULETTES
ROULS
ROUM
ROUMING
ROUMINGS
ROUMS
ROUNCE
ROUNCES
ROUNCEVAL
ROUNCEVALS
ROUNCIES
ROUNCY
ROUND
ROUNDARCH
ROUNDED
ROUNDEL
ROUNDELAY
ROUNDELAYS
ROUNDELS
ROUNDER
ROUNDERS
ROUNDEST
ROUNDHAND
ROUNDHANDS
ROUNDING
ROUNDINGS
ROUNDISH
ROUNDLE
ROUNDLES
ROUNDLET
ROUNDLETS
ROUNDLY
ROUNDNESS

ROUNDNESSES
ROUNDS
ROUNDSMAN
ROUNDSMEN
ROUNDURE
ROUNDURES
ROUP
ROUPED
ROUPIER
ROUPIEST
ROUPING
ROUPIT
ROUPS
ROUPY
ROUSANT
ROUSE
ROUSED
ROUSEMENT
ROUSEMENTS
ROUSER
ROUSERS
ROUSES
ROUSING
ROUSINGLY
ROUSSETTE
ROUSSETTES
ROUST
ROUSTED
ROUSTER
ROUSTERS
ROUSTING
ROUSTS
ROUT
ROUTE
ROUTED
ROUTEING
ROUTEMAN
ROUTEMEN
ROUTER
ROUTERS
ROUTES
ROUTH
ROUTHIE
ROUTHIER
ROUTHIEST
ROUTHS
ROUTINE
ROUTINEER
ROUTINEERS
ROUTINELY
ROUTINES
ROUTING
ROUTINGS
ROUTINISE
ROUTINISED
ROUTINISES
ROUTINISING
ROUTINISM
ROUTINISMS
ROUTINIST
ROUTINISTS
ROUTINIZE
ROUTINIZED
ROUTINIZES
ROUTINIZING
ROUTOUS
ROUTOUSLY
ROUTS
ROUX
ROVE

ROVED
ROVER
ROVERS
ROVES
ROVING
ROVINGLY
ROVINGS
ROW
ROWABLE
ROWAN
ROWANS
ROWBOAT
ROWBOATS
ROWDEDOW
ROWDEDOWS
ROWDIER
ROWDIES
ROWDIEST
ROWDILY
ROWDINESS
ROWDINESSES
ROWDY
ROWDYDOW
ROWDYDOWS
ROWDYISH
ROWDYISM
ROWDYISMS
ROWED
ROWEL
ROWELLED
ROWELLING
ROWELS
ROWEN
ROWENS
ROWER
ROWERS
ROWING
ROWINGS
ROWLOCK
ROWLOCKS
ROWME
ROWMES
ROWND
ROWNDED
ROWNDELL
ROWNDELLS
ROWNDING
ROWNDS
ROWS
ROWT
ROWTED
ROWTH
ROWTHS
ROWTING
ROWTS
ROYAL
ROYALET
ROYALETS
ROYALISE
ROYALISED
ROYALISES
ROYALISING
ROYALISM
ROYALISMS
ROYALIST
ROYALISTS
ROYALIZE
ROYALIZED
ROYALIZES
ROYALIZING

ROYALLER
ROYALLEST
ROYALLY
ROYALS
ROYALTIES
ROYALTY
ROYNE
ROYNED
ROYNES
ROYNING
ROYNISH
ROYST
ROYSTED
ROYSTER
ROYSTERED
ROYSTERER
ROYSTERERS
ROYSTERING
ROYSTERS
ROYSTING
ROYSTS
ROZELLE
ROZELLES
ROZET
ROZETED
ROZETING
ROZETS
ROZIT
ROZITED
ROZITING
ROZITS
ROZZER
ROZZERS
RUB
RUBAIYAT
RUBAIYATS
RUBATI
RUBATO
RUBATOS
RUBBED
RUBBER
RUBBERED
RUBBERING
RUBBERISE
RUBBERISED
RUBBERISES
RUBBERISING
RUBBERIZE
RUBBERIZED
RUBBERIZES
RUBBERIZING
RUBBERS
RUBBERY
RUBBET
RUBBING
RUBBINGS
RUBBISH
RUBBISHED
RUBBISHES
RUBBISHING
RUBBISHLY
RUBBISHY
RUBBIT
RUBBLE
RUBBLES
RUBBLY
RUBDOWN
RUBDOWNS
RUBE
RUBEFIED

RUBEFIES
RUBEFY
RUBEFYING
RUBELLA
RUBELLAN
RUBELLANS
RUBELLAS
RUBELLITE
RUBELLITES
RUBEOLA
RUBEOLAS
RUBES
RUBESCENT
RUBICELLE
RUBICELLES
RUBICON
RUBICONNED
RUBICONNING
RUBICONS
RUBICUND
RUBIDIUM
RUBIDIUMS
RUBIED
RUBIER
RUBIES
RUBIEST
RUBIFIED
RUBIFIES
RUBIFY
RUBIFYING
RUBIN
RUBINE
RUBINEOUS
RUBINES
RUBINS
RUBIOUS
RUBLE
RUBLES
RUBRIC
RUBRICAL
RUBRICATE
RUBRICATED
RUBRICATES
RUBRICATING
RUBRICIAN
RUBRICIANS
RUBRICS
RUBS
RUBSTONE
RUBSTONES
RUBY
RUBYING
RUC
RUCHE
RUCHED
RUCHES
RUCHING
RUCHINGS
RUCK
RUCKED
RUCKING
RUCKLE
RUCKLED
RUCKLES
RUCKLING
RUCKS
RUCKSACK
RUCKSACKS
RUCKUS
RUCKUSES

RUCS
RUCTATION
RUCTATIONS
RUCTION
RUCTIONS
RUD
RUDAS
RUDASES
RUDBECKIA
RUDBECKIAS
RUDD
RUDDED
RUDDER
RUDDERS
RUDDIED
RUDDIER
RUDDIES
RUDDIEST
RUDDILY
RUDDINESS
RUDDINESSES
RUDDING
RUDDLE
RUDDLED
RUDDLEMAN
RUDDLEMEN
RUDDLES
RUDDLING
RUDDOCK
RUDDOCKS
RUDDS
RUDDY
RUDDYING
RUDE
RUDELY
RUDENESS
RUDENESSES
RUDER
RUDERAL
RUDERALS
RUDERIES
RUDERY
RUDESBIES
RUDESBY
RUDEST
RUDIMENT
RUDIMENTS
RUDISH
RUDS
RUE
RUED
RUEFUL
RUEFULLY
RUEING
RUEINGS
RUELLE
RUELLES
RUELLIA
RUELLIAS
RUES
RUFESCENT
RUFF
RUFFE
RUFFED
RUFFES
RUFFIAN
RUFFIANED
RUFFIANING
RUFFIANLY
RUFFIANS

RUFFIN
RUFFING
RUFFINS
RUFFLE
RUFFLED
RUFFLER
RUFFLERS
RUFFLES
RUFFLING
RUFFLINGS
RUFFS
RUFOUS
RUG
RUGATE
RUGBIES
RUGBY
RUGGED
RUGGEDER
RUGGEDEST
RUGGEDISE
RUGGEDISED
RUGGEDISES
RUGGEDISING
RUGGEDIZE
RUGGEDIZED
RUGGEDIZES
RUGGEDIZING
RUGGEDLY
RUGGER
RUGGERS
RUGGIER
RUGGIEST
RUGGING
RUGGINGS
RUGGY
RUGOSE
RUGOSELY
RUGOSITIES
RUGOSITY
RUGOUS
RUGS
RUGULOSE
RUIN
RUINABLE
RUINATE
RUINATED
RUINATES
RUINATING
RUINATION
RUINATIONS
RUINED
RUINER
RUINERS
RUING
RUINGS
RUINING
RUININGS
RUINOUS
RUINOUSLY
RUINS
RUKH
RUKHS
RULABLE
RULE
RULED
RULELESS
RULER
RULERED
RULERING
RULERS

RULERSHIP
RULERSHIPS
RULES
RULESSE
RULIER
RULIEST
RULING
RULINGS
RULLION
RULLIONS
RULLOCK
RULLOCKS
RULY
RUM
RUMAL
RUMALS
RUMBA
RUMBAS
RUMBELOW
RUMBELOWS
RUMBLE
RUMBLED
RUMBLER
RUMBLERS
RUMBLES
RUMBLING
RUMBLINGS
RUMBLY
RUMBO
RUMBOS
RUME
RUMEN
RUMES
RUMINA
RUMINANT
RUMINANTS
RUMINATE
RUMINATED
RUMINATES
RUMINATING
RUMINATOR
RUMINATORS
RUMKIN
RUMKINS
RUMLY
RUMMAGE
RUMMAGED
RUMMAGER
RUMMAGERS
RUMMAGES
RUMMAGING
RUMMER
RUMMERS
RUMMEST
RUMMIER
RUMMIES
RUMMIEST
RUMMILY
RUMMINESS
RUMMINESSES
RUMMISH
RUMMY
RUMOR
RUMORED
RUMORING
RUMOROUS
RUMORS
RUMOUR
RUMOURED
RUMOURER

RUMOURERS
RUMOURING
RUMOURS
RUMP
RUMPED
RUMPING
RUMPLE
RUMPLED
RUMPLES
RUMPLESS
RUMPLING
RUMPS
RUMPUS
RUMPUSES
RUMS
RUN
RUNABOUT
RUNABOUTS
RUNAGATE
RUNAGATES
RUNAROUND
RUNAROUNDS
RUNAWAY
RUNAWAYS
RUNCH
RUNCHES
RUNCIBLE
RUNCINATE
RUND
RUNDALE
RUNDALES
RUNDLE
RUNDLED
RUNDLES
RUNDLET
RUNDLETS
RUNDOWN
RUNDOWNS
RUNDS
RUNE
RUNED
RUNES
RUNFLAT
RUNG
RUNGS
RUNIC
RUNKLE
RUNKLED
RUNKLES
RUNKLING
RUNLET
RUNLETS
RUNNABLE
RUNNEL
RUNNELS
RUNNER
RUNNERS
RUNNET
RUNNETS
RUNNIER
RUNNIEST
RUNNING
RUNNINGLY
RUNNINGS
RUNNION
RUNNIONS
RUNNY
RUNRIG
RUNRIGS
RUNS

RUNT
RUNTED
RUNTIER
RUNTIEST
RUNTISH
RUNTS
RUNTY
RUNWAY
RUNWAYS
RUPEE
RUPEES
RUPIA
RUPIAH
RUPIAHS
RUPIAS
RUPTURE
RUPTURED
RUPTURES
RUPTURING
RURAL
RURALISE
RURALISED
RURALISES
RURALISING
RURALISM
RURALISMS
RURALIST
RURALISTS
RURALITIES
RURALITY
RURALIZE
RURALIZED
RURALIZES
RURALIZING
RURALLY
RURALNESS
RURALNESSES
RURALS
RURP
RURPS
RUSA
RUSALKA
RUSALKAS
RUSAS
RUSCUS
RUSCUSES
RUSE
RUSES
RUSH
RUSHED
RUSHEN
RUSHER
RUSHERS
RUSHES
RUSHIER
RUSHIEST
RUSHINESS
RUSHINESSES
RUSHING
RUSHLIGHT
RUSHLIGHTS
RUSHY
RUSINE
RUSK
RUSKS
RUSMA
RUSMAS
RUSSEL
RUSSELS

RUSSET

RUSSET
RUSSETED
RUSSETING
RUSSETINGS
RUSSETS
RUSSETY
RUSSIA
RUSSIAS
RUST
RUSTED
RUSTIC
RUSTICAL
RUSTICALS
RUSTICATE
RUSTICATED
RUSTICATES
RUSTICATING
RUSTICIAL
RUSTICISE
RUSTICISED
RUSTICISES
RUSTICISING
RUSTICISM
RUSTICISMS
RUSTICITIES

RUSTICITY
RUSTICIZE
RUSTICIZED
RUSTICIZES
RUSTICIZING
RUSTICS
RUSTIER
RUSTIEST
RUSTILY
RUSTINESS
RUSTINESSES
RUSTING
RUSTINGS
RUSTLE
RUSTLED
RUSTLER
RUSTLERS
RUSTLES
RUSTLESS
RUSTLING
RUSTLINGS
RUSTRE
RUSTRED
RUSTRES
RUSTS

RUSTY
RUT
RUTABAGA
RUTABAGAS
RUTACEOUS
RUTH
RUTHENIC
RUTHENIUM
RUTHENIUMS
RUTHFUL
RUTHFULLY
RUTHLESS
RUTHS
RUTILANT
RUTILATED
RUTILE
RUTILES
RUTIN
RUTINS
RUTS
RUTTED
RUTTER
RUTTERS
RUTTIER
RUTTIEST

RUTTING
RUTTINGS
RUTTISH
RUTTY
RYA
RYAL
RYALS
RYAS
RYBAT
RYBATS
RYBAUDRYE
RYBAUDRYES
RYBAULD
RYBAULDS
RYE
RYEPECK
RYEPECKS
RYES
RYFE
RYKE
RYKED
RYKES
RYKING
RYMME
RYMMED

RYMMES
RYMMING
RYND
RYNDS
RYOKAN
RYOKANS
RYOT
RYOTS
RYOTWARI
RYOTWARIS
RYPE
RYPECK
RYPECKS
RYPER
RYTHME
RYTHMED
RYTHMES
RYTHMING
RYVE
RYVED
RYVES
RYVING

S

SAB
SABADILLA
SABADILLAS
SABATON
SABATONS
SABBAT
SABBATIC
SABBATINE
SABBATISE
SABBATISED
SABBATISES
SABBATISING
SABBATISM
SABBATISMS
SABBATIZE
SABBATIZED
SABBATIZES
SABBATIZING
SABBATS
SABELLA
SABELLAS
SABER
SABERED
SABERING
SABERS
SABIN
SABINS
SABLE
SABLED
SABLES
SABLING
SABOT
SABOTAGE
SABOTAGED
SABOTAGES
SABOTAGING
SABOTEUR
SABOTEURS
SABOTIER
SABOTIERS
SABOTS
SABRA
SABRAS
SABRE
SABRED
SABRES
SABRING
SABS
SABULOSE
SABULOUS
SABURRA
SABURRAL
SABURRAS
SAC
SACCADE
SACCADES
SACCADIC
SACCATE
SACCHARIC
SACCHARIN
SACCHARINS
SACCIFORM
SACCOI
SACCOS

SACCOSES
SACCULAR
SACCULE
SACCULES
SACCULI
SACCULUS
SACELLA
SACELLUM
SACHEM
SACHEMDOM
SACHEMDOMS
SACHEMS
SACHET
SACHETS
SACK
SACKAGE
SACKAGES
SACKBUT
SACKBUTS
SACKCLOTH
SACKCLOTHS
SACKED
SACKFUL
SACKFULS
SACKING
SACKINGS
SACKLESS
SACKS
SACLESS
SACQUE
SACQUES
SACRA
SACRAL
SACRALISE
SACRALISED
SACRALISES
SACRALISING
SACRALIZE
SACRALIZED
SACRALIZES
SACRALIZING
SACRAMENT
SACRAMENTED
SACRAMENTING
SACRAMENTS
SACRARIA
SACRARIUM
SACRED
SACREDLY
SACRIFICE
SACRIFICED
SACRIFICES
SACRIFICING
SACRIFIDE
SACRIFIED
SACRIFIES
SACRIFY
SACRIFYING
SACRILEGE
SACRILEGES
SACRING
SACRINGS
SACRIST
SACRISTAN

SACRISTANS
SACRISTIES
SACRISTS
SACRISTY
SACRUM
SACS
SAD
SADDEN
SADDENED
SADDENING
SADDENS
SADDER
SADDEST
SADDHU
SADDHUS
SADDISH
SADDLE
SADDLED
SADDLER
SADDLERIES
SADDLERS
SADDLERY
SADDLES
SADDLING
SADHU
SADHUS
SADISM
SADISMS
SADIST
SADISTIC
SADISTS
SADLY
SADNESS
SADNESSES
SAE
SAECULUM
SAECULUMS
SAETER
SAETERS
SAFARI
SAFARIED
SAFARIING
SAFARIS
SAFE
SAFED
SAFEGUARD
SAFEGUARDED
SAFEGUARDING
SAFEGUARDINGS
SAFEGUARDS
SAFELY
SAFENESS
SAFENESSES
SAFER
SAFES
SAFEST
SAFETIES
SAFETY
SAFFIAN
SAFFIANS
SAFFLOWER
SAFFLOWERS
SAFFRON
SAFFRONED

SAFFRONS
SAFFRONY
SAFING
SAFRANIN
SAFRANINE
SAFRANINES
SAFRANINS
SAFROLE
SAFROLES
SAG
SAGA
SAGACIOUS
SAGACITIES
SAGACITY
SAGAMAN
SAGAMEN
SAGAMORE
SAGAMORES
SAGAPENUM
SAGAPENUMS
SAGAS
SAGATHIES
SAGATHY
SAGE
SAGEBRUSH
SAGEBRUSHES
SAGELY
SAGENE
SAGENES
SAGENESS
SAGENESSES
SAGENITE
SAGENITES
SAGENITIC
SAGER
SAGES
SAGEST
SAGGAR
SAGGARD
SAGGARDS
SAGGARS
SAGGED
SAGGER
SAGGERS
SAGGIER
SAGGIEST
SAGGING
SAGGINGS
SAGGY
SAGIER
SAGIEST
SAGINATE
SAGINATED
SAGINATES
SAGINATING
SAGITTA
SAGITTAL
SAGITTARIES
SAGITTARY
SAGITTAS
SAGITTATE
SAGO
SAGOIN
SAGOINS

SAGOS
SAGOUIN
SAGOUINS
SAGS
SAGUARO
SAGUAROS
SAGUIN
SAGUINS
SAGUM
SAGY
SAHIB
SAHIBA
SAHIBAH
SAHIBAHS
SAHIBAS
SAHIBS
SAI
SAIBLING
SAIBLINGS
SAIC
SAICE
SAICES
SAICK
SAICKS
SAICS
SAID
SAIDEST
SAIDS
SAIDST
SAIGA
SAIGAS
SAIKEI
SAIKEIS
SAIKLESS
SAIL
SAILABLE
SAILBOARD
SAILBOARDS
SAILED
SAILER
SAILERS
SAILIER
SAILIEST
SAILING
SAILINGS
SAILLESS
SAILOR
SAILORING
SAILORINGS
SAILORLY
SAILORS
SAILPLANE
SAILPLANES
SAILS
SAILY
SAIM
SAIMIRI
SAIMIRIS
SAIMS
SAIN
SAINE
SAINED
SAINFOIN
SAINFOINS

SAINING	SALAD	SALIFYING	SALPICON	SALUKI
SAINS	SALADE	SALIGOT	SALPICONS	SALUKIS
SAINT	SALADES	SALIGOTS	SALPIFORM	SALUTARY
SAINTDOM	SALADING	SALIMETER	SALPINGES	SALUTE
SAINTDOMS	SALADINGS	SALIMETERS	SALPINX	SALUTED
SAINTED	SALADS	SALINA	SALPINXES	SALUTER
SAINTESS	SALAL	SALINAS	SALPS	SALUTERS
SAINTESSES	SALALS	SALINE	SALS	SALUTES
SAINTFOIN	SALAME	SALINES	SALSA	SALUTING
SAINTFOINS	SALAMI	SALINITIES	SALSAED	SALVABLE
SAINTHOOD	SALAMIS	SALINITY	SALSAFIES	SALVAGE
SAINTHOODS	SALAMON	SALIVA	SALSAFY	SALVAGED
SAINTING	SALAMONS	SALIVAL	SALSAING	SALVAGES
SAINTISH	SALANGANE	SALIVARY	SALSAS	SALVAGING
SAINTISM	SALANGANES	SALIVAS	SALSE	SALVARSAN
SAINTISMS	SALARIAT	SALIVATE	SALSES	SALVARSANS
SAINTLIER	SALARIATS	SALIVATED	SALSIFIES	SALVATION
SAINTLIEST	SALARIED	SALIVATES	SALSIFY	SALVATIONS
SAINTLIKE	SALARIES	SALIVATING	SALT	SALVATORIES
SAINTLING	SALARY	SALIX	SALTANDO	SALVATORY
SAINTLINGS	SALARYING	SALLAD	SALTANT	SALVE
SAINTLY	SALBAND	SALLADS	SALTANTS	SALVED
SAINTS	SALBANDS	SALLAL	SALTATE	SALVER
SAINTSHIP	SALCHOW	SALLALS	SALTATED	SALVERS
SAINTSHIPS	SALCHOWS	SALLE	SALTATES	SALVES
SAIQUE	SALE	SALLEE	SALTATING	SALVETE
SAIQUES	SALEABLE	SALLEES	SALTATION	SALVETES
SAIR	SALEABLY	SALLES	SALTATIONS	SALVIA
SAIRED	SALEP	SALLET	SALTATO	SALVIAS
SAIRER	SALEPS	SALLETS	SALTATORY	SALVIFIC
SAIREST	SALERATUS	SALLIED	SALTED	SALVING
SAIRING	SALERATUSES	SALLIES	SALTER	SALVINGS
SAIRS	SALES	SALLOW	SALTERN	SALVO
SAIS	SALESGIRL	SALLOWED	SALTERNS	SALVOES
SAIST	SALESGIRLS	SALLOWER	SALTERS	SALVOR
SAITH	SALESLADIES	SALLOWEST	SALTEST	SALVORS
SAITHE	SALESLADY	SALLOWING	SALTIER	SALVOS
SAITHES	SALESMAN	SALLOWISH	SALTIERS	SAM
SAITHS	SALESMEN	SALLOWS	SALTIEST	SAMAAN
SAJOU	SALET	SALLOWY	SALTILY	SAMAANS
SAJOUS	SALETS	SALLY	SALTINESS	SAMAN
SAKE	SALEWD	SALLYING	SALTINESSES	SAMANS
SAKER	SALEWORK	SALLYPORT	SALTING	SAMARA
SAKERET	SALEWORKS	SALLYPORTS	SALTINGS	SAMARAS
SAKERETS	SALFERN	SALMI	SALTIRE	SAMARIUM
SAKERS	SALFERNS	SALMIS	SALTIRES	SAMARIUMS
SAKES	SALIAUNCE	SALMON	SALTISH	SAMBA
SAKI	SALIAUNCES	SALMONET	SALTISHLY	SAMBAL
SAKIA	SALIC	SALMONETS	SALTLESS	SAMBALS
SAKIAS	SALICES	SALMONID	SALTLY	SAMBAR
SAKIEH	SALICET	SALMONIDS	SALTNESS	SAMBARS
SAKIEHS	SALICETA	SALMONOID	SALTNESSES	SAMBAS
SAKIS	SALICETS	SALMONOIDS	SALTO	SAMBO
SAKIYEH	SALICETUM	SALMONS	SALTOED	SAMBOS
SAKIYEHS	SALICETUMS	SALON	SALTOING	SAMBUCA
SAKKOI	SALICIN	SALONS	SALTOS	SAMBUCAS
SAKKOS	SALICINE	SALOON	SALTPETER	SAMBUR
SAKKOSES	SALICINES	SALOONIST	SALTPETERS	SAMBURS
SAKSAUL	SALICINS	SALOONISTS	SALTPETRE	SAME
SAKSAULS	SALICYLIC	SALOONS	SALTPETRES	SAMEL
SAL	SALIENCE	SALOOP	SALTS	SAMELY
SALAAM	SALIENCES	SALOOPS	SALTUS	SAMEN
SALAAMED	SALIENCIES	SALOP	SALTUSES	SAMENESS
SALAAMING	SALIENCY	SALOPETTE	SALTY	SAMENESSES
SALAAMS	SALIENT	SALOPETTES	SALUBRITIES	SAMES
SALABLE	SALIENTLY	SALOPIAN	SALUBRITY	SAMEY
SALABLY	SALIENTS	SALOPS	SALUE	SAMFOO
SALACIOUS	SALIFIED	SALP	SALUED	SAMFOOS
SALACITIES	SALIFIES	SALPIAN	SALUES	SAMFU
SALACITY	SALIFY	SALPIANS	SALUING	SAMFUS

SAMIEL
SAMIELS
SAMIER
SAMIEST
SAMISEN
SAMISENS
SAMITE
SAMITES
SAMIZDAT
SAMIZDATS
SAMLET
SAMLETS
SAMLOR
SAMLORS
SAMNITIS
SAMNITISES
SAMOSA
SAMOSAS
SAMOVAR
SAMOVARS
SAMP
SAMPAN
SAMPANS
SAMPHIRE
SAMPHIRES
SAMPI
SAMPIRE
SAMPIRES
SAMPIS
SAMPLE
SAMPLED
SAMPLER
SAMPLERIES
SAMPLERS
SAMPLERY
SAMPLES
SAMPLING
SAMPLINGS
SAMPS
SAMSHOO
SAMSHOOS
SAMSHU
SAMSHUS
SAMURAI
SAN
SANATIVE
SANATORIA
SANATORY
SANBENITO
SANBENITOS
SANCHO
SANCHOS
SANCTIFIED
SANCTIFIES
SANCTIFY
SANCTIFYING
SANCTIFYINGS
SANCTION
SANCTIONED
SANCTIONING
SANCTIONS
SANCTITIES
SANCTITY
SANCTUARIES
SANCTUARY
SANCTUM
SANCTUMS
SAND
SANDAL
SANDALLED

SANDALS
SANDARAC
SANDARACH
SANDARACHS
SANDARACS
SANDBAG
SANDBAGGED
SANDBAGGING
SANDBAGS
SANDED
SANDER
SANDERS
SANDERSES
SANDHI
SANDHIS
SANDIER
SANDIEST
SANDINESS
SANDINESSES
SANDING
SANDINGS
SANDIVER
SANDIVERS
SANDLING
SANDLINGS
SANDMAN
SANDMEN
SANDPAPER
SANDPAPERED
SANDPAPERING
SANDPAPERS
SANDPIPER
SANDPIPERS
SANDS
SANDSTONE
SANDSTONES
SANDWICH
SANDWICHED
SANDWICHES
SANDWICHING
SANDWORT
SANDWORTS
SANDY
SANDYISH
SANE
SANEI
SANEIS
SANELY
SANENESS
SANENESSES
SANER
SANEST
SANG
SANGAR
SANGAREE
SANGAREES
SANGARS
SANGFROID
SANGFROIDS
SANGLIER
SANGLIERS
SANGRIA
SANGRIAS
SANGS
SANGUIFIED
SANGUIFIES
SANGUIFY
SANGUIFYING
SANGUINE
SANGUINED

SANGUINER
SANGUINES
SANGUINEST
SANGUINING
SANICLE
SANICLES
SANIDINE
SANIDINES
SANIES
SANIFIED
SANIFIES
SANIFY
SANIFYING
SANIOUS
SANITARIA
SANITARY
SANITATE
SANITATED
SANITATES
SANITATING
SANITIES
SANITISE
SANITISED
SANITISES
SANITISING
SANITIZE
SANITIZED
SANITIZES
SANITIZING
SANITY
SANJAK
SANJAKS
SANK
SANKO
SANKOS
SANNUP
SANNUPS
SANNYASI
SANNYASIN
SANNYASINS
SANNYASIS
SANPAN
SANPANS
SANS
SANSA
SANSAS
SANSERIF
SANSERIFS
SANTAL
SANTALIN
SANTALINS
SANTALS
SANTIR
SANTIRS
SANTOLINA
SANTOLINAS
SANTON
SANTONICA
SANTONICAS
SANTONIN
SANTONINS
SANTONS
SANTOUR
SANTOURS
SANTUR
SANTURS
SAOUARI
SAOUARIS
SAP
SAPAJOU

SAPAJOUS
SAPAN
SAPANS
SAPEGO
SAPEGOES
SAPELE
SAPELES
SAPFUL
SAPHEAD
SAPHEADED
SAPHEADS
SAPID
SAPIDITIES
SAPIDITY
SAPIDLESS
SAPIENCE
SAPIENCES
SAPIENT
SAPIENTLY
SAPLESS
SAPLING
SAPLINGS
SAPODILLA
SAPODILLAS
SAPOGENIN
SAPOGENINS
SAPONIFIED
SAPONIFIES
SAPONIFY
SAPONIFYING
SAPONIN
SAPONINS
SAPONITE
SAPONITES
SAPOR
SAPOROUS
SAPORS
SAPOTA
SAPOTAS
SAPPAN
SAPPANS
SAPPED
SAPPER
SAPPERS
SAPPHIC
SAPPHICS
SAPPHIRE
SAPPHIRED
SAPPHIRES
SAPPHISM
SAPPHISMS
SAPPHIST
SAPPHISTS
SAPPIER
SAPPIEST
SAPPINESS
SAPPINESSES
SAPPING
SAPPLES
SAPPY
SAPRAEMIA
SAPRAEMIAS
SAPRAEMIC
SAPROBE
SAPROBES
SAPROLITE
SAPROLITES
SAPROPEL
SAPROPELS
SAPROZOIC

SAPS
SAPSAGO
SAPSAGOS
SAPSUCKER
SAPSUCKERS
SAPUCAIA
SAPUCAIAS
SAPWOOD
SAPWOODS
SAR
SARABAND
SARABANDS
SARAFAN
SARAFANS
SARANGI
SARANGIS
SARBACANE
SARBACANES
SARCASM
SARCASMS
SARCASTIC
SARCENET
SARCENETS
SARCOCARP
SARCOCARPS
SARCODE
SARCODES
SARCODIC
SARCOID
SARCOIDS
SARCOLOGIES
SARCOLOGY
SARCOMA
SARCOMAS
SARCOMATA
SARCOMERE
SARCOMERES
SARCOPTIC
SARCOUS
SARD
SARDANA
SARDANAS
SARDEL
SARDELLE
SARDELLES
SARDELS
SARDINE
SARDINES
SARDIUS
SARDIUSES
SARDONIAN
SARDONIC
SARDONYX
SARDONYXES
SARDS
SARED
SAREE
SAREES
SARGASSO
SARGASSOS
SARGE
SARGES
SARGO
SARGOS
SARGUS
SARGUSES
SARI
SARIN
SARING
SARINS

SARIS
SARK
SARKFUL
SARKFULS
SARKIER
SARKIEST
SARKING
SARKINGS
SARKS
SARKY
SARMENT
SARMENTA
SARMENTS
SARMENTUM
SARNEY
SARNEYS
SARNIE
SARNIES
SAROD
SARODS
SARONG
SARONGS
SARONIC
SAROS
SAROSES
SARPANCH
SARPANCHES
SARRASIN
SARRASINS
SARRAZIN
SARRAZINS
SARS
SARSA
SARSAS
SARSDEN
SARSDENS
SARSEN
SARSENET
SARSENETS
SARSENS
SARSNET
SARSNETS
SARTOR
SARTORIAL
SARTORIAN
SARTORII
SARTORIUS
SARTORIUSES
SARTORS
SARUS
SARUSES
SARZA
SARZAS
SASARARA
SASARARAS
SASH
SASHAY
SASHAYED
SASHAYING
SASHAYS
SASHED
SASHES
SASHIMI
SASHIMIS
SASHING
SASIN
SASINE
SASINES
SASINS
SASKATOON

SASKATOONS
SASQUATCH
SASQUATCHES
SASS
SASSABIES
SASSABY
SASSAFRAS
SASSAFRASES
SASSARARA
SASSARARAS
SASSE
SASSED
SASSES
SASSIER
SASSIEST
SASSING
SASSOLIN
SASSOLINS
SASSOLITE
SASSOLITES
SASSY
SASTRUGA
SASTRUGI
SAT
SATANIC
SATANICAL
SATANISM
SATANISMS
SATANITIES
SATANITY
SATARA
SATARAS
SATCHEL
SATCHELS
SATE
SATED
SATEDNESS
SATEDNESSES
SATEEN
SATEENS
SATELESS
SATELLES
SATELLITE
SATELLITED
SATELLITES
SATELLITING
SATES
SATI
SATIABLE
SATIATE
SATIATED
SATIATES
SATIATING
SATIATION
SATIATIONS
SATIETIES
SATIETY
SATIN
SATINED
SATINET
SATINETS
SATINETTA
SATINETTAS
SATINETTE
SATINETTES
SATING
SATINING
SATINS
SATINWOOD
SATINWOODS

SATINY
SATIRE
SATIRES
SATIRIC
SATIRICAL
SATIRISE
SATIRISED
SATIRISES
SATIRISING
SATIRIST
SATIRISTS
SATIRIZE
SATIRIZED
SATIRIZES
SATIRIZING
SATIS
SATISFIED
SATISFIER
SATISFIERS
SATISFIES
SATISFY
SATISFYING
SATIVE
SATORI
SATORIS
SATRAP
SATRAPAL
SATRAPIC
SATRAPIES
SATRAPS
SATRAPY
SATSUMA
SATSUMAS
SATURABLE
SATURANT
SATURANTS
SATURATE
SATURATED
SATURATES
SATURATING
SATURATOR
SATURATORS
SATURNIC
SATURNINE
SATURNISM
SATURNISMS
SATURNIST
SATURNISTS
SATYR
SATYRA
SATYRAL
SATYRALS
SATYRAS
SATYRESS
SATYRESSES
SATYRIC
SATYRICAL
SATYRID
SATYRIDS
SATYRISK
SATYRISKS
SATYRS
SAUBA
SAUBAS
SAUCE
SAUCED
SAUCEMAN
SAUCEMEN
SAUCEPAN
SAUCEPANS

SAUCER
SAUCERFUL
SAUCERFULS
SAUCERS
SAUCES
SAUCH
SAUCHS
SAUCIER
SAUCIEST
SAUCILY
SAUCINESS
SAUCINESSES
SAUCING
SAUCISSE
SAUCISSES
SAUCISSON
SAUCISSONS
SAUCY
SAUFGARD
SAUFGARDS
SAUGER
SAUGERS
SAUGH
SAUGHS
SAUL
SAULGE
SAULGES
SAULIE
SAULIES
SAULS
SAULT
SAULTS
SAUNA
SAUNAS
SAUNT
SAUNTED
SAUNTER
SAUNTERED
SAUNTERER
SAUNTERERS
SAUNTERING
SAUNTERINGS
SAUNTERS
SAUNTING
SAUNTS
SAUREL
SAURELS
SAURIAN
SAURIANS
SAURIES
SAUROID
SAUROPOD
SAUROPODS
SAURY
SAUSAGE
SAUSAGES
SAUT
SAUTÉ
SAUTÉD
SAUTED
SAUTÉED
SAUTÉING
SAUTÉS
SAUTING
SAUTOIR
SAUTOIRS
SAUTS
SAVABLE
SAVAGE
SAVAGED

SAVAGEDOM
SAVAGEDOMS
SAVAGELY
SAVAGER
SAVAGERIES
SAVAGERY
SAVAGES
SAVAGEST
SAVAGING
SAVAGISM
SAVAGISMS
SAVANNA
SAVANNAH
SAVANNAHS
SAVANNAS
SAVANT
SAVANTS
SAVARIN
SAVARINS
SAVATE
SAVATES
SAVE
SAVED
SAVEGARD
SAVEGARDED
SAVEGARDING
SAVEGARDS
SAVELOY
SAVELOYS
SAVER
SAVERS
SAVES
SAVEY
SAVEYED
SAVEYING
SAVEYS
SAVIN
SAVINE
SAVINES
SAVING
SAVINGLY
SAVINGS
SAVINS
SAVIOUR
SAVIOURS
SAVOR
SAVORED
SAVORIES
SAVORING
SAVOROUS
SAVORS
SAVORY
SAVOUR
SAVOURED
SAVOURIES
SAVOURILY
SAVOURING
SAVOURLY
SAVOURS
SAVOURY
SAVOY
SAVOYS
SAVVEY
SAVVEYED
SAVVEYING
SAVVEYS
SAVVIED
SAVVIES
SAVVY
SAVVYING

SAW
SAWAH
SAWAHS
SAWDER
SAWDERED
SAWDERING
SAWDERS
SAWDUST
SAWDUSTED
SAWDUSTING
SAWDUSTS
SAWDUSTY
SAWED
SAWER
SAWERS
SAWING
SAWINGS
SAWN
SAWNEY
SAWNEYS
SAWPIT
SAWPITS
SAWS
SAWYER
SAWYERS
SAX
SAXATILE
SAXAUL
SAXAULS
SAXES
SAXHORN
SAXHORNS
SAXIFRAGE
SAXIFRAGES
SAXITOXIN
SAXITOXINS
SAXONIES
SAXONITE
SAXONITES
SAXONY
SAXOPHONE
SAXOPHONES
SAY
SAYABLE
SAYED
SAYEDS
SAYER
SAYERS
SAYEST
SAYID
SAYIDS
SAYING
SAYINGS
SAYNE
SAYON
SAYONARA
SAYONARAS
SAYONS
SAYS
SAYST
SAYYID
SAYYIDS
SAZ
SAZERAC®
SAZERACS®
SAZES
SAZHEN
SAZHENS
SBIRRI
SBIRRO

SCAB
SCABBARD
SCABBARDED
SCABBARDING
SCABBARDS
SCABBED
SCABBIER
SCABBIEST
SCABBING
SCABBLE
SCABBLED
SCABBLES
SCABBLING
SCABBY
SCABIES
SCABIOUS
SCABIOUSES
SCABRID
SCABROUS
SCABS
SCAD
SCADS
SCAFF
SCAFFIE
SCAFFIES
SCAFFOLD
SCAFFOLDED
SCAFFOLDING
SCAFFOLDINGS
SCAFFOLDS
SCAFFS
SCAG
SCAGLIA
SCAGLIAS
SCAGLIOLA
SCAGLIOLAS
SCAGS
SCAIL
SCAILED
SCAILING
SCAILS
SCAITH
SCAITHED
SCAITHING
SCAITHS
SCALA
SCALADE
SCALADES
SCALADO
SCALADOS
SCALAE
SCALAR
SCALARS
SCALAWAG
SCALAWAGS
SCALD
SCALDED
SCALDER
SCALDERS
SCALDFISH
SCALDFISHES
SCALDIC
SCALDING
SCALDINGS
SCALDINI
SCALDINO
SCALDS
SCALE
SCALED

SCALELESS
SCALELIKE
SCALENE
SCALER
SCALERS
SCALES
SCALIER
SCALIEST
SCALINESS
SCALINESSES
SCALING
SCALINGS
SCALL
SCALLAWAG
SCALLAWAGS
SCALLED
SCALLION
SCALLIONS
SCALLOP
SCALLOPED
SCALLOPING
SCALLOPS
SCALLS
SCALLYWAG
SCALLYWAGS
SCALP
SCALPED
SCALPEL
SCALPELS
SCALPER
SCALPERS
SCALPING
SCALPLESS
SCALPRUM
SCALPRUMS
SCALPS
SCALY
SCAM
SCAMBLE
SCAMBLED
SCAMBLER
SCAMBLERS
SCAMBLES
SCAMBLING
SCAMBLINGS
SCAMEL
SCAMELS
SCAMMONIES
SCAMMONY
SCAMP
SCAMPED
SCAMPER
SCAMPERED
SCAMPERING
SCAMPERS
SCAMPI
SCAMPING
SCAMPINGS
SCAMPIS
SCAMPISH
SCAMPS
SCAMS
SCAN
SCAND
SCANDAL
SCANDALLED
SCANDALLING
SCANDALS
SCANDENT
SCANDIUM

SCANDIUMS
SCANNED
SCANNER
SCANNERS
SCANNING
SCANNINGS
SCANS
SCANSION
SCANSIONS
SCANT
SCANTED
SCANTER
SCANTEST
SCANTIER
SCANTIES
SCANTIEST
SCANTILY
SCANTING
SCANTITIES
SCANTITY
SCANTLE
SCANTLED
SCANTLES
SCANTLING
SCANTLINGS
SCANTLY
SCANTNESS
SCANTNESSES
SCANTS
SCANTY
SCAPA
SCAPAED
SCAPAING
SCAPAS
SCAPE
SCAPED
SCAPEGOAT
SCAPEGOATS
SCAPELESS
SCAPEMENT
SCAPEMENTS
SCAPES
SCAPHOID
SCAPHOIDS
SCAPHOPOD
SCAPHOPODS
SCAPI
SCAPING
SCAPOLITE
SCAPOLITES
SCAPPLE
SCAPPLED
SCAPPLES
SCAPPLING
SCAPULA
SCAPULAE
SCAPULAR
SCAPULARIES
SCAPULARS
SCAPULARY
SCAPULAS
SCAPUS
SCAR
SCARAB
SCARABEE
SCARABEES
SCARABOID
SCARABOIDS
SCARABS
SCARCE

SCARCELY
SCARCER
SCARCEST
SCARCITIES
SCARCITY
SCARE
SCARECROW
SCARECROWS
SCARED
SCAREDER
SCAREDEST
SCARER
SCARERS
SCARES
SCAREY
SCARF
SCARFED
SCARFING
SCARFINGS
SCARFISH
SCARFISHES
SCARFS
SCARFSKIN
SCARFSKINS
SCARIER
SCARIEST
SCARIFIED
SCARIFIER
SCARIFIERS
SCARIFIES
SCARIFY
SCARIFYING
SCARING
SCARIOUS
SCARLESS
SCARLET
SCARLETED
SCARLETING
SCARLETS
SCARMOGE
SCARMOGES
SCARP
SCARPED
SCARPER
SCARPERED
SCARPERING
SCARPERS
SCARPETTI
SCARPETTO
SCARPINES
SCARPING
SCARPINGS
SCARPS
SCARRE
SCARRED
SCARRES
SCARRIER
SCARRIEST
SCARRING
SCARRINGS
SCARRY
SCARS
SCART
SCARTED
SCARTH
SCARTHS
SCARTING
SCARTS
SCARVES
SCARY

SCAT
SCATCH
SCATCHES
SCATH
SCATHE
SCATHED
SCATHEFUL
SCATHES
SCATHING
SCATHS
SCATOLE
SCATOLES
SCATOLOGIES
SCATOLOGY
SCATS
SCATT
SCATTED
SCATTER
SCATTERED
SCATTERER
SCATTERERS
SCATTERING
SCATTERINGS
SCATTERS
SCATTERY
SCATTIER
SCATTIEST
SCATTING
SCATTS
SCATTY
SCAUD
SCAUDED
SCAUDING
SCAUDS
SCAUP
SCAUPER
SCAUPERS
SCAUPS
SCAUR
SCAURED
SCAURIES
SCAURING
SCAURS
SCAURY
SCAVAGE
SCAVAGER
SCAVAGERS
SCAVAGES
SCAVENGE
SCAVENGED
SCAVENGER
SCAVENGERED
SCAVENGERING
SCAVENGERINGS
SCAVENGERS
SCAVENGES
SCAVENGING
SCAVENGINGS
SCAW
SCAWS
SCAZON
SCAZONS
SCAZONTIC
SCAZONTICS
SCEAT
SCEATT
SCEATTAS
SCEDULE
SCEDULES
SCELERAT

SCELERATE
SCELERATES
SCELERATS
SCENA
SCENARIES
SCENARIO
SCENARIOS
SCENARISE
SCENARISED
SCENARISES
SCENARISING
SCENARIST
SCENARISTS
SCENARIZE
SCENARIZED
SCENARIZES
SCENARIZING
SCENARY
SCEND
SCENDED
SCENDING
SCENDS
SCENE
SCENED
SCENERIES
SCENERY
SCENES
SCENIC
SCENICAL
SCENING
SCENT
SCENTED
SCENTFUL
SCENTING
SCENTINGS
SCENTLESS
SCENTS
SCEPSES
SCEPSIS
SCEPSISES
SCEPTIC
SCEPTICAL
SCEPTICS
SCEPTRAL
SCEPTRE
SCEPTRED
SCEPTRES
SCEPTRY
SCERNE
SCERNED
SCERNES
SCERNING
SCHAPPE
SCHAPPED
SCHAPPES
SCHAPPING
SCHAPSKA
SCHAPSKAS
SCHECHITA
SCHECHITAS
SCHEDULE
SCHEDULED
SCHEDULES
SCHEDULING
SCHEELITE
SCHEELITES
SCHELLUM
SCHELLUMS
SCHELM
SCHELMS

SCHEMA
SCHEMATA
SCHEMATIC
SCHEME
SCHEMED
SCHEMER
SCHEMERS
SCHEMES
SCHEMING
SCHEMINGS
SCHERZI
SCHERZO
SCHERZOS
SCHIAVONE
SCHIAVONES
SCHIEDAM
SCHIEDAMS
SCHILLER
SCHILLERS
SCHILLING
SCHILLINGS
SCHIMMEL
SCHIMMELS
SCHISM
SCHISMA
SCHISMAS
SCHISMS
SCHIST
SCHISTOSE
SCHISTOUS
SCHISTS
SCHIZO
SCHIZOID
SCHIZOIDS
SCHIZONT
SCHIZONTS
SCHIZOPOD
SCHIZOPODS
SCHIZOS
SCHLÄGER
SCHLÄGERS
SCHLEMIEL
SCHLEMIELS
SCHLEMIHL
SCHLEMIHLS
SCHLEP
SCHLEPP
SCHLEPPED
SCHLEPPIER
SCHLEPPIEST
SCHLEPPING
SCHLEPPS
SCHLEPPY
SCHLEPS
SCHLICH
SCHLICHS
SCHLIEREN
SCHLOCK
SCHLOCKS
SCHLOSS
SCHLOSSES
SCHMALTZ
SCHMALTZES
SCHMALTZIER
SCHMALTZIEST
SCHMALTZY
SCHMELZ
SCHMELZES
SCHMO
SCHMOCK

SCHMOCKS
SCHMOE
SCHMOES
SCHMOOZE
SCHMOOZED
SCHMOOZES
SCHMOOZING
SCHMUCK
SCHMUCKS
SCHMUTTER
SCHMUTTERS
SCHNAPPER
SCHNAPPERS
SCHNAPPS
SCHNAPPSES
SCHNAPS
SCHNAPSES
SCHNAUZER
SCHNAUZERS
SCHNELL
SCHNITZEL
SCHNITZELS
SCHNOOK
SCHNOOKS
SCHNORKEL
SCHNORKELS
SCHNORR
SCHNORRED
SCHNORRER
SCHNORRERS
SCHNORRING
SCHNORRS
SCHNOZZLE
SCHNOZZLES
SCHOLAR
SCHOLARCH
SCHOLARCHS
SCHOLARLY
SCHOLARS
SCHOLIA
SCHOLIAST
SCHOLIASTS
SCHOLION
SCHOLIUM
SCHOOL
SCHOOLBAG
SCHOOLBAGS
SCHOOLBOY
SCHOOLBOYS
SCHOOLE
SCHOOLED
SCHOOLERIES
SCHOOLERY
SCHOOLES
SCHOOLING
SCHOOLINGS
SCHOOLMAN
SCHOOLMEN
SCHOOLS
SCHOONER
SCHOONERS
SCHORL
SCHORLS
SCHOUT
SCHOUTS
SCHTICK
SCHTICKS
SCHTIK
SCHTIKS
SCHTOOK

SCHTOOKS
SCHTOOM
SCHTUCK
SCHTUCKS
SCHUIT
SCHUITS
SCHUL
SCHULS
SCHUSS
SCHUSSED
SCHUSSES
SCHUSSING
SCHUYT
SCHUYTS
SCHWA
SCHWAS
SCIAENID
SCIAENOID
SCIAMACHIES
SCIAMACHY
SCIARID
SCIARIDS
SCIATIC
SCIATICA
SCIATICAL
SCIATICAS
SCIENCE
SCIENCED
SCIENCES
SCIENT
SCIENTER
SCIENTIAL
SCIENTISE
SCIENTISED
SCIENTISES
SCIENTISING
SCIENTISM
SCIENTISMS
SCIENTIST
SCIENTISTS
SCIENTIZE
SCIENTIZED
SCIENTIZES
SCIENTIZING
SCILICET
SCILLA
SCILLAS
SCIMITAR
SCIMITARS
SCINCOID
SCINTILLA
SCINTILLAS
SCIOLISM
SCIOLISMS
SCIOLIST
SCIOLISTS
SCIOLOUS
SCIOLTO
SCION
SCIONS
SCIOSOPHIES
SCIOSOPHY
SCIROC
SCIROCCO
SCIROCCOS
SCIROCS
SCIRRHOID
SCIRRHOUS
SCIRRHUS
SCIRRHUSES

SCISSEL
SCISSELS
SCISSIL
SCISSILE
SCISSILS
SCISSION
SCISSIONS
SCISSOR
SCISSORED
SCISSORER
SCISSORERS
SCISSORING
SCISSORS
SCISSURE
SCISSURES
SCIURINE
SCIUROID
SCLAFF
SCLAFFED
SCLAFFING
SCLAFFS
SCLATE
SCLATED
SCLATES
SCLATING
SCLAUNDER
SCLAUNDERS
SCLAVE
SCLAVES
SCLERA
SCLERAL
SCLERAS
SCLERE
SCLEREID
SCLEREIDE
SCLEREIDES
SCLEREIDS
SCLEREMA
SCLEREMAS
SCLERES
SCLERITE
SCLERITES
SCLERITIS
SCLERITISES
SCLEROID
SCLEROMA
SCLEROMAS
SCLEROSE
SCLEROSED
SCLEROSES
SCLEROSING
SCLEROSIS
SCLEROTAL
SCLEROTALS
SCLEROTIA
SCLEROTIC
SCLEROTICS
SCLEROUS
SCLIFF
SCLIFFS
SCLIM
SCLIMMED
SCLIMMING
SCLIMS
SCOFF
SCOFFED
SCOFFER
SCOFFERS
SCOFFING
SCOFFINGS

SCOFFLAW
SCOFFLAWS
SCOFFS
SCOG
SCOGGED
SCOGGING
SCOGS
SCOINSON
SCOINSONS
SCOLD
SCOLDED
SCOLDER
SCOLDERS
SCOLDING
SCOLDINGS
SCOLDS
SCOLECES
SCOLECID
SCOLECITE
SCOLECITES
SCOLECOID
SCOLEX
SCOLICES
SCOLIOMA
SCOLIOMAS
SCOLIOSES
SCOLIOSIS
SCOLIOTIC
SCOLLOP
SCOLLOPED
SCOLLOPING
SCOLLOPS
SCOLYTOID
SCOMBROID
SCOMFISH
SCOMFISHED
SCOMFISHES
SCOMFISHING
SCONCE
SCONCED
SCONCES
SCONCHEON
SCONCHEONS
SCONCING
SCONE
SCONES
SCONTION
SCONTIONS
SCOOG
SCOOGED
SCOOGING
SCOOGS
SCOOP
SCOOPED
SCOOPER
SCOOPERS
SCOOPFUL
SCOOPFULS
SCOOPING
SCOOPINGS
SCOOPS
SCOOT
SCOOTED
SCOOTER
SCOOTERS
SCOOTING
SCOOTS
SCOPA
SCOPAE
SCOPATE

SCOPE
SCOPES
SCOPULA
SCOPULAS
SCOPULATE
SCORBUTIC
SCORCH
SCORCHED
SCORCHER
SCORCHERS
SCORCHES
SCORCHING
SCORCHINGS
SCORDATO
SCORE
SCORED
SCORELINE
SCORELINES
SCORER
SCORERS
SCORES
SCORIA
SCORIAC
SCORIAE
SCORIFIED
SCORIFIER
SCORIFIERS
SCORIFIES
SCORIFY
SCORIFYING
SCORING
SCORINGS
SCORIOUS
SCORN
SCORNED
SCORNER
SCORNERS
SCORNFUL
SCORNING
SCORNINGS
SCORNS
SCORODITE
SCORODITES
SCORPER
SCORPERS
SCORPIO
SCORPIOID
SCORPION
SCORPIONS
SCORPIOS
SCORSE
SCORSED
SCORSER
SCORSERS
SCORSES
SCORSING
SCOT
SCOTCH
SCOTCHED
SCOTCHES
SCOTCHING
SCOTER
SCOTERS
SCOTIA
SCOTIAS
SCOTOMA
SCOTOMAS
SCOTOMATA
SCOTOMIES
SCOTOMY

SCOTOPIA
SCOTOPIAS
SCOTOPIC
SCOTS
SCOUG
SCOUGED
SCOUGING
SCOUGS
SCOUNDREL
SCOUNDRELS
SCOUP
SCOUPED
SCOUPING
SCOUPS
SCOUR
SCOURED
SCOURER
SCOURERS
SCOURGE
SCOURGED
SCOURGER
SCOURGERS
SCOURGES
SCOURGING
SCOURIE
SCOURIES
SCOURING
SCOURINGS
SCOURS
SCOURSE
SCOURSED
SCOURSES
SCOURSING
SCOUSE
SCOUSES
SCOUT
SCOUTED
SCOUTER
SCOUTERS
SCOUTH
SCOUTHER
SCOUTHERED
SCOUTHERING
SCOUTHERINGS
SCOUTHERS
SCOUTHERY
SCOUTHS
SCOUTING
SCOUTINGS
SCOUTS
SCOW
SCOWDER
SCOWDERED
SCOWDERING
SCOWDERINGS
SCOWDERS
SCOWL
SCOWLED
SCOWLING
SCOWLS
SCOWP
SCOWPED
SCOWPING
SCOWPS
SCOWRER
SCOWRERS
SCOWRIE
SCOWRIES
SCOWS
SCOWTH

SCOWTHER
SCOWTHERED
SCOWTHERING
SCOWTHERS
SCOWTHS
SCRAB
SCRABBED
SCRABBING
SCRABBLE
SCRABBLED
SCRABBLER
SCRABBLERS
SCRABBLES
SCRABBLING
SCRABS
SCRAE
SCRAES
SCRAG
SCRAGGED
SCRAGGIER
SCRAGGIEST
SCRAGGILY
SCRAGGING
SCRAGGLY
SCRAGGY
SCRAGS
SCRAICH
SCRAICHED
SCRAICHING
SCRAICHS
SCRAIGH
SCRAIGHED
SCRAIGHING
SCRAIGHS
SCRAM
SCRAMBLE
SCRAMBLED
SCRAMBLER
SCRAMBLERS
SCRAMBLES
SCRAMBLING
SCRAMBLINGS
SCRAMJET
SCRAMJETS
SCRAMMED
SCRAMMING
SCRAMS
SCRAN
SCRANCH
SCRANCHED
SCRANCHES
SCRANCHING
SCRANNEL
SCRANNY
SCRANS
SCRAP
SCRAPE
SCRAPED
SCRAPER
SCRAPERS
SCRAPES
SCRAPIE
SCRAPIES
SCRAPING
SCRAPINGS
SCRAPPED
SCRAPPIER
SCRAPPIEST
SCRAPPILY
SCRAPPING

SCRAPPY
SCRAPS
SCRAT
SCRATCH
SCRATCHED
SCRATCHER
SCRATCHERS
SCRATCHES
SCRATCHIER
SCRATCHIEST
SCRATCHING
SCRATCHINGS
SCRATCHY
SCRATS
SCRATTED
SCRATTING
SCRATTLE
SCRATTLED
SCRATTLES
SCRATTLING
SCRAUCH
SCRAUCHED
SCRAUCHING
SCRAUCHS
SCRAUGH
SCRAUGHED
SCRAUGHING
SCRAUGHS
SCRAW
SCRAWL
SCRAWLED
SCRAWLER
SCRAWLERS
SCRAWLIER
SCRAWLIEST
SCRAWLING
SCRAWLINGS
SCRAWLS
SCRAWLY
SCRAWM
SCRAWMED
SCRAWMING
SCRAWMS
SCRAWNIER
SCRAWNIEST
SCRAWNY
SCRAWS
SCRAY
SCRAYE
SCRAYES
SCRAYS
SCREAK
SCREAKED
SCREAKING
SCREAKS
SCREAKY
SCREAM
SCREAMED
SCREAMER
SCREAMERS
SCREAMING
SCREAMS
SCREE
SCREECH
SCREECHED
SCREECHER
SCREECHERS
SCREECHES
SCREECHIER
SCREECHIEST

SCREECHING
SCREECHY
SCREED
SCREEDED
SCREEDER
SCREEDERS
SCREEDING
SCREEDINGS
SCREEDS
SCREEN
SCREENED
SCREENER
SCREENERS
SCREENING
SCREENINGS
SCREENS
SCREES
SCREEVE
SCREEVED
SCREEVER
SCREEVERS
SCREEVES
SCREEVING
SCREEVINGS
SCREICH
SCREICHED
SCREICHING
SCREICHS
SCREIGH
SCREIGHED
SCREIGHING
SCREIGHS
SCREW
SCREWBALL
SCREWBALLS
SCREWED
SCREWER
SCREWERS
SCREWIER
SCREWIEST
SCREWING
SCREWINGS
SCREWS
SCREWTOP
SCREWTOPS
SCREWY
SCRIBABLE
SCRIBAL
SCRIBBLE
SCRIBBLED
SCRIBBLER
SCRIBBLERS
SCRIBBLES
SCRIBBLING
SCRIBBLINGS
SCRIBBLY
SCRIBE
SCRIBED
SCRIBER
SCRIBERS
SCRIBES
SCRIBING
SCRIBINGS
SCRIBISM
SCRIBISMS
SCRIECH
SCRIECHED
SCRIECHING
SCRIECHS
SCRIED

SCRIENE
SCRIENES
SCRIES
SCRIEVE
SCRIEVED
SCRIEVES
SCRIEVING
SCRIGGLE
SCRIGGLED
SCRIGGLES
SCRIGGLING
SCRIGGLY
SCRIKE
SCRIKED
SCRIKES
SCRIKING
SCRIM
SCRIMMAGE
SCRIMMAGED
SCRIMMAGES
SCRIMMAGING
SCRIMP
SCRIMPED
SCRIMPIER
SCRIMPIEST
SCRIMPILY
SCRIMPING
SCRIMPLY
SCRIMPS
SCRIMPY
SCRIMS
SCRIMSHAW
SCRIMSHAWED
SCRIMSHAWING
SCRIMSHAWS
SCRIMURE
SCRIMURES
SCRINE
SCRINES
SCRIP
SCRIPPAGE
SCRIPPAGES
SCRIPS
SCRIPT
SCRIPTED
SCRIPTING
SCRIPTORY
SCRIPTS
SCRIPTURE
SCRIPTURES
SCRITCH
SCRITCHED
SCRITCHES
SCRITCHING
SCRIVE
SCRIVED
SCRIVENER
SCRIVENERS
SCRIVES
SCRIVING
SCROBE
SCROBES
SCRODDLED
SCROFULA
SCROFULAS
SCROG
SCROGGIE
SCROGGIER
SCROGGIEST
SCROGGY

SCROGS
SCROLL
SCROLLED
SCROLLERIES
SCROLLERY
SCROLLING
SCROLLS
SCROOGE
SCROOGED
SCROOGES
SCROOGING
SCROOP
SCROOPED
SCROOPING
SCROOPS
SCROTAL
SCROTUM
SCROTUMS
SCROUGE
SCROUGED
SCROUGER
SCROUGERS
SCROUGES
SCROUGING
SCROUNGE
SCROUNGED
SCROUNGER
SCROUNGERS
SCROUNGES
SCROUNGING
SCROUNGINGS
SCROW
SCROWDGE
SCROWDGED
SCROWDGES
SCROWDGING
SCROWL
SCROWLE
SCROWLED
SCROWLES
SCROWLING
SCROWLS
SCROWS
SCROYLE
SCROYLES
SCRUB
SCRUBBED
SCRUBBER
SCRUBBERS
SCRUBBIER
SCRUBBIEST
SCRUBBING
SCRUBBINGS
SCRUBBY
SCRUBLAND
SCRUBLANDS
SCRUBS
SCRUFF
SCRUFFIER
SCRUFFIEST
SCRUFFS
SCRUFFY
SCRUM
SCRUMMAGE
SCRUMMAGED
SCRUMMAGES
SCRUMMAGING
SCRUMMED
SCRUMMIER
SCRUMMIEST

SCRUMMING
SCRUMMY
SCRUMP
SCRUMPED
SCRUMPIES
SCRUMPING
SCRUMPS
SCRUMPY
SCRUMS
SCRUNCH
SCRUNCHED
SCRUNCHES
SCRUNCHIER
SCRUNCHIEST
SCRUNCHING
SCRUNCHY
SCRUNT
SCRUNTS
SCRUNTY
SCRUPLE
SCRUPLED
SCRUPLER
SCRUPLERS
SCRUPLES
SCRUPLING
SCRUTABLE
SCRUTATOR
SCRUTATORS
SCRUTINIES
SCRUTINY
SCRUTO
SCRUTOIRE
SCRUTOIRES
SCRUTOS
SCRUZE
SCRUZED
SCRUZES
SCRUZING
SCRY
SCRYDE
SCRYER
SCRYERS
SCRYING
SCRYINGS
SCRYNE
SCRYNES
SCUBA
SCUBAS
SCUCHIN
SCUCHINS
SCUCHION
SCUCHIONS
SCUD
SCUDDALER
SCUDDALERS
SCUDDED
SCUDDER
SCUDDERS
SCUDDING
SCUDDLE
SCUDDLED
SCUDDLES
SCUDDLING
SCUDI
SCUDLER
SCUDLERS
SCUDO
SCUDS
SCUFF
SCUFFED

SCUFFIER	SCUMMED	SCUTCHES	SEADROME	SEARATS
SCUFFIEST	SCUMMER	SCUTCHING	SEADROMES	SEARCE
SCUFFING	SCUMMERS	SCUTCHINGS	SEAFARER	SEARCED
SCUFFLE	SCUMMIER	SCUTE	SEAFARERS	SEARCES
SCUFFLED	SCUMMIEST	SCUTELLA	SEAFARING	SEARCH
SCUFFLER	SCUMMING	SCUTELLAR	SEAFARINGS	SEARCHED
SCUFFLERS	SCUMMINGS	SCUTELLUM	SEAFOOD	SEARCHER
SCUFFLES	SCUMMY	SCUTES	SEAFOODS	SEARCHERS
SCUFFLING	SCUMS	SCUTIFORM	SEAGULL	SEARCHES
SCUFFS	SCUNCHEON	SCUTIGER	SEAGULLS	SEARCHING
SCUFFY	SCUNCHEONS	SCUTIGERS	SEAHORSE	SEARCING
SCUFT	SCUNGE	SCUTS	SEAHORSES	SEARE
SCUFTS	SCUNGED	SCUTTER	SEAL	SEARED
SCUG	SCUNGES	SCUTTERED	SEALANT	SEARER
SCUGGED	SCUNGIER	SCUTTERING	SEALANTS	SEARES
SCUGGING	SCUNGIEST	SCUTTERS	SEALCH	SEAREST
SCUGS	SCUNGING	SCUTTLE	SEALCHS	SEARING
SCUL	SCUNGY	SCUTTLED	SEALED	SEARINGS
SCULK	SCUNNER	SCUTTLER	SEALER	SEARNESS
SCULKED	SCUNNERED	SCUTTLERS	SEALERIES	SEARNESSES
SCULKING	SCUNNERING	SCUTTLES	SEALERS	SEARS
SCULKS	SCUNNERS	SCUTTLING	SEALERY	SEAS
SCULL	SCUP	SCUTUM	SEALGH	SEASATYR
SCULLE	SCUPPAUG	SCYBALA	SEALGHS	SEASATYRS
SCULLED	SCUPPAUGS	SCYBALOUS	SEALING	SEASCAPE
SCULLER	SCUPPER	SCYBALUM	SEALINGS	SEASCAPES
SCULLERIES	SCUPPERED	SCYE	SEALS	SEASD
SCULLERS	SCUPPERING	SCYES	SEALSKIN	SEASE
SCULLERY	SCUPPERS	SCYPHI	SEALSKINS	SEASED
SCULLES	SCUPS	SCYPHUS	SEALYHAM	SEASES
SCULLING	SCUR	SCYTALE	SEALYHAMS	SEASHELL
SCULLINGS	SCURF	SCYTALES	SEAM	SEASHELLS
SCULLION	SCURFIER	SCYTHE	SEAMAN	SEASHORE
SCULLIONS	SCURFIEST	SCYTHED	SEAMANLY	SEASHORES
SCULLS	SCURFS	SCYTHEMAN	SEAMARK	SEASICK
SCULP	SCURFY	SCYTHEMEN	SEAMARKS	SEASICKER
SCULPED	SCURRED	SCYTHER	SEAME	SEASICKEST
SCULPIN	SCURRIED	SCYTHERS	SEAMED	SEASIDE
SCULPING	SCURRIER	SCYTHES	SEAMEN	SEASIDES
SCULPINS	SCURRIERS	SCYTHING	SEAMER	SEASING
SCULPS	SCURRIES	SDAINE	SEAMERS	SEASON
SCULPSIT	SCURRIL	SDAINED	SEAMES	SEASONAL
SCULPT	SCURRILE	SDAINES	SEAMIER	SEASONED
SCULPTED	SCURRING	SDAINING	SEAMIEST	SEASONER
SCULPTING	SCURRIOUR	SDAYN	SEAMINESS	SEASONERS
SCULPTOR	SCURRIOURS	SDAINED	SEAMINESSES	SEASONING
SCULPTORS	SCURRY	SDAYNING	SEAMING	SEASONINGS
SCULPTS	SCURRYING	SDAYNS	SEAMLESS	SEASONS
SCULPTURE	SCURS	SDEIGNE	SEAMOUNT	SEASURE
SCULPTURED	SCURVIER	SDEIGNED	SEAMOUNTS	SEASURES
SCULPTURES	SCURVIES	SDEIGNES	SEAMS	SEAT
SCULPTURING	SCURVIEST	SDEIGNING	SEAMSTER	SEATED
SCULPTURINGS	SCURVILY	SDEIN	SEAMSTERS	SEATER
SCULS	SCURVY	SDEINED	SEAMY	SEATERS
SCUM	SCUSE	SDEINING	SEAN	SEATING
SCUMBAG	SCUSED	SDEINS	SÉANCE	SEATINGS
SCUMBAGS	SCUSES	SEA	SÉANCES	SEATLESS
SCUMBER	SCUSING	SEABED	SEANED	SEATS
SCUMBERED	SCUT	SEABEDS	SEANING	SEAWARD
SCUMBERING	SCUTA	SEABERRIES	SEANNACHIES	SEAWARDLY
SCUMBERS	SCUTAGE	SEABERRY	SEANNACHY	SEAWARDS
SCUMBLE	SCUTAGES	SEABOARD	SEANS	SEAWAY
SCUMBLED	SCUTAL	SEABOARDS	SEAPLANE	SEAWAYS
SCUMBLES	SCUTATE	SEABORNE	SEAPLANES	SEAWEED
SCUMBLING	SCUTCH	SEACOAST	SEAPORT	SEAWEEDS
SCUMBLINGS	SCUTCHED	SEACOASTS	SEAPORTS	SEAWORTHY
SCUMFISH	SCUTCHEON	SEACRAFT	SEAQUAKE	SEAZE
SCUMFISHED	SCUTCHEONS	SEACRAFTS	SEAQUAKES	SEAZED
SCUMFISHES	SCUTCHER	SEACUNNIES	SEAR	SEAZES
SCUMFISHING	SCUTCHERS	SEACUNNY	SEARAT	SEAZING

SEBACEOUS
SEBACIC
SEBATE
SEBATES
SEBESTEN
SEBESTENS
SEBIFIC
SEBUM
SEBUMS
SEBUNDIES
SEBUNDY
SEC
SECANT
SECANTS
SECATEUR
SECATEURS
SECCO
SECCOS
SECEDE
SECEDED
SECEDER
SECEDERS
SECEDES
SECEDING
SECERN
SECERNED
SECERNENT
SECERNENTS
SECERNING
SECERNS
SECESH
SECESHER
SECESHERS
SECESHES
SECESSION
SECESSIONS
SECKEL
SECKELS
SECLUDE
SECLUDED
SECLUDES
SECLUDING
SECLUSION
SECLUSIONS
SECLUSIVE
SECODONT
SECODONTS
SECOND
SECONDARIES
SECONDARY
SECONDE
SECONDED
SECONDEE
SECONDEES
SECONDER
SECONDERS
SECONDES
SECONDI
SECONDING
SECONDLY
SECONDO
SECONDS
SECRECIES
SECRECY
SECRET
SECRETA
SECRETAGE
SECRETAGES
SECRETARIES
SECRETARY

SECRETE
SECRETED
SECRETES
SECRETIN
SECRETING
SECRETINS
SECRETION
SECRETIONS
SECRETIVE
SECRETLY
SECRETORY
SECRETS
SECS
SECT
SECTARIAL
SECTARIAN
SECTARIANS
SECTARIES
SECTARY
SECTATOR
SECTATORS
SECTILE
SECTILITIES
SECTILITY
SECTION
SECTIONAL
SECTIONED
SECTIONING
SECTIONS
SECTOR
SECTORAL
SECTORED
SECTORIAL
SECTORIALS
SECTORING
SECTORS
SECTS
SECULAR
SECULARLY
SECULARS
SECULUM
SECULUMS
SECUND
SECUNDINE
SECUNDINES
SECUNDUM
SECURABLE
SECURANCE
SECURANCES
SECURE
SECURED
SECURELY
SECURER
SECURERS
SECURES
SECUREST
SECURING
SECURITAN
SECURITANS
SECURITIES
SECURITY
SED
SEDAN
SEDANS
SEDATE
SEDATED
SEDATELY
SEDATER
SEDATES
SEDATEST

SEDATING
SEDATION
SEDATIONS
SEDATIVE
SEDATIVES
SEDENT
SEDENTARY
SEDERUNT
SEDERUNTS
SEDES
SEDGE
SEDGED
SEDGELAND
SEDGELANDS
SEDGES
SEDGIER
SEDGIEST
SEDGY
SEDILE
SEDILIA
SEDIMENT
SEDIMENTED
SEDIMENTING
SEDIMENTS
SEDITION
SEDITIONS
SEDITIOUS
SEDUCE
SEDUCED
SEDUCER
SEDUCERS
SEDUCES
SEDUCING
SEDUCINGS
SEDUCTION
SEDUCTIONS
SEDUCTIVE
SEDUCTOR
SEDUCTORS
SEDULITIES
SEDULITY
SEDULOUS
SEDUM
SEDUMS
SEE
SEEABLE
SEECATCH
SEECATCHIE
SEED
SEEDBED
SEEDBEDS
SEEDBOX
SEEDBOXES
SEEDCAKE
SEEDCAKES
SEEDED
SEEDER
SEEDERS
SEEDIER
SEEDIEST
SEEDILY
SEEDINESS
SEEDINESSES
SEEDING
SEEDINGS
SEEDLESS
SEEDLING
SEEDLINGS
SEEDLIP
SEEDLIPS

SEEDNESS
SEEDNESSES
SEEDS
SEEDSMAN
SEEDSMEN
SEEDY
SEEING
SEEINGS
SEEK
SEEKER
SEEKERS
SEEKING
SEEKS
SEEL
SEELD
SEELED
SEELING
SEELINGS
SEELS
SEELY
SEEM
SEEMED
SEEMELESS
SEEMER
SEEMERS
SEEMING
SEEMINGLY
SEEMINGS
SEEMLESS
SEEMLESSE
SEEMLIER
SEEMLIEST
SEEMLIHED
SEEMLIHEDS
SEEMLY
SEEMLYHED
SEEMLYHEDS
SEEMS
SEEN
SEEP
SEEPAGE
SEEPAGES
SEEPED
SEEPIER
SEEPIEST
SEEPING
SEEPS
SEEPY
SEER
SEERESS
SEERESSES
SEERS
SEES
SEESAW
SEESAWED
SEESAWING
SEESAWS
SEETHE
SEETHED
SEETHER
SEETHERS
SEETHES
SEETHING
SEETHINGS
SEEWING
SEG
SEGAR
SEGARS
SEGGAR
SEGGARS

SEGHOL
SEGHOLATE
SEGHOLATES
SEGHOLS
SEGMENT
SEGMENTAL
SEGMENTED
SEGMENTING
SEGMENTS
SEGNO
SEGNOS
SEGO
SEGOL
SEGOLATE
SEGOLATES
SEGOLS
SEGOS
SEGREANT
SEGREGATE
SEGREGATED
SEGREGATES
SEGREGATING
SEGS
SEGUE
SEGUED
SEGUEING
SEGUES
SEI
SEICENTO
SEICENTOS
SEICHE
SEICHES
SEIF
SEIFS
SEIGNEUR
SEIGNEURS
SEIGNIOR
SEIGNIORIES
SEIGNIORS
SEIGNIORY
SEIGNORAL
SEIGNORIES
SEIGNORY
SEIL
SEILED
SEILING
SEILS
SEINE
SEINED
SEINER
SEINERS
SEINES
SEINING
SEININGS
SEIS
SEISE
SEISED
SEISES
SEISIN
SEISING
SEISINS
SEISM
SEISMAL
SEISMIC
SEISMICAL
SEISMISM
SEISMISMS
SEISMS
SEITIES
SEITY

SEIZABLE
SEIZE
SEIZED
SEIZER
SEIZERS
SEIZES
SEIZIN
SEIZING
SEIZINGS
SEIZINS
SEIZURE
SEIZURES
SEJANT
SEJEANT
SEKOS
SEKOSES
SEKT
SEKTS
SEL
SELACHIAN
SELACHIANS
SELADANG
SELADANGS
SELAH
SELAHS
SELCOUTH
SELD
SELDOM
SELDSEEN
SELDSHOWN
SELE
SELECT
SELECTED
SELECTING
SELECTION
SELECTIONS
SELECTIVE
SELECTOR
SELECTORS
SELECTS
SELENATE
SELENATES
SELENIC
SELENIDE
SELENIDES
SELENIOUS
SELENITE
SELENITES
SELENITIC
SELENIUM
SELENIUMS
SELENOUS
SELES
SELF
SELFED
SELFHOOD
SELFHOODS
SELFING
SELFISH
SELFISHLY
SELFISM
SELFISMS
SELFIST
SELFISTS
SELFLESS
SELFNESS
SELFNESSES
SELFS
SELICTAR
SELICTARS

SELKIE
SELKIES
SELL
SELLABLE
SELLE
SELLER
SELLERS
SELLES
SELLING
SELLOTAPE
SELLOTAPED
SELLOTAPES
SELLOTAPING
SELLS
SELS
SELTZER
SELTZERS
SELVA
SELVAGE
SELVAGED
SELVAGEE
SELVAGEES
SELVAGES
SELVAGING
SELVAS
SELVEDGE
SELVEDGED
SELVEDGES
SELVEDGING
SELVES
SEMANTEME
SEMANTEMES
SEMANTIC
SEMANTICS
SEMANTRA
SEMANTRON
SEMAPHORE
SEMAPHORED
SEMAPHORES
SEMAPHORING
SEMATIC
SEMBLABLE
SEMBLABLES
SEMBLABLY
SEMBLANCE
SEMBLANCES
SEMBLANT
SEMBLANTS
SEMBLE
SEMBLED
SEMBLES
SEMBLING
SEMÉ
SEMÉE
SEMEIA
SEMEION
SEMEIOTIC
SEMEIOTICS
SEMEME
SEMEMES
SEMEN
SEMENS
SEMESTER
SEMESTERS
SEMESTRAL
SEMI
SEMIANGLE
SEMIANGLES
SEMIBREVE
SEMIBREVES

SEMIBULL
SEMIBULLS
SEMICOLON
SEMICOLONS
SEMICOMA
SEMICOMAS
SEMIE
SEMIES
SEMIFINAL
SEMIFINALS
SEMIFLUID
SEMIFLUIDS
SEMILOG
SEMILOGS
SEMILUNE
SEMILUNES
SEMINAL
SEMINALLY
SEMINAR
SEMINARIES
SEMINARS
SEMINARY
SEMINATE
SEMINATED
SEMINATES
SEMINATING
SEMIOLOGIES
SEMIOLOGY
SEMIOTIC
SEMIOTICS
SEMIPED
SEMIPEDS
SEMIPLUME
SEMIPLUMES
SEMIS
SEMISES
SEMITAR
SEMITARS
SEMITAUR
SEMITAURS
SEMITONE
SEMITONES
SEMITONIC
SEMIVOWEL
SEMIVOWELS
SEMMIT
SEMMITS
SEMOLINA
SEMOLINAS
SEMPER
SEMPITERN
SEMPLE
SEMPLER
SEMPLEST
SEMPLICE
SEMPRE
SEMPSTER
SEMPSTERS
SEMSEM
SEMSEMS
SEMUNCIA
SEMUNCIAE
SEMUNCIAL
SEMUNCIAS
SEN
SENARIES
SENARII
SENARIUS
SENARY
SENATE

SENATES
SENATOR
SENATORS
SEND
SENDAL
SENDALS
SENDED
SENDER
SENDERS
SENDING
SENDINGS
SENDS
SENECIO
SENECIOS
SENEGA
SENEGAS
SENESCENT
SENESCHAL
SENESCHALS
SENGREEN
SENGREENS
SENILE
SENILITIES
SENILITY
SENIOR
SENIORITIES
SENIORITY
SENIORS
SENNA
SENNACHIE
SENNACHIES
SENNAS
SENNET
SENNETS
SENNIGHT
SENNIGHTS
SENNIT
SENNITS
SENS
SENSA
SENSATION
SENSATIONS
SENSE
SENSED
SENSEFUL
SENSELESS
SENSES
SENSIBLE
SENSIBLER
SENSIBLEST
SENSIBLY
SENSILE
SENSILLA
SENSILLUM
SENSING
SENSINGS
SENSISM
SENSISMS
SENSIST
SENSISTS
SENSITISE
SENSITISED
SENSITISES
SENSITISING
SENSITIVE
SENSITIVES
SENSITIZE
SENSITIZED
SENSITIZES
SENSITIZING

SENSOR
SENSORIAL
SENSORIES
SENSORIUM
SENSORIUMS
SENSORS
SENSORY
SENSUAL
SENSUALLY
SENSUALTIES
SENSUALTY
SENSUISM
SENSUISMS
SENSUIST
SENSUISTS
SENSUM
SENSUOUS
SENT
SENTED
SENTENCE
SENTENCED
SENTENCER
SENTENCERS
SENTENCES
SENTENCING
SENTIENCE
SENTIENCES
SENTIENCIES
SENTIENCY
SENTIENT
SENTIENTS
SENTIMENT
SENTIMENTS
SENTINEL
SENTINELLED
SENTINELLING
SENTINELS
SENTING
SENTRIES
SENTRY
SENTS
SENVIES
SENVY
SENZA
SEPAD
SEPADDED
SEPADDING
SEPADS
SEPAL
SEPALINE
SEPALODIES
SEPALODY
SEPALOID
SEPALOUS
SEPALS
SEPARABLE
SEPARABLY
SEPARATE
SEPARATED
SEPARATES
SEPARATING
SEPARATOR
SEPARATORS
SEPARATUM
SEPARATUMS
SEPHEN
SEPHENS
SEPIA
SEPIAS
SEPIMENT

SEPIMENTS	SEQUELS	SERES	SERIPHS	SERRAN
SEPIOLITE	SEQUENCE	SEREST	SERJEANCIES	SERRANID
SEPIOLITES	SEQUENCED	SERF	SERJEANCY	SERRANIDS
SEPIOST	SEQUENCES	SERFAGE	SERJEANT	SERRANOID
SEPIOSTS	SEQUENCING	SERFAGES	SERJEANTIES	SERRANOIDS
SEPIUM	SEQUENT	SERFDOM	SERJEANTS	SERRANS
SEPIUMS	SEQUENTS	SERFDOMS	SERJEANTY	SERRAS
SEPOY	SEQUESTER	SERFHOOD	SERK	SERRATE
SEPOYS	SEQUESTERED	SERFHOODS	SERKALI	SERRATED
SEPPUKU	SEQUESTERING	SERFISH	SERKALIS	SERRATES
SEPPUKUS	SEQUESTERS	SERFS	SERKS	SERRATING
SEPS	SEQUIN	SERFSHIP	SERMON	SERRATION
SEPSES	SEQUINS	SERFSHIPS	SERMONED	SERRATIONS
SEPSIS	SEQUOIA	SERGE	SERMONEER	SERRATURE
SEPT	SEQUOIAS	SERGEANCIES	SERMONEERS	SERRATURES
SEPTA	SERA	SERGEANCY	SERMONER	SERRATUS
SEPTAL	SÉRAC	SERGEANT	SERMONERS	SERRATUSES
SEPTARIA	SÉRACS	SERGEANTS	SERMONET	SERRE
SEPTARIAN	SERAFILE	SERGES	SERMONETS	SERRED
SEPTARIUM	SERAFILES	SERIAL	SERMONIC	SERREFILE
SEPTATE	SERAGLIO	SERIALISE	SERMONING	SERREFILES
SEPTATION	SERAGLIOS	SERIALISED	SERMONINGS	SERRES
SEPTATIONS	SERAI	SERIALISES	SERMONISE	SERRICORN
SEPTEMFID	SERAIL	SERIALISING	SERMONISED	SERRIED
SEPTEMVIR	SERAILS	SERIALISM	SERMONISES	SERRIES
SEPTEMVIRI	SERAIS	SERIALISMS	SERMONISH	SERRING
SEPTEMVIRS	SERAL	SERIALIST	SERMONISING	SERRS
SEPTENARIES	SERANG	SERIALISTS	SERMONIZE	SERRULATE
SEPTENARY	SERANGS	SERIALITIES	SERMONIZED	SERRY
SEPTENNIA	SERAPE	SERIALITY	SERMONIZES	SERRYING
SEPTET	SERAPES	SERIALIZE	SERMONIZING	SERUEWE
SEPTETS	SERAPH	SERIALIZED	SERMONS	SERUEWED
SEPTETT	SERAPHIC	SERIALIZES	SEROLOGIES	SERUEWES
SEPTETTE	SERAPHIM	SERIALIZING	SEROLOGY	SERUEWING
SEPTETTES	SERAPHIMS	SERIALLY	SERON	SERUM
SEPTETTS	SERAPHIN	SERIALS	SERONS	SERUMS
SEPTIC	SERAPHINE	SERIATE	SEROON	SERVAL
SEPTICITIES	SERAPHINES	SERIATED	SEROONS	SERVALS
SEPTICITY	SERAPHINS	SERIATELY	SEROSA	SERVANT
SEPTIFORM	SERAPHS	SERIATES	SEROSAE	SERVANTED
SEPTIMAL	SERASKIER	SERIATIM	SEROSAS	SERVANTING
SEPTIME	SERASKIERS	SERIATING	SEROSITIES	SERVANTRIES
SEPTIMES	SERDAB	SERIATION	SEROSITY	SERVANTRY
SEPTIMOLE	SERDABS	SERIATIONS	SEROTINE	SERVANTS
SEPTIMOLES	SERE	SERIC	SEROTINES	SERVE
SEPTLEVA	SERED	SERICEOUS	SEROTONIN	SERVED
SEPTLEVAS	SEREIN	SERICIN	SEROTONINS	SERVER
SEPTS	SEREINS	SERICINS	SEROTYPE	SERVERIES
SEPTUM	SERENADE	SERICITE	SEROTYPED	SERVERS
SEPTUOR	SERENADED	SERICITES	SEROTYPES	SERVERY
SEPTUORS	SERENADER	SERICITIC	SEROTYPING	SERVES
SEPTUPLE	SERENADERS	SERICON	SEROUS	SERVEWE
SEPTUPLED	SERENADES	SERICONS	SEROW	SERVEWED
SEPTUPLES	SERENADING	SERIEMA	SEROWS	SERVEWES
SEPTUPLET	SERENATA	SERIEMAS	SERPENT	SERVEWING
SEPTUPLETS	SERENATAS	SERIES	SERPENTED	SERVICE
SEPTUPLING	SERENATE	SERIF	SERPENTING	SERVICED
SEPULCHRE	SERENATES	SERIFS	SERPENTRIES	SERVICES
SEPULCHRED	SERENE	SERIGRAPH	SERPENTRY	SERVICING
SEPULCHRES	SERENED	SERIGRAPHS	SERPENTS	SERVIENT
SEPULCHRING	SERENELY	SERIN	SERPIGINES	SERVIETTE
SEPULTURE	SERENER	SERINETTE	SERPIGO	SERVIETTES
SEPULTURED	SERENES	SERINETTES	SERPIGOES	SERVILE
SEPULTURES	SERENESS	SERING	SERPULA	SERVILELY
SEPULTURING	SERENESSES	SERINGA	SERPULAE	SERVILES
SEQUACITIES	SERENEST	SERINGAS	SERPULITE	SERVILISM
SEQUACITY	SERENING	SERINS	SERPULITES	SERVILISMS
SEQUEL	SERENITIES	SERIOUS	SERR	SERVILITIES
SEQUELA	SERENITY	SERIOUSLY	SERRA	SERVILITY
SEQUELAE	SERER	SERIPH	SERRAE	SERVING

SERVINGS	SETUALE	SEXING	SFORZATO	SHAGGY
SERVITOR	SETUALES	SEXISM	SFORZATOS	SHAGREEN
SERVITORS	SETWALL	SEXISMS	SFUMATO	SHAGREENS
SERVITUDE	SETWALLS	SEXIST	SFUMATOS	SHAGROON
SERVITUDES	SEVEN	SEXISTS	SGRAFFITI	SHAGROONS
SERVO	SEVENFOLD	SEXLESS	SGRAFFITO	SHAGS
SESAME	SEVENS	SEXOLOGIES	SH	SHAH
SESAMES	SEVENTEEN	SEXOLOGY	SHABBIER	SHAHS
SESAMOID	SEVENTEENS	SEXPOT	SHABBIEST	SHAIKH
SESAMOIDS	SEVENTH	SEXPOTS	SHABBILY	SHAIKHS
SESE	SEVENTHLY	SEXT	SHABBLE	SHAIRN
SESELI	SEVENTHS	SEXTAN	SHABBLES	SHAIRNS
SESELIS	SEVENTIES	SEXTANS	SHABBY	SHAITAN
SESEY	SEVENTY	SEXTANSES	SHABRACK	SHAITANS
SESS	SEVER	SEXTANT	SHABRACKS	SHAKABLE
SESSA	SEVERABLE	SEXTANTAL	SHACK	SHAKE
SESSILE	SEVERAL	SEXTANTS	SHACKLE	SHAKEABLE
SESSION	SEVERALLY	SEXTET	SHACKLED	SHAKED
SESSIONAL	SEVERALS	SEXTETS	SHACKLES	SHAKEN
SESSIONS	SEVERALTIES	SEXTETT	SHACKLING	SHAKER
SESSPOOL	SEVERALTY	SEXTETTE	SHACKS	SHAKERISM
SESSPOOLS	SEVERANCE	SEXTETTES	SHAD	SHAKERISMS
SESTERCE	SEVERANCES	SEXTETTS	SHADBERRIES	SHAKERS
SESTERCES	SEVERE	SEXTILE	SHADBERRY	SHAKES
SESTERTIA	SEVERED	SEXTILES	SHADBUSH	SHAKIER
SESTET	SEVERELY	SEXTOLET	SHADBUSHES	SHAKIEST
SESTETS	SEVERER	SEXTOLETS	SHADDOCK	SHAKILY
SESTETT	SEVEREST	SEXTON	SHADDOCKS	SHAKINESS
SESTETTE	SEVERIES	SEXTONESS	SHADE	SHAKINESSES
SESTETTES	SEVERING	SEXTONESSES	SHADED	SHAKING
SESTETTO	SEVERITIES	SEXTONS	SHADELESS	SHAKINGS
SESTETTOS	SEVERITY	SEXTS	SHADES	SHAKO
SESTETTS	SEVERS	SEXTUOR	SHADIER	SHAKOES
SESTINA	SEVERY	SEXTUORS	SHADIEST	SHAKOS
SESTINAS	SEW	SEXTUPLE	SHADILY	SHAKT
SESTINE	SEWAGE	SEXTUPLED	SHADINESS	SHAKUDO
SESTINES	SEWAGES	SEXTUPLES	SHADINESSES	SHAKUDOS
SESTON	SEWED	SEXTUPLET	SHADING	SHAKY
SESTONS	SEWEL	SEXTUPLETS	SHADINGS	SHALE
SET	SEWELLEL	SEXTUPLING	SHADOOF	SHALED
SETA	SEWELLELS	SEXUAL	SHADOOFS	SHALES
SETACEOUS	SEWELS	SEXUALISE	SHADOW	SHALIER
SETAE	SEWEN	SEXUALISED	SHADOWED	SHALIEST
SETBACK	SEWENS	SEXUALISES	SHADOWER	SHALING
SETBACKS	SEWER	SEXUALISING	SHADOWERS	SHALL
SETNESS	SEWERAGE	SEXUALISM	SHADOWIER	SHALLI
SETNESSES	SEWERAGES	SEXUALISMS	SHADOWIEST	SHALLIS
SETON	SEWERED	SEXUALIST	SHADOWING	SHALLON
SETONS	SEWERING	SEXUALISTS	SHADOWINGS	SHALLONS
SETOSE	SEWERINGS	SEXUALITIES	SHADOWS	SHALLOON
SETS	SEWERS	SEXUALITY	SHADOWY	SHALLOONS
SETT	SEWIN	SEXUALIZE	SHADS	SHALLOP
SETTEE	SEWING	SEXUALIZED	SHADUF	SHALLOPS
SETTEES	SEWINGS	SEXUALIZES	SHADUFS	SHALLOT
SETTER	SEWINS	SEXUALIZING	SHADY	SHALLOTS
SETTERED	SEWN	SEXUALLY	SHAFT	SHALLOW
SETTERING	SEWS	SEXVALENT	SHAFTED	SHALLOWED
SETTERS	SEX	SEXY	SHAFTER	SHALLOWER
SETTING	SEXED	SEY	SHAFTERS	SHALLOWEST
SETTINGS	SEXENNIAL	SEYEN	SHAFTING	SHALLOWING
SETTLE	SEXER	SEYENS	SHAFTINGS	SHALLOWINGS
SETTLED	SEXERS	SEYS	SHAFTLESS	SHALLOWLY
SETTLER	SEXES	SEYSURE	SHAFTS	SHALLOWS
SETTLERS	SEXFID	SEYSURES	SHAG	SHALM
SETTLES	SEXFOIL	SEZ	SHAGEARED	SHALMS
SETTLING	SEXFOILS	SFERICS	SHAGGED	SHALOM
SETTLINGS	SEXIER	SFORZANDI	SHAGGIER	SHALOT
SETTLOR	SEXIEST	SFORZANDO	SHAGGIEST	SHALOTS
SETTLORS	SEXINESS	SFORZANDOS	SHAGGILY	SHALT
SETTS	SEXINESSES	SFORZATI	SHAGGING	SHALWAR

SHALWARS
SHALY
SHAM
SHAMA
SHAMAN
SHAMANIC
SHAMANISM
SHAMANISMS
SHAMANIST
SHAMANISTS
SHAMANS
SHAMAS
SHAMATEUR
SHAMATEURS
SHAMBLE
SHAMBLED
SHAMBLES
SHAMBLING
SHAMBLINGS
SHAMBOLIC
SHAME
SHAMED
SHAMEFAST
SHAMEFUL
SHAMELESS
SHAMER
SHAMERS
SHAMES
SHAMIANA
SHAMIANAH
SHAMIANAHS
SHAMIANAS
SHAMING
SHAMISEN
SHAMISENS
SHAMMED
SHAMMER
SHAMMERS
SHAMMIES
SHAMMING
SHAMMY
SHAMOY
SHAMOYED
SHAMOYING
SHAMOYS
SHAMPOO
SHAMPOOED
SHAMPOOER
SHAMPOOERS
SHAMPOOING
SHAMPOOS
SHAMROCK
SHAMROCKS
SHAMS
SHAMUS
SHAMUSES
SHAN
SHANACHIE
SHANACHIES
SHAND
SHANDIES
SHANDRIES
SHANDRY
SHANDS
SHANDY
SHANGHAI
SHANGHAIED
SHANGHAIING
SHANGHAIS
SHANK

SHANKED
SHANKING
SHANKS
SHANNIES
SHANNY
SHANS
SHANTIES
SHANTUNG
SHANTUNGS
SHANTY
SHANTYMAN
SHANTYMEN
SHAPABLE
SHAPE
SHAPEABLE
SHAPED
SHAPELESS
SHAPELIER
SHAPELIEST
SHAPELY
SHAPEN
SHAPER
SHAPERS
SHAPES
SHAPING
SHAPINGS
SHAPS
SHARD
SHARDED
SHARDS
SHARE
SHARECROP
SHARECROPPED
SHARECROPPING
SHARECROPS
SHARED
SHAREMAN
SHAREMEN
SHARER
SHARERS
SHARES
SHARESMAN
SHARESMEN
SHARIA
SHARIAS
SHARIAT
SHARIATS
SHARING
SHARINGS
SHARK
SHARKED
SHARKER
SHARKERS
SHARKING
SHARKINGS
SHARKS
SHARKSKIN
SHARKSKINS
SHARN
SHARNS
SHARNY
SHARP
SHARPED
SHARPEN
SHARPENED
SHARPENER
SHARPENERS
SHARPENING
SHARPENS
SHARPER

SHARPERS
SHARPEST
SHARPIE
SHARPIES
SHARPING
SHARPINGS
SHARPISH
SHARPLY
SHARPNESS
SHARPNESSES
SHARPS
SHASH
SHASHES
SHASHLIK
SHASHLIKS
SHASTER
SHASTERS
SHASTRA
SHASTRAS
SHAT
SHATTER
SHATTERED
SHATTERING
SHATTERS
SHATTERY
SHAUCHLE
SHAUCHLED
SHAUCHLES
SHAUCHLIER
SHAUCHLIEST
SHAUCHLING
SHAUCHLY
SHAVE
SHAVED
SHAVELING
SHAVELINGS
SHAVEN
SHAVER
SHAVERS
SHAVES
SHAVIE
SHAVIES
SHAVING
SHAVINGS
SHAW
SHAWED
SHAWING
SHAWL
SHAWLED
SHAWLING
SHAWLINGS
SHAWLLESS
SHAWLS
SHAWM
SHAWMS
SHAWS
SHAY
SHAYA
SHAYAS
SHAYS
SHCHI
SHCHIS
SHE
SHEA
SHEADING
SHEADINGS
SHEAF
SHEAFED
SHEAFIER
SHEAFIEST

SHEAFING
SHEAFS
SHEAFY
SHEAL
SHEALED
SHEALING
SHEALINGS
SHEALS
SHEAR
SHEARED
SHEARER
SHEARERS
SHEARING
SHEARINGS
SHEARLING
SHEARLINGS
SHEARMAN
SHEARMEN
SHEARS
SHEAS
SHEATH
SHEATHE
SHEATHED
SHEATHES
SHEATHIER
SHEATHIEST
SHEATHING
SHEATHINGS
SHEATHS
SHEATHY
SHEAVE
SHEAVED
SHEAVES
SHEAVING
SHEBANG
SHEBANGS
SHEBEEN
SHEBEENED
SHEBEENER
SHEBEENERS
SHEBEENING
SHEBEENINGS
SHEBEENS
SHECHITA
SHECHITAH
SHECHITAHS
SHECHITAS
SHED
SHEDDER
SHEDDERS
SHEDDING
SHEDDINGS
SHEDS
SHEEL
SHEELED
SHEELING
SHEELINGS
SHEELS
SHEEN
SHEENED
SHEENIER
SHEENIES
SHEENIEST
SHEENING
SHEENS
SHEENY
SHEEP
SHEEPDOG
SHEEPDOGS
SHEEPFOLD

SHEEPFOLDS
SHEEPIER
SHEEPIEST
SHEEPISH
SHEEPMEAT
SHEEPMEATS
SHEEPSKIN
SHEEPSKINS
SHEEPWALK
SHEEPWALKS
SHEEPY
SHEER
SHEERED
SHEERER
SHEEREST
SHEERING
SHEERLY
SHEERS
SHEET
SHEETED
SHEETIER
SHEETIEST
SHEETING
SHEETINGS
SHEETS
SHEETY
SHEHITA
SHEHITAH
SHEHITAHS
SHEHITAS
SHEIK
SHEIKDOM
SHEIKDOMS
SHEIKH
SHEIKHDOM
SHEIKHDOMS
SHEIKHS
SHEIKS
SHEILA
SHEILAS
SHEILING
SHEILINGS
SHEKEL
SHEKELS
SHELDDUCK
SHELDDUCKS
SHELDRAKE
SHELDRAKES
SHELDUCK
SHELDUCKS
SHELF
SHELFED
SHELFIER
SHELFIEST
SHELFING
SHELFROOM
SHELFROOMS
SHELFS
SHELFY
SHELL
SHELLAC
SHELLACKED
SHELLACKING
SHELLACKINGS
SHELLACS
SHELLBACK
SHELLBACKS
SHELLBARK
SHELLBARKS
SHELLDUCK

SHELLDUCKS
SHELLED
SHELLER
SHELLERS
SHELLFIRE
SHELLFIRES
SHELLFISH
SHELLFISHES
SHELLFUL
SHELLFULS
SHELLIER
SHELLIEST
SHELLING
SHELLINGS
SHELLS
SHELLWORK
SHELLWORKS
SHELLY
SHELTER
SHELTERED
SHELTERER
SHELTERERS
SHELTERING
SHELTERINGS
SHELTERS
SHELTERY
SHELTIE
SHELTIES
SHELTY
SHELVE
SHELVED
SHELVES
SHELVIER
SHELVIEST
SHELVING
SHELVINGS
SHELVY
SHEMOZZLE
SHEMOZZLED
SHEMOZZLES
SHEMOZZLING
SHEND
SHENDING
SHENDS
SHENT
SHEPHERD
SHEPHERDED
SHEPHERDING
SHEPHERDS
SHERBET
SHERBETS
SHERD
SHERDS
SHERE
SHEREEF
SHEREEFS
SHERIA
SHERIAS
SHERIAT
SHERIATS
SHERIF
SHERIFF
SHERIFFS
SHERIFIAN
SHERIFS
SHERRIES
SHERRIS
SHERRISES
SHERRY
SHES

SHET
SHETLAND
SHETS
SHETTING
SHEUCH
SHEUCHED
SHEUCHING
SHEUCHS
SHEUGH
SHEUGHED
SHEUGHING
SHEUGHS
SHEVA
SHEVAS
SHEW
SHEWBREAD
SHEWBREADS
SHEWED
SHEWEL
SHEWELS
SHEWING
SHEWN
SHEWS
SHIATSU
SHIATSUS
SHIBUICHI
SHIBUICHIS
SHICKER
SHICKERED
SHICKERS
SHICKSA
SHICKSAS
SHIDDER
SHIDDERS
SHIED
SHIEL
SHIELD
SHIELDED
SHIELDER
SHIELDERS
SHIELDING
SHIELDS
SHIELDUCK
SHIELDUCKS
SHIELED
SHIELING
SHIELINGS
SHIELS
SHIER
SHIERS
SHIES
SHIEST
SHIFT
SHIFTED
SHIFTER
SHIFTERS
SHIFTIER
SHIFTIEST
SHIFTILY
SHIFTING
SHIFTINGS
SHIFTLESS
SHIFTS
SHIFTY
SHIGELLA
SHIGELLAS
SHIITAKE
SHIKAR
SHIKAREE
SHIKAREES

SHIKARI
SHIKARIS
SHIKARS
SHIKSA
SHIKSAS
SHIKSE
SHIKSES
SHILL
SHILLABER
SHILLABERS
SHILLED
SHILLELAH
SHILLELAHS
SHILLING
SHILLINGS
SHILLS
SHILPIT
SHILY
SHIM
SHIMMER
SHIMMERED
SHIMMERING
SHIMMERINGS
SHIMMERS
SHIMMERY
SHIMMIED
SHIMMIES
SHIMMY
SHIMMYING
SHIMOZZLE
SHIMOZZLED
SHIMOZZLES
SHIMOZZLING
SHIMS
SHIN
SHINDIES
SHINDIG
SHINDIGS
SHINDY
SHINE
SHINED
SHINELESS
SHINER
SHINERS
SHINES
SHINESS
SHINESSES
SHINGLE
SHINGLED
SHINGLER
SHINGLERS
SHINGLES
SHINGLIER
SHINGLIEST
SHINGLING
SHINGLINGS
SHINGLY
SHINIER
SHINIEST
SHINING
SHININGLY
SHINNE
SHINNED
SHINNES
SHINNIED
SHINNIES
SHINNING
SHINNY
SHINNYING
SHINS

SHINTIES
SHINTY
SHINY
SHIP
SHIPBOARD
SHIPBOARDS
SHIPFUL
SHIPFULS
SHIPLAP
SHIPLAPPED
SHIPLAPPING
SHIPLAPS
SHIPLESS
SHIPMAN
SHIPMATE
SHIPMATES
SHIPMEN
SHIPMENT
SHIPMENTS
SHIPPED
SHIPPEN
SHIPPENS
SHIPPER
SHIPPERS
SHIPPING
SHIPPINGS
SHIPPO
SHIPPON
SHIPPONS
SHIPPOS
SHIPPOUND
SHIPPOUNDS
SHIPS
SHIPSHAPE
SHIPWRECK
SHIPWRECKED
SHIPWRECKING
SHIPWRECKS
SHIPYARD
SHIPYARDS
SHIR
SHIRALEE
SHIRALEES
SHIRE
SHIREMAN
SHIREMEN
SHIRES
SHIRK
SHIRKED
SHIRKER
SHIRKERS
SHIRKING
SHIRKS
SHIRR
SHIRRA
SHIRRAS
SHIRRED
SHIRRING
SHIRRINGS
SHIRRS
SHIRS
SHIRT
SHIRTED
SHIRTIER
SHIRTIEST
SHIRTING
SHIRTINGS
SHIRTLESS
SHIRTS
SHIRTY

SHIT
SHITE
SHITES
SHITING
SHITS
SHITTAH
SHITTAHS
SHITTIER
SHITTIEST
SHITTIM
SHITTIMS
SHITTING
SHITTY
SHIV
SHIVAREE
SHIVAREED
SHIVAREEING
SHIVAREES
SHIVE
SHIVER
SHIVERED
SHIVERING
SHIVERINGS
SHIVERS
SHIVERY
SHIVES
SHIVOO
SHIVOOS
SHIVS
SHIVVED
SHIVVING
SHLEMIEL
SHLEMIELS
SHLEP
SHLEPPED
SHLEPPING
SHLEPS
SHLIMAZEL
SHLIMAZELS
SHLOK
SHLOKS
SHMOOSE
SHMOOSED
SHMOOSES
SHMOOSING
SHMOOZE
SHMOOZED
SHMOOZES
SHMOOZING
SHOAL
SHOALED
SHOALER
SHOALEST
SHOALIER
SHOALIEST
SHOALING
SHOALINGS
SHOALNESS
SHOALNESSES
SHOALS
SHOALWISE
SHOALY
SHOAT
SHOATS
SHOCHET
SHOCHETIM
SHOCK
SHOCKED
SHOCKER
SHOCKERS

SHOCKING
SHOCKS
SHOD
SHODDIER
SHODDIES
SHODDIEST
SHODDILY
SHODDY
SHODER
SHODERS
SHOE
SHOEBLACK
SHOEBLACKS
SHOED
SHOEHORN
SHOEHORNED
SHOEHORNING
SHOEHORNS
SHOEING
SHOEINGS
SHOELESS
SHOEMAKER
SHOEMAKERS
SHOER
SHOERS
SHOES
SHOESHINE
SHOESHINES
SHOFAR
SHOFARS
SHOFROTH
SHOG
SHOGGED
SHOGGING
SHOGGLE
SHOGGLY
SHOGS
SHOGUN
SHOGUNAL
SHOGUNATE
SHOGUNATES
SHOGUNS
SHOJI
SHOJIS
SHOLA
SHOLAS
SHONE
SHOO
SHOOED
SHOOGIE
SHOOGIED
SHOOGIEING
SHOOGIES
SHOOGLE
SHOOGLED
SHOOGLES
SHOOGLIER
SHOOGLIEST
SHOOGLING
SHOOGLY
SHOOING
SHOOK
SHOOKS
SHOOL
SHOOLED
SHOOLING
SHOOLS
SHOON
SHOOS
SHOOT

SHOOTABLE
SHOOTER
SHOOTERS
SHOOTING
SHOOTINGS
SHOOTIST
SHOOTISTS
SHOOTS
SHOP
SHOPBOARD
SHOPBOARDS
SHOPE
SHOPFUL
SHOPFULS
SHOPHAR
SHOPHARS
SHOPHROTH
SHOPMAN
SHOPMEN
SHOPPED
SHOPPER
SHOPPERS
SHOPPIER
SHOPPIEST
SHOPPING
SHOPPINGS
SHOPPY
SHOPS
SHOPWORN
SHORAN
SHORANS
SHORE
SHORED
SHORELESS
SHORELINE
SHORELINES
SHOREMAN
SHOREMEN
SHORER
SHORERS
SHORES
SHORESMAN
SHORESMEN
SHOREWARD
SHOREWARDS
SHORING
SHORINGS
SHORN
SHORT
SHORTAGE
SHORTAGES
SHORTCAKE
SHORTCAKES
SHORTCUT
SHORTCUTS
SHORTED
SHORTEN
SHORTENED
SHORTENER
SHORTENERS
SHORTENING
SHORTENINGS
SHORTENS
SHORTER
SHORTEST
SHORTFALL
SHORTFALLS
SHORTGOWN
SHORTGOWNS
SHORTHAND

SHORTHANDS
SHORTIE
SHORTIES
SHORTING
SHORTISH
SHORTLY
SHORTNESS
SHORTNESSES
SHORTS
SHORTY
SHOT
SHOTE
SHOTES
SHOTFIRER
SHOTFIRERS
SHOTGUN
SHOTGUNS
SHOTMAKER
SHOTMAKERS
SHOTPROOF
SHOTS
SHOTT
SHOTTED
SHOTTEN
SHOTTING
SHOTTLE
SHOTTLES
SHOTTS
SHOUGH
SHOUGHS
SHOULD
SHOULDER
SHOULDERED
SHOULDERING
SHOULDERINGS
SHOULDERS
SHOULDEST
SHOULDST
SHOUT
SHOUTED
SHOUTER
SHOUTERS
SHOUTHER
SHOUTHERED
SHOUTHERING
SHOUTHERS
SHOUTING
SHOUTINGS
SHOUTS
SHOVE
SHOVED
SHOVEL
SHOVELER
SHOVELERS
SHOVELFUL
SHOVELFULS
SHOVELLED
SHOVELLER
SHOVELLERS
SHOVELLING
SHOVELS
SHOVER
SHOVERS
SHOVES
SHOVING
SHOW
SHOWBIZ
SHOWBIZZY
SHOWBREAD
SHOWBREADS

SHOWCARD
SHOWCARDS
SHOWCASE
SHOWCASED
SHOWCASES
SHOWCASING
SHOWED
SHOWER
SHOWERED
SHOWERFUL
SHOWERING
SHOWERINGS
SHOWERS
SHOWERY
SHOWGHE
SHOWGHES
SHOWGIRL
SHOWGIRLS
SHOWIER
SHOWIEST
SHOWILY
SHOWINESS
SHOWINESSES
SHOWING
SHOWINGS
SHOWMAN
SHOWMANLY
SHOWMEN
SHOWN
SHOWPIECE
SHOWPIECES
SHOWPLACE
SHOWPLACES
SHOWROOM
SHOWROOMS
SHOWS
SHOWY
SHRADDHA
SHRADDHAS
SHRANK
SHRAPNEL
SHRAPNELS
SHRED
SHREDDED
SHREDDER
SHREDDERS
SHREDDIER
SHREDDIEST
SHREDDING
SHREDDINGS
SHREDDY
SHREDLESS
SHREDS
SHREEK
SHREEKED
SHREEKING
SHREEKS
SHREIK
SHREIKED
SHREIKING
SHREIKS
SHREW
SHREWD
SHREWDER
SHREWDEST
SHREWDLY
SHREWED
SHREWING
SHREWISH
SHREWMICE

SHREWS
SHRIECH
SHRIECHED
SHRIECHES
SHRIECHING
SHRIEK
SHRIEKED
SHRIEKER
SHRIEKERS
SHRIEKING
SHRIEKINGS
SHRIEKS
SHRIEVAL
SHRIEVE
SHRIEVED
SHRIEVES
SHRIEVING
SHRIFT
SHRIFTS
SHRIGHT
SHRIGHTS
SHRIKE
SHRIKED
SHRIKES
SHRIKING
SHRILL
SHRILLED
SHRILLER
SHRILLEST
SHRILLING
SHRILLINGS
SHRILLS
SHRILLY
SHRIMP
SHRIMPED
SHRIMPER
SHRIMPERS
SHRIMPING
SHRIMPINGS
SHRIMPS
SHRINAL
SHRINE
SHRINED
SHRINES
SHRINING
SHRINK
SHRINKAGE
SHRINKAGES
SHRINKER
SHRINKERS
SHRINKING
SHRINKS
SHRITCH
SHRITCHED
SHRITCHES
SHRITCHING
SHRIVE
SHRIVED
SHRIVEL
SHRIVELLED
SHRIVELLING
SHRIVELS
SHRIVEN
SHRIVER
SHRIVERS
SHRIVES
SHRIVING
SHRIVINGS
SHROFF
SHROFFAGE

SHROFFAGES	SHUFFLING	SIB	SICKNESSES	SIEMENS
SHROFFED	SHUFFLINGS	SIBB	SICKNURSE	SIEN
SHROFFING	SHUFTI	SIBBS	SICKNURSES	SIENNA
SHROFFS	SHUFTIES	SIBILANCE	SICKROOM	SIENNAS
SHROUD	SHUFTIS	SIBILANCES	SICKROOMS	SIENS
SHROUDED	SHUFTY	SIBILANCIES	SICKS	SIENT
SHROUDIER	SHUL	SIBILANCY	SICLIKE	SIENTS
SHROUDIEST	SHULS	SIBILANT	SICS	SIERRA
SHROUDING	SHUN	SIBILANTS	SIDA	SIERRAN
SHROUDINGS	SHUNLESS	SIBILATE	SIDALCEA	SIERRAS
SHROUDS	SHUNNED	SIBILATED	SIDALCEAS	SIESTA
SHROUDY	SHUNNING	SIBILATES	SIDAS	SIESTAS
SHROVE	SHUNS	SIBILATING	SIDDHA	SIETH
SHROVED	SHUNT	SIBILOUS	SIDDHAS	SIETHS
SHROVES	SHUNTED	SIBLING	SIDDHI	SIEVE
SHROVING	SHUNTER	SIBLINGS	SIDDHIS	SIEVED
SHROW	SHUNTERS	SIBS	SIDDUR	SIEVERT
SHROWD	SHUNTING	SIBSHIP	SIDDURIM	SIEVERTS
SHROWED	SHUNTINGS	SIBSHIPS	SIDE	SIEVES
SHROWING	SHUNTS	SIBYL	SIDEARM	SIEVING
SHROWS	SHUSH	SIBYLS	SIDEARMS	SIFAKA
SHRUB	SHUSHED	SIC	SIDEBOARD	SIFAKAS
SHRUBBED	SHUSHES	SICCAN	SIDEBOARDS	SIFFLE
SHRUBBERIES	SHUSHING	SICCAR	SIDEBURNS	SIFFLED
SHRUBBERY	SHUT	SICCATIVE	SIDECAR	SIFFLES
SHRUBBIER	SHUTS	SICCATIVES	SIDECARS	SIFFLING
SHRUBBIEST	SHUTTER	SICCED	SIDED	SIFT
SHRUBBING	SHUTTERED	SICCING	SIDELIGHT	SIFTED
SHRUBBY	SHUTTERING	SICCITIES	SIDELIGHTS	SIFTER
SHRUBLESS	SHUTTERINGS	SICCITY	SIDELING	SIFTERS
SHRUBS	SHUTTERS	SICE	SIDELOCK	SIFTING
SHRUG	SHUTTING	SICES	SIDELOCKS	SIFTINGLY
SHRUGGED	SHUTTLE	SICH	SIDELONG	SIFTINGS
SHRUGGING	SHUTTLED	SICILIANA	SIDER	SIFTS
SHRUGS	SHUTTLES	SICILIANAS	SIDERAL	SIGH
SHRUNK	SHUTTLING	SICILIANE	SIDEREAL	SIGHED
SHRUNKEN	SHWA	SICILIANO	SIDERITE	SIGHER
SHTCHI	SHWAS	SICILIANOS	SIDERITES	SIGHERS
SHTCHIS	SHY	SICK	SIDERITIC	SIGHFUL
SHTETL	SHYER	SICKED	SIDEROSES	SIGHING
SHTETLS	SHYERS	SICKEN	SIDEROSIS	SIGHINGLY
SHTICK	SHYEST	SICKENED	SIDEROSISES	SIGHS
SHTICKS	SHYING	SICKENER	SIDERS	SIGHT
SHTOOK	SHYISH	SICKENERS	SIDES	SIGHTED
SHTOOKS	SHYLY	SICKENING	SIDESMAN	SIGHTER
SHTOOM	SHYNESS	SICKENINGS	SIDESMEN	SIGHTERS
SHTUCK	SHYNESSES	SICKENS	SIDESWIPE	SIGHTING
SHTUCKS	SHYSTER	SICKER	SIDESWIPES	SIGHTLESS
SHTUM	SHYSTERS	SICKERLY	SIDEWALK	SIGHTLIER
SHTUMM	SI	SICKEST	SIDEWALKS	SIGHTLIEST
SHUBUNKIN	SIAL	SICKIE	SIDEWARD	SIGHTLY
SHUBUNKINS	SIALIC	SICKIES	SIDEWARDS	SIGHTS
SHUCK	SIALOGRAM	SICKING	SIDEWAY	SIGHTSAW
SHUCKED	SIALOGRAMS	SICKISH	SIDEWAYS	SIGHTSEE
SHUCKER	SIALOID	SICKISHLY	SIDEWISE	SIGHTSEEING
SHUCKERS	SIALOLITH	SICKLE	SIDHA	SIGHTSEEINGS
SHUCKING	SIALOLITHS	SICKLED	SIDHAS	SIGHTSEEN
SHUCKINGS	SIALON	SICKLEMAN	SIDING	SIGHTSEER
SHUCKS	SIALONS	SICKLEMEN	SIDINGS	SIGHTSEERS
SHUDDER	SIALS	SICKLES	SIDLE	SIGHTSEES
SHUDDERED	SIAMANG	SICKLIED	SIDLED	SIGIL
SHUDDERING	SIAMANGS	SICKLIER	SIDLES	SIGILLARY
SHUDDERINGS	SIAMESE	SICKLIES	SIDLING	SIGILLATE
SHUDDERS	SIAMESED	SICKLIEST	SIEGE	SIGILS
SHUDDERY	SIAMESES	SICKLILY	SIEGED	SIGISBEI
SHUFFLE	SIAMESING	SICKLY	SIEGER	SIGISBEO
SHUFFLED	SIAMEZE	SICKLYING	SIEGERS	SIGLA
SHUFFLER	SIAMEZED	SICKMAN	SIEGES	SIGMA
SHUFFLERS	SIAMEZES	SICKMEN	SIEGING	SIGMAS
SHUFFLES	SIAMEZING	SICKNESS	SIELD	SIGMATE

SIGMATED
SIGMATES
SIGMATIC
SIGMATING
SIGMATION
SIGMATIONS
SIGMATISM
SIGMATISMS
SIGMATRON
SIGMATRONS
SIGMOID
SIGMOIDAL
SIGN
SIGNAL
SIGNALISE
SIGNALISED
SIGNALISES
SIGNALISING
SIGNALIZE
SIGNALIZED
SIGNALIZES
SIGNALIZING
SIGNALLED
SIGNALLER
SIGNALLERS
SIGNALLING
SIGNALLINGS
SIGNALLY
SIGNALMAN
SIGNALMEN
SIGNALS
SIGNARIES
SIGNARY
SIGNATORIES
SIGNATORY
SIGNATURE
SIGNATURES
SIGNBOARD
SIGNBOARDS
SIGNED
SIGNER
SIGNERS
SIGNET
SIGNETED
SIGNETS
SIGNEUR
SIGNEURIE
SIGNEURIES
SIGNIEUR
SIGNIEURS
SIGNIFICS
SIGNIFIED
SIGNIFIER
SIGNIFIERS
SIGNIFIES
SIGNIFY
SIGNIFYING
SIGNING
SIGNIOR
SIGNIORS
SIGNLESS
SIGNOR
SIGNORA
SIGNORAS
SIGNORE
SIGNORES
SIGNORI
SIGNORIA
SIGNORIAL
SIGNORIAS

SIGNORIES
SIGNORINA
SIGNORINAS
SIGNORS
SIGNORY
SIGNPOST
SIGNPOSTED
SIGNPOSTING
SIGNPOSTS
SIGNS
SIKA
SIKAS
SIKE
SIKES
SILAGE
SILAGED
SILAGES
SILAGING
SILANE
SILANES
SILASTIC
SILASTICS
SILD
SILDS
SILE
SILED
SILEN
SILENCE
SILENCED
SILENCER
SILENCERS
SILENCES
SILENCING
SILENE
SILENES
SILENS
SILENT
SILENTER
SILENTEST
SILENTLY
SILENTS
SILENUS
SILENUSES
SILER
SILERS
SILES
SILESIA
SILESIAS
SILEX
SILEXES
SILICA
SILICANE
SILICANES
SILICAS
SILICATE
SILICATED
SILICATES
SILICATING
SILICEOUS
SILICIC
SILICIDE
SILICIDES
SILICIFIED
SILICIFIES
SILICIFY
SILICIFYING
SILICIOUS
SILICIUM
SILICIUMS
SILICLE

SILICLES
SILICON
SILICONE
SILICONES
SILICONS
SILICOSES
SILICOSIS
SILICOTIC
SILICOTICS
SILICULA
SILICULAS
SILICULE
SILICULES
SILING
SILIQUA
SILIQUAS
SILIQUE
SILIQUES
SILIQUOSE
SILK
SILKED
SILKEN
SILKENED
SILKENING
SILKENS
SILKIE
SILKIER
SILKIES
SILKIEST
SILKILY
SILKINESS
SILKINESSES
SILKING
SILKS
SILKTAIL
SILKTAILS
SILKWEED
SILKWEEDS
SILKWORM
SILKWORMS
SILKY
SILL
SILLABUB
SILLABUBS
SILLADAR
SILLADARS
SILLER
SILLERS
SILLIER
SILLIES
SILLIEST
SILLILY
SILLINESS
SILLINESSES
SILLOCK
SILLOCKS
SILLS
SILLY
SILO
SILOED
SILOING
SILOS
SILPHIA
SILPHIUM
SILPHIUMS
SILT
SILTATION
SILTATIONS
SILTED
SILTIER

SILTIEST
SILTING
SILTS
SILTSTONE
SILTSTONES
SILTY
SILURID
SILURIDS
SILURIST
SILURISTS
SILUROID
SILUROIDS
SILVA
SILVAE
SILVAN
SILVANS
SILVAS
SILVATIC
SILVER
SILVERED
SILVERING
SILVERINGS
SILVERISE
SILVERISED
SILVERISES
SILVERISING
SILVERIZE
SILVERIZED
SILVERIZES
SILVERIZING
SILVERLY
SILVERN
SILVERS
SILVERY
SIM
SIMA
SIMAR
SIMARRE
SIMARRES
SIMARS
SIMAS
SIMI
SIMIAL
SIMIAN
SIMICUS
SIMILAR
SIMILARLY
SIMILE
SIMILES
SIMILISE
SIMILISED
SIMILISES
SIMILISING
SIMILIZE
SIMILIZED
SIMILIZES
SIMILIZING
SIMILOR
SIMILORS
SIMIOUS
SIMIS
SIMITAR
SIMITARS
SIMKIN
SIMKINS
SIMMER
SIMMERED
SIMMERING
SIMMERS
SIMNEL

SIMNELS
SIMONIAC
SIMONIACS
SIMONIES
SIMONIOUS
SIMONIST
SIMONISTS
SIMONY
SIMOOM
SIMOOMS
SIMOON
SIMOONS
SIMORG
SIMORGS
SIMP
SIMPAI
SIMPAIS
SIMPATICO
SIMPER
SIMPERED
SIMPERER
SIMPERERS
SIMPERING
SIMPERINGS
SIMPERS
SIMPKIN
SIMPKINS
SIMPLE
SIMPLED
SIMPLER
SIMPLERS
SIMPLES
SIMPLESSE
SIMPLESSES
SIMPLEST
SIMPLETON
SIMPLETONS
SIMPLEX
SIMPLICES
SIMPLIFIED
SIMPLIFIES
SIMPLIFY
SIMPLIFYING
SIMPLING
SIMPLINGS
SIMPLISM
SIMPLISMS
SIMPLIST
SIMPLISTE
SIMPLISTS
SIMPLY
SIMPS
SIMS
SIMULACRA
SIMULACRE
SIMULACRES
SIMULANT
SIMULANTS
SIMULAR
SIMULARS
SIMULATE
SIMULATED
SIMULATES
SIMULATING
SIMULATOR
SIMULATORS
SIMULCAST
SIMULCASTED
SIMULCASTING
SIMULCASTS

SIMULIUM
SIMULIUMS
SIMURG
SIMURGH
SIMURGHS
SIMURGS
SIN
SINAPISM
SINAPISMS
SINCE
SINCERE
SINCERELY
SINCERER
SINCEREST
SINCERITIES
SINCERITY
SINCIPUT
SINCIPUTS
SIND
SINDED
SINDING
SINDINGS
SINDON
SINDONS
SINDS
SINE
SINECURE
SINECURES
SINES
SINEW
SINEWED
SINEWING
SINEWLESS
SINEWS
SINEWY
SINFONIA
SINFONIAS
SINFUL
SING
SINGABLE
SINGE
SINGED
SINGEING
SINGER
SINGERS
SINGES
SINGING
SINGINGLY
SINGINGS
SINGLE
SINGLED
SINGLES
SINGLET
SINGLETON
SINGLETONS
SINGLETS
SINGLING
SINGLINGS
SINGLY
SINGS
SINGSONG
SINGSONGED
SINGSONGING
SINGSONGS
SINGSPIEL
SINGSPIELS
SINGULAR
SINGULARS
SINGULT
SINGULTS

SINGULTUS
SINGULTUSES
SINICAL
SINICISE
SINICISED
SINICISES
SINICISING
SINICIZE
SINICIZED
SINICIZES
SINICIZING
SINISTER
SINISTRAL
SINISTRALS
SINK
SINKAGE
SINKAGES
SINKER
SINKERS
SINKIER
SINKIEST
SINKING
SINKINGS
SINKS
SINKY
SINLESS
SINLESSLY
SINNED
SINNER
SINNERED
SINNERING
SINNERS
SINNET
SINNETS
SINNING
SINOEKETE
SINOEKETES
SINOPIA
SINOPIAS
SINOPIS
SINOPISES
SINOPITE
SINOPITES
SINS
SINOYNE
SINTER
SINTERED
SINTERING
SINTERS
SINTERY
SINUATE
SINUATED
SINUATELY
SINUATION
SINUATIONS
SINUITIS
SINUITISES
SINUOSE
SINUOSITIES
SINUOSITY
SINUOUS
SINUOUSLY
SINUS
SINUSES
SINUSITIS
SINUSITISES
SINUSOID
SINUSOIDS
SIP
SIPE

SIPED
SIPES
SIPHON
SIPHONAGE
SIPHONAGES
SIPHONAL
SIPHONATE
SIPHONED
SIPHONET
SIPHONETS
SIPHONIC
SIPHONING
SIPHONS
SIPHUNCLE
SIPHUNCLES
SIPING
SIPPED
SIPPER
SIPPERS
SIPPET
SIPPETS
SIPPING
SIPPLE
SIPPLED
SIPPLES
SIPPLING
SIPS
SIR
SIRCAR
SIRCARS
SIRDAR
SIRDARS
SIRE
SIRED
SIREN
SIRENE
SIRENES
SIRENIAN
SIRENIANS
SIRENIC
SIRENS
SIRES
SIRGANG
SIRGANGS
SIRI
SIRIASES
SIRIASIS
SIRIH
SIRIHS
SIRING
SIRIS
SIRKAR
SIRKARS
SIRLOIN
SIRLOINS
SIRNAME
SIRNAMED
SIRNAMES
SIRNAMING
SIROC
SIROCCO
SIROCCOS
SIROCS
SIRRAH
SIRRAHS
SIRRED
SIRREE
SIRREES
SIRRING
SIRS

SIRUP
SIRUPED
SIRUPING
SIRUPS
SIRVENTE
SIRVENTES
SIS
SISAL
SISALS
SISERARIES
SISERARY
SISES
SISKIN
SISKINS
SISS
SISSERARIES
SISSERARY
SISSES
SISSIER
SISSIES
SISSIEST
SISSOO
SISSOOS
SISSY
SIST
SISTED
SISTER
SISTERED
SISTERING
SISTERLY
SISTERS
SISTING
SISTRA
SISTRUM
SISTS
SIT
SITAR
SITARS
SITATUNGA
SITATUNGAS
SITCOM
SITCOMS
SITDOWN
SITDOWNS
SITE
SITED
SITES
SITFAST
SITFASTS
SITH
SITHE
SITHED
SITHEN
SITHENCE
SITHENS
SITHES
SITHING
SITING
SITIOLOGIES
SITIOLOGY
SITOLOGIES
SITOLOGY
SITREP
SITREPS
SITS
SITTAR
SITTARS
SITTER
SITTERS
SITTINE

SITTING
SITTINGS
SITUATE
SITUATED
SITUATES
SITUATING
SITUATION
SITUATIONS
SITULA
SITULAE
SITUS
SITUTUNGA
SITUTUNGAS
SITZKRIEG
SITZKRIEGS
SIVER
SIVERS
SIWASH
SIWASHES
SIX
SIXAINE
SIXAINES
SIXER
SIXERS
SIXES
SIXFOLD
SIXPENCE
SIXPENCES
SIXPENNIES
SIXPENNY
SIXSCORE
SIXSCORES
SIXTE
SIXTEEN
SIXTEENER
SIXTEENERS
SIXTEENMO
SIXTEENMOS
SIXTEENS
SIXTEENTH
SIXTEENTHS
SIXTES
SIXTH
SIXTHLY
SIXTHS
SIXTIES
SIXTIETH
SIXTIETHS
SIXTY
SIZABLE
SIZAR
SIZARS
SIZARSHIP
SIZARSHIPS
SIZE
SIZEABLE
SIZED
SIZEL
SIZELS
SIZER
SIZERS
SIZES
SIZIER
SIZIEST
SIZINESS
SIZINESSES
SIZING
SIZINGS
SIZY
SIZZLE

SIZZLED
SIZZLER
SIZZLERS
SIZZLES
SIZZLING
SIZZLINGS
SJAMBOK
SJAMBOKKED
SJAMBOKKING
SJAMBOKS
SKA
SKAIL
SKAILED
SKAILING
SKAILS
SKAITH
SKAITHED
SKAITHING
SKAITHS
SKALD
SKALDIC
SKALDS
SKART
SKARTH
SKARTHS
SKARTS
SKAS
SKAT
SKATE
SKATED
SKATER
SKATERS
SKATES
SKATING
SKATINGS
SKATOLE
SKATOLES
SKATOLOGIES
SKATOLOGY
SKATS
SKATT
SKATTS
SKAW
SKAWS
SKEAN
SKEANS
SKEAR
SKEARED
SKEARING
SKEARS
SKEARY
SKEDADDLE
SKEDADDLED
SKEDADDLES
SKEDADDLING
SKEELIER
SKEELIEST
SKEELY
SKEER
SKEERED
SKEERING
SKEERS
SKEERY
SKEESICKS
SKEET
SKEETER
SKEETERS
SKEETS
SKEG
SKEGGER

SKEGGERS
SKEGS
SKEIGH
SKEIGHER
SKEIGHEST
SKEIN
SKEINS
SKELDER
SKELDERED
SKELDERING
SKELDERS
SKELETAL
SKELETON
SKELETONS
SKELF
SKELFS
SKELLIE
SKELLIED
SKELLIER
SKELLIES
SKELLIEST
SKELLOCH
SKELLOCHED
SKELLOCHING
SKELLOCHS
SKELLUM
SKELLUMS
SKELLY
SKELLYING
SKELM
SKELMS
SKELP
SKELPED
SKELPING
SKELPINGS
SKELPS
SKELTER
SKELTERED
SKELTERING
SKELTERS
SKENE
SKENES
SKEO
SKEOS
SKEP
SKEPFUL
SKEPFULS
SKEPPED
SKEPPING
SKEPS
SKEPSES
SKEPSIS
SKEPTIC
SKEPTICS
SKER
SKERRED
SKERRICK
SKERRICKS
SKERRIES
SKERRING
SKERRY
SKERS
SKETCH
SKETCHED
SKETCHER
SKETCHERS
SKETCHES
SKETCHIER
SKETCHIEST
SKETCHILY

SKETCHING
SKETCHY
SKEW
SKEWBALD
SKEWBALDS
SKEWED
SKEWER
SKEWERED
SKEWERING
SKEWERS
SKEWEST
SKEWING
SKEWS
SKI
SKIABLE
SKIAGRAM
SKIAGRAMS
SKIAGRAPH
SKIAGRAPHS
SKIAMACHIES
SKIAMACHY
SKIASCOPIES
SKIASCOPY
SKIATRON
SKIATRONS
SKID
SKIDDED
SKIDDING
SKIDOO
SKIDOOS
SKIDPAN
SKIDPANS
SKIDS
SKIED
SKIER
SKIERS
SKIES
SKIEY
SKIEYER
SKIEYEST
SKIFF
SKIFFED
SKIFFING
SKIFFLE
SKIFFLES
SKIFFS
SKIING
SKIINGS
SKIJORING
SKIJORINGS
SKILFUL
SKILFULLY
SKILL
SKILLED
SKILLESS
SKILLET
SKILLETS
SKILLIER
SKILLIES
SKILLIEST
SKILLING
SKILLINGS
SKILLION
SKILLIONS
SKILLS
SKILLY
SKIM
SKIMMED
SKIMMER
SKIMMERS

SKIMMIA
SKIMMIAS
SKIMMING
SKIMMINGS
SKIMP
SKIMPED
SKIMPIER
SKIMPIEST
SKIMPILY
SKIMPING
SKIMPS
SKIMPY
SKIMS
SKIN
SKINFLICK
SKINFLICKS
SKINFLINT
SKINFLINTS
SKINFOOD
SKINFOODS
SKINFUL
SKINFULS
SKINHEAD
SKINHEADS
SKINK
SKINKED
SKINKER
SKINKERS
SKINKING
SKINKS
SKINLESS
SKINNED
SKINNER
SKINNERS
SKINNIER
SKINNIEST
SKINNING
SKINNY
SKINS
SKINT
SKINTER
SKINTEST
SKIO
SKIOS
SKIP
SKIPJACK
SKIPJACKS
SKIPPED
SKIPPER
SKIPPERED
SKIPPERING
SKIPPERS
SKIPPET
SKIPPETS
SKIPPING
SKIPPINGS
SKIPS
SKIRL
SKIRLED
SKIRLING
SKIRLINGS
SKIRLS
SKIRMISH
SKIRMISHED
SKIRMISHES
SKIRMISHING
SKIRMISHINGS
SKIRR
SKIRRED
SKIRRET

SKIRRETS
SKIRRING
SKIRRS
SKIRT
SKIRTED
SKIRTER
SKIRTERS
SKIRTING
SKIRTINGS
SKIRTLESS
SKIRTS
SKIS
SKIT
SKITE
SKITED
SKITES
SKITING
SKITS
SKITTER
SKITTERED
SKITTERING
SKITTERS
SKITTISH
SKITTLE
SKITTLED
SKITTLES
SKITTLING
SKIVE
SKIVED
SKIVER
SKIVERED
SKIVERING
SKIVERS
SKIVES
SKIVIE
SKIVIER
SKIVIEST
SKIVING
SKIVINGS
SKIVVIES
SKIVVY
SKIVY
SKLATE
SKLATED
SKLATES
SKLATING
SKLENT
SKLENTED
SKLENTING
SKLENTS
SKLIFF
SKLIFFS
SKLIM
SKLIMMED
SKLIMMING
SKLIMS
SKOAL
SKOFF
SKOFFED
SKOFFING
SKOFFS
SKOKIAAN
SKOKIAANS
SKOL
SKOLIA
SKOLION
SKOLLIE
SKOLLIES
SKOLLY
SKRAN

SKRANS
SKREAKY
SKREEN
SKREENE
SKREENES
SKREENS
SKREIGH
SKREIGHED
SKREIGHING
SKREIGHS
SKRIECH
SKRIECHED
SKRIECHING
SKRIECHS
SKRIED
SKRIEGH
SKRIEGHED
SKRIEGHING
SKRIEGHS
SKRIES
SKRIK
SKRIKS
SKRIMMAGE
SKRIMMAGED
SKRIMMAGES
SKRIMMAGING
SKRIMP
SKRIMPED
SKRIMPING
SKRIMPS
SKRUMP
SKRUMPED
SKRUMPING
SKRUMPS
SKRY
SKRYER
SKRYERS
SKRYING
SKUA
SKUAS
SKUDLER
SKUDLERS
SKUG
SKUGGED
SKUGGING
SKUGS
SKULK
SKULKED
SKULKER
SKULKERS
SKULKING
SKULKINGS
SKULKS
SKULL
SKULLCAP
SKULLCAPS
SKULLS
SKULPIN
SKULPINS
SKUMMER
SKUMMERED
SKUMMERING
SKUMMERS
SKUNK
SKUNKED
SKUNKING
SKUNKS
SKURRIED
SKURRIES
SKURRY

SKURRYING
SKUTTLE
SKUTTLED
SKUTTLES
SKUTTLING
SKY
SKYBORN
SKYCLAD
SKYER
SKYERS
SKYEY
SKYIER
SKYIEST
SKYING
SKYISH
SKYJACK
SKYJACKED
SKYJACKER
SKYJACKERS
SKYJACKING
SKYJACKINGS
SKYJACKS
SKYLARK
SKYLARKED
SKYLARKING
SKYLARKINGS
SKYLARKS
SKYLIGHT
SKYLIGHTS
SKYLINE
SKYLINES
SKYMAN
SKYMEN
SKYR
SKYRE
SKYRED
SKYRES
SKYRING
SKYROCKET
SKYROCKETED
SKYROCKETING
SKYROCKETS
SKYRS
SKYSAIL
SKYSAILS
SKYSCAPE
SKYSCAPES
SKYTE
SKYTED
SKYTES
SKYTING
SKYWARD
SKYWARDS
SKYWAY
SKYWAYS
SLAB
SLABBED
SLABBER
SLABBERED
SLABBERER
SLABBERERS
SLABBERING
SLABBERS
SLABBERY
SLABBIER
SLABBIEST
SLABBING
SLABBY
SLABS
SLABSTONE

SLABSTONES
SLACK
SLACKED
SLACKEN
SLACKENED
SLACKENING
SLACKENINGS
SLACKENS
SLACKER
SLACKERS
SLACKEST
SLACKING
SLACKLY
SLACKNESS
SLACKNESSES
SLACKS
SLADANG
SLADANGS
SLADE
SLADES
SLAE
SLAES
SLAG
SLAGGED
SLAGGIER
SLAGGIEST
SLAGGING
SLAGGY
SLAGS
SLAID
SLAIN
SLAINTE
SLAIRG
SLAIRGED
SLAIRGING
SLAIRGS
SLAISTER
SLAISTERED
SLAISTERIES
SLAISTERING
SLAISTERS
SLAISTERY
SLAKE
SLAKED
SLAKELESS
SLAKES
SLAKING
SLALOM
SLALOMED
SLALOMING
SLALOMS
SLAM
SLAMMAKIN
SLAMMAKINS
SLAMMED
SLAMMER
SLAMMERS
SLAMMING
SLAMS
SLANDER
SLANDERED
SLANDERER
SLANDERERS
SLANDERING
SLANDERS
SLANE
SLANES
SLANG
SLANGED
SLANGIER

SLANGIEST
SLANGILY
SLANGING
SLANGINGS
SLANGISH
SLANGS
SLANGULAR
SLANGY
SLANT
SLANTED
SLANTING
SLANTLY
SLANTS
SLANTWAYS
SLANTWISE
SLAP
SLAPJACK
SLAPJACKS
SLAPPED
SLAPPER
SLAPPERS
SLAPPING
SLAPS
SLAPSTICK
SLAPSTICKS
SLASH
SLASHED
SLASHER
SLASHERS
SLASHES
SLASHING
SLASHINGS
SLAT
SLATE
SLATED
SLATER
SLATERS
SLATES
SLATHER
SLATHERED
SLATHERING
SLATHERS
SLATIER
SLATIEST
SLATINESS
SLATINESSES
SLATING
SLATINGS
SLATS
SLATTED
SLATTER
SLATTERED
SLATTERING
SLATTERN
SLATTERNS
SLATTERS
SLATTERY
SLATTING
SLATY
SLAUGHTER
SLAUGHTERED
SLAUGHTERING
SLAUGHTERS
SLAVE
SLAVED
SLAVER
SLAVERED
SLAVERER
SLAVERERS
SLAVERIES

SLAVERING
SLAVERS
SLAVERY
SLAVEY
SLAVEYS
SLAVING
SLAVISH
SLAVISHLY
SLAVOCRAT
SLAVOCRATS
SLAW
SLAWS
SLAY
SLAYED
SLAYER
SLAYERS
SLAYING
SLAYS
SLEAVE
SLEAVED
SLEAVES
SLEAVING
SLEAZE
SLEAZES
SLEAZIER
SLEAZIEST
SLEAZILY
SLEAZY
SLED
SLEDDED
SLEDDING
SLEDDINGS
SLEDED
SLEDGE
SLEDGED
SLEDGER
SLEDGERS
SLEDGES
SLEDGING
SLEDGINGS
SLEDS
SLEE
SLEECH
SLEECHES
SLEECHY
SLEEK
SLEEKED
SLEEKEN
SLEEKENED
SLEEKENING
SLEEKENS
SLEEKER
SLEEKERS
SLEEKEST
SLEEKIER
SLEEKIEST
SLEEKING
SLEEKINGS
SLEEKIT
SLEEKLY
SLEEKNESS
SLEEKNESSES
SLEEKS
SLEEKY
SLEEP
SLEEPER
SLEEPERS
SLEEPERY
SLEEPIER

SLEEPIEST	SLICKNESSES	SLINKY	SLOBBIEST	SLOPPED
SLEEPILY	SLICKS	SLIP	SLOBBY	SLOPPIER
SLEEPING	SLID	SLIPE	SLOBLAND	SLOPPIEST
SLEEPINGS	SLIDDEN	SLIPES	SLOBLANDS	SLOPPILY
SLEEPLESS	SLIDDER	SLIPFORM	SLOBS	SLOPPING
SLEEPRY	SLIDDERED	SLIPPAGE	SLOCKEN	SLOPPY
SLEEPS	SLIDDERING	SLIPPAGES	SLOCKENED	SLOPS
SLEEPY	SLIDDERS	SLIPPED	SLOCKENING	SLOPWORK
SLEER	SLIDDERY	SLIPPER	SLOCKENS	SLOPWORKS
SLEEST	SLIDE	SLIPPERED	SLOE	SLOPY
SLEET	SLIDED	SLIPPERIER	SLOEBUSH	SLOSH
SLEETED	SLIDER	SLIPPERIEST	SLOEBUSHES	SLOSHED
SLEETIER	SLIDERS	SLIPPERING	SLOES	SLOSHES
SLEETIEST	SLIDES	SLIPPERS	SLOETHORN	SLOSHIER
SLEETING	SLIDING	SLIPPERY	SLOETHORNS	SLOSHIEST
SLEETS	SLIDINGLY	SLIPPIER	SLOETREE	SLOSHING
SLEETY	SLIDINGS	SLIPPIEST	SLOETREES	SLOSHY
SLEEVE	SLIER	SLIPPING	SLOG	SLOT
SLEEVED	SLIEST	SLIPPY	SLOGAN	SLOTH
SLEEVER	SLIGHT	SLIPRAIL	SLOGANEER	SLOTHED
SLEEVERS	SLIGHTED	SLIPRAILS	SLOGANEERED	SLOTHFUL
SLEEVES	SLIGHTER	SLIPS	SLOGANEERING	SLOTHING
SLEEVING	SLIGHTEST	SLIPSHOD	SLOGANEERINGS	SLOTHS
SLEEVINGS	SLIGHTING	SLIPSLOP	SLOGANEERS	SLOTS
SLEEZIER	SLIGHTISH	SLIPSLOPS	SLOGANISE	SLOTTED
SLEEZIEST	SLIGHTLY	SLIPT	SLOGANISED	SLOTTER
SLEEZY	SLIGHTS	SLIPWARE	SLOGANISES	SLOTTERS
SLEIDED	SLILY	SLIPWARES	SLOGANISING	SLOTTING
SLEIGH	SLIM	SLIPWAY	SLOGANISINGS	SLOUCH
SLEIGHED	SLIME	SLIPWAYS	SLOGANIZE	SLOUCHED
SLEIGHING	SLIMED	SLISH	SLOGANIZED	SLOUCHER
SLEIGHINGS	SLIMES	SLISHES	SLOGANIZES	SLOUCHERS
SLEIGHS	SLIMIER	SLIT	SLOGANIZING	SLOUCHES
SLEIGHT	SLIMIEST	SLITHER	SLOGANIZINGS	SLOUCHIER
SLEIGHTS	SLIMILY	SLITHERED	SLOGANS	SLOUCHIEST
SLENDER	SLIMINESS	SLITHERIER	SLOGGED	SLOUCHING
SLENDERER	SLIMINESSES	SLITHERIEST	SLOGGER	SLOUCHY
SLENDEREST	SLIMING	SLITHERING	SLOGGERS	SLOUGH
SLENDERLY	SLIMLINE	SLITHERS	SLOGGING	SLOUGHED
SLEPT	SLIMLY	SLITHERY	SLOGGORNE	SLOUGHIER
SLEUTH	SLIMMED	SLITS	SLOGGORNES	SLOUGHIEST
SLEUTHED	SLIMMER	SLITTER	SLOGHORNE	SLOUGHING
SLEUTHING	SLIMMERS	SLITTERS	SLOGHORNES	SLOUGHS
SLEUTHS	SLIMMEST	SLITTING	SLOGORNE	SLOUGHY
SLEW	SLIMMING	SLIVE	SLOGORNES	SLOVE
SLEWED	SLIMMINGS	SLIVED	SLOGS	SLOVEN
SLEWING	SLIMMISH	SLIVEN	SLOID	SLOVENLY
SLEWS	SLIMNESS	SLIVER	SLOIDS	SLOVENRIES
SLEY	SLIMNESSES	SLIVERED	SLOKEN	SLOVENRY
SLEYS	SLIMS	SLIVERING	SLOKENED	SLOVENS
SLICE	SLIMSY	SLIVERS	SLOKENING	SLOW
SLICED	SLIMY	SLIVES	SLOKENS	SLOWBACK
SLICER	SLING	SLIVING	SLOOM	SLOWBACKS
SLICERS	SLINGER	SLIVOVIC	SLOOMED	SLOWCOACH
SLICES	SLINGERS	SLIVOVICA	SLOOMING	SLOWCOACHES
SLICING	SLINGING	SLIVOVICAS	SLOOMS	SLOWED
SLICINGS	SLINGS	SLIVOVICS	SLOOMY	SLOWER
SLICK	SLINGSHOT	SLIVOVITZ	SLOOP	SLOWEST
SLICKED	SLINGSHOTS	SLIVOVITZES	SLOOPS	SLOWING
SLICKEN	SLINK	SLIVOWITZ	SLOOT	SLOWINGS
SLICKENED	SLINKER	SLIVOWITZES	SLOOTS	SLOWISH
SLICKENING	SLINKERS	SLOAN	SLOP	SLOWLY
SLICKENS	SLINKIER	SLOANS	SLOPE	SLOWNESS
SLICKER	SLINKIEST	SLOB	SLOPED	SLOWNESSES
SLICKERS	SLINKING	SLOBBER	SLOPES	SLOWPOKE
SLICKEST	SLINKS	SLOBBERED	SLOPEWISE	SLOWPOKES
SLICKING	SLINKSKIN	SLOBBERING	SLOPIER	SLOWS
SLICKINGS	SLINKSKINS	SLOBBERS	SLOPIEST	SLOYD
SLICKLY	SLINKWEED	SLOBBERY	SLOPING	SLOYDS
SLICKNESS	SLINKWEEDS	SLOBBIER	SLOPINGLY	SLUB

SLUBB
SLUBBED
SLUBBER
SLUBBERED
SLUBBERING
SLUBBERINGS
SLUBBERS
SLUBBIER
SLUBBIEST
SLUBBING
SLUBBINGS
SLUBBS
SLUBBY
SLUBS
SLUDGE
SLUDGES
SLUDGIER
SLUDGIEST
SLUDGY
SLUE
SLUED
SLUEING
SLUES
SLUG
SLUGFEST
SLUGFESTS
SLUGGABED
SLUGGABEDS
SLUGGARD
SLUGGARDS
SLUGGED
SLUGGER
SLUGGERS
SLUGGING
SLUGGISH
SLUGHORN
SLUGHORNE
SLUGHORNES
SLUGHORNS
SLUGS
SLUICE
SLUICED
SLUICES
SLUICIER
SLUICIEST
SLUICING
SLUICY
SLUIT
SLUITS
SLUM
SLUMBER
SLUMBERED
SLUMBERER
SLUMBERERS
SLUMBERING
SLUMBERINGS
SLUMBERS
SLUMBERY
SLUMBROUS
SLUMBRY
SLUMMED
SLUMMER
SLUMMERS
SLUMMIER
SLUMMIEST
SLUMMING
SLUMMINGS
SLUMMOCK
SLUMMOCKED
SLUMMOCKING

SLUMMOCKS
SLUMMY
SLUMP
SLUMPED
SLUMPIER
SLUMPIEST
SLUMPING
SLUMPS
SLUMPY
SLUMS
SLUNG
SLUNK
SLUR
SLURB
SLURBS
SLURP
SLURPED
SLURPING
SLURPS
SLURRED
SLURRIES
SLURRING
SLURRY
SLURS
SLUSE
SLUSES
SLUSH
SLUSHED
SLUSHES
SLUSHIER
SLUSHIEST
SLUSHING
SLUSHY
SLUT
SLUTS
SLUTTERIES
SLUTTERY
SLUTTISH
SLY
SLYBOOTS
SLYER
SLYEST
SLYISH
SLYLY
SLYNESS
SLYNESSES
SLYPE
SLYPES
SMA
SMACK
SMACKED
SMACKER
SMACKERS
SMACKING
SMACKINGS
SMACKS
SMAIK
SMAIKS
SMALL
SMALLAGE
SMALLAGES
SMALLED
SMALLER
SMALLEST
SMALLING
SMALLISH
SMALLNESS
SMALLNESSES
SMALLPOX
SMALLPOXES

SMALLS
SMALM
SMALMED
SMALMIER
SMALMIEST
SMALMILY
SMALMING
SMALMS
SMALMY
SMALT
SMALTI
SMALTITE
SMALTITES
SMALTO
SMALTOS
SMALTS
SMARAGD
SMARAGDS
SMARM
SMARMED
SMARMIER
SMARMIEST
SMARMILY
SMARMING
SMARMS
SMARMY
SMART
SMARTARSE
SMARTARSES
SMARTASS
SMARTASSES
SMARTED
SMARTEN
SMARTENED
SMARTENING
SMARTENS
SMARTER
SMARTEST
SMARTIE
SMARTIES
SMARTING
SMARTLY
SMARTNESS
SMARTNESSES
SMARTS
SMARTY
SMASH
SMASHED
SMASHER
SMASHEROO
SMASHEROOS
SMASHERS
SMASHES
SMASHING
SMASHINGS
SMATCH
SMATCHED
SMATCHES
SMATCHING
SMATTER
SMATTERED
SMATTERER
SMATTERERS
SMATTERING
SMATTERINGS
SMATTERS
SMEAR
SMEARED
SMEARIER
SMEARIEST

SMEARILY
SMEARING
SMEARS
SMEARY
SMEATH
SMEATHS
SMECTIC
SMEDDUM
SMEDDUMS
SMEE
SMEECH
SMEECHED
SMEECHES
SMEECHING
SMEEK
SMEEKED
SMEEKING
SMEEKS
SMEES
SMEETH
SMEETHS
SMEGMA
SMEGMAS
SMELL
SMELLED
SMELLER
SMELLERS
SMELLIER
SMELLIEST
SMELLING
SMELLINGS
SMELLS
SMELLY
SMELT
SMELTED
SMELTER
SMELTERIES
SMELTERS
SMELTERY
SMELTING
SMELTINGS
SMELTS
SMEUSE
SMEUSES
SMEW
SMEWS
SMICKER
SMICKERED
SMICKERING
SMICKERINGS
SMICKERS
SMICKET
SMICKETS
SMICKLY
SMIDDIES
SMIDDY
SMIDGEN
SMIDGENS
SMIDGEON
SMIDGEONS
SMIDGIN
SMIDGINS
SMIGHT
SMIGHTED
SMIGHTING
SMIGHTS
SMILAX
SMILAXES
SMILE
SMILED

SMILEFUL
SMILELESS
SMILER
SMILERS
SMILES
SMILET
SMILETS
SMILING
SMILINGLY
SMILINGS
SMILODON
SMILODONS
SMIR
SMIRCH
SMIRCHED
SMIRCHES
SMIRCHING
SMIRK
SMIRKED
SMIRKIER
SMIRKIEST
SMIRKING
SMIRKS
SMIRKY
SMIRR
SMIRRED
SMIRRIER
SMIRRIEST
SMIRRING
SMIRRS
SMIRRY
SMIRS
SMIT
SMITE
SMITER
SMITERS
SMITES
SMITH
SMITHED
SMITHERIES
SMITHERS
SMITHERY
SMITHIED
SMITHIES
SMITHING
SMITHS
SMITHY
SMITHYING
SMITING
SMITS
SMITTED
SMITTEN
SMITTING
SMITTLE
SMOCK
SMOCKED
SMOCKING
SMOCKINGS
SMOCKS
SMOG
SMOGGIER
SMOGGIEST
SMOGGY
SMOGS
SMOILE
SMOILED
SMOILES
SMOILING
SMOKABLE
SMOKE

SMOKED
SMOKELESS
SMOKER
SMOKERS
SMOKES
SMOKIER
SMOKIES
SMOKIEST
SMOKILY
SMOKINESS
SMOKINESSES
SMOKING
SMOKINGS
SMOKO
SMOKOS
SMOKY
SMOLDER
SMOLDERED
SMOLDERING
SMOLDERS
SMOLT
SMOLTS
SMOOCH
SMOOCHED
SMOOCHES
SMOOCHING
SMOOR
SMOORED
SMOORING
SMOORS
SMOOT
SMOOTED
SMOOTH
SMOOTHE
SMOOTHED
SMOOTHEN
SMOOTHENED
SMOOTHENING
SMOOTHENS
SMOOTHER
SMOOTHERS
SMOOTHES
SMOOTHEST
SMOOTHIE
SMOOTHIES
SMOOTHING
SMOOTHINGS
SMOOTHISH
SMOOTHLY
SMOOTHS
SMOOTING
SMOOTS
SMORBROD
SMORBRODS
SMORE
SMORED
SMORES
SMORING
SMORZANDO
SMORZATO
SMOTE
SMOTHER
SMOTHERED
SMOTHERER
SMOTHERERS
SMOTHERING
SMOTHERINGS
SMOTHERS
SMOTHERY
SMOUCH

SMOUCHED
SMOUCHES
SMOUCHING
SMOULDER
SMOULDERED
SMOULDERING
SMOULDERS
SMOULDRY
SMOUS
SMOUSE
SMOUSED
SMOUSER
SMOUSERS
SMOUSES
SMOUSING
SMOUT
SMOUTED
SMOUTING
SMOUTS
SMOWT
SMOWTS
SMOYLE
SMOYLED
SMOYLES
SMOYLING
SMUDGE
SMUDGED
SMUDGER
SMUDGERS
SMUDGES
SMUDGIER
SMUDGIEST
SMUDGILY
SMUDGING
SMUDGY
SMUG
SMUGGED
SMUGGER
SMUGGEST
SMUGGING
SMUGGLE
SMUGGLED
SMUGGLER
SMUGGLERS
SMUGGLES
SMUGGLING
SMUGGLINGS
SMUGLY
SMUGNESS
SMUGNESSES
SMUGS
SMUR
SMURRED
SMURRIER
SMURRIEST
SMURRING
SMURRY
SMURS
SMUT
SMUTCH
SMUTCHED
SMUTCHES
SMUTCHING
SMUTS
SMUTTED
SMUTTIER
SMUTTIEST
SMUTTILY
SMUTTING
SMUTTY

SMYTRIE
SMYTRIES
SNAB
SNABBLE
SNABBLED
SNABBLES
SNABBLING
SNABS
SNACK
SNACKED
SNACKING
SNACKS
SNAFFLE
SNAFFLED
SNAFFLES
SNAFFLING
SNAFU
SNAFUS
SNAG
SNAGGED
SNAGGIER
SNAGGIEST
SNAGGING
SNAGGY
SNAGS
SNAIL
SNAILED
SNAILERIES
SNAILERY
SNAILIER
SNAILIEST
SNAILING
SNAILS
SNAILY
SNAKE
SNAKEBIRD
SNAKEBIRDS
SNAKEBITE
SNAKEBITES
SNAKED
SNAKELIKE
SNAKEROOT
SNAKEROOTS
SNAKES
SNAKESKIN
SNAKESKINS
SNAKEWEED
SNAKEWEEDS
SNAKEWISE
SNAKEWOOD
SNAKEWOODS
SNAKIER
SNAKIEST
SNAKILY
SNAKINESS
SNAKINESSES
SNAKING
SNAKISH
SNAKY
SNAP
SNAPHANCE
SNAPHANCES
SNAPPED
SNAPPER
SNAPPERED
SNAPPERING
SNAPPERS
SNAPPIER
SNAPPIEST
SNAPPILY

SNAPPING
SNAPPINGS
SNAPPISH
SNAPPY
SNAPS
SNAPSHOT
SNAPSHOTS
SNAR
SNARE
SNARED
SNARER
SNARERS
SNARES
SNARIER
SNARIEST
SNARING
SNARINGS
SNARK
SNARKS
SNARL
SNARLED
SNARLER
SNARLERS
SNARLIER
SNARLIEST
SNARLING
SNARLINGS
SNARLS
SNARLY
SNARRED
SNARRING
SNARS
SNARY
SNASH
SNASHED
SNASHES
SNASHING
SNASTE
SNASTES
SNATCH
SNATCHED
SNATCHER
SNATCHERS
SNATCHES
SNATCHIER
SNATCHIEST
SNATCHILY
SNATCHING
SNATCHY
SNATH
SNATHE
SNATHES
SNATHS
SNAZZIER
SNAZZIEST
SNAZZY
SNEAD
SNEADS
SNEAK
SNEAKED
SNEAKER
SNEAKERS
SNEAKEUP
SNEAKEUPS
SNEAKIER
SNEAKIEST
SNEAKILY
SNEAKING
SNEAKISH
SNEAKS

SNEAKSBIES
SNEAKSBY
SNEAKY
SNEAP
SNEAPED
SNEAPING
SNEAPS
SNEATH
SNEATHS
SNEB
SNEBBE
SNEBBED
SNEBBES
SNEBBING
SNEBS
SNECK
SNECKED
SNECKING
SNECKS
SNED
SNEDDED
SNEDDING
SNEDS
SNEE
SNEED
SNEEING
SNEER
SNEERED
SNEERER
SNEERERS
SNEERIER
SNEERIEST
SNEERING
SNEERINGS
SNEERS
SNEERY
SNEES
SNEESH
SNEESHAN
SNEESHANS
SNEESHES
SNEESHIN
SNEESHING
SNEESHINGS
SNEESHINS
SNEEZE
SNEEZED
SNEEZER
SNEEZERS
SNEEZES
SNEEZIER
SNEEZIEST
SNEEZING
SNEEZINGS
SNEEZY
SNELL
SNELLED
SNELLER
SNELLEST
SNELLING
SNELLS
SNELLY
SNIB
SNIBBED
SNIBBING
SNIBS
SNICK
SNICKED
SNICKER
SNICKERED

SNICKERING	SNIPPER	SNOOKSES	SNOUTY	SNUFFIER
SNICKERS	SNIPPERS	SNOOL	SNOW	SNUFFIEST
SNICKET	SNIPPET	SNOOLED	SNOWBALL	SNUFFING
SNICKETS	SNIPPETS	SNOOLING	SNOWBALLED	SNUFFINGS
SNICKING	SNIPPETY	SNOOLS	SNOWBALLING	SNUFFLE
SNICKS	SNIPPIER	SNOOP	SNOWBALLS	SNUFFLED
SNIDE	SNIPPIEST	SNOOPED	SNOWCAP	SNUFFLER
SNIDELY	SNIPPING	SNOOPER	SNOWCAPS	SNUFFLERS
SNIDENESS	SNIPPINGS	SNOOPERS	SNOWDRIFT	SNUFFLES
SNIDENESSES	SNIPPY	SNOOPING	SNOWDRIFTS	SNUFFLING
SNIDER	SNIPS	SNOOPS	SNOWDROP	SNUFFLINGS
SNIDES	SNIPY	SNOOT	SNOWDROPS	SNUFFS
SNIDEST	SNIRT	SNOOTED	SNOWED	SNUFFY
SNIFF	SNIRTLE	SNOOTFUL	SNOWFALL	SNUG
SNIFFED	SNIRTLED	SNOOTFULS	SNOWFALLS	SNUGGED
SNIFFER	SNIRTLES	SNOOTIER	SNOWFLAKE	SNUGGER
SNIFFERS	SNIRTLING	SNOOTIEST	SNOWFLAKES	SNUGGERIES
SNIFFIER	SNIRTS	SNOOTING	SNOWFLECK	SNUGGERY
SNIFFIEST	SNITCH	SNOOTS	SNOWFLECKS	SNUGGEST
SNIFFILY	SNITCHED	SNOOTY	SNOWFLICK	SNUGGING
SNIFFING	SNITCHER	SNOOZE	SNOWFLICKS	SNUGGLE
SNIFFINGS	SNITCHERS	SNOOZED	SNOWIER	SNUGGLED
SNIFFLE	SNITCHES	SNOOZER	SNOWIEST	SNUGGLES
SNIFFLED	SNITCHING	SNOOZERS	SNOWILY	SNUGGLING
SNIFFLER	SNIVEL	SNOOZES	SNOWINESS	SNUGLY
SNIFFLERS	SNIVELLED	SNOOZING	SNOWINESSES	SNUGNESS
SNIFFLES	SNIVELLER	SNOOZLE	SNOWING	SNUGNESSES
SNIFFLING	SNIVELLERS	SNOOZLED	SNOWISH	SNUGS
SNIFFS	SNIVELLING	SNOOZLES	SNOWK	SNUSH
SNIFFY	SNIVELLY	SNOOZLING	SNOWKED	SNUSHED
SNIFT	SNIVELS	SNORE	SNOWKING	SNUSHES
SNIFTED	SNOB	SNORED	SNOWKS	SNUSHING
SNIFTER	SNOBBERIES	SNORER	SNOWLESS	SNUZZLE
SNIFTERED	SNOBBERY	SNORERS	SNOWLIKE	SNUZZLED
SNIFTERING	SNOBBIER	SNORES	SNOWLINE	SNUZZLES
SNIFTERS	SNOBBIEST	SNORING	SNOWLINES	SNUZZLING
SNIFTIER	SNOBBISH	SNORINGS	SNOWMAN	SO
SNIFTIEST	SNOBBISM	SNORKEL	SNOWMEN	SOAK
SNIFTING	SNOBBISMS	SNORKELS	SNOWS	SOAKAGE
SNIFTS	SNOBBY	SNORT	SNOWSCAPE	SOAKAGES
SNIFTY	SNOBLING	SNORTED	SNOWSCAPES	SOAKAWAY
SNIG	SNOBLINGS	SNORTER	SNOWSLIP	SOAKAWAYS
SNIGGED	SNOD	SNORTERS	SNOWSLIPS	SOAKED
SNIGGER	SNODDED	SNORTIER	SNOWSTORM	SOAKEN
SNIGGERED	SNODDING	SNORTIEST	SNOWSTORMS	SOAKER
SNIGGERER	SNODDIT	SNORTING	SNOWY	SOAKERS
SNIGGERERS	SNODS	SNORTINGS	SNUD	SOAKING
SNIGGERING	SNOEK	SNORTS	SNUBBE	SOAKINGLY
SNIGGERINGS	SNOEKS	SNORTY	SNUBBED	SOAKINGS
SNIGGERS	SNOG	SNOT	SNUBBER	SOAKS
SNIGGING	SNOGGED	SNOTS	SNUBBERS	SOAP
SNIGGLE	SNOGGING	SNOTTED	SNUBBES	SOAPBERRIES
SNIGGLED	SNOGS	SNOTTER	SNUBBIER	SOAPBERRY
SNIGGLER	SNOKE	SNOTTERED	SNUBBIEST	SOAPBOX
SNIGGLERS	SNOKED	SNOTTERIES	SNUBBING	SOAPBOXES
SNIGGLES	SNOKES	SNOTTERING	SNUBBINGS	SOAPED
SNIGGLING	SNOKING	SNOTTERS	SNUBBISH	SOAPIER
SNIGGLINGS	SNOOD	SNOTTERY	SNUBBY	SOAPIEST
SNIGS	SNOODED	SNOTTIER	SNUBS	SOAPILY
SNIP	SNOODING	SNOTTIES	SNUCK	SOAPINESS
SNIPE	SNOODS	SNOTTIEST	SNUDGE	SOAPINESSES
SNIPED	SNOOK	SNOTTILY	SNUDGED	SOAPING
SNIPER	SNOOKED	SNOTTING	SNUDGES	SOAPLESS
SNIPERS	SNOOKER	SNOTTY	SNUDGING	SOAPS
SNIPES	SNOOKERED	SNOUT	SNUFF	SOAPSTONE
SNIPIER	SNOOKERING	SNOUTED	SNUFFBOX	SOAPSTONES
SNIPIEST	SNOOKERS	SNOUTIER	SNUFFBOXES	SOAPWORT
SNIPING	SNOOKING	SNOUTIEST	SNUFFED	SOAPWORTS
SNIPINGS	SNOOKS	SNOUTING	SNUFFER	SOAPY
SNIPPED		SNOUTS	SNUFFERS	SOAR

SOARAWAY
SOARE
SOARED
SOARES
SOARING
SOARINGLY
SOARINGS
SOARS
SOB
SOBBED
SOBBING
SOBBINGLY
SOBBINGS
SOBEIT
SOBER
SOBERED
SOBERER
SOBEREST
SOBERING
SOBERISE
SOBERISED
SOBERISES
SOBERISING
SOBERIZE
SOBERIZED
SOBERIZES
SOBERIZING
SOBERLY
SOBERNESS
SOBERNESSES
SOBERS
SOBOLE
SOBOLES
SOBRIETIES
SOBRIETY
SOBRIQUET
SOBRIQUETS
SOBS
SOC
SOCAGE
SOCAGER
SOCAGERS
SOCAGES
SOCCAGE
SOCCAGES
SOCCER
SOCCERS
SOCIABLE
SOCIABLY
SOCIAL
SOCIALISE
SOCIALISED
SOCIALISES
SOCIALISING
SOCIALISM
SOCIALISMS
SOCIALIST
SOCIALISTS
SOCIALITE
SOCIALITES
SOCIALITIES
SOCIALITY
SOCIALIZE
SOCIALIZED
SOCIALIZES
SOCIALIZING
SOCIALLY
SOCIALS
SOCIATE
SOCIATES

SOCIATIVE
SOCIETAL
SOCIETARY
SOCIETIES
SOCIETY
SOCIOGRAM
SOCIOGRAMS
SOCIOLOGIES
SOCIOLOGY
SOCIOPATH
SOCIOPATHS
SOCK
SOCKED
SOCKER
SOCKERS
SOCKET
SOCKETED
SOCKETING
SOCKETS
SOCKEYE
SOCKEYES
SOCKING
SOCKO
SOCKS
SOCLE
SOCLES
SOCMAN
SOCMEN
SOCS
SOD
SODA
SODAIC
SODAIN
SODAINE
SODALITE
SODALITES
SODALITIES
SODALITY
SODAMIDE
SODAMIDES
SODAS
SODDED
SODDEN
SODDENED
SODDENER
SODDENEST
SODDENING
SODDENS
SODDIER
SODDIEST
SODDING
SODDY
SODGER
SODGERED
SODGERING
SODGERS
SODIC
SODIUM
SODIUMS
SODOMIES
SODOMISE
SODOMISED
SODOMISES
SODOMISING
SODOMITE
SODOMITES
SODOMITIC
SODOMIZE
SODOMIZED
SODOMIZES

SODOMIZING
SODOMY
SODS
SOEVER
SOFA
SOFAR
SOFARS
SOFAS
SOFFIONI
SOFFIT
SOFFITS
SOFT
SOFTA
SOFTAS
SOFTBACK
SOFTBACKS
SOFTBALL
SOFTBALLS
SOFTED
SOFTEN
SOFTENED
SOFTENER
SOFTENERS
SOFTENING
SOFTENINGS
SOFTENS
SOFTER
SOFTEST
SOFTHEAD
SOFTHEADS
SOFTIE
SOFTIES
SOFTING
SOFTISH
SOFTLING
SOFTLINGS
SOFTLY
SOFTNESS
SOFTNESSES
SOFTS
SOFTWARE
SOFTWARES
SOFTWOOD
SOFTWOODS
SOFTY
SOG
SOGER
SOGERED
SOGERING
SOGERS
SOGGED
SOGGIER
SOGGIEST
SOGGILY
SOGGINESS
SOGGINESSES
SOGGING
SOGGINGS
SOGGY
SOGS
SOH
SOHS
SOIGNÉ
SOIGNÉE
SOIL
SOILED
SOILIER
SOILIEST
SOILINESS
SOILINESSES

SOILING
SOILINGS
SOILLESS
SOILS
SOILURE
SOILURES
SOILY
SOIRÉE
SOIRÉES
SOJA
SOJAS
SOJOURN
SOJOURNED
SOJOURNER
SOJOURNERS
SOJOURNING
SOJOURNINGS
SOJOURNS
SOKE
SOKEMAN
SOKEMANRIES
SOKEMANRY
SOKEMEN
SOKEN
SOKENS
SOKES
SOL
SOLA
SOLACE
SOLACED
SOLACES
SOLACING
SOLACIOUS
SOLAH
SOLAHS
SOLAN
SOLAND
SOLANDER
SOLANDERS
SOLANDS
SOLANINE
SOLANINES
SOLANO
SOLANOS
SOLANS
SOLANUM
SOLANUMS
SOLAR
SOLARISE
SOLARISED
SOLARISES
SOLARISING
SOLARISM
SOLARIST
SOLARISTS
SOLARIUM
SOLARIUMS
SOLARIZE
SOLARIZED
SOLARIZES
SOLARIZING
SOLARS
SOLAS
SOLATION
SOLATIONS
SOLATIUM
SOLATIUMS
SOLD
SOLDADO
SOLDADOS

SOLDAN
SOLDANS
SOLDE
SOLDER
SOLDERED
SOLDERER
SOLDERERS
SOLDERING
SOLDERINGS
SOLDERS
SOLDES
SOLDI
SOLDIER
SOLDIERED
SOLDIERIES
SOLDIERING
SOLDIERINGS
SOLDIERLY
SOLDIERS
SOLDIERY
SOLDO
SOLDS
SOLE
SOLECISE
SOLECISED
SOLECISES
SOLECISING
SOLECISM
SOLECISMS
SOLECIST
SOLECISTS
SOLECIZE
SOLECIZED
SOLECIZES
SOLECIZING
SOLED
SOLEIN
SOLELY
SOLEMN
SOLEMNER
SOLEMNESS
SOLEMNESSES
SOLEMNEST
SOLEMNIFIED
SOLEMNIFIES
SOLEMNIFY
SOLEMNIFYING
SOLEMNISE
SOLEMNISED
SOLEMNISES
SOLEMNISING
SOLEMNITIES
SOLEMNITY
SOLEMNIZE
SOLEMNIZED
SOLEMNIZES
SOLEMNIZING
SOLEMNLY
SOLEN
SOLENESS
SOLENESSES
SOLENETTE
SOLENETTES
SOLENODON
SOLENODONS
SOLENOID
SOLENOIDS
SOLENS
SOLER
SOLERA

SOLERAS
SOLERS
SOLES
SOLEUS
SOLEUSES
SOLFATARA
SOLFATARAS
SOLFEGGI
SOLFEGGIO
SOLFERINO
SOLFERINOS
SOLI
SOLICIT
SOLICITED
SOLICITIES
SOLICITING
SOLICITINGS
SOLICITOR
SOLICITORS
SOLICITS
SOLICITY
SOLID
SOLIDARE
SOLIDARES
SOLIDARY
SOLIDATE
SOLIDATED
SOLIDATES
SOLIDATING
SOLIDER
SOLIDEST
SOLIDI
SOLIDIFIED
SOLIDIFIES
SOLIDIFY
SOLIDIFYING
SOLIDISH
SOLIDISM
SOLIDISMS
SOLIDIST
SOLIDISTS
SOLIDITIES
SOLIDITY
SOLIDLY
SOLIDNESS
SOLIDNESSES
SOLIDS
SOLIDUM
SOLIDUMS
SOLIDUS
SOLILOQUIES
SOLILOQUY
SOLING
SOLIPED
SOLIPEDS
SOLIPSISM
SOLIPSISMS
SOLIPSIST
SOLIPSISTS
SOLITAIRE
SOLITAIRES
SOLITARIES
SOLITARY
SOLITO
SOLITON
SOLITONS
SOLITUDE
SOLITUDES
SOLIVE
SOLIVES

SOLLAR
SOLLARS
SOLLER
SOLLERET
SOLLERETS
SOLLERS
SOLO
SOLOED
SOLOING
SOLOIST
SOLOISTS
SOLONCHAK
SOLONCHAKS
SOLONETS
SOLONETSES
SOLONETZ
SOLONETZES
SOLOS
SOLS
SOLSTICE
SOLSTICES
SOLUBLE
SOLUM
SOLUMS
SOLUS
SOLUTE
SOLUTES
SOLUTION
SOLUTIONED
SOLUTIONING
SOLUTIONS
SOLUTIVE
SOLVABLE
SOLVATE
SOLVATED
SOLVATES
SOLVATING
SOLVATION
SOLVATIONS
SOLVE
SOLVED
SOLVENCIES
SOLVENCY
SOLVENT
SOLVENTS
SOLVER
SOLVERS
SOLVES
SOLVING
SOMA
SOMAS
SOMASCOPE
SOMASCOPES
SOMATIC
SOMATISM
SOMATISMS
SOMATIST
SOMATISTS
SOMBRE
SOMBRED
SOMBRELY
SOMBRER
SOMBRERO
SOMBREROS
SOMBRES
SOMBREST
SOMBRING
SOMBROUS
SOME
SOMEBODIES

SOMEBODY
SOMEDAY
SOMEDEAL
SOMEDELE
SOMEGATE
SOMEHOW
SOMEONE
SOMEONES
SOMEPLACE
SOMERSET
SOMERSETS
SOMERSETTED
SOMERSETTING
SOMETHING
SOMETHINGS
SOMETIME
SOMETIMES
SOMEWAY
SOMEWAYS
SOMEWHAT
SOMEWHATS
SOMEWHEN
SOMEWHERE
SOMEWHILE
SOMEWHY
SOMEWISE
SOMITAL
SOMITE
SOMITES
SOMITIC
SOMMELIER
SOMMELIERS
SOMNIAL
SOMNIFIC
SOMNOLENT
SON
SONANCE
SONANCES
SONANCIES
SONANCY
SONANT
SONANTS
SONAR
SONARS
SONATA
SONATAS
SONATINA
SONATINAS
SONCE
SONCES
SONDAGE
SONDAGES
SONDE
SONDELI
SONDELIS
SONDES
SONE
SONERI
SONERIS
SONES
SONG
SONGBIRD
SONGBIRDS
SONGBOOK
SONGBOOKS
SONGCRAFT
SONGCRAFTS
SONGFUL
SONGFULLY
SONGLESS

SONGMAN
SONGMEN
SONGS
SONGSMITH
SONGSMITHS
SONGSTER
SONGSTERS
SONIC
SONICS
SONLESS
SONNE
SONNES
SONNET
SONNETARY
SONNETED
SONNETEER
SONNETEERED
SONNETEERING
SONNETEERINGS
SONNETEERS
SONNETING
SONNETINGS
SONNETISE
SONNETISED
SONNETISES
SONNETISING
SONNETIST
SONNETISTS
SONNETIZE
SONNETIZED
SONNETIZES
SONNETIZING
SONNETRIES
SONNETRY
SONNETS
SONNIES
SONNY
SONOBUOY
SONOBUOYS
SONOGRAPH
SONOGRAPHS
SONORANT
SONORANTS
SONORITIES
SONORITY
SONOROUS
SONSE
SONSES
SONSHIP
SONSHIPS
SONSIE
SONSIER
SONSIEST
SONSY
SONTAG
SONTAGS
SONTIES
SONUANCE
SONUANCES
SOOGEE
SOOGEED
SOOGEEING
SOOGEES
SOOGIE
SOOGIED
SOOGIEING
SOOGIES
SOOJEY
SOOJEYED

SOOJEYING
SOOJEYS
SOOK
SOOKS
SOOLE
SOOLED
SOOLES
SOOLING
SOOM
SOOMED
SOOMING
SOOMS
SOON
SOONER
SOONEST
SOOP
SOOPED
SOOPING
SOOPINGS
SOOPS
SOOPSTAKE
SOOT
SOOTE
SOOTED
SOOTERKIN
SOOTERKINS
SOOTES
SOOTFLAKE
SOOTFLAKES
SOOTH
SOOTHE
SOOTHED
SOOTHER
SOOTHERS
SOOTHES
SOOTHEST
SOOTHFAST
SOOTHFUL
SOOTHING
SOOTHINGS
SOOTHLICH
SOOTHLY
SOOTHS
SOOTHSAID
SOOTHSAY
SOOTHSAYING
SOOTHSAYINGS
SOOTHSAYS
SOOTIER
SOOTIEST
SOOTILY
SOOTINESS
SOOTINESSES
SOOTING
SOOTLESS
SOOTS
SOOTY
SOP
SOPH
SOPHA
SOPHAS
SOPHERIC
SOPHERIM
SOPHIA
SOPHIAS
SOPHIC
SOPHICAL
SOPHISM
SOPHISMS
SOPHIST

SOPHISTER	SORDA	SORORITIES	SOTTISHLY	SOUPSPOONS
SOPHISTERS	SORDES	SORORITY	SOTTISIER	SOUPY
SOPHISTIC	SORDID	SORORIZE	SOTTISIERS	SOUR
SOPHISTICS	SORDIDER	SORORIZED	SOU	SOURCE
SOPHISTRIES	SORDIDEST	SORORIZES	SOUARI	SOURCED
SOPHISTRY	SORDIDLY	SORORIZING	SOUARIS	SOURCES
SOPHISTS	SORDINE	SOROSES	SOUBISE	SOURCING
SOPHOMORE	SORDINES	SOROSIS	SOUBISES	SOURCINGS
SOPHOMORES	SORDINI	SOROSISES	SOUBRETTE	SOURDINE
SOPHS	SORDINO	SORPTION	SOUBRETTES	SOURDINES
SOPITE	SORDO	SORPTIONS	SOUCE	SOURDOUGH
SOPITED	SORDOR	SORRA	SOUCED	SOURDOUGHS
SOPITES	SORDORS	SORRAS	SOUCES	SOURED
SOPITING	SORDS	SORREL	SOUCHONG	SOURER
SOPOR	SORE	SORRELS	SOUCHONGS	SOUREST
SOPORIFIC	SORED	SORRIER	SOUCING	SOURING
SOPORIFICS	SOREDIA	SORRIEST	SOUCT	SOURINGS
SOPOROSE	SOREDIAL	SORRILY	SOUFFLE	SOURISH
SOPOROUS	SOREDIATE	SORRINESS	SOUFFLÉ	SOURISHLY
SOPORS	SOREDIUM	SORRINESSES	SOUFFLES	SOURLY
SOPPED	SOREE	SORROW	SOUFFLÉS	SOURNESS
SOPPIER	SOREES	SORROWED	SOUGH	SOURNESSES
SOPPIEST	SOREHEAD	SORROWER	SOUGHED	SOUROCK
SOPPILY	SOREHEADS	SORROWERS	SOUGHING	SOUROCKS
SOPPINESS	SOREHON	SORROWFUL	SOUGHS	SOURPUSS
SOPPINESSES	SOREHONS	SORROWING	SOUGHT	SOURPUSSES
SOPPING	SOREL	SORROWINGS	SOUK	SOURS
SOPPINGS	SORELL	SORROWS	SOUKS	SOURSE
SOPPY	SORELLS	SORRY	SOUL	SOURSES
SOPRA	SORELS	SORRYISH	SOULDAN	SOUS
SOPRANI	SORELY	SORT	SOULDANS	SOUSE
SOPRANINI	SORENESS	SORTABLE	SOULDIER	SOUSED
SOPRANINO	SORENESSES	SORTANCE	SOULDIERED	SOUSES
SOPRANINOS	SORER	SORTANCES	SOULDIERING	SOUSEWIFE
SOPRANIST	SORES	SORTATION	SOULDIERS	SOUSEWIVES
SOPRANISTS	SOREST	SORTATIONS	SOULED	SOUSING
SOPRANO	SOREX	SORTED	SOULFUL	SOUSINGS
SOPRANOS	SOREXES	SORTER	SOULFULLY	SOUSLIK
SOPS	SORGHO	SORTERS	SOULLESS	SOUSLIKS
SORA	SORGHOS	SORTES	SOULS	SOUT
SORAGE	SORGHUM	SORTIE	SOUM	SOUTACHE
SORAGES	SORGHUMS	SORTIED	SOUMED	SOUTACHES
SORAL	SORGO	SORTIEING	SOUMING	SOUTANE
SORAS	SORGOS	SORTIES	SOUMINGS	SOUTANES
SORB	SORI	SORTILEGE	SOUMS	SOUTAR
SORBARIA	SORICINE	SORTILEGES	SOUND	SOUTARS
SORBARIAS	SORICOID	SORTILEGIES	SOUNDED	SOUTENEUR
SORBATE	SORING	SORTILEGY	SOUNDER	SOUTENEURS
SORBATES	SORITES	SORTING	SOUNDERS	SOUTER
SORBED	SORITIC	SORTINGS	SOUNDEST	SOUTERLY
SORBENT	SORITICAL	SORTITION	SOUNDING	SOUTERS
SORBENTS	SORN	SORTITIONS	SOUNDINGS	SOUTH
SORBET	SORNED	SORTMENT	SOUNDLESS	SOUTHED
SORBETS	SORNER	SORTMENTS	SOUNDLY	SOUTHER
SORBING	SORNERS	SORTS	SOUNDNESS	SOUTHERED
SORBITOL	SORNING	SORUS	SOUNDNESSES	SOUTHERING
SORBITOLS	SORNINGS	SOS	SOUNDS	SOUTHERLY
SORBO	SORNS	SOSS	SOUP	SOUTHERN
SORBOS	SOROBAN	SOSSED	SOUPÇON	SOUTHERNS
SORBS	SOROBANS	SOSSES	SOUPÇONS	SOUTHERS
SORBUS	SOROCHE	SOSSING	SOUPER	SOUTHING
SORBUSES	SOROCHES	SOSSINGS	SOUPERS	SOUTHINGS
SORCERER	SORORAL	SOSTENUTO	SOUPIER	SOUTHLAND
SORCERERS	SORORATE	SOT	SOUPIEST	SOUTHLANDS
SORCERESS	SORORATES	SOTERIAL	SOUPLE	SOUTHMOST
SORCERESSES	SORORIAL	SOTS	SOUPLED	SOUTHPAW
SORCERIES	SORORISE	SOTTED	SOUPLES	SOUTHPAWS
SORCEROUS	SORORISED	SOTTING	SOUPLING	SOUTHRON
SORCERY	SORORISES	SOTTINGS	SOUPS	SOUTHRONS
SORD	SORORISING	SOTTISH	SOUPSPOON	SOUTHS

SOUTHSAID	SOWN	SPADEWORKS	SPALTED	SPARENESSES
SOUTHSAY	SOWND	SPADGER	SPALTING	SPARER
SOUTHSAYING	SOWNDED	SPADGERS	SPALTS	SPARERS
SOUTHSAYS	SOWNDING	SPADICES	SPAMMY	SPARES
SOUTHWARD	SOWNDS	SPADILLE	SPAN	SPAREST
SOUTHWARDS	SOWNE	SPADILLES	SPANAEMIA	SPARGE
SOUTS	SOWNES	SPADILLIO	SPANAEMIAS	SPARGED
SOUVENIR	SOWP	SPADILLIOS	SPANAEMIC	SPARGER
SOUVENIRED	SOWPS	SPADILLO	SPANCEL	SPARGERS
SOUVENIRING	SOWS	SPADILLOS	SPANCELLED	SPARGES
SOUVENIRS	SOWSE	SPADING	SPANCELLING	SPARGING
SOV	SOWSED	SPADIX	SPANCELS	SPARID
SOVENANCE	SOWSES	SPADO	SPANDREL	SPARIDS
SOVENANCES	SOWSING	SPADOES	SPANDRELS	SPARING
SOVEREIGN	SOWSSE	SPADONES	SPANDRIL	SPARINGLY
SOVEREIGNS	SOWSSED	SPADOS	SPANDRILS	SPARK
SOVIET	SOWSSES	SPADROON	SPANE	SPARKE
SOVIETIC	SOWSSING	SPADROONS	SPANED	SPARKED
SOVIETISE	SOWTER	SPAE	SPANES	SPARKES
SOVIETISED	SOWTERS	SPAED	SPANG	SPARKING
SOVIETISES	SOWTH	SPAEING	SPANGED	SPARKISH
SOVIETISING	SOWTHED	SPAEMAN	SPANGHEW	SPARKLE
SOVIETISM	SOWTHING	SPAEMEN	SPANGHEWED	SPARKLED
SOVIETISMS	SOWTHS	SPAER	SPANGHEWING	SPARKLER
SOVIETIZE	SOX	SPAERS	SPANGHEWS	SPARKLERS
SOVIETIZED	SOY	SPAES	SPANGING	SPARKLES
SOVIETIZES	SOYA	SPAEWIFE	SPANGLE	SPARKLESS
SOVIETIZING	SOYAS	SPAEWIVES	SPANGLED	SPARKLET
SOVIETS	SOYLE	SPAGERIC	SPANGLER	SPARKLETS
SOVRAN	SOYLED	SPAGERICS	SPANGLERS	SPARKLIES
SOVRANS	SOYLES	SPAGERIST	SPANGLES	SPARKLING
SOVRANTIES	SOYS	SPAGERISTS	SPANGLET	SPARKLINGS
SOVRANTY	SOZZLE	SPAGHETTI	SPANGLETS	SPARKLY
SOVS	SOZZLED	SPAGHETTIS	SPANGLIER	SPARKS
SOW	SOZZLES	SPAGIRIC	SPANGLIEST	SPARLING
SOWANS	SOZZLING	SPAGIRICS	SPANGLING	SPARLINGS
SOWAR	SOZZLY	SPAGIRIST	SPANGLINGS	SPAROID
SOWARREE	SPA	SPAGIRISTS	SPANGLY	SPAROIDS
SOWARREES	SPACE	SPAGYRIC	SPANGS	SPARRE
SOWARRIES	SPACED	SPAGYRICS	SPANIEL	SPARRED
SOWARRY	SPACELESS	SPAGYRIST	SPANIELLED	SPARRER
SOWARS	SPACEMAN	SPAGYRISTS	SPANIELLING	SPARRERS
SOWCE	SPACEMEN	SPAHEE	SPANIELS	SPARRES
SOWCED	SPACER	SPAHEES	SPANING	SPARRING
SOWCES	SPACERS	SPAHII	SPANK	SPARRINGS
SOWCING	SPACES	SPAHIS	SPANKED	SPARROW
SOWED	SPACESHIP	SPAIN	SPANKER	SPARROWS
SOWENS	SPACESHIPS	SPAINED	SPANKERS	SPARRY
SOWER	SPACEY	SPAING	SPANKING	SPARS
SOWERS	SPACIAL	SPAINGS	SPANKINGS	SPARSE
SOWF	SPACIER	SPAINING	SPANKS	SPARSEDLY
SOWFED	SPACIEST	SPAINS	SPANLESS	SPARSELY
SOWFF	SPACING	SPAIRGE	SPANNED	SPARSER
SOWFFED	SPACINGS	SPAIRGED	SPANNER	SPARSEST
SOWFFING	SPACIOUS	SPAIRGES	SPANNERS	SPARSITIES
SOWFFS	SPACY	SPAIRGING	SPANNING	SPARSITY
SOWFING	SPADASSIN	SPAKE	SPANS	SPART
SOWFS	SPADASSINS	SPALD	SPANSULE	SPARTAN
SOWING	SPADE	SPALDS	SPANSULES	SPARTEINE
SOWINGS	SPADED	SPALE	SPAR	SPARTEINES
SOWL	SPADEFUL	SPALES	SPARABLE	SPARTERIE
SOWLE	SPADEFULS	SPALL	SPARABLES	SPARTERIES
SOWLED	SPADEMAN	SPALLE	SPARAXIS	SPARTH
SOWLES	SPADEMEN	SPALLED	SPARAXISES	SPARTHE
SOWLING	SPADER	SPALLES	SPARD	SPARTHES
SOWLS	SPADERS	SPALLING	SPARE	SPARTHS
SOWM	SPADES	SPALLS	SPARED	SPARTS
SOWMED	SPADESMAN	SPALPEEN	SPARELESS	SPAS
SOWMING	SPADESMEN	SPALPEENS	SPARELY	SPASM
SOWMS	SPADEWORK	SPALT	SPARENESS	SPASMATIC

SPASMED	SPEAKERS	SPECTATED	SPEKBOOM	SPERMATICS
SPASMIC	SPEAKING	SPECTATES	SPEKBOOMS	SPERMATID
SPASMING	SPEAKINGS	SPECTATING	SPELAEAN	SPERMATIDS
SPASMODIC	SPEAKS	SPECTATOR	SPELD	SPERMIC
SPASMS	SPEAL	SPECTATORS	SPELDED	SPERMOUS
SPASTIC	SPEALS	SPECTER	SPELDER	SPERMS
SPASTICS	SPEAN	SPECTERS	SPELDERED	SPERRE
SPAT	SPEANED	SPECTRA	SPELDERING	SPERRED
SPATE	SPEANING	SPECTRAL	SPELDERS	SPERRES
SPATES	SPEANS	SPECTRE	SPELDIN	SPERRING
SPATFALL	SPEAR	SPECTRES	SPELDING	SPERSE
SPATFALLS	SPEARED	SPECTRUM	SPELDINGS	SPERSED
SPATHE	SPEARFISH	SPECULA	SPELDINS	SPERSES
SPATHED	SPEARFISHES	SPECULAR	SPELDRIN	SPERSING
SPATHES	SPEARHEAD	SPECULATE	SPELDRING	SPERST
SPATHIC	SPEARHEADED	SPECULATED	SPELDRINGS	SPERTHE
SPATHOSE	SPEARHEADING	SPECULATES	SPELDRINS	SPERTHES
SPATIAL	SPEARHEADS	SPECULATiNG	SPELDS	SPET
SPATIALLY	SPEARIER	SPECULUM	SPELEAN	SPETCH
SPÄTLESE	SPEARIEST	SPED	SPELIKIN	SPETCHES
SPÄTLESEN	SPEARING	SPEECH	SPELIKINS	SPETS
SPÄTLESES	SPEARMAN	SPEECHED	SPELK	SPETSNAZ
SPATS	SPEARMEN	SPEECHES	SPELKS	SPETSNAZES
SPATTED	SPEARMINT	SPEECHFUL	SPELL	SPETTING
SPATTEE	SPEARMINTS	SPEECHIFIED	SPELLABLE	SPETZNAZ
SPATTEES	SPEARS	SPEECHIFIES	SPELLBIND	SPETZNAZES
SPATTER	SPEARWORT	SPEECHIFY	SPELLBINDING	SPEW
SPATTERED	SPEARWORTS	SPEECHIFYING	SPELLBINDS	SPEWED
SPATTERING	SPEARY	SPEECHING	SPELLBOUND	SPEWER
SPATTERS	SPEAT	SPEED	SPELLDOWN	SPEWERS
SPATTING	SPEATS	SPEEDBALL	SPELLDOWNS	SPEWIER
SPATULA	SPEC	SPEEDBALLS	SPELLED	SPEWIEST
SPATULAR	SPECCIES	SPEEDED	SPELLER	SPEWINESS
SPATULAS	SPECCY	SPEEDER	SPELLERS	SPEWINESSES
SPATULATE	SPECIAL	SPEEDERS	SPELLFUL	SPEWING
SPATULE	SPECIALLY	SPEEDFUL	SPELLICAN	SPEWS
SPATULES	SPECIALS	SPEEDIER	SPELLICANS	SPEWY
SPAUL	SPECIALTIES	SPEEDIEST	SPELLIKIN	SPHACELUS
SPAULD	SPECIALTY	SPEEDILY	SPELLIKINS	SPHACELUSES
SPAULDS	SPECIATE	SPEEDING	SPELLING	SPHAER
SPAULS	SPECIATED	SPEEDINGS	SPELLINGS	SPHAERE
SPAVIE	SPECIATES	SPEEDLESS	SPELLS	SPHAERES
SPAVIES	SPECIATING	SPEEDO	SPELT	SPHAERITE
SPAVIN	SPECIE	SPEEDOS	SPELTER	SPHAERITES
SPAVINED	SPECIES	SPEEDS	SPELTERS	SPHAERS
SPAVINS	SPECIFIC	SPEEDSTER	SPELTS	SPHAGNOUS
SPAW	SPECIFICS	SPEEDSTERS	SPENCE	SPHEAR
SPAWL	SPECIFIED	SPEEDWAY	SPENCER	SPHEARE
SPAWLED	SPECIFIES	SPEEDWAYS	SPENCERS	SPHEARES
SPAWLING	SPECIFY	SPEEDWELL	SPENCES	SPHEARS
SPAWLS	SPECIFYING	SPEEDWELLS	SPEND	SPHENDONE
SPAWN	SPECIMEN	SPEEDY	SPENDABLE	SPHENDONES
SPAWNED	SPECIMENS	SPEEL	SPENDALL	SPHENE
SPAWNER	SPECIOUS	SPEELED	SPENDALLS	SPHENES
SPAWNERS	SPECK	SPEELER	SPENDER	SPHENIC
SPAWNING	SPECKED	SPEELERS	SPENDERS	SPHENODON
SPAWNINGS	SPECKIER	SPEELING	SPENDING	SPHENODONS
SPAWNS	SPECKIEST	SPEELS	SPENDINGS	SPHENOID
SPAWS	SPECKING	SPEER	SPENDS	SPHENOIDS
SPAY	SPECKLE	SPEERED	SPENT	SPHERAL
SPAYAD	SPECKLED	SPEERING	SPEOS	SPHERE
SPAYADS	SPECKLES	SPEERINGS	SPEOSES	SPHERED
SPAYD	SPECKLESS	SPEERS	SPERLING	SPHERES
SPAYDS	SPECKLING	SPEIR	SPERLINGS	SPHERIC
SPAYED	SPECKS	SPEIRED	SPERM	SPHERICAL
SPAYING	SPECKY	SPEIRING	SPERMARIA	SPHERICS
SPAYS	SPECS	SPEIRINGS	SPERMARIES	SPHERIER
SPEAK	SPECTACLE	SPEIRS	SPERMARY	SPHERIEST
SPEAKABLE	SPECTACLES	SPEISS	SPERMATIA	SPHERING
SPEAKER	SPECTATE	SPEISSES	SPERMATIC	SPHEROID

SPHEROIDS	SPIFF	SPINATE	SPIRAL	SPITEFULLER
SPHERULAR	SPIFFIER	SPINDLE	SPIRALISM	SPITEFULLEST
SPHERULE	SPIFFIEST	SPINDLED	SPIRALISMS	SPITES
SPHERULES	SPIFFING	SPINDLES	SPIRALIST	SPITFIRE
SPHERY	SPIFFY	SPINDLIER	SPIRALISTS	SPITFIRES
SPHINCTER	SPIGHT	SPINDLIEST	SPIRALITIES	SPITING
SPHINCTERS	SPIGHTED	SPINDLING	SPIRALITY	SPITS
SPHINGES	SPIGHTING	SPINDLINGS	SPIRALLED	SPITTED
SPHINGID	SPIGHTS	SPINDLY	SPIRALLING	SPITTEN
SPHINGIDS	SPIGNEL	SPINDRIFT	SPIRALLY	SPITTER
SPHINX	SPIGNELS	SPINDRIFTS	SPIRALS	SPITTERS
SPHINXES	SPIGOT	SPINE	SPIRANT	SPITTING
SPHYGMIC	SPIGOTS	SPINED	SPIRANTS	SPITTINGS
SPHYGMOID	SPIK	SPINEL	SPIRASTER	SPITTLE
SPHYGMUS	SPIKE	SPINELESS	SPIRASTERS	SPITTLES
SPHYGMUSES	SPIKED	SPINELS	SPIRATED	SPITTOON
SPIAL	SPIKELET	SPINES	SPIRATION	SPITTOONS
SPIALS	SPIKELETS	SPINET	SPIRATIONS	SPITZ
SPIC	SPIKENARD	SPINETS	SPIRE	SPITZES
SPICA	SPIKENARDS	SPINETTE	SPIREA	SPIV
SPICAS	SPIKES	SPINETTES	SPIREAS	SPIVS
SPICATE	SPIKIER	SPINIER	SPIRED	SPIVVERIES
SPICATED	SPIKIEST	SPINIEST	SPIRELESS	SPIVVERY
SPICCATO	SPIKILY	SPINIFEX	SPIREME	SPIVVIER
SPICCATOS	SPIKINESS	SPINIFEXES	SPIREMES	SPIVVIEST
SPICE	SPIKINESSES	SPINIFORM	SPIRES	SPIVVY
SPICED	SPIKING	SPININESS	SPIREWISE	SPLASH
SPICER	SPIKY	SPININESSES	SPIRIC	SPLASHED
SPICERIES	SPILE	SPINK	SPIRICS	SPLASHER
SPICERS	SPILED	SPINKS	SPIRIER	SPLASHERS
SPICERY	SPILES	SPINNAKER	SPIRIEST	SPLASHES
SPICES	SPILIKIN	SPINNAKERS	SPIRILLA	SPLASHIER
SPICIER	SPILIKINS	SPINNER	SPIRILLAR	SPLASHIEST
SPICIEST	SPILING	SPINNERET	SPIRILLUM	SPLASHILY
SPICILEGE	SPILINGS	SPINNERETS	SPIRING	SPLASHING
SPICILEGES	SPILITE	SPINNERIES	SPIRIT	SPLASHINGS
SPICILY	SPILITES	SPINNERS	SPIRITED	SPLASHY
SPICINESS	SPILITIC	SPINNERY	SPIRITFUL	SPLAT
SPICINESSES	SPILL	SPINNET	SPIRITING	SPLATCH
SPICING	SPILLAGE	SPINNETS	SPIRITINGS	SPLATCHED
SPICK	SPILLAGES	SPINNEY	SPIRITISM	SPLATCHES
SPICKER	SPILLED	SPINNEYS	SPIRITISMS	SPLATCHING
SPICKEST	SPILLER	SPINNIES	SPIRITIST	SPLATS
SPICKNEL	SPILLIKIN	SPINNING	SPIRITISTS	SPLATTED
SPICKNELS	SPILLIKINS	SPINNINGS	SPIRITOSO	SPLATTER
SPICKS	SPILLIKINS	SPINNY	SPIRITOUS	SPLATTERED
SPICS	SPILLIKINS	SPINODE	SPIRITS	SPLATTERING
SPICULA	SPILLING	SPINODES	SPIRITUAL	SPLATTERS
SPICULAR	SPILLINGS	SPINOSE	SPIRITUALS	SPLATTING
SPICULAS	SPILLOVER	SPINOSITIES	SPIRITUEL	SPLATTINGS
SPICULATE	SPILLOVERS	SPINOSITY	SPIRITUS	SPLAY
SPICULE	SPILLS	SPINOUS	SPIRITUSES	SPLAYED
SPICULES	SPILLWAY	SPINOUT	SPIRITY	SPLAYING
SPICULUM	SPILLWAYS	SPINOUTS	SPIRLING	SPLAYS
SPICY	SPILOSITE	SPINS	SPIRLINGS	SPLEEN
SPIDE	SPILOSITES	SPINSTER	SPIROID	SPLEENFUL
SPIDER	SPILT	SPINSTERS	SPIRT	SPLEENIER
SPIDERIER	SPILTH	SPINTEXT	SPIRTED	SPLEENIEST
SPIDERIEST	SPILTHS	SPINTEXTS	SPIRTING	SPLEENISH
SPIDERS	SPIN	SPINULATE	SPIRTLE	SPLEENS
SPIDERY	SPINA	SPINULE	SPIRTLES	SPLEENY
SPIE	SPINACH	SPINULES	SPIRTS	SPLENDENT
SPIED	SPINACHES	SPINULOSE	SPIRY	SPLENDID
SPIEL	SPINAE	SPINULOUS	SPIT	SPLENDOR
SPIELED	SPINAGE	SPINY	SPITAL	SPLENDORS
SPIELER	SPINAGES	SPIRACLE	SPITALS	SPLENDOUR
SPIELERS	SPINAL	SPIRACLES	SPITCHER	SPLENDOURS
SPIELING	SPINAR	SPIRACULA	SPITE	SPLENETIC
SPIELS	SPINARS	SPIRAEA	SPITED	SPLENETICS
SPIES	SPINAS	SPIRAEAS	SPITEFUL	SPLENIA

SPLENIAL
SPLENIC
SPLENII
SPLENITIS
SPLENITISES
SPLENIUM
SPLENIUMS
SPLENIUS
SPLENIUSES
SPLENT
SPLENTED
SPLENTING
SPLENTS
SPLEUCHAN
SPLEUCHANS
SPLICE
SPLICED
SPLICES
SPLICING
SPLIFF
SPLIFFS
SPLINE
SPLINED
SPLINES
SPLINING
SPLINT
SPLINTED
SPLINTER
SPLINTERED
SPLINTERING
SPLINTERS
SPLINTERY
SPLINTING
SPLINTS
SPLIT
SPLITS
SPLITTED
SPLITTER
SPLITTERS
SPLITTING
SPLODGE
SPLODGED
SPLODGES
SPLODGIER
SPLODGIEST
SPLODGILY
SPLODGING
SPLODGY
SPLORE
SPLORES
SPLOSH
SPLOSHED
SPLOSHES
SPLOSHING
SPLOTCH
SPLOTCHED
SPLOTCHES
SPLOTCHIER
SPLOTCHIEST
SPLOTCHING
SPLOTCHY
SPLURGE
SPLURGED
SPLURGES
SPLURGIER
SPLURGIEST
SPLURGING
SPLURGY
SPLUTTER
SPLUTTERED

SPLUTTERING
SPLUTTERINGS
SPLUTTERS
SPLUTTERY
SPODE
SPODES
SPODIUM
SPODIUMS
SPODUMENE
SPODUMENES
SPOFFISH
SPOFFY
SPOIL
SPOILAGE
SPOILED
SPOILER
SPOILERS
SPOILFUL
SPOILING
SPOILS
SPOILSMAN
SPOILSMEN
SPOILT
SPOKE
SPOKEN
SPOKES
SPOKESMAN
SPOKESMEN
SPOKEWISE
SPOLIATE
SPOLIATED
SPOLIATES
SPOLIATING
SPOLIATOR
SPOLIATORS
SPONDAIC
SPONDEE
SPONDEES
SPONDULIX
SPONDYL
SPONDYLS
SPONGE
SPONGED
SPONGEOUS
SPONGER
SPONGERS
SPONGES
SPONGIER
SPONGIEST
SPONGILY
SPONGIN
SPONGING
SPONGINS
SPONGIOSE
SPONGIOUS
SPONGOID
SPONGY
SPONSAL
SPONSALIA
SPONSIBLE
SPONSING
SPONSINGS
SPONSION
SPONSIONS
SPONSON
SPONSONS
SPONSOR
SPONSORED
SPONSORING
SPONSORS

SPONTOON
SPONTOONS
SPOOF
SPOOFED
SPOOFER
SPOOFERIES
SPOOFERS
SPOOFERY
SPOOFING
SPOOFS
SPOOK
SPOOKED
SPOOKERIES
SPOOKERY
SPOOKIER
SPOOKIEST
SPOOKILY
SPOOKING
SPOOKISH
SPOOKS
SPOOKY
SPOOL
SPOOLED
SPOOLER
SPOOLERS
SPOOLING
SPOOLS
SPOOM
SPOOMED
SPOOMING
SPOOMS
SPOON
SPOONBILL
SPOONBILLS
SPOONED
SPOONEY
SPOONEYS
SPOONFUL
SPOONFULS
SPOONIER
SPOONIES
SPOONIEST
SPOONILY
SPOONING
SPOONMEAT
SPOONMEATS
SPOONS
SPOONWAYS
SPOONWISE
SPOONY
SPOOR
SPOORED
SPOORER
SPOORERS
SPOORING
SPOORS
SPORADIC
SPORANGIA
SPORE
SPORES
SPORIDESM
SPORIDESMS
SPORIDIA
SPORIDIAL
SPORIDIUM
SPOROCARP
SPOROCARPS
SPOROCYST
SPOROCYSTS
SPOROGENIES

SPOROGENY
SPOROPHYL
SPOROPHYLS
SPORRAN
SPORRANS
SPORT
SPORTABLE
SPORTANCE
SPORTANCES
SPORTED
SPORTER
SPORTERS
SPORTFUL
SPORTIER
SPORTIEST
SPORTILY
SPORTING
SPORTIVE
SPORTLESS
SPORTS
SPORTSMAN
SPORTSMEN
SPORTY
SPORULAR
SPORULATE
SPORULATED
SPORULATES
SPORULATING
SPORULE
SPORULES
SPOSH
SPOSHES
SPOSHY
SPOT
SPOTLESS
SPOTLIGHT
SPOTLIGHTED
SPOTLIGHTING
SPOTLIGHTS
SPOTLIT
SPOTS
SPOTTE
SPOTTED
SPOTTER
SPOTTERS
SPOTTES
SPOTTIER
SPOTTIEST
SPOTTILY
SPOTTING
SPOTTINGS
SPOTTY
SPOUSAGE
SPOUSAGES
SPOUSAL
SPOUSALS
SPOUSE
SPOUSED
SPOUSES
SPOUSING
SPOUT
SPOUTED
SPOUTER
SPOUTERS
SPOUTIER
SPOUTIEST
SPOUTING
SPOUTLESS
SPOUTS
SPOUTY

SPRACK
SPRACKLE
SPRACKLED
SPRACKLES
SPRACKLING
SPRAD
SPRAG
SPRAGGED
SPRAGGING
SPRAGS
SPRAICKLE
SPRAICKLED
SPRAICKLES
SPRAICKLING
SPRAID
SPRAIN
SPRAINED
SPRAINING
SPRAINS
SPRAINT
SPRAINTS
SPRANG
SPRANGLE
SPRANGLED
SPRANGLES
SPRANGLING
SPRAT
SPRATS
SPRATTLE
SPRATTLED
SPRATTLES
SPRATTLING
SPRAUCHLE
SPRAUCHLED
SPRAUCHLES
SPRAUCHLING
SPRAUNCIER
SPRAUNCIEST
SPRAUNCY
SPRAWL
SPRAWLED
SPRAWLER
SPRAWLERS
SPRAWLIER
SPRAWLIEST
SPRAWLING
SPRAWLS
SPRAWLY
SPRAY
SPRAYED
SPRAYER
SPRAYERS
SPRAYEY
SPRAYIER
SPRAYIEST
SPRAYING
SPRAYS
SPREAD
SPREADER
SPREADERS
SPREADING
SPREADINGS
SPREADS
SPREAGH
SPREAGHS
SPREATHE
SPREATHED
SPREATHES
SPREATHING
SPREAZE

SPREAZED
SPREAZES
SPREAZING
SPRECHERIES
SPRECHERY
SPRECKLED
SPRED
SPREDD
SPREDDE
SPREDDEN
SPREDDES
SPREDDING
SPREDDS
SPREDS
SPREE
SPREED
SPREEING
SPREES
SPREETHE
SPREETHED
SPREETHES
SPREETHING
SPREEZE
SPREEZED
SPREEZES
SPREEZING
SPRENT
SPRIG
SPRIGGED
SPRIGGIER
SPRIGGIEST
SPRIGGING
SPRIGGY
SPRIGHT
SPRIGHTED
SPRIGHTING
SPRIGHTLIER
SPRIGHTLIEST
SPRIGHTLY
SPRIGHTS
SPRIGS
SPRING
SPRINGAL
SPRINGALD
SPRINGALDS
SPRINGALS
SPRINGBOK
SPRINGBOKS
SPRINGE
SPRINGED
SPRINGER
SPRINGERS
SPRINGES
SPRINGIER
SPRINGIEST
SPRINGILY
SPRINGING
SPRINGINGS
SPRINGLE
SPRINGLES
SPRINGLET
SPRINGLETS
SPRINGS
SPRINGY
SPRINKLE
SPRINKLED
SPRINKLER
SPRINKLERS
SPRINKLES
SPRINKLING

SPRINKLINGS
SPRINT
SPRINTED
SPRINTER
SPRINTERS
SPRINTING
SPRINTINGS
SPRINTS
SPRIT
SPRITE
SPRITEFUL
SPRITELY
SPRITES
SPRITS
SPRITSAIL
SPRITSAILS
SPRITZER
SPRITZERS
SPRITZIG
SPRITZIGS
SPROCKET
SPROCKETS
SPROD
SPRODS
SPROG
SPROGS
SPRONG
SPROUT
SPROUTED
SPROUTING
SPROUTINGS
SPROUTS
SPRUCE
SPRUCED
SPRUCELY
SPRUCER
SPRUCES
SPRUCEST
SPRUCING
SPRUE
SPRUES
SPRUG
SPRUGS
SPRUIK
SPRUIKED
SPRUIKER
SPRUIKERS
SPRUIKING
SPRUIKS
SPRUIT
SPRUITS
SPRUNG
SPRUSH
SPRUSHED
SPRUSHES
SPRUSHING
SPRY
SPRYER
SPRYEST
SPRYLY
SPRYNESS
SPRYNESSES
SPUD
SPUDDED
SPUDDIER
SPUDDIEST
SPUDDING
SPUDDINGS
SPUDDY
SPUDS

SPUE
SPUED
SPUEING
SPUES
SPUILZIE
SPUILZIED
SPUILZIEING
SPUILZIES
SPULE
SPULEBANE
SPULEBANES
SPULEBONE
SPULEBONES
SPULES
SPULYE
SPULYED
SPULYEING
SPULYES
SPULYIE
SPULYIED
SPULYIEING
SPULYIES
SPULZIE
SPULZIED
SPULZIEING
SPULZIES
SPUME
SPUMED
SPUMES
SPUMIER
SPUMIEST
SPUMING
SPUMOUS
SPUMY
SPUN
SPUNGE
SPUNGES
SPUNK
SPUNKED
SPUNKIE
SPUNKIER
SPUNKIEST
SPUNKING
SPUNKS
SPUNKY
SPUR
SPURGE
SPURGES
SPURIAE
SPURIOUS
SPURLESS
SPURLING
SPURLINGS
SPURN
SPURNE
SPURNED
SPURNER
SPURNERS
SPURNES
SPURNING
SPURNINGS
SPURNS
SPURRED
SPURRER
SPURRERS
SPURREY
SPURREYS
SPURRIER
SPURRIERS

SPURRIES
SPURRING
SPURRINGS
SPURRY
SPURS
SPURT
SPURTED
SPURTING
SPURTLE
SPURTLES
SPURTS
SPUTA
SPUTNIK
SPUTNIKS
SPUTTER
SPUTTERED
SPUTTERER
SPUTTERERS
SPUTTERING
SPUTTERINGS
SPUTTERS
SPUTTERY
SPUTUM
SPY
SPYAL
SPYALS
SPYGLASS
SPYGLASSES
SPYING
SPYINGS
SPYMASTER
SPYMASTERS
SPYRE
SPYRES
SQUAB
SQUABASH
SQUABASHED
SQUABASHES
SQUABASHING
SQUABBED
SQUABBER
SQUABBEST
SQUABBIER
SQUABBIEST
SQUABBING
SQUABBISH
SQUABBLE
SQUABBLED
SQUABBLER
SQUABBLERS
SQUABBLES
SQUABBLING
SQUABBY
SQUABS
SQUACCO
SQUACCOS
SQUAD
SQUADDIES
SQUADDY
SQUADRON
SQUADRONE
SQUADRONED
SQUADRONES
SQUADRONING
SQUADRONS
SQUADS
SQUAIL
SQUAILED
SQUAILER
SQUAILERS

SQUAILING
SQUAILINGS
SQUAILS
SQUALID
SQUALIDER
SQUALIDEST
SQUALIDLY
SQUALL
SQUALLED
SQUALLER
SQUALLERS
SQUALLIER
SQUALLIEST
SQUALLING
SQUALLINGS
SQUALLS
SQUALLY
SQUALOID
SQUALOR
SQUALORS
SQUAMA
SQUAMAE
SQUAMATE
SQUAME
SQUAMELLA
SQUAMELLAS
SQUAMES
SQUAMOSAL
SQUAMOSALS
SQUAMOSE
SQUAMOUS
SQUAMULA
SQUAMULAS
SQUAMULE
SQUAMULES
SQUANDER
SQUANDERED
SQUANDERING
SQUANDERINGS
SQUANDERS
SQUARE
SQUARED
SQUAREFLY
SQUARER
SQUARERS
SQUARES
SQUAREST
SQUARING
SQUARINGS
SQUARISH
SQUARROSE
SQUARSON
SQUARSONS
SQUASH
SQUASHED
SQUASHER
SQUASHERS
SQUASHES
SQUASHIER
SQUASHIEST
SQUASHILY
SQUASHING
SQUASHY
SQUAT
SQUATNESS
SQUATNESSES
SQUATS
SQUATTED
SQUATTER
SQUATTERED

SQUATTERING
SQUATTERS
SQUATTEST
SQUATTIER
SQUATTIEST
SQUATTING
SQUATTLE
SQUATTLED
SQUATTLES
SQUATTLING
SQUATTY
SQUAW
SQUAWK
SQUAWKED
SQUAWKER
SQUAWKERS
SQUAWKIER
SQUAWKIEST
SQUAWKING
SQUAWKINGS
SQUAWKS
SQUAWKY
SQUAWMAN
SQUAWMEN
SQUAWS
SQUEAK
SQUEAKED
SQUEAKER
SQUEAKERIES
SQUEAKERS
SQUEAKERY
SQUEAKIER
SQUEAKIEST
SQUEAKILY
SQUEAKING
SQUEAKINGS
SQUEAKS
SQUEAKY
SQUEAL
SQUEALED
SQUEALER
SQUEALERS
SQUEALING
SQUEALINGS
SQUEALS
SQUEAMISH
SQUEEDGE
SQUEEDGED
SQUEEDGES
SQUEEDGING
SQUEEGEE
SQUEEGEED
SQUEEGEEING
SQUEEGEES
SQUEEZE
SQUEEZED
SQUEEZER
SQUEEZERS
SQUEEZES
SQUEEZIER
SQUEEZIEST
SQUEEZING
SQUEEZINGS
SQUEEZY
SQUEG
SQUEGGED
SQUEGGER
SQUEGGERS
SQUEGGING
SQUEGGINGS

SQUEGS
SQUELCH
SQUELCHED
SQUELCHER
SQUELCHERS
SQUELCHES
SQUELCHIER
SQUELCHIEST
SQUELCHING
SQUELCHINGS
SQUELCHY
SQUIB
SQUIBBED
SQUIBBING
SQUIBBINGS
SQUIBS
SQUID
SQUIDDED
SQUIDDING
SQUIDGE
SQUIDGED
SQUIDGES
SQUIDGIER
SQUIDGIEST
SQUIDGING
SQUIDGY
SQUIDS
SQUIER
SQUIERS
SQUIFF
SQUIFFER
SQUIFFERS
SQUIFFIER
SQUIFFIEST
SQUIFFY
SQUIGGLE
SQUIGGLED
SQUIGGLES
SQUIGGLIER
SQUIGGLIEST
SQUIGGLING
SQUIGGLY
SQUILGEE
SQUILGEED
SQUILGEEING
SQUILGEES
SQUILL
SQUILLS
SQUINANCIES
SQUINANCY
SQUINCH
SQUINCHES
SQUINIED
SQUINIES
SQUINNIED
SQUINNIES
SQUINNY
SQUINNYING
SQUINT
SQUINTED
SQUINTER
SQUINTERS
SQUINTEST
SQUINTING
SQUINTINGS
SQUINTS
SQUINY
SQUINYING
SQUIRAGE
SQUIRAGES

SQUIRALTIES
SQUIRALTY
SQUIRARCH
SQUIRARCHS
SQUIRE
SQUIREAGE
SQUIREAGES
SQUIRED
SQUIREDOM
SQUIREDOMS
SQUIREEN
SQUIREENS
SQUIRELY
SQUIRES
SQUIRESS
SQUIRESSES
SQUIRING
SQUIRM
SQUIRMED
SQUIRMIER
SQUIRMIEST
SQUIRMING
SQUIRMS
SQUIRMY
SQUIRR
SQUIRRED
SQUIRREL
SQUIRRELLED
SQUIRRELLING
SQUIRRELS
SQUIRRELY
SQUIRRING
SQUIRRS
SQUIRT
SQUIRTED
SQUIRTER
SQUIRTERS
SQUIRTING
SQUIRTINGS
SQUIRTS
SQUISH
SQUISHED
SQUISHES
SQUISHIER
SQUISHIEST
SQUISHING
SQUISHY
SQUIT
SQUITCH
SQUITCHES
SQUITS
SRADDHA
SRADDHAS
ST
STAB
STABBED
STABBER
STABBERS
STABBING
STABBINGS
STABILE
STABILES
STABILISE
STABILISED
STABILISES
STABILISING
STABILITIES
STABILITY
STABILIZE
STABILIZED

STABILIZES
STABILIZING
STABLE
STABLED
STABLER
STABLERS
STABLES
STABLEST
STABLING
STABLINGS
STABLISH
STABLISHED
STABLISHES
STABLISHING
STABLY
STABS
STACCATO
STACCATOS
STACK
STACKED
STACKER
STACKERS
STACKET
STACKETS
STACKING
STACKINGS
STACKS
STACKYARD
STACKYARDS
STACTE
STACTES
STADDA
STADDAS
STADDLE
STADDLES
STADE
STADES
STADIA
STADIAL
STADIALS
STADIAS
STADIUM
STADIUMS
STAFF
STAFFAGE
STAFFAGES
STAFFED
STAFFER
STAFFERS
STAFFING
STAFFROOM
STAFFROOMS
STAFFS
STAG
STAGE
STAGED
STAGER
STAGERIES
STAGERS
STAGERY
STAGES
STAGEY
STAGGARD
STAGGARDS
STAGGED
STAGGER
STAGGERED
STAGGERER
STAGGERERS
STAGGERING

STAGGERINGS
STAGGERS
STAGGING
STAGHORN
STAGHORNS
STAGHOUND
STAGHOUNDS
STAGIER
STAGIEST
STAGILY
STAGINESS
STAGINESSES
STAGING
STAGINGS
STAGNANCIES
STAGNANCY
STAGNANT
STAGNATE
STAGNATED
STAGNATES
STAGNATING
STAGS
STAGY
STAID
STAIDER
STAIDEST
STAIDLY
STAIDNESS
STAIDNESSES
STAIG
STAIGS
STAIN
STAINED
STAINER
STAINERS
STAINING
STAININGS
STAINLESS
STAINS
STAIR
STAIRCASE
STAIRCASES
STAIRED
STAIRFOOT
STAIRFOOTS
STAIRHEAD
STAIRHEADS
STAIRS
STAIRWAY
STAIRWAYS
STAIRWISE
STAITH
STAITHE
STAITHES
STAITHS
STAKE
STAKED
STAKES
STAKING
STALACTIC
STALAG
STALAGMA
STALAGMAS
STALAGS
STALE
STALED
STALELY
STALEMATE
STALEMATED
STALEMATES

STALEMATING
STALENESS
STALENESSES
STALER
STALES
STALEST
STALING
STALK
STALKED
STALKER
STALKERS
STALKIER
STALKIEST
STALKING
STALKINGS
STALKLESS
STALKO
STALKOES
STALKS
STALKY
STALL
STALLAGE
STALLAGES
STALLED
STALLING
STALLINGS
STALLION
STALLIONS
STALLMAN
STALLMEN
STALLS
STALWART
STALWARTS
STALWORTH
STALWORTHS
STAMEN
STAMENED
STAMENS
STAMINA
STAMINAL
STAMINAS
STAMINATE
STAMINEAL
STAMINODE
STAMINODES
STAMINODIES
STAMINODY
STAMINOID
STAMMEL
STAMMELS
STAMMER
STAMMERED
STAMMERER
STAMMERERS
STAMMERING
STAMMERINGS
STAMMERS
STAMNOI
STAMNOS
STAMP
STAMPED
STAMPEDE
STAMPEDED
STAMPEDES
STAMPEDING
STAMPEDO
STAMPEDOED
STAMPEDOES
STAMPEDOING
STAMPER

STAMPERS
STAMPING
STAMPINGS
STAMPS
STANCE
STANCES
STANCH
STANCHED
STANCHEL
STANCHELLED
STANCHELLING
STANCHELS
STANCHER
STANCHERED
STANCHERING
STANCHERS
STANCHES
STANCHEST
STANCHING
STANCHINGS
STANCHION
STANCHIONED
STANCHIONING
STANCHIONS
STANCHLY
STANCK
STAND
STANDARD
STANDARDS
STANDEN
STANDER
STANDERS
STANDGALE
STANDGALES
STANDING
STANDINGS
STANDISH
STANDISHES
STANDS
STANE
STANED
STANES
STANG
STANGED
STANGING
STANGS
STANHOPE
STANHOPES
STANIEL
STANIELS
STANING
STANK
STANKS
STANNARIES
STANNARY
STANNATE
STANNATES
STANNATOR
STANNATORS
STANNEL
STANNELS
STANNIC
STANNITE
STANNITES
STANNOUS
STANYEL
STANYELS
STANZA
STANZAIC
STANZAS

STANZE
STANZES
STANZO
STANZOES
STANZOS
STAP
STAPEDES
STAPEDIAL
STAPEDII
STAPEDIUS
STAPEDIUSES
STAPELIA
STAPELIAS
STAPES
STAPH
STAPHS
STAPHYLE
STAPHYLES
STAPLE
STAPLED
STAPLER
STAPLERS
STAPLES
STAPLING
STAPPED
STAPPING
STAPPLE
STAPPLES
STAPS
STAR
STARAGEN
STARAGENS
STARBOARD
STARBOARDED
STARBOARDING
STARBOARDS
STARCH
STARCHED
STARCHER
STARCHERS
STARCHES
STARCHIER
STARCHIEST
STARCHILY
STARCHING
STARCHY
STARDOM
STARDOMS
STARE
STARED
STARER
STARERS
STARES
STARETS
STARETSES
STARETZ
STARETZES
STARFISH
STARFISHES
STARING
STARINGLY
STARINGS
STARK
STARKED
STARKEN
STARKENED
STARKENING
STARKENS
STARKER
STARKERS

STARKEST
STARKING
STARKLY
STARKNESS
STARKNESSES
STARKS
STARLESS
STARLET
STARLETS
STARLIGHT
STARLIGHTS
STARLIKE
STARLING
STARLINGS
STARLIT
STARN
STARNED
STARNIE
STARNIES
STARNING
STARNS
STAROSTA
STAROSTAS
STAROSTIES
STAROSTY
STARR
STARRED
STARRIER
STARRIEST
STARRILY
STARRING
STARRINGS
STARRS
STARRY
STARS
STARSHINE
STARSHINES
STARSPOT
STARSPOTS
START
STARTED
STARTER
STARTERS
STARTFUL
STARTING
STARTINGS
STARTISH
STARTLE
STARTLED
STARTLER
STARTLERS
STARTLES
STARTLING
STARTLINGS
STARTLISH
STARTLY
STARTS
STARVE
STARVED
STARVES
STARVING
STARVINGS
STARWORT
STARWORTS
STASES
STASH
STASHED
STASHES
STASHIE
STASHIES

STASHING
STASIDION
STASIDIONS
STASIMA
STASIMON
STASIS
STATABLE
STATAL
STATANT
STATE
STATED
STATEDLY
STATEHOOD
STATEHOODS
STATELESS
STATELIER
STATELIEST
STATELILY
STATELY
STATEMENT
STATEMENTS
STATER
STATEROOM
STATEROOMS
STATERS
STATES
STATESIDE
STATESMAN
STATESMEN
STATEWIDE
STATIC
STATICAL
STATICS
STATING
STATION
STATIONAL
STATIONED
STATIONER
STATIONERS
STATIONING
STATIONS
STATISM
STATISMS
STATIST
STATISTIC
STATISTICS
STATISTS
STATIVE
STATOCYST
STATOCYSTS
STATOLITH
STATOLITHS
STATOR
STATORS
STATUA
STATUARIES
STATUARY
STATUAS
STATUE
STATUED
STATUES
STATUETTE
STATUETTES
STATURE
STATURED
STATURES
STATUS
STATUTE
STATUTES
STATUTORY

STAUNCH
STAUNCHED
STAUNCHER
STAUNCHES
STAUNCHEST
STAUNCHING
STAUNCHLY
STAVE
STAVED
STAVES
STAVING
STAW
STAWED
STAWING
STAWS
STAY
STAYED
STAYER
STAYERS
STAYING
STAYINGS
STAYLESS
STAYNE
STAYNED
STAYNES
STAYNING
STAYRE
STAYRES
STAYS
STAYSAIL
STAYSAILS
STEAD
STEADED
STEADFAST
STEADIED
STEADIER
STEADIES
STEADIEST
STEADILY
STEADING
STEADINGS
STEADS
STEADY
STEADYING
STEAK
STEAKS
STEAL
STEALE
STEALED
STEALER
STEALERS
STEALES
STEALING
STEALINGS
STEALS
STEALT
STEALTH
STEALTHIER
STEALTHIEST
STEALTHS
STEALTHY
STEAM
STEAMBOAT
STEAMBOATS
STEAMED
STEAMER
STEAMERS
STEAMIE
STEAMIER
STEAMIES

STEAMIEST
STEAMILY
STEAMING
STEAMINGS
STEAMS
STEAMSHIP
STEAMSHIPS
STEAMY
STEAN
STEANE
STEANED
STEANES
STEANING
STEANINGS
STEANS
STEAR
STEARAGE
STEARAGES
STEARATE
STEARATES
STEARD
STEARE
STEARED
STEARES
STEARIC
STEARIN
STEARINE
STEARINES
STEARING
STEARINS
STEARS
STEARSMAN
STEARSMEN
STEATITE
STEATITES
STEATITIC
STEATOMA
STEATOMAS
STEATOSES
STEATOSIS
STED
STEDD
STEDDE
STEDDED
STEDDES
STEDDIED
STEDDIES
STEDDING
STEDDS
STEDDY
STEDDYING
STEDE
STEDED
STEDES
STEDFAST
STEDING
STEDS
STEED
STEEDED
STEEDIED
STEEDIES
STEEDING
STEEDS
STEEDY
STEEDYING
STEEK
STEEKING
STEEKIT
STEEKS
STEEL

STEELBOW
STEELBOWS
STEELD
STEELED
STEELIER
STEELIEST
STEELING
STEELINGS
STEELS
STEELWORK
STEELWORKS
STEELY
STEELYARD
STEELYARDS
STEEM
STEEMED
STEEMING
STEEMS
STEEN
STEENBOK
STEENBOKS
STEENBRAS
STEENBRASES
STEENED
STEENING
STEENINGS
STEENKIRK
STEENKIRKS
STEENS
STEEP
STEEPED
STEEPEN
STEEPENED
STEEPENING
STEEPENS
STEEPER
STEEPERS
STEEPEST
STEEPING
STEEPISH
STEEPLE
STEEPLED
STEEPLES
STEEPLY
STEEPNESS
STEEPNESSES
STEEPS
STEEPY
STEER
STEERABLE
STEERAGE
STEERAGES
STEERED
STEERER
STEERERS
STEERIES
STEERING
STEERINGS
STEERLING
STEERLINGS
STEERS
STEERSMAN
STEERSMEN
STEERY
STEEVE
STEEVED
STEEVELY
STEEVER
STEEVES
STEEVEST

STEEVING
STEEVINGS
STEGNOSES
STEGNOSIS
STEGNOTIC
STEGODON
STEGODONS
STEGODONT
STEGODONTS
STEGOMYIA
STEGOMYIAS
STEGOSAUR
STEGOSAURS
STEIL
STEILS
STEIN
STEINBOCK
STEINBOCKS
STEINED
STEINING
STEININGS
STEINS
STELA
STELAE
STELAR
STELE
STELENE
STELL
STELLAR
STELLATE
STELLATED
STELLED
STELLIFIED
STELLIFIES
STELLIFY
STELLIFYING
STELLIFYINGS
STELLING
STELLION
STELLIONS
STELLS
STELLULAR
STEM
STEMBOK
STEMBOKS
STEMBUCK
STEMBUCKS
STEME
STEMED
STEMES
STEMING
STEMLESS
STEMLET
STEMLETS
STEMMA
STEMMATA
STEMME
STEMMED
STEMMES
STEMMING
STEMPEL
STEMPELS
STEMPLE
STEMPLES
STEMS
STEMSON
STEMSONS
STEN
STENCH
STENCHED

STENCHES
STENCHIER
STENCHIEST
STENCHING
STENCHY
STENCIL
STENCILLED
STENCILLING
STENCILLINGS
STENCILS
STEND
STENDED
STENDING
STENDS
STENGAH
STENGAHS
STENLOCK
STENLOCKS
STENNED
STENNING
STENOPAIC
STENOSED
STENOSES
STENOSIS
STENOTIC
STENOTYPE
STENOTYPES
STENOTYPIES
STENOTYPY
STENS
STENT
STENTED
STENTING
STENTOR
STENTORS
STENTOUR
STENTOURS
STENTS
STEP
STEPBAIRN
STEPBAIRNS
STEPCHILD
STEPCHILDREN
STEPDAME
STEPDAMES
STEPHANE
STEPHANES
STEPNEY
STEPNEYS
STEPPE
STEPPED
STEPPER
STEPPERS
STEPPES
STEPPING
STEPS
STEPSON
STEPSONS
STEPT
STEPWISE
STERADIAN
STERADIANS
STERCORAL
STERCULIA
STERCULIAS
STERE
STEREO
STEREOED
STEREOING
STEREOME

STEREOMES	STEWARDRY	STICKS	STILLER	STINTEDLY
STEREOS	STEWARDS	STICKUP	STILLERS	STINTER
STERES	STEWARTRIES	STICKUPS	STILLEST	STINTERS
STERIC	STEWARTRY	STICKWORK	STILLIER	STINTIER
STERIGMA	STEWED	STICKWORKS	STILLIEST	STINTIEST
STERIGMATA	STEWER	STICKY	STILLING	STINTING
STERILE	STEWERS	STICKYING	STILLINGS	STINTINGS
STERILISE	STEWIER	STIDDIE	STILLION	STINTLESS
STERILISED	STEWIEST	STIDDIED	STILLIONS	STINTS
STERILISES	STEWING	STIDDIES	STILLNESS	STINTY
STERILISING	STEWINGS	STIDDYING	STILLNESSES	STIPA
STERILITIES	STEWPAN	STIE	STILLS	STIPAS
STERILITY	STEWPANS	STIED	STILLY	STIPE
STERILIZE	STEWPOND	STIEING	STILT	STIPEL
STERILIZED	STEWPONDS	STIES	STILTED	STIPELS
STERILIZES	STEWPOT	STIEVE	STILTEDLY	STIPEND
STERILIZING	STEWPOTS	STIEVELY	STILTER	STIPENDS
STERLET	STEWS	STIEVER	STILTERS	STIPES
STERLETS	STEWY	STIEVEST	STILTIER	STIPITATE
STERLING	STEY	STIFF	STILTIEST	STIPITES
STERLINGS	STEYER	STIFFED	STILTING	STIPPLE
STERN	STEYEST	STIFFEN	STILTINGS	STIPPLED
STERNAGE	STHENIC	STIFFENED	STILTISH	STIPPLER
STERNAGES	STIBBLE	STIFFENER	STILTS	STIPPLERS
STERNAL	STIBBLER	STIFFENERS	STILTY	STIPPLES
STERNEBRA	STIBBLERS	STIFFENING	STIME	STIPPLING
STERNEBRAE	STIBBLES	STIFFENINGS	STIMED	STIPPLINGS
STERNED	STIBIAL	STIFFENS	STIMES	STIPULAR
STERNER	STIBINE	STIFFER	STIMIE	STIPULARY
STERNEST	STIBINES	STIFFEST	STIMIED	STIPULATE
STERNING	STIBIUM	STIFFING	STIMIES	STIPULATED
STERNITE	STIBIUMS	STIFFISH	STIMING	STIPULATES
STERNITES	STIBNITE	STIFFLY	STIMULANT	STIPULATING
STERNITIC	STIBNITES	STIFFNESS	STIMULANTS	STIPULE
STERNLY	STICCADO	STIFFNESSES	STIMULATE	STIPULED
STERNMOST	STICCADOES	STIFFS	STIMULATED	STIPULES
STERNNESS	STICCADOS	STIFLE	STIMULATES	STIR
STERNNESSES	STICCATO	STIFLED	STIMULATING	STIRABOUT
STERNPORT	STICCATOES	STIFLER	STIMULI	STIRABOUTS
STERNPORTS	STICCATOS	STIFLERS	STIMULUS	STIRE
STERNS	STICH	STIFLES	STIMY	STIRED
STERNSON	STICHERON	STIFLING	STIMYING	STIRES
STERNSONS	STICHERONS	STIFLINGS	STING	STIRING
STERNUM	STICHIC	STIGMA	STINGAREE	STIRK
STERNUMS	STICHIDIA	STIGMAS	STINGAREES	STIRKS
STERNWARD	STICHOI	STIGMATA	STINGED	STIRLESS
STERNWARDS	STICHOS	STIGMATIC	STINGER	STIRP
STERNWAY	STICHS	STIGMATICS	STINGERS	STIRPES
STERNWAYS	STICK	STIGME	STINGIER	STIRPS
STEROID	STICKED	STIGMES	STINGIEST	STIRRA
STEROIDS	STICKER	STILB	STINGILY	STIRRAH
STEROL	STICKERS	STILBENE	STINGING	STIRRAHS
STEROLS	STICKFUL	STILBENES	STINGINGS	STIRRAS
STERVE	STICKFULS	STILBITE	STINGLESS	STIRRE
STERVED	STICKIED	STILBITES	STINGO	STIRRED
STERVES	STICKIER	STILBS	STINGOS	STIRRER
STERVING	STICKIES	STILE	STINGS	STIRRERS
STET	STICKIEST	STILED	STINGY	STIRRES
STETS	STICKILY	STILES	STINK	STIRRING
STETTED	STICKING	STILET	STINKARD	STIRRINGS
STETTING	STICKINGS	STILETS	STINKARDS	STIRRUP
STEVEDORE	STICKIT	STILETTO	STINKER	STIRRUPS
STEVEDORED	STICKJAW	STILETTOED	STINKERS	STIRS
STEVEDORES	STICKJAWS	STILETTOING	STINKHORN	STISHIE
STEVEDORING	STICKLE	STILETTOS	STINKHORNS	STISHIES
STEVEN	STICKLED	STILING	STINKING	STITCH
STEVENS	STICKLER	STILL	STINKINGS	STITCHED
STEW	STICKLERS	STILLAGE	STINKS	STITCHER
STEWARD	STICKLES	STILLAGES	STINT	STITCHERIES
STEWARDRIES	STICKLING	STILLED	STINTED	STITCHERS

STITCHERY	STODGY	STONECROP	STOOP	STORMY
STITCHES	STOEP	STONECROPS	STOOPE	STORNELLI
STITCHING	STOEPS	STONED	STOOPED	STORNELLO
STITCHINGS	STOGEY	STONEFISH	STOOPER	STORY
STITHIED	STOGEYS	STONEFISHES	STOOPERS	STORYETTE
STITHIES	STOGIE	STONEHAND	STOOPES	STORYETTES
STITHY	STOGIES	STONEHANDS	STOOPING	STORYING
STITHYING	STOGY	STONELESS	STOOPS	STORYINGS
STIVE	STOIC	STONEN	STOOR	STOT
STIVED	STOICAL	STONER	STOORS	STOTINKA
STIVER	STOICALLY	STONERN	STOOSHIE	STOTINKI
STIVERS	STOICISM	STONERS	STOOSHIES	STOTIOUS
STIVES	STOICISMS	STONES	STOP	STOTS
STIVING	STOIT	STONESHOT	STOPE	STOTTED
STIVY	STOITED	STONESHOTS	STOPED	STOTTER
STOA	STOITER	STONEWALL	STOPES	STOTTERED
STOAE	STOITERED	STONEWALLED	STOPING	STOTTERING
STOAI	STOITERING	STONEWALLING	STOPINGS	STOTTERS
STOAS	STOITERS	STONEWALLINGS	STOPLESS	STOTTING
STOAT	STOITING	STONEWALLS	STOPPAGE	STOUN
STOATS	STOITS	STONEWARE	STOPPAGES	STOUND
STOB	STOKE	STONEWARES	STOPPED	STOUNDED
STOBS	STOKED	STONEWORK	STOPPER	STOUNDING
STOCCADO	STOKEHOLD	STONEWORKS	STOPPERED	STOUNDS
STOCCADOS	STOKEHOLDS	STONEWORT	STOPPERING	STOUNING
STOCCATA	STOKER	STONEWORTS	STOPPERS	STOUNS
STOCCATAS	STOKERS	STONG	STOPPING	STOUP
STOCK	STOKES	STONIED	STOPPINGS	STOUPS
STOCKADE	STOKING	STONIER	STOPPLE	STOUR
STOCKADED	STOLA	STONIES	STOPPLED	STOURIER
STOCKADES	STOLAS	STONIEST	STOPPLES	STOURIEST
STOCKADING	STOLE	STONILY	STOPPLING	STOURS
STOCKED	STOLED	STONINESS	STOPS	STOURY
STOCKFISH	STOLEN	STONINESSES	STORABLE	STOUSH
STOCKFISHES	STOLES	STONING	STORAGE	STOUSHED
STOCKIER	STOLID	STONINGS	STORAGES	STOUSHES
STOCKIEST	STOLIDER	STONK	STORAX	STOUSHING
STOCKILY	STOLIDEST	STONKER	STORAXES	STOUT
STOCKINET	STOLIDITIES	STONKERED	STORE	STOUTEN
STOCKINETS	STOLIDITY	STONKERING	STORED	STOUTENED
STOCKING	STOLIDLY	STONKERS	STOREMAN	STOUTENING
STOCKINGS	STOLN	STONKS	STOREMEN	STOUTENS
STOCKISH	STOLON	STONN	STORER	STOUTER
STOCKIST	STOLONS	STONNE	STOREROOM	STOUTEST
STOCKISTS	STOMA	STONNED	STOREROOMS	STOUTH
STOCKLESS	STOMACH	STONNES	STORERS	STOUTHRIE
STOCKMAN	STOMACHAL	STONNING	STORES	STOUTHRIES
STOCKMEN	STOMACHED	STONNS	STOREY	STOUTHS
STOCKPILE	STOMACHER	STONY	STOREYED	STOUTISH
STOCKPILED	STOMACHERS	STONYING	STOREYS	STOUTLY
STOCKPILES	STOMACHIC	STOOD	STORGE	STOUTNESS
STOCKPILING	STOMACHICS	STOODEN	STORGES	STOUTNESSES
STOCKPILINGS	STOMACHING	STOOGE	STORIATED	STOUTS
STOCKS	STOMACHS	STOOGED	STORIED	STOVAINE
STOCKTAKE	STOMACHY	STOOGES	STORIES	STOVAINES
STOCKTAKES	STOMATA	STOOGING	STORIETTE	STOVE
STOCKWORK	STOMATAL	STOOK	STORIETTES	STOVED
STOCKWORKS	STOMATIC	STOOKED	STORING	STOVEPIPE
STOCKY	STOMODEA	STOOKER	STORK	STOVEPIPES
STOCKYARD	STOMODEUM	STOOKERS	STORKS	STOVER
STOCKYARDS	STOMODEUMS	STOOKING	STORM	STOVERS
STODGE	STOMP	STOOKS	STORMED	STOVES
STODGED	STOMPED	STOOL	STORMFUL	STOVIES
STODGER	STOMPING	STOOLBALL	STORMIER	STOVING
STODGERS	STOMPS	STOOLBALLS	STORMIEST	STOVINGS
STODGES	STOND	STOOLED	STORMILY	STOW
STODGIER	STONDS	STOOLIE	STORMING	STOWAGE
STODGIEST	STONE	STOOLIES	STORMINGS	STOWAGES
STODGILY	STONECHAT	STOOLING	STORMLESS	STOWAWAY
STODGING	STONECHATS	STOOLS	STORMS	STOWAWAYS

STOWDOWN	STRAINT	STRATEGICS	STREAMLET	STREWING
STOWDOWNS	STRAINTS	STRATEGIES	STREAMLETS	STREWINGS
STOWED	STRAIT	STRATEGY	STREAMS	STREWMENT
STOWER	STRAITED	STRATH	STREAMY	STREWMENTS
STOWERS	STRAITEN	STRATHS	STREEK	STREWN
STOWING	STRAITENED	STRATIFIED	STREEKED	STREWS
STOWINGS	STRAITENING	STRATIFIES	STREEKING	STREWTH
STOWLINS	STRAITENS	STRATIFY	STREEKS	STRIA
STOWN	STRAITER	STRATIFYING	STREEL	STRIAE
STOWND	STRAITEST	STRATONIC	STREELED	STRIATA
STOWNDED	STRAITING	STRATOSE	STREELING	STRIATE
STOWNDING	STRAITLY	STRATOUS	STREELS	STRIATED
STOWNDS	STRAITS	STRATUM	STREET	STRIATES
STOWNLINS	STRAK	STRATUS	STREETAGE	STRIATING
STOWRE	STRAKE	STRATUSES	STREETAGES	STRIATION
STOWRES	STRAKES	STRAUCHT	STREETED	STRIATIONS
STOWS	STRAMAÇON	STRAUCHTED	STREETFUL	STRIATUM
STRABISM	STRAMAÇONS	STRAUCHTER	STREETFULS	STRIATUMS
STRABISMS	STRAMASH	STRAUCHTEST	STREETIER	STRIATURE
STRACK	STRAMASHED	STRAUCHTING	STREETIEST	STRIATURES
STRAD	STRAMASHES	STRAUCHTS	STREETS	STRICH
STRADDLE	STRAMASHING	STRAUGHT	STREETWAY	STRICHES
STRADDLED	STRAMAZON	STRAUGHTED	STREETWAYS	STRICKEN
STRADDLES	STRAMAZONS	STRAUGHTER	STREETY	STRICKLE
STRADDLING	STRAMMEL	STRAUGHTEST	STREIGHT	STRICKLED
STRADIOT	STRAMMELS	STRAUGHTING	STREIGNE	STRICKLES
STRADIOTS	STRAMP	STRAUGHTS	STREIGNED	STRICKLING
STRADS	STRAMPED	STRAUNGE	STREIGNES	STRICT
STRAE	STRAMPING	STRAVAIG	STREIGNING	STRICTER
STRAES	STRAMPS	STRAVAIGED	STRELITZ	STRICTEST
STRAFE	STRAND	STRAVAIGING	STRELITZES	STRICTISH
STRAFED	STRANDED	STRAVAIGS	STRELITZI	STRICTLY
STRAFES	STRANDING	STRAW	STRENE	STRICTURE
STRAFF	STRANDS	STRAWED	STRENES	STRICTURES
STRAFFED	STRANGE	STRAWEN	STRENGTH	STRID
STRAFFING	STRANGELY	STRAWIER	STRENGTHS	STRIDDEN
STRAFFS	STRANGER	STRAWIEST	STRENUITIES	STRIDDLE
STRAFING	STRANGERED	STRAWING	STRENUITY	STRIDDLED
STRAG	STRANGERING	STRAWLESS	STRENUOUS	STRIDDLES
STRAGGLE	STRANGERS	STRAWN	STREP	STRIDDLING
STRAGGLED	STRANGEST	STRAWS	STREPENT	STRIDE
STRAGGLER	STRANGLE	STRAWY	STREPS	STRIDENCE
STRAGGLERS	STRANGLED	STRAY	STRESSED	STRIDENCES
STRAGGLES	STRANGLER	STRAYED	STRESSES	STRIDENCIES
STRAGGLIER	STRANGLES	STRAYER	STRESSFUL	STRIDENCY
STRAGGLIEST	STRANGLES	STRAYERS	STRESSFUL	STRIDENT
STRAGGLING	STRANGLING	STRAYING	STRESSING	STRIDES
STRAGGLINGS	STRANGURIES	STRAYINGS	STRESSOR	STRIDING
STRAGGLY	STRANGURY	STRAYLING	STRESSORS	STRIDLING
STRAGS	STRAP	STRAYLINGS	STRETCH	STRIDOR
STRAICHT	STRAPLESS	STRAYS	STRETCHED	STRIDORS
STRAICHTER	STRAPPADO	STREAK	STRETCHER	STRIDS
STRAICHTEST	STRAPPADOED	STREAKED	STRETCHERED	STRIFE
STRAIGHT	STRAPPADOING	STREAKER	STRETCHERING	STRIFEFUL
STRAIGHTED	STRAPPADOS	STREAKERS	STRETCHERS	STRIFES
STRAIGHTER	STRAPPED	STREAKIER	STRETCHES	STRIFT
STRAIGHTEST	STRAPPER	STREAKIEST	STRETCHIER	STRIFTS
STRAIGHTING	STRAPPERS	STREAKILY	STRETCHIEST	STRIG
STRAIGHTS	STRAPPING	STREAKING	STRETCHING	STRIGA
STRAIK	STRAPPINGS	STREAKINGS	STRETCHY	STRIGAE
STRAIKED	STRAPPY	STREAKS	STRETTA	STRIGATE
STRAIKING	STRAPS	STREAKY	STRETTE	STRIGGED
STRAIKS	STRAPWORT	STREAM	STRETTI	STRIGGING
STRAIN	STRAPWORTS	STREAMED	STRETTO	STRIGIL
STRAINED	STRASS	STREAMER	STREW	STRIGILS
STRAINER	STRASSES	STREAMERS	STREWAGE	STRIGINE
STRAINERS	STRATA	STREAMIER	STREWAGES	STRIGOSE
STRAINING	STRATAGEM	STREAMIEST	STREWED	STRIGS
STRAININGS	STRATAGEMS	STREAMING	STREWER	STRIKE
STRAINS	STRATEGIC	STREAMINGS	STREWERS	STRIKEOUT

STRIKEOUTS	STRODLING	STROW	STUBBLIEST	STUMER
STRIKER	STROKE	STROWED	STUBBLY	STUMERS
STRIKERS	STROKED	STROWER	STUBBORN	STUMM
STRIKES	STROKEN	STROWERS	STUBBORNED	STUMMED
STRIKING	STROKER	STROWING	STUBBORNING	STUMMEL
STRIKINGS	STROKERS	STROWINGS	STUBBORNS	STUMMELS
STRING	STROKES	STROWN	STUBBY	STUMMING
STRINGED	STROKING	STROWS	STUBS	STUMMS
STRINGENT	STROKINGS	STROY	STUCCO	STUMP
STRINGER	STROLL	STROYED	STUCCOED	STUMPAGE
STRINGERS	STROLLED	STROYING	STUCCOER	STUMPAGES
STRINGIER	STROLLER	STROYS	STUCCOERS	STUMPED
STRINGIEST	STROLLERS	STRUCK	STUCCOING	STUMPER
STRINGILY	STROLLING	STRUCKEN	STUCCOS	STUMPERS
STRINGING	STROLLINGS	STRUCTURE	STUCK	STUMPIER
STRINGINGS	STROLLS	STRUCTURED	STUCKS	STUMPIES
STRINGS	STROMA	STRUCTURES	STUD	STUMPIEST
STRINGY	STROMATA	STRUCTURING	STUDDED	STUMPILY
STRINKLE	STROMATIC	STRUDEL	STUDDEN	STUMPING
STRINKLED	STROMB	STRUDELS	STUDDING	STUMPS
STRINKLES	STROMBS	STRUGGLE	STUDDINGS	STUMPY
STRINKLING	STROMBUS	STRUGGLED	STUDDLE	STUMS
STRINKLINGS	STROMBUSES	STRUGGLER	STUDDLES	STUN
STRIP	STROND	STRUGGLERS	STUDENT	STUNG
STRIPE	STRONDS	STRUGGLES	STUDENTRIES	STUNK
STRIPED	STRONG	STRUGGLING	STUDENTRY	STUNKARD
STRIPES	STRONGARM	STRUGGLINGS	STUDENTS	STUNNED
STRIPEY	STRONGARMED	STRUM	STUDIED	STUNNER
STRIPIER	STRONGARMING	STRUMA	STUDIEDLY	STUNNERS
STRIPIEST	STRONGARMS	STRUMAE	STUDIER	STUNNING
STRIPING	STRONGER	STRUMATIC	STUDIERS	STUNNINGS
STRIPINGS	STRONGEST	STRUMITIS	STUDIES	STUNS
STRIPLING	STRONGISH	STRUMITISES	STUDIO	STUNSAIL
STRIPLINGS	STRONGLY	STRUMMED	STUDIOS	STUNSAILS
STRIPPED	STRONGMAN	STRUMMEL	STUDIOUS	STUNT
STRIPPER	STRONGMEN	STRUMMELS	STUDS	STUNTED
STRIPPERS	STRONGYLE	STRUMMING	STUDWORK	STUNTING
STRIPPING	STRONGYLES	STRUMOSE	STUDWORKS	STUNTMAN
STRIPPINGS	STRONTIA	STRUMOUS	STUDY	STUNTMEN
STRIPS	STRONTIAN	STRUMPET	STUDYING	STUNTS
STRIPY	STRONTIANS	STRUMPETED	STUFF	STUPA
STRIVE	STRONTIAS	STRUMPETING	STUFFED	STUPAS
STRIVED	STRONTIUM	STRUMPETS	STUFFER	STUPE
STRIVEN	STRONTIUMS	STRUMS	STUFFERS	STUPED
STRIVER	STROOK	STRUNG	STUFFIER	STUPEFIED
STRIVERS	STROOKE	STRUNT	STUFFIEST	STUPEFIER
STRIVES	STROOKEN	STRUNTED	STUFFILY	STUPEFIERS
STRIVING	STROOKES	STRUNTING	STUFFING	STUPEFIES
STRIVINGS	STROP	STRUNTS	STUFFINGS	STUPEFY
STROAM	STROPHE	STRUT	STUFFS	STUPEFYING
STROAMED	STROPHES	STRUTS	STUFFY	STUPENT
STROAMING	STROPHIC	STRUTTED	STUGGY	STUPES
STROAMS	STROPPED	STRUTTER	STULL	STUPID
STROBE	STROPPIER	STRUTTERS	STULLS	STUPIDER
STROBES	STROPPIEST	STRUTTING	STULM	STUPIDEST
STROBIC	STROPPING	STRUTTINGS	STULMS	STUPIDITIES
STROBILA	STROPPY	STRYCHNIA	STULTIFIED	STUPIDITY
STROBILAE	STROPS	STRYCHNIAS	STULTIFIES	STUPIDLY
STROBILE	STROSSERS	STRYCHNIC	STULTIFY	STUPIDS
STROBILES	STROUD	STRYFULL	STULTIFYING	STUPING
STROBILI	STROUDING	STUB	STUM	STUPOR
STROBILUS	STROUDINGS	STUBBED	STUMBLE	STUPOROUS
STRODDLE	STROUDS	STUBBIER	STUMBLED	STUPORS
STRODDLED	STROUP	STUBBIES	STUMBLER	STUPRATE
STRODDLES	STROUPS	STUBBIEST	STUMBLERS	STUPRATED
STRODDLING	STROUT	STUBBING	STUMBLES	STUPRATES
STRODE	STROUTED	STUBBLE	STUMBLIER	STUPRATING
STRODLE	STROUTING	STUBBLED	STUMBLIEST	STURDIED
STRODLED	STROUTS	STUBBLES	STUMBLING	STURDIER
STRODLES	STROVE	STUBBLIER	STUMBLY	STURDIES

STURDIEST	STYMYING	SUBBING	SUBERISING	SUBLIMATE
STURDILY	STYPSIS	SUBBINGS	SUBERIZE	SUBLIMATED
STURDY	STYPSISES	SUBBRANCH	SUBERIZED	SUBLIMATES
STURE	STYPTIC	SUBBRANCHES	SUBERIZES	SUBLIMATING
STURGEON	STYPTICAL	SUBBREED	SUBERIZING	SUBLIME
STURGEONS	STYPTICS	SUBBREEDS	SUBEROSE	SUBLIMED
STURMER	STYRAX	SUBCANTOR	SUBEROUS	SUBLIMELY
STURMERS	STYRAXES	SUBCANTORS	SUBERS	SUBLIMER
STURNINE	STYRE	SUBCAUDAL	SUBFAMILIES	SUBLIMES
STURNOID	STYRED	SUBCLASS	SUBFAMILY	SUBLIMEST
STURT	STYRENE	SUBCLASSES	SUBFEU	SUBLIMING
STURTED	STYRENES	SUBCLAUSE	SUBFEUED	SUBLIMINGS
STURTING	STYRES	SUBCLAUSES	SUBFEUING	SUBLIMISE
STURTS	STYRING	SUBCOSTA	SUBFEUS	SUBLIMISED
STUSHIE	SUABILITIES	SUBCOSTAL	SUBFLOOR	SUBLIMISES
STUSHIES	SUABILITY	SUBCOSTALS	SUBFLOORS	SUBLIMISING
STUTTER	SUABLE	SUBCOSTAS	SUBFUSC	SUBLIMITIES
STUTTERED	SUASIBLE	SUBDEACON	SUBFUSCS	SUBLIMITY
STUTTERER	SUASION	SUBDEACONS	SUBFUSK	SUBLIMIZE
STUTTERERS	SUASIONS	SUBDEAN	SUBFUSKS	SUBLIMIZED
STUTTERING	SUASIVE	SUBDEANS	SUBGENERA	SUBLIMIZES
STUTTERINGS	SUASIVELY	SUBDEW	SUBGENUS	SUBLIMIZING
STUTTERS	SUASORY	SUBDEWED	SUBGENUSES	SUBLINEAR
STY	SUAVE	SUBDEWING	SUBGRADE	SUBLUNAR
STYE	SUAVELY	SUBDEWS	SUBGRADES	SUBLUNARIES
STYED	SUAVER	SUBDIVIDE	SUBGROUP	SUBLUNARS
STYES	SUAVEST	SUBDIVIDED	SUBGROUPS	SUBLUNARY
STYING	SUAVITIES	SUBDIVIDES	SUBHUMAN	SUBLUNATE
STYLAR	SUAVITY	SUBDIVIDING	SUBIMAGINES	SUBMAN
STYLATE	SUB	SUBDOLOUS	SUBIMAGO	SUBMARINE
STYLE	SUBACID	SUBDUABLE	SUBIMAGOS	SUBMARINED
STYLED	SUBACRID	SUBDUAL	SUBINCISE	SUBMARINES
STYLELESS	SUBACT	SUBDUALS	SUBINCISED	SUBMARINING
STYLES	SUBACTED	SUBDUCE	SUBINCISES	SUBMEN
STYLET	SUBACTING	SUBDUCED	SUBINCISING	SUBMENTAL
STYLETS	SUBACTION	SUBDUCES	SUBITO	SUBMENTUM
STYLI	SUBACTIONS	SUBDUCING	SUBJACENT	SUBMENTUMS
STYLIFORM	SUBACTS	SUBDUCT	SUBJECT	SUBMERGE
STYLING	SUBACUTE	SUBDUCTED	SUBJECTED	SUBMERGED
STYLISE	SUBADAR	SUBDUCTING	SUBJECTING	SUBMERGES
STYLISED	SUBADARS	SUBDUCTS	SUBJECTS	SUBMERGING
STYLISES	SUBADULT	SUBDUE	SUBJOIN	SUBMERSE
STYLISH	SUBADULTS	SUBDUED	SUBJOINED	SUBMERSED
STYLISHLY	SUBAERIAL	SUBDUEDLY	SUBJOINING	SUBMERSES
STYLISING	SUBAGENCIES	SUBDUER	SUBJOINS	SUBMERSING
STYLIST	SUBAGENCY	SUBDUERS	SUBJUGATE	SUBMICRON
STYLISTIC	SUBAGENT	SUBDUES	SUBJUGATED	SUBMICRONS
STYLISTICS	SUBAGENTS	SUBDUING	SUBJUGATES	SUBMISS
STYLISTS	SUBAH	SUBDUPLE	SUBJUGATING	SUBMISSLY
STYLITE	SUBAHDAR	SUBEDAR	SUBLATE	SUBMIT
STYLITES	SUBAHDARIES	SUBEDARS	SUBLATED	SUBMITS
STYLIZE	SUBAHDARS	SUBEDIT	SUBLATES	SUBMITTED
STYLIZED	SUBAHDARY	SUBEDITED	SUBLATING	SUBMITTER
STYLIZES	SUBAHS	SUBEDITING	SUBLATION	SUBMITTERS
STYLIZING	SUBAHSHIP	SUBEDITOR	SUBLATIONS	SUBMITTING
STYLO	SUBAHSHIPS	SUBEDITORS	SUBLEASE	SUBMITTINGS
STYLOBATE	SUBALPINE	SUBEDITS	SUBLEASED	SUBMUCOSA
STYLOBATES	SUBALTERN	SUBENTIRE	SUBLEASES	SUBMUCOSAE
STYLOID	SUBALTERNS	SUBEQUAL	SUBLEASING	SUBMUCOUS
STYLOIDS	SUBAQUA	SUBER	SUBLESSEE	SUBNEURAL
STYLOS	SUBARCTIC	SUBERATE	SUBLESSEES	SUBNIVEAL
STYLUS	SUBARID	SUBERATES	SUBLESSOR	SUBNIVEAN
STYLUSES	SUBASTRAL	SUBERECT	SUBLESSORS	SUBNORMAL
STYME	SUBATOM	SUBEREOUS	SUBLET	SUBNORMALS
STYMED	SUBATOMIC	SUBERIC	SUBLETHAL	SUBOCTAVE
STYMES	SUBATOMICS	SUBERIN	SUBLETS	SUBOCTAVES
STYMIE	SUBATOMS	SUBERINS	SUBLETTER	SUBOCULAR
STYMIED	SUBBASAL	SUBERISE	SUBLETTERS	SUBOFFICE
STYMIES	SUBBASALS	SUBERISED	SUBLETTING	SUBOFFICES
STYMING	SUBBED	SUBERISES	SUBLETTINGS	SUBORDER

SUBORDERS	SUBSOILER	SUBTITLED	SUBZONE	SUCK
SUBORN	SUBSOILERS	SUBTITLES	SUBZONES	SUCKED
SUBORNED	SUBSOILING	SUBTITLING	SUCCADE	SUCKEN
SUBORNER	SUBSOILINGS	SUBTLE	SUCCADES	SUCKENER
SUBORNERS	SUBSOILS	SUBTLER	SUCCEED	SUCKENERS
SUBORNING	SUBSOLAR	SUBTLEST	SUCCEEDED	SUCKENS
SUBORNS	SUBSONIC	SUBTLETIES	SUCCEEDER	SUCKER
SUBOVATE	SUBSTAGE	SUBTLETY	SUCCEEDERS	SUCKERED
SUBOXIDE	SUBSTAGES	SUBTLIST	SUCCEEDING	SUCKERING
SUBOXIDES	SUBSTANCE	SUBTLISTS	SUCCEEDS	SUCKERS
SUBPHYLA	SUBSTANCES	SUBTLY	SUCCENTOR	SUCKET
SUBPHYLUM	SUBSTRACT	SUBTONIC	SUCCENTORS	SUCKETS
SUBPLOT	SUBSTRACTED	SUBTONICS	SUCCÈS	SUCKING
SUBPLOTS	SUBSTRACTING	SUBTOPIA	SUCCESS	SUCKINGS
SUBPOENA	SUBSTRACTS	SUBTOPIAN	SUCCESSES	SUCKLE
SUBPOENAED	SUBSTRATA	SUBTOPIAS	SUCCESSOR	SUCKLED
SUBPOENAING	SUBSTRATE	SUBTOTAL	SUCCESSORS	SUCKLER
SUBPOENAS	SUBSTRATES	SUBTOTALLED	SUCCI	SUCKLERS
SUBPRIOR	SUBSTRUCT	SUBTOTALLING	SUCCINATE	SUCKLES
SUBPRIORS	SUBSTRUCTED	SUBTOTALS	SUCCINATES	SUCKLING
SUBREGION	SUBSTRUCTING	SUBTRACT	SUCCINCT	SUCKLINGS
SUBREGIONS	SUBSTRUCTS	SUBTRACTED	SUCCINCTER	SUCKS
SUBROGATE	SUBSTYLAR	SUBTRACTING	SUCCINCTEST	SUCRASE
SUBROGATED	SUBSTYLE	SUBTRACTS	SUCCINIC	SUCRASES
SUBROGATES	SUBSTYLES	SUBTRIBE	SUCCINITE	SUCRE
SUBROGATING	SUBSULTUS	SUBTRIBES	SUCCINITES	SUCRES
SUBS	SUBSULTUSES	SUBTRIST	SUCCINUM	SUCRIER
SUBSACRAL	SUBSUME	SUBTROPIC	SUCCINUMS	SUCRIERS
SUBSCRIBE	SUBSUMED	SUBTROPICS	SUCCOR	SUCROSE
SUBSCRIBED	SUBSUMES	SUBTRUDE	SUCCORED	SUCROSES
SUBSCRIBES	SUBSUMING	SUBTRUDED	SUCCORIES	SUCTION
SUBSCRIBING	SUBSYSTEM	SUBTRUDES	SUCCORING	SUCTIONS
SUBSCRIBINGS	SUBSYSTEMS	SUBTRUDING	SUCCORS	SUCTORIAL
SUBSCRIPT	SUBTACK	SUBTYPE	SUCCORY	SUCTORIAN
SUBSCRIPTS	SUBTACKS	SUBTYPES	SUCCOSE	SUCTORIANS
SUBSEA	SUBTEEN	SUBUCULA	SUCCOTASH	SUCURUJÚ
SUBSECIVE	SUBTEENS	SUBUCULAS	SUCCOTASHES	SUCURUJÚS
SUBSELLIA	SUBTENANT	SUBULATE	SUCCOUR	SUD
SUBSERE	SUBTENANTS	SUBUNGUAL	SUCCOURED	SUDAMEN
SUBSERIES	SUBTEND	SUBUNIT	SUCCOURER	SUDAMINA
SUBSERVE	SUBTENDED	SUBUNITS	SUCCOURERS	SUDAMINAL
SUBSERVED	SUBTENDING	SUBURB	SUCCOURING	SUDANIC
SUBSERVES	SUBTENDS	SUBURBAN	SUCCOURS	SUDARIES
SUBSERVING	SUBTENSE	SUBURBANS	SUCCOUS	SUDARIUM
SUBSET	SUBTENSES	SUBURBIA	SUCCUBA	SUDARIUMS
SUBSETS	SUBTEXT	SUBURBIAS	SUCCUBAE	SUDARY
SUBSHRUB	SUBTEXTS	SUBURBS	SUCCUBAS	SUDATE
SUBSHRUBS	SUBTIL	SUBURSINE	SUCCUBI	SUDATED
SUBSIDE	SUBTILE	SUBVASSAL	SUCCUBINE	SUDATES
SUBSIDED	SUBTILELY	SUBVASSALS	SUCCUBOUS	SUDATING
SUBSIDES	SUBTILER	SUBVERSAL	SUCCUBUS	SUDATION
SUBSIDIES	SUBTILEST	SUBVERSALS	SUCCUBUSES	SUDATIONS
SUBSIDING	SUBTILETIES	SUBVERSE	SUCCULENT	SUDATORIES
SUBSIDISE	SUBTILETY	SUBVERSED	SUCCULENTS	SUDATORY
SUBSIDISED	SUBTILISE	SUBVERSES	SUCCUMB	SUDD
SUBSIDISES	SUBTILISED	SUBVERSING	SUCCUMBED	SUDDEN
SUBSIDISING	SUBTILISES	SUBVERST	SUCCUMBING	SUDDENLY
SUBSIDIZE	SUBTILISING	SUBVERT	SUCCUMBS	SUDDENTIES
SUBSIDIZED	SUBTILIST	SUBVERTED	SUCCURSAL	SUDDENTY
SUBSIDIZES	SUBTILISTS	SUBVERTER	SUCCURSALS	SUDDER
SUBSIDIZING	SUBTILITIES	SUBVERTERS	SUCCUS	SUDDERS
SUBSIDY	SUBTILITY	SUBVERTING	SUCCUSS	SUDDS
SUBSIST	SUBTILIZE	SUBVERTS	SUCCUSSED	SUDOR
SUBSISTED	SUBTILIZED	SUBVIRAL	SUCCUSSES	SUDORAL
SUBSISTING	SUBTILIZES	SUBWARDEN	SUCCUSSING	SUDORIFIC
SUBSISTS	SUBTILIZING	SUBWARDENS	SUCH	SUDORIFICS
SUBSIZAR	SUBTILLY	SUBWAY	SUCHLIKE	SUDOROUS
SUBSIZARS	SUBTILTIES	SUBWAYS	SUCHNESS	SUDORS
SUBSOIL	SUBTILTY	SUBZERO	SUCHNESSES	SUDS
SUBSOILED	SUBTITLE	SUBZONAL	SUCHWISE	SUDSER

SUDSERS
SUDSIER
SUDSIEST
SUDSY
SUE
SUEABLE
SUED
SUEDE
SUÉDE
SUEDED
SUÈDED
SUEDES
SUÈDES
SUEDETTE
SUEDETTES
SUEDING
SUÈDING
SUER
SUERS
SUES
SUET
SUETS
SUETTY
SUETY
SUFFER
SUFFERED
SUFFERER
SUFFERERS
SUFFERING
SUFFERINGS
SUFFERS
SUFFETE
SUFFETES
SUFFICE
SUFFICED
SUFFICER
SUFFICERS
SUFFICES
SUFFICING
SUFFIX
SUFFIXAL
SUFFIXED
SUFFIXES
SUFFIXING
SUFFLATE
SUFFLATED
SUFFLATES
SUFFLATING
SUFFOCATE
SUFFOCATED
SUFFOCATES
SUFFOCATING
SUFFOCATINGS
SUFFRAGAN
SUFFRAGANS
SUFFRAGE
SUFFRAGES
SUFFUSE
SUFFUSED
SUFFUSES
SUFFUSING
SUFFUSION
SUFFUSIONS
SUGAR
SUGARED
SUGARIER
SUGARIEST
SUGARING
SUGARINGS
SUGARLESS

SUGARS
SUGARY
SUGGEST
SUGGESTED
SUGGESTER
SUGGESTERS
SUGGESTING
SUGGESTS
SUI
SUICIDAL
SUICIDE
SUICIDES
SUIDIAN
SUILLINE
SUING
SUINGS
SUINT
SUINTS
SUIT
SUITABLE
SUITABLY
SUITE
SUITED
SUITES
SUITING
SUITINGS
SUITOR
SUITORED
SUITORING
SUITORS
SUITRESS
SUITRESSES
SUITS
SUIVEZ
SUJEE
SUJEED
SUJEEING
SUJEES
SUK
SUKH
SUKHS
SUKIYAKI
SUKIYAKIS
SUKS
SULCAL
SULCALISE
SULCALISED
SULCALISES
SULCALISING
SULCALIZE
SULCALIZED
SULCALIZES
SULCALIZING
SULCATE
SULCATED
SULCATION
SULCATIONS
SULCI
SULCUS
SULFA
SULFATE
SULFATED
SULFATES
SULFATING
SULFUR
SULFURED
SULFURING
SULFURS
SULK
SULKED

SULKIER
SULKIES
SULKIEST
SULKILY
SULKINESS
SULKINESSES
SULKING
SULKS
SULKY
SULLAGE
SULLAGES
SULLEN
SULLENER
SULLENEST
SULLENLY
SULLENS
SULLIED
SULLIES
SULLY
SULLYING
SULPHA
SULPHATE
SULPHATED
SULPHATES
SULPHATIC
SULPHATING
SULPHIDE
SULPHIDES
SULPHITE
SULPHITES
SULPHONE
SULPHONES
SULPHONIC
SULPHUR
SULPHURED
SULPHURET
SULPHURETS
SULPHURIC
SULPHURING
SULPHURS
SULPHURY
SULTAN
SULTANA
SULTANAS
SULTANATE
SULTANATES
SULTANESS
SULTANESSES
SULTANIC
SULTANS
SULTRIER
SULTRIEST
SULTRILY
SULTRY
SUM
SUMAC
SUMACH
SUMACHS
SUMACS
SUMATRA
SUMATRAS
SUMLESS
SUMMA
SUMMAE
SUMMAND
SUMMANDS
SUMMAR
SUMMARIES
SUMMARILY
SUMMARISE

SUMMARISED
SUMMARISES
SUMMARISING
SUMMARIST
SUMMARISTS
SUMMARIZE
SUMMARIZED
SUMMARIZES
SUMMARIZING
SUMMARY
SUMMAS
SUMMAT
SUMMATE
SUMMATED
SUMMATES
SUMMATING
SUMMATION
SUMMATIONS
SUMMATIVE
SUMMATS
SUMMED
SUMMER
SUMMERED
SUMMERIER
SUMMERIEST
SUMMERING
SUMMERINGS
SUMMERLY
SUMMERS
SUMMERSET
SUMMERSETS
SUMMERSETTED
SUMMERSETTING
SUMMERY
SUMMING
SUMMINGS
SUMMIST
SUMMISTS
SUMMIT
SUMMITRIES
SUMMITRY
SUMMITS
SUMMON
SUMMONED
SUMMONER
SUMMONERS
SUMMONING
SUMMONS
SUMMONSED
SUMMONSES
SUMMONSING
SUMO
SUMOS
SUMP
SUMPH
SUMPHISH
SUMPHS
SUMPIT
SUMPITAN
SUMPITANS
SUMPITS
SUMPS
SUMPSIMUS
SUMPSIMUSES
SUMPTER
SUMPTERS
SUMPTUARY
SUMPTUOUS
SUMS
SUN

SUNBATH
SUNBATHE
SUNBATHED
SUNBATHER
SUNBATHERS
SUNBATHES
SUNBATHING
SUNBATHINGS
SUNBATHS
SUNBEAM
SUNBEAMED
SUNBEAMS
SUNBEAMY
SUNBED
SUNBEDS
SUNBELT
SUNBELTS
SUNBLOCK
SUNBLOCKS
SUNBOW
SUNBOWS
SUNBRIGHT
SUNBURN
SUNBURNED
SUNBURNING
SUNBURNS
SUNBURNT
SUNBURST
SUNBURSTS
SUNDAE
SUNDAES
SUNDARI
SUNDARIS
SUNDER
SUNDERED
SUNDERER
SUNDERERS
SUNDERING
SUNDERINGS
SUNDERS
SUNDIAL
SUNDIALS
SUNDOWN
SUNDOWNS
SUNDRA
SUNDRAS
SUNDRI
SUNDRIES
SUNDRIS
SUNDRY
SUNFAST
SUNFLOWER
SUNFLOWERS
SUNG
SUNGAR
SUNGARS
SUNGLASS
SUNGLASSES
SUNGLOW
SUNGLOWS
SUNHAT
SUNHATS
SUNK
SUNKEN
SUNKET
SUNKETS
SUNKIE
SUNKIES
SUNKS
SUNLESS

SUNLIGHT
SUNLIGHTS
SUNLIKE
SUNLIT
SUNN
SUNNED
SUNNIER
SUNNIEST
SUNNILY
SUNNINESS
SUNNINESSES
SUNNING
SUNNS
SUNNY
SUNPROOF
SUNRAY
SUNRAYS
SUNRISE
SUNRISES
SUNRISING
SUNRISINGS
SUNS
SUNSET
SUNSETS
SUNSHINE
SUNSHINES
SUNSHINY
SUNSPOT
SUNSPOTS
SUNSTONE
SUNSTONES
SUNSTROKE
SUNSTROKES
SUNSTRUCK
SUNSUIT
SUNSUITS
SUNTAN
SUNTANNED
SUNTANS
SUNTRAP
SUNTRAPS
SUNWARD
SUNWARDS
SUNWISE
SUP
SUPAWN
SUPAWNS
SUPER
SUPERABLE
SUPERABLY
SUPERADD
SUPERADDED
SUPERADDING
SUPERADDS
SUPERATE
SUPERATED
SUPERATES
SUPERATING
SUPERB
SUPERBER
SUPERBEST
SUPERBITIES
SUPERBITY
SUPERBLY
SUPERCOLD
SUPERCOOL
SUPERCOOLED
SUPERCOOLING
SUPERCOOLS
SUPERED

SUPERETTE
SUPERETTES
SUPERFINE
SUPERFLUX
SUPERFLUXES
SUPERFUSE
SUPERFUSED
SUPERFUSES
SUPERFUSING
SUPERGLUE
SUPERGLUES
SUPERHEAT
SUPERHEATED
SUPERHEATING
SUPERHEATS
SUPERHET
SUPERHETS
SUPERHIVE
SUPERHIVES
SUPERING
SUPERIOR
SUPERIORS
SUPERMAN
SUPERMART
SUPERMARTS
SUPERMEN
SUPERNAL
SUPERNOVA
SUPERNOVAE
SUPERNOVAS
SUPERPLUS
SUPERPLUSES
SUPERPOSE
SUPERPOSED
SUPERPOSES
SUPERPOSING
SUPERS
SUPERSALT
SUPERSALTS
SUPERSEDE
SUPERSEDED
SUPERSEDES
SUPERSEDING
SUPERSTAR
SUPERSTARS
SUPERTAX
SUPERTAXES
SUPERVENE
SUPERVENED
SUPERVENES
SUPERVENING
SUPERVISE
SUPERVISED
SUPERVISES
SUPERVISING
SUPINATE
SUPINATED
SUPINATES
SUPINATING
SUPINATOR
SUPINATORS
SUPINE
SUPINELY
SUPINES
SUPPAWN
SUPPAWNS
SUPPEAGO
SUPPEAGOES
SUPPED
SUPPER

SUPPERED
SUPPERING
SUPPERS
SUPPING
SUPPLANT
SUPPLANTED
SUPPLANTING
SUPPLANTS
SUPPLE
SUPPLED
SUPPLER
SUPPLES
SUPPLEST
SUPPLIAL
SUPPLIALS
SUPPLIANT
SUPPLIANTS
SUPPLICAT
SUPPLICATS
SUPPLIED
SUPPLIER
SUPPLIERS
SUPPLIES
SUPPLING
SUPPLY
SUPPLYING
SUPPORT
SUPPORTED
SUPPORTER
SUPPORTERS
SUPPORTING
SUPPORTINGS
SUPPORTS
SUPPOSAL
SUPPOSALS
SUPPOSE
SUPPOSED
SUPPOSER
SUPPOSERS
SUPPOSES
SUPPOSING
SUPPOSINGS
SUPPRESS
SUPPRESSED
SUPPRESSES
SUPPRESSING
SUPPURATE
SUPPURATED
SUPPURATES
SUPPURATING
SUPREMACIES
SUPREMACY
SUPRÊME
SUPREME
SUPREMELY
SUPREMER
SUPREMES
SUPRÊMES
SUPREMEST
SUPREMITIES
SUPREMITY
SUPREMO
SUPREMOS
SUPS
SUQ
SUQS
SUR
SURA
SURAH
SURAHS

SURAL
SURANCE
SURANCES
SURAS
SURAT
SURATS
SURBASE
SURBASED
SURBASES
SURBATE
SURBATED
SURBATES
SURBATING
SURBED
SURBEDDED
SURBEDDING
SURBEDS
SURBET
SURCEASE
SURCEASED
SURCEASES
SURCEASING
SURCHARGE
SURCHARGED
SURCHARGES
SURCHARGING
SURCINGLE
SURCINGLED
SURCINGLES
SURCINGLING
SURCOAT
SURCOATS
SURCULI
SURCULOSE
SURCULUS
SURCULUSES
SURD
SURDITIES
SURDITY
SURDS
SURE
SURED
SURELY
SURENESS
SURENESSES
SURER
SURES
SUREST
SURETIED
SURETIES
SURETY
SURETYING
SURF
SURFACE
SURFACED
SURFACER
SURFACERS
SURFACES
SURFACING
SURFACINGS
SURFBOARD
SURFBOARDS
SURFED
SURFEIT
SURFEITED
SURFEITER
SURFEITERS
SURFEITING
SURFEITINGS
SURFEITS

SURFER
SURFERS
SURFICIAL
SURFIER
SURFIEST
SURFING
SURFINGS
SURFMAN
SURFMEN
SURFS
SURFY
SURGE
SURGED
SURGEFUL
SURGELESS
SURGENT
SURGEON
SURGEONCIES
SURGEONCY
SURGEONS
SURGERIES
SURGERY
SURGES
SURGICAL
SURGING
SURGINGS
SURGY
SURICATE
SURICATES
SURING
SURLIER
SURLIEST
SURLILY
SURLINESS
SURLINESSES
SURLOIN
SURLOINS
SURLY
SURMASTER
SURMASTERS
SURMISAL
SURMISALS
SURMISE
SURMISED
SURMISER
SURMISERS
SURMISES
SURMISING
SURMISINGS
SURMOUNT
SURMOUNTED
SURMOUNTING
SURMOUNTINGS
SURMOUNTS
SURMULLET
SURMULLETS
SURNAME
SURNAMED
SURNAMES
SURNAMING
SURPASS
SURPASSED
SURPASSES
SURPASSING
SURPLICE
SURPLICED
SURPLICES
SURPLUS
SURPLUSES
SURPRISAL

SURPRISALS
SURPRISE
SURPRISED
SURPRISER
SURPRISERS
SURPRISES
SURPRISING
SURPRISINGS
SURQUEDIES
SURQUEDRIES
SURQUEDRY
SURQUEDY
SURRA
SURRAS
SURREAL
SURREBUT
SURREBUTS
SURREBUTTED
SURREBUTTING
SURREINED
SURREJOIN
SURREJOINED
SURREJOINING
SURREJOINS
SURRENDER
SURRENDERED
SURRENDERING
SURRENDERS
SURRENDRIES
SURRENDRY
SURREY
SURREYS
SURROGATE
SURROGATES
SURROUND
SURROUNDED
SURROUNDING
SURROUNDINGS
SURROUNDS
SURROYAL
SURROYALS
SURTAX
SURTAXED
SURTAXES
SURTAXING
SURTOUT
SURTOUTS
SURUCUCU
SURUCUCUS
SURVEILLE
SURVEILLED
SURVEILLES
SURVEILLING
SURVEW
SURVEWE
SURVEWED
SURVEWES
SURVEWING
SURVEWS
SURVEY
SURVEYAL
SURVEYALS
SURVEYED
SURVEYING
SURVEYINGS
SURVEYOR
SURVEYORS
SURVEYS
SURVIEW
SURVIEWED

SURVIEWING
SURVIEWS
SURVIVAL
SURVIVALS
SURVIVE
SURVIVED
SURVIVES
SURVIVING
SURVIVOR
SURVIVORS
SUS
SUSCEPTOR
SUSCEPTORS
SUSCITATE
SUSCITATED
SUSCITATES
SUSCITATING
SUSHI
SUSHIS
SUSLIK
SUSLIKS
SUSPECT
SUSPECTED
SUSPECTING
SUSPECTS
SUSPENCE
SUSPEND
SUSPENDED
SUSPENDER
SUSPENDERS
SUSPENDING
SUSPENDS
SUSPENS
SUSPENSE
SUSPENSES
SUSPENSOR
SUSPENSORS
SUSPICION
SUSPICIONED
SUSPICIONING
SUSPICIONS
SUSPIRE
SUSPIRED
SUSPIRES
SUSPIRING
SUSS
SUSSARARA
SUSSARARAS
SUSSED
SUSSES
SUSSING
SUSTAIN
SUSTAINED
SUSTAINER
SUSTAINERS
SUSTAINING
SUSTAININGS
SUSTAINS
SUSTINENT
SUSURRANT
SUSURRUS
SUSURRUSES
SUTILE
SUTLER
SUTLERIES
SUTLERS
SUTLERY
SUTOR
SUTORIAL
SUTORIAN

SUTORS
SUTRA
SUTRAS
SUTTEE
SUTTEEISM
SUTTEEISMS
SUTTEES
SUTTLE
SUTTLED
SUTTLES
SUTTLETIE
SUTTLETIES
SUTTLING
SUTURAL
SUTURALLY
SUTURE
SUTURED
SUTURES
SUTURING
SUVERSED
SUZERAIN
SUZERAINS
SVASTIKA
SVASTIKAS
SVELTE
SVELTER
SVELTEST
SWAB
SWABBED
SWABBER
SWABBERS
SWABBING
SWABS
SWACK
SWAD
SWADDIES
SWADDLE
SWADDLED
SWADDLER
SWADDLERS
SWADDLES
SWADDLING
SWADDY
SWADS
SWAG
SWAGE
SWAGED
SWAGES
SWAGGED
SWAGGER
SWAGGERED
SWAGGERER
SWAGGERERS
SWAGGERING
SWAGGERINGS
SWAGGERS
SWAGGIE
SWAGGIES
SWAGGING
SWAGING
SWAGMAN
SWAGMEN
SWAGS
SWAGSHOP
SWAGSHOPS
SWAGSMAN
SWAGSMEN
SWAIN
SWAINING
SWAININGS

SWAINISH
SWAINS
SWALE
SWALED
SWALES
SWALIER
SWALIEST
SWALING
SWALINGS
SWALLET
SWALLETS
SWALLOW
SWALLOWED
SWALLOWER
SWALLOWERS
SWALLOWING
SWALLOWS
SWALY
SWAM
SWAMI
SWAMIS
SWAMP
SWAMPED
SWAMPER
SWAMPERS
SWAMPIER
SWAMPIEST
SWAMPING
SWAMPLAND
SWAMPLANDS
SWAMPS
SWAMPY
SWAN
SWANG
SWANHERD
SWANHERDS
SWANK
SWANKED
SWANKER
SWANKERS
SWANKEST
SWANKEY
SWANKEYS
SWANKIER
SWANKIES
SWANKIEST
SWANKING
SWANKS
SWANKY
SWANLIKE
SWANNERIES
SWANNERY
SWANNIER
SWANNIEST
SWANNY
SWANS
SWANSDOWN
SWANSDOWNS
SWAP
SWAPPED
SWAPPER
SWAPPERS
SWAPPING
SWAPPINGS
SWAPS
SWAPT
SWARAJ
SWARAJES
SWARAJISM
SWARAJISMS

SWARAJIST
SWARAJISTS
SWARD
SWARDED
SWARDING
SWARDS
SWARDY
SWARE
SWARF
SWARFED
SWARFING
SWARFS
SWARM
SWARMED
SWARMER
SWARMERS
SWARMING
SWARMINGS
SWARMS
SWART
SWARTH
SWARTHIER
SWARTHIEST
SWARTHS
SWARTHY
SWARTNESS
SWARTNESSES
SWARTY
SWARVE
SWARVED
SWARVES
SWARVING
SWASH
SWASHED
SWASHER
SWASHERS
SWASHES
SWASHIER
SWASHIEST
SWASHING
SWASHINGS
SWASHWORK
SWASHWORKS
SWASHY
SWASTIKA
SWASTIKAS
SWAT
SWATCH
SWATCHES
SWATH
SWATHE
SWATHED
SWATHES
SWATHIER
SWATHIEST
SWATHING
SWATHS
SWATHY
SWATS
SWATTED
SWATTER
SWATTERED
SWATTERING
SWATTERS
SWATTING
SWAY
SWAYBACK
SWAYBACKS
SWAYED
SWAYER

SWAYERS	SWEETEST	SWIFTLET	SWINGS	SWOBBERS
SWAYING	SWEETFISH	SWIFTLETS	SWINGTREE	SWOBBING
SWAYINGS	SWEETFISHES	SWIFTLY	SWINGTREES	SWOBS
SWAYL	SWEETIE	SWIFTNESS	SWINISH	SWOLLEN
SWAYLED	SWEETIES	SWIFTNESSES	SWINISHLY	SWOLN
SWAYLING	SWEETING	SWIFTS	SWINK	SWONE
SWAYLINGS	SWEETINGS	SWIG	SWINKED	SWONES
SWAYLS	SWEETISH	SWIGGED	SWINKING	SWOON
SWAYS	SWEETLY	SWIGGER	SWINKS	SWOONED
SWEAL	SWEETMEAL	SWIGGERS	SWIPE	SWOONING
SWEALED	SWEETMEAT	SWIGGING	SWIPED	SWOONINGS
SWEALING	SWEETMEATS	SWIGS	SWIPER	SWOONS
SWEALINGS	SWEETNESS	SWILL	SWIPERS	SWOOP
SWEALS	SWEETNESSES	SWILLED	SWIPES	SWOOPED
SWEAR	SWEETPEA	SWILLER	SWIPEY	SWOOPING
SWEARD	SWEETPEAS	SWILLERS	SWIPING	SWOOPS
SWEARDS	SWEETS	SWILLING	SWIPPLE	SWOOSH
SWEARER	SWEETWOOD	SWILLINGS	SWIPPLES	SWOOSHED
SWEARERS	SWEETWOODS	SWILLS	SWIRE	SWOOSHES
SWEARING	SWEETY	SWIM	SWIRES	SWOOSHING
SWEARINGS	SWEIR	SWIMMABLE	SWIRL	SWOP
SWEARS	SWEIRNESS	SWIMMER	SWIRLED	SWOPPED
SWEAT	SWEIRNESSES	SWIMMERET	SWIRLIER	SWOPPER
SWEATED	SWEIRT	SWIMMERETS	SWIRLIEST	SWOPPERS
SWEATER	SWELCHIE	SWIMMERS	SWIRLING	SWOPPING
SWEATERS	SWELCHIES	SWIMMIER	SWIRLS	SWOPPINGS
SWEATIER	SWELL	SWIMMIEST	SWIRLY	SWOPS
SWEATIEST	SWELLDOM	SWIMMING	SWISH	SWOPT
SWEATING	SWELLDOMS	SWIMMINGS	SWISHED	SWORD
SWEATINGS	SWELLED	SWIMMY	SWISHER	SWORDED
SWEATS	SWELLER	SWIMS	SWISHERS	SWORDER
SWEATY	SWELLERS	SWIMSUIT	SWISHES	SWORDERS
SWEDE	SWELLEST	SWIMSUITS	SWISHEST	SWORDFISH
SWEDES	SWELLING	SWIMWEAR	SWISHIER	SWORDFISHES
SWEE	SWELLINGS	SWINDGE	SWISHIEST	SWORDING
SWEED	SWELLISH	SWINDGED	SWISHING	SWORDLESS
SWEEING	SWELLS	SWINDGES	SWISHINGS	SWORDMAN
SWEEL	SWELT	SWINDGING	SWISHY	SWORDMEN
SWEELED	SWELTED	SWINDLE	SWISSING	SWORDPLAY
SWEELING	SWELTER	SWINDLED	SWISSINGS	SWORDPLAYS
SWEELS	SWELTERED	SWINDLER	SWITCH	SWORDS
SWEENEY	SWELTERING	SWINDLERS	SWITCHED	SWORDSMAN
SWEENEYS	SWELTERINGS	SWINDLES	SWITCHEL	SWORDSMEN
SWEENIES	SWELTERS	SWINDLING	SWITCHELS	SWORE
SWEENY	SWELTING	SWINDLINGS	SWITCHES	SWORN
SWEEP	SWELTRIER	SWINE	SWITCHING	SWOT
SWEEPBACK	SWELTRIEST	SWINEHERD	SWITCHINGS	SWOTS
SWEEPBACKS	SWELTRY	SWINEHERDS	SWITCHMAN	SWOTTED
SWEEPER	SWELTS	SWINEHOOD	SWITCHMEN	SWOTTER
SWEEPERS	SWEPT	SWINEHOODS	SWITCHY	SWOTTERS
SWEEPIER	SWERF	SWINERIES	SWITH	SWOTTING
SWEEPIEST	SWERFED	SWINERY	SWITHER	SWOTTINGS
SWEEPING	SWERFING	SWINEY	SWITHERED	SWOUN
SWEEPINGS	SWERFS	SWING	SWITHERING	SWOUND
SWEEPS	SWERVE	SWINGBOAT	SWITHERS	SWOUNDED
SWEEPY	SWERVED	SWINGBOATS	SWITS	SWOUNDING
SWEER	SWERVER	SWINGE	SWITSES	SWOUNDS
SWEERED	SWERVERS	SWINGED	SWIVEL	SWOUNE
SWEERT	SWERVES	SWINGEING	SWIVELLED	SWOUNED
SWEES	SWERVING	SWINGER	SWIVELLING	SWOUNES
SWEET	SWERVINGS	SWINGERS	SWIVELS	SWOUNING
SWEETED	SWEVEN	SWINGES	SWIZ	SWOUNS
SWEETEN	SWEVENS	SWINGING	SWIZZES	SWOWND
SWEETENED	SWIES	SWINGINGS	SWIZZLE	SWOWNDS
SWEETENER	SWIFT	SWINGISM	SWIZZLED	SWOWNE
SWEETENERS	SWIFTED	SWINGISMS	SWIZZLES	SWOWNES
SWEETENING	SWIFTER	SWINGLE	SWIZZLING	SWUM
SWEETENINGS	SWIFTERS	SWINGLED	SWOB	SWUNG
SWEETENS	SWIFTEST	SWINGLES	SWOBBED	SWY
SWEETER	SWIFTING	SWINGLING	SWOBBER	SYBARITE
		SWINGLINGS		

SYBARITES
SYBARITIC
SYBBE
SYBBES
SYBIL
SYBILS
SYBO
SYBOE
SYBOES
SYBOTIC
SYBOTISM
SYBOTISMS
SYBOW
SYBOWS
SYCAMINE
SYCAMINES
SYCAMORE
SYCAMORES
SYCE
SYCEE
SYCEES
SYCES
SYCOMORE
SYCOMORES
SYCONIUM
SYCONIUMS
SYCOPHANT
SYCOPHANTS
SYCOSES
SYCOSIS
SYE
SYED
SYEING
SYEN
SYENITE
SYENITES
SYENITIC
SYENS
SYES
SYKE
SYKER
SYKES
SYLLABARIES
SYLLABARY
SYLLABI
SYLLABIC
SYLLABICS
SYLLABIFIED
SYLLABIFIES
SYLLABIFY
SYLLABIFYING
SYLLABISE
SYLLABISED
SYLLABISES
SYLLABISING
SYLLABISM
SYLLABISMS
SYLLABIZE
SYLLABIZED
SYLLABIZES
SYLLABIZING
SYLLABLE
SYLLABLED
SYLLABLES
SYLLABLING
SYLLABUB
SYLLABUBS
SYLLABUS
SYLLABUSES
SYLLEPSES

SYLLEPSIS
SYLLEPTIC
SYLLOGISE
SYLLOGISED
SYLLOGISES
SYLLOGISING
SYLLOGISM
SYLLOGISMS
SYLLOGIZE
SYLLOGIZED
SYLLOGIZES
SYLLOGIZING
SYLPH
SYLPHID
SYLPHIDE
SYLPHIDES
SYLPHIDS
SYLPHINE
SYLPHISH
SYLPHS
SYLVA
SYLVAE
SYLVAN
SYLVANITE
SYLVANITES
SYLVANS
SYLVAS
SYLVATIC
SYLVIA
SYLVIAS
SYLVIINE
SYLVINE
SYLVINES
SYLVINITE
SYLVINITES
SYLVITE
SYLVITES
SYMAR
SYMARS
SYMBION
SYMBIONS
SYMBIONT
SYMBIONTS
SYMBIOSES
SYMBIOSIS
SYMBIOTIC
SYMBOL
SYMBOLE
SYMBOLES
SYMBOLIC
SYMBOLICS
SYMBOLISE
SYMBOLISED
SYMBOLISES
SYMBOLISING
SYMBOLISM
SYMBOLISMS
SYMBOLIST
SYMBOLISTS
SYMBOLIZE
SYMBOLIZED
SYMBOLIZES
SYMBOLIZING
SYMBOLLED
SYMBOLLING
SYMBOLOGIES
SYMBOLOGY
SYMBOLS
SYMITAR
SYMITARE

SYMITARES
SYMITARS
SYMMETRAL
SYMMETRIC
SYMMETRIES
SYMMETRY
SYMPATHIES
SYMPATHY
SYMPHILE
SYMPHILES
SYMPHILIES
SYMPHILY
SYMPHONIC
SYMPHONIES
SYMPHONY
SYMPHYSES
SYMPHYSIS
SYMPHYTIC
SYMPLOCE
SYMPLOCES
SYMPODIA
SYMPODIAL
SYMPODIUM
SYMPOSIA
SYMPOSIAC
SYMPOSIAL
SYMPOSIUM
SYMPTOM
SYMPTOMS
SYMPTOSES
SYMPTOSIS
SYMPTOTIC
SYNAGOGAL
SYNAGOGUE
SYNAGOGUES
SYNANGIA
SYNANGIUM
SYNANGIUMS
SYNANTHIC
SYNANTHIES
SYNANTHY
SYNAPHEA
SYNAPHEAS
SYNAPHEIA
SYNAPHEIAS
SYNAPSE
SYNAPSES
SYNAPSIS
SYNAPTASE
SYNAPTASES
SYNAPTE
SYNAPTES
SYNAPTIC
SYNARCHIES
SYNARCHY
SYNASTRIES
SYNASTRY
SYNAXES
SYNAXIS
SYNC
SYNCARP
SYNCARPIES
SYNCARPS
SYNCARPY
SYNCED
SYNCH
SYNCHED
SYNCHING
SYNCHRONIES
SYNCHRONY

SYNCHS
SYNCHYSES
SYNCHYSIS
SYNCING
SYNCLINAL
SYNCLINALS
SYNCLINE
SYNCLINES
SYNCOPAL
SYNCOPATE
SYNCOPATED
SYNCOPATES
SYNCOPATING
SYNCOPE
SYNCOPES
SYNCOPIC
SYNCOPTIC
SYNCRETIC
SYNCS
SYNCYTIA
SYNCYTIAL
SYNCYTIUM
SYNCYTIUMS
SYND
SYNDACTYL
SYNDED
SYNDESES
SYNDESIS
SYNDET
SYNDETIC
SYNDETS
SYNDIC
SYNDICAL
SYNDICATE
SYNDICATED
SYNDICATES
SYNDICATING
SYNDICS
SYNDING
SYNDINGS
SYNDROME
SYNDROMES
SYNDROMIC
SYNDS
SYNE
SYNECHIA
SYNECTIC
SYNECTICS
SYNED
SYNEDRIA
SYNEDRIAL
SYNEDRION
SYNEDRIUM
SYNERESES
SYNERESIS
SYNERGIC
SYNERGID
SYNERGIDS
SYNERGIES
SYNERGISM
SYNERGISMS
SYNERGIST
SYNERGISTS
SYNERGY
SYNES
SYNESES
SYNESIS
SYNGAMIC
SYNGAMIES

SYNGAMOUS
SYNGAMY
SYNGRAPH
SYNGRAPHS
SYNING
SYNIZESES
SYNIZESIS
SYNOD
SYNODAL
SYNODALS
SYNODIC
SYNODICAL
SYNODS
SYNODSMAN
SYNODSMEN
SYNOECETE
SYNOECETES
SYNOECISE
SYNOECISED
SYNOECISES
SYNOECISING
SYNOECISM
SYNOECISMS
SYNOECIZE
SYNOECIZED
SYNOECIZES
SYNOECIZING
SYNOICOUS
SYNONYM
SYNONYMIC
SYNONYMIES
SYNONYMS
SYNONYMY
SYNOPSES
SYNOPSIS
SYNOPTIC
SYNOPTIST
SYNOPTISTS
SYNOVIA
SYNOVIAL
SYNOVIAS
SYNOVITIS
SYNOVITISES
SYNTACTIC
SYNTAGMA
SYNTAGMATA
SYNTAN
SYNTANS
SYNTAX
SYNTAXES
SYNTECTIC
SYNTEXIS
SYNTEXISES
SYNTHESES
SYNTHESIS
SYNTHETIC
SYNTHETICS
SYNTONIC
SYNTONIES
SYNTONIN
SYNTONINS
SYNTONISE
SYNTONISED
SYNTONISES
SYNTONISING
SYNTONIZE
SYNTONIZED
SYNTONIZES
SYNTONIZING
SYNTONOUS

SYNTONY
SYPE
SYPED
SYPES
SYPHILIS
SYPHILISE
SYPHILISED
SYPHILISES
SYPHILISING
SYPHILIZE
SYPHILIZED
SYPHILIZES
SYPHILIZING
SYPHILOID

SYPHILOMA
SYPHILOMAS
SYPHON
SYPHONED
SYPHONING
SYPHONS
SYPING
SYREN
SYRENS
SYRINGA
SYRINGAS
SYRINGE
SYRINGEAL
SYRINGED

SYRINGES
SYRINGING
SYRINX
SYRINXES
SYRLYE
SYRPHID
SYRPHIDS
SYRTES
SYRTIS
SYRUP
SYRUPED
SYRUPING
SYRUPS
SYRUPY

SYSSITIA
SYSTALTIC
SYSTEM
SYSTEMED
SYSTEMIC
SYSTEMISE
SYSTEMISED
SYSTEMISES
SYSTEMISING
SYSTEMIZE
SYSTEMIZED
SYSTEMIZES
SYSTEMIZING
SYSTEMS

SYSTOLE
SYSTOLES
SYSTOLIC
SYSTYLE
SYSTYLES
SYTHE
SYTHES
SYVER
SYVERS
SYZYGIAL
SYZYGIES
SYZYGY

T

TA	TABOGGANING	TACHOGRAMS	TADPOLES	TAIGAS
TAAL	TABOGGANS	TACHYLITE	TADS	TAIGLE
TAALS	TABOO	TACHYLITES	TADVANCE	TAIGLED
TAB	TABOOED	TACHYLYTE	TAE	TAIGLES
TABANID	TABOOING	TACHYLYTES	TAED	TAIGLING
TABANIDS	TABOOS	TACHYON	TAEDIUM	TAIL
TABARD	TABOR	TACHYONS	TAEDIUMS	TAILARD
TABARDS	TABORED	TACIT	TAEING	TAILARDS
TABARET	TABORER	TACITLY	TAEL	TAILBACK
TABARETS	TABORERS	TACITNESS	TAELS	TAILBACKS
TABASHEER	TABORET	TACITNESSES	TAENIA	TAILED
TABASHEERS	TABORETS	TACITURN	TAENIAE	TAILING
TABASHIR	TABORIN	TACK	TAENIAS	TAILINGS
TABASHIRS	TABORING	TACKED	TAENIASES	TAILLESS
TABBED	TABORINS	TACKER	TAENIASIS	TAILLEUR
TABBIED	TABORS	TACKERS	TAENIATE	TAILLEURS
TABBIES	TABOUR	TACKET	TAENIOID	TAILLIE
TABBINET	TABOURED	TACKETS	TAES	TAILLIES
TABBINETS	TABOURET	TACKETY	TAFFEREL	TAILOR
TABBING	TABOURETS	TACKIER	TAFFERELS	TAILORED
TABBOULEH	TABOURIN	TACKIEST	TAFFETA	TAILORESS
TABBOULEHS	TABOURING	TACKINESS	TAFFETAS	TAILORESSES
TABBY	TABOURINS	TACKING	TAFFETASES	TAILORING
TABBYHOOD	TABOURS	TACKINGS	TAFFETIES	TAILORINGS
TABBYHOODS	TABRERE	TACKLE	TAFFETY	TAILORS
TABBYING	TABRERES	TACKLED	TAFFIES	TAILPIECE
TABEFIED	TABRET	TACKLER	TAFFRAIL	TAILPIECES
TABEFIES	TABRETS	TACKLERS	TAFFRAILS	TAILPLANE
TABEFY	TABS	TACKLES	TAFFY	TAILPLANES
TABEFYING	TABU	TACKLING	TAFIA	TAILRACE
TABELLION	TABUED	TACKLINGS	TAFIAS	TAILRACES
TABELLIONS	TABUING	TACKS	TAG	TAILS
TABERDAR	TABULA	TACKSMAN	TAGETES	TAILSKID
TABERDARS	TABULAE	TACKSMEN	TAGGED	TAILSKIDS
TABES	TABULAR	TACKY	TAGGER	TAILYE
TABESCENT	TABULARLY	TACO	TAGGERS	TAILYES
TABETIC	TABULATE	TACONITE	TAGGING	TAILZIE
TABID	TABULATED	TACONITES	TAGHAIRM	TAILZIES
TABINET	TABULATES	TACOS	TAGHAIRMS	TAINT
TABINETS	TABULATING	TACT	TAGLIONI	TAINTED
TABLA	TABULATOR	TACTFUL	TAGLIONIS	TAINTING
TABLAS	TABULATORS	TACTFULLY	TAGMEME	TAINTLESS
TABLATURE	TABUN	TACTIC	TAGMEMES	TAINTS
TABLATURES	TABUNS	TACTICAL	TAGMEMIC	TAINTURE
TABLE	TABUS	TACTICIAN	TAGMEMICS	TAINTURES
TABLEAU	TACAHOUT	TACTICIANS	TAGRAG	TAIPAN
TABLEAUX	TACAHOUTS	TACTICITIES	TAGRAGS	TAIPANS
TABLED	TACAMAHAC	TACTICITY	TAGS	TAIRA
TABLEFUL	TACAMAHACS	TACTICS	TAGUAN	TAIRAS
TABLEFULS	TACE	TACTILE	TAGUANS	TAIS
TABLELAND	TACES	TACTILIST	TAHA	TAISCH
TABLELANDS	TACET	TACTILISTS	TAHAS	TAISCHES
TABLES	TACH	TACTILITIES	TAHINA	TAISH
TABLET	TACHE	TACTILITY	TAHINAS	TAISHES
TABLETED	TACHES	TACTION	TAHINI	TAIT
TABLETING	TACHISM	TACTIONS	TAHINIS	TAITS
TABLETS	TACHISME	TACTISM	TAHR	TAIVER
TABLEWISE	TACHISMES	TACTISMS	TAHRS	TAIVERED
TABLING	TACHISMS	TACTLESS	TAHSIL	TAIVERING
TABLINGS	TACHIST	TACTS	TAHSILDAR	TAIVERS
TABLOID	TACHISTE	TACTUAL	TAHSILDARS	TAIVERT
TABLOIDS	TACHISTES	TACTUALLY	TAHSILS	TAJ
TABOGGAN	TACHISTS	TAD	TAI	TAJES
TABOGGANED	TACHOGRAM	TADPOLE	TAIGA	TAK

TAKA	TALIPES	TALUK	TAMMIES	TANGLES
TAKABLE	TALIPOT	TALUKDAR	TAMMY	TANGLIER
TAKAHE	TALIPOTS	TALUKDARS	TAMP	TANGLIEST
TAKAHEA	TALISMAN	TALUKS	TAMPED	TANGLING
TAKAHEAS	TALISMANS	TALUS	TAMPER	TANGLINGS
TAKAHES	TALK	TALUSES	TAMPERED	TANGLY
TAKAMAKA	TALKABLE	TALWEG	TAMPERER	TANGO
TAKAMAKAS	TALKATHON	TALWEGS	TAMPERERS	TANGOED
TAKAS	TALKATHONS	TAM	TAMPERING	TANGOING
TAKE	TALKATIVE	TAMABLE	TAMPERINGS	TANGOIST
TAKEABLE	TALKED	TAMAL	TAMPERS	TANGOISTS
TAKEN	TALKER	TAMALE	TAMPING	TANGOS
TAKEOVER	TALKERS	TAMALES	TAMPINGS	TANGRAM
TAKEOVERS	TALKFEST	TAMALS	TAMPION	TANGRAMS
TAKER	TALKFESTS	TAMANDUA	TAMPIONS	TANGS
TAKERS	TALKIE	TAMANDUAS	TAMPON	TANGUN
TAKES	TALKIES	TAMANOIR	TAMPONADE	TANGUNS
TAKIN	TALKING	TAMANOIRS	TAMPONADES	TANGY
TAKING	TALKINGS	TAMANU	TAMPONAGE	TANIST
TAKINGLY	TALKS	TAMANUS	TAMPONAGES	TANISTRIES
TAKINGS	TALL	TAMARA	TAMPONED	TANISTRY
TAKINS	TALLAGE	TAMARACK	TAMPONING	TANISTS
TAKS	TALLAGED	TAMARACKS	TAMPONS	TANK
TAKY	TALLAGES	TAMARAS	TAMPS	TANKA
TALA	TALLAGING	TAMARI	TAMS	TANKAGE
TALAK	TALLAT	TAMARILLO	TAN	TANKAGES
TALAKS	TALLATS	TAMARILLOS	TANA	TANKARD
TALANT	TALLBOY	TAMARIN	TANADAR	TANKARDS
TALANTS	TALLBOYS	TAMARIND	TANADARS	TANKAS
TALAPOIN	TALLENT	TAMARINDS	TANAGER	TANKED
TALAPOINS	TALLENTS	TAMARINS	TANAGERS	TANKER
TALAQ	TALLER	TAMARIS	TANAGRA	TANKERS
TALAQS	TALLEST	TAMARISK	TANAGRAS	TANKFUL
TALAR	TALLET	TAMARISKS	TANAGRINE	TANKFULS
TALARIA	TALLETS	TAMASHA	TANAISTE	TANKIA
TALARS	TALLIABLE	TAMASHAS	TANAISTES	TANKIAS
TALAS	TALLIATE	TAMBER	TANAS	TANKING
TALAUNT	TALLIATED	TAMBERS	TANDEM	TANKINGS
TALAUNTS	TALLIATES	TAMBOUR	TANDEMS	TANKS
TALAYOT	TALLIATING	TAMBOURA	TANDOORI	TANLING
TALAYOTS	TALLIED	TAMBOURAS	TANDOORIS	TANLINGS
TALBOT	TALLIER	TAMBOURED	TANE	TANNA
TALBOTS	TALLIERS	TAMBOURIN	TANG	TANNABLE
TALBOTYPE	TALLIES	TAMBOURING	TANGA	TANNAGE
TALBOTYPES	TALLITH	TAMBOURINS	TANGAS	TANNAGES
TALC	TALLITHS	TAMBOURS	TANGED	TANNAH
TALCKY	TALLNESS	TAMBURA	TANGELO	TANNAHS
TALCOSE	TALLNESSES	TAMBURAS	TANGELOS	TANNAS
TALCOUS	TALLOT	TAMBURIN	TANGENCIES	TANNATE
TALCS	TALLOTS	TAMBURINS	TANGENCY	TANNATES
TALCUM	TALLOW	TAME	TANGENT	TANNED
TALCUMS	TALLOWED	TAMEABLE	TANGENTS	TANNER
TALE	TALLOWING	TAMED	TANGERINE	TANNERIES
TALEFUL	TALLOWISH	TAMELESS	TANGERINES	TANNERS
TALEGALLA	TALLOWS	TAMELY	TANGHIN	TANNERY
TALEGALLAS	TALLOWY	TAMENESS	TANGHININ	TANNEST
TALENT	TALLY	TAMENESSES	TANGHININS	TANNIC
TALENTED	TALLYING	TAMER	TANGHINS	TANNIN
TALENTS	TALLYMAN	TAMERS	TANGIBLE	TANNING
TALES	TALLYMEN	TAMES	TANGIBLES	TANNINGS
TALESMAN	TALLYSHOP	TAMEST	TANGIBLY	TANNINS
TALESMEN	TALLYSHOPS	TAMIN	TANGIE	TANREC
TALI	TALMA	TAMINE	TANGIER	TANRECS
TALION	TALMAS	TAMINES	TANGIES	TANS
TALIONIC	TALON	TAMING	TANGIEST	TANSIES
TALIONS	TALONED	TAMINGS	TANGING	TANSY
TALIPAT	TALONS	TAMINS	TANGLE	TANTALATE
TALIPATS	TALPA	TAMIS	TANGLED	TANTALATES
TALIPED	TALPAE	TAMISE	TANGLER	TANTALIC
TALIPEDS	TALPAS	TAMISES	TANGLERS	TANTALISE

TANTALISED	TAPETI	TARBOOSH	TARRAS	TARTLETS
TANTALISES	TAPETIS	TARBOOSHES	TARRASES	TARTLY
TANTALISING	TAPETS	TARBOUSH	TARRE	TARTNESS
TANTALISINGS	TAPETUM	TARBOUSHES	TARRED	TARTNESSES
TANTALISM	TAPEWORM	TARBUSH	TARRES	TARTRATE
TANTALISMS	TAPEWORMS	TARBUSHES	TARRIANCE	TARTRATES
TANTALITE	TAPING	TARCEL	TARRIANCES	TARTS
TANTALITES	TAPIOCA	TARCELS	TARRIED	TARTY
TANTALIZE	TAPIOCAS	TARDIED	TARRIER	TARWEED
TANTALIZED	TAPIR	TARDIER	TARRIERS	TARWEEDS
TANTALIZES	TAPIROID	TARDIES	TARRIES	TARWHINE
TANTALIZING	TAPIRS	TARDIEST	TARRIEST	TARWHINES
TANTALIZINGS	TAPIS	TARDILY	TARRINESS	TASAR
TANTALUM	TAPISES	TARDINESS	TARRINESSES	TASARS
TANTALUMS	TAPIST	TARDINESSES	TARRING	TASH
TANTALUS	TAPISTS	TARDIVE	TARRINGS	TASHED
TANTALUSES	TAPLASH	TARDY	TARROCK	TASHES
TANTARA	TAPLASHES	TARDYING	TARROCKS	TASHING
TANTARARA	TAPPA	TARE	TARROW	TASIMETER
TANTARARAS	TAPPAS	TARED	TARROWED	TASIMETERS
TANTARAS	TAPPED	TARES	TARROWING	TASK
TANTI	TAPPER	TARGE	TARROWS	TASKED
TANTIVIES	TAPPERS	TARGED	TARRY	TASKER
TANTIVY	TAPPET	TARGES	TARRYING	TASKERS
TANTO	TAPPETS	TARGET	TARS	TASKING
TANTONIES	TAPPICE	TARGETED	TARSAL	TASKINGS
TANTONY	TAPPICED	TARGETEER	TARSALGIA	TASKS
TANTRA	TAPPICES	TARGETEERS	TARSALGIAS	TASLET
TANTRAS	TAPPICING	TARGETING	TARSALS	TASLETS
TANTRIC	TAPPING	TARGETS	TARSEL	TASS
TANTRUM	TAPPINGS	TARGING	TARSELS	TASSE
TANTRUMS	TAPPIT	TARIFF	TARSI	TASSEL
TANYARD	TAPROOM	TARIFFED	TARSIA	TASSELL
TANYARDS	TAPROOMS	TARIFFING	TARSIAS	TASSELLED
TAOISEACH	TAPROOT	TARIFFS	TARSIER	TASSELLING
TAOISEACHS	TAPROOTS	TARING	TARSIERS	TASSELLINGS
TAP	TAPS	TARLATAN	TARSIOID	TASSELLS
TAPA	TAPSMAN	TARLATANS	TARSUS	TASSELLY
TAPACOLO	TAPSMEN	TARMAC	TART	TASSELS
TAPACOLOS	TAPSTER	TARMACKED	TARTAN	TASSES
TAPACULO	TAPSTERS	TARMACKING	TARTANA	TASSET
TAPACULOS	TAPSTRIES	TARMACS	TARTANAS	TASSETS
TAPADERA	TAPSTRY	TARN	TARTANE	TASSIE
TAPADERAS	TAPU	TARNAL	TARTANED	TASSIES
TAPADERO	TAPUS	TARNATION	TARTANES	TASSWAGE
TAPADEROS	TAR	TARNISH	TARTANS	TASTABLE
TAPAS	TARA	TARNISHED	TARTAR	TASTE
TAPE	TARAKIHI	TARNISHER	TARTARE	TASTED
TAPED	TARAKIHIS	TARNISHERS	TARTARES	TASTEFUL
TAPELESS	TARAND	TARNISHES	TARTARIC	TASTELESS
TAPELINE	TARANDS	TARNISHING	TARTARISE	TASTER
TAPELINES	TARANTARA	TARNS	TARTARISED	TASTERS
TAPEN	TARANTARAED	TARO	TARTARISES	TASTES
TAPER	TARANTARAING	TAROC	TARTARISING	TASTEVIN
TAPERED	TARANTARAS	TAROCS	TARTARIZE	TASTEVINS
TAPERER	TARANTAS	TAROK	TARTARIZED	TASTIER
TAPERERS	TARANTASES	TAROKS	TARTARIZES	TASTIEST
TAPERING	TARANTASS	TAROS	TARTARIZING	TASTILY
TAPERINGS	TARANTASSES	TAROT	TARTARLY	TASTING
TAPERNESS	TARANTISM	TAROTS	TARTARS	TASTINGS
TAPERS	TARANTISMS	TARP	TARTER	TASTY
TAPERWISE	TARANTULA	TARPAN	TARTEST	TAT
TAPES	TARANTULAS	TARPANS	TARTIER	TATAMI
TAPESTRIED	TARAS	TARPAULIN	TARTIEST	TATAMIS
TAPESTRIES	TARAXACUM	TARPAULINS	TARTINE	TATE
TAPESTRY	TARAXACUMS	TARPON	TARTINES	TATER
TAPESTRYING	TARBOGGIN	TARPONS	TARTINESS	TATERS
TAPET	TARBOGGINED	TARPS	TARTINESSES	TATES
TAPETA	TARBOGGINING	TARRAGON	TARTISH	TATH
TAPETAL	TARBOGGINS	TARRAGONS	TARTLET	TATHED

TATHING	TAUS	TAXAMETER	TEAED	TEAZELED
TATHS	TAUT	TAXAMETERS	TEAGLE	TEAZELING
TATIE	TAUTED	TAXATION	TEAGLED	TEAZELLED
TATIES	TAUTEN	TAXATIONS	TEAGLES	TEAZELLING
TATLER	TAUTENED	TAXATIVE	TEAGLING	TEAZELS
TATLERS	TAUTENING	TAXED	TEAING	TEAZES
TATOU	TAUTENS	TAXER	TEAK	TEAZING
TATOUS	TAUTER	TAXERS	TEAKS	TEAZLE
TATS	TAUTEST	TAXES	TEAL	TEAZLED
TATT	TAUTING	TAXI	TEALS	TEAZLES
TATTED	TAUTIT	TAXIARCH	TEAM	TEAZLING
TATTER	TAUTLY	TAXIARCHS	TEAMED	TEBBAD
TATTERED	TAUTNESS	TAXICAB	TEAMER	TEBBADS
TATTERING	TAUTNESSES	TAXICABS	TEAMERS	TECH
TATTERS	TAUTOG	TAXIDERMIES	TEAMING	TECHIER
TATTERY	TAUTOGS	TAXIDERMY	TEAMINGS	TECHIEST
TATTIE	TAUTOLOGIES	TAXIED	TEAMS	TECHNIC
TATTIER	TAUTOLOGY	TAXIES	TEAMSTER	TECHNICAL
TATTIES	TAUTOMER	TAXIMAN	TEAMSTERS	TECHNICS
TATTIEST	TAUTOMERS	TAXIMEN	TEAMWISE	TECHNIQUE
TATTILY	TAUTONYM	TAXIMETER	TEAMWORK	TECHNIQUES
TATTINESS	TAUTONYMS	TAXIMETERS	TEAMWORKS	TECHS
TATTINESSES	TAUTS	TAXING	TEAPOT	TECHY
TATTING	TAVER	TAXINGS	TEAPOTS	TECKEL
TATTINGS	TAVERED	TAXIS	TEAPOY	TECKELS
TATTLE	TAVERING	TAXIWAY	TEAPOYS	TECTIFORM
TATTLED	TAVERN	TAXIWAYS	TEAR	TECTONIC
TATTLER	TAVERNA	TAXMAN	TEARAWAY	TECTONICS
TATTLERS	TAVERNAS	TAXMEN	TEARAWAYS	TECTORIAL
TATTLES	TAVERNER	TAXON	TEARER	TECTRICES
TATTLING	TAVERNERS	TAXONOMER	TEARERS	TECTRIX
TATTLINGS	TAVERNS	TAXONOMERS	TEARFUL	TED
TATTOO	TAVERS	TAXONOMIC	TEARFULLY	TEDDED
TATTOOED	TAVERT	TAXONOMIES	TEARIER	TEDDER
TATTOOER	TAW	TAXONOMY	TEARIEST	TEDDERS
TATTOOERS	TAWDRIER	TAXOR	TEARING	TEDDIES
TATTOOING	TAWDRIES	TAXORS	TEARLESS	TEDDING
TATTOOIST	TAWDRIEST	TAXYING	TEARS	TEDDY
TATTOOISTS	TAWDRILY	TAYBERRIES	TEARY	TEDESCA
TATTOOS	TAWDRY	TAYBERRY	TEAS	TEDESCHE
TATTOW	TAWED	TAYRA	TEASE	TEDESCHI
TATTOWED	TAWER	TAYRAS	TEASED	TEDESCO
TATTOWING	TAWERIES	TAZZA	TEASEL	TEDIOSITIES
TATTOWS	TAWERS	TAZZAS	TEASELED	TEDIOSITY
TATTS	TAWERY	TAZZE	TEASELER	TEDIOUS
TATTY	TAWIE	TCHICK	TEASELERS	TEDIOUSLY
TATU	TAWING	TCHICKED	TEASELING	TEDISOME
TATUED	TAWINGS	TCHICKING	TEASELINGS	TEDIUM
TATUING	TAWNEY	TCHICKS	TEASELLED	TEDIUMS
TATUS	TAWNEYS	TE	TEASELLER	TEDS
TAU	TAWNIER	TEA	TEASELLERS	TEDY
TAUBE	TAWNIES	TEABERRIES	TEASELLING	TEE
TAUBES	TAWNIEST	TEABERRY	TEASELLINGS	TEED
TAUGHT	TAWNINESS	TEACH	TEASELS	TEEHEE
TAULD	TAWNINESSES	TEACHABLE	TEASER	TEEHEED
TAUNT	TAWNY	TEACHER	TEASERS	TEEHEEING
TAUNTED	TAWPIE	TEACHERS	TEASES	TEEHEES
TAUNTER	TAWPIES	TEACHES	TEASING	TEEING
TAUNTERS	TAWS	TEACHIE	TEASINGLY	TEEL
TAUNTING	TAWSE	TEACHING	TEASINGS	TEELS
TAUNTINGS	TAWSES	TEACHINGS	TEASPOON	TEEM
TAUNTS	TAWT	TEACHLESS	TEASPOONS	TEEMED
TAUPE	TAWTED	TEACUP	TEAT	TEEMER
TAUPES	TAWTIE	TEACUPFUL	TEATED	TEEMERS
TAUPIE	TAWTING	TEACUPFULS	TEATIME	TEEMFUL
TAUPIES	TAWTS	TEACUPS	TEATIMES	TEEMING
TAUREAN	TAX	TEAD	TEATS	TEEMLESS
TAURIC	TAXA	TEADE	TEAZE	TEEMS
TAURIFORM	TAXABLE	TEADES	TEAZED	TEEN
TAURINE	TAXABLY	TEADS	TEAZEL	TEENAGE

TEENAGED	TEHEES	TELEPHEMES	TELLURIAN	TEMPO
TEENAGER	TEHR	TELEPHONE	TELLURIANS	TEMPORAL
TEENAGERS	TEHRS	TELEPHONED	TELLURIC	TEMPORALS
TEEND	TEIL	TELEPHONES	TELLURIDE	TEMPORARIES
TEENDED	TEILS	TELEPHONIES	TELLURIDES	TEMPORARY
TEENDING	TEIND	TELEPHONING	TELLURION	TEMPORE
TEENDS	TEINDED	TELEPHONY	TELLURIONS	TEMPORISE
TEENE	TEINDING	TELERGIC	TELLURISE	TEMPORISED
TEENED	TEINDS	TELERGIES	TELLURISED	TEMPORISES
TEENES	TEKNONYMIES	TELERGY	TELLURISES	TEMPORISING
TEENIER	TEKNONYMY	TELESALE	TELLURISING	TEMPORISINGS
TEENIEST	TEKTITE	TELESALES	TELLURITE	TEMPORIZE
TEENING	TEKTITES	TELESCOPE	TELLURITES	TEMPORIZED
TEENS	TEL	TELESCOPED	TELLURIUM	TEMPORIZES
TEENSIER	TELA	TELESCOPES	TELLURIUMS	TEMPORIZING
TEENSIEST	TELAE	TELESCOPIES	TELLURIZE	TEMPORIZINGS
TEENSY	TELAMON	TELESCOPING	TELLURIZED	TEMPOS
TEENTIER	TELAMONES	TELESCOPY	TELLURIZES	TEMPS
TEENTIEST	TELARY	TELESEME	TELLURIZING	TEMPT
TEENTSIER	TELD	TELESEMES	TELLUROUS	TEMPTABLE
TEENTSIEST	TELECAST	TELESES	TELLY	TEMPTED
TEENTSY	TELECASTED	TELESIS	TELOPHASE	TEMPTER
TEENTY	TELECASTING	TELESM	TELOPHASES	TEMPTERS
TEENY	TELECASTS	TELESMS	TELOS	TEMPTING
TEEPEE	TELECHIR	TELESTIC	TELOSES	TEMPTINGS
TEEPEES	TELECHIRS	TELESTICH	TELPHER	TEMPTRESS
TEER	TELECINE	TELESTICHS	TELPHERS	TEMPTRESSES
TEERED	TELECINES	TELETEX	TELS	TEMPTS
TEERING	TELECOM	TELETEXES	TELSON	TEMPURA
TEERS	TELECOMS	TELETEXT	TELSONS	TEMPURAS
TEES	TELEDU	TELETEXTS	TELT	TEMS
TEETER	TELEDUS	TELETHON	TEMBLOR	TEMSE
TEETERED	TELEFILM	TELETHONS	TEMBLORES	TEMSED
TEETERING	TELEFILMS	TELETRON	TEME	TEMSES
TEETERS	TELEGA	TELETRONS	TEMED	TEMSING
TEETH	TELEGAS	TELEVIEW	TEMENOS	TEMULENCE
TEETHE	TELEGENIC	TELEVIEWED	TEMENOSES	TEMULENCES
TEETHED	TELEGONIES	TELEVIEWING	TEMERITIES	TEMULENCIES
TEETHES	TELEGONY	TELEVIEWS	TEMERITY	TEMULENCY
TEETHING	TELEGRAM	TELEVISE	TEMEROUS	TEMULENT
TEETHINGS	TELEGRAMS	TELEVISED	TEMES	TEN
TEETOTAL	TELEGRAPH	TELEVISES	TEMP	TENABLE
TEETOTALS	TELEGRAPHED	TELEVISING	TEMPED	TENACE
TEETOTUM	TELEGRAPHING	TELEVISOR	TEMPER	TENACES
TEETOTUMS	TELEGRAPHS	TELEVISORS	TEMPERA	TENACIOUS
TEF	TELEMARK	TELEX	TEMPERAS	TENACITIES
TEFF	TELEMARKED	TELEXED	TEMPERATE	TENACITY
TEFFS	TELEMARKING	TELEXES	TEMPERATED	TENACULUM
TEFS	TELEMARKS	TELEXING	TEMPERATES	TENACULUMS
TEG	TELEMETER	TELIC	TEMPERATING	TENAIL
TEGG	TELEMETERED	TELL	TEMPERED	TENAILLE
TEGGS	TELEMETERING	TELLABLE	TEMPERER	TENAILLES
TEGMEN	TELEMETERS	TELLAR	TEMPERERS	TENAILLON
TEGMENTAL	TELEMETRIES	TELLARED	TEMPERING	TENAILLONS
TEGMENTUM	TELEMETRY	TELLARING	TEMPERINGS	TENAILS
TEGMENTUMS	TELEOLOGIES	TELLARS	TEMPERS	TENANCIES
TEGMINA	TELEOLOGY	TELLER	TEMPEST	TENANCY
TEGS	TELEONOMIES	TELLERED	TEMPESTED	TENANT
TEGUEXIN	TELEONOMY	TELLERING	TEMPESTING	TENANTED
TEGUEXINS	TELEOSAUR	TELLERS	TEMPESTS	TENANTING
TEGULA	TELEOSAURS	TELLIES	TEMPI	TENANTRIES
TEGULAE	TELEOST	TELLING	TEMPING	TENANTRY
TEGULAR	TELEOSTS	TELLINGLY	TEMPLAR	TENANTS
TEGULARLY	TELEPATH	TELLINGS	TEMPLATE	TENCH
TEGULATED	TELEPATHED	TELLS	TEMPLATES	TENCHES
TEGUMENT	TELEPATHIES	TELLTALE	TEMPLE	TEND
TEGUMENTS	TELEPATHING	TELLTALES	TEMPLED	TENDANCE
TEHEE	TELEPATHS	TELLURAL	TEMPLES	TENDANCES
TEHEED	TELEPATHY	TELLURATE	TEMPLET	TENDED
TEHEEING	TELEPHEME	TELLURATES	TEMPLETS	TENDENCE

TENDENCES
TENDENCIES
TENDENCY
TENDENZ
TENDENZEN
TENDER
TENDERED
TENDERER
TENDERERS
TENDEREST
TENDERING
TENDERINGS
TENDERISE
TENDERISED
TENDERISES
TENDERISING
TENDERIZE
TENDERIZED
TENDERIZES
TENDERIZING
TENDERLY
TENDERS
TENDING
TENDINOUS
TENDON
TENDONS
TENDRE
TENDRES
TENDRIL
TENDRILS
TENDRON
TENDRONS
TENDS
TENE
TENEBRAE
TENEBRIO
TENEBRIOS
TENEBRISM
TENEBRISMS
TENEBRIST
TENEBRISTS
TENEBRITIES
TENEBRITY
TENEBROSE
TENEBROUS
TENEMENT
TENEMENTS
TENENDUM
TENENDUMS
TENES
TENESMUS
TENESMUSES
TENET
TENETS
TENFOLD
TENIA
TENIAE
TENIAS
TENIOID
TENNÉ
TENNER
TENNERS
TENNÉS
TENNIS
TENNISES
TENON
TENONED
TENONER
TENONERS
TENONING

TENONS
TENOR
TENORIST
TENORISTS
TENORITE
TENORITES
TENOROON
TENOROONS
TENORS
TENOTOMIES
TENOTOMY
TENOUR
TENOURS
TENPENCE
TENPENCES
TENPENNY
TENPINS
TENREC
TENRECS
TENS
TENSE
TENSED
TENSELY
TENSENESS
TENSENESSES
TENSER
TENSES
TENSEST
TENSIBLE
TENSILE
TENSILITIES
TENSILITY
TENSING
TENSION
TENSIONS
TENSITIES
TENSITY
TENSIVE
TENSON
TENSONS
TENSOR
TENSORS
TENT
TENTACLE
TENTACLED
TENTACLES
TENTACULA
TENTAGE
TENTAGES
TENTATION
TENTATIONS
TENTATIVE
TENTED
TENTER
TENTERED
TENTERING
TENTERS
TENTFUL
TENTFULS
TENTH
TENTHLY
TENTHS
TENTIE
TENTIER
TENTIEST
TENTIGO
TENTIGOS
TENTING
TENTINGS
TENTORIA

TENTORIAL
TENTORIUM
TENTORIUMS
TENTS
TENTWISE
TENTY
TENUE
TENUES
TENUIOUS
TENUIS
TENUITIES
TENUITY
TENUOUS
TENUOUSLY
TENURABLE
TENURE
TENURES
TENURIAL
TENUTO
TENZON
TENZONS
TEOCALLI
TEOCALLIS
TEOSINTE
TEOSINTES
TEPAL
TEPALS
TEPEE
TEPEES
TEPEFIED
TEPEFIES
TEPEFY
TEPEFYING
TEPHIGRAM
TEPHIGRAMS
TEPHRA
TEPHRAS
TEPHRITE
TEPHRITES
TEPHRITIC
TEPHROITE
TEPHROITES
TEPID
TEPIDER
TEPIDEST
TEPIDITIES
TEPIDITY
TEPIDLY
TEPIDNESS
TEPIDNESSES
TEQUILA
TEQUILAS
TEQUILLA
TEQUILLAS
TERAI
TERAIS
TERAKIHI
TERAKIHIS
TERAPH
TERAPHIM
TERAPHIMS
TERAS
TERATA
TERATISM
TERATISMS
TERATOGEN
TERATOGENS
TERATOID
TERATOMA
TERATOMATA

TERBIC
TERBIUM
TERBIUMS
TERCE
TERCEL
TERCELET
TERCELETS
TERCELS
TERCES
TERCET
TERCETS
TERCIO
TERCIOS
TEREBENE
TEREBENES
TEREBINTH
TEREBINTHS
TEREBRA
TEREBRAE
TEREBRANT
TEREBRANTS
TEREBRAS
TEREBRATE
TEREBRATED
TEREBRATES
TEREBRATING
TEREDINES
TEREDO
TEREDOS
TEREFA
TEREFAH
TEREK
TEREKS
TERETE
TERF
TERFE
TERFES
TERFS
TERGAL
TERGITE
TERGITES
TERGUM
TERGUMS
TERIYAKI
TERIYAKIS
TERM
TERMAGANT
TERMAGANTS
TERMED
TERMER
TERMERS
TERMINAL
TERMINALS
TERMINATE
TERMINATED
TERMINATES
TERMINATING
TERMINER
TERMINERS
TERMING
TERMINI
TERMINISM
TERMINISMS
TERMINIST
TERMINISTS
TERMINUS
TERMINUSES
TERMITARIES
TERMITARY
TERMITE

TERMITES
TERMLESS
TERMLIES
TERMLY
TERMOR
TERMORS
TERMS
TERN
TERNAL
TERNARIES
TERNARY
TERNATE
TERNATELY
TERNE
TERNED
TERNES
TERNING
TERNION
TERNIONS
TERNS
TERPENE
TERPENES
TERPENOID
TERPENOIDS
TERPINEOL
TERPINEOLS
TERRA
TERRACE
TERRACED
TERRACES
TERRACING
TERRACINGS
TERRAE
TERRAIN
TERRAINS
TERRAMARA
TERRAMARE
TERRANE
TERRANES
TERRAPIN
TERRAPINS
TERRARIA
TERRARIUM
TERRARIUMS
TERRAS
TERRASES
TERRAZZO
TERRAZZOS
TERREEN
TERREENS
TERRELLA
TERRELLAS
TERRENE
TERRENELY
TERRENES
TERRET
TERRETS
TERRIBLE
TERRIBLES
TERRIBLY
TERRICOLE
TERRICOLES
TERRIER
TERRIERS
TERRIES
TERRIFIC
TERRIFIED
TERRIFIES
TERRIFY
TERRIFYING

TERRINE
TERRINES
TERRIT
TERRITORIES
TERRITORY
TERRITS
TERROR
TERRORISE
TERRORISED
TERRORISES
TERRORISING
TERRORISM
TERRORISMS
TERRORIST
TERRORISTS
TERRORIZE
TERRORIZED
TERRORIZES
TERRORIZING
TERRORS
TERRY
TERSE
TERSELY
TERSENESS
TERSENESSES
TERSER
TERSEST
TERSION
TERSIONS
TERTIA
TERTIAL
TERTIALS
TERTIAN
TERTIANS
TERTIARIES
TERTIARY
TERTIAS
TERTIUS
TERTIUSES
TERTS
TERVALENT
TERZETTA
TERZETTAS
TERZETTI
TERZETTO
TERZETTOS
TES
TESLA
TESLAS
TESSELLA
TESSELLAE
TESSELLAR
TESSERA
TESSERACT
TESSERACTS
TESSERAE
TESSERAL
TESSITURA
TESSITURAS
TEST
TESTA
TESTABLE
TESTACIES
TESTACY
TESTAMENT
TESTAMENTS
TESTAMUR
TESTAMURS
TESTAS
TESTATE

TESTATION
TESTATIONS
TESTATOR
TESTATORS
TESTATRIX
TESTATRIXES
TESTATUM
TESTATUMS
TESTE
TESTED
TESTEE
TESTEES
TESTER
TESTERN
TESTERNED
TESTERNING
TESTERNS
TESTERS
TESTES
TESTICLE
TESTICLES
TESTIER
TESTIEST
TESTIFIED
TESTIFIER
TESTIFIERS
TESTIFIES
TESTIFY
TESTIFYING
TESTILY
TESTIMONIED
TESTIMONIES
TESTIMONY
TESTIMONYING
TESTINESS
TESTINESSES
TESTING
TESTINGS
TESTIS
TESTON
TESTONS
TESTOON
TESTOONS
TESTRIL
TESTRILL
TESTRILLS
TESTRILS
TESTS
TESTUDINES
TESTUDO
TESTUDOS
TESTY
TETANAL
TETANIC
TETANIES
TETANISE
TETANISED
TETANISES
TETANISING
TETANIZE
TETANIZED
TETANIZES
TETANIZING
TETANOID
TETANUS
TETANUSES
TETANY
TETCHIER
TETCHIEST
TETCHILY

TETCHY
TÊTE
TÊTES
TETHER
TETHERED
TETHERING
TETHERS
TETRA
TETRACID
TETRACT
TETRACTS
TETRAD
TETRADIC
TETRADITE
TETRADITES
TETRADS
TETRAGON
TETRAGONS
TETRAGRAM
TETRAGRAMS
TETRALOGIES
TETRALOGY
TETRAPLA
TETRAPLAS
TETRAPOD
TETRAPODIES
TETRAPODS
TETRAPODY
TETRARCH
TETRARCHIES
TETRARCHS
TETRARCHY
TETRAS
TETRAXON
TETRAXONS
TETRODE
TETRODES
TETRONAL
TETRONALS
TETROXIDE
TETROXIDES
TETRYL
TETRYLS
TETTER
TETTERED
TETTERING
TETTEROUS
TETTERS
TETTIX
TETTIXES
TEUCH
TEUCHAT
TEUCHATS
TEUCHER
TEUCHEST
TEUCHTER
TEUCHTERS
TEUGH
TEUGHER
TEUGHEST
TEW
TEWART
TEWARTS
TEWED
TEWEL
TEWELS
TEWHIT
TEWHITS
TEWING
TEWIT

TEWITS
TEWS
TEXAS
TEXASES
TEXT
TEXTBOOK
TEXTBOOKS
TEXTILE
TEXTILES
TEXTORIAL
TEXTS
TEXTUAL
TEXTUALLY
TEXTUARIES
TEXTUARY
TEXTURAL
TEXTURE
TEXTURED
TEXTURES
TEXTURING
TEXTURISE
TEXTURISED
TEXTURISES
TEXTURISING
TEXTURIZE
TEXTURIZED
TEXTURIZES
TEXTURIZING
THACK
THACKS
THAE
THAGI
THAGIS
THAIM
THAIRM
THAIRMS
THALAMI
THALAMIC
THALAMUS
THALASSIC
THALER
THALERS
THALIAN
THALLI
THALLIC
THALLINE
THALLIUM
THALLIUMS
THALLOID
THALLOUS
THALLUS
THALLUSES
THALWEG
THALWEGS
THAN
THANA
THANADAR
THANADARS
THANAGE
THANAGES
THANAH
THANAHS
THANAS
THANATISM
THANATISMS
THANATIST
THANATISTS
THANATOID
THANE
THANEDOM

THANEDOMS
THANEHOOD
THANEHOODS
THANES
THANESHIP
THANESHIPS
THANK
THANKED
THANKEE
THANKER
THANKERS
THANKFUL
THANKING
THANKINGS
THANKLESS
THANKS
THANNA
THANNAH
THANNAHS
THANNAS
THAR
THARS
THAT
THATAWAY
THATCH
THATCHED
THATCHER
THATCHERS
THATCHES
THATCHING
THATCHINGS
THATCHT
THATNESS
THATNESSES
THAUMATIN
THAUMATINS
THAW
THAWED
THAWER
THAWERS
THAWIER
THAWIEST
THAWING
THAWINGS
THAWLESS
THAWS
THAWY
THE
THEACEOUS
THEANDRIC
THEARCHIC
THEARCHIES
THEARCHY
THEATER
THEATERS
THEATRAL
THEATRE
THEATRES
THEATRIC
THEATRICS
THEAVE
THEAVES
THEBAINE
THEBAINES
THECA
THECAE
THECAL
THECATE
THECODONT
THECODONTS

THEE
THEED
THEEING
THEEK
THEEKED
THEEKING
THEEKS
THEES
THEFT
THEFTBOOT
THEFTBOOTS
THEFTBOTE
THEFTBOTES
THEFTS
THEFTUOUS
THEGITHER
THEGN
THEGNS
THEIC
THEICS
THEINE
THEINES
THEIR
THEIRS
THEISM
THEISMS
THEIST
THEISTIC
THEISTS
THELEMENT
THELEMENTS
THELF
THELVES
THELYTOKIES
THELYTOKY
THEM
THEMA
THEMATA
THEMATIC
THEME
THEMED
THEMES
THEMING
THEN
THENABOUT
THENABOUTS
THENAR
THENARS
THENCE
THENS
THEOCRACIES
THEOCRACY
THEOCRASIES
THEOCRASY
THEOCRAT
THEOCRATS
THEODICIES
THEODICY
THEOGONIC
THEOGONIES
THEOGONY
THEOLOGER
THEOLOGERS
THEOLOGIC
THEOLOGIES
THEOLOGUE
THEOLOGUES
THEOLOGY
THEOMACHIES
THEOMACHY

THEOMANCIES
THEOMANCY
THEOMANIA
THEOMANIAS
THEONOMIES
THEONOMY
THEOPATHIES
THEOPATHY
THEOPHAGIES
THEOPHAGY
THEOPHANIES
THEOPHANY
THEORBIST
THEORBISTS
THEORBO
THEORBOS
THEOREM
THEOREMS
THEORETIC
THEORETICS
THEORIC
THEORICS
THEORIES
THEORIQUE
THEORIQUES
THEORISE
THEORISED
THEORISER
THEORISERS
THEORISES
THEORISING
THEORIST
THEORISTS
THEORIZE
THEORIZED
THEORIZER
THEORIZERS
THEORIZES
THEORIZING
THEORY
THEOSOPH
THEOSOPHIES
THEOSOPHS
THEOSOPHY
THEOTOKOS
THEOW
THEOWS
THERALITE
THERALITES
THERAPIES
THERAPIST
THERAPISTS
THERAPSID
THERAPSIDS
THERAPY
THERBLIG
THERBLIGS
THERE
THEREAT
THEREAWAY
THEREBY
THEREFOR
THEREFORE
THEREFROM
THEREIN
THEREINTO
THERENESS
THERENESSES
THEREOF
THEREON

THEREOUT
THERES
THERETO
THEREUNTO
THEREUPON
THEREWITH
THERIAC
THERIACA
THERIACAL
THERIACAS
THERIACS
THERM
THERMAE
THERMAL
THERMALLY
THERMALS
THERMIC
THERMICAL
THERMION
THERMIONS
THERMITE
THERMITES
THERMOS
THERMOSES
THERMOTIC
THERMOTICS
THERMS
THEROID
THEROLOGIES
THEROLOGY
THEROPOD
THEROPODS
THESAURUS
THESAURUSES
THESE
THESES
THESIS
THESPIAN
THESPIANS
THETA
THETAS
THETCH
THETCHED
THETCHES
THETCHING
THETE
THETES
THETHER
THETIC
THETICAL
THEURGIC
THEURGIES
THEURGIST
THEURGISTS
THEURGY
THEW
THEWED
THEWES
THEWIER
THEWIEST
THEWLESS
THEWS
THEWY
THEY
THIAMIN
THIAMINE
THIAMINES
THIAMINS
THIASUS
THIASUSES

THIAZIDE
THIAZIDES
THIBET
THIBETS
THIBLE
THIBLES
THICK
THICKED
THICKEN
THICKENED
THICKENER
THICKENERS
THICKENING
THICKENINGS
THICKENS
THICKER
THICKEST
THICKET
THICKETED
THICKETS
THICKETY
THICKHEAD
THICKHEADS
THICKING
THICKISH
THICKLY
THICKNESS
THICKNESSES
THICKO
THICKOES
THICKOS
THICKS
THICKSET
THICKSETS
THICKSKIN
THICKSKINS
THICKY
THIEF
THIEVE
THIEVED
THIEVERIES
THIEVERY
THIEVES
THIEVING
THIEVINGS
THIEVISH
THIG
THIGGER
THIGGERS
THIGGING
THIGGINGS
THIGGIT
THIGH
THIGHS
THIGS
THILK
THILL
THILLER
THILLERS
THILLS
THIMBLE
THIMBLED
THIMBLES
THIMBLING
THIN
THINE
THING
THINGAMIES
THINGAMY
THINGHOOD

THINGHOODS
THINGIES
THINGNESS
THINGNESSES
THINGS
THINGUMMIES
THINGUMMY
THINGY
THINK
THINKABLE
THINKER
THINKERS
THINKING
THINKINGS
THINKS
THINLY
THINNED
THINNER
THINNERS
THINNESS
THINNESSES
THINNEST
THINNING
THINNINGS
THINNISH
THINS
THIOL
THIOLS
THIOUREA
THIOUREAS
THIR
THIRAM
THIRAMS
THIRD
THIRDED
THIRDING
THIRDINGS
THIRDLY
THIRDS
THIRDSMAN
THIRDSMEN
THIRL
THIRLAGE
THIRLAGES
THIRLED
THIRLING
THIRLS
THIRST
THIRSTED
THIRSTER
THIRSTERS
THIRSTFUL
THIRSTIER
THIRSTIEST
THIRSTILY
THIRSTING
THIRSTS
THIRSTY
THIRTEEN
THIRTEENS
THIRTIES
THIRTIETH
THIRTIETHS
THIRTY
THIRTYISH
THIS
THISNESS
THISNESSES
THISTLE
THISTLES

THISTLY	THOWELS	THREEPS	THRIVES	THRUMMERS
THITHER	THOWL	THREES	THRIVING	THRUMMING
THIVEL	THOWLESS	THREESOME	THRIVINGS	THRUMMINGS
THIVELS	THOWLS	THREESOMES	THRO	THRUMMY
THLIPSES	THRAE	THRENE	THROAT	THRUMS
THLIPSIS	THRALDOM	THRENES	THROATED	THRUSH
THLIPSISES	THRALDOMS	THRENETIC	THROATIER	THRUSHES
THO	THRALL	THRENODE	THROATIEST	THRUST
THOFT	THRALLDOM	THRENODES	THROATILY	THRUSTED
THOFTS	THRALLDOMS	THRENODIC	THROATS	THRUSTER
THOLE	THRALLED	THRENODIES	THROATY	THRUSTERS
THOLED	THRALLING	THRENODY	THROB	THRUSTING
THOLES	THRALLS	THRENOS	THROBBED	THRUSTINGS
THOLI	THRANG	THRENOSES	THROBBING	THRUSTS
THOLING	THRANGED	THREONINE	THROBBINGS	THRUTCH
THOLOBATE	THRANGING	THREONINES	THROBLESS	THRUTCHED
THOLOBATES	THRANGS	THRESH	THROBS	THRUTCHES
THOLOI	THRAPPLE	THRESHED	THROE	THRUTCHING
THOLOS	THRAPPLED	THRESHEL	THROED	THRUWAY
THOLUS	THRAPPLES	THRESHELS	THROEING	THRUWAYS
THON	THRAPPLING	THRESHER	THROES	THRYMSA
THONDER	THRASH	THRESHERS	THROMBI	THRYMSAS
THONG	THRASHED	THRESHES	THROMBIN	THUD
THONGED	THRASHER	THRESHING	THROMBINS	THUDDED
THONGS	THRASHERS	THRESHINGS	THROMBOSE	THUDDING
THORACES	THRASHES	THRESHOLD	THROMBOSED	THUDS
THORACIC	THRASHING	THRESHOLDS	THROMBOSES	THUG
THORAX	THRASHINGS	THRETTIES	THROMBOSING	THUGGEE
THORAXES	THRASONIC	THRETTY	THROMBUS	THUGGEES
THORITE	THRAVE	THREW	THRONE	THUGGERIES
THORITES	THRAVES	THRICE	THRONED	THUGGERY
THORIUM	THRAW	THRID	THRONES	THUGGISM
THORIUMS	THRAWARD	THRIDACE	THRONG	THUGGISMS
THORN	THRAWART	THRIDACES	THRONGED	THUGS
THORNBACK	THRAWING	THRIDDED	THRONGFUL	THUJA
THORNBACKS	THRAWN	THRIDDING	THRONGING	THUJAS
THORNED	THRAWS	THRIDS	THRONGINGS	THULIA
THORNIER	THREAD	THRIFT	THRONGS	THULIAS
THORNIEST	THREADED	THRIFTIER	THRONING	THULITE
THORNING	THREADEN	THRIFTIEST	THROPPLE	THULITES
THORNLESS	THREADER	THRIFTILY	THROPPLED	THULIUM
THORNS	THREADERS	THRIFTS	THROPPLES	THULIUMS
THORNSET	THREADIER	THRIFTY	THROPPLING	THUMB
THORNTREE	THREADIEST	THRILL	THROSTLE	THUMBED
THORNTREES	THREADING	THRILLANT	THROSTLES	THUMBIER
THORNY	THREADS	THRILLED	THROTTLE	THUMBICOT
THORON	THREADY	THRILLER	THROTTLED	THUMBING
THORONS	THREAP	THRILLERS	THROTTLER	THUMBKINS
THOROUGH	THREAPING	THRILLING	THROTTLERS	THUMBLESS
THOROUGHER	THREAPIT	THRILLS	THROTTLES	THUMBLING
THOROUGHEST	THREAPS	THRILLY	THROTTLING	THUMBLINGS
THOROUGHS	THREAT	THRIMSA	THROTTLINGS	THUMBNAIL
THORP	THREATED	THRIMSAS	THROUGH	THUMBNAILS
THORPE	THREATEN	THRIP	THROUGHLY	THUMBPOT
THORPES	THREATENED	THRIPS	THROVE	THUMBPOTS
THORPS	THREATENING	THRIPSES	THROW	THUMBS
THOSE	THREATENINGS	THRISSEL	THROWE	THUMBY
THOTHER	THREATENS	THRISSELS	THROWER	THUMP
THOTHERS	THREATFUL	THRIST	THROWERS	THUMPED
THOU	THREATING	THRISTED	THROWES	THUMPER
THOUGH	THREATS	THRISTING	THROWING	THUMPERS
THOUGHT	THREAVE	THRISTLE	THROWINGS	THUMPING
THOUGHTED	THREAVES	THRISTLES	THROWN	THUMPS
THOUGHTEN	THREE	THRISTS	THROWS	THUNDER
THOUGHTS	THREEFOLD	THRISTY	THROWSTER	THUNDERED
THOUING	THREENESS	THRIVE	THROWSTERS	THUNDERER
THOUS	THREENESSES	THRIVED	THRU	THUNDERERS
THOUSAND	THREEP	THRIVEN	THRUM	THUNDERING
THOUSANDS	THREEPING	THRIVER	THRUMMED	THUNDERINGS
THOWEL	THREEPIT	THRIVERS	THRUMMER	THUNDERS

THUNDERY
THUNDROUS
THURIBLE
THURIBLES
THURIFER
THURIFERS
THURIFIED
THURIFIES
THURIFY
THURIFYING
THUS
THUSES
THUSNESS
THUSNESSES
THUSWISE
THWACK
THWACKED
THWACKER
THWACKERS
THWACKING
THWACKINGS
THWACKS
THWAITE
THWAITES
THWART
THWARTED
THWARTER
THWARTERS
THWARTING
THWARTINGS
THWARTLY
THWARTS
THY
THYINE
THYLACINE
THYLACINES
THYLOSE
THYLOSES
THYLOSIS
THYME
THYMES
THYMIDINE
THYMIDINES
THYMIER
THYMIEST
THYMINE
THYMINES
THYMOCYTE
THYMOCYTES
THYMOL
THYMOLS
THYMUS
THYMUSES
THYMY
THYRATRON
THYRATRONS
THYREOID
THYREOIDS
THYRISTOR
THYRISTORS
THYROID
THYROIDS
THYROXIN
THYROXINE
THYROXINES
THYROXINS
THYRSE
THYRSES
THYRSI
THYRSOID

THYRSUS
THYSELF
TI
TIAR
TIARA
TIARAED
TIARAS
TIARS
TIBIA
TIBIAE
TIBIAL
TIBIAS
TIC
TICAL
TICALS
TICCA
TICE
TICED
TICES
TICH
TICHES
TICHIER
TICHIEST
TICHY
TICING
TICK
TICKED
TICKEN
TICKENS
TICKER
TICKERS
TICKET
TICKETED
TICKETING
TICKETS
TICKEY
TICKEYS
TICKIES
TICKING
TICKINGS
TICKLE
TICKLED
TICKLER
TICKLERS
TICKLES
TICKLIER
TICKLIEST
TICKLING
TICKLINGS
TICKLISH
TICKLY
TICKS
TICKY
TICS
TID
TIDAL
TIDBIT
TIDBITS
TIDDIES
TIDDLE
TIDDLED
TIDDLER
TIDDLERS
TIDDLES
TIDDLEY
TIDDLIER
TIDDLIES
TIDDLIEST
TIDDLING
TIDDLY

TIDDY
TIDE
TIDED
TIDELESS
TIDEMARK
TIDEMARKS
TIDEMILL
TIDEMILLS
TIDES
TIDIED
TIDIER
TIDIES
TIDIEST
TIDILY
TIDINESS
TIDINESSES
TIDING
TIDINGS
TIDIVATE
TIDIVATED
TIDIVATES
TIDIVATING
TIDS
TIDY
TIDYING
TIE
TIED
TIELESS
TIER
TIERCE
TIERCÉ
TIERCEL
TIERCELET
TIERCELETS
TIERCELS
TIERCERON
TIERCERONS
TIERCES
TIERED
TIERING
TIERS
TIES
TIETAC
TIETACK
TIETACKS
TIETACS
TIFF
TIFFANIES
TIFFANY
TIFFED
TIFFIN
TIFFING
TIFFINGS
TIFFINS
TIFFS
TIFT
TIFTED
TIFTING
TIFTS
TIG
TIGE
TIGER
TIGERISH
TIGERISM
TIGERISMS
TIGERLY
TIGERS
TIGERY
TIGES
TIGGED

TIGGING
TIGHT
TIGHTEN
TIGHTENED
TIGHTENER
TIGHTENERS
TIGHTENING
TIGHTENS
TIGHTER
TIGHTEST
TIGHTISH
TIGHTLY
TIGHTNESS
TIGHTNESSES
TIGHTS
TIGHTWAD
TIGHTWADS
TIGLON
TIGLONS
TIGON
TIGONS
TIGRESS
TIGRESSES
TIGRINE
TIGRISH
TIGROID
TIGS
TIKA
TIKAS
TIKE
TIKES
TIKI
TIKIS
TIL
TILAPIA
TILAPIAS
TILBURIES
TILBURY
TILDE
TILDES
TILE
TILED
TILEFISH
TILEFISHES
TILER
TILERIES
TILERS
TILERY
TILES
TILING
TILINGS
TILL
TILLABLE
TILLAGE
TILLAGES
TILLED
TILLER
TILLERED
TILLERS
TILLIER
TILLIEST
TILLING
TILLINGS
TILLITE
TILLITES
TILLS
TILLY
TILS
TILT
TILTABLE

TILTED
TILTER
TILTERS
TILTH
TILTHS
TILTING
TILTINGS
TILTS
TIMARIOT
TIMARIOTS
TIMBAL
TIMBALE
TIMBALES
TIMBALS
TIMBER
TIMBERED
TIMBERING
TIMBERINGS
TIMBERS
TIMBÓ
TIMBÓS
TIMBRE
TIMBREL
TIMBRELS
TIMBRES
TIME
TIMED
TIMELESS
TIMELIER
TIMELIEST
TIMELY
TIMENOGUY
TIMENOGUYS
TIMEOUS
TIMEOUSLY
TIMEPIECE
TIMEPIECES
TIMER
TIMERS
TIMES
TIMESCALE
TIMESCALES
TIMETABLE
TIMETABLED
TIMETABLES
TIMETABLING
TIMID
TIMIDER
TIMIDEST
TIMIDITIES
TIMIDITY
TIMIDLY
TIMIDNESS
TIMIDNESSES
TIMING
TIMINGS
TIMIST
TIMISTS
TIMOCRACIES
TIMOCRACY
TIMON
TIMONEER
TIMONEERS
TIMONS
TIMOROUS
TIMORSOME
TIMOTHIES
TIMOTHY
TIMOUS
TIMOUSLY

TIMPANI	TINKERED	TIPPERS	TIRRIVIE	TITRATE
TIMPANIST	TINKERING	TIPPET	TIRRIVIES	TITRATED
TIMPANISTS	TINKERINGS	TIPPETS	TIRRS	TITRATES
TIMPANO	TINKERS	TIPPIER	TIS	TITRATING
TIMPS	TINKING	TIPPIEST	TISANE	TITRATION
TIN	TINKLE	TIPPING	TISANES	TITRATIONS
TINAJA	TINKLED	TIPPINGS	TISICK	TITRE
TINAJAS	TINKLER	TIPPLE	TISICKS	TITRES
TINAMOU	TINKLERS	TIPPLED	TISSUE	TITS
TINAMOUS	TINKLES	TIPPLER	TISSUED	TITTED
TINCAL	TINKLIER	TIPPLERS	TISSUES	TITTER
TINCALS	TINKLIEST	TIPPLES	TISSUING	TITTERED
TINCHEL	TINKLING	TIPPLING	TISWAS	TITTERER
TINCHELS	TINKLINGS	TIPPY	TISWASES	TITTERERS
TINCT	TINKLY	TIPS	TIT	TITTERING
TINCTED	TINKS	TIPSIER	TITAN	TITTERINGS
TINCTING	TINMAN	TIPSIEST	TITANATE	TITTERS
TINCTS	TINMEN	TIPSIFIED	TITANATES	TITTIES
TINCTURE	TINNED	TIPSIFIES	TITANIC	TITTING
TINCTURED	TINNER	TIPSIFY	TITANITE	TITTIVATE
TINCTURES	TINNERS	TIPSIFYING	TITANITES	TITTIVATED
TINCTURING	TINNIE	TIPSILY	TITANIUM	TITTIVATES
TIND	TINNIER	TIPSINESS	TITANIUMS	TITTIVATING
TINDAL	TINNIES	TIPSINESSES	TITANOUS	TITTLE
TINDALS	TINNIEST	TIPSTAFF	TITANS	TITTLEBAT
TINDED	TINNING	TIPSTAFFS	TITBIT	TITTLEBATS
TINDER	TINNINGS	TIPSTAVES	TITBITS	TITTLED
TINDERS	TINNITUS	TIPSTER	TITCH	TITTLES
TINDERY	TINNITUSES	TIPSTERS	TITCHES	TITTLING
TINDING	TINNY	TIPSY	TITE	TITTUP
TINDS	TINPOT	TIPT	TITELY	TITTUPED
TINE	TINPOTS	TIPTOE	TITER	TITTUPING
TINEA	TINS	TIPTOED	TITERS	TITTUPS
TINEAS	TINSEL	TIPTOEING	TITFER	TITTUPY
TINED	TINSELLED	TIPTOES	TITFERS	TITTY
TINEID	TINSELLING	TIPTOP	TITHABLE	TITUBANCIES
TINEIDS	TINSELLY	TIPTOPS	TITHE	TITUBANCY
TINES	TINSELRIES	TIPULA	TITHED	TITUBANT
TINFOIL	TINSELRY	TIPULAS	TITHER	TITUBATE
TINFOILS	TINSELS	TIRADE	TITHERS	TITUBATED
TINFUL	TINSEY	TIRADES	TITHES	TITUBATES
TINFULS	TINSEYS	TIRASSE	TITHING	TITUBATING
TING	TINOMITII	TINASSES	TITHINGS	TITULAR
TINGE	TINSMITHS	TIRE	TITI	TITULARIES
TINGED	TINSNIPS	TIRED	TITIAN	TITULARLY
TINGES	TINSTONE	TIREDER	TITIANS	TITULARS
TINGING	TINSTONES	TIREDEST	TITILLATE	TITULARY
TINGLE	TINT	TIREDNESS	TITILLATED	TITULE
TINGLED	TINTED	TIREDNESSES	TITILLATES	TITULED
TINGLER	TINTER	TIRELESS	TITILLATING	TITULES
TINGLERS	TINTERS	TIRELING	TITIS	TITULING
TINGLES	TINTIER	TIRELINGS	TITIVATE	TITUP
TINGLIER	TINTIEST	TIRES	TITIVATED	TITUPED
TINGLIEST	TINTINESS	TIRESOME	TITIVATES	TITUPING
TINGLING	TINTINESSES	TIRING	TITIVATING	TITUPPED
TINGLINGS	TINTING	TIRINGS	TITLARK	TITUPPING
TINGLISH	TINTINGS	TIRL	TITLARKS	TITUPS
TINGLY	TINTLESS	TIRLED	TITLE	TITUPY
TINGS	TINTS	TIRLING	TITLED	TIZWAS
TINGUAITE	TINTY	TIRLS	TITLELESS	TIZWASES
TINGUAITES	TINTYPE	TIRO	TITLER	TIZZ
TINHORN	TINTYPES	TIROES	TITLERS	TIZZES
TINHORNS	TINWARE	TIROS	TITLES	TIZZIES
TINIER	TINWARES	TIRR	TITLING	TIZZY
TINIEST	TINY	TIRRED	TITLINGS	TMESES
TININESS	TIP	TIRRING	TITMICE	TMESIS
TINING	TIPI	TIRRIT	TITMOSE	TO
TINK	TIPIS	TIRRITS	TITMOUSE	TOAD
TINKED	TIPPED	TIRRIVEE	TITOKI	TOADFISH
TINKER	TIPPER	TIRRIVEES	TITOKIS	TOADFISHES

TOADFLAX
TOADFLAXES
TOADGRASS
TOADGRASSES
TOADIED
TOADIES
TOADRUSH
TOADRUSHES
TOADS
TOADSTOOL
TOADSTOOLS
TOADY
TOADYING
TOADYISH
TOADYISM
TOADYISMS
TOAST
TOASTED
TOASTER
TOASTERS
TOASTIE
TOASTIES
TOASTING
TOASTINGS
TOASTS
TOASTY
TOAZE
TOAZED
TOAZES
TOAZING
TOBACCO
TOBACCOES
TOBACCOS
TOBIES
TOBOGGAN
TOBOGGANED
TOBOGGANING
TOBOGGANINGS
TOBOGGANS
TOBOGGIN
TOBOGGINED
TOBOGGINING
TOBOGGINS
TOBRAKE
TOBY
TOCCATA
TOCCATAS
TOCCATINA
TOCCATINAS
TOCHER
TOCHERED
TOCHERING
TOCHERS
TOCO
TOCOLOGIES
TOCOLOGY
TOCOS
TOCSIN
TOCSINS
TOD
TODAY
TODAYS
TODDE
TODDED
TODDES
TODDIES
TODDING
TODDLE
TODDLED
TODDLER

TODDLERS
TODDLES
TODDLING
TODDY
TODIES
TODS
TODY
TOE
TOECAP
TOECAPS
TOECLIP
TOECLIPS
TOED
TOEING
TOENAIL
TOENAILS
TOES
TOFF
TOFFEE
TOFFEES
TOFFIER
TOFFIES
TOFFIEST
TOFFISH
TOFFS
TOFFY
TOFORE
TOFT
TOFTS
TOFU
TOFUS
TOG
TOGA
TOGAED
TOGAS
TOGATE
TOGATED
TOGE
TOGED
TOGES
TOGETHER
TOGGED
TOGGERIES
TOGGERY
TOGGING
TOGGLE
TOGGLED
TOGGLES
TOGGLING
TOGS
TOGUE
TOGUES
TOHEROA
TOHEROAS
TOHO
TOHOS
TOIL
TOILE
TOILED
TOILER
TOILERS
TOILES
TOILET
TOILETED
TOILETING
TOILETRIES
TOILETRY
TOILETS
TOILETTE
TOILETTES

TOILFUL
TOILINET
TOILINETS
TOILING
TOILINGS
TOILLESS
TOILS
TOILSOME
TOISE
TOISEACH
TOISEACHS
TOISECH
TOISECHS
TOISES
TOISON
TOISONS
TOKAMAK
TOKAMAKS
TOKE
TOKED
TOKEN
TOKENED
TOKENING
TOKENISM
TOKENISMS
TOKENS
TOKES
TOKING
TOKO
TOKOLOGIES
TOKOLOGY
TOKOLOSHE
TOKOLOSHES
TOKOS
TOLA
TOLAS
TOLBOOTH
TOLBOOTHS
TOLD
TOLE
TOLED
TOLERABLE
TOLERABLY
TOLERANCE
TOLERANCES
TOLERANT
TOLERATE
TOLERATED
TOLERATES
TOLERATING
TOLERATOR
TOLERATORS
TOLES
TOLING
TOLINGS
TOLL
TOLLABLE
TOLLAGE
TOLLAGES
TOLLBOOTH
TOLLBOOTHS
TOLLDISH
TOLLDISHES
TOLLED
TOLLER
TOLLERS
TOLLGATE
TOLLGATES
TOLLING
TOLLINGS

TOLLMAN
TOLLMEN
TOLLS
TOLSEL
TOLSELS
TOLSEY
TOLSEYS
TOLT
TOLTER
TOLTERED
TOLTERING
TOLTERS
TOLTS
TOLU
TOLUATE
TOLUATES
TOLUENE
TOLUENES
TOLUIC
TOLUIDINE
TOLUIDINES
TOLUOL
TOLUOLS
TOLUS
TOLZEY
TOLZEYS
TOM
TOMAHAWK
TOMAHAWKED
TOMAHAWKING
TOMAHAWKS
TOMALLEY
TOMALLEYS
TOMAN
TOMANS
TOMATO
TOMATOES
TOMB
TOMBAC
TOMBACS
TOMBAK
TOMBAKS
TOMBED
TOMBIC
TOMBING
TOMBLESS
TOMBOC
TOMBOCS
TOMBOLA
TOMBOLAS
TOMBOLO
TOMBOLOS
TOMBOY
TOMBOYISH
TOMBOYS
TOMBS
TOMBSTONE
TOMBSTONES
TOME
TOMENTOSE
TOMENTOUS
TOMENTUM
TOMENTUMS
TOMES
TOMFOOL
TOMFOOLED
TOMFOOLING
TOMFOOLS
TOMIAL
TOMIUM

TOMIUMS
TOMMIED
TOMMIES
TOMMY
TOMMYING
TOMOGRAM
TOMOGRAMS
TOMOGRAPH
TOMOGRAPHS
TOMORROW
TOMORROWS
TOMPION
TOMPIONS
TOMPON
TOMPONS
TOMS
TOMTIT
TOMTITS
TON
TONAL
TONALITE
TONALITES
TONALITIES
TONALITY
TONANT
TONDI
TONDINI
TONDINO
TONDINOS
TONDO
TONDOS
TONE
TONED
TONELESS
TONEME
TONEMES
TONEMIC
TONES
TONETIC
TONEY
TONG
TONGA
TONGAS
TONGS
TONGUE
TONGUED
TONGUELET
TONGUELETS
TONGUES
TONGUING
TONGUINGS
TONIC
TONICITIES
TONICITY
TONICS
TONIER
TONIES
TONIEST
TONIGHT
TONIGHTS
TONING
TONISH
TONISHLY
TONITE
TONITES
TONK
TONKED
TONKER
TONKERS
TONKING

363

TOSHERS

TONKS
TONLET
TONLETS
TONNAG
TONNAGE
TONNAGES
TONNAGS
TONNE
TONNEAU
TONNEAUS
TONNELL
TONNELLS
TONNES
TONNISH
TONNISHLY
TONOMETER
TONOMETERS
TONOMETRIES
TONOMETRY
TONS
TONSIL
TONSILLAR
TONSILS
TONSOR
TONSORIAL
TONSORS
TONSURE
TONSURED
TONSURES
TONTINE
TONTINER
TONTINERS
TONTINES
TONUS
TONUSES
TONY
TOO
TOOART
TOOARTS
TOOK
TOOL
TOOLBAG
TOOLBAGS
TOOLBOX
TOOLBOXES
TOOLED
TOOLER
TOOLERS
TOOLHOUSE
TOOLHOUSES
TOOLING
TOOLINGS
TOOLKIT
TOOLKITS
TOOLMAKER
TOOLMAKERS
TOOLMAN
TOOLMEN
TOOLROOM
TOOLROOMS
TOOLS
TOOM
TOOMED
TOOMER
TOOMEST
TOOMING
TOOMS
TOON
TOONS
TOORIE

TOORIES
TOOT
TOOTED
TOOTER
TOOTERS
TOOTH
TOOTHACHE
TOOTHACHES
TOOTHCOMB
TOOTHCOMBS
TOOTHED
TOOTHFUL
TOOTHFULS
TOOTHIER
TOOTHIEST
TOOTHING
TOOTHLESS
TOOTHPICK
TOOTHPICKS
TOOTHS
TOOTHSOME
TOOTHWASH
TOOTHWASHES
TOOTHWORT
TOOTHWORTS
TOOTHY
TOOTING
TOOTLE
TOOTLED
TOOTLES
TOOTLING
TOOTS
TOOTSIE
TOOTSIES
TOOTSY
TOP
TOPARCH
TOPARCHIES
TOPARCHS
TOPARCHY
TOPAZ
TOPAZES
TOPAZINE
TOPCOAT
TOPCOATS
TOPE
TOPECTOMIES
TOPECTOMY
TOPED
TOPEE
TOPEES
TOPEK
TOPEKS
TOPER
TOPERS
TOPES
TOPFULL
TOPHI
TOPHUS
TOPI
TOPIARIAN
TOPIARIES
TOPIARIST
TOPIARISTS
TOPIARY
TOPIC
TOPICAL
TOPICALLY
TOPICS
TOPING

TOPIS
TOPKNOT
TOPKNOTS
TOPLESS
TOPLOFTY
TOPMAKER
TOPMAKERS
TOPMAKING
TOPMAKINGS
TOPMAN
TOPMAST
TOPMASTS
TOPMEN
TOPMINNOW
TOPMINNOWS
TOPMOST
TOPOI
TOPOLOGIC
TOPOLOGIES
TOPOLOGY
TOPONYM
TOPONYMAL
TOPONYMIC
TOPONYMICS
TOPONYMIES
TOPONYMS
TOPONYMY
TOPOS
TOPPED
TOPPER
TOPPERS
TOPPING
TOPPINGLY
TOPPINGS
TOPPLE
TOPPLED
TOPPLES
TOPPLING
TOPS
TOPSAIL
TOPSAILS
TOPSIDE
TOPOIDEO
TOPSMAN
TOPSMEN
TOPSPIN
TOPSPINS
TOQUE
TOQUES
TOR
TORAN
TORANA
TORANAS
TORANS
TORBANITE
TORBANITES
TORC
TORCH
TORCHED
TORCHER
TORCHÈRE
TORCHÈRES
TORCHERS
TORCHES
TORCHING
TORCHON
TORCHONS
TORCS
TORCULAR
TORCULARS

TORDION
TORDIONS
TORE
TOREADOR
TOREADORS
TORERO
TOREROS
TORES
TOREUTIC
TOREUTICS
TORGOCH
TORGOCHS
TORI
TORIC
TORII
TORIIS
TORMENT
TORMENTED
TORMENTIL
TORMENTILS
TORMENTING
TORMENTINGS
TORMENTOR
TORMENTORS
TORMENTS
TORMENTUM
TORMENTUMS
TORMINA
TORMINAL
TORMINOUS
TORN
TORNADE
TORNADES
TORNADIC
TORNADO
TORNADOES
TOROID
TOROIDAL
TOROIDS
TORPEDO
TORPEDOED
TORPEDOER
TORPEDOERS
TORPEDOES
TORPEDOING
TORPEDOS
TORPEFIED
TORPEFIES
TORPEFY
TORPEFYING
TORPID
TORPIDITIES
TORPIDITY
TORPIDLY
TORPIDS
TORPITUDE
TORPITUDES
TORPOR
TORPORS
TORQUATE
TORQUATED
TORQUE
TORQUED
TORQUES
TORR
TORREFIED
TORREFIES
TORREFY
TORREFYING
TORRENT

TORRENTS
TORRET
TORRETS
TORRID
TORRIDER
TORRIDEST
TORRIDITIES
TORRIDITY
TORRS
TORS
TORSADE
TORSADES
TORSE
TORSEL
TORSELS
TORSES
TORSION
TORSIONAL
TORSIONS
TORSIVE
TORSK
TORSKS
TORSO
TORSOS
TORT
TORTE
TORTEN
TORTES
TORTILE
TORTILITIES
TORTILITY
TORTILLA
TORTILLAS
TORTIOUS
TORTIVE
TORTOISE
TORTOISES
TORTRICES
TORTRICID
TORTRICIDS
TORTRIX
TORTS
TORTUOUS
TORTURE
TORTURED
TORTURER
TORTURERS
TORTURES
TORTURING
TORTURINGS
TORTUROUS
TORUFFLED
TORULA
TORULAS
TORULIN
TORULINS
TORULOSE
TORULOSES
TORULOSIS
TORULUS
TORULUSES
TORUS
TOSE
TOSED
TOSES
TOSH
TOSHACH
TOSHACHS
TOSHED
TOSHERS

TOSHES	TOTTIE	TOURNEYED	TOWMONDS	TOXOCARAS
TOSHIER	TOTTIER	TOURNEYER	TOWMONS	TOXOID
TOSHIEST	TOTTIES	TOURNEYERS	TOWMONT	TOXOIDS
TOSHING	TOTTIEST	TOURNEYING	TOWMONTS	TOXOPHILIES
TOSHY	TOTTING	TOURNEYS	TOWN	TOXOPHILY
TOSING	TOTTINGS	TOURNURE	TOWNEE	TOY
TOSS	TOTTY	TOURNURES	TOWNEES	TOYED
TOSSED	TOUCAN	TOURS	TOWNHOUSE	TOYER
TOSSEN	TOUCANET	TOUSE	TOWNHOUSES	TOYERS
TOSSER	TOUCANETS	TOUSED	TOWNIE	TOYING
TOSSERS	TOUCANS	TOUSER	TOWNIER	TOYINGS
TOSSES	TOUCH	TOUSERS	TOWNIES	TOYISH
TOSSIER	TOUCHABLE	TOUSES	TOWNIEST	TOYISHLY
TOSSIEST	TOUCHÉ	TOUSING	TOWNISH	TOYLESOME
TOSSILY	TOUCHED	TOUSINGS	TOWNLAND	TOYLSOM
TOSSING	TOUCHER	TOUSLE	TOWNLANDS	TOYMAN
TOSSINGS	TOUCHERS	TOUSLED	TOWNLING	TOYMEN
TOSSPOT	TOUCHES	TOUSLES	TOWNLINGS	TOYS
TOSSPOTS	TOUCHIER	TOUSLING	TOWNLY	TOYSHOP
TOSSY	TOUCHIEST	TOUSTIE	TOWNS	TOYSHOPS
TOST	TOUCHILY	TOUSY	TOWNSCAPE	TOYSOME
TOT	TOUCHING	TOUT	TOWNSCAPED	TOYWOMAN
TOTAL	TOUCHINGS	TOUTED	TOWNSCAPES	TOYWOMEN
TOTALISE	TOUCHLESS	TOUTER	TOWNSCAPING	TOZE
TOTALISED	TOUCHWOOD	TOUTERS	TOWNSCAPINGS	TOZED
TOTALISER	TOUCHWOODS	TOUTIE	TOWNSFOLK	TOZES
TOTALISERS	TOUCHY	TOUTIER	TOWNSFOLKS	TOZIE
TOTALISES	TOUGH	TOUTIEST	TOWNSHIP	TOZIES
TOTALISING	TOUGHEN	TOUTING	TOWNSHIPS	TOZING
TOTALITIES	TOUGHENED	TOUTS	TOWNSKIP	TRABEATE
TOTALITY	TOUGHENER	TOUZE	TOWNSKIPS	TRABEATED
TOTALIZE	TOUGHENERS	TOUZED	TOWNSMAN	TRABECULA
TOTALIZED	TOUGHENING	TOUZES	TOWNSMEN	TRABECULAE
TOTALIZER	TOUGHENINGS	TOUZING	TOWNY	TRACE
TOTALIZERS	TOUGHENS	TOUZLE	TOWPATH	TRACEABLE
TOTALIZES	TOUGHER	TOUZLED	TOWPATHS	TRACEABLY
TOTALIZING	TOUGHEST	TOUZLES	TOWROPE	TRACED
TOTALLED	TOUGHIE	TOUZLING	TOWROPES	TRACELESS
TOTALLING	TOUGHIES	TOVARISH	TOWS	TRACER
TOTALLY	TOUGHISH	TOVARISHES	TOWSE	TRACERIED
TOTALS	TOUGHLY	TOW	TOWSED	TRACERIES
TOTARA	TOUGHNESS	TOWAGE	TOWSER	TRACERS
TOTARAS	TOUGHNESSES	TOWAGES	TOWSERS	TRACERY
TOTE	TOUGHS	TOWARD	TOWSES	TRACES
TOTED	TOUK	TOWARDLY	TOWSING	TRACHEA
TOTEM	TOUKED	TOWARDS	TOWSY	TRACHEAE
TOTEMIC	TOUKING	TOWBAR	TOWT	TRACHEAL
TOTEMISM	TOUKS	TOWBARS	TOWTED	TRACHEARIES
TOTEMISMS	TOUN	TOWED	TOWTING	TRACHEARY
TOTEMIST	TOUNS	TOWEL	TOWTS	TRACHEATE
TOTEMISTS	TOUPEE	TOWELLED	TOWY	TRACHEID
TOTEMS	TOUPEES	TOWELLING	TOWZE	TRACHEIDE
TOTES	TOUPET	TOWELLINGS	TOWZED	TRACHEIDES
TOTHER	TOUPETS	TOWELS	TOWZES	TRACHEIDS
TOTHERS	TOUR	TOWER	TOWZING	TRACHITIS
TOTIENT	TOURACO	TOWERED	TOXAEMIA	TRACHITISES
TOTIENTS	TOURACOS	TOWERIER	TOXAEMIAS	TRACHOMA
TOTING	TOURED	TOWERIEST	TOXAEMIC	TRACHOMAS
TOTITIVE	TOURER	TOWERING	TOXAPHENE	TRACHYTE
TOTITIVES	TOURERS	TOWERLESS	TOXAPHENES	TRACHYTES
TOTS	TOURING	TOWERS	TOXIC	TRACHYTIC
TOTTED	TOURINGS	TOWERY	TOXICAL	TRACING
TOTTER	TOURISM	TOWHEE	TOXICALLY	TRACINGS
TOTTERED	TOURISMS	TOWHEES	TOXICANT	TRACK
TOTTERER	TOURIST	TOWING	TOXICANTS	TRACKAGE
TOTTERERS	TOURISTIC	TOWINGS	TOXICITIES	TRACKAGES
TOTTERING	TOURISTS	TOWLINE	TOXICITY	TRACKED
TOTTERINGS	TOURISTY	TOWLINES	TOXIN	TRACKER
TOTTERS	TOURNEDOS	TOWMON	TOXINS	TRACKERS
TOTTERY	TOURNEY	TOWMOND	TOXOCARA	TRACKING

TRACKINGS	TRAGI	TRAMPLINGS	TRANSFUSES	TRANSUMPTS
TRACKLESS	TRAGIC	TRAMPOLIN	TRANSFUSING	TRANSVEST
TRACKMAN	TRAGICAL	TRAMPOLINS	TRANSHIP	TRANSVESTED
TRACKMEN	TRAGOPAN	TRAMPS	TRANSHIPPED	TRANSVESTING
TRACKROAD	TRAGOPANS	TRAMS	TRANSHIPPING	TRANSVESTS
TRACKROADS	TRAGULE	TRAMWAY	TRANSHIPPINGS	TRANT
TRACKS	TRAGULES	TRAMWAYS	TRANSHIPS	TRANTED
TRACKWAY	TRAGULINE	TRANCE	TRANSHUME	TRANTER
TRACKWAYS	TRAGUS	TRANCED	TRANSHUMED	TRANTERS
TRACT	TRAHISON	TRANCEDLY	TRANSHUMES	TRANTING
TRACTABLE	TRAHISONS	TRANCES	TRANSHUMING	TRANTS
TRACTATE	TRAIK	TRANCHE	TRANSIENT	TRAP
TRACTATES	TRAIKED	TRANCHES	TRANSIENTS	TRAPAN
TRACTATOR	TRAIKING	TRANCHET	TRANSIRE	TRAPANNED
TRACTATORS	TRAIKIT	TRANCHETS	TRANSIRES	TRAPANNING
TRACTED	TRAIKS	TRANCING	TRANSIT	TRAPANS
TRACTILE	TRAIL	TRANECT	TRANSITS	TRAPE
TRACTING	TRAILED	TRANECTS	TRANSITTED	TRAPED
TRACTION	TRAILER	TRANGAM	TRANSITTING	TRAPES
TRACTIONS	TRAILERED	TRANGAMS	TRANSLATE	TRAPESED
TRACTIVE	TRAILERING	TRANGLE	TRANSLATED	TRAPESES
TRACTOR	TRAILERS	TRANGLES	TRANSLATES	TRAPESING
TRACTORS	TRAILING	TRANKUM	TRANSLATING	TRAPESINGS
TRACTRIX	TRAILS	TRANKUMS	TRANSMEW	TRAPEZE
TRACTRIXES	TRAIN	TRANNIE	TRANSMEWED	TRAPEZED
TRACTS	TRAINABLE	TRANNIES	TRANSMEWING	TRAPEZES
TRACTUS	TRAINED	TRANNY	TRANSMEWS	TRAPEZIA
TRACTUSES	TRAINEE	TRANQUIL	TRANSMIT	TRAPEZIAL
TRAD	TRAINEES	TRANQUILLER	TRANSMITS	TRAPEZING
TRADABLE	TRAINER	TRANQUILLEST	TRANSMITTED	TRAPEZIUM
TRADE	TRAINERS	TRANSACT	TRANSMITTING	TRAPEZIUMS
TRADEABLE	TRAINING	TRANSACTED	TRANSMOVE	TRAPEZIUS
TRADED	TRAININGS	TRANSACTING	TRANSMOVED	TRAPEZIUSES
TRADEFUL	TRAINS	TRANSACTS	TRANSMOVES	TRAPEZOID
TRADELESS	TRAIPSE	TRANSAXLE	TRANSMOVING	TRAPEZOIDS
TRADEMARK	TRAIPSED	TRANSAXLES	TRANSMUTE	TRAPING
TRADEMARKS	TRAIPSES	TRANSCEND	TRANSMUTED	TRAPPEAN
TRADENAME	TRAIPSING	TRANSCENDED	TRANSMUTES	TRAPPED
TRADENAMES	TRAIPSINGS	TRANSCENDING	TRANSMUTING	TRAPPER
TRADER	TRAIT	TRANSCENDS	TRANSOM	TRAPPERS
TRADERS	TRAITOR	TRANSE	TRANSOMS	TRAPPIER
TRADES	TRAITORLY	TRANSECT	TRANSONIC	TRAPPIEST
TRADESMAN	TRAITORS	TRANSECTED	TRANSONICS	TRAPPING
TRADESMEN	TRAITRESS	TRANSECTING	TRANSPIRE	TRAPPINGS
TRADING	TRAITRESSES	TRANSECTS	TRANSPIRED	TRAPPY
TRADINGS	TRAITS	TRANSENNA	TRANSPIRES	TRAPS
TRADITION	TRAJECT	TRANSENNAS	TRANSPIRING	TRAPUNTO
TRADITIONS	TRAJECTED	TRANSEPT	TRANSPORT	TRAPUNTOS
TRADITIVE	TRAJECTING	TRANSEPTS	TRANSPORTED	TRASH
TRADITOR	TRAJECTS	TRANSES	TRANSPORTING	TRASHED
TRADITORS	TRAM	TRANSFARD	TRANSPORTINGS	TRASHERIES
TRADS	TRAMMEL	TRANSFECT	TRANSPORTS	TRASHERY
TRADUCE	TRAMMELLED	TRANSFECTED	TRANSPOSE	TRASHES
TRADUCED	TRAMMELLING	TRANSFECTING	TRANSPOSED	TRASHIER
TRADUCER	TRAMMELS	TRANSFECTS	TRANSPOSES	TRASHIEST
TRADUCERS	TRAMP	TRANSFER	TRANSPOSING	TRASHILY
TRADUCES	TRAMPED	TRANSFERRED	TRANSPOSINGS	TRASHING
TRADUCING	TRAMPER	TRANSFERRING	TRANSSHIP	TRASHTRIE
TRADUCINGS	TRAMPERS	TRANSFERS	TRANSSHIPPED	TRASHTRIES
TRAFFIC	TRAMPET	TRANSFIX	TRANSSHIPPING	TRASHY
TRAFFICKED	TRAMPETS	TRANSFIXED	TRANSSHIPS	TRASS
TRAFFICKING	TRAMPETTE	TRANSFIXES	TRANSUDE	TRASSES
TRAFFICKINGS	TRAMPETTES	TRANSFIXING	TRANSUDED	TRATTORIA
TRAFFICS	TRAMPING	TRANSFORM	TRANSUDES	TRATTORIAS
TRAGEDIAN	TRAMPLE	TRANSFORMED	TRANSUDING	TRATTORIE
TRAGEDIANS	TRAMPLED	TRANSFORMING	TRANSUME	TRAUCHLE
TRAGEDIES	TRAMPLER	TRANSFORMINGS	TRANSUMED	TRAUCHLED
TRAGEDY	TRAMPLERS	TRANSFORMS	TRANSUMES	TRAUCHLES
TRAGELAPH	TRAMPLES	TRANSFUSE	TRANSUMING	TRAUCHLING
TRAGELAPHS	TRAMPLING	TRANSFUSED	TRANSUMPT	TRAUMA

TRAUMAS	TREADLER	TREFOIL	TRENCHES	TRIABLE
TRAUMATA	TREADLERS	TREFOILED	TRENCHING	TRIACID
TRAUMATIC	TREADLES	TREFOILS	TREND	TRIACT
TRAVAIL	TREADLING	TREGETOUR	TRENDED	TRIACTINE
TRAVAILED	TREADLINGS	TREGETOURS	TRENDIER	TRIAD
TRAVAILING	TREADMILL	TREHALA	TRENDIES	TRIADIC
TRAVAILS	TREADMILLS	TREHALAS	TRENDIEST	TRIADIST
TRAVE	TREADS	TREILLAGE	TRENDING	TRIADISTS
TRAVEL	TREAGUE	TREILLAGES	TRENDS	TRIADS
TRAVELLED	TREAGUES	TREILLE	TRENDY	TRIAGE
TRAVELLER	TREASON	TREILLES	TRENISE	TRIAGES
TRAVELLERS	TREASONS	TREK	TRENISES	TRIAL
TRAVELLING	TREASURE	TREKKED	TRENTAL	TRIALISM
TRAVELLINGS	TREASURED	TREKKER	TRENTALS	TRIALISMS
TRAVELS	TREASURER	TREKKERS	TREPAN	TRIALIST
TRAVERSAL	TREASURERS	TREKKING	TREPANG	TRIALISTS
TRAVERSALS	TREASURES	TREKS	TREPANGS	TRIALITIES
TRAVERSE	TREASURIES	TREKSHUIT	TREPANNED	TRIALITY
TRAVERSED	TREASURING	TREKSHUITS	TREPANNER	TRIALLIST
TRAVERSER	TREASURY	TRELLIS	TREPANNERS	TRIALLISTS
TRAVERSERS	TREAT	TRELLISED	TREPANNING	TRIALOGUE
TRAVERSES	TREATABLE	TRELLISES	TREPANNINGS	TRIALOGUES
TRAVERSING	TREATED	TRELLISING	TREPANS	TRIALS
TRAVERSINGS	TREATER	TREMA	TREPHINE	TRIANGLE
TRAVERTIN	TREATERS	TREMAS	TREPHINED	TRIANGLED
TRAVES	TREATIES	TREMATIC	TREPHINES	TRIANGLES
TRAVESTIED	TREATING	TREMATODE	TREPHINING	TRIAPSAL
TRAVESTIES	TREATINGS	TREMATODES	TREPID	TRIARCH
TRAVESTY	TREATISE	TREMATOID	TREPIDANT	TRIARCHIES
TRAVESTYING	TREATISES	TREMATOIDS	TREPIDER	TRIARCHS
TRAVIS	TREATMENT	TREMBLANT	TREPIDEST	TRIARCHY
TRAVISES	TREATMENTS	TREMBLE	TREPONEMA	TRIATHLON
TRAVOIS	TREATS	TREMBLED	TREPONEMAS	TRIATHLONS
TRAWL	TREATY	TREMBLER	TREPONEMATA	TRIATIC
TRAWLED	TREBLE	TREMBLERS	TRESPASS	TRIATICS
TRAWLER	TREBLED	TREMBLES	TRESPASSED	TRIATOMIC
TRAWLERS	TREBLES	TREMBLIER	TRESPASSES	TRIAXIAL
TRAWLING	TREBLING	TREMBLIEST	TRESPASSING	TRIAXIALS
TRAWLINGS	TREBLY	TREMBLING	TRESS	TRIAXON
TRAWLS	TREBUCHET	TREMBLINGS	TRESSED	TRIAXONS
TRAY	TREBUCHETS	TREMBLY	TRESSEL	TRIBADE
TRAYBIT	TRECENTO	TRÉMIE	TRESSELS	TRIBADES
TRAYBITS	TRECENTOS	TREMIE	TRESSES	TRIBADIC
TRAYFUL	TRECK	TREMIES	TRESSIER	TRIBADIES
TRAYFULS	TRECKED	TRÉMIES	TRESSIEST	TRIBADISM
TRAYNE	TRECKING	TREMOLANT	TRESSING	TRIBADISMS
TRAYNED	TRECKS	TREMOLANTS	TRESSURE	TRIBADY
TRAYNES	TREDDLE	TREMOLITE	TRESSURED	TRIBAL
TRAYNING	TREDDLED	TREMOLITES	TRESSURES	TRIBALISM
TRAYS	TREDDLES	TREMOLO	TRESSY	TRIBALISMS
TREACHER	TREDDLING	TREMOLOS	TRESTLE	TRIBALIST
TREACHERIES	TREDILLE	TREMOR	TRESTLES	TRIBALISTS
TREACHERS	TREDILLES	TREMORS	TRET	TRIBALLY
TREACHERY	TREDRILLE	TREMULANT	TRETS	TRIBASIC
TREACHOUR	TREDRILLES	TREMULANTS	TREVALLIES	TRIBBLE
TREACHOURS	TREE	TREMULATE	TREVALLY	TRIBBLES
TREACLE	TREED	TREMULATED	TREVIS	TRIBE
TREACLED	TREEING	TREMULATES	TREVISES	TRIBELESS
TREACLES	TREELESS	TREMULATING	TREVISS	TRIBES
TREACLIER	TREEN	TREMULOUS	TREVISSES	TRIBESMAN
TREACLIEST	TREENAIL	TRENAIL	TREW	TRIBESMEN
TREACLING	TREENAILS	TRENAILS	TREWS	TRIBLET
TREACLY	TREENS	TRENCH	TREWSMAN	TRIBLETS
TREAD	TREES	TRENCHAND	TREWSMEN	TRIBOLOGIES
TREADER	TREESHIP	TRENCHANT	TREY	TRIBOLOGY
TREADERS	TREESHIPS	TRENCHARD	TREYBIT	TRIBRACH
TREADING	TREETOP	TRENCHARDS	TREYBITS	TRIBRACHS
TREADINGS	TREETOPS	TRENCHED	TREYS	TRIBUNAL
TREADLE	TREF	TRENCHER	TREZ	TRIBUNALS
TREADLED	TREFA	TRENCHERS	TREZES	TRIBUNATE

TRIBUNATES	TRICORN	TRIGAMY	TRIMARAN	TRIPEMAN
TRIBUNE	TRICORNE	TRIGGED	TRIMARANS	TRIPEMEN
TRIBUNES	TRICORNES	TRIGGER	TRIMER	TRIPERIES
TRIBUTARIES	TRICORNS	TRIGGERED	TRIMERIC	TRIPERY
TRIBUTARY	TRICOT	TRIGGERING	TRIMEROUS	TRIPES
TRIBUTE	TRICOTS	TRIGGERS	TRIMERS	TRIPEWIFE
TRIBUTER	TRICROTIC	TRIGGEST	TRIMESTER	TRIPEWIVES
TRIBUTERS	TRICUSPID	TRIGGING	TRIMESTERS	TRIPHONE
TRIBUTES	TRICYCLE	TRIGLOT	TRIMETER	TRIPHONES
TRICAR	TRICYCLED	TRIGLOTS	TRIMETERS	TRIPITAKA
TRICARS	TRICYCLER	TRIGLY	TRIMETHYL	TRIPLANE
TRICE	TRICYCLERS	TRIGLYPH	TRIMETRIC	TRIPLANES
TRICED	TRICYCLES	TRIGLYPHS	TRIMLY	TRIPLE
TRICEPS	TRICYCLIC	TRIGNESS	TRIMMED	TRIPLED
TRICEPSES	TRICYCLING	TRIGNESSES	TRIMMER	TRIPLES
TRICERION	TRICYCLINGS	TRIGON	TRIMMERS	TRIPLET
TRICERIONS	TRIDACNA	TRIGONAL	TRIMMEST	TRIPLETS
TRICES	TRIDACNAS	TRIGONIC	TRIMMING	TRIPLEX
TRICHINA	TRIDACTYL	TRIGONOUS	TRIMMINGS	TRIPLEXES
TRICHINAE	TRIDARN	TRIGONS	TRIMNESS	TRIPLIED
TRICHINAS	TRIDARNS	TRIGRAM	TRIMNESSES	TRIPLIES
TRICHITE	TRIDE	TRIGRAMS	TRIMS	TRIPLING
TRICHITES	TRIDENT	TRIGRAPH	TRIN	TRIPLINGS
TRICHITIC	TRIDENTAL	TRIGRAPHS	TRINAL	TRIPLOID
TRICHOID	TRIDENTED	TRIGS	TRINARY	TRIPLOIDIES
TRICHOME	TRIDENTS	TRIGYNIAN	TRINDLE	TRIPLOIDY
TRICHOMES	TRIDUAN	TRIGYNOUS	TRINDLED	TRIPLY
TRICHORD	TRIDUUM	TRIHEDRAL	TRINDLES	TRIPLYING
TRICHORDS	TRIDUUMS	TRIHEDRALS	TRINDLING	TRIPOD
TRICHOSES	TRIDYMITE	TRIHEDRON	TRINE	TRIPODAL
TRICHOSIS	TRIDYMITES	TRIHEDRONS	TRINED	TRIPODIES
TRICHROIC	TRIE	TRIHYBRID	TRINES	TRIPODS
TRICHROME	TRIECIOUS	TRIHYBRIDS	TRINGLE	TRIPODY
TRICING	TRIED	TRIHYDRIC	TRINGLES	TRIPOLI
TRICK	TRIENNIAL	TRIKE	TRINING	TRIPOLIS
TRICKED	TRIER	TRIKED	TRINITIES	TRIPOS
TRICKER	TRIERARCH	TRIKES	TRINITRIN	TRIPOSES
TRICKERIES	TRIERARCHS	TRIKING	TRINITRINS	TRIPPANT
TRICKERS	TRIERS	TRILBIES	TRINITY	TRIPPED
TRICKERY	TRIES	TRILBY	TRINKET	TRIPPER
TRICKIER	TRIETERIC	TRILBYS	TRINKETED	TRIPPERS
TRICKIEST	TRIETHYL	TRILD	TRINKETER	TRIPPERY
TRICKILY	TRIFACIAL	TRILEMMA	TRINKETERS	TRIPPET
TRICKING	TRIFECTA	TRILEMMAS	TRINKETING	TRIPPETS
TRICKINGS	TRIFECTAS	TRILINEAR	TRINKETINGS	TRIPPING
TRICKISH	TRIFFID	TRILITH	TRINKETRIES	TRIPPINGS
TRICKLE	TRIFFIDS	TRILITHIC	TRINKETRY	TRIPPLE
TRICKLED	TRIFFIDY	TRILITHON	TRINKETS	TRIPPLED
TRICKLES	TRIFID	TRILITHONS	TRINKUM	TRIPPLER
TRICKLESS	TRIFLE	TRILITHS	TRINKUMS	TRIPPLERS
TRICKLET	TRIFLED	TRILL	TRINOMIAL	TRIPPLES
TRICKLETS	TRIFLER	TRILLED	TRINOMIALS	TRIPPLING
TRICKLIER	TRIFLERS	TRILLING	TRINS	TRIPS
TRICKLIEST	TRIFLES	TRILLINGS	TRIO	TRIPSES
TRICKLING	TRIFLING	TRILLION	TRIODE	TRIPSIS
TRICKLINGS	TRIFOCAL	TRILLIONS	TRIODES	TRIPTANE
TRICKLY	TRIFOCALS	TRILLIUM	TRIOLET	TRIPTANES
TRICKS	TRIFOLIES	TRILLIUMS	TRIOLETS	TRIPTOTE
TRICKSIER	TRIFOLIUM	TRILLO	TRIONES	TRIPTOTES
TRICKSIEST	TRIFOLIUMS	TRILLOES	TRIONYM	TRIPTYCH
TRICKSOME	TRIFOLY	TRILLS	TRIONYMAL	TRIPTYCHS
TRICKSTER	TRIFORIA	TRILOBATE	TRIONYMS	TRIPTYQUE
TRICKSTERS	TRIFORIUM	TRILOBE	TRIOR	TRIPTYQUES
TRICKSY	TRIFORM	TRILOBED	TRIORS	TRIPUDIUM
TRICKY	TRIFORMED	TRILOBES	TRIOS	TRIPUDIUMS
TRICLINIC	TRIG	TRILOBITE	TRIOXIDE	TRIQUETRA
TRICOLOR	TRIGAMIES	TRILOBITES	TRIOXIDES	TRIQUETRAS
TRICOLORS	TRIGAMIST	TRILOGIES	TRIP	TRIRADIAL
TRICOLOUR	TRIGAMISTS	TRILOGY	TRIPE	TRIREME
TRICOLOURS	TRIGAMOUS	TRIM	TRIPEDAL	TRIREMES

TRISAGION	TRIUMPHERS	TROG	TROPED	TROUPING
TRISAGIONS	TRIUMPHING	TROGGED	TROPES	TROUSE
TRISECT	TRIUMPHINGS	TROGGING	TROPHESIES	TROUSERED
TRISECTED	TRIUMPHS	TROGGS	TROPHESY	TROUSERS
TRISECTING	TRIUMVIR	TROGGSES	TROPHI	TROUSES
TRISECTOR	TRIUMVIRI	TROGON	TROPHIC	TROUSSEAU
TRISECTORS	TRIUMVIRIES	TROGONS	TROPHIED	TROUSSEAUS
TRISECTS	TRIUMVIRS	TROGS	TROPHIES	TROUSSEAUX
TRISEME	TRIUMVIRY	TROIKA	TROPHY	TROUT
TRISEMES	TRIUNE	TROIKAS	TROPHYING	TROUTER
TRISEMIC	TRIUNES	TROILISM	TROPIC	TROUTERS
TRISHAW	TRIUNITIES	TROILISMS	TROPICAL	TROUTFUL
TRISHAWS	TRIUNITY	TROILIST	TROPICS	TROUTIER
TRISKELE	TRIVALENT	TROILISTS	TROPING	TROUTIEST
TRISKELES	TRIVALVE	TROILITE	TROPISM	TROUTING
TRISKELIA	TRIVALVED	TROILITES	TROPISMS	TROUTINGS
TRISMUS	TRIVALVES	TROKE	TROPIST	TROUTLESS
TRISMUSES	TRIVET	TROKED	TROPISTIC	TROUTLET
TRISOME	TRIVETS	TROKES	TROPISTS	TROUTLETS
TRISOMES	TRIVIA	TROKING	TROPOLOGIES	TROUTLING
TRISOMIC	TRIVIAL	TROLL	TROPOLOGY	TROUTLINGS
TRISOMIES	TRIVIALLY	TROLLED	TROPPO	TROUTS
TRISOMY	TRIVIUM	TROLLER	TROSSERS	TROUTY
TRIST	TRIVIUMS	TROLLERS	TROT	TROUVÈRE
TRISTE	TRIZONAL	TROLLEY	TROTH	TROUVÈRES
TRISTFUL	TRIZONE	TROLLEYS	TROTHED	TROUVEUR
TRISTICH	TRIZONES	TROLLIES	TROTHFUL	TROUVEURS
TRISTICHS	TROAD	TROLLING	TROTHING	TROVER
TRISUL	TROADE	TROLLINGS	TROTHLESS	TROVERS
TRISULA	TROADES	TROLLOP	TROTHS	TROW
TRISULAS	TROADS	TROLLOPED	TROTLINE	TROWED
TRISULS	TROAT	TROLLOPEE	TROTLINES	TROWEL
TRITE	TROATED	TROLLOPEES	TROTS	TROWELLED
TRITELY	TROATING	TROLLOPING	TROTTED	TROWELLER
TRITENESS	TROATS	TROLLOPS	TROTTER	TROWELLERS
TRITENESSES	TROCAR	TROLLOPY	TROTTERS	TROWELLING
TRITER	TROCARS	TROLLS	TROTTING	TROWELS
TRITES	TROCHAIC	TROLLY	TROTTINGS	TROWING
TRITEST	TROCHAL	TROMBONE	TROTTOIR	TROWS
TRITHEISM	TROCHE	TROMBONES	TROTTOIRS	TROWSERS
TRITHEISMS	TROCHEE	TROMINO	TROTYL	TROY
TRITHEIST	TROCHEES	TROMINOES	TROTYLS	TROYS
TRITHEISTS	TROCHES	TROMINOS	TROUBLE	TRUANCIES
TRITIATE	TROCHI	TROMMEL	TROUBLED	TRUANCY
TRITIATED	TROCHILIC	TROMMELS	TROUBLER	TRUANT
TRITIATES	TROCHILUS	TROMP	TROUBLERS	TRUANTED
TRITIATING	TROCHILUSES	TROMPE	TROUBLES	TRUANTING
TRITICAL	TROCHISK	TROMPES	TROUBLING	TRUANTRIES
TRITICALE	TROCHISKS	TROMPS	TROUBLINGS	TRUANTRY
TRITICALES	TROCHITE	TRON	TROUBLOUS	TRUANTS
TRITICISM	TROCHITES	TRONA	TROUGH	TRUCAGE
TRITICISMS	TROCHLEA	TRONAS	TROUGHS	TRUCAGES
TRITIDE	TROCHLEAR	TRONC	TROULE	TRUCE
TRITIDES	TROCHLEAS	TRONCS	TROULED	TRUCELESS
TRITIUM	TROCHOID	TRONE	TROULES	TRUCES
TRITIUMS	TROCHOIDS	TRONES	TROULING	TRUCHMAN
TRITON	TROCHUS	TRONS	TROUNCE	TRUCHMANS
TRITONE	TROCHUSES	TROOLIE	TROUNCED	TRUCHMEN
TRITONES	TROCK	TROOLIES	TROUNCER	TRUCIAL
TRITONIA	TROCKED	TROOP	TROUNCERS	TRUCK
TRITONIAS	TROCKING	TROOPED	TROUNCES	TRUCKAGE
TRITONS	TROCKS	TROOPER	TROUNCING	TRUCKAGES
TRITURATE	TROD	TROOPERS	TROUNCINGS	TRUCKED
TRITURATED	TRODDEN	TROOPIAL	TROUPE	TRUCKER
TRITURATES	TRODE	TROOPIALS	TROUPED	TRUCKERS
TRITURATING	TRODES	TROOPING	TROUPER	TRUCKING
TRIUMPH	TRODS	TROOPS	TROUPERS	TRUCKINGS
TRIUMPHAL	TROELIE	TROPARIA	TROUPES	TRUCKLE
TRIUMPHED	TROELIES	TROPARION	TROUPIAL	TRUCKLED
TRIUMPHER	TROELY	TROPE	TROUPIALS	TRUCKLER

TRUCKLERS	TRUNDLES	TSADDIQS	TUBERCLED	TUG
TRUCKLES	TRUNDLING	TSAMBA	TUBERCLES	TUGGED
TRUCKLING	TRUNK	TSAMBAS	TUBERCULE	TUGGER
TRUCKLINGS	TRUNKED	TSAR	TUBERCULES	TUGGERS
TRUCKMAN	TRUNKFISH	TSARDOM	TUBEROSE	TUGGING
TRUCKMEN	TRUNKFISHES	TSARDOMS	TUBEROUS	TUGGINGLY
TRUCKS	TRUNKFUL	TSAREVICH	TUBERS	TUGGINGS
TRUCULENT	TRUNKFULS	TSAREVICHES	TUBES	TUGRIK
TRUDGE	TRUNKING	TSAREVNA	TUBFAST	TUGRIKS
TRUDGED	TRUNKINGS	TSAREVNAS	TUBFASTS	TUGS
TRUDGEN	TRUNKS	TSARINA	TUBFISH	TUI
TRUDGENS	TRUNNION	TSARINAS	TUBFISHES	TUILLE
TRUDGEON	TRUNNIONS	TSARISM	TUBFUL	TUILLES
TRUDGEONS	TRUQUAGE	TSARISMS	TUBFULS	TUILLETTE
TRUDGER	TRUQUAGES	TSARIST	TUBICOLAR	TUILLETTES
TRUDGERS	TRUQUEUR	TSARISTS	TUBICOLE	TUILYIE
TRUDGES	TRUQUEURS	TSARITSA	TUBICOLES	TUILYIED
TRUDGING	TRUSS	TSARITSAS	TUBIFORM	TUILYIEING
TRUDGINGS	TRUSSED	TSARS	TUBING	TUILYIES
TRUE	TRUSSER	TSESSEBE	TUBINGS	TUILZIE
TRUED	TRUSSERS	TSESSEBES	TUBS	TUILZIED
TRUEING	TRUSSES	TSETSE	TUBULAR	TUILZIEING
TRUEMAN	TRUSSING	TSETSES	TUBULATE	TUILZIES
TRUEMEN	TRUSSINGS	TSIGANE	TUBULATED	TUIS
TRUENESS	TRUST	TSIGANES	TUBULATES	TUISM
TRUENESSES	TRUSTED	TSOTSI	TUBULATING	TUISMS
TRUEPENNIES	TRUSTEE	TSOTSIS	TUBULE	TUITION
TRUEPENNY	TRUSTEES	TSUBA	TUBULES	TUITIONAL
TRUER	TRUSTER	TSUBAS	TUBULOUS	TUITIONS
TRUES	TRUSTERS	TSUNAMI	TUCHUN	TULAREMIA
TRUEST	TRUSTFUL	TSUNAMIS	TUCHUNS	TULAREMIAS
TRUFFLE	TRUSTIER	TUAN	TUCK	TULAREMIC
TRUFFLED	TRUSTIES	TUANS	TUCKAHOE	TULBAN
TRUFFLES	TRUSTIEST	TUART	TUCKAHOES	TULBANS
TRUG	TRUSTILY	TUARTS	TUCKED	TULCHAN
TRUGS	TRUSTING	TUATARA	TUCKER	TULCHANS
TRUING	TRUSTLESS	TUATARAS	TUCKERBAG	TULE
TRUISM	TRUSTS	TUATERA	TUCKERBAGS	TULES
TRUISMS	TRUSTY	TUATERAS	TUCKERBOX	TULIP
TRUISTIC	TRUTH	TUATH	TUCKERBOXES	TULIPANT
TRULL	TRUTHFUL	TUATHS	TUCKERED	TULIPANTS
TRULLS	TRUTHLESS	TUB	TUCKERING	TULIPS
TRULY	TRUTHLIKE	TUBA	TUCKERS	TULLE
TRUMEAU	TRUTHS	TUBAE	TUCKET	TULLES
TRUMEAUX	TRUTHY	TUBAGE	TUCKETS	TULWAR
TRUIMP	TRY	TUBAGES	TUCKING	TULWARS
TRUMPED	TRYE	TUBAL	TUCKS	TUM
TRUMPERIES	TRYER	TUBAR	TUCOTUCO	TUMBLE
TRUMPERY	TRYERS	TUBAS	TUCOTUCOS	TUMBLED
TRUMPET	TRYING	TUBATE	TUCUTUCO	TUMBLER
TRUMPETED	TRYINGLY	TUBBED	TUCUTUCOS	TUMBLERS
TRUMPETER	TRYINGS	TUBBER	TUFA	TUMBLES
TRUMPETERS	TRYP	TUBBERS	TUFACEOUS	TUMBLING
TRUMPETING	TRYPS	TUBBIER	TUFAS	TUMBLINGS
TRUMPETINGS	TRYPSIN	TUBBIEST	TUFF	TUMBREL
TRUMPETS	TRYPSINS	TUBBINESS	TUFFE	TUMBRELS
TRUMPING	TRYPTIC	TUBBINESSES	TUFFES	TUMBRIL
TRUMPINGS	TRYSAIL	TUBBING	TUFFET	TUMBRILS
TRUMPS	TRYSAILS	TUBBINGS	TUFFETS	TUMEFIED
TRUNCAL	TRYST	TUBBISH	TUFFS	TUMEFIES
TRUNCATE	TRYSTED	TUBBY	TUFT	TUMEFY
TRUNCATED	TRYSTER	TUBE	TUFTED	TUMEFYING
TRUNCATES	TRYSTERS	TUBECTOMIES	TUFTER	TUMESCE
TRUNCATING	TRYSTING	TUBECTOMY	TUFTERS	TUMESCED
TRUNCHEON	TRYSTS	TUBED	TUFTIER	TUMESCENT
TRUNCHEONED	TSADDIK	TUBEFUL	TUFTIEST	TUMESCES
TRUNCHEONING	TSADDIKIM	TUBEFULS	TUFTING	TUMESCING
TRUNCHEONS	TSADDIKS	TUBELESS	TUFTINGS	TUMID
TRUNDLE	TSADDIQ	TUBER	TUFTS	TUMIDITIES
TRUNDLED	TSADDIQIM	TUBERCLE	TUFTY	TUMIDITY

TUMIDLY	TUNNAGE	TURBOPROPS	TURNDUNS	TUSKIEST
TUMIDNESS	TUNNAGES	TURBOS	TURNED	TUSKING
TUMIDNESSES	TUNNED	TURBOT	TURNER	TUSKLESS
TUMMIES	TUNNEL	TURBOTS	TURNERIES	TUSKS
TUMMY	TUNNELLED	TURBULENT	TURNERS	TUSKY
TUMOR	TUNNELLER	TURCOPOLE	TURNERY	TUSSAH
TUMOROUS	TUNNELLERS	TURCOPOLES	TURNING	TUSSAHS
TUMORS	TUNNELLING	TURD	TURNINGS	TUSSAL
TUMOUR	TUNNELLINGS	TURDINE	TURNIP	TUSSEH
TUMOURS	TUNNELS	TURDION	TURNIPED	TUSSEHS
TUMP	TUNNIES	TURDIONS	TURNIPING	TUSSER
TUMPED	TUNNING	TURDOID	TURNIPS	TUSSERS
TUMPHIES	TUNNINGS	TURDS	TURNKEY	TUSSIS
TUMPHY	TUNNY	TUREEN	TURNKEYS	TUSSISES
TUMPING	TUNS	TUREENS	TURNOFF	TUSSIVE
TUMPS	TUNY	TURF	TURNOFFS	TUSSLE
TUMPY	TUP	TURFED	TURNOVER	TUSSLED
TUMS	TUPEK	TURFEN	TURNOVERS	TUSSLES
TUMULAR	TUPEKS	TURFIER	TURNPIKE	TUSSLING
TUMULARY	TUPELO	TURFIEST	TURNPIKES	TUSSOCK
TUMULI	TUPELOS	TURFINESS	TURNROUND	TUSSOCKS
TUMULT	TUPIK	TURFINESSES	TURNROUNDS	TUSSOCKY
TUMULTED	TUPIKS	TURFING	TURNS	TUSSORE
TUMULTING	TUPPED	TURFINGS	TURNSKIN	TUSSORES
TUMULTS	TUPPENCE	TURFITE	TURNSKINS	TUT
TUMULUS	TUPPENCES	TURFITES	TURNSOLE	TUTANIA
TUN	TUPPENNIES	TURFMAN	TURNSOLES	TUTANIAS
TUNA	TUPPENNY	TURFMEN	TURNSPIT	TUTEE
TUNABLE	TUPPING	TURFS	TURNSPITS	TUTEES
TUNABLY	TUPS	TURFY	TURNSTILE	TUTELAGE
TUNAS	TUPTOWING	TURGENT	TURNSTILES	TUTELAGES
TUNBELLIES	TUQUE	TURGENTLY	TURNSTONE	TUTELAR
TUNBELLY	TUQUES	TURGID	TURNSTONES	TUTELARIES
TUND	TURACIN	TURGIDITIES	TURNTABLE	TUTELARS
TUNDED	TURACINS	TURGIDITY	TURNTABLES	TUTELARY
TUNDING	TURACO	TURGIDLY	TURPETH	TUTENAG
TUNDRA	TURACOS	TURGOR	TURPETHS	TUTENAGS
TUNDRAS	TURBAN	TURGORS	TURPITUDE	TUTIORISM
TUNDS	TURBAND	TURION	TURPITUDES	TUTIORIST
TUNDUN	TURBANDS	TURIONS	TURPS	TUTIORISTS
TUNDUNS	TURBANED	TURKEY	TURQUOISE	TUTMAN
TUNE	TURBANS	TURKEYS	TURQUOISES	TUTMEN
TUNEABLE	TURBANT	TURKIES	TURRET	TUTOR
TUNED	TURBANTS	TURKIESES	TURRETED	TUTORAGE
TUNEFUL	TURBARIES	TURKIS	TURRETS	TUTORAGES
TUNEFULLY	TURBARY	TURKISES	TURRIBANT	TUTORED
TUNELESS	TURBID	TURLOUGH	TURRIBANTS	TUTORESS
TUNER	TURBIDITE	TURLOUGHS	TURTLE	TUTORESSES
TUNERS	TURBIDITES	TURM	TURTLED	TUTORIAL
TUNES	TURBIDITIES	TURME	TURTLER	TUTORIALS
TUNESMITH	TURBIDITY	TURMERIC	TURTLERS	TUTORING
TUNESMITHS	TURBIDLY	TURMERICS	TURTLES	TUTORINGS
TUNGSTATE	TURBINAL	TURMES	TURTLING	TUTORISE
TUNGSTATES	TURBINALS	TURMOIL	TURTLINGS	TUTORISED
TUNGSTEN	TURBINATE	TURMOILED	TURVES	TUTORISES
TUNGSTENS	TURBINE	TURMOILING	TUSCHE	TUTORISING
TUNIC	TURBINED	TURMOILS	TUSCHES	TUTORISM
TUNICATE	TURBINES	TURMS	TUSH	TUTORISMS
TUNICATED	TURBIT	TURN	TUSHED	TUTORIZE
TUNICATES	TURBITH	TURNABOUT	TUSHERIES	TUTORIZED
TUNICIN	TURBITHS	TURNABOUTS	TUSHERY	TUTORIZES
TUNICINS	TURBITS	TURNAGAIN	TUSHES	TUTORIZING
TUNICKED	TURBO	TURNAGAINS	TUSHING	TUTORS
TUNICLE	TURBOCAR	TURNBACK	TUSK	TUTORSHIP
TUNICLES	TURBOCARS	TURNBACKS	TUSKAR	TUTORSHIPS
TUNICS	TURBOFAN	TURNCOAT	TUSKARS	TUTRESS
TUNIER	TURBOFANS	TURNCOATS	TUSKED	TUTRESSES
TUNIEST	TURBOND	TURNCOCK	TUSKER	TUTRIX
TUNING	TURBONDS	TURNCOCKS	TUSKERS	TUTRIXES
TUNINGS	TURBOPROP	TURNDUN	TUSKIER	TUTS

TUTSAN
TUTSANS
TUTTED
TUTTI
TUTTIES
TUTTING
TUTTIS
TUTTY
TUTU
TUTUS
TUTWORK
TUTWORKER
TUTWORKERS
TUTWORKS
TUXEDO
TUXEDOES
TUXEDOS
TUYÈRE
TUYÈRES
TUZZ
TUZZES
TWA
TWADDLE
TWADDLED
TWADDLER
TWADDLERS
TWADDLES
TWADDLING
TWADDLINGS
TWADDLY
TWAE
TWAES
TWAFALD
TWAIN
TWAINS
TWAITE
TWAITES
TWAL
TWALHOURS
TWALPENNIES
TWALPENNY
TWALS
TWANG
TWANGED
TWANGIER
TWANGIEST
TWANGING
TWANGINGS
TWANGLE
TWANGLED
TWANGLES
TWANGLING
TWANGLINGS
TWANGS
TWANGY
TWANK
TWANKAY
TWANKAYS
TWANKS
TWAS
TWASOME
TWASOMES
TWAT
TWATS
TWATTLE
TWATTLED
TWATTLER
TWATTLERS
TWATTLES
TWATTLING

TWATTLINGS
TWAY
TWAYS
TWEAK
TWEAKED
TWEAKING
TWEAKS
TWEE
TWEED
TWEEDIER
TWEEDIEST
TWEEDLE
TWEEDLED
TWEEDLES
TWEEDLING
TWEEDS
TWEEDY
TWEEL
TWEELED
TWEELING
TWEELS
TWEELY
TWEENESS
TWEENESSES
TWEENIES
TWEENY
TWEER
TWEERED
TWEERING
TWEERS
TWEEST
TWEET
TWEETED
TWEETER
TWEETERS
TWEETING
TWEETS
TWEEZE
TWEEZED
TWEEZERS
TWEEZES
TWEEZING
TWELFTH
TWELFTHLY
TWELFTHS
TWELVE
TWELVEMO
TWELVEMOS
TWELVES
TWENTIES
TWENTIETH
TWENTIETHS
TWENTY
TWENTYISH
TWERP
TWERPS
TWIBILL
TWIBILLS
TWICE
TWICER
TWICERS
TWICHILD
TWICHILDREN
TWIDDLE
TWIDDLED
TWIDDLER
TWIDDLERS
TWIDDLES
TWIDDLIER
TWIDDLIEST

TWIDDLING
TWIDDLINGS
TWIDDLY
TWIER
TWIERS
TWIFOLD
TWIFORKED
TWIFORMED
TWIG
TWIGGED
TWIGGEN
TWIGGER
TWIGGERS
TWIGGIER
TWIGGIEST
TWIGGING
TWIGGY
TWIGHT
TWIGHTED
TWIGHTING
TWIGHTS
TWIGS
TWIGSOME
TWILIGHT
TWILIGHTED
TWILIGHTING
TWILIGHTS
TWILIT
TWILL
TWILLED
TWILLIES
TWILLING
TWILLS
TWILLY
TWILT
TWILTED
TWILTING
TWILTS
TWIN
TWINE
TWINED
TWINER
TWINERS
TWINES
TWINGE
TWINGED
TWINGES
TWINGING
TWINIER
TWINIEST
TWINING
TWININGLY
TWININGS
TWINK
TWINKED
TWINKING
TWINKLE
TWINKLED
TWINKLER
TWINKLERS
TWINKLES
TWINKLING
TWINKLINGS
TWINKS
TWINLING
TWINLINGS
TWINNED
TWINNING
TWINNINGS
TWINS

TWINSHIP
TWINSHIPS
TWINTER
TWINTERS
TWINY
TWIRE
TWIRED
TWIRES
TWIRING
TWIRL
TWIRLED
TWIRLER
TWIRLERS
TWIRLIER
TWIRLIEST
TWIRLING
TWIRLS
TWIRLY
TWIRP
TWIRPS
TWISCAR
TWISCARS
TWIST
TWISTABLE
TWISTED
TWISTER
TWISTERS
TWISTIER
TWISTIEST
TWISTING
TWISTINGS
TWISTS
TWISTY
TWIT
TWITCH
TWITCHED
TWITCHER
TWITCHERS
TWITCHES
TWITCHIER
TWITCHIEST
TWITCHING
TWITCHINGS
TWITCHY
TWITE
TWITES
TWITS
TWITTED
TWITTEN
TWITTENS
TWITTER
TWITTERED
TWITTERER
TWITTERERS
TWITTERING
TWITTERINGS
TWITTERS
TWITTERY
TWITTING
TWITTINGS
TWIZZLE
TWIZZLED
TWIZZLES
TWIZZLING
TWO
TWOER
TWOERS
TWOFOLD
TWONESS
TWONESSES

TWOPENCE
TWOPENCES
TWOPENNIES
TWOPENNY
TWOS
TWOSEATER
TWOSEATERS
TWOSOME
TWOSOMES
TWOSTROKE
TWYER
TWYERE
TWYERES
TWYERS
TWYFOLD
TWYFORKED
TWYFORMED
TYCHISM
TYCHISMS
TYCOON
TYCOONATE
TYCOONATES
TYCOONERIES
TYCOONERY
TYCOONS
TYDE
TYE
TYED
TYEING
TYES
TYG
TYGS
TYING
TYKE
TYKES
TYKISH
TYLECTOMIES
TYLECTOMY
TYLER
TYLERS
TYLOPOD
TYLOPODS
TYLOSES
TYLOSIS
TYLOTE
TYLOTES
TYMBAL
TYMBALS
TYMP
TYMPAN
TYMPANA
TYMPANAL
TYMPANI
TYMPANIC
TYMPANICS
TYMPANIES
TYMPANIST
TYMPANISTS
TYMPANO
TYMPANS
TYMPANUM
TYMPANY
TYMPS
TYND
TYNDE
TYNE
TYNED
TYNES
TYNING
TYPAL

TYPE
TYPECAST
TYPECASTING
TYPECASTS
TYPED
TYPES
TYPEWRITE
TYPEWRITES
TYPEWRITING
TYPEWRITINGS
TYPEWRITTEN
TYPEWROTE
TYPHLITIC
TYPHLITIS
TYPHLITISES
TYPHOID
TYPHOIDAL
TYPHOIDS
TYPHON
TYPHONIAN
TYPHONIC

TYPHONS
TYPHOON
TYPHOONS
TYPHOUS
TYPHUS
TYPHUSES
TYPIC
TYPICAL
TYPICALLY
TYPIFIED
TYPIFIER
TYPIFIERS
TYPIFIES
TYPIFY
TYPIFYING
TYPING
TYPINGS
TYPIST
TYPISTS
TYPO
TYPOLOGIES

TYPOLOGY
TYPOMANIA
TYPOMANIAS
TYPOS
TYPTO
TYPTOED
TYPTOING
TYPTOS
TYRAMINE
TYRAMINES
TYRAN
TYRANNE
TYRANNED
TYRANNES
TYRANNESS
TYRANNESSES
TYRANNIC
TYRANNIES
TYRANNING
TYRANNIS
TYRANNISE

TYRANNISED
TYRANNISES
TYRANNISING
TYRANNIZE
TYRANNIZED
TYRANNIZES
TYRANNIZING
TYRANNOUS
TYRANNY
TYRANS
TYRANT
TYRANTED
TYRANTING
TYRANTS
TYRE
TYRED
TYRELESS
TYRES
TYRO
TYROES
TYRONES

TYROSINE
TYROSINES
TYSTIE
TYSTIES
TYTE
TYTHE
TYTHED
TYTHES
TYTHING
TZADDIK
TZADDIKIM
TZADDIKS
TZADDIQ
TZADDIQIM
TZADDIQS
TZAR
TZARS
TZIGANIES
TZIGANY
TZIMMES

U

UAKARI
UAKARIS
UBEROUS
UBERTIES
UBERTY
UBIETIES
UBIETY
UBIQUE
UBIQUITIES
UBIQUITY
UDAL
UDALLER
UDALLERS
UDALS
UDDER
UDDERED
UDDERFUL
UDDERLESS
UDDERS
UDO
UDOMETER
UDOMETERS
UDOMETRIC
UDOS
UDS
UEY
UEYS
UFO
UFOLOGIES
UFOLOGIST
UFOLOGISTS
UFOLOGY
UFOS
UG
UGGED
UGGING
UGH
UGHS
UGLI
UGLIED
UGLIER
UGLIES
UGLIEST
UGLIFIED
UGLIFIES
UGLIFY
UGLIFYING
UGLILY
UGLINESS
UGLINESSES
UGLIS
UGLY
UGLYING
UGS
UGSOME
UHLAN
UHLANS
UHURU
UHURUS
UINTAHITE
UINTAHITES
UINTAITE
UINTAITES
UITLANDER

UITLANDERS
UKASE
UKASES
UKELELE
UKELELES
UKULELE
UKULELES
ULCER
ULCERATE
ULCERATED
ULCERATES
ULCERATING
ULCERED
ULCERING
ULCEROUS
ULCERS
ULE
ULEMA
ULEMAS
ULES
ULEX
ULEXES
ULICHON
ULICHONS
ULICON
ULICONS
ULIGINOUS
ULIKON
ULIKONS
ULITIS
ULITISES
ULLAGE
ULLAGED
ULLAGES
ULLAGING
ULLING
ULLINGS
ULMACEOUS
ULMIN
ULMING
ULNA
ULNAE
ULNAR
ULNARE
ULNARIA
ULOSES
ULOSIS
ULOTRICHIES
ULOTRICHY
ULSTER
ULSTERED
ULSTERS
ULTERIOR
ULTIMA
ULTIMACIES
ULTIMACY
ULTIMAS
ULTIMATA
ULTIMATE
ULTIMATES
ULTIMATUM
ULTIMO

ULTION
ULTIONS
ULTRA
ULTRAISM
ULTRAISMS
ULTRAIST
ULTRAISTS
ULTRARED
ULTRAS
ULULANT
ULULATE
ULULATED
ULULATES
ULULATING
ULULATION
ULULATIONS
ULYIE
ULYIES
ULZIE
ULZIES
UM
UMBEL
UMBELLAR
UMBELLATE
UMBELLULE
UMBELLULES
UMBELS
UMBER
UMBERED
UMBERING
UMBERS
UMBERY
UMBILICAL
UMBILICI
UMBILICUS
UMBILICUSES
UMBLES
UMBO
UMBONAL
UMBONATE
UMBONES
UMBOS
UMBRA
UMBRAE
UMBRAGE
UMBRAGED
UMBRAGES
UMBRAGING
UMBRAL
UMBRAS
UMBRATED
UMBRATIC
UMBRATILE
UMBRE
UMBREL
UMBRELLA
UMBRELLAS
UMBRELLO
UMBRELLOES
UMBRELLOS
UMBRELS
UMBRERE
UMBRERES
UMBRES

UMBRETTE
UMBRETTES
UMBRIERE
UMBRIERES
UMBRIL
UMBRILS
UMBROSE
UMBROUS
UMIAK
UMIAKS
UMLAUT
UMLAUTED
UMLAUTING
UMLAUTS
UMPH
UMPIRAGE
UMPIRAGES
UMPIRE
UMPIRED
UMPIRES
UMPIRING
UMPTEEN
UMPTEENTH
UMPTIETH
UMPTY
UMQUHILE
UMWHILE
UN
UNABASHED
UNABATED
UNABLE
UNACCUSED
UNACHING
UNACTABLE
UNACTED
UNACTIVE
UNADAPTED
UNADMIRED
UNADOPTED
UNADORED
UNADORNED
UNADVISED
UNAFRAID
UNAIDABLE
UNAIDED
UNAIMED
UNAIRED
UNAKING
UNALIGNED
UNALIKE
UNALIST
UNALISTS
UNALIVE
UNALLAYED
UNALLIED
UNALLOYED
UNALTERED
UNAMAZED
UNAMENDED
UNAMERCED
UNAMIABLE
UNAMUSED
UNAMUSING
UNANCHOR

UNANCHORED
UNANCHORING
UNANCHORS
UNANELED
UNANIMITIES
UNANIMITY
UNANIMOUS
UNANXIOUS
UNAPPAREL
UNAPPARELLED
UNAPPARELLING
UNAPPARELS
UNAPPLIED
UNAPT
UNAPTLY
UNAPTNESS
UNAPTNESSES
UNARGUED
UNARISEN
UNARM
UNARMED
UNARMING
UNARMS
UNARTFUL
UNASHAMED
UNASKED
UNASSAYED
UNASSUMED
UNASSURED
UNATONED
UNATTIRED
UNAU
UNAUS
UNAVENGED
UNAVOIDED
UNAVOWED
UNAWARE
UNAWARES
UNAWED
UNBACKED
UNBAFFLED
UNBAG
UNBAGGED
UNBAGGING
UNBAGS
UNBAITED
UNBAKED
UNBALANCE
UNBALANCED
UNBALANCES
UNBALANCING
UNBANDED
UNBANKED
UNBAPTISE
UNBAPTISED
UNBAPTISES
UNBAPTISING
UNBAPTIZE
UNBAPTIZED
UNBAPTIZES
UNBAPTIZING
UNBAR
UNBARBED
UNBARE

UNBARED	UNBIASSED	UNBOWED	UNCANDOUR	UNCHOSEN
UNBARES	UNBIASSING	UNBOX	UNCANDOURS	UNCHRISOM
UNBARING	UNBID	UNBOXED	UNCANNIER	UNCHURCH
UNBARK	UNBIDDEN	UNBOXES	UNCANNIEST	UNCHURCHED
UNBARKED	UNBIND	UNBOXING	UNCANNILY	UNCHURCHES
UNBARKING	UNBINDING	UNBRACE	UNCANNY	UNCHURCHING
UNBARKS	UNBINDINGS	UNBRACED	UNCANONIC	UNCI
UNBARRED	UNBINDS	UNBRACES	UNCAP	UNCIAL
UNBARRING	UNBISHOP	UNBRACING	UNCAPABLE	UNCIALS
UNBARS	UNBISHOPED	UNBRAIDED	UNCAPE	UNCIFORM
UNBASHFUL	UNBISHOPING	UNBRASTE	UNCAPED	UNCINATE
UNBATED	UNBISHOPS	UNBRED	UNCAPES	UNCINATED
UNBATHED	UNBITT	UNBREECH	UNCAPING	UNCINI
UNBE	UNBITTED	UNBREECHED	UNCAPPED	UNCINUS
UNBEAR	UNBITTING	UNBREECHES	UNCAPPING	UNCIPHER
UNBEARDED	UNBITTS	UNBREECHING	UNCAPS	UNCIPHERED
UNBEARING	UNBLAMED	UNBRIDGED	UNCAREFUL	UNCIPHERING
UNBEARS	UNBLENDED	UNBRIDLE	UNCARING	UNCIPHERS
UNBEATEN	UNBLENT	UNBRIDLED	UNCART	UNCIVIL
UNBED	UNBLESS	UNBRIDLES	UNCARTED	UNCIVILLY
UNBEDDED	UNBLESSED	UNBRIDLING	UNCARTING	UNCLAD
UNBEDDING	UNBLESSES	UNBRIZZED	UNCARTS	UNCLAIMED
UNBEDS	UNBLESSING	UNBROKE	UNCASE	UNCLASP
UNBEEN	UNBLEST	UNBROKEN	UNCASED	UNCLASPED
UNBEGET	UNBLIND	UNBRUISED	UNCASES	UNCLASPING
UNBEGETS	UNBLINDED	UNBRUSED	UNCASHED	UNCLASPS
UNBEGETTING	UNBLINDING	UNBRUSHED	UNCASING	UNCLASSED
UNBEGGED	UNBLINDS	UNBUCKLE	UNCATE	UNCLE
UNBEGOT	UNBLOCK	UNBUCKLED	UNCAUGHT	UNCLEAN
UNBEGOTTEN	UNBLOCKED	UNBUCKLES	UNCAUSED	UNCLEANED
UNBEGUILE	UNBLOCKING	UNBUCKLING	UNCE	UNCLEANER
UNBEGUILED	UNBLOCKS	UNBUDDED	UNCEASING	UNCLEANEST
UNBEGUILES	UNBLOODED	UNBUILD	UNCERTAIN	UNCLEANLY
UNBEGUILING	UNBLOODY	UNBUILDING	UNCES	UNCLEAR
UNBEGUN	UNBLOTTED	UNBUILDS	UNCESSANT	UNCLEARED
UNBEING	UNBLOWED	UNBUILT	UNCHAIN	UNCLEARER
UNBEINGS	UNBLOWN	UNBUNDLE	UNCHAINED	UNCLEAREST
UNBEKNOWN	UNBLUNTED	UNBUNDLED	UNCHAINING	UNCLEARLY
UNBELIEF	UNBODIED	UNBUNDLES	UNCHAINS	UNCLED
UNBELIEFS	UNBODING	UNBUNDLING	UNCHANCIER	UNCLENCH
UNBELIEVE	UNBOLT	UNBUNDLINGS	UNCHANCIEST	UNCLENCHED
UNBELIEVED	UNBOLTED	UNBURDEN	UNCHANCY	UNCLENCHES
UNBELIEVES	UNBOLTING	UNBURDENED	UNCHANGED	UNCLENCHING
UNBELIEVING	UNBOLTS	UNBURDENING	UNCHARGE	UNCLES
UNBELOVED	UNBONE	UNBURDENS	UNCHARGED	UNCLESHIP
UNBELT	UNBONED	UNBURIED	UNCHARGES	UNCLESHIPS
UNBELTED	UNBONES	UNBURIES	UNCHARGING	UNCLEW
UNBELTING	UNBONING	UNBURNED	UNCHARITIES	UNCLEWED
UNBELTS	UNBONNET	UNBURNT	UNCHARITY	UNCLEWING
UNBEND	UNBONNETED	UNBURROW	UNCHARM	UNCLEWS
UNBENDED	UNBONNETING	UNBURROWED	UNCHARMED	UNCLING
UNBENDING	UNBONNETS	UNBURROWING	UNCHARMING	UNCLIPPED
UNBENDS	UNBOOKED	UNBURROWS	UNCHARMS	UNCLIPT
UNBENIGN	UNBOOKISH	UNBURTHEN	UNCHARNEL	UNCLOAK
UNBENT	UNBOOT	UNBURTHENED	UNCHARNELED	UNCLOAKED
UNBEREFT	UNBOOTED	UNBURTHENING	UNCHARNELLING	UNCLOAKING
UNBERUFEN	UNBOOTING	UNBURTHENS	UNCHARNELS	UNCLOAKS
UNBESEEM	UNBOOTS	UNBURY	UNCHARTED	UNCLOG
UNBESEEMED	UNBORE	UNBURYING	UNCHARY	UNCLOGGED
UNBESEEMING	UNBORN	UNBUSY	UNCHASTE	UNCLOGGING
UNBESEEMS	UNBORNE	UNBUTTON	UNCHECK	UNCLOGS
UNBESPEAK	UNBOSOM	UNBUTTONED	UNCHECKED	UNCLOSE
UNBESPEAKING	UNBOSOMED	UNBUTTONING	UNCHECKING	UNCLOSED
UNBESPEAKS	UNBOSOMER	UNBUTTONS	UNCHECKS	UNCLOSES
UNBESPOKE	UNBOSOMERS	UNCAGE	UNCHEERED	UNCLOSING
UNBESPOKEN	UNBOSOMING	UNCAGED	UNCHEWED	UNCLOTHE
UNBIAS	UNBOSOMS	UNCAGES	UNCHILD	UNCLOTHED
UNBIASED	UNBOUGHT	UNCAGING	UNCHILDED	UNCLOTHES
UNBIASES	UNBOUND	UNCALLED	UNCHILDING	UNCLOTHING
UNBIASING	UNBOUNDED	UNCANDID	UNCHILDS	UNCLOUD

UNCLOUDED
UNCLOUDING
UNCLOUDS
UNCLOUDY
UNCLOVEN
UNCLUTCH
UNCLUTCHED
UNCLUTCHES
UNCLUTCHING
UNCO
UNCOCK
UNCOCKED
UNCOCKING
UNCOCKS
UNCOIL
UNCOILED
UNCOILING
UNCOILS
UNCOINED
UNCOLT
UNCOLTED
UNCOLTING
UNCOLTS
UNCOMBED
UNCOMBINE
UNCOMBINED
UNCOMBINES
UNCOMBINING
UNCOMELY
UNCOMMON
UNCOMMONER
UNCOMMONEST
UNCONCERN
UNCONCERNS
UNCONFINE
UNCONFINED
UNCONFINES
UNCONFINING
UNCONFORM
UNCONGEAL
UNCONGEALED
UNCONGEALING
UNCONGEALS
UNCOOKED
UNCOOL
UNCOPE
UNCOPED
UNCOPES
UNCOPING
UNCORD
UNCORDED
UNCORDIAL
UNCORDING
UNCORDS
UNCORK
UNCORKED
UNCORKING
UNCORKS
UNCORRUPT
UNCOS
UNCOSTLY
UNCOUNTED
UNCOUPLE
UNCOUPLED
UNCOUPLES
UNCOUPLING
UNCOURTLY
UNCOUTH
UNCOUTHER
UNCOUTHEST

UNCOUTHLY
UNCOVER
UNCOVERED
UNCOVERING
UNCOVERS
UNCOWL
UNCOWLED
UNCOWLING
UNCOWLS
UNCOYNED
UNCRATE
UNCRATED
UNCRATES
UNCRATING
UNCREATE
UNCREATED
UNCREATES
UNCREATING
UNCROPPED
UNCROSS
UNCROSSED
UNCROSSES
UNCROSSING
UNCROWDED
UNCROWN
UNCROWNED
UNCROWNING
UNCROWNS
UNCRUDDED
UNCRUMPLE
UNCRUMPLED
UNCRUMPLES
UNCRUMPLING
UNCTION
UNCTIONS
UNCTUOUS
UNCULLED
UNCURABLE
UNCURBED
UNCURDLED
UNCURED
UNCURIOUS
UNCURL
UNCURLED
UNCURLING
UNCURLS
UNCURRENT
UNCURSE
UNCURSED
UNCURSES
UNCURSING
UNCURTAIN
UNCURTAINED
UNCURTAINING
UNCURTAINS
UNCUS
UNCUT
UNDAM
UNDAMAGED
UNDAMMED
UNDAMMING
UNDAMNED
UNDAMPED
UNDAMS
UNDASHED
UNDATE
UNDATED
UNDAUNTED
UNDAWNING
UNDAZZLE

UNDAZZLED
UNDAZZLES
UNDAZZLING
UNDE
UNDÉ
UNDEAD
UNDEAF
UNDEAFED
UNDEAFING
UNDEAFS
UNDEALT
UNDEAR
UNDEBASED
UNDECAYED
UNDECEIVE
UNDECEIVED
UNDECEIVES
UNDECEIVING
UNDECENT
UNDECIDED
UNDECIMAL
UNDECK
UNDECKED
UNDECKING
UNDECKS
UNDEE
UNDÉE
UNDEEDED
UNDEFACED
UNDEFIDE
UNDEFIED
UNDEFILED
UNDEFINED
UNDEIFIED
UNDEIFIES
UNDEIFY
UNDEIFYING
UNDELAYED
UNDELIGHT
UNDELIGHTS
UNDELUDED
UNDER
UNDERACT
UNDERACTING
UNDERACTS
UNDERARM
UNDERBEAR
UNDERBEARING
UNDERBEARINGS
UNDERBEARS
UNDERBID
UNDERBIDDING
UNDERBIDS
UNDERBIT
UNDERBITE
UNDERBITES
UNDERBITING
UNDERBITTEN
UNDERBORE
UNDERBORNE
UNDERBOUGHT
UNDERBRED
UNDERBUSH
UNDERBUSHED
UNDERBUSHES
UNDERBUSHING
UNDERBUY
UNDERBUYING
UNDERBUYS

UNDERCARD
UNDERCARDS
UNDERCART
UNDERCARTS
UNDERCAST
UNDERCASTS
UNDERCLAD
UNDERCLAY
UNDERCLAYS
UNDERCLUB
UNDERCLUBBED
UNDERCLUBBING
UNDERCLUBS
UNDERCOAT
UNDERCOATS
UNDERCOOK
UNDERCOOKS
UNDERCOOL
UNDERCOOLED
UNDERCOOLING
UNDERCOOLS
UNDERCUT
UNDERCUTS
UNDERCUTTING
UNDERDECK
UNDERDECKS
UNDERDID
UNDERDO
UNDERDOER
UNDERDOERS
UNDERDOES
UNDERDOG
UNDERDOGS
UNDERDOING
UNDERDONE
UNDERDRAW
UNDERDRAWING
UNDERDRAWINGS
UNDERDRAWN
UNDERDRAWS
UNDERDREW
UNDERFED
UNDERFEED
UNDERFEEDING
UNDERFEEDS
UNDERFELT
UNDERFELTS
UNDERFIRE
UNDERFIRED
UNDERFIRES
UNDERFIRING
UNDERFLOW
UNDERFLOWS
UNDERFONG
UNDERFONGED
UNDERFONGING
UNDERFONGS
UNDERFOOT
UNDERFOOTED
UNDERFOOTING
UNDERFOOTS
UNDERFUR
UNDERFURS
UNDERGIRD
UNDERGIRDED
UNDERGIRDING
UNDERGIRDS
UNDERGO
UNDERGOES
UNDERGOING

UNDERGONE
UNDERGOWN
UNDERGOWNS
UNDERGRAD
UNDERGRADS
UNDERHAND
UNDERHANDS
UNDERHUNG
UNDERKEEP
UNDERKEEPING
UNDERKEEPS
UNDERKEPT
UNDERKING
UNDERKINGS
UNDERLAID
UNDERLAIN
UNDERLAP
UNDERLAPPED
UNDERLAPPING
UNDERLAPS
UNDERLAY
UNDERLAYING
UNDERLAYS
UNDERLET
UNDERLETS
UNDERLETTING
UNDERLETTINGS
UNDERLIE
UNDERLIES
UNDERLINE
UNDERLINED
UNDERLINES
UNDERLING
UNDERLINGS
UNDERLINING
UNDERLIP
UNDERLIPS
UNDERLYING
UNDERMAN
UNDERMANNED
UNDERMANNING
UNDERMANS
UNDERMEN
UNDERMINE
UNDERMINED
UNDERMINING
UNDERMININGS
UNDERMOST
UNDERN
UNDERNOTE
UNDERNOTED
UNDERNOTES
UNDERNOTING
UNDERNS
UNDERPAID
UNDERPASS
UNDERPASSES
UNDERPAY
UNDERPAYING
UNDERPAYS
UNDERPEEP
UNDERPEEPED
UNDERPEEPING
UNDERPEEPS
UNDERPIN
UNDERPINNED
UNDERPINNING
UNDERPINNINGS
UNDERPINS

UNDERPLAY
UNDERPLAYED
UNDERPLAYING
UNDERPLAYS
UNDERPLOT
UNDERPLOTS
UNDERPROP
UNDERPROPPED
UNDERPROPPING
UNDERPROPS
UNDERRAN
UNDERRATE
UNDERRATED
UNDERRATES
UNDERRATING
UNDERRUN
UNDERRUNNING
UNDERRUNNINGS
UNDERRUNS
UNDERSAID
UNDERSAY
UNDERSAYE
UNDERSAYES
UNDERSAYING
UNDERSAYS
UNDERSEA
UNDERSEAL
UNDERSEALED
UNDERSEALING
UNDERSEALINGS
UNDERSEALS
UNDERSELF
UNDERSELL
UNDERSELLING
UNDERSELLS
UNDERSELVES
UNDERSET
UNDERSETS
UNDERSETTING
UNDERSHOT
UNDERSIDE
UNDERSIDES
UNDERSIGN
UNDERSIGNED
UNDERSIGNING
UNDERSIGNS
UNDERSKIES
UNDERSKY
UNDERSOIL
UNDERSOILS
UNDERSOLD
UNDERSONG
UNDERSONGS
UNDERTAKE
UNDERTAKEN
UNDERTAKES
UNDERTAKING
UNDERTAKINGS
UNDERTANE
UNDERTIME
UNDERTIMES
UNDERTINT
UNDERTINTS
UNDERTONE
UNDERTONES
UNDERTOOK
UNDERTOW
UNDERTOWS
UNDERUSE
UNDERUSED

UNDERUSES
UNDERUSING
UNDERVEST
UNDERVESTS
UNDERWAY
UNDERWEAR
UNDERWEARS
UNDERWENT
UNDERWING
UNDERWINGS
UNDERWIT
UNDERWITS
UNDERWOOD
UNDERWOODS
UNDERWORK
UNDERWORKED
UNDERWORKING
UNDERWORKS
UNDESERT
UNDESERTS
UNDESERVE
UNDESERVED
UNDESERVES
UNDESERVING
UNDESIRED
UNDEVOUT
UNDID
UNDIES
UNDIGHT
UNDIGHTING
UNDIGHTS
UNDIGNIFIED
UNDIGNIFIES
UNDIGNIFY
UNDIGNIFYING
UNDILUTED
UNDIMMED
UNDINE
UNDINES
UNDINISM
UNDINISMS
UNDINTED
UNDIPPED
UNDIVIDED
UNDIVINE
UNDO
UNDOCK
UNDOCKED
UNDOCKING
UNDOCKS
UNDOER
UNDOERS
UNDOES
UNDOING
UNDOINGS
UNDONE
UNDOOMED
UNDOUBLE
UNDOUBLED
UNDOUBLES
UNDOUBLING
UNDOUBTED
UNDRAINED
UNDRAPED
UNDRAW
UNDRAWING
UNDRAWN
UNDRAWS
UNDREADED
UNDREAMED

UNDREAMT
UNDRESS
UNDRESSED
UNDRESSES
UNDRESSING
UNDRESSINGS
UNDREST
UNDREW
UNDRIED
UNDRILLED
UNDRIVEN
UNDROSSY
UNDROWNED
UNDRUNK
UNDUBBED
UNDUE
UNDUG
UNDULANCIES
UNDULANCY
UNDULANT
UNDULATE
UNDULATED
UNDULATES
UNDULATING
UNDULLED
UNDULOSE
UNDULOUS
UNDULY
UNDUTEOUS
UNDUTIFUL
UNDYED
UNDYING
UNDYINGLY
UNEARED
UNEARNED
UNEARTH
UNEARTHED
UNEARTHING
UNEARTHLIER
UNEARTHLIEST
UNEARTHLY
UNEARTHS
UNEASE
UNEASES
UNEASIER
UNEASIEST
UNEASILY
UNEASY
UNEATABLE
UNEATEN
UNEATH
UNEATHES
UNEDGE
UNEDGED
UNEDGES
UNEDGING
UNEDITED
UNEFFACED
UNELATED
UNELECTED
UNEMPTIED
UNENDING
UNENDOWED
UNENGAGED
UNENTERED
UNENVIED
UNENVIOUS
UNENVYING
UNEQUABLE
UNEQUAL

UNEQUALLY
UNEQUALS
UNERRING
UNESPIED
UNESSAYED
UNESSENCE
UNESSENCED
UNESSENCES
UNESSENCING
UNETH
UNETHICAL
UNEVEN
UNEVENER
UNEVENEST
UNEVENLY
UNEXALTED
UNEXCITED
UNEXPIRED
UNEXPOSED
UNEXTINCT
UNEYED
UNFABLED
UNFACT
UNFACTS
UNFADABLE
UNFADED
UNFADING
UNFAILING
UNFAIR
UNFAIRED
UNFAIRER
UNFAIREST
UNFAIRING
UNFAIRLY
UNFAIRS
UNFAITH
UNFAITHS
UNFALLEN
UNFAMED
UNFANNED
UNFASTEN
UNFASTENED
UNFASTENING
UNFASTENS
UNFAULTY
UNFAZED
UNFEARED
UNFEARFUL
UNFEARING
UNFED
UNFEED
UNFEELING
UNFEIGNED
UNFELLED
UNFELT
UNFENCED
UNFETTER
UNFETTERED
UNFETTERING
UNFETTERS
UNFEUDAL
UNFEUED
UNFIGURED
UNFILDE
UNFILED
UNFILIAL
UNFILLED
UNFILMED
UNFINE
UNFIRED

UNFIRM
UNFISHED
UNFIT
UNFITLY
UNFITNESS
UNFITNESSES
UNFITS
UNFITTED
UNFITTER
UNFITTEST
UNFITTING
UNFIX
UNFIXED
UNFIXES
UNFIXING
UNFIXITIES
UNFIXITY
UNFLAWED
UNFLEDGED
UNFLESH
UNFLESHED
UNFLESHES
UNFLESHING
UNFLESHLY
UNFLOORED
UNFLUSH
UNFLUSHED
UNFLUSHES
UNFLUSHING
UNFOCUSED
UNFOLD
UNFOLDED
UNFOLDER
UNFOLDERS
UNFOLDING
UNFOLDINGS
UNFOLDS
UNFOOL
UNFOOLED
UNFOOLING
UNFOOLS
UNFOOTED
UNFORBID
UNFORCED
UNFORGED
UNFORGOT
UNFORM
UNFORMAL
UNFORMED
UNFORMING
UNFORMS
UNFORTUNE
UNFORTUNES
UNFOUGHT
UNFOUND
UNFOUNDED
UNFRAMED
UNFRANKED
UNFRAUGHT
UNFRAUGHTED
UNFRAUGHTING
UNFRAUGHTS
UNFREE
UNFREEMAN
UNFREEMEN
UNFREEZE
UNFREEZES
UNFREEZING
UNFRETTED
UNFRIEND

UNFRIENDS	UNGLUES	UNHANDING	UNHELED	UNHUSKING
UNFROCK	UNGLUING	UNHANDLED	UNHELES	UNHUSKS
UNFROCKED	UNGOD	UNHANDS	UNHELING	UNI
UNFROCKING	UNGODDED	UNHANDY	UNHELM	UNIAXIAL
UNFROCKS	UNGODDING	UNHANG	UNHELMED	UNICITIES
UNFROZE	UNGODLIER	UNHANGED	UNHELMING	UNICITY
UNFROZEN	UNGODLIEST	UNHANGING	UNHELMS	UNICOLOR
UNFUELLED	UNGODLIKE	UNHANGS	UNHELPED	UNICOLOUR
UNFUMED	UNGODLILY	UNHAPPIED	UNHELPFUL	UNICORN
UNFUNDED	UNGODLY	UNHAPPIER	UNHEPPEN	UNICORNS
UNFUNNY	UNGODS	UNHAPPIES	UNHEROIC	UNICYCLE
UNFURL	UNGORD	UNHAPPIEST	UNHERST	UNICYCLES
UNFURLED	UNGORED	UNHAPPILY	UNHEWN	UNIDEAL
UNFURLING	UNGORGED	UNHAPPY	UNHIDDEN	UNIFIABLE
UNFURLS	UNGOT	UNHAPPYING	UNHINGE	UNIFIC
UNFURNISH	UNGOTTEN	UNHARBOUR	UNHINGED	UNIFIED
UNFURNISHED	UNGOWN	UNHARBOURED	UNHINGES	UNIFIER
UNFURNISHES	UNGOWNED	UNHARBOURING	UNHINGING	UNIFIERS
UNFURNISHING	UNGOWNING	UNHARBOURS	UNHIP	UNIFIES
UNFURRED	UNGOWNS	UNHARDY	UNHIRED	UNIFILAR
UNGAIN	UNGRACED	UNHARMED	UNHITCH	UNIFORM
UNGAINFUL	UNGRADED	UNHARMFUL	UNHITCHED	UNIFORMED
UNGAINLIER	UNGRASSED	UNHARMING	UNHITCHES	UNIFORMING
UNGAINLIEST	UNGRAVELY	UNHARNESS	UNHITCHING	UNIFORMLY
UNGAINLY	UNGRAZED	UNHARNESSED	UNHIVE	UNIFORMS
UNGALLANT	UNGROOMED	UNHARNESSES	UNHIVED	UNIFY
UNGALLED	UNGROUND	UNHARNESSING	UNHIVES	UNIFYING
UNGARBLED	UNGROWN	UNHASP	UNHIVING	UNIFYINGS
UNGAUGED	UNGRUDGED	UNHASPED	UNHOARD	UNILLUMED
UNGAZED	UNGUAL	UNHASPING	UNHOARDED	UNILOBAR
UNGEAR	UNGUARD	UNHASPS	UNHOARDING	UNILOBED
UNGEARED	UNGUARDED	UNHASTING	UNHOARDS	UNIMBUED
UNGEARING	UNGUARDING	UNHASTY	UNHOLIER	UNIMPEDED
UNGEARS	UNGUARDS	UNHAT	UNHOLIEST	UNIMPOSED
UNGENIAL	UNGUENT	UNHATCHED	UNHOLILY	UNINCITED
UNGENTEEL	UNGUENTS	UNHATS	UNHOLPEN	UNINDEXED
UNGENTLE	UNGUES	UNHATTED	UNHOLY	UNINJURED
UNGENTLY	UNGUESSED	UNHATTING	UNHOMELY	UNINSURED
UNGENUINE	UNGUIDED	UNHATTINGS	UNHONEST	UNINURED
UNGERMANE	UNGUIFORM	UNHAUNTED	UNHOOD	UNINVITED
UNGET	UNGUILTY	UNHEAD	UNHOODED	UNION
UNGETS	UNGUIS	UNHEADED	UNHOODING	UNIONISE
UNGETTING	UNGULA	UNHEADING	UNHOODS	UNIONISED
UNGHOSTLY	UNGULAE	UNHEADS	UNHOOK	UNIONISES
UNGIFTED	UNGULATE	UNHEAL	UNHOOKED	UNIONISING
UNGILD	UNGULATES	UNHEALED	UNHOOKING	UNIONISM
UNGILDED	UNGULED	UNHEALING	UNHOOKS	UNIONISMS
UNGILDING	UNGUM	UNHEALS	UNHOOP	UNIONIST
UNGILDS	UNGUMMED	UNHEALTH	UNHOOPED	UNIONISTS
UNGILT	UNGUMMING	UNHEALTHIER	UNHOOPING	UNIONIZE
UNGIRD	UNGUMS	UNHEALTHIEST	UNHOOPS	UNIONIZED
UNGIRDED	UNGYVE	UNHEALTHS	UNHOPED	UNIONIZES
UNGIRDING	UNGYVED	UNHEALTHY	UNHOPEFUL	UNIONIZING
UNGIRDS	UNGYVES	UNHEARD	UNHORSE	UNIONS
UNGIRT	UNGYVING	UNHEARSE	UNHORSED	UNIPAROUS
UNGIRTH	UNHABLE	UNHEARSED	UNHORSES	UNIPED
UNGIRTHED	UNHACKED	UNHEARSES	UNHORSING	UNIPEDS
UNGIRTHING	UNHAILED	UNHEARSING	UNHOUSE	UNIPLANAR
UNGIRTHS	UNHAIR	UNHEART	UNHOUSED	UNIPOD
UNGIVING	UNHAIRED	UNHEARTED	UNHOUSES	UNIPODS
UNGLAD	UNHAIRING	UNHEARTING	UNHOUSING	UNIPOLAR
UNGLAZED	UNHAIRS	UNHEARTS	UNHUMAN	UNIQUE
UNGLOSSED	UNHALLOW	UNHEATED	UNHUMBLED	UNIQUELY
UNGLOVE	UNHALLOWED	UNHEDGED	UNHUNG	UNIQUER
UNGLOVED	UNHALLOWING	UNHEEDED	UNHUNTED	UNIQUES
UNGLOVES	UNHALLOWS	UNHEEDFUL	UNHURRIED	UNIQUEST
UNGLOVING	UNHALSED	UNHEEDILY	UNHURT	UNIRONED
UNGLUE	UNHAND	UNHEEDING	UNHURTFUL	UNIS
UNGLUED	UNHANDED	UNHEEDY	UNHUSK	UNISERIAL
UNGLUEING	UNHANDILY	UNHELE	UNHUSKED	UNISEX

UNISEXUAL
UNISON
UNISONAL
UNISONANT
UNISONOUS
UNISONS
UNIT
UNITAL
UNITARIAN
UNITARIANS
UNITARY
UNITE
UNITED
UNITEDLY
UNITER
UNITERS
UNITES
UNITIES
UNITING
UNITINGS
UNITION
UNITIONS
UNITISE
UNITISED
UNITISES
UNITISING
UNITIVE
UNITIVELY
UNITIZE
UNITIZED
UNITIZES
UNITIZING
UNITS
UNITY
UNIVALENT
UNIVALENTS
UNIVALVE
UNIVALVES
UNIVERSAL
UNIVERSALS
UNIVERSE
UNIVERSES
UNIVOCAL
UNIVOCALS
UNJADED
UNJEALOUS
UNJOINT
UNJOINTED
UNJOINTING
UNJOINTS
UNJOYFUL
UNJOYOUS
UNJUST
UNJUSTER
UNJUSTEST
UNJUSTLY
UNKED
UNKEMPT
UNKENNED
UNKENNEL
UNKENNELLED
UNKENNELLING
UNKENNELS
UNKENT
UNKEPT
UNKET
UNKID
UNKIND
UNKINDER
UNKINDEST

UNKINDLED
UNKINDLIER
UNKINDLIEST
UNKINDLY
UNKING
UNKINGED
UNKINGING
UNKINGLIER
UNKINGLIEST
UNKINGLY
UNKINGS
UNKISS
UNKISSED
UNKISSES
UNKISSING
UNKNELLED
UNKNIGHT
UNKNIGHTED
UNKNIGHTING
UNKNIGHTS
UNKNIT
UNKNITS
UNKNITTED
UNKNITTING
UNKNOT
UNKNOTS
UNKNOTTED
UNKNOTTING
UNKNOWING
UNKNOWN
UNKNOWNS
UNLACE
UNLACED
UNLACES
UNLACING
UNLADE
UNLADED
UNLADEN
UNLADES
UNLADING
UNLADINGS
UNLAID
UNLASH
UNLASHED
UNLASHES
UNLASHING
UNLAST
UNLASTE
UNLATCH
UNLATCHED
UNLATCHES
UNLATCHING
UNLAW
UNLAWED
UNLAWFUL
UNLAWING
UNLAWS
UNLAY
UNLAYING
UNLAYS
UNLEAD
UNLEADED
UNLEADING
UNLEADS
UNLEAL
UNLEARN
UNLEARNED
UNLEARNING
UNLEARNS
UNLEARNT

UNLEASED
UNLEASH
UNLEASHED
UNLEASHES
UNLEASHING
UNLED
UNLESS
UNLET
UNLICH
UNLICKED
UNLID
UNLIDDED
UNLIDDING
UNLIDS
UNLIGHTED
UNLIKABLE
UNLIKE
UNLIKELIER
UNLIKELIEST
UNLIKELY
UNLIKES
UNLIMBER
UNLIMBERED
UNLIMBERING
UNLIMBERS
UNLIME
UNLIMED
UNLIMES
UNLIMING
UNLIMITED
UNLINE
UNLINEAL
UNLINED
UNLINES
UNLINING
UNLINK
UNLINKED
UNLINKING
UNLINKS
UNLISTED
UNLIT
UNLIVABLE
UNLIVE
UNLIVED
UNLIVELY
UNLIVES
UNLIVING
UNLOAD
UNLOADED
UNLOADER
UNLOADERS
UNLOADING
UNLOADINGS
UNLOADS
UNLOCATED
UNLOCK
UNLOCKED
UNLOCKING
UNLOCKS
UNLOGICAL
UNLOOKED
UNLOOSE
UNLOOSED
UNLOOSEN
UNLOOSENED
UNLOOSENING
UNLOOSENS
UNLOOSES
UNLOOSING
UNLOPPED

UNLORD
UNLORDED
UNLORDING
UNLORDLY
UNLORDS
UNLOSABLE
UNLOST
UNLOVABLE
UNLOVE
UNLOVED
UNLOVELY
UNLOVES
UNLOVING
UNLUCKIER
UNLUCKIEST
UNLUCKILY
UNLUCKY
UNMADE
UNMAILED
UNMAIMED
UNMAKABLE
UNMAKE
UNMAKES
UNMAKING
UNMAKINGS
UNMAN
UNMANACLE
UNMANACLED
UNMANACLES
UNMANACLING
UNMANAGED
UNMANLIER
UNMANLIEST
UNMANLIKE
UNMANLY
UNMANNED
UNMANNING
UNMANS
UNMANTLE
UNMANTLED
UNMANTLES
UNMANTLING
UNMANURED
UNMARD
UNMARKED
UNMARRED
UNMARRIED
UNMARRIES
UNMARRY
UNMARRYING
UNMASK
UNMASKED
UNMASKER
UNMASKERS
UNMASKING
UNMASKS
UNMATCHED
UNMATED
UNMATURED
UNMEANING
UNMEANT
UNMEEK
UNMEET
UNMEETLY
UNMELTED
UNMERITED
UNMET
UNMETED
UNMEW
UNMEWED

UNMEWING
UNMEWS
UNMILKED
UNMILLED
UNMINDED
UNMINDFUL
UNMINGLED
UNMIRY
UNMISSED
UNMIXED
UNMIXEDLY
UNMOANED
UNMODISH
UNMONEYED
UNMONIED
UNMOOR
UNMOORED
UNMOORING
UNMOORS
UNMORAL
UNMOTIVED
UNMOULD
UNMOULDED
UNMOULDING
UNMOULDS
UNMOUNT
UNMOUNTED
UNMOUNTING
UNMOUNTS
UNMOURNED
UNMOVABLE
UNMOVABLY
UNMOVED
UNMOVEDLY
UNMOVING
UNMOWN
UNMUFFLE
UNMUFFLED
UNMUFFLES
UNMUFFLING
UNMUSICAL
UNMUZZLE
UNMUZZLED
UNMUZZLES
UNMUZZLING
UNMUZZLINGS
UNNAIL
UNNAILED
UNNAILING
UNNAILS
UNNAMABLE
UNNAMED
UNNANELD
UNNATIVE
UNNATURAL
UNNEATH
UNNEEDED
UNNEEDFUL
UNNERVE
UNNERVED
UNNERVES
UNNERVING
UNNEST
UNNESTED
UNNESTING
UNNESTS
UNNETHES
UNNETTED
UNNOBLE
UNNOBLED

UNNOBLES
UNNOBLING
UNNOTED
UNNOTICED
UNOBEYED
UNOBVIOUS
UNOFFERED
UNOFTEN
UNOILED
UNOPENED
UNOPPOSED
UNORDER
UNORDERED
UNORDERING
UNORDERLY
UNORDERS
UNOWED
UNOWNED
UNPACK
UNPACKED
UNPACKER
UNPACKERS
UNPACKING
UNPACKINGS
UNPACKS
UNPAGED
UNPAID
UNPAINED
UNPAINFUL
UNPAINT
UNPAINTED
UNPAINTING
UNPAINTS
UNPAIRED
UNPALSIED
UNPANEL
UNPANELLED
UNPANELLING
UNPANELS
UNPANGED
UNPANNEL
UNPANNELLED
UNPANNELLING
UNPANNELS
UNPAPER
UNPAPERED
UNPAPERING
UNPAPERS
UNPARED
UNPARTIAL
UNPATHED
UNPAVED
UNPAY
UNPAYABLE
UNPAYING
UNPAYS
UNPEELED
UNPEERED
UNPEG
UNPEGGED
UNPEGGING
UNPEGS
UNPEN
UNPENNED
UNPENNIED
UNPENNING
UNPENS
UNPENT
UNPEOPLE
UNPEOPLED

UNPEOPLES
UNPEOPLING
UNPERCH
UNPERCHED
UNPERCHES
UNPERCHING
UNPERFECT
UNPERPLEX
UNPERPLEXED
UNPERPLEXES
UNPERPLEXING
UNPERSON
UNPERSONED
UNPERSONING
UNPERSONS
UNPERVERT
UNPERVERTED
UNPERVERTING
UNPERVERTS
UNPICK
UNPICKED
UNPICKING
UNPICKS
UNPIERCED
UNPILOTED
UNPIN
UNPINKED
UNPINKT
UNPINNED
UNPINNING
UNPINS
UNPITIED
UNPITIFUL
UNPITYING
UNPLACE
UNPLACED
UNPLACES
UNPLACING
UNPLAGUED
UNPLAINED
UNPLAIT
UNPLAITED
UNPLAITING
UNPLAITS
UNPLANKED
UNPLANNED
UNPLANTED
UNPLEASED
UNPLEATED
UNPLEDGED
UNPLIABLE
UNPLIABLY
UNPLIANT
UNPLUCKED
UNPLUG
UNPLUGGED
UNPLUGGING
UNPLUGS
UNPLUMB
UNPLUMBED
UNPLUMBING
UNPLUMBS
UNPLUME
UNPLUMED
UNPLUMES
UNPLUMING
UNPOETIC
UNPOINTED
UNPOISED
UNPOISON

UNPOISONED
UNPOISONING
UNPOISONS
UNPOLICED
UNPOLISH
UNPOLISHED
UNPOLISHES
UNPOLISHING
UNPOLITE
UNPOLITIC
UNPOLLED
UNPOPE
UNPOPED
UNPOPES
UNPOPING
UNPOPULAR
UNPOSED
UNPOSTED
UNPOTABLE
UNPRAISE
UNPRAISED
UNPRAISES
UNPRAISING
UNPRAY
UNPRAYED
UNPRAYING
UNPRAYS
UNPREACH
UNPREACHED
UNPREACHES
UNPREACHING
UNPRECISE
UNPREDICT
UNPREDICTED
UNPREDICTING
UNPREDICTS
UNPREPARE
UNPREPARED
UNPREPARES
UNPREPARING
UNPRESSED
UNPRETTY
UNPRICED
UNPRIEST
UNPRIESTED
UNPRIESTING
UNPRIESTS
UNPRIMED
UNPRINTED
UNPRISON
UNPRISONED
UNPRISONING
UNPRISONS
UNPRIZED
UNPROP
UNPROPER
UNPROPPED
UNPROPPING
UNPROPS
UNPROVED
UNPROVEN
UNPROVIDE
UNPROVIDED
UNPROVIDES
UNPROVIDING
UNPROVOKE
UNPROVOKED
UNPROVOKES
UNPROVOKING
UNPRUNED

UNPULLED
UNPURGED
UNPURSE
UNPURSED
UNPURSES
UNPURSING
UNPURSUED
UNQUALIFIED
UNQUALIFIES
UNQUALIFY
UNQUALIFYING
UNQUEEN
UNQUEENED
UNQUEENING
UNQUEENLIER
UNQUEENLIEST
UNQUEENLY
UNQUEENS
UNQUELLED
UNQUIET
UNQUIETED
UNQUIETING
UNQUIETLY
UNQUIETS
UNQUOTE
UNQUOTED
UNQUOTES
UNQUOTING
UNRACED
UNRACKED
UNRAISED
UNRAKE
UNRAKED
UNRAKES
UNRAKING
UNRATED
UNRAVEL
UNRAVELLED
UNRAVELLING
UNRAVELLINGS
UNRAVELS
UNRAZORED
UNREACHED
UNREAD
UNREADIER
UNREADIEST
UNREADILY
UNREADY
UNREAL
UNREALISE
UNREALISED
UNREALISES
UNREALISING
UNREALISM
UNREALISMS
UNREALITIES
UNREALITY
UNREALIZE
UNREALIZED
UNREALIZES
UNREALIZING
UNREALLY
UNREAPED
UNREASON
UNREASONS
UNREAVE
UNREAVED
UNREAVES
UNREAVING
UNREBATED

UNREBUKED
UNRECKED
UNRED
UNREDREST
UNREDUCED
UNREEL
UNREELED
UNREELING
UNREELS
UNREEVE
UNREEVED
UNREEVES
UNREEVING
UNREFINED
UNREFUTED
UNREIN
UNREINED
UNREINING
UNREINS
UNRELATED
UNRELAXED
UNREMOVED
UNRENEWED
UNRENT
UNREPAID
UNREPAIR
UNREPAIRS
UNRESERVE
UNRESERVES
UNREST
UNRESTFUL
UNRESTING
UNRESTS
UNREVISED
UNREVOKED
UNRHYMED
UNRIBBED
UNRID
UNRIDABLE
UNRIDDEN
UNRIDDLE
UNRIDDLED
UNRIDDLER
UNRIDDLERS
UNRIDDLES
UNRIDDLING
UNRIFLED
UNRIG
UNRIGGED
UNRIGGING
UNRIGHT
UNRIGHTS
UNRIGS
UNRIMED
UNRINGED
UNRIP
UNRIPE
UNRIPENED
UNRIPER
UNRIPEST
UNRIPPED
UNRIPPING
UNRIPPINGS
UNRIPS
UNRISEN
UNRIVEN
UNRIVET
UNRIVETED
UNRIVETING
UNRIVETS

UNROBE
UNROBED
UNROBES
UNROBING
UNROLL
UNROLLED
UNROLLING
UNROLLS
UNROOF
UNROOFED
UNROOFING
UNROOFS
UNROOST
UNROOSTED
UNROOSTING
UNROOSTS
UNROOT
UNROOTED
UNROOTING
UNROOTS
UNROPE
UNROPED
UNROPES
UNROPING
UNROSINED
UNROTTED
UNROTTEN
UNROUGED
UNROUGH
UNROUND
UNROUNDED
UNROUNDING
UNROUNDS
UNROUSED
UNROYAL
UNROYALLY
UNRUBBED
UNRUDE
UNRUFFE
UNRUFFLE
UNRUFFLED
UNRUFFLES
UNRUFFLING
UNRULE
UNRULED
UNRULES
UNRULIER
UNRULIEST
UNRULY
UNRUMPLED
UNS
UNSADDLE
UNSADDLED
UNSADDLES
UNSADDLING
UNSAFE
UNSAFELY
UNSAFER
UNSAFEST
UNSAFETIES
UNSAFETY
UNSAID
UNSAILED
UNSAINED
UNSAINT
UNSAINTED
UNSAINTING
UNSAINTLIER
UNSAINTLIEST
UNSAINTLY

UNSAINTS
UNSALABLE
UNSALTED
UNSALUTED
UNSAPPED
UNSASHED
UNSATABLE
UNSATED
UNSATIATE
UNSATING
UNSAVED
UNSAVOURY
UNSAY
UNSAYABLE
UNSAYING
UNSAYS
UNSCALE
UNSCALED
UNSCALES
UNSCALING
UNSCANNED
UNSCARRED
UNSCATHED
UNSCENTED
UNSCOURED
UNSCREW
UNSCREWED
UNSCREWING
UNSCREWS
UNSCYTHED
UNSEAL
UNSEALED
UNSEALING
UNSEALS
UNSEAM
UNSEAMED
UNSEAMING
UNSEAMS
UNSEASON
UNSEASONED
UNSEASONING
UNSEASONS
UNSEAT
UNSEATED
UNSEATING
UNSEATS
UNSECRET
UNSECULAR
UNSECURED
UNSEDUCED
UNSEEABLE
UNSEEDED
UNSEEING
UNSEEL
UNSEELED
UNSEELING
UNSEELS
UNSEEMING
UNSEEMINGS
UNSEEMLIER
UNSEEMLIEST
UNSEEMLY
UNSEEN
UNSEENS
UNSEIZED
UNSELDOM
UNSELF
UNSELFED
UNSELFING
UNSELFISH

UNSELFS
UNSELVES
UNSENSE
UNSENSED
UNSENSES
UNSENSING
UNSENT
UNSERIOUS
UNSET
UNSETS
UNSETTING
UNSETTLE
UNSETTLED
UNSETTLES
UNSETTLING
UNSEVERED
UNSEW
UNSEWED
UNSEWING
UNSEWN
UNSEWS
UNSEX
UNSEXED
UNSEXES
UNSEXING
UNSEXIST
UNSEXUAL
UNSHACKLE
UNSHACKLED
UNSHACKLES
UNSHACKLING
UNSHADED
UNSHADOW
UNSHADOWED
UNSHADOWING
UNSHADOWS
UNSHAKED
UNSHAKEN
UNSHALE
UNSHALED
UNSHALES
UNSHALING
UNSHAMED
UNSHAPE
UNSHAPED
UNSHAPELIER
UNSHAPELIEST
UNSHAPELY
UNSHAPEN
UNSHAPES
UNSHAPING
UNSHARED
UNSHAVED
UNSHAVEN
UNSHEATHE
UNSHEATHED
UNSHEATHES
UNSHEATHING
UNSHED
UNSHELL
UNSHELLED
UNSHELLING
UNSHELLS
UNSHENT
UNSHEWN
UNSHIP
UNSHIPPED
UNSHIPPING
UNSHIPS
UNSHOCKED

UNSHOD
UNSHOE
UNSHOED
UNSHOEING
UNSHOES
UNSHOOT
UNSHOOTED
UNSHOOTING
UNSHOOTS
UNSHORN
UNSHOT
UNSHOUT
UNSHOUTED
UNSHOUTING
UNSHOUTS
UNSHOWN
UNSHRIVED
UNSHRIVEN
UNSHROUD
UNSHROUDED
UNSHROUDING
UNSHROUDS
UNSHRUBD
UNSHUNNED
UNSHUT
UNSHUTS
UNSHUTTER
UNSHUTTERED
UNSHUTTERING
UNSHUTTERS
UNSHUTTING
UNSICKER
UNSICKLED
UNSIFTED
UNSIGHING
UNSIGHT
UNSIGHTED
UNSIGHTLIER
UNSIGHTLIEST
UNSIGHTLY
UNSIGNED
UNSINEW
UNSINEWED
UNSINEWING
UNSINEWS
UNSISTING
UNSIZABLE
UNSIZED
UNSKILFUL
UNSKILLED
UNSKIMMED
UNSKINNED
UNSLAIN
UNSLAKED
UNSLING
UNSLINGING
UNSLINGS
UNSLUICE
UNSLUICED
UNSLUICES
UNSLUICING
UNSLUNG
UNSMART
UNSMILING
UNSMITTEN
UNSMOOTH
UNSMOOTHED
UNSMOOTHING
UNSMOOTHS
UNSMOTE

UNSNAP
UNSNAPPED
UNSNAPPING
UNSNAPS
UNSNARL
UNSNARLED
UNSNARLING
UNSNARLS
UNSNECK
UNSNECKED
UNSNECKING
UNSNECKS
UNSNUFFED
UNSOAPED
UNSOCIAL
UNSOCKET
UNSOCKETED
UNSOCKETING
UNSOCKETS
UNSOD
UNSODDEN
UNSOFT
UNSOILED
UNSOLACED
UNSOLD
UNSOLDER
UNSOLDERED
UNSOLDERING
UNSOLDERS
UNSOLEMN
UNSOLID
UNSOLIDLY
UNSOLVED
UNSONSY
UNSOOTE
UNSORTED
UNSOUGHT
UNSOUL
UNSOULED
UNSOULING
UNSOULS
UNSOUND
UNSOUNDED
UNSOUNDER
UNSOUNDEST
UNSOUNDLY
UNSOURCED
UNSOURED
UNSOWN
UNSPAR
UNSPARED
UNSPARING
UNSPARRED
UNSPARRING
UNSPARS
UNSPEAK
UNSPEAKING
UNSPEAKS
UNSPED
UNSPELL
UNSPELLED
UNSPELLING
UNSPELLS
UNSPENT
UNSPHERE
UNSPHERED
UNSPHERES
UNSPHERING
UNSPIDE
UNSPIED

UNSPILLED
UNSPILT
UNSPOILED
UNSPOILT
UNSPOKE
UNSPOKEN
UNSPOTTED
UNSPRUNG
UNSPUN
UNSQUARED
UNSTABLE
UNSTABLER
UNSTABLEST
UNSTACK
UNSTACKED
UNSTACKING
UNSTACKS
UNSTAID
UNSTAINED
UNSTAMPED
UNSTARCH
UNSTARCHED
UNSTARCHES
UNSTARCHING
UNSTATE
UNSTATED
UNSTATES
UNSTATING
UNSTAYED
UNSTAYING
UNSTEADIED
UNSTEADIER
UNSTEADIES
UNSTEADIEST
UNSTEADY
UNSTEADYING
UNSTEEL
UNSTEELED
UNSTEELING
UNSTEELS
UNSTEP
UNSTEPPED
UNSTEPPING
UNSTEPS
UNSTERILE
UNSTICK
UNSTICKING
UNSTICKS
UNSTIFLED
UNSTILLED
UNSTINTED
UNSTITCH
UNSTITCHED
UNSTITCHES
UNSTITCHING
UNSTOCK
UNSTOCKED
UNSTOCKING
UNSTOCKS
UNSTOP
UNSTOPPED
UNSTOPPER
UNSTOPPERED
UNSTOPPERING
UNSTOPPERS
UNSTOPPING
UNSTOPS
UNSTOW
UNSTOWED
UNSTOWING

UNSTOWS
UNSTRAP
UNSTRAPPED
UNSTRAPPING
UNSTRAPS
UNSTRING
UNSTRINGED
UNSTRINGING
UNSTRINGS
UNSTRIP
UNSTRIPED
UNSTRIPPED
UNSTRIPPING
UNSTRIPS
UNSTRUCK
UNSTRUNG
UNSTUCK
UNSTUDIED
UNSTUFFED
UNSTUFFY
UNSTUFT
UNSUBDUED
UNSUBJECT
UNSUBTLE
UNSUCCESS
UNSUCCESSES
UNSUCKED
UNSUIT
UNSUITED
UNSUITING
UNSUITS
UNSULLIED
UNSUMMED
UNSUNG
UNSUNNED
UNSUNNY
UNSUPPLE
UNSURE
UNSURED
UNSURER
UNSUREST
UNSUSPECT
UNSWADDLE
UNSWADDLED
UNSWADDLES
UNSWADDLING
UNSWATHE
UNSWATHED
UNSWATHES
UNSWATHING
UNSWAYED
UNSWEAR
UNSWEARING
UNSWEARINGS
UNSWEARS
UNSWEET
UNSWEPT
UNSWORE
UNSWORN
UNTACK
UNTACKED
UNTACKING
UNTACKLE
UNTACKLED
UNTACKLES
UNTACKLING
UNTACKS
UNTAILED
UNTAINTED
UNTAKEN

UNTAMABLE
UNTAMABLY
UNTAME
UNTAMED
UNTAMES
UNTAMING
UNTANGLE
UNTANGLED
UNTANGLES
UNTANGLING
UNTANNED
UNTAPPED
UNTARRED
UNTASTED
UNTAUGHT
UNTAX
UNTAXED
UNTAXES
UNTAXING
UNTEACH
UNTEACHES
UNTEACHING
UNTEAM
UNTEAMED
UNTEAMING
UNTEAMS
UNTEMPER
UNTEMPERED
UNTEMPERING
UNTEMPERS
UNTEMPTED
UNTENABLE
UNTENANT
UNTENANTED
UNTENANTING
UNTENANTS
UNTENDED
UNTENDER
UNTENT
UNTENTED
UNTENTING
UNTENTS
UNTENTY
UNTESTED
UNTETHER
UNTETHERED
UNTETHERING
UNTETHERS
UNTHANKED
UNTHATCH
UNTHATCHED
UNTHATCHES
UNTHATCHING
UNTHAW
UNTHAWED
UNTHAWING
UNTHAWS
UNTHINK
UNTHINKING
UNTHINKS
UNTHOUGHT
UNTHREAD
UNTHREADED
UNTHREADING
UNTHREADS
UNTHRIFT
UNTHRIFTS
UNTHRIFTY
UNTHRONE
UNTHRONED

UNTHRONES
UNTHRONING
UNTIDIED
UNTIDIER
UNTIDIES
UNTIDIEST
UNTIDILY
UNTIDY
UNTIDYING
UNTIE
UNTIES
UNTIL
UNTILE
UNTILED
UNTILES
UNTILING
UNTILLED
UNTIMELIER
UNTIMELIEST
UNTIMELY
UNTIMEOUS
UNTIN
UNTINGED
UNTINNED
UNTINNING
UNTINS
UNTIRABLE
UNTIRED
UNTIRING
UNTITLED
UNTO
UNTOILING
UNTOLD
UNTOMB
UNTOMBED
UNTOMBING
UNTOMBS
UNTONED
UNTORN
UNTOUCHED
UNTOWARD
UNTRACE
UNTRACED
UNTRACES
UNTRACING
UNTRACKED
UNTRADED
UNTRAINED
UNTREAD
UNTREADING
UNTREADS
UNTREATED
UNTRESSED
UNTRIDE
UNTRIED
UNTRIM
UNTRIMMED
UNTRIMMING
UNTRIMS
UNTROD
UNTRODDEN
UNTRUE
UNTRUER
UNTRUEST
UNTRUISM
UNTRUISMS
UNTRULY
UNTRUSS
UNTRUSSED

UNTRUSSER
UNTRUSSERS
UNTRUSSES
UNTRUSSING
UNTRUSSINGS
UNTRUST
UNTRUSTS
UNTRUSTY
UNTRUTH
UNTRUTHS
UNTUCK
UNTUCKED
UNTUCKING
UNTUCKS
UNTUMBLED
UNTUNABLE
UNTUNABLY
UNTUNE
UNTUNED
UNTUNEFUL
UNTUNES
UNTUNING
UNTURBID
UNTURF
UNTURFED
UNTURFING
UNTURFS
UNTURN
UNTURNED
UNTURNING
UNTURNS
UNTUTORED
UNTWINE
UNTWINED
UNTWINES
UNTWINING
UNTWIST
UNTWISTED
UNTWISTING
UNTWISTINGS
UNTWISTS
UNTYING
UNTYINGS
UNTYPABLE
UNTYPICAL
UNURGED
UNUSABLE
UNUSABLY
UNUSED
UNUSEFUL
UNUSHERED
UNUSUAL
UNUSUALLY
UNUTTERED
UNVAIL
UNVAILE
UNVAILED
UNVAILES
UNVAILING
UNVAILS
UNVALUED
UNVARIED
UNVARYING
UNVEIL
UNVEILED
UNVEILER
UNVEILERS
UNVEILING
UNVEILINGS
UNVEILS

UNVENTED
UNVERSED
UNVEXED
UNVIABLE
UNVIEWED
UNVIRTUE
UNVIRTUES
UNVISITED
UNVISOR
UNVISORED
UNVISORING
UNVISORS
UNVITAL
UNVIZARD
UNVIZARDED
UNVIZARDING
UNVIZARDS
UNVOCAL
UNVOICE
UNVOICED
UNVOICES
UNVOICING
UNVOICINGS
UNVULGAR
UNWAGED
UNWAKED
UNWAKENED
UNWALLED
UNWANTED
UNWARDED
UNWARE
UNWARELY
UNWARES
UNWARIE
UNWARIER
UNWARIEST
UNWARILY
UNWARLIKE
UNWARMED
UNWARNED
UNWARPED
UNWARY
UNWASHED
UNWASHEN
UNWASTED
UNWASTING
UNWATCHED
UNWATER
UNWATERED
UNWATERING
UNWATERS
UNWATERY
UNWAYED
UNWEAL
UNWEALS
UNWEANED
UNWEAPON
UNWEAPONED
UNWEAPONING
UNWEAPONS
UNWEARIED
UNWEARY
UNWEAVE
UNWEAVED
UNWEAVES
UNWEAVING
UNWEBBED
UNWED
UNWEDDED
UNWEEDED

UNWEENED
UNWEETING
UNWEIGHED
UNWELCOME
UNWELDY
UNWELL
UNWEPT
UNWET
UNWETTED
UNWHIPPED
UNWHIPT
UNWIELDIER
UNWIELDIEST
UNWIELDY
UNWIFELIER
UNWIFELIEST
UNWIFELY
UNWIGGED
UNWILFUL
UNWILL
UNWILLED
UNWILLING
UNWILLS
UNWIND
UNWINDING
UNWINDINGS
UNWINDS
UNWINGED
UNWINKING
UNWIPED
UNWIRE
UNWIRED
UNWIRES
UNWIRING
UNWISDOM
UNWISDOMS
UNWISE
UNWISELY
UNWISER
UNWISEST
UNWISH
UNWISHED
UNWISHES
UNWISHFUL
UNWISHING
UNWIST
UNWIT
UNWITCH
UNWITCHED
UNWITCHES
UNWITCHING
UNWITS
UNWITTED
UNWITTILY
UNWITTING
UNWITTY
UNWIVE
UNWIVED
UNWIVES
UNWIVING
UNWOMAN
UNWOMANED
UNWOMANING
UNWOMANLIER
UNWOMANLIEST
UNWOMANLY
UNWOMANS
UNWON
UNWONT
UNWONTED

UNWOODED
UNWOOED
UNWORDED
UNWORK
UNWORKED
UNWORKING
UNWORKS
UNWORLDLIER
UNWORLDLIEST
UNWORLDLY
UNWORMED
UNWORN
UNWORRIED
UNWORTH
UNWORTHIER
UNWORTHIEST
UNWORTHS
UNWORTHY
UNWOUND
UNWOUNDED
UNWOVEN
UNWRAP
UNWRAPPED
UNWRAPPING
UNWRAPS
UNWREAKED
UNWREATHE
UNWREATHED
UNWREATHES
UNWREATHING
UNWRINKLE
UNWRINKLED
UNWRINKLES
UNWRINKLING
UNWRITE
UNWRITES
UNWRITING
UNWRITTEN
UNWROTE
UNWROUGHT
UNWRUNG
UNYEANED
UNYOKE
UNYOKED
UNYOKES
UNYOKING
UNZEALOUS
UNZIP
UNZIPPED
UNZIPPING
UNZIPS
UNZONED
UP
UPADAISY
UPAITHRIC
UPAS
UPASES
UPBEAR
UPBEARING
UPBEARS
UPBEAT
UPBEATS
UPBIND
UPBINDING
UPBINDS
UPBLEW
UPBLOW
UPBLOWING
UPBLOWN
UPBLOWS

UPBOIL
UPBOILED
UPBOILING
UPBOILS
UPBORE
UPBORNE
UPBOUND
UPBOUNDEN
UPBRAID
UPBRAIDED
UPBRAIDER
UPBRAIDERS
UPBRAIDING
UPBRAIDINGS
UPBRAIDS
UPBRAST
UPBRAY
UPBRAYED
UPBRAYING
UPBRAYS
UPBREAK
UPBREAKING
UPBREAKS
UPBRING
UPBRINGING
UPBRINGINGS
UPBRINGS
UPBROKE
UPBROKEN
UPBROUGHT
UPBUILD
UPBUILDING
UPBUILDINGS
UPBUILDS
UPBUILT
UPBURNING
UPBURST
UPBURSTING
UPBURSTS
UPBY
UPBYE
UPCAST
UPCASTING
UPCASTS
UPCATCH
UPCATCHES
UPCATCHING
UPCAUGHT
UPCHEARD
UPCHEER
UPCHEERED
UPCHEERING
UPCHEERS
UPCLIMB
UPCLIMBED
UPCLIMBING
UPCLIMBS
UPCLOSE
UPCLOSED
UPCLOSES
UPCLOSING
UPCOAST
UPCOIL
UPCOILED
UPCOILING
UPCOILS
UPCOME
UPCOMES
UPCURL
UPCURLED

UPCURLING
UPCURLS
UPCURVED
UPDATE
UPDATED
UPDATES
UPDATING
UPDRAG
UPDRAGGED
UPDRAGGING
UPDRAGS
UPDRAW
UPDRAWING
UPDRAWN
UPDRAWS
UPDREW
UPFILL
UPFILLED
UPFILLING
UPFILLINGS
UPFILLS
UPFLOW
UPFLOWED
UPFLOWING
UPFLOWS
UPFLUNG
UPFOLLOW
UPFOLLOWED
UPFOLLOWING
UPFOLLOWS
UPFRONT
UPFURL
UPFURLED
UPFURLING
UPFURLS
UPGANG
UPGANGS
UPGATHER
UPGATHERED
UPGATHERING
UPGATHERS
UPGAZE
UPGAZED
UPGAZES
UPGAZING
UPGO
UPGOES
UPGOING
UPGOINGS
UPGONE
UPGRADE
UPGRADED
UPGRADES
UPGRADING
UPGREW
UPGROW
UPGROWING
UPGROWINGS
UPGROWN
UPGROWS
UPGROWTH
UPGROWTHS
UPGUSH
UPGUSHED
UPGUSHES
UPGUSHING
UPHAND
UPHANG
UPHANGING
UPHANGS

UPHAUD
UPHAUDED
UPHAUDING
UPHAUDS
UPHEAP
UPHEAPED
UPHEAPING
UPHEAPINGS
UPHEAPS
UPHEAVAL
UPHEAVALS
UPHEAVE
UPHEAVED
UPHEAVES
UPHEAVING
UPHELD
UPHILD
UPHILL
UPHILLS
UPHOARD
UPHOARDED
UPHOARDING
UPHOARDS
UPHOIST
UPHOISTED
UPHOISTING
UPHOISTS
UPHOLD
UPHOLDER
UPHOLDERS
UPHOLDING
UPHOLDINGS
UPHOLDS
UPHOLSTER
UPHOLSTERED
UPHOLSTERING
UPHOLSTERS
UPHOORD
UPHOORDED
UPHOORDING
UPHOORDS
UPHROE
UPHROES
UPHUNG
UPHURL
UPHURLED
UPHURLING
UPHURLS
UPJET
UPJETS
UPJETTED
UPJETTING
UPKEEP
UPKEEPS
UPKNIT
UPKNITS
UPKNITTED
UPKNITTING
UPLAID
UPLAND
UPLANDER
UPLANDERS
UPLANDISH
UPLANDS
UPLAY
UPLAYING
UPLAYS
UPLEAD
UPLEADING
UPLEADS

UPLEAN
UPLEANED
UPLEANING
UPLEANS
UPLEANT
UPLEAP
UPLEAPED
UPLEAPING
UPLEAPS
UPLEAPT
UPLED
UPLIFT
UPLIFTED
UPLIFTER
UPLIFTERS
UPLIFTING
UPLIFTINGS
UPLIFTS
UPLIGHTED
UPLIGHTER
UPLIGHTERS
UPLOCK
UPLOCKED
UPLOCKING
UPLOCKS
UPLOOK
UPLOOKED
UPLOOKING
UPLOOKS
UPLYING
UPMAKE
UPMAKER
UPMAKERS
UPMAKES
UPMAKING
UPMAKINGS
UPMOST
UPON
UPPED
UPPER
UPPERMOST
UPPERS
UPPILED
UPPING
UPPINGS
UPPISH
UPPISHLY
UPPITY
UPRAISE
UPRAISED
UPRAISES
UPRAISING
UPRAN
UPRATE
UPRATED
UPRATES
UPRATING
UPREAR
UPREARED
UPREARING
UPREARS
UPREST
UPRESTS
UPRIGHT
UPRIGHTED
UPRIGHTING
UPRIGHTLY
UPRIGHTS
UPRISAL
UPRISALS

UPRISE
UPRISEN
UPRISES
UPRISING
UPRISINGS
UPRIST
UPRISTS
UPRIVER
UPROAR
UPROARED
UPROARING
UPROARS
UPROLL
UPROLLED
UPROLLING
UPROLLS
UPROOT
UPROOTAL
UPROOTALS
UPROOTED
UPROOTER
UPROOTERS
UPROOTING
UPROOTINGS
UPROOTS
UPROSE
UPROUSE
UPROUSED
UPROUSES
UPROUSING
UPRUN
UPRUNNING
UPRUNS
UPRUSH
UPRUSHED
UPRUSHES
UPRUSHING
UPRYST
UPS
UPSEE
UPSEES
UPSEND
UPSENDING
UPSENDS
UPSENT
UPSET
UPSETS
UPSETTER
UPSETTERS
UPSETTING
UPSETTINGS
UPSEY
UPSEYS
UPSHOOT
UPSHOOTING
UPSHOOTS
UPSHOT
UPSHOTS
UPSIDE
UPSIDES
UPSIES
UPSILON
UPSILONS
UPSITTING
UPSITTINGS
UPSPAKE
UPSPEAK
UPSPEAKING
UPSPEAKS
UPSPEAR

UPSPEARED
UPSPEARING
UPSPEARS
UPSPOKE
UPSPOKEN
UPSPRANG
UPSPRING
UPSPRINGING
UPSPRINGS
UPSPRUNG
UPSTAGE
UPSTAGED
UPSTAGES
UPSTAGING
UPSTAIR
UPSTAIRS
UPSTAND
UPSTANDING
UPSTANDS
UPSTARE
UPSTARED
UPSTARES
UPSTARING
UPSTART
UPSTARTED
UPSTARTING
UPSTARTS
UPSTATE
UPSTAY
UPSTAYED
UPSTAYING
UPSTAYS
UPSTOOD
UPSTREAM
UPSTREAMED
UPSTREAMING
UPSTREAMS
UPSTROKE
UPSTROKES
UPSURGE
UPSURGED
UPSURGES
UPSURGING
UPSWARM
UPSWARMED
UPSWARMING
UPSWARMS
UPSWAY
UPSWAYED
UPSWAYING
UPSWAYS
UPSWEEP
UPSWEEPS
UPSWELL
UPSWELLED
UPSWELLING
UPSWELLS
UPSWEPT
UPSWING
UPSWINGS
UPSY
UPTAK
UPTAKE
UPTAKEN
UPTAKES
UPTAKING
UPTAKS
UPTEAR
UPTEARING
UPTEARS

UPTHREW
UPTHROW
UPTHROWING
UPTHROWN
UPTHROWS
UPTHRUST
UPTHRUSTED
UPTHRUSTING
UPTHRUSTS
UPTHUNDER
UPTHUNDERED
UPTHUNDERING
UPTHUNDERS
UPTIE
UPTIED
UPTIES
UPTIGHT
UPTIGHTER
UPTIGHTEST
UPTILT
UPTILTED
UPTILTING
UPTILTS
UPTOOK
UPTORE
UPTORN
UPTOWN
UPTOWNS
UPTRAIN
UPTRAINED
UPTRAINING
UPTRAINS
UPTREND
UPTRENDS
UPTRILLED
UPTURN
UPTURNED
UPTURNING
UPTURNINGS
UPTURNS
UPTYING
UPVALUE
UPVALUED
UPVALUES
UPVALUING
UPWAFT
UPWAFTED
UPWAFTING
UPWAFTS
UPWARD
UPWARDLY
UPWARDS
UPWELL
UPWELLED
UPWELLING
UPWELLINGS
UPWELLS
UPWENT
UPWHIRL
UPWHIRLED
UPWHIRLING
UPWHIRLS
UPWIND
UPWINDING
UPWINDS
UPWOUND
UPWROUGHT
UR
URACHUS
URACHUSES

URACIL	URCHINS	URINATED	URSONS	USURESSES
URACILS	URD	URINATES	URTICA	USURIES
URAEMIA	URDÉ	URINATING	URTICANT	USURING
URAEMIAS	URDEE	URINATION	URTICARIA	USURIOUS
URAEMIC	URDÉE	URINATIONS	URTICARIAS	USUROUS
URAEUS	URDS	URINATIVE	URTICAS	USURP
URAEUSES	URDY	URINATOR	URTICATE	USURPED
URALI	URE	URINATORS	URTICATED	USURPEDLY
URALIS	UREA	URINE	URTICATES	USURPER
URALITE	UREAL	URINED	URTICATING	USURPERS
URALITES	UREAS	URINES	URUBU	USURPING
URALITIC	UREDIA	URINING	URUBUS	USURPS
URALITISE	UREDINE	URINOLOGIES	URUS	USURY
URALITISED	UREDINES	URINOLOGY	URUSES	USWARD
URALITISES	UREDINIA	URINOUS	URVA	USWARDS
URALITISING	UREDINIAL	URITE	URVAS	UT
URALITIZE	UREDINIUM	URITES	US	UTAS
URALITIZED	UREDINOUS	URMAN	USABLE	UTASES
URALITIZES	UREDIUM	URMANS	USAGE	UTE
URALITIZING	UREDO	URN	USAGER	UTENSIL
URANIAN	UREIDE	URNAL	USAGERS	UTENSILS
URANIC	UREIDES	URNED	USAGES	UTERI
URANIDE	UREMIA	URNFIELD	USANCE	UTERINE
URANIDES	UREMIAS	URNFIELDS	USANCES	UTERITIS
URANIN	UREMIC	URNFUL	USE	UTERITISES
URANINITE	URENA	URNFULS	USED	UTEROTOMIES
URANINITES	URENAS	URNING	USEFUL	UTEROTOMY
URANINS	URENT	URNINGS	USEFULLY	UTERUS
URANISCUS	URES	URNS	USELESS	UTES
URANISCUSES	URESES	UROCHORD	USELESSLY	UTILE
URANISM	URESIS	UROCHORDS	USER	UTILISE
URANISMS	URETER	UROCHROME	USERS	UTILISED
URANITE	URETERAL	UROCHROMES	USES	UTILISER
URANITES	URETERIC	URODELAN	USHER	UTILISERS
URANITIC	URETERS	URODELANS	USHERED	UTILISES
URANIUM	URETHAN	URODELE	USHERESS	UTILISING
URANIUMS	URETHANE	URODELES	USHERESSES	UTILITIES
URANOLOGIES	URETHANES	URODELOUS	USHERETTE	UTILITY
URANOLOGY	URETHANS	UROGRAPHIES	USHERETTES	UTILIZE
URANOUS	URETHRA	UROGRAPHY	USHERING	UTILIZED
URANYL	URETHRAE	UROKINASE	USHERINGS	UTILIZER
URANYLS	URETHRAL	UROKINASES	USHERS	UTILIZERS
URAO	URETHRAS	UROLAGNIA	USHERSHIP	UTILIZES
URAOS	URETIC	UROLAGNIAS	USHERSHIPS	UTILIZING
URARI	URGE	UROLITH	USING	UTIS
URARIS	URGED	UROLITHS	USNEA	UTISES
URATE	URGENCE	UROLOGIC	USNEAS	UTMOST
URATES	URGENCES	UROLOGIES	USTION	UTMOSTS
URBAN	URGENCIES	UROLOGIST	USTIONS	UTOPIA
URBANE	URGENCY	UROLOGISTS	USUAL	UTOPIAN
URBANELY	URGENT	UROLOGY	USUALLY	UTOPIANS
URBANER	URGENTLY	UROMERE	USUALNESS	UTOPIAS
URBANEST	URGER	UROMERES	USUALNESSES	UTOPIAST
URBANISE	URGERS	UROPOD	USUALS	UTOPIASTS
URBANISED	URGES	UROPODS	USUCAPION	UTOPISM
URBANISES	URGING	UROPYGIAL	USUCAPIONS	UTOPISMS
URBANISING	URGINGS	UROPYGIUM	USUCAPT	UTOPIST
URBANITE	URIAL	UROPYGIUMS	USUCAPTED	UTOPISTS
URBANITES	URIALS	UROSCOPIES	USUCAPTING	UTRICLE
URBANITIES	URIC	UROSCOPY	USUCAPTS	UTRICLES
URBANITY	URICASE	UROSES	USUFRUCT	UTRICULAR
URBANIZE	URICASES	UROSIS	USUFRUCTED	UTRICULI
URBANIZED	URIDINE	UROSOME	USUFRUCTING	UTRICULUS
URBANIZES	URIDINES	UROSOMES	USUFRUCTS	UTS
URBANIZING	URINAL	UROSTEGE	USURE	UTTER
URCEOLATE	URINALS	UROSTEGES	USURED	UTTERABLE
URCEOLI	URINANT	UROSTYLE	USURER	UTTERANCE
URCEOLUS	URINARIES	UROSTYLES	USURERS	UTTERANCES
URCEOLUSES	URINARY	URSINE	USURES	UTTERED
URCHIN	URINATE	URSON	USURESS	UTTERER

UTTERERS
UTTEREST
UTTERING
UTTERINGS
UTTERLESS
UTTERLY
UTTERMOST

UTTERNESS
UTTERNESSES
UTTERS
UTU
UTUS
UVA
UVAROVITE

UVAROVITES
UVAS
UVEA
UVEAL
UVEAS
UVEITIS
UVEITISES

UVULA
UVULAE
UVULAR
UVULARLY
UVULAS
UVULITIS
UVULITISES

UXORIAL
UXORICIDE
UXORICIDES
UXORIOUS

V

VAC
VACANCE
VACANCES
VACANCIES
VACANCY
VACANT
VACANTLY
VACATE
VACATED
VACATES
VACATING
VACATION
VACATIONED
VACATIONING
VACATIONS
VACATUR
VACATURS
VACCINAL
VACCINATE
VACCINATED
VACCINATES
VACCINATING
VACCINE
VACCINES
VACCINIA
VACCINIAL
VACCINIAS
VACCINIUM
VACCINIUMS
VACHERIN
VACHERINS
VACILLANT
VACILLATE
VACILLATED
VACILLATES
VACILLATING
VACKED
VACKING
VACS
VACUA
VACUATE
VACUATED
VACUATES
VACUATING
VACUATION
VACUATIONS
VACUIST
VACUISTS
VACUITIES
VACUITY
VACUOLAR
VACUOLATE
VACUOLE
VACUOLES
VACUOUS
VACUOUSLY
VACUUM
VACUUMED
VACUUMING
VACUUMS
VADE
VADED
VADES
VADING

VAE
VAES
VAGABOND
VAGABONDED
VAGABONDING
VAGABONDS
VAGAL
VAGARIES
VAGARIOUS
VAGARISH
VAGARY
VAGI
VAGILE
VAGILITIES
VAGILITY
VAGINA
VAGINAE
VAGINAL
VAGINALLY
VAGINANT
VAGINAS
VAGINATE
VAGINATED
VAGINITIS
VAGINITISES
VAGINULA
VAGINULAE
VAGINULE
VAGINULES
VAGITUS
VAGITUSES
VAGRANCIES
VAGRANCY
VAGRANT
VAGRANTS
VAGROM
VAGROMS
VAGUE
VAGUED
VAGUELY
VAGUENESS
VAGUENESSES
VAGUER
VAGUES
VAGUEST
VAGUING
VAGUS
VAHINE
VAHINES
VAIL
VAILED
VAILING
VAILS
VAIN
VAINER
VAINESSE
VAINESSES
VAINEST
VAINGLORIED
VAINGLORIES
VAINGLORY
VAINGLORYING
VAINLY
VAINNESS

VAINNESSES
VAIR
VAIRÉ
VAIRS
VAIRY
VAIVODE
VAIVODES
VAKASS
VAKASSES
VAKEEL
VAKEELS
VAKIL
VAKILS
VALANCE
VALANCED
VALANCES
VALE
VALENCE
VALENCES
VALENCIES
VALENCY
VALENTINE
VALENTINES
VALERIAN
VALERIANS
VALES
VALET
VALETA
VALETAS
VALETE
VALETED
VALETES
VALETING
VALETINGS
VALETS
VALGOUS
VALGUS
VALGUSES
VALI
VALIANCE
VALIANCES
VALIANCIES
VALIANCY
VALIANT
VALIANTLY
VALIANTS
VALID
VALIDATE
VALIDATED
VALIDATES
VALIDATING
VALIDER
VALIDEST
VALIDITIES
VALIDITY
VALIDLY
VALIDNESS
VALIDNESSES
VALINE
VALINES
VALIS
VALISE
VALISES
VALLAR

VALLARY
VALLECULA
VALLECULAE
VALLEY
VALLEYS
VALLONIA
VALLONIAS
VALLUM
VALLUMS
VALONEA
VALONEAS
VALONIA
VALONIAS
VALORISE
VALORISED
VALORISES
VALORISING
VALORIZE
VALORIZED
VALORIZES
VALORIZING
VALOROUS
VALOUR
VALOURS
VALSE
VALSED
VALSES
VALSING
VALUABLE
VALUABLES
VALUABLY
VALUATE
VALUATED
VALUATES
VALUATING
VALUATION
VALUATIONS
VALUATOR
VALUATORS
VALUE
VALUED
VALUELESS
VALUER
VALUERS
VALUES
VALUING
VALUTA
VALUTAS
VALVAL
VALVAR
VALVASSOR
VALVASSORS
VALVATE
VALVE
VALVED
VALVELESS
VALVELET
VALVELETS
VALVES
VALVING
VALVULA
VALVULAE
VALVULAR
VALVULE

VALVULES
VAMBRACE
VAMBRACED
VAMBRACES
VAMOOSE
VAMOOSED
VAMOOSES
VAMOOSING
VAMOSE
VAMOSED
VAMOSES
VAMOSING
VAMP
VAMPED
VAMPER
VAMPERS
VAMPING
VAMPINGS
VAMPIRE
VAMPIRED
VAMPIRES
VAMPIRIC
VAMPIRING
VAMPIRISE
VAMPIRISED
VAMPIRISES
VAMPIRISING
VAMPIRISM
VAMPIRISMS
VAMPIRIZE
VAMPIRIZED
VAMPIRIZES
VAMPIRIZING
VAMPISH
VAMPLATE
VAMPLATES
VAMPS
VAN
VANADATE
VANADATES
VANADIC
VANADIUM
VANADIUMS
VANADOUS
VANDAL
VANDALISE
VANDALISED
VANDALISES
VANDALISING
VANDALISM
VANDALISMS
VANDALIZE
VANDALIZED
VANDALIZES
VANDALIZING
VANDALS
VANDYKE
VANDYKED
VANDYKES
VANDYKING
VANE
VANED
VANELESS
VANES

VANESSA	VAPOROUS	VARIOLATED	VASSAIL	VAURIEN
VANESSAS	VAPORS	VARIOLATES	VASSAILS	VAURIENS
VANG	VAPOUR	VARIOLATING	VASSAL	VAUS
VANGS	VAPOURED	VARIOLE	VASSALAGE	VAUT
VANGUARD	VAPOURER	VARIOLES	VASSALAGES	VAUTE
VANGUARDS	VAPOURERS	VARIOLITE	VASSALED	VAUTED
VANILLA	VAPOURING	VARIOLITES	VASSALESS	VAUTES
VANILLAS	VAPOURINGS	VARIOLOID	VASSALESSES	VAUTING
VANILLIN	VAPOURISH	VARIOLOUS	VASSALING	VAUTS
VANILLINS	VAPOURS	VARIORUM	VASSALRIES	VAVASORIES
VANISH	VAPOURY	VARIORUMS	VASSALRY	VAVASORY
VANISHED	VAPULATE	VARIOUS	VASSALS	VAVASOUR
VANISHER	VAPULATED	VARIOUSLY	VAST	VAVASOURS
VANISHERS	VAPULATES	VARISCITE	VASTER	VAWARD
VANISHES	VAPULATING	VARISCITES	VASTEST	VAWARDS
VANISHING	VAQUERO	VARISTOR	VASTIDITIES	VAWTE
VANISHINGS	VAQUEROS	VARISTORS	VASTIDITY	VAWTED
VANITAS	VARA	VARIX	VASTIER	VAWTES
VANITASES	VARACTOR	VARLET	VASTIEST	VAWTING
VANITIES	VARACTORS	VARLETESS	VASTITIES	VEAL
VANITORIES	VARAN	VARLETESSES	VASTITUDE	VEALE
VANITORY	VARANS	VARLETRIES	VASTITUDES	VEALES
VANITY	VARAS	VARLETRY	VASTITY	VEALIER
VANNED	VARDIES	VARLETS	VASTLY	VEALIEST
VANNER	VARDY	VARLETTO	VASTNESS	VEALS
VANNERS	VARE	VARLETTOS	VASTNESSES	VEALY
VANNING	VAREC	VARMENT	VASTS	VECTOR
VANNINGS	VARECH	VARMENTS	VASTY	VECTORED
VANQUISH	VARECHS	VARMINT	VAT	VECTORIAL
VANQUISHED	VARECS	VARMINTS	VATFUL	VECTORING
VANQUISHES	VARES	VARNA	VATFULS	VECTORINGS
VANQUISHING	VAREUSE	VARNAS	VATIC	VECTORS
VANS	VAREUSES	VARNISH	VATICIDE	VEDALIA
VANT	VARGUEÑO	VARNISHED	VATICIDES	VEDALIAS
VANTAGE	VARGUEÑOS	VARNISHER	VATICINAL	VEDETTE
VANTAGED	VARIABLE	VARNISHERS	VATMAN	VEDETTES
VANTAGES	VARIABLES	VARNISHES	VATMEN	VEDUTA
VANTAGING	VARIABLY	VARNISHING	VATS	VEDUTE
VANTBRACE	VARIANCE	VARNISHINGS	VATTED	VEDUTISTA
VANTBRACES	VARIANCES	VARROA	VATTING	VEDUTISTI
VANTS	VARIANT	VARROAS	VAU	VEE
VANWARD	VARIANTS	VARSAL	VAUDOO	VEENA
VAPID	VARIATE	VARSITIES	VAUDOOS	VEENAS
VAPIDER	VARIATED	VARSITY	VAUDOUX	VEER
VAPIDEST	VARIATES	VARTABED	VAULT	VEERED
VAPIDITIES	VARIATING	VARTABEDS	VAULTAGE	VEERIES
VAPIDITY	VARIATION	VARUS	VAULTAGES	VEERING
VAPIDLY	VARIATIONS	VARUSES	VAULTED	VEERINGLY
VAPIDNESS	VARIATIVE	VARVE	VAULTER	VEERINGS
VAPIDNESSES	VARICELLA	VARVED	VAULTERS	VEERS
VAPOR	VARICELLAS	VARVEL	VAULTING	VEERY
VAPORABLE	VARICES	VARVELLED	VAULTINGS	VEES
VAPORED	VARICOSE	VARVELS	VAULTS	VEG
VAPORETTI	VARIED	VARVES	VAULTY	VEGA
VAPORETTO	VARIEDLY	VARY	VAUNCE	VEGAN
VAPORETTOS	VARIEGATE	VARYING	VAUNCED	VEGANIC
VAPORIFIC	VARIEGATED	VARYINGS	VAUNCES	VEGANISM
VAPORING	VARIEGATES	VAS	VAUNCING	VEGANISMS
VAPORISE	VARIEGATING	VASA	VAUNT	VEGANS
VAPORISED	VARIER	VASAL	VAUNTAGE	VEGAS
VAPORISER	VARIERS	VASCULA	VAUNTAGES	VEGETABLE
VAPORISERS	VARIES	VASCULAR	VAUNTED	VEGETABLES
VAPORISES	VARIETAL	VASCULUM	VAUNTER	VEGETABLY
VAPORISING	VARIETIES	VASCULUMS	VAUNTERIES	VEGETAL
VAPORIZE	VARIETY	VASE	VAUNTERS	VEGETALS
VAPORIZED	VARIFORM	VASECTOMIES	VAUNTERY	VEGETANT
VAPORIZER	VARIOLA	VASECTOMY	VAUNTFUL	VEGETATE
VAPORIZERS	VARIOLAR	VASES	VAUNTING	VEGETATED
VAPORIZES	VARIOLAS	VASIFORM	VAUNTINGS	VEGETATES
VAPORIZING	VARIOLATE	VASOMOTOR	VAUNTS	VEGETATING

VEGETATINGS
VEGETE
VEGETIVE
VEGETIVES
VEGGIE
VEGGIES
VEGIE
VEGIES
VEHEMENCE
VEHEMENCES
VEHEMENCIES
VEHEMENCY
VEHEMENT
VEHICLE
VEHICLES
VEHICULAR
VEHM
VEHME
VEHMIC
VEHMIQUE
VEIL
VEILED
VEILIER
VEILIEST
VEILING
VEILINGS
VEILLESS
VEILLEUSE
VEILLEUSES
VEILS
VEILY
VEIN
VEINED
VEINIER
VEINIEST
VEINING
VEININGS
VEINLET
VEINLETS
VEINOUS
VEINS
VEINSTONE
VEINSTONES
VEINSTUFF
VEINSTUFFS
VEINY
VELA
VELAMEN
VELAMINA
VELAR
VELARIA
VELARIC
VELARISE
VELARISED
VELARISES
VELARISING
VELARIUM
VELARIZE
VELARIZED
VELARIZES
VELARIZING
VELARS
VELATE
VELATED
VELATURA
VELD
VELDS
VELDSKOEN
VELDSKOENS
VELDT

VELDTS
VELE
VELES
VELETA
VELETAS
VELIGER
VELIGERS
VELL
VELLEITIES
VELLEITY
VELLENAGE
VELLENAGES
VELLET
VELLETS
VELLICATE
VELLICATED
VELLICATES
VELLICATING
VELLON
VELLONS
VELLS
VELLUM
VELLUMS
VELOCE
VELOCITIES
VELOCITY
VELODROME
VELODROMES
VELOUR
VELOURS
VELOUTÉ
VELOUTÉS
VELOUTINE
VELOUTINES
VELSKOEN
VELSKOENS
VELUM
VELURE
VELURED
VELURES
VELURING
VELVERET
VELVERETS
VELVET
VELVETED
VELVETEEN
VELVETEENS
VELVETING
VELVETINGS
VELVETS
VELVETY
VENA
VENAE
VENAL
VENALITIES
VENALITY
VENALLY
VENATIC
VENATICAL
VENATION
VENATIONS
VENATOR
VENATORS
VEND
VENDACE
VENDACES
VENDAGE
VENDAGES
VENDANGE
VENDANGES

VENDED
VENDEE
VENDEES
VENDER
VENDERS
VENDETTA
VENDETTAS
VENDEUSE
VENDEUSES
VENDIBLE
VENDIBLES
VENDIBLY
VENDING
VENDIS
VENDISES
VENDISS
VENDISSES
VENDITION
VENDITIONS
VENDOR
VENDORS
VENDS
VENDUE
VENDUES
VENEER
VENEERED
VENEERER
VENEERERS
VENEERING
VENEERINGS
VENEERS
VENEFIC
VENEFICAL
VENERABLE
VENERABLY
VENERATE
VENERATED
VENERATES
VENERATING
VENERATOR
VENERATORS
VENEREAL
VENEREAN
VENEREANS
VENEREOUS
VENERER
VENERERS
VENERIES
VENERY
VENEWE
VENEWES
VENEY
VENEYS
VENGE
VENGEABLE
VENGEABLY
VENGEANCE
VENGEANCES
VENGED
VENGEFUL
VENGEMENT
VENGEMENTS
VENGER
VENGERS
VENGES
VENGING
VENIAL
VENIALITIES
VENIALITY
VENIALLY

VENIN
VENINS
VENIRE
VENIREMAN
VENIREMEN
VENIRES
VENISON
VENISONS
VENITE
VENITES
VENNEL
VENNELS
VENOM
VENOMED
VENOMING
VENOMOUS
VENOMS
VENOSE
VENOSITY
VENOUS
VENT
VENTAGE
VENTAGES
VENTAIL
VENTAILE
VENTAILES
VENTAILS
VENTANA
VENTANAS
VENTAYLE
VENTAYLES
VENTED
VENTER
VENTERS
VENTIDUCT
VENTIDUCTS
VENTIFACT
VENTIFACTS
VENTIGE
VENTIGES
VENTIL
VENTILATE
VENTILATED
VENTILATES
VENTILATING
VENTILS
VENTING
VENTINGS
VENTOSE
VENTOSITIES
VENTOSITY
VENTRAL
VENTRALLY
VENTRALS
VENTRE
VENTRED
VENTRES
VENTRICLE
VENTRICLES
VENTRING
VENTROUS
VENTS
VENTURE
VENTURED
VENTURER
VENTURERS
VENTURES
VENTURI
VENTURING
VENTURINGS

VENTURIS
VENTUROUS
VENUE
VENUES
VENULE
VENULES
VENUS
VENUSES
VENVILLE
VENVILLES
VERACIOUS
VERACITIES
VERACITY
VERANDA
VERANDAH
VERANDAHS
VERANDAS
VERATRIN
VERATRINE
VERATRINES
VERATRINS
VERATRUM
VERATRUMS
VERB
VERBAL
VERBALISE
VERBALISED
VERBALISES
VERBALISING
VERBALISM
VERBALISMS
VERBALIST
VERBALISTS
VERBALITIES
VERBALITY
VERBALIZE
VERBALIZED
VERBALIZES
VERBALIZING
VERBALLED
VERBALLING
VERBALLY
VERBALS
VERBARIAN
VERBARIANS
VERBATIM
VERBENA
VERBENAS
VERBERATE
VERBERATED
VERBERATES
VERBERATING
VERBIAGE
VERBIAGES
VERBICIDE
VERBICIDES
VERBLESS
VERBOSE
VERBOSELY
VERBOSER
VERBOSEST
VERBOSITIES
VERBOSITY
VERBS
VERDANCIES
VERDANCY
VERDANT
VERDANTLY
VERDELHO
VERDELHOS

VERDERER
VERDERERS
VERDEROR
VERDERORS
VERDET
VERDETS
VERDICT
VERDICTS
VERDIGRIS
VERDIGRISED
VERDIGRISES
VERDIGRISING
VERDIT
VERDITER
VERDITERS
VERDITS
VERDOY
VERDURE
VERDURED
VERDURES
VERDUROUS
VERECUND
VERGE
VERGED
VERGENCIES
VERGENCY
VERGER
VERGERS
VERGES
VERGING
VERGLAS
VERGLASES
VERIDICAL
VERIER
VERIEST
VERIFIED
VERIFIER
VERIFIERS
VERIFIES
VERIFY
VERIFYING
VERILY
VERISM
VERISMO
VERISMOS
VERISMS
VERIST
VERISTIC
VERISTS
VERITABLE
VERITABLY
VERITIES
VERITY
VERJUICE
VERJUICED
VERJUICES
VERKRAMP
VERLIG
VERLIGTE
VERLIGTES
VERMEIL
VERMEILED
VERMEILING
VERMEILLE
VERMEILLES
VERMEILS
VERMELL
VERMELLS
VERMES
VERMIAN

VERMICIDE
VERMICIDES
VERMICULE
VERMICULES
VERMIFORM
VERMIFUGE
VERMIFUGES
VERMIL
VERMILIES
VERMILION
VERMILIONED
VERMILIONING
VERMILIONS
VERMILS
VERMILY
VERMIN
VERMINATE
VERMINATED
VERMINATES
VERMINATING
VERMINED
VERMINOUS
VERMINS
VERMINY
VERMIS
VERMISES
VERMOUTH
VERMOUTHS
VERNAL
VERNALISE
VERNALISED
VERNALISES
VERNALISING
VERNALITIES
VERNALITY
VERNALIZE
VERNALIZED
VERNALIZES
VERNALIZING
VERNALLY
VERNANT
VERNATION
VERNATIONS
VERNICLE
VERNICLES
VERNIER
VERNIERS
VERONICA
VERONICAS
VERONIQUE
VERQUERE
VERQUERES
VERQUIRE
VERQUIRES
VERREL
VERRELS
VERREY
VERRUCA
VERRUCAE
VERRUCAS
VERRUCOSE
VERRUCOUS
VERRUGA
VERRUGAS
VERRY
VERS
VERSAL
VERSALS
VERSANT
VERSANTS

VERSATILE
VERSE
VERSED
VERSELET
VERSELETS
VERSER
VERSERS
VERSES
VERSET
VERSETS
VERSICLE
VERSICLES
VERSIFIED
VERSIFIER
VERSIFIERS
VERSIFIES
VERSIFORM
VERSIFY
VERSIFYING
VERSIN
VERSINE
VERSINES
VERSING
VERSINGS
VERSINS
VERSION
VERSIONAL
VERSIONER
VERSIONERS
VERSIONS
VERSO
VERSOS
VERST
VERSTS
VERSUS
VERSUTE
VERT
VERTEBRA
VERTEBRAE
VERTEBRAL
VERTED
VERTEX
VERTICAL
VERTICALS
VERTICES
VERTICIL
VERTICILS
VERTICITIES
VERTICITY
VERTIGINES
VERTIGO
VERTIGOES
VERTIGOS
VERTING
VERTIPORT
VERTIPORTS
VERTS
VERTU
VERTUE
VERTUES
VERTUOUS
VERTUS
VERVAIN
VERVAINS
VERVE
VERVEL
VERVELLED
VERVELS
VERVEN
VERVENS

VERVES
VERVET
VERVETS
VERY
VESICA
VESICAE
VESICAL
VESICANT
VESICANTS
VESICATE
VESICATED
VESICATES
VESICATING
VESICLE
VESICLES
VESICULA
VESICULAE
VESICULAR
VESPA
VESPAS
VESPER
VESPERAL
VESPERS
VESPIARIES
VESPIARY
VESPINE
VESPOID
VESSAIL
VESSAILS
VESSEL
VESSELS
VEST
VESTA
VESTAL
VESTALS
VESTAS
VESTED
VESTIARIES
VESTIARY
VESTIBULE
VESTIBULED
VESTIBULES
VESTIBULING
VESTIGE
VESTIGES
VESTIGIA
VESTIGIAL
VESTIGIUM
VESTIMENT
VESTIMENTS
VESTING
VESTINGS
VESTITURE
VESTITURES
VESTMENT
VESTMENTS
VESTRAL
VESTRIES
VESTRY
VESTRYMAN
VESTRYMEN
VESTS
VESTURAL
VESTURE
VESTURED
VESTURER
VESTURERS
VESTURES
VESTURING
VESUVIAN

VESUVIANS
VET
VETCH
VETCHES
VETCHIER
VETCHIEST
VETCHLING
VETCHLINGS
VETCHY
VETERAN
VETERANS
VETIVER
VETIVERS
VETKOEK
VETKOEKS
VETO
VETOED
VETOES
VETOING
VETS
VETTED
VETTING
VETTURA
VETTURAS
VETTURINI
VETTURINO
VEX
VEXATION
VEXATIONS
VEXATIOUS
VEXATORY
VEXED
VEXEDLY
VEXEDNESS
VEXEDNESSES
VEXER
VEXERS
VEXES
VEXILLA
VEXILLARIES
VEXILLARY
VEXILLUM
VEXING
VEXINGLY
VEXINGS
VEZIR
VEZIRS
VIA
VIABILITIES
VIABILITY
VIABLE
VIADUCT
VIADUCTS
VIAL
VIALFUL
VIALFULS
VIALLED
VIALS
VIAMETER
VIAMETERS
VIAND
VIANDS
VIAS
VIATICA
VIATICALS
VIATICUM
VIATICUMS
VIATOR
VIATORIAL
VIATORS

VIBE	VICINITY	VIED	VILDNESSES	VIMS
VIBES	VICIOSITIES	VIELLE	VILE	VIN
VIBEX	VICIOSITY	VIELLES	VILELY	VINA
VIBICES	VICIOUS	VIER	VILENESS	VINACEOUS
VIBIST	VICIOUSLY	VIERS	VILENESSES	VINAL
VIBISTS	VICOMTE	VIES	VILER	VINAS
VIBRACULA	VICOMTES	VIEW	VILEST	VINASSE
VIBRAHARP	VICTIM	VIEWABLE	VILIACO	VINASSES
VIBRAHARPS	VICTIMISE	VIEWDATA	VILIACOES	VINCA
VIBRANCIES	VICTIMISED	VIEWDATAS	VILIACOS	VINCAS
VIBRANCY	VICTIMISES	VIEWED	VILIAGO	VINCIBLE
VIBRANT	VICTIMISING	VIEWER	VILIAGOES	VINCULA
VIBRATE	VICTIMIZE	VIEWERS	VILIAGOS	VINCULUM
VIBRATED	VICTIMIZED	VIEWIER	VILIFIED	VINDALOO
VIBRATES	VICTIMIZES	VIEWIEST	VILIFIER	VINDALOOS
VIBRATILE	VICTIMIZING	VIEWINESS	VILIFIERS	VINDEMIAL
VIBRATING	VICTIMS	VIEWINESSES	VILIFIES	VINDICATE
VIBRATION	VICTOR	VIEWING	VILIFY	VINDICATED
VIBRATIONS	VICTORESS	VIEWINGS	VILIFYING	VINDICATES
VIBRATIVE	VICTORESSES	VIEWLESS	VILIPEND	VINDICATING
VIBRATO	VICTORIA	VIEWLY	VILIPENDED	VINE
VIBRATOR	VICTORIAS	VIEWPHONE	VILIPENDING	VINED
VIBRATORS	VICTORIES	VIEWPHONES	VILIPENDS	VINEGAR
VIBRATORY	VICTORINE	VIEWPOINT	VILL	VINEGARED
VIBRATOS	VICTORINES	VIEWPOINTS	VILLA	VINEGARING
VIBRIO	VICTORS	VIEWS	VILLADOM	VINEGARS
VIBRIOS	VICTORY	VIEWY	VILLADOMS	VINEGARY
VIBRIOSES	VICTRESS	VIFDA	VILLAGE	VINER
VIBRIOSIS	VICTRESSES	VIFDAS	VILLAGER	VINERIES
VIBRISSA	VICTRIX	VIGESIMAL	VILLAGERIES	VINERS
VIBRISSAE	VICTRIXES	VIGIA	VILLAGERS	VINERY
VIBRONIC	VICTUAL	VIGIAS	VILLAGERY	VINES
VIBS	VICTUALLED	VIGIL	VILLAGES	VINEW
VIBURNUM	VICTUALLING	VIGILANCE	VILLAGIO	VINEWED
VIBURNUMS	VICTUALS	VIGILANCES	VILLAGIOS	VINEWING
VICAR	VICUÑA	VIGII ANT	VILLAGREE	VINEWS
VICARAGE	VICUÑAS	VIGILANTE	VILLAGREES	VINEYARD
VICARAGES	VIDAME	VIGILANTES	VILLAIN	VINEYARDS
VICARATE	VIDAMES	VIGILS	VILLAINIES	VINIER
VICARATES	VIDE	VIGNERON	VILLAINS	VINIEST
VICARESS	VIDELICET	VIGNERONS	VILLAINY	VINING
VICARESSES	VIDENDA	VIGNETTE	VILLAN	VINO
VICARIAL	VIDENDUM	VIGNETTED	VILLANAGE	VINOLENT
VICARIATE	VIDEO	VIGNETTER	VILLANAGES	VINOLOGIES
VICARIATES	VIDEODISC	VIGNETTERS	VILLANIES	VINOLOGY
VICARIES	VIDEODISCS	VIGNETTES	VILLANOUS	VINOS
VICARIOUS	VIDEOED	VIGNETTING	VILLANS	VINOSITIES
VICARS	VIDEOFIT	VIGOR	VILLANY	VINOSITY
VICARSHIP	VIDEOFITS	VIGORISH	VILLAR	VINOUS
VICARSHIPS	VIDEOGRAM	VIGORISHES	VILLAS	VINS
VICARY	VIDEOGRAMS	VIGORO	VILLATIC	VINT
VICE	VIDEOING	VIGOROS	VILLEIN	VINTAGE
VICED	VIDEOS	VIGOROUS	VILLEINS	VINTAGED
VICENARY	VIDEOTAPE	VIGORS	VILLENAGE	VINTAGER
VICENNIAL	VIDEOTAPES	VIGOUR	VILLENAGES	VINTAGERS
VICEREINE	VIDEOTEX	VIGOURS	VILLI	VINTAGES
VICEREINES	VIDEOTEXES	VIHARA	VILLIAGO	VINTAGING
VICEROY	VIDEOTEXT	VIHARAS	VILLIAGOES	VINTAGINGS
VICEROYS	VIDEOTEXTS	VIHUELA	VILLIAGOS	VINTED
VICES	VIDETTE	VIHUELAS	VILLIFORM	VINTING
VICESIMAL	VIDETTES	VIKING	VILLOSE	VINTNER
VICIATE	VIDIMUS	VIKINGISM	VILLOSITIES	VINTNERS
VICIATED	VIDIMUSES	VIKINGISMS	VILLOSITY	VINTRIES
VICIATES	VIDUAGE	VIKINGS	VILLOUS	VINTRY
VICIATING	VIDUAGES	VILAYET	VILLS	VINTS
VICINAGE	VIDUAL	VILAYETS	VILLUS	VINY
VICINAGES	VIDUITIES	VILD	VIM	VINYL
VICINAL	VIDUITY	VILDE	VIMANA	VINYLS
VICING	VIDUOUS	VILDLY	VIMANAS	VIOL
VICINITIES	VIE	VILDNESS	VIMINEOUS	VIOLA

VIOLABLE
VIOLABLY
VIOLAS
VIOLATE
VIOLATED
VIOLATES
VIOLATING
VIOLATION
VIOLATIONS
VIOLATIVE
VIOLATOR
VIOLATORS
VIOLD
VIOLENCE
VIOLENCES
VIOLENT
VIOLENTED
VIOLENTING
VIOLENTLY
VIOLENTS
VIOLER
VIOLERS
VIOLET
VIOLETS
VIOLIN
VIOLINIST
VIOLINISTS
VIOLINS
VIOLIST
VIOLISTS
VIOLONE
VIOLONES
VIOLS
VIPER
VIPERINE
VIPERISH
VIPEROUS
VIPERS
VIRAEMIA
VIRAEMIAS
VIRAEMIC
VIRAGO
VIRAGOES
VIRAGOISH
VIRAGOS
VIRAL
VIRANDA
VIRANDAS
VIRANDO
VIRANDOS
VIRELAY
VIRELAYS
VIREMENT
VIREMENTS
VIRENT
VIREO
VIREOS
VIRES
VIRESCENT
VIRETOT
VIRETOTS
VIRGA
VIRGAS
VIRGATE
VIRGATES
VIRGE
VIRGER
VIRGERS
VIRGES
VIRGIN

VIRGINAL
VIRGINALLED
VIRGINALLING
VIRGINALS
VIRGINING
VIRGINITIES
VIRGINITY
VIRGINIUM
VIRGINIUMS
VIRGINLY
VIRGINS
VIRGULATE
VIRGULE
VIRGULES
VIRICIDAL
VIRICIDE
VIRICIDES
VIRID
VIRIDIAN
VIRIDIANS
VIRIDITE
VIRIDITES
VIRIDITIES
VIRIDITY
VIRILE
VIRILISED
VIRILISM
VIRILISMS
VIRILITIES
VIRILITY
VIRILIZED
VIRION
VIRIONS
VIRL
VIRLS
VIROGENE
VIROGENES
VIROID
VIROIDS
VIROLOGIES
VIROLOGY
VIROSE
VIROSES
VIROSIS
VIROUS
VIRTU
VIRTUAL
VIRTUALLY
VIRTUE
VIRTUES
VIRTUOSA
VIRTUOSE
VIRTUOSI
VIRTUOSIC
VIRTUOSO
VIRTUOSOS
VIRTUOUS
VIRTUS
VIRUCIDAL
VIRUCIDE
VIRUCIDES
VIRULENCE
VIRULENCES
VIRULENCIES
VIRULENCY
VIRULENT
VIRUS
VIRUSES
VIS
VISA

VISAED
VISAGE
VISAGED
VISAGES
VISAGIST
VISAGISTE
VISAGISTES
VISAGISTS
VISAING
VISAS
VISCACHA
VISCACHAS
VISCERA
VISCERAL
VISCERATE
VISCERATED
VISCERATES
VISCERATING
VISCID
VISCIDITIES
VISCIDITY
VISCIN
VISCINS
VISCOSE
VISCOSES
VISCOSITIES
VISCOSITY
VISCOUNT
VISCOUNTIES
VISCOUNTS
VISCOUNTY
VISCOUS
VISCUM
VISCUMS
VISCUS
VISE
VISÉ
VISED
VISÉED
VISÉING
VISES
VISÉS
VISIBLE
VISIBLES
VISIBLY
VISIE
VISIED
VISIEING
VISIER
VISIERS
VISIES
VISILE
VISILES
VISING
VISION
VISIONAL
VISIONARIES
VISIONARY
VISIONED
VISIONER
VISIONERS
VISIONING
VISIONINGS
VISIONIST
VISIONISTS
VISIONS
VISIT
VISITABLE
VISITANT
VISITANTS

VISITATOR
VISITATORS
VISITE
VISITED
VISITEE
VISITEES
VISITER
VISITERS
VISITES
VISITING
VISITINGS
VISITOR
VISITORS
VISITRESS
VISITRESSES
VISITS
VISIVE
VISNE
VISNES
VISNOMIE
VISNOMIES
VISNOMY
VISON
VISONS
VISOR
VISORED
VISORING
VISORS
VISTA
VISTAED
VISTAING
VISTAL
VISTALESS
VISTAS
VISTO
VISTOS
VISUAL
VISUALISE
VISUALISED
VISUALISES
VISUALISING
VISUALIST
VISUALISTS
VISUALITIES
VISUALITY
VISUALIZE
VISUALIZED
VISUALIZES
VISUALIZING
VISUALLY
VISUALS
VITA
VITAE
VITAL
VITALISE
VITALISED
VITALISER
VITALISERS
VITALISES
VITALISING
VITALISM
VITALISMS
VITALIST
VITALISTS
VITALITIES
VITALITY
VITALIZE
VITALIZED
VITALIZER
VITALIZERS

VITALIZES
VITALIZING
VITALLY
VITALS
VITAMIN
VITAMINE
VITAMINES
VITAMINS
VITASCOPE
VITASCOPES
VITATIVE
VITE
VITELLARY
VITELLI
VITELLIN
VITELLINE
VITELLINES
VITELLINS
VITELLUS
VITEX
VITEXES
VITIABLE
VITIATE
VITIATED
VITIATES
VITIATING
VITIATION
VITIATIONS
VITIATOR
VITIATORS
VITICETA
VITICETUM
VITICETUMS
VITICIDE
VITICIDES
VITILIGO
VITILIGOS
VITIOSITIES
VITIOSITY
VITRAGE
VITRAGES
VITRAIL
VITRAIN
VITRAINS
VITRAUX
VITREOUS
VITREUM
VITREUMS
VITRIC
VITRICS
VITRIFIED
VITRIFIES
VITRIFORM
VITRIFY
VITRIFYING
VITRINE
VITRINES
VITRIOL
VITRIOLIC
VITRIOLS
VITTA
VITTAE
VITTATE
VITTLE
VITTLES
VITULAR
VITULINE
VIVA
VIVACE
VIVACIOUS

VIVACITIES	VIZIRATES	VOGUES	VOLED	VOLUTE
VIVACITY	VIZIRIAL	VOGUEY	VOLENS	VOLUTED
VIVAED	VIZIRS	VOGUING	VOLERIES	VOLUTES
VIVAING	VIZIRSHIP	VOGUISH	VOLERY	VOLUTIN
VIVAMENTE	VIZIRSHIPS	VOICE	VOLES	VOLUTINS
VIVANDIER	VIZOR	VOICED	VOLET	VOLUTION
VIVANDIERS	VIZORED	VOICEFUL	VOLETS	VOLUTIONS
VIVARIA	VIZORING	VOICELESS	VOLING	VOLUTOID
VIVARIES	VIZORS	VOICER	VOLITANT	VOLVA
VIVARIUM	VIZSLA	VOICERS	VOLITATE	VOLVAS
VIVARIUMS	VIZSLAS	VOICES	VOLITATED	VOLVATE
VIVARY	VIZY	VOICING	VOLITATES	VOLVE
VIVAS	VIZZIE	VOICINGS	VOLITATING	VOLVED
VIVAT	VIZZIED	VOID	VOLITIENT	VOLVES
VIVDA	VIZZIES	VOIDABLE	VOLITION	VOLVING
VIVDAS	VIZZYING	VOIDANCE	VOLITIONS	VOLVULUS
VIVE	VLEI	VOIDANCES	VOLITIVE	VOLVULUSES
VIVELY	VLEIS	VOIDED	VOLITIVES	VOMER
VIVENCIES	VLIES	VOIDEE	VOLKSRAAD	VOMERINE
VIVENCY	VLY	VOIDEES	VOLKSRAADS	VOMERS
VIVER	VOAR	VOIDER	VOLLEY	VOMICA
VIVERRINE	VOARS	VOIDERS	VOLLEYED	VOMICAS
VIVERS	VOCABLE	VOIDING	VOLLEYING	VOMIT
VIVES	VOCABLES	VOIDINGS	VOLLEYS	VOMITED
VIVESES	VOCABULAR	VOIDNESS	VOLOST	VOMITING
VIVIANITE	VOCAL	VOIDNESSES	VOLOSTS	VOMITINGS
VIVIANITES	VOCALIC	VOIDS	VOLPINO	VOMITIVE
VIVID	VOCALION	VOILA	VOLPINOS	VOMITIVES
VIVIDER	VOCALIONS	VOILE	VOLPLANE	VOMITO
VIVIDEST	VOCALISE	VOILES	VOLPLANED	VOMITORIES
VIVIDITIES	VOCALISED	VOISINAGE	VOLPLANES	VOMITORY
VIVIDITY	VOCALISER	VOISINAGES	VOLPLANING	VOMITOS
VIVIDLY	VOCALISERS	VOITURE	VOLS	VOMITS
VIVIDNESS	VOCALISES	VOITURES	VOLT	VOODOO
VIVIDNESSES	VOCALISING	VOITURIER	VOLTA	VOODOOED
VIVIFIC	VOCALISM	VOITURIERS	VOLTAGE	VOODOOING
VIVIFIED	VOCALISMS	VOIVODE	VOLTAGES	VOODOOISM
VIVIFIER	VOCALIST	VOIVODES	VOLTAIC	VOODOOISMS
VIVIFIERS	VOCALISTS	VOL	VOLTAISM	VOODOOIST
VIVIFIES	VOCALITIES	VOLA	VOLTAISMS	VOODOOISTS
VIVIFY	VOCALITY	VOLABLE	VOLTE	VOODOOS
VIVIFYING	VOCALIZE	VOLAE	VOLTES	VOR
VIVIPARIES	VOCALIZED	VOLAGE	VOLTIGEUR	VORACIOUS
VIVIPARY	VOCALIZER	VOLAGEOUS	VOLTIGEURS	VORACITIES
VIVISECT	VOCALIZERS	VOLANT	VOLTINISM	VORACITY
VIVISECTED	VOCALIZES	VOLANTE	VOLTINISMS	VORAGO
VIVISECTING	VOCALIZING	VOLANTES	VOLTMETER	VORAGOES
VIVISECTS	VOCALLY	VOLAR	VOLTMETERS	VORANT
VIVO	VOCALNESS	VOLARIES	VOLTS	VORPAL
VIVRES	VOCALNESSES	VOLARY	VOLUBIL	VORTEX
VIXEN	VOCALS	VOLATIC	VOLUBLE	VORTEXES
VIXENISH	VOCATION	VOLATILE	VOLUBLY	VORTICAL
VIXENLY	VOCATIONS	VOLATILES	VOLUCRINE	VORTICES
VIXENS	VOCATIVE	VOLCANIAN	VOLUME	VORTICISM
VIZAMENT	VOCATIVES	VOLCANIC	VOLUMED	VORTICISMS
VIZAMENTS	VOCES	VOLCANISE	VOLUMES	VORTICIST
VIZARD	VOCODER	VOLCANISED	VOLUMETER	VORTICISTS
VIZARDED	VOCODERS	VOLCANISES	VOLUMETERS	VORTICITIES
VIZARDING	VOCULAR	VOLCANISING	VOLUMINAL	VORTICITY
VIZARDS	VOCULE	VOLCANISM	VOLUMING	VORTICOSE
VIZCACHA	VOCULES	VOLCANISMS	VOLUMIST	VOTARESS
VIZCACHAS	VODKA	VOLCANIST	VOLUMISTS	VOTARESSES
VIZIER	VODKAS	VOLCANISTS	VOLUNTARIES	VOTARIES
VIZIERATE	VOE	VOLCANIZE	VOLUNTARY	VOTARIST
VIZIERATES	VOES	VOLCANIZED	VOLUNTEER	VOTARISTS
VIZIERIAL	VOGIE	VOLCANIZES	VOLUNTEERED	VOTARY
VIZIERS	VOGIER	VOLCANIZING	VOLUNTEERING	VOTE
VIZIES	VOGIEST	VOLCANO	VOLUNTEERS	VOTED
VIZIR	VOGUE	VOLCANOES	VÖLUSPA	VOTEEN
VIZIRATE	VOGUED	VOLE	VÖLUSPAS	VOTEENS

VOTELESS
VOTER
VOTERS
VOTES
VOTING
VOTIVE
VOUCH
VOUCHED
VOUCHEE
VOUCHEES
VOUCHER
VOUCHERS
VOUCHES
VOUCHING
VOUCHSAFE
VOUCHSAFED
VOUCHSAFES
VOUCHSAFING
VOUDOU
VOUDOUED
VOUDOUING
VOUDOUS
VOUGE
VOUGES
VOULGE
VOULGES
VOULU
VOUSSOIR
VOUSSOIRED
VOUSSOIRING
VOUSSOIRS
VOUTSAFE
VOUTSAFED
VOUTSAFES

VOUTSAFING
VOW
VOWED
VOWEL
VOWELISE
VOWELISED
VOWELISES
VOWELISING
VOWELIZE
VOWELIZED
VOWELIZES
VOWELIZING
VOWELLED
VOWELLESS
VOWELLING
VOWELLY
VOWELS
VOWESS
VOWESSES
VOWING
VOWS
VOX
VOYAGE
VOYAGED
VOYAGER
VOYAGERS
VOYAGES
VOYAGEUR
VOYAGEURS
VOYAGING
VOYEUR
VOYEURISM
VOYEURISMS
VOYEURS

VRAIC
VRAICKER
VRAICKERS
VRAICKING
VRAICKINGS
VRAICS
VRIL
VRILS
VROOM
VROOMED
VROOMING
VROOMS
VROUW
VROUWS
VUG
VUGGY
VUGS
VULCAN
VULCANIAN
VULCANIC
VULCANISE
VULCANISED
VULCANISES
VULCANISING
VULCANISM
VULCANISMS
VULCANIST
VULCANISTS
VULCANITE
VULCANITES
VULCANIZE
VULCANIZED
VULCANIZES
VULCANIZING

VULCANS
VULGAR
VULGARER
VULGAREST
VULGARIAN
VULGARIANS
VULGARISE
VULGARISED
VULGARISES
VULGARISING
VULGARISM
VULGARISMS
VULGARITIES
VULGARITY
VULGARIZE
VULGARIZED
VULGARIZES
VULGARIZING
VULGARLY
VULGARS
VULGATE
VULGATES
VULGO
VULGUS
VULGUSES
VULN
VULNED
VULNERARIES
VULNERARY
VULNERATE
VULNERATED
VULNERATES
VULNERATING
VULNING

VULNS
VULPICIDE
VULPICIDES
VULPINE
VULPINISM
VULPINISMS
VULPINITE
VULPINITES
VULSELLA
VULSELLAE
VULSELLUM
VULTURE
VULTURES
VULTURINE
VULTURISH
VULTURISM
VULTURISMS
VULTURN
VULTURNS
VULTUROUS
VULVA
VULVAL
VULVAR
VULVAS
VULVATE
VULVIFORM
VULVITIS
VULVITISES
VUM
VUMMED
VUMMING
VUMS
VYING
VYINGLY

W

WABAIN	WAEFUL	WAGON	WAISTS	WALIES
WABAINS	WAENESS	WAGONAGE	WAIT	WALIEST
WABBLE	WAENESSES	WAGONAGES	WAITE	WALING
WABBLED	WAESOME	WAGONED	WAITED	WALIS
WABBLER	WAESUCKS	WAGONER	WAITER	WALISE
WABBLERS	WAFER	WAGONERS	WAITERAGE	WALISES
WABBLES	WAFERED	WAGONETTE	WAITERAGES	WALK
WABBLING	WAFERING	WAGONETTES	WAITERING	WALKABLE
WABBLY	WAFERS	WAGONFUL	WAITERINGS	WALKABOUT
WABOOM	WAFERY	WAGONFULS	WAITERS	WALKABOUTS
WABOOMS	WAFF	WAGONING	WAITES	WALKED
WABSTER	WAFFED	WAGONS	WAITING	WALKER
WABSTERS	WAFFING	WAGS	WAITINGLY	WALKERS
WACKE	WAFFLE	WAGTAIL	WAITINGS	WALKING
WACKES	WAFFLED	WAGTAILS	WAITRESS	WALKINGS
WACKIER	WAFFLES	WAHINE	WAITRESSES	WALKS
WACKIEST	WAFFLING	WAHINES	WAITS	WALKWAY
WACKINESS	WAFFS	WAHOO	WAIVE	WALKWAYS
WACKINESSES	WAFT	WAHOOS	WAIVED	WALL
WACKY	WAFTAGE	WAID	WAIVER	WALLA
WAD	WAFTAGES	WAIDE	WAIVERS	WALLABA
WADD	WAFTED	WAIF	WAIVES	WALLABAS
WADDED	WAFTER	WAIFED	WAIVING	WALLABIES
WADDIE	WAFTERS	WAIFING	WAIVODE	WALLABY
WADDIED	WAFTING	WAIFS	WAIVODES	WALLAH
WADDIES	WAFTINGS	WAIFT	WAIWODE	WALLAHS
WADDING	WAFTS	WAIFTS	WAIWODES	WALLAROO
WADDINGS	WAFTURE	WAIL	WAKE	WALLAROOS
WADDLE	WAFTURES	WAILED	WAKED	WALLAS
WADDLED	WAG	WAILER	WAKEFUL	WALLED
WADDLES	WAGE	WAILERS	WAKEFULLY	WALLER
WADDLING	WAGED	WAILFUL	WAKELESS	WALLERS
WADDS	WAGELESS	WAILING	WAKEMAN	WALLET
WADDY	WAGENBOOM	WAILINGLY	WAKEMEN	WALLETS
WADDYING	WAGENBOOMS	WAILINGS	WAKEN	WALLFISH
WADE	WAGER	WAILS	WAKENED	WALLFISHES
WADED	WAGERED	WAIN	WAKENER	WALLIER
WADER	WAGERER	WAINAGE	WAKENERS	WALLIES
WADERS	WAGERERS	WAINAGES	WAKENING	WALLIEST
WADES	WAGERING	WAINED	WAKENINGS	WALLING
WADI	WAGERS	WAINING	WAKENS	WALLINGS
WADIES	WAGES	WAINS	WAKER	WALLOP
WADING	WAGGED	WAINSCOT	WAKERIFE	WALLOPED
WADINGS	WAGGERIES	WAINSCOTED	WAKERS	WALLOPER
WADIS	WAGGERY	WAINSCOTING	WAKES	WALLOPERS
WADMAAL	WAGGING	WAINSCOTINGS	WAKIKI	WALLOPING
WADMAALS	WAGGISH	WAINSCOTS	WAKIKIS	WALLOPINGS
WADMAL	WAGGISHLY	WAINSCOTTED	WAKING	WALLOPS
WADMALS	WAGGLE	WAINSCOTTING	WAKINGS	WALLOW
WADMOL	WAGGLED	WAINSCOTTINGS	WALD	WALLOWED
WADMOLL	WAGGLES	WAIST	WALDFLUTE	WALLOWER
WADMOLLS	WAGGLING	WAISTBAND	WALDFLUTES	WALLOWERS
WADMOLS	WAGGLY	WAISTBANDS	WALDGRAVE	WALLOWING
WADS	WAGGON	WAISTBELT	WALDGRAVES	WALLOWINGS
WADSET	WAGGONED	WAISTBELTS	WALDHORN	WALLOWS
WADSETS	WAGGONER	WAISTBOAT	WALDHORNS	WALLPAPER
WADSETT	WAGGONERS	WAISTBOATS	WALDS	WALLPAPERS
WADSETTED	WAGGONING	WAISTCOAT	WALE	WALLS
WADSETTER	WAGGONS	WAISTCOATS	WALED	WALLSEND
WADSETTERS	WAGHALTER	WAISTED	WALER	WALLSENDS
WADSETTING	WAGHALTERS	WAISTER	WALERS	WALLWORT
WADSETTS	WAGING	WAISTERS	WALES	WALLWORTS
WADY	WAGMOIRE	WAISTLINE	WALI	WALLY
WAE	WAGMOIRES	WAISTLINES	WALIER	WALLYDRAG

WALLYDRAGS	WANGLINGS	WAPINSHAW	WARHEADS	WARRANDS
WALNUT	WANGS	WAPINSHAWS	WARIER	WARRANED
WALNUTS	WANGUN	WAPITI	WARIEST	WARRANING
WALRUS	WANGUNS	WAPITIS	WARILY	WARRANS
WALRUSES	WANHOPE	WAPPED	WARIMENT	WARRANT
WALTY	WANHOPES	WAPPEND	WARIMENTS	WARRANTED
WALTZ	WANIER	WAPPER	WARINESS	WARRANTEE
WALTZED	WANIEST	WAPPERED	WARINESSES	WARRANTEES
WALTZER	WANIGAN	WAPPERING	WARING	WARRANTER
WALTZERS	WANIGANS	WAPPERS	WARISON	WARRANTERS
WALTZES	WANING	WAPPING	WARISONS	WARRANTIES
WALTZING	WANINGS	WAPS	WARK	WARRANTING
WALTZINGS	WANK	WAR	WARKS	WARRANTINGS
WALY	WANKED	WARATAH	WARLIKE	WARRANTOR
WAMBLE	WANKER	WARATAHS	WARLING	WARRANTORS
WAMBLED	WANKERS	WARBLE	WARLINGS	WARRANTS
WAMBLES	WANKING	WARBLED	WARLOCK	WARRANTY
WAMBLIER	WANKLE	WARBLER	WARLOCKRIES	WARRAY
WAMBLIEST	WANKS	WARBLERS	WARLOCKRY	WARRAYED
WAMBLING	WANLE	WARBLES	WARLOCKS	WARRAYING
WAMBLINGS	WANLY	WARBLING	WARLORD	WARRAYS
WAMBLY	WANNED	WARBLINGS	WARLORDS	WARRE
WAME	WANNEL	WARBY	WARM	WARRED
WAMED	WANNER	WARD	WARMAN	WARREN
WAMEFUL	WANNESS	WARDED	WARMBLOOD	WARRENER
WAMEFULS	WANNESSES	WARDEN	WARMBLOODS	WARRENERS
WAMES	WANNEST	WARDENED	WARMED	WARRENS
WAMMUS	WANNING	WARDENING	WARMEN	WARREY
WAMMUSES	WANNISH	WARDENRIES	WARMER	WARREYED
WAMPEE	WANS	WARDENRY	WARMERS	WARREYING
WAMPEES	WANT	WARDENS	WARMEST	WARREYS
WAMPISH	WANTAGE	WARDER	WARMING	WARRIGAL
WAMPISHED	WANTAGES	WARDERED	WARMINGS	WARRIGALS
WAMPISHES	WANTED	WARDERING	WARMLY	WARRING
WAMPISHING	WANTER	WARDERS	WARMNESS	WARRIOR
WAMPUM	WANTERS	WARDING	WARMNESSES	WARRIORS
WAMPUMS	WANTHILL	WARDINGS	WARMONGER	WARRISON
WAMPUS	WANTHILLS	WARDOG	WARMONGERS	WARRISONS
WAMPUSES	WANTIES	WARDOGS	WARMS	WARS
WAMUS	WANTING	WARDRESS	WARMTH	WARSHIP
WAMUSES	WANTINGS	WARDRESSES	WARMTHS	WARSHIPS
WAN	WANTON	WARDROBE	WARN	WARSLE
WANCHANCY	WANTONED	WARDROBER	WARNED	WARSLED
WAND	WANTONER	WARDROBERS	WARNER	WARSLES
WANDER	WANTONEST	WARDROBES	WARNERS	WARSLING
WANDERED	WANTONING	WARDROP	WARNING	WARST
WANDERER	WANTONISE	WARDROPS	WARNINGLY	WARSTED
WANDERERS	WANTONISED	WARDS	WARNINGS	WARSTING
WANDERING	WANTONISES	WARDSHIP	WARNS	WARSTS
WANDERINGS	WANTONISING	WARDSHIPS	WARP	WART
WANDEROO	WANTONIZE	WARE	WARPATH	WARTED
WANDEROOS	WANTONIZED	WARED	WARPATHS	WARTIER
WANDERS	WANTONIZES	WAREHOUSE	WARPED	WARTIEST
WANDLE	WANTONIZING	WAREHOUSED	WARPER	WARTIME
WANDOO	WANTONLY	WAREHOUSES	WARPERS	WARTIMES
WANDOOS	WANTONS	WAREHOUSING	WARPING	WARTLESS
WANDS	WANTS	WAREHOUSINGS	WARPINGS	WARTS
WANE	WANTY	WARELESS	WARPLANE	WARTWEED
WANED	WANWORDY	WARES	WARPLANES	WARTWEEDS
WANES	WANWORTH	WARFARE	WARPS	WARTWORT
WANEY	WANY	WARFARED	WARRAGAL	WARTWORTS
WANG	WANZE	WARFARER	WARRAGALS	WARTY
WANGAN	WANZED	WARFARERS	WARRAGLE	WARWOLF
WANGANS	WANZES	WARFARES	WARRAGLES	WARWOLVES
WANGLE	WANZING	WARFARIN	WARRAGUL	WARY
WANGLED	WAP	WARFARING	WARRAGULS	WAS
WANGLER	WAPENSHAW	WARFARINGS	WARRAN	WASE
WANGLERS	WAPENSHAWS	WARFARINS	WARRAND	WASES
WANGLES	WAPENTAKE	WARHABLE	WARRANDED	WASH
WANGLING	WAPENTAKES	WARHEAD	WARRANDING	WASHABLE

WASHED
WASHEN
WASHER
WASHERED
WASHERIES
WASHERING
WASHERMAN
WASHERMEN
WASHERS
WASHERY
WASHES
WASHIER
WASHIEST
WASHINESS
WASHINESSES
WASHING
WASHINGS
WASHLAND
WASHLANDS
WASHROOM
WASHROOMS
WASHY
WASP
WASPIE
WASPIER
WASPIES
WASPIEST
WASPISH
WASPISHLY
WASPS
WASPY
WASSAIL
WASSAILED
WASSAILER
WASSAILERS
WASSAILING
WASSAILINGS
WASSAILRIES
WASSAILRY
WASSAILS
WASSERMAN
WASSERMEN
WAST
WASTAGE
WASTAGES
WASTE
WASTED
WASTEFUL
WASTEFULL
WASTEL
WASTELAND
WASTELANDS
WASTELS
WASTENESS
WASTENESSES
WASTER
WASTERED
WASTERFUL
WASTERIES
WASTERIFE
WASTERIFES
WASTERING
WASTERS
WASTERY
WASTES
WASTING
WASTINGS
WASTNESS
WASTNESSES
WASTREL

WASTRELS
WASTRIES
WASTRY
WASTS
WAT
WATCH
WATCHABLE
WATCHCASE
WATCHCASES
WATCHED
WATCHER
WATCHERS
WATCHES
WATCHET
WATCHETS
WATCHFUL
WATCHING
WATCHMAN
WATCHMEN
WATCHWORD
WATCHWORDS
WATE
WATER
WATERAGE
WATERAGES
WATERED
WATERER
WATERERS
WATERFALL
WATERFALLS
WATERIER
WATERIEST
WATERING
WATERINGS
WATERISH
WATERLESS
WATERLILIES
WATERLILY
WATERLOG
WATERLOGGED
WATERLOGGING
WATERLOGS
WATERMAN
WATERMARK
WATERMARKED
WATERMARKING
WATERMARKS
WATERMEN
WATERS
WATERSHED
WATERSHEDS
WATERSIDE
WATERSIDES
WATERWAY
WATERWAYS
WATERWORK
WATERWORKS
WATERY
WATS
WATT
WATTAGE
WATTAGES
WATTER
WATTEST
WATTLE
WATTLED
WATTLES
WATTLING
WATTLINGS
WATTMETER

WATTMETERS
WATTS
WAUCHT
WAUCHTED
WAUCHTING
WAUCHTS
WAUFF
WAUFFED
WAUFFING
WAUFFS
WAUGH
WAUGHED
WAUGHING
WAUGHS
WAUGHT
WAUGHTED
WAUGHTING
WAUGHTS
WAUK
WAUKED
WAUKING
WAUKRIFE
WAUKS
WAUL
WAULED
WAULING
WAULINGS
WAULK
WAULKED
WAULKING
WAULKS
WAULS
WAUR
WAURST
WAURSTED
WAURSTING
WAURSTS
WAVE
WAVEBAND
WAVEBANDS
WAVED
WAVEFORM
WAVEFORMS
WAVEFRONT
WAVEFRONTS
WAVEGUIDE
WAVEGUIDES
WAVELESS
WAVELET
WAVELETS
WAVELIKE
WAVELLITE
WAVELLITES
WAVEMETER
WAVEMETERS
WAVER
WAVERED
WAVERER
WAVERERS
WAVERING
WAVERINGS
WAVEROUS
WAVERS
WAVERY
WAVES
WAVESHAPE
WAVESHAPES
WAVESON
WAVESONS
WAVEY

WAVEYS
WAVIER
WAVIES
WAVIEST
WAVINESS
WAVINESSES
WAVING
WAVINGS
WAVY
WAW
WAWE
WAWES
WAWL
WAWLED
WAWLING
WAWLINGS
WAWLS
WAWS
WAX
WAXBERRIES
WAXBERRY
WAXBILL
WAXBILLS
WAXED
WAXEN
WAXER
WAXERS
WAXES
WAXIER
WAXIEST
WAXINESS
WAXINESSES
WAXING
WAXINGS
WAXWING
WAXWINGS
WAXWORK
WAXWORKER
WAXWORKERS
WAXWORKS
WAXY
WAY
WAYBREAD
WAYBREADS
WAYED
WAYFARE
WAYFARED
WAYFARER
WAYFARERS
WAYFARES
WAYFARING
WAYFARINGS
WAYGONE
WAYGOOSE
WAYGOOSES
WAYING
WAYLAID
WAYLAY
WAYLAYER
WAYLAYERS
WAYLAYING
WAYLAYS
WAYLESS
WAYMARK
WAYMARKED
WAYMARKING
WAYMARKS
WAYMENT
WAYMENTED
WAYMENTING

WAYMENTS
WAYS
WAYSIDE
WAYSIDES
WAYWARD
WAYWARDLY
WAYWISER
WAYWISERS
WAYWORN
WAYZGOOSE
WAYZGOOSES
WAZIR
WAZIRS
WE
WEAK
WEAKEN
WEAKENED
WEAKENER
WEAKENERS
WEAKENING
WEAKENS
WEAKER
WEAKEST
WEAKFISH
WEAKFISHES
WEAKLIER
WEAKLIEST
WEAKLING
WEAKLINGS
WEAKLY
WEAKNESS
WEAKNESSES
WEAL
WEALD
WEALDS
WEALS
WEALSMAN
WEALSMEN
WEALTH
WEALTHIER
WEALTHIEST
WEALTHILY
WEALTHS
WEALTHY
WEAMB
WEAMBS
WEAN
WEANED
WEANEL
WEANELS
WEANER
WEANERS
WEANING
WEANLING
WEANLINGS
WEANS
WEAPON
WEAPONED
WEAPONRIES
WEAPONRY
WEAPONS
WEAR
WEARABLE
WEARED
WEARER
WEARERS
WEARIED
WEARIER
WEARIES
WEARIEST

WEARIFUL
WEARILESS
WEARILY
WEARINESS
WEARINESSES
WEARING
WEARINGS
WEARISH
WEARISOME
WEARS
WEARY
WEARYING
WEASAND
WEASANDS
WEASEL
WEASELED
WEASELER
WEASELERS
WEASELING
WEASELLED
WEASELLER
WEASELLERS
WEASELLING
WEASELLY
WEASELS
WEATHER
WEATHERED
WEATHERING
WEATHERINGS
WEATHERLY
WEATHERS
WEAVE
WEAVED
WEAVER
WEAVERS
WEAVES
WEAVING
WEAVINGS
WEAZAND
WEAZANDS
WEAZEN
WEAZENED
WEAZENING
WEAZENS
WEB
WEBBED
WEBBIER
WEBBIEST
WEBBING
WEBBINGS
WEBBY
WEBER
WEBERS
WEBS
WEBSTER
WEBSTERS
WEBWHEEL
WEBWHEELS
WEBWORM
WEBWORMS
WECHT
WECHTS
WED
WEDDED
WEDDING
WEDDINGS
WEDELN
WEDELNED
WEDELNING
WEDELNS

WEDGE
WEDGED
WEDGES
WEDGEWISE
WEDGIE
WEDGIES
WEDGING
WEDGINGS
WEDLOCK
WEDLOCKS
WEDS
WEE
WEED
WEEDED
WEEDER
WEEDERIES
WEEDERS
WEEDERY
WEEDICIDE
WEEDICIDES
WEEDIER
WEEDIEST
WEEDINESS
WEEDINESSES
WEEDING
WEEDINGS
WEEDLESS
WEEDS
WEEDY
WEEING
WEEK
WEEKDAY
WEEKDAYS
WEEKE
WEEKEND
WEEKENDS
WEEKES
WEEKLIES
WEEKLY
WEEKNIGHT
WEEKNIGHTS
WEEKS
WEEL
WEELS
WEEM
WEEN
WEENED
WEENIER
WEENIEST
WEENING
WEENS
WEENY
WEEP
WEEPER
WEEPERS
WEEPHOLE
WEEPHOLES
WEEPIE
WEEPIER
WEEPIES
WEEPIEST
WEEPING
WEEPINGLY
WEEPINGS
WEEPS
WEEPY
WEER
WEES
WEEST

WEET
WEETE
WEETEN
WEETING
WEETINGLY
WEETLESS
WEEVER
WEEVERS
WEEVIL
WEEVILED
WEEVILLED
WEEVILLY
WEEVILS
WEEVILY
WEFT
WEFTAGE
WEFTAGES
WEFTE
WEFTED
WEFTES
WEFTING
WEFTS
WEID
WEIDS
WEIGELA
WEIGELAS
WEIGH
WEIGHABLE
WEIGHAGE
WEIGHAGES
WEIGHED
WEIGHER
WEIGHERS
WEIGHING
WEIGHINGS
WEIGHS
WEIGHT
WEIGHTED
WEIGHTIER
WEIGHTIEST
WEIGHTILY
WEIGHTING
WEIGHTINGS
WEIGHTS
WEIGHTY
WEIL
WEILS
WEIR
WEIRD
WEIRDED
WEIRDER
WEIRDEST
WEIRDIE
WEIRDIES
WEIRDING
WEIRDLY
WEIRDNESS
WEIRDNESSES
WEIRDO
WEIRDOS
WEIRDS
WEIRED
WEIRING
WEIRS
WEISE
WEISED
WEISES
WEISING
WEIZE
WEIZED

WEIZES
WEIZING
WEKA
WEKAS
WELAWAY
WELCH
WELCHED
WELCHER
WELCHERS
WELCHES
WELCHING
WELCOME
WELCOMED
WELCOMER
WELCOMERS
WELCOMES
WELCOMING
WELD
WELDABLE
WELDED
WELDER
WELDERS
WELDING
WELDINGS
WELDLESS
WELDMENT
WELDMENTS
WELDMESH
WELDMESH®
WELDMESHES
WELDMESHES®
WELDOR
WELDORS
WELDS
WELFARE
WELFARES
WELFARISM
WELFARISMS
WELFARIST
WELFARISTS
WELK
WELKE
WELKED
WELKES
WELKIN
WELKING
WELKINS
WELKS
WELKT
WELL
WELLADAY
WELLANEAR
WELLAWAY
WELLED
WELLIE
WELLIES
WELLING
WELLINGS
WELLS
WELLY
WELSH
WELSHED
WELSHER
WELSHERS
WELSHES
WELSHING
WELT
WELTED
WELTER
WELTERED

WELTERING
WELTERS
WELTING
WELTS
WEM
WEMB
WEMBS
WEMS
WEN
WENCH
WENCHED
WENCHER
WENCHERS
WENCHES
WENCHING
WEND
WENDED
WENDIGO
WENDIGOS
WENDING
WENDS
WENNIER
WENNIEST
WENNISH
WENNY
WENS
WENT
WENTS
WEPT
WERE
WEREGILD
WEREGILDS
WEREWOLF
WEREWOLVES
WERGILD
WERGILDS
WERNERITE
WERNERITES
WERSH
WERSHER
WERSHEST
WERT
WERWOLF
WERWOLVES
WESAND
WESANDS
WEST
WESTBOUND
WESTED
WESTER
WESTERED
WESTERING
WESTERINGS
WESTERLIES
WESTERLY
WESTERN
WESTERNER
WESTERNERS
WESTERNS
WESTERS
WESTING
WESTINGS
WESTLIN
WESTMOST
WESTS
WESTWARD
WESTWARDS
WET
WETBACK
WETBACKS

WETHER	WHANGS	WHEELWORK	WHEREON	WHIFFLES
WETHERS	WHAP	WHEELWORKS	WHEREOUT	WHIFFLING
WETLAND	WHAPPED	WHEELY	WHERES	WHIFFLINGS
WETLANDS	WHAPPING	WHEEN	WHERESO	WHIFFS
WETLY	WHAPS	WHEENGE	WHERETO	WHIFFY
WETNESS	WHARE	WHEENGED	WHEREUNTO	WHIFT
WETNESSES	WHARES	WHEENGES	WHEREUPON	WHIFTS
WETS	WHARF	WHEENGING	WHEREVER	WHIG
WETTED	WHARFAGE	WHEENS	WHEREWITH	WHIGGED
WETTER	WHARFAGES	WHEEPLE	WHERRET	WHIGGING
WETTEST	WHARFED	WHEEPLED	WHERRETED	WHIGS
WETTING	WHARFING	WHEEPLES	WHERRETING	WHILE
WETTISH	WHARFINGS	WHEEPLING	WHERRETS	WHILED
WEX	WHARFS	WHEESHT	WHERRIES	WHILES
WEXE	WHARVE	WHEESHTED	WHERRY	WHILING
WEXED	WHARVES	WHEESHTING	WHERRYMAN	WHILK
WEXES	WHAT	WHEESHTS	WHERRYMEN	WHILLIED
WEXING	WHATEN	WHEEZE	WHET	WHILLIES
WEY	WHATEVER	WHEEZED	WHETHER	WHILLY
WEYARD	WHATNA	WHEEZES	WHETS	WHILLYING
WEYS	WHATNESS	WHEEZIER	WHETSTONE	WHILLYWHA
WEYWARD	WHATNESSES	WHEEZIEST	WHETSTONES	WHILLYWHAED
WEZAND	WHATNOT	WHEEZILY	WHETTED	WHILLYWHAING
WEZANDS	WHATNOTS	WHEEZING	WHETTER	WHILLYWHAS
WHACK	WHATS	WHEEZINGS	WHETTERS	WHILOM
WHACKED	WHATSIS	WHEEZLE	WHETTING	WHILST
WHACKER	WHATSIT	WHEEZLED	WHEUGH	WHIM
WHACKERS	WHATSITS	WHEEZLES	WHEUGHED	WHIMBREL
WHACKIER	WHATSO	WHEEZLING	WHEUGHING	WHIMBRELS
WHACKIEST	WHATTEN	WHEEZY	WHEUGHS	WHIMMED
WHACKING	WHAUP	WHEFT	WHEW	WHIMMIER
WHACKINGS	WHAUPS	WHEFTS	WHEWED	WHIMMIEST
WHACKO	WHAUR	WHELK	WHEWING	WHIMMING
WHACKOES	WHAURS	WHELKED	WHEWS	WHIMMY
WHACKOS	WHEAL	WHELKIER	WHEY	WHIMPER
WHACKS	WHEALS	WHELKIEST	WHEYEY	WHIMPERED
WHACKY	WHEAR	WHELKS	WHEYISH	WHIMPERER
WHAISLE	WHEARE	WHELKY	WHEYS	WHIMPERERS
WHAISLED	WHEAT	WHELM	WHICH	WHIMPERING
WHAISLES	WHEATEAR	WHELMED	WHICHEVER	WHIMPERINGS
WHAISLING	WHEATEARS	WHELMING	WHICKER	WHIMPERS
WHAIZLE	WHEATEN	WHELMS	WHICKERED	WHIMPLE
WHAIZLED	WHEATS	WHELP	WHICKERING	WHIMPLED
WHAIZLES	WHEE	WHELPED	WHICKERS	WHIMPLES
WHAIZLING	WHEECH	WHELPING	WHID	WHIMPLING
WHALE	WHEECHED	WHELPS	WHIDAH	WHIMS
WHALEBONE	WHEECHING	WHEMMLE	WHIDAHS	WHIMSEY
WHALEBONES	WHEECHS	WHEMMLED	WHIDDED	WHIMSEYS
WHALED	WHEEDLE	WHEMMLES	WHIDDER	WHIMSICAL
WHALER	WHEEDLED	WHEMMLING	WHIDDERED	WHIMSIES
WHALERIES	WHEEDLER	WHEN	WHIDDERING	WHIMSILY
WHALERS	WHEEDLERS	WHENAS	WHIDDERS	WHIMSY
WHALERY	WHEEDLES	WHENCE	WHIDDING	WHIN
WHALES	WHEEDLING	WHENCES	WHIDS	WHINCHAT
WHALING	WHEEDLINGS	WHENCEVER	WHIFF	WHINCHATS
WHALINGS	WHEEL	WHENEVER	WHIFFED	WHINE
WHALLY	WHEELBASE	WHENS	WHIFFER	WHINED
WHAM	WHEELBASES	WHERE	WHIFFERS	WHINER
WHAMMED	WHEELED	WHEREAS	WHIFFET	WHINERS
WHAMMING	WHEELER	WHEREAT	WHIFFETS	WHINES
WHAMPLE	WHEELERS	WHEREBY	WHIFFIER	WHINGE
WHAMPLES	WHEELIE	WHEREFOR	WHIFFIEST	WHINGED
WHAMS	WHEELIER	WHEREFORE	WHIFFING	WHINGEING
WHANG	WHEELIES	WHEREFORES	WHIFFINGS	WHINGEINGS
WHANGAM	WHEELIEST	WHEREFROM	WHIFFLE	WHINGER
WHANGAMS	WHEELING	WHEREIN	WHIFFLED	WHINGERS
WHANGED	WHEELINGS	WHEREINTO	WHIFFLER	WHINGES
WHANGEE	WHEELMAN	WHERENESS	WHIFFLERIES	WHINIARD
WHANGEES	WHEELMEN	WHERENESSES	WHIFFLERS	WHINIARDS
WHANGING	WHEELS	WHEREOF	WHIFFLERY	WHINIER

WHINIEST	WHIRRED	WHITED	WHIZZED	WHORESONS
WHININESS	WHIRRET	WHITEFISH	WHIZZER	WHORING
WHININESSES	WHIRRETED	WHITEFISHES	WHIZZERS	WHORISH
WHINING	WHIRRETING	WHITEHEAD	WHIZZES	WHORISHLY
WHININGLY	WHIRRETS	WHITEHEADS	WHIZZING	WHORL
WHININGS	WHIRRIED	WHITELY	WHIZZINGS	WHORLED
WHINNIED	WHIRRIES	WHITEN	WHO	WHORLS
WHINNIES	WHIRRING	WHITENED	WHOA	WHORT
WHINNY	WHIRRINGS	WHITENER	WHODUNNIT	WHORTS
WHINNYING	WHIRRS	WHITENERS	WHODUNNITS	WHOSE
WHINS	WHIRRY	WHITENESS	WHOEVER	WHOSEVER
WHINSTONE	WHIRRYING	WHITENESSES	WHOLE	WHOSO
WHINSTONES	WHIRS	WHITENING	WHOLEFOOD	WHOSOEVER
WHINY	WHIRTLE	WHITENINGS	WHOLEFOODS	WHOT
WHINYARD	WHIRTLES	WHITENS	WHOLEMEAL	WHOW
WHINYARDS	WHISH	WHITER	WHOLEMEALS	WHUMMLE
WHIP	WHISHED	WHITES	WHOLENESS	WHUMMLED
WHIPBIRD	WHISHES	WHITEST	WHOLENESSES	WHUMMLES
WHIPBIRDS	WHISHING	WHITEWALL	WHOLES	WHUMMLING
WHIPCAT	WHISHT	WHITEWALLS	WHOLESALE	WHUNSTANE
WHIPCATS	WHISHTED	WHITEWARE	WHOLESALES	WHUNSTANES
WHIPCORD	WHISHTING	WHITEWARES	WHOLESOME	WHY
WHIPCORDS	WHISHTS	WHITEWASH	WHOLESOMER	WHYDAH
WHIPCORDY	WHISK	WHITEWASHED	WHOLESOMEST	WHYDAHS
WHIPJACK	WHISKED	WHITEWASHES	WHOLISM	WHYEVER
WHIPJACKS	WHISKER	WHITEWASHING	WHOLISMS	WICK
WHIPLASH	WHISKERED	WHITEWING	WHOLISTIC	WICKED
WHIPLASHED	WHISKERS	WHITEWINGS	WHOLLY	WICKEDER
WHIPLASHES	WHISKERY	WHITEWOOD	WHOM	WICKEDEST
WHIPLASHING	WHISKET	WHITEWOODS	WHOMBLE	WICKEDLY
WHIPLIKE	WHISKETS	WHITEY	WHOMBLED	WICKEN
WHIPPED	WHISKEY	WHITEYS	WHOMBLES	WICKENS
WHIPPER	WHISKEYS	WHITHER	WHOMBLING	WICKER
WHIPPERS	WHISKIES	WHITHERED	WHOMEVER	WICKERED
WHIPPET	WHISKING	WHITHERING	WHOMMLE	WICKERS
WHIPPETS	WHISKS	WHITHERS	WHOMMLED	WICKET
WHIPPIER	WHISKY	WHITIER	WHOMMLES	WICKETS
WHIPPIEST	WHISPER	WHITIEST	WHOMMLING	WICKIES
WHIPPING	WHISPERED	WHITING	WHOOBUB	WICKING
WHIPPINGS	WHISPERER	WHITINGS	WHOOBUBS	WICKS
WHIPPY	WHISPERERS	WHITISH	WHOOP	WICKY
WHIPS	WHISPERING	WHITLING	WHOOPED	WIDDIES
WHIPSTAFF	WHISPERINGS	WHITLINGS	WHOOPEE	WIDDLE
WHIPSTAFFS	WHISPERO	WHITLOW	WHOOPEES	WIDDLED
WHIPSTALL	WHISPERY	WHITLOWS	WHOOPER	WIDDLES
WHIPSTALLED	WHISS	WHITRET	WHOOPERS	WIDDLING
WHIPSTALLING	WHISSED	WHITRETS	WHOOPING	WIDDY
WHIPSTALLS	WHISSES	WHITS	WHOOPINGS	WIDE
WHIPSTER	WHISSING	WHITSTER	WHOOPS	WIDELY
WHIPSTERS	WHIST	WHITSTERS	WHOOSH	WIDEN
WHIPT	WHISTED	WHITTAW	WHOOSHED	WIDENED
WHIPWORM	WHISTING	WHITTAWER	WHOOSHES	WIDENER
WHIPWORMS	WHISTLE	WHITTAWERS	WHOOSHING	WIDENERS
WHIR	WHISTLED	WHITTAWS	WHOOT	WIDENESS
WHIRL	WHISTLER	WHITTER	WHOOTED	WIDENESSES
WHIRLBAT	WHISTLERS	WHITTERED	WHOOTING	WIDENING
WHIRLBATS	WHISTLES	WHITTERING	WHOOTS	WIDENS
WHIRLED	WHISTLING	WHITTERS	WHOP	WIDER
WHIRLER	WHISTLINGS	WHITTLE	WHOPPED	WIDES
WHIRLERS	WHISTS	WHITTLED	WHOPPER	WIDEST
WHIRLIGIG	WHIT	WHITTLER	WHOPPERS	WIDGEON
WHIRLIGIGS	WHITE	WHITTLERS	WHOPPING	WIDGEONS
WHIRLING	WHITEBAIT	WHITTLES	WHOPPINGS	WIDGET
WHIRLINGS	WHITEBAITS	WHITTLING	WHOPS	WIDGETS
WHIRLPOOL	WHITEBASS	WHITTLINGS	WHORE	WIDISH
WHIRLPOOLS	WHITEBASSES	WHITTRET	WHORED	WIDOW
WHIRLS	WHITEBEAM	WHITTRETS	WHOREDOM	WIDOWED
WHIRLWIND	WHITEBEAMS	WHITY	WHOREDOMS	WIDOWER
WHIRLWINDS	WHITECAP	WHIZ	WHORES	WIDOWERS
WHIRR	WHITECAPS	WHIZZ	WHORESON	WIDOWHOOD

WIDOWHOODS
WIDOWING
WIDOWS
WIDTH
WIDTHS
WIDTHWAYS
WIDTHWISE
WIEL
WIELD
WIELDABLE
WIELDED
WIELDER
WIELDERS
WIELDIER
WIELDIEST
WIELDING
WIELDLESS
WIELDS
WIELDY
WIELS
WIFE
WIFEHOOD
WIFEHOODS
WIFELESS
WIFELIER
WIFELIEST
WIFELY
WIG
WIGAN
WIGANS
WIGEON
WIGEONS
WIGGED
WIGGERIES
WIGGERY
WIGGING
WIGGINGS
WIGGLE
WIGGLED
WIGGLER
WIGGLERS
WIGGLES
WIGGLIER
WIGGLIEST
WIGGLING
WIGGLY
WIGHT
WIGHTED
WIGHTING
WIGHTLY
WIGHTS
WIGLESS
WIGS
WIGWAG
WIGWAGGED
WIGWAGGING
WIGWAGS
WIGWAM
WIGWAMS
WILCO
WILD
WILDCAT
WILDCATS
WILDCATTED
WILDCATTING
WILDER
WILDERED
WILDERING
WILDERS
WILDEST

WILDFIRE
WILDFIRES
WILDGRAVE
WILDGRAVES
WILDING
WILDINGS
WILDISH
WILDLIFE
WILDLY
WILDNESS
WILDNESSES
WILDOAT
WILDOATS
WILDS
WILE
WILED
WILEFUL
WILES
WILFUL
WILFULLY
WILI
WILIER
WILIEST
WILILY
WILINESS
WILINESSES
WILING
WILIS
WILL
WILLABLE
WILLED
WILLEMITE
WILLEMITES
WILLERS
WILLET
WILLETS
WILLEY
WILLEYED
WILLEYING
WILLEYS
WILLIE
WILLIED
WILLIES
WILLING
WILLINGLY
WILLIWAW
WILLIWAWS
WILLOW
WILLOWED
WILLOWING
WILLOWISH
WILLOWS
WILLOWY
WILLS
WILLY
WILLYARD
WILLYART
WILLYING
WILT
WILTED
WILTING
WILTS
WILY
WIMBLE
WIMBLED
WIMBLES
WIMBLING
WIMBREL
WIMBRELS
WIMP

WIMPIER
WIMPIEST
WIMPISH
WIMPLE
WIMPLED
WIMPLES
WIMPLING
WIMPS
WIMPY
WIN
WINCE
WINCED
WINCER
WINCERS
WINCES
WINCEY
WINCEYS
WINCH
WINCHED
WINCHES
WINCHING
WINCHMAN
WINCHMEN
WINCING
WINCINGS
WINCOPIPE
WINCOPIPES
WIND
WINDAC
WINDACS
WINDAGE
WINDAGES
WINDAS
WINDASES
WINDBLOW
WINDBLOWS
WINDBURN
WINDBURNS
WINDED
WINDER
WINDERS
WINDFALL
WINDFALLS
WINDIER
WINDIEST
WINDIGO
WINDIGOS
WINDILY
WINDINESS
WINDINESSES
WINDING
WINDINGLY
WINDINGS
WINDLASS
WINDLASSED
WINDLASSES
WINDLASSING
WINDLE
WINDLES
WINDLESS
WINDMILL
WINDMILLED
WINDMILLING
WINDMILLS
WINDOCK
WINDOCKS
WINDORE
WINDORES
WINDOW
WINDOWED

WINDOWING
WINDOWINGS
WINDOWS
WINDPIPE
WINDPIPES
WINDRING
WINDROSE
WINDROSES
WINDROW
WINDROWED
WINDROWING
WINDROWS
WINDS
WINDSES
WINDSHIP
WINDSHIPS
WINDSTORM
WINDSTORMS
WINDSURF
WINDSURFED
WINDSURFS
WINDSWEPT
WINDTHROW
WINDTHROWS
WINDWARD
WINDWARDS
WINDY
WINE
WINED
WINERIES
WINERY
WINES
WINEY
WING
WINGBEAT
WINGBEATS
WINGDING
WINGDINGS
WINGE
WINGED
WINGEDLY
WINGEING
WINGER
WINGERS
WINGES
WINGIER
WINGIEST
WINGING
WINGLESS
WINGLET
WINGLETS
WINGS
WINGSPAN
WINGSPANS
WINGY
WINIER
WINIEST
WINING
WINK
WINKED
WINKER
WINKERS
WINKING
WINKINGLY
WINKINGS
WINKLE
WINKLER
WINKLERS
WINKLES
WINKS

WINN
WINNA
WINNABLE
WINNER
WINNERS
WINNING
WINNINGLY
WINNINGS
WINNLE
WINNLES
WINNOCK
WINNOCKS
WINNOW
WINNOWED
WINNOWER
WINNOWERS
WINNOWING
WINNOWINGS
WINNOWS
WINNS
WINO
WINOS
WINS
WINSEY
WINSEYS
WINSOME
WINSOMELY
WINSOMER
WINSOMEST
WINTER
WINTERED
WINTERIER
WINTERIEST
WINTERING
WINTERISE
WINTERISED
WINTERISES
WINTERISING
WINTERIZE·
WINTERIZED
WINTERIZES
WINTERIZING
WINTERLY
WINTERS
WINTERY
WINTLE
WINTLED
WINTLES
WINTLING
WINTRIER
WINTRIEST
WINTRY
WINY
WINZE
WINZES
WIPE
WIPED
WIPEOUT
WIPEOUTS
WIPER
WIPERS
WIPES
WIPING
WIPINGS
WIRE
WIRED
WIREDRAW
WIREDRAWING
WIREDRAWINGS
WIREDRAWN

WIREDRAWS
WIREDREW
WIRELESS
WIRELESSED
WIRELESSES
WIRELESSING
WIREPHOTO
WIREPHOTOS
WIRER
WIRERS
WIRES
WIRETAP
WIRETAPPED
WIRETAPPING
WIRETAPS
WIREWORK
WIREWORKS
WIREWOVE
WIRIER
WIRIEST
WIRILY
WIRINESS
WIRINESSES
WIRING
WIRINGS
WIRRICOW
WIRRICOWS
WIRY
WIS
WISARD
WISARDS
WISDOM
WISDOMS
WISE
WISEACRE
WISEACRES
WISECRACK
WISECRACKED
WISECRACKING
WISECRACKS
WISED
WISELING
WISELINGS
WISELY
WISENESS
WISENESSES
WISENT
WISENTS
WISER
WISES
WISEST
WISH
WISHBONE
WISHBONES
WISHED
WISHER
WISHERS
WISHES
WISHFUL
WISHFULLY
WISHING
WISHINGS
WISING
WISKET
WISKETS
WISP
WISPED
WISPIER
WISPIEST
WISPING

WISPS
WISPY
WIST
WISTARIA
WISTARIAS
WISTED
WISTERIA
WISTERIAS
WISTFUL
WISTFULLY
WISTING
WISTITI
WISTITIS
WISTLY
WISTS
WIT
WITAN
WITCH
WITCHED
WITCHEN
WITCHENS
WITCHERIES
WITCHERY
WITCHES
WITCHETTIES
WITCHETTY
WITCHING
WITCHINGS
WITCHKNOT
WITCHKNOTS
WITE
WITED
WITELESS
WITES
WITGAT
WITGATS
WITH
WITHAL
WITHDRAW
WITHDRAWING
WITHDRAWN
WITHDRAWS
WITHDREW
WITHE
WITHED
WITHER
WITHERED
WITHERING
WITHERINGS
WITHERITE
WITHERITES
WITHERS
WITHES
WITHHAULT
WITHHELD
WITHHOLD
WITHHOLDING
WITHHOLDS
WITHIER
WITHIES
WITHIEST
WITHIN
WITHING
WITHOUT
WITHOUTEN
WITHS
WITHSTAND
WITHSTANDING
WITHSTANDS
WITHSTOOD

WITHWIND
WITHWINDS
WITHY
WITHYWIND
WITHYWINDS
WITING
WITLESS
WITLESSLY
WITLING
WITLINGS
WITLOOF
WITLOOFS
WITNESS
WITNESSED
WITNESSER
WITNESSERS
WITNESSES
WITNESSING
WITS
WITTED
WITTER
WITTERED
WITTERING
WITTERS
WITTICISM
WITTICISMS
WITTIER
WITTIEST
WITTILY
WITTINESS
WITTINESSES
WITTING
WITTINGLY
WITTINGS
WITTOL
WITTOLLY
WITTOLS
WITTY
WITWALL
WITWALLS
WITWANTON
WITWANTONED
WITWANTONING
WITWANTONS
WIVE
WIVED
WIVEHOOD
WIVEHOODS
WIVERN
WIVERNS
WIVES
WIVING
WIZARD
WIZARDLY
WIZARDRIES
WIZARDRY
WIZARDS
WIZEN
WIZENED
WIZENING
WIZENS
WIZIER
WIZIERS
WO
WOAD
WOADED
WOADS
WOBBEGONG
WOBBEGONGS
WOBBLE

WOBBLED
WOBBLER
WOBBLERS
WOBBLES
WOBBLIER
WOBBLIES
WOBBLIEST
WOBBLING
WOBBLINGS
WOBBLY
WOBEGONE
WOCK
WOCKS
WODGE
WODGES
WOE
WOEBEGONE
WOEFUL
WOEFULLER
WOEFULLEST
WOEFULLY
WOEFULNESS
WOEFULNESSES
WOES
WOESOME
WOFUL
WOFULLY
WOFULNESS
WOFULNESSES
WOG
WOGGLE
WOGGLES
WOGS
WOIWODE
WOIWODES
WOK
WOKE
WOKEN
WOKS
WOLD
WOLDS
WOLF
WOLFED
WOLFER
WOLFERS
WOLFING
WOLFINGS
WOLFISH
WOLFISHLY
WOLFKIN
WOLFKINS
WOLFLING
WOLFLINGS
WOLFRAM
WOLFRAMS
WOLFS
WOLFSDANE
WOLFSBANES
WOLLIES
WOLLY
WOLVE
WOLVED
WOLVER
WOLVERENE
WOLVERENES
WOLVERINE
WOLVERINES
WOLVERS
WOLVES
WOLVING

WOLVINGS
WOLVISH
WOLVISHLY
WOMAN
WOMANED
WOMANHOOD
WOMANING
WOMANISE
WOMANISED
WOMANISER
WOMANISERS
WOMANISES
WOMANISH
WOMANISING
WOMANIZE
WOMANIZED
WOMANIZER
WOMANIZERS
WOMANIZES
WOMANIZING
WOMANKIND
WOMANLIER
WOMANLIEST
WOMANLY
WOMANS
WOMB
WOMBAT
WOMBATS
WOMBED
WOMBING
WOMBS
WOMBY
WOMEN
WOMENFOLK
WOMENFOLKS
WOMENKIND
WOMERA
WOMERAS
WON
WONDER
WONDERED
WONDERER
WONDERERS
WONDERFUL
WONDERING
WONDERINGS
WONDEROUS
WONDERS
WONDRED
WONDROUS
WONGA
WONGAS
WONING
WONINGS
WONKIER
WONKIEST
WONKY
WONNED
WONNING
WONS
WONT
WONTED
WONTING
WONTLESS
WONTS
WOO
WOOBUT
WOOBUTS
WOOD
WOODBIND

WOODBINDS	WOOFIER	WORCESTER	WORLDLIEST	WORTHIER
WOODBINE	WOOFIEST	WORCESTERS	WORLDLING	WORTHIES
WOODBINES	WOOFS	WORD	WORLDLINGS	WORTHIEST
WOODBLOCK	WOOFY	WORDAGE	WORLDLY	WORTHILY
WOODBLOCKS	WOOING	WORDAGES	WORLDS	WORTHING
WOODCHIP	WOOINGLY	WORDBOOK	WORLDWIDE	WORTHLESS
WOODCHIPS	WOOINGS	WORDBOOKS	WORM	WORTHS
WOODCHUCK	WOOL	WORDBOUND	WORMED	WORTHY
WOODCHUCKS	WOOLD	WORDED	WORMER	WORTHYING
WOODCOCK	WOOLDED	WORDIER	WORMERIES	WORTLE
WOODCOCKS	WOOLDER	WORDIEST	WORMERS	WORTLES
WOODCRAFT	WOOLDERS	WORDILY	WORMERY	WORTS
WOODCRAFTS	WOOLDING	WORDINESS	WORMIER	WOS
WOODCUT	WOOLDINGS	WORDINESSES	WORMIEST	WOSBIRD
WOODCUTS	WOOLDS	WORDING	WORMING	WOSBIRDS
WOODED	WOOLFAT	WORDINGS	WORMS	WOST
WOODEN	WOOLFATS	WORDISH	WORMWOOD	WOT
WOODENER	WOOLFELL	WORDLESS	WORMWOODS	WOTCHER
WOODENEST	WOOLFELLS	WORDS	WORMY	WOTS
WOODENLY	WOOLLED	WORDSMITH	WORN	WOTTED
WOODHOUSE	WOOLLEN	WORDSMITHS	WORRAL	WOTTEST
WOODHOUSES	WOOLLENS	WORDY	WORRALS	WOTTETH
WOODIE	WOOLLIER	WORE	WORREL	WOTTING
WOODIER	WOOLLIES	WORE WORN	WORRELS	WOUBIT
WOODIES	WOOLLIEST	WORK	WORRICOW	WOUBITS
WOODIEST	WOOLLY	WORKABLE	WORRICOWS	WOULD
WOODINESS	WOOLMAN	WORKADAY	WORRIED	WOULDS
WOODINESSES	WOOLMEN	WORKBOAT	WORRIER	WOULDST
WOODING	WOOLS	WORKBOATS	WORRIERS	WOUND
WOODLAND	WOOLSACK	WORKBOOK	WORRIES	WOUNDABLE
WOODLANDS	WOOLSACKS	WORKBOOKS	WORRIMENT	WOUNDED
WOODLESS	WOOLSEY	WORKED	WORRIMENTS	WOUNDER
WOODLICE	WOOLSEYS	WORKER	WORRISOME	WOUNDERS
WOODLOUSE	WOOLWARD	WORKERIST	WORRIT	WOUNDILY
WOODMAN	WOOLWORK	WORKERISTS	WORRITED	WOUNDING
WOODMEN	WOOLWORKS	WORKERS	WORRITING	WOUNDINGS
WOODMICE	WOOMERA	WORKFOLK	WORRITS	WOUNDLESS
WOODMOUSE	WOOMERANG	WORKFOLKS	WORRY	WOUNDS
WOODNESS	WOOMERANGS	WORKFORCE	WORRYCOW	WOUNDWORT
WOODNESSES	WOOMERAS	WORKFORCES	WORRYCOWS	WOUNDWORTS
WOODRUFF	WOON	WORKFUL	WORRYGUTS	WOUNDY
WOODRUFFS	WOONED	WORKHORSE	WORRYING	WOURALI
WOODS	WOONING	WORKHORSES	WORRYINGS	WOURALIS
WOODSHED	WOONS	WORKHOUSE	WORRYWART	WOVE
WOODSHEDDED	WOORALI	WORKHOUSES	WORRYWARTS	WOVEN
WOODSHEDDING	WOORALIS	WORKING	WORSE	WOW
WOODSHEDS	WOORARA	WORKINGS	WORSED	WOWED
WOODSIER	WOORARAS	WORKLESS	WORSEN	WOWEE
WOODSIEST	WOOS	WORKLOAD	WORSENED	WOWF
WOODSMAN	WOOSEL	WORKLOADS	WORSENESS	WOWFER
WOODSMEN	WOOSELL	WORKMAN	WORSENESSES	WOWFEST
WOODSY	WOOSELLS	WORKMANLY	WORSENING	WOWING
WOODWALE	WOOSELS	WORKMEN	WORSENS	WOWS
WOODWALES	WOOSH	WORKPIECE	WORSER	WOWSER
WOODWARD	WOOSHED	WORKPIECES	WORSES	WOWSERS
WOODWARDS	WOOSHES	WORKPLACE	WORSHIP	WOX
WOODWIND	WOOSHING	WORKPLACES	WORSHIPPED	WOXEN
WOODWINDS	WOOT	WORKROOM	WORSHIPPING	WRACK
WOODWORK	WOOTZ	WORKROOMS	WORSHIPS	WRACKED
WOODWORKS	WOOTZES	WORKS	WORSING	WRACKFUL
WOODWOSE	WOOZIER	WORKSHOP	WORST	WRACKING
WOODWOSES	WOOZIEST	WORKSHOPS	WORSTED	WRACKS
WOODY	WOOZILY	WORKSOME	WORSTEDS	WRAITH
WOOED	WOOZINESS	WORKTOP	WORSTING	WRAITHS
WOOER	WOOZINESSES	WORKTOPS	WORSTS	WRANGLE
WOOERS	WOOZY	WORKWEAR	WORT	WRANGLED
WOOF	WOP	WORKWEARS	WORTH	WRANGLER
WOOFED	WOPPED	WORLD	WORTHED	WRANGLERS
WOOFER	WOPPING	WORLDED	WORTHFUL	WRANGLES
WOOFERS	WOPS	WORLDLIER	WORTHIED	WRANGLING

WRANGLINGS	WREAKLESS	WRETHE	WRITABLE	WRYEST
WRAP	WREAKS	WRETHED	WRITATIVE	WRYING
WRAPOVER	WREATH	WRETHES	WRITE	WRYLY
WRAPOVERS	WREATHE	WRETHING	WRITER	WRYNECK
WRAPPAGE	WREATHED	WRICK	WRITERESS	WRYNECKS
WRAPPAGES	WREATHEN	WRICKED	WRITERESSES	WRYNESS
WRAPPED	WREATHER	WRICKING	WRITERLY	WRYNESSES
WRAPPER	WREATHERS	WRICKS	WRITERS	WRYTHEN
WRAPPERS	WREATHES	WRIED	WRITES	WUD
WRAPPING	WREATHIER	WRIER	WRITHE	WUDDED
WRAPPINGS	WREATHIEST	WRIES	WRITHED	WUDDING
WRAPROUND	WREATHING	WRIEST	WRITHEN	WUDS
WRAPROUNDS	WREATHS	WRIGGLE	WRITHES	WULFENITE
WRAPS	WREATHY	WRIGGLED	WRITHING	WULFENITES
WRAPT	WRECK	WRIGGLER	WRITHINGS	WULL
WRASSE	WRECKAGE	WRIGGLERS	WRITHLED	WULLED
WRASSES	WRECKAGES	WRIGGLES	WRITING	WULLING
WRAST	WRECKED	WRIGGLIER	WRITINGS	WULLS
WRASTED	WRECKER	WRIGGLIEST	WRITS	WUNNER
WRASTING	WRECKERS	WRIGGLING	WRITTEN	WUNNERS
WRASTS	WRECKFISH	WRIGGLINGS	WRIZLED	WURLEY
WRATE	WRECKFISHES	WRIGGLY	WROATH	WURLEYS
WRATH	WRECKFUL	WRIGHT	WROATHS	WURLIES
WRATHED	WRECKING	WRIGHTS	WROKE	WURST
WRATHFUL	WRECKINGS	WRING	WROKEN	WURSTS
WRATHIER	WRECKS	WRINGED	WRONG	WURTZITE
WRATHIEST	WREN	WRINGER	WRONGED	WURTZITES
WRATHILY	WRENCH	WRINGERS	WRONGER	WUSHU
WRATHING	WRENCHED	WRINGING	WRONGERS	WUSHUS
WRATHLESS	WRENCHES	WRINGINGS	WRONGEST	WUTHER
WRATHS	WRENCHING	WRINGS	WRONGFUL	WUTHERED
WRATHY	WRENCHINGS	WRINKLE	WRONGING	WUTHERING
WRAWL	WRENS	WRINKLED	WRONGLY	WUTHERS
WRAWLED	WREST	WRINKLES	WRONGNESS	WUZZLE
WRAWLING	WRESTED	WRINKLIER	WRONGNESSES	WUZZLED
WRAWLS	WRESTER	WRINKLIES	WRONGOUS	WUZZLES
WRAXLE	WRESTERS	WRINKLIEST	WRONGS	WUZZLING
WRAXLED	WRESTING	WRINKLING	WROOT	WYANDOTTE
WRAXLES	WRESTLE	WRINKLY	WROOTED	WYANDOTTES
WRAXLING	WRESTLED	WRIST	WROOTING	WYE
WRAXLINGS	WRESTLER	WRISTBAND	WROOTS	WYES
WREAK	WRESTLERS	WRISTBANDS	WROTE	WYND
WREAKE	WRESTLES	WRISTIER	WROTH	WYNDS
WREAKED	WRESTLING	WRISTIEST	WROUGHT	WYTE
WREAKER	WRESTLINGS	WRISTLET	WRUNG	WYTED
WREAKERS	WRESTS	WRISTLETS	WRY	WYTES
WREAKES	WRETCH	WRISTS	WRYDILL	WYTING
WREAKFUL	WRETCHED	WRISTY	WRYBILLS	WYVERN
WREAKING	WRETCHES	WRIT	WRYER	WYVERNS

X

XANTHATE	XENOLITHS	XERASIAS	XOANON	XYLOMAS
XANTHATES	XENOMANIA	XERIC	XOANONS	XYLOMETER
XANTHEIN	XENOMANIAS	XEROCHASIES	XYLEM	XYLOMETERS
XANTHEINS	XENOMENIA	XEROCHASY	XYLEMS	XYLONIC
XANTHENE	XENOMENIAS	XERODERMA	XYLENE	XYLONITE
XANTHENES	XENON	XERODERMAS	XYLENES	XYLONITES
XANTHIC	XENONS	XEROMA	XYLENOL	XYLOPHAGE
XANTHIN	XENOPHILE	XEROMAS	XYLENOLS	XYLOPHAGES
XANTHINE	XENOPHILES	XEROMORPH	XYLIC	XYLOPHONE
XANTHINES	XENOPHOBE	XEROMORPHS	XYLITOL	XYLOPHONES
XANTHINS	XENOPHOBES	XEROPHAGIES	XYLITOLS	XYLORIMBA
XANTHOMA	XENOPHOBIES	XEROPHAGY	XYLOCARP	XYLORIMBAS
XANTHOMAS	XENOPHOBY	XEROPHILIES	XYLOCARPS	XYLOSE
XANTHOUS	XENOPHYA	XEROPHILY	XYLOGEN	XYLOSES
XEBEC	XENOPHYAS	XEROPHYTE	XYLOGENS	XYLYL
XEBECS	XENOTIME	XEROPHYTES	XYLOGRAPH	XYLYLS
XENIA	XENOTIMES	XEROSES	XYLOGRAPHS	XYST
XENIAL	XENURINE	XEROSIS	XYLOID	XYSTER
XENIAS	XERAFIN	XEROSTOMA	XYLOIDIN	XYSTERS
XENIUM	XERAFINS	XEROSTOMAS	XYLOIDINE	XYSTI
XENOCRYST	XERANSES	XEROTES	XYLOIDINES	XYSTOI
XENOCRYSTS	XERANSIS	XEROTESES	XYLOIDINS	XYSTOS
XENOGAMIES	XERANTIC	XEROTIC	XYLOL	XYSTOSES
XENOGAMY	XERAPHIM	XI	XYLOLOGIES	XYSTS
XENOGRAFT	XERAPHIMS	XIPHOID	XYLOLOGY	XYSTUS
XENOGRAFTS	XERARCH	XIPHOIDAL	XYLOLS	XYSTUSES
XENOLITH	XERASIA	XIS	XYLOMA	

Y

YABBER	YANK	YARTO	YEADS	YELLOWEST
YABBERED	YANKED	YARTOS	YEAH	YELLOWING
YABBERING	YANKER	YASHMAK	YEALDON	YELLOWISH
YABBERS	YANKERS	YASHMAKS	YEALDONS	YELLOWS
YABBIE	YANKIE	YATAGAN	YEALM	YELLOWY
YABBIES	YANKIES	YATAGANS	YEALMED	YELLS
YABBY	YANKING	YATAGHAN	YEALMING	YELM
YACCA	YANKS	YATAGHANS	YEALMS	YELMED
YACCAS	YAOURT	YATE	YEAN	YELMING
YACHT	YAOURTS	YATES	YEANED	YELMS
YACHTED	YAP	YATTER	YEANING	YELP
YACHTER	YAPOCK	YATTERED	YEANLING	YELPED
YACHTERS	YAPOCKS	YATTERING	YEANLINGS	YELPER
YACHTING	YAPOK	YATTERINGS	YEANS	YELPERS
YACHTINGS	YAPOKS	YATTERS	YEAR	YELPING
YACHTS	YAPON	YAUD	YEARD	YELPINGS
YACHTSMAN	YAPONS	YAUDS	YEARDED	YELPS
YACHTSMEN	YAPP	YAULD	YEARDING	YELT
YACK	YAPPED	YAUP	YEARDS	YELTS
YACKED	YAPPER	YAUPON	YEARLIES	YEN
YACKER	YAPPERS	YAUPONS	YEARLING	YENNED
YACKERS	YAPPING	YAW	YEARLINGS	YENNING
YACKING	YAPPS	YAWED	YEARLONG	YENS
YACKS	YAPO	YAWEY	YEARLY	YENTA
YAFF	YAPSTER	YAWING	YEARN	YENTAS
YAFFED	YAPSTERS	YAWL	YEARNED	YEOMAN
YAFFING	YARD	YAWLED	YEARNING	YEOMANLY
YAFFLE	YARDAGE	YAWLING	YEARNINGS	YEOMANRIES
YAFFLES	YARDAGES	YAWLS	YEARNS	YEOMANRY
YAFFS	YARDANG	YAWN	YEARS	YEOMEN
YAGER	YARDANGS	YAWNED	YEAS	YEP
YAGERS	YARDED	YAWNIER	YEAST	YEPS
YAGGER	YARDING	YAWNIEST	YEASTED	YERBA
YAGGERS	YARDLAND	YAWNING	YEASTIER	YERBAS
YAH	YARDLANDS	YAWNINGLY	YEASTIEST	YERD
YAHOO	YARDMAN	YAWNINGS	YEASTING	YERDED
YAHOOS	YARDMEN	YAWNS	YEASTS	YERDING
YAK	YARDS	YAWNY	YEASTY	YERDS
YAKHDAN	YARDSTICK	YAWP	YEDE	YERK
YAKHDANS	YARDSTICKS	YAWPED	YEDES	YERKED
YAKKA	YARDWAND	YAWPER	YEED	YERKING
YAKKAS	YARDWANDS	YAWPERS	YEEDS	YERKS
YAKKED	YARE	YAWPING	YEGG	YERSINIA
YAKKER	YARELY	YAWPS	YEGGMAN	YERSINIAE
YAKKERS	YARER	YAWS	YEGGMEN	YERSINIAS
YAKKING	YAREST	YAWY	YEGGS	YES
YAKS	YARFA	YBET	YELD	YESES
YAKUZA	YARFAS	YBLENT	YELDRING	YESHIVA
YALD	YARMULKA	YBORE	YELDRINGS	YESHIVAH
YALE	YARMULKAS	YBOUND	YELDROCK	YESHIVAHS
YALES	YARMULKE	YBOUNDEN	YELDROCKS	YESHIVAS
YAM	YARMULKES	YBRENT	YELK	YESHIVATH
YAMEN	YARN	YCLAD	YELKS	YESHIVOTH
YAMENS	YARNED	YCLED	YELL	YESK
YAMMER	YARNING	YCLEEPE	YELLED	YESKED
YAMMERED	YARNS	YCLEPED	YELLING	YESKING
YAMMERING	YARPHA	YCLEPT	YELLINGS	YESKS
YAMMERINGS	YARPHAS	YCOND	YELLOCH	YESSES
YAMMERS	YARR	YDRAD	YELLOCHED	YEST
YAMS	YARROW	YDRED	YELLOCHING	YESTER
YAMULKA	YARROWS	YE	YELLOCHS	YESTERDAY
YAMULKAS	YARRS	YEA	YELLOW	YESTERDAYS
YANG	YARTA	YEAD	YELLOWED	YESTEREVE
YANGS	YARTAS	YEADING	YELLOWER	YESTEREVES

YESTERN
YESTREEN
YESTS
YESTY
YET
YETI
YETIS
YETT
YETTS
YEUK
YEUKED
YEUKING
YEUKS
YEVE
YEVEN
YEVES
YEVING
YEW
YEWEN
YEWS
YEX
YEXED
YEXES
YEXING
YFERE
YGLAUNST
YGO
YGOE
YIBBLES
YIELD
YIELDABLE
YIELDED
YIELDER
YIELDERS
YIELDING
YIELDINGS
YIELDS
YIKKER
YIKKERED
YIKKERING
YIKKERS
YILL
YILLS
YIN
YINCE
YINS
YIP
YIPPED
YIPPEE
YIPPIES
YIPPING
YIPPY
YIPS
YIRD
YIRDED
YIRDING
YIRDS
YIRK
YIRKED
YIRKING
YIRKS
YITE
YITES
YLEM
YLEMS
YLIKE

YLKE
YMOLT
YMOLTEN
YMPE
YMPES
YMPING
YMPT
YNAMBU
YNAMBUS
YO
YOB
YOBBISH
YOBBISHLY
YOBBO
YOBBOES
YOBBOS
YOBS
YOCK
YOCKED
YOCKING
YOCKS
YOD
YODE
YODEL
YODELLED
YODELLER
YODELLERS
YODELLING
YODELS
YODLE
YODLED
YODLER
YODLERS
YODLES
YODLING
YOGA
YOGAS
YOGH
YOGHOURT
YOGHOURTS
YOGHS
YOGHURT
YOGHURTS
YOGI
YOGIC
YOGIN
YOGINI
YOGINIS
YOGINS
YOGIS
YOGISM
YOGISMS
YOGURT
YOGURTS
YOHIMBINE
YOHIMBINES
YOICK
YOICKED
YOICKING
YOICKS
YOICKSED
YOICKSES
YOICKSING
YOJAN
YOJANA
YOJANAS

YOJANS
YOK
YOKE
YOKED
YOKEL
YOKELISH
YOKELS
YOKES
YOKING
YOKINGS
YOKKED
YOKKING
YOKS
YOKUL
YOLD
YOLDRING
YOLDRINGS
YOLK
YOLKED
YOLKIER
YOLKIEST
YOLKS
YOLKY
YOMP
YOMPED
YOMPING
YOMPS
YON
YOND
YONDER
YONGTHLY
YONI
YONIS
YONKER
YONKERS
YONKS
YONT
YOOP
YOOPS
YOPPER
YOPPERS
YORE
YORES
YORK
YORKED
YORKER
YORKERS
YORKIE
YORKIES
YORKING
YORKS
YOS
YOU
YOUK
YOUKED
YOUKING
YOUKS
YOUNG
YOUNGER
YOUNGEST
YOUNGISH
YOUNGLING
YOUNGLINGS
YOUNGLY
YOUNGNESS
YOUNGNESSES

YOUNGSTER
YOUNGSTERS
YOUNGTH
YOUNGTHLY
YOUNGTHS
YOUNKER
YOUNKERS
YOUR
YOURN
YOURS
YOURSELF
YOURSELVES
YOURT
YOURTS
YOUTH
YOUTHFUL
YOUTHHEAD
YOUTHHEADS
YOUTHHOOD
YOUTHHOODS
YOUTHIER
YOUTHIEST
YOUTHLY
YOUTHS
YOUTHSOME
YOUTHY
YOW
YOWE
YOWES
YOWIE
YOWIES
YOWL
YOWLED
YOWLEY
YOWLEYS
YOWLING
YOWLINGS
YOWLS
YOWS
YPIGHT
YPLAST
YPLIGHT
YPSILOID
YPSILON
YPSILONS
YRAPT
YRAVISHED
YRENT
YRIVD
YSAME
YSHEND
YSHENDING
YSHENDS
YSHENT
YSLAKED
YTOST
YTTERBIA
YTTERBIAS
YTTERBIUM
YTTERBIUMS
YTTRIA
YTTRIAS
YTTRIC
YTTRIOUS
YTTRIUM
YTTRIUMS

YU
YUAN
YUCA
YUCAS
YUCCA
YUCCAS
YUCK
YUCKED
YUCKER
YUCKERS
YUCKIER
YUCKIEST
YUCKING
YUCKS
YUCKY
YUFT
YUFTS
YUG
YUGA
YUGAS
YUGS
YUK
YUKE
YUKED
YUKES
YUKIER
YUKIEST
YUKING
YUKKIER
YUKKIEST
YUKKY
YUKS
YUKY
YULAN
YULANS
YULE
YULES
YULETIDE
YULETIDES
YUMMIER
YUMMIEST
YUMMY
YUMP
YUMPIE
YUMPIES
YUMPS
YUNX
YUNXES
YUP
YUPON
YUPONS
YUPPIE
YUPPIES
YUPPY
YUPS
YURT
YURTS
YUS
YWIS
YWRAKE
YWROKE
YWROKEN

Z

ZABAIONE
ZABAIONES
ZABETA
ZABETAS
ZABRA
ZABRAS
ZABTIEH
ZABTIEHS
ZACK
ZACKS
ZADDIK
ZADDIKIM
ZADDIKS
ZAFFER
ZAFFERS
ZAFFRE
ZAFFRES
ZAG
ZAGGED
ZAGGING
ZAGS
ZAIRE
ZAKUSKA
ZAKUSKI
ZAMAN
ZAMANG
ZAMANGS
ZAMANS
ZAMARRA
ZAMARRAS
ZAMARRO
ZAMARROS
ZAMBO
ZAMBOMBA
ZAMBOMBAS
ZAMBOORAK
ZAMBOORAKS
ZAMBOS
ZAMIA
ZAMIAS
ZAMINDAR
ZAMINDARI
ZAMINDARIS
ZAMINDARS
ZAMOUSE
ZAMOUSES
ZAMPOGNA
ZAMPOGNAS
ZANDER
ZANDERS
ZANELLA
ZANELLAS
ZANIED
ZANIER
ZANIES
ZANIEST
ZANJA
ZANJAS
ZANJERO
ZANJEROS
ZANTE
ZANTES
ZANY
ZANYING
ZANYISM

ZANYISMS
ZANZE
ZANZES
ZAP
ZAPATEADO
ZAPATEADOS
ZAPOTILLA
ZAPOTILLAS
ZAPPED
ZAPPIER
ZAPPIEST
ZAPPING
ZAPPY
ZAPS
ZAPTIAH
ZAPTIAHS
ZAPTIEH
ZAPTIEHS
ZARAPE
ZARAPES
ZARATITE
ZARATITES
ZAREBA
ZAREBAS
ZAREEBA
ZAREEBAS
ZARF
ZARFS
ZARIBA
ZARIBAS
ZARNEC
ZARNECS
ZARNICH
ZARNICHS
ZARZUELA
ZARZUELAS
ZASTRUGA
ZASTRUGI
ZATI
ZATIO
ZAX
ZAXES
ZEA
ZEAL
ZEALANT
ZEALANTS
ZEALFUL
ZEALLESS
ZEALOT
ZEALOTISM
ZEALOTISMS
ZEALOTRIES
ZEALOTRY
ZEALOTS
ZEALOUS
ZEALOUSLY
ZEALS
ZEAS
ZEBEC
ZEBECK
ZEBECKS
ZEBECS
ZEBRA
ZEBRAS
ZEBRASS

ZEBRASSES
ZEBRINE
ZEBRINNIES
ZEBRINNY
ZEBROID
ZEBRULA
ZEBRULAS
ZEBRULE
ZEBRULES
ZEBU
ZEBUB
ZEBUBS
ZEBUS
ZECCHINE
ZECCHINES
ZECCHINI
ZECCHINO
ZECCHINOS
ZED
ZEDOARIES
ZEDOARY
ZEDS
ZEE
ZEES
ZEIN
ZEINS
ZEITGEIST
ZEITGEISTS
ZEK
ZEKS
ZEL
ZELANT
ZELANTS
ZELOSO
ZELOTYPIA
ZELOTYPIAS
ZELS
ZEMINDAR
ZEMINDARI
ZEMINDARIES
ZEMINDARIS
ZEMINDARS
ZEMINDARY
ZEMSTVO
ZEMSTVOS
ZENANA
ZENANAS
ZENDIK
ZENDIKS
ZENITH
ZENITHAL
ZENITHS
ZEOLITE
ZEOLITES
ZEOLITIC
ZEPHYR
ZEPHYRS
ZEPPELIN
ZEPPELINS
ZERDA
ZERDAS
ZEREBA
ZEREBAS
ZERIBA
ZERIBAS

ZERO
ZEROED
ZEROING
ZEROS
ZEROTH
ZERUMBET
ZERUMBETS
ZEST
ZESTFUL
ZESTFULLY
ZESTIER
ZESTIEST
ZESTS
ZESTY
ZETA
ZETAS
ZETETIC
ZETETICS
ZEUGMA
ZEUGMAS
ZEUGMATIC
ZEUXITE
ZEUXITES
ZEZE
ZEZES
ZHO
ZHOMO
ZHOMOS
ZHOS
ZIBELINE
ZIBELINES
ZIBELLINE
ZIBELLINES
ZIBET
ZIBETS
ZIFF
ZIFFIUS
ZIFFIUSES
ZIFFS
ZIG
ZIGAN
ZIGANKA
ZIGANKAS
ZIGANS
ZIGGED
ZIGGING
ZIGGURAT
ZIGGURATS
ZIGS
ZIGZAG
ZIGZAGGED
ZIGZAGGING
ZIGZAGGY
ZIGZAGS
ZIKKURAT
ZIKKURATS
ZILA
ZILAS
ZILCH
ZILCHES
ZILLAH
ZILLAHS
ZILLION
ZILLIONS
ZILLIONTH

ZILLIONTHS
ZIMB
ZIMBI
ZIMBIS
ZIMBS
ZIMMER
ZIMMERS
ZIMOCCA
ZIMOCCAS
ZINC
ZINCED
ZINCIER
ZINCIEST
ZINCIFIED
ZINCIFIES
ZINCIFY
ZINCIFYING
ZINCING
ZINCITE
ZINCITES
ZINCKED
ZINCKIER
ZINCKIEST
ZINCKIFIED
ZINCKIFIES
ZINCKIFY
ZINCKIFYING
ZINCKING
ZINCKY
ZINCO
ZINCODE
ZINCODES
ZINCOID
ZINCOS
ZINCOUS
ZINCS
ZINCY
ZINEB
ZINEBS
ZINFANDEL
ZINFANDELS
ZING
ZINGED
ZINGEL
ZINGELS
ZINGIBER
ZINGIBERS
ZINGIER
ZINGIEST
ZINGING
ZINGS
ZINGY
ZINKE
ZINKED
ZINKENITE
ZINKENITES
ZINKES
ZINKIER
ZINKIEST
ZINKIFIED
ZINKIFIES
ZINKIFY
ZINKIFYING
ZINKING
ZINKY

ZINNIA
ZINNIAS
ZIP
ZIPPED
ZIPPER
ZIPPERED
ZIPPERS
ZIPPIER
ZIPPIEST
ZIPPING
ZIPPY
ZIPS
ZIPTOP
ZIRCALLOY
ZIRCALLOYS
ZIRCON
ZIRCONIA
ZIRCONIAS
ZIRCONIC
ZIRCONIUM
ZIRCONIUMS
ZIRCONS
ZIT
ZITHER
ZITHERN
ZITHERNS
ZITHERS
ZITS
ZIZ
ZIZEL
ZIZELS
ZIZZ
ZIZZED
ZIZZES
ZIZZING
ZLOTY
ZLOTYS
ZO
ZOA
ZOARIUM
ZOARIUMS
ZOBO
ZOBOS
ZOBU
ZOBUS
ZOCCOLO
ZOCCOLOS
ZOCCOS
ZODIAC
ZODIACAL
ZODIACS
ZOEA
ZOEAE
ZOEAL
ZOEAS
ZOECHROME
ZOECHROMES
ZOEFORM
ZOETIC
ZOETROPE
ZOETROPES
ZOETROPIC
ZOIATRIA
ZOIATRIAS
ZOIATRICS
ZOIC
ZOISITE
ZOISITES
ZOISM
ZOISMS

ZOIST
ZOISTS
ZOMBI
ZOMBIE
ZOMBIES
ZOMBIISM
ZOMBIISMS
ZOMBIS
ZOMBORUK
ZOMBORUKS
ZONA
ZONAE
ZONAL
ZONARY
ZONATE
ZONATED
ZONATION
ZONATIONS
ZONDA
ZONDAS
ZONE
ZONED
ZONELESS
ZONES
ZONING
ZONINGS
ZONKED
ZONOID
ZONULA
ZONULAR
ZONULAS
ZONULE
ZONULES
ZONULET
ZONULETS
ZOO
ZOOBIOTIC
ZOOBLAST
ZOOBLASTS
ZOOCHORE
ZOOCHORES
ZOOCHORIES
ZOOCHORY
ZOOCYTIA
ZOOCYTIUM
ZOOEA
ZOOEAE
ZOOEAL
ZOOEAS
ZOOECIA
ZOOECIUM
ZOOGAMETE
ZOOGAMETES
ZOOGAMIES
ZOOGAMOUS
ZOOGAMY
ZOOGENIC
ZOOGENIES
ZOOGENOUS
ZOOGENY
ZOOGLOEA
ZOOGLOEAS
ZOOGLOEIC
ZOOGONIES
ZOOGONOUS
ZOOGONY
ZOOGRAFT
ZOOGRAFTS
ZOOGRAPHIES
ZOOGRAPHY
ZOOID

ZOOIDAL
ZOOIDS
ZOOKS
ZOOLATER
ZOOLATERS
ZOOLATRIA
ZOOLATRIAS
ZOOLATRIES
ZOOLATRY
ZOOLITE
ZOOLITES
ZOOLITH
ZOOLITHIC
ZOOLITHS
ZOOLITIC
ZOOLOGIES
ZOOLOGIST
ZOOLOGISTS
ZOOLOGY
ZOOM
ZOOMANCIES
ZOOMANCY
ZOOMANTIC
ZOOMED
ZOOMETRIC
ZOOMETRIES
ZOOMETRY
ZOOMING
ZOOMORPH
ZOOMORPHIES
ZOOMORPHS
ZOOMORPHY
ZOOMS
ZOON
ZOONAL
ZOONIC
ZOONITE
ZOONITES
ZOONITIC
ZOONOMIA
ZOONOMIAS
ZOONOMIC
ZOONOMIES
ZOONOMIST
ZOONOMISTS
ZOONOMY
ZOONOSES
ZOONOSIS
ZOONOTIC
ZOONS
ZOOPATHIES
ZOOPATHY
ZOOPERAL
ZOOPERIES
ZOOPERIST
ZOOPERISTS
ZOOPERY
ZOOPHAGAN
ZOOPHAGANS
ZOOPHILE
ZOOPHILES
ZOOPHILIA
ZOOPHILIAS
ZOOPHILIES
ZOOPHILY
ZOOPHOBIA
ZOOPHOBIAS
ZOOPHORIC
ZOOPHORUS
ZOOPHORUSES
ZOOPHYTE

ZOOPHYTES
ZOOPHYTIC
ZOOPLASTIES
ZOOPLASTY
ZOOS
ZOOSCOPIC
ZOOSCOPIES
ZOOSCOPY
ZOOSPERM
ZOOSPERMS
ZOOSPORE
ZOOSPORES
ZOOSPORIC
ZOOTAXIES
ZOOTAXY
ZOOTECHNIES
ZOOTECHNY
ZOOTHECIA
ZOOTHEISM
ZOOTHEISMS
ZOOTHOME
ZOOTHOMES
ZOOTOMIC
ZOOTOMIES
ZOOTOMIST
ZOOTOMISTS
ZOOTOMY
ZOOTOXIN
ZOOTOXINS
ZOOTROPE
ZOOTROPES
ZOOTROPHIES
ZOOTROPHY
ZOOTYPE
ZOOTYPES
ZOOTYPIC
ZOOZOO
ZOOZOOS
ZOPILOTE
ZOPILOTES
ZOPPO
ZORGITE
ZORGITES
ZORIL
ZORILLE
ZORILLES
ZORILLO
ZORILLOS
ZORILS
ZORINO
ZORINOS
ZORRO
ZORROS
ZOS
ZOSTER
ZOSTERS
ZOUNDS
ZOUNDSES
ZOWIE
ZUCCHETTO
ZUCCHETTOS
ZUCCHINI
ZUCCHINIS
ZUCHETTA
ZUCHETTAS
ZUCHETTO
ZUCHETTOS
ZUFFOLI
ZUFFOLO
ZUFOLI
ZUFOLO

ZUGZWANG
ZUGZWANGS
ZULU
ZULUS
ZUMBOORUK
ZUMBOORUKS
ZUPA
ZUPAN
ZUPANS
ZUPAS
ZURF
ZURFS
ZUZ
ZUZES
ZYGAENID
ZYGAENINE
ZYGAENOID
ZYGAL
ZYGANTRA
ZYGANTRUM
ZYGANTRUMS
ZYGODONT
ZYGOMA
ZYGOMAS
ZYGOMATIC
ZYGON
ZYGONS
ZYGOPHYTE
ZYGOPHYTES
ZYGOSE
ZYGOSES
ZYGOSIS
ZYGOSPERM
ZYGOSPERMS
ZYGOSPORE
ZYGOSPORES
ZYGOTE
ZYGOTES
ZYGOTIC
ZYLONITE
ZYLONITES
ZYMASE
ZYMASES
ZYME
ZYMES
ZYMIC
ZYMITE
ZYMITES
ZYMOGEN
ZYMOGENIC
ZYMOGENS
ZYMOID
ZYMOLITIC
ZYMOLOGIC
ZYMOLOGIES
ZYMOLOGY
ZYMOLYSES
ZYMOLYSIS
ZYMOME
ZYMOMES
ZYMOMETER
ZYMOMETERS
ZYMOSES
ZYMOSIS
ZYMOTIC
ZYMURGIES
ZYMURGY
ZYTHUM
ZYTHUMS